PRACTICE AND PROCEDURE IN LABOR ARBITRATION

PRACTICE AND PROCEDURE
IN
LABOR ARBITRATION

SECOND EDITION

OWEN FAIRWEATHER

The Bureau of National Affairs, Inc., Washington, D.C.

Library of Congress Cataloging in Publication Data

Fairweather, Owen.
  Practice and procedure in labor arbitration.

  Includes bibliographical references and index.
  1. Arbitration, Industrial—United States.
I. Title.
KF3424.F35 1981   344.73'0189143   81-10089
ISBN 0-87179-365-2   347.304189143   AACR2

KF
3424
.F35
1983X

International Standard Book Number: 0-87179-365-2
Printed in the United States of America

Preface

Beginning in about 1938, when labor arbitration agreements began to include an arbitration procedure, the courts started out misunderstanding the process and frowned upon it; later they began to protect it and enforced the awards; then they began to supervise it. An increasing variety of various types of Section 301 suits have been filed in courts to obtain vacations, revisions, and *de novo* appellate reviews of awards which are now essentially attaching labor arbitration to the bottom of the judicial process, increasing formalism and costs and stretching out resolution time.

In the beginning, when a labor agreement was a relatively primitive document, many arbitrators considered themselves to be private mediators. At the time, arbitrators subscribed to the cliché that arbitration was an informal process in which external rules of practice and procedure were out of place and that the parties had granted to the arbitrator the authority to make whatever rules he believed he needed. The arbitrators quite naturally nurtured this view and when the cliché was operating, courts rarely pried into practice and procedure matters.

When the first edition of this book was assembled in the late sixties the procedural variations in what arbitrators actually did were catalogued. The author said in the preface that he was concerned for fear that cataloguing of the variations in procedures would tend to set up rigidities that might dampen an arbitrator's freedom. He said:

> The process of cataloguing started in various legal memoranda, but the attempt to make a reasonably complete catalogue began in 1967. As material was collected, the risk involved in cataloguing became quite clear. A practice or procedure that is reported might be considered to be endorsed as the preferred practice or procedure. Partly for this reason, an effort was made to report the variety that exists with a conscious effort to avoid editorial identification of the "best" procedure. Some of the flexibility so valuable to the labor arbitration process might inadvertently be damaged if one procedure or another were considered "best."

Beginning in the mid-sixties, statutes and regulations governing the employer-employee relationship came into being and became more complex and pervasive. Matters once regulated by collective bargaining or, in default, left to management decision, became subject to constitutional or statutory command.

These statutes, and the regulations adopted pursuant to their authority, introduced legal principles as the basis for the rights of individual employees, and these rights can be vindicated in courts as well as in arbitration. As arbitration procedures became more formal, arbitration became more expensive. But even the most costly arbitration proceedings are economical by comparison with the cost of the trial of a lawsuit with similar issues. Judge Alvin Rubin of the Fifth Circuit has stated:

> It seems to me that arbitration is not only a just means of resolving disputes, but that even the most formal arbitration proceeding is much faster, less expensive, and more responsive to industrial needs than the best-run courts available today. It is a myth that access to justice must mean access to the courts, especially the federal courts.[1]

In the late seventies, more procedural rigidities sprang up, not because the practices and procedures of arbitrators had been catalogued, but because the Supreme Court in a series of decisions passed on to the trial courts the duty of reviewing arbitration awards if they "touched the law." Chief Justice Warren Burger, a member of the Supreme Court when it contributed to the trend moving grievance cases into courts, explained: "Remedies for personal wrongs that once were considered the responsibility of institutions other than the courts are now boldly asserted as legal entitlements."[2]

When a Section 301 suit starts up a review of an award the case will have no priority, unless an injunction is sought and, as Judge Rubin explained, the case "dawdles on the calendar. It is not unusual for [such a] case to linger four years before final decision."[3]

No longer is there any concern because the cataloguing of procedures might reduce the "flexibility so valuable to the labor arbitration process." The concern is now the reverse. Will labor arbitrators absorb the simple yet sound legal procedures fast enough to cause courts and agencies to accept the awards without relitigating them, slowing down the resolution of many types of grievances that once were considered the labor arbitrator's exclusive campgrounds?

Chief Justice Burger is now a champion to reverse the trend. He said arbitration awards should again be considered final and binding.

---

[1]Rubin, *Arbitration: Toward a Rebirth*, TRUTH, LIE DETECTORS, AND OTHER PROBLEMS IN LABOR ARBITRATION, Proceedings of the Thirty-First Annual Meeting, National Academy of Arbitrators, J. Stern and B. Dennis, eds. (Washington: BNA Books, 1979), p. 30.
[2]Burger, *Isn't There a Better Way?* (1982 report on the state of the judiciary), 68 ABA J. 274.
[3]Rubin, note 1 *supra*, at p. 34.

[A]rbitration procedures [should] become a realistic alternative rather than an additional step in an already prolonged process. For this reason, if a system of voluntary arbitration is to be truly effective, it should be final and binding, without a provision for *de novo* trial or review.[4]

Judge Rubin adds to Chief Justice Burger's comments a pragmatic suggestion:

[W]e should ... consider making it possible by statute for unions and employers to agree on the resolution by arbitration of many of the issues that are governed by both statute and agreement. Many issues of employment discrimination, equal pay, age discrimination, and the like could be decided as well or better by an arbitrator as by a federal judge.[5]

Labor arbitrators are good public servants. They are good scholars, and they work hard. However, if they are to help reverse the trend as urged by Chief Justice Burger, Judge Rubin, and others, they and the representatives on both sides must watch carefully: many courts and agencies are standing ready to accept an award for review if the arbitrator has lowered his or her guard and provides them any reason to do so.

Judge Harry T. Edwards, once an active arbitrator and now a busy member of the District of Columbia Circuit Court, believes the trend toward the use of a court to resolve disputes is harmful because "The judicial process is heavily steeped in procedures. Many cases may be won or lost on 'procedural' points that have nothing whatsoever to do with the merits of the case." Thus, he urges arbitrators, who must focus on the growing appellate review, to avoid developing a "magistrate mentality."

[T]he potential hazard of judicial review is that it will likely result in arbitrators deciding cases and writing opinions in such a way as to insulate their awards against judicial reversal.... If the arbitrator adopts a "magistrate mentality," and performs only as if he or she is "the first link in one or more appellate chains," then it is entirely possible that no one will ever concentrate fully on the merits of the case. Indeed, if arbitrators in any sector begin to think of themselves as magistrates rather than arbitrators, the advantages of the arbitral process will be lost.[6]

I am deeply indebted to Eileen Hickey, my secretary, who also poured effort into the first book. The real backup on the team, how-

---

[4]Burger, note 2 *supra*, at p. 277.

[5]Rubin, note 1 *supra*, at pp. 37-38.

[6]Edwards, *Advantages of Arbitration Over Litigation: Reflections of a Judge,* ARBITRATION 1982: CONDUCT OF THE HEARING, Proceedings of the Thirty-Fifth Annual Meeting, National Academy of Arbitrators, B. Dennis and J. Stern, eds. (Washington: BNA Books, 1983).

ever, has been Tim Darby, a tireless, dedicated, skilled editor, who goes farther than do most editors—and he has been a good challenger, a needed member of any team.

OWEN FAIRWEATHER

January 1983

Table of Contents

CHAPTER I

Source of Law
in Labor Arbitration

A discussion of practice and procedure in labor arbitration includes the manner in which a labor arbitration case is initiated, how the hearing proceeds, and what happens after the hearing is concluded and the award issued. When labor arbitration began to grow in the United States as a result of the rapid unionization of major industries in the early 1930s most of the practice and procedure in labor arbitration was established and developed by the arbitrator. He used, as his basic standards, the needs and desires of the parties he was servicing, since labor arbitration was considered a completely private process.

The view that labor arbitration should be controlled or formalized by any body of law made by judges or legislators was repugnant not only to the early arbitrators but also to the parties submitting disputes to arbitration. They rather uniformly believed that judges, legislators, and lawyers did not understand the pragmatic and fast-moving nature of the labor arbitration process and that, if the law crept in, it would generate rigidities which would make the labor arbitration process less satisfactory to the parties.

Later, however, the law began to flow over the labor arbitration process like a tidal wave. At first, much of this law involved procedural matters; later, federal laws began to have a strong impact on arbitration. One reason there was so little law surrounding labor arbitration in its infancy was that the courts initially made no effort to accommodate the process. They considered labor arbitration to be a process competitive with the court system, and therefore a process that should be thwarted and discouraged.[1]

In the early days of labor arbitration, courts ruled that an agree-

---

[1]*See generally* Sturges and Reckeson, *Common Law and Statutory Arbitration: Problems Arising From Their Coexistence,* 46 Minn. L. Rev. 819 (1962); 6A A. Corbin, Contracts § 1443 at 388 (1962, Supp. 1964) ("A general agreement to arbitrate all future disputes is contrary to public policy and void"); *United Steelworkers v. Warrior & Gulf Navigation Co.,* 363 U.S. 574, 586-87, 46 LRRM 2416 (1960) (dissenting opinion); *Marchant v. Mead-Morrison Mfg. Co.,* 252 N.Y. 284, 299, 169 N.E. 386, 391 (1929); *Continental Milling & Feed Co. v. Doughnut Co.,* 186 Md. 669, 676, 48 A.2d 447, 450 (1946); *U.S. v. Moorman,* 338 U.S. 457, 462 (1950).

ment to submit a dispute to arbitration could be revoked at will by either party, even after the arbitration hearing, if the revocation occurred prior to the entry of an award. Agreements to arbitrate were revocable even when they contained an express covenant that neither party to the agreement could revoke them because, the courts held, parties could not make irrevocable agreements about matters legally revocable.[2]

The courts' jealousy of arbitration as a competing process and their refusal to enforce agreements to arbitrate on the theory that one or the other party could revoke them disappeared as the state legislatures began to enact arbitration statutes. Before Congress gave legal recognition to labor arbitration, at least 29 states had arbitration statutes specifically applicable to controversies arising out of labor agreements or specific agreements to arbitrate a labor dispute[3] and at least 19 states had general arbitration statutes construed to be applicable to disputes arising out of labor agreements.[4]

---

[2]*See, e.g., Baltimore and Ohio R. Co. v. Standard,* 56 Ohio St. 224, 46 N.E. 577 (1897).

[3]Alabama (Ala. Code tit. 26, §§ 338 to 342 (1958)); Alaska (Alaska Stat. § 23.05.060 (1962)); Arkansas (Ark. Stat. Ann. § 81-107 (1960)); Colorado (Colo. Rev. Stat. Ann. §§ 80-4-10, 80-4-11 (1963)); Connecticut (Conn. Gen. Stat. Rev. § 31-117 (1968)); Illinois (Ill. Ann. Stat. ch. 10, §§ 20 to 30 (Smith-Hurd, 1966), *as amended* (Supp. 1970)); Iowa (Iowa Code Ann. §§ 90.1 to 90.14 (1949)); Kentucky (Ky. Rev. Stat. §§ 336.140, 336.150 (1962)); Louisiana (La. Rev. Stat. Ann. §§ 23:861 to 23:876 (1964)); Maine (Me. Rev. Stat. Ann. §§ 881 to 960 (1964)); Maryland (Md. Ann. Code art. 89, §§ 3 to 13 (1969)); Massachusetts (Mass. Ann. Laws ch. 150C, §§ 1 to 16 (1965)); Michigan (Mich. Stat. Ann. § 17.454 (10.3) (1968)); Minnesota (Minn. Stat. Ann. § 179.09 (Supp. 1970)); Montana (Mont. Rev. Codes Ann. §§ 41-901 to 41-909 (1961)); Nevada (Nev. Rev. Stat. §§ 614.010 to 614.080 (1967)); New Hampshire (N.H. Rev. Stat. Ann. §§ 273:12 to 273:27 (1966)); New Jersey (N.J. Rev. Stat. §§ 34-13-1 to 34-13-9 (1965)); North Carolina (N.C. Gen. Stat. §§ 95-36.1 to 95-36.9 (1965)); Ohio (Ohio Rev. Code Ann. §§ 4129.01 to 4129.12 (1965)); Oregon (Ore. Rev. Stat. §§ 662.405 to 662.455 (1967)); Pennsylvania (Pa. Stat. Ann. tit. 43, §§ 211.31 to 211.39 (1964)); Rhode Island (R. I. Gen. Laws Ann. §§ 28-9-1 to 28-9-26 (1968)); South Carolina (S.C. Code Ann. §§ 40-301 to 40-307 (1962)); Texas (Tex. Rev. Civ. Stat. Ann. arts. 239 to 249 (1959)); Utah (Utah Code Ann. § 35-1-16 (1953)); Vermont (Vt. Stat. Ann. tit. 21, §§ 501 to 513 (1967)); Washington (Wash. Rev. Code Ann. §§ 49-08.010 to 49-08.060 (1962)); Wisconsin (Wis. Stat. Ann. § 111.10 (1957)).

[4]Delaware (Del. Code Ann. tit. 10 §§ 5701 to 5706 (1953)); Florida (Fla. Stat. Ann. §§ 682.01 to 682.22 (Supp. 1969)); Georgia (Ga. Code Ann. §§ 7-201 to 7-224 (1953)); Hawaii (Hawaii Rev. Laws §§ 658-1 to 658-15 (1968)); Idaho (Idaho Code Ann. §§ 7-901 to 7-910 (1948)); Kansas (Kan. Stat. Ann. §§ 5-201 to 5-213 (1963)); Mississippi (Miss. Code Ann. §§ 279 to 297 (1956)); Missouri (Mo. Ann. Stat. §§ 435.010 to 435.280 (1950)); Nebraska (Neb. Rev. Stat. §§ 25-2103 to 25-2120 (1943)); Nevada (Nev. Rev. Stat. §§ 38.010 to 38.240 (1967)); New Mexico (N.M. Stat. Ann. §§ 22-3-1 to 22-3-8 (1953)); New York (N.Y. Civ. Prac. §§ 7501 to 7514 (McKinney, 1963)); North Dakota (N.D. Cent. Code §§ 32-29-01 to 32-29-21 (1960)); Tennessee (Tenn. Code Ann. §§ 23-501 to 23-519 (1955)); Virginia (Va. Code Ann. §§ 8-503 to 8-507 (1950) *as amended.* § 8-503 (Supp. 1968)); West Virginia (W. Va. Code Ann. §§ 55-10-1 to 55-10-8 (1966)). Indiana and Wyoming have enacted the Uniform Arbitration Act supplemented by language making it expressly applicable to labor arbitration: Indiana (Ind. Ann. Stat. §§ 3-227 to 3-248 (Supp. 1970)); Wyoming (Wyo. Stat. Ann. §§ 1-1048.1 to 1-1048.21 (Supp. 1969)). The California statute (Cal. Civ. Proc. Code §§ 1280-1294 (West, 1955)) excepting from arbitration contracts "pertaining to labor" has been construed to except only contracts relating to the actual hiring of labor and not collective bargaining agreements. *Ulene v. Murray Millman of California,* 175 Cal. App.2d 655, 346 P.2d 494 (1959).

On the federal side of the ledger, Congress had enacted in 1925 the United States Arbitration Act,[5] a statute to enforce commercial agreements to arbitrate,[6] and parties to labor agreements began to predicate enforcement suits on this Act.

Then after enactment of Section 301 of the Labor Management Relations Act in 1964,[7] there developed considerable confusion in the lower federal courts as to whether Section 301 or the U.S. Arbitration Act conferred jurisdiction upon federal courts to compel or stay labor arbitration and to enforce or vacate awards.[8] In *Textile Workers Union v. American Thread Co.*,[9] Judge Wyzanski held that an agreement to arbitrate a dispute concerning the interpretation and application of a labor agreement could be enforced under Section 301, but that the practice under the U.S. Arbitration Act should be "a guiding analogy."[10]

Subsequently, in *Textile Workers Union v. Lincoln Mills,*[11] the Supreme Court for the first time clearly identified Section 301 as the source of all law, substantive and procedural, for labor arbitration. In that case, the Fifth Circuit had held that an agreement to arbitrate could not be enforced[12] because there was no federal or state common law or statute that required or permitted the enforcement of such an agreement. The Supreme Court, however, reversed and enforced the agreement. Justice Douglas, writing the majority opinion, did not refer to the U.S. Arbitration Act, but he did say that the Supreme Court's construction of Section 301 was in accord with Judge Wyzanski's decision in *American Thread.*[13] It was interpreted that the Supreme Court had accepted the arbitration practice under the U.S. Arbitration Act "as a guiding analogy"[14] to be followed as the procedural law applicable to labor arbitration developed.

Then the Supreme Court clearly said in *General Electric Co. v. Local 205, United Electrical Workers,*[15] that the procedural law developed under the U.S. Arbitration Act was to be "a guiding analogy." It enforced, under Section 301, an agreement to arbitrate which

---

[5]9 U.S.C. § 1, *et seq.* (1947).

[6]The U.S. Arbitration Act, as Judge Wyzanski observed, "was drafted a generation ago, prior not only to the Taft-Hartley Act but also the labor situation that has developed since the 1930's." *Textile Workers Union v. American Thread Co.,* 113 F. Supp. 137, 142, 32 LRRM 2205, 2209 (D. Mass. 1953).

[7]29 U.S.C. § 185 (1964). Generally referred to in this text as Section 301.

[8]*See generally* Cox, *Grievance Arbitration in the Federal Courts,* 67 Harv. L. Rev. 591 (1956).

[9]113 F. Supp. 137, 32 LRRM 2205 (D. Mass. 1953).

[10]*Id.* at 142, 32 LRRM at 2209.

[11]353 U.S. 448, 40 LRRM 2113 (1957).

[12]*Lincoln Mills v. Textile Workers Union,* 230 F.2d 81, 37 LRRM 2462 (5th Cir. 1956).

[13]353 U.S. at 451, 40 LRRM at 2114 (1957).

[14]*See* Smith and Jones, *Arbitration and the Courts,* 63 Mich. L. Rev. 751, 801-2 n. 120 (1965).

[15]353 U.S. 547, 40 LRRM 2119 (1957).

the Second Circuit had enforced under the U.S. Arbitration Act, noting that the Second Circuit had taken "a different path . . . though we reach the same result."[16] Despite this, in a companion case, *Goodall-Sanford, Inc. v. United Textile Workers Local 1802,*[17] the Supreme Court counselled against too full an application of the U.S. Arbitration Act as "a guiding analogy." It held, under Section 301, that an order directing arbitration was a "final decision" that could be appealed; this decision was contrary to rulings by lower courts based on the U.S. Arbitration Act. Thus, the U.S. Arbitration Act was not to be exclusively the source of procedural answers in labor arbitration cases, but only the "guiding analogy."

Fourteen years later a district court absorbed some procedural law into Section 301 from state law. A subpoena for the appearance of a witness and for the production of certain records issued under a state statute in a labor arbitration proceeding was enforced by the court.[18] While the court said it was acting *sua sponte* and added the requirement that the records called for by the subpoena were to be examined by the arbitrator *in camera,* its authority came from a combination of the state statute, the U.S. Arbitration Act, and Section 301.

In spite of the uneasy status of state statutory law in suits to compel or stay arbitration, or to enforce or vacate awards, state courts frequently rely on state arbitration statutes in denying requested relief.[19] For example, a request for vacation of an award was denied by a Minnesota court under a provision of a Minnesota statute. The argument that the Minnesota statutory law was not applicable to block the vacation was rejected by the court with this observation: "[T]he controlling substantive law is Federal law," but "state law, if compatible with the purposes of § 301, may be resorted to in order to find the rule that will best effectuate the Federal policy."[20]

---

[16]*Id.* at 548, 40 LRRM at 2119 (1957).

[17]353 U.S. 550, 40 LRRM 2118 (1957). *See also Aircraft Lodge 703 v. Curtiss-Wright Corp.,* 169 F. Supp. 837, 43 LRRM 2525 (D. N.J. 1959); *MacNeish v. New York Typographical Union No. 6,* 205 F. Supp. 558, 50 LRRM 2361 (S.D. N.Y. 1962); *Pock v. New York Typographical Union No. 6,* 223 F. Supp. 181, 54 LRRM 2666 (S.D. N.Y. 1963); *Austin Mailers Union No. 136 v. Newspapers, Inc.,* 226 F. Supp. 600 (W. D. Tex. 1963), *aff'd,* 329 F.2d 312, 55 LRRM 2693 (5th Cir. 1964). *cert. denied,* 377 U.S. 985, 76 LRRM 2544 (1964); *cf. Western Automatic Machine Screw Co. v. UAW,* 335 F.2d 103, 56 LRRM 2978 (6th Cir. 1964); *Local 1645, UAW v. Torrington Co.,* 242 F. Supp. 813, 59 LRRM 2267 (D. Conn. 1965); *aff'd,* 358 F.2d 103, 62 LRRM 2011 (2d Cir. 1966).

[18]*Local Lodge 1746, IAM v. United Aircraft Corp.,* 329 F. Supp. 283, 77 LRRM 2596 (D. Conn. 1971).

[19]*See generally* Comment, *The Applicability of State Arbitration Statutes to Proceedings Subject to LMRA Section 301,* 21 Ohio State L.J. 692 (1966); *Local 2131, United Bhd. of Carpenters & Joiners v. Aetna Steel Products Corp.,* 56 Sch. L.R. 141, 36 LA 717 (C.P. Schuylkill Co., Pa. 1960).

[20]*Fischer v. Guaranteed Concrete Co.,* 276 Minn. 510, 514, 151 N.W.2d 266, 269, 65 LRRM 2493, 2495. (1967).

Following this same easy rationale, many state and federal district courts have required strict compliance with the procedural requirements of the state or federal arbitration statutes.[21] For example, a New York court held that a motion to compel arbitration must be served on the other party in technical compliance with the state statutory requirements.[22] Further, a New York federal court held that an action to stay must be filed within the state statutory time limits.[23]

Some litigants began to use a "shotgun" approach, basing jurisdiction on both Section 301 and the U.S. Arbitration Act.[24] Other litigants used Section 301 as the jurisdictional base and then asked the court to invoke remedies found in the U.S. Arbitration Act. A Connecticut district court in *Metal Products Workers Union, Local 1645, UAW v. Torrington Co.*[25] found its jurisdiction in Section 301, but its authority to apply remedies in the U.S. Arbitration Act.[26] A Wisconsin district court in *Operating Engineers, Local 139 v. Carl A. Morse, Inc.*[27] followed this reasoning, finding its jurisdiction in Section 301

[21] *Cf. IAM v. General Electric Co.,* 406 F.2d 1046, 70 LRRM 2477 (2d. Cir. 1969). (Commencement of action to compel arbitration by petition under Section 4 of the U.S. Arbitration Act instead of by a complaint under Section 301 is valid in that the Arbitration Act has been recognized as applicable to labor cases.)

[22] *2166 Bronx Park East, Inc. v. Local 32E, Building Service Employees,* 45 Misc.2d 492, 257 N.Y.S.2d 192, 193, 58 LRRM 2143, 2144 (Sup. Ct. 1965) ("Although service by certified mail is permitted for notice of intention to arbitrate and for an application to stay arbitration within 10 days after service of such notice (CPLR 7503 [c]), an application to compel arbitration is the commencement of a special proceeding (CPLR 7502[a]) and must be instituted by service in the same manner as a summons (CPLR 403[c])."); *cf. DeLorto v. United Parcel Service, Inc.,* 401 F. Supp. 408, 90 LRRM 3312 (D. Mass. 1975); *UMW v. Jones & Laughlin Steel Corp.,* 378 F Supp. 1206, 86 LRRM 3089 (W.D. Pa. 1974); *Hill v. Avco Corp.,* 275 F. Supp. 482, 67 LRRM 2037 (N.D. Ohio 1967).

[23] *IAM v. General Electric Co.,* 282 F. Supp. 413, 67 LRRM 2817 (N.D. N.Y. 1968), *aff'd,* 406 F.2d 1046, 70 LRRM 2477 (2d Cir. 1969).

[24] *See Garlick Funeral Homes, Inc. v. Local 100, AFL-CIO,* 413 F. Supp. 130, 92 LRRM 2482 (S.D. N.Y. 1976); *Lucas v. Philco-Ford Corp.,* 399 F. Supp. 1184, 90 LRRM 2122 (E.D. Pa. 1975); *MacNeish v. New York Typographical Union,* 205 F. Supp. 558, 50 LRRM 2361 (S.D. N.Y. 1962), wherein jurisdiction was based on both Section 301 of the Labor-Management Relations Act and Section 1 of the Arbitration Act.

[25] 242 F. Supp. 813, 59 LRRM 2267 (D. Conn. 1965), *aff'd,* 362 F.2d 677, 62 LRRM 2495 (2d Cir. 1966).

[26] *In Torrington, supra,* the court said:
Although the Arbitration Act itself confers no jurisdiction upon this Court, "it does provide an additional procedure and remedy in the federal courts where jurisdiction already exists." The Court, having determined that Section 301(a) independently establishes its jurisdiction of the parties and the subject matter of the action, find that procedures authorized by the Arbitration Act, including the three month limitation period, were available to the Union.
242 F. Supp. at 819, 59 LRRM at 2270 (footnotes omitted). *See, e.g., Bell Aerospace Co. v Local 516, International Union, etc.,* 500 F.2d 921, 86 LRRM 3240 (2d Cir. 1974); *Chattanooga Mailers Union, Local 92 v. Chattanooga News-Free Press Co.,* 524 F.2d 1305, 90 LRRM 3000 (6th Cir. 1975); *Pietro Scalzitti Co. v. International Union of Engineers, Local No. 150,* 351 F.2d 576, 60 LRRM 2222 (7th Cir. 1965); *Pepsico, Inc. v. Brewery Workers Local 812, Soft Drink Workers Union,* 89 LRRM 2541 (E.D. N.Y. 1975).

[27] 387 F. Supp. 153, 88 LRRM 2145 (E.D. Wis. 1974), *aff'd,* 529 F.2d 574, 91 LRRM 2415 (7th Cir. 1976).

and its procedural rules "governed by the terms of 9 U.S.C. § 4" (U.S. Arbitration Act).[28] District and circuit courts want clear rules, and they began to discard the view that the U.S. Arbitration Act was merely a "guiding analogy."

In *Bell Aerospace Co. v. International Union, etc., Local 516*,[29] the Second Circuit indicated that the U.S. Arbitration Act was more than a guide when it held that "[a] federal court may vacate the award of an arbitrator only on the ground specified in 9 U.S.C. § 10 (1970)."[30] A decision by the First Circuit followed, stating that the court must follow the U.S. Arbitration Act precisely.[31]

The conclusion of these courts that they are bound by the exact language of the Arbitration Act when procedural rules were being applied seems contrary to the Supreme Court's holding in *Lincoln Mills*[32] that that Act was to be used as a "guiding analogy" rather than to be mandatorily followed. Nevertheless, many courts have said that since the U.S. Arbitration Act is the only statement by Congress on arbitration procedure, its rules should be followed exactly. Therefore, litigants should determine whether the particular court considers itself *bound* or *guided* by the U.S. Arbitration Act in procedural matters if and when procedure questions arise, unless some procedural variation has been absorbed under Section 301 by the applicable court. The litigant is wise to follow the U.S. Arbitration Act rule *with one very important exception.*

The statute of limitations applicable to litigation growing out of a labor agreement cannot be absorbed from the U.S. Arbitration Act because that act specifically provides that the 90-day litigation rule is not applicable to labor agreements (not applicable to employees in interstate commerce).

Because of this apparent vacuum in the U.S Arbitration Act for limitations for labor arbitration litigation, no limitation could be absorbed from the Act into Section 301. The Supreme Court in 1966

[28]387 F. Supp. at 161, 88 LRRM at 2150. An unusual aberration developed in *Falls Stamping and Welding Co. v. International Union, etc.*, 416 F. Supp. 574, 93 LRRM 2546 (N.D. Ohio 1976), wherein the plaintiff initiated an action pursuant to Section 10 of the Arbitration Act and the arbitrator's award was vacated without any reference to Section 301. Thus, some courts may go further than applying the Arbitration Act once jurisdiction is found under Section 301, and may instead base jurisdiction on the Arbitration Act alone.

[29]500 F.2d 921, 86 LRRM 3240 (2d Cir. 1974).

[30]*Id.* at 923, 86 LRRM at 3241. *To the same effect, Metal Products Workers Union, Local 1645, UAW v. Torrington Co.*, note 25 *supra.*

[31]*Local 251, Teamsters v. Narragansett Improvement Co.*, 503 F.2d 309, 311-12, 87 LRRM 2279, 2280 (1st Cir. 1974), wherein the court said it " 'must grant ... an order [to confirm an award] unless the award is vacated, modified, or corrected as prescribed in sections 10 and 11 of the Arbitration Act' 9 U.S.C. § 9 (1970)."

[32]*Textile Workers Union v. Lincoln Mills*, 353 U.S. 448, 456-57, 40 LRRM 2113, 2116. (1957).

filled the vacuum by holding in *UAW v. Hoosier Cardinal*[33] that the appropriate state statute of limitations should be used. The Supreme Court explained that using the appropriate state statute of limitations would not impair the goal of uniformity enunciated as a labor policy.[34] The limitation statutes are different in various states, and in some states there are several such statutes.

The Second Circuit Court in *West Rock Lodge No. 2120, IAM v. Geometric Tool Co.*,[35] on the other hand, bent the *Hoosier-Cardinal* rule by refusing to absorb the Connecticut statute of limitations into Section 301, even though the district court had done so. The Circuit Court said the Connecticut rule requiring an arbitration award to be rendered within 60 days after the close of a hearing was incompatible with national labor policy. The rule was considered to be too strict.

Then in 1981, the Supreme Court began to shake its 1966 *Hoosier-Cardinal* rule quite hard. A car washer had been discharged for falsifying time cards and the arbitrator had sustained the discharge. The grievant's personal lawyer then filed under Section 301 a fair representation suit 17 months after the award had been issued. The claim in the suit was that the grievant's rights under the labor agreement had been breached both by the union and by the employer. In *United Parcel Service, Inc. v. Mitchell,*[36] the Second Circuit had felt obligated to apply the New York breach-of-contract statute of limitations which permitted suits to be filed for six years after the alleged breach occurred. This decision was then reviewed by the Supreme Court. The Court reversed the court below (in an opinion written by Justice Rehnquist), holding that use of the six-year limitation, although technically correct under *Hoosier-Cardinal,* would keep arbitration awards in limbo for up to six years and could easily cause labor arbitration to "become unworkable."[37] The Supreme Court, therefore, selected another statute of limitations rule it found in New York; the Court barred the fair representation suit[38] by applying a 90-day limitation

---

[33]383 U.S. 696, 61 LRRM 2545 (1966). *See also Howerton v. J. Christenson Co.,* 76 LRRM 2937 (N.D. Calif. 1971).

[34]The difficulty with the *Hoosier Cardinal* rule began at its inception. Time periods in statutes of limitations applying to breaches of written contracts are longer than those in rules used when the agreements are oral. However, even though labor agreements are written, the shorter period applicable to oral agreements is used. In a subsequent case, the Supreme Court commented:

We said in *Hoosier Cardinal* that one of the leading federal policies in this area is the "relatively rapid disposition of labor disputes." 383 U.S. at 707. ... This policy was one of the reasons the Court in *Hoosier Cardinal* chose the generally shorter period for actions based on an *oral contract* rather than that for actions upon a *written contract.* [Emphasis added.]

[35]406 F.2d 284, 70 LRRM 2228 (2d Cir. 1968).

[36]*United Parcel Service, Inc. v. Mitchell,* 624 F.2d 394, 105 LRRM 2301 (2d Cir. 1980).

[37]*United Parcel Service, Inc. v. Mitchell,* 451 U.S. 56, 107 LRRM 2001 (1981).

[38]*See* Chapter XXIII, Fair Representation Obligations.

that technically was applicable not to breach-of-contract actions but to suits for vacation of awards.

This switch from the technically correct six-year limitation rule to the 90-day limitation rule caused Justices Blackmun, Stewart and Stevens to assert in their separate opinions in *United Parcel Service, Inc. v. Mitchell* that the *Hoosier-Cardinal* rule that had been established in 1966 should be abandoned and the National Labor Relations Act six-month limitation rule (Section 10 (b)) should be absorbed into Section 301, so that suits under that section could have a uniform limitations rule. Justice Stewart explained that the six-month rule contained in Section 10(b) was undoubtedly the limitation desired by Congress because the six months rule had been set forth "to protect the collective bargaining systems from delayed attack."[39]

Since three Supreme Court justices have become critical both of the lack of uniformity and of the difficulty in applying the *Hoosier-Cardinal* rule, and believe a uniform federal rule should be used, a change may occur in the future. Litigants, therefore, should be on the alert, since the *Hoosier-Cardinal* rule in effect for 15 years has been challenged in *United Parcel Service, Inc.*

The confusion in the application of the *Hoosier-Cardinal* rule was also revealed in *Sine v. Teamsters, Local 992*,[40] decided by the Fourth Circuit. Ronald Sine and another grievant had brought a fair representation suit under Section 301[41] and the U.S. Arbitration Act.[42] A private lawyer was asking for the back pay not granted by the arbitrator. The Fourth Circuit did not even discuss the breach-of-contract statute of limitations, even though the Second Circuit in *United Parcel Service, Inc.* had chosen that rule, believing it was the proper one to be applied to the same type of suit under the *Hoosier-Cardinal* rule. The Maryland limitation rule selected by the Fourth Circuit barred a fair representation suit after 30 days following issuance of the award, rather than after 90 days (the New York rule selected by the Supreme Court) or 2,190 days (the New York rule selected by the Second Circuit).

The Fourth Circuit barred the fair representation suit because:

> The award here was issued on August 22, 1978 .... Plaintiffs filed the present action on November 20, 1978, which is more than thirty days after they received the award; thus, the action is untimely ....[43]

---

[39]451 U.S. at 68, 107 LRRM at 2005.

[40]644 F.2d 997, 107 LRRM 2089 (4th Cir. 1981). *See also Liotta v. National Forge Co.,* 629 F.2d 903, 105 LRRM 2636 (3d Cir. 1980), *cert. denied,* 451 U.S. 970, 107 LRRM 2144 (1981).

[41]29 U.S.C. § 185 (1964).

[42]9 U.S.C. § 1 *et. seq.* (1947).

[43]644 F.2d at 1002-03, 107 LRRM at 2093.

The great variation in state limitation rules which can be selected under the *Hoosier-Cardinal* rule may possibly cause the National Labor Relations Act rule to be established as a uniform rule even though the *Hoosier-Cardinal* rule has been the rule for years; the *caveat* that a change may be made should not be ignored.

CHAPTER II

The Submission of a Case to Arbitration

A case is submitted to arbitration either pursuant to a provision of a labor agreement which provides that future disputes will be submitted to arbitration, or pursuant to a separate agreement to submit a particular dispute to arbitration.

SUBMISSION OF A DISPUTE UNDER THE ARBITRATION PROVISIONS OF A LABOR AGREEMENT

Generally, the obligation to arbitrate is found in a clause in a labor agreement that provides that disputes which cannot be resolved by agreement will be resolved by arbitration. The initiation of arbitration is usually by a "demand," normally in letter form, requesting that a particular grievance be submitted to, and resolved by, arbitration.

This normal practice has been codified in Rule 7 of the Voluntary Labor Arbitration Rules of the American Arbitration Association as follows:

> 7. *Initiation Under an Arbitration Clause in a Collective Bargaining Agreement*—Arbitration under an arbitration clause in a collective bargaining agreement under these Rules may be initiated by either party in the following manner:
>
> (a) By giving written notice to the other party of intention to arbitrate (Demand), which notice shall contain a statement setting forth the nature of the dispute and the remedy sought, and
>
> (b) By filing at any Regional Office of the AAA three copies of said notice, together with a copy of the collective bargaining agreement, or such parts thereof as relate to the dispute, including the arbitration provisions. After the Arbitrator is appointed, no new or different claim may be submitted, except with the consent of the Arbitrator and all other parties.[1]

The party receiving the demand typically responds by complying with the contractual procedures for selecting an arbitrator[2] or by submitting the grievance to a previously agreed upon arbitrator.

---

[1] American Arbitration Association, *Voluntary Labor Arbitration Rules,* Rule 7, as amended, 1979.

[2] The process of selecting the arbitrator or the board of arbitration to whom the grievance claim will be submitted is discussed in detail in Chapter V.

The submission of a particular grievance claim often takes the form of a joint letter asking the arbitrator to determine the merits of the grievance, citing the specific provision of the labor agreement in dispute, and, by reference to the arbitration clause in the labor agreement, advising the arbitrator of the scope of his or her authority.[3]

In many instances the statement of the grievance, as originally written by the employee or the union steward, will be a claim of a violation of a provision in the labor agreement. This original written statement may be very poorly worded. A problem arises when the representatives from both parties are unable to agree among themselves on a revised statement which would pose a more precise question for the arbitrator. The failure of parties to frame issues more precisely at this stage seems due to a fear that the representatives on the side that loses will be blamed for the loss because of the revision in the wording of the grievance.[4]

Arbitrator Joseph Brandschain has examined the reasons for the lack of precision in grievance formulation:

> In some cases ... the company, through its foreman, shop superintendent, or general manager, may have answered the grievance by letter or put its position in writing on the grievance form, giving reasons for the denial of the complaint. The company may have restated or revised that position through two, three, or four subsequent steps of the grievance procedure.[5]

Some arbitrators, in an effort to clarify the grievance, shift the issue and the award is subject to vacation. In *International Union, United Automobile, Aerospace and Agricultural Implement Workers of America and Its Local 800 v. Sivyer Steel Castings Co.*,[6] the United States District Court for the Northern District of Illinois rendered a very brief decision vacating an award by Arbitrator Robert Howlett (the Chairman of the Arbitration Board in this case):

> Defendant's motion for summary judgment sustained for the reason that the arbitrator exceeded the authority granted by the Collective Bargaining Agreement between the parties and also the issues submitted to him for determination. Plaintiff's cross motion for summary judgment is denied.

---

[3]Russell, RUSSELL ON ARBITRATION, Seventeenth Edition, A. Walton, ed. (London: Stevens, 1963), p. 158; Prasow and Peters, ARBITRATION AND COLLECTIVE BARGAINING (New York: McGraw-Hill, 1970), pp. 17–24; Merrill, *A Labor Arbitrator Views His Work*, 10 VANDERBILT L. REV. 789, 793 (1957); Kagel, *Labor and Commercial Arbitration Under the California Arbitration Statute*, 38, CALIF. L. REV. 799, 804–805 (1950). *See also* Davey, *Hazards in Labor Arbitration*, 1 IND. & LAB. REL. REV. 386, 398 (1948).

[4]Mentschikoff, *The Significance of Arbitration—A Preliminary Inquiry*, 17 LAW & CONTEMP. PROB. 698, 705 (1952).

[5]Brandschain, *Preparation and Trial of a Labor Arbitration Case*, THE PRACTICAL LAWYER, Vol. 18, No. 7 (Nov. 1972).

[6]Case No. 63-C-1991 (N.D. Ill. Aug. 26, 1965).

In *Local 791, International Union of Electrical, Radio and Machine Workers, AFL-CIO v. Magnavox Co.,*[7] the Sixth Circuit affirmed the District Court's order setting aside an arbitration award because the arbitrator had exceeded the authority conferred on him by the labor agreement.

SUBMISSION OF A DISPUTE BY A SUBMISSION AGREEMENT

Sometimes, where the labor agreement provides for submission of future disputes to arbitration, the dispute to be submitted is identified on a "submission agreement."[8] Such an agreement is always necessary where the contract does not provide for submission of future disputes to arbitration or where it provides for arbitration of a dispute only if the parties agree to submit a specific dispute.

The "submission agreement" sets forth the question to be resolved, the relief desired, and identifies the arbitrator or the arbitration board that the parties have selected.[9] It usually grants the arbitrator or board jurisdiction over the subject of the dispute and empowers the arbitrator or board to decide conclusively all questions of law or fact which must be decided to resolve the dispute.

Arbitrator Joseph Brandschain explained the wisdom of using agreed stipulations of facts and questions to be decided. The procedure resembles a combination of a complaint and answer in court litigation. Brandschain wrote: "[I]n view of the formlessness of the grievance, it would be well worthwhile to obtain, before going to the hearing, an agreed stipulation of the facts or questions that the arbitrator is to decide. This would be the ideal situation. However, experience has shown that many fruitless hours are wasted in attempts to reach such stipulations, the agreement usually being frustrated by objections of one party or the other to particular words or phrases."[10] (It should be remembered again that often we are dealing with lay "lawyers" on one or both sides.)

---

[7]286 F.2d 465, 47 LRRM 2296 (6th Cir. 1960).

[8]Goldberg, A Lawyer's Guide to Commercial Arbitration, Second Edition, (Philadelphia: ALI-ABA Committee on Continuing Professional Education, 1977).

[9]Six state statutes require that the submission agreement name the arbitrator or arbitrators. Colorado (Colo. Rev. Stat. Ann. ch. 18, Rule 109(b) (Rules of Civ. Pro. 1970)); Georgia (Ga. Code Ann. § 7-201 (1936)); Iowa (Iowa Code Ann. § 679.2 (1950)); Kentucky (Ky. Rev. Stat. § 417.020 (1962)); Nebraska (Neb. Rev. Stat. § 25-2104 (1943)); and Tennessee (Tenn. code Ann. § 23-504 (1955)).

[10]Brandschain, *Preparation and Trial of a Labor Arbitration Case,* The Practical Lawyer, Vol. 18, No. 7 (Nov. 1972).

In *E. I. du Pont de Nemours & Co.*, [11] Arbitrator Begley wrote:

> This Board recognizes that a submission agreement is controlling upon the scope of arbitration and limits the jurisdiction of the Board to an answer to the sole question contained therein. This principle is well established in numerous judicial decisions, e.g., National Cash Register Co., 25 LA 313 (N.Y.S. Ct.); Farson vs. United Press Association, 27 LA 18 (N.Y.S. Ct.) . . . .

That awards should be vacated when the arbitrator resolves issues not presented in a stipulated question is now clear law. For example, in *Local 1078, United Automobile, Aircraft and Agricultural Implement Workers of America, AFL-CIO v. Anaconda American Brass Co.*, [12] the award was vacated because the arbitrator did not confine his award to a simple "yes" or "no" answer. The arbitrator developed a different question and then ruled on it, thereby exceeding the scope of the question. Likewise, in *Sperry Division, Sperry Rand Corp. v. Int'l. Union of Electrical Workers, Local 445*, [13] the award was vacated because the arbitrator did not confine his award to the questions submitted for decision. He also developed a different question and then ruled upon it, thereby exceeding the scope of the parties' submission.

A court vacated another award when the arbitrator departed from the issue presented for reasons of sympathy. The court held that the issue presented to the arbitrator was whether stealing is "just cause" for discharge. The arbitrator did not answer this specific question; instead, he reinstated an employee who had been discharged for stealing four cans of crabmeat. The Third Circuit pointed out that the question submitted to the arbitrator was very limited and that the arbitrator did not have the authority to consider the value of the theft as a mitigating circumstance. Once the act of stealing was proven and no longer in dispute, the "just cause" for discharge was proven. *Amalgamated Food & Allied Workers Union, Local 56 v. Great Atlantic and Pacific Tea Co.* [14]

Where the jurisdiction and/or remedial powers of the arbitrator or board are limited in the labor agreement, care must be exercised not to incorporate broader definitions in the submission agreement, since the submission agreement will control. For example, in *Railway Clerks v. Universal Carloading*, [15] the labor agreement provided that if

---

[11] 39 LA 1083, 1084 (Begley, 1962).
[12] 149 Conn. 687, 182 A.2d 623, 625 (1962).
[13] 33 N.Y.2d 517, 85 LRRM 2256 (1974).
[14] 415 F.2d 185, 71 LRRM 2966 (3d Cir. 1969).
[15] 1 Cal. App. 3d 145, 72 LRRM 2798 (1969). *See also Capital City Telephone Co. v. CWA*, 575 F.2d 655, 98 LRRM 2438 (8th Cir. 1978); *International Union of Electrical and Machine Workers of America, Local 1140, Inc. v. Portec*, 228 N.W.2d 239, 89 LRRM 2288 (Minn. 1975). A stipulation may turn out to be too narrow. In *Timm Industries, Inc.*, 9 LA 642 (Prasow, 1948),

the charges against the employee were not sustained, the employee shall be reinstated and paid for all time lost. The arbitrator ordered reinstatement, but declined to award back pay. In refusing the union's petition to correct the award, the court held that since the questions submitted to the arbitrator in the submission agreement were whether the company had acted properly when it terminated the employee and "[i]f not, what remedy is ordered?" the submission agreement superseded the labor agreement and the union could not object that no back pay was awarded or that the remedy was not to its liking. On the other hand, in *Food Workers v. A & P Tea Co.,*[16] the court vacated an award which did not reinstate an employee on the ground that the arbitrator's authority had been limited by a letter between the parties; the court held that the submission agreement, rather than the letter, determined the authority of the arbitrator.

EFFECT OF THE FAILURE TO BE SPECIFIC

A state court has stayed an arbitration proceeding until the specific issues to be arbitrated were made clear on the ground that the employer is entitled to be apprised of the specific provisions of the agreement sought to be enforced and the nature of the employer's breach.[17]

---

the stipulation limited the arbitrator to the consideration of one particular section of the collective agreement in determining the disposition to be made of the grievance. The company based its case on the management rights section, but the arbitrator stated that the introduction of the management rights provision was extraneous to the issue, as defined in the submission agreement, and he made his decision solely on the basis of the one section specified by the parties in the submission agreement. In *Michigan Consolidated Gas Co.,* 58 LA 1058 (Shister, 1972), the sole determination that the employer and union sought at the hearing was the constitutionality and/or legality of the company's action of putting into effect grooming standards governing the appearance of its employees while at work. The contract provided that, "Employees shall be as neat and clean of person as the job will permit." The union argued that the Company's implementation of that provision through the grooming standards was unreasonable, but the arbitrator determined that he could not rule whether the implementation was reasonable since the parties did not address themselves to that question. *See also Delta Lines v. Teamsters, Local 468,* 95 LRRM 2498 (Cal. Ct. App. 1977) (arbitrator who was called upon to decide sole issue whether employer had just cause under collective bargaining contract to discharge employee who failed to report for work exceeded his power in ordering employee's reinstatement with back pay); *Centre Stage Dinner Playhouse,* 67 LA 792 (Graham, 1976) (employer was not entitled to arbitrate issues arising after date of appointment of arbitrator, in the absence of the union's consent, where the contract provided that controversies shall be submitted to arbitration pursuant to the rules of the American Arbitration Association, which rules state that "after the arbitrator is appointed no new or different claim may be submitted to him except with the consent of the arbitrator and all other parties."); *League of Voluntary Hospitals,* 67 LA 293 (Gootnick, 1976) (arbitrator did not have authority to rule on union's demand for ruling on language of management rights clause of contract, which union presented for the first time in its post-hearing brief, under the parties' stipulation limiting the arbitrator's authority to "all of the written demands which have been presented by the parties.")

[16]415 F.2d 185, 71 LRRM 2966 (3d Cir. 1969).

[17]*Unipak Aviation Corp. v. Mantell,* 20 Misc.2d 1078, 196 N.Y.S.2d 126 (1959).

On the other hand, an arbitrator has ruled that where a violation of two clauses is alleged but only one clause was found to be involved, no basis for a claim of nonarbitrability existed.[18] Another arbitrator ruled that it was proper in a particular dispute to redefine the issue after the evidence was presented where such *post hoc* redefinition would not be an "expansion of the issue" that would "prejudice the company by a surprise presentation for which it was unprepared."[19]

Where the statement of the grievance is ambiguous, the arbitrator will sometimes clarify the issue to be determined. For instance, an arbitrator ruled that a claim by a company in its answer to a grievance that the union had violated the agreement by engaging in an illegal work stoppage was an issue in the case, in spite of the union's contention that this claim raised in the answer was a "new and separate matter," not part of the grievance. The arbitrator said:

> "Judged by any reasonable standard of grievance interpretation, the company was quite justified in treating the written grievance as having raised two problems, and in seeking to answer both complaints .... The company certainly had the right to explain the foreman-refusal to discuss the answer and claim that the men who had shut down their machines to seek such discussion were thereby in violation of the contract. To expect any closer relationship between a grievance and a grievance answer would be to attempt to bestow upon the labor-management grievance procedure a technical character which would equal or exceed even the highly complex struggle over pleadings in court cases, and I do not believe this is either intended or desirable."[20]

In *Procter & Gamble Co. v. Ind. Oil Workers*,[21] the court held that an arbitrator did not exceed his powers when he issued an award requiring an employer to reinstate with back pay a discharged employee, even though the section of the agreement under which the violation was found was not cited in the union's stipulation, since the section was cited by the employer as an affirmative defense.

Similarly, where an arbitration hearing was held even though the issues submitted were vague, the Sixth Circuit held that a federal district court had erred when it vacated the award on the grounds that the statement of the issue submitted was too vague.[22]

The need for specificity in the statement of the issue in dispute, however, was underscored by the Supreme Court's decision in *Boys*

---

[18] *Textile Paper Products Co.*, AAA Case No. 88-14 (Sanders, 1966).
[19] *Continental Can Co.*, AAA Case No. 45-17 (Sugerman, 1962).
[20] *Champion Spark Plug Co.*, AAA Case No. 41-17 (Rock, 1961).
[21] 386 F. Supp. 213, 87 LRRM 3179 (D.C. Md. 1974).
[22] *Kroger Co. v. Teamsters Local 661*, 380 F.2d 728, 65 LRRM 2573 (6th Cir. 1967).

Markets, Inc. v. Retail Clerks Union, Local 770.[23] There, the Court held that a federal district court may enjoin a strike in violation of a no-strike clause if the dispute involved is one that can be submitted to an arbitrator under the labor agreement. This means that before an injunction will issue to enjoin the strike action, a court is required to determine if the issue in dispute is one within the scope of the commitment to arbitrate in the labor agreement.[24]

This new involvement of courts in questions of labor agreement interpretation has also involved the courts in the process of clarification of issues for resolution by arbitrators. For example, the Second Circuit in *Ice Cream Drivers Local 757 v. Borden, Inc.*[25] held, relying specifically on *Boys Markets,* that the district court could rephrase and broaden the statement of the issue to be arbitrated to include " 'the disputes between [Borden and the union] arising out of Borden, Inc.'s closing of its manufacturing operations ... ' "[26] so that the dispute causing the strike which the court enjoined would find its resolution through arbitration.

In addition, the desired relief should be clearly requested in the submission presented to the arbitrator. The problem that can arise when the relief requested is not clear is illustrated by a decision of the Eighth Circuit in *Luggage & Novelty Workers Local 66 v. Neevel Luggage Mfg. Co., Inc.*[27] affirming a trial court's denial of enforcement of an award because the arbitrator granted relief beyond that requested by the submission. The question submitted was whether the layoff of certain employees was "improper under the terms of the contract between the parties." The arbitrator determined that the layoff was improper but then ordered that the employees be reinstated and paid for time lost. The trial court had denied enforcement of that part of the award granting back pay because the question of back pay was not

---

[23]398 U.S. 235, 74 LRRM 2257 (1970).

[24]The Supreme Court, in *Boys Markets,* neglected to articulate the standards to be applied by lower courts in determining whether a particular dispute is, in fact, subject to the mandatory grievance provisions of a specific collective bargaining agreement. Following the Court's decision, the Circuit Courts divided over the question whether a sympathy strike was over an "arbitrable grievance" and hence within the narrow exception to the Norris-LaGuardia Act established in *Boys Markets.* In *Buffalo Forge Co. v. Steelworkers,* 428 U.S. 397, 92 LRRM 3032 (1976), the Supreme Court held that its decision in *Boys Markets* was inapplicable to a case involving a refusal by a union, that had negotiated a no-strike agreement with the employer, to cross the picket lines of a sister local, since the strike was not over any dispute between the union and the employer that was even remotely subject to the arbitration provisions of the contract.

[25]433 F.2d 41, 75 LRRM 2481 (2d Cir. 1970), *cert. denied,* 401 U.S. 940, 76 LRRM 2576 (1971).

[26]433 F.2d at 46, 75 LRRM at 2484 (2d Cir. 1970).

[27]325 F.2d 992, 55 LRRM 2153 (8th Cir. 1964). *But see American Bosch Arma Corp. v. International Union of Elec. Workers Local 794,* 243 F. Supp. 493, 59 LRRM 2798 (N.D. Miss. 1965). Moreover, the Eighth Circuit decision should not cause one to conclude that an arbitrator does not have broad remedial powers, a topic fully discussed in Chapter XVIII.

"specifically submitted for arbitration." In affirming, the court of appeals relied on the *Steelworkers Trilogy,* [28] holding that a party cannot be required to submit to arbitration any dispute which it has not agreed so to submit. [29]

Arbitrators as well as courts have pointed out the need for care in stating the relief desired in the submission. For example, Arbitrator Whitley P. McCoy held in *International Harvester Company, Springfield Works*[30] that a request for retroactive pay for all men in a department affected by a particular breach of contract was too general to permit an award of back pay. McCoy held that if an employee felt he was denied pay, he was required to file a claim for the specific sum he believed was due and to support the claim with evidence. In *Lindell II,*[31] Arbitrator Torosian held that he could not grant a union's request that an employee be made whole for lost earnings, since the employer and the union, in framing the issue to be decided by the arbitrator, limited it to whether the employee quit his employment or was discharged by the employer.

While not conclusive, these cases highlight the fact that if care is not exercised in drafting the question to be resolved and the relief requested, the award may not resolve the dispute and the stage may be set for additional litigation.

SUBMISSION OF MULTIPLE GRIEVANCES TO ONE ARBITRATOR

When a union attempts to submit two or more nonrelated grievances to the same arbitrator in the same hearing,[32] a procedural issue

---

[28]*United Steelworkers of America v. American Mfg. Co.,* 363 U.S. 564, 46 LRRM 2414 (1960); *United Steelworkers of America v. Warrior & Gulf Navigation Co.,* 363 U.S. 574, 46 LRRM 2416 (1960); *United Steelworkers of America v. Enterprise Wheel & Car Corp.,* 363 U.S. 593, 46 LRRM 2423 (1960).

[29]325 F.2d 992, 994, 55 LRRM 2153 (8th Cir. 1964). *See also Retail Store Employees Union Local 782 v. Sav-On Groceries,* 508 F.2d 500, 88 LRRM 3205 (10th Cir. 1975); *Delta Lines, Inc. v. Teamsters, Local 85,* 409 F. Supp. 873, 93 LRRM 2037 (N.D. Cal. 1976).

[30]Case No. 28 (McCoy, 1949) (unpublished). *See also Geneva Industries, Inc.,* 66-3 ARB ¶ 8852 (Davis, 1966); *Caterpillar Tractor Co.,* 65-1 ARB ¶ 8187 (Dworkin, 1964); *Greer Steel Company,* 68-1 ARB ¶ 8366 (McIntosh, 1968); *United Engineering & Foundry Co.,* 70-2 ARB ¶ 8644 (Dybeck, 1970); *General Dynamics Corp.,* 59 LA 1175 (Gentile, 1972); *United Telephone System,* 64 LA 525 (Cohen, 1975). *But see Bethlehem Steel Corp.,* 54 LA 445 (Gill, 1969); *General Services Administration,* 63 LA 487 (Lippman, 1974).

[31]58 LA 391 (Torosian, 1972).

[32]The term "multiple grievance arbitration" must be distinguished from the term "multiple grievants" which refers to a single grievance involving two or more employees directly affected by a single management action (*e.g.,* assignment of a low-seniority employee to a vacancy when several other employees with higher seniority have bid for the vacancy), or where two or more employees are affected by what is asserted to be the same management action occurring at different times (*e.g.,* temporary transfer of three different employees to the same lower-rated job on three different days).

often arises. If the labor agreement expressly provides that more than
one grievance may be submitted at one hearing to one arbitrator, the
answer is found in the agreement. But where the labor agreement is
silent or vague on this matter, arbitrators examine the more general
language relating to the grievance procedure to find the answer and
generally permit a group of grievances, absent other controlling factors,[33] to be submitted at one time.

Arbitrator John F. Sullivan, in *Automatic Division of Yale &
Towne,*[34] held that more than one grievance could be submitted to a
single arbitrator where the contractual procedure stated that it was intended "to settle grievances in an orderly and expeditious manner."
Likewise, Arbitrator Robben Fleming in *Standard Oil Co.*[35] said that
a party is required to submit more than one issue in a single arbitration if the other party so desires, where the contract does not specifically deal with arbitration of multiple grievances and where "there is
nothing in the past practice of the parties which furnishes a reliable
guideline for reaching a decision as to what the parties intended." The
fact that the grievance procedure section of the contract referred to "a
question" and "the subject" in the singular "does not indicate that
single, rather than multiple, issues were to be heard in the actual arbitration proceeding." Fleming went on to say that where neither the
contract nor past practice provides a "satisfactory guide," it is fair to
assume:

> [T]hat the parties intended their arbitration clause to have the interpreta-
> tion commonly accorded such clauses in the day-to-day practice of the in-
> dustrial relations world. This practice is clearly in favor of multiple issues
> in a single arbitration proceeding. This practice is so universal that a con-
> trary result should only be reached where the contract specifically indicates

---

[33]*Standard Oil Co.*, AAA Case No. 3-3 (Fleming, 1959) (multiple grievances allowed since
there was no past practice furnishing a reliable guideline); *West Va. Pulp & Paper Co.*, 71-1
ARB ¶ 8086 (Seinsheimer, 1971) (multiple grievances allowed, but arbitrator noted that a
technical case may arise which would require a specially experienced arbitrator and thus would
not be subject to combination); *Chamberlain Corp.*, 49 LA 355 (Duff, 1967) (multiple
grievances must be submitted jointly unless the contract or past practice requires a contrary procedure). *See also Modine Manufacturing Company*, (Smith, 1971) (unpublished); *Crown Zellerbach Corp.*, 65-2 ARB ¶ 8573 (Carmichael, 1965); *see also Amarlite, Division of Anaconda
Aluminum Co.*, 65-2 ARB ¶ 8729 (Ray, 1965).

[34]*F.M. & C.S.* No. 63A/1969 (Sullivan, 1963) (unpublished). *See also Pittsburgh
Metallurgical Co., Inc.*, AAA Case No. 6-7 (Luskin, 1959) where it was held that even when the
term "grievance" was used in the singular, a union had the right to combine grievances in the
absence of express language to the contrary. *But cf. American Mach. & Foundry Co.*, AAA Case
No. 28-9 (Norton, 1961) involving the term "grievance" in the singular, but buttressed by a past
practice of submitting only one case at a time.

[35]*Standard Oil Co.*, AAA Case No. 3-3 (Fleming, 1959).

that such was the intention of the parties. This contract does not express any such intent.[36]

In *Perfection Biscuit Co.*,[37] on the other hand, Arbitrator O'Malley held that where the labor agreement referred to the processing "of a grievance" to arbitration, more than one grievance could not be submitted simultaneously to one arbitrator over the employer's objection. Similarly, in *Longview Fibre Co.*,[38] Arbitrator Smith held that he did not have the authority to decide the merits of two grievances in addition to another grievance before him since the employer agreed to submit only the one grievance for arbitration. Arbitrator Smith so held notwithstanding the fact that it appeared evident to the arbitrator that the three grievances were sufficiently identical that they could be resolved as one grievance and covered within a single submission agreement.

In *Monongahela Power Co.*,[39] Arbitrator Blue held that in deciding the merits of one grievance, he did not have the authority to declare that two other grievances be forfeited in future arbitrations since the union had refused to submit any grievances other than the main grievance. Arbitrator Blue stated that he "can rule only that there was no unanimity of agreement as to the scope of this arbitration or his jurisdiction,"[40] and concluded that the issue of whether the union's failure to submit the other two grievances constituted a bar to arbitration is to be resolved by another arbitrator.[41]

---

[36]*Id. See also Pittsburgh Metallurgical Co.*, AAA Case No. 6-7 (Luskin, 1959); *Hamilton Cosco*, AAA Case No. 32-5 (Fisher, 1961); *Anaconda American Brass Co.*, AAA Case No. 130-16 (Keffe, 1969); *Waller Bros. Stone Co.*, AAA Case No. 22-13 (Luskin, 1960); *Dragon Cement Co.*, AAA Case No. 48-3 (Zack, 1962); *Fuller Co.*, AAA Case No. 63-20 (Unterberger, 1963); *Goodman Mfg. Co.*, AAA Case No. 64-15 (Jaffee, 1963); *Cleveland Pneumatic Tool Co.*, 54 LA 371 (Belkin, 1970).

[37]*F.M. & C.S. No.* 64A/1921 (O'Malley, 1963) (unpublished). *See also Phillips Fibers Corp.*, 71-2 ARB ¶ 8450 (Amis, 1971); *Charles Taylor Sons Co.*, 70-2 ARB ¶ 8607 (Volz, 1970); *American Metal Climax, Inc.*, 69-2 ARB ¶ 8855 (Dworkin, 1969); *Agrico Chemical Co.*, 51 LA 1001 (Traynor, 1968); *Wilcox Electric Co.*, 68-2 ARB ¶ 8608 (Solomon, 1968); *Day & Zimmerman, Inc.*, 51 LA 215 (Marshall, 1968); *Crown Zellerbach Corp.*, 21 ALAA ¶ 72,508 (Larson, 1964); *Remington Rand Univac*, 42 LA 65 (Lockhart, 1964); *Anaconda American Brass Co.*, AAA Case No. 51-12 (Turkus, 1962); *Erwin Mills*, AAA Case No. 88-10 (Porter, 1966); *Macy's New York*, AAA Case No. 91-8 (Rubin, 1966).

[38]63 LA 529 (Smith, 1974).

[39]64 LA 1210 (Blue, 1975).

[40]*Id.* at 1214.

[41]In *Wagner Castings Company* (Malinowski, 1972) (unpublished), the arbitrator held that an employer was not obligated to submit multiple grievances where there was no specific language in the contract obligating the Company to present more than one grievance and no such obligation could be found from the parties' prior course of conduct. The arbitrator noted that on those occasions when multiple grievances were presented to the same arbitrator it was a matter of mutual consent and agreement and not a matter of unilateral right in one party. The arbitrator also noted as significant that the parties used the singular form of the noun "grievance."

Some arbitrators have permitted more than one grievance to be presented over the objection of the employer if the grievances were all processed through the steps of the grievance procedure simultaneously and reached arbitration at the same time.[42] Yet another arbitrator, to the contrary, said that simultaneous processing does not authorize the submission of a group of grievances to one arbitrator.[43] Similarly, a court directed that three factually unrelated grievances should be submitted to three different arbitration boards:

> To permit an accumulation of disputes and then require that one board pass on all would be like requiring three unrelated matters in court litigation be tried by the same jury. ... If complaints are of sufficient importance to require arbitration, the saving of some expense cannot outweigh the importance of having experienced and satisfactory arbitrators in each specific problem which they will be summoned to consider.[44]

Generally, courts hold that the arbitrability of multiple disputes before a single arbitrator is an issue which must be resolved by the arbitrator.[45] In *UAW v. Robertshaw Controls Co.*,[46] the court refused to grant the UAW's request for an order directing the employer to submit several unrelated grievances to a single arbitrator on the ground that an arbitrator had previously held that the applicable labor agreement did not require that result.

Likewise, in *American Can Co. v. Papermakers, Local 412*,[47] the court held that an employer was not entitled to an order vacating an arbitrator's determination that the labor agreement permitted the hearing of multiple grievances by a single arbitrator, since the question was one of procedure to be determined by an arbitrator and not by the court. In *Chemical Workers v. Imco Container Co.*,[48] the court

---

[42]*Koppers Co.*, 33 LA 392 (Schedler, 1959); *Armstrong Cork Co.*, 23 LA 13 (Williams, 1954); *W. Va. Pulp & Paper Co.*, 71-1 ARB ¶ 8086 (Seinsheimer, 1970).

[43]*Cit-Con Oil Corp.*, 24 LA 186 (Morvant, 1955).

[44]*Parker White Metal Co. v. Mine Workers Union*, 45 Erie Co. L.J. 315, 54 LRRM 2797 (C.P. Erie Co., Pa. 1962).

[45]That questions of procedural arbitrability are for the arbitrator and not the court is settled by *John Wiley & Sons, Inc. v. Livingston*, 376 U.S. 543, 55 LRRM 2769 (1964), a case that will be frequently cited throughout this book. Of course, the question of what is substantive and what is procedural has always plagued courts, and its resolution is no less difficult in this area than it is elsewhere. Several lower courts have held that whether or not multiple grievances should be arbitrated jointly before a single arbitrator or separately in different arbitration proceedings is a procedural matter of contract interpretation and is for the arbitrator and not the court to decide. *American Sterilizer Co. v. International U. UAW, Local 832*, 341 F. Supp. 522, 80 LRRM 2319 (W.D. Pa. 1972); *Fitchburg Paper Company v. MacDonald*, 242 F. Supp. 502, 60 LRRM 2217 (D. Mass. 1965); *Teamsters Local 469 v. Hess Oil & Chem. Corp.*, 226 F. Supp. 452, 55 LRRM 2475 (D. N.J. 1964); *Traylor Eng. & Mfg. Div. of Fuller Co. v. United Steelworkers*, 220 F. Supp. 896, 54 LRRM 2106 (E.D. Pa. 1963); *Avon Products, Inc. v. International U. UAW, Local 710*, 386 F.2d 651, 67 LRRM 2001 (8th Cir. 1961).

[46]63 LRRM 2348 (S.D. Ohio 1966).

[47]356 F. Supp. 495, 82 LRRM 3055 (E.D. Pa. 1973).

[48]78 LRRM 2014 (S.D. Ind. 1971).

held that an arbitration award that determined more than one issue in a single hearing was not violative of a clause in the labor agreement if the arbitrator can "find his decision within the terms of this agreement," even though the arbitrator's decision was based both on the experience of others and his own general background in labor law and arbitration.

Similarly, in *Fitchburg Paper Co. v. MacDonald*[49] and *Teamsters Local 469 v. Hess Oil & Chemical Corp.*,[50] the courts ruled that the procedural issue in dispute was one for an arbitrator, not for the court, to resolve and accordingly ordered the issue to be arbitrated. In *American Sterilizer Co. v. Auto Workers*,[51] the court held that a dispute over the submission of multiple grievances is for an arbitrator, not for a court to determine. The fact that the contract speaks only in the singular when using the term "grievance" is not controlling.

While one court took judicial notice of the convenience and expediency with which one arbitrator could hear and resolve a series of grievances, it similarly ruled that the issue was one for the arbitrator to resolve.[52] In another case, however, the court ordered that all arbitration proceedings instituted by a union should be consolidated into one proceeding on the ground that the interests of all the parties involved were common. All the grievances involved an interpretation of a consumer price index contract provision.[53]

Arbitrator Turkus in *Anaconda American Brass Co.*[54] decided against multiple grievance arbitration where the union had submitted nine separate and different grievances to a single arbitrator and where the individual grievances had arisen at various times over an 11-month period. He held that the resolution of the procedural issue required the arbitrator to ascertain the parties' contractual intent; he rejected the view that consideration of efficiency, expedition, and economy should be controlling. He found that one arbitrator did not have authority to hear multiple grievances because (i) references in the grievance procedure were in the singular; (ii) a special procedure was established for "technical" disputes and disputes relating to discharge and discipline cases (indicating the parties did not want those kinds of cases, at least, to be arbitrated with other types of disputes); and (iii) the parties' consistent past practice had been to arbitrate cases separately and individually. While noting that the parties had, on one occasion, mutually agreed to submit multiple cases to arbitration, he

---

[49]242 F. Supp. 502, 60 LRRM 2217 (D. Mass. 1965).

[50]226 F. Supp. 452, 55 LRRM 2475 (D. N.J. 1964).

[51]341 F. Supp. 522, 80 LRRM 2319 (W.D. Pa. 1972).

[52]*Traylor Eng. & Mfg. Div. of Fuller Co. v. United Steelworkers of America*, 220 F. Supp. 896, 54 LRRM 2106 (E.D. Pa. 1963).

[53]*American Broadcasting Co. v. Brandt*, 72 LRRM 2210 (N.Y. Sup. Ct. 1969).

[54]39 LA 814 (Turkus, 1962).

ruled that this one exception did not change the understood practice without a specific mutual agreement.

In *Harshaw Chemical*,[55] Arbitrator Seinsheimer decided that multiple grievances could be decided in a single proceeding if (i) the grievances to be arbitrated all reached the arbitration stage at the same time and (ii) they involved issues which were not so dissimilar as to affect the parties' selection of the arbitrator. Likewise, Arbitrator Dworkin in *Johnson Bronze Co.*[56] required the employer to present multiple grievances to arbitration where the grievances were not numerous and were processed at approximately the same time. Arbitrator Dworkin went on to say, however, that the union waived its right to insist on multiple grievance arbitration when it sent separate submission letters to the Federal Mediation and Conciliation Service for each grievance. In *American Metal Climax, Inc.*,[57] Arbitrator Dworkin held that considerable weight should be given to past practices and, in the absence of such past practice, the controlling question should be whether a party is unduly prejudiced by the multiple grievance procedure. He held in that case that three "run-of-the-mill" disciplinary cases were sufficiently similar and that it would not be "burdensome" to the employer to arbitrate them together.

In *Vancouver Plywood Co.*,[58] Arbitrator Emery decided that the company improperly refused to agree to arbitrate the timeliness and the merits of the same grievance in the same hearing even though the arbitration provision plainly stated that "not more than one grievance shall be presented at any arbitration hearing unless the same principle in the application of the contract is involved." The arbitrator reasoned that even though timeliness and the case on the merits do not involve "the same principle," the Supreme Court in *John Wiley & Sons, Inc. v. Livingston*[59] has stated that the policy behind federal labor law is to regard procedural questions as aspects of the dispute and not as a separate issue.

THE SIGNIFICANCE OF THE AGREEMENT TO BE BOUND BY THE AWARD

The statutes of five states require that the parties specifically agree, either in the labor agreement or in the submission agreement, to be

---

[55] 44 LA 97 (Seinsheimer, 1965).
[56] 41 LA 961 (Dworkin, 1963).
[57] 69-2 ARB ¶ 8855 (Dworkin, 1969).
[58] 62 LA 592 (Emery, 1974).
[59] 376 U.S. 543, 55 LRRM 2769 (1964).

bound by the award,[60] and in one state it is required that the parties post bonds to guarantee compliance with the award.[61] However, the most important reason why the parties should specifically agree to be bound by the arbitrator's decision is to avoid relitigation of the same issue by the National Labor Relations Board (NLRB). In fact, the Board has announced that it will refrain from asserting its jurisdiction, even though a charge is filed raising an issue within the Board's jurisdiction, where an arbitrator's award has adequately resolved the issue.[62] More recently, the Board has specifically held that the federal labor law requires the parties to a contract to honor their contractual obligation to arbitrate rather than to ignore their agreed-upon procedure for the sake of pursuing other legal remedies under the LMRA.[63] This deference to arbitration, however, is contingent upon the parties having agreed to be bound by the award. This requirement that there be an agreement to be bound is one of the so-called *Spielberg* requirements set up by the Board in its *Spielberg* decision.[64]

The agreement to be bound can either be in writing in the labor agreement or in the submission agreement, or it can be implied from a uniform practice of submitting disputes to arbitration and complying with them.[65] Where a "claim of reservation" is made by a party about compliance with an award, the Board will not defer to the award.

---

[60]Colorado (COLO. REV. STAT. ANN. ch. 18, Rule 109(b) (Rules of Civ. Pro. 1970)); Kentucky (KY. REV. STAT. ¶ 417.020 (1962)); Michigan (MICH. STAT. ANN. ¶ 417.454 (10.3) (1968)); New Mexico (N.M. STAT. ANN. ¶ 22-3-4 (1953)); and Texas (TEX. REV. CIV. STAT. ANN. art. 242 (1959)).

[61]South Carolina (S. C. CODE ANN. § 10-1901 (1962)).

[62]Section 10(a) of the LMRA provides that the NLRB is empowered to prevent any person from engaging in an unfair labor practice and that this power shall not be affected by any other means of adjustment or prevention established by agreement. However, the Act also provides in Section 203(d) that "[f]inal adjustment by a method agreed upon by the parties is hereby declared to be the desirable method for settlement of grievance disputes arising over the application or interpretation of an existing collective-bargaining agreement." The Board has a problem of harmonizing its obligation under Section 10(a) to prevent unfair labor practices with its obligation to promote the private resolution of grievance disputes over matters such as discharges, which may involve matters which might well be considered an unfair labor practice. The balance between these two statutory objectives has been obtained by the development of a Board policy of deferring to an arbitration award previously issued by an arbitrator involving conduct which might constitute an unfair labor practice under Section 8 if the Board finds that the arbitration procedure was fair and regular, that all parties agreed to be bound by the award, and the decision of the arbitrator was not repugnant to the purposes of the Act. These three standards generate procedural considerations in arbitration and are referred to in various places in this study as the Spielberg requirements because the case in which they were first enunciated was *Spielberg Mfg. Co.*, 112 NLRB 1080, 36 LRRM 1152 (1955).

[63]*Collyer Insulated Wire*, 192 NLRB 150, 77 LRRM 1931 (1971).

[64]*Spielberg Mfg. Co.*, 112 NLRB 1080, 36 LRRM 1152 (1955).

[65]In *Denver-Chicago Trucking Co.*, 132 NLRB 1416, 1421, 48 LRRM 1524 (1961), the Board based its finding that the parties had agreed to be bound by a Joint Grievance Committee's statement that the parties had followed the contractual grievance procedure for 18 years, and that no "claim of reservation" had ever been made by any party. *See also Local 18, Operating Engineers*, 145 NLRB 1492, 55 LRRM 1188 (1964).

Thus, in *Hershey Chocolate Corp.*,[66] an attorney for some of the grievants advised the arbitrator of his intention to seek "other legal recourse" should the award be unfavorable, and hence the Board refused to defer to it because the employees had not agreed to be bound by it.

The Third Circuit, however, questioned the Board's refusal in *Hershey Chocolate* to defer, saying it doubted "whether the Board in this instance wisely rejected the arbitrator's decision."[67] Since that decision, the Board has deferred to awards even where one party asserted that the award was "tainted" by the unwillingness of the other party to be completely bound.[68] However, in a more recent decision, the Board, in *Jacobs Transfer, Inc.*,[69] refused to defer to an award where the grievant did not voluntarily submit to be bound by the arbitration procedures.

SECURING PARTICIPATION OF ALL INTERESTED PARTIES

Although most disputes submitted to arbitration are bilateral, in some situations a union not a party to the collective bargaining agreement from which the arbitration arose has a direct and substantial interest in the outcome of the proceeding. A court has denied enforcement of an award adversely affecting the interests of a nonparticipating union[70] and arbitrators have discussed cases on the ground that a binding award could not issue unless another union was a party.[71] Also, the NLRB now states it will not defer to an award if the rights of a union not a party to the arbitration would be affected.[72]

The most common examples of such trilateral controversies are

---

[66]129 NLRB 1052, 47 LRRM 1130 (1960), *enforcement denied,* 297 F.2d 286, 48 LRRM 2173 (3d Cir. 1961).

[67]*NLRB v. Hershey Chocolate Corp.,* 297 F.2d 286, 293, 48 LRRM 2173 (3d Cir. 1961).

[68]*Edward Axel Roffman Associates, Inc.,* 147 NLRB 717, 724, 56 LRRM 1268 (1964); *Insulation & Specialties, Inc.,* 144 NLRB 1540, 1543-1544, 54 LRRM 1306 (1963).

[69]201 NLRB 210, 82 LRRM 1360 (1973).

[70]*See, e.g., Jennings v. M. & M. Transportation Co.,* 104 N.J. 265, 249 A.2d 631, 70 LRRM 2581 (Super. Ct. 1969). (After arbitration award giving one local a certain work assignment, a second local claimed the work. The International Union then made a jurisdictional award to the second local. The court held the second award would be controlling.)

[71]*Ametek, Inc.,* AAA Case No. 62-6 (Loucks, 1963) (Disputed work assignment was not within the jurisdiction of the arbitrator because the work in dispute had been assigned to a member of union which did not participate in the arbitration.); *Pottstown Metal Products-Division of Cochrane Corp.,* AAA Case No. 12-21 (Crawford, 1959). (Grievance concerned promotion to a position in a unit represented by a union other than that to which the grievant belonged. The other union had declined to participate in the arbitration.)

[72]*Warm Springs Lumber Co.,* 181 NLRB 600, 73 LRRM 1429 (1970); *Horn & Hardart Co.,* 173 NLRB 1077, 69 LRRM 1522 (1968), *aff'd,* 439 F.2d 674 (2d Cir. 1971).

"jurisdictional disputes."[73] In *Carey v. Westinghouse Electric Corp.*,[74] the Supreme Court ruled that the absence of one of the unions involved in a jurisdictional dispute does not affect the arbitrability of the claim of one of the disputants. As the Court noted, absent the participation of the other union, "an adjudication of the arbiter might not put an end to the dispute. ... [But it] may as a practical matter end the controversy or put into movement forces that will resolve it."[75] Justice Black dissented in *Carey,* stating that the lack of the second union as a party placed the employer in a "helpless position":

> He is trapped in a cross-fire between unions. All he can do is guess as to which union's members he will be required by an arbitrator, the Labor Board, or a court to assign to the disputed jobs. If he happens to guess wrong, he is liable to be mulcted in damages. ... [T]he employer cannot make a choice which will be binding on either an arbitrator, the Board, or a court. The Court's holding, thus subjecting an employer to damages when he has done nothing wrong, seems to me contrary to the National Labor Relations Act as well as to the basic principles of common everyday justice.[76]

Black's supposition proved correct in *Carey,* because the NLRB subsequently declined to defer to the arbitration award stemming from the Court's decision in *Carey.*[77] In subsequent decisions, the Board has declined to defer to an arbitration award when a party affected by the arbitration award was not a party to the arbitration proceeding.[78] However, several arbitrators have relied on the Supreme Court's decision in *Carey* to hold that arbitrators have the authority to

---

[73]The term "jurisdictional dispute," as discussed in *Carey v. Westinghouse Electric Corp.*, 375 U.S. 261, 263, 55 LRRM 2042 (1964), includes: "(1) a controversy as to whether certain work should be performed by workers in one bargaining unit or those in another; or (2) a controversy as to which union should represent the employees doing particular work." *See generally* Comment, *The Employer As a Necessary Party to Voluntary Settlement of Work Assignment Disputes Under Section 10(k) of the NLRA,* 38 U. CHI. L. REV. 389 (1971), which deals with the question as to the necessity for an employer to be a party to a type (1) jurisdictional dispute.

[74]375 U.S. 261, 55 LRRM 2042 (1964).

[75]*Id.* at 265, 55 LRRM at 2044.

[76]*Id.* at 275, 55 LRRM at 2048.

[77]*Westinghouse Electric Corp.,* 162 NLRB 768, 64 LRRM 1082 (1967). The arbitration award which the Board did not follow is *Westinghouse Electric Corp.,* 45 LA 161 (Feinberg, 1965). The cross-fire in which an employer can be caught when the issue in arbitration is a claim of a union to certain work when the other union is not a party is also illustrated by cases such as *American Sterilizer Co. v. Local 832, UAW,* 278 F. Supp. 637, 67 LRRM 2894 (W.D. Pa. 1968), where two separate arbitration proceedings under separate collective bargaining agreements resulted in opposite interpretations of identical language in the two contracts. *See also Local 1505, Electrical Workers v. Local 1836, Machinists,* 304 F.2d 365, 50 LRRM 2337 (1st Cir. 1962), *vacated,* 372 U.S. 523, 52 LRRM 2672 (1963), with directions to dismiss the cause as moot.

[78]*TIME-DC, Inc.,* 225 NLRB 1175, 93 LRRM 1270 (1976); *Retail Clerks Union,* 206 NLRB 931, 84 LRRM 1431 (1973).

make an award in a jurisdictional work assignment dispute even though the union to which the disputed work was assigned is not a party to the arbitration proceedings. [79]

In *Lockheed-California Co.*, [80] Arbitrator Block ruled that he had authority under the agreement between the employer and the International Association of Machinists (IAM) to offer the United Welders Union, over IAM's objection, an opportunity to join as a party the arbitration of IAM's claim over work which the employer had assigned to the United Welders. Upon the Welders' acceptance of the offer, the arbitrator ruled that a "new" agreement for arbitration would arise, under which the substantive provisions of both unions' contracts with the employer would be applicable and would be harmonized and adjudicated by the arbitrator.

However, in a later case between the same employer and union, [81] Arbitrator Jones ruled that he had no authority, in a claim by the IAM that the employer had violated the agreement by assigning work to the Engineers and Scientists Guild, to invite the Guild to participate in the proceedings. Although the arbitrator's award in favor of the IAM did affect the Guild, he felt that he lacked authority under the agreement or state or federal law to join a party not a signatory to the arbitration agreement.

In *National Steel & Shipbuilding Co.*, [82] Union A grieved about work the company had assigned to members of Union B. The company argued that the dispute was not arbitrable because Arbitrator Jones could not issue an effective remedy unless Union B either was a party to the arbitration or indicated to the arbitrator that it would defer to Union A's claim if it was sustained. Arbitrator Jones issued an award holding the dispute was not arbitrable unless either the employer, Union A, or Union B moved to incorporate Union B into the proceeding as a third party. Union A made the motion and Arbitrator Jones then issued an "arbitral interpleader order." He held that the order was not self-executing, but would be binding on Union B if that union agreed to be bound or if a court compelled Union B to participate under Section 301. If neither event occurred, the arbitration would then proceed bilaterally. Union B refused to consent and neither the company nor Union A attempted to obtain an interpleader order. Arbitrator Jones dismissed the grievance as not arbitrable. [83]

---

[79] *Marion Power Shovel Co.*, 61 LA 914 (Gibson, 1973); *General Dynamics Corp.*, 59 LA 1175 (Gentile, 1972); *National Steel & Ship Building Co.*, 56 LA 353 (Block, 1971).

[80] 46 LA 865 (Block, 1966).

[81] 49 LA 981 (Jones, 1967).

[82] 40 LA 625 (Jones, 1963); 40 LA 631 (Jones, 1963); 40 LA 838 (Jones, 1963); 40 LA 841 (Jones, 1963).

[83] *See* Jones, *Autobiography of a Decision; The Function of Innovation in Labor Arbitration and the National Steel Orders of Joinder and Interpleader,* 10 U.C.L.A. L. REV. 987 (1963);

This was the first effort by an arbitrator to use an interpleader order, but since this case it has been used successfully by Arbitrator Jones in three cases;[84] Arbitrator Sembower has also entered a similar order.[85] Other arbitrators have declined to issue such an order when requested by one party to do so.[86]

The power of a court to order the interpleading of a third party in arbitration was recognized in *Columbia Broadcasting System, Inc. v. American Recording and Broadcasting Association.*[87] There the employer sued under Section 301 to compel joint arbitration (interpleader order) of the two unions' claims with the employer. The Second Circuit found the language of Section 301 broad enough to grant the employer's request.

In *Window Glass Cutters League v. American St. Gobian Corp.,*[88] the employer followed a different procedure but achieved the same result. Instead of asking a court for an interpleader order under Section 301, the employer refused to process a grievance of one union challenging a work assignment made to members of another union. The union then sued under Section 301 to compel the processing of its grievance. The employer then moved to join as an indispensable party the other union claiming the work. The court granted the motion under Rule 19(a)(2)(ii) of the Federal Rules of Civil Procedure, stating that the employer would otherwise be subjected to the possibility of incurring inconsistent obligations to each union.

The basic objection to an interpleader order in an arbitration proceeding is that it vitiates the consensual nature of arbitration. Specifically, it is argued that the union which is the object of the joinder has no effective control over the decision to initiate the arbitra-

---

Jones, *An Arbitral Answer to a Judicial Dilemma; The Carey Decision and Trilateral Arbitration of Judicial Disputes,* 11 U.C.L.A. L. REV. 327 (1964). *See also* Bernstein, *On Nudging and Shoving all Parties to a Jurisdictional Dispute into Arbitration; The Dubious Procedure of National Steel,* 78 HARV. L. REV. 784 (1965). For Jones' response to this criticism, *see* Jones, *On Nudging and Shoving the National Steel Arbitration into a Dubious Procedure,* 79 HARV. L. REV. 327 (1965). *See also* Bernstein and Jones, *Jurisdictional Dispute Arbitration: The Jostling Professors,* 14 U.C.L.A. L. REV. 347 (1966).

[84] *Mayfair Markets, Inc.,* 42 LA 14 (Jones, 1964); 42 LA 702 (Jones, 1964); *Lockheed Aircraft Corp., Lockheed-California Co.,* 49 LA 981 (Jones, 1967); *Stardust Hotel,* 50 LA 1186 (Jones, 1968).

[85] *Marvell-Schebler Div.,* 54 LA 24 (Sembower, 1969).

[86] *Union Tank Car Co.,* 55 LA 170 (Platt, 1970); *General Dynamics,* 51 LA 902 (Hebling, 1968); *Lockheed Aircraft Corp., Lockheed-California Co.,* 46 LA 865 (Block, 1966); *Westinghouse Electric Corp.,* 45 LA 161 (Feinberg, 1965); *Thorsen Mfg. Co.,* 44 LA 1049 (Koven, 1965); *E. R. Wagner Co.,* 43 LA 210 (Fleming, 1964); *Philco Corp.,* 42 LA 604 (Lazarus, 1963); *Crown Cork & Seal Co.,* 41 LA 665 (Schedler, 1963).

[87] 293 F. Supp. 1400, 69 LRRM 2914 (S.D. N.Y. 1968), *aff'd,* 414 F.2d 1326, 72 LRRM 2140 (2d Cir. 1969); *see also Operating Engineers v. Corley Builders,* 76 LRRM 3005 (N.D. Ill. 1971).

[88] 47 F.R.D. 255, 71 LRRM 3173 (W.D. Pa. 1969), *aff'd,* 428 F.2d 353, 74 LRRM 2749 (3d Cir. 1970).

tion and the choice of the arbitrator. Furthermore, some have asserted that Section 8(b)(4)(D) of the Labor Management Relations Act (LMRA)[89] and the injunctive procedures of Section 10(1),[90] as well as arbitral institutions such as the AFL-CIO Internal Disputes Plan, are adequate tools to remedy the two-union work jurisdictional problems.[91] Proponents of this view do not see the problems of duplicative proceedings and inconsistent determinations as critical enough to interject the element of compulsion involved in an interpleader order.

The problems discussed above involve the need for participation of a different union, if its rights or the rights of its members will be affected by the award of the arbitrator. Related to these problems is the need for participation of individuals whose rights may be affected by the award. *Clark v. Hein-Werner Corp.*[92] was a case where a group of supervisors brought an action to enjoin the enforcement of an award that held that the supervisors could not displace employees in the unit in a work force reduction causing them to be laid off. The court enjoined the enforcement of the award on the ground that the supervisors were not represented in the arbitration hearing.

Arbitrators who have reacted to this court-announced view have pointed out that arbitration awards sustaining a claim by one employee that the employee's seniority rights were violated would become invalid unless the junior employee and possibly everyone junior to the grievant received notice of the hearing and was given a right to appear.[93]

The Supreme Court in *Humphrey v. Moore*[94] determined that the relative seniority rights of large numbers of employees can be determined with the union representative without involvement of the individual in an arbitration proceeding. Where the rights affected are between individuals represented by the same union, such a view is consistent with the Supreme Court's views expressed in *J. I. Case*[95] that exclusive representational rights have been granted the union by the National Labor Relations Act. However, this rationale does not completely resolve the problems that confronted the court in *Hein-Werner.*

---

[89] 29 U.S.C. § 158(b)(4)(D).

[90] 29 U.S.C. § 160(1).

[91] *See* note 83 *supra.*

[92] 8 Wisc. 2d 264, 99 N.W.2d 132 (1959), *cert. denied,* 362 U.S. 962 (1960).

[93] *Quality Aluminum Casting Co.,* 41 LA 580 (Marshall, 1963).

[94] 375 U.S. 335, 55 LRRM 2031 (1964).

[95] *J. I. Case Co. v. NLRB,* 321 U.S. 332, 14 LRRM 501 (1944).

CHAPTER III

Enforcement of Agreements to Arbitrate

Enforcement of an agreement to arbitrate, whether expressed in the collective bargaining contract or in a special submission agreement, would in all likelihood be sought by a suit under Section 301 of the LMRA,[1] in either federal or state court. While a 301 enforcement proceeding is of primary importance because of the broad coverage of that section, arbitration agreements may also be enforced under provisions of state arbitration statutes[2] or the U.S. Arbitration Act.[3] As pointed out in Chapter I, however, state and federal arbitration statutes are applicable in enforcement proceedings only to the extent that such statutes are compatible with the body of federal substantive law created under Section 301. This chapter deals with the manner in which courts handle actions brought to enforce arbitration agreements.[4]

AN AGREEMENT TO ARBITRATE MUST BE ESTABLISHED

In any proceeding to compel arbitration, it must be established that there exists a valid and enforceable arbitration agreement. The burden of proof rests on the party urging the existence of such an agree-

---

[1] 29 U.S.C. § 185 (1978).

[2] States which have made arbitration clauses binding and enforceable, under either general arbitration statutes or statutes specifically enacted for labor disputes under union contracts, include: California, Colorado, Connecticut, Florida, Louisiana, Maine, Massachusetts, Minnesota, New Hampshire, New Jersey, New York, North Carolina, Ohio, Pennsylvania, Rhode Island, Washington and Wyoming. Wisconsin, while specifically excluding union contracts from the scope of its general arbitration statute, has included provisions in its state labor relations act making the refusal to arbitrate an unfair labor practice. *See, e.g., Kiekhaefer Corp. v. Wisconsin Employment Relations Board,* 43 LRRM 2520 (Wisc. Cir. Ct. 1958).

[3] 9 U.S.C. § 1, *et seq.* (1964).

[4] When it is claimed in an enforcement proceeding that the issue is not encompassed by the agreement to arbitrate, the defense is that of nonarbitrability. This defense is also dealt with in the next chapter, since the granting of a stay for lack of arbitrability of the subject matter often involves the same considerations that are involved in the denial of the enforcement of an alleged obligation to arbitrate.

ment.[5] For example, where an employer sought to compel a union to arbitrate, a court denied the request on the basis that the union's negotiator did not possess the power to bind the union to the purported agreement.[6] In another case, a clause in a labor agreement stating that when the grievance procedure is exhausted without satisfaction the parties "shall further make an effort to agree to dispose of the difference or grievance by means of arbitration" was held not enforceable as an agreement to arbitrate.[7] A union sought to impel a company to arbitrate under a provision that when a dispute remained unsettled, "the issue in dispute may be submitted to an impartial arbitrator." The company had argued that the clause included the word "may" and not "shall." The court responded with a rule of construction: when two interpretations are reasonably permissible, the court will adopt the one which renders a contract valid and effectual. This means the word "may" means the same as "shall."[8] A court also has held that a provision in a labor agreement providing that in the event the "no strike" provision is breached, the employer may request the American Arbitration Association to appoint an arbitrator "does not mean that the employer's remedy is limited to arbitration and that the employer cannot seek remedy in a court."[9]

Similarly, a company's promise to execute a labor agreement which would contain an agreement to arbitrate was found not to be an enforceable agreement to arbitrate. Concerning the union's demand for arbitration, the court said "the union was seeking arbitration under a collective agreement that was never consummated."[10] Likewise, a company's written assent to be bound by an association agreement

---

[5]*United Steelworkers of America v. Warrior & Gulf Nav. Co.*, 363 U.S. 564, 583, n. 7, 46 LRRM 2414 (1960); *Atkinson v. Sinclair Refining Co.*, 370 U.S. 238, 241, 50 LRRM 2433 (1962). In *Drake Bakeries v. Local 50*, 370 U.S. 254, 256, 50 LRRM 2440 (1962), the Court held:

> As was true in *Atkinson, supra,* the issue of arbitrability is a question for the courts and is to be determined by the contract entered into by the parties.

John Wiley & Sons, Inc. v. Livingston, 376 U.S. 543, 546 n. 1, 55 LRRM 2769 (1964); *Int'l Union of Operating Engineers, Local 150 v. Flair Builders, Inc.,* 406 U.S. 487, 80 LRRM 2441 (1972); *Torrington Co. v. Metal Products Workers Union, Local 1645,* 347 F.2d 93, 59 LRRM 2588 (2d Cir. 1965), *cert. denied,* 382 U.S. 940, 60 LRRM 2512 (1965); *Bethlehem Mines Corp. v. United Mine Workers,* 344 F. Supp. 1161, 80 LRRM 3069 (D. Pa. 1972).

[6]*Warrior Constructors, Inc. v. Operating Engineers, Local 926,* 383 F.2d 700, 66 LRRM 2220 (5th Cir. 1967).

[7]*Steelworkers, Local 4264 v. New Park Mining Co.,* 169 F. Supp. 107, 43 LRRM 2277 (D. Utah 1958), *aff'd,* 273 F.2d 352, 43 LRRM 2281 (10th Cir. 1959). *See also Fredriksen v. Bornscheuer,* 213 N.Y.S.2d 799 (Sup. Ct. 1961); *Oil, Chemical and Atomic Workers, Local 8-831 v. Mobil Oil Corp.,* 441 F.2d 651, 77 LRRM 2062 (3d Cir. 1971).

[8]*Service Employees International Union Local 18, AFL-CIO v. American Building Maintenance Company,* 29 Cal. App. 3d 356, 105 Cal. Rptr. 564, 82 LRRM 2785 (Ct. App. 1972).

[9]*Lynchburg Foundry Co. v. Patternmakers, Lynchburg Div.,* 597 F.2d 384, 101 LRRM 2047 (4th Cir. 1979).

[10]*In re Luggage Workers Union, Local 60,* 11 App. Div.2d 668, 45 LRRM 3086 (N.Y. 1960).

that had expired did not obligate the company to arbitrate a dispute under a subsequent agreement to which it had not signed a written assent.[11]

An agreement separate from the collective bargaining contract must be clearly incorporated by reference into the contract before an agreement to arbitrate contained in the basic agreement applies to disputes over the interpretation of the separate agreement.[12] For example, in a memorandum of agreement which provided that "the employer agrees to continue the pension plan in the form presently in existence," this language was held not to be a sufficient reference to show a clear intention of the parties to arbitrate grievances arising under the pension plan:

> Inasmuch as the pension plan is not incorporated into the collective bargaining agreement, the grievance concerning the administration of its pension plan ... does not fall within the ambit of paragraph 18 of the collective bargaining agreement which provides that arbitration is to be had concerning "all grievances *hereunder.* "[13] [Emphasis in original.]

Similarly, where the dispute arose over sick leave payments from a welfare fund, no agreement to arbitrate was established because the provisions establishing welfare benefits were not in the collective agreement.[14]

More recent cases, however, indicate that the law is taking a different turn in this area; the courts, in emphasizing that labor peace is promoted by agreements to arbitrate,[15] have been prone to look more carefully for the existence of such agreements. For example, the Eighth Circuit[16] decided that a statement in a letter from an employer to a union, when withdrawing its proposals during negotiations, saying that "[W]e will continue handling any grievances that may arise in accordance with the procedure set forth [in the draft agreement]" established an agreement to arbitrate a discharge grievance arising nearly a year later. When the union sought to arbitrate the discharge

---

[11]*Local 11, IBEW v. Jandon Electric Co.,* 429 F.2d 584, 74 LRRM 2892 (9th Cir. 1970).

[12]*United Steelworkers of America, Local No. 1617 v. The General Fireproofing Company,* 464 F.2d 726, 80 LRRM 3113 (6th Cir. 1972).

[13]*In re New York Racing Ass'n. Inc.,* 32 Misc.2d 867, 869, 224 N.Y.S.2d 784, 786, 49 LRRM 2574, 2575 (Sup. Ct. 1962).

[14]*Pittsburgh Railways Co. v. Amal. Ass'n of Street, Electric Railway and Motor Coach Employees of America, Division 85,* 176 F. Supp. 16, 44 LRRM 2790 (W.D. Pa. 1959).

[15]*Retail Clerks v. Lion Dry Goods, Inc.,* 369 U.S. 17 (1962); *Monroe Sander Corp. v. Livingston,* 377 F.2d 6, 9-10, 65 LRRM 2273 (2d Cir.), *cert. denied,* 389 U.S. 831, 66 LRRM 2308 (1967); *Columbian Carbon Co. v. International Union of Operating Engineers, Local No. 405,* 360 F.2d 1018, 62 LRRM 2292 (5th Cir. 1966); *IUE v. General Electric Co.,* 332 F.2d 485, 56 LRRM 2289 (2d Cir.), *cert. denied,* 379 U.S. 928, 57 LRRM 2608 (1964). *See* discussion under "Stays Granted for Nonarbitrability of Subject Matter" in Chapter IV.

[16]*Taft Broadcasting Co., WDAF AM-FM-TV v. NLRB,* 441 F.2d 1382, 77 LRRM 2257 (8th Cir. 1971).

case, the employer replied that no agreement to arbitrate existed. The court, however, found that the letter to the union 10 months earlier constituted an interim agreement that the company would arbitrate grievance cases even though there had been no final agreement between the parties on the terms of the contract.

Similarly, the Second Circuit reversed the district court's denial of a union's petition to compel arbitration on the question of whether an employer violated a collective bargaining agreement by closing its plant and terminating employees without notifying and bargaining with the union.[17] The court rejected the employer's contention that the termination of its business in effect terminated its obligations under the agreement, including the agreement to arbitrate. The court also referred to arbitration the question of whether the employer violated the employees' rights by unilaterally terminating their pension plan upon closing the plant, although the pension plan contained a separate arbitration procedure and specifically excluded "the provisions" of the plan and "the meaning, application or performance hereof" from arbitration under the collective bargaining contract. The court acknowledged that arbitrability of the pension plan presented a much closer question but, again relying on the arbitration clause in the labor agreement, stated that doubt should be resolved in favor of arbitration.

In 1971, a ventilation structure at the Gateway Coal mine reduced the airflow, creating some hazard to the miners. The three assistant foremen in the area did not promptly make entries in the required airflow logbook,[18] causing a delay in the repair. Since these assistant foremen increased the period of the safety hazard, a strike was called to force their exclusion. The district court enjoined the strike and directed prompt arbitration.[19] The Third Circuit reversed and then the Supreme Court reversed the Third Circuit,[20] concluding that safety disputes should be submitted to arbitration and strike action over safety issues prohibited.

The Supreme Court announced a "presumption of arbitrability" over safety matters because "industrial strife can result from unresolved controversies over safety matters" and resolution through the "special expertise of the labor arbitrator" was a more effective method of resolving safety problems than battling over them under pressure of a strike.

[17]*Bressette v. International Talc Co.,* 527 F.2d 211, 91 LRRM 2077 (2d Cir. 1975). *See also Carpenters Dist. Council of Denver v. Brady Corp.,* 513 F.2d 1, 88 LRRM 3281 (10th Cir. 1975); *Local 103, IUE v. RCA Corp.,* 516 F.2d 1336, 89 LRRM 2487 (3d Cir. 1975).

[18]*Gateway Coal Co. v. United Mine Workers of America,* 466 F.2d 1157, 80 LRRM 3153 (3d Cir. 1972); *rev'd,* 414 U.S. 368, 85 LRRM 2049 (1974).

[19]*Gateway Coal Co. v. United Mine Workers of America,* 80 LRRM 2633 (D.C. Pa. 1971).

[20]*Gateway Coal Co.,* note 18 *supra.*

ENFORCEMENT OF AN AGREEMENT TO ARBITRATE NEED NOT DETERMINE THE MERITS

In an action to compel arbitration, the function of the court should be confined to ascertaining whether the party seeking arbitration is making a claim which is governed by the contract. This was made clear by the Supreme Court in the *Steelworkers Trilogy*[21] where it was held:

The function of the court is very limited when the parties have agreed to submit all questions of contract interpretation to the arbitrator. It is confined to ascertaining whether the party seeking arbitration is making a claim which on its face is governed by the contract. Whether the moving party is right or wrong is a question of contract interpretation for the arbitrator. In these circumstances the moving party should not be deprived of the arbitrator's judgment, when it was his judgment and all that it connotes that was bargained for.[22]

The Fifth Circuit, reflecting on the *Steelworkers Trilogy,* stated:

The merits of a suit to compel arbitration, of course, do not include the determination (1) of the underlying facts and (2) what the ultimate outcome of the controversy will be. These, if the matter is arbitrable, are for the determination of the arbitrator. What and all that we must pass on here is the correctness of the district court's determination that an arbitrable controversy is presented.[23]

Arbitrator Joseph Brandschain restated the views of the court:[24]

For arbitration is a matter of contract and a party cannot be required to submit to arbitration any dispute which he has not agreed to submit. Yet, to be consistent with congressional policy in favor of settlement of disputes by the parties through the machinery of arbitration, the judicial inquiry under § 301 must be strictly confined to the question whether the reluctant party did agree to arbitrate the grievance.

. . .

In cases where one side refuses to arbitrate, whether on the ground of non-arbitrability, stare decisis, or pure orneriness, resort would normally be to the courts for a mandatory order.

---

[21]*United Steelworkers of America v. American Mfg. Co.,* 363 U.S. 564, 46 LRRM 2414 (1960); *United Steelworkers of America v. Warrior & Gulf Navigation Co.,* 363 U.S. 574, 46 LRRM 2416 (1960); *United Steelworkers of America v. Enterprise Wheel & Car Corp.,* 363 U.S. 593, 46 LRRM 2423 (1960).

[22]363 U.S. at 567-68, 46 LRRM at 2415.

[23]*Gulf Oil Corp. v. Operating Engineers, Local 715,* 279 F.2d 533, 535, 46 LRRM 2499 (5th Cir. 1960).

[24]Brandschain, *Preparation and Trial of a Labor Arbitration Case,* THE PRACTICAL LAWYER, Vol. 18, No. 7 (Nov. 1972).

Where a company was ordered to arbitrate, one court rejected the company's plea that the court delineate the precise issue to be determined, stating that such an intrusion into the arbitration process by the court would be against "the more advanced thinking on arbitration," but others have concluded that delineation is a court's function where the issue is unclear.[25]

COMPLIANCE WITH THE GRIEVANCE PROCEDURE AS A PREREQUISITE FOR ENFORCEMENT

Questions of procedural requirements under the grievance procedure are to be determined by the arbitrator. While, at one time, there was variance among many courts as to the resolution of this issue, the Supreme Court, in *John Wiley & Sons, Inc. v. Livingston,* [26] made clear that "procedural questions which grow out of the dispute and bear on its final disposition should be left to the arbitrator."

Thus, courts have consistently followed *Wiley's* dictate that arbitrators, not courts, should decide whether or not procedural prerequisites to arbitration have been satisfied.[27]

For example, on the question of timeliness, in *Local 51, IBEW v. Illinois Power Co.,* [28] the Seventh Circuit was faced with the issue of whether a union waived its rights to the grievance and arbitration procedure under the collective bargaining contract by not filing its grievance against the employer within the specific time limit provided

---

[25]Courts should not delineate: *Retail Shoe & Textile Salesmen's Union, Local 410 v. Sears, Roebuck & Co.,* 185 F. Supp. 558, 46 LRRM 2758 (N.D. Cal. 1960); *see also General Tire & Rubber Co. v. Local 512, United Rubber Workers,* 191 F. Supp. 911, 49 LRRM 2001 (D. R.I. 1961). Courts should delineate: *John Wiley & Sons, Inc. v. Livingston,* 376 U.S. 543, 546–47, 55 LRRM 2769, 2771-2 (1964); *Local 616, IUE v. Byrd Plastics, Inc.,* 428 F.2d 23, 74 LRRM 2550 (3rd Cir. 1970); *Piano & Musical Instrument Workers v. W. W. Kimball Co.,* 239 F. Supp. 523, 58 LRRM 2752 (N.D. Ill. 1965). The Illinois court said the arbitrator could not second guess the court on arbitrability determination, but arbitrators have not felt so constrained. *Wilshire Oil Co. of California,* AAA Case No. 65-9 (Roberts, 1964); *Socony Mobil Oil Co.,* AAA Case No. 72-14 (Turkus, 1965); *Hughes Tool Co.,* AAA Case No. 26-1 (Aaron, 1960); *Berkshire Hathaway Co.,* AAA Case No. 41-1 (Healy, 1961); *Macy's New York,* AAA Case No. 43-6 (Schmertz, 1962); *Celanese Corp. of America,* AAA Case No. 19-4 (Kahn, 1960).

[26]376 U.S. 543, 557 (1964).

[27]*See, e.g., Radiator Corp. v. Operative Potters,* 358 F.2d 455, 61 LRRM 2664 (6th Cir. 1966); *Avon Products, Inc. v. UAW,* 386 F.2d 651, 67 LRRM 2001 (8th Cir. 1967); *Palestine Telephone Co. v. Local 1506, IBEW,* 279 F.2d 234, 65 LRRM 2776 (5th Cir. 1967). See also *International Union of Operating Engineers, Local 150 v. Flair Builders, Inc.,* 406 U.S. 487, 80 LRRM 2441 (1972); *Local 611 Hotel, Restaurant Employees v. Harry M. Stevens, Inc.,* 89 LRRM 2016 (S.D. N.Y. 1975); *Amalgamated Meat Cutters v. Servomation Corp.,* 402 F. Supp. 1058, 90 LRRM 3028 (M.D. Pa. 1975); *Office & Professional Employees Local 9 v. Allied Industrial Workers,* 397 F. Supp. 688, 90 LRRM 2129 (E.D. Wis. 1975).

[28]357 F.2d 916, 61 LRRM 2613 (7th Cir. 1966), *cert. denied,* 385 U.S. 850, 63 LRRM 2235 (1966).

for in the contract. On this rehearing of the case the court specifically held that *Wiley* was controlling and that the issue as to timeliness of the grievance was solely for the arbitrator. The same issue was posed in *Teamsters Local 776 v. Standard Motor Freight, Inc.* [29] and in *Chambers v. Beaunit Corp.* [30] In both those cases, the district courts similarly held that the issue of timeliness was for the arbitrator.

A question left unanswered by *Wiley* is whether a court should vacate an award where the arbitrator's procedural ruling is particularly egregious. This question arose in *Farkash v. Brach,* [31] which predated *Wiley.* In *Farkash,* the contract provided that if the parties could not agree on a hearing date, the arbitrator could call a hearing on "such notice as he deems appropriate." The day set by the arbitrator for the hearing fell on a religious holiday for the employer. In spite of this, the arbitrator held the hearing. The court vacated the award on the grounds that due process required that the employer be given a chance to attend the arbitration and present his case. Such a court decision appropriately requires that an arbitrator's procedural ruling be in accordance with due process. As such, the court decision was eminently correct.

Enforcement likewise was denied for an arbitrator's award which permitted an individual grievance to be expanded into a class action and made provision for attorneys' fees, costs and punitive damages. The treatment of the grievance as a class action, as well as the remedies sought, had not been raised in the grievance procedures; all were presented for the first time at the arbitration hearing. While the court acknowledged that such matters might be appropriate for arbitral consideration if brought into issue at the initial stages of the grievance, it held that since these matters were not properly before the arbitrator in this case, the award exceeded the scope of his authority.

The line between substance and procedure, of course, has never been an easy one to draw, and this is no less true in applying the *Wiley* rule. [32] For example, where the contract specifically excluded from arbitration disputes over "standards of production established or changed by management," a grievance charge that a production standard was improperly changed by the company was held not arbitrable. The court rejected the union's contention that the provision in the agreement specifying that "[a]ny case appealed to the arbitrator over which he has no power to rule shall be referred back to the parties without

---

[29] 260 F. Supp. 269, 63 LRRM 2385 (M.D. Pa. 1966).

[30] 278 F. Supp. 62, 67 LRRM 2316 (E.D. Tenn. 1967), *aff'd,* 404 F.2d 128, 69 LRRM 2732 (6th Cir. 1968).

[31] 52 LRRM 2334 (N.Y. Sup. Ct. 1963). *See also Hall v. Eastern Air Lines, Inc.,* 511 F.2d 663, 89 LRRM 2111 (5th Cir. 1975).

[32] *See* notes 81–82 *infra* and accompanying text.

decision," excluded the question of arbitrability from court determination.[33]

Where a union waited several years before taking action to challenge an employer's alleged violations of a contract, the union was held by the Supreme Court not to have deprived itself of the right to compel arbitration. Reversing the Seventh Circuit, the Court explained that, while a court has the responsibility to determine whether a union and employer have agreed to arbitration, a claim that particular grievances are barred by laches is an arbitrable question.[34] In dissent, Justice Powell, joined by Chief Justice Burger, argued that the equitable defense of laches, like fraud or duress in the inception of the contract, is a question properly within the province of courts to decide.[35]

However, the lower courts have not uniformly followed the Supreme Court's decision that the issue of laches should be referred to arbitration. The Sixth Circuit, for example, has expressly stated that in that circuit the rule is that laches is an equitable defense to be determined by the court, rather than a procedural question to be decided by the arbitrator.[36] Other courts, however, have held that a claim that a particular grievance is barred by laches is itself an arbitrable question.[37] The principal argument, in the Fourth Circuit's view, for leaving the issue to the arbitrator is that court litigation involves an inordinate delay which is inconsistent with the national labor policy of speedy resolution of employee grievances.[38]

EFFECT OF TERMINATION OF THE COLLECTIVE AGREEMENT ON ENFORCEMENT ACTION

As noted earlier, an obligation to arbitrate must be established before a court will order arbitration. Where the grievance arose during

---

[33]*Local 73, Amalgamated Meatcutters and Butcher Workmen v. Fred Rueping Leather Co.,* 282 F. Supp. 653, 67 LRRM 3045 (E.D. Wis. 1968). *See also Beckley Mfg. Corp. v. Electrical Workers, Local 2011,* 296 F. Supp. 117, 70 LRRM 2689 (D.C. W. Va. 1969).

[34]*International Union of Operating Engineers v. Flair Builders, Inc.,* 406 U.S. 487, 80 LRRM 2441 (1972). *But cf. Clothing Workers v. Ironall Factories Co.,* 386 F.2d 586, 67 LRRM 2093 (6th Cir. 1967).

[35]406 U.S. at 492, 80 LRRM at 2442.

[36]*Chattanooga Mailers Local 92 v. Chattanooga News-Free Press Co.,* 524 F.2d 1305, 90 LRRM 3000 (6th Cir. 1975).

[37]*See, e.g., Controlled Sanitation Corp. v. District 128, IAM,* 524 F.2d 1324, 90 LRRM 2892 (3d Cir. 1975), *cert. denied,* 424 U.S. 915, 91 LRRM 2410 (1976); *Int'l Union, UAW v. Int'l Telephone & Telegraph Corp.,* 508 F.2d 1309, 88 LRRM 2213 (8th Cir. 1975); *General Dynamics Corp. v. Local 5, Industrial Workers of America,* 469 F.2d 848, 81 LRRM 2746 (1st Cir. 1972); *Marine Engineers v. Noank Nav. Inc.,* 94 LRRM 2887 (S.D. N.Y. 1977); *Reid Burton Construction, Inc. v. Carpenters Dist. Council of Southern Colorado,* 535 F.2d 598, 92 LRRM 2321 (10th Cir. 1976), *cert. denied,* 429 U.S. 907, 93 LRRM 2512 (1976); *Welded Tube Co. v. UE Local 168,* 91 LRRM 2027 (E.D. Pa. 1975).

[38]*Tobacco Workers v. Lorillard Corp.,* 448 F.2d 949, 78 LRRM 2273 (4th Cir. 1971).

the life of the collective agreement, but the demand to arbitrate occurs after the agreement expires, an order to arbitrate will usually issue,[39] for otherwise "a party [could] simply . . . stall the arbitration hearing until after the expiration of the contract and thus not be bound by the award."[40] Where it is not clear that the operative event took place during the term of the agreement, courts have refused to order arbitration.[41] Where four employees were discharged for activities in connection with a strike during a hiatus between two agreements, grievances over the discharges were held arbitrable because:

> The grievance was action of the Employer in terminating the contractual right to present and future employment. It was these actions by the Employer after the new contract became effective that for the first time had any adverse effect upon the four employees. This was the action complained of, not the reasons given by the Employer for the disciplinary discharge.[42]

A dispute over a lockout which occurred during the period between two agreements, however, was not one that could be arbitrated because no agreement was in force when the dispute arose. The court said: "Whether such a contract exists . . . must be decided by the Court before any authority is conferred upon the arbitrator."[43] Finding no agreement in existence at the time of the grievance, the Sixth Circuit refused to order arbitration. Arbitration also was denied where the activity on which discipline was based, the discipline complained

[39]*UAW v. White Motor Corp.*, 374 F. Supp. 421, 81 LRRM 2222 (Minn. 1972); *Honeywell, Inc. v. United Instrument Workers*, 307 F. Supp. 1126, 73 LRRM 2210 (E.D. Pa. 1970); *Piano & Musical Instrument Workers, Local 2549 v. W. W. Kimball Co.*, 221 F. Supp. 461, 54 LRRM 2212 (N.D. Ill. 1963), *rev'd*, 333 F.2d 761, 56 LRRM 2644 (7th Cir.), *rev'd*, 379 U.S. 357, 57 LRRM 2628 (1964); *Machinists, Lodge 2116 v. Buffalo Eclipse Corp.*, 12 App. Div. 2d 875, 210 N.Y.S.2d 214, 36 LA 117 (1961); *Textile Workers Union v. Newton & Co.*, 394 Pa. 422, 147 A.2d 155, 31 LA 766 (1958); *Potoker v. Brooklyn Eagle*, 2 N.Y.S.2d 553, 28 LA 344 (1957).

[40]*Piper v. Meco, Inc.*, 302 F. Supp. 926, 927 (N.D. Ohio 1968), *aff'd*, 412 F.2d 752, 71 LRRM 2655 (6th Cir. 1969); *United Steelworkers of America v. Enterprise Wheel & Car Corp.*, 363 U.S. 593, 46 LRRM 2423 (1960).

[41]*Teamsters v. Kroger Co.*, 411 F.2d 1191, 71 LRRM 2479 (3d Cir. 1969); *Austin Mailers Union No. 136 v. Newspapers, Inc.*, 226 F. Supp. 600 (W.D. Tex. 1963), *aff'd*, 329 F.2d 312, 55 LRRM 2693 (5th Cir.), *petition for cert. dismissed*, 377 U.S. 985, 56 LRRM 2544 (1964). *See also Machinists Lodge 2369 v. Oxco Brush Div. of Vistron Corp.*, 517 F.2d 239, 89 LRRM 2341 (6th Cir. 1975); *Chattanooga Mailers Local 92 v. Chattanooga News-Free Press Co.*, note 36 *supra*.

[42]*Boeing Co. v. IAM*, 381 F.2d 119, 122, 65 LRRM 2961 (5th Cir. 1967). *Contra, IBEW v. Wadsworth Electric Mfg. Co.*, 240 F. Supp. 292, 58 LRRM 2861 (E.D. Ky. 1965).

[43]*Local 998, UAW v. B & T Metals Co.*, 315 F.2d 432, 436, 52 LRRM 2787 (6th Cir. 1963). *See also Hilton Davis Chemical Co., Div. of Sterling Drug, Inc.*, 185 NLRB No. 58, 75 LRRM 1036 (1970); *Teamsters, Local 996, Hawaii Teamsters v. Honolulu Rapid Transit Co., Ltd.*, 343 F. Supp. 419, 80 LRRM 2758 (D. Hawaii 1972); *Oil Chemical and Atomic Workers v. American Maize Products Co.*, 492 F.2d 409, 86 LRRM 2438 (7th Cir. 1974). A union can waive the arbitration of pending grievances in the course of negotiating a new labor agreement; *Public Service, Production & Maintenance Employees, Local 1057 v. Transit Management of Laredo, Inc.*, 86 LC ¶ 11,365 (S.D. Tex. 1979).

of, and the filing of grievances over such discipline all occurred during the hiatus.[44] But if the parties agree to arbitrate grievances which arise during the interval, they must do so.[45]

If, however, employee rights such as severance payments upon termination had been established in a labor agreement, and if then the agreement expired and thereafter the employees were terminated, the Supreme Court in *Nolde*[46] continued in effect the obligation to arbitrate because the severance payments had become "vested." There is a presumption that rights continue beyond the expiration of the labor agreement unless a clear negation to such continuation has been incorporated into the agreement or arises from a clear implication.[47] In *Nolde*, the company had argued that the duty to arbitrate was strictly a contractual obligation and since the dispute over severance pay did not arise until after expiration of the labor agreement, there continued no obligation to arbitrate. The Supreme Court said "No," and directed arbitration.

In *UAW v. Tri-State Plastic Molding Co.*,[48] even when the expired agreement did not expressly include a severance pay provision as in *Nolde*, the District Court[49] found that severance payment was customary and, since no express exclusion of the severance pay benefit had been included in the subsequent agreement, the court ordered arbitration of the issue. In *Union v. Helio San Jeronimo Corp.*,[50] however, when the parties negotiated a settlement agreement concurrent with the plant closing after expiration of the labor agreement, the court found that settlement negotiations made it understood that severance payments were not contemplated, meeting the *Nolde* negative criterion, and refused to order arbitration.

---

[44]*Procter & Gamble Independent Union of Port Ivory, N.Y. v. Procter & Gamble Mfg. Co.*, 312 F.2d 181, 51 LRRM 2752 (2d Cir. 1962), *cert. denied*, 374 U.S. 830, 53 LRRM 2544 (1963). The NLRB has held that it is not a violation of Section 8(a)(5) to refuse to process a grievance to arbitration which arose during a period between old and new contracts. *Hilton-Davis Chemical Co.*, 185 NLRB No. 58, 75 LRRM 1036 (1970). *See also* cases cited in note 32 *supra*.

[45]*Taft Broadcasting Co.*, 185 NLRB No. 68, 75 LRRM 1076 (1970), *enf'd*, 441 F.2d 1382, 77 LRRM 2257 (8th Cir. 1971).

[46]*Nolde Brothers, Inc. v. Local 358, Bakery and Confectionery Workers*, 430 U.S. 243, 94 LRRM 2753 (1977). *See also Federated Metals Corp. v. United Steelworkers*, 648 F.2d 856, 107 LRRM 2271 (3d Cir. 1981). The court said it would enforce the arbitration of claims of early retirement benefits, even though these had accrued after the expiration of the agreement, on the basis of the *Nolde Brothers* decision.

[47]430 U.S. at 252, 94 LRRM at 2756.

[48]95 LRRM 2116 (W.D. Ky. 1977); *see also Local 35, Washington Baltimore Newspaper Guild v. The Washington Post Co.*, 442 F.Supp. 1060, 96 LRRM 3138 (D. D.C. 1977); *Halstead Industries, Inc. v. Steelworkers*, 432 F.Supp. 109, 95 LRRM 2756 (W.D. Pa. 1977); *Steelworkers v. U.S. Steel Corp.*, 96 LRRM 2622 (D. Minn. 1977); *Bohack Corp. v. Truck Drivers Local Union No. 807*, 431 F.Supp. 646, 95 LRRM 3031 (E.D. N.Y. 1977).

[49]96 LRRM 2279 (D. P.R. 1977).

[50]*Union de Trabajadores, etc. v. Helio, etc.*, 434 F. Supp. 643, 96 LRRM 2279 (D. P.R. 1977).

Where there is an agreement to arbitrate disputes over the terms of a new contract, the Fourth Circuit, in *Winston Salem Printing Pressmen v. Piedmont Publishing Co.*, [51] found it enforceable even though the agreement containing the commitment to arbitrate the new terms had expired prior to receipt of the demand for arbitration. The court acknowledged that its opinion was in conflict with the First Circuit's holding in *Boston Printing Pressmen's Union No. 67 v. Potter Press* [52] that such disputes are not arbitrable after the expiration of the contract, but held that *Potter Press* no longer represented an accurate interpretation of Section 301 in light of *Lincoln Mills* [53] and later Supreme Court decisions, such as *Wiley* and the *Steelworkers Trilogy*.

ENFORCEMENT BY THE SIGNATORY UNION

Generally speaking, the only parties entitled to invoke enforcement of an agreement to arbitrate are the parties to the agreement. [54] In many instances, the union will be the sole enforcer because many collective agreements do not allow the employer to present a grievance for arbitration.

In *United Electrical Workers v. Star Expansion Industries,* [55] the court held that a union which was decertified after it had initiated the arbitration of a discharge dispute retained the right to process the grievance to a conclusion. The motion of the newly certified union for an injunction restraining the employer and the decertified union from proceeding with the arbitration was denied. The court noted that the arbitrator, when representatives of the newly certified union appeared at the hearing, ruled that the union which had initiated the arbitration could process the grievance to conclusion because "the duty to arbitrate is of contractual origin," and the successor union had no agreement when the grievance arose. "No legal theory is suggested which can permit [the successor union] to assert rights under a contract to

---

[51] 393 F.2d 221, 67 LRRM 2939 (4th Cir. 1968). *See also Div. No. 892, Amalgamated Ass'n Street, Electric Railway & Motor Coach v. MK&O Transit Lines,* 210 F. Supp. 351, 51 LRRM 2470 (N.D. Okla. 1962). *Also, Nashville Printing Pressmen's Union, Local 50 v. Newspaper Printing Corp.,* 518 F.2d 351, 89 LRRM 2861 (6th Cir. 1975); *State Ass'n of Homes for Adults, Inc. v. Local 1115, Nursing Home & Hotel Employees,* 90 LRRM 2908 (S.D. N.Y. 1975).

[52] 141 F. Supp. 553, 38 LRRM 2211 (D. Mass. 1956), *aff'd,* 241 F.2d 787, 39 LRRM 2524 (1st Cir. 1957), *cert. denied,* 355 U.S. 817, 40 LRRM 2680 (1957).

[53] *Textile Workers of America v. Lincoln Mills,* 353 U.S. 448, 40 LRRM 2113 (1957).

[54] *See, e.g., Local 13, Int. Longshoremen's & W.U. v. Pacific Mar. Ass'n,* 441 F.2d 1061, 77 LRRM 2160 (9th Cir. 1971), *cert. denied,* 404 U.S. 1016, 79 LRRM 2182 (1972); *Vaca v. Sipes* 386 U.S. 171, 64 LRRM 2369 (1967); *Black-Clawson Co. v. Machinists,* 313 F.2d 179, 52 LRRM 2038 (2d Cir. 1962); *Ostrofsky v. Steelworkers,* 171 F. Supp. 782, 43 LRRM 2744 (D. Md. 1959), *aff'd,* 273 F.2d 614, 45 LRRM 2486 (4th Cir. 1960), *cert. denied,* 363 U.S. 849 (1960).

[55] 246 F. Supp. 400, 56 LRRM 2286 (S.D. N.Y. 1946). *See also A. Seltzer & Co. v. Livingston,* 253 F. Supp. 509, 61 LRRM 2581 (S.D. N.Y. 1966).

which it is a complete stranger."[56] Moreover, "[T]o thrust upon the courts ... a matter already decided by the arbitrator would be productive of delay and confusion and impair the federal policy in favor of arbitration."[57] It would better serve the "promotion and maintenance of industrial peace and stabilization" to permit the instant arbitration to "proceed untrammeled" to a conclusion.[58]

Likewise, the arbitrator in *Trumbull Asphalt Co.*[59] found that a decertified union retains standing to process grievances to arbitration after its decertification where the grievances arose and were initiated prior thereto.

The Second Circuit, however, in *McGuire v. Humble Oil & Refining Co.*,[60] has suggested that the continuing right of a signatory or a predecessor union to arbitrate grievances will not be enforced when a merger of bargaining units has occurred and further processing of grievances by the displaced union could adversely affect the ongoing bargaining agent's authority. Similarly, in *Glendale Mfg. Co. v. Local No. 520, ILGWU*,[61] the Fourth Circuit refused to enforce an arbitration award which required an employer to negotiate with a union pursuant to a wage reopening clause. In this case, several days after the arbitrator rendered the award, the union was decertified. A month later, when the union requested the employer to negotiate in accordance with the award, the employer refused. Upholding this refusal, the court held that to require the employer to abide by the award would be equivalent to ordering him to violate Section 8(a) (2) of the LMRA by bargaining with a minority union. Since it could not force the employer to commit an unfair labor practice, the court denied enforcement of the award.

ENFORCEMENT BY THE SIGNATORY EMPLOYER

If a labor agreement provides that either the company or the union may appeal a case to arbitration, then the company has the same standing to enforce an agreement to arbitrate as the union.[62] In some

---

[56]246 F. Supp. at 401, 56 LRRM at 2287.

[57]*Id.* at 402, 56 LRRM at 2287-88.

[58]*Id.*, 56 LRRM at 2288.

[59]38 LA 1093 (Elson, 1962).

[60]355 F.2d 352, 61 LRRM 2410 (2d Cir. 1966), *cert. denied,* 384 U.S. 988, 62 LRRM 2339 (1966).

[61]283 F.2d 936, 47 LRRM 2152 (4th Cir. 1960).

[62]*Kentile Floors, Inc.,* AAA Case No. 103-3 (Sovern, 1967); *Kentile Floors, Inc.,* AAA Case No. 141-15 (Hill, 1967); *The National Cash Register Co.,* AAA Case No. 92-10 (Brandschain, 1966); *Chase Bag Co.,* AAA Case No. 61-15 (Elkouri, 1963); *see also Controlled Sanitation Corp. v. Dist. 128, International Association of Machinists,* 524 F.2d 1324, 90 LRRM 2892 (3d Cir. 1975), *cert. denied,* 96 S. Ct. 1114, 91 LRRM 2410 (1976); *Reid Burton Construction, Inc.,* 535 F.2d 598, 92, LRRM 2321 (10th Cir. 1976).

agreements the employer acquires the right to move a grievance up to arbitration even though the employer does not have a right to file a grievance. For example, in *Local 463, United Papermakers v. Federal Paper Board Co.,* [63] the labor agreement provided that a grievance may be filed by an "aggrieved employee" or the union but after the grievance reaches the fourth step "either party to the dispute may call upon the American Arbitration Association to select an arbitrator." The court ruled that under this language the company could proceed to arbitration.

On the other hand, a federal court in Connecticut enforced the demand of United Aircraft Corporation that the union proceed to arbitrate a dispute over a one-day suspension of a union steward when the union had refused the employer's request to arbitrate and had taken the case to the NLRB. [64] The court said that compelling the union to honor its contractual duty to arbitrate with the Company would not frustrate, invade, or otherwise interfere with the Board's investigation of the charge that the company engaged in an unfair labor practice.

One question posed is whether an employer signatory can seek relief from the courts rather than file a grievance over a dispute with the union. Very often an employer may have a dispute with a union over damages incurred as the result of the union's breach of a no-strike clause. In such circumstances, the employer is usually foreclosed from seeking damages in a court suit under Section 301. Courts have ruled that the employer is limited solely to seeking redress under a contract's arbitration procedure,[65] unless it can be said with "positive assurance"[66] that the employer is barred from the contract's grievance procedure. This standard of "positive assurance" has led most courts to require arbitration of an employer's claim for damages resulting from a union's breach of its no-strike clause.[67]

---

[63]239 F. Supp. 45, 58 LRRM 2593 (D. Conn. 1965).

[64]*United Aircraft Corp. v. Canel Lodge 700, IAM,* 314 F. Supp. 371, 74 LRRM 2518 (D. Conn. 1970), *aff'd,* 436 F.2d 1, 76 LRRM 2111 (1970), *cert. denied,* 402 U.S. 908, 76 LRRM 3028 (1971).

[65]*Drake Bakeries v. Local 50, American Bakery & Confectionery Workers,* 370 U.S. 254, 50 LRRM 2440 (1962).

[66]*Atkinson v. Sinclair Refining Co.,* 370 U.S. 238, 50 LRRM 2433 (1962); *see also United Steelworkers of America v. Warrior & Gulf Navigation Co.,* 363 U.S. 574, 46 LRRM 2416 (1960); *see also Local No. 358, Bakery Workers v. Nolde Brothers, Inc.,* 530 F.2d 548, 91 LRRM 2570 (4th Cir. 1975), *aff'd,* 430 U.S. 243, 94 LRRM 2753 (1977); *Lever Bros. v. International Chemical Workers Union,* 554 F.2d 115, 93 LRRM 2961 (4th Cir. 1976); *Gangime v. General Electric Co.,* 532 F.2d 861, 91 LRRM 3081 (2d Cir. 1976); *California Trucking Ass'n v. Corcoran,* 74 F.R.D. 534, 95 LRRM 2315 (N.D. Cal. 1977).

[67]*See, e.g., ITT World Communications, Inc. v. Communications Workers of America,* 422 F.2d 77, 73 LRRM 2244 (2d Cir. 1970); *H. K. Porter Co. v. Local 37, United Steelworkers of America,* 400 F.2d 691, 69 LRRM 2246 (4th Cir. 1968); *IAM v. General Electric Co.,* 406 F.2d 1046, 70 LRRM 2477 (2d Cir. 1969); *Alloy Cast Steel Co. v. United Steelworkers of America,* 429 F. Supp. 445, 95 LRRM 2033 (N.D. Ohio 1977).

Courts have, however, even under the "positive assurance" standard, determined that an employer was barred from the contract's grievance and arbitration procedures. For example, in *G. T. Schjeldahl Co. v. Local 1680, IAM*[68] and *Boeing Co. v. UAW,*[69] the arbitrability of an employer's claim for damages for breach of a no-strike clause was litigated. While the courts in both cases recognized the strong national labor policy favoring arbitration, they also recognized that a claim for arbitration must be premised on a contractual provision. Reviewing the arbitration clauses in dispute, both courts concluded that they were "employee oriented" and hence did not allow an employer to demand arbitration.

In *Boeing,*[70] the Third Circuit noted:

> Despite this liberal rule of construction a reluctant party may not be compelled to submit a controversy to arbitration unless under a fair construction of the agreement he is bound to do so. ... Absent a contractual obligation to the contrary, a reluctant party is free to pursue any available legal remedy to redress its grievances. [Citations omitted.]
> . . .
> It is apparent from a reading of the contract that the grievance procedure is employee oriented. The grievance procedure is available only to the employees as "the exclusive remedy for the disposition of any claim, dispute or grievance of any kind ... AGAINST THE COMPANY." (Emphasis supplied). Article VI, § 7. The only arbitrable grievances are those "involving the interpretation or application of the provisions of [the] agreement which [have] been processed through Step 4 of the grievance procedure," supra. The entire procedural structure is designed to resolve only the employees' grievances against the company. This seems obvious from a consideration of Article V-A (Grievance Procedure) and Article VI (Arbitration) in their entirety.
> It is our opinion that we have before us a case in which "it may be said with positive assurance," as in *Atkinson,* supra, that the arbitration clause is not susceptible of a construction that the plaintiff was bound to arbitrate the issues involved in its action for damages."

Similarly, the First Circuit held in *G. T. Schjeldahl Co.:*[71]

> We recognize that the strong policy favoring labor arbitration requires doubts to be resolved in favor of arbitration. ... However, where the

[68] 393 F.2d 502, 67 LRRM 3042 (1st Cir. 1968); *see also ITT World Communications v. Communications Workers,* 422 F.2d 77, 73 LRRM 2244 (2d Cir. 1970), wherein the court held that doubt should be resolved in favor of arbitrability; *Blake Construction Co. v. Laborers International Union,* 511 F.2d 324, 88 LRRM 3443 (DDC 1975).
[69] 370 F.2d 969, 64 LRRM 2208 (3d Cir. 1967); *see also U.S. Steel Corp. v. United Mine Workers,* 394 F. Supp. 345, 90 LRRM 2067 (W.D. Pa. 1975).
[70] 370 F.2d at 970-71, 64 LRRM at 2209.
[71] 393 F.2d at 504-05, 67 LRRM at 3043. *See also* cases refusing to compel an employer to arbitrate when the grievance procedure is "employee-oriented" including: *Friedrich v. Local 780,*

undertaking in question was in all other respects oriented towards employee grievances only, the mere fact that the agreement contains a clause which might be more broadly construed if it were not limited by specific provisions is not a sufficient ambiguity. Nor is the belief that it would be preferable had the agreement been broader sufficient reason to make it so. That only employee grievances should be arbitrated is not a result absurd on its face. Cf. Boeing Co. v. International Union, 3 Cir., 1967, 370 F.2d 969, 64 LRRM 2208. Our duty to determine whether under a proper construction of the agreement the parties agreed to arbitrate ... does not require us to do violence to principles of contract interpretation."

These two cases represent an interesting base point for analysis of collective bargaining contracts which, while not specifically excluding an employer's right to arbitrate, can be construed as such. Moreover, they are consistent with the Supreme Court's constant declarations that arbitration, while the preferable forum to resolve industrial disputes, is still only required where the contract so permits. [72]

Where a union had ordered employees to refuse to work overtime and the employer could not, under the labor agreement, submit a grievance objecting to this union conduct, an injunction was held to be proper even though the union claimed that the employer's failure to submit the issue to arbitration should cause a *Boys Markets*[73] type of injunction not to issue.[74] The Third Circuit in *Avco Corp. v. Local 787, UAW*[75] said that all that is required for a *Boys Markets* type of injunction is that both parties be contractually bound to arbitrate, and that *Boys Markets* does not require that both parties be capable of initiating arbitration.

Another case posing the problem of who can enforce an agreement to arbitrate arose in the context of an employers' association.[76] There, a federal district court held that the association had standing to invoke arbitration on behalf of the member employers. Since the association was the employers' agent in contract negotiations and, therefore, a party to the agreement, the court said it could properly institute arbitration proceedings under a clause stating that either "the Employer or the Union shall submit the grievance to the [arbitration] committee."

IUE, 515 F.2d 225, 89 LRRM 2846 (5th Cir. 1975); *Faultless Division v. Lodge 2040, IAM*, 513 F.2d 987, 88 LRRM 3531 (7th Cir. 1975); *Welded Tube Co. v. UE Local 168*, 91 LRRM 2027 (E.D. Pa. 1975).

[72]*See, e.g., Atkinson v. Sinclair Refining Co.*, 370 U.S. 238, 50 LRRM 2433 (1962).

[73]*Boys Markets, Inc. v. Retail Clerks Union Local 770*, 398 U.S. 235, 74 LRRM 2257 (1970).

[74]The union's claim that the *Boys Markets* type of injunction could not issue was sustained in the district court in *Avco Corp. v. UAW Local 787*, 325 F. Supp. 588, 77 LRRM 2014 (D.C. Pa. 1971). *See also Stroehmann Bros. v. Bakery Workers Local 1427*, 315 F. Supp. 647, 74 LRRM 2957 (D.C. Pa. 1970).

[75]459 F.2d 968, 80 LRRM 2290 (3d Cir. 1972).

[76]*Connecticut Labor Relations Division of New England Road Builders Ass'n v. Hoisting &*

ENFORCEMENT BY A UNION THAT IS A PREDECESSOR, SUCCESSOR, OR A LOCAL

The right of a successor union to represent employees in an arbitration initiated by the predecessor union became the issue in *United Electrical Workers v. Star Expansion Industries, Inc.*[77] The predecessor union had filed a grievance protesting the discharge of an employee; an arbitrator was appointed and a hearing set. The labor agreement with the predecessor union then expired and the predecessor was displaced through a representation election. The successor union, relying on its certification as the bargaining representative, sought to displace the predecessor union as the representative of the dischargee. The arbitrator refused intervention by the successor union and the district court affirmed, saying that the certification of the successor gave the successor no rights under the predecessor's expired contract with the employer since there is "no legal theory . . . which can permit it to assert rights under a contract to which it is a complete stranger."[78]

Quite to the contrary, in *Brewery Workers v. Stigmaier Brewing Co.,*[79] another district court held that a union that was displaced by a successor union in an NLRB election had no standing to bring a suit to compel arbitration of a demand to liquidate a pension plan established under an agreement with the predecessor union, because the successor union, upon certification, became the representative of all the employees and was therefore entitled to all rights and assumed all representational obligations under the pension plan.[80]

A related problem exists where the local of the union desires to proceed to arbitration and the international does not, or vice versa. One court has held that a local union has no standing to compel arbitration under a labor agreement executed by the international union "on behalf of" the local,[81] since the agreement is between the international union and the employer. Another district court, however, declared that a dispute over whether a local union, whose request for the ap-

---

Portable Engineers, Local 478 of Operating Engineers, 285 F. Supp. 311, 68 LRRM 2537 (D. Conn. 1968).

[77]Note 55 *supra; contra, Duralite Co. v. Local 485 IUE,* 207 F. Supp. 273, 50 LRRM 2556 (E.D. N.Y. 1962).

[78]246 F. Supp. at 401, 56 LRRM at 2287.

[79]338 F. Supp. 1137, 79 LRRM 2765 (D.C. Pa. 1972).

[80]*Id.* at 1137, 79 LRRM at 2765.

[81]*Local 12405, District 50 UMW v. Martin Marietta Corp.,* 328 F.2d 945, 55 LRRM 2592 (7th Cir. 1964), *cert. denied,* 379 U.S. 880, 57 LRRM 2276 (1964); *see also Dist. 100 International Ass'n of Machinists v. Compagnie Nationale Air France,* 414 F. Supp. 538, 92 LRRM 3240 (E.D. N.Y. 1976), wherein the court dismissed a local union's suit seeking an order compelling the employer to process a grievance on the basis that the collective bargaining agreement was between the employer and the international union and not the local union.

pointment of an arbitrator was endorsed by the multi-union unit, is the proper party to represent an aggrieved employee is a procedural question to be decided by the arbitrator and not the court.[82]

ENFORCEMENT BY AND AGAINST A
SUCCESSOR EMPLOYER

In *John Wiley & Sons v. Livingston,*[83] the Supreme Court established that a successor company is bound by the arbitration provisions of a predecessor's contract. In *Wiley,* Interscience Publishers, Inc., a relatively small firm whose employees were represented by an AFL-CIO local, was merged into a significantly larger publishing house, John Wiley & Sons. Interscience was completely liquidated as a result of the merger and its employees were transferred to the Wiley Company. After the merger, the union which had represented the Interscience workers argued that John Wiley & Sons was obligated to honor certain arbitration provisions of the union contract which Interscience had signed before the merger. The Wiley firm resisted the union's claim against it on the grounds that the contract in question was between the union and Interscience, that Interscience no longer existed as a corporate entity, and that Wiley was not obligated to honor the contract to which Interscience had agreed.

The Supreme Court held that, on the facts of the case, Wiley was Interscience's "successor" and therefore bound by the arbitration provisions of the Interscience contract. Such successorship existed, the Court reasoned, because of the "substantial continuity of identity in the business enterprise" from Interscience to Wiley. Such continuity was held to result from "the wholesale transfer of Interscience employees to the Wiley plant."[84] As the Court stated:

> The preference of national labor policy for arbitration as a substitute for tests of strength between contending forces could be overcome only if other considerations compellingly so demanded. We find none. While the principles of law governing ordinary contracts would not bind to a contract an unconsenting successor to a contracting party, a collective bargaining agreement is not an ordinary contract. ... Central to the peculiar status and the function of a collective bargaining agreement is the fact, dictated both by circumstance ... and by the requirements of the National Labor Relations Act, that it is not in any real sense the simple product of a consensual relationship. Therefore, although the duty to arbitrate ... must be

---

[82]*Electric Boat Div., General Dynamics Corp. v. Bhd. of Carpenters and Joiners, Local 1302,* 242 F. Supp. 617, 59 LRRM 2623 (D. Conn. 1965). *See also U.S. v. Pilot Freight Carriers, Inc.,* 54 F.R.D. 519 (D. N.C. 1972).

[83]376 U.S. 543, 55 LRRM 2769 (1964).

[84]*Id.* at 551, 55 LRRM at 2773.

founded on a contract, the impressive policy considerations favoring arbitration are not wholly overborne by the fact that Wiley did not sign the contract being construed.[85]

Whether *Wiley* always requires a successor employer to honor the substantive terms of the predecessor's contract was re-examined by the Supreme Court in *NLRB v. Burns Security Services.*[86] In this case, the Burns private police agency was awarded a contract for maintaining security at an industrial plant previously served by another private security company, the Wackenhut Corporation. To staff its new account, Burns hired twenty-seven of the guards who had worked at that industrial location for Wackenhut before Wackenhut was replaced by Burns. In addition, Burns brought in fifteen of its own people to meet its manpower needs at the plant. The question which the Supreme Court confronted was whether Burns was required by Section 8(a)(5) to bargain with the union which had represented the security guards at the location when the location had been served by Wackenhut. The Supreme Court concluded that Burns was Wackenhut's "successor" and was therefore bound by Wackenhut's preexisting duty to bargain with the union. Such successorship existed because, among other things, (1) Burns " 'had in its employ a majority of Wackenhut's former employees' " and (2) "these employees had already expressed their choice of a bargaining representative in an election held a short time before."[87] The Court further concluded:

> [Burns' duty as a successor] arose when it selected as its work force the employees of the previous employer to perform the same tasks at the same place they had worked in the past. ... In an election held but a few months before, the union had been designated bargaining agent for the employees in the unit and a majority of these employees had been hired by Burns for work in the identical unit. ... It has been consistently held that a mere change of employers or of ownership in the employing industry is not such an "unusual circumstance" as to affect the force of the Board's certification [of a union] within the normal operative period if a majority of employees after the change of ownership or management were employed by the preceding employer.[88]

While the Supreme Court in *Burns* determined that a successor employer may be bound to recognize and bargain with a predecessor's union, the Court also determined that successor employers "are not bound by the substantive provisions of a collective-bargaining contract

---

[85]*Id.* at 549–50, 55 LRRM at 2772–73.
[86]406 U.S. 272, 80 LRRM 2225 (1972).
[87]*Id.* at 278, 80 LRRM at 2227.
[88]*Id.* at 278–79, 80 LRRM at 2227.

negotiated by their predecessors but not agreed to or assumed by them."[89] In this regard, the Court distinguished *Wiley:*

> The Court held in *Wiley* that although the predecessor employer which had signed a collective bargaining contract with the union had disappeared by merger with the successor, the union could compel the successor to arbitrate the extent to which the successor was obligated under the collective-bargaining agreement. . . .
>
> We do not find *Wiley* controlling in the circumstances here. *Wiley* arose in the context of a § 301 suit to compel arbitration, not in the context of an unfair labor practice proceeding where the board is expressly limited by the provisions of § 8(d). . . .
>
> *Wiley's* limited accommodation between the legislative endorsement of freedom of contract and the judicial preference for peaceful arbitral settlement of labor disputes does not warrant the Board's holding that the employer commits an unfair labor practice unless he honors the substantive terms of the preexisting contract. The present case does not involve a § 301 suit; nor does it involve the duty to arbitrate. Rather, the claim is that Burns must be held bound by the contract executed by Wackenhut, whether Burns has agreed to it or not and even though Burns made it perfectly clear that it had no intention of assuming that contract. *Wiley* suggests no such open-ended obligation. Its narrower holding dealt with a merger occurring against a background of state law that embodied the general rule that in merger situations the surviving corporation is liable for the obligations of the disappearing corporation. See N. Y. Stock Corporation Law § 90 (1951); 15 W. Fletcher, Private Corporations, § 7121 (1961 rev. ed.). Here there was no merger or sale of assets, and there were no dealings whatsoever between Wackenhut and Burns. On the contrary, they were competitors for the same work, each bidding for the service contract at Lockheed.[90]

The Supreme Court further qualified a successor's duty to arbitrate under a predecessor's contract in *Howard Johnson Co. v. Hotel Employees.*[91] In this case, the national hotel and restaurant company assumed direct operation of an establishment previously run by local franchise holders. The national corporation purchased all of the personal property held by the local owners and agreed to lease the motel and restaurant buildings as well. As part of its takeover, the national company fired the supervisory personnel who had managed the establishment for the local owners. Howard Johnson also replaced most of the nonsupervisory employees with new personnel of its own choosing. After this takeover and reorganization, the union, which had represented the fired employees while the franchise was still in local hands,

[89]*Id.* at 284, 80 LRRM at 2230.
[90]*Id.* at 285-86, 80 LRRM at 2230.
[91]417 U.S. 249, 86 LRRM 2449 (1974).

attempted to assert contractual arbitration rights against the national Howard Johnson Company. In the union's view, the national corporation was the "successor" to the local owners and therefore bound by the contract signed by the union and the local franchisers. The union sought an order under Section 301 compelling the local franchise holder and Howard Johnson to arbitrate the extent of their obligations to the old employees under the bargaining agreements.

The district court ordered the franchise holder and Howard Johnson to arbitrate the extent of their obligations. The Supreme Court revised the district court's order with regard to Howard Johnson. The Court reasoned that successorship arose in *Wiley* and *Burns* only because of the continuity of the work force. In *Wiley*, virtually all of the predecessor's employees worked for the new corporation. In *Burns*, a majority did. But in *Howard Johnson*, only a small fraction of the labor force employed by the old owners continued to work for the national corporation. Hence, there was no continuity of work force and no successorship. Thus, when a new owner hires a substantially different group of employees, there is ordinarily no successorship and the new owner cannot be bound by any of the obligations placed upon the previous owner, including the obligation to bargain with a particular union. The Court, however, noted the scope of its ruling:

> Thus, our holding today is that Howard Johnson was not required to arbitrate with the Union representing the former Grissom employees in the circumstances of this case. We necessarily do not decide whether Howard Johnson is or is not a "successor employer" for any other purpose.[92]

Cases decided subsequent to *Burns* and *Howard Johnson* have held that a union is not entitled to specific performance of the substantive provisions of a predecessor's contract by a successor employer who did not assume the obligations of the agreement and was not a party to it. There remains, however, some uncertainty as to whether a successor employer may be obligated to arbitrate the extent of its obligations under the predecessors' contract or whether it assumed any obligations. For example, in *Bartenders and Culinary Workers Union v. Howard Johnson Co.*,[93] the Ninth Circuit, leaving open the question of whether a successor would have been obligated to arbitrate the extent of its obligations under the contract, concluded that in a Section 301 action:

> *NLRB v. Burns International Security Service, Inc.*, 406 U.S. 272, 92 S.Ct. 152, 32 L.Ed.2d 61 (1972), held that the Board may not order a successor employer to abide by the substantive provisions of a collective

---

[92]417 U.S. at 262, n. 9, 86 LRRM at 2454, n. 9.
[93]535 F.2d 1160, 92 LRRM 2525 (9th Cir. 1976).

bargaining contract negotiated by its predecessor but not agreed to or assumed by the successor employer. *Howard Johnson Co. v. Hotel Employees,* 417 U.S. 249, 94 S.Ct. 2236, 41 L.Ed.2d 46 (1974), held that the fundamental policies outlined in *Burns* cannot be disregarded in a court proceeding under section 301. Courts and secondary authorities alike are virtually unanimous in the view that a court may not impose the substantive provisions of a collective bargaining contract, as distinguished from the obligation to arbitrate, upon a nonconsenting successor employer. . . .

The Union rests upon *John Wiley & Sons,* arguing that it remains good law despite the subsequent decisions in *Burns International Security Service* and *Howard Johnson Co.,* and on the facts of this case, requires the court to impose the full collective bargaining agreement upon the Company. We need not decide whether *Wiley* survived *Burns* and *Howard Johnson;* nor need we decide whether, if *Wiley* survived, it is distinguishable from the case before us. As the Supreme Court noted in *Burns* (406 U.S. at 286, 92 S.Ct. at 1581, 32 L.Ed.2d at 72), *Wiley* did not impose the full collective bargaining agreement upon the successor employer. On the contrary, the successor was compelled only to arbitrate. Whether any of the substantive terms of the agreement were binding upon the successor was left to the arbitrator to determine. 376 U.S. at 555, 84 S.Ct. at 917, 11 L.Ed.2d at 907.[94]

In *Russom v. Sears, Roebuck & Co.,*[95] the district court concluded that *Burns* imposes upon a successor employer the duty to bargain or to arbitrate with the existing union but not the obligation to be bound to the substantive provisions of the collective bargaining agreement. Similarly, in *Local 1115 v. B&K Investments, Inc.,*[96] the district court held that a successor company may be compelled to arbitrate the extent of its obligation under its predecessor's contract. In this case the court ruled that whether or not the successor is bound by any or all of the substantive provisions of their predecessor's contracts is a question for the arbitrator, in the first instance, to decide subject to judicial review.

---

[94]*Id.* at 1162-63, 92 LRRM at 2527.

[95]415 F. Supp. 792, 94 LRRM 2882 (E.D. Mo. 1976), *aff'd,* 558 F.2d 439, 95 LRRM 2914 (8th Cir. 1977), *cert. denied.* 434 U.S. 955, 96 LRRM 2921 (1977). *See* Summers, *Individual Rights in Collective Agreements and Arbitration,* 37 N.Y.U.L. REV. 362, 384 (1962). *See Serra v. Pepsi-Cola General Bottlers, Inc.,* 248 F. Supp. 684, 61 LRRM 2080 (N.D. Ill. 1965), as an example of one of the few cases which adopted this view.

[96]*Local 1115 v. B & K Investments, Inc.,* 436 F. Supp. 1203, 96 LRRM 2348 (S.D. Fla. 1977); *see also United Steelworkers of America v. Unites States Gypsum Co.,* 492 F.2d 713, 85 LRRM 2962 (5th Cir. 1974). *Note Boeing Company v. International Association of Machinists.* 504 F.2d 307, 87 LRRM 2865 (5th Cir. 1974); *United Paperworkers v. Penntech Papers, Inc.,* 439 F. Supp. 610, 96 LRRM 2910, *aff'd,* 583 F.2d 33, 96 LRRM 2910 (D.C. Me. 1977); *Lathers Local 104 v. McGlynn Plastering, Inc.,* 91 LRRM 3000 (W.D. Wash. 1976). *See also* Lewis, *Fair Representation in Grievance Arbitration: Vaca v. Sipes,* THE SUPREME COURT REVIEW 81 (1967); Clark, *The Duty of Fair Representation: A Theoretical Structure,* 51 TEXAS L. REV. 1119 (1973).

Whether or not an employer is a successor has been held by some courts to be a question to be resolved by the court and thus the question of the obligation to arbitrate could also be a matter for the court.[97] Other courts have said the question is to be resolved by the arbitrator.[98] Where the question is whether the agreement grants arbitration rights to employees in plants in only one division or in any plant in the company where the union represents the employees, courts have held this to be a question to be decided by the arbitrator.[99]

Where the successor is a trustee in bankruptcy, the trustee has been held not bound by the agreement to arbitrate contained in an agreement between the union and the bankrupt employer. For example, the Sixth Circuit said that enforcement of arbitration of a grievance claim that vacation amounts due were to increase as if the employer were still in business was not required. The bankruptcy court held that it was not obligated to surrender jurisdiction to the arbitrator on such a claim since "labor peace was not an issue" and that the employees would be given a chance to prove their grievance claim in the bankruptcy court.[100]

Similarly, the Ninth Circuit approved the dissolution by a federal district court of a state court order compelling arbitration where the employer was bankrupt and its business was terminated. The court said that while federal policy favors arbitration of "ordinary" labor disputes, the bankruptcy court is resolving various controversies between various creditors of a debtor, and the employees' claim is another such claim and not "the type of grievance which is ordinarily the subject of arbitration under a collective bargaining agreement enforced pursuant to § 301(a)."[101]

---

[97]*Monroe Sander Corp. v. Livingston*, 377 F.2d 67, 65 LRRM 2273 (2d Cir. 1967); *Office Employees Int'l Union, Local 153 v. Ward Garcia Corp.*, 190 F. Supp. 448, 47 LRRM 2780 (S.D. N.Y. 1961); *Retail Clerks Union, Local 428 v. L. Bloom Sons*, 173 Cal. App. 2d 701, 344 P.2d 511, 33 LA 273 (1959).

[98]*U.S. Gypsum v. United Steelworkers*, 384 F.2d 38, 66 LRRM 2232 (5th Cir. 1967). Subsequently, Arbitrator Rolf Valtin held U.S. Gypsum a successor and obligated to arbitrate under the predecessor's labor agreement. *See United States Gypsum Co.*, 56 LA 363 (Valtin, 1971); *United Electrical Workers v. Star Expansion Industries, Inc.*, 246 F. Supp. 400, 56 LRRM 2286 (S.D. N.Y. 1964).

[99]*Teamsters Local 745 v. Braswell Motor Freight Lines, Inc.*, 392 F.2d 1, 68 LRRM 2143 (5th Cir. 1968).

[100]*Muskegon Motor Specialties Co. v. Davis*, 313 F.2d 841, 52 LRRM 2541 (6th Cir. 1963). *Cf. Koven & Bro. v. United Steelworkers Local 5767*, 381 F.2d 196, 65 LRRM 2201 (3d Cir. 1967).

[101]*Johnson v. England*, 356 F.2d 44, 61 LRRM 2635 (9th Cir.), *cert. denied*, 384 U.S. 961, 62 LRRM 2231 (1966); *Riker v. Browne*, 204 N.Y. S.2d 60, 62 (Sup. Ct. 1960) ("A provisional receiver is born by order of the court. ... He may affirm or reject the rights and obligations of the interest he is caretaking, and it would be inconsistent to compel arbitration ... against him on obligations antedating his creation."); *Eastern Freight Ways, Inc. v. Local 707, Teamsters*, 300 F. Supp. 1289, 71 LRRM 2631 (S.D. N.Y. 1969).

ENFORCEMENT BY AN AGGRIEVED EMPLOYEE

The enforcement of an award is no longer under the union's exclusive control. If the aggrieved employee is disappointed with the decision, the employee may retain a private attorney and initiate various "second chance" procedures through a private suit.

Often the private attorney can file a suit under Section 301 and convince a judge and jury that the union representative, either before or after the grievance reached arbitration, was guilty of a significant negligence and that the award should be vacated and the grievance retried in the federal court. The time limits set out in the labor agreement are lifted for such a suit, but the suit must be started within 90 days after the issuance of the award.[102] This "second chance" procedure through a private suit filed against both the union and the company is not only slow and difficult but expensive.

Another large number of grievants who get a "second chance" are those in cases that involve awards that can be shown by the private attorney to have some "edge" or aspect related to the Civil Rights Act (Title VII) or the Fair Labor Standards Act. The automatic review of awards by a federal judge when the grievant is disappointed[103] may well be sought successfully by private attorneys when the award touches some public law.[104]

Some grievances have a factual base covered in a particular statute, such as the Employment Retirement Security Act (ERISA), and private attorneys for a disappointed grievant may find a right in the statute to have the award reviewed by the federal court.[105]

Other grievants get a "second chance" when the private attorney urges a Labor Department lawyer to prosecute a suit in the district court to seek a vacation or revision of the award.[106]

The disappointed grievant may also have a private attorney review the award before the NLRB by filing an unfair labor practice charge claiming that the award is inconsistent with Board law, and if this is established, the Board will vacate the award under the *Spielberg* procedures.[107]

Other aggrieved employees have had private attorneys file suits to enforce a grievance under a labor agreement under Section 301 when

---

[102] *See* discussion of statute of limitations applicable to litigation growing out of a labor agreement (Chapter I) and discussion of fair representation suits (Chapter XXIII).

[103] *See* discussion in Chapter XXII.

[104] *See* discussion in Chapter XXII.

[105] *See* discussion in Chapter XXII.

[106] *See* discussion in Chapter XXII.

[107] Discussed in Chapter XXII.

the labor agreement did not contain an arbitration procedure[108] or to have a grievance determined by the court when the employer refused to process the grievance under the contractual procedure and has, in effect, repudiated that procedure:

> An obvious situation in which the employee should not be limited to the exclusive remedial procedures established by the contract occurs when the conduct of the employer amounts to a repudiation of those contractual procedures. Cf. *Drake Bakeries, Inc. v. Local 50, Am. Bakery, etc., Workers,* 370 U.S. 254, 260–263. See generally 6A Cordin Contracts § 1443 (1962). In such a situation (and there may of course be others), the employer is estopped by his own conduct to rely on the unexhausted grievance and arbitration procedures as a defense to the employee's cause of action.[109]

ENFORCEMENT BY THIRD PARTIES

In many instances, persons other than employees may be indirectly affected by the terms of the labor agreement and therefore may desire to raise a complaint under it. Generally, as noted earlier, persons not parties to the agreement have no standing to compel arbitration under the agreement. For example, persons promised benefits by an employer at a time before they transferred into the bargaining unit[110] and retirees[111] have no standing to seek arbitration either independently or through the union.[112]

The same type of analysis denies to civil rights groups and "outside" interest groups any right to submit grievances on behalf of employees and process them to arbitration, or to represent employees in arbitration when the employees are already covered by an existing labor agreement and represented by a union. To recognize such a group as an employee's representative would be inconsistent with the legal rights of the certified union.[113]

---

[108]*Oil, Chemical and Atomic Workers v. American Maize Products Co.,* 429 F.2d 409, 86 LRRM 2438 (7th Cir. 1974). A union can waive the arbitration of pending grievances in the course of negotiating a new labor agreement; *Public Service, Production & Maintenance Employees, Local 157 v. Transit Management of Laredo, Inc.,* 86 LC ¶ 11,365 (D. Tex. 1979).

[109]*Vaca v. Sipes,* 386 U.S. 171, 185, 64 LRRM 2369, 2374 (1967).

[110]*J. I. Case Co. v. NLRB,* 321 U.S. 332, 14 LRRM 501 (1944); *Ranco, Inc.,* 68-1 ARB ¶ 9197 (Klein, 1968). In *Ranco,* the arbitrator denied standing to arbitrate to employees who sought enforcement of a promise of a gift of tools if they transferred into the bargaining unit.

[111]In *Van Dyne-Crotty, Inc.,* 46 LA 338 (Teple, 1966), the arbitrator denied standing to a "voluntary retiree" to compel arbitration of a grievance which arose after retirement.

[112]*Flambeau Paper Co.,* 68-2 ARB ¶ 8404 (Hart, 1968).

[113]*Hotel Employers Ass'n of San Francisco,* 47 LA 873 (Burns, 1966), where the arbitrator determined that the employer violated the collective bargaining agreement by arbitrating a dispute with a civil rights group since the union, not the civil rights group, was the employees' bargaining representative.

ENFORCEMENT BY THE NLRB

The National Labor Relations Board had maintained that an employer commits an unfair labor practice if it refuses to arbitrate grievances which request reinstatement of strikers discharged for engaging in picketing misconduct.[114] The Board's position was reversed by the Fourth Circuit in 1971 in *NLRB v. Community Motor Bus Co.*[115]

The Fourth Circuit determined that the agreement which ended the strike did not include a provision relating to arbitration of disputes over reinstatement of strikers guilty of misconduct and, thus, the employer's refusal to arbitrate the cases was not an unfair labor practice. In later cases, the Board has concluded that enforcement of agreements to arbitrate is a matter for the courts, not the Board. In *Hilton-Davis Chemical Co.,*[116] the Board quoted with approval the following from a Second Circuit opinion:

> The duty to arbitrate is wholly contractual and the courts have the obligation to determine whether there is a contract imposing such a duty.[117]

---

[114]*Community Motor Bus Co.,* 180 NLRB 677, 73 LRRM 1223 (1970).

[115]*NLRB v. Community Motor Bus Co.,* 439 F.2d 965, 76 LRRM 2844 (4th Cir. 1971).

[116]185 NLRB 241, 75 LRRM 1036 (1970).

[117]*Procter & Gamble Ind. U. v. Procter & Gamble Mfg. Co.,* 312 F.2d 181, 184, 51 LRRM 2752, 2753 (2nd Cir. 1962), *cert. denied*, 374 U.S. 830, 53 LRRM 2544 (1963); *see also International Union, United Automobile, Aerospace and Agricultural Implement Workers of America v. International Telephone and Telegraph Corporation,* 508 F.2d 1309, 88 LRRM 2213 (8th Cir. 1975); *National Marine Engineers Beneficial Ass'n. v. Globe Seaways, Inc.,* 451 F.2d 1159, 79 LRRM 2067 (2d Cir. 1971).

CHAPTER IV

Stays of Arbitration

In the prior chapter, actions to enforce an agreement to arbitrate were considered. Closely related are actions to stay an arbitration.[1] If a request for an order to arbitrate is not granted, the effect is a stay. If the request for a stay is not granted, the effect is an order to arbitrate.[2] In this chapter, we are concerned with what the courts do when claims of procedural deficiency or of nonarbitrability are presented.

REQUEST FOR STAYS BECAUSE OF PROCEDURAL DEFICIENCY

When confronted with the claim of lack of arbitrability because of procedural deficiencies, courts have held that under the Supreme Court's decision in *John Wiley & Sons, Inc. v. Livingston*,[3] questions of procedural arbitrability should be resolved by the arbitrator.[4]

---

[1]Zalusky, *Arbitration: Updating a Vital Process, AFL-CIO,* AMERICAN FEDERATIONIST, Vol. 83, No. 11 (Nov. 1976).

[2]Murray and Griffin, *Expedited Arbitration of Discharge Cases,* THE ARBITRATION JOURNAL, Vol. 31, No. 4, (Dec. 1976).

[3]376 U.S. 543, 557, 55 LRRM 2769, 2771 (1964).

[4]*Meat Cutters Local 405 v. Tennessee Dressed Beef Co.,* 428 F.2d 797, 74 LRRM 2722 (6th Cir. 1970); *UAW Local 864 v. Daniel Radiator Corp. of Texas,* 328 F.2d 614, 55 LRRM 3001 (5th Cir. 1964). *United States ex rel. Madison v. Rundle,* 422 F.2d 49 (3d Cir. 1970); *Bevington & Basile Wholesalers, Inc. v. Brewery Workers Local 46,* 330 F.2d 202, 55 LRRM 2976 (8th Cir. 1964); *Meat Cutters Local 195 v. Way,* 238 F. Supp. 726, 58 LRRM 2308 (E.D. Pa. 1965); *Western Automatic Machine Screw Co. v. UAW Local 101,* 335 F.2d 103, 56 LRRM 2978 (6th Cir. 1964); *Teamsters Local 776 v. Standard Motor Freight, Inc.,* 260 F. Supp. 269, 63 LRRM 2385 (M.D. Pa. 1966); *Trailways of New England, Inc. v. Amalgamated Ass'n of Street, Electric Railway and Motor Coach Employees, Div. 1318,* 343 F.2d 815, 58 LRRM 2848 (1st Cir. 1965); *Rochester Tel. Corp. v. Communications Workers,* 340 F.2d 237, 58 LRRM 2223 (2d Cir. 1964); *Long Island Lumber Co. v. Martin,* 15 N.Y.2d 380, 259 N.Y.S.2d 142, 59 LRRM 2237 (1965); *Local 1401, Retail Clerks Int'l Ass'n v. Woodman's Food Mkt., Inc.,* 371 F.2d 199, 63 LRRM 2568 (7th Cir. 1966); *Brewery Workers Local 366 v. Adolph Coors Co.,* 240 F. Supp. 279, 59 LRRM 2950 (D. Colo. 1964); *International Union of Operating Engineers, Local 150, AFL-CIO v. Flair Builders, Inc.,* 406 U.S. 487, 80 LRRM 2441, 92 S. Ct. 1710 (1972); *Local 771, IATSE, AFL-CIO v. RKO General, Inc., WOR Division,* 546 F.2d 1107, 94 LRRM 2928 (2d Cir. 1977); *Hotel & Restaurant Employees & Bartenders International Union, AFL-CIO v. Michelson's Food Services, Inc.,* 545 F.2d 1248, 94 LRRM 2014 (9th Cir. 1976); *Bressette v. In-*

Even prior to *Wiley,* courts recognized that "the essence of arbitration [is] that it be speedy, . . . and . . . if procedural questions are to be passed on by the court it would open the door to all sorts of technical obstructionism."[5] The rule that the arbitrator, rather than the courts, should decide the procedural deficiency questions has been held not to apply to commercial arbitration where the special reasons for expeditious procedure are not present to the same degree as they are in labor arbitration.[6]

In a case concerning whether an employer had waived contractual time limits in the agreement by prior conduct, a federal court held that it was a question of procedural arbitrability which should be decided by an arbitrator, not the court.[7] The court noted that it was "unnecessary" to determine whether there were exceptions to the *Wiley* doctrine. To decide in a court what procedural questions are "strictly procedural" would be reopening the door closed by the *Wiley* decision.

On the other hand, courts have dismissed arbitration requests where the procedural defect is so clear that to refer the matter to an arbitrator would be an imposition on all concerned.[8] Where a party admittedly has not complied with plain contractual time limits and has neither offered mitigating facts nor cited contributory conduct by the opposing side as a defense, the Sixth Circuit in a post-*Wiley* decision has held that it would still be within the court's jurisdiction to bar

---

ternational Talc Co., Inc., 527 F.2d 211, 91 LRRM 2077 (2d Cir. 1975); *United Electrical Radio and Machine Workers of America v. Honeywell,* 522 F.2d 1221, 90 LRRM 2193 (7th Cir. 1975); *Local 81, American Federation of Technical Engineers, AFL-CIO v. Western Electric Co.,* 508 F.2d 106, 88 LRRM 2067 (7th Cir. 1974); *Barrett v. Manufacturers Railway Company,* 453 F.2d 1305, 79 LRRM 2411 (8th Cir. 1972); *Board of Education v. Bellmore,* 39 N.Y.2d 167, 383 N.Y.S.2d 242, 347 N.E.2d 603, 92 LRRM 2244 (1976); *Nationwide Insurance v. Investors,* 37 N.Y.2d 91, 371 N.Y.S.2d 463, 332 N.E.2d 333 (1975); *Mtr. City School District, Poughkeepsie,* 35 N.Y.2d 599, 364 N.Y.S.2d 492, 324 N.E.2d 144, 89 LRRM 3012 (1974).

[5]*Local 748, IUE v. Jefferson City Cabinet Co.,* 314 F.2d 192, 195, 52 LRRM 2513 (6th Cir. 1963).

[6]*Long Island Lumber Co. v. Martin,* 15 N.Y.2d 380, 259 N.Y.S.2d 142 (1965).

[7]*Brewery Workers Local 366 v. Adolph Coors Co.,* 240 F. Supp. 279, 59 LRRM 2950 (D. Colo. 1964).

[8]*See, e.g., Boilermakers Local 483 v. Shell Oil Co.,* 369 F.2d 526, 63 LRRM 2173 (7th Cir. 1966); *Boeing Co. v. UAW Local 1069,* 349 F.2d 412, 59 LRRM 2988 (3d Cir. 1965). *See also Western Metal Specialty Div.,* 53 LA 878 (Solomon, 1969); *Ranco, Inc.,* 50 LA 269 (Klein, 1968); *Local 13, International Federation of Professional & Technical Engineers, AFL-CIO v. General Electric Co.,* 531 F.2d 1178, 91 LRRM 2471, 91 LRRM 3088 (3d Cir. 1976); *Local 210 International Printing Pressmen & Assistants Union v. Times World Corp.,* 381 F. Supp. 149, 87 LRRM 3009 (D.C. Va. 1974); *Local No. 644, United Brotherhood of Carpenters & Joiners of America, AFL-CIO v. Walsh Construction Co.,* 79 LRRM 2150 (S.D. Ill. 1972); *District 2, Marine Engineers Beneficial Association, AFL-CIO v. Falcon Carriers, Inc.,* 374 F. Supp. 1342, 86 LRRM 2121 (D.C. N.Y. 1974).

recourse to arbitration.[9] However, the better view is that both the failure to comply with contractual time limits and so-called extrinsic defenses to arbitration like laches should be referred to the arbitrator for resolution.[10]

A unique procedural question was decided by the court in *Local 616, IUE v. Byrd Plastics, Inc.*[11] An initial arbitration had been dismissed by the arbitrator on the ground that the employee had not signed the grievance form as required by the contract. The grievance was then refiled over the signature of the employee. The employer refused to participate in the second arbitration on the ground that the first arbitration had disposed of the grievance and discharged the employer's duty to arbitrate. The second arbitrator disagreed with this argument and decided on the merits for the employee. The district court denied enforcement, but the circuit court reversed, analogizing the result of the first arbitration to a dismissal without prejudice. Although the court agreed with the finding of the second arbitrator that the grievance remained arbitrable, the court did not defer to his decision but reexamined the issue for itself.

STAYS BECAUSE OF CONFLICT WITH
THE NLRA AND FLSA

Where the NLRB is involved, courts have issued stays of an arbitration proceeding to avoid a possible conflict between the decision of the Board and the award of the arbitrator. For example, a court has ruled that an arbitrator may not determine which of two rival unions is entitled to disputed work when that issue is pending before the Board.[12] There, an employer had filed a charge with the Board alleging that both unions had threatened to strike if their members were not assigned certain work and were, therefore, violating the National Labor Relations Act. One union petitioned the court to compel the employer

---

[9]*ACWA v. Ironall Factories Co.,* 386 F.2d 586, 67 LRRM 2093 (6th Cir. 1967); *International Union of Operating Engineers Local 150 v. Flair Builders, Inc.,* 440 F.2d 557, 76 LRRM 2595 (7th Cir. 1971); *Amalgamated Clothing Workers of America v. Ironall Factories Co.,* 386 F.2d 586, 67 LRRM 2093 (6th Cir. 1967); *Chattanooga Mailers v. Chattanooga News-Free Press,* 524 F.2d 1305, 90 LRRM 3000 (6th Cir. 1975). *Contra, Tobacco Workers International Union Local 317 v. Lorillard Corporation,* 448 F.2d 949, 78 LRRM 2273 (4th Cir. 1971).

[10]*International Union of Operating Engineers Local 150 v. Flair Builders, Inc.,* 406 U.S. 487, 80 LRRM 2441 (1972); *Tobacco Workers v. Lorillard Corp.,* 448 F.2d 949, 78 LRRM 2273 (4th Cir. 1971); *Davis v. Pro Basketball, Inc.,* 381 F. Supp. 1, 87 LRRM 2285 (D.C. N.Y. 1974); *Halcon International, Inc. v. Monsanto Australia Ltd.,* 446 F.2d 156 (7th Cir. 1971); *Lodge 1327, International Association of Machinists & A. W. v. Fraser & Johnston Co.,* 454 F.2d 88, 79 LRRM 2118 (9th Cir. 1971).

[11]428 F.2d 23, 74 LRRM 2550 (3d Cir. 1970).

[12]*New York Mailers' Union No. 6 v. New York Times Co.,* 32 Misc.2d 60, 222 N.Y.S.2d 1000, 49 LRRM 2233 (Sup. Ct. 1961).

to arbitrate the dispute over the work assignment, and the company asked that the petition be dismissed on the ground that the NLRB had exclusive jurisdiction over the issue. The court agreed with the employer, holding:

> [T]he Board possesses the sole and exclusive jurisdiction to decide which of the rival unions is entitled to an assignment of the work forming the basis of the controversy between them, and that the provisions of the collective bargaining agreements with the unions, though among the factors to be considered by the Board, are not conclusive upon it and may be disregarded by it. It must follow that even if arbitration were ordered, pursuant to the collective bargaining agreement, any award made by the arbitrators would not be binding upon the Board, which alone has the jurisdiction to decide what union is entitled to the work. Permitting arbitration to proceed would undoubtedly lead, in many cases, to an award requiring an employer to assign work to one union, only to have the Board direct that the work be assigned to a rival union.[13]

The issue of whether a union was entitled to recognition as the bargaining representative of employees in a store was held not arbitrable where a second union was seeking recognition of the same unit of employees under NLRB procedures.[14] The first union had a labor agreement with the employer in which it was designated the exclusive representative of the employees; after entering into this agreement, the employer contracted to supervise operation of a second store. The other union filed a petition with the NLRB seeking an election in the second store to determine whether it should be the bargaining representative. When the first union requested arbitration of this issue, the court said:

> Such matters cannot be ultimately decided through the grievance resolving procedure of collective bargaining agreement where the rights of third persons, not parties to the agreement, are involved. Therefore, the relief requested by plaintiff cannot be granted by this court.[15]

Similarly, arbitration was enjoined pending conclusion of proceedings before the NLRB where the trial examiner made a preliminary finding on the very question to be arbitrated.[16] The union initiated an arbitration through the procedures of the Federal Mediation and Con-

---

[13]32 Misc.2d at 62, 222 N.Y.S.2d at 1002, 49 LRRM at 2234.

[14]*Local 1357, Retail Clerks Int'l Ass'n v. Food Fair Stores, Inc.*, 202 F.Supp. 322, 48 LRRM 2284 (E.D. Pa. 1961). *See also Amperex Electronic Corp. v. Rugen*, 284 App. Div. 808, 132 N.Y.S.2d 93, 22 LA 694 (1954); *Int'l Ass'n of Machinists v. Howmet Corp.*, 466 F.2d 1249, 81 LRRM 2289 (9th Cir. 1972).

[15]202 F. Supp. at 324, 48 LRRM at 2285.

[16]*Kentile, Inc. v. Local 457, United Rubber, Cork, Linoleum & Plastics Workers*, 228 F. Supp. 541, 55 LRRM 3011 (E.D.N.Y. 1964); *Colonie Hill, Ltd. v. Local 164, Bartenders, Hotel & Restaurant Employees Union*, 343 F. Supp. 986, 80 LRRM 2745 (D.C. N.Y. 1972). *But see*

ciliation Service (FMCS) as specified in the collective bargaining agreement. The employer instituted a Section 301 suit to enjoin the arbitration. The court, granting the injunction, held that it would be repetitious to arbitrate the very same issue which the trial examiner had decided. Likewise, a court ruled that an arbitration initiated by a union would be stayed where the issue to be referred to the arbitrator had been ruled on by the Board, for otherwise there might be conflicting decisions on the same issue.[17] And, in *Lanco Coal Co. v. Southern Labor Union, Local 250,*[18] the court refused to enjoin a wildcat strike and compel arbitration of the dispute, notwithstanding the broad contractual arbitration provisions and the *Boys Markets* decision,[19] because the dispute was primarily a representation case involving the employees' dissatisfaction with their union and thus one "where the priority position of the National Labor Relations Board should be protected."[20]

At first glance, these decisions would seem to conflict with *Carey v. Westinghouse Electric Corp.*[21] where the Supreme Court was confronted with a dispute involving a claim by a union that its members should do certain work while the same work was being claimed by another union for its members. The company had refused to arbitrate the claim of one of the unions on the ground that the dispute presented a matter within the jurisdiction of the NLRB. The lower court refused to compel arbitration, but the Supreme Court, in reversing, noted that no matter how the dispute was characterized, arbitration should be held because of the strong federal policy favoring arbitration. Moreover, the Court noted, the NLRB's superior power could always be invoked thereafter. The Court articulated its rationale as follows:

> However the dispute be considered—whether one involving work assignment or one concerning representation—we see no barrier to use of the arbitration procedure. If it is a work assignment dispute, arbitration conveniently fills a gap and avoids the necessity of a strike to bring the matter to the Board. If it is a representation matter, resort to arbitration may have a pervasive, curative effect even though one union is not a party.
>
> By allowing the dispute to go to arbitration its fragmentation is avoided to a substantial extent; and those conciliatory measures which Congress

---

International Tel. & Tel. Corp. v. Local 400, IUE, 248 F. Supp. 949, 950-51, 59 LRRM 3033, 3035 (D.N.J. 1965) where the court said:
    The commencement of arbitration will not interfere with the pending decertification proceeding. . . . If the decision on decertification changes the representative status of the Union the matter may be corrected upon suit to enforce the award.
[17]*Blue Bird Knitwear Co. v. Livingston,* 54 LRRM 2476 (N.Y. Sup. Ct. 1963).
[18]320 F. Supp. 273, 76 LRRM 2249 (N.D. Ala. 1970).
[19]*Boys Markets, Inc. v. Retail Clerks Union, Local 770,* 398 U.S. 235, 74 LRRM 2257 (1970).
[20]*United States v. Partin,* 320 F. Supp. at 275.
[21]372 U.S. 261, 55 LRRM 2042 (1964).

deemed vital to "industrial peace" . . . and which may be dispositive of the entire dispute, are encouraged. The superior authority of the Board may be invoked at any time. Meanwhile the therapy of arbitration is brought to bear in a complicated and troubled area. [22]

While there may appear to be tension between *Carey* and the decisions referred to previously, the latter are generally distinguishable from *Carey* because in the cases where the stays of arbitration were issued by the courts, the superior authority of the Board had already been invoked, thus rendering any arbitration meaningless; whereas, in *Carey*, the superior authority of the Board had not yet been invoked. [23] As for *Lanco Coal Co., supra,* this can be distinguished on the grounds that, unlike in *Carey*, the court felt that arbitration could serve no useful purpose because of the peculiar circumstances present there.

Where the NLRB has already decided the issue, the policy considerations for granting a stay of a demand for arbitration on the same issue are, of course, different. [24] For example, after two unions and the employer had joined in a petition to the NLRB for a unit clarification, the Seventh Circuit refused to compel arbitration of a dispute over the unit because the Board's determination of the unit, adverse to the position of the union petitioning for an order compelling arbitration, fully disposed of the issue. In upholding a lower court's refusal to order arbitration, the court in *Smith Steel Workers v. A. O. Smith Corp.* stated:

> Arbitration provides an alternative means of resolving disputes over the appropriate representational unit, but it does not control the Board in subsequent proceedings. . . . The court could compel neither arbitration nor enforce any arbiter's award in conflict with the Board's order. [25]

In a situation where the arbitration agreement precluded the filing of unfair labor practices, a court refused to stay the action before the

---

[22]*Id.* at 272, 55 LRRM at 2047. *See also International Union of Operating Engineers, Local 279 v. Sid Richardson Carbon Company,* 471 F.2d 1175, 82 LRRM 2403 (5th Cir. 1973).

[23]The superior power of the Board, however, was eventually invoked and its decision was contrary to that of the arbitrator. *Westinghouse Electric Corp.,* 162 NLRB 768, 64 LRRM 1082 (1967).

[24]*Buchholz v. Local 463, IUE,* 15 App.Div.2d 394, 224 N.Y.S.2d 638, 49 LRRM 2743 (1962), *aff'd,* 15 N.Y.2d 181, 257 N.Y.S.2d 134, 58 LRRM 2462 (1965). Of course, where the issues before the Board and the arbitrator differ, even though they are related, prior Board action is not a bar to a subsequent arbitration petition. *See Local 12934 of International Union, District 50, United Mine Workers of America v. Dow Corning Co.,* 459 F.2d 221, 80 LRRM 2218 (6th Cir. 1972).

[25]420 F.2d 1, 7, 73 LRRM 2028, 2031 (7th Cir. 1969). *See also Local 464, American Bakery and Confectionery Workers International Union, AFL-CIO v. Hershey Chocolate Corp.,* 310 F. Supp. 1182, 73 LRRM 2538 (M.D. Pa. 1970).

Board, holding that the agreement was unenforceable.[26] This dispute concerned the misconduct of strikers. The union objected to the company action concerning the strikers and it was agreed that the dispute should be arbitrated. The union then filed an unfair labor practice charge with the NLRB, which the company claimed the union could not do under the agreement. The Second Circuit rejected the company's contentions, holding that such an agreement does not waive the union's right to file unfair labor practices because the rights under the National Labor Relations Act are public ones that cannot be impaired by a private agreement.[27]

Related to the decisions refusing to grant a stay where a claim could be submitted to the NLRB and granting a stay when it has been are the cases where the stay of arbitration is requested because the claim could be processed under the Fair Labor Standards Act. The Third Circuit, in a decision which the Supreme Court declined to review,[28] held that arbitration would not be prohibited merely because a claim could be brought under the Fair Labor Standards Act. In a different context, the Sixth Circuit ruled that arbitration was mandatory despite the fact that the plaintiff-employee had a cause of action under the Kentucky workmen's compensation statute. The court found that the claim was clearly governed by the labor contract and as such was to be treated as arising under the Labor Management Relations Act. Accordingly, the court held that arbitration should have been attempted prior to the filing of the suit.[29]

STAYS GRANTED FOR LACK OF A GRIEVANCE

A stay was granted where a dispute had not yet crystallized and any award the arbitrator rendered would have been a request for an ad-

---

[26]*IAM Lodge 743 v. United Aircraft Corp.,* 337 F.2d 5, 57 LRRM 2245 (2d Cir. 1964), *cert. denied,* 380 U.S. 908, 58 LRRM 2496 (1965). *See also United Aircraft Corporation v. Canel Lodge No. 700, IAM & AW,* 314 F. Supp. 371, 74 LRRM 2518 (D.C. Conn. 1970); *International Association, Etc., Local 395 v. Lake County, Indiana Council, Etc.,* 347 F. Supp. 1377, 82 LRRM 2363 (D.C. Ind. 1972).

[27]*E.g., Hribar Trucking, Inc.,* 166 NLRB 745, 65 LRRM 1555 (1967); *Breitling Bros. Construction Co.,* 153 NLRB 685, 59 LRRM 1540 (1965); *Great Lakes Carbon Corp.,* 152 NLRB 988, 59 LRRM 1266 (1965).

[28]*Watkins v. Hudson Coal Co.,* 151 F.2d 311, 5 WH Cases 565 (3d Cir. 1945), *cert. denied,* 327 U.S. 777, 5 WH Cases 864 (1946). *See also State v. Berry,* 434 P.2d 471 (Ore. Sup. Ct. 1968); *Andacht v. William Andacht, Inc.,* 183 N.Y.S.2d 62 (1958); *U.S. Bulk Carriers v. Arguelles,* 400 U.S. 351, 76 LRRM 2161 (1971); *Iowa Beef Packers, Inc. v. Thompson, cert. dismissed,* 405 U.S. 228 (1972).

[29]*R. F. Rhine v. Union Carbide Corp.,* 343 F.2d 12, 58 LRRM 2724 (6th Cir. 1965), *rev'g* 221 F. Supp. 701 (W.D. Ky. 1963).

visory opinion.[30] In that case, a union had petitioned to compel arbitration to determine whether the labor agreement should cover vessels which were to be transferred to a company in which the employer owned 26 percent of the stock. At the time the demand was made, the transfer was still contingent on government approval. The court said that the matter was not arbitrable because "it merely calls for an advisory opinion."

A union received a stay of an arbitration claim that the increase in the union's dues and initiation fee was discriminatory and excessive on the ground that the claim did not establish any issue of discrimination against the employer.[31] When an employer contended, however, that the union violated the collective agreement when it disciplined a foreman who was also a union member, and the union in reply contended its disciplinary procedures were internal union concerns, the court concluded there was sufficient merit in both contentions that arbitration should be directed.[32]

Similarly, there was no recognizable grievance against an employer's successor over a vacation pay claim where the union had executed and had delivered a general release discharging the employer and its successor and assigns from all actions in law or in equity which the union "ever had, now has or ... hereafter can, shall or may have," save one claim unrelated to the controversy.[33] Where a claim is discharged by operation of law, the court held it "may not be subject to arbitration as it is not arbitrable under the collective bargaining agreement."[34] In contrast, another court held that it was for the arbitrator, not the court, to determine whether a controversy was moot due to an alleged accord and satisfaction.[35]

A court has also examined a union's compliance with the time limits for appeal because under many collective agreements the failure of the union to process the grievance within a time limit is evidence that the union accepted the last answer of the employer, and if acceptance has

---

[30]*District 2, Marine Engineers Beneficial Ass'n v. Isbrandtsen Co.*, 226 N.Y.S.2d 883, 50 LRRM 2795 (Sup. Ct. 1962). *See also Lempco Automotive, Inc. v. IAM Local 1444*, 184 F. Supp. 114, 46 LRRM 2951 (N.D. Ohio 1960), where settlement of the grievance caused the action to stay arbitration to become moot.

[31]*Stamford Transit Co. v. Teamsters Local 145*, 146 Conn. 467, 152 A.2d 502, 32 LA 634 (1959).

[32]*Pock v. New York Typographical Union No. 6*, 223 F. Supp. 181, 54 LRRM 2666 (S.D. N.Y. 1963); *see also Houston Chronicle Publishing Co. v. Houston Typographical Union No. 87*, 272 F. Supp. 974 (S.D. Tex. 1966); *Macneish v. New York Typographical Union No. 6*, 205 F. Supp. 558, 50 LRRM 2361 (S.D. N.Y. 1962).

[33]*L. O. Koven & Bro. v. Local 5767, Steelworkers*, 250 F. Supp. 810 (D. N.J. 1966).

[34]*Id.* at 815.

[35]*Galveston Maritime Ass'n v. South Atlantic & Gulf Coast Dist., Int'l Longshoremen's Ass'n, Local 307*, 234 F. Supp. 250 (S.D. Tex. 1964).

in fact occurred, no grievance remains to be arbitrated.[36] Such a holding, of course, raises serious questions as to whether the court is entangling itself in a procedural matter, contrary to *Wiley.*

In another case where a stay was granted for lack of a grievance, the grievant claimed that his layoff was inconsistent with his seniority layoff rights.[37] However, the new labor agreement had omitted the layoff provisions of the prior agreement and a letter accompanying the agreement explained that a joint study committee would be appointed to negotiate a mutually acceptable layoff plan by an agreed date or economic sanctions could be invoked. Since the parties were unable to agree on a layoff plan by the agreed date, a strike ensued. The court rejected the argument that the provision of the old agreement remained in effect during the negotiation period and thus denied the request for arbitration.

Likewise, an injunction was granted against the arbitration of a grievance brought by the union where the employer showed that the grievance was the same as a prior one earlier decided by a joint area committee.[38]

EFFECT OF A WILDCAT STRIKE ON THE DUTY TO ARBITRATE

Where there has been a strike in violation of the agreement, employers have often requested a stay of arbitration on the basis that the union's pledge not to strike was the *quid pro quo* for the right to arbitrate and the fundamental breach, caused by the strike, terminated the employer's obligation to arbitrate.[39] This view had little acceptance and the Supreme Court has expressly held in *Drake Bakeries*[40] and *Needham Packing*[41] that arbitration rights under a collective agreement are not forfeited by the breach of the no-strike clause of the

[36]*Hall v. Sperry Gyroscope Co.*, 26 Misc.2d 566, 208 N.Y.S.2d 63, 35 LA 363, 447 (Sup. Ct. 1960).

[37]*Radio Corp. of America v. Ass'n of Scientists & Professional Engineering Personnel,* 414 F.2d 893, 71 LRRM 3196 (3d Cir. 1969). *See also City of Hartford, Conn.,* 71-1 ARB ¶ 8090 (Johnson, 1971).

[38]*Drake Motor Lines v. Highway Truck Drivers,* 343 F. Supp. 1130, 80 LRRM 3003 (E.D. Pa. 1972). *See Signal Delivery Service, Inc. v. Teamsters Local 107, Highway Truck Drivers & Helpers,* 345 F. Supp. 697, 80 LRRM 3222 (D. Pa. 1972).

[39]The Supreme Court has held that an agreement to arbitrate is the *quid pro quo* for a no-strike commitment. *Lucas Flour v. Teamsters Local 174,* 369 U.S. 95, 105, 49 LRRM 2717, 2721-22(1962).

[40]*Drake Bakeries v. Local 50, American Bakery & Confectionery Workers,* 370 U.S. 254, 50 LRRM 2440 (1962).

[41]*Local 721, United Packinghouse, Food and Allied Workers v. Needham Packing Co.,* 376 U.S. 247, 55 LRRM 2580 (1964).

agreement. Courts have also refused to stay arbitration of grievances over the seniority rights of wildcat strikers[42] or the discharge of employees who participated in such a strike.[43]

The Second Circuit reexamined the effect of a strike in violation of a no-strike clause upon the right of a union to invoke the arbitration clause in light of, and after, the Supreme Court's decision in *Boys Markets*[44] and concluded that the strike did not cause a forfeiture of such rights.[45] However, there must always be a finding on arbitrability before a *Boys Markets* injunction will issue.[46]

STAYS GRANTED FOR NONARBITRABILITY OF SUBJECT MATTER

Before the *Steelworkers Trilogy*[47] there were many attempts to persuade courts to deny arbitration on the ground that the subject matter

---

[42]*Wright Steel & Wire Co. v. Steelworkers,* 346 F.2d 928, 59 LRRM 2574 (1st Cir. 1965); *Local 120, Textile Workers v. Newberry Mills, Inc.,* 315 F.2d 217, 52 LRRM 2650 (4th Cir. 1963); *Local 748, IUE v. Jefferson City Cabinet Co.,* 314 F.2d 192, 52 LRRM 2513 (6th Cir. 1963); *Retail, Wholesale Department Store Union, Local 1085 v. Vaughn's Sanitary Bakery, Inc.,* 196 F. Supp. 633, 48 LRRM 2963 (M.D. Pa. 1961); *U.S. Pipe & Foundry Co. v. Steelworkers Local 2026, et al,* 67 N.J. Super. 384, 170 A.2d 505, 50 LRRM 2283 (1961); *Local 239, Molders & Foundry Workers v. Susquehanna Casting Co.,* 283 F.2d 80, 46 LRRM 3079 (3d Cir. 1960); *National Cash Register Co. v. Wilson,* 7 App. Div.2d 550, 184 N.Y.S.2d 957, 32 LA 410 (1959).

[43]*Trailways of New England, Inc. v. Motor Coach Employees, Div. 1318,* 343 F.2d 815, 58 LRRM 2848 (1st Cir. 1965), *aff'g* 232 F. Supp. 608, 56 LRRM 2186 (D. Mass. 1964); *Teamsters Local 677 v. Trudon & Platt Motor Lines, Inc.,* 146 Conn. 17, 147 A.2d 484, 31 LA 685 (1958); *Armstrong-Norwalk Rubber Corp. v. Local 283, Rubber Workers,* 167 F. Supp. 817, 43 LRRM 2098 (D. Conn. 1958).

[44]*See* note 19 *supra.*

[45]*Teamsters Local 757 v. Borden, Inc.,* 433 F.2d 41, 75 LRRM 2481 (2d Cir. 1970); *Ice Cream Drivers & Employees Union Local 757 v. Borden, Inc.,* 312 F. Supp. 549, 74 LRRM 3020 (D.C. N.Y. 1970); *Edward Nezelek, Inc. v. Local Union No. 294,* 342 F. Supp. 507, 80 LRRM 3459 (D.C. N.Y. 1972). Also, in *Nezelek* the court held that an employer's good faith refusal to arbitrate in the belief that a jurisdictional dispute existed for the NLRB was not fatal to the future arbitrability of the dispute.

[46]*Parade Publications, Inc. v. Philadelphia Mailers Union Local 14,* 459 F.2d 369, 80 LRRM 2264 (3d Cir. 1972); *United Steelworkers of America, AFL-CIO-CLC v. National Labor Relations Board,* 530 F.2d 266, 91 LRRM 2275 (3rd Cir. 1976), *cert. denied,* 429 U.S. 834, 93 LRRM 2363; *United States Steel Corporation v. United Mine Workers of America,* 519 F.2d 1236, 90 LRRM 2539 (5th Cir. 1975), *cert. denied,* 428 U.S. 910, 92 LRRM 3006; *Plain Dealer Publishing Company v. Cleveland Typographical Union #53,* 520 F.2d 1220, 90 LRRM 2110 (6th Cir. 1975), *cert. denied,* 428 U.S. 909, 92 LRRM 3006, *Island Creek Coal Company v. United Mine Workers,* 507 F.2d 650, 88 LRRM 2364 (3rd Cir. 1975), *cert. denied,* 423 U.S. 877, 90 LRRM 2554, *rehearing denied,* 423 U.S. 1009; *Napa Pittsburgh, Inc. v. Automotive Chauffers, Local Union No. 926,* 502 F.2d 321, 87 LRRM 2044 (3rd Cir. 1974), *cert. denied,* 419 U.S. 1049, 87 LRRM 3035 (1974); *Transway Corporation v. Hawaii Teamsters & Allied Workers, Local 996, IBT,* 411 F. Supp. 299, 91 LRRM 2910 (D.C. Hawaii 1976).

[47]*Steelworkers v. Warrior & Gulf Navigation Co.,* 363 U.S. 574, 46 LRRM 2416 (1960); *Steelworkers v. Enterprise Wheel & Car Corp.,* 363 U.S. 593, 46 LRRM 2423 (1960); *Steelworkers v. American Mfg. Co.,* 363 U.S. 564, 46 LRRM 2414 (1960).

or issue presented in the grievance claim was one over which the arbitrator had no jurisdiction because it raised an issue which did not involve the interpretation or application of the labor agreement. What the courts have been doing since the *Trilogy* when a request for denial of arbitration is presented depends on the scope of the arbitration clause.[48]

The typical arbitration clause authorizing the arbitrator to decide questions of interpretation and application of the labor agreement is referred to as a "broad clause." Clauses which specifically exclude certain subjects from arbitration are referred to as "exclusion clauses." There are some unique cases under each heading. Arbitrator Joseph Brandschain explained the different language in labor agreements concerning the scope of the arbitration clause:[49]

> Some collective bargaining agreements specify what may be arbitrated. More often they specify a limited number of specific types of matters that may not be arbitrated—such as incentive rates or the ability of specific employees, for instance—because management took the position, when it negotiated the contract, that these were matters within its absolute discretion, and the union so agreed.
>
> Usually, however, there are no specific subjects stated in the agreement to be arbitrable or nonarbitrable. Instead the agreement may contain either:
>
> (1) A broad, general clause stating that any dispute or difference between the parties may be arbitrated;
>
> (2) A narrower, more restrictive clause stating that "only matters arising under this agreement may be arbitrated"; or
>
> (3) An even more restrictive clause stating that only "matters of construction or interpretation of this agreement may be arbitrated."

---

[48] In cases dealing with collective bargaining agreements in the public sector, courts have not only looked to the scope of the arbitration clause in determining whether or not to grant a stay of arbitration, but have also examined the statutes under which the public employer operates to determine whether or not the employer may delegate decision-making authority on the subject matter of the dispute to an arbitrator. In *Board of Education v. Rockford Education Assoc.*, 3 Ill. App.3d 1090, 280 N.E.2d 286, 80 LRRM 2592 (App. Ct. 1972), for example, the court granted a stay of arbitration because under the school code only the school board had the authority to determine who should be appointed to a job. Thus, no arbitrator could decide whether or not the grievant should have been promoted to a vacant position because the school board could not, by contract, bargain away its discretion in such matters. *See also, Board of Trustees of Junior College District No. 508 v. Cook County Teachers Union, Local 1600, et al.*, 62 Ill.2d 470, 343 N.E.2d 473, 92 LRRM 2380 (Ill. 1976); *Morris Central School District v. Morris Education Assoc.*, 84 Misc.2d 675, 376 N.Y.S.2d 376, 91 LRRM 2770 (Sup. Ct. 1975).

[49] Brandschain, *Preparation and Trial of a Labor Arbitration Case*, THE PRACTICAL LAWYER, Vol. 18, No. 7 (Nov. 1972), p. 38.

Stays Granted Under Broad Clauses

Courts have generally been reluctant to issue stays since the *Steel-workers Trilogy.*[50] In rare cases, however, stays have been granted. For example, a court has issued a stay in a case where an employee objected to a retirement consistent with a uniform twelve-year practice never previously challenged.[51]

When one court examined the specific clauses of a labor agreement and the rights reserved to the management by the agreement, an arbitration was denied.[52] The agreement gave the employer the right to reduce the work force for a short period without considering seniority, and the grievants objected to the employer's disregard of seniority during a short-period layoff. In affirming the district court's declaratory judgment that the grievance over the layoff was not arbitrable, the Third Circuit found that the layoff was an authorized exercise of rights specifically reserved to management and, consequently, an objection to it was not an issue to be submitted to arbitration.[53]

On the other hand, a management rights clause providing that an insurance company had the exclusive right to determine the types and classes of policies to be sold did not prevent arbitration of a union's grievance over the company's elimination of certain insurance policies and the substitution of others.[54] The federal district court added that if an arbitrator should decide in favor of the union, the arbitrator

---

[50]*See* note 47 *supra.* Some commentators have viewed these three decisions as a reaction to the growing "rush to the court" whenever a colorable claim of doubt as to arbitrability was present. Freidin, LABOR ARBITRATION IN THE COURTS, (Philadelphia: Univ. of Pa. Press, 1952), p. 20. For a general discussion of these cases, *see* Smith and Jones, *The Supreme Court and Labor Dispute Arbitration: The Emerging Federal Law,* 63 MICH. L. REV. 751, 755 (1965); Levitt, *The Supreme Court and Arbitration,* 14 N.Y.U. CONF. LAB. 217 (1961). "[B]oth the number and the success of challenges to the [enforcement of the obligation to arbitrate] declined." ABA Section of Labor Relations Law, *Report on the Committee on Labor Arbitration and the Law of Collective Bargaining,* PROGRAM OF THE 1968 ANNUAL MEETING, AMERICAN BAR ASSOCIATION, p. 161. *See also* Snyder, *What Has the Supreme Court Done to Arbitration,* 12 LAB. L.J. 93 (1961); St. Antoine, *Contract Enforcement and the Courts, Labor Contracts in the Courts,* 15 LAB. L.J. 583 (1964); Davey, *Discussion: Arbitrability and the Arbitrator's Jurisdiction,* MANAGEMENT RIGHTS AND THE ARBITRATION PROCESS, Proceedings of the Ninth Annual Meeting, National Academy of Arbitrators, J. McKelvey, ed. (Washington: BNA Books, 1956), p. 34.

[51]*Local 30, Philadelphia Leather Workers' Union of Meat Cutters v. Brodsky & Son,* 243 F. Supp. 728, 56 LRRM 2121 (E.D. Pa. 1964).

[52]*Halsted & Mitchell Co. v. Steelworkers Local 7032,* 421 F.2d 1191, 72 LRRM 2915 (3d Cir. 1969).

[53]*See* related discussion under "Enforcement of an Agreement to Arbitrate Need Not Determine the Merits" in Chapter III.

[54]*United Insurance Co. of America v. Insurance Workers Int'l Union,* 315 F. Supp. 1133, 75 LRRM 2053 (E.D. Pa. 1970).

could grant relief other than requiring the reinstatement of the old policies.

Where no language in the agreement can be identified as applicable to the dispute and the arbitrator's jurisdiction is limited to interpretation and application of the agreement, some courts have issued stays,[55] while others have referred the matter to the arbitrator.[56]

Stays Denied Under Broad Clauses

Under broad clauses, courts have referred to arbitration grievances over the omission of names from a seniority list;[57] establishment of new job classifications;[58] the obligation to retire and the right to a pension;[59] promotions and reassignments;[60] the right to holiday and vacation pay after a plant closing;[61] failure to pay overtime premiums;[62] in-

---

[55]*Radio Corp. of America v. Ass'n of Scientists & Professional Engineering Personnel,* 414 F.2d 893, 71 LRRM 3196 (3d Cir. 1969); *Boilermakers Local 483 v. Shell Oil Co.,* 369 F.2d 526, 63 LRRM 2173 (7th Cir. 1966); *Boeing Co. v. UAW Local 1069,* 349 F.2d 412, 59 LRRM 2988 (3d Cir. 1965); *Torrington Co. v. Metal Products Workers Local 1645,* 347 F.2d 93, 59 LRRM 2588 (2d Cir. 1965); *UMW Dist. 50 v. Matthiessen & Hegeler Zinc Co.,* 291 F. Supp. 578, 69 LRRM 2403 (N.D. W.Va. 1968); *District 2, Marine Engineers Beneficial Assoc., AFL-CIO v. Falcon Carriers, Inc.,* 374 F. Supp. 1342, 86 LRRM 2121 (S.D. N.Y. 1974).

[56]*Local 12934, District 50 UMWA v. Dow Corning Corp.,* 69 L.C. § 13,045, 80 LRRM 2214 (E.D. Mich. 1971); *Monroe Sander Corp. v. Livingston,* 377 F.2d 6, 65 LRRM 2273 (2d Cir. 1967); *Local 1401, Retail Clerks v. Woodman's Food Market,* 371 F.2d 199, 63 LRRM 2568 (7th Cir. 1966); *Local 1416, IAM v. Jostens, Inc.,* 250 F. Supp. 496 (D. Minn. 1966); *A.S. Abell Co. v. Baltimore Typographical Union No. 12,* 338 F.2d 190, 57 LRRM 2480 (4th Cir. 1964); *IBEW Local 702 v. Central Illinois Public Service Co.,* 324 F.2d 920, 54 LRRM 2589 (7th Cir. 1963); *Fitzgerald v. General Electric Co.,* 23 App. Div.2d 288, 260 N.Y.S.2d 470, 59 LRRM 2500 (1965); *Board of Education Union Free School District No. 7 v. Great Neck Teachers Assoc.,* 332 N.Y.S.2d 326, 80 LRRM 2969 (Sup. Ct. 1972), *aff'd,* 338 N.Y.S.2d 400, 84 LRRM 2400 (App. Div. 1972).

[57]*United Furniture Workers Local 402 v. Mohawk Flush Door Corp.,* 212 F. Supp. 933, 52 LRRM 2209 (M.D. Pa. 1963). *See also Southwestern Electric Power Co. v. IBEW Local 738,* 293 F.2d 929, 48 LRRM 2960 (5th Cir. 1961).

[58]*Carey v. General Electric Co.,* 213 F. Supp. 276, 50 LRRM 2119 (S.D. N.Y. 1962); *Cutting Room Appliances Corp. v. FLM Joint Board, United Mechanics, 150 Div.,* 75 LRRM 2288 (N.Y. Sup. Ct. 1970).

[59]*Butchers Union Local 229 v. Cudahy Packing Co.,* 488 P.2d 849, 59 Cal. Rptr. 713, 65 LRRM 2820 (Cal. 1967); *United Saw, File & Steel Products Workers of America, Federal Labor Union 22254 v. H. K. Porter Co.,* 190 F. Supp. 407, 35 LA 59 (E.D. Pa. 1960); *International Tel. & Tel. Corp. v. Local 400 Professional, Technical and Salaried Div., IUE,* 290 F.2d 581, 48 LRRM 2217 (3d Cir. 1961); *Communications Workers v. Southwestern Bell Tel. Co.,* 415 F.2d 35, 71 LRRM 3025 (5th Cir. 1969); *Chemical Workers Local 19 v. Jefferson Lake Sulphur Co.,* 197 F. Supp. 155, 48 LRRM 2974 (S.D. Tex. 1961).

[60]*Palestine Tel. Co. v. IBEW Local 1506,* 379 F.2d 234, 65 LRRM 2776 (5th Cir. 1967); *In re Rollway Bearing Co.,* 11 App. Div.2d 753, 201 N.Y.S.2d 648 (1960); *Communications Workers v. Bell Tel. Laboratories, Inc.,* 349 F.2d 398, 59 LRRM 2954 (3d Cir. 1965).

[61]*IBEW v. Westinghouse Electric Corp.,* 198 F. Supp. 817, 49 LRRM 2059 (E.D. Pa. 1961); *Posner v. Grunwald-Marx, Inc.,* 56 Cal.2d 162, 363 P.2d 313, 14 Cal. Rptr. 297 (Cal. 1961).

[62]*Philadelphia Photo-Engravers' Union 7 v. Parade Publications, Inc.,* 202 F. Supp. 685, 49 LRRM 2726 (E.D. Pa. 1962); *United Brick & Clay Workers v. A.P. Green Fire Brick Co.,* 343 F.2d 590, 58 LRRM 2837 (8th Cir. 1965).

stallation of new equipment;[63] wage payments;[64] discharge of an employee at the request of the government;[65] the role of supervision in employment procedures;[66] eligibility of a discharged employee for employment;[67] discharge of an employee where there is no reference to discharge in the agreement;[68] discharge of a probationary employee;[69] improper classification of an employee;[70] refusal to reinstate a disabled employee;[71] refusal to displace replacements of strikers desiring to return;[72] assignments of work to an employee in another union;[73] walking off the job;[74] new time value for an incentive standard;[75] refusal of the employer to train an employee for a new skill;[76] the scope of the appropriate unit;[77] refusal to pay fringe benefit;[78] lack of work due to suspension of operations because of a strike of another union;[79] discontinuance of employee discounts;[80] readjustment of delivery routes;[81] refusal to increase pension benefits;[82] termination of

---

[63]*Taft Broadcasting Co. v. Radio Broadcast Technicians Local 253,* 298 F.2d 707, 49 LRRM 2572 (5th Cir. 1962); *Cuneo Eastern Press, Inc. of Pa. v. Bookbinders & Bindery Women's Union Local 2,* 176 F. Supp. 956, 44 LRRM 2919 (E.D. Pa. 1959); *Bhd. of Locomotive Firemen & Enginemen Lodge 844 v. Kennecott Copper Corp.,* 338 F.2d 224, 57 LRRM 2530 (10th Cir. 1964).

[64]*Socony Vacuum Tanker Men's Ass'n v. Socony Mobil Oil Co.,* 254 F. Supp. 897, 63 LRRM 2037 (S.D. N.Y. 1966); *Columbian Carbon Co. v. Operating Engineers Local 405,* 360 F.2d 1018, 62 LRRM 2292 (5th Cir. 1966).

[65]*IAM Local 2003 v. Hayes Corp.,* 296 F.2d 238, 49 LRRM 2210 (5th Cir. 1961).

[66]*IAM Local 1416 v. Jostens, Inc.,* 250 F. Supp. 496 (D. Minn. 1966).

[67]*Teamsters Local 782 v. Blue Cab Co.,* 353 F.2d 687, 60 LRRM 2491 (7th Cir. 1965).

[68]*Local 156, Packinghouse Workers v. Du Quoin Packing Co.,* 337 F.2d 419, 57 LRRM 2268 (7th Cir. 1964); *IAM Lodge 12, District 37 v. Cameron Iron Works, Inc.,* 183 F. Supp. 144, 46 LRRM 2086 (S.D. Tex. 1960).

[69]*Local 702, United Ass'n of Journeymen & Apprentices of the Plumbing and Pipe Fitting Industry v. Nashville Gas Co.,* 76 LRRM 2417 (D.C. Tenn. 1970).

[70]*Acme Markets, Inc. v. Retail Clerks Union Local 1357,* 235 F. Supp. 814, 58 LRRM 2374 (E.D. Pa. 1964).

[71]*Carey v. General Electric Co.,* 213 F. Supp. 276, 50 LRRM 2119 (S.D. N.Y. 1962).

[72]*IAM Lodge 1652 v. International Aircraft Services, Inc.,* 302 F.2d 808, 49 LRRM 2976 (4th Cir. 1962).

[73]*Carey v. General Electric Co.,* 213 F. Supp. 276, 50 LRRM 2119 (S.D. N.Y. 1962).

[74]*International Molders & Foundry Workers Union Local 239 v. Susquehanna Casting Co.,* 184 F. Supp. 543, 46 LRRM 2484 (M.D. Pa. 1960).

[75]*IUE v. Westinghouse Electric Corp.,* 268 F.2d 352, 44 LRRM 2369 (3d Cir. 1959).

[76]*Local 459, IUE v. Remington Rand,* 191 N.Y.S.2d 876, 44 LRRM 2897 (Sup. Ct. 1959).

[77]*Clanebach, Inc. v. Las Vegas Local Joint Executive Bd. of Culinary Workers and Bartenders,* 388 F.2d 766, 67 LRRM 2498 (9th Cir. 1968).

[78]*Fruit & Vegetable Packers & Warehousemen Local 760 v. California Packing Corp.,* 54 LRRM 2625 (E.D. Wash. 1963).

[79]*IBEW Local 24 v. Hearst Corp.,* 352 F.2d 957, 60 LRRM 2401 (4th Cir. 1965).

[80]*IBEW Local 702 v. Central Illinois Public Service Co.,* 324 F.2d 920, 54 LRRM 2589 (7th Cir. 1963).

[81]*F & M Schaefer Brewing Co. v. Local 49, Brewery Workers,* 420 F.2d 854, 73 LRRM 2298 (2d Cir. 1970).

[82]*Westvaco Corp. v. United Paperworkers International Union, Local 1388, AFL-CIO,* 424 F. Supp. 250, 94 LRRM 2332 (S.D. N.Y. 1976).

manufacturing operations;[83] subcontracting;[84] and the closing of a plant.[85]

Disputes over nonpayment or reduced payment of a small financial bonus, or failure to provide a turkey at Thanksgiving or Christmas, however, have been held to be nonarbitrable issues under a broad clause.[86] The court explained its reasoning thus:

> [T]he employer paid the Christmas bonus uninterruptedly over a period of years; yet neither the current collective bargaining agreement nor any of its predecessors mentions a bonus or binds the employer to continue it. . . . There is no mention anywhere of bonus or the slightest suggestion that either party contemplated that the Christmas bonus paid voluntarily by the employer was within the provisions of the agreement. It clearly was not and, therefore, may not be made the subject of an arbitrable dispute under it.[87]

On the other hand, the failure to pay a Christmas bonus has been held by other courts to be an arbitrable grievance under a broad arbitration clause.[88]

The courts have adopted some general tests to determine whether the subject matter of a dispute is arbitrable. Interpreting a contract which excluded from arbitration all questions "involving changes in the terms and provisions of this agreement," the First Circuit held that it would not deny arbitration under such contract language unless it could say " 'with positive assurance' that a decision in the union's

---

[83]*Paramount Bag Manufacturing Co., Inc. v. Rubberized Novelty and Plastic Fabric Workers' Union, Local 98, ILGWU,* 353 F. Supp. 1131, 82 LRRM 2583 (E.D. N.Y. 1973).

[84]*UAW Local 463 v. Weatherhead Co.,* 203 F. Supp. 612, 49 LRRM 3036 (N.D. Ohio 1962); *Westinghouse Electric Corp. v. IAM Local 1790, Dist. 38,* 304 F.2d 449, 50 LRRM 2247 (1st Cir. 1962); *United Cement, Lime & Gypsum Workers Local 206 v. Celotex Corp.,* 205 F. Supp. 957, 50 LRRM 2233 (E.D. Pa. 1962); *Application of Morten, Inc.,* 216 N.Y.S.2d 825 (Sup. Ct. 1961); *IUE v. General Electric Co.,* 332 F.2d 485, 56 LRRM 2289 (2d Cir. 1964); *Cluett, Peabody & Co. v. Clothing Workers,* 17 Misc.2d 582, 188 N.Y.S.2d 695, 32 LA 269 (Sup. Ct. 1959).

[85]*Bressette v. International Tole Company, Inc.,* 527 F.2d 211, 91 LRRM 2077 (2d Cir. 1975).

[86]*Boeing Co. v. UAW Local 1069,* 349 F.2d 412, 59 LRRM 2988 (3d Cir. 1965). *Accord, Progress Bulletin Publishing Co.,* 182 NLRB No. 135, 74 LRRM 1237 (1970) (contract silent on Christmas bonus, so solution to the dispute does not turn on interpretation of contract).

[87]*Supreme Knitting Machine Co. v. Amalgamated Machine Metal and Instrument Local 485,* 32 Misc.2d 1010, 224 N.Y.S.2d 45, 49 LRRM 2668 (Sup. Ct. 1962).

[88]*Newspaper Guild of Buffalo Local 26 v. Tonawanda Publishing Co.,* 20 App. Div.2d 211, 245 N.Y.S.2d 832, 55 LRRM 2222 (1964); *Hirt v. N.Y. Automatic Canteen Corp.,* 295 N.Y.S.2d 142, 70 LRRM 2485 (Sup. Ct. 1968); *Akron Typographical Union No. 182 v. Beacon Journal Publishing Co.,* 72 LRRM 2362 (N.D. Ohio 1968), *aff'd,* 416 F.2d 969, 72 LRRM 2368 (6th Cir.) *cert. denied,* 396 U.S. 959, 72 LRRM 2866 (1969); *Harris Structural Steel Co. v. Steelworkers Local 3682,* 298 F.2d 363, 49 LRRM 2472 (3d Cir. 1962).

favor would necessarily constitute a change in the terms of the agreement."[89]

Another general test involves the use of bargaining history. Courts generally hold that where bargaining history must be referred to in an effort to prove the nonarbitrability of the subject matter, the language of the agreement is not clear enough to foreclose arbitration and the question of arbitrability should be referred to the arbitrator.[90] At least one appellate court, however, has remanded a case to the trial court with instructions to hold a hearing to receive evidence concerning the bargaining history of disputed contract language, stating that this was appropriate because the history could determine the arbitrability of the grievance.[91]

There have been post-*Trilogy* decisions in several circuit courts which exemplify that a strict reading of the labor agreement, even under a broad arbitration clause, will lead to a conclusion that a claim is nonarbitrable. In *Independent Petroleum Workers of America, Inc. v. American Oil Co.*,[92] the collective bargaining agreement provided that "questions directly involving or arising from applications, interpretations or alleged violations of the terms of this agreement," were subject to arbitration. The Seventh Circuit held that the employer was not required to arbitrate a dispute concerning the subcontracting out of certain work because there was no clause referring to subcontracting and "the mere allegation that the agreement has been violated" did not entitle a party to submit a dispute to arbitration. According to the court, the bargaining history of the parties demonstrated that the

---

[89]*Camden Industries Co. v. Carpenters, Local 1688,* 353 F.2d 178, 180, 60 LRRM 2525, 2526 (1st Cir. 1965).

[90]*IUE v. General Electric Co.,* 332 F.2d 485, 490, 56 LRRM 2289 (2d Cir. 1964). *See also Communications Workers v. Southwestern Bell Tel. Co.,* 415 F.2d 35, 71 LRRM 3025 (5th Cir. 1969); *Order of Repeatermen and Toll Test-Boardmen Local 1011, IBEW v. Bell Tel. Co. of Nevada,* 254 F. Supp. 462, 63 LRRM 2167 (D. Nev. 1966); *Local 483, Boilermakers v. Shell Oil Co.,* 369 F.2d 526, 63 LRRM 2173 (7th Cir. 1966); *Insurance Workers Int'l Union v. Home Life Insurance Co.,* 255 F. Supp. 926, 62 LRRM 2694 (E.D. Pa. 1966); *Communications Workers v. Bell Tel. Laboratories, Inc.,* 349 F.2d 398, 59 LRRM 2954 (3d Cir. 1965); *Acme Markets, Inc., v. Retail Clerks Union Local 1357,* 235 F. Supp. 814, 58 LRRM 2374 (E.D. Pa. 1964); *A.S. Abell Co. v. Baltimore Typographical Union No. 12,* 338 F.2d 190, 57 LRRM 2480 (4th Cir. 1964); *Ass'n of Westinghouse Salaried Employees v. Westinghouse Electric Corp.,* 283 F.2d 93, 46 LRRM 3084 (3d Cir. 1960).

[91]*Local 81, American Federation of Technical Engineers, AFL-CIO v. Western Electric Co., Inc.,* 508 F.2d 106, 88 LRRM 2081 (7th Cir. 1974).

[92]324 F.2d 903, 54 LRRM 2598 (7th Cir. 1963), *aff'd* by an equally divided court, 379 U.S. 130, 57 LRRM 2512 (1964). *Accord, Teamsters v. Blue Cab Co.,* 353 F.2d 687, 60 LRRM 249 (7th Cir. 1964); *Pacific Northwest Bell Tel. Co. v. Communications Workers,* 310 F.2d 244, 51 LRRM 2405 (9th Cir. 1962); *Independent Soap Workers v. Procter & Gamble,* 314 F.2d 38, 52 LRRM 2528 (9th Cir.), *cert. denied,* 374 U.S. 807, 53 LRRM 2468 (1963); *Columbian Carbon Co. v. IUE Local 405,* 360 F.2d 1018, 62 LRRM 2292 (5th Cir. 1966). *See Boilermakers v. Shell Oil Co.,* 369 F.2d 526, 63 LRRM 2173 (7th Cir. 1966).

union had been unsuccessful in attempting to prohibit the company's right to contract out work.

The *American Oil* case was relied on by the Seventh Circuit in *Local 483, International Brotherhood of Boilermakers v. Shell Oil Co.* [93] The court, in discussing its prior opinion, stated:

> But fundamentally the question decided there, and here, is that when arbitration is limited in the bargaining agreement to questions involving the application and interpretation of the agreement, and the agreement does not limit the freedom of the employer to contract out work, a court should not compel arbitration. This court there considered the Supreme Court cases (the *Steelworkers Trilogy*) relied upon here and found that those cases did not change the principle "that compulsory arbitration cannot be properly awarded absent a contract between the parties agreeing thereto." 324 F.2d at 906. The court there considered as having "some significance" the bargaining history between the parties, which showed the Union's lack of success in gaining an agreement prohibiting or limiting the company's right to contract out work, and the silence of the contract on the point. [94]

Along these same lines, the Second Circuit said it was an error to refuse to accept evidence of bargaining history where the meaning of an exclusionary clause was the issue before the district court. [95]

Stays Granted Under Exclusionary Clauses

A clause excluding a subject matter from arbitration can be construed as an instruction to the arbitrator as well as to a court. When the matter comes first to the court, the courts have stated that where the issue is clearly one excluded from arbitration by a specific exclusion clause, the party asking for the stay order should receive it so as not to be required to go through an arbitration when it bargained not to be so required.

A trial court properly enjoined the union's attempt to arbitrate the gas prices paid by employee drivers but permitted arbitration of "pay off" adjustments because the parties had agreed to arbitrate this issue. Such a definition of the issues could be considered a determination on the merits. [96]

In *Playboy Clubs International v. Hotel & Restaurant Employees & Bartenders Union,* [97] the employer moved for a preliminary injunction staying arbitration proceedings arising from the discharge of "Bun-

---

[93] 369 F.2d 526, 63 LRRM 2173 (7th Cir. 1966). *See also Associated Milk Dealers, Inc. v. Milk Drivers Union,* 422 F.2d 546, 73 LRRM 2435 (7th Cir. 1970).

[94] 369 F.2d at 529, 63 LRRM at 2175.

[95] *Strauss v. Silvercup Bakers, Inc.,* 353 F.2d 555, 61 LRRM 2001 (2d Cir. 1965).

[96] *Cabs, Inc. v. IBT Local 435,* 82 LC ¶ 55,084 (Colo. Ct. App. 1977).

[97] 321 F. Supp. 704, 76 LRRM 2419 (S.D. N.Y. 1971).

nies" for "lack of Bunny image" because the labor agreement (i) restricted arbitration to discharge for union activity and (ii) provided a
special three-step procedure, in which the executive vice president of
the employer had the right to make the final decision with respect to
discharge for any other reason including the failure to maintain "the
Bunny image." The court found that there was no claim by the union
that the 13 discharges in issue were for union activity. The court
granted the employer's motion to stay the arbitration proceedings.

Similarly, in *Cook v. Gristede Bros.* [98] the court granted the union's
petition for a stay of arbitration in a case involving a change in the
company's method of buying products and product lines because the
labor agreement provided for arbitration only in cases of discharge for
"just cause." In so holding, the court stated that "the fact that the
parties in unambiguous fashion expressed their intent by making specific provision for arbitration applicable only in a clearly defined area
is evidence sufficiently forceful to declare their purpose to exclude
other grievances therefrom." [99]

When a party argues that grievances over certain subjects cannot be
appealed to arbitration because of a clause excluding the subject matter, the party making the argument must realize that the merits of the
claim may then be decided by the court. If the arbitrator cannot interpret and apply the agreement, courts do not conclude that an alleged
violation of the agreement has no remedy, but rather hold that the
court can determine the dispute. [100] In *UAW Local 391 v. Webster
Electric Co.,* [101] the employer contracted out janitorial work and
thereby displaced three employees. The court held that since there was
no arbitration clause, the question of contracting out was for the judiciary and not for an arbitrator. The court concluded by finding that
the employer's action violated the union shop provision of the collective bargaining agreement.

In another case, a stay was granted in a dispute over a promotion
when the agreement said "in no event" shall a dispute arising out of
the promotion clause "be subject to arbitration." The court said the
exclusionary language foreclosed arbitration in spite of the Supreme
Court decisions establishing a "strong presumption" in favor of arbi-

---

[98] 359 F. Supp. 906, 84 LRRM 2173 (S.D. N.Y. 1973).

[99] *Id.* at 908, 84 LRRM at 2175.

[100] *See, e.g., Oil, Chemical and Atomic Workers International Union, Local 1-124 v.
American Oil Co.,* 387 F. Supp. 796, 89 LRRM 2167 (D. Wyo. 1975), *aff'd,* 528 F.2d 252, 91
LRRM 2202 (10th Cir. 1976).

[101] 299 F.2d 195, 49 LRRM 2592 (7th Cir. 1962). *See also American Motors Corporation v.
Wisconsin Employment Relations Board,* 145 N.W.2d 137, 63 LRRM 2226 (Wis. Sup. Ct.
1966); *Allied Oil Workers Union v. Ethyl Corp.,* 341 F.2d 47, 58 LRRM 2267 (5th Cir. 1965);
Telephone Workers v. New England Telephone & Telegraph Co., 240 F. Supp. 431, 59 LRRM
2006 (D. Mass. 1965).

tration because "it is difficult to imagine a clearer or more direct exclusionary clause."[102]

A change in the method of payment from an incentive to a time basis was held not arbitrable since the wage plan agreement provided that the company may cancel production standards or incentive application when changed circumstances "make it impracticable, in the Company's judgment, to accurately measure the operation for incentive application."[103]

When the management rights clause reserved to management a specific authority such as "the right to ... subcontract work" and the arbitration clause excluded from arbitration the exercise by management of its reserved rights, a grievance protesting the subcontracting of work was held not arbitrable.[104] The court distinguished *Warrior & Gulf*,[105] stating that in *Warrior* the clause excluded matters "which are strictly a function of management" from arbitration without identifying subcontracting as one of those matters, while the instant contract specifically barred subcontracting from the grievance procedure and arbitration.

Similarly, where the management rights clause had been interpreted by the parties to exclude from arbitration subcontracting, except disputes over the subcontracting of maintenance work, a dispute over the transfer of work to another plant was held not arbitrable.[106]

One federal district court has held that where it was the established policy to contract out maintenance work and the agreement gave the company the right to continue such policy while excluding from arbitration disputes over the exercise of such policies, a dispute over contracting out was not arbitrable.[107] The court said that in *Warrior & Gulf* the exclusions from arbitration were vague, whereas in the case under consideration "contracting out of maintenance work was a policy of the respondent; ... the written contract permitted the Company to exercise and continue such policy; and ... the same was not arbi-

---

[102]*Communications Workers v. New York Tel. Co.*, 327 F.2d 94, 96, 55 LRRM 2275 (2d Cir. 1964). *See also Desert Coca-Cola Bottling Co. v. General Sales Drivers, Delivery Drivers, and Helpers Local 14*, 335 F.2d 198, 56 LRRM 2933 (9th Cir. 1964); *Order of Repeatermen and Toll Test-Boardmen Local 1011 v. Bell Tel. Co. of Nev.*, 254 F. Supp. 462, 63 LRRM 2167 (D. Nev. 1966).

[103]*General Drivers, Warehousemen & Helpers Local 89 v. American Radiator & Standard Sanitary Corp.*, 309 F.2d 434, 51 LRRM 2456 (6th Cir. 1962).

[104]*Rochester Independent Workers Local 1 v. General Dynamics/Electronic Div.*, 54 Misc.2d 470, 282 N.Y.S.2d 804 (Sup. Ct. 1967). *See also Radio Corp. of America v. Ass'n of Scientists & Professional Engineering Personnel*, 414 F.2d 893, 71 LRRM 3196 (3d Cir. 1969).

[105]*Steelworkers v. Warrior & Gulf Navigation Co.*, 363 U.S. 574, 46 LRRM 2416 (1960).

[106]*Boeing Co. v. Local 1069, UAW*, 234 F. Supp. 404, 57 LRRM 2125 (E.D. Pa. 1964).

[107]*Local 725, IUE v. Standard Oil Co. of Ind.*, 186 F. Supp. 895, 46 LRRM 2997 (D. N.D. 1960).

trable but was specifically excluded from the scope of arbitration."[108] The court's evaluation of *Warrior & Gulf* is not inconsistent with the Supreme Court's decision, for as the Court noted there:

> A specific collective bargaining agreement may exclude contracting out from the grievance procedure. ... In such a case a grievance based solely on contracting out would not be arbitrable. Here, however, there is no such provision. ... In the absence of any express provisions excluding a particular grievance from arbitration, we think only the most forceful evidence of a purpose to exclude the claim from arbitration can prevail ....
> ... Whether contracting out in the present case violated the agreement ... is a question for the arbiter, not for the courts.[109]

Two cases illustrate the diversity of views taken by the courts in deciding whether or not a stay of arbitration should be issued if the contract contains an exclusion clause. In *Local 103, International Union of Electrical, Radio and Machine Workers, AFL-CIO v. RCA Corporation,* [110] the labor agreement provided that " 'In no event ... shall the same question [or issue] be the subject of arbitration more than once.' "[111] The union sought a stay of arbitration contending that a 1946 arbitrator's decision bound the company regarding the pending grievance. After a lengthy discussion, the court held that the broad language of the arbitration clause of the contract required that an arbitrator, rather than the court, decide

> the relevance and effect of the 1946 arbitration award and opinion; it is for him to decide whether it qualified "in industrial common law," through "experience developed by reason and reason tried and tested by experience," as the "same question or issue" presented by the immediate grievance which therefore may not "be the subject of arbitration more than once." [Footnote omitted.][112]

In another case decided within the same jurisdiction, *Halstead Industries, Inc. v. United Steelworkers of America and Local No. 7032,* [113] the labor agreement provided that the "Rights of Management" clause would not be subject to arbitration. The company contended that a grievance regarding its refusal to assign leadmen to work in specific areas was within the management rights clause and there-

---

[108]*Id.* at 902, 46 LRRM at 3002.

[109]363 U.S. at 584-85, 46 LRRM at 2420-2421. *See also Local 1912, IAM v. United States Potash Co.,* 270 F.2d 496, 44 LRRM 2861 (10th Cir. 1959); *UAW Local 463 v. Weatherhead Co.,* 203 F. Supp. 612, 49 LRRM 3036 (N.D. Ohio 1962); *IUE v. General Electric Co.,* 148 Conn. 693, 174 A.2d 298 (1961).

[110]516 F.2d 1336, 89 LRRM 2487 (3d Cir. 1975).

[111]*Id.* at 1338, 89 LRRM at 2488.

[112]*Id.* at 1340-41, 89 LRRM at 2490.

[113]432 F. Supp. 109, 95 LRRM 2756 (W.D. Pa. 1977).

fore not arbitrable. The union contended that the management rights clause was subordinate to other provisions of the contract, including those relating to safety, job classifications and seniority, and that the pending grievance was, therefore, arbitrable. After a lengthy discussion, the court held that since the management rights clause reserved to the employer the right "to assign work" and "change work schedules and assignments," the grievance was not arbitrable.

Where the agreement specifically excluded from arbitration disputes involving individuals who had been permanently replaced during a strike, a dispute involving such employees was held not arbitrable. The court said that an order to arbitrate would be "a perversion of the grievance procedure and an effort by the union to get through the grievance machinery new employment for those persons whose claims were expressly excluded from it."[114] In other similar cases, courts have granted stays of arbitration because the contract specifically excluded from the arbitration or grievance procedures the subject matter of the pending dispute. Such cases have involved the selection of sabbatical leave candidates,[115] subcontracting,[116] and employee benefits.[117]

Because of the presumption in favor of arbitrability, courts have held the following cases to be arbitrable: a dispute over vacation pay where the agreement provided for arbitration of "any dispute or grievance excepting wages";[118] a dispute over a "time value" where the agreement excluded disputes over the job incentive system;[119] a dispute over a change from incentive to time payment for certain work where the agreement excluded disputes over the establishment or changing of wage rates;[120] a dispute over a layoff where the agreement excluded disputes over the company's right to schedule shutdowns;[121]

[114]*IUE Local 787 v. Collins Radio Co.*, 317 F.2d 214, 220, 53 LRRM 2140 (5th Cir. 1963). *See also Storck v. Quaker Oats*, 85 Ill.App.2d 399, 228 N.E.2d 752, 66 LRRM 2318 (1967).

[115]*Board of Education, Somers Central School District v. Somers Faculty Ass'n*, 48 App. Div. 2d 872, 369 N.Y.S.2d 753, 90 LRRM 2106 (App. Div. 1975).

[116]*Sperry Rand Corp. v. Engineers Union, International Union of Electrical, Radio and Machine Workers*, 85 LRRM 2615 (S.D. N.Y. 1974).

[117]*Oil, Chemical and Atomic Workers, International Union Local 2-124 v. American Oil Co.*, 387 F. Supp. 796, 89 LRRM 2167 (D. Wyo. 1975), *aff'd*, 528 F.2d 252, 91 LRRM 2202 (10th Cir. 1976).

[118]*Nafi Corp. v. Textile Workers Local 981*, 196 N.E.2d 598, 55 LRRM 2086 (Ohio Ct. App. 1963).

[119]*IUE v. Westinghouse Electric Corp.*, 169 F. Supp. 798, 43 LRRM 2457 (W.D. Pa. 1958), *aff'd*, 268 F.2d, 352, 44 LRRM 2369 (3d Cir. 1959). *See also Steelworkers Local 4377 v. General Electric Co.*, 211 F. Supp. 562 (N.D. Ohio 1962), 51 LRRM 2531, *aff'd*, 327 F.2d 853, 55 LRRM 2519 (6th Cir. 1964).

[120]*Steelworkers Local 4377 v. General Electric Co.*, 327 F.2d 853, 55 LRRM 2519 (6th Cir. 1964). *See also Local 490, Rubber Workers v. Kirkhill Rubber Co.*, 367 F.2d 956, 63 LRRM 2196 (9th Cir. 1966).

[121]*Local 967, IAM v. General Electric Co.*, 282 F. Supp. 413, 67 LRRM 2817 (N.D. N.Y. 1968), *aff'd*, 406 F.2d 1046, 70 LRRM 2477 (2d Cir. 1969).

a dispute over a discharge for insubordination where the agreement said the employer was to be the sole judge of qualifications;[122] a dispute over a promotion where the agreement said the "employer has discretion and authority in filling job openings";[123] and a dispute over the denial of merit increases where the agreement provided that "[the] arbitrator shall have no authority to change wage rates."[124]

Also notable within this area is *Gateway Coal Co. v. United Mine Workers of America, et al.*,[125] in which the Supreme Court held that the "presumption of arbitrability" articulated in the *Trilogy* cases and broad arbitration language contained in the labor agreement applied to mine safety disputes, and that the strike resulting from alleged unsafe working conditions could be enjoined even though the contract provided that the employer must close down the mine if the safety committee believed an immediate danger existed. It should be noted here that courts will not generally enjoin a strike alleged to be in violation of an existing labor agreement unless the dispute underlying the strike is subject to a contractual arbitration procedure.[126] Thus, the strike action in *Gateway Coal* would not have been enjoined if the Court had found that mine safety disputes were not subject to the arbitration provision.[127]

Where there was language that could be construed as barring the arbitrator from establishing or modifying wage rates or job classifications, a court held that grievances relating to those matters should be arbitrated because:

> [T]he canons for construing labor agreements, as set down by the Supreme Court, require that such a broad-reaching exclusion as is urged by the Company should be garbed in unmistakably clear language.
> . . .
> . . . Should [the arbitrator's] decision or the remedy exceed the bounds of his authority as established by the collective bargaining agreement, that abuse of authority is remediable in an action to vacate the award.[128]

Significantly, the court was saying that if after the court's referral of the dispute to arbitration the arbitrator exceeded his jurisdiction when

---

[122]*Operating Engineers Local 3 v. Crooks Bros. Tractor Co.*, 295 F.2d 282, 48 LRRM 2988 (9th Cir. 1961).

[123]*Nepco Unit of Local 95, Office Employees Union v. Nekoosa-Edwards Paper Co.*, 287 F.2d 452, 47 LRRM 2647 (7th Cir. 1961).

[124]*Radio Corp. of America v. Ass'n of Professional Engineering Personnel*, 291 F.2d 105, 48 LRRM 2270 (3d Cir. 1961). *See also Cleveland Federation of Musicians Local 4 v. Musical Arts Ass'n*, 71 LRRM 2855 (N.D. Ohio 1969).

[125]414 U.S. 368, 85 LRRM 2049 (1974).

[126]*Boys Markets, Inc. v. Retail Clerks Union*, 398 U.S. 235, 74 LRRM 2257 (1970).

[127]*Gateway Coal Co. v. United Mine Workers of America, et al.*, 466 F.2d 1157, 80 LRRM 3153 (3d Cir. 1972), *rev'd*, 414 U.S. 368, 85 LRRM 2049 (1974).

[128]*Carey v. General Electric Co.*, 315 F.2d 499, 507-08, 52 LRRM 2662 (2d Cir. 1963).

he rendered his award, the court could review the correctness of the arbitrator's award in an action to vacate.[129] This would mean that the standards used to determine, in an action to vacate, whether the arbitrator determined the jurisdiction question correctly are different from those used to determine whether a stay should or should not be issued in the first instance.

On the other hand, some courts hold that the arbitrator's determination that a dispute is arbitrable is binding on the court in an action to vacate even if the reviewing court disagrees with the arbitrator's finding, unless that finding can be shown to be arbitrary and capricious.[130] Another court went so far as to say that a finding by the arbitrator that the arbitrator has jurisdiction is "insulated from subsequent judicial review."[131]

Stays of Claims for Damages for Contract Breach Strikes Denied Under Broad Clauses

Numerous broad arbitration clauses have supported an employer's petition for an order to arbitrate the employer's claim for damages resulting from violation of a no-strike clause or an employer's petition for denial of the union's request for a stay order to prevent submission of such a claim to arbitration.[132] Similarly, court actions by employers for damages for a contract breach strike have been denied on the ground that the employer should have taken the claim for damages to the arbitrator.[133] Courts, however, have been willing to grant em-

[129]*Accord, Foodhandlers Local 425, Meat Cutters v. Pluss Poultry, Inc.*, 260 F.2d 835, 43 LRRM 2090 (8th Cir. 1958). But see *Meat Cutters Local 385 v. Penobscot Poultry Co.*, 200 F. Supp. 879, 49 LRRM 2241 (D. Me. 1961); *Local 149, Boot & Shoe Workers v. Faith Shoe Co.*, 201 F. Supp. 234, 49 LRRM 2424 (M.D. Pa. 1962).
[130]*Federal Labor Union 18887 v. Midvale-Heppenstall Co.*, 421 F.2d 1289, 73 LRRM 2384 (3d Cir. 1970).
[131]*Camden Industries Co. v. Carpenters Local 1688*, 353 F.2d 178, 60 LRRM 2525 (1st Cir. 1965).
[132]*Johnson Builders v. Carpenters Local 1095*, 422 F.2d 137, 73 LRRM 2664 (10th Cir. 1970); *Howard Electric Co. v. IBEW Local 570*, 423 F.2d 164, 73 LRRM 2785 (9th Cir. 1970); *ITT World Communications v. Communications Workers*, 422 F.2d 77, 73 LRRM 2244 (2d Cir. 1970); *H.K. Porter Co. v. Steelworkers Local 37*, 400 F.2d 691, 69 LRRM 2246 (4th Cir. 1968); *United States Steel Corp. v. Seafarers International Union*, 237 F. Supp. 529, 58 LRRM 2344 (E.D. Pa. 1965); *Teamsters Local 70 v. Consolidated Freightways Corp.*, 335 F.2d 642, 56 LRRM 3033 (9th Cir. 1964); *Fifth Avenue Coach Lines, Inc. v. Transport Workers Local 100*, 235 F. Supp. 842, 57 LRRM 2528 (S.D. N.Y. 1964); *Yale & Towne Mfg. Co. v. Local 1717, IAM*, 299 F.2d 882, 49 LRRM 2652 (3d Cir. 1962); *Tenney Engineering, Inc. v. IUE Local 437*, 174 F. Supp. 878, 44 LRRM 2422 (D. N.J. 1959).
[133]*Local 463, Papermakers v. Federal Paper Board Co.*, 239 F. Supp. 45, 58 LRRM 2593 (D. Conn. 1965); *Franchi Const. Co. v. Local 560 Hod Carriers*, 248 F. Supp. 134, 60 LRRM 2561 (D. Mass. 1965); *Minn. Joint Board, ACWA v. United Garment Mfg. Co.*, 338 F.2d 195, 57 LRRM 2521 (8th Cir. 1964); *Evans-Amityville Dairy, Inc. v. Kelly*, 214 F. Supp. 951, 52 LRRM

ployers damages when they are procedurally foreclosed from seeking relief through the arbitration process on their own initiation.

One court mixed the issue of arbitrability and nonarbitrability of various questions arising out of a contract breach strike in an interesting way. The issue of whether the strike was a contract violation is for the arbitrator, the court held, but if the arbitrator found that the strike was a violation, the issue of damages was for the court.[134]

STAY OF ARBITRATION BECAUSE OF BANKRUPTCY

Where there is a clear showing that a claimant in arbitration has been adjudicated a bankrupt and that a trustee has been appointed, the claimant has no standing to maintain the arbitration proceeding. In such a case the court granted the petitioner's motion for a permanent stay of arbitration.[135]

APPEALS AND REMOVALS IN STAY LITIGATION

If an appeal is taken after a stay of arbitration has been denied, the district court should temporarily enjoin the arbitration to permit the appeal to be completed. The motion for a stay of arbitration pending appeal is made under Rule 65(c) of the Federal Rules of Civil Procedure.

An application for a stay of arbitration can be removed to a federal court by a defendant if the requirements for removal are met,[136] but a union which represented the grievant in an arbitration case and filed an application for a stay in a state court could not remove to the federal court because the federal statute authorizing removal of a civil action permits removal only by a defendant.[137]

2583 (E.D. N.Y. 1963); *Gilmour v. Wood, Wire and Metal Lathers Int'l Union Local 74*, 223 F. Supp. 236, 54 LRRM 2457 (N.D. Ill. 1963); *Drake Bakeries, Inc. v. Local 50, American Bakery & Confectionery Workers*, 370 U.S. 254, 50 LRRM 2440 (1962); *Controlled Sanitation Corp. v. District 128*, 524 F.2d 1324, 91 LRRM 2240 (3d Cir. 1975), *cert. denied*, 424 U.S. 915, 90 LRRM 2892.

[134]*Los Angeles Paper Bag Co. v. Printing Specialties & Paper Products Union, Dist. Council 2*, 345 F.2d 757, 59 LRRM 2427 (9th Cir. 1965). *See Dist. 50 IAM v. Chris-Craft Corp.*, 385 F.2d 946, 67 LRRM 2124 (6th Cir. 1967); *Tenney Engineering, Inc. v. UE Local 437*, 174 F. Supp. 878, 44 LRRM 2422 (D. N.J. 1959).

[135]*Pantana, Inc. v. Dust Glow Fabrics*, N.Y.L.J. March 14, 1975, Sup. Ct., N.Y. Cty.

[136]28 U.S.C. § 1441(a) (1971). *See also Avco Corp. v. IAM Aero Lodge 735*, 390 U.S. 557, 67 LRRM 2881 (1968), holding a § 301 action to be removable from state to federal court.

[137]*Hall v. Sperry Gyroscope Co.*, 183 F. Supp. 891, 46 LRRM 2215 (S.D. N.Y. 1960). *See In re Rosenthal-Block China Corp.*, 278 F.2d 713, 714 (2d Cir. 1960); *Old Dutch Farms, Inc. v. Milk Drivers & Dairy Employees Local 584*, 222 F. Supp. 125, 54 LRRM 2387 (E.D. N.Y. 1963).

The enjoining of contemplated action by an employer until the arbitration of a dispute over the action was completed occurred in a dispute over contracting out work. A district court concluded that the union was entitled to an order restraining the company from subcontracting the work until the merits of the dispute were determined by an arbitrator because there were 60 man-days of work involved.[138]

---

[138]*IUE Local 103 v. Radio Corp. of America,* 77 LRRM 2201 (D. N.J. 1971); *see Lever Brothers Co. v. International Chemical Workers Union, Local 217,* 554 F.2d 115, 93 LRRM 2961 (4th Cir. 1976); *contra, Detroit Newspaper Publishers Ass'n. v. Detroit Typographical Union No. 18, Intern. Typographical Union,* 471 F.2d 872, 82 LRRM 2332 (6th Cir. 1972), *cert. denied,* 411 U.S. 967, 83 LRRM 2039 (1973); *see Amalgamated Transit Union, Division 1384 et al. v. Greyhound Lines, Inc.,* 550 F.2d 1237, 95 LRRM 2097 (9th Cir. 1977), *cert. denied,* 434 U.S. 837, 96 LRRM 2514.

CHAPTER V

Selection of the Arbitrator or the Board

If a party intends to object to a demand for arbitration, that party may waive the objection by participation in the selection of an arbitrator or board,[1] but a request for an extension of time within which to select an arbitrator does not waive this objection and a party may thereafter move a court for an order to stay the arbitration.[2]

The different available forms of arbitration have been succinctly explained by Arbitrator Brandschain:

> In many industries there are impartial arbitrators or umpires designated in collective bargaining agreements to hear all grievances that reach arbitration. Such agreements may be either between the union and a single company or between the union and a number of employers who have banded together in an employer association for labor relations and arbitration purposes. Generally, however, you will be faced with the selection of an ad hoc arbitrator who will serve only for the pending case or group of cases.[3]

PROCEDURES FOR SELECTION OF AN ARBITRATOR OR A BOARD OF ARBITRATORS

Where the procedure for selecting an arbitrator or a board of arbitrators specified by the agreement or by a statute is not the procedure actually used and there has been no agreement to a variation in procedure or to a waiver, an award rendered by the arbitrator or board may be set aside by a court.[4] The more common selection procedures

---

[1]*In re New York Shipping Ass'n,* 54 LRRM 2680 (N.Y. Sup. Ct. 1963); *Frank Chevrolet Corp. v. UAW Local 259,* 33 Misc.2d 12, 228 N.Y.S.2d 692 (1962).

[2]*Dana Realty Corp. v. Consolidated Electric Construction Co.,* 21 App. Div. 2d 769, 250 N.Y.S.2d 784 (1964).

[3]Brandschain, *Preparation and Trial of a Labor Arbitration Case,* THE PRACTICAL LAWYER, Vol. 18, No. 7 (Nov. 1972), p. 27.

[4]*Order of Railway Conductors & Brakemen v. Clinchfield Railroad Co.,* 278 F. Supp. 322, 67 LRRM 2318 (E.D. Tenn. 1967); *Edmund E. Garrison, Inc. v. Local 137, IUOE,* 283 F. Supp. 771, 68 LRRM 2249 (S.D. N.Y. 1968) (Employer was not entitled to select himself and his attorney as arbitrators under agreements providing that arbitration boards would be composed of two representatives of each party and that parties could not be arbitrators. In so holding, the court noted "[C]ustom in arbitration proceedings dictates that a party may not appoint himself." (283 F. Supp. at 773, 68 LRRM at 2250)).

are by mutual agreement, through use of an agency, or through use of an arbitration board.

Selection by Mutual Agreement

Approximately 68 percent of those labor agreements providing for selection of an arbitrator for each dispute (*ad hoc* arbitration) provide that the arbitrator shall be selected by mutual agreement.[5] One observer described the process involved in selecting *ad hoc* arbitrators as follows:

> It is frequently standard operating procedure when a case arises for each side to scurry about making telephone calls to parties who have appeared in cases before particular arbitrators under consideration, to read all obtainable decisions previously rendered by such arbitrators, to check "confidential" reports kept by services maintained for the purpose of keeping tab on arbitrators and to check "black lists" and "approved" lists of arbitrators maintained by various sources. This hapazard, hit or miss procedure is not only burdensome, time-consuming and frequently ineffective, but it also tends to degrade arbitration and the arbitration process.[6]

Arbitrator Brandschain advised representatives of both sides:

> Arbitration is probably the only kind of adversary, judicial, or quasi-judicial proceeding in which parties litigant have a voice in the selection of the "judge," who will sit in judgment on their actions and decide their rights. Since this is part of the rules of the game, it is "fair game" to take advantage of arbitrators' known or presumed attitudes towards certain types of cases and thus to try to select an arbitrator who will decide the case for your side. In any event, you want to prevent the selection of an arbitrator whose background, prior decisions, or other history indicates a bias that is adverse to your position.
>
> While each party can affect the choice, he cannot "dictate" it. However, he can in most instances veto the selection of those persons under consideration who are the most unacceptable.
>
> At a preliminary or *in limine* stage of the preparation for the hearing, it may be necessary for you to assist your client in the selection of the arbitrator. While such selection may have been agreed to by the client before counsel entered the case, it is preferable that the client be advised that he not make the selection without the advice and assistance of counsel, who may be able to aid in making the choice.

---

[5]BASIC PATTERNS IN UNION CONTRACTS, Ninth Edition (Washington: BNA Books, 1979), p. 16. This computerized BNA survey analyzed a sample of 400 labor agreements constituting a cross-section of industries, unions, number of employees covered, and geographical areas; the sample was taken from BNA's file of over 5,000 labor agreements.

[6]Levitt, *Lawyers, Legalism, and Labor Arbitration,* 6 N.Y.L. FORUM 379 (1960).

He further observed that:

> [I]f one side suggests arbitrator A, the other side is afraid that he may be in the suggesting side's corner. Frequently an expeditious way to bridge this dilemma is for one or both sides to name several names that would be acceptable, and to tell the other side to pick any one of these. This is an effective procedure, and one that fairly well assures the designation of a not unsatisfactory arbitrator.[7]

In the event the parties deadlock and cannot agree upon an arbitrator, some states allow court appointment of the arbitrator upon application of one of the parties.[8] On the other hand, several states have statutory provisions preventing court appointment of arbitrators.[9] Quite obviously, in such states, the labor agreement should provide a *final* method for selecting the arbitrator to avoid the risk of a deadlock.

Approximately six percent of the labor agreements in the United States provide for a permanent arbitrator.[10] This procedure, of course, avoids the delays involved in selecting an arbitrator each time a grievance or group of grievances reaches the arbitration step of the grievance procedure and, of course, carries no risk of deadlock and possible court intervention. The permanent arbitrator usually serves only as long as the individual is acceptable to both parties.

A permanent arbitrator is desirable where the agreement covers a large number of employees and it is anticipated that a significant number of grievances will go to arbitration during the term of the

---

[7]Brandschain, note 3 *supra* at pp. 27-29.

[8]State statutes providing for court appointment of the arbitrator are: ALASKA STAT. § 9.43.030 (1968); ARIZ. REV. STAT. ANN. § 12-1503 (Supp. 1965); ARK. STAT. ANN. § 34-513 (1969); CAL. CIV. PROC. § 1281.6 (Supp. 1965); CONN. GEN. STAT. § 52-411 (1958); DEL. CODE tit. 10, § 5704 (1953); FLA. STAT. ANN. § 682.04 (Supp. 1969); HAW. REV. STAT. § 658-4 (1955); IDAHO CODE § 7-903 (1975); ILL. ANN. STAT. (Smith-Hurd) ch. 10 § 213 (malpractice arbitration only in health care area); IND. CODE ANN. (Burns) § 34-4-2-4 (1969); KANSAS GEN. STAT. ANN. § 5-403 (1973); LA. REV. STAT. § 9:4204 (1950); MASS. GEN. LAWS ANN. ch. 251, § 3 (1960); MD. [CTS. & JUD. PROC.] CODE ANN. § 3-211(c) (1974); ME. REV. STAT. ANN. tit. 26, § 954 (1964); MICH. STAT. ANN. § 600.5015 (1963); MINN. STAT. ANN. § 572.10 (Supp. 1965); NEV. REV. STAT. § 38.055 (1963); N.H. REV. STAT. ANN. § 542:4 (1955); N.J. REV. STAT. § 2A:24-5 (1952); N.M. STAT. ANN. § 22-3-11 (1971); N.Y. CIV. PRAC. LAW § 7504 (McKinney, 1963); N.C. GEN. STAT. § 1-567.4 (1973); OHIO REV. CODE ANN. § 2711.04 (Page, 1953); ORE. REV. STAT. § 33.250 (1963); PA. STAT. ANN. tit. 5, § 164 (1963); R.I. GEN. LAWS ANN. § 10-3-6 (1956); S.D. COMPILED LAWS ANN. § 21-25A-9 (1976); TENN. CODE ANN. § 23-504 (1955); TEX. REV. CIV. STAT. ANN. art. 226 (Supp. 1965); UTAH CODE ANN. § 78-31-4 (1953); WASH. REV. CODE § 7.04.050 (1961); WIS. STAT. ANN. § 298.04 (1975); WYO. STAT. ANN. § 1-1048.5 (Supp. 1963).

[9]*See, e.g.,* ALA. CODE. tit. 7, §§ 829, 830 (1958) (the arbitrator is to be chosen by the parties); ILL. ANN. STAT. ch. 10, § 103 (Smith-Hurd, Supp. 1964) ("if the method of appointment of arbitrators is not specified in the agreement and cannot be agreed upon by the parties, the entire arbitration agreement shall terminate"); S.C. CODE ANN. § 10-1902 (1962) (the arbitrator shall be chosen by the parties).

[10]BASIC PATTERNS IN UNION CONTRACTS, note 5 *supra* at p. 16.

agreement. The steel and automotive industries have made extensive use of permanent arbitrators. Stability is sought through a consistency in decisions permitting the parties to anticipate more accurately the nature of the award, causing, it is hoped, the withdrawal of grievances as they approach the hearing stage.[11]

A few labor agreements contain a list of several arbitrators from which the parties make a selection in rotation.[12] In some cases, the parties agree to use one of the arbitrators to hear all cases unless that individual is unavailable, in which case the second arbitrator on the list is called. This method, like the naming of a permanent arbitrator, speeds up the selection process.

Selection Through Use of Agency Procedures

A common method of selecting an arbitrator is an agreement to utilize the services of an impartial agency, usually either the American Arbitration Association (AAA) or the Federal Mediation and Conciliation Service (FMCS). Arbitrator Brandschain holds that agency procedures are preferred over selection by mutual agreement:

> The union's representatives may believe that their members may be distrustful of such a privately agreed selection and would therefore prefer that the appointment have an aura of "official" endorsement and impartiality. Sometimes the employer also prefers an impartial selection, either because he distrusts anyone suggested by the union, or he feels that the employees will be impressed thereby and thus perhaps more readily accept an unfavorable decision.[13]

One survey reported that, in approximately 43 percent of labor agreements containing arbitration procedures, the arbitrator is selected on a case-by-case (*ad hoc*) basis by the parties, while in 21 percent the arbitrator is selected on an *ad hoc* basis through the facilities of an impartial agency (generally from a list of arbitrators submitted by the impartial agency). An impartial agency is used to select the arbitrator in 62 percent of the labor agreements specifying the selection process when the parties reach an impasse in the selection process, or if the chosen arbitrator cannot serve, with the parties either ranking their choices from the agency's list and permitting the agency to select an arbitrator acceptable to both parties, or striking names in rotation.

---

[11] A court maintained consistency by reappointment of an arbitrator after a lapse in his term in *William Faehndrich, Inc.*, 15 Misc.2d 370, 181 N.Y.S.2d 918, 31 LA 874 (Sup. Ct. 1959).

[12] *See, e.g.,* Killingsworth, *Arbitration: Its Uses in Industrial Relations,* 21 LA 859, 860 (1963); Basic Patterns in Union Contracts, note 5 *supra* at p. 16.

[13] Brandschain, note 3 *supra* at p. 29.

The most frequently used impartial agency is the FMCS (50 percent), followed by the AAA (36 percent). A small number of contracts specify other impartial agencies (for example, state or federal judges or deans of law or labor relations schools).[14] The AAA maintains a national panel or roster whose members have been selected for their experience, competence, and impartiality.[15]

Effective April 15, 1979, the Federal Mediation and Conciliation Service amended its regulations on arbitration. The changes strengthen the Service's policy against having advocates listed on the Roster of Arbitrators, and spell out certain due process procedures to be followed in connection with the removal of arbitrators from the roster. In addition, an Arbitrator Review Board was established to assist the Director.

The FMCS has clarified the term "advocacy" to make it easier to establish whether or not a prospective arbitrator is an advocate and to help implement its policy of keeping advocates off the roster. A "grandfather clause," however, has been included which allows advocates listed before November 17, 1976, to remain on the roster. Certain due process procedures have been established to be used in connection with the removal of a listing from the roster.

The FMCS[16] and the AAA maintain rosters of approved arbitrators. The AAA and the FMCS normally will submit lists of arbitrators who are near the location of the parties and who possess special technical

---

[14]BASIC PATTERNS IN UNION CONTRACTS, note 5 *supra* at p. 16.

[15]A relatively small percentage of the arbitrators listed do the bulk of the arbitration work. For example, a search of the American Arbitration Association's unpublished records in 1981 revealed that of approximately 3,000 arbitrators listed with the AAA, only 1,036 had handled a case the previous year, and only 739 had handled more than one case.

[16]Under 29 C.F.R. §§ 140.5 (1980), "Listing on the Roster; Criteria for listing and retention," it is specified:

(a) *General Criteria.* Applicants for the Roster will be listed on the Roster upon a determination that they:

(1) Are experienced, competent and acceptable in decision-making rules in the resolution of labor relations disputes; or

(2) Have extensive experience in relevant positions in collective bargaining; and

(3) Are capable of conducting an orderly hearing, can analyze testimony and exhibits and can prepare clear and concise findings and awards within reasonable time limits.

Upon joint request FMCS will supply the parties with the names of seven arbitrators unless the applicable collective bargaining agreement provides for a different number, or unless the parties themselves request a different number (29 C.F.R. § 1404.12 (1980)). FMCS will supply a list of arbitrators upon request of one party; however " ... any submission of a panel should not be construed as anything more than compliance with a request, and does not necessarily reflect the contractual requirements of the parties" and "in no way constitutes a determination by the Service that the parties are obligated to arbitrate the dispute in question." 29 C.F.R. §§ 1404.10(a), 1404.13(c) (1980).

knowledge, if so requested by the parties.[17] The AAA charges $75 to each party, whereas the FMCS furnishes panels without charge.[18]

Under the AAA procedures, it is important to distinguish between a simple request for an arbitration panel and agreement of the parties to proceed under the agency's Voluntary Labor Arbitration Rules. Once the parties agree to be bound by these rules, greater authority resides in the AAA administrator to appoint an arbitrator if the normal procedure does not result in a satisfactory choice. The full procedure is:

> 12. **Appointment from Panel**—If the parties have not appointed an Arbitrator and have not provided any other method of appointment, the Arbitrator shall be appointed in the following manner: Immediately after the filing of the demand or submission, the AAA shall submit simultaneously to each party an identical list of names of persons chosen from the Labor Panel [the AAA National Panel of Labor Arbitrators]. Each party shall have seven days from the mailing date in which to cross off any names objected to, number the remaining names indicating the order of preference, and return the list to the AAA. If a party does not return the list within the time specified, all persons named therein shall be deemed acceptable. From among the persons who have been approved on both lists, and in accordance with the designated order of mutual preference, the AAA shall invite the acceptance of an Arbitrator to serve. If the parties fail to agree upon any of the persons named or if those named decline or are unable to act, or if for any other reason the appointment cannot be made from the submitted lists, the Administrator shall have the power to make the appointment from other members of the Panel without the submission of any additional lists.[19]

A party cannot delay an arbitration hearing under the AAA rules by refusing to select an arbitrator.[20]

The FMCS procedural rules suggests that, where a contract is silent as to the manner of selecting arbitrators, the parties may wish to consider one of two methods most commonly utilized for selection of an arbitrator from a panel. The FMCS provides the panel and the parties may either (1) select an arbitrator by alternately striking names from the submitted panel until one remains (usually done at a joint meeting between the parties) or (2) rank the arbitrators on the panel in

---

[17] FMCS regulations provide that the selection of names for inclusion on a panel will consider many factors, "but agreed upon wishes of the parties are paramount." Special qualifications of arbitrators experienced in certain issues, industries, or background may be taken into consideration at the parties' request. 29 C.F.R. § 1404.12(c) (1980).

[18] The AAA's fee covers all panel lists provided to the parties in the particular case, in addition to the use of a conference room at the AAA's Regional Office for the hearing. There is an extra charge for additional hearings or postponements. Many state agencies, such as the state department of labor or a state employment relations board, also provide lists of arbitrators.

[19] American Arbitration Association, *Voluntary Labor Arbitration Rules,* Rule 12 (1979).

[20] *Id.,* Rules 13, 27.

preference order in which case the FMCS will appoint the individual whose name has the lowest accumulated numerical number.[21]

Selection of an Arbitration Board

Some labor agreements provide that each party is to appoint one arbitrator and that the two appointed arbitrators are to select the impartial arbitrator or chairperson. In Georgia, this procedure is incorporated into a statute requiring that "every arbitration under this Chapter shall be composed of three arbitrators, one of whom shall be chosen by each of the parties and one by the arbitrators chosen by the parties."[22] This statutory procedure was held not to be satisfied where the dispute was submitted to two arbitrators who were given the power to select a third should they disagree.[23] The Texas statute provides for the selection of a five-person board of arbitration, two by each party and the fifth selected by the other four.[24] The South Carolina statute calls upon each party to select a "discreet person, both of whom then select the third member of the board."[25] Even a bipartite board can be an arbitration board if the parties so agree. Furthermore, the participation of a party in an arbitration before a board which was not composed of the number of arbitrators specified in the Railway Labor Act constituted a waiver of that party's right to object to an award rendered by that board.[26]

A study of 1,717 labor agreements by the Bureau of Labor Statistics of the United States Department of Labor revealed that 46 percent of the agreements studied provided for tripartite arbitration boards in 1952, but that the percentage had declined to 39 percent by 1962 and to 38 percent by 1965.[27] More recent statistics are not available; however, according to one FMCS official, requests for arbitrators to serve as members of tripartite panels are few.

The risk of deadlock exists where the appointed arbitrators cannot agree on an impartial arbitrator or chairperson, and the applicable

---

[21]29 C.F.R. § 1404.13(b) (1980); Finnegan, *Federal Mediation and Conciliation Service*, MANAGEMENT RIGHTS AND THE ARBITRATION PROCESS, Proceedings of the Ninth Annual Meeting, National Academy of Arbitrators, J. McKelvey, ed. (Washington: BNA Books, 1956), p. 96.

[22]GA. CODE ANN. § 7-202 (1936).

[23]*Osborn & Walcott Mfg. Co. v. Blanton,* 109 Ga. 196, 34 S.E. 306 (1899) (refusal to enforce award).

[24]TEX. REV. CIV. STAT. ANN. art. 239 (1959).

[25]S.C. CODE OF LAWS § 15-47-20 (1976).

[26]*Order of Railway Conductors v. Clinchfield R.R. Co.,* 407 F.2d 985, 70 LRRM 3076 (6th Cir. 1969)

[27]U.S. Bureau of Labor Statistics, Dept. of Labor, Bulletin No. 1425-26, MAJOR COLLECTIVE BARGAINING AGREEMENTS 36 (1966).

labor agreement fails to provide a method for breaking the deadlock.[28] In some states, courts will appoint the arbitrator upon application of one of the parties; in others they will not.[29]

In spite of the risk of deadlock, the usual practice is for each party to nominate an arbitrator and for the two arbitrators to choose a third, the impartial chairperson. There has been considerable controversy as to whether the two arbitrators chosen by the parties are expected to maintain the same degree of impartiality as the impartial chairperson or whether they may assume the role of advocates for their nominators.[30] Early guidelines on this question were provided in *American Eagle Fire Insurance Co. v. New Jersey Insurance Co.,*[31] where the court held:

> [T]he practice of arbitrators conducting themselves as champions of their nominators is to be condemned as contrary to the purpose of arbitrations and as calculated to bring the system of enforced arbitrations into disrepute.... [The arbitrator] should keep his own counsel and not run to his nominator for advice when he sees that he may be in a minority. When once he enters into an arbitration, he ceases to act as agent of the party who appoints him. He must lay aside all bias and approach the case with a mind open to conviction and without regard to his previously formed opinions as to the merits of the party or the cause. He should sedulously refrain from any conduct which might justify even the inference that either party is the special recipient of his solicitude or favor....[32]

This approach was the basis for many early awards.[33]

The trend, however, has been toward relaxation of strict standards of impartiality for party-nominated arbitrators. For example, in one case the arbitration clause—which required each party to select one member "not associated with the Company or the Union," the two so named then to select the chairperson from a list furnished by the American Arbitration Association—was interpreted not to disqualify

---

[28]The NLRB has the power to order a union to arbitrate claims involving conflicting interpretations of provisions of its labor agreements concerning the impartial resolution of the merits of grievances, *See NLRB v. Food Store Employees Union, Local 347, etc.,* 417 U.S. 1, 86 LRRM 2209 (1974); *NLRB v. Local 485, Int'l Union of Electrical, R & M Wkrs.,* 454 F.2d 17, 79 LRRM 2278 (2d Cir. 1972); *Phelps Dodge v. NLRB,* 313 U.S. 177, 8 LRRM 439 (1941); *NLRB v. Local Union 396, International Brotherhood of Teamsters, Chauffeurs, Warehousemen and Helpers of America,* 509 F.2d 1075, 88 LRRM 2589 (9th Cir. 1975).

[29]*See* notes 8 and 9 *supra.*

[30]*See In re M.A.G. Prod. (Motion Picture Management Corp.),* 3 A.D.2d 660 (1st Dept. 1957); *Grainger v. Shea Enterprises,* 162 N.Y.S.2d 673 (N.Y. County 1957); *Dresdner v. Czeisler,* 33 Misc.2d 578 (Kings County 1962); *Tave Constr. Co., Inc. v. Wiesenfeld,* 82 N.J. Super. 562 (1964), *aff'd,* 217 A.2d 140 (App. Div. 1966); and *American Home Assurance Co. v. American Fidelity,* 261 F. Supp. 734 (S.D. N.Y. 1966).

[31]240 N.Y. 398, 148 N.E. 562 (1925).

[32]240 N.Y. at 405, 148 N.E. at 564.

[33]*See, e.g., Wheeling Gas v. The City of Wheeling,* 5 W.Va. 448 (1872).

an attorney "most of [whose] clients are labor organizations," who had been counsel for the union on "isolated occasions," and who had served as a union appointee to arbitration panels for the same parties.[34] Arbitrator Crane said:

> General experience with tripartite arbitration boards indicates that it is the impartial chairman who decides the disputed issue and that a party-appointed member either concurs or dissents, depending upon whether or not the decision is favorable to the party which appointed him.[35]

New York Civil Practice Law and Rules were specifically amended to provide that only the partiality of an arbitrator appointed as a neutral is a basis for vacating an award.[36] This change "takes cognizance of the common practice of each party appointing his own arbitrator who is not individually expected to be neutral."[37]

This approach was upheld in *Astoria Medical Group v. Health Insurance Plan of Greater New York.*[38] There, it was held that an arbitrator appointed by the parties may be partisan, but he may not be dishonest by being "deaf to the testimony or blind to the evidence presented."[39] The use of nonneutral arbitrators was found not to be objectionable since the arbitration is not strictly a judicial remedy.[40] A motion to vacate, the court held, must be based on "some misconduct on the part of an arbitrator and not simply on his interest in the subject matter or the controversy of his relationship to the party who selected him."[41]

The manner in which the arbitration board is selected is important when the General Counsel of the NLRB determines whether to dismiss the charge and defer to arbitration. General Counsel Peter Nash said:[42]

> Unfair labor practice charges will not be deferred for arbitration unless the applicable contract procedures for the resolution of disputes provides for

---

[34]*Columbus & Southern Ohio Electric Co.*, AAA Case No. 31-13 (Crane, 1961).

[35]*Id.*

[36]*New York Civil Practice Law and Rules*, Section 7511(b) (ii) (as amended 1963).

[37]N.Y.S. LEGISLATIVE DOCUMENT No. 13 at 146 (1958).

[38]11 N.Y.2d 128, 227 N.Y.S.2d 401, 182 N.E.2d 85 (1962). *See also Associated General Contractors, Evansville Chapter, Inc. v. NLRB*, 465 F.2d 327, 80 LRRM 3157 (7th Cir. 1972); *Stef Shipping Corp. v. Norris Grain Co.*, 209 F. Supp. 249 (S.D. N.Y. 1962).

[39]11 N.Y.2d at 137.

[40]*Id.* at 136.

[41]*Id.* at 137. *See Brenan v. Stewarts Pharmacies, Ltd.*, 1st Cir Ct. of Hawaii, S.P. No. 3897, Nov. 20, 1975 (award set aside where party-appointed arbitrator had acted as negotiator for principal); *Federico v. Frick*, Cal. App. 3d 872, 84 Cal. Rptr. 74, 73 LRRM 2810 (2d Dist., Div. 3, 1970).

[42]Nash, *Revised Memorandum of NLRB General Counsel On Processing of Deferral to Arbitration Cases* (Official Text), 90 DLR F-1 (May 9, 1973). (The following three footnotes taken from Nash text.)

"arbitration." In determining whether the person, persons or body provided in the contract for the last-stage resolution of the dispute are arbitrators or arbitral bodies, and that the contract therefore provides for "arbitration," the criteria for this determination which have been developed by the Board in the application of the *Spielberg*[43] policy should be employed. Thus, the absence of a neutral member on a bipartite panel would not necessarily preclude deferral.[44] But where, in addition, it appears that all members of the bipartite panel are or would be arrayed in interest against the charging party, deferral would not be appropriate.[45]

The NLRB (over persistent dissents by Member Jenkins) has consistently followed the General Counsel's Memorandum in finding deferral appropriate where the arbitration mechanism has consisted of a bipartite panel which may not have a strictly neutral member, provided *Spielberg* standards of fairness have been met.

The management and union representatives on a tripartite board are actually advocates for the respective parties.[46] To label the management and union representatives on the board as "arbitrators" is not only a misnomer, but also raises serious ethical and legal questions.[47] The occasional use of tripartite boards of arbitration sometimes creates special problems. Under law, the award must be supported by at least a majority. The difficulty is that the two party-appointed arbitrators may regard themselves as advocates of their sides, rather than impartial adjudicators, which may make it difficult

---

[43]*Spielberg Manufacturing Co.*, 112 NLRB 1080, 36 LRRM 1152 (1955).

[44]*Denver-Chicago Trucking Co.*, 132 NLRB 1416, 48 LRRM 1524 (1961); *Modern Motor Express Inc.*, 149 NLRB 1507, 58 LRRM 1005 (1964). The Board's reference in *Tulsa-Whisenhunt Funeral Homes, Inc.*, 195 NLRB 106, 79 LRRM 1265 (1972), n. 1, to "a forum of third parties" was not deemed sufficient to infer Board rejection of the relevance of the *Denver-Chicago* principle to the Collyer deferral policy (*Collyer Insulated Wire*, 192 NLRB 837, 77 LRRM 1931 (1971)). See *Great Coastal Express, Inc.*, 196 NLRB 871, 80 LRRM 1097 (1972); *National Biscuit Co.*, 198 NLRB 552, 80 LRRM 1727 (1972); *Tyee Construction Co.*, 202 NLRB 307, 82 LRRM 1548 (1973).

[45]*Jacobs Transfer, Inc.*, 201 NLRB 210, 82 LRRM 1360 (1973); *Youngstown Cartage Co.*, 146 NLRB 305, 55 LRRM 1301 (1964); *Roadway Express, Inc.*, 145 NLRB 513, 54 LRRM 1419 (1963). *Cf. United Parcel Service, Inc.*, 232 NLRB 1114, 96 LRRM 1288 (1977); *Automotive Transport, Inc.*, 223 NLRB 217 (1976); *Kansas Meat Packers*, 198 NLRB 543, 80 LRRM 1743 (1972); *Terminal Transport Co., Inc.*, 185 NLRB 672, 75 LRRM 1130 (1970).

[46]See *United Ass'n of Journeymen, Plumbing and Pipe Fitting Industry Local 525 v. Eighth Judicial District Court of Nevada*, 412 P.2d 352, 62 LRRM 2126 (Nev. Sup. Ct. 1966) (where the contract between a union and a contractors' association provided for a tripartite board composed of two members designated by each side and a neutral chairman, the lower court was in error in vacating award of the arbitration board so established on the basis that it was not composed of five unbiased, neutral members). See also *Palizzotto v. Teamsters Local 641*, 67 N.J. Super. 145, 170 A.2d 57, 36 LA 828 (1961); *Div. 1223, Street, Electric Railway & Motor Coach Employees v. Council of Western Greyhound*, 56 LRRM 2712 (Calif. Dist. Ct. App. 1964); *Johnson v. Jahncke Service, Inc.*, 52 LRRM 2194 (La. Ct. App. 1962).

[47]See Levitt, *Lawyers, Legalism, and Labor Arbitration*, note 6 *supra*, at 397.

for the impartial arbitrator to get the support of one of the others for a majority award. Parties often resolve this difficulty by empowering the third arbitrator to render a decision without the concurrence of the others. This may be done either in the arbitration clause or, in the event of deadlock, by later stipulation of the parties. When this is done, the third arbitrator is in a better position to rule on the issues as the arbitrator sees them without having to compromise a position for the sake of a majority award. For example, the Committee on Ethics of the National Academy of Arbitrators questioned the wisdom of labeling all of the members of such tripartite boards arbitrators, as follows:

> If arbitration is a judicial process, the use of tripartite boards of arbitration to determine questions of contract interpretation may involve a problem of ethical content. . . . It is common knowledge that the members designated by the parties almost invariably view the case as partisans, though purporting to sit as impartial judges. . . .
>
> Is this an "ethical" arrangement? Whether it is or not, if the decision is to be made by majority vote, it often puts the neutral arbitrator in an impossible position if his function is to decide the case "judicially." Yet the parties may have entered into such an arrangement in perfect good faith. They may have sound practical reasons for preferring such an arrangement, uppermost of which is the fear of having an arbitrator unfamiliar with the mores of the particular company-union relationship go off "half-cocked." When it is realized that an award in a labor dispute is not merely the decision of a legal issue but may materially affect the day-to-day relationship of an employer and his employees for an indefinite period in the future, the concern of the parties is understandable. Yet serious questions exist as to the propriety of tripartite arbitration in the interpretation of labor contracts—if the arbitration and the judicial processes are indistinguishable.[48]

---

[48]*Standards of Conduct for Labor Arbitrators*, THE PROFESSION OF LABOR ARBITRATION, Selected Proceedings of the First Seven Annual Meetings, National Academy of Arbitrators, J. McKelvey, ed. (Washington: BNA Books, 1957), pp. 143–44 quoted in *Associated General Contractors of America, Evansville Chapter, Inc. v. NLRB*, 465 F.2d 327, 80 LRRM 3157 (7th Cir. 1972). This cautious approach to the characterization of management and union representatives on tripartite boards was formalized in the *Code of Professional Responsibility for Arbitrators of Labor-Management Disputes*, approved by the National Academy of Arbitrators at its Annual Meeting on April 28, 1975, and also approved by AAA and FMCS, which are parties to the Code. Thus, the preamble to the Code defines an "arbitrator" as used therein as "any *impartial* person, irrespective of specific title, who serves in a labor-management dispute procedure in which there is conferred authority to decide issues or to make formal recommendations." (Emphasis added.) The preamble goes on to provide specifically that the Code "does *not* apply to partisan representatives on tripartite boards." (Emphasis added.) ARBITRATION—1975, Proceedings of the Twenty-Eighth Annual Meeting, National Academy of Arbitrators, B. Dennis and G. Somers, eds. (Washington: BNA Books, 1976), p. 219; 64 LA 1317 (1975).

Absence of one of the three arbitrators from the hearing, unless absence is waived, is grounds for vacating the award.[49] The death of a party appointed as arbitrator after the hearings but before the decision is also grounds for vacating the award.[50] If a party-appointed arbitrator, however, withdraws after the proceedings begin, the remaining two can render the award.[51]

After the hearing, the board members meet in an executive session to review the evidence and the two partisan members attempt to ensure that the neutral chairperson understands the position of the party each represents and their views as to the weight and significance of the evidence. Sometimes the executive session is held after the neutral chairperson has prepared a draft of the award, and the partisan members are then given an opportunity to correct factual errors and suggest changes in language.

DUTY OF THE ARBITRATOR TO DISCLOSE

Arbitrators who have been selected to arbitrate a labor dispute have a duty to disclose to the parties certain types of information concerning their backgrounds, associations, and relationships. Section II. B—Required Disclosures—of the Code Of Professional Responsibility For Arbitrators Of Labor-Management Disputes, approved jointly in

---

[49]*West Towns Bus Co. v. Div. 241, Amalgamated Ass'n of Street, Electric Ry. and Motor Coach Employees,* 26 Ill. App.2d 398, 168 N.E.2d 473 (1960); *Knickerbocker Textile Corp. v. Donath,* 22 Misc.2d 1056, 205 N.Y.S.2d 408 (Sup. Ct.), *aff'd,* 282 App. Div. 680 (1953); *Turner v. Cox,* 16 Cal. Rptr. 644 (Ct. App. 1961); *Bluhm v. Perenia,* 75 N.Y.S.2d 170 (Sup. Ct. 1946).

[50]*Fromer Foods, Inc. v. Edelstein Foods, Inc.,* 181 N.Y.S.2d 352, 353 (Sup. Ct. 1958):

"In most instances an award by two arbitrators is binding even though a third withdraws before the award is rendered. This is not so, however, when one of the arbitrators dies after the hearing but before the decision has been made or the award rendered. The deceased arbitrator cannot be deemed to be a mere dissenter...."

See also Cia De Navegacion Omsil, S.A. v. Hugo Neu Corporation, 359 F. Supp. 898 (S.D. N.Y. 1973); *Mitchell v. Alfred Hofmann, Inc.,* 48 N.J. Super. 396, 137 A.2d 569 (App. Div. 1958). *See related matters, In re Karpinecz (Marshall),* 48 Misc.2d 8 (Nassau County 1965), (substitution of another arbitrator permitted); *Ench Equipment Corp. v. Enkay Foods, Inc.,* 43 N.J. Super. 500, 129 A.2d 313 (App. Div. 1957) (resignation of three arbitrators and turning matter back to court not permitted).

[51]*In re Publishers' Ass'n of New York City,* 15 Misc.2d 931, 934, 181 N.Y.S.2d 527, 530, 31 LA 87, 873 (Sup. Ct. 1959):

"Obviously the Union's withdrawal from the arbitration during its progress, because the impartial chairman did not agree with its contentions, may not be permitted to defeat the award. Arbitration would be completely undermined if awards could be nullified by such strategy."

See also Amalgamated Ass'n of Street, Electric Ry. & Motor Coach Employees v. Connecticut Co., 24 LA 107 (Conn. Sup. Ct. Err. 1955); *Sam Kane Packing Co. v. Amalgamated Meat Cut. & B.W.,* 477 F.2d 1128, 83 LRRM 2298 (5th Cir. 1973), *cert. denied,* 414 U.S. 1001, 84 LRRM 2606; *Fuller v. Pepsi-Cola Bottling Co. of Lexington, Ky.,* 406 S.W.2d 416, 63 LRRM 2220 (Ky. 1966).

1975 by the National Academy of Arbitrators, American Arbitration Association, and Federal Mediation and Conciliation Service, as parties thereto, elaborates in the following terms the substance of an arbitrator's ethical disclosure obligation:

Required Disclosures

1. Before accepting an appointment, an arbitrator must disclose directly or through the administrative agency involved, any current or past managerial, representational, or consultative relationship with any company or union involved in a proceeding in which he or she is being considered for appointment or has been tentatively designated to serve. Disclosure must also be made of any pertinent pecuniary interest.

a. The duty to disclose includes membership on a Board of Directors, full-time or part-time service as a representative or advocate, consultation work for a fee, current stock or bond ownership (other than mutual fund shares or appropriate trust arrangements) or any other pertinent form of managerial, financial or immediate family interest in the company or union involved.

2. When an arbitrator is serving concurrently as an advocate for or representative of other companies or unions in labor relations matters, or has done so in recent years, he or she must disclose such activities before accepting appointment as an arbitrator.

An arbitrator must disclose such activities to an administrative agency if he or she is on that agency's active roster or seeks placement on a roster. Such disclosure then satisfies this requirement for cases handled under that agency's referral.

a. It is not necessary to disclose names of clients or other specific details. It is necessary to indicate the general nature of the labor relations advocacy or representational work involved, whether for companies or unions or both, and a reasonable approximation of the extent of such activity.

b. *An arbitrator on an administrative agency's roster has a continuing obligation to notify the agency of any significant changes pertinent to this requirement.*

c. When an administrative agency is not involved, an arbitrator must make such disclosure directly unless he or she is certain that both parties to the case are fully aware of such activities.

3. An arbitrator must not permit personal relationships to affect decision-making.

Prior to acceptance of an appointment, an arbitrator must disclose to the parties or to the administrative agency involved any close personal relationship or other circumstance, in addition to those specifically mentioned earlier in this section, which might reasonably raise a question as to the arbitrator's impartiality.

a. Arbitrators establish personal relationships with many company and union representatives, with fellow arbitrators, and with fellow members of various professional associations. There should be no attempt to be secretive about such friendships or acquaintances but disclosure is not necessary unless some feature of a particular relationship might reasonably appear to impair impartiality.

4. If the circumstances requiring disclosure are not known to the arbitrator prior to acceptance of appointment, disclosure must be made when such circumstances become known to the arbitrator.

5. The burden of disclosure rests on the arbitrator. After appropriate disclosure, the arbitrator may serve if both parties so desire. If the arbitrator believes or perceives that there is a clear conflict of interest, he or she should withdraw, irrespective of the expressed desires of the parties.[52]

The Code clearly rests the burden of withdrawal from a case because of a perceived conflict of interest on the arbitrator, regardless of the interests or desires of the respective parties.

In addition, the American Arbitration Association's 1979 Voluntary Labor Arbitration Rules provide in Rule 11 that "No person shall serve as a neutral arbitrator in any arbitration in which that person has any financial or personal interest in the result of the arbitration, unless the parties, in writing, waive such disqualification."[53] And Rule 17 reads as follows:

Prior to accepting appointment, the prospective neutral Arbitrator shall disclose any circumstances likely to create a presumption of bias or which he believes might disqualify him as an impartial Arbitrator. Upon receipt of such information, the AAA shall immediately disclose it to the parties. If either party declines to waive the presumptive disqualification, the vacancy thus created shall be filled in accordance with the applicable provisions of these Rules."[54]

On its face, this Rule does not appear to cover a problem of disclosure which arises subsequent to acceptance of the appointment by the arbitrator, but Rule 46 provides that "The Arbitrator shall interpret and apply these Rules [including Rule 11] insofar as they relate to the Arbitrator's power and duties."[55]

As noted above, the Federal Mediation and Conciliation Service has adopted, in the Code of Federal Regulations, the Code of Professional Responsibility for Arbitrators for Labor-Management Disputes, discussed *supra,* for arbitrators whose services are obtainable through FMCS.[56] The FMCS also has adopted, in the Code of Federal Regulations, the Code of Professional Conduct for Labor Mediators for its arbitrators:

[52]*Code of Professional Responsibility for Arbitrators of Labor-Management Disputes,* ARBITRATION—1975, note 48 *supra* at pp. 222–225, 64 LA 1317, 1321 (1975).
[53]American Arbitration Association, *Voluntary Labor Arbitration Rules,* Rule 11, 1979.
[54]*Id.,* Rule 17.
[55]*Id.,* Rule 46.
[56]29 C.F.R. § 1404.4(b) (1980).

The practice of mediation is a profession with ethical responsibilities and duties. Those who engage in the practice of mediation must be dedicated to the principles of free and responsible collective bargaining. They must be aware that their duties and obligations relate to the parties who engage in collective bargaining, to every other mediator, to the agencies which administer the practice of mediation, and to the general public.[57]

The Code of Professional Conduct proscribes certain activities:

The mediator should not use his position for private gain or advantage, nor should he engage in any employment, activity or enterprise which will conflict with his work as a mediator, nor should he accept any money, or thing of value for the performance of his duties—other than his regular salary—or incur obligations to any party which might interfere with the impartial performance of his duties.[58]

The Code of Federal Regulations more specifically indicates the reasons for which a member may be cancelled from the service by the Director:

Notice of cancellation may be given to the member whenever the member:
(1) No longer meets the criteria for admission;
(2) Has been repeatedly and flagrantly delinquent in submitting awards;
(3) Has refused to make reasonable and periodic reports to FMCS, as required in Subpart C of this part, concerning activities pertaining to arbitration;
(4) Has been the subject of complaints by parties who use FMCS facilities and the Director, after appropriate inquiry, concludes that just cause for cancellation has been shown;
(5) Is determined by the Director to be unacceptable to the parties who use FMCS arbitration facilities; the Director may base a determination of unacceptability on FMCS records showing the number of times the arbitrator's name has been proposed to the parties and the number of times it has been selected.[59]

In 1925, Congress adopted the United States Arbitration Act.[60] Whether this statute applies to arbitration of a dispute under a labor agreement has been discussed in various contexts in this volume. Nevertheless, for arbitration of controversies coming within its terms, Section 10 provides that an award may be vacated "where there was evident partiality . . . in the arbitrators."[61]

---

[57] 29 C.F.R. § 1400.735-20 (1980) and Appendix cited therein.
[58] Appendix to 29 C.F.R. Part 1400 (1980).
[59] 29 C.F.R. § 1404.5(d) (1980).
[60] Act of February 12, 1925, c. 213, 43 Stat. 883, *reenacted into positive law,* Act of July 30, 1947, c. 392, § 1, 61 Stat. 669 (codified at 9 U.S.C. §§ 1–14 (1976)).
[61] 9 U.S.C. § 10 (1976).

An arbitrator's failure to disclose his previous association with the union was held by a court to be grounds for vacating an award since such nondisclosure deprived the employer of its rightful opportunity to make a knowledgeable selection of an impartial arbitrator.[62] The facts showed that: (1) the arbitrator was employed as an attorney for the respondent union for a period of several years; (2) less than six months prior to the hearing he listed his address as that of the union; and (3) in 1967 he had been paid over $10,000 by the union for his services. "On this record," the court concluded, "it is reasonable to infer that the prior relationship between the arbitrator and the [union] constituted partiality."[63]

In *Commonwealth Coatings Corp. v. Continental Casualty Co.,*[64] the Supreme Court vacated an arbitration award in a commercial arbitration case. The majority of the Court found that the award should be set aside under Section 10 of the U. S. Arbitration Act because the neutral member of an arbitration board failed to disclose that he had received $12,000 in consultant's fees from one of the parties over a period of four to five years. The neutral arbitrator, in fact, had rendered service as a consultant on the very projects which became involved in arbitration. Justices Harlan, Stewart, and Fortas pointed out in a dissent that the award in question was unanimously adopted by the panel, which included an arbitrator chosen by the subcontractor, and that there was no claim that the neutral arbitrator actually was partial. The dissent believed that the majority of the court adopted a *per se* rule that if an arbitrator had any prior business relations with one of the parties of which he fails to inform the other party, however innocently, the arbitration award is always subject to being set aside.

It should be noted that there are a number of cases decided prior to *Commonwealth* in which the courts have vacated an award because of a failure to disclose a prior business relationship.[65] Although a determination of what is partiality and bias is difficult, a number of clearly disqualifying criteria have emerged in a few decisions involving labor arbitration. In some cases, courts have found that the relationship between an arbitrator and one of the parties was significant enough to justify vacating the award.

---

[62]*Colony Liquor Distributors, Inc. v. Teamsters Local 669,* 34 App. Div.2d 1060, 312 N.Y.S.2d 403, 74 LRRM 2945 (1970).

[63]34 App. Div.2d at 1062, 312 N.Y.S.2d at 405. *See also Sanko S.S. Co., Ltd. v. Cook Industries, Inc.,* 495 F.2d 1260 (2d Cir. 1973); *Reed & Martin, Inc. v. Westinghouse Electric Corp.,* 439 F.2d 1268 (2d Cir. 1971); *In re United Culinary Bar & Grill Employees Union of New York, Local 923,* 11 LA 1119 (N.Y. Sup. Ct. 1949).

[64]393 U.S. 145 (1968).

[65]*See In re Siegel,* 153 N.Y.S.2d 673, 26 LA 499 (Sup. Ct. N.Y. County, 1956). *In re Friedman,* 213 N.Y.S. 369 (1st Dept. 1926); *Petroleum Cargo Carriers Ltd. v. Unitas, Inc.,* 220 N.Y.S.2d 724, *aff'd,* 224 N.Y.S.2d 654 (1st Dept. 1962).

In *Labor Relations Sec. of Northern New York Building Exchange, Inc. v. Gordon,* [66] the award was vacated because the arbitrator failed to disclose that he was a member of the Civil Service Employees Association. If disclosure is made during or prior to the hearing and the parties continue with the arbitrator, the courts have held that the parties have waived their right to object.

Removal of a party-appointed arbitrator is generally refused. *Astoria Medical Group v. Health Ins. Plans of Greater New York* [67] held that where there is a tripartite arbitration there can be no objection to the "partisan" arbitrator's relationship with his designee. In *Cecil v. Bank of America Nat. Trust & Savings Association,* [68] it was held that when a tripartite panel is being used a party may appoint his attorney as arbitrator.

DUTY OF THE APPOINTING AGENCY TO DISCLOSE

An appointing agency has a duty to disclose to the parties facts which may determine the qualification of an arbitrator. A federal district court in *Rogers v. Schering Corp.* [69] said:

> [W]hen the Association is informed by a prospective arbitrator in response to its inquiry, of circumstances which are "likely to create a presumption of bias," nothing less than a prompt communication of such disclosure to the parties, even where the filling of a vacancy is concerned, provides the affected party with an opportunity to challenge "for cause." Nor is it sufficient for the Association to take the position that *it* weighed the disclosure and concluded that it did not affect the eligibility of the proposed arbitrator. [Emphasis in original.]
>   . . .
> The failure of the Administrator to communicate to the parties [such] information . . . is more than a loose procedural informality. It goes to the heart of a body designed to resolve controversy—its integrity. In this instance it fails to protect what might be termed "due arbitration process." [70]

In that case an arbitration panel had rendered an award concerning the royalty value of a drug patent. Prior to the award and during the hearing one of the parties to the arbitration discovered that a member of the panel had done business with the other party to the arbitration.

---

[66] 335 N.Y.S.2d 624 (Sup. Ct., Onondaga County, 1972).

[67] 11 N.Y.2d 128, 227 N.Y.S.2d 401 (1962).

[68] 236 P.2d 408 (Cal. 1951).

[69] 165 F. Supp. 295 (D. N.J. 1958), *aff'd,* 271 F.2d 266 (3d Cir. 1959), *cert. denied,* 359 U.S. 991 (1959).

[70] 165 F. Supp. at 300-01. *See also Advance Trucking Corp. v. Teamsters, Local 807,* 38 Misc.2d 618, 240 N.Y.S.2d 203, 52 LRRM 2365 (Sup. Ct. 1963).

This information had been disclosed to the American Arbitration Association, which had selected the panel, but had not been relayed to the parties. An objection was raised at the hearing but no change in the make-up of the panel resulted. The court considered the lack of notification irregular and illegal and vacated the award.

LIABILITY OF THE ARBITRATOR

It was early established that judges should be immune to civil liability for acts performed in accordance with their duties.[71] This immunity has also been extended to arbitrators. For example, in *Jones v. Brown*,[72] it was held that an arbitrator could not be sued for damages as a result of a fraudulent and corrupt act or award. An arbitrator as a quasi-judicial officer has immunity from testifying as to reasons for the award and, therefore, cannot be examined in order to impeach the award.[73] In *Hill v. Aro Corp.*,[74] an employee sued an arbitrator who had decided the employee's grievance against the employee. The employee claimed that the arbitrator had engaged in misconduct during the hearing. The court granted the arbitrator's motion to dismiss:

> If national policy encourages arbitration and if arbitrators are indispensable agencies in the furtherance of that policy, then it follows that the common law rule protecting arbitrators from suit ought not only to be affirmed, but, if need be, expanded.[75]

Injured parties are, however, not completely without remedy. In *Beaver v. Brown*[76] the court said that while judicial immunity protects arbitrators from civil liability, "it does not allow them compensation for an act rendered useless by their willful misconduct." Evidence of such misconduct could be used to defeat a motion by the arbitrator to recover for his or her services.

---

[71]*See, e.g., Bradley v. Fisher,* 80 U.S. 335 (1872).

[72]54 Iowa 74 (1880). *See also Babylon Milk & Cream Co. v. Horvitz,* 151 N.Y.S.2d 221, 26 LA 121 (Sup. Ct. 1956); *Cahn v. ILGWU,* 203 F. Supp. 191, 49 LRRM 2850 (E.D. Pa.), *aff'd,* 311 F.2d 113 (3d Cir. 1962); *Kenney v. McLean Trucking Co.,* 54 N.J. 533, 149 A.2d 606, 32 LA 323 (N.J. Super. Ct. 1959).

[73]*Grambling v. Food Machinery & Chem. Corp.,* 151 F. Supp. 853, 860–61 (W.D. S.C. 1957) and *Fukaya Trading Co., S.A. v. Eastern Marine Corp.,* 322 F. Supp. 278, 279–80 (E.D. La. 1971). *Morysville Body Works, Inc. v. United Steelworkers,* Civil Action No. 75-2498, Oct. 8, 1976 (E.D. Pa.).

[74]263 F. Supp. 324, 64 LRRM 2315 (N.D. Ohio 1967).

[75]*Id.* at 326, 64 LRRM at 2317.

[76]56 Iowa 565 (1881).

CHAPTER VI

The Challenges to the Arbitrator
That a Dispute Is Not Arbitrable

This chapter considers the authority or jurisdiction of the arbitrator to determine a particular dispute. Stated another way, it reports what arbitrators do when a claim is made that a particular grievance should be dismissed because it is not arbitrable under the labor agreement.

What courts do concerning claims that a particular grievance is not arbitrable has been reported in Chapters III and IV. Often, courts resolve a claim that a particular grievance is not arbitrable by referring the dispute to arbitration, unless the lack of arbitrability is absolutely clear.

The first situation to be examined is where a court refers a dispute to arbitration after one party has claimed before the court that the dispute is not arbitrable, and the claim, rejected by the court, is again made to the arbitrator. Is the arbitrator bound to find the dispute arbitrable because a court has referred the dispute to arbitration, or can the arbitrator examine the claim of nonarbitrability anew?

The contention that the arbitrator cannot reexamine the claim of nonarbitrability once a court has referred a dispute to arbitration was discussed by Arbitrator Thomas T. Roberts. The Supreme Court of California had referred a case claimed to be nonarbitrable to arbitration, and, over the objection of the union, Roberts held that the court's order directing arbitration did not preclude the company from again raising the question of arbitrability before the arbitrator.[1] Arbitrator Turkus has said that it would be "utterly inconsistent with the very doctrine or overriding theme upon which the [*Warrior & Gulf*] decision is predicated," and an "abdication of responsibility and independence of judgment" if the arbitrator were to hold a grievance arbitrable merely because under the Supreme Court view it should not be withheld from arbitration.[2] In a like vein, Arbitrator Benjamin

---

[1] *Wilshire Oil Co. of California,* AAA Case No. 65-9, 42 LA 315 (Roberts, 1964).
[2] *Socony Mobil Oil Co.,* AAA Case No. 72-14 (Turkus, 1965).

Aaron explained that the import of the *Steelworkers Trilogy* is that those cases do not require a finding of arbitrability by arbitrators:

> "Those cases all dealt ... with the power of federal courts, rather than with the discretion of arbitrators. Construing those cases in a way most favorable to the Union here involved would lead at most to the conclusion that if the parties had litigated this issue in federal court instead of submitting it to private arbitration, the court would have ruled that the issue was arbitrable; or that, conversely, if the arbitration decision in this case were in favor of arbitrability, the court would decline to vacate it on review. Neither of those contingencies has occurred. The parties elected to resolve this dispute through arbitration, and the decision rests upon the judgment of a majority of the three Arbitrators selected to hear the case. In exercising that judgment we should not, in my opinion, be influenced by any calculation of what a court might do if confronted by the same problem. The dominant theme of the Supreme Court decision referred to above is that courts typically lack the specialized knowledge, experience, and insight to deal wisely with these problems. Whether either this assumption, or the corresponding one that arbitrators typically possess such expertise, is correct is, to put it mildly, a question on which there is considerable disagreement. In any case, the doctrine enunciated in the Supreme Court to uphold claims of arbitrability solely on the ground that a court would do so in like circumstances must be resisted; for to yield would be to abdicate the assumed independence of judgment based on specialized knowledge and experience upon which the Supreme Court doctrine is predicated."[3]

Similarly, Arbitrator James J. Healy has said that when the labor agreement provided for arbitration of "any dispute ... of any nature or character," and even though there " 'probably' was a basis for finding arbitrability ... under ... *Warrior & Gulf Navigation Co.*, the union's request for establishment of a differential ... when certain tasks are performed was not arbitrable."[4] The arbitrator interpreted the decision of the Supreme Court to mean that the union could establish a *"prima facie case"* in a court for its right to proceed to arbitration, but that it still remained for the arbitrator to determine whether to proceed "to the pure merits" of the claim or to dismiss the claim for lack of an arbitral issue.

Arbitrator Eric J. Shertz said that a determination by an arbitrator that a grievance is arbitrable does not mean that the grievance has merit:

> The arbitrability of an issue does not require it to be meritorious. A grievance, though wholly lacking in merit, may be arbitrable because it involves as its subject matter a term or condition of employment encompassed by the Collective Bargaining Agreement.[5]

---

[3]*Hughes Tool Co.*, AAA Case No. 26-1, 36 LA 1125 (Aaron, 1960).
[4]*Berkshire Hathaway Co.*, AAA Case No. 41-1 (Healy, 1961).
[5]*Macy's New York*, AAA Case No. 43-6 (Schmertz, 1962).

In a similar vein, Arbitrator Mark L. Kahn explained that parties often confuse lack of merit of a grievance as a basis for a claim of nonarbitrability:

> I find that the Company in this case has similarly (but erroneously) derived a conclusion as to arbitrability from its appraisal of the merits. If the action of the Company that gave rise to this proceeding was within its rights and did not violate either the Agreement or any binding joint understanding then the grievance should be denied—not because it is not arbitrable but because it lacks merit.[6]

Arbitrator Brandschain suggested that the arbitrable questions should be handled separately from the merit questions.[7] Often, the two questions are considered the opposite sides of the same coin. Unless the procedural question is handled first and separately, however, it will be confused with the substantive questions. If the arbitrator decides that the grievance is not sustainable, and gives no clear-cut answer to the arbitrability question, it may leave the parties in the dark when a similar question arises in the future.[8] On the other hand, since the arbitrability issue is so closely intertwined with the merits, it is often impossible to distinguish arbitrability from substance.

Claims of nonarbitrability must turn on the particular provisions of the agreement in issue. There are, however, particular provisions in any agreement which generate disputes over claims of nonarbitrability. For example, the definition of a "grievance" in the labor agreement may create restrictions on the arbitrator's authority. Commonly, the arbitrator is limited to deciding grievances which in turn are defined as claims that a provision of the agreement has been violated by some management action. In such circumstances, a grievance that does not allege some violation of the labor agreement itself will produce a challenge that the arbitrator has no jurisdiction over the matter.

Generally, labor agreements do not provide that management may file a grievance.[9] Hence, arbitrators often do not have authority to

---

[6]*Celanese Corp. of America,* AAA Case No. 19-4 (Kahn, 1960).

[7]Brandschain, *Preparation & Trial of a Labor Arbitration Case,* THE PRACTICAL LAWYER, Vol. 18, No. 7 (Nov. 1972).

[8]*Playboy Clubs Int'l, Inc. v. Hotel & Restaurant Employees Union,* 321 F. Supp 704, 76 LRRM 2419 (S.D. N.Y. 1971).

[9]An exception was the agreement in *Drake Bakeries, Inc. v. Local 50, Bakery and Confectionery Workers,* 370 U.S. 254, 257, 50 LRRM 2440, 2441, (1962), which provided:
"The parties agree that they will promptly attempt to adjust all complaints, disputes or grievances arising between them involving questions of interpretation or application of any clause or matter covered by this contract or any act or conduct in relations between the parties hereto, directly or indirectly."
The arbitration provision gave "either party" the right to refer an unsettled matter to arbitration. The Supreme Court held that this language required the employer to arbitrate a claim against the union based on an alleged breach of the no-strike clause.

hear a claim by management that the union or an employee has violated the agreement. In some labor agreements, however, there are special arbitration procedures by which the employer can submit a grievance concerning a violation of the no-strike clause.[10]

The contractual grievance procedure establishes the manner in which a grievance is initiated, the number of steps or union-management conferences through which the grievance is processed, and the time limits between the various steps. These "procedural details" vary greatly in different labor agreements. Nonetheless, failure to follow the procedures will usually provide a basis for an objection to any attempt to present the grievance case to arbitration on the ground that the arbitrator cannot assert jurisdiction over the grievance since it is not properly before him or her.

In addition to restrictions on arbitral authority contained in the definition of a grievance, labor agreements typically contain express limitations on the arbitrator's authority. The arbitrator is commonly confined to the resolution of grievances or disputes as to "the interpretation or application of the agreement," or of claims of "violation of the agreement." Frequently, the arbitrator is further enjoined not to "add to, subtract from, or modify any of the terms of the agreement."[11] In a *Ford Motor Company* agreement, the arbitrator is admonished also that he has "no power to substitute his discretion for the company's discretion in cases where the company is given discretion" by the agreement and no power "to provide agreement for the parties in those cases where they have in their contract agreed that further negotiations shall or may provide for certain contingencies."[12] If the responding party, usually the company, believes the claim presented would require the arbitrator to exceed these or similar limitations, a challenge to the arbitrator's jurisdiction to hear and render an award is often made.

Below some of the various types of challenges to the jurisdiction of the arbitrator are discussed by arbitrators.

---

[10]*See* discussion of special arbitration procedures involving violations of the no-strike clause under "Injunctive Relief to Halt Violation of the No-Strike Clause" in Chapter XVIII.

[11]It is not uncommon for an agreement to provide that disputes over wage rates, production standards, safety, or other specified matters may not be presented to arbitration, and a right of the union to strike over such disputes is reserved to the union; in others, it is not. Where the issue is not one over which the union can arbitrate, it is one that can be submitted to a court even though this would likely surprise the party, usually the management, that demanded the specific exclusion from arbitration. *See* Schulman, *Reason, Contract and Law in Labor Relations*, 68 HARV. L. REV. 999, 1004–05 (1955).

[12]Agreement between Ford Motor Company and UAW, Article VII, § 56 (1976).

LACK OF JURISDICTION DUE TO
PROCEDURAL DEFECTS, AND THEIR WAIVER

Late Filing of the Grievance

When a grievance has not been filed within the time limits set forth in the collective bargaining agreement, the arbitrator generally will dismiss the claim as nonarbitrable[13] unless the opposing party has waived this procedural defect. Since the parties have limited the cases which they agree to arbitrate according to the terms of their agreement, the arbitrator has no authority to hear a claim presented too late, because it has not properly entered the procedure and hence has not reached the arbitration "step." Arbitrators have supported the dismissal not only on the ground that the arbitrator must receive authority to hear the grievance claim from the agreement, but also on the ground that the establishment of a time limit reflects the parties' recognition that grievance matters should be heard promptly and not allowed to fester for long periods permitting evidence to be lost and recollections to be dimmed.[14] Where the agreement requires that grievances be filed "promptly," the arbitrator has a more difficult task in determining whether this standard has been met.[15]

---

[13]*See, e.g., Anaconda Aluminum Co.,* 57 LA 900 (Allen, 1971); *Allied Paper, Inc.,* 71-1 ARB ¶ 8173 (Davis, 1971); *Specialty Paper Box Co.,* 50 LA 1220 (Nathanson, 1968); *Ekco Products Co.,* 40 LA 1339 (Duff, 1963); *American Metallurgical Products Co.,* 34 LA 311 (McDermott, 1959); *Creamery Package Mfg. Co.,* 31 LA 917 (Kelliher, 1958); *Mosaic Tile Co.,* 13 LA 949 (Cornsweet, 1950); *Walker Country Hosiery Mills,* 13 LA 387 (Holden, 1949); *Firestone Tire & Rubber Co.,* 9 LA 518 (Rader, 1948); *Standard-Coose-Thatcher Co.,* 4 LA 79 (McCoy, 1946). *See also* related cases in which new issue could not be raised because of expiration of time limits: *Du-Wel Products, Inc.,* 55 LA 891 (Walsh, 1970); *Darlington Fabrics,* AAA Case No. 92-12 (Rose, 1966); *Quinn Wire & Iron Works,* 64-1 ARB ¶ 8400 (Doyle, 1964); *Continental Can,* AAA Case No. 58-16 (Green, 1963); *Witco Chemical Co.,* AAA Case No. 14-12 (Wirtz, 1959); *Tappan Co.,* AAA Case No. 9-14 (Kabaker, 1959); *R. H. Osbrink Mfg. Co.,* 28 LA 88 (Phelps, 1957); *U.S. Rubber Co.,* 28 LA 704 (Livengood, 1957); *John Deere Tractor Works,* 18 LA 497 (Davey, 1952). The Eighth Circuit held that the five-year Missouri contract statute of limitations was applicable to arbitration and the limitation starts to run when the grievance claim is rejected. *Warren v. Teamsters,* 544 F.2d 334, 93 LRRM 2734 (8th Cir. 1976). Tort action statute of limitations for arbitrations. *Howard v. Aluminum Workers,* 418 F. Supp. 1058, 93 LRRM 2385 (E.D. Va. 1976); *Pesola v. Inland Tool & Manufacturing, Inc.,* 93 LRRM 2458 (E.D. Mich. 1976); *Glowacki v. Motor Wheel Corp.,* 241 N.W. 2d 240, 92 LRRM 2769 (Mich. Ct. App. 1976); *Morin v. Buick Motor Division,* 91 LRRM 2578 (E.D. Mich. 1976); *Smart v. Ellis Trucking Co.,* 91 LRRM 2587 (E.D. Mich. 1976); *DeVries v. Interstate Motor Freight System,* 91 LRRM 2764 (N.D. Ohio, 1976) (six years but statute tolled by union's false assurance); *Vandever v. Bell Helicopter Co.,* 93 LRRM 2235 (N.D. Tex. 1976) (two years to union and two years to employer).

[14]*See, e.g., Precision Extrusions, Inc.,* 49 LA 338 (Stouffer, 1967); *Kennecott Copper Corp.,* 35 LA 412 (Ross, 1960); *National Basketball Association (Pro Basketball, Inc.), Portland Trail Blazers,* June 19, 1975 (Seitz, 1975).

[15]*See, e.g., Jones & Laughlin Steel Corp.,* 30 LA 432 (Cahn, 1958); *Management Services, Inc.,* 26 LA 505 (Williams, 1956); *Combustion Engineering Co.,* 20 LA 416 (McCoy, 1953); *Barbet Mills, Inc.,* 19 LA 677 (Maggs, 1952); *but see North American Refractories,* AAA Case No. 84-13 (Teple, 1955); *Celanese Corp. of America,* AAA Case No. 32-22, 37 LA 707 (Dunau, 1961).

In cases where the delay in filing the grievance is not substantial, arbitrators have shown great reluctance to dismiss a claim and have taken considerable pains to find a construction favorable to timely filing. For example, under a provision that "all grievances and differences of opinion must be mentioned within 15 days after they are first known to exist," intervening holidays were held not included in the calculation since the policy in favor of prompt settlement of grievances is not compromised by their exclusion.[16] Also, days not worked because of a strike have not been counted on the ground that normal grievance processing is suspended during the strike.[17]

Furthermore, some arbitrators, by analogy to the familiar case law concerning the application of statutes of limitation to fraudulent actions, hold that time limits on filing run only from the time the grievant became aware of or should have become aware of a claim. For example, an employee who was terminated from employment while on sick leave and hence had no opportunity to learn of his termination until he attempted to return to work was not barred under a time limit period running from the date of termination.[18] "However, even though the Arbitrator may excuse late filing due to lack of knowledge, backpay may be denied the grievant for failure to diligently advance his interests."[19] Arbitrators have generally felt that grievants should have full awareness of their injury before the time limit should start running, but this awareness is held to occur with the first clear and overt act sufficient to give such notice.[20]

Lack of awareness, however, that there exist time limits within which a grievance may be filed does not excuse late filing, since a grievant provided with a copy of the labor agreement is conclusively presumed to be aware of the existence of the time limits.[21] As with all

---

[16]*Eimco Corp.*, 41 LA 1184 (Dykstra, 1963); *see also Schneider's Modern Bakery, Inc.*, 44 LA 574 (Hon, 1965).

[17]*Airco Alloys & Carbide Co.*, 50 LA 1223 (Kesselman, 1968).

[18]*E. F. Hausermann Co.*, 42 LA 1076 (Klein, 1964). *See also Garvin's Jersey Farms, Inc.*, 41 LA 927 (Stouffer, 1963); *but see Durez Plastics Div. Hooker Chemical Corp.*, AAA Case No. 146-9 (Scheib, 1970); *Standard Steel Treating Co.*, AAA Case No. 146-8 (Walt, 1970); *Singer Co.*, 46 LA 382 (Cahn, 1966); *Robertshaw-Fulton Controls Co.*, AAA Case No. 58-16 (Green, 1963); *National Dairy Products*, AAA Case No. 40-20 (Miller, 1962); *United States Pipe & Foundry Co.*, AAA Case No. 33-9 (Seibel, 1961); *E. W. Bliss Co.*, AAA Case No. 19-7 (Teple, 1960). *See also Portland Associated Morticians, Inc.*, 58 LA 49 (Wren, 1971); *Du-Wel Products, Inc.*, 55 LA 891 (Walsh, 1970); *Rockwell Mfg. Co.*, 56 LA 492 (Kates, 1971).

[19]*Chicago Electrotypers Division, Electrographic Corporation*, 51 LA 197 (Sembower, 1968).

[20]*See, e.g., Tin Processing Corp.*, 26 LA 732 (Morvant, 1956) (union could not object to layoff of an employee according to an erroneous seniority list posted three years earlier); *Ekco Products Co.*, 40 LA 1339, 1341 (Duff, 1963) ("Whether or not Union officials had knowledge of the facts concerning Miss N____'s dismissal, Miss N____ knew all the relevant facts, and could have brought them to the attention of the Union.").

[21]*Research Parts & Engineering Corp.*, 48 LA 594 (Krinsky, 1967). *See also Watson v. Teamsters Local 728*, 399 F.2d 875, 69 LRRM 2099 (5th Cir. 1968) wherein the grievants claimed lack of awareness of the fact of their having been hired as "casuals" to explain their failure to file a

general rules, exceptions have been created. Thus, in *Mutual Plastics Mold Corp.,* [22] an employee disqualified from working by the company's doctor filed an untimely grievance asserting her failure to file earlier should be excused because she did not know until she later discussed the matter with a union representative that a grievance could be filed on the subject. Accepting this contention, the arbitrator said:

> Under most circumstances, the employee is presumed to know that actions of management are subject to review through the grievance and arbitration procedure. The specific facts of this case, however, render the normal presumption inapplicable. In the Arbitrator's opinion, a reasonable construction of the three day time limit for filing a grievance as applied to this case is that the time did not begin to run until the Union or employee concerned became aware of the right to file a grievance. [23]

When the running of a time limit on filing starts with "the alleged incident," "cause," or "event," ambiguities in the language exist which require interpretation. A grievant might argue, for instance, that the act of actually filling a job vacancy with another employee, rather than the rejection of the grievant's own bid for the vacancy, was the incident that started the time limit running. [24] In one case (a grievance claiming pay for work the employee should have been assigned), it was held that the "event" was the date management refused to allow the grievant work rather than the date it refused his subsequent demand for pay—an interpretation which tightened the time restriction. [25]

If the alleged violation can be considered to impose a continuing injury to the grievant, the arbitrator may find that the grievance is a continuing one and that the time limit on the filing of a grievance recommences each day and, hence, a filing of a grievance is never precluded. Damages or back pay in such a case, however, will be awarded only from the date the grievance was filed. A company's failure to discharge an employee who does not join the union within 31 days is never barred because the failure remains as a "continuing viola-

---

grievance protesting that status or to demand seniority status after 30 days employment as provided in the contract. The court concluded it to be highly unlikely that the grievants were actually unaware and, in any event, paid no heed to their subjective state of mind; *Corn Products Co.,* AAA Case No. 103-9 (Edes, 1967); *American Enka Corp.,* AAA Case No. 88-12, 49 LA 615 (Steele, 1966).

[22]48 LA 2 (Block, 1967).

[23]*Id.* at 8.

[24]*Joy Mfg. Co.,* 44 LA 304 (Sembower, 1965) (the act starting the limitation was the unequivocal rejection of employee's bid); *Heckethorn Mfg. & Supply Co.,* 61-1 ARB ¶ 8255 (Warns, 1960) (the "occurrence" was the layoff of the senior, not the recall of a junior, employee).

[25]*Bethlehem Steel Corp.,* 46 LA 767 (Strongin, 1966).

tion."[26] The most frequent use of the "continuing violation" doctrine occurs in claims for damages as a result of the employer's failure to pay an employee at the rate established for the classification to which the employee is assigned or the failure to grant a merit increase.[27]

In addition, arbitrators will not bar a grievance because of late filing if conduct by a management representative makes it unjust or unreasonable to do so on the grounds of estoppel. For example, if the delay in filing was occasioned by an offer by the management representative to settle the claim, not yet formally filed, or to make certain evidence available which the employee claims is needed to file a proper claim, the employer will be estopped from setting up the contractual time limit as a bar.[28] Similarly, where the parties have not observed time limits in the past, this history, together with evidence that the employer was aware that a grievance filing was contemplated, may bar the employer's objection that the grievance was not filed on time.[29] Arbitrators also hold that the time limit objection is waived by the employer if the grievance is processed through the preliminary steps of the grievance procedure without timeliness being asserted as a defense.[30]

Arbitrator Clair Duff explained that a grievance over establishment of an incentive rate was not barred from arbitration because it was not filed promptly. Since the employer continued to revise the procedures, the facts basic to the grievance did not become static. He said:

> Contractual time limits cannot be stringently applied to facts that are shifting. Until the incentive plan applicable to this crew was developed in its final form, and its impact on the earning ability of the employees in-

---

[26]*Kerr-McGee Oil Industries, Inc.,* 44 LA 701 (Hayes, 1965); *Sargent Engineering Corp.,* 43 LA 1165 (McNaughton, 1964); *Standard Oil Co. of Calif.,* AAA Case No. 70-4 (Burns, 1964); *American Meter Co.,* AAA Case No. 61-17 (Teple, 1963).

[27]*See, e.g., Allegheny Cigarette Service Company,* 58 LA 1259 (Kates, 1972); *Dayton Tire & Rubber Co.,* 48 LA 83 (Dworkin, 1967); *Steel Warehouse Co.,* 45 LA 357 (Dolnick, 1965); *Taylor-Winfield Corp.,* 45 LA 153 (Kates, 1965); *Avco Corp. Lycoming Div.,* 43 LA 765 (Kornblum, 1964). *See also Miss. Structural Steel Co.,* 55 LA 23 (Boothe, 1970); *Nashville Bridge Co.,* 48 LA 44 (Williams, 1967); *Combustion Engineering, Inc.,* 46 LA 289 (Murphy, 1966).

[28]*Quality Electric Steel Castings, Inc.,* 62 LA 1157 (Ruiz, 1974); *Weirton Steel Co.,* 54 LA 1049 (Kates, 1970); *Interscience Encyclopedia, Inc.,* 55 LA 210 (Roberts, 1970); *Russ Maita Distributors,* 51 LA 861 (Koven, 1968); *Sanna Dairies, Inc.,* 43 LA 16 (Rice, 1964); *Celanese Corp. of America,* AAA Case No. 14-11 (Schedler, 1959).

[29]*Dockside Machine & Boiler Works, Inc.,* 55 LA 1221 (Block, 1970); *City Transportation Co.,* AAA Case No. 88-11 (Williams, 1966); *Borg-Warner Corp.,* AAA Case No. 84-21 (Lennard, 1965); *Ward Foods, Inc., Bell Bakeries Div.,* 43 LA 608 (Dworet, 1964); *Eastern Racing Association,* AAA Case No. 72-9 (MacLeod, 1964).

[30]*American Smelting and Refining Co.,* 65 LA 328 (Ray, 1975); *Dept. of the Army,* 63 LA 924 (Ferguson, 1974); *Concrete Products,* 70-2 ARB ¶ 8873 (Erbs, 1970); *The General Tire & Rubber Company,* 68-1 ARB ¶ 8186 (Crawford, undated); *Billingsley, Inc.,* 48 LA 802 (Krinsky, 1967); *but see Deep Rock Oil Corp.,* 6 ALAA ¶ 69,376, 20 LA 865 (Emery, 1953). *But see* awards listed in note 32.

volved could be reliably determined, the dispute was inchoate. Under such circumstances, the "grievance occurred" when the final impact of the new incentive could be measured with accuracy which certainly was some weeks after the final revision was adopted.[31]

On the other hand, arbitrators hold that a discussion of a grievance claim on its merits in a preliminary step of the grievance procedure will not waive an objection based on failure to file the grievance within the time limit if the objection is raised by the employer at the first opportunity.[32] Arbitrators usually hold that before they will find a waiver of the objection to their jurisdiction, the waiver must be established by clear and substantial evidence. For example, in *Firestone Tire & Rubber Co.*[33] the agreement provided that a written grievance must be filed with the company's labor relations department within three days after a discharge or suspension. The union charged that the company had waived the formal filing within this time limit, since its representatives were aware of the discharge and had discussed it with union representatives, leading them to believe that the management was reconsidering the discharge. Arbitrator Rader held the evidence of waiver was insufficient.

> There is no question legally but that the parties to the contract can waive provisions in it, but this cannot be done by implication unless it be that the implications are of such a nature to create a legal and positive presumption that the same were waived. Otherwise it is necessary that there be a direct waiving by both parties to any given provision in a contract.... To rule, without the strongest provocation, that [a] provision of a grievance section of a contract has been waived would be establishment of a precedent which might have far-reaching effects. To use an illustration, it would be like the neglecting of a leak in the dikes of Holland....[34]

Tardy Processing Through Grievance Steps

After a grievance has been properly filed, failure to process the grievance to the next higher step of the procedure is also often asserted as a bar to arbitration of the grievance on the basis that arbitrators have no jurisdiction to hear and determine a grievance not properly

[31]*H. K. Porter Co.*, AAA Case No. 54-12 (Duff, 1963).
[32]*Elicon Detroit, Inc.*, AAA Case No. 54-30-0384 (Walt, 1972); *Pennsylvania Steel Foundry & Machine Co.*, AAA Case No. 94-19 (Boyer, 1966); *Chase Bag Co.*, 42 LA 153 (Elkouri, 1963); *American Metallurgical Products Co.*, 34 LA 311 (McDermott, 1959).
[33]9 LA 518 (Rader, 1948).
[34]*Id.* at 521, 522. See also *Ravenna Arsenal, Inc.*, 70-1 ARB ¶ 8325 (Dworkin, 1970); *Mosaic Tile Co.*, 13 LA 949, 950 (Cornsweet, 1950) ("Since the agreement is the 'constitution' of the parties and written by them after negotiation, any waiver of one of its provisions must be proven by clear, convincing and definite evidence."); *Phillips Petroleum Co.*, 7 LA 595 (Rader, 1947).

before them.[35] Often this procedural defect will occur prior to arbitration and after the grievance has been processed through all conference steps.[36]

Where a telegram appealing a grievance to arbitration was sent one day late, Arbitrator Lewis M. Gill held the grievance was not arbitrable. Rejecting the union's contention that knowledge by the company of the union's dissatisfaction because of comments at a grievance meeting constituted notice of appeal, Gill noted that such an argument had "a great deal of persuasiveness." He held, however:

> The question before me at this point is quite different; it is whether I have any authority to rule that the grievances are arbitrable under these circumstances, and if so whether I should do so. It seems perfectly clear that I have no such authority. The time limit in question is very plain and unambiguous, and it was unquestionably past by the time the Union's telegram was sent and received. The parties can waive a contractual provision by mutual agreement, but an arbitrator cannot.[37]

Arbitrators dismiss grievances when there is a failure to respect time limits for appeals on policy grounds as well as on the ground of lack of jurisdiction or authority. Arbitrator Stouffer said:

> The principal reason for strict adherence to contractual time limitations for processing of grievances is so that the grievances will be quickly and efficiently processed. Any relaxation of the time requirements, rather than benefiting any of the parties, actually leads to the ultimate destruction of the utility of the grievance procedure.
>
> The Company and the Union in consummating the currently-effective Collective Bargaining Agreement expressly agreed to the time limits for processing grievances, and also that an arbitrator would have no authority to add to, subtract from, or change the Agreement....[38]

In *John Deere Tractor Co.*,[39] Arbitrator Clarence M. Updegraff also explained the benefits of time limits:

> The union is well-manned by some able full-time and some similarly able part-time officers. If they abandon a grievance at any step, it may well be

[35]*Abex Corp.*, 53 LA 79 (Stouffer, 1969); *Chase Bag Co.*, 53 LA 612 (Larson, 1969); *Diamond Power Specialty Corp.*, 44 LA 878 (Dworkin, 1964).
[36]*Purex Corp.*, 58 LA 760 (Cummins, 1972); *Frolic Footwear, Inc.*, 53 LA 353 (Seinsheimer, 1969); *Forest City Foundries Co.*, 69-1 ARB ¶ 8315 (Uible, 1968); *Precision Extrusions, Inc.*, 49 LA 338 (Stouffer, 1967) (and numerous cases cited herein); *Erwin Mills, Inc.*, 47 LA 606 (Stark, 1966); *Management Services, Inc.*, 20 LA 34 (McCoy, 1963); *International Harvester Co.*, 10 LA 525 (Kelliher, 1948). *See also Massey-Ferguson*, AAA Case No. 84-8 (Cole, 1965); *Cleveland Pneumatic Tool Co.*, 43 LA 869 (Dworkin, 1964); *Foster Refrigerator Corp.*, AAA Case No. 56-14 (Santer, 1963).
[37]*Lancaster Malleable Castings Co.*, AAA Case No. 9-10 (Gill, 1959).
[38]*Precision Extrusions, Inc.*, 49 LA 338, 341 (Stouffer, 1967).
[39]3 LA 737 (Updegraff, 1946).

inferred that they have become convinced of its lack of merit. The time limitations have a part to play similar to those in adjustment of legal rights. Statutes of limitations exist to limit or terminate all sorts of legal rights and procedures since, though "the law abhors forfeitures" it proceeds upon the principle that, if rights are not pursued while the disputes are reasonably recent or fresh, justice may fail because evidence has disappeared, witnesses have moved off and been lost, or collateral rights entitled to recognition have appeared which rest upon the established status quo.[40]

Arbitrator Byron R. Abernethy discussed the lack of timely filing of grievances in *Bliss & Laughlin Steel Company* (Houston, Texas plant):[41]

> The first question to be resolved here is that of the arbitrability of this grievance. It seems clear that the grievance filed ... was not timely filed under ... the Agreement, which requires the filing of a grievance in the case of a discharge within two (2) working days of the discharge or "of the date" the Grievant *"becomes aware,* or should become *aware* of the event." [Emphasis added.] The record here is clear that, regardless of the fact that the Postal Service was unable to deliver the termination letters to the Grievant, he was in fact "aware ... of the event"—his discharge—not later than December 18, 1974. By his own admission his brother had made him aware of that fact by then.... If the matter stopped here, the Arbitrator would have to hold, as the Company urges, that the time limits fixed in the Working Agreement are mandatory and must be enforced, and that the grievance must therefore be dismissed.
>
> But, as the Union urges, the record here is unmistakably clear that, despite its tardy filing, this grievance was accepted by the Company as a valid grievance and it was processed through all of the earlier steps of the grievance procedure on its merits without any objection whatever by any Company official at any time prior to the arbitration hearing that this was an untimely and procedurally defective grievance which would not be entertained and handled on its merits. Quite clearly this defense was raised for the first time at the arbitration hearing.... Did the Company, by handling the grievance up to this point on the merits only without ever challenging the timeliness of its filing, in effect waive its objection to the Grievant's failure to comply with the contractual two-day time limit *requirement*? It appears to this Arbitrator that it did.[42] [Emphasis added.]

As with the initial filing of a grievance, arbitrators have demonstrated a similar reluctance to bar a grievance for failure to appeal within a time limit and thus have found, for example, the employer estopped to assert the lack of timely appeal when the union has in the

---

[40]*Id.* at 743.

[41]*Bliss & Laughlin Steel Company* (Abernethy, Sept. 9, 1975) (private, unpublished award).

[42]*To the same effect, see Denver Post,* 41 LA 200 (Gorsuch, 1963); *Ironrite, Inc.,* 28 LA 398 (Whiting, 1956); *Produce, Inc.,* 50 LA 453 (Keefe, 1968); *contra, Joy Manufacturing Company,* 44 LA 304 (Sembower, 1965); *Publisher's Assn. of New York,* 39 LA 379 (Schmertz, 1962).

past failed to conform to the time limit on appeal requirements without objection from the management,[43] or where company representatives gave the union representatives reason to believe there would be another hearing at which an international representative of the union would be present,[44] or where the delay in filing the demand for arbitration was occasioned by the parties' attempt, at the company's suggestion, to formulate the issue.[45]

Some arbitrators have found a waiver where the objection to jurisdiction is based on a failure to appeal a grievance from the last step to arbitration within the time limits, unless the objection is raised before the commencement of the arbitration hearing.[46] Others, however, have held that where time limits on appeal are clear and compliance with these limitations has been required in the past, a party is not obligated to raise an objection before the hearing starts. Arbitrator John Sembower discussed the reasons for such a view in *Joy Manufacturing Co.*:[47]

[I]t is regrettable that the timeliness of the grievance should arise for the first time in arbitration, but still it has to be considered because it is universally held that the jurisdiction of the arbitrator may be questioned at any point, just as may the jurisdiction of a court of law, unless the issue has been expressly waived.

---

[43]*Coca Cola Co., Foods Division,* 65 LA 165 (Crane, 1975); *Kankakee Electric Steel Co.,* 53 LA 178 (Sembower, 1969); *E. W. Bliss Co.,* 45 LA 1000 (Lehoczky, 1965); *Collis Co.,* 50 LA 1157 (Doyle, 1968). See also *Penn Jersey Boiler & Construction Co.,* 50 LA 177 (Buckwalter, 1967); *General Precision, Inc.,* 42 LA 589 (Roberts, 1964); *E. J. Lavino Co.,* AAA Case No. 7-15 (Valtin, 1959).

[44]*Southland Paper Mills,* AAA Case No. 32-3 (Singletary, 1961).

[45]*Hammermill Paper Co.,* AAA Case No. 62-22 (Shister, 1963); *Royal McBee Corp.,* AAA Case No. 16-7 (Healy, 1959); *but see Federal-Mogul-Bower Bearings, Inc.,* AAA Case No. 14-20 (Seibel, 1959).

[46]*United States Plywood-Champion Papers, Inc.,* 60 LA 443 (Warns, 1973); *Lectromelt Corporation,* 58 LA 463 (McDermott, 1972); *American Air Filter Co.,* 54 LA 1251 (Dolnick, 1970); *Badger Concrete Co.,* 50 LA 901 (Krinsky, 1968); *Produce, Inc.,* 50 LA 453 (Keefe, 1968); *United Engineering & Foundry Co.,* 49 LA 1036 (Wagner, 1967); *United States Steel Corp.,* 48 LA 1085 (Dybeck, 1967); *Plasti-Line, Inc.,* AAA Case No. 88-16 (King, 1966); *The General Refractories Co.,* AAA Case No. 48-6 (Miller, 1962).

[47]44 LA 304, 306-07 (Sembower, 1965). See also *Textile Paper Products,* 51 LA 385 (Herbert, Imp. Arb., 1967); *Nashville Bridge Co.,* 48 LA 44 (Williams, 1967); *Erwin Mills,* AAA Case No. 90-5, 47 LA 606 (Stark, 1966); *Lake Shore Coach Co.,* 44 LA 1190 (Geissinger, 1965); *Wyandotte Chemicals Corp.,* 35 LA 783 (Wollett, 1960) (no waiver although the defense of nonarbitrability was not raised until the third step); *American Metallurgical Products Co.,* 34 LA 311 (McDermott, 1959) (no waiver since timeliness issue was raised prior to arbitration, although not discussed); *Deep Rock Oil Corp.,* 20 LA 865 (Emery, 1953) (no waiver was found where the sole grounds for inferring a waiver was the company's failure to raise earlier its objections to an untimely demand for arbitration); *Management Services, Inc.,* 20 LA 34 (McCoy, 1953); *Consolidated Vultee Aircraft Corp.,* 12 LA 786, 793 (Aaron, 1949) ("The first two steps are at the shop level; and it would appear to be sound policy to try to settle even untimely grievances on their merits at that stage"); *Columbian Carbon Co.,* 8 LA 634 (Potter, 1947) (no waiver merely because company failed to raise a defense for timeliness at the earliest possible moment).

Aware that parties usually prefer their disputes to be decided upon the so-called merits rather than technicalities, arbitrators usually are rather lenient if there are no specific time elements spelled out in the contract. But it is different if the parties had agreed upon deadlines, because these are, in effect, self-imposed "statutes of limitations." . . .

One possible basis for deviation is if the parties have allowed their schedule to fall into disuse, and both are guilty of repeatedly letting things slide and not living up to the time requirements. . . . However, in this instance there is no evidence of anything but a policy of strict compliance on the part of both parties. . . .

Under a clause which stated that unsettled grievances "will be considered closed" if not filed for arbitration within 60 days of the origin of the grievance, a grievance was held to be not arbitrable four months after it arose, despite the fact that it was still being negotiated in the grievance procedure.[48] The union's argument that it would be "bizarre" to demand arbitration before it was known that negotiations would be fruitless relates to, Arbitrator Ellmann said, "the wisdom" of the clause the parties had agreed upon, but does not give the arbitrator the right to disregard that clause. The parties saw fit to impose a time limit "from the time the grievance arose." As this language is "unambiguous and emphatic," Arbitrator Ellmann held, he "may not uphold the right to arbitrate and disregard the condition qualifying the right which the parties saw fit to state so clearly."[49]

An exception to the more general rule, however, appears to arise when one party appeals a grievance to arbitration after permitting an earlier but identical grievance to be barred by failure to appeal it to arbitration within the time limit. Arbitrator Killingsworth held the objection to the second grievance must be raised prior to the arbitration hearing, or it is waived:

By any realistic standard, the present grievance is the same as Grievance No. 22-67. Precisely the same reassignment of functions provides the basis for both grievances. Therefore, the Company could have refused to consider the present grievance in the grievance procedure on the ground that the Union's failure to appeal Grievance No. 22-67 to arbitration had settled that grievance on the basis of the Company's Step 4 answer, which denied the grievance. Or the Company could have discussed the whole matter once again, while specifically reserving the right to object to the appeal of the present grievance to arbitration. The Company in fact did

[48]*Booth Broadcasting Co.*, AAA Case No. 52-14 (Ellmann, 1962).

[49]*In FMC Corp.*, 54 LA 807 (Whyte, 1970), time limits arose in a different context. There, the contract required an award to be issued within 15 days "after the matter is finally submitted." When the company requested a stenographic transcript and permission to file a brief, the arbitrator ruled the requests proper and concluded that the 15 days began only after the briefs were filed.

neither of these things.... In other words, it appears that the Company raised this jurisdictional point for the first time at the arbitration hearing.[50]

LACK OF JURISDICTION BECAUSE OF THE PASSAGE OF TIME

Arbitrators have sometimes held that an alleged offense cannot be processed to arbitration because it has been barred by the passage of time.[51] This concept, known as laches, may be a rationale by the arbitrator for a decision on the merits and may not be a true procedural rule. However, the concept of laches is close enough to a procedural rule to deserve mention. Some arbitrators are actually imposing a "reasonable time" requirement within which grievances must be filed by adopting the equitable principle of laches.[52]

A decision by Arbitrator Raymond R. Roberts illustrates how considerations of laches enter a consideration of the merits.[53] An employee, hired in 1968, stated on his employment application that he had been self-employed at farming since 1961. Two years later, the employer learned that the employee had been working for another company at the time he filled out the application and that the prior employer was not satisfied with his work performance. When this discovery was made, the employee was discharged for violation of the rule against falsification of employment applications. The union protested, claiming that the discharge was improper because it was based on a cause which had occurred two years before. The company argued that the employee would not have been hired if his prior employment had been known and the prior employer's assessment obtained. Arbitrator Roberts upheld the discharge. Roberts noted that essentially two lines

---

[50]*General American Transportation Corp.*, Grievance No. 16-68, pp. 5-6 (Killingsworth, 1970) (unreported). *See also IUE Local 616 v. Byrd Plastics, Inc.*, 428 F.2d 23, 74 LRRM 2550 (3d Cir. 1971); *Miehle-Goss-Dexter, Inc.*, AAA Case No. 97-17 (Davis, 1966); *United States Steel Corp.*, 11 STEEL ARB. 8311 (Florey, 1963); *United States Steel Corp.*, 5 STEEL ARB. 2861 (Garnett, 1955).

[51]*Acme Hamilton Manufacturing Corp.*, AAA Case No. 86-8, 46 LA 845 (Dash, 1965); *P. R. Mallory & Co.*, AAA Case No. 19-23 (Stark, 1960).

[52]*Northorp Corp., Electronics Division*, 70-2 ARB ¶ 8543 (Block, 1970); *Mt. Elliott Cemetery Assn.*, 70-2 ARB ¶ 8861 (Walsh, 1970); *Dayton Tire & Rubber Co.*, 48 LA 83 (Dworkin, 1967); *Huber Pontiac, Inc.*, 63-3 ARB ¶ 9021 (Traynor, 1966); *New York Racing Ass'n.*, 43 LA 129 (Scheiber, 1964); *Bethlehem Steel Co.*, 37 LA 956 (Seward, 1961); *Warner Electric Brake & Clutch Co.*, 31 LA 219 (Kelliher, 1958) (failure to file a grievance promptly cut off back pay even though the grievance was brought within the period of time specified in the agreement); *Rockwell Mfg. Co.*, 25 LA 534 (Duff, 1955) (analogy drawn to equitable doctrine of laches); *Hinson Mfg. Co.*, 20 LA 688 (Davey, 1953) (a grievance filed six months after the action was barred by laches).

[53]*Tiffany Metal Products Mfg. Co.*, 56 LA 135 (Roberts, 1971).

of cases have emerged among arbitrators in dealing with problems of this kind—the first, applying limitation periods when the misrepresentation was not serious or ceased to be relevant or material to the employment; the second, where the misrepresentation was serious and of continuing importance to employment, applying no limitation period. Applying the standard to the instant case, Roberts found the misrepresentation to be deliberate and material to the employee's continuing employment since his record with the company was seen as an extension of previous actions with his former employer.

Similarly, Arbitrator Albert Epstein upheld the discharge of a drill press operator who had failed to indicate on an employment application executed eight months earlier that she had a college degree and had been discharged by her last employer. The arbitrator found that the omission was intentional and sustained the discharge.[54]

On the other hand, it was held in *Dayton Malleable Iron Co.*[55] that the employee was improperly discharged where the asserted falsity consisted of failing to reveal that he had earlier been employed by the employer. On the facts, said Arbitrator Howlett, it must be found that the claimed falsity was not willful. The employee had also been with the company approximately four years before the falsification was discovered and that falsification consisted of not revealing in his application that he had worked some 25 days for the company previously before quitting. Moreover, the arbitrator found the falsification not to be a material one.

The defense of laches has barred back pay even in situations where the grievance is continuing and hence is not barred. In such a case, Arbitrator Teple said:[56]

"Although the union testified that it was not previously aware of the company's failure to pay the bonus, it cannot be denied that it failed to investigate the matter over an extended period of years .... So far as any earlier period is concerned, the defense of laches is applicable." However, "the breach of the agreement has been a continuing one, ... occurring at the end of each payroll period, and it cannot be said that the present grievance was untimely filed...." In view of the "lack of attention" to this matter on the part of the union for so long a period, ... back pay was awarded only to the date of the grievance.

---

[54]*Powers Regulator Co.*, 56 LA 11 (Epstein, 1970). *See also Tiffany Metal Products Mfg. Co., supra; Thorsen Mfg. Co.*, 55 LA 581 (Koven, 1970); *Midland-Ross Corp.*, 55 LA 258 (McNaughton, 1970); *General Cable Corp.*, 54 LA 696 (Updegraff, 1970); *Westinghouse Corp.*, AAA Case No. 146-2 (Schmertz, 1970); *Henry Vogt Machine Co.*, AAA Case No. 90-6, 46 LA 654 (Stouffer, 1966); *Rexall Drug Co.*, AAA Case No. 47-6, 39 LA 142 (Dworkin, 1962); *General Electric Co.*, AAA Case No. 5-22 (Brown, 1959).

[55]54 LA 1192 (Howlett, 1970).

[56]*American Meter Co.*, AAA Case No. 61-17 (Teple, 1963).

LACK OF JURISDICTION OVER A CHANGED ISSUE

Some arbitrators have held that their authority is limited to a determination of the merits of the claim of contract violation alleged in the submitted grievance. For example, in *National Lead Co.*, Arbitrator Joseph G. Stashower said:

> When the dispute is submitted to the Arbitrator, as a result of the appeal of the grievance, the only items which the Administrator may consider are those mentioned in the grievance, unless the parties have by stipulation extended the scope of the Arbitrator's authority to consider additional items not mentioned in the grievance. Therefore, it must be held in this dispute, that the only items which the Arbitrator may consider are those mentioned in Grievance No. 712.[57]

If the union representatives attempt to broaden the scope of the claim by asserting a different or additional violation at the arbitration hearing, the arbitrator may well hold that a new grievance is being submitted in a manner inconsistent with the agreed upon procedure. Both jurisdictional grounds and policy considerations require that a hearing on such new claims be disallowed.[58] In *Allis-Chalmers Mfg. Co.*,[59] Arbitrator Elmer E. Hilpert succinctly expressed the underlying rationale:

> [T]he Referee does not treat a grievance, written at the "shop level," as a "pleading" in a court of law. Hence, if any time prior to the Hearing of the matter ... the Union has "cured," or "corrected" the "defects," or deficiencies, in its allegations of necessary facts, in a grievance, the Referee would treat this as a processable grievance, subject only to the postponements necessary to enable the Company to meet the Union's case. However, if the union changes its whole theory of recovery when it comes before the Referee, such a "new" grievance must obviously be returned to the prior steps in the parties' "Complaint and Grievance Procedure." ...[60]

---

[57]30 LA 893, 897 (Stashower, 1958).

[58]*John Morrell & Co.*, 65 LA 933 (Davis, 1975); *Business Forms, Inc.*, 65 LA 1031 (McDermott, 1975); *Perfex Plastics, Inc.*, 68-2 ARB ¶ 8638 (Malinowski, 1968); *Lithonia Lighting, Inc.*, 67-1 ARB ¶ 8043 (Holly, 1967); *Decar Plastics Corp.*, 66-3 ARB ¶ 8810 (Solomon, 1966); *Chrysler Corp.*, 1 ALAA ¶ 67,258 (Wolff, 1964); *Tenn-Flake, Inc.*, 60-1 ARB ¶ 8178 (Alexander, 1960); *Bethlehem Steel Co.*, 8 Steel Arb. 5515, 5519, 29 LA 418, 30 LA 428 (Stark, 1959); *National Lead Co.*, 30 LA 893 (Stashower, 1958); *Bridgeport Brass Co.*, 30 LA 622 (Donnelly Chm., 1958); *American Airlines, Inc.*, 27 LA 448 (Wolff, 1956); *Bethlehem Steel Co.*, 5 Steel Arb. 3419 (Seward, 1956); *Bethlehem Steel Co.*, 4 Steel Arb. 2373 (Platt, 1954); *Bethlehem Steel Co.*, 2 Steel Arb. 1293, 19 LA 561, 20 LA 38, 87 (Seward, 1953); *Bethlehem Steel Co.*, 17 LA 295, 300 (Selekman, 1951); *General Motors*, Umpire Decision No. E-276 (Alexander, 1949); *Chrysler Corp.*, 1 ALAA ¶ 67,258 (Wolff, 1944).

[59]Referee Case No. 57 (Hilpert, 1958) (unpublished).

[60]*Id.* at 16.

Similarly, where the union submitted to the arbitrator an issue different from the one discussed in the grievance procedure and set forth in the union's demand for arbitration, Arbitrator James Artieri ruled that he had no jurisdiction to hear the union's new issue. The labor agreement stated that only "such grievance" as has not been "satisfactorily settled" in the grievance procedure "may be appealed to an impartial umpire."

> It seems clear that the only question properly before the undersigned is whether the employer as charged, has assigned bargaining unit work to nonbargaining unit personnel. However, the union is presently specifically contending that by reason of the regular performance of experimental work by [the nonbargaining unit employee] he is not outside the bargaining unit, as the grievance alleges, but, to the contrary, is part of it. The union therefore is no longer protesting that the company is assigning bargaining unit work to a nonbargaining unit employee.... The arbitrator has no authority to render declaratory judgment on a claim that asserts no specific violation and that has not been processed through the grievance procedure to arbitration.[61]

When an employer reassigned certain duties between classifications and a grievance was filed claiming that the reassignment violated the local working conditions provision, and then in its prehearing brief (submitted just prior to the arbitration hearing) the union for the first time raised a claim that the reassignment violated the seniority article, Arbitrator David Miller refused to consider the union's new seniority claim because it had not been raised in the prior steps of the grievance procedure:

> Under the Agreement an issue brought to arbitration is framed by the original grievance statement and the facts, arguments and allegations raised by either party in the pre-arbitration steps of the grievance procedure. Unquestionably the obligation for early disclosure of all main facts and pertinent arguments is designed to permit settlement of the issue by the parties and to prevent surprise in the event the matter is submitted to arbitration. The purpose is evident throughout the provisions for "Adjustment of Grievance"—Section 6. And it is emphasized in the Arbitration Procedure "ground rules" mutually adopted by the parties' representatives on September 17, 1962. This does not mean that obviously inherent facts and arguments should be excluded from consideration in arbitration by overtechnical appraisal of the presentations in the earlier steps of the procedure. It does mean, however, that either party is entitled to know and consider, in the pre-arbitration steps of the grievance procedure, the essential claims and arguments upon which the other relies.
> . . .

---

[61]*John Bath & Co.*, AAA Case No. 86-9 (Altieri, 1965).

It is my conclusion that this late submission of the question with respect to whether a seniority violation occurred raises a serious procedural issue. Of the several arguments raised by the Union in this case, that alleging violation of Section 12 could conceivably be the most important. To permit its inclusion at this juncture would be to entertain a major alteration in position without benefit of prearbitration discussion of the issue by the parties. And to do so would be a disservice to the purposes of Section 6 procedures. The ruling is, therefore, that the matter of violation of Section 12—Seniority is not properly before me.[62]

Similarly, in *E. B. Bliss,*[63] Arbitrator Di Leone ruled that although the union could refer to new sections of the contract in the fourth step of the grievance procedure, additional sections may not be referred to during the arbitration proceedings.

When a union raised a grievance with respect to certain employees, claiming damages at the hearing for other employees similarly situated but not mentioned in the original grievance, Arbitrator Morvant excluded the claims of the unnamed grievants. The company had had no opportunity to either investigate those claims or to attempt their settlement.[64]

The desire to have both parties deal fully and honestly with each other from the start of the grievance process has been emphasized by many arbitrators as the rationale for refusing to hear an issue that has not been processed through the grievance procedure. Arbitrator David Wolff observed in an early case:

Under a strict, but fair, interpretation of the grievance procedure provided in the contract, the Chairman can find that the Union is bound by, and limited to, the matters contained in the original grievance, inasmuch as any material extension, amendment or modification results, in fact, in another or different grievance. Such a change or shift in position at a date later than the original grievance may not permit either side a fair and full use of the grievance procedure. Not only does it weaken the procedure, but the knowledge that such a loose practice was permitted could easily even-

[62]*United States Steel Corp.,* 12 STEEL ARB. 8490, 8491 (Miller, 1964).

[63]7 STEEL ARB. 4781, 4783 (Di Leone, 1958). *See* Elkouri and Elkouri, HOW ARBITRATION WORKS, Third Edition (Washington: BNA Books, 1973), pp. 196–97:

[I]f a deviation from what occurred at the pre-arbitral stage actually constitutes the addition of a new issue or dispute that has not been previously discussed by the parties, or the addition of a claim that has not been filed as required by the collective agreement, and if this by-passing of the grievance procedure is objected to by one of the parties, the arbitrator will ordinarily refuse to dispose of the new matter in his award.

See also Whirlwind, Inc., 68-2 ARB ¶ 8525, 50 LA 888 (Solomon, 1968); *Bethlehem Steel Corp.,* 13 STEEL ARB. 9896 (Porter, 1966).

[64]*See, e.g., Geigy Chemical Corp.,* 34 LA 102 (Morvant, 1959); *Swift & Co.,* 17 LA 537 (Seward, 1951). *Compare International Harvester Co.,* 14 LA 756 (Seward, 1950) (arbitrator found the abstract contract interpretation arbitrable but would not award back pay for unnamed grievants).

tually void the good results which may be expected in the preliminary steps of a well functioning grievance system.[65]

More recently, Arbitrator Arthur Malinowski refused to consider an issue not raised in the prior steps of the grievance procedure, and said:

> Arbitrators have long held that the procedural steps of the grievance procedure provide an opportunity for possible settlement of the controversies which may arise between the Parties. It is in the atmosphere of discussion, offer and counter-offer that the Parties may resolve their differences in a manner not to interfere with production. The parties in Article II have provided for an elaborate grievance procedure and have further clearly limited the Arbitrator's authority to those matters which have been properly carried through the grievance and arbitration procedure.[66]

Perhaps the most exhaustive discussion of this problem was by Arbitrator Bernard Meltzer in *Borg-Warner Corp.*[67] The union had challenged the company's right to downgrade an employee. At the hearing, it argued that even if the employee had been properly downgraded, the company should have permitted him to bump into a job for which he qualified. Arbitrator Meltzer refused to consider the bumping argument on the ground that the issue had not been raised in prior steps of the grievance procedure and, therefore, was not ripe for arbitration. His analysis is particularly lucid:

> The arbitrator recognizes that a grievance should not be read like a technical instrument or a common law pleading. Nevertheless, the arbitrator is persuaded that in this case important legal and practical considerations require him to limit the issue to be determined solely to that raised by the written grievance initially signed by the grievant and the Union Steward.
>
> Under the contract, arbitration is the final step in a complex and formal grievance procedure. Accordingly, the arbitrator's authority to determine a grievance not processed in accordance with the contract is open to serious question. While the parties may waive compliance with the prescribed grievance procedure and alter the original grievance in the course of processing it, the vague and inconclusive evidence regarding a statement concerning "juggling," which did not operate as adequate notice of the issues to be raised, is not a sufficient basis, in the circumstances of this case, for finding a waiver.
>
> These legal considerations reflect and are reenforced by strong practical considerations. Arbitration is a supplement to, and not a substitute for, the grievance process. The arbitrator's function is "to decide questions

---

[65]*Chrysler Corp.*, 1 ALAA ¶ 67,258, (Wolff, 1944); *see also Bethlehem Steel Co.*, 4 STEEL ARB. 2373 (Platt, 1954); *Bethlehem Steel Co.*, 17 LA 295, 300 (Selekman, 1951); *General Motors Corp.*, Umpire Decision No. E-276 at 638 (Wallen, 1949).

[66]*Perfex Plastics, Inc.*, 68-2 ARB ¶ 8638 at 5218 (Malinowski, 1968).

[67]27 LA 580 (Meltzer, 1956).

which the parties themselves have tried to settle without success." To treat
these two processes as the same is to threaten the integrity and usefulness
of both of them. Where, as in this case, there is a multi-step grievance procedure, one of the resultant advantages is that it brings to bear on the solution of a grievance with general implications the different kinds of know-
how which exist at different echelons of the Union and the Company. But
this advantage is lost or diluted where a new issue is formulated for the
first time at the arbitration stage.

These generalities operate with particular force in this case. The issues
in question, crystallized only at the arbitration stage, involve a complex
seniority system created by contractual language which is not altogether
clear. Witnesses who might have testified as to past practices were either
not available at the hearing, or when available, had not collected data
which might have been relevant. Under all these circumstances, there is a
danger that a determination of these issues in this arbitration might create
difficulties which have not been fully explored because of the failure
to process these issues through the grievance procedure. [Citations omitted.][68]

Unless the parties have thoroughly explored an issue in the lower
stages of the grievance procedure, it cannot be said to have been
"referred" or "appealed" to arbitration. In other words, the determination of the arbitrator's jurisdiction is for the parties and is not
subject to the latitude normally given to an arbitrator concerning
other matters. This rule was stated by Arbitrator Howlett:

> While arbitrators are not bound by the technical procedural rules of the
> common law or chancery courts . . ., the flexibility afforded an arbitrator
> in procedure and deciding a case on the merits does not apply to decision
> of the issue or issues before the arbitrator.[69]

On the other hand, arbitrators seldom refuse jurisdiction of a grievance because the grievant or the union representative failed to cite the
correct labor agreement provision in support of a claim, even where
the agreement so provides, or altered the theories underlying the
claim, so long as the company was not misled by this failure or
change.[70] If the grievance clearly states the relevant facts, arbitrators
generally hold that adequate notice concerning the claim has been
given, even if the basis for the claim at the hearing varies from the
claim asserted at the first step.[71]

---

[68]*Id.* at 584.

[69]*Wyandotte Chemicals Corp.*, 38 LA 808, 817 (Howlett, 1962).

[70]*Anderson Clayton Foods Co.*, 54 LA 551 (Feller, 1970); *Hupp Corp.*, 48 LA 524 (Hayes,
1967); *Olin Mathieson Chemical Corp.*, 67-1 ARB ¶ 8292 (Getman, undated); *Montgomery
Ward & Co.*, 48 LA 429 (Gorsuch, 1967); *Package Machinery Co.*, 41 LA 47, 48 (Altieri, 1963).

[71]*Monroe Concrete Co.*, 56 LA 15 (Weckstein, 1971); *Colson Co.*, 54 LA 896 (Roberts, 1970);
Lockheed Aircraft Corp., 55 LA 14 (Krimsly, 1970).

LACK OF AN AGGRIEVED

Where the agreement required "the aggrieved" to present the grievance orally in the first step and then to sign a written statement of it in the second step, a grievance signed by the chief steward challenged as nonarbitrable was said by Arbitrator Gross in *Interlake Iron Corp.*[72] to be arbitrable because the steward was the employee's representative. However, where the requirement was that the aggrieved employee sign the grievance and there was evidence the employee refused to do so, Arbitrator McIntosh in *Symington Wayne Corp.*[73] held he had no jurisdiction to hear the grievance. Similarly, where eight members of the union committee, none of whom was the aggrieved, signed the grievance, the requirement in the labor agreement that a grievance "be reduced to writing and signed by the aggrieved" as a condition for proceeding from the first to the second step of the grievance procedure made the grievance not arbitrable, Arbitrator Loucks in *Masell Manufacturing Corp.*[74] explained:

It is perfectly clear that, unless the matter is in writing and is "signed by the aggrieved," there is nothing which can proceed from [the first step] onward through the subsequent steps of the grievance procedure of which arbitration is the final step.

Where the grievance was over a demotion, but the grievant had been discharged for other reasons after the grievance was filed but before the arbitration, and its arbitrability was challenged on the ground there was no longer an employee-grievant, Arbitrator Robert McIntosh in *Kelsey-Hayes Co.*[75] said an arbitrable issue was presented:

At the time the grievance was filed, [an employer-employee relationship] existed. That being so, the necessary jurisdiction was established.... Certainly an employee who has begun proceedings to clear his employment record is entitled to pursue his remedy until he has exhausted all available avenues and through all available tribunals.

Arbitrator Bert Luskin in *The Electric Storage Battery Co.*[76] ex-

[72]AAA Case No. 76-6 (Gross, 1964); *see also Flexsteel Industries,* AAA Case No. 68-6 (Abersold, 1964).
[73]AAA Case No. 104-8 (Dash, 1967); *see also Howell Electric Motors Co.,* AAA Case No. 36-22, 38 LA 580 (Kahn, 1961).
[74]AAA Case No. 14-1 (Loucks, 1959). *See also Combustion Engineering, Inc.,* 54 LA 1118 (Erbs, 1970).
[75]AAA Case No. 40-5 (McIntosh, 1961).
[76]AAA Case No. 17-13 (Luskin, 1959); *see also American Bosch Arma Corp.,* AAA Case No. 66-2 (Greene, 1964).

plained that where the dischargee was a probationary employee a grievance over his discharge presented an arbitrable issue because:

> The issue in question involves the interpretation and application of provisions of the collective bargaining agreement, and to that extent the grievance is arbitrable. A distinction must be made between issues which, by their nature, fall outside the scope of the arbitrator's authority in areas which would prohibit the issuance of an award in cases where the application or interpretation of provisions of the agreement are not involved. The fact that provisions of the agreement permit the Company to exercise its right to terminate a probationary employee would constitute a good and sufficient defense to the claim of the discharged employee; but the issue, however, may be the subject of a grievance with the terminal point of arbitration, since it does in fact involve the application and interpretation of specific provisions of the collective bargaining agreement.

A grievance claiming reinstatement of an individual who had accepted retirement checks was arbitrable because the question of whether the grievant had actually retired, losing rights under the agreement, was a question of interpretation.[77]

Arbitrator Ralph Seward in *Swift & Company*[78] found the employer had violated a no-discrimination clause by refusing to hire qualified Negro job applicants, but stated that his award could be applied only to named grievants and could not be extended to additional grievants whose names were furnished to the employer for the first time at the arbitration hearing. He stated in part:

> The arbitrator's award does not cover the five negro women whose names were first given to the company at the arbitration hearing. The scope of this grievance and of the union's claim for relief was defined when the union furnished the company with the names of thirteen negro women who had allegedly been the victims of discrimination. This list purported to be complete. Prior to the hearing there was no suggestion that additional women might be involved. In the opinion of the arbitrator the union's attempt to expand the grievance at the arbitration hearing to include additional grievants was improper and must fail.[79]

In *Geigy Chemical Corp.*,[80] an employee filed a written grievance on a formal grievance report form and said 10 employees were involved. In rejecting jurisdiction over the claims of the unnamed grievants, Arbitrator Horvant explained:

---

[77]*Schnadig Corp.*, AAA Case No. 78-12 (Abersold, 1965).

[78]17 LA 537 (Seward, 1951).

[79]*Id.* at 540. *See also City of Hartford, Conn.*, 71-1 ARB ¶ 8090 (Johnson, 1971) (a vague claim of racial discrimination without specifying incidents and grievants did not present an arbitrable issue).

[80]34 LA 102 (Morvant, 1959).

On the other hand, it is a misuse of the grievance procedure to permit a brother member to file a grievance and not identify oneself with that grievance if the same injury is suffered. It is wrong because (1) it is unfair to expect one man to carry the fight for others who remain in the background anonymously, (2) it is unfair to the Company because they cannot evaluate the grievance as to a possible compromise settlement when they are ignorant as to how many employees are involved, and (3) it is unfair to the grievance procedure because it was never intended that one of the parties may withhold important facts concerning a dispute while it is being considered in the grievance steps. The primary purpose of the grievance procedure is to settle disputes, and it is only possible to achieve a settlement when all of the facts are known and can be evaluated. Unless both parties are aware of all facts concerning a dispute, which includes the names of the people involved, how then can it be said that all efforts have been exhausted to effect a settlement? By withholding facts the parties are also withholding effort towards reaching a settlement.[81]

However, Arbitrator Benjamin Wolf in *A. P. Smith Valve Division*[82] said that where one member of a group signed and the grievance was filed within the time limit, the claims of other employees in the group were not defeated when their names were added after the grievance filing time had elapsed.

One purpose of the signature requirement is to prevent a grievance from being filed against the employee's wishes. Another is to prevent the filing of a grievance by a person not authorized to do so. In this case, neither of these circumstances applies.

Since the objection raised by the Employer would foreclose the right of an employee to be heard on the merits of his grievance, any doubt with respect to the formality of the filing should be resolved in favor of permitting the grievance to have a hearing on the merits. For this reason, I find that the original grievance was properly signed in detail within the meaning of [the contract].

Finally, the delayed signing by some of the grievants was explained by the fact that the employer had said that if the union were serious about the complaints, each individual ought to sign it. Thus, "these grievances were corrected amendments of the original grievances" and the fact that the individual signing occurred after the five day period does not "nullify the timeliness."

Where four employees signed the grievance and there was no evidence that a fifth withheld his signature because he acknowledged the propriety of the company's action, Arbitrator Brecht in *National Vulcanized Fibre Co.*[83] permitted the fifth to join as a grievant.

---

[81]*Id.* at 104–05.

[82]*A. P. Smith Valve Division of U.S. Pipe & Foundry,* AAA Case No. 139-1 (Wolf, 1970).

[83]AAA Case No. 83-6 (Brecht, 1965). *See also Bethlehem Steel Corp.,* 54 LA 445 (Gill, 1969).

Although an "aggrieved employee" was needed to get a case before the arbitrator and ten employees signed the grievance, Arbitrator Walt in *Smith Plastics, Inc.*[84] permitted three additional grievants to be added at the hearing where the issues involved were the same, saying:

> Since the company is not faced with defending any new or different factual allegations, I see no harm in considering the thirteen grievances as a single question.

Normally a grievance cannot be filed against a rule *per se*, because the arbitrator has no grievant. Instead, the grievance must be filed against the disciplining of an employee when he or she violates the rule. This was illustrated when the Aluminum Company of America set up a plan to curb excessive absenteeism among employees and the union filed a grievance claiming the new rule could not be issued. Judge Kennedy of the Ninth Circuit said that because the new rule had not yet resulted in any disciplinary action against any employee, the grievance filed against the rule was nonarbitrable, notwithstanding the possiblity that in the future a grievance might arise when some employee who violated the rule was disciplined.[85]

The manager responsible for directing a work force will set up many rules. Some of these have a penalty attached stating, for example, that if an employee violates a given rule, the employee may be discharged by the company. Sometimes arbitrators have concluded that the discipline attached to the rule is unreasonable and therefore is not a "just" discipline, whether it be suspension or discharge. The lack of a "just" discipline attachment to a rule was explained by Arbitrator Harry Burns in *Schmidt Cabinet Co., Inc.*[86] The company had instituted a rule requiring employees to "punch" the time clock, recording time spent on all visits to the rest room. Even though the employer testified that the establishment of the rule had increased production, Arbitrator Burns said that he was not prepared to sustain the rule at the expense of the employees' dignity.

LACK OF JURISDICTION BECAUSE THE CLAIM IS SETTLED

Where the grievance is merely a refining of a grievance that was settled previously, arbitrators hold that the second grievance is not arbitrable, even where "both the Union and Company testimony, and

---

[84] AAA Case No. 105-10 (Walt, 1967).
[85] *Aluminum Company of America v. United Auto Workers,* 630 F.2d 1340, 105 LRRM 2390 (9th Cir. 1980).
[86] 75 LA 397 (Burns, 1980). *To the same effect, Gremar Mfg. Co.*, 46 LA 215 (Teele, 1956).

documents available at the hearing, support the Grievant's claim" that the work he performed entitled him to an evaluation equal to that of the setup man. Arbitrator Cummins "[found] the issue closed" because of the settlement of an earlier grievance involving the same basic claim.[87] This rationale involves the application in labor arbitration of the principle of *res judicata,* long established in the law, that if the identical claim was previously settled it cannot be relitigated. Even resubmission of a grievance that was continuing in nature after a prior identical grievance was "considered settled," because it was not appealed within the specified time limit, caused Arbitrator Cole to hold that the "new grievance was nonarbitrable."[88]

Where the requested relief had been granted, even though the parties still disputed the appropriate interpretation of the labor agreement, the grievance was dismissed. This is the application of the legal principle that matters that have become *moot* should not be litigated. Arbitrator Eckhardt explained his lack of authority to render an award after the "demand" was "paid off" to make the issue *moot*:

> Until an actual dispute arises together with the related, specific facts, neither party has a right to demand arbitration. For this purpose, the dispute cannot be theoretical and will exist only when one party is demanding some benefit or condition which the other party refuses to give.
>
> Furthermore, even though such a dispute does exist at some time, there is no basis for arbitration unless the dispute continues at the time of the award of the arbitrator. A withdrawal or an abandonment of the demand by the one party or the acceding to that demand by the other will terminate the dispute and leave no issue for arbitration. This is true despite the fact that, even at that point, the parties are not in agreement on the interpretation of the clause which gave rise to the dispute.
>
> To provide an adequate basis for arbitration, a grievance must be more than an argument over interpretation. It must be also a request for action. Without a demand for relief, there is no reason for arbitration. Those executing the Agreement controlling this arbitration surely so intended when they provided for arbitration as a method of settling "grievances." . . .[89]

Likewise, when a union advised a company that a grievance was settled and hence withdrawn from the grievance procedure, the grievance became nonarbitrable even when the union membership by vote attempted to reverse this decision. Arbitrator Wallen said that the withdrawal was a "commitment to a third party, in this case the company," and the failure of the membership to ratify could not have the

---

[87] *Penn-Union Machine Corp.,* AAA Case No. 15-14 (Cummins, 1959). *Brown Co.,* 59 LA 235 (Bloch, 1972); *Bethlehem Mines Corp.,* 70-1 ARB ¶ 8307 (Lugar, 1969). *See* text associated with note 50 *supra,* and cases cited therein.

[88] *Farrel Corp.,* AAA Case No. 84-8 (Cole, 1965).

[89] *Inland Container Corp.,* 29 LA 861 (Eckhardt, 1957).

effect of "rescinding" that action. "The withholding of approval in such circumstances merely constitutes notice of the Executive Board that the membership does not agree with the course it has taken...."[90]

On the other hand, withdrawal of a grievance protesting the company's announcement that a job would be awarded to a junior bidder (grievance No. 15) did not bar arbitration of the same grievance (grievance No. 21) several months later when the job actually was filled by the junior. Arbitrator Ryder said:

> It can fairly be said that grievance No. 15 was only grieving an event that might happen. This event did not happen while grievance No. 15 was in active process. Hence, since the event conceivably also might not happen, the grievance complained of contractual hurt and loss ... where no such hurt and loss yet existed or might ever come to exist.... It is the arbitrator's opinion that grievance No. 15 was filed anticipatorily, pressing a grievance of employees who then had no basis yet to grieve. Not only was their grieving untimely at the time of filing but their grieving remained untimely all the time the grievance progressed through the appellate steps of the grievance procedure until they were exhausted. The selection of [the junior] became grievable when in fact the company acted on its announced selection.... Then a grievance could be properly filed—and it was in the form of instant grievance No. 21.[91]

Similarly, Arbitrator Healy ruled that when a grievance was withdrawn and corrected to refer to a violation of a different clause of the labor agreement and then refiled, the grievance was arbitrable because the union was not acting capriciously and that:

> The position taken by the company would seem to be unreasonably inflexible, given the language of the relevant contract provisions. This is not tantamount to a legal case of *res adjudicata*. It is simply a matter of a union having decided that its appellate claim, as originally advanced, was ill-founded. As the contract is written, ... the union is privileged to alter its allegation and introduce what it deems to be the most valid basis for its complaint. True, the union cannot be allowed to alter capriciously its basis for complaint. Were this to be allowed the company is correct in stating that what it had a right to consider a resolved grievance could be kept alive indefinitely by the union's capricious change of its grievance-basis claim. In the present case, however, there is no reason to conclude that the revised grievance placed the company in any greater jeopardy or that it was

---

[90]*General Cable Corp.*, AAA Case No. 36-14 (Wallen, 1961); *Midland-Ross Corp.*, 53 LA 113 (Dyke, 1969).

[91]*Allied Products Corp.*, AAA Case No. 26-20 (Ryder, 1960); *Hess Oil & Chemical Corp.*, 51 LA 445 (Gould, 1968).

otherwise affected adversely by the grievance based on a different contract clause.[92]

Although a failure on the part of the union to properly advance the grievance claim to arbitration may cause the arbitrator to rule he or she has no jurisdiction to grant the claim,[93] failure of the company to comply with a procedural requirement of the agreement does not similarly cause arbitrators to find that a "settlement" favorable to the claimant has occurred. For example, Arbitrator John McGury held that the failure of the company to comply with a requirement in the labor agreement that parties submit a written statement of their positions at the arbitration hearing did not justify the union's request that its holiday pay grievance be granted for that reason alone. "Forfeitures are to be avoided whenever possible in all legal relationships. This is especially true where the parties have a continuing interest in the resolution of problems on their merits, rather than by deadlines or technicalities." The critical question is whether the party guilty of the procedural defeat thereby gained an advantage "in presenting the substantive aspects of the case." In this case, despite the fault, "both parties are able to stand on equal terms in presenting their case at the time of the hearing."[94]

Furthermore, where a procedural defect can be cured, the arbitrator should cure it, not generate a forfeiture. For example, where the union contended that arbitration of the employer's complaint was barred by the fact that no conference between the parties over the alleged violation of the agreement had taken place, Arbitrator Michael Sovern ruled that at most "the union would be entitled to a stay of these proceedings for the holding of the omitted conference. But the union did not request such relief and little purpose would be served by tendering it the opportunity to do so now. I conclude the dispute is arbitrable."[95]

LACK OF AN AGREEMENT TO INTERPRET

Challenges to the arbitrator based on the contention that a document other than the labor agreement governs the outcome of the claim often arise in the employee benefits area. Many labor bargaining agreements refer to the establishment or maintenance of employee benefits, such as insurance or pension benefits, which are governed by

---

[92]*Chapman Valve Manufacturing Co.,* AAA Case No. 41-11 (Healy, 1961).

[93]See *"Tardy Processing Through Grievance Steps,"* supra, in this chapter.

[94]*Borg-Warner Corp.,* AAA Case No. 62-5 (McGury, 1964).

[95]*Kentile Floors, Inc.,* AAA Case No. 103-3 (Sovern, 1967).

separate documents and administered by parties other than those subject to the labor agreement. Whether claims pertaining to the proper
administration of such benefit programs will be considered to be arbitrable depends on the wording of the collective bargaining agreement. In some cases, such claims may be specifically excluded from
arbitration. For example, in *New England Telephone & Telegraph
Co.*,[96] the labor agreement specifically excluded from arbitration
questions "arising in connection with the Plan for Employees' Pen-
sions, Disability Benefits and Death Benefits." The reason for the exclusion was that the Plan had traditionally been administered by a
joint employer-employee Benefits Committee, rather than by the
employer. Accordingly, Arbitrator Sander held that a claim of a
failure to pay disability benefits to a pregnant employee was not arbitrable.

In *Anchor Coupling Co.*[97] Arbitrator Kates held he had authority to
consider the merits of a pension claim made under the labor agreement but based on an auxiliary document. The labor agreement contained a provision setting forth the parties' intent to negotiate a pension plan. The plan itself provided that the union reserved the right to
"test" the effective date of the plan through an "appropriate legal procedure." The arbitrator held that since arbitration was an "appropriate legal procedure," he had the authority under the labor
agreement to determine the effective date of the pension plan.

Where the contract neither explicitly excludes from arbitration nor
expressly or impliedly includes as arbitrable disputes regarding employee benefits or their administration, the arbitrability of such
disputes apparently hinges in part on the specificity of the contract
provision dealing with the benefit. If the labor agreement provides
only that the company will maintain a particular insurance policy, Arbitrators Ryder, Larkin and Volz have held that disputes relating to
coverage or levels of benefits are not arbitrable. Such matters are between the employer and the insurance carrier and involve interpretation of the insurance contract rather than the labor agreement.[98] If,
however, the dispute involves whether the company has provided the
insurance coverage contemplated by the labor agreement, the dispute
may be held to be arbitrable.[99] This is especially true where the labor
agreement specifically lists the benefits to be provided to employees.[100]

Perhaps the most fundamental challenge to arbitrability that can be

---

[96]62 LA 216 (Sander, 1973).

[97]64 LA 205 (Kates, 1974).

[98]*Louisville Cooperage Co.*, 63 LA 165 (Volz, 1974); *Stewart-Warner Corp.*, 54 LA 931 (Larkin, 1970); *Whitehead & Kales Co.*, 49 LA 1128 (Ryder, 1968).

[99]*Barber-Greene Co.*, 54 LA 933 (Sembower, 1970).

[100]*Gilbert & Bennett Mfg. Co.*, 58 LA 815 (Larkin, 1972).

raised before an arbitrator is the claim that there is no valid labor agreement between the parties, either because it has never been entered into or because a prior agreement has expired. While the issue of *contract expiration* has generally been held to be one for judicial resolution,[101] the issue of the existence of a valid contract has been determined by arbitrators. Arbitrator Rolf Valtin, in *United States Gypsum,*[102] held that Gypsum, as a successor employer, was bound by the dues checkoff and wage reopener provisions of its predecessor's labor agreement. After its acquisition of a lime plant formerly owned by United Cement Company, Gypsum refused to check off dues or to meet with the Steelworkers to negotiate wages under the wage reopener provisions of United's contract with the Steelworkers. After Gypsum also refused to arbitrate the question of the applicability of these provisions, the Steelworkers filed suit to compel arbitration. In May 1966, the district court ordered arbitration; but before any proceeding could be held, the Union was decertified. In February 1971, Arbitrator Valtin held that the United contract was binding on Gypsum from April 1, 1965 until December 2, 1966. He ordered, *inter alia,* that the company retroactively make dues checkoff payments to the union without deductions from employees' wages. He also ordered the company to pay to the employees a retroactive ten cents per hour increase under the reopener provision. This was based on his opinion that Gypsum would have agreed to such an increase, if it had negotiated with the Steelworkers. Valtin's award was enforced by the Fifth Circuit, with the exception of his imposition of substantive contract terms upon the parties.[103] On appeal, the Fifth Circuit upheld the entire award, and the Supreme Court twice declined to review this decision.

A similar award by Arbitrator David M. Helfeld occurred in *Negco Enterprises, Inc.*[104] Arbitrator Helfeld determined that the employer was bound by a company official's oral agreement to accept the predecessor's labor agreement with the union, on the ground that the company was the *alter ego* of its predecessor. Accordingly, Arbitrator Helfeld stated that he had jurisdiction to hear the union's breach of contract claims on the merits.

---

[101]*See, e.g., International Union, United Automobile, Aerospace and Agricultural Implement Workers of America, UAW v. International Telephone and Telegraph Corporation, Thermotech Division,* 508 F.2d 1309, 88 LRRM 2213 (8th Cir. 1975) and cases cited therein. *See also* Chapter III, *supra.*

[102]*United States Gypsum Co.,* 56 LA 363 (Valtin, 1971).

[103]*United Steelworkers of America v. United States Gypsum Co.,* 492 F.2d 713, 85 LRRM 2962 (5th Cir. 1974), *aff'g in part, rev'g in part, and remanding* 339 F. Supp. 302, 79 LRRM 2833 (D. Ala. 1972); *rehearing denied,* 498 F.2d 334, 87 LRRM 2075 (5th Cir. 1974); *cert. denied,* 419 U.S. 998, 87 LRRM 2658 (1974); *reconsideration denied,* 419 U.S. 1097 (1974).

[104]68 LA 633 (Helfeld, 1976).

The authority of the arbitrator to make this type of substantive determination is unclear. The question of whether an employer is the legal successor to a predecessor would seem to be one for judicial resolution under the Supreme Court's decisions in *NLRB v. Burns International Security Services*,[105] and *Howard Johnson Co., Inc. v. Hotel and Restaurant Employees*.[106] Similarly, the question of whether an employer is legally bound to arbitrate claims arising under an expired agreement would seem also to be reserved for judicial resolution under the Supreme Court's holding in *Nolde Brothers, Inc. v. Local No. 358, Bakery & Confectionery Workers Union*[107] and its prior decision in *John Wiley & Sons v. Livingston*.[108] Additionally, the "alter ego" concept applied by Arbitrator Helfeld in the *Negco Enterprises* case is a doctrine utilized by the NLRB in interpreting obligations arising under the Act[109] rather than an arbitral concept. Yet the *U.S. Gypsum* case, *supra*, illustrates that the arbitrator obviously has some authority to make a threshold determination concerning the existence of an agreement to interpret.

The question of how far the arbitrator may go in taking cognizance of the law in this area requires some very fine line-drawing. Arbitrator Hogan's decision in *J. J. O'Donnell Woolens, Inc.*[110] is an example of an award which attempts to allocate judicial and arbitral responsibility. He determined that the employer had assumed certain obligations under its predecessor's labor agreement and had not voluntarily assumed others, including disputed vacation pay and retirement separation pay clauses. He declined, however, to determine whether the successor was *legally obligated* to assume the disputed clauses. The resolution of that issue depended not on an interpretation of the labor agreement but on an interpretation of the court decisions relating to successorship. In reserving that question for a court of competent jurisdiction, the arbitrator applied the following standard:

> Where the fundamental dispute is over the meaning of the Contract in relation to the facts the dispute should be resolved at arbitration but when the dispute is over the meaning or application of Court decisions the question should go to a court of competent jurisdiction unless the arbitrator finds that prior court decisions are clear and unambiguous *when applied to the facts of his particular case*.[111] [Emphasis in original.]

---

[105]406 U.S. 272, 80 LRRM 2225 (1972).
[106]417 U.S. 249, 86 LRRM 2449 (1974).
[107]430 U.S. 243, 94 LRRM 2753 (1977); *rehearing denied,* 430 U.S. 988.
[108]376 U.S. 543, 55 LRRM 2769 (1964).
[109]*See, e.g., P. A. Hayes, Inc. and P & H Mechanical Corp.*, 226 NLRB No. 39 (1976).
[110]61 LA 739 (Hogan, 1972).
[111]*Id.* at 744.

Using this standard, the arbitrator determined that the law was sufficiently clear for him to determine that the company was a successor to
its predecessor, but insufficiently clear and unambiguous to allow him
to determine the legal effect of successorship with respect to the two
disputed provisions.

LACK OF JURISDICTION OVER THE SUBJECT MATTER

Collective bargaining agreements establish a set of usually generalized rules to resolve future specific disputes. In this context, no
amount of care can eliminate potential ambiguity. If the parties were
to attempt to anticipate all variations, negotiations would be endless
and even to make the effort would, under most circumstances, be unwise because of the innumerable agreements that would be needed to
settle matters that might not arise, thus increasing the chance of deadlock.

The absence of specific language relating to the management conduct complained of in a grievance often leads to the challenge that the
grievance involves no issue of contract interpretation over which the
arbitrator has either jurisdiction or authority to resolve the particular
grievance claim.[112] For example, a grievance requesting that the company fill an assistant foreman's job during his vacation did not present
an arbitrable issue where the collective bargaining agreement contained no provision concerning the wages, hours, and conditions of
employment of supervisory personnel, and the arbitrator "cannot
order the company to reactivate a position outside the bargaining
unit."[113]

In a case involving the company's right to require employees to take
their vacations during a period of plant shutdown and where the labor
agreement excluded "any matters of general management questions,
management policy, business requirements [or] operations" from arbitration, the arbitrator found that the union's contention that the exclusionary clause did not apply would have merit if the union could
demonstrate the company's action was not predicated on operational
requirements, but was arbitrarily based on unrelated considerations.
However, the arbitrator held that the burden of demonstrating bad

---

[112]*See, e.g., T & M Rubber Specialties Co., Inc.*, 54 LA 292 (Sembower, 1970); *Arrow
Newaygo Foundry Co.*, AAA Case No. 105-5 (Rogers, 1967); *Anaconda American Brass Co.*,
AAA Case No. 69-15 (Davis, 1964); *Bell Telephone Co. of Pa.*, AAA Case No. 40-6 (Duff, 1962);
but see Capital Times Co., 65 LA 348 (Lee, 1975); *Louisville Cooperage Co.*, 63 LA 165 (Volz,
1974); *Eagle-Picher Industries, Inc.*, 63 LA 713 (Marshall, 1974); *William H. Haskell Mfg. Div.
of Easco Corp.*, AAA Case No. 141-13 (Yagoda, 1970); *Ostendorf-Morris Co.*, AAA Case No.
35-23 (Teple, 1961).
[113]*American Enka Corp.*, AAA Case No. 84-9 (Holly, 1965).

faith on the company's part had not been met, and hence, "[t]he dispute would seem to fall four square within the scope of the exclusionary language leaving matters of business requirements, operations, and general management questions outside of the competence of the arbitrator to pass upon."[114] It is submitted that the discussion by Arbitrator Altieri, leading to the conclusion that the dispute was not arbitrable, could easily be the reasoning establishing why the grievance should be denied on its merits, except for the fact that the clause of the agreement involved was expressed as an exclusion of subject matter from arbitration.

Similarly, a grievance against the issuance of a memorandum to supervisors setting forth guidelines for determining improper absenteeism did not present an arbitrable grievance,[115] as it did not relate to any provision of the labor agreement.

In another case, a claim against a company for reimbursement for damage to an employee's tool box was held not arbitrable by Arbitrator Samuel Edes. He said:

> I cannot relate, directly or indirectly, the practice upon which the Union relies to any express provision of the contract.[116]

Edes explained the relationship of lack of jurisdiction to resolve a grievance and the parol evidence rule discussed in Chapter X when he rejected the union's contention that the company's past practice with respect to repair or replacement of tools made such benefits an "integral part of the contract." "I do not find it necessary," the arbitrator said, "in this case to pass upon whether the past practice of the Company was such as to encompass the replacement of [the grievant's] tool box." Evidence of past practice would be persuasive in interpreting an "ambiguous" or "inept" provision of a contract, but in the absence of any contract provision dealing with the subject matter of the grievance, the arbitrator "cannot decide a controversy based entirely upon practices and customs outside of the obligations assumed in the written terms of the agreement."[117]

However, a grievance by a discharged foreman who had formerly been in the unit but was not retransferred upon his termination was an arbitrable one because the issue

> posed by the parties on the merits sufficiently involves the possible interpretation and application of [the clause governing return to the bargaining unit] to warrant careful consideration by an arbitrator. Should the em-

---

[114]*E. R. Squibb Co.*, AAA Case No. 30-4 (Altieri, 1961).

[115]*Boston Edison Co.*, AAA Case No. 132-2 (Rubin, 1969).

[116]*Borg-Warner Corp.*, AAA Case No. 14-21 (Edes, 1959).

[117]*Id.*

ployee have been retransferred to a position in the bargaining unit? Are [the recognition clause] and [the clause governing retransfers] entirely consistent? The issue on the merits is not immediately, obviously and grossly beyond the scope of [the retransfer clause]. This is not to say that the grievance . . . and the remedy requested need to have a *prima facie* case but only that it may possibly involve, in a serious way, the interpretation and application of provisions of the agreement.[118]

Where a labor agreement provided for the negotiation of the revisions in base rates during its term, and also provided that "all claims, disputes or differences arising out of the terms of this agreement shall be settled in accordance with the procedure provided by the agreement," the inability of the parties to agree on new base rates did not present an arbitrable issue. "The arbitration of basic wage rates is uncommon in most industries, including aircraft and electronics; it seems most unlikely, therefore, that the parties would have contemplated the arbitration of a wage reopening dispute and yet not have provided specifically in the Agreement for such an eventuality."[119]

Arbitrators do not conclude that merely because the issue in dispute could become a matter of concern under the National Labor Relations Act they do not have jurisdiction if an interpretation and application of the agreement is involved. Concurrent jurisdiction of the NLRB and an arbitrator was asserted by Arbitrator Melvin Lennard[120] when he refused to stay a decision of a submitted dispute because the same issue was pending before the NLRB.

Similarly, Arbitrator David Helfeld declined to stay until such time as the NLRB could rule on a pending de-authorization petition, a decision on a union's claim that the employer had violated the "recognition clause" of the contract by discouraging union activity.[121]

Every decision by an arbitrator denying a grievance on the ground that there is no contractual restriction on the right of management to take the action complained of, is, in fact, a ruling that the subject matter was not covered by the agreement. When the subject matter is not covered, the non-arbitrability claim is not waived by a failure to raise this claim during the processing of the grievance. For example, Arbitrator G. Allen Dash said that where the labor agreement required the parties "to attempt in good faith to adjust all grievances" under methods provided for in the agreement, the employer was "obliged to consider [a grievance] on its merits through the several

---

[118]*Landers, Frary & Clark,* AAA Case No. 75-7 (Dunlop, 1964).

[119]*Hughes Tool Co.,* AAA Case No. 26-1 (Aaron, 1960).

[120]*Burgmaster Corp.,* AAA Case No. 85-11, 46 LA 746, 750 (Lennard, 1965). *Accord, Aeroil Products Co.,* AAA Case No. 65-18 (Stark, 1964); *Nicolet Industries,* AAA Case No. 18-11 (Rock, 1960).

[121]*Sonic Knitting Industries, Inc.,* 65 LA 453 (Helfeld, 1975).

steps of the Grievance Procedure" and did not forfeit its right to assert the defense of "non-arbitrability" by having failed to question arbitrability during the grievance procedure:

> There is no need, and there would be no point, for the Company to raise the issue of arbitrability during the several steps of the Grievance Procedure at which the Company is obligated to consider the merits of the grievance.[122]

Furthermore, the employer's right to dispute arbitrability for the first time at the hearing was not affected, as the union asserted, by the failure to make this defense in the statement answering the demand for arbitration:

> Under the contract and under the Rules of the American Arbitration Association, the participation of the Company in selecting an Arbitrator to hear a particular grievance does not require it to divulge its defense of non-arbitrability in advance of the arbitration proceedings.... By participation in the selection of the Arbitrator to hear and decide a particular grievance, the Company and the Union do commit themselves to having the question of arbitrability decided by the Arbitrator (if that question is raised as a defense by either party), but they do not thereby automatically commit themselves to arbitrate the grievance on its merits unless the Arbitrator rules that the grievance is arbitrable.[123]

Similarly, Arbitrator S. Harry Galfand pointed out that a party can waive a procedural defect which, if not waived, would bar arbitration on the merits, but it cannot waive a lack of jurisdiction over subject matter to create in the arbitrator jurisdiction which does not exist. He said that the failure of the company to indicate in advance its intention to contest arbitrability did not prevent such a claim from being made. "It is a question of whether the arbitrator has the power of jurisdiction to consider the question." If he lacks that power, that lack cannot be overcome, no matter when the defense of nonarbitrability is raised:

> The doctrine of estoppel—perhaps applicable to the failure to take advantage of a procedural failure—cannot, in my opinion, be applied to the fundamental question of the arbitrator's jurisdiction. It is certainly helpful to harmonious labor-management relations, and courteous to advise that a position of nonarbitrability will be taken, but I cannot hold that the failure to do so constitutes a fatal or disabling defect.[124]

A challenge to the arbitrator's jurisdiction on a subject-matter basis is generally handled as a preliminary matter before a decision on the merits. Since jurisdiction over subject matter and the merits of the

[122]*Celanese Corp. of America,* AAA Case No. 10-21 (Dash, 1959). *Accord: Mobil Chemical Co.,* 64 LA 10 (Naehring, 1974).
[123]*Id.*
[124]*Bally Case & Cooler Co.,* AAA Case No. 93-10 (Galfand, 1966).

claim are very often closely related,[125] and the prevailing view among arbitrators appears to be that a grievance claim will be considered within their jurisdiction if based upon an alleged violation of the agreement[126] and involving an issue not completely foreign to the traditional scope of labor agreements and arbitration,[127] a challenge to the jurisdiction of the arbitrator to hear the matter creates a risk. If the arbitrator finds jurisdiction to hear the case on the merits, he or she may feel compelled to find some provision of the agreement from which to imply a restriction when deciding the grievance on the merits. In view of this, an attack on grounds of subject matter jurisdiction may be inadvisable because the same consideration can be raised when the grievance is being considered on its merits, *i.e.*, does it present a factual basis for finding of a contract violation?

The risks of attacking subject-matter jurisdiction of the arbitrator are not limited solely to this consideration, however. As one arbitrator noted when he ruled that a grievance not signed by an aggrieved employee was not within his jurisdiction, this meant that the dispute became one over which the union could conduct an authorized strike under a clause permitting strikes over matters not subject to grievance procedure.[128] This is also underscored by the rule announced by the Supreme Court in *Boys Markets, Inc. v. Retail Clerks Union, Local 770*,[129] which produces an often unexpected consequence when the employer wins on a procedural objection basis. Thus, a strike in violation of the agreement over the dispute would not be enjoinable because the grievance is not subject to resolution by arbitration.

An employer may similarly achieve a questionable victory where it prevails on an arbitrability claim in a case subject to deferral by the NLRB under its *Collyer* doctrine,[130] which specifies the transfer of arbitration matters from the NLRB to an arbitrator. An arbitration award which does not reach the merits will not moot an unfair labor practice charge under the Board's *Spielberg* standards.[131] Indeed, the

---

[125]In *Sun Oil Co.*, Arbitrator Byron Abernethy says there may be only a "semantic difference" between ruling that a claim is unarbitrable and ruling that it is an arbitrable claim which is utterly without merit. But he says the union grievance raises a question of application of the agreement to promotions to supervisory status. He decides this is an issue which, "under the terms of this agreement, the union is entitled to have resolved." *Sun Oil Co.*, 52 LA 463, 467 (Abernethy, 1969).

[126]A claim based upon an agreement unrelated to the collective agreement and the arbitration provision contained therein is generally held by arbitrators to be not properly before them. *See, e.g., Ranco, Inc.*, 50 LA 269 (Klein, 1968).

[127]*Ethyl Corp.*, 50 LA 322 (Dworkin, 1968); *Great Atlantic & Pacific Tea Co.*, 49 LA 515 (Crawford, 1967); *New Hotel Showboat, Inc.*, 48 LA 240 (Jones, 1967).

[128]*Lummis & Co.*, AAA Case No. 32-22 (Kahn, 1961).

[129]398 U.S. 235 (1970). *See also Buffalo Forge Co. v. United Steelworkers of America*, 428 U.S. 397, 92 LRRM 3032, (1976).

[130]*Collyer Insulated Wire*, 192 NLRB 837, 77 LRRM 1931 (1971).

[131]*Spielberg Manufacturing Co.*, 112 NLRB 1080, 36 LRRM 1152 (1955).

Board as a matter of practice routinely requires employers to agree that the arbitration claim may be heard on its merits before staying its hand pursuant to *Collyer.*

THE PROCEDURE USED TO RAISE A CHALLENGE
TO THE ARBITRATOR'S JURISDICTION

A claim that the arbitrator has no jurisdiction over the subject matter or that the grievance is not properly before the arbitrator because of a procedural defect, such as untimely filing or appeal, can be presented in one of two ways. The claim may be presented in a separate and advance hearing, where a ruling on jurisdiction is requested. More commonly, the lack of jurisdiction contention is presented as the first part of a hearing on the merits.[132] Unless the parties specifically agree to submit the issue of arbitrability in a separate advance hearing, the arbitrator usually asks both parties to proceed on the merits after the party has presented its jurisdictional objection, deferring a ruling as to jurisdiction until after the record on both the jurisdiction and merits has been completed.[133]

In this connection, courts have held that a defense of nonarbitrability is not lost because the party asserting it participated in a hearing on the merits of the grievance, as long as the party asserts and preserves the defense of nonarbitrability.[134] Some arbitrators, however, are less sure about the effect participation in a hearing on the merits has upon the nonarbitrability defense.[135] Since the issue of nonarbitrability goes to the issue of the arbitrator's jurisdiction, the better rule would appear to be that participation in the arbitration does not constitute waiver. Such a rule would conform to the general judicial rule that lack of subject-matter jurisdiction is never waived.[136]

---

[132]Smith and Jones, *The Impact of the Emerging Federal Law of Grievance Arbitration on Judges, Arbitrators and Parties,* 52 VA. L. REV. 831, 871 (1966); Elkouri and Elkouri, HOW ARBITRATION WORKS, Third Edition (Washington: BNA Books, 1973); pp. 169-180; Collins, *Arbitrability and Arbitrators,* 13 N.Y.U. CONF. LAB. 449, 451 (1960).

[133]For an example of a preliminary ruling procedure, *see Central Transformer Corp., Moloney Electric Co. Div.,* 50 LA 927 (Lehoczyky, 1967). *See generally* Fuller, *Collective Bargaining and the Arbitrator,* WIS. L. REV. 3, 13-18 (1963).

[134]*Bakery & Confectionery Workers Local 719 v. National Biscuit Co.,* 378 F.2d 918, 65 LRRM 2482 (3d Cir. 1967) (objection at hearing preserves defense); *Humble Oil & Refining Co. v. Teamsters Local 866,* 271 F. Supp. 281, 65 LRRM 3016 (S.D. N.Y. 1967) (participation in hearing does not bar defense). However, where a party participates in a hearing without raising an arbitrability defense, the party may be barred from subsequently raising the defense in a post-hearing brief (*Ajax Forging and Casting Co.,* 64 LA 1309 (Haughton, 1975)) or in a court action to enforce or vacate the resulting award (*Atomic Uniform Corp. v. ILGWU,* 86 LRRM 2331 (S.D. N.Y. 1973)).

[135]*Phoenix Closures, Inc.,* 49 LA 874 (Sembower, 1967) (proceedings on merits renders defense moot); *City of Meriden,* 48 LA 137 (Summers, 1967) (arbitrator unsure of effect of award upon reviewing court).

[136]Wright, FEDERAL COURTS (St. Paul: West Pub. Co., 1963), p. 244.

CHAPTER VII

Obtaining the Evidence

In modern litigation, court procedures permit wide use of pretrial discovery to compel production of records and witnesses for depositions.[1] In general, evidence obtained from a party during discovery may be used in a trial[2] for any purpose.[3] Depositions of a person not a party may be used only for impeachment[4] if that person is a witness and in certain limited circumstances as testimony where the deponent is unavailable as a witness at the trial.[5]

In arbitration, formal prehearing discovery procedures are very limited. Labor arbitrators are sensitive to the need for cautious discovery in the collective bargaining relationship because of the potentially adverse effect which broad discovery rules could have where parties deal with each other on a daily basis. An awareness of this unique relationship was recognized in this statement of Arbitrator Edgar Jones:

> The needs of the managerial process require a different and more cautious approach than the broad license to probe embodied in the Federal Rules. Furthermore, the constituent nature of a labor union, its political structure, means that discovery without "good cause" shown would be un-

---

[1]Fed. R. Civ. P. 26(b) (*Depositions Pending Action*) provides:
Any party may take the testimony of any person, including a party, by deposition upon oral examination or by written interrogatories, for the purpose of discovery or for the use as evidence or both.
See also id. at 33 (*Interrogatories to Parties*); *id.* at 35 (*Physical and Mental Examination of Persons*); and *id.* at 36 (*Admission of Facts and of Genuineness of Documents*).
[2]Fed. R. Civ. P. 26(d) and Fed. R. Civ. P. 33 provide that the rules of evidence govern admissibility.
[3]*Id.* 26(d) (2).
[4]*Id.* 26(d) (1).
[5]*Id.* 26(d) (3) provides:
The deposition of a witness, whether or not a party, may be used by any party for any purpose if the court finds: 1) that the witness is dead; or 2) that the witness is at a greater distance than 100 miles from the place of trial or hearing, or is out of the United States, unless is appears that the absence of the witness was procured by the party offering the deposition; or 3) that the witness is unable to attend or testify because of age, sickness, infirmity or imprisonment; or 4) that the party offering the deposition has been unable to procure the attendance of the witness by subpoena; or 5) upon application and notice, that such exceptional circumstances exist as to make it desirable, in the interest of justice and with due regard to the importance of presenting the testimony of witnesses orally in open court, to allow the deposition to be used.

wise in those situations in which the union is the object rather than the in-
itiator of discovery remedies. The underlying psychology looks much the
same in either case. A certain amount of inscrutability is needed on each
side for an effective continuing bargaining relationship to function.[6]

This is not to say, however, that discovery is either unknown or unworkable in arbitration. Quite the contrary. A free flow of information
between the parties is needed to enable them to better evaluate their
respective positions and perhaps avoid arbitration altogether. This
chapter will examine such arbitral procedures used to obtain evidence
and the attendant problems which have arisen.

INFORMAL DISCOVERY ENFORCED BY REMANDS TO THE GRIEVANCE PROCEDURE

The grievance procedure moves the grievance up toward arbitration
through a series of discussions, and during these meetings bits of documentary evidence that would not be admissible in a court of law are
exchanged and become part of the grievance procedure evidence:

> Either of the parties may also ... put in various bits of documentary
> evidence that would not be admissible in a court of law—such as doctors'
> certifications as to their treatment of employees for absences or their abil-
> ity to return to work, notices to appear in court, and letters from lawyers,
> collection agencies, and others. In most cases the nonlawyer and even the
> lawyer arbitrator will receive such doubtfully admissible material.... [7]

Perhaps the most common form of arbitral discovery is the informal, through exchanges of information as the grievance claim proceeds through the grievance procedure. This greatly reduces the need
for court-sanctioned discovery procedures in labor arbitration.[8]

Some collective agreements specifically recognize that full exchange
of information on an informal, but complete, basis is important. For
example, the United States Steel Corporation labor agreement with
the United Steelworkers provides:

> At all steps in the grievance procedure, and particularly at the 3rd Step
> and above, the grievant and the Union representative should disclose to
> the Company representatives a full and detailed statement of the facts
> relied upon, the remedy sought, and the provision of the Agreement relied

[6]Jones, *Labor Board, the Courts and Arbitration—A Feasibility Study of Tribunal Interaction in Grievable Refusals to Disclose*, 116 U. PA. L. REV. 1185, 1224 (1968).

[7]Brandschain, *Preparation and Trial of a Labor Arbitration Case*, THE PRACTICAL LAWYER, Vol. 18, No. 7 (Nov. 1972), p. 36.

[8]*See generally* Bernstein and Northrop, *Annotation, Discovery in Aid of Arbitration Proceedings*, 98 A.L.R. 2d 1247 (1963).

upon. In the same manner, company representatives should disclose all the pertinent facts relied upon by the Company.[9]

Only when both sides know all the facts can either be expected to commit itself to an early settlement. As in collective bargaining, a party must know the facts before consenting to be bound. Arbitrator Jones explained the need for free but informal exchange of information in the grievance procedure:

> It is obvious that a major purpose of the usual multi-step grievance procedure is to achieve the earliest possible disclosure of the operative facts of the dispute and the dispositive contractual provisions....
>
> Disclosure is thus a normal characteristic of a properly functioning grievance procedure.... The whole thrust of the grievance procedure is toward early and complete disclosure so that settlement can ensue.[10]

Thus, the parties generally will have obtained knowledge of facts by an informal discovery process prior to the arbitration hearing. If certain required information is not initially available at the hearing, arbitrators frequently suggest "informal" discovery:

> It is quite common for an arbitrator to suggest in the course of the morning, what we might call, rhetorically, "lunchbreak discovery"; "Why don't you dig that out during the lunchbreak and make it available." The parties generally comply and disclosure is routine when the hearing resumes after luncheon.[11]

Arbitrator Gabriel Alexander explained the policy considerations behind informal discovery in grievance processing:

> [S]ound collective bargaining requires frank and candid disclosure at the earliest opportunity of all the facts known to each party. There will undoubtedly be times when facts are not discovered, and therefore not disclosed, until after the grievance has been partially processed, and problem enough is created by those instances. There is not a scintilla of justification for the withholding of information by either party from and after the time it is discovered.[12]

Arbitrators have responded to these considerations, to the extent that the "general rule" is usually stated as being that new evidence or argument will not be admitted at the arbitration hearing unless some

---

[9]Section 6(D)(1), *General Provisions Applying to Grievances,* UNITED STATES STEEL CORP. AND UNITED STEELWORKERS OF AMERICA AGREEMENT (August 1, 1980).

[10]Jones, *The Accretion of Federal Power in Labor Arbitration—The Example of Arbitral Discovery,* 116 U. PA. L. REV. 830, 836 (1968).

[11]*Id.* at 842.

[12]*Decisions of the Impartial Umpire, General Motors Corp.,* No. F-97 (Alexander, 1950). In the General Motors arbitration practice, the arbitrator does not permit evidence to be submitted at the hearing that was not reported to the other side at the second step.

special reason is shown for its not having been brought out before.[13] If the evidence is of a type that should have been exchanged, arbitrators sometimes will remand the case to the grievance procedure for reconsideration in light of the new evidence without the participation of the arbitrator.[14]

These views were reiterated by Arbitrator Bert Luskin when he explained at a *Rockford Clutch Division*[15] arbitration hearing his position concerning information exchange:

> [I]n the grievance procedure, gentlemen, you ought to put all your cards on the table, and both sides should be aware of what the theories of the other are.
>
> I object strongly to the "ace-in-the-sleeve" technique. I think it is wrong. I think it inhibits the grievance procedure....
>
> ... [I]f your grievance procedure is going to work, both sides must know in advance what the other is going to say in arbitration. Both should have been able, in the grievance procedure, to explore the whole thing, and everybody should know what is going to come forward.

When, however, new evidence that a party desires to introduce merely grows out of a deeper investigation prior to the arbitration hearing, the policy of encouraging a free exchange of facts in the lower steps of the procedure is not applicable and arbitrators do not return the case to the grievance procedure.[16]

Although the exchange of information is usually encouraged by arbitrators, some arbitrators have been reluctant to order witnesses to appear for questioning. In *Menasco Mfg. Co.,*[17] the grievant argued that he should be reinstated to work rather than remaining on a medical leave of absence with disability pay. At the third step of the grievance procedure, the company, referring to a contract clause stating that each party should be given the facts by the other before the hearing, asked to have the grievant produced for questioning at the third step. The union representative refused to direct the grievant to

---

[13]Wirtz, *Due Process of Arbitration,* THE ARBITRATOR AND THE PARTIES, Proceedings of the Eleventh Annual Meeting, National Academy of Arbitrators, J. McKelvey, ed. (Washington: BNA Books, 1958), pp. 1, 14, 15.

[14]*Bethlehem Steel Co.,* 18 LA 366 (Feinberg, 1951).

[15]Excerpts from transcript of grievance arbitration, *Rockford Clutch Division and UAW,* September 30, 1971.

[16]*See, e.g., Standard Oil Company (Ohio),* 68-1 ARB ¶ 8305 (Anrod, 1968); *United Parcel Service, Inc.,* 66-2 ARB ¶ 8703 (Dolson, 1966); *Pittsburgh Steel Co.,* XI STEEL ARB ¶ 8131 (McDermott, 1963); *North American Aviation, Inc.,* 17 LA 183 (Komaroff, 1951); *Texas Co.,* 7 LA 75 (Carmichael, 1947); *Bethlehem Steel Co.,* 6 LA 617 (Wyckoff, 1947); *American Steel and Wire Co.,* 5 LA 193 (Blumer, 1946). Wirtz, note 13 *supra,* at 1, 15:

> [U]nless some deliberate attempt to mislead the other party is disclosed, and particularly if the "new" evidence or argument appears substantially material, most arbitrators will be disinclined to rule the matter out of the proceedings.

[17]65-2 ARB ¶ 8834 (Boles, 1965).

attend. Arbitrator Boles did not order that the grievant appear for questioning, stating that at that level of discussion the company representatives already had knowledge of all of the relevant facts. [18]

When the shoe was on the other foot in *Acme Boot Co.* [19] and the union was seeking information, Arbitrator Oppenheim likewise did not order production. The union claimed that the denial of requested information denied "procedural due process" to a union steward discharged following a contract breach strike. The arbitrator said that the company's termination letter gave the grievant the desired information—*i.e.*, that the grievant was being penalized for "participation, leadership, and support of an illegal work stoppage." Moreover, the arbitrator said, everyone was aware that the grievant alone rejected a company request to return to work as a cue for rank-and-file strikers to do the same. Since all information had been disclosed, there could be no doubt in the minds of the union representatives as to why the grievant was singled out for discharge. [20]

THE ARBITRATOR'S AUTHORITY TO ORDER FORMAL DISCOVERY

If the labor agreement is silent on the authority of the arbitrator with respect to discovery, the arbitrator's authority arises (1) from a particular state arbitration act, (2) from the rules of the American Arbitration Association, if the parties have agreed to them, [21] (3) from the

---

[18]*Id.* at 6047.

[19]52 LA 585 (Oppenheim, 1969).

[20]*See, e.g.,* American Arbitration Association, *Voluntary Labor Arbitration Rules,* Rule 28 (1979) which states:

28. **Evidence**—The parties may offer such evidence as they desire and shall produce such additional evidence as the Arbitrator may deem necessary to an understanding and determination of the dispute. When the Arbitrator is authorized by law to subpoena witnesses and documents, he may do so upon his own initiative or upon the request of any party. The Arbitrator shall be the judge of the relevancy and materiality of the evidence offered and conformity to legal rules of evidence shall not be necessary. All evidence shall be taken in the presence of all of the Arbitrators and all of the parties except where any of the parties is absent in default or has waived his right to be present.

[21] See discussion in Chapter I and Jones, note 10 *supra.* The arguments surrounding this problem are premised, in the first instance, by the decision in *NLRB v. Acme Industrial Co.*, 385 U.S. 432, 64 LRRM 2069 (1967) where the Supreme Court upheld a Board decision requiring that information sought by a union from an employer should be made available so that the union could determine whether to grieve. Thus, given the right of discovery, the Court's decision in *UAW v. Hoosier Cardinal Corp.*, 383 U.S. 696, 61 LRRM 2545 (1966) that state statutes of limitation are to govern § 301 actions, indicates that the dichotomy between substance and procedure—*see, e.g., Hannah v. Plumer,* 380 U.S. 460 (1965); *Byrd v. Blue Ridge Rural Electric Co-op, Inc.,* 356 U.S. 525 (1958); *Guaranty Trust Co. of New York v. York,* 326 U.S. 99 (1945); *Erie R. Co. v. Tompkins,* 304 U.S. 64 (1938)—exists under national labor policy and, hence, state law is controlling. It is argued, however, that these state laws are, under *Textile Workers Union v. Lincoln Mills,* 353 U.S. 448, 40 LRRM 2113 (1957), merged into a uniform federal

state statutory discovery procedures on the ground that they are merged into the emerging federal law on labor arbitration,[22] or (4) on an *ad hoc* basis derived from the arbitrator's authority to rule on procedural questions.

Arbitrator Mark Kahn, in *Pennsalt Chemical Corp.*,[23] without relying on any authority other than his right to rule on procedural questions, said that under a labor agreement the union, "by use of grievance procedure and arbitration," has the right to review the company's determination of evaluation points for new or changed jobs and hence the company was obligated to give the union representative the point ratings for each factor of the job involved and the points for other related jobs. He rejected the company's contention that under the labor agreement it was required only to explain to the union representatives the basis for its determination of the evaluation points and did not have to provide the actual number of points:

> Since job evaluation is designed to provide a systematic basis for the establishment of an internal wage structure, the point rating received by a particular job, for each of the factors involved in the plan, can only be appraised intelligently on the basis of the point rating assigned to other jobs for these same five factors under the particular plan in effect.... It would seem to be necessary ... that selected factor point ratings for other jobs in which the respective factors rank close to the factors for the job in dispute be supplied.

Thus, in a federal case,[24] a district court held that under *Wiley*, procedural matters such as discovery, including subpoena of records, were to be decided by the arbitrator.[25]

It is interesting to note that while Arbitrator Kahn would thus appear to have inherent powers to order delivery of substantial infor-

---

law. In *Local Lodge 1746, IAM v. United Aircraft*, 329 F. Supp. 283, 77 LRRM 2596 (D. Conn. 1971) the court enforced a subpoena for the appearance of a witness and production of certain records issued under a state statute on the basis of the authority vested in the court by the U.S. Arbitration Act.

[22]*Teamsters Local 757 v. Borden, Inc.*, 78 LRRM 2398 (S.D. N.Y. 1971); *John Wiley & Sons v. Livingston*, 376 U.S. 543, 555-59, 55 LRRM 2769, 2775-76 (1964); *Great Scott Supermarkets, Inc. v. Local Union No. 337, Teamsters*, 363 F. Supp. 1351, 84 LRRM 2514 (E.D. Mich. 1973). *See generally* Fleming, The Labor Arbitration Process (Ann Arbor: Univ. of Mich. Press, 1965), pp. 170-75; Jones, note 10 *supra.*

[23]AAA Case No. 16-15 (Kahn, 1961).

[24]*Great Scott Supermarkets, Inc. v. Local Union No. 337, Teamsters*, 363 F. Supp. 1351, 84 LRRM 2514 (E.D. Mich. 1973). *See also Teamsters Local 757 v. Borden, Inc.*, 78 LRRM 2398 (S.D. N.Y. 1971), in which a district court ruled that an employer was not required to comply with a subpoena *duces tecum* obtained from a state court.

[25]*Cf. Tappan Co.*, 49 LA 922 (Dworkin, 1967), where the arbitrator held that his authority on procedural matters extended to a determination of the proper form in which relevant data on incentive standards and rates should be submitted to the union, even though another arbitrator had denied the union's contention in a previous grievance and no specific challenge to the incentive rates was presented to this arbitrator.

mation, the more formalized rules such as those of the American Arbitration Association (AAA) do not appear to support a full range of discovery procedures.[26] The following decision involved prehearing discovery under Rule 30 of the AAA Commercial Arbitration Rules; that rule is identical to the parallel rule (No. 28) in the Voluntary AAA Labor Arbitration Rules.[27] A federal district court held that Rule 30 did not give a party the right to take a discovery deposition of the other party:[28]

Respondent urges that it is entitled to avail itself of the discovery rules because, save for the agreement to arbitrate, the federal courts would have jurisdiction of the subject matter of a suit arising out of the controversy between the parties and in such a suit the federal discovery rules would obtain. The argument contains its own answer. By voluntarily becoming a party to a contract in which arbitration was the agreed mode for settling disputes thereunder respondent chose to avail itself of procedures peculiar to the arbitral process rather than those used in judicial determination. "A main object of a voluntary submission to arbitration is the avoidance of formal and technical preparation of a case for the usual procedure of a judicial trial." 1 Wigmore, *Evidence* Section 4(e) (3d ed. 1940). Arbitration may well have advantages but where the converse results a party having chosen to arbitrate cannot then vacillate and successfully urge a preference for a unique combination of litigation and arbitration. . . .

The fundamental differences between the fact-finding process of a judicial tribunal and those of a panel of arbitrators demonstrate the need of pretrial discovery in the one and its superfluity and utter incompatibility in the other.

In addition, the court rejected the argument that Rule 81 (a) (3)[29] of the Federal Rules of Civil Procedure permitted one party to take a formal discovery deposition of the other party to an arbitration proceeding. Similarly, in another commercial case the plaintiff's request for a pre-arbitration discovery deposition under the AAA rules was rejected:

---

[26]The AAA Rules do, however, show the arbitrator as able to "subpoena witnesses and documents" when authorized by state law. *See* note 20 *supra. See also* "The Subpoena of Documents and Other Evidence," *infra,* in this chapter.

[27]*See* note 20 *supra.*

[28]*Commercial Solvents Corp. v. Louisiana Liquid Fertilizer Co.,* 20 F.R.D. 359, 361–362 (S.D. N.Y. 1957).

[29]FED. R. CIV. P. 81(a) (3) provides:

(3) In proceedings under Title 9, U.S.C., relating to arbitration, or under the Act of May 20, 1926, ch. 347, § 9 (44 Stat. 585), U.S.C., Title 45 § 159, relating to boards of arbitration of railway labor disputes, these rules apply only to the extent that matters of procedure are not provided for in those statutes. These rules apply to proceedings to compel the giving of testimony or production of documents in accordance with a subpoena issued by an officer or agency of the United States under any statute of the United States except as otherwise provided by statute or by rules of the district court or by order of the court in the proceedings.

[I]n a proceeding before arbitrators neither the statute [U. S. Arbitration Act] nor the rules make available to any party thereto the discovery procedures provided in the Federal Rules of Civil Procedure.[30]

The Pennsylvania Supreme Court[31] also held that the AAA rules did not permit prehearing discovery, even though the state law did.[32] The parties had submitted a dispute under the AAA Commercial Arbitration Rules and the arbitrator ruled that under those rules a set of interrogatories submitted by one party to the other need not be answered. The court affirmed the ruling of the arbitrator, stating that the arbitrator had properly ruled that the other party "was not entitled to discovery under the arbitration rules." The issue, the court said, was:

[W]hether pretrial discovery or "pre-hearing" discovery under the Procedural Rules is available in an arbitration proceeding instituted in accordance with the provisions of the ... rules of the American Arbitration Association.[33]

The court observed that:

Appellant knew full well that those [AAA] rules did *not* provide for any pretrial discovery as in action at law.[34] [Emphasis added.]

Although noting that the Pennsylvania statute[35] allowed for depositions in arbitration, the court added:

When appellant, by its own contract, agreed to abide by the rules of the American Arbitration Association, it voluntarily surrendered the right to invoke any of the procedural devices which would be available in an action at law. The right to discovery is one of these devices which is not obligatory as an essential of due process to a valid arbitration proceeding.[36]

In a case where the parties had agreed that the rules of the American Arbitration Association would prevail, Arbitrator Albert Epstein, in *AFTRA ex. rel. Howard Miller and Westinghouse Broadcasting*

---

[30]*Foremost Yarn Mills, Inc. v. Rose Mills, Inc.*, 25 F.R.D. 9, 11 (E.D. Pa. 1960). On the other hand, at least one court has held that F.R.C.P. Rule 42(a) authorizing consolidation of actions is applicable to arbitration proceedings. *Robinson v. Warner*, 370 F. Supp. 828 (D. R.I. 1974).

[31]*Harleysville Mutual Casualty Co. v. Adair*, 421 Pa. 141, 218 A.2d 791 (1966).

[32]The AAA rules expressly grant to the arbitrator the power to subpoena documents and witnesses where such power is granted by state law, but the rules do not grant the power to the arbitrator to require prehearing depositions even where such power is granted by state or federal laws to courts. *See* note 20, *supra*.

[33]421 Pa. at 143–44, 218 A.2d at 793.

[34]*Id.* at 144, 218 A.2d at 794.

[35]PA. STAT. ANN. tit. 5, § 167 (1963).

[36]421 Pa. at 145, 218 A.2d at 794.

Co.,[37] denied a request for leave to take a prehearing deposition but did so as an interpretation of the state law:

I am denying the application for leave to take depositions at this time, under the authority vested in me by the terms of Chapter 10, Section 107 of the Illinois Revised Statutes. There has been no showing at this time that the applicant requires depositions for use as evidence relevant to the proceedings, and counsel for the Company has indicated that upon direction by the Arbitrator during the hearing, the witnesses whose depositions are being sought, will be available to testify at the hearing.

Hence, Arbitrator Epstein did not conclude that the AAA rules should be the exclusive source of procedural rights as did the Pennsylvania court, but he nonetheless reached the same conclusion: The use of formal discovery procedures generally is not compatible with the arbitration process.[38]

However, more recent court decisions evidence greater willingness to allow formal discovery in arbitration where exceptional circumstances exist. In *Vespe Contracting Co. v. Anvan Corp.*,[39] a court allowed pre-trial discovery under the Federal Rules of Civil Procedure after granting a stay of court proceedings pending arbitration of the underlying dispute. The court reasoned:

While the court, in making available this additional opportunity for discovery, does not wish to bestow upon plaintiff more rights in the arbitral process than the contract provided for, such action seems appropriate in this case in order to insure that any delay which may occur will not work undue hardship. As progress continues at the construction site, evidence of Vespe's performance of the concrete work is "disappearing" behind the hotel's interior and exterior wall coverings.... In light of the peculiar circumstances here, we think it proper to allow discovery to proceed at this time.[40]

Thus, formal discovery may be provided where speed is necessary.[41]

---

[37]AAA Case No. 51-30-0174-68 (Epstein, 1968).

[38]This incompatibility is seen in a different light in *De Sapio v. Kohlmeyer*, 35 N.Y. 2d 402, 321 N.E.2d 770 (1974), in which a defendant in a damage action was held to have waived his right to arbitration where he procured a deposition of plaintiff.

[39]399 F. Supp. 516 (E.D. Pa. 1975).

[40]399 F. Supp. at 522. For a contrary finding based on the facts presented, *see Levin v. Ripple Twist Mills, Inc.*, 416 F. Supp. 876 (E.D. Pa. 1976).

[41]"Necessity rather than convenience should be the test." *In re Katz*, 160 N.Y.S. 2d 159 (A.D. 1st Dept. 1957). In *Bergen Shipping Co., Ltd. v. Japan Marine Services, Ltd.*, 386 F. Supp. 430 (S.D. N.Y. 1974), the court found the test of necessity met where one party sought to take the depositions of a ship's crew members who were about to be reassigned to vessels leaving the country. Similarly, in *Ferro Union Corp. v. S.S. Ionic Coast*, 43 F.R.D. 11 (S.D. Texas 1967), the court held that exceptional circumstances allowing discovery were present in the fact that the vessel sought to be inspected would be in port for only four days and would thereafter sail for parts unknown.

And one court had held that formal discovery may be had on the threshold issue of arbitrability.[42]

Some cases have gone even further than the "necessity" exception. In a labor arbitration case arising from the Fifth Circuit, *Asbestos Workers Local 166 v. Leona Lee Corp.*,[43] the parties had entered into a settlement agreement resolving two lawsuits and an NLRB proceeding which the union later claimed was breached by the company. The union then brought suit to have the question of the breach resolved under the arbitration clause of the parties' labor agreement. In granting the union's request, the district court also ordered formal discovery:

> To the extent necessary for the presentation of the matter submitted for trade board and arbitration determination, the discovery process of this Court pursuant to the Federal Rules of Civil Procedure shall be available and enforceable in the Court.[44]

The court of appeals in affirming held:

> Also, the District Court did not err when it specifically made available to the parties federal discovery procedures "to the extent necessary for the presentation of matters submitted for Trade Board and Arbitration determination." Such order is consistent with the District Court's retention of jurisdiction and effectuates the policy favoring arbitration.[45]

This is certainly a curious order because there appears to be, from the reported facts, no compelling circumstances to justify resort to formal discovery procedures. How such an order "effectuates the policy favoring arbitration" was not articulated but generally an "over use" of discovery procedures has been seriously questioned in labor arbitration.

However, another court was somewhat more successful in justifying its similar conclusion.[46] While recognizing that discovery in arbitration cases is not favored by the courts, the court noted that the criticism of the lack of discovery in arbitration is a throw-back to the outmoded "sporting theory" of justice:

> Under the principles outlined above, the court believes that it should exercise discretion to permit discovery in this case because (1) discovery is particularly necessary in a case where the claim is for payment for work done and virtually completed, and the nature of any defense is unknown; (2) the

---

[42]*International Union of Electrical, Radio and Machine Workers and Westinghouse Electric Corp.*, 48 F.R.D. 298 (S.D. N.Y. 1969). *But see International Components Corp. v. Klaiber*, 387 N.Y.S.2d 253 (A.D. 1st Dept. 1976).

[43]76 LRRM 2024 (W.D. Tex. 1969), *aff'd*, 434 F.2d 192, 76 LRRM 2026 (5th Cir. 1970).

[44]76 LRRM at 2025.

[45]434 F.2d at 194, 76 LRRM at 2027.

[46]*Bigge Crane and Rigging Co. v. Docutel Corp.*, 371 F. Supp. 240 (E.D. N.Y. 1973).

amounts involved are so substantial that any expense in taking depositions is relatively small; (3) the action has proceeded to such a point that the taking of depositions can probably be accomplished without delaying the arbitration; and (4) only one of the five defendants has joined in the motion to stay the trial.[47]

In any event, the court in *Leona* apparently limits the scope of discovery procedures in terms of relevance and materiality, a standard which has been used *vis-a-vis* subpoenas in labor arbitration.[48] That it is the court, rather than the arbitrator, which determines the issues of relevance and materiality seems at odds with other case law,[49] and is a surprising result emanating from this generally surprising case.

In *IAM Local Lodge 1746 v. United Aircraft Corp.*,[50] a federal district court had to determine whether an arbitrator, at the request of the union, had the power to deliver to the union certain investigation records in connection with a discharge case and to subpoena a company official to the hearing. The court ruled that under the U.S. Arbitration Act[51] the court had the authority to enforce a subpoena of a witness and deliver records even though the subpoena had been issued under a state law. The court, however, put limitations on the process:

> This Federal Court does have concurrent enforcement jurisdiction and possesses the necessary statutory authority (9 U.S.C. § 7) to enforce the procedures attendant upon the orderly consummation of this arbitration hearing.... Under this aegis, it will act *sua sponte* to sever the Gordian knot which created the impasse. The defendant shall produce forthwith the disputed file material for an *in camera* inspection by the arbitrator.
>
> Such a procedure will, of course, deny to the plaintiff-Union its claim of a *carte blanche* discovery privilege, to peruse the employer's file....
> . . .
> It must be assumed that the presiding arbitrator is an experienced person well versed in evaluating the alleged claims of the employer, that some files contain classified security information involving national defense or plant security, personal health records and other similar confidential data. All of this should be screened from the file, except where the arbitrator determines it to be relevant evidence in the dispute. Even in the latter instances, proper safeguards should be ordered, such as sealing the record or limiting its access to counsel only, so that no unnecessary harm or prejudice or unnecessary embarrassment may be caused to anyone.

---

[47]*Id.* at 245, 246. Note the court's confusion of "particular" necessity with ordinary lack of information. One district court in the Fifth Circuit thought so little of *Bigge* and *Leona* that it refused to follow them even though the *Leona* case was presumably controlling precedent in that court. *See Mississippi Power Co. v. Peabody Coal Co.*, 69 F.R.D. 558 (S.D. Miss. 1976).

[48]*See, e.g., IAM Local Lodge 1746 v. United Aircraft Corp.*, 329 F. Supp. 283, 77 LRRM 2596 (D. Conn. 1971); *Teamsters Local 757 v. Borden, Inc.*, 78 LRRM 2398 (S.D. N.Y. 1971).

[49]*Id.*

[50]329 F. Supp. 283, 77 LRRM 2596 (D. Conn. 1971).

[51]9 U.S.C. § 7 (1970).

"Once it is determined, as we have, that the parties are obligated to submit the subject matter of a dispute to arbitration, procedural questions
which grow out of the dispute and bear on its final deposition should be
left to the arbitrator." John Wiley and Sons, Inc. v. Livingston, 376 U.S.
543, 557, 84 S. Ct. 909, 918, 11 L.Ed.2d 898, aff'g 313 F.2d 52, 52
LRRM 2223 (2d Cir. 1964).[52]

Another federal court reached a contrary result in a case involving a
state-issued subpoena *duces tecum*.[53] In denying enforcement of the
state-issued subpoena, however, the court, as did the court in *United
Aircraft*, recognized the primary role of the arbitrator in determining
such disputes.

In this latter case, after a court had ordered Borden, Inc.[54] to arbitrate disputes arising out of the closing of a manufacturing facility,
the union informally demanded of Borden certain books and records.
Production was refused and the union asked the arbitrator to issue a
subpoena to compel their production. Before acting on the request,
the arbitrator took the matter under advisement to determine the relevancy of the requested documents. The union then asked a state court
to issue a subpoena pursuant to state statute. Borden then had the
case removed to a federal district court. That court held that it was up
to the arbitrator to issue the subpoena if the arbitrator determined
that the documents asked for would be relevant. The court explained
that the arbitrator derives the necessary power not from the state statute or from the U.S. Arbitration Act, but from the emerging federal
law developing under Section 301. The court held:

> It is § 301 itself which mandates the application of federal law to this
> case. In *Textile Workers Union of America v. Lincoln Mills*, 353 U.S. 448,
> 40 LRRM 2113 (1957), the Court made abundantly clear the principle that
> federal law is to govern the enforcement of collective bargaining agree-
> ments pursuant to § 301...
>
> Given the applicability of federal law, we now turn to a clear and consis-
> tent line of federal cases holding that it is, at least in the first instance, the
> duty of the arbitrator to make procedural decisions in the course of an ar-
> bitration....
>
> . . .
>
> The arbitrator in this action has already devoted time and energy to the
> resolution of this dispute. In so doing he has become familiar with the
> substantive issues in the case and, under the Labor Management Relations
> Act and the decisions which have construed it, it is properly his function to
> determine the relevancy and materiality of the documents requested and

[52]329 F. Supp. at 286-87.
[53]*Teamsters Local 757 v. Borden, Inc.*, 78 LRRM 2398 (S.D. N.Y. 1971).
[54]*Ice Cream Drivers and Employees Union Local 757 v. Borden, Inc.*, 312 F. Supp. 549, 74
LRRM 3020 (S.D. N.Y. 1970), *aff'd*, 433 F.2d 41, 75 LRRM 2481 (2d Cir. 1970).

whether production should be ordered. The intervention of this court sought by the applicant here *in medias res* can only serve to impair the integrity of the arbitration process.[55]

It should be noted that the American Arbitration Rules are, of course, binding on the arbitrator only if they are made applicable by the labor agreement.[56] Nevertheless, these limited rules reflect the notion that arbitration is a quite different forum from a court with respect to discovery—a notion that a growth of formal prehearing discovery procedures might chill the free flow of information that now operates in the grievance procedure itself. It should be emphasized that while court litigation is often the terminal point of a relationship between parties, arbitration is only a part of a continuing collective bargaining relationship. Arbitration may indeed be an adversary proceeding, but it is one where the adversaries must keep a watchful eye lest they, by overformalism, endanger the parties' larger relationship.[57]

A body of federal law and rules which has a bearing on arbitral discovery includes a section of the United States Arbitration Act, 29 U.S.C.A.

---

[55]78 LRRM at 2399-2400.

[56]In *Penn Tanker Co. of Delaware v. C.H.Z. Rolimplex, Warszawa,* 199 F. Supp. 716 (S.D. N.Y. 1961), discovery procedures by oral depositions and written interrogatories were held inappropriate in arbitration proceedings commenced under the U.S. Arbitration Act:

It is true that in *Commercial Solvents* it does not appear that there was any proceeding instituted under 9 U.S.C. § 8, as there is here, with the Court retaining jurisdiction to direct arbitration. But this would not seem to change the basic policy considerations. The purpose of 9 U.S.C. § 8 is "to allow an aggrieved party the benefit of security obtained by attachment." ... Thus, in *Empresa Maritima de Transportes, S.A. v. Transatlantic and Pacific Corp.,* Admiralty No. 197-220 (S.D. N.Y. 1959), a libel had also been commenced under 9 U.S.C. § 8. Thereafter, libelant sought to use discovery and inspection procedure otherwise available in admiralty proceedings. In denying the motion, this Court made clear that a party who elects to arbitrate may not simultaneously invoke the discovery procedure of this Court....

...

Title 9 does not deal in terms with discovery although sections thereof do deal with "matters of procedure"; *e.g.,* §§ 4 and 7. An argument could be made that the Federal Rules should be applied to proceedings under Title 9 to the extent to which they are mutually consistent. It may be that there is a limited area for application of discovery procedures to proceedings under Title 9; *e.g.,* on the issue of whether there was an agreement to arbitrate which the Court must decide under § 4 before directing the parties to proceed to arbitration.... But I do not think that Rule 81(a) (3) is designed to allow judicially imposed and controlled discovery as to the merits of a controversy which will be referred to arbitration under 9 U.S.C. § 4, except, perhaps, upon a showing of true necessity because of an exceptional situation—which this case does not appear to be. [Citations omitted.]

[57]In *Kallus v. Ideal Novelty and Toy Co.,* 45 N.Y.S. 2d 554 (Sup. Ct. 1943), the court denied petitioner's request for pretrial deposition on the basis that such a pretrial examination of witnesses is "utterly incompatible with arbitration." In *Stiller Fabrics v. Michael Saphier Assoc.,* 148 N.Y.S.2d 591 (Sup. Ct. 1956), the court denied a request for leave to conduct a prehearing examination, saying that such pretrial procedures are not compatible with "the whole purpose and methods of procedure in arbitration." *See also In re Katz,* 3 App. Div.2d 238, 160 N.Y.S.2d 159 (1957); *In re Schwartz,* 127 Misc. 452, 217 N.Y.S. 233 (Sup. Ct. 1925). In another case, the use of discovery in arbitration proceedings about to be commenced under

§ 7, which grants the arbitrator the right to summon any person as witness and compel that person to produce any material document, record, book, or paper; and Section 301 of the Labor Management Relations Act, 29 U.S.C.A. § 185, which states that a suit for violation of a collective bargaining agreement may be brought in federal district court without respect to amount or regard to diversity of citizenship.

DEPOSITIONS USED AS EVIDENCE

Section 7(b) of the Uniform Arbitration Act[58] provides:

(b) On application of a party and for use as evidence, the arbitrators may permit a deposition to be taken, in the manner and upon the terms designated by the arbitrators, of a witness who cannot be subpoenaed or is unable to attend the hearing.

Thus, this authority would permit an arbitrator to grant an application[59] for the taking of evidentiary depositions of witnesses. An evidentiary deposition, in contrast to a discovery deposition,[60] is taken to preserve evidence and is only permitted after it has been shown a necessary procedure and that the evidence sought is relevant. To this extent, it is compatible with effective grievance procedures and practices, and hence is also compatible with the "emerging federal law."

That the arbitrator may require a showing of the relevancy of the evidence sought is illustrated by a commerical arbitration case where an application to take depositions to preserve evidence was denied because there was no showing of the relevance of the evidence:[61]

The arbitrators ruled that before they would allow the issuance of commissions to take such depositions, appellant would have to submit some *prima*

---

the rules of the New York Stock Exchange was denied on the ground it would handicap those proceedings. The Massachusetts court stated:

We also feel that arbitration, once undertaken, should continue freely without being subjected to a judicial restraint which would tend to render the proceedings neither one thing nor the other, but transform them into a hybrid, part judicial and part arbitrational. We also might add that it seems somewhat incongruous to resort to judicial help for pre-hearing discovery after a voluntary understanding had left the entire matter to the determination of arbitrators.

Cavanaugh v. McConnell & Co., 357 Mass. 452, 258 N.E.2d 561 (1970). *But see, e.g., Bigge Crane and Rigging Co. v. Docutel Corp.,* 371 F. Supp. 240 (E.D. N.Y. 1973).

[58]UNIFORM ARBITRATION ACT § 7(b); *see, e.g.,* PA. STAT. ANN. tit. 5, § 167 (1963).

[59]Unlike federal practice, the party must obtain leave of the presiding authority (the arbitrator) before taking a deposition. *See* FED. R. CIV. P. 26(d) (3), note 5 *supra,* which operates after the deposition has been taken.

[60]For an example explaining the difference, *see* Illinois Supreme Court Rules 202 and 212, ILL. REV. STAT. ch. 110A §§ 202 and 212 (1971).

[61]*Kemikalija Import-Export v. Associated Metals and Minerals Corp.,* 19 App. Div. 2d 868, 244 N.Y.S.2d 115, 116 (1963).

facie proof of the existence of [the relevant information sought] a sufficient showing to warrant the taking of depositions. Until it did so, the materiality and relevance of the proposed testimony would not be established.

THE SUBPOENA OF DOCUMENTS AND OTHER EVIDENCE

Occasionally during an arbitration proceeding, evidence essential to a party's case requires a subpoena to bring it before the arbitrator either in documentary form or in the person of a recalcitrant witness.[62] Many states have statutes allowing the arbitrator to require the production of specified documents or the attendance of specified persons as witnesses.[63] If the arbitrator's request is ignored, enforcement is then available through the courts, not as an enforcement of subpoena powers created by the state statute or by the U.S. Arbitration Act, but as an enforcement of the arbitrator's power to compel production of material evidence under Section 301.[64]

Although federal labor law has largely preempted state labor law, some states have modern arbitration acts which generally are applicable to labor, as well as commercial arbitration. By far the most modern and important of these is the Uniform Arbitration Act. About a dozen states have adopted this Act with relatively little modification. Section 7 of this Act provides that arbitrators may issue subpoenas for

---

[62]The UNIFORM ARBITRATION ACT, § 7, for example, provides:

§ 7. Witnesses, Subpoenas, Depositions.

(a) The arbitrators may issue (cause to be issued) subpoenas for the attendance of witnesses and for the production of books, records, documents and other evidence, and shall have the power to administer oaths. Subpoenas so issued shall be served, and upon application to the Court by a party or the arbitrators, enforced, in the manner provided by law for the service and enforcement of subpoenas in a civil action.

(b) On application of a party and for use as evidence, the arbitrators may permit a deposition to be taken, in the manner and upon the terms designated by the arbitrators, or a witness who cannot be subpoenaed or is unable to attend the hearing.

(c) All provisions of law compelling a person under subpoena to testify are applicable.

(d) Fees for attendance as a witness shall be the same as for a witness in the ... Court.

[63]Indiana [IND. ANN. STAT. §§ 3-227 to 3-248 (Supp. 1970)]; Maine [ME. REV. STAT. ANN. tit. 14 §§ 14-5927 to 14-5949 (Supp. 1970)]; Maryland [MD. ANN. CODE art. 7, §§ 1 to 23 (1968)]; Massachusetts [MASS. ANN. LAWS ch. 1500, §§ 1 to 16 (1965)]; Minnesota [MINN. STAT. ANN. §§ 572.08 to 572.30 (Supp. 1970)]; Wyoming [WYO. STAT. ANN. §§ 1-1048.1 to 1-1048.21 (Supp. 1969)]. For other state statutes permitting use of subpoenas, see CAL. CIV. PROC. CODE § 1282.6 (West, Supp. 1965); N.Y. CIV. PRAC. § 7505 (McKinney, 1963); PA. STAT. ANN. tit. 5, § 166 (1963).

[64]See *Teamsters Local 757 v. Borden, Inc.,* 78 LRRM 2398 (S.D. N.Y. 1971); *Great Scott Supermarkets, Inc. v. Local U. No. 337, Teamsters,* 363 F. Supp. 1351, 84 LRRM 2514 (E.D. Mich. 1973). Crucial to the arbitrator's § 301 power, of course, is the existence of an agreement to arbitrate. Thus, in *University of California,* 63 LA 314 (Jacobs, 1974), the arbitrator rescinded a subpoena *duces tecum* on the ground that the grievance procedure leading to arbitration was a unilateral undertaking by the employer and not the result of a mutual agreement.

the attendance of witnesses and for the production of books, records, documents, and other evidence.[65]

Only three states have modified the Uniform Arbitration Act to any real degree when the state statutes were adopted. For example, Indiana provides that an arbitrator cannot subpoena financial data; Texas specifically permits the arbitrator to authorize depositions of adverse witnesses for discovery purposes because all discovery provisions available in court are available to the parties in arbitration. Does the federal labor law preempt the variations of the Uniform Arbitration Act?[66] There are no decisions on this question. *UAW v. Hoosier Cardinal Corp.,*[67] however, is worth consideration. In that decision the U. S. Supreme Court applied a state statute of limitations to a suit brought under Section 301 of the LMRA. The Court declined to create a uniform rule on the basis that "The need for uniformity, then, is greatest where its absence would threaten the smooth functioning of those consensual processes that federal labor law is chiefly designed to promote—the formation of the collective agreement and the private settlement of disputes under it."[68] Whether the Court would hold that state court discovery procedures for Texas, for example, would "threaten the smooth functioning" is impossible to say. The Court could find that Section 7 of the Uniform Arbitration Act encourages the smooth functioning of the grievance procedure; it must be noted, however, that the Court has a long history of deferring to state statutes of limitations in the absence of a federal statute.

The normal process for the exchange of information commences with the requirement that the party seeking the information make a written demand on the other. If the party with the information refuses to disclose it, the requesting party would apply to the arbitrator for an order compelling disclosure, detailing the information sought and a description of the records or witnesses necessary to obtain the information. The requesting party would thereupon have to show good cause. The withholding party could, if it chooses, present arguments to show the lack of good cause.

Although not used extensively at present, a pre-hearing conference could be used to resolve various requests for information. At this conference the parties would present to the arbitrator basic information concerning the case and the lingering discovery problems that must be

---

[65]*See* note 62 *supra.*

[66]The limitations being imposed on information delivery by the Privacy Act are in sharp contrast to the OSHA regulations which require employers to provide union representatives (1) employee medical records, (2) data on toxic or harmful substances, and (3) analytical medical and engineering reports based on such records or data. OSHA Regulation, 29 C.F.R. § 1910.20.

[67]383 U.S. 696, 61 LRRM 2545 (1966).

[68]*Id.* at 702, 61 LRRM at 2548.

resolved by the arbitrator. The arbitrator could also help the parties frame the issue if they have not yet explored the possibilities for settlement. Professor R. W. Fleming[69] suggested that new or apprentice arbitrators be used to conduct pre-hearing conferences if needed. They might be paid a lower *per diem* fee and work under the supervision of an experienced arbitrator. This would have the dual effect of relieving pressure on the experienced arbitrator, plus giving new arbitrators an opportunity to obtain experience and to be exposed to the parties who are often involved in arbitrations.

If the request for production of books is considered too broad by the arbitrator and/or the courts, the subpoena scope may be restricted.[70] Arbitrator Jules Justin, for example, refused in *I. Hirst Enterprises, Inc.,*[71] to grant a request for any part of the subpoena *duces tecum* because the purpose was either a fishing expedition or a harassment. In *C.&P. Telephone Co. of W. Va.,*[72] Arbitrator Dworkin interpreted the scope of an arbitrator's subpoena power under Rule 28 of the American Arbitration Association Rules:

> A party may at any time prior to the conclusion of the hearing make a written request to the arbitrator for the production, disclosure and inspection of specific documents and other writings in possession and control of a party to the dispute, which request may be granted by such arbitrator if he determines that the request is proper and that the information requested is relevant and material to the issues in dispute.[73]

Arbitrator Dworkin did grant the union's subpoena request, but limited the scope:

> [I]t should extend only to such documents and writings which appear to be relevant and pertinent to the issues presented for ultimate determination. The exercise of the arbitrator's authority should be reasonable, and the party is entitled to be protected against "fishing expeditions" and the examination of files and records which may not be considered as being pertinent. . . .
>
> Accordingly, the request for the disclosure of the employment application is denied, as is the request for the reports of the supervisors on the ground that such records would not be of any probative value, and would involve the disclosure of confidential reports, including personal opinions. . . .[74]

---

[69]Fleming, THE LABOR ARBITRATION PROCESS (Ann Arbor: Univ. of Mich. Press, 1965).

[70]*Local 99, ILGWU v. Clarise Sportswear Co.,* 44 Misc.2d 913, 255 N.Y.S.2d 282 (Sup. Ct. 1964). There it was held that the union's right to investigate payroll records and cash disbursements of employer "pertaining to employees" did not give the arbitrator authority to issue a subpoena to produce books and records for information as to merchandise manufactured.

[71]24 LA 444–47 (Justin, 1954).

[72]21 LA 367 (Dworkin, 1953).

[73]*Id.* at 371.

[74]*Id.*

In *Automatic Electric Co.*[75] the dispute concerned incentive rates. The union sought advance data concerning allowances for personal needs, fatigue or rest. Arbitrator Sembower held the request had sufficient particularity and materiality to overrule the employer's motion to quash a subpoena *duces tecum* issued pursuant to the Illinois statute, saying that the statutory requirement of "precise designation" had been met and that the request was not a "dragnet" or "shotgun" request for records.[76]

In *Milliken Woolens v. Weber Knit Sportswear,*[77] the arbitrator had issued a subpoena for production of certain books and records but later concluded that the subpoenaed books and records were not material or relevant and modified their order so the production was not required. The court said:

> It is elementary that "mere refusal to receive evidence is not sufficient to vacate; the evidence excluded must be shown to be clearly relevant to the disputed issue.[78]

DISCOVERY UNDER SECTION 8(a)(5) OF THE NLRA

Although informal discovery as a case proceeds up through the grievance procedure is widespread, cases do arise where disclosure of information is refused by either the company or the union. Discovery has been limited by courts for policy reasons (explained in "The Arbitrator's Authority To Order Formal Discovery" in this chapter, *supra*) but is less limited when discovery is sought under the National Labor Relations Act by the filing of a Section 8(a)(5) charge.

In *NLRB v. Acme Industrial Co.,*[79] the Supreme Court upheld an NLRB decision ordering an employer to supply information to the union because it was needed to evaluate the requested facts to determine whether or not certain arbitrable grievances did exist. The court established a "discovery-type standard"—"The probability that the desired information was relevant"[80]—and held that it was proper for the Board to make a "threshold determination of the potential

---

[75]42 LA 1056 (Sembower, 1964).

[76]*Id. See also Food Employer Council, Inc.,* 197 NLRB No. 98, 80 LRRM 1440 (1972), where the Board laid down guidelines within the boundaries of good faith and common sense to be followed in giving the union the information requested.

[77]20 Misc.2d 504, 192 N.Y.S.2d 408 (Sup. Ct. 1959); *but see Heck Elevator Maintenance, Inc.,* 197 NLRB No. 20, 80 LRRM 1448 (1972), where the Board held that a union was entitled to request information about a company's relationships to and arrangements with a second company so the union could determine whether it should pursue grievances over the alleged performance of contract work by nonmember employees of this second employer.

[78]20 Misc.2d at 506, 192 N.Y.S.2d at 411 (citations omitted).

[79]385 U.S. 432, 64 LRRM 2069 (1967).

[80]*Id.* at 437, 64 LRRM at 2071.

relevance"[81] of the data and order delivery of the data if it was relevant. Standards set out in *Acme Industrial* are now examined by the NLRB in demand-for-disclosure cases.[82] A ruling that a disclosure of data should be made is not a determination by the Board on the merits of the dispute, as one court noted:

> In ordering the employer to furnish requested information under [the *Acme Industrial* standards], the Board does not make a binding construction of the contract but leaves the question of definite and detailed interpretation to the parties' grievance machinery or to the arbitrator.[83]

At least one court prior to *Acme Industrial* held that the NLRB may not determine whether the employer's refusal to furnish economic data to the union constituted bargaining in bad faith where that determination would require a decision on the merits of an arbitrable grievance. The court said:

> Where the parties have prescribed a voluntary grievance procedure for settlement of such controversies, courts are to (a) enforce them fully and (b) stay out of the determination of the intrinsic merits under the guise of determining arbitrability.... The courthouse ... is not the place to work out industrial disputes when arbitration has been prescribed and is available.[84]

Unfortunately, these disclosure disputes are not usually disposed of in an expeditious manner. They are raised in an 8(a)(5) charge proceeding and hence thwart the entire grievance arbitration information exchange process, which was designed to put emphasis on prompt settlements. Arbitrator Jones persuasively argues that the NLRB disclosure procedure is too slow, too expensive, and too cumbersome:

---

[81]*Id. See also NLRB v. Rockwell-Standard Corp.*, 410 F.2d 953, 71 LRRM 2328 (6th Cir. 1969).

[82]*See, e.g., United States Steel Corp.*, 178 NLRB 444, 73 LRRM 1137 (1969); *P.R. Mallory & Co.*, 171 NLRB 457, 68 LRRM 1097 (1968), *enforced sub nom. P.R. Mallory & Co. v. NLRB*, 411 F.2d 948, 71 LRRM 2412 (7th Cir. 1969). *See also IT&T Corp. v. NLRB*, 382 F.2d 366, 65 LRRM 3002 (3d Cir. 1967); *American Oil Co.*, 164 NLRB 29, 65 LRRM 1022 (1967), where blanket requests for information were denied enforcement.

[83]*P.R. Mallory & Co. v. NLRB*, 411 F.2d 948, 954, 71 LRRM 2412, 2416 (7th Cir. 1969). In *Fafnir Bearing Co. v. NLRB*, 362 F.2d 716, 62 LRRM 2415 (2d Cir. 1966) the court held that where the labor contract was silent, the union had a right to have its timestudy expert make a study of an incentive rate involved in a grievance.

[84]*Sinclair Refining Co. v. NLRB*, 306 F.2d 569, 50 LRRM 2830 (5th Cir. 1962). In *Timken Roller Bearing v. NLRB*, 325 F.2d 746, 752–53, 54 LRRM 2785, 2791 (6th Cir. 1963), the Sixth Circuit distinguished *Sinclair* on the grounds that in the latter, the cease-and-desist order was not enforced because the ordered action was not within the subject matter of the collective bargaining agreement, whereas in *Timken* the ordered action was explicitly a part of the collective bargaining agreement. Therefore, the court enforced the Board's order. In *IAM v. United Aircraft Corp.*, 337 F.2d 5, 10 n. 4, 57 LRRM 2245, 2249 (2d Cir. 1964), a case concerned with an attempt to preclude resort to the NLRB through limitations on the right to arbitrate, the Second Circuit said the *Sinclair* case "concerned a dispute over the relevance of information sought by the Union, and not a waiver of the Union's right to admittedly relevant information."

[T]he Board ... simply does not have at its disposal the remedy of discovery.[85]

He proposes that the Board refrain from using Section 8(a)(5) as a discovery procedure in connection with grievance arbitrations and states that arbitrators should have the authority to approve prehearing discovery procedures, thus shifting such procedure back from the NLRB to the arbitrator and speeding up the arbitration process now being slowed down when the Board discovery process is used.

The arbitrator cannot, by using a loose relevancy standard, direct a company to deliver any and all information specifically requested. The Second Circuit said that an employer is not required to furnish any and all information which the union thinks might be "helpful" in processing grievances[86] but in balance the Fourth Circuit said that the employer must furnish information which is relevant to the processing of a grievance.[87] Wage and other information relating to terms and conditions of employment for employees in the bargaining unit is information that has been held to be presumptively relevant.[88]

Cases in which no Section 8(a)(5) violation has been found as far as relevant information is concerned generally reveal an interplay of three factors: (1) the employer had *bona fide* objections to providing the information in the precise form requested,[89] (2) the employer attempted to accommodate the union by providing information in a mutually satisfactory form,[90] and (3) the union unreasonably resisted the employer's attempts to agree on a mutually satisfactory arrangement.[91]

The Board developed a *per se* approach to a company's refusal to disclose "relevant data," and the Second Circuit[92] enforced the Board's finding. Such cases have been the springboard for discovery orders where information is requested by the union. Cases in this area are grounded by a single principle: a union must have access to sufficient information to enable it to "intelligently" represent the employees for whom it acts as exclusive bargaining representative. The

[85]Jones, note 10 *supra*, at 1196, 1211–18.
[86]*Puerto Rico Telephone Co. v. NLRB*, 359 F.2d 983, 62 LRRM 2069 (1966).
[87]*NLRB v. Whitin Machine Works*, 217 F.2d 593, 35 LRRM 2215 (4th Cir. 1954), *cert. denied*, 349 U.S. 905, 35 LRRM 2730 (1955).
[88]*Curtiss-Wright Corp., Wright Aeronautical Division v. NLRB*, 347 F.2d 61, 59 LRRM 2433 (3rd Cir. 1965).
[89]*Westinghouse Electric Corp.*, 129 NLRB 850, 47 LRRM 1072 (1960).
[90]*Shell Oil Co. v. NLRB*, 457 F.2d 615, 79 LRRM 2997 (9th Cir. 1972).
[91]*Emeryville Research Center, Shell Department Co. v. NLRB*, 441 F.2d 880, 77 LRRM 2043 (9th Cir. 1971).
[92]*NLRB v. Yawman & Erbe Mfg. Co.*, 187 F.2d 947, 27 LRRM 2524 (2d Cir. 1951).

Board related the standard of relevance established in modern codes—a legal standard. The Second Circuit stated:[93]

> The rule governing disclosure of data of this kind is not unlike that prevailing in discovery procedures under modern codes. There the information must be disclosed unless it plainly appears irrelevant. . . .

The collection of relevant information tends to be more limited in *ad hoc* arbitration procedures because a specific grievance must start through the grievance procedure before a request for information is filed with the employer and then, if the information is not delivered, the request is presented to the arbitrator *after his or her selection.* Refusal to deliver requested information after the arbitrator directs delivery would support a Section 8(a)(5) charge, but using this route for enforcement *after the arbitrator has been selected* would make use of the Board's procedures even slower than moving the arbitration order up to the federal court for enforcement with or without modification. Since a permanent umpire supervises the grievance handling process, in some multiplant situations, it is sometimes possible to request the umpire to direct the company to deliver information to the union which could be considered relevant to *future* grievances and use this information to develop grievances. In *Westinghouse*[94] and *East Dayton Tool*[95] the Board held that the employers violated Section 8(a)(5) of the Act by refusing to provide, at the union's request, a wide variety of information relating to fair employment practices.

In *Westinghouse,* the union asked for (1) a wide array of statistical data specifiying the race, sex and national origin of employees, broken down by labor grade, classification and wage rate, whether day work or incentive, seniority statute, the number of new hires in each classification, and the number of promotions; (2) all state and federal Equal Employment Opportunity (EEO) charges and complaints filed against the company; and (3) affirmative action plans and accompanying work force analyses.[96] The company argued that the disclosure request should be limited because of the nature of the charges, com-

---

[93]*Id. See also Boston Herald-Traveler Corp.,* 110 NLRB 2097, 35 LRRM 1309 (1954), enforced, 223 F.2d 58, 36 LRRM 2220 (1st Cir. 1955); *Curtiss-Wright Corp., Wright Aeronautical Division v. NLRB,* 347 F.2d 61, 59 LRRM 2433 (3d Cir. 1965); *Texaco, Inc. v. NLRB,* 407 F.2d 754, 70 LRRM 2728 (7th Cir. 1969). There is no requirement that the union first conduct an independent investigation before seeking to obtain the information from the employer. *AMCAR Division, ACF Industries,* 231 NLRB 83, 96 LRRM 1291 (1977). Finally, even the employer's good-faith belief that it is not legally required to produce the information requested will not preclude a finding of an 8(a)(5) violation. *Emeryville Research Center, Shell Development Co. v. NLRB,* 441 F.2d 880, 77 LRRM 2043 (9th Cir. 1971).

[94]239 NLRB No. 19, 99 LRRM 1482 (1978).

[95]239 NLRB No. 20, 99 LRRM 1499 (1978).

[96]Reverse Freedom of Information Act (FOIA) Orders and their effect on arbitration are discussed in the next section in this chapter.

plaints and the confidentiality guarantees in Title VII[97] and in the Equal Employment Opportunity Commission (EEOC) regulations.[98] The majority of the Board[99] rejected these contentions, noting that the confidential provisions are binding only on information accumulated by the government agencies and does not prevent orders disclosing the same information from one private party to another. Accordingly, the Board ordered disclosure of all complaints and charges after the identities of the charging parties were deleted. The minority of the Board said the majority's analysis was weak because the disclosure order required the company to deliver information prepared for the EEOC which the EEOC could not deliver to the Board.

In the *East Dayton Tool* case the union sought applicant flow, hire data, and insurance information to establish discrimination claims that the company had employed too few blacks and women. The Board issued an order delivering the information on the number of minorities and females, but denied copies of the master insurance plans. The majority of the Board concluded that information on applicant flow and hire data was relevant to the union's effort to eliminate discriminatory hiring practices. The Board also held that the union was entitled to the information before discrimination grievances were filed and even though the underlying subject—hiring practices—was not a mandatory subject of collective bargaining and hence not a subject for a grievance.[100] However, the Board majority did agree that the union was not entitled to copies of the affirmative action plans and work force analyses because the documents contained confidential and commercial information and because the disclosure would contravene the confidentiality policy of the Office of Federal Contract Compliance Programs. In addition, the majority of the Board concluded that the goals and timetables were not necessary to enable the union to administer the labor agreement. Since the NLRB did not order disclosure of the affirmative action plans, work force analyses, projections, goals, and timetables, the Board decision did not face the claim that such requests would violate the Trade Secrets Act.[101] The Board's view, expressed in *East Dayton* and *Westinghouse,* suggests that information prepared by a company at the request of the EEOC could be obtained by the union directly from the company by a Board

[97]42 U.S.C. §§ 2000e-8(e).
[98]29 C.F.R. § 1601.20.
[99]Member Murphy did not even address the issue of relevance, choosing to dissent on the issue of confidentiality alone. She contended that confidentiality of the identity of charging parties could not be assured merely by deleting names from the text of the charge.
[100]*Tanner Motor Livery, Ltd.,* 148 NLRB 1402, 1404, 57 LRRM 1170 (1964), *enforcement denied on other grounds,* 419 F.2d 216, 72 LRRM 2866 (9th Cir. 1969).
[101]18 U.S.C. § 1905.

order, even though it was prepared and delivered to the Commission on the understanding that the information was confidential.

Later, the Supreme Court in *Detroit Edison v. NLRB*[102] further limited the breadth of information standard first set up in *Acme Industrial*.[103] In *Detroit Edison* the company had set up and validated some aptitude tests to screen out applicants for the job classification of "Instrument Man B"; applicants who took the test had been advised that their test scores would remain confidential. Ten bargaining unit employees applied for Instrument Man B openings but none of them were selected, and non-unit applicants were then hired. The union filed grievances on behalf of the ten and asked for the test scores. The employer refused to release them because they were considered confidential and the NLRB held that the refusal was a violation of Section 8(a)(5).[104] The Supreme Court, however, held that this order by the Board was an abuse of its "arguably relevant" remedial discretion. Quite significantly, the Court also emphasized that a union's bare assertion that it needs information that might be helpful to form or process a grievance does not automatically oblige the employer to supply it.

To illustrate the increased limitations on information delivery which are affecting arbitration, the NLRB dismissed unfair labor practice charges filed by the union in *Anheuser-Busch, Inc.*[105] In this case the union asked for some written witness statements prepared by the company in connection with its suspension of a grievant who had been involved in a number of altercations and who used some "threatening and abusive" language reported in the statements. The company refused to provide the statements to the union because those who signed statements had been assured their names would not be disclosed before the hearing, to avoid possible harassment.

FREEDOM OF INFORMATION ACT LIMITATIONS

The Freedom of Information Act (FOIA) amendments, as modified by the Sunshine Act,[106] made more documents available to the public.

---

[102]440 U.S. 301, 100 LRRM 2728 (1979). The NLRB's general counsel has issued a memorandum (No. 79-22) outlining expanded investigation procedures applicable in cases where the charged party contends that relevant information is confidential, sensitive, or otherwise privileged. Although the memorandum opines that *Detroit Edison* "may ultimately be confined to its precise facts," the general counsel does not accept its rationale as requiring more extensive investigation into similar cases in the future.

[103]385 U.S. 432, 64 LRRM 2069 (1967).

[104]*Detroit Edison*, 218 NLRB 1024, 89 LRRM 1515, *enforced sub nom. NLRB v. Detroit Edison Co.*, 560 F.2d 722, 95 LRRM 3341 (6th Cir. 1977).

[105]237 NLRB No. 146, 99 LRRM 1174 (1978); *see also C & P Telephone Co. v. NLRB*, 687 F.2d 633, 111 LRRM 2165 (2d Cir. 1982).

[106]Pub. L. 94-409, § 5(b), Sept. 13, 1976, 90 Stat. 1247.

An information-collecting procedure that developed enabled unions to collect extensive data before a grievance was filed; the legal staff could then prepare meaningful grievances to be filed against the employer. Unions found that filing unfair labor practice charges against employers to obtain information prior to the filing of a grievance was a slow process. The employer could refuse the information request. When the 8(a)(5) charge was filed, it would first have to be analyzed, then converted into an unfair labor practice complaint, then processed through the hearing stage before an administrative law judge, then through the review stage before a Board panel, and, finally, to an order by a circuit court.

In 1974, union representatives began to use the Freedom of Information Act to collect and process information much faster. Unions requested copies of the extensive information filed by employers with various agencies: Equal Employment Opportunity Reports (EEO-Is) and Affirmative Action Plans (AAPs) filed by federal contractors with 16 federal departments under the requirements of Executive Order 11246, and Occupational Safety and Health Investigation Reports. By dissecting these reports, the union's legal staff could obtain data concerning job titles; advancements; the number of incumbents; the number of males and females; the number of blacks, Spanish-surnamed Americans, American Indians and Orientals; and pay scales.[107]

There was a strong reaction against this flood of requests for information prepared by the employer and, now, to be used against the employer. The Freedom of Information Act had two basic exemptions to the obligation to release information, No. 3 and 4, and a series of suits for injunctions was filed under these exemptions.

Under Exception No. 3, disclosure of information was enjoined if the desired information was "specifically exempted from disclosure by statute."[108] The Supreme Court[109] construed "Exemption 3" broadly. Administrators have been given substantial discretionary authority to withhold requested information.[110] After the Supreme Court decision, every limitation on disclosure contained in approximately 100 statutes was listed in the legislative history. After the Supreme Court broadened "Exemption 3," employers had argued that AAPs and EEO-1 reports fell within the scope of the exemption of disclosure.

---

[107]*Local 2047, Am. Federation v. Defense General Supply Center,* 573 F.2d 184, 97 LRRM 3207 (4th Cir. 1978), *aff'g* 432 F. Supp. 481, 94 LRRM 2058 (E.D. Va. 1976).

[108]5 U.S.C.A. § 552(b)(3) (Supp. 1977).

[109]*Administrator, FAA v. Robertson,* 422 U.S. 255 (1975).

[110]The purpose of the Sunshine Act, Pub. L. No. 94-409, § 5(b), Sept. 13, 1976, 90 Stat. 1247 (codified at 5 U.S.C.A. § 552 (Supp. 1977) effective March 22, 1977) was to narrow Exemption 3, making more documents available to the public and to overrule *Robertson, supra.*

Exemption 4 was intended to protect employers from turning over information which could reveal a competitive position. The Privacy Act[111] added emphasis to these limitations.

Title 18, Section 1905 of the United States Code made it a criminal offense for government employees to disclose trade secrets. Statistical data has been called a trade secret. Commercial information was twice held by the District of Columbia Circuit not to be within Exemption 3 of the Freedom of Information Act.[112] The Fourth Circuit[113] expressly held that Section 1905 falls within that exemption. The Supreme Court, however, refused to review this decision.

Suits raised under Exemptions 3 and 4 of the Freedom of Information Act, with the aid of Section 1905 of Title 18 of the United States Code, and under the Privacy Act have caused a series of injunctions to be issued against various governmental agencies ordering them *not* to turn over requested information. These orders are called "Reverse FOIAs"—restraints on easy access to information.

Injunctions now exist to prevent release of information that could reveal labor costs, new products, competitive bid strategies, processes, production capabilities, customer names, consumption needs, minority hiring quotas, and technological risks taken related to the purchase of capital equipment.[114] "Sanitized" information release is common—removing names and releasing aggregate rather than individual compensation data.[115]

Limitations on information exchange are growing; this may introduce complications into the labor arbitration process. If an arbitrator ignores a reverse FOIA injunctive order, the employer's

[111]5 U.S.C. § 552a.

[112]*National Parks & Conservation Ass'n v. Kleppe*, 547 F.2d 673, 686-87 (D.C. Cir. 1976); *Charles River Park "A", Inc. v. HUD*, 519 F.2d 935, 941 n. 7 (D.C. Cir. 1975); *Grumman Aircraft Eng'r Corp. v. Renegotiation Bd.*, 425 F.2d 578, 580 n. 5 (D.C. Cir. 1970). *See also Pharmaceutical Mfrs. Ass'n v. Weinberger*, 401 F. Supp. 444, 446 n. 1 (D. D.C. 1975); *Ditlow v. Volpe*, 362 F. Supp. 1321, 1323 (D. D.C. 1973), *rev'd sub nom. Ditlow v. Brinegar*, 494 F.2d 1073 (D.C. Cir.), *cert. denied*, 419 U.S. 974 (1974).

[113]*Westinghouse Elec. Corp. v. Schlesinger*, 392 F. Supp. 1246, 7 FEP Cases 682 (E.D. Va. 1974), *aff'd*, 542 F.2d 1190, 13 FEP Cases 868 (4th Cir. 1976), *cert. denied*, 431 U.S. 924, 14 FEP Cases 1686 (1977).

[114]*Westinghouse Elec. Corp. v. Schlesinger*, 392 F. Supp. 1246, 7 FEP Cases 682 (E.D. Va. 1974), *aff'd*, 542 F.2d 1190, 13 FEP Cases 868 (4th Cir. 1976), *cert. denied*, 431 U.S. 924, 14 FEP Cases 1686 (1977).

[115]*Chrysler Corp. v. Schlesinger*, 412 F. Supp. 171, 176 (D. Del. 1976); *Westinghouse Elec. Corp. v. Schlesinger*, 392 F. Supp. 1246, 7 FEP Cases 682 (E.D. Va. 1974), *aff'd*, 542 F.2d 1190, 13 FEP Cases 868 (4th Cir. 1976), *cert. denied*, 431 U.S. 924, 14 FEP Cases 1686 (1977); *United States Steel Corp. v. Schlesinger*, 8 FEP Cases 923, 924, (E.D. Va. 1974); *Metropolitan Life Ins. Co. v. Usery*, 426 F. Supp. 150, 160 (D. D.C. 1976), *cert. denied*, 97 S. Ct. 2198 (1977). *But see Hughes Aircraft Co. v. Schlesinger*, 384 F. Supp. 292, 297-98, 8 FEP Cases 1163 (C.D. Cal. 1974). *See also American Federation of Government Employees v. Defense General Supply Center* 573 F.2d 184, 97 LRRM 3027 (4th Cir. 1978); *Press Democrat Publishing Co. v. NLRB*, 629 F.2d 1320, 105 LRRM 3046 (9th Circuit 1980).

challenge may proceed to federal court. The employer may argue that the arbitrator should not override the limitations on government disclosure of information established in the previous injunction.

FEDERAL RULE 34 MAY MAKE DOCUMENT DELIVERY UNDER SECTION 301 MORE USABLE

Arbitrators have been told that under Section 301 they have the authority to cause documents to be exchanged between parties prior to the hearing. Rule 34 of the Federal Rules of Civil Procedure adds this detail into the general authority: the word "document" includes "writings, drawings, graphs, charts, photographs, phonorecords, and other data compilations." Information storage techniques have become increasingly more sophisticated and some "documents" are difficult to understand unless there is some translation of the basic material into a usable form.[116] Section 8(a)(5) of the National Labor Relations Act denies the obligation of a company to translate information from one form to another for the convenience of the union in an arbitration hearing. Revised Rule 34[117] requires necessary translations. The obligation to translate undoubtedly increases when the basic information is found on a computer tape.[118] A court ordered United Aircraft Corporation[119] to translate electronic records so the data delivered to the union would be in usable form.

In addition, the court added that the conclusions and the basis for the conclusions reached by expert witnesses should be delivered under Rule 34. For example, in *Quadrini v. Sikorsky Aircraft Division, United Aircraft Corp.,*[120] which involved a helicopter crash, one party requested the other to furnish the following information under Rule 34:

All reports, memoranda, papers, notes, studies, graphs, charts, tabulations, analyses, summaries, data sheets, statistical or informational accumulations, data processing cards or worksheets, and computer generated documents, including drafts or preliminary revisions of any of the above, prepared in connection with this litigation by or under the direction or super-

---

[116]Wright and Miller, FEDERAL PRACTICE AND PROCEDURE (St. Paul: West Pub. Co., 1970), 2206 at 609.

[117]FED. R. CIV. P. 34.

[118]*United States v. Davey,* 404 F. Supp. 1283 (S.D. N.Y. 1975); *Adams v. Dan River Mills, Inc.,* 54 F.R.D. 220, 4 FEP Cases 523 (W.D. Va. 1972).

[119]*Local 743 IAM v. United Aircraft Corp.,* 220 F. Supp. 19, 53 LRRM 2904 (D. Conn. 1963).

[120]74 F.R.D. 594 (D. Conn. 1977).

vision of any witness whom you expect to call as an expert witness at the trial of this matter.[121]

In granting this request, the court noted:

> Though the usual application of [Rule 26(b)(4)(ii)] is in ordering depositions of an expert, I see no reason not to apply the rule in the context of a Rule 34 document production request as well. [Citations omitted.][122]

Federal Rule 34 may, however, create some limitation on arbitrator observations. The claimed need for entry into various locations in a plant has often arisen in arbitration cases, particularly when grievances involve safety or ecology. Arbitrators have often visited plants to make a personal inspection. However, limitations on such visits may grow. In *Belcher v. Bassett Furniture Industries,*[123] the court held that such visits: (1) generate unreliable hearsay evidence; (2) result in some disruption of production; and (3) create a safety hazard when the visit is a wide-ranging tour of the plant. The court pointed out that the benefit from such a tour was conjectural and the oral statements made during such a tour would be unsworn and unrecorded testimony.

---

[121]*Id.* at 594.

[122]*Id.* at 595.

[123]588 F.2d 904, 18 FEP Cases 1078 (4th Cir. 1978).

CHAPTER VIII

The Hearing

An opportunity to present evidence and arguments and to cross-examine witnesses is a fundamental part of the grievance and arbitration process. Many state statutes expressly require a hearing in an arbitration proceeding[1] and other state statutes provide that an arbitrator's refusal to hear all evidence is grounds for the vacation of an award, thereby recognizing that a hearing is essential.[2]

---

[1]The following statutes expressly protect a party's right to a hearing: ALA. CODE tit. 7, § 832 (1958); ALASKA STAT. 09.43.050 (1968); ARIZ. REV. STAT. § 12-1505 (1965); ARK. STAT. ANN. § 34-507 (1960); CAL. CIV. PROC. CODE § 1282.2 (1961); DEL. CODE tit. 10, § 5706 (1972); FLA. STAT. ANN. §§ 682.06(2) and 682.13(d)(Supp. 1969); IDAHO CODE § 7-905 (1975); ILL. REV. STAT. ch. 10, § 105(b)(1971); IND. CODE § 34-4-2-6 (1971); KAN. GEN. STAT. ANN. § 5-405(b)(1973); KY. REV. STAT. § 417.030 (1962); ME. REV. STAT. ANN. tit. 14, §§ 5931(a) and 5938(1)(D)(Supp. 1970); Md. [CTS. & JUD. PROC.] CODE ANN. § 3-214 (1974); MASS. GEN. LAWS ANN. ch. 251 § 5 (1960); MICH. STAT. ANN. § 17.454 (10.3)(3)(1968); MINN. STAT. ANN. § 572.12(b)(Supp. 1970); MISS. CODE ANN. § 11-15-5 (1972); MONT. REV. CODES ANN. §§ 93-201-5 and 93-201-7 (1964); NEV. REV. STAT. § 38-075 (1969); N.J. REV. STAT. § 2A:24-8(c)(1965); N.M. STAT. ANN. § 22-3-13 (1971); N.Y. CIV. PRAC. art. 75, § 7506(c) (McKinney, 1963); OHIO REV. CODE ANN. § 2711.10 (1969); PA. STAT. ANN. tit. 5, § 166 (1963); R.I. GEN. LAWS ANN. § 28-9-8 (1968); TEX. REV. CIV. STAT. ANN. art. 228 (1966); WASH. REV. CODE § 7.04.070 (1961); WYO. STAT. ANN. § 1-1031 (Supp. 1969). Two states provide that their court rules will apply to arbitration procedure: COLO. REV. STAT. ANN. § 80-4-10 (1964); GA. CODE ANN. § 7-210 (1953).

[2]CAL. CIV. PRO. CODE § 1288(c)(West, 1955); CONN. GEN. STAT. REV. § 52-418(c) (1968); HAW. REV. STAT. § 658-9 (1955); LA. REV. STAT. ANN. § 9:4210(c)(1964); MISS. CODE ANN. § 11-15-23 (1972); MO. ANN. STAT. § 435.100(a)(3)(1952); N.C. GEN. STAT. § 1-567.13(4) (1973); N.D. CENT. CODE § 32-29-08(3)(1960); PA. STAT. ANN. tit. 5, § 170(c)(1963); S.D. COMPILED LAWS ANN. § 21-25A-24 (1976); UTAH CODE ANN. § 78-31-16(3) (1953); WIS. STAT. ANN. § 298.10 (1975); WYO. STAT. ANN. § 1-1041(c)(Supp. 1969). Numerous other states also require that arbitrators take oaths that they will act fairly and in an unbiased way. A challenge to the absence of a hearing could be made through these clauses. States that have arbitrator's oaths are: ALA. CODE tit. 7, 836 (1958); ARK. STAT. ANN. § 34.503 (1960); CONN. GEN. STAT. REV. § 52-414 (1968); GA. CODE ANN. § 7-207 (1953); KY. REV. STAT. § 417.012 (1962); MISS. CODE ANN. § 11-15-9 (1972); MO. ANN. STAT. § 435.030 (1952); MONT. REV. CODE ANN. § 93-201-5 (1964); N.D. CENT. CODE § 32-29-04 (1960); N.Y. CIV. PRAC. art. 75, § 7506(a)(McKinney, 1963); R.I. GEN. LAWS ANN. § 28-9-10 (1968) (can be waived by consent of parties); S.C. CODE § 15-47-20 (1972).

THE ARBITRATOR'S CONTROL OF THE HEARING

Generally, it has been held that the arbitrator is in control of all facets of the hearing. Attempts to wrest control of the hearing from an arbitrator have met with mixed success. For example, even upon a showing of misconduct by the arbitrator, some courts have refused to grant a stay once the proceedings have commenced,[3] but other courts have not felt so constrained.[4]

In *In re IAM Republic Lodge No. 1987 and Republic Aviation Corp.*,[5] the court intervened on the union's petition in a proceeding and issued an order that a grievance concerning vacations be heard promptly, ahead of 15 pending grievances. This was in order to have the issue decided before the deadline for taking vacations arrived. The court did not rely on Section 301 of the LMRA, but said that under New York state law it had authority to order an expedited proceeding in view of its power to compel arbitration. In other situations courts have held that a union may not withdraw from an arbitration proceeding it has instituted, absent the arbitrator's consent. To do so, one court said, would "destroy the whole warp and woof of arbitration."[6]

LOCATION OF THE HEARING

As a general rule, selection of the hearing site is left to the parties. Rule 10 of the American Arbitration Association's Voluntary Labor Arbitration Rules provides that "The parties may mutually agree upon the locale where the arbitration is to be held." Sometimes the parties select a "neutral" site (removed from the plant premises) at which to hold the hearing,[7] but often they prefer that the hearing be held at the plant so that needed records can be quickly obtained.

To prevent a stalemate from occurring over a disagreement on a hearing site, a number of state statutes give the arbitrator the ultimate

---

[3]*Lipman v. Haeuser Shellac Co., Inc.*, 263 App. Div. 880, 32 N.Y.S.2d 351 (1942); *In re Nadalen Full Fashion Knitting Mills, Inc. and Barbizon Knitwear Corp.*, 206 Misc. 757, 134 N.Y.S.2d 612 (Sup. Ct. 1954).

[4]*Astoria Medical Group v. Health Insurance Plan of Greater New York*, 13 App. Div. 2d 288, 216 N.Y.S.2d 906 (1961), where the court removed a party-appointed arbitrator prior to the award, saying "[I]t is inconceivable that a court of equity must sit idly by and permit an arbitration proceeding to continue where, by reason of the surrounding circumstances, any award made in favor of one party is preordained to be vacated. The courts are not that impotent."

[5]41 Misc. 2d 279, 245 N.Y.S.2d 900 (Sup. Ct. 1963).

[6]*Simons v. New York Herald Tribune, Inc.*, 15 Misc. 2d 116, 152 N.Y.S.2d 13 (Sup. Ct. 1956).

[7]To help parties find a "neutral" site, both the American Arbitration Association and the Federal Mediation and Conciliation Service maintain hearing rooms in several cities. American Arbitration Association, *Procedural Aspects of Labor-Management Arbitration*, 28 LA 933, 943 (1957); 29 C.F.R. § 1404.12 (1980).

right to determine the site.[8] Furthermore, the same power can be inferred from more general provisions of various state statutes.[9] Of course, these statutes are the guides. The rules contained therein become the rules in labor arbitration only when they are adopted by the court as being compatible with the procedural law of labor arbitration under Section 301. Rule 10 of the American Arbitration Association's Voluntary Labor Arbitration Rules directs in part:

> [If] the locale is not designated in the collective bargaining agreement or Submission, and if there is a dispute as to the appropriate locale, the AAA shall have the power to determine the locale and its decision shall be binding.[10]

However, one court has overruled the AAA locale determination and granted a motion to change the venue of an arbitration because moving the locale from Buffalo, New York to New York City, where one party's business records were located, would reduce needless expenses to the parties and witnesses.[11]

Arbitrator Brandschain described an effective table arrangement.[12]

> It is best to have tables arranged in either a "T" or "U" shape, with the arbitrator sitting at the head and the parties at the sides. There should be a functional seating arrangement for witnesses, designed to render their testimony clearly audible, with provision for the verbatim reporter, if one is used. These arrangements are preferable to the parties sitting around a single table, where there is a tendency for them to crowd each other and the arbitrator, to get their exhibits and papers and his intermingled, and to invade the privacy of his notes.
>
>   . . .

---

[8]ALA. CODE tit. 7, 832 (1958); ALASKA STAT. § 09.43.050 (1968); ARIZ. REV. STAT. § 12-1505 (1965); CAL. CIV. PROC. CODE § 1282.2 (1961); CONN. GEN. STAT. ANN. § 52-413 (1968); DEL. CODE tit. 10, § 5706 (1972); FLA. STAT. ANN. § 682.06 (1969); GA. CODE ANN. § 7-204 (1953); IDAHO CODE § 7-905 (1975); ILL. ANN. STAT. ch. 10 § 105 (1966); IND. CODE § 34-4-2-6 (1971); KAN. GEN. STAT. ANN. § 5-405(a)(1973); ME. REV. STAT. ANN. tit. 14 § 5931 (Supp. 1970); MD. [CTS. & JUD. PROC.] CODE ANN. § 3-213 (1974); MASS. GEN. LAWS ANN. ch. 251, § 5 (1960); MINN. STAT. ANN. § 572.12 (Supp. 1970); MISS. CODE ANN. § 11-15-5 (1972); MONT. REV. CODES ANN. § 93-201-4 (1964); NEV. REV. STAT. § 38.075 (1969); N.M. STAT. ANN. § 22-3-13 (1971); N.Y. CIV. PRAC. § 3-29-03 (1960); N.C. GEN. STAT. § 1-567.6 (1973); OHIO REV. CODE ANN. § 2711.06 (Supp. 1969); R. I. GEN. LAWS ANN. § 28-9-8 (1968); S.D. COMPILED LAWS ANN. § 21-25A-11 (1975); TEX. REV. CIV. STAT. ANN. art. 228 (1966); UTAH CODE ANN. § 78-31-6 (1953); VT. STAT. ANN. tit. 21, § 507 (1967); WASH. REV. CODE § 7.04.070 (1961); WYO. STAT. ANN. § 1-1031 (Supp. 1969).

[9]ARK. STAT. ANN. § 34-507 (1960); KY. REV. STAT. § 417.016 (1962); MICH. STAT. ANN. § 17.454 (10.3)(1968).

[10]See also Note, Labor Arbitration in New Jersey, 14 RUTGERS L. REV. 143, 173 (1959); Braman, The 1943 Washington Arbitration Act, 4 ARB J. (n.s.) 217, 221 (1949); Sterm and Troetschel, The Role of Modern Arbitration in the Progressive Development of Florida Law, 7 MIAMI L.Q. 205, 208 (1953).

[11]D.M.C. Construction Corp. v. A. Leo Nash Steel Corp., 381 N.Y.S.2d 325 (1976).

[12]Brandschain, Preparation and Trial of a Labor Arbitration Case, THE PRACTICAL LAWYER, Vol. 18, No. 7 (Nov. 1972).

Arbitration hearings are not normally held in courtrooms but in plant offices, hotel or motel conference rooms, or lawyers' offices. This makes it necessary to improvise some sort of hearing setting, so that the advocates and the arbitrator will have enough table space to spread their papers and exhibits.

NOTICE OF THE HEARING TO THE REPRESENTATIVE AND THE RIGHT OF THE GRIEVANT TO BE PRESENT

When the location has been determined, the parties must be notified of the time and place of the hearing. Many state statutes require a formal notice.[13] Some statutes expressly provide that an objection to lack of formal notice is waived when a party appears at the proper time and place.[14] Rule 19 of the Voluntary Labor Arbitration Rules of the AAA requires prior notification to both parties of the hearing.

The NLRB has also set some guidelines concerning notice of hearing. It has ruled that if an issue which could have been brought before the Board is submitted to arbitration, the Board will defer to the resulting award if certain standards of procedural regularity and fairness are met. These guidelines are commonly referred to as the *Spielberg* standards.[15] One of these guidelines requires that notice of the time and location of the hearing must have been given to the individual grievant, unless it can be shown that the individual grievant's

---

[13]Ala. Code tit. 7, § 832 (1958); Alaska Stat. § 09.43.050 (1968); Ariz. Rev. Stat. § 12-1505 (1965); Ark. Stat. Ann. § 34-507 (1960); Cal. Civ. Proc. Code § 12822 (1961); Colo. Rev. Stat. Ann. § 80-4-10 (1964); Conn. Gen. Stat. Rev. § 52-413 (1968); Del. Code tit. 10, § 5706 (1972); Fla. Stat. Ann. § 682.06 (1969); Ga. Code Ann. § 7-204 (1953); Idaho Code § 7-905 (1975); Ill. Ann. Stat. ch. 10, § 105(a)(1966); Ind. Code § 34-4-2-6 (1971); Kan. Gen. Stat. Ann. § 5-405(a)(1973); Ky. Rev. Stat. § 417.030 (1962); Me. Rev. Ann. tit. 14, § 5931(a) (Supp. 1970); Md. [Cts. & Jud. Proc.] Code Ann. § 3-213 (1974); Mass. Gen. Laws Ann. ch. 251, § 5 (1960); Mich. Stat. Ann. § 17.454 (10.3)(3) (1968); Minn. Stat. Ann. § 572.12(a) (1968); Miss. Code Ann. § 11-15-7 (1972); Mo. Ann. Stat. § 435.050 (1952); Nev. Rev. Stat. § 38.075 (1969); N.M. Stat. Ann. § 22-3-13 (1971); N.Y. Civ. Prac. art. 75, § 7506(b)(McKinney, 1963); N.C. Gen. Stat. § 1-567.6 (1973); N.D. Cent. Code § 32-29-03 (1960); R. I. Gen. Laws Ann. § 28-9-8 (1968); S. D. Compiled Laws Ann. § 21-25A-11 (1975); Tenn. Code Ann. § 23-507 (1955); Tex. Rev. Civ. Stat. Ann. art. 228 (1966); Utah Code Ann. § 78-31-6 (1953); Vt. Stat. Ann. tit. 21, § 507 (1967); Wash. Rev. Code § 7.04.070 (1961).

[14]Alaska Stat. § 09.43.050 (1968); Ariz. Rev. Stat. § 12-1505 (1965); Cal. Civ. Proc. Code § 1282.2 (1961); Del. Code tit. 10, § 5706 (1972); Fla. Stat. Ann. § 682.06 (1969); Idaho Code § 7-905 (1975); Ill. Rev. Stat. ch. 10, § 105(a) (1971); Ind. Code § 34-4-2-6 (1971); Kan. Gen. Stat. Ann. § 5-405(a) (1973); Me. Rev. Stat. Ann. tit. 14, § 5931 (Supp. 1970); Md. [Cts. & Jud. Proc.] Code Ann. § 3-213 (1974); Mass. Gen. Laws Ann. ch. 251, § 5 (1960); Minn. Stat. Ann. § 572.12(a) (Supp. 1970); Miss. Code Ann. § 11-15-7 (1972); Nev. Rev. Stat. § 38.075 (1969) N.M. Stat. Ann. § 22-3-13 (1971); N.C. Gen. Stat. § 1-567.6 (1973); S.D. Compiled Laws Ann. § 21-25A-11 (1975); Tex. Rev. Civ. Stat. Ann. art. 228 (1966).

[15]*Spielberg Manufacturing Co.*, 112 NLRB 1080, 36 LRRM 1152 (1955).

interests were fully and adequately represented at the hearing. In *International Harvester Company*, [16] the grievant was not present but the company representative was considered to have been sufficiently articulate in the defense of the employee during the arbitration hearing. The union wanted to have the employee discharged for failure to pay union dues. The arbitrator held that Harvester had violated the union security provision by refusing to discharge the employee for nonpayment of dues. The Board found that the arbitration award satisfied the *Spielberg* requirements:

> [The employee's] interests were vigorously defended there by the Company, which had at all times supported [the employee's] position that he was not legally required to maintain his union membership and stubbornly resisted the Union's efforts to secure his removal from his job. For these reasons, we find no serious procedural infirmities in the arbitration proceedings which warrant disregarding the arbitrator's award. After all is said and done, "procedural regularity [is] not . . . an end in itself, but [is] . . . a means of defending substantive interest."[17]

The court of appeals agreed:

> There is no statutory or constitutional right of an employee to be present at an arbitration hearing. It appears that the company fully and adequately defended petitioner's position at the hearing.[18]

Similarly, in *Eazor Express, Inc.* [19] the Board deferred to a decision of a joint grievance committee, upholding a discharge despite the grievant's absence from the hearing on the ground that the employee's interest was adequately represented by the union. If, on the other hand, the dischargee's position is not sufficiently presented by the union representative, the Board will not defer to an award adverse to the employee.[20]

One arbitrator, however, has concluded that *Spielberg* also requires that a grievant must be allowed to attend all sessions of the hearing if the grievant so chooses. In *International Smelting and Refining Co.*, [21] Arbitrator Kornblum said the employer could not properly exclude the grievant from the hearing except during the time he was testifying,

---

[16]138 NLRB 923, 51 LRRM 1155 (1962), *enforced sub nom. Ramsey v. NLRB*, 327 F.2d 784, 55 LRRM 2441 (7th Cir. 1964).

[17]138 NLRB at 928, 51 LRRM at 1157.

[18]327 F.2d at 788, 55 LRRM at 2443.

[19]172 NLRB 1705, 69 LRRM 1081 (1968).

[20]*Roadway Express, Inc.*, 145 NLRB 513, 54 LRRM 1419 (1963); *Precision Fittings, Inc.*, 141 NLRB 1034, 52 LRRM 1443 (1963); *Gateway Transportation Co.*, 134 NLRB 1763, 50 LRRM 1495 (1962); *Ford Motor Co.*, 131 NLRB 1462, 48 LRRM 1280 (1961); *Hamilton-Scheu and Walsh Shoe Co.*, 80 NLRB 1496, 23 LRRM 1263 (1948).

[21]45 LA 885 (Kornblum, 1965).

even though the labor agreement provides that witnesses at any step of the grievance procedure "shall appear separately and remain present solely to be heard as witnesses." Arbitrator Daniel Kornblum relied, *inter alia,* upon the fact that under the *Spielberg* doctrine, the award emanating from such a hearing might not be accepted by the NLRB:

> [S]uch an exclusion would seemingly run counter to the proviso to Section 9(a) of the Labor Management Relations Act, giving an "individual employee" the qualified right to present his own grievance to his employer. It is well known that the National Labor Relations Board will not honor arbitration awards where, among other things, it is convinced that the arbitration proceedings are not "fair and regular" or the result is "clearly repugnant to the purposes of the Act."[22] [Cites omitted.]

Arbitrator Howlett reopened a closed hearing in *Eaton Corporation*[23] because the grievant was not present at the arbitration hearing. The absence of the grievant does not make the hearing *ex parte* if the union representatives are present, but in spite of this representation the arbitrator said a "question of due persons" is raised when the dischargee is not present even if the dischargee is represented. Arbitrator Howlett, because of his concerns, decided to write the grievant after the hearing had been closed and offered him another hearing, explaining he would play the tapes he took at the previous hearing and the grievant could add his testimony after hearing the testimony already given. Rather than taking up his offer, the grievant wrote Arbitrator Howlett a letter which was accepted into the record, and Howlett said this new evidence justified converting the discharge into a reinstatement without back pay.

> I am conscious of the need for due process—as are all arbitrators. Because Grievant was not present at the hearing, and was not given written notice thereof, I have decided to issue an unusual award.

He said he believed he should:

> direct that Grievant have an opportunity to return to work if he desires to do so within a specified time after receiving a copy of my opinion and award. If he wishes to have another chance, he will have an opportunity to prove that he can be a good employee. He must realize, however, that actions of the type described by witnesses Mulski and Scott are grounds for discharge; and it appears likely that had Grievant's poor attendance record continued, he could have been discharged for absenteeism. If Grievant does return he must further realize that he cannot expect support from his Union if he engages in any misfeasance, malfeasance or nonfeasance. The Union representatives did all they could for Grievant at the hearing in this case.

---

[22]*Id.* at 886.
[23]73 LA 403 (Howlett, 1979).

If such an absent grievant is reinstated by *ex parte* letters because of "due process" concerns by the arbitrator, no grievant should attend a discharge arbitration and expose his testimony to cross-examination, but should merely write a personal letter to the arbitrator stating that "he wishes to have another chance . . . to prove that he can be a good employee."

RIGHT OF A PARTY TO A CONTINUANCE

Closely related to the questions of notice and personal presence is the right of a party to a continuance of the hearing for proper cause. Generally the arbitrator is considered to have exclusive authority over the granting or refusing of requests for adjournments of the hearing.[24]

But in the Uniform Arbitration Act, the granting of a continuance or postponement is required upon a showing of necessity or good cause. The Act specifically recites that an award may be vacated by the court if the arbitrator refused to postpone a hearing upon sufficient cause being shown.

One arbitrator has indicated that requests for continuances by grievants may be more favorably construed than similar requests made by an employer. In *Bamberger's*,[25] the employer requested a continuation in a discharge hearing pending the trial of a criminal case involving the same offense alleged in the discharge case. The employer's request was premised upon the local prosecutor's request that a certain witness not be called at the arbitration hearing prior to the criminal trial. The arbitrator denied the continuance, holding that the grievant was entitled to a reasonably prompt hearing to resolve his job status and economic rights irrespective of the criminal charges pending against him.

Failure to grant a party's request for an adjournment or a continuance can cause the NLRB to disregard the award under the *Spielberg* tests.

An arbitrator's refusal of a postponement requested by the com-

---

[24]*Kool Air Systems, Inc. v. Syossett Institutional Builders, Inc.*, 22 App. Div. 2d 672, 253 N.Y.S.2d 346 (1964).

[25]59 LA 879 (Glushien, 1972). *See Automobile Mech., Local 701 v. Holiday Oldsmobile*, 356 F. Supp. 1325, 84 LRRM 2200 (N.D. Ill. 1972); *Local Union No. 251 v. Narragansett Improvement Co.*, 503 F.2d 309, 87 LRRM 2279 (1st Cir. 1974); *Steward M. Muller Constr. Co. v. Clement Ferdinand & Co.*, 36 A.D.2d 814, 320 N.Y.S.2d 277 (1st Dept. 1971); *Shammas v. National Telefilm Associates, Inc.*, 11 Cal. App. 3d 1050, 90 Cal Rptr. 119 (2d Dist. Div. 2, 1970); *Walter Kidde Constructors, Inc. v. Morris A. Fierberg Co.*, 169 Conn. 640, 363 A.2d 1118 (1975), *aff'g* No. 139616 (Sup. Ct. Hartford County, 1974); *Lighting Unlimited, Inc. v. Unger Const. Co.*, 217 Pa. Super. 252, 269 A.2d 368 (1970); *Krakauer v. Rotmil*, N.Y.L.J., July 27, 1971, p.2., col. 2 (Sup. Ct. N.Y. County).

pany's representative was found by a court to be unjustified when the company's administrative assistant became noticeably ill at the hearing and was taken directly from the hearing to the hospital. The arbitrator had permitted union witnesses to present their testimony. The court said that the arbitrator had abused his discretion in not granting an adjournment.[26]

In another court, the award was vacated and the matter remitted for a hearing before a different arbitrator when a request for an adjournment so a material witness could be present was denied.[27]

An award sustaining the discharge of an employee who received only two days' notice before the arbitration hearing and was denied an adjournment to arrange for the presence of certain witnesses was not deferred to by the Board because "such a procedure . . . does not satisfy the required standards of fairness and regularity."[28] The Board also refused to defer to an arbitration award because one of the grievants had been denied an adjournment of substantial duration requested because of her illness, the arbitrator having granted an adjournment of only one day.[29]

In a case similar to *Bamberger's, supra,* the postponement of the arbitration hearing was sought not to facilitate the taking of evidence, but to await the outcome of a criminal proceeding involving the same subject matter.[30] The arbitrator said the result of the criminal proceeding would not control his award and did not grant an adjournment. The New York Appellate Court upheld the award. Its determination was later affirmed by the Court of Appeals, and an application to the Supreme Court for *certiorari* was unsuccessful.

---

[26]*See Allendale Nursing Home, Inc. v. Local 1115, Joint Board,* 377 F. Supp. 1208, 87 LRRM 2498 (S.D. N.Y. 1974). Other awards have been vacated when the arbitrator unjustifiably failed to adjourn the hearing. *See Woodco Mfg. Corp. v. G.R. & R. Mfg., Inc.,* 51 A.D.2d 531, 378 N.Y.S.2d 504 (3d Dept. 1976). The New York Supreme Court vacated the award and directed a rehearing before the *same* arbitrator. The Appellate Division found the "misconduct" such as to require a hearing before a *new* arbitrator. It wrote (378 N.Y.S.2d at 505):

> Where refusal to grant an adjournment results in the foreclosure of the presentation of material and pertinent evidence, such refusal constitutes sufficient misconduct to vitiate the award.

[27]*Ceseretti v. Trans-Air System, Inc.,* 22 A.D.2d 27, 253 N.Y.S.2d 409 (1964), *aff'd,* 15 N.Y.2d 844, 257 N.Y.S.2d 950, 205 N.E.2d 871 (1965). *See also Lorenzo v. Beauty Culturists Union Local 150A,* 79 LRRM 2431 (N.Y. Sup. Ct. Bronx County, 1971).

[28]*Gateway Transportation Co.,* 137 NLRB 1763, 50 LRRM 1495 (1962).

[29]*Raytheon Co.,* 140 NLRB 883, 52 LRRM 1129 (1963), *enforcement denied on other grounds,* 326 F.2d 471, 55 LRRM 2101 (1st Cir. 1964).

[30]*See Langemeyer v. Campbell,* 27 A.D.2d 942, 279 N.Y.S.2d 41 (2d Dept. 1967), *aff'd,* 21 N.Y.2d 796, 288 N.Y.S.2d 629 (1968), *cert. denied,* 393 U.S. 934 (1968); *see also Local 964, United Bro. of Carpenters and Joiners of America v. Giresi,* 29 A.D.2d 768, 287 N.Y.S.2d 854 (2d Dept. 1968).

THE PARTIES' AND AGGRIEVED EMPLOYEES' RIGHTS TO SELECT COUNSEL

The principle that both parties to an arbitration proceeding have the right to be represented by counsel of their own choosing is well established. This right is expressed in the rules of the American Arbitration Association[31] and is usually protected by the state statute.[32] The employees in a California arbitration case attempted to have a court appoint counsel to bring suit to set aside an arbitration award. The court refused to do so because there was no precedent supporting the employees' "unique" request.[33]

An employee has a right to independent counsel in an arbitration case where the employee makes a claim and showing of proof that the union will not provide fair representation.[34]

One court held that a representative of an independent employee group could intervene in an arbitration proceeding between the union and the company because the court concluded that the union had a history of collusion with the employer.[35] Such collusion cases are rare, however, and in the absence of clear evidence that the grievant will not be fairly represented by the union, the grievant may not retain outside counsel to prosecute a claim.[36]

---

[31] American Arbitration Association, *Voluntary Labor Arbitration Rules*, Rule 20 (1979).

[32] Some states provide an unwaivable right to an attorney. Ill. Rev. Stat. ch. 10, § 106 (1966); N.Y. Civ. Prac. art. 75, § 7506(d)(McKinney, 1963); Wash. Rev. Code § 7.04.100 (1961). Other state statutes provide a right to an attorney and further say that a prior waiver of that right is ineffective. Alaska Stat. 09.43.060 (1968); Ariz. Rev. Stat. § 12-1507 (1965); Cal. Civ. Proc. Code § 1282.4 (1961); Del. Code tit. 10, § 5707 (1972); Fla. Stat. Ann. § 682.07 (1969); Idaho Code § 7-906 (1975); Ind. Code § 34-4-2-6 (1971); Kansas Gen. Stat. Ann. § 5-406 (1973); Me. Rev. Stat. Ann. tit. 14, § 5932 (Supp. 1970); Md. [Cts. & Jud. Proc.] Code Ann. § 3-216 (1974); Mass. Gen. Laws Ann. ch. 251, 6 (1960); Minn. Stat. Ann. § 572.13 (Supp. 1970); Nev. Rev. Stat. § 38.085 (1969); N.M. Stat. Ann. § 22-3-14 (1971); N.C. Gen. Stat. § 1-567.7 (1973); Tex. Rev. Civ. Stat. Ann. art. 229 (1966). Other statutes provide that only the grievant, employee, or a lawyer can represent parties in arbitrations but do not guarantee the right to an attorney at such. Utah Code Ann. § 78-31-9 (1953); Wyo. Stat. Ann. § 1-1031 (1957).

[33] *Archuleta v. Grand Lodge of IAM*, 262 Cal. App. 2d 202, 68 Cal. Rptr. 694, 68 LRRM 2442 (1968). *See also An Outline of Procedure Under the New York Arbitration Law*, 20 Arb. J. (n.s.) 73, 89 (1965); Falls, *Arbitration Under the New Civil Practice Law and Rules in New York*, 17 Arb. J. (n.s.) 197, 210–11 (1962).

[34] *See* "Enforcement by Third Parties," Chapter III, *supra*.

[35] *Iroquois Beverage Corp. v. Int'l Union of United Brewery, Flour, Cereal, Soft Drink and Distillery Workers*, 14 Misc. 2d 290, 159 N.Y.S.2d 256 (Sup. Ct. 1955).

[36] *See, e.g., Yale Transport, Inc.*, 41 LA 736 (Kerrison, 1963); *but see Clark v. Hein-Werner Corp.*, 8 Wis. 2d 264, 99 N.W.2d 132, 45 LRRM 2137 (1959) which has been greatly criticized since *Vaca v. Sipes*, 386 U.S. 171, 64 LRRM 2369 (1967). *See also* Fleming, *Some Problems of Due Process and Fair Procedure in Labor Arbitration*, 13 Stan. L. Rev. 235, 237–38 (1961). *See also United States v. Brotherhood of Railroad Trainmen*, 96 F. Supp. 428, 27 LRRM 2308 (N.D. Ill. 1951):

    As long as the Union functions as a Union the Union is responsible for the mass actions of its members. That means this, that when the members go out and act in a concerted fashion

Where the individual employee's interest does not coincide with those of the union, giving rise to a question of the adequacy of the union's representation of the employee, the NLRB will not defer to the arbitration award unless the employee had the right to be independently represented by his or her own counsel. When the employee leading a movement to replace the incumbent president of the local union was discharged, a grievance protesting the discharge was processed to arbitration. At the hearing, the dischargee objected to being represented by the attorney for the incumbent president of the local union and asked to be represented by his own attorney. When this request was denied, the dischargee and his attorney left the hearing. The arbitrator upheld the discharge, but the Board refused to defer to the award because of the arbitrator's failure to permit the employee's counsel to participate.[37] The Wisconsin Employment Relations Board refused to enforce an award reinstating a discharged employee because the employer's counsel was excluded from the hearing before a board which issued the reinstatement order:

> Tribunals set up by contract to administer and dispense "industrial justice" must comport to certain customary and traditional standards of

---

and do an illegal act the Union is responsible. They just can't say, "Oh, well, we didn't do that as Union members."

If they are members of the Union, then they do act in concerted fashion under the decision of the courts in this country; if it is a mass action the Union is responsible for that sort of an action.

. . .

Now, can the Union escape responsibility under that sort of a situation? Let us admit Mr. Kennedy did what he says he did, all he says he did, and these officers did all they say they did. Yet, the great mass of the Union stayed out. They said, "We refuse to work. We are sick." And they carried on what it is admitted was an unauthorized work stoppage or unauthorized strike. That is admitted.

In a strike in breach of agreement case, the same presumption was adopted to hold a union responsible for a strike in breach of a no-strike pledge. In *United Textile Workers v. Newberry Mills, Inc.*, 238 F. Supp. 366, 59 LRRM 2305 (W.D. S.C. 1965), the court stated:

As long as a union is functioning as a union it must be held responsible for the mass action of its members. It is perfectly obvious not only in objective reasoning but because of experience that men don't act collectively without leadership. The idea of suggesting that the number of people who went on strike would all get the same idea at once, independently of leadership, and walk out of defendant's mill "is of course simply ridiculous." A union that is functioning must be held responsible for the mass action of its members. The above stated principles of law will preserve the union, "because if the plan is adopted throughout the country of trying to use a wink, a nod, a code, instead of the word 'strike,' and if that sort of a maneuver is recognized as valid by the Courts" then we "will have among the unions lawlessness, chaos, and ultimate anarchy. And then the unions will have to be socialized. In other words, they will have to be destroyed." United States v. International Union, U.M.W. of A., 77 F. Supp. 563, 21 LRRM 2721 (D.C. D.C. 1948), aff'd, 85 U.S. App. D.C. 149, 177 F.2d 29, 24 LRRM 2111 (1949), *cert. denied*, 338 U.S. 871, 25 LRRM 2038 (1949).

[37]164 NLRB 563, 65 LRRM 1127 (1967), *enforced sub nom. United Electrical Workers v. NLRB*, 409 F.2d 150, 70 LRRM 2529 (D.C. Cir. 1969).

fair play in their dispensation thereof. This we believe to be especially true when the decisions of such tribunals are to be given finality.[38]

As the right to private counsel has become more clearly defined in recent years, some of the opposition to the use of lawyers in labor arbitration has disappeared. Lawyers with experience in labor arbitration realize that the relationship between employer and employees is "necessarily a continuing one, and that to win a point in ... arbitration by taking a technical or legalistic position may be as hollow a victory as winning a lawsuit against your wife for bending the fender."[39] Arbitrator Elmer Hilpert said much the same thing:

> But above all, an arbitration is a "family affair"; and the general demeanor toward the opposite party, or his witnesses, should be such as not to "win a battle and lose a war."[40]

Arbitrator Benjamin Aaron, after observing the representatives in many arbitration hearings, said that lawyers can add much to the quality of arbitration. Lawyers are trained to outline disputes clearly and simply, to come directly to the point at issue, to present evidence in an orderly fashion and to sum up arguments, relating them to the record made at the hearing.[41] Similarly, Arbitrator Sylvester Garrett explained that when lawyers are the representatives in arbitration, the facts are usually promptly elicited through effective examination and cross-examination of witnesses.[42] In fact, several arbitrators have pointed out that lay representatives tend to be more "legalistic" and technical than lawyers. For example, Arbitrator Maurice Merrill stated:

> Too many laymen think they are acting like lawyers when they resort to pettifogging objections or fight to the last ditch over each minor incident. The lawyers who have appeared before me have manifested an appreciation of the broader aspects of labor-management relationship, a fairness, and adaptability and a resourcefulness that rebuts completely the objections which some have raised against participation by lawyers in the arbitral process. So far from obstructing it with undue technicality and belligerence, they have helped it to run smoothly. I hope that we shall have increasing use of lawyers as representatives of both sides in labor arbitration.[43]

---

[38]*William O'Donell, Inc.*, 54 LRRM 1375, 1376 (Wis. Employ. Rel. Bd., 1963), *aff'd*, 26 Wis. 2d 1, 131 N.W.2d 352, 58 LRRM 2073 (1964).

[39]Livengood, *The Lawyer's Role in Grievance and Arbitration*, 9 Lab. L.J. 495, 499 (1958).

[40]Hilpert, The Arbitration Process, Labor Law Institute, Missouri Bar Ass'n, October 4, 1956 (unpublished).

[41]Aaron, *Some Procedural Problems in Arbitration*, 10 Vand. L. Rev. 733 (1957).

[42]Garrett, *Are Lawyers Necessarily an Evil in Grievance Arbitration?*, 8 U.C.L.A. L. Rev. 535 (1961).

[43]Merrill, *A Labor Arbitrator Views His Work*, 10 Vand. L. Rev. 789, 794 (1957).

EX PARTE PROCEEDINGS

It sometimes happens that, although legally bound to proceed to the arbitration hearing, one party to the dispute will refuse to participate. In such instances, arbitrators are extremely reluctant to conduct an *ex parte* proceeding and prefer to find some way of arranging to hear both parties to the dispute. For example, if one party refuses to appear because it feels the issue is not arbitrable, the arbitrator might try to circumvent the problem by inducing the unwilling party to enter a "special appearance" to be heard only on the issue of arbitrability.

The reasons for the general reluctance to proceed in the absence of one party to a dispute are obvious. Arbitrators draw their authority to hear grievance disputes from the parties themselves. If one party refuses to submit the dispute to arbitration, doubts necessarily are raised concerning the validity of the arbitrator's power to proceed.[44]

Arbitrator Jaffee explained that the absence of one party makes the arbitrator's task much more difficult. The case presented by the willing party will more than likely be slanted; the arbitrator will not have the benefit of opposing evidence and counsel's cross-examination. Thus, the arbitrator's evaluation of evidence and testimony is made more difficult.[45]

In some instances, however, arbitrators have concluded that they must overlook these difficulties and go forward with *ex parte* proceedings.[46] A general arbitration clause in an agreement would be rendered meaningless if a party could prevent its implementation by

---

[44]Such doubts formed the basis of Arbitrator Whelan's refusal to proceed in an *ex parte* hearing in *A.B.C. Cartage & Trucking Co.*, 42 LA 55 (Whelan, 1963).

[45]*See Aleo Mfg. Co.*, 15 LA 715, 721 (Jaffee, 1950). *See also* note 52, *infra*.

[46]*See, e.g., Thompson Fuel Service*, 42 LA 62 (Kerrison, 1964); *Velvet Textile Corp.*, 7 LA 685 (Pope, 1947). In *Amal. Meat Cutters & Butcher Workmen v. Penobscot Poultry Co.*, 200 F. Supp. 879, 49 LRRM 2241 (D. Me. 1961), when the parties could not agree on an arbitrator within 10 days, the designation, according to the contract, was to be made by the state board of conciliation and arbitration and that board made an appropriate appointment. Both parties were then notified of the hearings, but the company representatives informed the arbitrator they would not attend as they did not consider the disputed questions arbitrable. When an award was rendered *ex parte* in favor of the union, the court was asked to compel the company to comply with the award. The court granted this relief, saying: "Defendant was provided full opportunity to appear before the arbitrator and to be heard. It cannot now complain that it chose to stay away." *See also Joint Bd. of Cloak, Shirt and Dressmakers Union v. Senco, Inc.*, 289 F. Supp. 513, 69 LRRM 2142 (D. Mass. 1968) where an *ex parte* arbitration was enforced in part. The court refused to enforce the monetary damages part of the award because the records necessary to determine such award were in the sole possession of the defaulting party, but the court did enforce the arbitrator's order concerning liquidated damages, fund contributions, relocation of part of the company, and access to certain company records. The arbitrator's finding that the company had violated the labor agreement by dealing with jobbers not under contract with the union was upheld.

refusing to appear at the hearing. Arbitrator Liston Pope in *Velvet Textile Corp.*,[47] stated:

> The Arbitrator regrets that the representative of the corporation did not see fit to present evidence on the union demand. As a result of this failure, there may well be factors in the corporation's situation of which the arbitrator is not cognizant, which would have modified his decision had they been made known. But it is incumbent on an arbitrator to rule in terms of the evidence presented, and the failure of either party to take advantage of the opportunity offered to present its case does not vitiate or invalidate the arbitration procedure. A general arbitration clause in a contract would be rendered meaningless if its implementation depended on the willingness of each party to the contract to present its case, as the party desiring no change in relationships could nullify arbitration simply by refusing to make an appearance.

A federal district court approved the use of an *ex parte* procedure rather than to seek a court order compelling an employer to be present and proceed to arbitration. The court stated that any award resulting from the *ex parte* hearing would be enforceable in an action brought under Section 301, as long as the arbitrator was designated according to the procedure specified in the labor agreement, and the employer was given full opportunity to appear and be heard.[48] A clear notice of the time and place of the hearing must be given to the party who does not participate.[49] Without such notice of the opportunity to be heard, courts will not enforce an *ex parte* award.[50]

[47] *Velvet Textile Corp.*, 7 LA 685 (Pope, 1947).

[48] *Amal. Meat Cutters & Butcher Workmen v. Penobscot Poultry Co.*, 200 F. Supp. 879, 49 LRRM 2241 (D. Me. 1961). *See also* discussion of this case in note 47 *supra.* To the same effect see *Ulene v. La Vida Sportswear Co.*, 220 Cal. App. 2d 335, 34 Cal. Rptr. 36, 58 LRRM 2582 (1963); *Retail Clerks International Ass'n, Local 1207 v. Seattle Department Stores Ass'n, Inc.*, 62 LRRM 2706 (W.D. Wash. 1966). Where the contractual method for selecting the arbitrator requires the cooperation of both parties, a court refused to enforce an *ex parte* award in *Fuller v. Pepsi Cola Bottling Co. of Lexington, Kentucky*, 406 S.W.2d 419, 63 LRRM 2220 (Ky. Ct. App. 1966), saying:
> The contract is silent as to the procedure to be followed in the event either party failed to appoint its arbitrator. In such a situation, the remedy of the party not in default was a suit to enforce arbitration, not a suit to enforce a unilateral arbitration award not provided for in the contract.

[49] In *Farkash v. Brach*, 52 LRRM 2334 (N.Y. Sup. Ct. 1963), an *ex parte* award was vacated because the arbitrator called a hearing for a time he knew one party would not be present because his attorney would be out of the state due to observance of a religious holiday. In *Smith v. Campbell & Facciolla, Inc.*, 20 Cal. App. 2d 134, 20 Cal. Rptr. 606 (1962), an arbitrator rendered an award in favor of one party without giving notice of the hearing to the other side. The court vacated the award, noting that *ex parte* arbitrations are permissible but due notice of the proceedings is required. *See also United Steelworkers v. Danville Foundry Corp.*, 52 LRRM 2584 (M.D. Pa. 1963).

[50] *In re N.Y. Shipping Ass'n.*, 32 LA 696 (N.Y. Sup. Ct. 1959); *Food Handlers, Local 425 v. Pluss Poultry, Inc.*, 260 F.2d 835, 43 LRRM 2090 (8th Cir. 1958). In *Mercuri v. Ligar*, 225 Cal. App. 2d 327, 37 Cal. Rptr. 306 (1964), the court held that failure to give personal service of notice of a motion to vacate defeats the attempt to vacate. The absence of the grievant does not cause the arbitration hearing to be *ex parte* when the union representative is present and acts as the grievant's representative.

Rule 27 of the Voluntary Labor Arbitration Rules of the American Arbitration Association[51] provides:

27. **Arbitration in the Absence of a Party**—Unless the law provides to the contrary, the arbitration may proceed in the absence of any party, who, after due notice, fails to be present or fails to obtain an adjournment. An award shall not be made solely on the default of a party. The Arbitrator shall require the other party to submit such evidence as he may require for the making of an award.[52]

It should be emphasized, as the rule notes, that an award cannot be granted if a default alone occurred. Rather, the arbitrator must obtain from the party who does participate adequate evidence to meet the appropriate burden of proof.[53] Since in an arbitration proceeding there are no pleadings upon which an arbitrator could adjudge the merits of the dispute, and given the usual generality of the statement of the issue in requests for arbitration, this requirement seems to be an absolute necessity.

Some labor agreements have a provision which specifically determines what should happen if one of the parties refuses to appear at an arbitration hearing. For example, Arbitrator Singer noted in the *Bronx County Pharmaceutical Association*[54] award that the agreement stated "in the event of a willful default by any of the parties hereto in appearing before the arbitrator after due written notice shall have been given, the arbitrator is hereby authorized to render a decision upon the testimony of the party appearing . . . ." Arbitrator Singer said that since the sole reason advanced by the union representatives for not appearing was that they would not appear in the same room with counsel for the association, their refusal to attend was willful,

---

[51] Rule 27 was relied upon in *Aleo Mfg. Co.*, 15 LA 715 (Jaffee, 1950), where the arbitrator proceeded to conduct a hearing even though the employer was not present. *Ex parte* awards, based upon Rule 27 of the *AAA Voluntary Labor Arbitration Rules* have been enforced in several cases. *See Steelworkers v. Danville Foundry Corp.*, 52 LRRM 2584 (M.D. Pa. 1963); *Local 149, Boot and Shoe Workers v. Faith Shoe Co.*, 201 F. Supp. 234, 49 LRRM 2424 (M.D. Pa. 1962); *U.S. Pipe & Foundry Co. v. Am. Arb. Assn. & United Steelworkers Local 2021*, 67 N.J. Super. 384, 170 A.2d 505, 36 LA 1153 (App. Div. 1961); *UAW v. Waltham Screw Co.*, 47 LRRM 2196 (D. Mass. 1960).

[52] American Arbitration Association, *Voluntary Labor Arbitration Rules*, Rule 27 (1979).

[53] *Dessy-Atco, Inc. v. Youngset Fashions, Inc.*, 205 N.Y.S.2d 577 (Sup. Ct. 1960).

[54] 16 LA 85 (Singer, 1951). In *Fuller v. Pepsi-Cola Bottling Co.*, 406 S.W.2d 416, 63 LRRM 2220 (Ky. Ct. App. 1961), an *ex parte* award of a union-appointed arbitrator ordering a reinstatement of a discharged employee, made after a failure of employer to appoint an arbitrator, was found not enforceable where a collective bargaining agreement did not contain a provision permitting a party-appointed arbitrator to proceed *ex parte* and did not provide an alternative plan of arbitration should one party fail to appoint an arbitrator. In so ruling, the court relied on *Harbison-Walker Refractories v. United Brick & Clay Workers*, 339 S.W.2d 933, 47 LRRM 2077 (Ky. Ct. App. 1960), where the union had a right, if the employer refused to appoint an arbitrator, to request appointment of an arbitrator by the American Arbitration Association—clearly an alternative plan of arbitration.

and he had jurisdiction to hear the testimony *ex parte* and issue an award on that testimony.[55]

USE OF TRANSCRIPTS AND TAPES IN ARBITRATION HEARINGS

The Voluntary Labor Arbitration Rules of the American Arbitration Association provide that a stenographic record may be taken.[56] Arbitrator Samuel Jaffee explained that providing a transcript makes the arbitration proceeding more accurate for the arbitrator:

> Of course, where there is no reporter, it means that the arbitrator has to work harder at taking notes. It also means that a party's representative or attorney may be somewhat inconvenienced in his own notetaking, especially when he himself is asking the witness questions....[57]

Arbitrator Elmer Hilpert said concerning transcripts:

> Their value in complex cases hardly needs to be stressed .... Their value to the parties in their subsequent dealings is beginning to be recognized. They have the added value in arbitration cases of assisting in maintaining order.[58]

Arbitrator Benjamin Aaron explained that where there are credibility issues, a transcript enables the arbitrator to observe the demeanor of witnesses free from the distraction of notetaking[59] and permits the conflicts in testimony to be recorded for later comparisons.

Arbitrator Arthur Ross explained that transcripts are taken more frequently when attorneys present the case because they usually prepare post-hearing briefs and want their presentation to be accurate. He further stated that:

> Certainly I would not argue that attorneys, transcripts and briefs should be avoided because they use more time. The advantages of professional handling cannot be gainsaid, especially when significant issues and interests are involved.[60]

If an arbitration award is submitted to a court for enforcement, vacation, or modification, it is often necessary that a full record be

---

[55]*See generally Pacific Maritime Ass'n,* 52 LA 1189 (Kagel, 1969); *Rides Food Shop,* 4 LA 719 (Baskind, 1946).

[56]American Arbitration Association, *Voluntary Labor Arbitration Rules,* Rule 21 (1979).

[57]Jaffee, *Battle Report: The Problems of Stenograph Records in Arbitration,* 20 ARB J. (n.s.) 97 (1965).

[58]Hilpert, *The Arbitration Process,* Labor Law Institute, Missouri Bar Ass'n, October 4, 1956 (unpublished).

[59]Aaron, *Labor Arbitration and Its Critics,* 10 LAB. L.J. 605, 607 (1959).

[60]Ross, *The Well-Aged Arbitration Case,* 11 IND. & LAB. REL. REV. 262, 267 (1958).

made available to the court to resolve the conflicting arguments about what transpired at the arbitration hearing.[61]

The importance of meeting the *Spielberg* standards to permit an award to be deferred to by the NLRB also makes the use of transcripts in arbitration hearings more important. The Board has said it will defer to an arbitrator's ruling, even where it might have reached a different result, if the arbitrator was presented with the unfair labor practice issue[62] but will not defer if the statutory questions were ignored or dealt with only superficially.[63] As Board Member Brown observed, the major problem in applying this standard is the difficulty in determining whether an arbitrator fully considered the unfair labor practice issue before rendering the award.[64] One obvious aid in resolving this question is a transcript of the arbitration proceeding, and trial examiners will frequently refer to the fact that they have examined a transcript in determining whether or not the statutory issues had been raised and submitted to the arbitrator.[65] Of course, it is even more helpful when the arbitrators specifically note in their written decisions that they have considered statutory as well as contractual issues.[66] Thus, parties interested in avoiding the possibility of a second hearing involving the same factual situation, and the risk of an inconsistent result, would find it in their best interests to have a transcript taken at the arbitration hearing.

Some local unions which have opposed the use of transcripts assert that their principal objections are that transcripts increase the cost of

[61]Jaffee, note 53 *supra* at 98.

[62]*Howard Electric Co.*, 166 NLRB 338, 341, 65 LRRM 1577 (1967); *Schott's Bakery, Inc.*, 164 NLRB 332, 334-35, 65 LRRM 1180 (1967); *Modern Motor Express, Inc.*, 149 NLRB 1507, 1511, 58 LRRM 1005 (1964); *I. Oscherwitz & Sons*, 130 NLRB 1078, 1079, 47 LRRM 1415 (1961).

[63]*Milne Truck Lines*, 171 NLRB 226, 69 LRRM 1109 (1968); *John Klann Moving & Trucking Co.*, 170 NLRB 1207, 67 LRRM 1585 (1968); *Illinois Ryan Transport Corp.*, 165 NLRB 227, 232, 65 LRRM 1296 (1967), *rev'd on other grounds*, 404 F.2d 274, 69 LRRM 2761 (8th Cir. 1968); *D. C. International, Inc.*, 162 NLRB 1383, 64 LRRM 1177 (1967); *Dubo Mfg. Co.*, 148 NLRB 1114, 1116, 57 LRRM 1111 (1964); *Schreiber Trucking Co.*, 148 NLRB 697, 705, 57 LRRM 1070 (1964); *Raytheon Co.*, 140 NLRB 883, 884-85, 52 LRRM 1129 (1963), *enforcement denied on other grounds*, 326 F.2d 471, 55 LRRM 2101 (1st Cir. 1964); *Ford Motor Co.*, 131 NLRB 1462, 1463-64, 1492, 48 LRRM 1280 (1961); *IBEW Local 340*, 131 NLRB 260, 48 LRRM 1022 (1961), *enforced*, 301 F.2d 824, 49 LRRM 3159 (9th Cir. 1962); *Monsanto Chem. Co.*, 130 NLRB 1097, 1098-99, 47 LRRM 1451 (1961).

[64]Brown, *The National Labor Policy, the NLRB, and Arbitration*. DEVELOPMENTS IN AMERICAN AND FOREIGN ARBITRATION, Proceedings of the Twenty-first Annual Meeting, National Academy of Arbitrators, C. Rehmus, ed. (Washington: BNA Books, 1968), p. 85.

[65]*John Klann Moving & Trucking Co.*, 170 NLRB 1207, 67 LRRM 1585 (1968); *D. C. International, Inc.*, 162 NLRB 1383, 64 LRRM 1177 (1967); *IBEW, Local 340*, 131 NLRB 260, 48 LRRM 1022 (1961), *enforced*, 301 F.2d 824, 49 LRRM 3159 (9th Cir. 1962).

[66]In *Monsanto Chem. Co.*, 130 NLRB 1097, 1099 n. 7, 47 LRRM 1451, 1452 (1961), the Board, in refusing to defer to an award, pointed to the arbitrator's specific statement in his award that he had ignored any alleged statutory violations. *See also Airco Industrial Gases-Pacific Div. of Air Reduction Co., Inc.*, 195 NLRB 676, 79 LRRM 1467 (1972).

arbitration proceedings and cause needless delay. The first objection is not valid because the cost of a transcript should be borne by the party ordering it. Only when both parties order copies is the cost shared by both parties. Rule 21 of the AAA Voluntary Labor Arbitration Rules specifically provide that the party or parties requesting a stenographic record of the proceedings shall pay the cost of such transcript. Thus, if only the company orders a transcript, the union does not incur any additional expense.

The objection that delay results when a transcript is taken is also not necessarily valid. While the typing of a transcript may delay a proceeding from two days to two weeks, such a delay is not great when considered as part of the total time elapsed between the filing of the grievance and the issuance of an award. Arbitrators often take longer to write an award when they must rely on notes and hesitate to deal with credibility questions when they have no testimony to review.

The making of a record in an arbitration hearing, like the making of a record in any other procedure, tends to eliminate duplication of statements, repetition of questions and shortens answers.

A common problem that occurs in hearings is referred to as "overlapping"—when more than one person speaks at a time. When a record is being made by a reporter, the reporter will reduce "overlapping" by advising the parties that it is not possible to report when two persons speak.

Another common problem develops when a discussion called "off the record" continues into significant matters and the important statements are not recorded, leaving a blank in the record. When counsel wishes to "go off the record," the request should always be made to the arbitrator and not directly to the reporter. Arbitrators rarely permit the discussion of pertinent information off the record. If this occurs, the party purchasing the transcript should register a formal objection with the arbitrator.

Electronic tapes are used in some arbitration hearings to reduce costs. Arbitrator Robert Howlett in *Eaton Corp., Kalamazoo Plant*[67] referred to the tapes he uses at hearings in connection with his offer to allow an absent grievant to hear the prior testimony before adding his own testimony:

> I stated that I would retain my cassettes of the hearing; and write to the Grievant to offer him an opportunity for another hearing. At such hearing, if held, I would play the tapes so Grievant would have the advantage of hearing the evidence offered at the June 29 hearing.

---

[67]*Eaton Corporation Transmission Division, Kalamazoo Plant and Allied Industrial Workers,* 73 LA 403, 404 (Howlett, 1979).

CHAPTER IX

The Witnesses

The function of an arbitration hearing is to gather the facts needed by an arbitrator to properly resolve the dispute. The most common method by which evidence concerning the facts is presented is through the oral testimony of witnesses. This chapter deals with practices concerning witnesses appearing in arbitration proceedings.

SUBPOENA OF WITNESSES

It is not common to subpoena witnesses in arbitration cases. However, employees are sometimes subpoenaed by the employer to protect them from the accusation that they appeared voluntarily as witnesses for the employer.[1]

Subpoenas ordering witnesses to appear at an arbitration hearing have been issued by courts under state statutes. One federal court enforced an arbitrator's subpoena for the appearance of a witness under a state statute on the basis of the authority vested in the court by the Federal Arbitration Act,[2] considering that Act to be the "guiding analogy" for the law emerging through Section 301 of the Labor Management Relations Act, 1947, on procedural matters mentioned by the Supreme Court.[3] However, enforcement was properly denied in a case in which an arbitrator was already acting but had not yet ruled on the propriety of the subpoena.[4] Both decisions are compatible with the counsel by the Supreme Court in *Goodall-Sanford, Inc. v. United Textile Workers, Local 1802*[5] that procedural rules contained in state

---

[1]*See* "Employees as Company Witnesses" *infra.*

[2]*Local Lodge 1746 v. United Aircraft Corp.*, 329 F. Supp. 283, 77 LRRM 2596 (D. Conn. 1971). *But see Washington-Baltimore Newspaper Guild v. Washington Post Co.*, 76 LRRM 2274, 442 F.2d 1234 (D.C. Cir. 1971), which asserts in a *dictum* that subpoenas are not available in private arbitration proceedings. However, the award was sustained.

[3]*Textile Workers Union v. Lincoln Mills*, 353 U.S. 448, 451, 40 LRRM 2113, 2114 (1957).

[4]*Teamsters Local 757 v. Borden, Inc.*, 78 LRRM 2398 (S.D. N.Y. 1971). The party preparing the subpoena had arranged for its issuance under the general state statute without any action by the arbitrator.

[5]353 U.S. 550 (1957).

or federal arbitration statutes must often be retailored before being incorporated into the procedural law emerging through Section 301.[6]

It would seem to be clear that the arbitrator, without need of any specific statutory power, can issue a subpoena for the attendance of a witness which would be enforced by a federal court under Section 301. In Chapter VII the control that arbitrators have placed on pretrial discovery procedures through their right to determine the relevancy was explained.[7] Arbitrators usually determine the relevancy of the information sought in advance so as to avoid harassment of one party by another through "fishing expeditions." Placing control of the subpoena of witnesses to an arbitration proceeding in the hands of the arbitrator, rather than in the hands of a court under a state or federal statute, should be preferred by both parties.

PRIVACY OF ARBITRATION

Arbitrators have, on occasion, been asked by one party to instruct the other parties and witnesses not to engage in public discussion concerning the matter in dispute. Arbitration, as a process, is private; this is an advantage it has over court litigation.

The Code of Professional Responsibility for Arbitrators of Labor-Management Disputes, prepared by the American Arbitration Association and the National Academy of Arbitrators, states in paragraph 39 that:

> 1. **All significant aspects of an arbitration proceeding must be treated by the arbitrator as confidential unless this requirement is waived by both parties or disclosure is required or permitted by law.**[8]

One party should not be permitted to subvert the clear intent of these rules by intentionally appealing to the mass media over the objections of the other.

The American Arbitration Association explains one important reason for the privacy of arbitration:

> The good name of a company and the reputation of its product are often its most valuable assets, representing heavy outlays for advertising. These

---

[6]See "Subpoena of Documents and Other Evidence" in Chapter VII and *Comment, The Applicability of State Arbitration Statutes to Proceedings Subject to LMRA Section 301,* 27 OHIO ST. L.J. 692, 705–08 (1966).

[7]See "Subpoena of Documents and Other Evidence" in Chapter VII.

[8]ARBITRATION—1975, Proceedings of the Twenty-Eighth Annual Meeting, National Academy of Arbitrators, B. Dennis and G. Somers, eds. (Washington: BNA Books, 1976). p. 224, 64 LA 1317, 1321 (1975).

may be lost if, as a result of public trial, the firm's credit standing or business ethics are cast in doubt. Differences are resolved through arbitration with less danger that the parties may be hurt by publicity.[9]

Publicity may affect not only the employer but employees as well. In a discharge case involving behavior such as drunkenness or fighting, any publication of the grievant's name could have an adverse impact on the employee's reputation, community standing, and the like. It is not surprising then that in published awards, employees' names are usually omitted.

In *AFTRA ex rel. Miller and Westinghouse Broadcasting Co.*,[10] the arbitrator made the following response to a request, known as a sequester order, for no public discussion of the matters involved in the arbitration proceeding:

> Counsel for Westinghouse Broadcasting Company, Inc., presented a motion for a ruling by the arbitrator that the arbitration proceedings are to be considered private and that there shall be no public comments by any of the parties or statements made for the purpose of reporting by news media, relating to the issues involved in this proceeding.
>
> I make no formal ruling in this regard, but under the *Procedural Standards and Code of Ethics of the American Arbitration Association,* the arbitration proceedings are considered private and the parties are requested to maintain the privacy of the proceedings until the hearings have been completed and an Award is issued.[11]

The view that the employee involved in a labor arbitration is obligated to respect the private nature of the proceeding is related to the rule that all employees owe a duty of loyalty to their employer which is violated when an employee releases statements which would be embarrassing or would expose the employer to ridicule.[12]

---

[9]American Arbitration Association, THE LAWYER AND ARBITRATION 5 (1960).

[10]AAA Case No. 51-30-0174-68 (Epstein, 1968).

[11]*Id.*

[12]Although arbitrators have recognized the employee's duty of loyalty in other factual situations, their enforcement of that duty has been quite limited. *Southern Bell Tel. Co.,* 69 LA 582 (Rimer, 1977) (unauthorized disclosure of company procedures); *Appalachian Power Co.,* 73-2 ARB ¶ 8496 (McDermott, 1973) (misleading statements about rate case issues); *North Carolina State AFL-CIO,* 70-2 ARB ¶ 8508 (Calhoun, 1970); *Anthony Co.,* 69-2 ARB 8699 (Cohen, 1969) (inspector embarrassed his company without good cause); *Thiokol Chemical Corp.,* 52 LA 1254 (Williams, 1969) (very large number of groundless grievances); *Los Angeles Herald-Examiner,* 49 LA 453 (Jones, 1967) (duty breached by informing a rival newspaper of an embarrassing ethical dispute); *Maier Brewing Co.,* 66-2 ARB ¶ 8605 (Somers, 1966) (employee posted a notice criticizing an employer's decision); *General Electric Co.,* 40 LA 1126 (Davey, 1963) (printing article accusing employer of "insisting on bad parts"); *Sinclair Oil & Gas Co.,* 39 LA 508 (Abernathy, 1962) (organizing a boycott of employer's product).

OPENING STATEMENTS

Before witnesses are called to the witness stand, it is wise for the representative to "prepare a short opening statement in the form of a trial brief defining the issues before the arbitrator and laying out what is intended to be proved."[13] In connection therewith, provisions of the labor agreement basic to the grievance should be set forth and explained so the arbitrator will have the necessary background. The different points of view in the two opening statements will sharpen up the differences which led to the dispute. Arbitrator Brandschain went on to explain:

> [I]n each case the specific terms of relevant contract provisions are very important to the trial ... of the case. What may be even more important is what the contract does not say on the point, ... the question may be governed by the residual rights of management, the broad terms of a management rights clause, or the broad terms of a recognition or seniority clause.[14]

SWEARING OF WITNESSES

The chief argument in favor of swearing witnesses is to impress upon them the importance of honesty. If the oath helps to encourage veracity, it may be of particular value where the issue in controversy centers on the credibility of certain witnesses.

Where an oath is not required by statute,[15] the decision on whether or not to swear witnesses is generally left by the arbitrator to the parties, and the arbitrator will usually accede to their request.[16] Ar-

---

[13]Brandschain, *Preparation and Trial of a Labor Arbitration Case,* THE PRACTICAL LAWYER, Vol. 18, No. 7 (Nov. 1972).

[14]*Id.*

[15]A few states directly require that all witnesses in an arbitration hearing be under oath. *See* KAN. STAT. ANN. § 5-206 (1975); MISS. CODE ANN. § 11-15-13 (1972); PA. STAT. ANN. tit. 5 § 166 (1963). Numerous states give arbitrators the power to administer oaths but in no way require them to do so. CAL. CIV. PROC. CODE § 1282.8 (West, 1972); ILL. REV. STATS. ch. 10, § 107(a) (1975); N.Y. CONSOL. LAWS vol. 4, § 7505 (1976); OHIO REV. CODE ANN. § 2711.06 (1954), are typical.

[16]Rule 24 of the *Voluntary Labor Arbitration Rules of the American Arbitration Association* (1979) provides in part, "The Arbitrator has discretion to require witnesses to testify under oath administered by any duly qualified person, and if required by law or requested by either party, shall do so." The Association's rules for expedited labor arbitration merely allow the arbitrator to require an oath. Arbitrator Maurice Merrill has stated: "The testimonial oath is desired by some parties and considered unimportant by others. My habit is to follow the wishes of the parties as to whether an oath should be administered to the witnesses." Merrill, *A Labor Arbitrator Views His Work,* 10 VAND. L. REV. 789, 795 (1957). *See also* Kagel, *Labor and Commercial Arbitration Under the California Arbitration Statute,* 38 CALIF. L. REV. 799, 822 (1950): "[I]f the arbitrator is requested to administer oaths he should accede. Absent such request the right is considered to be waived."

bitrator Marion Beatty has concluded: "If either side for any reason wants the witness sworn to tell the truth there can be little argument sufficient to warrant a refusal."[17] The oath generally used is: "Do you swear [or affirm] to tell the truth, the whole truth and nothing but the truth?"

If there is no statutory authority in the particular state for the swearing of witnesses, no prosecution for perjury can be maintained merely because the arbitrator or a notary public, usually the reporter, has administered the oath.[18] In any event, prosecution for perjury in a labor arbitration case is most unlikely.

ORDER AND NUMBER OF WITNESSES

Wide latitude is afforded the parties in the selection of evidence and the manner in which evidence is presented through witnesses. Indeed, if the arbitrator imposes too strict a limitation on the presentation of witnesses by a party, the award can be invalidated. For example, in *Harvey Aluminum, Inc. v. United Steelworkers,*[19] the court denied enforcement of an arbitration award because the arbitrator had disregarded material testimony of a witness on the ground that the testimony was introduced in rebuttal and should have been introduced during the proponent's principal case. The court stated:

> The refusal by the Arbitrator to hear all of the testimony of Officer Gottesman or to consider his testimony in making his Award turned on a rule of evidence which the court concludes should not have been binding on petitioner in the absence of some warning by the Arbitrator as to the evidentiary rules to be followed. The failure to receive and consider the material and pertinent testimony in the circumstances appears to have denied to the petitioner a fair hearing.[20]

---

[17]Beatty, LABOR-MANAGEMENT ARBITRATION MANUAL (New York: E. E. Eppler, 1960), p. 73.

[18]*See generally U.S. v. Curtis,* 107 U.S. 671 (1883); 70 C.J.S. 476.

[19]263 F. Supp. 488, 64 LRRM 2580 (C.D. Calif. 1967).

[20]263 F. Supp. at 493, 64 LRRM at 2583. *Cf. Local Union No. 251 v. Narragansett Improvement Co.,* 503 F.2d 309, 87 LRRM 2279 (1st Cir. 1974) (denial of postponement did not prevent enforcement); *Newark Stereotypers' Union v. Newark Morning Ledger,* 397 F.2d 594, 600 (3d Cir. 1968), *cert. denied,* 393 U.S. 954 (1968) (arbitrator's error must "affect the fairness of the proceeding" to prevent enforcement); *Eckert v. Budd Co.,* 88 LRRM 2979 (E.D. Pa. 1975) (claim of unfairness should have been made in the arbitration proceedings); *Lucas v. Philco-Ford Corp.,* 399 F. Supp. 1184, 90 LRRM 2122 (E.D. Pa. 1975) (failure of employer's doctor to appear in response to a subpoena was not prejudicial); *Teamsters Local 560 v. Eazor Express, Inc.,* 95 N.J. Super. 219, 230 A.2d 521, 65 LRRM 2647 (1967) (where a party requests a substantial departure from the normal procedure without stating a reason, the arbitrator is within his authority in denying the request).

The practicalities of the arbitral process limit the number of witnesses a party will call. There sometimes is a strong temptation to overwhelm the opposition by sheer weight of numbers, but this usually is a dangerous practice. One arbitrator has noted:

> In actual practice, the technique of parading witnesses testifying to a particular event or incident frequently boomerangs on the party using it. The opposing party, if he is skilled in cross-examination, can produce and then highlight conflicts in the witnesses' testimony, thus casting doubt on the credibility of all.[21]

But another arbitrator has pointed out, "The more serious danger is not that the arbitrator will hear too much irrelevancy, but rather that he will not hear enough of the relevant."[22]

EMPLOYEES AS COMPANY WITNESSES

Although few restraints are exercised by arbitrators over a party's choice of witnesses and the order of their appearance, some practical limitations are imposed by the cohesiveness of any employee group. As noted by one arbitrator:

> Experienced practitioners in the field of industrial relations accept without rancor, whether they approve or not, the so-called "code" which estops one member of an organization and frequently one member of an unorganized working force from testifying against another. Whatever the merit of elements such as these, they exist, and their presence cannot come as a shock in trying to elicit facts.[23]

Consequently, employers will often refrain from calling members of a bargaining unit, except the grievant, as witnesses in grievance arbitrations. But while employers may be reluctant to do so, they do have the right to call employees and union officials as witnesses. The duty to furnish information is especially clear if the employee's regular work relates to prevention of the misconduct in question, as in the case of a guard or storekeeper.[24]

In *Jaeger Machine Co.*,[25] Arbitrator Theodore High held that the company had a right to call union officials as witnesses, noting: "There is, of course, no property right in witnesses and anyone who is

---

[21]Davey, *The Arbitrator Speaks on Discharge and Discipline,* 17 Arb. J. 97, 102 (1962).

[22]Shulman, *Reason, Contract and Law in Labor Relations,* 68 Harv. L. Rev. 999, 1017 (1955).

[23]*General Motors Corp.,* 2 LA 491, 502 (Hotchkiss, 1938).

[24]*Lockheed Aircraft Corp.,* 27 LA 709 (Maggs, 1956); *C. & P. Telephone Co.,* 51 LA 457 (Seibel, 1968); Craver, *The Inquisitorial Process in Private Employment,* 63 Corn. L. Rev. 2, 7 (1977).

[25]55 LA 850 (High, 1970).

in the hearing room may be called by either party."[26] When the union officials refused to testify on the basis of the union's instructions, the arbitrator ruled that their refusal could be construed as supporting the company's contentions.

Employers do not call as witnesses employees who are members of the unit for another very significant reason. Many employees will report information to the employer with the understanding that they will not be involved as witnesses and that the fact that they "informed" on a fellow employee will be kept confidential. This often generates a real problem for employers. They may be certain that one of their employees stole a fellow employee's property or was selling hard drugs to fellow employees because they have been so informed by credible witnesses, but they also know they will be unable to prove their *prima facie* case in arbitration to support a discharge because they are committed not to call the informers as witnesses. Sometimes an informing employee will testify without objection if he or she is subpoenaed, thereby removing the label "company witness." On some occasions an employer who knows the facts is driven to employing undercover investigators who can make the necessary observations and then testify; however, such a procedure is expensive and an investigator can obtain evidence only if the improper conduct is continuing.

PROTECTING INFORMANTS FROM REPRISAL

In many situations, a witness will refuse to appear at an arbitration hearing for fear of reprisal. For this reason attempts are often made by the employer to submit the testimony of an informer to the arbitrator, yet keep the identity of the informer secret. Such efforts raise a myriad of evidentiary, procedural, and due process questions for the arbitrator, and no uniform response to such efforts has occurred.

Some arbitrators have summarily rejected the attempt to have statements of an informer accepted as evidence when the informer is not present at the hearing. In *A. C. and C. Co.,*[27] Arbitrator Israel Ben Scheiber held that the discharge of an employee, based on the confidential telephone calls of a fellow employee who did not appear at the hearing, could not be sustained. He emphasized:

[U]nder our American System of Jurisprudence where these two men could not be convicted of even such minor charges as spitting on the sidewalk or of passing through a red light, without having the chance to face and cross examine the witness to these acts, "confidential telephone calls" are certainly less than sufficient evidence, on which to base reprimands

[26]*Id.* at 852.
[27]24 LA 538 (Scheiber, 1955).

which might at a later date contribute to both their discharge, and to their difficulty in getting future employment.

The livelihood of a worker should certainly not be placed at the mercy of an informer, who because of his personal dislike of the man whom he accuses, or because of the informer's desire to improve his seniority status by the discharge of an accused employee, makes a "confidential telephone call" secure in the knowledge that he will not have to face the man whom he accuses, because of a Company policy not to embarrass him by compelling him to repeat his charges under oath, in the presence of, and to submit to cross-examination by, the man whom he has accused.[28]

Arbitrators have also declined to uphold disciplinary action based on statements of an informer who does not testify. They hold that such statements are hearsay and lack probative value because the correctness of the statement cannot be tested by cross-examination.[29] The requirement does not apply to the grievance hearings preceding the arbitration, especially as to witnesses not under the employer's control.[30] The same rule should apply to union witnesses not presented for cross-examination.[31]

In *Great Atlantic & Pacific Tea Co.*[32] the arbitrator was apparently convinced that the employer's version of the facts resulting in discharge was correct, but since it was founded on hearsay he ordered reinstatement for "one more chance" but without back pay.

On the other hand, some arbitrators have recognized the practical

---

[28]*Id.* at 540. *See also Twin City Rapid Transit Co.,* 37 LA 748 (Levinson, 1961); *Hooker Chemical Corp.,* 36 LA 857 (Kates, 1961); *Bower Roller Bearing Co.,* 22 LA 320 (Bowles, 1954); *Lockheed Aircraft Corp.,* 13 LA 433 (Aaron, 1949); *Murray Corp. of America,* 8 LA 713 (Wolff, 1947); Fleming, THE LABOR ARBITRATION PROCESS (Ann Arbor: Univ. of Mich. Press, 1965), pp. 177 *et seq.* where the author compares such arbitration cases to Supreme Court cases dealing with the dismissal of government employee for alleged security reasons. *But cf. Morton Int'l, Inc.,* 62 ARB ¶ 8423 (Merrill, 1967) (right to confront one's accuser does not guarantee right of a grievant to be present at a grievance meeting between the company and the union, but that right existed in that case for other reasons).

[29]*See e.g., Bamberger's,* 59 LA 879 (Glushien, 1972); *Curtis Mathes Mfg. Co.,* 70-2 ARB 855 (Ray, 1970); *Armstrong Cork Co.,* 53 LA 1112 (Williams, 1969); *Michigan Standard Alloy, Inc.,* 53 LA 511 (Forsythe, 1969); *Pick-N-Pay Supermarkets, Inc.,* 52 LA 832 (Houghton, 1969); *Owens-Corning Fiberglass Corp.,* 48 LA 1089 (Doyle, 1967).

[30]*Bel Air Markets,* 70-2 ARB ¶ 8530 (Eaton, 1970); *Allied Maintenance Co.,* 55 LA 731 (Sembower, 1970); *Purex Corp.,* 53 LA 841 (Sembower, 1969); *Grand Union Co.,* 48 LA 812 (Schieber, 1967); *Cleaners Hangers Co.,* 39 LA 661 (Klein, 1962). Evidence not disclosed in the grievance hearing may still be used in the arbitration hearing in the absence of any specific contractual restriction. *Inland Steel Container Co.,* 60 LA 536 (Marcus, 1973). *And see Stokely-Van Camp, Inc.,* 59 LA 655 (Griffin, 1972).

[31]In *Rich Manufacturing Co.,* 46 LA 154 (Block, 1966), a statement signed by 52 employees was received in evidence over the employer's objection, but was given "very little weight" by the arbitrator. The portion of the grievance to which the statement related was denied. In such a case any practical difference between excluding the evidence and receiving it "for what it is worth" disappears. Some arbitrators may well favor the latter ruling as being less likely to provoke controversy.

[32]53 LA 639 (Kornblum, 1969). *Cf. Norris Industries,* 71-2 ARB ¶ 8494 (Gentile, 1971).

need for keeping the identity of informers secret and have upheld discharges based on reports of undisclosed informers. The leading case in this area is *Los Angeles Transit Lines* where undercover "spotters" were hired to ride on buses to determine whether drivers were depositing fares into the fare box or were stealing the money. Arbitrator George Hildebrand noted evidence from such investigators was acceptable; he said "[t]he system may be odious, but there is no practical alternative."[33]

Arbitrators Willard Wirtz and Robben Fleming have both described procedures devised to bridge the gap between the protective value of cross-examination and the practical need to keep the identity of employee-informers secret.[34] One procedure allows the informant to be cross-examined behind a screen or by conference telephone, but permits the arbitrator to interview the witness face to face. Such a procedure has not always proven satisfactory. Arbitrator Ralph Seward has noted:

> When I first went to General Motors in 1944, I found that they were accustomed—in certain discharge cases where the company was afraid to call members of the bargaining unit as witnesses for fear of what might happen to them—to have the arbitrator interview such witnesses in private. I changed the rule a bit by requiring some showing of danger to witnesses who testified openly at the hearing, but with this change I went along with the procedure for a time. This made me of course, an independent investigator as well as a trier of the facts. I now think it was an unsound and dangerous procedure even though I am sure that it enabled me to get closer to the truth in some cases than I could otherwise have done.[35]

A variation of some interest occurred in *Walker Mfg. Co. (Harrisonburg, Va.)*.[36] The company had information that two employees were promoting a slowdown in production. The informing employees feared harassment if the fact they had informed became general knowledge. Wishing to prevent retaliation against the informers, the company withheld their identity from the union until the hearing. However, to prevent a charge of unfair surprise, copies of the informants'

---

[33]25 LA 740, 741 (Hildebrand, 1955). *Accord, Shenango Valley Transportation Co.*, 23 LA 362 (Brecht, 1954). *See generally* Fleming, *Due Process in Arbitration*, 13 STAN. L. REV. 235, 245–48 (1961); Carlson and Phillips, *Due Process Considerations in Grievance Arbitration Proceedings*, 2 HASTINGS CON L.Q. 519, 536–38 (1975).

[34]Fleming, note 33 *supra;* Fleming, note 28 *supra*, at 179–81; Wirtz, *Due Process of Arbitration*, THE ARBITRATOR AND THE PARTIES, Proceedings of the Eleventh Annual Meeting, National Academy of Arbitrators, J. McKelvey, ed. (Washington: BNA Books, 1958), p. 19.

[35]Wirtz, note 34 *supra*, at n. 18. *See also Lockheed Aircraft Corp.*, 13 LA 433, 434 (Aaron, 1949) (employer's proposal of independent investigation by arbitrator rejected).

[36]FMCS File 69A/3891 (Ludenberg, 1969) (unpublished). *Accord, Max Factor & Co.*, 61 LA 886 (Jones, 1973) (identity of an adverse witness withheld until the hearing; home and work addresses withheld at the hearing).

affidavits (with the signatures obliterated) were given to the union and at the hearing the informers appeared as witnesses and were subject to cross-examination. The arbitrator felt that this procedure did not violate the rights of the grievants because the grievants knew what charges were against them and what evidence the company had to support the charges.

Where an informer asked for $50 to reveal a thievery ring, and was paid that sum, the arbitrator sustained his suspension until he revealed the names. The arbitrator did, however, require the company to promise to protect the informer from liability if the information was misused.[37]

In *Kelsey-Hayes,* [38] the company offered an employee's written statement as an exhibit, but was reluctant to call her as a witness. When Arbitrator Keefe attempted to call the employee as his own witness, it was revealed that she had been indirectly threatened by the grievant; the company then imposed thirty-day suspension in addition to the suspension being reviewed by Arbitrator Keefe because of the threat, and the arbitrator sustained the total discipline.

For reasons related to the protection of informers, a court, when it enforced an arbitrator's subpoena of company investigation records in a discharge case, specified that the records would be delivered *in camera* for inspection by the arbitrator. The court made this a condition so as not to expose to the union representatives generally any statements from one employee reporting on a fellow employee.[39]

It is firmly established that union or management retaliation against employees who file complaints or testify before the NLRB is illegal.[40] In *Ebasco Services, Inc.,* [41] however, the Board broadened its rule against retaliation to cover witnesses in arbitration hearings. There, three foremen were demoted because they took time off to appear before a permanent arbitration board that was investigating a grievance. The trial examiner pointed out that the Board's policy was to encourage the use of deferring to arbitration awards. That the law as administered by the Board should give witnesses in arbitration proceedings the same protection they would receive if they had been witnesses in a Board proceeding was held to be a reasonable intention of congressional policy to encourage grievance proceedings. Thus, the employer was held to have violated Section 8(a)(1) of the National Labor Relations Act by disciplining these foremen for appearing at the

---

[37]*Eisen Merchantile, Inc.,* 58 LA 340 (Madden, 1972).

[38]65 LA 987 (Keefe, 1975).

[39]*Local Lodge 1746 v. United Aircraft Corp.,* 329 F. Supp. 283, 77 LRRM 2596 (D. Conn. 1971).

[40]*See generally NLRB v. Scrivener,* 405 U.S. 11 (1972).

[41]181 NLRB 768 (1970). *See also Dugal, Ltd.,* 196 NLRB 511 (1972).

hearing. A union-imposed fine of $25 against an employee who testified against a fellow employee's interests in an arbitration proceeding was also found by the NLRB to be coercive and a violation of the National Labor Relations Act.[42]

The Board also found that an employer's action in changing an employee's assignment was unlawfully motivated because he had received an award from an arbitrator for more pay.[43] In a two-to-one decision the Board found that the reassignment was punishment for successfully pursuing a grievance. The fact that the employer might have had to pay more because of the award was no defense for the reassignment. The Board refused to defer action pending a court review of the arbitration award because it said that the discontinuance of the assignment occurred after the award and, therefore, this action by the employer was not before the arbitrator.

The arbitrator also has an obligation to protect witnesses from undue influence and to protect parties from testimony that is distorted by improper influence. One court had held that an arbitration hearing will not be stayed where witnesses were alleged to have been tampered with or subjected to undue influence.[44] The court said that the witnesses would be available at the arbitration hearing and evidence of the alleged undue influence could be presented to the arbitrator.

THE GRIEVANT AS AN ADVERSE WITNESS

The grievant in a disciplinary case is an exception to the view that an employer should rarely use bargaining unit employees as witnesses. Some employers prefer to initiate a disciplinary case by calling the grievant as an adverse witness. This tactic enables the arbitrator to draw conclusions at the outset from the grievant's demeanor on the stand,[45] and also prevents the grievant from adjusting testimony in light of facts presented as part of the employer's initial case.[46] The grievant is asserting a contract right, and should be subjected to the same questions as if he or she were the plaintiff in a civil suit. Further-

---

[42]*Teamsters Local 788,* 190 NLRB 24, 77 LRRM 1458 (1971).

[43]*Mrs. Baird's Bakeries, Inc.,* 189 NLRB 606 (1971), *enforced,* 79 LRRM 2944 (5th Cir. 1972).

[44]*Application of WMCA,* 23 Misc. 2d 1014, 207 N.Y.S. 321 (N.Y. Sup. Ct. 1960). As in *Diebold, Inc.,* 48 LA 893 (Bradley, 1967) and *Clark Grave Vault Co.,* 47 LA 381 (McCoy, 1966).

[45]Elkouri and Elkouri, How ARBITRATION WORKS, Third Edition (Washington: BNA Books, 1973), p. 266; Fleming, THE LABOR ARBITRATION PROCESS (Ann Arbor: Univ. of Mich. Press, 1965), pp. 181–86; Edwards, *Due Process Considerations in Labor Arbitration.* 25 ARB. J. 141 (1970); Stone, *Due Process in Labor Arbitration.* PROCEEDINGS OF NEW YORK UNIVERSITY TWENTY-FOURTH ANNUAL CONFERENCE ON LABOR (1972), p. 11.

[46]In *International Smelting & Refining Co.,* 45 LA 885, (Kornblum, 1965), the arbitrator would not allow the grievant to be excluded from the hearing at any time.

more, if the grievant flatly refuses to testify, it will usually be impracticable to compel the individual to do so. The principal sanction will be the negative inferences which the arbitrator might draw from the grievant's silence.

Two cases decided by Arbitrator Whitley P. McCoy illustrate the problem. In *Southern Bell Tel. Co.*[47] he found no credible evidence connecting the grievant with violence, and refused to infer guilt solely from the refusal to testify. But in another case from the same strike there was a *prima facie* case against both grievants, and he drew an adverse inference from their failure "to disclose all the facts."[48]

As Arbitrator Russell A. Smith has said, "... I would like to see the grievant on the stand at some point during the proceeding, and I feel a little uncomfortable, frankly, when he is not."[49] And in *Tectum Corp.*[50] the arbitrator permitted the company to call the grievant as a witness over the union's objection, stating:

> This arbitrator's ruling that the grievant should submit to questioning by the Company ... was based upon the arbitrator's opinion that neither the Company nor the union should be allowed to withhold relevant and material testimony or other evidence except possibly in special circumstances not here involved such as possible criminal incrimination, trade secrets and classified Defense matters.[51]

In 1966, several tripartite committees made reports to the annual meeting of the National Academy of Arbitrators on various problems of proof in labor arbitration. The New York Tripartite Committee found nothing objectionable about calling witnesses from the opposing side, which would include calling the grievant as a witness at the opening of evidence in a disciplinary case. The committee said:

> It is permissible for a party to call witnesses from the opposing side. The witness may be treated as a hostile witness, but it is incumbent on the ar-

---

[47]25 LA 270 (McCoy, 1955), joined in by Arbitrators Schedler and Alexander. But in a similar case, back pay was denied because the employee could have avoided the grievance by denying the rule violation during the employer's investigation. *Exact Weight Scale Co.*, 50 LA 8 (McCoy, 1967). *See also Bamberger's*, 59 LA 879 (Glushien, 1972).

[48]26 LA 742 (1956), joined in by Arbitrators Alexander, Schedler and Whiting. The award also drew an adverse inference from the union's failure to call the grievants' wives as witnesses on an alibi issue. *Accord, NRM Corp.*, 51 LA 177 (Teple, 1968); *Guerin Special Motor Freight, Inc.*, 48 LA 1036 (Hardy, 1967).

[49]*Problems of Proof in the Arbitration Process: A Workshop on West Coast Tripartite Committee Report*, PROBLEMS OF PROOF IN ARBITRATION, Proceedings of the Nineteenth Annual Meeting, National Academy of Arbitrators, D. Jones, ed. (Washington: BNA Books, 1967), p. 232. Most of the arbitrators who heard his statement agreed.

[50]37 LA 807 (Autrey, 1961).

[51]*Id.* at 810. For interesting discussions of the admissibility of confessions by grievants *see Lucky Stores*, 53 LA 1274 (Eaton, 1969); *Anchor Hocking Corp.*, 66 LA 480 (Emerson, 1976); Craver, *The Inquisitorial Process in Private Employment*, 63 CORN. L. REV. 2, 11 (1977); Edwards, *Due Process Considerations in Labor Arbitration*, 35 ARB. J. 141 (1970).

bitrator to insure that the direct examination is proper and that the witness is protected against unfair tactics. (Some members do not consider an adverse witness, *per se*, to be hostile.)[52]

The Pittsburgh Tripartite Committee said:

> We see no reason why an adverse witness or party cannot be called, subject, however, to the right of the opposite side to examine the witness on *voir dire* before the witness testifies. We believe that the party calling the witness should be bound by the testimony of that witness.
>
> An arbitrator is called upon to make findings of fact and in order to perform his tasks properly all known facts should be presented to him. Hence, there should be no objection to calling witnesses from "the other side."
>
> An exception to this general rule, in the opinion of the Labor Members of our Committee, should exist in discipline cases. They insist that the burden should be on the employer to prove his case without having the right to call the grievant as a witness. Based on facts known to the employer, the decision to discipline was made. Hence, the grievant should be allowed to decide whether he desires to testify at a hearing involving discipline meted out to him. Management members argue that the general rule should prevail.[53]

The Chicago Tripartite Committee, on the other hand, was critical of calling the grievant as the first witness in a discharge or disciplinary case:

> Except for unusual cases, such as the situation where the grievant knows best what occurred and the circumstances surrounding the occurrence, an arbitrator should rule that the grievant may not be called as a witness at the outset of the case in a discharge or disciplinary matter. Except for this limitation, no other limitations should be placed by the arbitrator on the parties calling witnesses from the other side.[54]

So arbitrators and attorneys are not unanimous on this point.[55]

In *Douglas Aircraft Co.*,[56] the employer did not call the grievant as an adverse witness, but merely asked that he testify as the first witness in the hearing. This was denied.

---

[52]*Problems of Proof in the Arbitration Process: Report of the New York Tripartite Committee*, PROBLEMS OF PROOF IN ARBITRATION, note 49 *supra* at p. 301.

[53]*Problems of Proof in the Arbitration Process: Report of the Pittsburgh Tripartite Committee, Id.* at p. 258. Most management attorneys would deny any duty to be bound by the grievant's testimony.

[54]*Problems of Proof in the Arbitration Process: Report of the Chicago Area Tripartite Committee, Id.* at p. 99.

[55]One of the employer attorney members of the Chicago committee contended that the grievant could be called in any case. *Problems of Proof in the Arbitration Process: A Workshop on Chicago Tripartite Committee Report, Id.* at p. 145.

[56]28 LA 198 (Jones, 1957).

EXCLUSION OF WITNESSES DURING TESTIMONY BY OTHERS

Sometimes one or both parties will request that witnesses be excluded from the hearing room while other witnesses are testifying. This practice, which is sanctioned by the AAA rules, prevents the testimony of a witness from being influenced by the statements of others.[57] However, arbitrators are seldom willing to exclude the grievant,[58] and for this reason, as explained in the prior section, the grievant is often called as the employer's initial witness. Arbitrator Daniel Kornblum refused to apply a specific requirement of the agreement that witnesses "shall appear separately and remain present solely to be heard as witnesses" to a dischargee-grievant, saying:[59]

> In a discharge case, as here, exclusion of the aggrieved employee at this terminal stage of the grievance procedure would be tantamount to a denial of due process. It would be akin to excluding a defendant in a criminal proceeding from his own trial.

Similarly, in *Douglas Aircraft Co.*[60] the company moved to have the grievant excluded from the arbitration hearing on the ground that it is poor industrial relations practice to allow the grievant to hear adverse testimony by fellow unit employees and the supervisor. Arbitrator Edgar A. Jones, Jr. denied the motion, saying that the grievant had a legal right to be present in the hearing.

A sequester order is sometimes impossible to enforce. One was issued to witnesses by the arbitration board in the hearing leading to *Transport Workers Union v. Philadelphia Transportation Co.*,[61] but was violated by both the company and an outside witness. Because of this, it was contended that the testimony should have been excluded, but the court denied the request, saying:

> Although arbitration hearings are of a quasijudicial nature, the prime virtue of arbitration is its informality, and it would be inappropriate for courts to mandate rigid compliance with procedural rules such as sequestration....
>   ... In effect the petitioner is attacking the credibility of the witnesses

---

[57]American Arbitration Association, *Voluntary Labor Arbitration Rules,* Rule 22 (1979) cited and discussed in Note, *Labor Arbitration in New Jersey,* 14 RUTGERS L. REV. 143, 176 (1959). One arbitrator, commenting on this procedure, states: "On several occasions, I have observed the effectiveness of this safeguard...." Merrill, *A Labor Arbitrator Views His Work,* 10 VAND. L. REV. 789, 795 (1957). But a refusal to exclude witnesses does not require that the award be set aside. *Cf. Transport Workers Union v. Philadelphia Transportation Co.,* 283 F. Supp. 597, 68 LRRM 2094 (E.D. Pa. 1968).

[58]*See, e.g., Tectum Corp.,* 37 LA 807 (Autrey, 1961).

[59]*International Smelting & Refining Co.,* AAA Case No. 86-17 (Kornblum, 1965).

[60]28 LA 198 (Jones, 1957).

[61]283 F. Supp. 597, 68 LRRM 2094 (E.D. Pa. 1968). *See also McKinney Drilling Co. v. Mach I Limited Partnership,* 359 A.2d 100 (Md. 1976).

and this is a matter peculiarly suitable for the final judgment of the arbitrator. . . .

This Court has reached its decision reluctantly for it believes that the Board's failure to enforce its own Order could only serve to weaken its image as an impartial, judicial tribunal. Notwithstanding the Board's failure in this respect its decision is amply supported by the record as a whole. . . . [62]

CROSS-EXAMINATION

Cross-examination has been relied on to probe a witness' testimony, to make it more complete, or to expose it as false or distorted. It is a procedure that is essential to a fair hearing. The Uniform Arbitration Act provides that "the parties are entitled . . . to cross-examine witnesses appearing at the hearing," [63] and the American Arbitration Association's procedures recognize the right of parties to cross-examine witnesses. [64] Also, the arbitrator may examine a witness when necessary. [65] Indeed the failure of an arbitrator to ask questions when he or she needs more information has been called a "mortal sin." [66]

The New York Tripartite Committee concluded that the scope of the cross-examination need not be limited to the scope of direct examination, but that the arbitrator has discretion to confine the examination when the range of inquiry becomes excessive:

> Cross-examination need not be restricted to the scope of the direct examination, but the arbitrator should exercise reasonable discretion in this regard. If the questions are related directly or indirectly to the issue or to credibility, a reasonable latitude should be permitted. [67]

The committee added these observations:

> The arbitrator is responsible for conducting an orderly hearing and should exercise initiative to that end. Since the principal purpose of the hearing is to provide the arbitrator with relevant and admissible evidence necessary to resolve the issue in an expeditious manner, he should not permit personal attacks, outbursts, argumentative, loud or abusive questioning, hectering, badgering, refusing to let the witness answer the question, or like behavior.

---

[62]283 F. Supp. at 600, 68 LRRM at 2096.

[63]Uniform Arbitration Act § 5(b).

[64]American Arbitration Association, LABOR ARBITRATION PROCEDURES AND TECHNIQUES (1961), p. 18.

[65]*See e.g., Code of Professional Responsibility for Arbitrators of Labor-Management Disputes,* Part V, A. 1, b, ARBITRATION—1975, note 8 *supra* at p. 233, 64 LA at 1326.

[66]Davey, *Situation Ethics and the Arbitrator's Role,* ARBITRATION OF INTEREST DISPUTES, Proceedings of the Twenty-Sixth Annual Meeting, National Academy of Arbitrators, B. Dennis and G. Somers, eds. (Washington: BNA Books, 1974), p. 170.

[67]*See note 52 supra.*

The arbitrator must afford each party an adequate opportunity to present its case by evidence and argument. He must determine, in individual situations, how much leeway should be given a witness or representative in testifying or presenting his case. However, he should not permit the hearing to bog down with irrelevant matter or repetitious evidence or argument.[68]

The Chicago Tripartite Committee said:

We do not, in general, believe that the scope of cross-examination should be restricted to the scope of direct. Where the cross-examination appears to be getting into irrelevant matters, and objection is made, the arbitrator would do well to ask for an explanation of the purpose of the questions. Sometimes the zeal of an advocate may take him far afield and he may appreciate being guided back to the issue.

It is difficult to generalize as to the allowable latitude. Cross examination should not be interfered with unless it appears obvious that the questions have no bearing on the issues before the arbitrator or that the witness is not competent to answer the questions.[69]

It was pointed out that improper cross-examination tactics should be prevented by the arbitrator:

The arbitrator plays a crucial role in the proceedings. He should discourage and shut off improper tactics such as redundant cross examination, abuse or intimidation of witnesses by threats or otherwise, the putting of involved questions not susceptible of intelligent response, shouting at witnesses, standing over witnesses, and the making of unseemly gestures.

In certain situations where tense emotional attitudes develop, it may be necessary for the arbitrator to overlook an emotional outburst. But in general it is the arbitrator's responsibility to prevent the proceedings from degenerating into a donnybrook....[70]

Where a grievant was not present at an arbitration hearing, one arbitrator refused to rule on the grievance on the ground that the record was incomplete and procedural due process had been denied the employer.[71] There are, however, divergent views concerning the effect of denial of cross-examination. In *Sewanee Silica Co.*[72] the arbitrator admitted that the union's failure to produce witnesses deprived the employer of its right to cross-examine but concluded that this did not deprive the employer of a fair hearing, stating:

At several points in the Company's post-hearing brief ... the Company noted that the Union presented no witnesses, contenting itself with state-

---

[68]*Id.* at 303–4.

[69]*See* note 54 *supra,* at 102.

[70]*Id.* .

[71]*Vickers, Inc.* 39 LA 614, 621 (Prasow, 1962). *Contra, American Standard, Inc.,* 70-1 ARB ¶ 8420 (Marshall, 1970).

[72]47 LA 282 (Greene, 1966).

ments and exhibits, and thus that the Company had no opportunities for cross-examination. I wish to reject any possible implication of unfairness here.... An arbitration hearing is not a court; one of its principal values lies in its wide-ranging informality, free from the irksome encrustations of jury procedure. No party has an obligation to present witnesses, or to choose any particular form of procedure other than general decorum and order.[73]

However, the grievance was denied on the merits.

When a union officer testified in *Berg Airlectro Products Co.*,[74] he was directed by the arbitrator to answer certain questions on cross-examination for the names of the employees. He refused, and no serious sanction was imposed for that refusal.[75]

Where the employer fails to produce a witness and attempts to submit written reports or affidavits, arbitrators have held the evidence inadmissible on the grounds that if admitted the union would be denied its right to cross-examination, unless the reports or affidavits merely corroborate testimony which was subject to cross-examination. In *Armstrong Cork Corp.*[76] Arbitrator Ralph Roger Williams said:

> While the Company's statements taken from witnesses are entitled to weight, the Union had no opportunity to cross-examine these accusing witnesses
> . . .
> Those discharged are entitled to confront their accusers at the arbitration hearing, and to cross-examine them.... Signed statements of employees charging another employee with an offense are not conclusive evidence and must be supported by proof.... A written statement which is not supported by the testimony of its maker may be used to corroborate other evidence that was subject to cross-examination, but it should not be considered where it only produces novel evidence, because one test which may be used to determine the credibility of a witness is the demeanor of the witness while he is testifying at the hearing.[77]

But in *South Haven Rubber Co.*[78] an arbitrator received an affidavit of an attorney who died during the proceedings, relying primarily on an ambiguous Michigan statute and allowing the other party time to file its own affidavits. And in *U.S. Steel Corp.*,[79] fifteen signed

[73]*Id.* at 283.

[74]46 LA 668 (Sembower, 1966).

[75]*Id.* at 672, 675-76.

[76]70-1 ARB ¶ 8186 (Williams, 1969) (citations omitted): *but cf. Block Pontiac, Inc. v. Candando,* 274 F. Supp. 1014, 66 LRRM 2371 (E.D. Pa. 1967) (receipt of affidavits by arbitrator not grounds for invalidating award).

[77]53 LA 1112, 1113.

[78]54 LA 653 (Sembower, 1970). *Accord, U.S. Plywood-Champion Papers, Inc.,* 70-1 ARB ¶ 8340 (Hon, 1970).

[79]58 LA 694 (Kreimer, approved by Garrett, 1972). Conversely, an affidavit not previously shown to the union was excluded in *Minnesota Mining & Mfg. Co.,* 71-1 ARB ¶ 8250 (Jacobs, 1971).

statements by eyewitnesses had been taken in the presence of a union representative. Copies were given to the union during the grievance procedure although no cross-examination ever occurred. Two of the fifteen were brought to the arbitration hearing by the union but were not called by either side. The arbitrator admitted all of the statements as a part of the grievance minutes, although it does not appear that his decision would have been different without them.

IMPEACHING THE WITNESS

The New York Tripartite Report states:

> To impeach a witness is to call into question his veracity by means of evidence adduced for that purpose, or the adducing of proof that a witness is unworthy of belief. Ordinarily, a party may not impeach its own witness through his own testimony, except where he is a hostile witness or his testimony can be shown to constitute a surprise. (A hostile witness is one who manifests so much hostility or prejudice under examination that the party who has called him is allowed to cross-examine him, i.e., to treat him as though he had been called by the opposite party.) It is not improper to adduce evidence from other witnesses which contradicts or is inconsistent with the testimony of a prior witness called by the same party. It is not proper to introduce evidence or testimony concerning facts not relevant to the proceeding in order to discredit a witness except evidence of a conviction for perjury.[80]

The Chicago Tripartite Committee said:

> There should be no limitation in efforts to impeach a witness, particularly where cross examination is used to establish facts which are to be followed up by direct testimony. But impeachment does not mean harassment—and an arbitrator has an obligation to protect a witness from excessive badgering or repetitive examination on the same subject matter.[81]

False testimony by an employee may be just cause by itself for discharge.[82] And a false report by an employer for unemployment insurance purposes was treated as an admission against interest and good ground for questioning the credibility of the company officers.[83] The testimony of an undercover agent has been held to be in balance to grievant's denials where there was no other evidence on either side.[84]

---

[80]See note 52 supra, at 302.

[81]See note 54 supra, at 103. See also Friden Calculating Machine Co., 27 LA 496, 500-01 (Justin, 1956).

[82]Aristocrat Travel Products, Inc., 52 LA 314 (Koven, 1968).

[83]Koenig Trucking Co., 60 LA 899 (Howlett, 1973).

[84]General Portland, Inc., 62 LA 709 (Autrey, 1974). But discharges were sustained with comparatively little additional proof supporting the investigator in American Air Filter Co., Inc., 64 LA 404 (Hilpert, 1975).

The U.S. Court of Appeals at New Orleans said that the NLRB was justified in denying an employer's motion to reopen the record in an unfair labor practice proceeding to reassess the credibility of employee witnesses who later had been jailed after pleading guilty to federal charges of possession of drugs. The court also said the Board could rely on the idea that it could exclude all convictions for any crimes other than those involving dishonesty or false statements without balancing probative value, and prejudice was misplaced. Rule 609(a) of the Federal Rules of Evidence directs that evidence that a witness "has been convicted of a crime shall be admitted" for the purpose of attacking the credibility of the witness.

The court held that the Board did not abuse its discretion by refusing to reopen the record because its decision agrees with principles developed under the Federal Rules of Civil Procedure. It points out that neither of the employee witnesses had been convicted at the time of the hearing and that their later convictions could not be termed "newly discovered" evidence. The court adds that the evidence produced by the employer was merely impeaching, and "It is well settled that 'newly discovered evidence, the effect of which is merely to discredit, contradict or impeach a witness, does not afford a basis for the granting of a new trial.'"[85]

THE ADVOCATE-WITNESS RULE

Court decisions, particularly those announced by the Supreme Court which have been discussed in various subsequent chapters, have speeded up change in labor arbitration practice and procedure.[86] No longer can an arbitrator simply consider his or her desire and the desires of the parties while shaping the procedural rules to be applied in the arbitration hearings. This is partly because private attorneys are studying arbitrators' rulings recorded in transcripts, looking for "grist" for a challenge of the award before a district court or the NLRB.[87] For this reason, the arbitrator must mentally try to place a district judge or an administrative law judge in his or her place when making a ruling in an attempt to render a procedural ruling that either of them would accept. In addition, many more disputes can now be initiated either with a complaint at the district court office or with a

---

[85]*NLRB v. Decker and Sons,* 569 F.2d 357, 365, 97 LRRM 3179, 3184 (5th Cir. 1978), quoting *NLRB v. Sunrise Lumber & Trim Corporation,* 241 F.2d 620, 625–26, 39 LRRM 2441, 2444 (2d Cir. 1957), *cert. denied,* 355 U.S. 818, 40 LRRM 2680 (1957) (quoting *Davis v. Yellow Cab Company of St. Petersburg, Inc.,* 220 F.2d 790, 792 (5th Cir. 1955)).

[86]*See* particularly Chapters XI, XIII, XV, XVI, XVII, XVIII, XXI, XXII, and XXIII.

[87]*See* vacation of awards discussed in Chapter XXI, the *de novo* reviews of awards discussed in Chapter XXII, fair representation suits discussed in Chapter XXIII, and also the vacation of awards by suits of various agencies after release of the award, discussed in other chapters.

charge at the NLRB regional office[88] or by a grievance. Since resolution of such disputes can now be sought in different forums, the procedural rulings that affect the results are constantly being reviewed and the differences are debated.

In some arbitration hearings some party will quite certainly present a formal motion to the arbitrator that the advocate on the other side should be excluded from the hearing or that at least some advocate's testimony should be stricken (expunged) from the record because he or she has become either a formal or informal witness in the arbitration hearing. Basic to this motion would be the decision by the California Supreme Court in *Comden v. Superior Court*[89] under the California Professional Conduct Rule 2-111 (A)(4). That decision has created a furor since its release in 1978. The rule is not limited to California. The American Bar Association has the same rule now listed under Canon 5 as DR 5-101(B) and DR 5-102(A) and DR 5-102(B),[90] which applies in all states except California where the state's own similar rule is in effect as indicated. Courts in various jurisdictions have enforced the same rule.[91]

In *Comden,* a motion was made by the defendant's counsel at the trial court level to have the plaintiff's counsel displaced and excluded from the proceeding because another lawyer in the same law firm would certainly testify later in the litigation. This other lawyer had prepared an attached affidavit filed with the court in support of the request for a temporary injunction to cause the defendant to stop using the plaintiff's name in a distribution business. The defendant's counsel moved to have the plaintiff's counsel removed under the California Rule of Professional conduct, Rule 2-111(A)(4), and the trial judge granted the motion and then the Supreme Court of California approved the trial judge's exclusion.

A representative, consultant, or lawyer involved in an arbitration hearing either representing the company or the union often has negoti-

---

[88] Awards that have been released but involve, or should involve, some NLRB policy matters can be vacated by the process of nondeferral. *See* Chapter XXI.

[89] 20 Cal. 3d 906 (dissent at 919) 145 Cal. Rptr. 9, 576 P.2d 971 (1978), *cert. denied,* 439 U.S. 981, 99 S.Ct. 568 (1978). *See also* Marovich, *The Applicability of the Attorney-Witness Rule to Labor Arbitration,* THE ARBITRATION JOURNAL, Vol. 35, No. 1 (March, 1980). In *People v. Superior Court,* 84 Cal. App.3d 491, 148 Cal. Rptr. 704 (1978) which followed on the heels of *Comden,* the court of appeals held that a pretrial hearing in a criminal case is not a "trial" for purposes of the attorney withdrawal rule.

[90] ABA Code of Professional Responsibility, DR 5-101(B), DR 5-102(A) and DR 5-102(B). An attorney may testify, however, to prevent a "failure of justice," *Connolly v. Straw,* 53 Wis. 645, 649, 11 N.W. 17, 19 (1881), or to prevent a "miscarriage of justice." *Schwartz v. Wenger,* 267 Minn. 40, 43–44, 124 N.W.2d 489, 492 (1963).

[91] *Cornell v. Clairol, Inc.,* 440 F. Supp. 17 (N.D. Ga. 1977); *Supreme Beef Processors, Inc. v. American Consumer Industries, Inc.,* 441 F. Supp. 1064 (N.D. Tex. 1977); *American Dredging Co. v. City of Philadelphia,* 480 Pa. 177, 389 A.2d 568 (1978); *Universal Athletic Sales v. American Gym,* 546 F.2d 530, (3d Cir. 1976), *cert. denied,* 430 U.S. 984.

ated the terms of the labor agreement and/or the grievance disputes in
the various steps of the procedure. These advocates, either formally or
informally, often in connection with the questioning of other witnesses,
will orally give meaning to the words in the agreement or to the scope of
the grievance dispute. And their explanations will become part of the
record, all to be evaluated by the arbitrator. Should such testimony
support a motion to the arbitrator to have the advocate excluded or
have the advocate's testimony expunged from the arbitration record?

One response to an "advocate-witness" challenge in an arbitration
hearing is that given a number of years ago by Justice Traynor, then a
leading justice of the California Supreme Court, who said that in arbitration proceedings "all relevant evidence may be freely admitted and
rules of judicial procedure need not be observed *so long as the hearing
is fairly conducted.*"[92] [Emphasis added.] This comment from Judge
Traynor actually begs the question: To fairly conduct a labor arbitration hearing is it necessary that the rules of professional conduct (fair
conduct) be applied just as in all judicial hearings? This rule is now
more significant in view of the rules announced by the Supreme Court
and discussed in Chapter XXIII.

A careful review of the underlying rationale of the rules applicable
to judicial hearings reveals that the advocate-witness exclusion rationale is not applicable to labor arbitration proceedings. In labor arbitration there are no jurors who could become confused if a trial counsel becomes a witness and then again becomes the trial counsel, etc.
Furthermore, labor arbitrations are private, reducing the risk of confusion from role changing. In addition, one of the skills of labor arbitrators is the ferreting out of the truth, and changing roles would not
cause an arbitrator to become confused.

These differences between legal and arbitration proceedings insofar
as the application of this rule is concerned appear to be sound. The
most satisfactory reason for nonapplication that would be available to
a labor arbitrator, if the arbitrator must make a prompt ruling on an
advocate-witness challenge, is found in two rulings by administrative
law judges on such challenges in NLRB hearings.

In *Local Union No. 9, Operating Engineers,*[93] a challenge was presented to Administrative Law Judge James T. Rasbury and he denied
a motion to expunge the testimony of the advocate on the other side.
He then presented, in his report to the NLRB, his view that the advocate-witness' testimony was highly credible and important and hence
should not be excluded. Since Judge Rasbury specifically referred his

---

[92]*Sapp v. Barenfield,* 34 Cal. 2d 515, 520, 212 P.2d 233 (1949).
[93]210 NLRB 129 (1974), citing *French v. Hall,* 199 U.S. 152 (1886) and *Southern Beverage
Co.,* 171 NLRB 926, 71 LRRM 1429 (1968), *enforced,* 423 F.2d 720, 73 LRRM 2415 (5th Cir.
1970).

ruling to the Board, the Board considered it and affirmed it in a foot-note, stating:

> In our view, it is not our function or responsibility to pass on the ethical propriety of a decision by counsel to testify in one of our proceedings. When, as here, the testimony is otherwise proper and competent, it should be accepted in evidence.[94]

Later Judge Jerrold H. Shapiro in *Adolph Coors*[95] was presented with the same request to expunge the advocate's testimony under the ABA rule, and he dismissed the motion and proceeded to hear the tes-timony.[96] Judge Shapiro wrote to the Board that he considered that the advocate-witness' testimony should not be expunged because it was the *most* credible and he referred in his opinion to the Board's rul-ing on Judge Rasbury's questions in 1974.[97]

Arbitrator Harold W. Davey in *Needham Packing Co.*[98] dealt with this issue in passing (before the advocate-witness rules became so rigid) in response to the union's contention in a post-hearing brief that "the dual role of [one of the company's attorneys at the arbitration pro-ceeding] as both witness and attorney ... should operate to discount his testimony and render his credibility suspect...."[99] The advocate-witness had recorded some telephone conversations on a tape between himself and the union representative and the advocate wanted to intro-duce the tapes as evidence. The union representative after the hearing raised the advocate-witness issue. Arbitrator Davey, however, acting as chairman of a panel, did not expunge the testimony, standing by his ruling that even though the tapes would not be accepted, the advocate could testify as a witness and record his best recollection of the conver-sations subject to cross-examination. Although Arbitrator Davey did not discuss the advocate-witness rule specifically because the award was prior to *Alexander v. Gardner-Denver*,[100] he respected the view that a technical advocate rule should not act adversely to a current ar-bitration collection of information.

---

[94]210 NLRB 129 at n. 1.
[95]235 NLRB 271, 98 LRRM 1539 (1977).
[96]*Id.* at 273, n. 4.
[97]*Id.*
[98]44 LA 1057 (Davey, 1965).
[99]*Id.* at 1088.
[100]415 U.S. 36, 7 FEP Cases 81 (1974).

CHAPTER X

"Parol Evidence," "Residual Management Rights," and "Just Cause"

At the very heart of labor arbitration practice are the contract construction principles. These are used by arbitrators to construe the provisions and significant language in labor agreements that approve or limit management action—the source of the grievances that provide grist for their mills. Some arbitrators clearly use jurisdictional limits on their construction activity and some do not.

THE PAROL EVIDENCE RULE

The parole evidence rule, in its classic form, holds that evidence, whether oral or otherwise, cannot be admitted for the purpose of varying or contradicting written language recording the agreement between two parties.[1] This rule has sometimes been called a rule of substantive law because it causes the rights of the parties to be determined by an interpretation of the words in a written document rather than by evidence outside that document.

In labor arbitration the parol evidence rule is a construction doctrine which is closely related to the view that the scope of an arbitrator's jurisdiction is limited to disputes which involve the interpretation and application of a provision of the written agreement between the parties. In addition, the parol evidence rule is also closely related to the reserved rights construction doctrine which holds that management is restricted by the commitments it has made and recorded within the four corners of the written labor agreement, and that unless so restricted the basic managerial authority remains unrestricted.

The policy considerations fundamental to a strict application of

---

[1]*See* 3 A. Corbin, CONTRACTS § 573, 180–81 (rev. ed. 1960); 4 S. Williston, CONTRACTS § 631 (3d ed., W. Jaeger 1961); 9 J. Wigmore, EVIDENCE § 2425 (3d ed. 1940).

the parol evidence rule in labor arbitration were explained by Arbitrator Archibald Cox in *United Drill & Tool Corp.*:[2]

[T]he rule is bottomed on common sense. Many business transactions require long and complicated negotiations during the course of which the parties present many arguments and offer a wide variety of proposals and counterproposals. At the end, if a bargain is struck, both parties may want to be able to draw up a writing setting forth their undertakings so that each can say with assurance, "This is it. Here is the agreement setting forth our obligations." Business transactions would be unstable gambles indeed if this could not be done—if either party were subject to the risk of having a judge or jury go back over all the give-and-take of the prior negotiations and then tell him that it was not enough to carry out the writing. The parol evidence rule makes it possible for the parties to eliminate the uncertainty, if they wish, by adopting the writing as the complete and final expression of their agreement.

Arbitrator Peter Kelliher in *Pillsbury Mills*[3] explained what would happen if the parol evidence rule were not respected in construing labor agreements:

[T]here would be no point in reducing contract terms to writing. This is not simply a technical rule, but has a long range importance in the maintenance of good relations between the parties. The collective bargaining agreements between the parties are arrived at only after extended negotiations and create an understanding that covers a suitable

---

[2]28 LA 677, 679-80 (Cox, 1957). Arbitrator Cox made this additional observation in another context:

Possibly it is only lawyers who feel misgivings on observing the tendency of some labor arbitrators to receive testimony from the parties as to what they thought and said during the negotiation of the contract which an arbitrator is seeking to interpret. It is easy to brush aside a principle called the parol evidence rule with the explanation that you are getting to the bottom of the problem. Yet behind the technical label lies the policy of enabling men who sign written undertakings to rely on the pretty plain meaning of an agreement which purports to speak for itself, without speculating as to what a judge or arbitrator will conclude after hearing conflicting testimony on the claims, demands or understanding of this and that party prior to the contract's execution.

Cox, *The Place of Law in Labor Arbitration*, THE PROFESSION OF LABOR ARBITRATION, Selected Papers from the First Seven Annual Meetings of the National Academy of Arbitrators, 1948-1954, J. McKelvey, ed. (Washington: BNA Books, 1957), p. 86. *See also Columbian Carbon Co.*, 70-1 ARB ¶ 8100, 3354 (Brown, 1969); *Hoffman-Taft, Inc.*, 69-2 ARB ¶ 8481, 4640-41 (Roberts, 1969); *Bloomfield Hills Bd. of Educ.*, 52 LA 338 (Casselman, 1969); *Great Lakes Pipeline Co.*, 26 LA 100, 102 (Beatty, 1956); *Tennessee Valley Furniture Indus., Inc.*, 21 LA 781, 784 (Sanders, 1953).

[3]14 LA 1045, 1048-49 (Kelliher, 1950). It should be noted that the rule, in its classical application, does not apply to agreements concluded after the written agreement in question. In *United Shoe Workers of America v. Le Danne Footwear, Inc.*, 83 F. Supp. 714, 24 LRRM 2021 (D.C. Mass. 1949), a suit was brought to enforce an oral agreement between the parties made subsequent to their Labor Agreement. *See also American Machine & Foundry Co.*, 61-3 ARB ¶ 8730, 6358 (Sembower, 1961).

period of time. Alleged oral agreements cannot be permitted to vary the terms or to serve as amendments to written agreements.

Similarly, Arbitrator Newton Margulies in *Armstrong Rubber Mfg.*[4] said:

> The oral agreement [sought to be established by one party] is in flat contradiction of the Main Contract. If the existence of the Oral Contract were to have been proved, its terms would mean that the principal substance of the Main Contract was written for little purpose and the Supplemental Contract was written for no purpose. This is a conclusion which does not recommend itself to any arbitrator interested in sound labor relations. Written contracts should seldom if ever be considered to have been drafted, in part or in whole, for the purpose of misleading employees, management and insurance companies.

Parol Evidence Is Admissible to Construe Ambiguous Language

Parol evidence can be considered if the party offering it can establish as threshold conditions, (1) that the relevant language in the labor agreement is ambiguous and (2) that such language controls the disputed issue. Arbitrator Thomas Tongue in *B. J. Furniture Corp.*[5] stated this rule as follows:

> There are ... situations in which verbal discussions can be considered in determining the meaning of terms in contracts, if ambiguous.... But in such cases the verbal discussions can only be considered in determining the meaning of such terms and not to reach a result in any way inconsistent with the terms of the contract.

---

[4]19 LA 683, 685 (Margulies, 1952). *Accord, Sperry Gyroscope Co.*, 18 LA 916, 918 (Cole, 1952); *Miller's Furniture Mkt., Inc.*, 10 LA 577, 578 (Cahn, 1948). *See also Sun Rubber Co.*, 28 LA 362, 368 (Dworkin, 1957); *Price-Pfister Brass Mfg. Co.*, 25 LA 398, 404 (Prasow, 1955); *Bethlehem Steel Co.*, 21 LA 579, 582 (Seward, 1953); *Tide Water Oil Co.*, 17 LA 829, 833 (Wyckoff, 1952). *See also* the celebrated case of *Western Union Telegraph Co. v. American Communications Ass'n*, 299 N.Y. 177, 86 N.E.2d 162 (1949). *Accord, Teamsters, Local 986 v. Sears, Roebuck & Co.*, 79 LRRM 2907, 68 L.C. ¶ 12,633 (D.C. Calif. 1972). *E.g., Caribe Circuit Breaker Co.*, 63 LA 261, 262 (Pollock, 1974); *Wen Products, Inc.*, 54 LA 1029, 1034 (Sullivan, 1970); *Container Corp.*, 51 LA 1146, 1149 (Morris, 1969); *Del E. Webb*, 48 LA 164, 167 (Koven, 1967); *Univac-San Francisco, a Division of Sperry Rand Corp.*, 66-2 ARB ¶ 8503 (Burns, 1966); *Pana Refining Co.*, 47 LA 193 (Traynor, 1966); *Warwick Electronics, Inc.*, 46 LA 95 (Daugherty, 1966); *The Euclid Electric & Manufacturing Co.*, 65-2 ARB ¶ 8767 (Kates, 1965); *Delta Match Corp.*, 65-2 ARB ¶ 8613 (Abernethy, 1965); *B. J. John Furniture Corp.*, 32 LA 708, 711-12 (Tongue, 1959); *Grennan Bakeries, Inc.*, 1 LA 311, 313 (Whiting, 1956); *Tennessee Valley Furniture Industries, Inc.*, 21 LA 781, 783–84 (Sanders, 1953); *Luce Mfg. Co.*, 14 LA 628 (Arthur, 1950); *Wolverine Shoe & Tanning Corp.*, 15 LA 195, 200 (Platt, 1950); *Miller's Furniture Market*, 10 LA 577, 578 (Cahn, 1948); *Hanscom Baking Co.*, 8 LA 314, 315–16 (Feinberg, 1947); *Terre Haute Water Works Corp.*, 5 LA 747, 749 (Updegraff, 1946). *Contra, see* note 71 *infra*.

[5]*B. J. Furniture Corp.*, 32 LA 708, 711 (Tongue, 1959).

Similarly, Arbitrator Reynolds C. Seitz held in *Tecumseh Products Co.*:[6]

> In the face of such clear language general principles dictate against the admission of any parol evidence. In the absence of any written agreement signed by the parties as an indication of an intent to amend the clear language, general principles would require acceptance of the clear language as written. General principles indicate that past practice is most reliable only when language in the Agreement is very general, indefinite or ambiguous.

What Is Ambiguous Language?

The question of whether relevant language is ambiguous rests on the facts of each particular case. As a general rule, Arbitrator Walter Boles in *American Oil Co.*[7] explained that:

> Ambiguous language is language which could reasonably be given more than one meaning by reasonable men.

Interestingly, Arbitrator Benjamin Roberts in *Bell Laboratories*[8] found an ambiguity in language despite both parties' contentions that the contract language was clear:

> [C]ontradictory unanimity [on a proposition that the contract is unambiguous] does not establish the absence of an ambiguity.

To the contrary is a decision of a court that an agreement by the parties that a contract is unambiguous precludes introduction of parol evidence.[9]

Conversely, Arbitrator George Cheney in *Andrew Williams Meat Co.*[10] found a contract term unambiguous notwithstanding the parties' stipulation that it was ambiguous:

> Both the company and the union take the view that the Collective Bargaining Agreements are ambiguous with respect to the subject matter mentioned in Section X. The Arbiter is unable to concur in this view.... After a full and fair consideration, if the forum charged with the construction and interpretation is able to declare with certainty what the intention of the parties was from the writing itself, no matter how difficult this task may be, the instrument is not ambiguous, and the interpreter may not go

---

[6]65 LA 762, 763 (Seitz, 1975); *see also Construction Industry Committee*, 69 LA 14, 17 (Mansfield, 1977); *Hoover Ball & Bearing Co.*, 64 LA 63, 65 (Kelman, 1975); *Ralph's Grocery Co.*, 63 LA 845, 847 (Petrie, 1974); *Sperry Rand Corp.*, 69-2 ARB ¶ 8477, 4621 (Jenkins, 1969); *Joseph H. Reinfield, Inc.*, 61-3 ARB ¶ 8760, 6484–85 (Scheiber, 1961).

[7]*American Oil Co.*, 62-1 ARB ¶ 8073, 3279 (Boles, 1961).

[8]*Bell Tel. Laboratories*, 39 LA 1191, 1204 (Roberts, 1962).

[9]*Pacific Tel. & Tel. Co. v Communications Workers*, 199 F. Supp. 689, 50 LRRM 2086 (D. Ore. 1961), *rev'd on other grounds*, 310 F.2d 244, 51 LRRM 2405 (9th Cir. 1962).

[10]8 LA 518, 524 (Cheney, 1947).

outside the four corners of the documents to ascertain the intentions of the parties. It is only where the document contains conflicting and inconsistent provisions on a given subject that it is ambiguous and extrinsic circumstances can be availed of in ascertaining the intention of the parties. If the plain and unambiguous wording of a contract permits a complete fulfill-.ment of the obligations assumed, then that construction is to be preferred to one dependent upon forced addition to, or elimination of, the terms of the agreement.

Arbitrator Zane Lumbley in *Klopfenstein's*[11] held that where the meaning of the agreement is clear and unambiguous on its face, it is improper for an arbitrator to vary its terms based on the parties' bargaining history, even when that history had an informal written pre-contract agreement.

Rules Used to Construe Ambiguous Language

Before resorting to consideration of evidence outside the four corners of the document to construe ambiguous language, arbitrators often rely on various construction principles to clarify language.

The first principle holds that the ambiguous language must be construed so as to be compatible with the language in other provisions of the agreement. This well-known principle was stated by Arbitrator C. G. Hampton in *Buffalo-Springfield Roller Co.:*[12]

In any interpretation of a Contract, the Contract should be viewed as a whole, not in isolated parts. . . .

In *Birmingham Post,*[13] Arbitrator Whitley P. McCoy said:

It is an elementary principle of law that contracts are to be construed, if at all possible, in such a way as to give effect to every provision. Any interpretation which would result in nullifying completely a provision of the contract is to be avoided.

Similarly, Arbitrator Harry Platt in *Riley Stoker Corp.*[14] said:

The primary rule in construing a written instrument is to determine, not alone from a single word or phrase, but from the instrument as a whole, the true intent of the parties, and to interpret the meaning of a questioned

---

[11]75 LA 1224 (Lumbley, 1981). *See also Evidence in Arbitration,* M. Hill and A. Sinicropi, (Washington: BNA Books, 1980) pp. 50–53.

[12]*Buffalo-Springfield Roller Co.,* 5 LA 391, 394 (Hampton, 1946). *See also Longview Fibre Co.,* 63 LA 529, 534 (Smith, 1974); *Wilson Oak Flooring Co.,* 73-1 ARB ¶ 8163, 3600 (Ray, 1973).

[13]4 LA 310, 313 (McCoy, 1946). *See also Fulton Sylphon Co.,* 2 LA 116, 118 (McCoy, 1946).

[14]7 LA 764, 767 (Platt, 1947). *See also John Deere Tractor Co.,* 5 LA 631 (Updegraff, 1946); *Great Lakes Dredge and Dock Co.,* 5 LA 409 (Kelliher, 1946); *Metal & Thermit Corp.,* 1 LA 417 (Gilden, 1946).

word, or part, with regard to the connection in which it is used, the subject matter and its relation to all other parts or provisions.

A second construction principle often relied on by arbitrators to avoid reference outside of parol evidence holds that ambiguous language should be construed against the drafter. Arbitrator Russell Smith in *Timken Detroit Axle*[15] explained:

> On this record, and following an established canon of contract interpretation, the Arbitrator is of the opinion that the ambiguity in question should be resolved against the Company. As the proponent of the contract provision, it was incumbent upon the Company either to explain clearly what was contemplated or to use language which would not leave the matter in doubt.

Arbitrator James J. Healy in *Brown and Sharpe Mfg.*[16] relied on the same principle:

> It is an established principle of contract law that since the person who is doing the writing can, by exactness of expression, more easily prevent mistakes in meaning than the party with whom he is dealing, the doubts arising from ambiguity of language should be resolved against the former in favor of the latter.

One other construction rule often relied upon was referred to by Arbitrator Peter M. Kelliher in *John Deere Harvester Works:*[17]

> It is a universal rule of contract interpretation that a more specific provision takes precedence over a more general provision, particularly where the specific provision follows the general language. Inasmuch as the phrase in Section 3-B broadly construed is general enough to cover both returned material that is defective and returned material that is not defective and because Section 3-C relates only to defective work, which is the type of work here considered, the Arbitrator must find that the facts of this case are clearly governed by Section 3-C. The Arbitrator is not reading out of the contract the phrase "to rework returned material" because there are instances where material is returned for rework where the original performance was not defective, such as the cases cited where there has been a change in engineering requirements or customer demand.

Arbitrator Arthur A. Malinowski in *Ordnance Mfg. Div., Whirlpool Corp., Evansville*[18] has summarized the main rules used to clarify meaning in the order of their application, pointing out that they should be used before evidence external to the agreement is examined:

---

[15] 21 LA 197, 198 (Smith, 1953).
[16] 11 LA 228, 233 (Healy, 1948). Arbitrator Healy relied on the same construction principle in *Federal Paper Board Co.*, AAA Case No. 50-16 (Healy, 1962).
[17] 4 ALAA ¶ 68,773 (Kelliher, 1951).
[18] AAA Case No. 52-30 0298-70 (Malinowski, 1971). *See also Tribune-Star Publishing Co.*, 62 LA 544, 545 (Belshaw, 1974).

Inasmuch as the dispute concerned the interpretation of the terms in the Labor Agreement, the Arbitrator holds that the generally accepted rules of Contract Law will apply. Among these cardinal rules of interpretation are the following: (1) Every part of a Contract is to be interpreted, if possible, so as to carry out its general purpose, (2) The Contract is to be interpreted in such a way as to effectuate the intention of the Parties and where this intention clearly appears from the words used, there is no need to go further, for in such cases the words must govern and (3) Words used in a Contract will be given their ordinary meaning where nothing appears to show that they were used in a different sense or have a technical meaning, and where no unreasonable consequences will result from doing so.

Evidence External to the Agreement Used to Interpret Ambiguous Language

Past Practice

Evidence of the manner in which the parties to a labor agreement have carried out the terms of the agreement is indicative of the interpretation that should be given to an ambiguous provision. However, the term "past practice" is often misunderstood. Arbitrators frequently have cautioned, for example, that there must be such consistency in the practice as to leave no doubt of the parties' intent. Arbitrator Joseph I. Lewis in *Castle Rubber Co.*[19] has said:

> While it is true that a course of conduct so continuous and uninterrupted as to become an essential part of a given job classification, may be created, it is necessary to supply factors of mutual acceptance and reciprocity over a period of years so that both parties accept the practice as part of the job routine....

In *Sheller Manufacturing Corp.,*[20] Arbitrator Robert Matthews said:

> [T]he practice must be of sufficient generality and duration to imply acceptance of it as an authentic construction of the contract.

Arbitrators often reject evidence of past practice as evidence of the meaning of some ambiguous language in the labor agreement if there is no uniformity and the alleged practice is disputed. As noted by Arbitrator Paul Hebert in *Columbian Carbon Co.:*[21]

---

[19]63 LA 789, 791 (Lewis, 1974). *See also New Brighton Area School District*, 77-1 ARB ¶ 8035, 3153 (LeWinter, 1977); *McLouth Steel Corp.*, 77-1 ARB ¶ 8008, 3043 (Lipson, 1976); *Midwest Glasco*, 63 LA 869, 875 (Roberts, 1974).

[20]10 LA 617 (Matthews, 1948). *See also Chevron Chemical Co.*, 67 LA 920, 925 (Williams, 1976); *Albertson's, Inc.*, 74-1 ARB ¶ 8135, 3494 (Sutermeister, 1974).

[21]27 LA 762, 766–67 (Hebert, 1956). *See also Alameda Contra-Costa Transit District*, 77-1 ARB ¶ 8101, 3458 (Koven, 1977); *B. F. Goodrich Chemical Co.*, 64 LA 889, 891 (Dolson, 1975); *Reliance Steel Prods. Co.*, 24 LA 30 (Lehoczky, 1954).

The past practice under a disputed contract provision is not controlling where the interpretation of the clause has been the subject of dispute between the parties.

Arbitrator Clarence Updegraff in *Weaver Mfg. Co.*[22] has reached the same conclusion:

> [Since] the matter has been subject to some dispute throughout the period,... the practice ... has therefore not attained the standing of a mutual interpretation of the part of the contract in dispute....

Where the language in the labor agreement clearly specifies a right, the mere non-use of that right is not evidence that by practice the employer or the union has abandoned the right. The reason for this rule was stated by Arbitrator McCoy in *Latrobe Steel Co.*:[23]

> But if mere non-use resulted in the loss of a contract right, employees might be denied rights, for example overtime pay, merely because they had never through the years received any overtime pay. The Union would not want any such principle as that established. The Union argues that the Company has always sought agreement with the Union in the past. That is merely good labor relations. If seeking agreement, and abstaining from a right merely for lack of agreement, is going to result in losing the right, Management would be less likely in the future to practice good labor relations.

However, where the language is ambiguous and where the right in question is one which would be expected to be vigorously enforced, the non-exercise of claimed rights may be a relevant factor. Arbitrator James J. Healy in *Federal Paper Board*[24] explained:

> [I]t is a widely accepted principle that a party that has "slept on its claimed rights" over a sustained period may thereby have lost those rights. This would not necessarily be the case if the contract were explicit and unambiguous. But it is particularly applicable in a case such as this because the union waited three and a half years before claiming a violation. "In that period, embracing two separate contract negotiations, it never once raised a grievance nor did it suggest impropriety in company behavior during negotiations."

The readoption of ambiguous language is generally regarded as being evidence of an agreement to follow earlier practices established under such language, especially if such language has been construed by an interpreter. Arbitrator McCoy noted in *Swift & Co.*:[25]

---

[22] 11 LA 825, 826 (Updegraff, 1948).

[23] 34 LA 34, 36 (McCoy, 1960). *See also Kroehler Manufacturing Co.*, 17 LA 391 (Lapp, 1951); *Gibson Refrigerator Co.*, 17 LA 313, 317 (Platt, 1951).

[24] AAA Case No. 50-16 (Healy, 1962).

[25] 67-2 ARB ¶ 8399, 4440–41 (McCoy, 1967). *See also Kennecott Copper Co.*, 32 LA 646 (Ross, 1959); *Bethlehem Steel Co.*, 20 LA 87 (Seward, 1953); *cf. A. O. Smith Corp.*, 23 LA 27, 32 (Prasow, 1954).

When contract language has been interpreted, and the parties readopt the identical language in a renewal contract, they readopt that language with the meaning already established, whether it was established by court decision, by arbitration decision, by grievance settlements, by practice, by verbal agreement, or by written agreement.

Bargaining History

Another form of parol evidence relied upon by arbitrators to interpret ambiguous language is evidence of bargaining history.[26] Such evidence may be oral[27] or documentary,[28] but whatever its form, such bargaining history may be quite helpful in construing ambiguous language. Arbitrator Gundermann in *Milwaukee Spring Co.*[29] noted:

> While parties attempt to express their intent in collective bargaining agreements, occasionally ambiguity does occur. When such ambiguity arises, documents such as proposals and counterproposals may be helpful in determining the intent of the parties.

Where the evidence demonstrates that one party attempted during bargaining to obtain agreement on specific contract language but was unsuccessful and is urging the arbitrator to interpret ambiguous language in such a way as to obtain what it did not obtain across the bargaining table, arbitrators often reject the suggested interpretation. For example, Arbitrator Jaffee in *Consolidated Paper Box Mfg. Co.*[30] rejected a union's contention that ambiguous language should be construed to credit any unworked but paid holiday hours toward the 40 hours needed for weekly overtime because the union had attempted unsuccessfully during bargaining to obtain a commitment that such hours should be counted in calculating overtime:

> Accordingly ... I have no alternative, in the light of the practice and the negotiations, but to reject the Union's argument that a paid but unworked holiday counts toward the forty hours.

Arbitrator Dudley Whiting agrees in *General Aniline & Film Corp.*:[31]

---

[26] *See, e.g., Southwest Ornamental Iron Co.*, 38 LA 1025 (Murphy, 1962); *California Elec. Power Co.*, 21 LA 704 (Grant, 1953); *North American Aviation, Inc.*, 19 LA 138 (Kamaroff, 1952); *Kohlenberger Eng'r. Corp.*, 12 LA 380 (Prasow, 1949); *G. C. Hussey & Co.*, 5 LA 446 (Blair, 1946); *Western Pa. Motor Carriers Ass'n., Inc.*, 1 LA 190 (Guild, 1945).

[27] *Colonial Baking Co.*, 36 LA 1130 (Dworet, 1961); *American Can Co.*, 33 LA 809 (Bothwell, 1959); *Bethlehem Supply Co.*, 17 LA 632 (Emery, 1951); *Borden's Farm Products, Inc.*, 3 LA 401 (Burke, 1945).

[28] *Geneva Steel Co.*, 15 LA 834 (Garrett, 1950); *National Malleable & Steel Castings Co.*, 4 LA 110 (Blair, 1946); *Hershey Chocolate Corp.*, 1 LA 165 (McCoy, 1944).

[29] 39 LA 1270, 1272 (Gundermann, 1962). *See also Chevron Chemical Co.*, 67 LA 920, 925 (Williams, 1976).

[30] 27 LA 126, 128 (Jaffee, 1956). *See also Castle Rubber Co.*, 63 LA 789, 791 (Lewis, 1974); *Joseph T. Ryerson & Son*, 68-1 ARB ¶ 8038 (Roberts, 1968); *New Britain Machine Co.*, 45 LA 993 (McCoy, 1965); *Koppers Co.*, 21 LA 699, 702-03 (Meredith, 1953).

[31] AAA Case No. 36-7 (Whiting, 1962). *See also Tecumseh Products Co.*, 65 LA 762, 763 (Seitz, 1975); *Philadelphia Steel & Wire Corp.*, AAA Case No. 93-2 (Short, 1966).

When a matter has been the subject of negotiation and one party has been unsuccessful in obtaining a desired provision, it is wholly improper for an arbitrator to award that party the same result as a necessary implication of other contract provisions.

Similarly, Arbitrator William Murphy in *Southwest Ornamental Iron Co.*[32] held:

[I]t is also recognized that bargaining history and pre-contract negotiations between the parties are valuable and proper sources from which to ascertain the meaning and proper interpretation of the language of the contract. Where a specific provision has been regarded as an appropriate one for negotiations, and where one party has attempted but failed to get the provision included in the contract, an arbitrator should not thereafter read such provision into the contract through the guise of interpretation. In this case, the bargaining history of the parties and the negotiations preceding the current contract reveal clearly the Union's continuing dissatisfaction with the long-standing plant practice under which tackwelding was performed by helpers rates, and also the Union's persistent efforts to effectuate a change in this situation through the bargaining process. This repeated resort to the bargaining process to change the situation by changing the contract constitutes a recognition on the part of the Union that the practice was not in violation of the contract.

And, in *Joseph T. Ryerson and Son, Inc.*,[33] Arbitrator Roberts stated:

It may be seen from the foregoing that the Union now asks in arbitration precisely what it has been unsuccessful in obtaining during earlier negotiations. This effort must be rejected. If the Agreement is to be changed, that change must take place at the bargaining table and not in arbitration.

Finally, Arbitrator Jules J. Justin in *American Machine & Foundry Co.*[34] has taken the same approach, holding:

The Union raised the question during the negotiations leading to the present contract. It was then bargained out. It cannot be "bargained in" by way of an arbitration, under the guise of interpreting or construing other contract clauses, however related.

---

[32]38 LA 1025, 1028–29 (Murphy, 1962). *See also Higgins, Inc.*, 24 LA 224, 228 (Reynard, 1955); *S. Austin Bicking Paper Mfg. Co.*, 8 LA 987, 989 (Brandschain, 1947). As was stated in Elkouri and Elkouri, How ARBITRATION WORKS, Third Edition (Washington: BNA Books, 1973), p. 314:

If a party attempts but fails, in contract negotiations, to include a specific provision in the agreement, many arbitrators will hesitate to read such provision into the agreement through the process of interpretation.

[33]68-1 ARB ¶ 8038 at 3130 (Roberts, 1967).
[34]4 ALAA ¶ 68,697 (Justin, 1950). *See also Rohr Industries, Inc.*, 65 LA 1024, 1028 (Kaufman, 1975); *Consolidated Paper & Box Mfg. Co., Inc.*, 27 LA 126 (Jaffee, 1956); *Bethlehem Steel Co.*, 12 LA 588, 591 (Selekman, 1949); *West Virginia Pulp & Paper Co.*, 12 LA 391 (Copelof, 1949); *Harley Davidson Motor Co.*, 6 LA 395 (Lappin, 1947); *Pantasote Co.*, 3 LA 545 (Cole, 1946).

The "bargaining history" rule also works in reverse. Where one party proposes that a certain clause be removed from the agreement, arbitrators usually will not construe an ambiguous term in such a manner as to remove the obligation the party attempted to bargain out. Thus, in *Pittsburgh Plate Glass Co.,*[35] Arbitrator Philip G. Marshall noted:

> The Company showed conclusively that down through the years the Union had made efforts to delete or change the present contractual definition of "continuous processes" and to make all such employees eligible for overtime benefits on the same basis as employees working on non-continuous operations. They were unsuccessful in such efforts. In view of the clear collective bargaining history of Section 20 no proper question of interpretation or application is involved and hence the Arbitrator is without authority to entertain the request for relief sought by the Union. The grievances are therefore denied.

In *Red Owl Stores, Inc.,*[36] a grievance was filed claiming that under some ambiguous words the employees had the right to prepare all meat sold by the stores. However, in practice, the company had long received certain presliced meats. In the most recent labor agreement negotiations preceding the grievance, the union had attempted to get a strong jurisdictional clause but had failed. In rejecting the grievance, Arbitrator Arvid Anderson emphasized:

> The Union should have been clearly on notice during the negotiations that, if it intended to change the Company's pre-pricing practice, and to obtain exclusive jurisdiction over pricing ... it should have negotiated a specific limitation on such practice in the contract. The testimony of the representatives indicates that the Union was on notice and did intend to change the practice, if it could do so by a change in the contract provision. Having failed to secure such change in the negotiations, the Board of Arbitration has concluded that the practice of pre-pricing must not be disturbed in this arbitration.

However, when management had merely attempted to negotiate a clarification of its right to subcontract work during labor negotiations and union proposals were not accepted, Arbitrator Edwin Teple said in *Broughton's Farm Dairy, Inc.:*[37]

> It is well known that collective bargaining agreements frequently need clarification or elucidation and the parties may endeavor to strengthen their position on either side of the table by language which is designed to explain, clarify or specifically reaffirm a point notwithstanding the propos-

---

[35]14 LA 1 (Marshall, 1950).

[36]62-3 ARB ¶ 8938 at 6410-11 (Anderson, 1962). *See also FMC Corp.,* 45 LA 293 (McCoy, 1965).

[37]41 LA 1189, 1198 (Teple, 1963). *See also American Can Co.,* 33 LA 809, 812 (Bothwell, 1959); *Goodyear Tire & Rubber Co.,* 1 LA 556 (McCoy, 1946).

ing party's conviction that it is already covered by general terms, necessary implication, or an understanding based upon past practice.

Similarly, Arbitrator Barrett in *Westinghouse Electric Corp.* [38] said:

> When a party requests a modification of a contract, such request often constitutes decisive evidence that the modification was not previously contained in the contract. Such a rule may not be invariably applied, however, inasmuch as the party who requests the modification may in fact already possess the modification which he seeks.

THE "RESIDUAL RIGHTS" CONSTRUCTION PRINCIPLE: THE SUBSTANTIVE APPLICATION OF THE PAROL EVIDENCE RULE

The "Residual Rights" construction principle is very closely related to the parol evidence rule. The policy reasons for the principle are similar. The residual rights—often called "management rights"—construction principle is the simple view that management had all rights necessary to manage the plant and direct the working forces before the union became the employees' representative and negotiated a contract, and that unless management limited its managerial rights by a specific term of the agreement, those rights did not evaporate and hence are still retained by management after the labor agreement is signed.

Arbitrator Orville E. Andrews stated the rule very clearly in *Power-matic/Houdaille, Inc.:* [39]

> It is now a well established generalization that employers, except to the extent limited by contract or statute, retain all power to manage a plant, make rules, and set working hours. This is so even if the agreement does not list all of the rights that have been retained by management or has no management rights clause at all. The collective bargaining agreement operates as a limitation upon the right of the employer to establish working conditions only to the extent that such conditions of employment are covered by the agreement. The pre-existing rights of the employer still continue as to all matters not covered in the agreement. If the agreement is completely silent about a matter, then the employer is free to make unilateral changes if such changes are not inconsistent with the provisions of the current agreement. . . .

Arbitrator Wayne Quinlan in *American Sugar Refining Co.* [40] explained that this construction principle was generally accepted by arbitrators:

---

[38] AAA Case No. 47-10 (Barrett, 1962). *See also Construction Industry Committee*, 69 LA 14, 18 (Mansfield, 1977).

[39] 63 LA 1, 2 (Andrews, 1974).

[40] 38 LA 714, 718 (Quinlan, 1961). This principle is established "by an overwhelming weight of authority," *Sommers & Adams Co.*, 6 LA 283 (Whiting, 1947) and "uniformly acknowledged," *Great Lakes Carbon Corp.*, 19 LA 797 (Wettach, 1953).

The generally accepted view among arbitrators, to which this Arbitrator subscribes, is that management rights are limited only to the extent specified in the Working Agreement. Here, as we have seen, there is no contractual limitation of the type that would take away any of those rights generally and ordinarily considered as inherent in management.

Many other experienced arbitrators have articulated this construction principle during the many years that labor arbitration has been developing in the United States.[41] It is a principle which has been recognized by European observers as a basic reason management in the United States has often been able to make rapid changes in manufacturing methods to increase productivity.[42]

When an arbitrator construes a labor agreement provision under the residual rights doctrine or the parol evidence rule, he or she will hold that, if there is no negotiated written provision restricting management's right to take specific action, then there is no restriction on management's action.[43]

---

[41] *San Antonio Packing Co.*, 68 LA 893 (Bailey, 1977); *Walnut Development Co.*, 77-1 ARB ¶ 8296, 4276 (Gibson, 1977); *Longview Fibre Co.*, 63 LA 529, 536 (Smith, 1974); *Greyhound Lines-East*, 73-2 ARB ¶ 8519, 4931 (Rimer, 1973); *William L. Bonnell Co.*, 73-2 ARB ¶ 8428, 4576 (Rutherford, 1973); *Owens-Illinois, Inc.*, 70-2 ARB ¶ 8606, 5000 (Stouffer, 1970); *FMC Corp.*, 70-2 ARB ¶ 8594, 4951 (Whyte, 1970); *Whittaker Corp.*, 70-1 ARB ¶ 8302, 4001 (Geissinger, 1970); *Colson Co.*, 54 LA 896, 900 (Roberts, 1970); *Wahl Clipper Corp.*, 69-2 ARB ¶ 8610 (Gaff, 1969); *Corn Products Co.*, 50 LA 741 (Kates, 1968); *Packaging Corp. of America*, 68-2 ARB ¶ 8813 (Bauder, 1968); *Olin-Mathieson Chem. Corp.*, 68-2 ARB ¶ 8494 (Talent, 1968); *Goodrich Chem. Co.*, 67-1 ARB ¶ 8178 (McIntosh, 1967); *Bard Mfg. Co.*, 65-2 ARB ¶ 8796 (Uible, 1965); *Olin-Mathieson Chem. Corp.*, 42 LA 1025, 1040 (Klamon, 1964); *Union Mills Paper Mfg. Co.*, 64-1 ARB ¶ 8287 (Horlacher, 1963); *Mississippi Steel & Iron Co.*, 63-1 ARB ¶ 8391 (Mitchell, 1963); *KVP Sutherland Paper Co.*, 40 LA 737 (Kadish, 1963); *American Sugar Refining Co.*, 38 LA 714, 718 (Quinlan, 1961); *Harnishfeger Corp.*, 37 LA 685 (Young, 1961); *Texas Portland Cement Co.*, 36 LA 1257 (Autrey, 1961); *American Sugar Refining Co.*, 61-1 ARB ¶ 8137 (Singletary, 1961); *Colorado Fuel & Iron Corp.*, 9 STEEL ARB. 5603, 5604 (Alexander, 1959); *Celanese Corp. of America*, 30 LA 705 (Reid, 1958); *Diamond Milk Products, Inc.*, 28 LA 429 (Stouffer, 1957); *Monsanto Chemical Co.*, 27 LA 736, 743 (Roberts, 1956); *Babcock & Wilcox Co.*, 26 LA 172, 175 (Kates, 1956); *United Wallpaper, Inc.*, 25 LA 188, 191 (Sembower, 1955); *Reynolds Metals Co.*, 25 LA 44, 49 (Prasow, 1955); *Armstrong Rubber Mfg. Co.*, 24 LA 721, 722-23 (McCoy, 1955); *Celotex Corp.*, 24 LA 369, 371 (Reynard, 1955); *National Fireworks Ordnance Corp.*, 23 LA 349 (Larson, 1954); *Stewart-Warner Corp.*, 22 LA 547, 551 (Burns, 1954); *Lone Star Steel Co.*, 20 LA 710 (Smith, 1953); *Great Lakes Carbon Co.*, 19 LA 797, 799 (Wettach, 1953); *McKinney Mfg. Co.*, 19 LA 291, 293 (Reid, 1952); *Graham Bros.*, 16 LA 83 (Cheney, 1951); *Illinois Bell Tel. Co.*, 15 LA 274, 280 (Davis, 1950); *Blackhawk Mfg. Co.*, 7 LA 943, 945 (Updegraff, 1947); *Sommers & Adams Co.*, 6 LA 283 (Whiting, 1947); *Novelty Shawl Co.*, 4 LA 655, 656 (Wallen, 1946); *Merck & Co., Inc.*, 1 LA 430 (Korey, 1946). *See, e.g.*, *National Distillers Products Corp.*, 24 LA 500 (Delehanty, 1953); *Donaldson Co.*, 20 LA 826 (Louisell, 1953); *New York Trap Rock Corp.*, 19 LA 421 (Giardino, 1952); *Byerlite Corp.*, 12 LA 641 (Day, 1949); *M. T. Stevens & Sons Co.*, 7 LA 585 (Copelof, 1947).

[42] Fairweather, *A Comparison of British and American Grievance Handling*, DEVELOPMENTS IN AMERICAN AND FOREIGN ARBITRATION, Proceedings of the Twenty-First Annual Meeting, National Academy of Arbitrators, C. Rehmus, ed. (Washington: BNA Books, 1968), pp. 1–18.

[43] The residual rights construction principle is also consistent with the scope of the arbitrator's jurisdiction. It is ordinarily limited to the application of the terms of the written agreement to the facts of a particular grievance. There is usually an express proviso that the arbitrator does not have the power to add to, subtract from, or modify the agreement. *See e.g.*, *Mallinckrodt Chem. Works*, 38 LA 267, 268 (Hilpert, 1961).

The residual rights doctrine has been relied on in numerous grievance situations where managerial change has occurred and a grievance has been filed. For example, Arbitrator Wayne Quinlan in *Phillips Petroleum Co.*[44] applied the principle to a controversy over the establishment of a new job classification not included in the current agreement, holding:

> While fully understanding and appreciating the contentions of the Union relative to this new job classification being an alteration of the agreement between the parties, still it must be remembered that it has been generally accepted throughout the United States that management's rights not specifically surrendered in collective bargaining agreement are reserved to management.

Similarly, Arbitrator John A. Bailey in *Firestone Tire & Rubber Co.*[45] held when a grievance challenged the employer's right to unilaterally establish an absentee control program:

> [T]he company had the right to unilaterally establish the absentee control program. Nothing in the contract prevented it. The contract impliedly as well as expressly reserved certain rights to management. The right to develop internal procedures and records systems would seem to be among such impliedly reserved management rights. Developing standard operating procedures for managerial personnel to follow also would appear to be a prerogative impliedly reserved to management.
>
> . . .
>
> I conclude that the Company's unilateral establishment of the absentee control program was not prohibited by the contract, and that it was a proper exercise of a reserved management right to manage the plant efficiently.

Arbitrator James A. Doyle in *Omaha Cold Storage Terminal,*[46] referring to a union claim that there were implied limitations on the management rights to assign job duties, said:

> Such a limitation should not be lightly inferred. One arbitrator said the limitation must be express. Others have said it must be specific. Still another said the limitation must be a clear and forceful statement. In *Congoleum-Nairn, Inc., supra,* the arbitrator stated that, where the company's right to eliminate classifications has been limited, "the limitation has been expressly spelled out in clear fashion, *e.g.,* existing job classifications shall remain unchanged for the life of the agreement."
>
> In the present Agreement there is no express, specific or clear and force-

---

[44] 33 LA 379, 384 (Quinlan, 1960).

[45] 64 LA 1283, 1288 (Bailey, 1975). *See also Celotex Corp.*, 24 LA 369 (Reynard, 1955); *Stewart-Warner Corp.*, 22 LA 547, 551 (Burns, 1954).

[46] 48 LA 24, 31 (Doyle, 1967). *See also Colorado Fuel & Iron Corp.*, 9 STEEL ARB. 6697, 6699 (Valtin, 1961); *Great Lakes Steel Corp.*, 8STEEL ARB. 5603 (Alexander, 1959); *Reynolds Metals Co.*, 25 LA 44 (Prasow, 1958); *Armstrong Rubber Mfg. Co.*, 24 LA 721 (McCoy, 1955).

ful statement to the effect that the Company may not, during the life of the Agreement, eliminate a classification and assign the duties formerly performed by employees in that occupation to other classifications.

In a case involving a claim that members of the supervising force could not perform production work, Arbitrator Joseph M. Klamon in *Olin Mathieson Chemical Corp.*[47] stated:

> The review of administrative and legal cases and authorities, which appear in the Company Brief, would alone seem to be conclusive on this point, namely that the recognition of the Union as the proper bargaining agent for its members in no way supports an implied abridgement of the right of the Company to assign work. This is one of the fundamental rights of management, and can only be limited or restricted in direct contract negotiations. Moreover, such a restriction must be stated in the clearest of terms and even then extends only as far as is clearly stated. In this case the Company has agreed in the contract to certain restrictions on supervisory officials performing production work. As indicated, this of course binds the Company as far as the contract language goes and no further.

Arbitrators have pointed out that the residual rights construction principle operates even where there is no clause in the agreement specifically reserving to management the right to manage. In *International Shoe Co.*,[48] Arbitrator Raymond R. Roberts said:

> Even without a specific retention of management rights in a collective bargaining agreement, it is generally regarded that management retains all of its rights as a common law employer, including those necessary to the operation of its business, except to the extent that these rights have been bargained away in the collective bargaining agreement.

THE "ARBITRATOR'S JURISDICTION" CONSTRUCTION PRINCIPLE

The parol evidence rule and the residual rights doctrine are further articulations of the arbitrator's jurisdiction and authority. The arbitrator must find a restriction imposed on management contained within the four corners of the agreement, simply because the arbitrator has been hired to interpret the terms of the written labor agreement and prescribe how they are to be applied to resolve a particular grievance.[49]

Most labor agreements expressly provide that the arbitrator does not have the authority to add to, subtract from, or modify the agreement.

---

[47]42 LA 1025, 1040 (Klamon, 1964). *See also Texas-Portland Cement Co.*, 61-2 ARB ¶ 8343 (Autrey, 1961); *Monsanto Chemical Co.*, 27 LA 736, 743 (Roberts, 1956); *McKinney Mfg. Co.*, 19 LA 291 (Reid, 1952).

[48]77-1 ARB ¶ 8121, 3538–39 (Roberts, 1977).

[49]*See* related discussion of the jurisdictional limitations imposed on arbitrators in Chapter VI.

For example, in *Mallinckrodt Chemical Works,*[50] Arbitrator Elmer Hilpert held that these limitations on his jurisdiction precluded him from creating new terms or restricting otherwise unrestricted managerial rights:

> An arbitrator may give effect to, and, thus, compel continued adherence to, a "past practice," under a collective bargaining agreement, by "interpreting" a term, or provision, in such agreement in conformity with such "past practice," only when such term, or provision, is *ambiguous* (*i.e.,* is susceptible to either of the two contended-for meanings); but an arbitrator—whose authority, or "jurisdiction," is limited, by such agreement, to applying the terms, or provisions, thereof, or to interpret(ing) existing provisions of the Agreement and apply(ing) them to the specific facts of the grievance dispute—may not compel continued adherence to a "past practice," *as such.*
>
> Confusion, in this area of labor-management law, arises from a failure to see the distinction between *statutory-administrative* "terms and conditions of employment," which are under the jurisdiction of the National Labor Relations Board, and the terms, or provisions, of a collective bargaining agreement, which, usually, are all that is under the "jurisdiction" of an arbitrator. [Footnote omitted. Emphasis in original.]

Arbitrator Marion Beatty similarly observed in *American Sugar Refining Co.:*[51]

> In grievance arbitration, arbitrators are employed to interpret contracts, not to write them, add to them or modify them. If they are to be modified, that has to be done at the bargaining table. If this Union is to have "jurisdiction over work," it must obtain this at the bargaining table in language that fairly imports this.
>
> Arbitrators are not soothsayers and "wise men" employed to dispense equity and good will according to their own notions of what is best for the parties, nor are they kings like Solomon with unlimited wisdom or courts of unlimited jurisdiction. Arbitrators are employed to interpret the working agreement as the parties themselves wrote it. In contract interpretation, we are trying to ascertain the mutual intention of the parties. We must be guided primarily by the language used. Admittedly, certain inferences may be read into it, but they should be only those inferences which clearly and logically follow from the language used and which reasonable men must have mutually intended. To go far afield in search of veiled inferences or ethereal or celestial factors is a mistake, I believe. Labor contracts are much more earthy; they are not written in fancy language purposely containing hidden meanings.

[50]38 LA 267, 268 (Hilpert, 1961). *See also Central Telephone Co. of Virginia,* 68 LA 957, 961 (Whyte, 1977); *Independent Machine Co.,* 62 LA 824, 827 (Rybolt, 1974); *Arkansas Chemicals, Inc.,* 73-1 ARB ¶ 8175, 3650 (Holly, 1973); *Western Greyhound Lines,* 33 LA 157 (Kliensorge, 1959); *Coca-Cola Bottling Company,* 31 LA 697 (Conn. Bd. of Mediation and Arbitration, 1958).
[51]37 LA 334, 337 (Beatty, 1961).

And in *Ethyl Visqueen,*[52] Arbitrator Fred Witney said:

> In short, what the Union requests here is for the Arbitrator to read language into Article V which is not expressed in its terms. No arbitrator worthy of the obligations of his office may add to or subtract from express language agreed to by employers and unions.

Even where the labor agreement is silent on the scope of the arbitrator's jurisdiction, arbitrators usually do not hesitate to imply such limitations. Arbitrator Maxwell Copelof, in *Selby Shoe Co.,*[53] restricting his own jurisdiction in the absence of a jurisdictional provision, held:

> While this contract does not specifically say so, it is the Arbitrator's well-considered judgment that as Arbitrator he should not assume any powers of in any way modifying an existing contract. This is clearly stated in many of the contracts between unions and companies, and while not clearly stated in the contract with [naming the company and the union] the Arbitrator is convinced were he to assume any such authority, both the Union and the Company would strenuously object to his so doing, and rightfully so.

Such self-restriction reflects the obvious and well-understood distinction between the parties' right to bargain their own contract, and the parties' right to enforce what they have bargained for. The grievance-arbitration process obviously has to do with the latter, not the former. Arbitrators who, on occasion, forget this principle and attempt to impose on the parties their own ideas of what the contract should provide often find themselves no longer being commissioned and have received harsh remonstrance from the courts (the *Steelworkers Trilogy.*[54])

CLOTHING PRACTICE WITH CONTRACTUAL STATUS

Diametrically opposed to those arbitrators who (1) apply the parol evidence rule so as to require that the claimed right or duty be found within the four corners of the collective agreement, (2) find no limitation on the management's right to take managerial action unless the limitation was agreed on and expressed in the agreement, and (3) conclude an arbitrator only has jurisdictional authority to find that the

---

[52] 73-2 ARB ¶ 8345 at 4268 (Witney, 1973). *See also Bucyrus-Erie Co.*, 69 LA 93, 99 (Lipson, 1977).

[53] 9 LA 721, 723 (Copelof, 1948).

[54] *United Steelworkers of America v. American Mfg. Co.*, 363 U.S. 564, 46 LRRM 2414, (1960); *United Steelworkers of America v. Warrior & Gulf Navigation Co.*, 363 U.S. 574, 46 LRRM 2416 (1960); *United Steelworkers of America v. Enterprise Wheel & Car Co.*, 363 U.S. 593, 46 LRRM 2423 (1960).

rights and obligations assumed by one or the other party in the written agreement can be established by the process of interpreting and applying its terms, are those arbitrators who, by one of several various theories, find that unexpressed conditions of employment, referred to as "past practices," obtain contractual status. In this sense, the so-called practice is construed to be an actual contract enforceable apart from any other provision, and not merely evidence of what other provisions were intended to mean. Use of past practice as a contract was contrasted with the residual rights construction principle by Arbitrator Malcolm D. Talbott in *General Aniline & Film Corp.*:[55]

> Many representatives of Management consider a labor contract to be an instrument by which the Union and the employers secure specifically ceded defined rights in derogation of Management's once absolute prerogatives. Thus Management would retain all but the specifically ceded powers. Unilateral action by Management without consultation with the Union could modify or terminate existing plans or establish new plans not covered by the agreement, at will, under this view.
>
> . . .
>
> An expression of this view, and the one adopted here, is that parties to a comprehensive labor contract, where no evidence appears to the contrary, are to be presumed to have entered in such a contract with the understanding that major conditions of employment, even though not covered by the agreement expressly, will by implied consent of the parties remain *status quo* unless they are changed by mutual agreement.
>
> To support this, we acknowledge that parties contract with reference to an existing set of practices even if they are not mentioned in the contract. . . . Matters not covered by the contract may be part of the "context" of the agreement in holding major working conditions as they were.
>
> . . .
>
> A collective bargain is, under the view adopted here, a complete settlement and stabilizing of issues involving cost to Management and income to employees for these are certainly *major* conditions. Thus, the intent of such a comprehensive agreement may fairly be said to be to continue existing conditions.
>
> . . .
>
> New action may be taken only by mutual agreement of the parties or at the time of negotiation to accomplish such fundamental changes. [Emphasis in original.]

An expression of this view—rejecting the parol evidence, residual

---

[55] 19 LA 628, 629 (Talbott, 1952). The view expressed in this opinion results in an obligation to consult and reach agreement before making changes, which slows down the rate of change. The deleterious effects of such a view on the rate of productivity improvement in England was explained by H. J. Hebden before the Royal Commission on Trade Unions and Employers' Associations, Minutes of Evidence 1004, Her Majesty's Stationery Office, 1966, quoted in LABOR LAW DEVELOPMENTS, Proceedings of the Seventeenth Annual Institute on Labor Law (New York: Matthew Bender, 1971), pp. 218-19.

rights, or jurisdiction principles—is shown by Arbitrator Robert P. Brecht in the *Sylvania Electric Products, Inc.,*[56] ruling on a union claim for restrictions on management's right to schedule overtime.:

> Under an agreement use of the term "right" conveys a technical sanction. Therefore, the Company's right to require employees to work on regularly scheduled overtime Saturdays must stem from its Agreement with the Union. The definition of Company rights under an agreement is determined in one of three ways: (1) by specific sanction or prohibition, (2) by reasonable inference from expressed clauses, or (3) by what may be called the principle of residual rights stemming from a management clause such as Article 1, Section 2 of the present Agreement between the parties.
>
> This last basis is simply that when an area of control or management right has not been identified in the minds of the parties when the collective bargaining agreement was reached it is a right that remains with management if it is a reasonable extension of the management function as granted in the agreement.
>
> The Company, quite obviously, has relied upon interpretation of somewhat related provisions, upon the management clause, and upon its vocal insistence in negotiations to defend its claim that it has the right to require employees to work on regularly scheduled overtime Saturdays.
>
> It is generally conceded that the present Agreement contains no provision which specifically grants the right in question to the Company or specifically prohibits that right to the Company.
>
> ... Were this the *first time* the issue was raised under a new Agreement or under a series of consecutive Agreements, the principle of residual rights would be entirely persuasive. If the parties for reasons of their own will not through either positive sanctions or negative prohibitions define management's rights, it can be fairly assumed that any right *not specifically identified* will remain a part of managerial prerogative so long as it represents a legitimate extension of functions necessary to operate the business. But this condition in the present case is most emphatically absent. The parties in negotiations wrestled with the precise right in issue. It is true, of course, that the Company never yielded in its belief that the right in question belonged legitimately among its family of prerogatives; but it is equally true that the Union, pointedly and consistently, refused to concede the point by agreement and insisted that the Agreement as written did not grant positively the right to the Company....
>
> The conclusion, therefore, is inescapable that the Agreement as written does not cover the point in issue. This question, then, must be settled on its merits.... [Emphasis in original.]

Arbitrator Irvine Kerrison in *Kiamesha Concord, Inc.,*[57] elevated practice to contractual status because there was no relevant language in the agreement:

[56]24 LA 199, 208 (Brecht, 1954). *See also Midwest Glasco,* 63 LA 869, 874 (Roberts, 1974).
[57]69-2 ARB ¶ 8586, 5003 (Kerrison, 1969). *See Shell Oil Company,* 24 LA 748, 749 (Jones, 1955).

[W]here a contract is silent on a matter at issue, . . . past practice carries most weight.

Arbitrator Merrill in *Phillips Petroleum*[58] said that practice attains contractual status when the practice has been in effect under various labor agreements:

> In the light of the decisions, as recited above, it seems to me that the current of opinion has set strongly in favor of the position that existing practices, in respect to major conditions of employment, are to be regarded as included within a collective bargaining contract, negotiated after the practice has become established, and not repudiated or limited by it.

Arbitrator Theodore Dyke in *Sani-Clean Service, Inc.*[59] implied that past practice attains contractual status simply because it has been in effect for a long period of time:

> However, it would seem rather patent that the program established by the Company, though unilaterally and voluntarily, without any Union participation, in 1948 and continued on up to the present time without any interruption or innovation . . . has become an entrenched condition of employment. It's like the proverbial turkey at Christmas time. Once the Company gives the bird to its employees, especially where it is over a period of time, it's theirs, and the Company can't thereafter unilaterally take away that bird. It's a condition of employment. It's an emolument having a dollar value like wages which is a part of the Contract.

Arbitrator Turkus in *Jacob Ruppert*[60] outlined the factors he relies on to give prior practice contractual status:

1. Does the practice concern a major condition of employment?
2. Was it established unilaterally?
3. Was it administered unilaterally?
4. Did either of the parties seek to incorporate it into the body of the written agreement?
5. What is the frequency of repetition of the "practice"?
6. Is the "practice" a long-standing one?
7. Is it specific and detailed?
8. Do the employees rely on it?

---

[58]24 LA 191, 194 (Merrill, 1955). *Accord, Kennecott Copper Co.*, 32 LA 646 (Ross, 1958); *Minneapolis-Moline Co.*, 17 LA 497, 503 (Lockhart, 1951). *See also Akron City Hospital*, 74-1 ARB ¶ 8098, 3367 (Kates, 1974); *Fruehauf Trailer Co.*, 29 LA 372 (Jones, 1957); *Morris P. Kirk & Son, Inc.*, 27 LA 6 (Prasow, 1956); *E. W. Bliss Co.*, 24 LA 614 (Dworkin, 1955); *Northland Greyhound Lines, Inc.*, 23 LA 277 (Levinson, 1954); *International Harvester Co.*, 20 LA 276 (Wirtz, 1953); *American Seating Co.*, 16 LA 115 (Whiting, 1951); *California Cotton Mills Co.*, 14 LA 377 (Marshall, 1950); *Franklin Ass'n of Chicago*, 7 LA 614 (Gilden, 1947).
[59]63 LA 810, 813-14 (Dyke, 1974).
[60]35 LA 503, 504 (Turkus, 1960). *See also McCall Printing Co.*, 63 LA 627 (McDermott, 1974).

Arbitrator Irvine Kerrison in *American Air Compressor Corp.*[61] applied similar criteria to require the payment of a year-end bonus:

> Payment of such a [year-end] bonus had been long-established practice and, in the absence of contract language that says or implies to the contrary, such practice becomes contractual and binding and one party may expect it to continue if it has become such a practice that he has a right to rely upon it, a practice understood and mutually accepted and so treated by one party that the other has a right to expect it as part of his bargain.

The reasoning relied on by arbitrators who espouse the view that past practice *per se* attains contractual status begins with a proposition once expressed by Archibald Cox that the parties, when they negotiate a labor agreement "cannot reduce all the rules governing a community like an industrial plant to fifteen or even fifty pages."[62] They therefore conclude that the agreement includes not just the written provisions stated therein, but also the conditions and practices that have been applied. Hence, if a particular practice or condition is not repudiated during negotiations, these arbitrators find implied from the silence of the negotiators that when the agreement was signed they also agreed to a tacit understanding that all practices or conditions then operating would continue in force. For example, Arbitrator Douglas B. Brown said:

> The agreement, no matter how short, does provide a guide to modes of procedure and to the rights of the parties on *all* matters affecting the conditions of employment. Where explicit provisions are made, the question is relatively simple. But even where the agreement is silent, the parties have, by their silence, given assent to a continuation of the existing modes of procedure.[63] [Emphasis in original.]

This implication, of course, should not be possible if it conflicts with the express language of the agreement. For example, if the agreement said "the written provisions constitute the entire agreement of the parties," it would seem to be improper to imply that the parties meant to make practices and conditions not recorded in the agreement a part of the agreement.

Arbitrator Harry Shulman espoused a contrary view. He viewed as unrealistic the assumption that parties by their silence agree to freeze all practices and conditions of employment:

---

[61] 74-1 ARB ¶ 8074, 3278 (Kerrison, 1974).

[62] Cox, *Reflections Upon Labor Arbitration*, 72 HARV. L. REV. 1482, 1499 (1959).

[63] Brown, *Management Rights and the Collective Agreement*, PROCEEDINGS OF THE FIRST ANNUAL MEETING OF THE INDUSTRIAL RELATIONS RESEARCH ASSOCIATION (Champaign: IRRA, 1949), pp. 145-55.

It is more than doubtful that there is any general understanding among employers and unions as to the viability of existing practices during the term of a collective agreement.... I venture to guess that in many enterprises the execution of a collective agreement would be blocked if it were insisted that it contain a broad provision that "all existing practices, except as modified by this agreement, shall be continued for the life thereof, unless changed by mutual consent." ... The reasons for the block would be, of course, the great uncertainty as to the nature and extent of the commitment, and the relentless search for cost-saving changes....[64]

Therefore, in Shulman's view the Archibald Cox implication theory was invalid. He elaborated his view in a Ford Motor Co. award:

But there are ... practices which are ... more happenstance, that is, methods that developed without design or deliberation. Or they may be choices by Management in the exercise of managerial discretion as to convenient methods at the time. In such cases there is no thought of obligation or commitment for the future. Such practices are merely present ways, not prescribed ways, of doing things. The relevent item of significance is not the nature of the particular method but the managerial freedom with respect to it. Being the product of managerial determination in its permitted discretion such practices are, in the absence of contractual provision to the contrary, subject to change in the same discretion.... But there is no requirement of mutual agreement as a condition precedent to a change of a practice of this character.

A contrary holding would place past practice on a par with written agreement and create the anomaly that, while the parties expend great energy and time in negotiating the details of the Agreement, they unknowingly and unintentionally commit themselves to unstated and perhaps more important matters which in the future may be found to have been past practice.[65]

Arbitrator Russell Smith appears to align himself with those arbitrators who adopt the Archibald Cox assumption that the parties intended to contractually freeze the status quo—i.e., all past practices and conditions—when they entered into a labor agreement.[66] Smith, however, recognizes that under such an assumption, the union is given a veto over all changes, including those management would make to improve productivity.[67] Arbitrator Smith placed some limitations on

---

[64]Shulman, *Reason, Contract and Law in Labor Relations*, 68 HARV. L. REV. 999, 1011 (1955).

[65]*Ford Motor Co.*, 19 LA 237, 242 (Shulman, 1952). *See also International Harvester Co.*, 20 LA 276 (Wirtz, 1953).

[66]Smith, Merrifield and Rothschild, COLLECTIVE BARGAINING AND LABOR ARBITRATION (Indianapolis: Bobbs-Merrill Co., 1970).

[67]An observer from Great Britain reported to a Royal Commission the effect on national productivity that can be found in the manner in which labor agreements are construed:

The major difference between the [industrial relations] system in North America and the system in the U.K. is that the method of collective bargaining in North America assigns to management a precise and specific management function which it may exercise during the

the Cox "assumption implication theory" in order to avoid situations which would contractually freeze the status quo:

> Think of the difficulty one might encounter in trying to establish that the unstated assumption of the negotiators on both sides of the table was to continue existing practices. The majority [Archibald Cox] approach, on the other hand, comes close to engrafting a "past practice" clause onto the typical collective agreement without regard to the actual assumptions of the negotiators. Their silence at the bargaining table is presumed to constitute assent to existing conditions, whether they thought of this or not.
>
> . . .
>
> . . . Those of us who accept the principle that an agreement may require the continuance of existing practice recognize that this principle cannot be allowed to freeze *all* existing conditions. For instance, the long-time use of hand-controlled grinding machines could hardly be regarded as a practice prohibiting the introduction of automatic grinding machines. Or the long-time use of pastel colors in painting plant interiors could not preclude management from changing to a different color scheme. Plainly, not all practices can be considered binding conditions of employment. Thus, while we are willing to imply that practices are a part of the agreement, we are apprehensive of the breadth of the implication. What seems correct from a theoretical point of view does not always make sense from a practical point of view. Arbitrators, accordingly, have accepted the implication but sought to limit it to just certain kinds of practices. The difficulty is to determine what kind of rational line, if any, can be drawn between those practices which may be incorporated into the agreement and those which may not.[68] [Emphasis in original.]

Arbitrator Smith, seeking to find some limitations on the status quo freeze that would prevent needed change, stated that the past practice concept would apply to only "major practices" as contrasted to "minor conditions."[69] However, Arbitrator Smith did point out the weakness in the "major-minor" distinction:

> What is *major* to one group of employees may be *minor* to all the others; what is *major* from the standpoint of morale may be *minor* from the stand-

---

term of the contract, subject only to the right of the union to file grievances for processing by the grievance procedure culminating in arbitration. . . .

The effect is that . . . management is able to produce change at a much faster rate than we are able to do in this country. For example, any change consistent with the terms of the contract may be introduced by management immediately. . . . In the U.K. because there is no enforceable recognition of management's specific functions, management must be prepared to negotiate every time it wishes to make a change. The result is that we tend to have to bargain under pressure all the time. . . . Because of this there is a tendency for the U.K. compromise to be less efficient than the North American equivalent action by management. . . . Great Britain, Royal Commission on Trade Unions and Employers' Associations, Minutes of Evidence 25, *Witness: Massey-Ferguson (U.K.), Ltd.* (London: Her Majesty's Stationery Office, 1966), p.1004, Testimony of H. J. Hebden.

[68]*See* note 66 *supra,* at 256-57.

[69]*See* note 66 *supra,* at 258.

point of earnings and job security. There is no logical basis for distinguishing between *major* and *minor* conditions.... More important, this kind of
test encourages arbitrators "to commence their thinking with what they
consider a desirable decision and then work backward to appropriate
premises, devising syllogisms to justify that decision...."[70] That is, if an
arbitrator decides to enforce the practice he calls it a *major* condition, and
if he decides otherwise he calls it a *minor* condition. To this extent, the test
provides us with a rationalization rather than a reason for our ruling.[71]
[Emphasis added.]

Arbitrator Edgar A. Jones in *General Controls Corp.*,[72] carried the
"practice obtains contractual status" theory so far that when the practice was contrary to the clear words of the agreement he concluded
that the written agreement should be amended or reformed to conform to the practice:

> Even language which by its clear terms brooks no interpretation but one
> can be effectively amended, even repealed, by a course of contrary inter-
> pretation indulged by the parties over a significant period of time.

The view that a practice in conflict with clear language should be
considered an amendment to the agreement, a "status quo" or past
practice freeze, was sharply criticized by Arbitrator Saul Wallen:[73]

> The proposition that past practice can be used "to modify or amend
> what is seemingly unambiguous" rests on a ... dubious foundation. Those
> who argue that it is often permissible, when an arbitrator is confronted
> with a conflict between an established practice and a seemingly clear and
> unambiguous contract provision, to regard the practice as an amendment
> to the agreement rest their argument on the legal theory of reformation.
> They maintain that the parties' day-to-day actions, when they run counter

---

[70]Frank, *Experimental Jurisprudence and the New Deal*, 78 CONG. REG. 12412, 12413
(1934).

[71]For a selection of cases involving these "major-minor" distinctions, *see Pan Am Southern
Corp.*, 25 LA 611, 613 (Reynard, Chm., 1955); *Phillips Petroleum Co.*, 24 LA 191, 194 (Merrill,
1955); *Continental Baking Co.*, 20 LA 309, 311 (Updegraff, 1953); *General Aniline & Film
Corp.*, 19 LA 628, 629 (Talbott, Chm., 1952). *See* Cox and Dunlop, *The Duty to Bargain Collectively During the Term of an Existing Agreement*, 63 HARV. L. REV. 1097, 1116, 1117 (1950).

[72]31 LA 240 (Jones, 1958). To the same effect, *see Borg-Warner Corp.*, 36 LA 961 (Mishne,
1961); *Smith Display Service*, 17 LA 524 (Sherbow, 1951); *International Shoe Co.*, 2 LA 201
(Klamon, 1946). *Contra, National Lead Co.*, 28 LA 470, 474 (Roberts, 1957); *Metropolitan
Coach Lines*, 27 LA 376, 383 (Lennard, 1956); *Smith Display Service*, 17 LA 524, 526 (Sherbow,
1951); *Gibson Refrigerator Co.*, 17 LA 313, 318 (Platt, 1951); *Texas-New Mexico Pipe Line Co.*,
17 LA 90 (Emory, 1951); *Bethlehem Steel Co.*, 13 LA 556, 560 (Killingsworth, 1949); *Merrill-
Stevens Dry Dock & Repair Co.*, 10 LA 562, 563 (Douglas, 1948); *Pittsburgh Plate Glass Co.*, 8
LA 317, 322 (Blair, 1947).

[73]Wallen, *The Silent Contract v. Express Provisions: The Arbitration of Local Working Conditions*, COLLECTIVE BARGAINING AND THE ARBITRATOR'S ROLE, Proceedings of the Fifteenth
Annual Meeting, National Academy of Arbitrators, M. Kahn, ed. (Washington: BNA Books,
1962), pp. 121-22. *See* Arbitrator Wallen's holding in *United States Steel Corp.*, 40 LA 636
(Wallen, 1963).

to the plain meaning of the contract's words, evidence an intent to substitute that which they actually do for that which they said in writing they
would do. . . .

But this approach, it seems to me, is in derogation of an important function of the collective bargaining agreement. . . .

. . .

. . . [T]here is much to be said for the idea that the collective agreement's
clear language should be considered as the lodestar that enables the top
management of the company or the union to correct the deviations from
course introduced by subordinates during their day-to-day operations. If
the deviations are regarded as evidence of an intent to modify the clear
terms of the agreement, the agreement's value as an instrument of control
is thereby diminished.

The tension between the theories that "past practice" is contractually frozen and the traditional view that the arbitrator's authority is
limited to enforcement of the written agreement is, of course, substantial. As noted by Arbitrator George Cheney in *Inspiration Consolidated Copper Co.*[74] when all past practice is given contractual
status, the parol evidence rule is emasculated.

Furthermore, evidence of usage and custom is not permissible to restrict
or enlarge the explicit terms of an instrument or otherwise control the apparent intention of the parties. It is recognized that to permit a written and
express contract to be thus controlled, varied, or contradicted by a usage
or custom would not only amount to admitting parol evidence to vary a
written instrument but also would allow more presumptions or implications arising, in the absence of positive proof expressions of intention, to
control, vary, or even contradict the most formal and written declarations
of the parties.

Arbitrator Carl Warns in *Kroger Co.*[75] said that giving contractual
status to prior practice *per se* can be a violation of the arbitrator's
jurisdictional limitations:

Where as in this case the contract is completely silent on job assignments there is nothing for the practice (the grievance settlement) to relate
to or for the history of the negotiations to clarify. In other words, for me to
use the settlement of grievance No. 1113 as a principle upon which to resolve the issue before me would be to "add" to the contract which is not
within my authority to do. . . . [A]s arbitrator authorized only to construe
an existing contract and without authority to make one for the parties, I
can consider what the parties have done since the signing of the contract
only as an aid in resolving ambiguities in negotiated language. In other
words, where written language is not clear, as pointed out, I can consider

---

[74] 7 LA 86, 88 (Cheney, 1947).
[75] 31 LA 82, 84 (Warns, 1968). To the same effect, *see Mallinckrodt Chemical Works*, 38 LA
267, 268 (Hilpert, 1961).

bargain table statements and practices including the settlement of grievances as aids to interpretation. But I cannot without exceeding my authority accept such evidence to add duties and responsibilities which the parties did not agree to at the bargaining table.

And Arbitrator Harold W. Davey in *John Deere Des Moines Works*[76] explained another incongruous result that occurs when prior practice is given contractual status.

> In other words, the Company's past practice (which has been discontinued and which the Union seeks to have restored) was in my judgment contrary to both the letter and the spirit of (the contract). Therefore, it cannot be argued successfully that a change of practice which in effect brings it into line with contract requirements is at the same time a violation of the contract.

There are, of course, many labor agreements that contain a clause giving contractual status to practices beneficial to the employee so long as the underlying conditions basic to the practice remain unchanged. The famous 2B Clause, known as the "local working conditions clause," in the basic steel agreements is an example. Decisions of arbitrators under such clauses are not, of course, examples of the elevation of past practice to contractual status because in such agreements past practice has been given contractual status by an agreement of the parties.[77] The significance that the lack of a "past practice clause" in the agreement has on a grievance claim was pointed out by Arbitrator Bert L. Luskin in *The Maytag Company:*[78]

> The Collective Bargaining Agreement does not contain a "local working conditions" clause that would give contractual status to an established practice. There are specific terms and provisions of the Agreement that govern the matter of lunch periods. The payment of lunch money to a Driver is not a matter of contract, and a practice in that respect cannot achieve contractual status.

THE "TENSION" BETWEEN "MANAGEMENT RIGHTS" AND "JUST CAUSE" ADJUSTS DISCIPLINE

The Law of the Shop is Related to Residual Management Rights

In the *Steelworkers Trilogy*[79] the phrase "law of the shop" was used to explain that arbitrators rather than judges acquire an expertise in

[76]22 LA 628, 631 (Davey, 1954). *Accord, Carnegie Illinois Steel Corp.*, 12 LA 217 (Seward, 1949).
[77]A typical interpretation of 2B is found in *National Tube Division, United States Steel Co.*, 2 STEEL ARB. 1187 (Garrett, 1953).
[78]*The Maytag Company*, Grievance No. P1-D18-3-65 (Luskin, 1966).
[79]*United Steelworkers of America v. American Mfg. Co.*, 363 U.S. 564, 46 LRRM 2414 (1960); *United Steelworkers of America v. Warrior & Gulf Navigation Co.*, 363 U.S. 574, 46

labor relations matters. One of the clearest expositions of this type of "law" was reported by the Seventh Circuit in *S. J. Groves & Sons Co. v. Int'l Brotherhood of Teamsters, Local 627.*[80] The court carefully reviewed several arbitration awards in which "just cause" for discharge was discussed and concluded that discharge was now the "law" when one employee violently attacks another in the plant:

> "A dispute developed over Bower's (another laborer) use of [Grievant B——'s] personal automobile in this work and led to a heated verbal argument and an exchange of profanity and insult between [A——] and [B——]. [B——] swung at [A——] who blocked the blow. [A——] kicked [B——] below the stomach, leaving bruises. [B——] went to the truck, returned with a three-foot 'Maddox' handle and struck [A——] twice, first, on the back which knocked him to the ground and then again on his legs. Both [B——] and [A——] were discharged for fighting on the job." It was also stipulated that prior to this incident [B——] had not been disciplined by the company in three years of employment.[81]

The Seventh Circuit strongly upheld the district court's decision:

> The issue at trial was whether the employer breached the collective bargaining provision authorizing the employer to discharge employees for just cause when it discharged [B——] for fighting on the job site during working hours. Summary judgments are properly granted where there is no genuine issue of material fact and the moving party is entitled to *judgment as a matter of law.*[82] [Emphasis added.]

The Seventh Circuit went on to explain why approval of the discharge of a grievant who had attacked another in the work place is appropriate:

> The rationale for allowing employers to discharge employees for fighting is that such violence threatens the employer's legitimate concerns in job safety and in employee discipline and morale.[83]

The significance of the court's determination that violence warrants "just cause" for discharge cannot be emphasized too strongly.[84] Poor safety, poor employee discipline, and poor morale obviously reduce efficiency and productivity. Managers have the duty to plan and direct employees effectively; from that duty evolves a corollary right to discharge.

This analysis of the rights collected as residual rights is often summarized in the "management" provision of the labor agreement. This

---

LRRM 2416 (1960); *United Steelworkers of America v. Enterprise Wheel & Car Co.*, 363 U.S. 593, 46 LRRM 2423 (1960).

[80]581 F.2d 1241 (7th Cir. 1978), 99 LRRM 2623.

[81]*Id.* at 1244, 99 LRRM at 2625.

[82]*Id.*

[83]*Id.* at 1245, 99 LRRM at 2625.

[84]*Id. See* "The Margin Increases When the Discharge Is Work-Related," *infra.*

summary does not create rights but is merely descriptive of the rights which managers had before the labor agreement was executed.

The one important provision in a labor agreement that is not simply a recitation of reserved rights is the typical statement that "An employee may be discharged for just cause." These words are related to the residual rights of management to discharge employees, but the word "just cause" establishes limits which have been debated by analysts.

Some analysts have asserted that management's residual rights include the right to discharge employees if the discharge is not inconsistent with either statutory law or with a specific limitation agreed upon by the manager-owner and the union. Since it is the manager-owner who initially hires the individual employee, the manager-owner can release that employee at any time, unless the release is in contravention to one of the described limits. This concept of the "prerogative of ownership" had its origin in the feudal system of property.

Other analysts assert that management's residual rights have a functional base. An award in *Wright Aeronautical Corp.*[85] contains this view:

> ... It is management who is responsible for results. This being so, the management should be free to manage. To permit compulsory arbitration in matters affecting ... the selection of men to direct the execution of these policies, would force upon management judgment of persons chosen as arbitrators who may know little or nothing about the business and plant problems involved and who bear no personal responsibility for the consequences of their errors. The operation of a great industrial plant ... is a task which can be performed only by men familiar with its organization and skilled in the work that is done. Tampering with the machine by unskilled hands would be a dangerous procedure and is not to be encouraged.

The idea of "just cause" is that management retains the right to determine discipline, but only so long as such action sustains operational efficiency. This elusive contractual standard reflects itself in three different ways—the "functional test," the "management margin," and the "corrective discipline test."

The Functional Test

Industrial discipline rests upon the straightforward definition of management as the group of individuals with the duty of maintaining efficient plant operation. Since operating an efficient plant is its prime responsibility, management must have the concomitant right to

---

[85] 13 LRRM 2580, 2582 (1943) (arbitrator not indicated).

discharge that responsibility. This simple functional interpretation of management's rights and employees' duties was explained by Arbitrator Harry Shulman in *Ford Motor Company:*[86]

> But an industrial plant is not a debating society. Its object is production. When a controversy arises, production cannot wait for exhaustion of the grievance procedure. While that procedure is being pursued, production must go on. And someone must have the authority to direct the manner in which it is to go on until the controversy is settled. That authority is vested in supervision. It must be vested there because the responsibility for production is also vested there; and responsibility must be accompanied by authority. It is fairly vested there because the grievance procedure is capable of adequately recompensing employees for abuse of authority by supervision.

Arbitrator Albert Cornsweet made a similar observation in *Mosaic Tile Company:*[87]

> Now it is well established and universally accepted practice in labor-management relations that management has the right to direct the working forces and operate the plant efficiently.... Chaos would result if an employee could refuse to do work directed and this position spread through a vital department. An employee or group of employees cannot take matters into their own hands.

The right to impose discipline for failure to follow instructions is an inherent right of management. Arbitrator Clarence M. Updegraff recognized this fundamental principle in *John Deere Tractor Co:* [88]

> If one man may refuse to obey reasonable orders given to him within the scope of his duties without being discharged, all others may do so. All discipline would disappear and the production might well meet the vanishing point.... It is not a proper course of procedure for any man in a plant organized and under contract ... to refuse to do work directly ordered by his foreman when the same is within the line of his usual duties or is otherwise a reasonable direction from Management. The worker who feels his rights are being invaded, to avoid insubordination, should carry out the direction of a superior in the organization of the Company and report his contention promptly to the steward of his department.

The functional approach is easily defined: (1) the main responsibility of management is to properly direct the work force, and (2) when an employee engages in conduct which interferes with the fulfillment of management's duty to operate an efficient work force, management has the just right to impose discipline to either stop that conduct or if necessary to exclude the employee from the work force. Application of

---

[86]3 LA 779, 781 (Shulman, 1944).
[87]9 LA 625, 627 (Cornsweet, 1948).
[88]5 LA 561, 563 (Updegraff, 1946).

the functional approach to specific situations is often difficult. The following are comparative examples of what is a necessary functional action and what is not.

As a hypothetical example, an owner-manager with strong beliefs about morality observes two unmarried employees, male and female, together in an automobile near a country dance hall and discharges them. In a second example the owner-manager observes a couple together in a rarely-used room within the plant during working hours and takes the same action. An arbitrator could quite properly reinstate the two discharged employees in the first situation and not in the second. The manager has no functional purpose for imposing his standards of morality on employees. However, if this action occurs in the plant during working hours, there is a functional reason for enforcing the management prerogative to discipline for just cause.

A second frequent contrasting situation occurs when an employee is discharged for the use of profane language against a supervisor. The contrast can be best explained by two illustrations in a plant containing a labor agreement which lists causes for discharge, one being "employees shall not use profane language toward a supervisor." In the first situation, the employee says the profane words to the foreman at the start of the workday so loudly that other employees who are gathered around him can hear the words; in the second, the employee says the same words to the foreman when instructed to climb back up into a crane cab to continue operating it over a hot steel mill soaking pit because the relief worker did not report. The words in the first situation would constitute serious insubordination because if they are condoned, the efficiency within the work group would be reduced; whereas in the second situation the use of the profane words was primarily a reaction from fatigue and hence quite understandable, and they were not communicated to other employees as a threat to the supervisor's authority. The point at which a situation involving profanity becomes insubordination is not easily determined because it occurs when authority is being challenged. The total setting must be evaluated.

Arbitrator Kelliher in *Del Monte Corp., Midwest Division*[89] dealt with a case where an employee poured beer on the sleeve of an assistant plant manager's jacket while the assistant plant manager was standing near the bar at a party in honor of the retirement of three employees, attended by about 100 employees. Only one other employee observed the action, which was not accompanied by any abusive statement. The assistant manager did testify that he had

---

[89]*Del Monte Corporation, Midwest Division and Retail, Wholesale & Department Store Union, AFL-CIO Local No. 17* (Kelliher, Nov. 19, 1980) (Unpublished).

heard a "vocal disturbance" at the table where the employee concerned was seated when he delivered the invocation, and one cannery supervisor sitting at that table heard the employee say that if anybody would give her some money she would "pour a beer on Dick's head."

Arbitrator Kelliher evaluated the setting in making his determination as to whether the event was insubordination. In doing so he tested the effect of the events on the managerial ability to direct the other employees if the employee was not excluded from the work group. His pertinent observation follows:

> The Grievant made no abusive or threatening statements to Mr. [K———]. Only one other person was present and aware of the incident. . . . Not every such incident will adversely affect a Supervisor's ability to direct the workers. This principle was recognized by Arbitrator Bowles in his Award in General Telephone Co. of Kentucky, 69 LA 351, wherein he stated:
>> "In the cases, too, is recognition that an Arbitrator must assess the fact of the incident upon the employment relationship and particularly the future good will between the parties. There are those incidents that flare up that really will not affect future relations in any way."
>
> The Arbitrator does not believe that Ms. [P———'s] actions would have seriously affected the future relationship of the parties or have jeopardized Mr. [K———'s] ability to supervise the employees. The Arbitrator does not think that Mr. [K———] would have been intimidated by the Grievant or held in lesser esteem by other employees because of the incident. Based upon the particular facts and circumstances of this case, the Arbitrator cannot find that discharge was the appropriate penalty.

The Sixth Circuit[90] vacated an arbitration award that had reinstated an employee who had been discharged for insubordination. The arbitrator had determined that the discharge was too severe a penalty for the insubordination which involved the calling of a supervisor a "son-of-a-bitch" in the presence of the division manager and other employees. The Sixth Circuit found that when the arbitrator finds that the employee was insubordinate (which was not the finding by Arbitrator Kelliher on this particular issue) and when the collective bargaining agreement spells out "discharge" as the appropriate penalty for insubordination, the arbitrator is not free to dispense his own brand of industrial justice and reinstate the dischargee. The court went on to hold that management must retain the right to evaluate the point at which insubordination cannot be condoned; the arbitrator cannot easily second guess management's decision:

> The arbitrator states, after quoting Article XII of the collective bargaining agreement: "Thus, it appears in the collective bargaining agreement

---

[90]*International Brotherhood of Firemen and Oilers, Local 935-B v. The Nestle Co.*, 630 F.2d 474, 105 LRRM 2715 (6th Cir. 1980), *rev'g* 462 F. Supp. 94, 100 LRRM 2927.

that insubordination *may* be just cause for discharge." The collective bargaining agreement, however, uses the word "shall" rather than "may."

In the closing paragraph of his award, the arbitrator makes the following incredible statement:

"Because of the seniority of the grievant and because of lack of proof of threats or swearing above and beyond one name-calling of 'a son-of-a-bitch' there is insufficient proof in the record to make me believe that the grievant was, in fact, guilty of the vulgarities and threats as alluded to by the Company. For that reason I am going to give the grievant some relief.

IV AWARD

"The grievant shall be reinstated to his employment but without any back pay whatsoever and without loss of his seniority or contractual benefits."

Thus the arbitrator ignored his previous specific findings of insubordination by the grievant in his refusal to obey three orders of his foreman and the grievant's fabrication of his real defense, and then because the Company did not corroborate additional items of swearing, vile language and threats of violence, the arbitrator excuses the grievant's insubordination by declining to enforce the discharge provisions in the collective bargaining agreement.

A discharge for "just cause" inherently means exclusion of an employee from the work force for functional reasons and not as punishment by the employer for some "fault." This concept is most clearly articulated in awards by arbitrators when they approve the exclusion of employees as discharge for "just cause" in circumstances in which the employee is clearly not acting even negligently and certainly without any fault.

Arbitrator Yaeger in *Weber Mfg. Co., Inc.*[91] upheld a discharge for "just cause" because the grievant, while experiencing an epileptic seizure, had thrashed about in the midst of moving machinery. Obviously, the grievant's action was not premeditated; but the risk of injury to himself and to fellow employees was sufficient to justify exclusion. The arbitrator explained:

[A]n employee may be terminated for cause on account of circumstances that are beyond the control of said employee, and render him unemployable either in his present position or in another position.

... The Union believes the Employer's failure to require the Grievant to submit to a medical examination, subsequent to his second in-plant seizure and before the decision to discharge, establishes the discharge to be without cause....

. . .

In the instant case, there is no medical evidence to support a conclusion that the Grievant will not suffer an in-plant seizure in the future which would endanger both his safety and that of his fellow employees.

---

[91] 63 LA 56, 58–59 (Yaeger, 1974).

In *Du Pont (Netpreme Craftsmen)*[92] Arbitrator Epstein sustained the discharge of an employee who went to sleep while assigned as a watchman where welders were working in a closed tank. The grievant's responsibility as watchman was of some import. His alarm would both alert rescue crews to remove any welders who had fainted from the chemical fumes sometimes generated by the heat of the welding and warn all other welders to evacuate the area. The discharge was upheld as an action for "just cause" even though the sleeping was the employee's first such event. Since welding in such enclosures is an operational necessity, management must be certain that each employee understands that sleeping when acting as a watchman will result in automatic exclusion.

Similarly, Arbitrator Peter J. Kelliher stated in *Maremont Automotive Products:*[93]

> The Arbitrator is unable to find here that the Company did not act "in good faith" in relieving this employee from duty based upon the legitimate reason that competent medical opinion held that a failure to do so might lead to injury to the Grievant or to her fellow employees.

Arbitrator Robert G. Howlett in *E. I. Du Pont*[94] departed from the functional standard and adopted certain criminal law standards. On the basis that the grievant was temporarily insane when he viciously assaulted two employees and damaged property in the company's chemical plant, the arbitrator reinstated him.

> I have reached the conclusion that, in this case, the discharge should be set aside.
> The evidence establishes that Grievant suffered a mental or emotional breakdown when he assaulted the two employees and damaged Company property. The evidence does not persuade that Grievant was "at fault" to the extent that he abused or misused drugs which caused his behavior on the morning of December 26 as the Company asserts.
> ... Danger to Company employees and property does not outweigh the failure to establish just cause for discharge.

In sharp contrast, Arbitrator Davis in *Silas Mason Co.*[95] approved

[92] AAA Case No. 52-30-0049-77 (Epstein, 1978) (unpublished).
[93] 37 LA 175, 176 (Kelliher, 1961). *See also Arandell Corp.*, 56 LA 832 (Hazelwood, 1971).
[94] *E. I. duPont de Nemours & Co., East Chicago Plant* (Howlett, Sept. 1979) (unpublished). Arbitrator Klein in *B. F. Goodrich Co.*, 77-2 ARB ¶ 8561 (1977) reinstated the grievant and had him placed on sick leave retroactively because he decided the grievant was mentally ill when he struck a co-worker in the truckers' room, breaking the co-worker's nose and inflecting a facial gash requiring medical treatment at a hospital. The arbitrator said: "Simply stated, as a matter of equity, fundamental justice and common sense, it would be unfair and unjust to hold a person responsible for an act of misconduct committed at a time when that person was not only unable to control his actions but was mentally incapable of comprehending the culpable nature thereof." 77-2 ARB at 5426.
[95] 59 LA 197, 199 (Davis, 1972).

the discharge of an employee working in a munition plant when management found the employee "emotionally unstable." The arbitrator held that such an individual "simply cannot be infused into prime munitions manufacturing conditions. The company concluded that it could no longer take the risk of precipitous action by the grievant which might lose the lives of numerous employees as well as her own."

The Manager's Margin and the Arbitrator

Arbitrator William Stix in *Lever Bros.*[96] said he did not have the authority to substitute his discretion for that of the employer when an employee was discharged after being found "passed-out and blue" in the plant because of drug use. Stix also said he was unwilling to "second guess" the supervision. The employee had appealed to the Drug Addiction Committee (a union/management committee) and asserted that he would seek and accept help; because of his statements, a grievance was filed seeking reinstatement. The view of Stix is a clear expression of the view that an arbitrator should not upset a management determination unless it was "unreasonable, arbitrary or capricious" and that excluding an employee who was found "passed-out" in spite of the intention to seek help the grievant stated to a committee, does not meet this decription. This view sets up the "Manager's Margin" that causes the arbitrator not to be a "review manager without responsibility."

Arbitrator Marion Beatty explained in *Trans World Airlines, Inc.,*[97] why a labor arbitrator should not become an independent judge (even though he was for years the District Judge in the Third Judicial District in Topeka, Kansas). He explained that when he was acting as a labor arbitrator he was performing a different function—*i.e.* reviewing the manager's action:

> Under the generally accepted rule, if management's original decision in the matter was not arbitrary, capricious or unreasonable, or based on mistake of fact, its decision should stand. Furthermore, the boundaries of reasonableness should not be so narrowly drawn that management's judgment must coincide exactly with the arbitrator's judgment. If the penalty imposed is within the bounds of what the arbitrator can accept as a range of reasonableness, it should not be disturbed.
>
> A common mistake of some employees is the belief that they can, by appealing the disputed matter to arbitration, take the matter completely away from management and place it into the hands of a third party or

---

[96]70 LA 75, 76 (Stix, 1977). *See also Southern Iron & Equipment Co.*, 65 LA 694 (Rutherford, 1975).
[97]41 LA 142, 144 (Beatty, 1963).

board for an independent decision, based on sympathy or on standards different from those customarily used in industrial relations.

The comment by Arbitrator Beatty gains significance because, as a federal district judge who always acts as a third party, he can describe the contrasting role of a labor arbitrator with such precision.

The "Unreasonable, Arbitrary, or Capricious" Test

The general limitation on reduction of discipline imposed is the principle that an arbitrator should not substitute his or her judgment for that of management as to the appropriate penalty unless the arbitrator can find that the discipline imposed was "arbitrary, capricious, or discriminatory."[98] This limitation on the reduction of discipline was succinctly set forth in a frequently cited award by Arbitrator Whitley P. McCoy in *Stockham Pipe Fittings Co.*:[99]

> Where an employee has violated a rule or engaged in conduct meriting disciplinary action, it is primarily the function of management to decide upon the proper penalty. If management acts in good faith upon a fair investigation and fixes a penalty not inconsistent with that imposed in other like cases, an arbitrator should not disturb it. The mere fact that management has imposed a somewhat different penalty or a somewhat more severe penalty than the arbitrator would have, if he had had the decision to make originally, is no justification for changing it. The minds of equally reasonable men differ. A consideration which would weigh heavily with one man will seem of less importance to another. A circumstance which highly aggravates an offense in one man's eyes may be only slight aggravation to another. If an arbitrator could substitute his judgment and discretion for the judgment and discretion honestly exercised by management, then the functions of management would have been abdicated, and unions would take every case to arbitration. The result would be as intolerable to employees as to management. The only circumstances under which a penalty imposed by management can be rightfully set aside by an arbitrator are those where discrimination, unfairness, or capricious and arbitrary action are proved—in other words, where there has been abuse of discretion.

Arbitrator Stouffer said in *S. A. Shenk & Co.*[100] that the company's

---

[98] For a few of the numerous decisions where this principle is explained, *see Kaiser Aluminum & Chemical Corp.*, 48 LA 449 (Koven, 1967); *Randall Co.*, 66-2 ARB ¶ 8692 (Wissner, 1966); *West Virginia Pulp & Paper Co.*, 45 LA 515 (Daugherty, 1965); *Union-Tribune Publishing Co.*, 64-2 ARB ¶ 8626 (Prasow, 1964); *Baugh & Sons Co. of Ohio*, 62-3 ARB ¶ 8771 (Baldwin, 1962); *Davison Chemical Co.*, 31 LA 920 (McGuinness, 1959); *S.A. Shenk & Co.*, 24 LA 458 (Hays, 1955); *Bauer Bros. Co.*, 23 LA 696 (Dworkin, 1954); *Corn Products Refining Co.*, 21 LA 105 (Gilden, 1953).
[99] 1 LA 160, 162 (McCoy, 1945).
[100] 26 LA 395, 397 (Stouffer, 1956). *See also Hawaiian Telephone Co.*, 43 LA 1218, 1224-25 (Tsukiyama, 1964).

determination of the appropriate disciplinary action should not be redetermined by the arbitrator once it is found that the penalty was not "discriminatory, unfair, capricious or arbitrary," or in contravention of the terms of the labor agreement.

> The mere fact that Management had imposed somewhat different or more severe penalty than this Arbitrator might have fixed had he had the decision to make originally is no justification for this Arbitrator to change the penalty, that being primarily a function of Management....
>
> The only circumstances under which a penalty imposed by Management can rightfully be set aside by an Arbitrator are where discrimination, unfairness or capricious and arbitrary action are proved; i.e., where there has been abuse of discretion or in contravention of the terms of an existing Labor Contract.

This principle has been followed by several courts in vacating reinstatement awards when the arbitrators did not find that the management's determination was "arbitrary and capricious."[101]

Arbitrator Bert Luskin in the *Southwestern Bell Telephone Co.*[102] award said:

> The Arbitrator, however, cannot agree with the contention of the Company that the application of the standards of "just cause" would permit an arbitrator to indiscriminately substitute his judgment for that of the Company in all instances. In effect, the action taken by the Company must be examined in the light of the basis upon which the Company made its determination; and if the events would indicate that the Company determination was based upon the exercise of reason, judgment and discretion, the action of the Company must be sustained, unless it can be demonstrated that the decision was either discriminatory, arbitrary, capricious or based upon error of fact. The Arbitrator should not lightly disturb the Company's determination merely because he does not personally agree with the judgment exercised by the Company; nor should he substitute his judgment for that of the Company on the basis that different persons exercising judgment and discretion based upon the same facts might come to a different conclusion.

Arbitrator Clark Kerr, in *Wholesale Bakers Association of Sacramento*,[103] applied the view that the company has the initial right to determine discipline and it is presumed that the disciplinary action is correct:

---

[101] *Truck Drivers and Helpers, Local 784 v. Ulry-Talbert Co.*, 330 F.2d 562 (8th Cir. 1964). *See also Textile Workers v. American Thread Company*, 291 F.2d 894 (4th Cir. 1961); *Amanda Bent Bolt Co. v. UAW, Local 1549*, 451 F.2d 1277 (6th Cir. 1971); *Swerdlove v. Karlan and Bleicher, Inc.*, 41 LA 1064 (N.Y. Sup. Ct. 1963).

[102] AAA Case No. L-25262 DAL-L33-59 (Luskin, 1960) (unpublished), at 6.

[103] 4 ALAA ¶ 68,641 (Kerr, 1950).

The company has the basic right to discharge. The union may challenge discharges on the grounds that there was no adequate cause. If the union makes no challenge, the action of the company stands. If the union does make a challenge, it must show why the challenge is a merited one. There is no presumption that the action of the company is wrong until proved right; but quite the contrary. The contract does not read: "The company may not discharge until cause for discharge has been proved." If the contract did read that way, then the company would need to carry the burden of proof.

In *Kellogg Co.*,[104] Arbitrator Meltzer stated the same principle:

> Where, as in this case, there has been a fair hearing and a good-faith consideration of all the circumstances by management, management's determination as to the appropriate penalty should not be disturbed unless it was clearly unreasonable. The question involved is not whether the Board would have imposed the same penalty. The question is whether the penalty is within the reasonable range of discretion which management must have in order to discharge its primary responsibility for safe and efficient operations. . . .

Arbitrator Thomas Reynolds discussed these fundamentals in *Hercules Powder Co.*,[105] which involved a determination of the ability of two employees:

> Who shall decide that the difference between two employees is great, or is so small as to make them equal for all practical purposes? The instant case perfectly illustrates the dilemma. The Union complains that, besides seniority, there is no objective yardstick which can be applied to measure relative ability and aptitude. The Company agrees that these matters cannot be measured with perfect objectivity, but insists that experienced supervisors can reliably judge men. . . . [T]o accept the Union's thesis here would amount to saying . . . that when the Union disagrees with the Company's judgment it may have the decision reviewed by a third party. This way lies general confusion. Aside from its internal contradiction, the proposition is defective in its faulty assumption that outside parties, unfamiliar with the employees involved, could make better judgments as to their relative abilities and aptitudes than could the supervisors (assuming good faith on the part of the latter).

Since, as Arbitrator Reynolds observed, an arbitrator, as a third party, is generally incapable of being as sensitive to legitimate managerial needs as is the management, arbitrators typically will not reverse a management determination unless it is shown to be arbitrary, capricious, and without reasonable foundation, or so clearly erroneous as to suggest reliance upon invidious factors.

---

[104] 28 LA 303, 308–09 (Meltzer, 1957).
[105] *Hercules Powder Co.*, 10 LA 624, 626 (Reynolds, 1948).

Arbitrator Lichliter in *Hershey Chocolate Co.*[106] said:

The employer is best fitted to judge in such matters which employee is more valuable to him, and the Arbitrator does not believe that he should substitute his own judgment therefor in the absence of any evidence that the employer's determination was exercised arbitrarily or capriciously.

Arbitrators have followed this standard in other types of cases. For example, in a case involving work assignments, Arbitrator Vernon Stouffer in *Green River Steel Corp.*[107] held:

Management is entitled in the first instance to determine whether it has the required machinery, tools and equipment to perform a job.... If it be ultimately found that Management's judgment was arbitrary, capricious, unreasonable or made in bad faith, then its decision may be set aside. However, a mere error in judgment is not in itself sufficient reason to set the same aside, provided it is made in good faith.

Similarly, in regard to incentive standard and job evaluation cases, Arbitrator Schmidt in *Kroger Co.*[108] said:

It is, of course, true that ordinarily when a job rate is determined by a formalized classification and evaluation procedure the results of the evaluation as made by management should not be overridden or changed by an arbitrator in the absence of clear proof of arbitrariness....

Some arbitrators do not accept this limitation on their right to modify the amount of discipline. Instead, they hold that where the agreement does not impose a clear limitation on the arbitrator's power, they may substitute their own judgment concerning the amount of discipline and modify the amount of discipline even without finding management's determination to be arbitrary, capricious, or discriminatory.

As a practical matter, arbitrators who recognize the management margin with the view that the arbitrator will not upset the manager's decision unless the manager's action was "arbitrary and capricious"

[106]*Hershey Chocolate Co.*, 1 ALAA 67,169 at 67,361 (Lichliter, 1946). *See also Christy Vault Co.*, 42 LA 1093 (Koven, 1964); *General Box Co.*, 35 LA 867 (Caraway, 1960); *Allied Chemical & Dye Corp.*, 29 LA 395 (Reid, 1957); *Weber Showcase & Fixture Co.*, 27 LA 40 (Prasow, 1956); *Ingram-Richardson Mfg. Co.*, 3 LA 482 (Whiting, 1945). *See* Updegraff, ARBITRATION AND LABOR RELATIONS, Third Edition of ARBITRATION OF LABOR DISPUTES (Washington: BNA Books, 1970), pp. 304–05:

Arbitrators quite generally . . . hold that the decision of such a matter is one primarily for management, subject to being set aside only upon satisfactory proof that the decision was not a *bona fide* exercise of judgment and discretion but was the result of bias, favoritism, anti-union prejudice, or such like matter, or was the result of a clear mistake.

[107]*Green River Steel Corp.*, 41 LA 132, 136 (Stouffer, 1963). *See also United States Steel Corp.*, 41 LA 777 (Florey, 1963).
[108]*Kroger Co.*, 33 LA 296, 298 (Schmidt, 1959).

may produce different awards.[109] Arbitrator Elmer Hilpert in *Aladdin Industries, Inc.*,[110] clearly summarized this approach as follows:

> Arbitrators vary in the matter in which they state the limits, if any, that exist on their exercise of *their* discretion in this matter. Some apparently believe that *they* are possessed of power to apply the Gilbert & Sullivan principle that the "punishment should be made to fit the crime"; others, while adhering to that same principle, grant that the initial discretion, as to the severity of the penalty to impose, rests with the employer but claim the power to reverse, by modification, employer "abuses of discretion" in that regard; while still others insist they are to sustain the penalty imposed by the employer, unless to do so would "shock his [the arbitrator's] conscience." We believe precise *verbal* formula to be applied to be unimportant, for some arbitrators' consciences "shock" more readily, and some less readily, than others. [Emphasis in original.]

Studies classifying the types of arbitration awards indicate that the highest percentage involve discharges (exclusions). In such cases, the grievant will claim the discharge was not for "just cause"; management will say the "cause" is one typical in discharge action and the action is not an arbitrary, capricious, or discriminatory action.

The Courts Hold Back to Protect Arbitration

Sometimes the manager strongly believes that the arbitrator has entered the management's preserve when the arbitrator upsets the manager's action. This sometimes causes a suit to be filed for vacation of the award. What does the court do then? One circuit court in *Kewanee Machinery Div., Chromalloy American Corp. v. Teamsters Local 21*[111] discussed in its opinion why the arbitrator upset the management's action, why the district court vacated the award, and why the circuit court reinstated the award. This discussion explained the reasons for considering "the manager's 'margin' and the arbitrator." The arbitrator had reinstated the employee, stating the discharge was without a sound functional reason. The arbitrator said:

> If the just cause standard is to have any real meaning in contract administration, Management cannot abdicate its responsibility to undertake the onerous task of distinguishing between wrongful conduct meriting discipline and unfortunate circumstances, which despite production exigencies, demand a limited forebearance.[112]

---

[109] A good example of this type of reasoning may be seen in *Fruehauf Trailer Co.*, 16 LA 666 (Spaulding, 1951). *See also MetroFlight Airlines, Inc.*, 65 LA 925, 928 (Bailey, 1975).
[110] 61 LA 896, 898 (Hilpert, 1973).
[111] 593 F.2d 314, 100 LRRM 2845 (8th Cir. 1979), *rev'g* 450 F. Supp. 1074, 98 LRRM 2550. (E.D. Mo. 1978).
[112] *Id.* at 316, 100 LRRM at 2846.

The arbitrator further noted:

> Failure to distinguish between legitimate excuses for absence and reprehensible misconduct is repugnant to fundamental notions of fair play whenever it results in an employee whose absence is for legitimate reason beyond his control being treated as harshly as a deliberate wrongdoer.[113]

The arbitrator had to interpret these contrasting provisions:

> The company retains ... the sole right to ... discharge employees....
>
> . . .
>
> ... Seniority shall be broken and all employment relations terminated when an employee ... is discharged for proper cause.[114]

The district court had vacated the award and then the Eighth Circuit reversed the court below, explaining:

> The principal question before us is whether the arbitrator's award drew its essence from the collective bargaining agreement. *If it did, the District Court must be reversed....*
>
> . . .
>
> ... [T]he agreement before us contains two clauses governing the discharge of employees, one which provides that discharges be only upon proper cause. Thus, an arbitrator could hold that Kewanee does not retain complete control over discharges. In so holding, the arbitrator's award took its essence from the collective bargaining agreement.
>
> . . .
>
> ... It is a question of interpretation and construction under the facts—what relationship exists between the two provisions. We cannot interfere with the arbitrator's award "unless it can be said with positive assurance that the contract is not susceptible of the arbitrator's interpretation." Intern. Broth. of Elect. Wkers. v. Prof. Hole, 574 F.2d 497, 503, 98 LRRM 2407 (10th Cir. 1978). See also Ludwig Honold Mfg. Co. v. Fletcher, 405 F.2d 1123, 70 LRRM 2368 (3d Cir. 1969). This cannot be said here.[115] [Emphasis added. Footnotes omitted.]

In another example of a situation where a company sought a vacation of an award, believing that the arbitrator went beyond the "management margin" and substituted himself for the manager, the company's claim to "management margin" collided in court with the strong federal policy that arbitration awards should not be easily upset. The Flight Attendant System Board of Adjustment,[116] with Arbitrator Harry T. Edwards acting as the neutral chairman, ordered

---

[113]*Id.* at 317, n.4, 100 LRRM at 2846, n.4.

[114]*Id.* at 317, 100 LRRM at 2845–46.

[115]*Id.* at 316–18, 100 LRRM at 2846–47.

[116]*United Airlines* (Madigan Case, MEL 9-78, and Edwards Case, MEL 12-78) Flight Attendant System Board of Adjustment (Arb. Harry T. Edwards, Chairman, November 27, 1978) (unpublished).

United Airlines to reinstate two flight attendents to flight service, even after both had experienced major epileptic seizures, one occurring in 1975 at the Seattle, Washington airport and the other in 1976 at a Denver, Colorado department store. Arbitrator Edwards' award was released on November 27, 1978, because no epileptic events had been reported by either attendant since their most recent reported seizures. The expert testimony on both sides was in agreement that epilepsy cannot be so controlled by medical treatment that the patient will be free of risk of seizure and the chief medical officer of United explained that such individuals "cannot be counted on in emergency situations" because "pressures in an emergency situation might trigger a disabling convulsion." The company medical policy on epilepsy was:

> No flight attendant or driver of a Company vehicle will be returned to work with a diagnosis of epilepsy or disturbance of consciousness.

While there was a legal responsibility on United Airlines to perform "its services with the highest possible degree of safety in the public interest...."[117] Arbitrator Harry Edwards wrote:

> No conclusive facts have been presented to the Board on recurrence rates generally, frequency of recurrence or triggers inherent in the job in question. Therefore a generalized fear of incapacity is insufficient to support a change in policy which would deprive these grievants of their jobs.[118]

The District Court for the Eastern District of New York[119] then explained that the court should not upset the award because the federal policy of resolving labor differences by arbitration is, in this situation, not outweighed by the federal policy of safety during air travel:

> United claims that the Board lacked jurisdiction to overturn United's decision to remove [M——] and [E——] from flight status because of their epileptic conditions.... United asserts that nowhere in the collective bargaining agreement are there set forth standards of medical fitness for flight attendants, and because the establishment of medical standards is not a matter of contract, the Board is without power to revise the standards established by United....
>
> In support of its argument, United places great reliance on *World Airways, Inc. v. International Brotherhood of Teamsters,* 578 F.2d 800 (9th Cir. 1978). In that case, World Airways had suspended and demoted ... one of its pilots who had exhibited poor judgment in the performance of his flight duties. The individual filed a grievance ... and ... the ar-

---

[117]Federal Aviation Act of 1958, § 601(b), 49 U.S.C. § 1421(b).

[118]The grievants had been offered ground jobs. Arbitrator Edwards did discuss the difference in the risks involved if a pilot had momentary loss of control due to an epileptic seizure and if a flight attendant had such a seizure on the plane.

[119]*Association of Flight Attendants v. United Airlines, Inc.*, No. 79 C 44 (E.D. N.Y., August 23, 1979).

bitrator ... ordered the airline to retrain the individual and give him the opportunity to requalify as a pilot.

The district court granted the airline's petition to vacate that portion of the award, and the Ninth Circuit affirmed the decision, holding that federal law places upon the airlines the responsibility of determining whether or not an individual possesses the judgment to serve as a pilot and that the arbitrator had usurped this responsibility. Under those "unusual circumstances," the court found that the federal policy in ensuring the safety of air travel outweighed the policy of resolving labor differences by arbitration.

The court finds that the circumstances of this case are sufficiently distinguishable from those in *World Airways, Inc. v. International Brotherhood of Teamsters, supra,* to warrant a different result from that reached in that case. Here the court finds that the federal policy of resolving labor differences by arbitration is not outweighed by the policy of ensuring safety in air travel. In *World Airways* the court found that the arbitrator's award contravened 14 C.F.R. § 121.413(4)(ii) which establishes the duty of an air carrier to take into account "personal characteristics that could adversely affect safety" when determining the competency of its pilots. Here, the Board's award contravenes no such regulation. And while flight attendants have responsibilities relating to the safety of airline passengers, ... those responsibilities are nowhere near as great as those placed upon airline pilots. Therefore the weight to be accorded the policy of ensuring safety in air travel is not as great here as it was in *World Airways.*

The District Court distinguished the grounding of a pilot and a flight attendant and refused to cause the award reinstating the flight attendants to be upset because it decided that the tipping point between risk to passenger safety and the policy not to upset arbitration awards had not been reached.

The Margin Increases When the Discharge is Work-Related

Arbitrator Robert Howlett in *Valley Steel Casting Co.*[120] said that arbitrators are less prone to upset a discharge when the employee was discharged for misconduct specifically related to work rather than for events not work-connected. Arbitrator Howlett had sustained the discharge of an employee for careless welding, saying:

> In the arbitrator's opinion a distinction must be made between those situations in which an employee is guilty of misconduct or errors which are *not directly* connected with production and acts of misfeasance or nonfeasance which are *directly* related to the production of the Company's product. An arbitrator has a wider discretion in situations involving such issues as intoxication, bringing liquor into a plant, altercations with super-

---

[120]22 LA 520, 524–25 (Howlett, 1954).

visors, tardiness, overstaying leaves of absence and similar rule infractions which involve the personal behavior of employees. These are situations in which the relationship involved is between the employee and his employer....

Where, however, the disputed factual situation involves work on the product manufactured the relationship ceases to be solely an intraplant matter, but involves the company and its customers. In such situations the manufacturing concern must be in a position to protect its reputation and the quality of its product. A company's failure to do so would redound to the detriment of all persons connected with the enterprise—owners, management and employees. The union, which is the collective bargaining representative, also has, as an entity, an interest in the continued welfare of the company in its relationship with the customer and the public. In those situations where the manufacture of a company's product is concerned the arbitrator, in applying standards of "proper cause" and "injustice" and similar provisions of collective bargaining agreements, should be more hesitant in over-ruling a management's decision than in those cases where general patterns of human behavior are in dispute. [Footnotes omitted. Emphasis in original.]

Arbitrator Howlett summarized opinions from other arbitrators who strongly supported his conclusion that a discharge action by the management should rarely be upset if the reasons for the discharge are work-related. He reported that Arbitrator Maxwell Copelof in *Auto Lite Battery Corp.* [121] was faced with the problem of a repairman who had been warned, together with all repairmen, about faulty work following customer complaints. The repairman repaired only a part of a machine and was discharged because of this omission. Arbitrator Copelof, in upholding the discharge, said:

It ... became necessary for management to protect itself against further criticism and loss of patronage by removing this employee from its staff. [122]

Arbitrator Robert Brecht in *Glen L. Martin Co.,* [123] upheld the discharge where a riveter's helper did not buck a rivet properly in an aircraft wing assembly and, when it became necessary to remove the rivet, the riveter did not call her supervisor as required by the work procedures but instead attempted to correct the mistake herself. She could not, and ultimately the wing had to be scrapped, resulting not only in the loss of the wing but in an added delay while a replacement was made.

Arbitrator Jack Day in *Byerlite Corporation* [124] upheld the discharge of an employee assigned to watch an oxidizer tank; the employee told

---

[121] 3 LA 122 (Copelof, 1946).
[122] *Id.* at 125.
[123] 6 LA 500 (Brecht, 1947).
[124] 12 LA 641 (Day, 1949).

a supervisor he would watch the tank and then wandered off. The tank overflowed because of the employee's absence, and he was discharged.

Arbitrator Howlett inserted another conclusion from his review of such cases:[125]

> In all of these cases, activities of a grievant were involved which were concerned directly with the manufacturing operations in the plant. In such instances an arbitrator should not substitute his judgment for that of management unless management is at fault....

In *Standard Oil Co.*,[126] Arbitrator Harry Platt explained the risks to others when he sustained the discharge of a pumper, guilty of his first negligence, who loaded gasoline into the furnace oil compartment of a tank truck:

> There can be no question but that the safety of its employees, its customers, and the public in general is a proper concern of the Company and it naturally should not be hindered or discouraged from attempting to bring about safe working conditions in its plant and from enforcing all reasonable and necessary safety rules....
> ... It is our considered opinion that under all the circumstances of this case, we should not attempt to substitute our own judgment for that of Management's expert knowledge and judgment on a matter that may so vitally affect the future health and safety of its employees and the public and we accordingly must sustain the discharge of Mr. [P——].

The Corrective Discipline Test

Superimposed upon the functional test to determine whether management had just cause for the exclusion of an employee is a test to determine whether the employee's improper actions could be corrected by using corrective discipline or less discipline than exclusion. Arbitrator Seward explained the corrective approach to discipline as he sustained a discharge in *International Harvester Co.*:[127]

> The Arbitrator agrees that the Company's action in this case should be upheld.... It is clear that the Company was applying to R—— and his fellows the principles of corrective rather than retributive discipline. Under this concept, plant discipline, properly exercised, involves more than the mere matching penalties with offenses. ... Its purpose is not to "get even" with the employee but to influence his future conduct.

Corrective discipline is compatible with good management: to hire and train an employee costs money so, economically, correction is less

---

[125] *Valley Steel Castings Co.*, 22 LA 520, 527 (Howlett, 1954).
[126] 14 LA 516, 520–21 (Platt, 1950).
[127] Case No. 3-3070C (Seward, 1949) (private award).

expensive than exclusion. Also, normal corrective efforts involve low productivity levels or poor attendance.

Corrective discipline has a definite progression: oral warning, written warning, suspension, and exclusion. This corrective process, however, even in negligence cases, should not be hardened into routine. Management must be able to protect employees and the plant through the exclusion of a negligent employee on the first event. Arbitrator Harry Platt in *Standard Oil Co., supra,* said that when risk of injury to others arises from negligent conduct of an employee, managers should not consider themselves obligated to attempt to correct the negligent performance.

Certain types of conduct are beyond the correction limits. An employee discharged for stealing from a fellow employee's locker should not be reinstated on the premise that his or her "light finger" techniques will disappear, many employers believe. No employee has one "free steal"—a theft without discharge.

If an employee has been discharged for insubordination, the arbitrator may wonder whether some milder form of discipline would have caused the employee to obey instructions in the future. This doubt will be resolved if the employee was not discharged merely for refusal to follow instructions. Management has an alternative option in cases which could involve discharge for insubordination: the employee is afforded an opportunity to impose his or her own corrective discipline and follow the supervisor's directions. If the employee does not correct the behavior, the employee, in effect, discharges himself or herself. Arbitrator McCoy explained the effect of an alternative in *International Harvester Co.*:[128]

> [D]espite explicit warning that he would be discharged, he persisted in his refusal. It is not unfair to say, as counsel for the Company said, "He discharged himself." ... Discharge is not beyond the limits of reasonableness for the offense of flat refusal to work, particularly where the employee has been warned of discharge and given the opportunity to heed the warning. This principle has been quite generally recognized, as shown by the many decisions cited by the company including those of David A. Wolff in cases between Chrysler Corporation and this union and of Harry Shulman in cases between Ford Company and this union.

The manager has the duty to direct the work force and must have the right to use discipline. The arbitrator is always testing to find out if management's action was an "unnecessary, arbitrary or capricious" act. When the employee has clearly discharged himself, the question of corrective discipline is precluded.

---

[128]*International Harvester Co.,* Case No. 1-1106A (McCoy, 1948) (private award).

CHAPTER XI

Amount of Proof

Arbitrators articulate in their opinions legal principles that they borrow from trial court practice. Their use of the borrowed doctrines of "burden of proof" and the "quantum of proof" required to satisfy the burden of proof is reported in this chapter because the different articulations used by arbitrators sharply affect the outcome of arbitration proceedings.

Some arbitrators are not as prone to borrow from court practice as are others. Their reluctance may well stem from an instinctive worry that the analogy between what a trial judge does and what they, as arbitrators, do is not close enough to permit them to borrow the trial court principles indiscriminately and without some reshaping. However, other arbitrators also seeking proper results report that they do act sometimes as a trial judge and sometimes as an appellate judge, but never as a criminal judge who has the power to punish violators with fines or incarcerations.[1]

APPELLATE REVIEW OR TRIAL *DE NOVO?*

When the union is asking that a managerial determination be upset, as explained in the prior chapter, arbitrators will quite often state that management's determination will be approved unless the union can show that the determination was "unreasonable, arbitrary and capricious."[2] The arbitrator sets up such a test because he or she believes an arbitrator is not a review "manager without personal responsibility." Most arbitrators respect the managerial process and do not want to become "super-managers" yet they also believe that they can properly protect the interests of the individual employee against "unreasonable, arbitrary, or capricious" managing.[3]

---

[1]When labor arbitrators set out in their awards restitution for income loss or reinstatement of employment, they are acting as a civil court. The remedy by criminal judges is punishment (fines and incarceration). *See* Chapter XVIII, "Remedies."

[2]*See* discussion under "The 'Unreasonable, Arbitrary, or Capricious' Test" in Chapter X.

[3]*See* discussion under "The 'Residual Rights' Construction Principle: The Substantive Application of the Parol Evidence Rule" in Chapter X.

These arbitrators are seeking a balance. In doing so they are convinced that where managers have collected and weighed *all* evidence and have made a determination free of any prejudice, arbitrators should accept the management determination. By doing this, they are acting as an appellate judge, who accepts the determination of the trial judge, unless the determination is "clearly erroneous."[4] (A test essentially the same as the "unreasonable, arbitrary, or capricious" test applied by various labor arbitrators.)

Arbitrator Carroll Daugherty explained why the arbitrator can assume the role of an appellate judge: The arbitrator finds whether (1) *all* the pertinent evidence has been received by the management and carefully evaluated before the determination is finalized and (2) whether *all* the pertinent pro and con evidence has been exchanged between the parties during the various steps in the grievance procedure to sift out possible error.

The important role of the labor arbitrator is to hear the arguments about the significance of the evidence examined and asserted evidentiary conflicts, and to review the management determinations of these matters under the proper tests. Arbitrator Daugherty has commented:

> The arbitrator's hearing is an appeals proceeding designed to learn ... whether the employer, as a sort of trial court, had conducted, before making his decision, a full and fair inquiry into the employee's alleged "crime"; whether from the inquiry said trial court had obtained substantial evidence of the employee's guilt; whether the employer, in reaching his verdict and in deciding on the degree of discipline to be imposed, had acted in an even-handed, non-discriminatory manner; and whether the degree of discipline imposed by the employer was reasonably related to the seriousness of the proven offense and to the employee's previous record. In short, an arbitrator "tries" the employer to discover whether the latter's own "trial" and treatment of the employee was proper.[5]

Daugherty explains why he, like an appellate judge, is concerned with the evidentiary record compiled before management made its determination:

> Note 2: The company's investigation must normally be made *before* its disciplinary decision is made. If the company fails to do so, its failure may not normally be excused on the ground that the employee will get his day in court through the grievance procedure after the exaction of discipline.[6] [Emphasis in original.]

---

[4]Appellate courts sustain trial court determinations unless the determination is "clearly erroneous."

[5]*Whirlpool Corp.*, 58 LA 421, 427 (Daugherty, 1972); *Alby Asphalt & Refining Co.*, 34 LA 83 (Daugherty, 1960).

[6]58 LA at 429. *But see New York Telephone Co.*, 66 LA 1037, 1041–42 (Markowitz, 1976),

Daugherty's concern that management's determination be supported by substantial evidence is similar to the concern of an appellate judge that the trial judge's determination be supported by substantial evidence. His concern is reflected in these words:

Note 5: At his hearing the management "judge" should actively search out witnesses and evidence, not just passively take what participants or "volunteer" witnesses tell him.

5. At the investigation did the company "judge" obtain substantial and compelling evidence or proof that the employee was guilty as charged?

Note 1: It is not required that the evidence be fully conclusive or "beyond all reasonable doubt." But, the evidence must be truly weighty and substantial and not flimsy or superficial.[7]

Daugherty explained that the arbitrator should sometimes return to the role of a trial judge after listening to the testimony and evaluate the evidentiary value of the testimony as a trial judge would—but only when the arbitrator is not satisfied that management's determination was made after *all* available evidence was carefully reviewed and dispassionately evaluated.

Of course where the determination involves contractual interpretation, Daugherty's appellate judge analogy is not applicable. The arbitrator's role there is analogous to the role of a trial judge rendering a declaratory judgement. This last variation is mentioned here to emphasize the need for care when court practice and procedure concepts are borrowed, introduced, and squeezed into a labor arbitration proceeding.

The problems that occur if a strict trial court proof and procedure process or *de novo* appellate court procedure[8] is adopted by a skilled arbitrator can be illustrated by *Bethlehem Steel Corp.*[9] A female employee was discharged because she had administered a brutal beating to a fellow female employee in the shower room. The two women who found the victim on the floor and helped her to the dispensary, and the nurse who treated her wounds, made written statements during the investigation and reported the concurrent hearsay statements identifying the attacker. The victim was carefully questioned by an investigator and signed statements identifying the attacker; the victim's statements were tested by a polygraph examination and the examiner concluded the victim was telling the truth when she identified the attacker. After

---

where the arbitrator used evidence relating to the basis of discipline that was discovered after the discipline was imposed.

[7]58 LA at 429.

[8]"A new trial or retrial had in an appellate court in which the whole case is gone into as if no trial whatsoever had been had in the court below." BLACK'S LAW DICTIONARY 1677 (4th ed., 1968).

[9]68 LA 581 (Seward, 1977).

this investigation was completed the attacker was discharged, at which point she filed a grievance which was processed up through the various steps of the grievance procedure with full disclosure of the company's investigations to the union representatives. At the arbitration hearing before Arbitrator Seward, the victim refused to testify. In contrast, the grievant testified and denied being in the shower room when the beating took place. Several of her friends corrobated her testimony, explaining that she had showered at a time different from the one recorded in the company's investigation record. Arbitrator Seward reinstated the grievant primarily because he, as the trial judge, had not had the opportunity to hear the testimony of the victim and thereby make his personal judgment as to her truthfulness vs. the truthfulness of the grievant and her corroberating witnesses. He said:

> On this state of the record, the Impartial Chairman holds that the discharge of B—— simply cannot be upheld. He holds this despite the clear recognition that B—— may well have been guilty of the assault with which she had been charged and that she and other women who had been with her in the [shower] room may well have been lying about what went on.... The point is that the identification of B—— as A——'s assailant rests in the last analysis on hearsay—on what A—— said to other people about the assault—and there is no testimony in the record from A—— herself.... The failure of A—— to appear and testify at the arbitration hearing ... means that B—— has not had the opportunity to confront her accuser, hear her testimony and, through the union, to cross-examine her and directly challenge or reply to her account of the assault.[10]

Employees who occupy a job within the bargaining unit (and who therefore are represented by the union) and give damaging information to a manager will sometimes refuse to act as company witnesses before the arbitrator.[11] Imposing strict rules requiring *confrontation of one's accuser* in an open arbitration hearing, as if such a hearing were a criminal case, can mean the rejection of all evidence carefully collected by the company investigators and basic to the determination that is being reviewed, and may well generate a miscarriage of justice when at the last minute the "informer" refuses to testify and the investigation result is rejected as hearsay.[12]

Another example of a reinstatement because of the use of technical trial practice rules occurred in *Pacific Telephone and Telegraph Co.*[13] after an operator had been discharged. A company manager, in the

---

[10]*Id.* at 584.
[11]*See* "Employees As Company Witnesses" and "Protecting Informants from Reprisal" in Chapter IX.
[12]*See* discussion of the view that hearsay evidence can be accepted and then weighed by the arbitrator under "Admission of Hearsay" in Chapter XII.
[13]77-2 ARB ¶ 8416 (Fogel, 1977).

course of a review on the performance of operators, heard a conversation in which an operator was discourteous to a customer. Because of this the operator was terminated. The management believed this action was necessary to protect the company's reputation and to make it clear to all other operators that courteous conduct would be insisted upon. At the arbitration hearing before Arbitrator Fogel, the precise words used by the operator and the name of the customer to whom they were addressed were not presented because state regulations prohibited disclosure of telephone conversations and the names of the persons involved. The discourteous conduct was summarized, but the investigation details had to be sealed away from the arbitrator by state law; in the arbitrator's opinion the summary did not suffice, and the grievant was reinstated.

The appellate review analysis presented by Arbitrator Daugherty, *supra,* and the use of the "unreasonable, arbitrary and capricious" test by many arbitrators has an echo in the well-known presumption first announced by Arbitrator Harry Schulman.[14] He said that when there is a direct conflict in the testimony between a grievant seeking reinstatement and a supervisor who determined that the misconduct required termination, the testimony of the supervisor should be accepted because the supervisor is under financial pressure to retain trained employees except where misconduct requires termination, whereas the grievant has a financial incentive to be untruthful in the denial of the conduct which led to the discharge.

In contrast to the reluctance to use investigation information as a basis for a decision shown by arbitrators in some of the cases discussed above, is the willingness to examine and accept the investigation information presented by management, shown by Arbitrator Alex J. Simon in *Walter Manufacturing Co.*[15] He sustained the discharge of a 32-year-old employee who had been harassing a 59-year-old employee by warning him that if he continued to use the plant food machines he would be physically beaten. The older employee explained to his tormentor that he had to obtain food from the machines because his wife, who normally prepared the food, was in the hospital. The older employee complained of the threat to his foreman and an investigation was commenced. The company found that the younger employee had harassed others by threatening activity and that there were records of disciplinary warnings in the employee's folder, whereas the harassed older employee had a clean record. The younger employee was discharged and became the grievant.

---

[14]*Ford Motor Co.,* 1 ALAA ¶ 67,274 (Shulman, 1945). *See also* "Presumptions Concerning Credibility" in Chapter XII.
[15]60 LA 645 (Simon, 1973). *See also Combustion Engineering, Inc.,* 42 LA 807 (Daugherty, 1964).

Arbitrator Alex J. Simon sustained the discharge, explaining that while no third-party witness testified as to the harassment, the grievant's denial still was not accepted because the employer had thoroughly and objectively investigated the grievant's conduct and had obtained sufficient evidence to establish his guilt.

Arbitrator Updegraff in *Kraft Foods Co.*[16] was asked to reinstate an employee, but he did not do so because (1) the management determined that the female grievant harassed another female employee with foul language and blows, and (2) since the employer had the obligation to maintain working conditions in which female employees would not be harassed by such occurrences in their presence and the termination of the trained employee was a financial loss, the discharge must be considered a determination based on sufficient evidence to support the action as a termination for just cause.

> In respect to the question of "sufficient cause" the arbitrator recognizes the obligation of the employer to maintain working conditions in which its female employees will not be harassed and worried by the use of foul language and the exchange of blows. If such an atmosphere became common, the more orderly type of woman, the more valuable, useful, and respected employee would scarcely desire to remain upon the payroll. In the defense of its own interests and in the protection of its other desirable employees, therefore, it would seem that under the circumstances appearing in this case the discharge was for "sufficient cause."

Exacting proof of actual theft is not needed, said Arbitrator Charles Gregory in *Swift & Co.,*[17] to establish just cause to exclude an employee when management has made the determination in order to protect the reputation of the company. This case clearly illustrates that a labor arbitrator does not step into the shoes of a criminal judge but is reviewing a management determination.

> It seems that [H—— N——], the employee in question, who was a member of the militarized police guard necessary at the plant during the war, was apprehended on May 15, 1945, on the suspicion of having committed a burglary in a store in Omaha and was bound over on $1000.00 bond to the District Court for trial before a petit jury for having committed the alleged offense. The company, having learned of this, discharged him on May 16, 1945, as no longer suitable for plant-protection purposes with this cloud over his head. Indeed, the military authorities gave the company no option in this respect; and they apparently had the last word on matters of this sort.

The union representative argued that Arbitrator Gregory should base his decision on criminal standards:

---

[16]9 LA 397 (Updegraff, 1947).
[17]5 LA 702 (Gregory, 1946).

The theory of the union's present case is that the company did not discharge Mr. [N——] for proper cause, he being entitled to the presumption of innocence until proved guilty. Of course, he had not been proven guilty yet, since he has not even been tried as yet. The union claims that the burden of proving proper cause for the discharge is on the company and that it has not discharged this burden.

But Arbitrator Gregory concluded:

As to the merits of the case before the arbitrator, it appears to him, beyond any shadow of doubt, that the company discharged [N——] because it was convinced that he was no longer suitable to hold the job of a plant armed guard. Of course, *the company does not know that [N——] committed the felony* of which he has been charged; but the fact remains that *the company is entitled to make its own judgments on such matters as this in administering a large packing business involving a considerable investment....* The arbitrator thinks it had plenty of reason to discharge him, under the circumstances of this case. He does not think it of any great importance what the company would have done had [N——] been, say, a beef boner. The fact remains that retention in a position of trust as a plant-protection agent, [of] one who has been arrested and bound over for trial as a burglar, is asking a good deal. [Emphasis added.]

THE BURDEN OF PROOF

Another borrowing from court practice occurs when labor arbitrators set up a "burden of proof" and then determine whether the party who has the burden has presented sufficient evidence to overcome that burden. Arbitrators Clarence Updegraff and Whitley McCoy in their early joint book released in 1946 said concerning the concept of evidentiary burdens, "This is so sensible and logical a principle that no one, understanding it, would disagree."[18] They merely explained that "the party holding the affirmative of an issue must produce sufficient evidence to prove the facts essential to his claim."[19]

Some arbitrators have pointed out that setting out a burden of proof and then determining whether the burden has been met is not as easy as might be believed. The burden of proof is sometimes referred to as the burden of proceeding with further evidence. These burdens will typically shift. Arbitrator Hugh Babb explained this in *Allis Chalmers Mfg. Co.:*[20]

---

[18]Updegraff and McCoy, ARBITRATION OF LABOR DISPUTES, (Washington: BNA Books, 1946), p. 97.
[19]*Id.* at 161.
[20]29 LA 356, 358 (Babb, 1957). *See also Cleveland-Cliffs Iron Co.,* 51 LA 174 (Dunne, 1967) (burden shifts throughout case but ultimately rests with party that initially possessed it).

> While the *burden of proof* remains on the party affirming a fact in support of his case and does not change in any aspect of the cause, the *weight of the evidence* shifts from side to side as the hearing proceeds, according to the nature and strength of the proofs. [Emphasis in original.]

Then it was explained that burden of proof is, in reality a composite of "the burden of proceeding" and "the burden of persuasion" and there must be sufficient proof—called the "quantum of proof"—to shift the burden to the other side. Also, complicating the situation even more, presumptions may be relied upon by the party charged with any one of the above burdens.[21] For example, it is usually presumed that when company property is found hidden in an employee's automobile, basement, or garage, he or she put it there but such a presumption, usually part of a theft case, can be rebutted.[22]

Finally Arbitrator Joseph Brandschain, a pragmatic practitioner, wrote:

> Often the presentation of the case appears to be topsy-turvy.... Sometimes the side that logically has the burden of proof does not go first.
> Such a reversed order of presentation has become almost a universally accepted rule in discipline cases, because practice has demonstrated that this appears to be the expedient and sensible way to proceed. But it also raises the question of whether this shift in order of proceeding also shifts the burden of proof.[23]

Arbitrator Robben W. Fleming, former president of the University of Michigan, said that quibbling over who has the burden of producing evidence is an unrewarding argument. There is logic though to the employer's producing evidence first in a discipline case, for instance, because it may be that only management has the needed information.[24]

Some arbitrators do not express the concepts of burden of proof in their awards because they believe these concepts are too complex for labor arbitration. However one critic of the labor arbitration process, a defector from the ranks of the professional arbitrators, Judge Paul R. Hays, believes that even though some arbitrators do not talk about their use of burden of proof due to their preoccupation with avoiding legalisms, in actuality they use it:

---

[21] Updegraff, ARBITRATION AND LABOR RELATIONS, Third Edition of ARBITRATION OF LABOR DISPUTES (Washington: BNA Books, 1970), pp. 225, 251-53; Chambers, *Burden of Proof in Labor Arbitration*, 3 DUKE L.J. 127, 128 (1953); Beck, *Evidence, Burden and Quantum of Proof,* WASH. U. L. Q. 85, 89 (1949).

[22] *See* "Presumptions in Theft Cases" in Chapter XII and "Polygrapher Testimony to Corroborate or Impeach Testimony" in Chapter XIV.

[23] Brandschain, *Preparation and Trial of a Labor Arbitration Case,* THE PRACTICAL LAWYER, Vol. 18, No. 17 (Nov. 1972), p. 34.

[24] Fleming, THE LABOR ARBITRATION PROCESS (Ann Arbor: Univ. of Mich. Press, 1965), p. 69

But surely it is impossible for any adversary system to operate without such a rule. What the arbitrators are doing is failing to announce the rule, though they must use it. The failure to announce the rules seems unfair to the parties. It also may lead arbitrators, particularly those without legal training, to render compromise awards, as in a discharge case to order reinstatement without back pay because the arbitrator is not quite sure ... whether or not the employee was guilty of the offense with which he was charged.[25]

Placing the Burden on the Union

The general rule, followed by arbitrators in nondisciplinary proceedings, is that the grieving party, typically the union, bears the initial burden of presenting sufficient evidence to prove its contention. It is therefore usually up to the union to demonstrate that the action taken by the management is inconsistent with some limitation, contractual or otherwise, in the labor agreement. Arbitrator F. M. Ingle in *Combustion Engineering Co.*[26] explained:

The doctrine of burden of proof simply means that the party who asserts a claim or right against another party has the burden or responsibility of proving it. That is true in this case. The Union recognizes that the Company may have to make layoffs from time to time because of lack of work. Since it must be conceded that the Company has the right to lay off employees and to determine the respective ability of such employees, then their decision stands until such time as the aggrieved employee has produced evidence which would show that the employer or Company had abused the right, had discriminated against an employee or had not acted in good faith in the layoff.

In *International Minerals & Chemicals Corporation,*[27] the union grieved over the company's assignment of maintenance work to members in another classification. Arbitrator Sears found no basis to sustain the union's grievance:

This discussion of burden of proof should not be viewed by the parties as a mere academic exercise having no bearing on the merits of the present

---

[25]Hays, LABOR ARBITRATION: A DISSENTING VIEW, (New Haven: Yale Univ. Press, 1966), p. 70.

[26]9 LA 515, 517 (Ingle, 1948). *See also Local 761, International Union of Electrical Workers v. General Electric Co.,* 80 LRRM 2530 (W.D. Ky. 1972) where the court affirmed a previous arbitration award wherein the arbitrator imposed upon the union the burden of proving that a strike, precipitated by 63 maintenance employees, was legal. *See, e.g.,* Updegraff, note 21 *supra,* at p. 253: "The logical method of proceeding is for one who has advanced the grievance to state it and prove it."

[27]62-1 ARB ¶ 8284 at 4074 (Sears, 1962). *See also Petroleum Co.,* 69-2 ARB ¶ 8532 (Ray, 1969); *RCA Communications, Inc.,* 46 LA 833 (Shipman, 1966); *I. Hirst Enterprises, Inc.,* 24 LA 44, 47 (Justin, 1954); *McKinney Manufacturing Co.,* 19 LA 291 (Reid, 1952); *Combustion Engineering Co.,* 9 LA 515 (Ingle, 1948).

controversy. On the contrary, it is very important to the disposition of this case. "Burden of proof" really means that the party which has that burden must produce at the hearing MORE evidence than the party which does not have that burden. It is rather rare to find a discussion of burden of proof in the reported arbitration cases, except in discharge or disciplinary cases. However, the Arbitrator firmly believes that most arbitrators, at least subconsciously, are of the opinion that in contract interpretation cases, such as this, the grieving party has the burden of persuading the arbitrator that its position is the correct one.

Similarly, Arbitrator Vernon Stouffer wrote in *Columbus Bottlers, Inc.*:[28]

Nothing is found in the Agreement charging the employer with the responsibility of bearing the burden of proof and showing that its closing of the Plant is or was for lack of work. The Union is the complaining party and in the absence of provisions to the contrary, it follows that the burden of proof rests with it to show that the Employer's closing of the Plant constituted a violation of the Agreement or an abuse of discretion.

Arbitrator Paul Hebert explained that the burden is placed on the Union when it is attempting to upset a management determination because the management has the right to initiate determinations—the essence of management.

Since Management is responsible for running the plant and for seeing that it is operated productively, economically and efficiently, contract provisions such as here involved have been interpreted to mean that the initial determination as to the qualifications of an employee for a job must be made by Management. The decision of Management on the matter of qualifications will be upheld if it is reasonably supported by the evidence and if the initial decision is not arbitrary, capricious, or made in bad faith. . . .

After Management has made its determination on the issue of qualifications the burden of proof is on the Union to upset it by proving that the Company acted arbitrarily, capriciously, acted with discrimination or made an error in judgment.[29]

Similarly, in *Corn Products Co.*,[30] Arbitrator Harold Gilden said:

---

[28]44 LA 397, 400 (Stouffer, 1965). *See also United States Steel Corp. (Fairless Works)*, XIX STEEL ARB. 14, 403 (Klaus, 1975) (union has burden of proving existence of local working condition).

[29]*Koppers Co., Inc.*, 63-1 ARB ¶ 8376 at 4241 (Hebert, 1963). *National Broadcasting Co.*, 61 LA 872 (Nye, 1973) (union has burden of proof in layoff seniority grievance to show contract violation, but company has burden of proof to show junior employee had greater ability). *But see Pittsburgh-Des Moines Steel Co.*, 71-2 ARB ¶ 8028 (Cahn, 1970) (once union shows arbitrary decision in relative ability case, burden shifts to company to justify action). *But see, contra, American Air Filter Co., Inc.*, 77-2 ARB ¶ 8440 (Dolson, 1977).

[30]14 LA 620, 622 (Gilden, 1950). Other cases in which the above principle is restated include: *Celotex Corp.*, 66-2 ARB ¶ 8523 (Boothe, 1966); *Christy Vault Co.*, 42 LA 1093 (Koven, 1964);

Where, as here, the Union questions the Company's appraisal of an employee's competency for a given task, the Union has the burden of supporting such allegation by clear and convincing proof.

The Exception to the General Rule

When the company makes a determination that becomes an exception to the general rule set forth in the labor agreement, the burden of proof is often placed on the company on the ground that the company should prove the exception. For example, when a provision in the labor agreement states that employees will be paid a daily minimum wage when they report to work and find no work available except in certain special situations such as a strike in violation of the agreement, an act of God (flood, fire, public power loss), etc., the company must prove the exception or pay.[31]

Also, the typical labor agreement expressly, or impliedly, creates in the seniority provision a right to employment unless the employee engages in conduct justifying discharge for "cause" or "just cause" or "proper cause." The termination of an employee because of misconduct (a discharge) is an act which is an exception to this normal contractual right generated by length of service. Accordingly, many labor arbitrators require management to establish with adequate proof the cause for the discharge determination. One can argue that technically the burden of proof always remains on the party charging that the labor agreement was violated (the grievant) but the presumption of continued employment unless there is a "just cause" for discharge shifts the burden of proceeding to the company.[32]

Arbitrator McGury for example stated:

> In a discharge case, it is usually assumed that the company has the burden of proving a reasonable cause for the discharge under the contract. . . . [If] the Company has made the necessary minimal showing of adequate cause . . . [and] the grievant makes no response at all, . . . the Company's original case must stand and the discharge must be upheld.[33]

Green River Steel Co., 41 LA 132, 136 (Stouffer, 1963); United States Steel Corp., 41 LA 777 (Florey, 1963); Great Atlantic & Pacific Tea Co., 61-1 ARB ¶ 8034 (McCoy, 1961); General Box Co., 35 LA 867, 869 (Caraway, 1960); Standard Oil Co., 34 LA 285, 290 (Anrod, 1959); Kroger Co., 32 LA 296 (Schmidt, 1959); Allied Chemical & Dye Co., 29 LA 395 (Reid, 1957); Weber Showcase Co., 27 LA 40 (Prasow, 1956); Avco Mfg. Co., 24 LA 268 (Holly, 1955); Fruehauf Trailer Co., 11 LA 295 (Whiting, 1948); Merrill Stevens Drydock & Repair Co., 6 LA 838 (Marshall, 1947).

[31] Walworth Co., AAA Case No. 58-15 (James, 1963); see also Southwestern Bell Telephone Co., AAA Case No. 58-18 (Oppenheim, 1963).

[32] See Fed. R. Evid. § 301.

[33] American Maize Products Co., 39 LA 1165, 1168 (McGury, 1963). See also, Urickway Pressed Metals, 69 LA 64 (Mullaly, 1977); Koenig Trucking Co., 60 LA 899 (Howlett, 1973); Whirlpool Corp., 58 LA 421 (Daugherty, 1972); Chemical Leaman Tank Lines, 55 LA 435 (Roh-

Similarly, Arbitrator John Larkin noted that "It is generally held by arbitrators that the burden of proceeding first, to establish proof of cause for discharge, [is] upon the Company."[34]

Once the company has introduced sufficient "just cause" for the discharge, the burden of proceeding passes to the union which must then, if it is to prevail, successfully rebut the management's case, as Arbitrator McCoy explained in *Southern Bell Tel. & Tel.*:[35]

> While we have held that the burden of first proceeding, and the burden of proof, are upon the company to prove a reasonable cause for discharge, the making of a *prima facie* case discharged the burden of first proceeding and cast upon the union a burden of rebutting that *prima facie* case.

Similarly in *Ingersoll Products Div.*[36] Arbitrator Larkin explained:

> In the instant case the Company made the necessary showing that the grievants illegally walked off the job. Having established this fact, the burden of proving that there were mitigating circumstances passed to the grievants and the Union.

In *Mississippi Lime Co.*,[37] Arbitrator Clarence Updegraff stated:

> As a preliminary matter it should be stated that while the burden of proof is on an Employer to prove a discharge was justified when it occurs under a contract that the Employer will not terminate an Employee, "without just cause" ..., the claim that a man was wrongfully discharged despite making "reasonable requests" and "excuses" requires that he establish the reasonableness of his requests and the truth of his excuses for being absent from work. It would be obviously wrong to require that the employer disprove a vague and undefined claim of sickness by an employee. The latter, having affirmatively asserted sickness under all rules of procedure must be expected and required to offer proof of it. To hold otherwise would permit the absent employee to assert any fantastic reason for absence which might occur to the imagination and challenge the Employer to disprove it. To require the employee to establish that his claim of illness is well founded is only to require proof of the person likely to be in touch with all the evidence and able to produce it, if his claim is correct. He is likely to be defeated on such an endeavor only if his claim is not correct.

---

man, 1970); *Exact Weight Scale Co.*, 50 LA 8 (McCoy, 1967); *DuMont Laboratories*, 44 LA 1143 (Wildebush, 1965); *Geo. H. Dentler & Sons*, 42 LA 954 (Boles, 1964); *Borg-Warner Corp.*, 27 LA 148 (Dworkin, 1956); *Celotex Corp.*, 24 LA 36 (Reynard, 1955); *National Carbide Co.*, 24 LA 804 (Warns, 1955); *American Optical Company*, 4 LA 288, 292 (Whitton, 1946).

[34]*Ingersoll Products Div.*, 49 LA 882, 886 (Larkin, 1967). *See also Avco Mfg. Co.*, 24 LA 268 (Holly, 1955); Gorske, *Burden of Proof in Grievance Arbitration*, 43 MARQ. L. REV. 135 (1959).

[35]26 LA 742, 746 (McCoy, Chm., 1956). *See Hawaiian Telephone Co.*, 59 LA 930 (Gilson, 1972) (burden of proof shifted to union in discharge case when refusal to perform work was stipulated at hearing).

[36]49 LA 882, 886 (Larkin, 1967). *See also Western Greyhound Lines*, 36 LA 261 (Lennard, 1960).

[37]29 LA 559, 561 (Updegraff, 1957).

Clearly, this is why it is established procedure to require the absentee employee to prove his excuse when its correctness is challenged.

There are arbitrators, however, who maintain, even where a discharge has been challenged, that the burden of proof is initially on the union. For example, Arbitrator Clark Kerr in *Wholesale Bakers Ass'n.*[38] has held that unions challenging a discharge or other disciplinary action must affirmatively establish lack of cause, or risk denial of the grievance.

> The Company has the basic right to discharge. The Union may challenge discharges on the grounds that there was no adequate cause, or that proper notice was not given. If the Union makes no challenge, the action of the Company stands. If the Union does make a challenge, it must show why the challenge is a merited one. There is no presumption that the action of the Company is wrong until proved right; but quite the contrary. The contract does not read: "The Company may not discharge until cause for discharge has been proved." If the contract did read that way, then the Company would need to carry the burden of proof.

Where the discipline is less severe than discharge, various arbitrators have said the burden clearly rests on the Union[39] because there is no general rule that employees will not be disciplined. However, the clear weight of authority is that management bears the initial burden to establish the "cause" for its disciplinary action.[40]

In a case involving a grievant who had been suspended for one week for negligent driving, the testimony of the grievant's foreman and a fellow employee was insufficient to prove the employer's *prima facie* case for discipline. Arbitrator Davey in *John Deere Tractor Co., Waterloo Works*[41] said, "I do not find the proof sufficient to sustain the specific charge L—— was driving recklessly and that his truck was out of control."

ARTICULATING QUANTUM OF PROOF

Some arbitrators go beyond statements about the burden of proof and the point at which the burden shifts to the other side and make statements about the *amount* of proof that must be provided. Such a statement is termed an "articulation"—the collection of words that describes the quality and amount of proof (called the "quantum of

---

[38]4 ALAA 86, 641 at 71,433 (Kerr, 1950).

[39]*Dayton Malleable Iron Co.*, 27 LA 242 (Warns, 1956); *Walter Butler Shipbuilders, Inc.*, 2 LA 633 (Gorder, 1944).

[40]*See, e.g., Lockheed Aircraft Corp.*, 27 LA 709 (Maggs, 1956); *St. Joseph Lead Co.*, 16 LA 138 (Hilpert, 1951); *Armen Berry Casting Co.*, 17 LA 179 (Smith, 1950).

[41]20 LA 583 (Davey, 1953).

proof") required by the arbitrator before he or she is satisfied something is "proved." The words are sometimes from criminal or civil trial practice, and may well cause the arbitrator to grant or deny a grievance. Hence some cataloging of these articulations is appropriate.

Proof of guilt in criminal practice starts with the principle that the accused must be considered innocent until the evidence proves the accused to be guilty "beyond a reasonable doubt." Sometimes it is said that the guilt "must be so conclusive that impartial, reasonable and experienced persons would be morally certain of the guilt of the accused."[42] Thus if there is any doubt in the mind of the juror or the judge about the guilt the accused must be acquitted. In addition the accused must engage in the criminal conduct consciously—that is, not while unconscious, i.e., asleep or insane.[43]

In civil court practice the plaintiff is seeking damages from a defendant; the civil judge cannot assess a fine or incarcerate the accused found guilty. The fact of financial injury to the plaintiff by the defendant is proved differently than in criminal practice. If the evidence of financial injury is greater than the evidence of no financial injury—this is called a preponderance of evidence—the plaintiff wins relief.[44] In addition if an insane person injures another individual, the insane person is not excused—the insane person must pay.[45]

Since the basic articulations of quantum of proof in criminal and civil practice are so different, any borrowing of terms from either in arbitration should occur only after careful consideration, if at all. Arbitrator Benjamin Aaron set out this caveat:

> [I]t may be wise to warn inexperienced attorneys not to rely upon certain words of the art that arbitrators use carelessly in their opinions. When an arbitrator writes that the company or the union has proved a particular point "by a preponderance of the evidence," he may be implying the conscious application of a standard of proof; much more likely, however, he is simply using an expression which comes trippingly off the tongue and which has no real connection with the degree of proof he will require in future cases of the same type.[46]

In spite of Arbitrator Aaron's recommendation of caution when

---

[42]22A C.J.S. *Criminal Law* § 566 (1961).

[43]22A C.J.S. *Criminal Law* § 56 (1961).

[44]32A C.J.S. *Evidence* § 1019 (1964).

[45]Prosser, HANDBOOK OF THE LAW OF TORTS, Fourth Edition (St. Paul: West Pub. Co., 1971), Ch. 26, § 135. Arbitrator Howlett in *E. I. duPont* reinstated an employee who struck a supervisor and a fellow employee and ran about naked through some dangerous chemical pumps, ruling that because the misconduct was so excessive, the grievant must have been temporarily insane. *See* note 94 and related discussion in Chapter X.

[46]Aaron, *Symposium on Arbitration: Some Procedural Problems in Arbitration,* 10 VAND. L. REV. 649, 743 (1957).

criminal and civil practice concepts are borrowed, Arbitrator Laughlin in *Daystrom Furniture Co.*[47] employed the criminal practice concept out of his concern that discharge is "tantamount to economic death particularly when the discharge is for dishonesty because such a discharge greatly reduces the dischargee's opportunity for reemployment." Stolen company property was found in the grievant's automobile and he could not explain its presence in his possession, nor would he cooperate with a polygraph examination. The arbitrator then applied criminal standards and concluded that the grievant's apparent possession of the goods did not prove beyond a reasonable doubt that he was involved with the theft. The grievant was reinstated.[48]

Likewise, Arbitrator Ralph Hon in *National Bedding and Furniture Industries, Inc.,*[49] because of his sympathy for anyone discharged, borrowed criminal standards which caused him to reinstate the grievant.

> More specifically, to uphold a discharge on grounds which will not only terminate an employee's present means of livelihood but may well affect his chances of obtaining a job with another employer in his line of work, arbitrators insist that the employer prove his case beyond a reasonable doubt. Where this burden is sustained, the employee may be discharged in order to protect the interest of the Company, fellow employees and society. Where the burden is not sustained, the discharge is likely to be revoked. In other words, in order for the discharge to be upheld, the proof must be so conclusive that impartial, reasonable and experienced persons would be morally certain of the guilt of the accused. Dishonesty cannot be assumed, it must be proved.

Again, the criminal standards were borrowed by Arbitrators Laughlin and Hon because of the intense social stigma on, and ostracism of, an individual discharged for theft. As Arbitrator Murray M. Rohman put it, "[O]ne who faces social stigma and ostracism for the commission of an act is entitled to all the safeguards which industrial jurisprudence has established. Perhaps not the strictest proof of 'beyond reasonable doubt' as contrasted with the 'preponderance of evidence'—but very little short of it."[50]

Where some kind of criminal or reprehensible conduct is involved some other arbitrators also follow the criminal law standard.[51] Ar-

---

[47]*Daystrom Furniture Co.*, 65 LA 1157 (Laughlin, undated).

[48]*See* note 22 *supra.*

[49]67-1 ARB ¶ 8356 at 4283 (Hon, 1967).

[50]*Braniff Airways, Inc.*, 44 LA 417, 420-21 (Rohman, 1965).

[51]*Geo. H. Dentler & Sons,* 42 LA 954 (Boles, 1964); *see also Ames Harris Neville Co.,* 42 LA 803 (Koven, 1964); *American Smelting & Refining Co.,* 7 LA 147 (Wagner, 1947); *Bethlehem Steel Co.,* 2 LA 194 (Shipman, 1945). A district court held the "reasonable doubt" standard was met in a discharge case in *Alonso v. Kaiser Aluminum,* 345 F. Supp. 1356, 81 LRRM 2054 (S.D. W. Va. 1971), *aff'd,* 81 LRRM 2057 (4th Cir., Aug. 15, 1972).

bitrator Lesser in *Amelia Earhart Luggage Co.*[52] also believed the requirement for a greater amount of proof is proper if the misconduct basic to the discharge has a social stigma.

> It is not alone a question of breaking the plant rules, the customary type of case dealt with in labor arbitration, but also the breaking of the law of society against taking someone else's money. It follows, therefore, that a decision against the individual would have more far-reaching results than breaking plant rules, in that it would brand her for the rest of her life as an ordinary thief before her associates, friends and neighbors. Considering the gravity of the consequences, it follows logically to my mind that the evidence should not leave the shadow of reasonable doubt in order to rule against Mrs. Z.

Arbitrator Burton Turkus in *Great Atlantic & Pacific Tea Co.*[53] contrasted the two quanta of proof he employed as misconduct moved toward moral turpitude.

> The proof upon which the discharge is predicated, when grievous misconduct involving moral turpitude ... is the basis, should establish guilt thereof beyond a reasonable doubt.
> In other types of overt misconduct such as (a) illegal strikes ...; (b) refusal to perform job assignments...; (c) fighting ... and (d) other offenses likewise constituting a breach of peace inside the plant or other challenge to the authority of management and its right to maintain morale, discipline and efficiency in the work force, the requisite quantum of proof may not fall short of a clear and convincing demonstration of the commission of the offense....
> The dereliction relied upon for termination of employment may, of course, be predicated upon less dramatic forms of misconduct such as (a) incompetence ..., (b) absenteeism ..., (c) loafing,... intoxication or gambling on Company time, and (d) violation of safety or other reasonable rules or regulations. In such instance the degree of proof required must likewise achieve the requisite clear and convincing demonstration of the commission of the misconduct, offense or dereliction of duty upon which the discharge is predicated.

Arbitrator Lubow also increased the amount of proof he required as the level of moral turpitude involved rose. In *United Parcel Service*[54] he said the company must prove its case "beyond a reasonable doubt [the criminal quantum], since the allegations made would also constitute a crime."

Even in the narrow area of moral turpitude, however, there is not

---

[52]11 LA 301, 302 (Lesser, 1949); *see also Braniff Airways, Inc.* 44 LA 417, 420-21 (Rohman, 1965).

[53]63-1 ARB ¶ 8027 at 3089 (Turkus, 1962). *See, e.g., Allied Chemical Corp.*, 50 LA 616 (Turkus, 1968); *Service Trucking Co.*, 41 LA 377 (Turkus, 1963).

[54]67 LA 861, 865 (Lubow, 1976).

universal acceptance of "proof beyond a reasonable doubt" as the proper standard. When Arbitrator Russell A. Smith adopted this criminal standard in a case he heard involving moral turpitude, he admitted "there is no certainty that this is the prevailing view among arbitrators."[55]

Arbitrator Maurice Benewitz finds such differing standards of proof unpalatable from the viewpoint of the employer:

> If most or many arbitrators require a lesser degree of proof to sustain noncriminal discharges, this may result in an employer's inability to separate those whose retention is least desirable. Those employees whose continuance affects the possible safety of others as well as production have, under these standards, a higher degree of protection from an identical penalty than do those whose activity is entirely non-criminal although it may be objectionable.[56]

Arbitrator Martin in *Olin Corp.*[57] emphasized the unfairness of equating a company with the government by requiring such a high standard of proof:

> The concept in criminal law is that the "People" must never overwhelm the rights of the "person." In each criminal case, it is the rights and interests of the "People" which come in conflict with the rights of the "person." The level of proof is accordingly very high before the "People" can prevail over a "person."
>
> . . .
>
> . . . The Company cannot be put in the position of the "People" because the Company exists as a "person" under the law. The judgment must invariably be made upon the same basis that any suit is determined when it is between "persons"; the measure of proof must be "the preponderance of the evidence," not a level of proof "beyond reasonable doubt."

Arbitrators who articulate the criminal rather than the civil standard for the quantum of proof should review the appellate court opinion in *NLRB v. Blevins Popcorn Co.*[58] In reviewing a court-appointed

---

[55]*Kroger Co.*, 25 LA 906, 908 (Smith, 1955).
[56]*Discharge, Arbitration and the Quantum of Proof*, ARB. J., June 28, 1973.
[57]*Olin Corp.*, 63 LA 952, 955–56 (Martin, 1974).
[58]659 F.2d 1173, 107 LRRM 3108 (D.C. Cir. 1981). In *Neuhoff Bros. Packers, Inc.*, the arbitrator ordered the employee reinstated with back pay because the employer did not prove the theft "beyond a reasonable doubt" (the criminal standard). The employer would not reinstate the grievant and the union sued for enforcement. The trial court refused to enforce, holding that introducing "beyond a reasonable doubt" was changing the employer's management rights by making an employer unable to discharge unless the employee's discharge can be proved by the employer as if it were a crime. The appellate court reversed, holding that an arbitrator was not amending the agreement when he selected the proof standard he did, and that the court should not review the legal adequacy of the arbitrator's evidentiary rulings. *Meat Cutters, Local 540 v. Neuhoff Bros. Packers, Inc.*, 481 F.2d 817, 83 LRRM 2652 (5th Cir. 1973).

special master's determination[59] the court stated that he improperly used the criminal standard of "beyond a reasonable doubt" in a civil contempt proceeding, even though fines could be assessed. The court said that the special master had correctly used the "clear and convincing" test in the second stage of the civil contempt proceeding but had erroneously applied the "beyond a reasonable doubt" test at the third stage. Even though a fine can be assessed, the "clear and convincing" test should always be used in civil cases of all types.

Other arbitrators believe labor arbitrators should not borrow principles and concepts from the criminal law and practice because a labor arbitrator, in interpreting and ensuring a labor agreement, is not punishing individuals who are guilty of crimes. Arbitrator Simkin stated the difference clearly in *Westinghouse Electric Corp.*:[60]

> A court decision is a finding as to whether an individual is guilty or innocent of violation of some particular statute. This is not the issue in these proceedings. The question here is whether there is "just cause" for discharge or suspension.

Arbitrator Seidenberg in *Morgan Millwork Co.*[61] emphasized the difference by pointing out that a court decision would not resolve the arbitration case:

> We are constrained to state as a preliminary matter, that neither the acquittal nor the conviction of the Grievant in a court of law would have been dispositive of the issue before us for determination. Such matters as the burden of proof and the rules of evidence are different than those which guide a third party neutral interpreting a voluntary agreed upon collective bargaining contract.

Various arbitrators emphasize the strong similarity of arbitration cases involving disciplinary actions to court cases alleging tortious conduct between individuals where, even if a crime is in issue, only a "preponderance of evidence" standard is used:

> The standard of proof in civil litigation when commission of a crime is directly in issue is proof by a preponderance of the evidence.... An employer who could successfully sue an employee for an intentional conversion of the employer's property should probably not be required to re-

[59]*See* "Arbitrators Have Been Appointed As Masters" in Chapter XXII for a discussion of the relationship between a labor arbitrator and a special master to the federal judge whenever the grievance involves private law.
[60]26 LA 836, 842 (Simkin, 1956).
[61]62-2 ARB ¶ 8557 at 5084 (Seidenberg, 1962). *See also Youngstown Sheet & Tube Co.*, (Indiana Harbor), XIX STEEL ARB. 14,620 (Mittenthal, 1976) (acquittal in criminal case is not controlling); *Kast Metals Corp.*, 65 LA 783 (Davis, 1975); *Madison Gas & Electric Company*, 69-2 ARB ¶ 8094 (Slavney, 1969); *Hennis Freight Lines*, 44 LA 711 (McGury, 1965); *Sun Drugs Co., Inc.*, 31 LA 191 (Marcus, 1958).

tain the individual in his employ merely because a case cannot be proved beyond a reasonable doubt.[62]

Another criticism of the standard of "beyond a shadow of doubt" in a labor arbitration situation brought a strong statement of disapproval from the court of appeals in *Western Electric Co., Inc. v. Communication Equipment Workers, Inc.:*[63] "The imposition of a burden that in many, if not most, cases is simply impossible to sustain by either side can hardly be said to square with a fair system of dispute resolution."

The civil quantum of proof that is used by many arbitrators is called a "preponderance of the evidence."[64] Abstractly, this test requires the party bearing the burden of persuasion to convince the tribunal that, more likely than not, its version of the facts is correct. This test has been applied in a great many arbitral contexts, and appears to be the criterion employed in the countless cases wherein burden of proof is never mentioned.

Some arbitrators have articulated a quantum of proof that sounds like a compromise between "preponderance of the evidence" and "beyond a reasonable doubt." They say the correct test should be "clear and convincing evidence." Arbitrator Platt said this in *McLouth Steel Co.*[65] when the grievant wanted to upset a management selection:

It should be clear to all that, in order to decide a factual question such as the one above stated, an Arbitrator must be furnished with something more than protestations and mere assertions of an employee's general ability to work in a plant and that what is necessary in a case of this kind is

---

[62]Gorske, *Burden of Proof in Grievance Arbitration,* 43 MARQ. L. REV. 135, 138–39, 156 (1959). For a detailed exposition of these issues as they are treated in court proceedings, *see* 9 J. Wigmore, EVIDENCE 2497 (3d ed. 1940).

[63]554 F.2d 134, 138, 95 LRRM 2268, 2270 (4th Cir. 1977).

[64]Other standards have also been used: *General Telephone Co. of Calif.,* 73 LA 531 (Richman, 1979); *Braniff Airways, Inc.,* 73 LA 304 (Ray, 1979); *Keystone Steel & Wire Co.,* 72 LA 780 (Elson, 1979); *Casting Engineers,* 71 LA 949 (Petersen, 1978); *Helo Coast Processing Co.,* 77-2 ARB ¶ 8453 (Tsukeyama, 1977); *TRW, Inc.,* 69 LA 214 (Burris, 1977); *K.L.M. Royal Dutch Airlines,* 66 LA 547 (Kupsinel, 1975); *American Air Filter Co.,* 64 LA 404 (Hilpert, 1975); *Macnaughton-Brooks, Inc.,* 60 LA 125 (Shister, 1973); *Southwestern Bell Telephone,* 59 LA 709 (Kates, 1972); *Kroger Co.,* 25 LA 906 (Smith, 1955).

[65]11 LA 805, 809 (Platt, 1948) ("'clear' or 'substantial' preponderance of the credible evidence" required in a discharge case, *Coastal Resin Co.,* 61 LA 686 (Jenkins, 1973)). *See Jos. Schlitz Brewing Co.,* 51 LA 731 (Madden, 1968) ("clear and convincing proof by a preponderance of the evidence"). *See also Olin Corp.,* 63 LA 952 (Martin, 1974) (there is a higher intermediate burden of proof for discharges than for suspensions, although both are higher than "preponderance" standards and both are lower than "reasonable doubt" standards). *Accord, Youngstown Sheet & Tube Co.,* (Indiana Harbor), XIX STEEL ARB. 14,620 (Mittenthal, 1976) (clear and convincing standard applied to discharge for theft); *Timken Co.,* (Canton, Ohio), XIX STEEL ARB. 14,744 (Leb, 1976) (same standard in discharge for smoking dope). Two other cases where the standard was used in a discharge case are *Zinsco Electrical Products,* 64 LA 107 (Caraway, 1975), and *Bethlehem Steel Corp. (Bethlehem),* XVII STEEL ARB. 14,054 (Strongin, 1975).

that there be clear and convincing evidence which relates to the grievant's capacity for the specific job to which he seeks promotion.

Other arbitrators believe articulations of the quantum of proof this or that party should produce are courtroom criteria that may well set up unwise rigidities. Arbitrator Block wrote in *Flintkote Co.*:[66]

> In weighing the evidence, however, the Arbitrator sees no reason to adopt a Courtroom criterion as to the quantum of proof required. He seeks only to determine whether the evidence is convincing to him that the Company did or did not have "just and sufficient cause" to discharge the Grievant for the alleged act of theft.

Still other arbitrators say that proof standards are not very relevant in a labor arbitration proceeding. And some arbitrators consciously refuse to apply any standard to the quantum of proof issue. Arbitrator Samuel S. Kates, for example, often argues "that technical rules concerning burden of proof should not be applied in a labor arbitration case, but rather that the Arbitrator should rule in favor of whichever party he is persuaded by the evidence, viewed as a whole in the light of any applicable contract provisions, has acted correctly."[67]

---

[66]49 LA 810, 814 (Block, 1967). *See also Southern Greyhound Lines,* 43 LA 113 (Black, 1964).

[67]*Van Huffel Tube Corp.,* XVII STEEL ARB. 123,067 (Kates, 1973). *Accord, Weirton Steel Company,* 68-1 ARB ¶ 8249 (Kates, 1968). *See also Milgram Food Stores, Inc.,* 68-2 ARB ¶ 8622 (Murphy, 1968) ("[L]egal concepts of proof—from a 'preponderance of the evidence' to 'beyond a reasonable doubt'—are not very relevant to an arbitration proceeding. What is necessary is that the arbitrator be sufficiently convinced of the truth of the facts." 68-2 ARB at 5159).

CHAPTER XII

Rules of Evidence

Labor arbitrators usually adopt a liberal attitude toward the admission of evidence. There are various reasons for this. One is that there is no named jury in arbitration, making the need for legal roles less pressing; another is the theory that testimony from various witnesses without interruption has a "cathartic value." Since the parties are involved in a continuing relationship, the therapeutic result is to allow them to "get things off their chests." This theory has been well articulated by Arbitrator William E. Simkin:

> One of the fundamental purposes of an arbitration hearing is to let people get things off their chest, regardless of the decision. The arbitration proceeding is the opportunity for a third party, an outside party, to come in and act as a sort of father confessor to the parties, to let them get rid of their troubles, get them out in the open, and have a feeling of someone hearing their troubles. Because I believe so strongly that this is one of the fundamental purposes of arbitration, I don't think you ought to use any rules of evidence. You have to make up your own mind as to what is pertinent or not in the case. Lots of times I have let people talk for five minutes, when I knew all the time that they were talking it had absolutely nothing to do with the case—just completely foreign to it. But there was a fellow testifying, either as a worker or a company representative, who had something that was important for him to get rid of. It was a good time for him to get rid of it.[1]

A third reason is that, according to Gerald Asken, the "refusal to hear material evidence, and proper objection thereto, may constitute grounds for vacation the award."[2]

As mentioned above, many arbitrators believe that the therapeutic aspect of the arbitration process is enhanced if witnesses are allowed

---

[1] *Transcript of Proceedings,* CONFERENCE ON TRAINING OF LAW STUDENTS IN LABOR RELATIONS, Vol. 3 (1947) as quoted in Elkouri and Elkouri, HOW ARBITRATION WORKS, Third Edition (Washington: BNA Books, 1973), p. 254.

[2] Asken, *The Law of Labor Arbitration,* ARBITRATION CASES, N. Levin et al., eds. (New York: Practicing Law Institute, 1974), p. 36. *See Problems of Proof in the Arbitration Process: Report of the West Coast Tripartite Committee,* PROBLEMS OF PROOF IN ARBITRATION, Proceedings of the Nineteenth Annual Meeting, National Academy of Arbitrators, D. Jones, ed. (Washington: BNA Books, 1967), p. 167.

to tell their story freely, and that strict rules of evidence are applied in court cases, as opposed to arbitration hearings, to keep improper evidence away from juries because they lack the training both to weigh evidence carefully and to disregard evidence that should be ignored. Many arbitrators, however, believe they can properly sort out the evidence. One arbitrator, in urging others not to freely accept material which would not be accepted in a court, said:

> The nonlawyer arbitrator often is uncertain and loose in his treatment of the rules of evidence. For instance, when confronted with an objection to the introduction of a specific piece of evidence, the arbitrator usually admits the evidence with a comment that has become a standard cliche— namely, that he will "take it for what it's worth."
>
> A serious difficulty with such a nonlegal approach to evidence is that it may put the opposing lawyer in a quandary about how to evaluate "what it is worth" in order to determine how to proceed further with the case, whether to offer counter evidence or argument or how to treat the point in a post-hearing brief.[3]

One guideline used in the arbitration process is the Code of Professional Responsibility for Arbitrators of Labor-Management Disputes, prepared and approved by the American Arbitration Association, The National Academy of Arbitrators, and the Federal Mediation & Conciliation Service. The Code states in pertinent part:

> **An arbitrator must provide a fair and adequate hearing which assures that both parties have sufficient opportunity to present their respective evidence and argument.**[4]

The Code cautions arbitrators that within the limits of this responsibility, they should conform to the various types of hearing procedures desired by the parties. No express rule regarding exclusion of evidence, however, is contained in the rules of the Code.

The Voluntary Labor Arbitration Rules of the American Arbitration Association contain another well-recognized guideline:

> **Evidence**—The parties may offer such evidence as they desire and shall produce such additional evidence as the Arbitrator may deem necessary to an understanding and determination of the dispute. When the Arbitrator is authorized by law to subpoena witnesses and documents, he may do so upon his own initiative or upon the request of any party. The Arbitrator shall be the judge of the relevancy and materiality of the evidence offered

---

[3]Brandschain, *Preparation and Trial of a Labor Arbitration Case*, THE PRACTICAL LAWYER, Vol. 18, No. 7, p. 36 (Nov. 1972).

[4]Code of Professional Responsibility For Arbitrators of Labor-Management Disputes, Section V(A)(1) (1975), ARBITRATION—1975, Proceedings of the Twenty-Eighth Annual Meeting, National Academy of Arbitrators, B. Dennis and G. Somers, eds. (Washington: BNA Books, 1976), p. 232, 64 LA 1317, 1325–26 (1975).

and conformity to legal rules of evidence shall not be necessary. All evidence shall be taken in the presence of all of the Arbitrators and all of the parties except where any of the parties is absent in default or has waived his right to be present.[5]

Courts have held that arbitrators are not bound by the rules of evidence controlling judges in state or federal courts[6] and have rejected attempts to vacate awards on the ground that the arbitrator did not follow court rules concerning the admission or exclusion of evidence.[7] On the other hand, where there has been an exclusion of evidence which has, in the opinion of the reviewing court, denied a party a fair hearing, awards have been set aside. For example, in a case involving misconduct on a picket line[8] the company representative asked a police officer to testify about some rock throwing. The arbitrator refused to hear the testimony, asserting that it should have been part of the company's "case-in-chief," but the reviewing court rejected this technical ruling and vacated the award, quoting Arbitrator Benjamin Aaron:

> Despite the generally accepted principle that arbitration procedures are necessarily more informal than those in a court of law, objections to evidence on such grounds that it is hearsay, not the best evidence, or contrary to the parol evidence rule, are still frequently raised in *ad hoc* arbitration. To the extent that these and similar objections are intended to exclude proffered evidence, they generally fail. *The arbitrator is interested in gathering all the relevant facts he can, his principle objective is to render a viable decision, and any information that adds to his knowledge of the total situation will almost always be admitted.*[9] [Emphasis added in decision.]

When an objection is raised, the arbitrator will usually ask the party raising the objection to explain on what grounds the objection is offered. It is at this point that the advocate must state, with some clarity,

[5]American Arbitration Association, *Voluntary Labor Arbitration Rules*, Rule 28 (1979).

[6]*Newark Stereotypers' Union No. 18 v. Newark Morning Ledger Co.*, 397 F.2d 594, 599, 68 LRRM 2561, 2564 (3d Cir. 1968), *cert. denied*, 393 U.S. 954, 69 LRRM 2653 (1968).

[7]*Ficek v. Southern Pac. Co.*, 338 F.2d 655, 657, 57 LRRM 2573, 2575 (9th Cir. 1964), *cert. denied*, 380 U.S. 988, 60 LRRM 2284 (1965); *Western Oil Fields, Inc. v. Rathbun*, 250 F.2d 69, 71 (10th Cir. 1958).

[8]*Harvey Aluminum, Inc. v. United Steelworkers of America*, 263 F. Supp. 488, 64 LRRM 2580 (C.D. Cal. 1967). The court vacated the award on the ground that the arbitrator's exclusion of certain evidence as "cumulative" denied a fair hearing to the party presenting the evidence, even though the exclusion would have been proper in a judicial proceeding. The court noted that the arbitrator had not announced, prior to the hearing, that traditional rules of evidence would be followed nor did the parties' agreement to arbitrate specify that legal rules would be followed. *See also Smaglio v. Firemen's Fund Ins. Co.*, 432 Pa. 133, 247 A.2d 577 (1968).

[9]263 F. Supp. at 491, 64 LRRM at 2581-82, quoting from Aaron, *Some Procedural Problems in Arbitration*, 10 VAND. L. REV. 733, 743-44 (1957).

force and logic, a reason or reasons why the arbitrator should exclude the evidence. The arbitrator may accept the evidence with the caution that acceptance is only "for what it is worth." The arbitrator may urge an advocate not to present evidence that the arbitrator believes can be given little weight. This is both to speed up the presentation process and to protect the arbitrator from confusion. When an advocate believes evidence or an argument to be improper, an objection can serve the useful purpose of pointing out to the arbitrator the advocate's concern with the proffered material. But noting the general rule toward admissibility in arbitration, the advocate's objection is usually intended not so much to discourage admissibility as to encourage the arbitrator not to give the evidence significant weight. Sam Kagel has observed that objections "may be used as a signal to the arbitrator, when he is studying the award, that in the opinion of the objecting party the particular evidence is either irrelevant or entitled to very little weight."[10]

Raising an objection to bring something to the attention of the arbitrator—the unreliability of hearsay in a particular case, the irrelevancy of certain material to the controversy, or the fact that, since the contract is clear, parol evidence should not be relied upon in the arbitral setting—may serve to allay the advocate's concern as much as a declaration of inadmissibility by the arbitrator. Of course, there are circumstances, for example those involving offers of a compromise, discused later in this chapter, when an objection will lead to evidence being declared inadmissible.

Arbitrator Clarence Updegraff offers one warning in regard to the use of objections: they should not be repetitious and they should be plausible.

> Do not make captious, whimsical or unnecessary objections to testimony or arguments of the other party. Such interruptions are likely to waste time and confuse issues. The arbitrator, no doubt, will realize without having the matter expressly mentioned more than once, when he is hearing weak testimony....[11]

Because arbitrators are not legally required to admit or exclude evidence under rules of evidence,[12] some observers label all such rules "legalisms" which have no place in arbitration. The use of the cliché "legalism" to describe such rules conjures up visions of complicated

---

[10]Kagel, *Anatomy of a Labor Arbitration* (Washington: BNA Books, 1961), p. 79.

[11]Updegraff, *Preparation for Arbitration*, 22 LA 889-90 (1954).

[12]*Newark Stereotypers' Union No. 18 v. Newark Morning Ledger Co.*, 261 F. Supp. 832 (D. N. J. 1966), *aff'd*, 397 F.2d 594, 68 LRRM 2561 (3d Cir. 1968), *cert. denied*, 393 U.S. 954, 69 LRRM 2653 (1968); *Isbrandtsen Tankers, Inc. v. National Marine Engineers' Beneficial Assn'n*, 236 N.Y.S. 2d 808 (1962); FMCS Procedures, 29 C.F.R. § 1404.14 (1980); American Arbitration Associations *Voluntary Labor Arbitration Rules*, Rules 28-30 (1979).

technical maneuvers, frustrated witnesses, surprise evidence, court-room stage play, and the like. No one, of course, would seriously advocate that such matters should be introduced into labor arbitration hearings. Certain tested legal principles, however, have been followed by many arbitrators to introduce order, clarity, and simplicity into arbitration proceedings. The logic underlying adoption of some elements of the rules of evidence is as follows:

> The rules are based on many generations of judicial experience. They have as their primary objective the search for truth and generally the seeking to confine evidence so as to remove confusion, irrelevancy and manufactured facts. The significant consideration to bear in mind in relation to these rules is that they all have an underpinning of reason. They are not whimsical or arbitrary. Their objective is to encourage the process of unemotional and objective reasoning with the sole purpose to get at the truth.[13]

Rules of evidence should not be condemned merely because these principles have been borrowed from rules used in the courts. The principles behind many such rules are grounded in time-tested experience. Arbitrator Archibald Cox explained:

> When legal principles are invoked in arbitration proceedings it is well not to brush them aside impatiently but to recall, that behind them lies the weight of thought tested by experience. If the policy behind the legal rule holds true, the case should turn upon it. If a policy is unimportant, the legal law may safely be disregarded.[14]

As mentioned at the beginning of this chapter, some arbitrators assert that evidence rules have been developed to keep evidence from a jury that would have difficulty evaluating it, and that evidence need not be excluded in arbitration because the arbitrator is acting without a jury and can properly evaluate the evidence. These are only general assertions. Actually some technical evidence rules are used by arbitrators, as this chapter will attempt to show. For example, Arbitrator C. Chester Brisco in *Phillips Painting Contractors*[15] was reviewing a union claim that the employer had *willfully* failed to make some contractually required health and welfare fund payments. If the company had the necessary funds in its bank account at the date the money should have been paid in and failed to do so, the failure would be considered *willful* and a crime under the state law.

The union spokesman asked the company representatives to report

---

[13]*Problems of Proof in the Arbitration Process: Report of the Chicago Area Tripartite Committee,* PROBLEMS OF PROOF IN ARBITRATION, note 1 *supra,* at p. 89.

[14]Cox, *The Place of Law in Labor Arbitration,* THE PROFESSION OF LABOR ARBITRATION, Selected Papers From the First Seven Annual Meetings of the National Academy of Arbitrators, J. McKelvey, ed. (Washington: BNA Books, 1957), p. 86.

[15]72 LA 16 (Brisco, 1978). To the same effect *see Publishers' Ass'n. of New York City,* 43 LA 400 (Altieri, 1964).

to the union and the arbitrator the amount of money in the company's bank account on the pay-in date to determine whether the failure to pay was willful. The company representative refused, invoking the privilege of avoiding self-incrimination. The union's representative then answered that the use of this privilege had no place in the arbitration process and that refusal to turn over the information generated an adverse inference demonstrating that the company had sufficient funds to pay the needed amounts on the required date. The company's representative in turn asserted that arbitrators permitted witnesses to invoke the privilege when the answer could reveal a violation of a criminal statute and that, furthermore, the doctrine of adverse inference was inapplicable in the arbitration case because that principle can only be asserted *after* the other side has presented enough evidence to make a *prima facie* case, not before. Arbitrator Brisco held that since the union had failed to establish a *prima facie* case, the adverse inference doctrine could not be used to fill in the needed evidence. The union failed in its attempt to have the arbitrator order delivery of the information it requested—the employer's bank balance on a certain date.

Evidentiary principles utilized by arbitrators are noted below.

COLLATERAL ESTOPPEL

"Collateral Estoppel" is a doctrine which is as appropriate in arbitration as it is in courts to prevent introduction of evidence to prove that a determination of the same factual issue in a prior proceeding was incorrect.[16] Lord Kenyon, in his explanation of the legal maxim that "one alleging contrary or contradictory things is not to be heard," said:

> [A] man should not be permitted "to blow hot and cold" with reference to the same transaction, or insist, at different times, on the truth of each of two conflicting allegations, according to the promptings of private interest.[17]

In *Lockheed Aircraft Corp.*[18] Arbitrator James Willingham applied the principle of "collateral estoppel" to a case where an employee had

---

[16]*Res judicata* does not apply to prior arbitral findings when these are reviewed by courts (no collateral estoppel), said the Supreme Court, because "the fact-finding process in arbitration usually is not equivalent to judicial fact finding." *Alexander v. Gardner-Denver Company*, 415 U.S. 36, 57, 7 FEP Cases 81, 89 (1974). However, *res judicata* (collateral estoppel) does apply to state court holdings barring a Title VII suit. *Bennun v. Bd. of Governors of Rutgers*, 413 F. Supp. 1274, 12 FEP Cases 1393 (D. N.J. 1976). This view of the differences between fact-finding in arbitration awards and in state court decisions should cause fact-finding in arbitration to improve.

[17]H. Broom, A SELECTION OF LEGAL MAXIMS (2d ed. 1850).

[18]28 LA 411 (Willingham, 1957).

two garnishment judgments against him and was discharged for violating a plant rule:

> Although the grievant may not in fact have owed the bill, it is an elementary principle of law that a judgment cannot be attacked collaterally.... [19]

In *Wheeling Steel Corp.*[20] Arbitrator Mitchell Shipman stated that he was compelled as a matter of law to accept the findings of the Industrial Commission concerning the physical condition of the grievant:

> Accepting the Industrial Commission's findings and decision that the grievant's disability did not arise out of or in the course of his employment with the Company, which must, from the state of record proof, be done, the Umpire would, were he to find that the grievant continued physically unable to return to work on April 16, 1954, be required to hold that his employee status terminated on said date.
>
> Examining all of the other evidence in the case, certain parts of it stand out as most persuasive against the grievant's claim. One of them is his workmen's compensation claim application of February 26, 1954, wherein he affirms that as of that date, he continued to have "a temporary total disability." It is difficult, indeed to square these statements of the grievant with his contention that he was, on January 8, 1954, physically able to return to work.... [T]he only conclusion that can fairly and properly be reached is that he was not physically able to return to work on each of the dates of his request for reemployment or on April 16, 1954, the end of the one year period of his absence. Such a finding would on all sound and accepted principles of evidence, be mandatory.... [21]

Arbitrator Lennart Larson in *General American Transportation Corporation*[22] excused a grievant whose testimony during the arbitration hearing differed from his testimony in the workmen's compensation case:

> When a claim for permanent disability under a workmen's compensation act is made, the employee is likely to find himself in a position where his interests conflict. He wants to receive all the compensation that he is entitled to, and he states fully his pains and disabilities. At the same time, in

---

[19]*Id.* at 413.

[20]25 LA 68 (Shipman, 1955). *See also Odanah Iron Co.*, 24 LA 299 (Graff, 1955); *Missouri Water Co.*, 7 ALAA ¶ 69,979 (Beatty, 1955); *Jersey Central Power & Light Co.*, 7 LA 560 (Copelof, 1947).

[21]25 LA at 73.

[22]*General American Transportation Corp.*, (Larson, 1957) (unpublished). *See also Zellerbach Paper Co.*, 68 LA 69 (Stashower, 1977), which held that an employer cannot rely on a disability finding of a workmen's compensation appeals board in discharging an employee for physical inability to do the job. The arbitrator noted therein that to rule otherwise would be to undermine the entire workmen's compensation procedure, because the more forcefully an injured employee pressed his claim, the more he would jeopardize his future employment. *But see Sinclair Refining Co.*, (Hebert, 1957) (unpublished); *Great Atlantic & Pacific Tea Co.*, 6 ALAA ¶ 69,810 at 74,480 (Baskind, 1955).

most cases, he wants to get back to work as soon as possible. In pursuing this interest he must say that he is able to perform his job. He knows that returning to work is material evidence bearing on the degree of incapacity eventually found.

. . .

The Company has argued at length that the doctrine of collateral estoppel defeats [B——'s] grievance. The proposition is that [B——], having obtained a verdict and judgment for 50% permanent partial disability because of injury to his back, is estopped to deny that he is disabled from performing the blacksmith helper's job. . . .

. . .

The Arbitrator appreciates fully the merits and policy behind the doctrine of collateral estoppel. But the doctrine cannot be held to operate in the present proceeding. The lawsuit and the arbitration hearing dealt with different fact issues. In the lawsuit the issue was the degee to which [B——] had suffered depreciation in his earning capacity. In the arbitration proceeding the question was whether [B——] could do his job as blacksmith helper in a satisfactory manner without unreasonable risk to his well being and safety.

Arbitrator Ben Roberts evaluated a discharge of a grievant who had been working in the composing room of *The New York Times*.[23] He determined that the acquittal of the grievant following an arrest and criminal trial over his gambling operations in the composing room did not determine the outcome of the grievance over the discharge. The Arbitrator explained that the acquittal may have resulted from the fact that certain evidence presented at the arbitration hearing was omitted from the prosecution's case. Criminal cases are directed toward punishment; the discharge being imposed was not "punishment" but was enforced in order to improve the operation of the company's composing room.

The Court of Special Sessions made its findings under the criminal code. . . . The arbitrator must make his findings under the contract and within the rules of the forum over which he presides. He cannot be limited to the acceptance of the court's holding or acquittal as dispositive of the issues before him. It can well be that one may not be guilty of a crime and yet have conducted himself in a manner that has given sufficient cause for discharge under the collective bargaining agreement. There can be situations of conviction of criminal conduct which may not be sufficient to justify sustaining a dismissal under a collective contract. The company in the former and the collective bargaining representative in the latter cannot be denied the opportunity to present its own case in arbitration and as a

---

[23]*The New York Times*, (Roberts, Sept. 8, 1976) (unpublished private award). *See also Flintkote Co.*, 49 LA 810 (Block, 1967); *Service Trucking Co.*, 41 LA 377 (Turkus, 1963); *Publishers' Ass'n. of New York City*, 32 LA 44 (Simkin, 1959); *Kaiser Steel Corp.*, 31 LA 674 (Grant, 1958).

matter of contract application under the criteria agreed upon by the parties.

ADMISSION OF HEARSAY

"Hearsay evidence," as classically defined, is the report of a statement (written or oral) made by a person who is not a witness in the proceeding and introduced to prove the truth of what is asserted.[24]

The hearsay evidence rule is not an absolute rule even in courts and exceptions are made if there are special circumstances surrounding a particular declaration which render the statements more reliable.[25] One example of an exception is testimony which was given under oath at a prior proceeding where the parties and issues were the same. The assumption here is that the opposing party already had the opportunity to cross-examine. Admissions of an individual or a representative (assuming that person is a party to the suit in the same capacity) are admissible on the theory that it would be incongruous for a party to challenge the truthfulness of his or her own declaration.[26] Business records and oral reports that are made to a superior in the regular course of business are regarded as reliable on the theory that the need for regularity in the business will act as a check on their accuracy.[27]

Arbitrator Brandschain, who is also an attorney, made the following comment concerning "lay lawyers" and the introduction of hearsay evidence:

---

[24]J. Wigmore, *Evidence* § 1361 (3d ed. 1940).

[25]*See, e.g.,* Faribault State Hospital, 68 LA 713 (Lipson, 1977), where the arbitrator admitted hearsay declarations as *res gestae* statements.

[26]Courts and arbitrators generally refuse to receive evidence of compromise offers, for a purely policy reason: the parties should not be discouraged from attempting to settle. Elkouri and Elkouri, HOW ARBITRATION WORKS, note 1 *supra,* at pp. 288–89. This exception to the hearsay rule is frequently confused with the exception related to out-of-court declarations of a nonparty witness against the interest of the witness. *See also* note 24 *supra,* at 1445-57. *Cf. General Motors Corp.,* 2 LA 491, 503 (Hotchkiss, 1938). The NLRB decided in *Alvin J. Bart & Co., Inc. and New York Printing Pressmen,* 236 NLRB 242, 98 LRRM 1257 (1978), that evidence which would be inadmissible in federal court as hearsay would nevertheless be admitted in administrative proceedings and given whatever weight an administrative law judge considered justified. The Board found that sworn statements given by a witness during an investigation by a Board agent may be entitled to more evidentiary weight than the witness' subsequent testimony under oath before the administrative law judge. *See* Member Murphy dissented, warning against the agency's reliance on pretrial statements given to a Board agent as the sole basis for finding a violation, indicating that in the absence of counsel, the witness may have failed to grasp the serious nature of the affidavit. The dissent acknowledged that the affidavits could be used at trial for purposes of impeachment. Murphy submitted, however, that their use as substantive evidence is improper. She concluded that the holding ran afoul of Section 10(b) of the National Labor Relations Act, which requires the agency to apply Federal Rules of Evidence "so far as practicable."

[27]*See* note 24 *supra,* at 1370-71, at §§ 1386-89.

The general practitioner may be shocked, or even amused, at the behavior of the "lay lawyers" at the hearing. They habitually try to introduce hearsay and incompetent evidence—many times successfully—and ask questions in a manner that results in "counsel" making statements and even, in effect, testifying.[28]

Labor arbitrators are not constrained by the same strict rules of evidence that are followed by the courts and they seldom reject any evidence that is relevant to a material issue in the case.[29] The receipt of hearsay evidence may be necessary for the arbitrator to get a full understanding of the facts in issue.[30]

Some disagreement exists over the extent to which hearsay evidence, inadmissible in courts, should be admitted in labor arbitration. The New York Tripartite Committee report stated:

a. Any evidence qualifying in courts of law as an exception to the hearsay rule should be admissible in arbitration.

b. In addition, hearsay may be admitted by the arbitrator, at his discretion, if there are persuasive reasons for not requiring the presence of persons quoted and if there is reasonable ground to believe that the statement quoted is trustworthy and if the evidence is of a nature that can be readily refuted if contested.

(Some members would state instead: "In addition, hearsay may be admitted by the arbitrator, at his discretion, in exceptional cases, if there is powerful reason for not requiring the presence of the person quoted, and if there is reason to believe that the statement quoted is trustworthy.")[31]

The informality and speed of the arbitration process would suffer if the introduction of hearsay evidence were limited as tightly as it is in a court. Longer periods of preparation would be required; more witnesses would be needed; and lawyers who are familiar with the hearsay rules would be needed to prepare and present arbitration cases.

Though the rules of evidence should concededly be applied more liberally in arbitration cases, reasonable limits should be imposed on the use of hearsay evidence in order that the opposing party may have an adequate opportunity to rebut statements made in the absence of direct testimony:

[A] practice which deserves some comment is the acceptance of evidence by the arbitrator, "for what it is worth." When evidence is accepted "for

[28]Brandschain, note 3 *supra*, at 24.

[29]Shulman, *Reason, Contract and Law in Labor Relations*, 68 Harv. L. Rev. 999, 1017 (1955).

[30]*See Fenwick Fashion, Inc.*, 42 LA 582 (Elbert, undated). *See also United Instrument Workers Local 116 v. Minneapolis-Honeywell Regulator Co.*, 54 LRRM 2660 (E.D. Pa. 1963); *Chippewa Valley Board of Education*, 62 LA 409 (McCormick, 1974).

[31]*Problems of Proof in the Arbitration Process: Report of the New York Tripartite Committee*, Problems of Proof in Arbitration, *note 1 supra*, at 297-98.

what it is worth," it adds incaculable components. The opposing counsel, not knowing what worth the arbitrator will put upon the evidence, is compelled to explore every ramification of the testimony. In reply, the other similarly must counter the opposing evidence and argument. It frequently imposes an unproductive exercise for both parties. It may mean that the hearings are unnecessarily extended. It is suggested that this acceptance of proof "for what it is worth" be avoided.[32]

Arbitrator Clarence Updegraff takes a different view of this problem:

[T]he usual practice, where the evidence sought to be elicited is clearly hearsay, is to rule that it will be admitted "for what it is worth." Such ruling usually satisfies both parties: It satisfies the offerer of the testimony because he is getting the evidence in; it satisfies the objector because of the clear implication that the arbitrator knows the worthlessness, in most instances of pure hearsay.[33]

Arbitrator Aaron has drawn some general boundaries to the phrase "for what it's worth":

[A] competent arbitrator may be depended upon substantially to discount some kinds of hearsay evidence that he has admitted over objection. He will do so selectively, however, and not on the assumption that hearsay evidence, as such, is not to be credited. If, for example, a newly appointed personnel manager, or a recently elected business agent, offers a letter to his predecessor from a third party, the arbitrator is likely to ignore the fact that the evidence is hearsay; if satisfied that the document is genuine, he will give it such weight as its relevancy dictates. On the other hand, hearsay testimony about statements allegedly made by "the boys in the shop" or by executives in the "front office," though perhaps not excluded from the record by the arbitrator, probably will have no effect on his decision.[34]

Arbitrator Rauch in *Babcock & Wilcox Co.* has noted, furthermore, that "when hearsay evidence conflicts with uncontested evidence based on first-hand knowledge, the latter will generally prevail."[35]

Arbitrators, while accepting hearsay testimony, often wonder why better evidence is not brought forward, and when an arbitrator finds

[32] Roberts, *Precedent and Procedure in Arbitration Cases,* PROCEEDINGS OF NEW YORK UNIVERSITY SIXTH ANNUAL CONFERENCE ON LABOR, E. Stein, ed. (New York: Matthew Bender, 1953), p. 156.

[33] Updegraff, ARBITRATION AND LABOR RELATIONS, Third Edition of ARBITRATION OF LABOR DISPUTES (Washington: BNA Books, 1970), p. 256. *See also* American Arbitration Association, A MANUAL FOR COMMERCIAL ARBITRATORS (1980); Aaron, *Some Procedural Problems in Arbitration,* 10 VAND L. REV. 733 (1957); *Commercial National Bank,* 67 LA 163 (Lubow, 1976); the preference given to first-hand testimony over hearsay evidence is an important *caveat* to the general rule that hearsay evidence is admissable.

[34] Aaron, note 33 *supra,* at 744.

[35] 72-1 ARB ¶ 8367 (Rauch, 1972).

the hearsay evidence unpersuasive, the arbitrator should advise the parties of this fact and ask for better evidence. In *General Tire & Rubber Co.*[36] Arbitrator Donald Crawford noted:

> The Company relies on [A——'s] account of what [T——] said to the State Police when they interviewed the grievant and [T——]. The Union objected strenuously to the introduction of this hearsay testimony. The important point in arbitration is not whether the hearsay is admitted but its criticalness and what, if any, weight is given to it. (The parties are entitled to know the arbitrator's weighing of the hearsay.) In this case the hearsay could have been critical to the decision because its purpose was to establish the grievant's intent to participate in a theft. The Company was therefore asked to get the direct evidence.

Affidavits of individuals not attending the hearing and hence not subject to cross-examination are sometimes introduced as evidence in arbitrations and are often admitted subject to the same limitations that apply to all hearsay evidence.[37] In disciplinary cases, however, arbitrators often rule that affidavits are inadmissible because they deprive one of the parties of the right to cross-examination in a situation where careful evaluation of evidence is important.[38] At least one arbitrator has held that an affidavit of a nonwitness could be introduced to corroborate other evidence that was subject to cross-examination, but was inadmissible if it produced new evidence not testified to by other witnesses.[39]

In *Western Electric Co., Hawthorne Works,*[40] Arbitrator Dudley Whiting did accept some recorded testimony from an individual who would have been a witness had she not resigned. Pictures of her in the nude, taken "at the home of a girl friend," had found their way into the plant and were being sold there. As the individual's husband and her brother-in-law both worked in the plant as well, management wanted the person selling the pictures excluded from the plant to prevent repetition of what it considered an explosive situation. The individual who had been photographed said "she did not know how the pictures got into the plant" and that they had been distributed without her consent. An investigator wrote up a statement and read it to her and then had it typed by a stenographer, after which the individual

---

[36]68-1 ARB ¶ 8186 at 3649 (Crawford, 1968).

[37]*See, e.g., Imperial Glass Corp.*, 61 LA 1180 (Gibson, 1973); *Borden Co.*, 20 LA 483 (Rubin, 1953); Updegraff note 33 *supra*, at 256, 264.

[38]*Neuhoff Bros. Packers, Inc.*, 71-1 ARB ¶ 8179 (Ray, 1971); *Quaker State Oil Refining Corp.*, 68-1 ARB ¶ 8313 (Wood, 1968); *Jessop Steel Co.*, 68-1 ARB ¶ 8004 (Wood, 1967); *Ward Baking Co.*, 33 LA 791 (Marcus, 1959).

[39]*Milgram Food Stores, Inc.*, 68-2 ARB ¶ 8622 (Murphy, 1968).

[40]*Western Electric Company, Hawthorne Works, and International Brotherhood of Electrical Workers, AFL-CIO, Local 1859* (Whiting, 1966) (unpublished). *See* discussion of *Baker Marine Corp.*, 77 LA 721 (Marlatt, 1981) (acceptability of reports by investigator who had left employment out of fear for personal safety) under "Is Acceptance of Polygraph Evidence Beneficial or Detrimental to the Trier of Fact?" in Chapter XIV.

signed it. The statement was in the form of a deposition and said in part:

"I, [E—— S——], hereby and voluntarily without threat or promise make the following statement:
...
... During the course of my visit my girl friend and I thought it would be a lot of fun to have our pictures taken in the nude. That my girl friend took about five or six pictures of me and since then I had not given this incident much thought.... [T]hese pictures were taken with my consent, and I was not under the influence of drugs or liquor at the time.... That I am making this statement freely and voluntarily and solely for the purpose of fully informing the officials of the Western Electric Company, Incorporated, as to my acts as above described.

Before the statement was taken down, E—— S—— had asked to talk to her department chief alone. She said she was afraid that the pictures might be seen by her husband and that she had had an intimate relationship with the person who took the pictures but that "the intimacies with L—— were terminated." Her supervisor asked if she wanted to resign and she said she did. She said she and her husband and brother-in-law all worked in close proximity and she recognized that the situation was very explosive.

Medical evidence is often presented in the form of affidavits or certificates. Full weight, in the absence of contradictory evidence, is often given to such evidence.[41] Where, however, the medical condition of the grievant is the central point of the case, less weight should be given to an affidavit than to the testimony of a doctor who is exposed to cross-examination.

PRESUMPTIONS CONCERNING CREDIBILITY

In disciplinary cases, many arbitrators have resolved conflicts between testimony of the grievant and that of the supervisor (managerial representative) by use of a presumption that the supervisor has no intention of distorting the truth whereas the grievant has. Arbitrator William Dolson in *United Parcel Service, Inc.*[42] explained the underlying reasons for this presumption:

---

[41] *White Motor Co.*, 28 LA 823 (Lazarus, 1957); *Southern Cotton Oil Co.*, 26 LA 353 (Kelliher, 1956).

[42] 66-2 ARB ¶ 8703 at 5432 (Dolson, 1966), quoting Stessin, EMPLOYEE DISCIPLINE 44 (1960), paraphrasing the rule in *Ford Motor Co.*, 1 ALAA ¶ 67,274 (Shulman, 1945). *See also Herrud and Co.*, 77-2 ARB ¶ 8410 (Daniel, 1977); *Campbell Indus.*, 72-1 ARB ¶ 8120 (Block, 1972); *Washington, D.C. Publishers Ass'n.*, 67-1 ARB ¶ 8060 (Whyte, undated); *George A. Hormel & Co.*, 65-2 ARB ¶ 8562 (Boles, 1965); *Trailmobile, Inc.*, 28 LA 710 (Coffey, 1957); *Texas Electric Steel Casting Co.*, 28 LA 757 (Abernethy, 1957); *Standard Oil Co. (Indiana)*, 19 LA 795 (Naggi, 1952).

With respect to the problem where it is the supervisor's word against the grievant's, Arbitrator Harry Shulman at Ford Motor Co., laid down the following rule followed by many arbitrators:

"[A]n accused employee is presumed to have an incentive for not telling the truth and that when his testimony is contradicted by one who has nothing to gain or lose, the latter is to be believed."

Similarly, Arbitrator Earl Miller in *Cadillac Gage Co.*[43] held:

It was not probable that Foreman [M——] would have made up this story out of whole cloth and promptly reported it to Superintendent [X——]. The normal policy of a young foreman is to avoid antagonizing the men under him. Concocting such a lie against a Union member would be the worst way to achieve his own success. Furthermore, there was no background of trouble between Foreman [M——] and the grievant, which would have established a motive for such action.

Arbitrator Robert Mueller in *Western Condensing Co.*[44] also recognized the validity of this presumption:

Another criterion employed to a large extent by arbitrators, is to assess the motives to be served by the respective witnesses. The following example illustrates the general application of this criterion in a discharge case: G, the grievant, testifies that fact X did not exist. F, the foreman, testifies contra that fact X did exist. Solely on these facts, the testimony of grievant would not be afforded as much credibility as the foreman's testimony because the grievant would be more likely to perjure himself to save his job. Grievant has more at stake and therefore the motive is greater. The foreman, on the other hand, *prima facie,* has no motive to testify one way or the other, and presumably would not be inclined to perjure himself. If a strong motive can be shown on the part of the foreman or that the foreman harbors ill-will or malice toward the grievant, the findings more often will be for the grievant.

Arbitrator Arthur Ross said in *Pacific Gas & Electric Co.:*[45]

Considerable weight should be given to bona fide conclusions of supervisors when supported by factual evidence. In the first place, a supervisor is responsible for the efficient performance of his unit and has a legitimate concern that employees be properly assigned to achieve this objective. In the second place, he has a deeper and more intimate acquaintance with the men under his charge than an arbitrator is able to acquire in a brief hearing.

---

[43] 66-3 ARB ¶ 8969 at 6381 (Miller, 1966).

[44] 37 LA 912 (Mueller, 1962). *See also Jones & Laughlin Steel Corp.,* 8 STEEL ARB. 5885, 5886 (Alexander, 1960); *Firestone Tire & Rubber Co.,* 33 LA 206 (McCoy, 1959); *Pennsylvania Greyhound Lines, Inc.,* 19 LA 210 (Seward, 1952).

[45] 23 LA 556, 558 (Ross, 1954). *See also Hercules Powder Co.,* 10 LA 624, 625 (Reynolds, 1948).

Arbitrator Harold H. Leeper said in *Furr's, Inc.*:[46]

In view of the conflicting testimony between the Company's witnesses and the Union's witnesses as to some of the events which occurred on the morning of December 27, 1978, it is necessary for the Arbitrator to reach a conclusion as to the credibility of those witnesses. His observation of the eye-witnesses to the incident in the Manager's office ... indicates that their testimony was entirely credible.... On the other hand, we have the testimony of the Grievant and the other Union Steward. The latter was not a particularly impressive witness. He mumbled, appeared to evade some of the questions, and generally did not convince the undersigned that his testimony deserved much weight....[47]

...

Considering the Arbitrator's evaluation of the credibility of the witnesses, and the presumptions discussed above, it is concluded that the testimony of the Management witnesses is more likely to be accurate than that of the Grievant, as to his conduct in the office....

Accordingly, when there is a conflict in the stories told by the grievant and the managerial witness, the presumption will cause the managerial story to be adopted by the arbitrator unless the grievant's testimony is clearly corroborated.[48]

PRESUMPTIONS IN THEFT CASES

The amount of theft of company and fellow employee property by employees is reaching staggering totals each year.[49] Since managers have a duty to reduce the amount of theft, employees suspected of be-

---

[46]72 LA 960, 965 (Leeper, 1979).

[47]The court expressed a similar idea in *State Farm Life Insurance Company v. Smith*, 363 N.E.2d 785, 795 (S. Ct. 1977), quoting *Creamer v. Bivert*, 214 Mo. 473, 479, 113 S.W. 1118, 1120 (Sup. Ct. 1908):

Truth does not always stalk bodily forth naked, but modest withal, in a printed abstract in a court of last resort. She oft hides in nooks and crannies visible only to the mind's eye of the judge who tries the case. To him appears the furtive glance, the blush of conscious shame, the hesitation, the sincere or the flippant or sneering tone, the heat, the calmness, the yawn, the sigh, the candor or lack of it, the scant or full realization of the solemnity of an oath, the carriage and mien. The brazen face of the liar, the glibness of the schooled witness in reciting a lesson or the itching over-eagerness of the swift witness, as well as the honest face of the truthful one, are alone seen by him.

[48]This presumption has been applied by arbitrators to resolve conflicts between testimonies of management representatives and discharged grievants in many cases where use of the presumptions is not reported in the award. Since grievants often have no alibi witness available to rebutt the presumptions, some grievants who seriously believe the management representative is mistaken in his or her observations, etc., have asked to have their conflicting testimony subjected to a polygraph test. *See* "Polygrapher Testimony to Corroborate or Impeach Testimony" in Chapter XIV.

[49]Department of Commerce, *The Cost of Crimes Against Business*, cited by Reid and Inbau in *Truth and Deception*, Second Edition (Baltimore: Williams and Wilkins, 1977).

ing involved are often discharged. Grievances are then filed and processed to arbitration, and the company representative will present evidence to establish the *prima facie* case which usually will include the factual basis for a presumption.[50] Arbitrator Seidenberg in *Morgan Millwork Company*[51] said that when an employee has possession of stolen property, a presumption develops that the employee was involved with the theft. If the employee failed to advise the management of the property in the employee's possession, the presumption is essentially irrefutable. The employer need not prove that the grievant actually stole the property to support the discharge. In addition, the presumption is not rebutted when the grievant is acquitted of larceny in a state court:

> It is not unreasonable for the employer to conclude, especially during a period when it is suffering substantial losses of merchandise, that [in the case of] an employee whom the Police have detected possessing property bearing the stamp of the employer, without any claim or color of right on the part of the employee, that the prudent interests of the Company demanded the severance of the employment relationship.

Then the grievant, through his or her representative, will attempt to rebut the presumptions basic to the discharge.[52] The most common presumption in theft cases involves the possession of stolen items in automobiles,[53] homes,[54] lockers,[55] lunch boxes,[56] and large purses.[57]

These presumptions are not rebutted by directing the grievant to "take the Fifth" (an expression that is not appropriate in labor arbitration, but which means to remain mute).[58] Rarely can a grievant locate an alibi witness who will testify that the grievant was "framed" and that someone else, to frame the grievant, put the item in the grievant's automobile, home, etc. However, some rather spectacular rebuttals to the possession presumption have succeeded; Arbitrator Fred E. Kindig reinstated an employee who had been discharged by a refinery after guards found a substantial collection of valuable company prop-

---

[50]Hill and Sinicropi, EVIDENCE IN ARBITRATION (Washington: BNA Books, 1980), p. 24.

[51]62-2 ARB ¶ 8557 (Seidenberg, 1962). 52A C.J.S. *Larceny* ¶ 105 (1968). *See also* the decision in the *General Tire and Rubber Co.* case discussed by W. Willard Wirtz in *Due Process of Arbitration*, THE ARBITRATOR AND THE PARTIES, Proceedings of the Eleventh Annual Meeting of the National Academy of Arbitrators, J. McKelvey, ed. (Washington: BNA Books, 1958), p. 20.

[52]*See* note 50 *supra*, at p. 30.

[53]*Golden Pride, Inc.*, 68 LA 1232 (Jaffe, 1977); *Owens-Corning Fiberglass Corp.*, 67-1 ARB ¶ 8278 (Doyle, 1967); *Eastern Airlines*, 46 LA 549 (Seidenberg, 1965), *Allen Industries*, 26 LA 363 (Klamon, 1956).

[54]*Weirton Steel Co.*, 68-1 ARB ¶ 8249 (Kates, 1968).

[55]*International Nickel Co.*, 50 LA 65 (Shister, 1967).

[56]*Fruehauf Corp.*, 49 LA 89 (Daugherty, 1967).

[57]*Alden's, Inc.*, 6802 ARB ¶ 8814 (Kelliher, 1968). Contrasting is *Martin-Bower Co.*, 78 LA 236 (Role, 1982).

[58]*Simoniz Co.*, 44 LA 658 (McGury, 1964).

erty in the grievant's home.[59] The grievant's ex-wife had telephoned the guards, reporting that company property was in the grievant's garage, two days after the grievant had started eviction proceedings to remove her from the house. There was testimony to the effect that the grievant's wife and her boyfriend made daily trips to the refinery, allegedly making deliveries. The arbitrator rejected the normal presumption of theft that had arisen out of the "possession" of property in the grievant's house, stating in this case "it is entirely possible that said items [company property] could have been obtained even by the grievant's wife." A polygraph test might well have increased the chances of a favorable decision for the union member.[60]

PRESUMPTIONS OFTEN USED

Arbitrator Sinicropi explained the many "presumptions" and "inferences" that operate against grievants in arbitration:

> In the arbitral and judicial settings, presumptions have come into existence primarily because factfinders have believed that, absent evidence to the contrary, reason, logic, and human experience render the existence of one fact probable once another fact has been proven. Thus, to cite an example, Arbitrator Geissinger, in *FMC Corp.*, held that evidence that obscene phone calls were made from the grievant's home was sufficient to support a presumption of fact (or inference) that the calls were instigated by the grievant. . . .
>
> . . .
>
> It is important to note that the use of presumptions in both the legal and arbitral setting is generally only a means of shifting the burden of producing evidence to the party against whom the presumption operates.[61] [Footnotes omitted.]

Without cataloging the many presumptions that set up a *prima facie* case and then shift the burden of proof, it is still possible to discuss various presumptions that are used in labor arbitration to reduce long and tedious fact presentations.

Knowledge of Rules, Practices, and Policies

Often a critical facet of the management's *prima facie* case in a disciplinary proceeding is proof that the employee had knowledge of the rule he or she allegedly violated. Generally, however, arbitrators indulge in an evidentiary presumption of knowledge if the rule vio-

---

[59] *Standard of Ohio (Lima Refinery)* (Kindig) (unpublished).
[60] *Id. See also* note 48 *supra.*
[61] *See* note 50 *supra,* at pp. 24–25.

lated is one of common knowledge or the rules have been distributed. Thus, Arbitrator Milton Schmidt in *Ross Gear & Tool Co.*[62] noted:

> It is implicit in the employer-employee relationship that an employee must conform to certain well known, commonly accepted, standards of reasonable discipline and proper conduct while engaged in his work.... Among these obligations are the duty to perform his work as directed and to remain in his work station instead of wandering around ..., the duty to explain his absence from his work station for an unreasonably long period of time upon inquiry from a management representative, the duty to refrain from the use of foul abusive and profane language, particularly directed toward supervisory personnel....
>
> Published rules and regulations are not necessary to inform an employee that misconduct of the nature above described may subject him to discharge from the company's employ. Every employee ... is presumed to know that the [business] cannot operate without a reasonable measure of discipline....

As to the effect of published rules and regulations, Arbitrator Robert Howlett in *Valley Steel Casting Co.*[63] has held:

> [I]n the arbitrator's opinion a conscious remembering of a rule at the time an act is taken is not necessary in order that a discharge may be for proper cause. If such were the rule every discharge could be reversed by the testimony of a grievant (necessarily a subjective test) that he did not remember the rule which he was violating at the time he did so. The test with respect to a rule clearly communicated to employees must, of necessity, be determined by objective evidence. Unless strong reason is shown, every employee should be charged with knowledge of rules clearly communicated, whether he actually remembers them or not.

And Arbitrator Donald Lee in *Badger Concrete Co.*[64] commented on the effect of prior warnings:

> The written warnings placed both the grievant and the Union on notice that drastic action might follow. No appeal was taken from these notices; consequently, the Employer could rightfully assume that the grievant and the Union were fully aware of the situation.

Similarly, as to provisions of the collective bargaining agreement, Arbitrator Vernon Stouffer in *A. O. Smith Corp.*[65] noted:

> If any education regarding the contents of the Agreement is necessary, that is the duty of the Union, which is recognized and acts as the Bargaining Agent for all unit employees. Ignorance of provisions of the Agreement is not an acceptable reason or excuse for not calling to report absences.

---

[62]35 LA 293, 295–96 (Schmidt, 1960).
[63]22 LA 520, 527 (Howlett, 1954).
[64]64-3 ARB ¶ 9145 at 6962 (Lee, 1964).
[65]66-3 ARB ¶ 8848 at 5937 (Stouffer, 1966).

Finally, as to past practices and policies, Arbitrator Sam Tatum in *Chattanooga Box and Lumber Co.*[66] held:

[The Company] has consistently since 1947 refused to permit a leave for this purpose, and it has only permitted one who had gone out for maternity reasons to return as a new employee. To this the Union has acquiesced until the filing of this grievance. The argument by the Union [stated] that it did not know of the practice of the Company because such had not been communicated to it by the members. It must be concluded that the employees through the years have known of the policy of the Company and the knowledge of the employee must be the knowledge of the Union; and, too, in the plant the Union has its officials or committeemen who are in daily contact with the employees. Therefore, through the years the committeemen must have known of the position of the Company. The knowledge of the committeemen must be the knowledge of the Union.

Presumptions to Establish Responsibility for a Contract Violation Strike

Arbitrators, following the lead of Judge Goldsborough in *United States v. United Mine Workers,*[67] have used a presumption in lieu of evidence to determine the leadership of and responsibility for a strike in violation of a no-strike pledge. For example, in *General American Transportation Corp.*[68] Arbitrator Harry Pollock wrote:

It is generally safe to say that members of unions do not act in concert without leadership. This rule is proven by experience. Since this local was

---

[66]44 LA 373, 376 (Tatum, 1965). *See also Bell Aircraft Corp.*, 9 LA 65, 66 (Jaffee, 1947):
[I]n a matter so open and so universal as vacation pay, at least the Union's leadership is charged with knowledge of how the contract is being administered.
But see Olson v. Mall Tool Co., 346 Ill. App. 9, 104 N.E.2d 665 (1952), where it was held that a rule disqualifying an employee for vacation pay for quitting immediately after a vacation and before receiving her pay was not binding on the employee unless there was evidence that the employee had read the rule booklet or had been instructed to do so.
[67]77 F. Supp. 563, 566-67, 21 LRRM 2721, 2724 and 22 LRRM 2005 (D. D.C. 1948) (*aff'd in part and appeal dismissed in part*, 177 F.2d 29, 24 LRRM 2111 (D.C. Cir. 1949), *cert. denied*, 338 U.S. 871, 25 LRRM 2038 (1949)):
[T]he Court thinks the principle is this: that as long as a union is functioning as a union it must be held responsible for the mass action of its members. It is perfectly obvious not only in objective reasoning but because of experience that men don't act collectively without leadership. The idea of suggesting that from 250,000 to 350,000 men would all get the same idea at once, independently of leadership, and walk out of the mines, is of course simply ridiculous.
So that, in general, this Court announces a principle of law. The Court has no means of knowing whether higher courts will adopt the principle or not, but the Court has no doubt about its soundness, not any—that a union that is functioning must be held responsible for the mass action of its members.
See also United Textile Workers v. Newberry Mills, Inc., 238 F. Supp. 366, 373, 59 LRRM 2305, 2310 (W.D. S.C. 1965); *Operating Engineers, Local 926*, 196 NLRB 629 (1972), 80 LRRM 1126, *enforced*, 488 F.2d 979, 85 LRRM 2351 (5th Cir. 1974). *See also* note 36 in Chapter VIII. A concerted refusal to work overtime when it had been previously regularly scheduled and worked is presumptively strike action. *Elevator Mfr.'s Ass'n. v. Elevator Constructors*, 342 F. Supp. 372, 80 LRRM 2165, 2166 (S.D. N.Y. 1972).
[68]42 LA 142, 143-44 (Pollack, 1964).

functioning and there was apparently no schism, the union leadership must be held responsible for the acts of its members.

Arbitrator Barnett M. Goodstein in *National Homes Mfg.*[69] is among those arbitrators who place financial responsibility upon a Union when the members engage in a breach of the no-strike provision of the labor agreement. This financial penalty grows out of the Goldsborough presumption. The Union representatives argued that no official had encouraged the members to honor or to dishonor picket lines and that the members did not cross because of their personal convictions:[70]

> In this argument, the Union attempts to disassociate itself from its members whom it represents and on whose behalf it gave up the right to cross a picket line of a stranger union. This it cannot do. *The Union is responsible for the actions of its members, at least until it has made a good faith effort to get the members to honor their Contract.* In this case, the Union admits that it has done nothing to convince the employees that they should honor the no-strike, no-work stoppage clause of the Contract. Instead, in violation of the Contract, it has left the question of whether the Contract should be honored or violated up to the individual conscience of each individual member of the Union. In this action, the Union is saying that, when it serves our purpose, we will represent the interests of our members; however, when it is to our advantage not to do so, we will let them act as individuals, rather than as Union members. In order to obtain the benefits of their Contract, the Union and its members must accept its obligations. [Emphasis added.]

Some courts did not adopt the "mass action" presumption, believing that to hold the Union responsible some actual proof of union instigation is necessary. This need for verification proof evolved from the following language in Section 6 of the Norris LaGuardia Act, 29 U.S.C.A. § 106:

> [N]o association or organization participating or interested in a labor dispute, shall be held responsible or liable in any court of the United States for the unlawful acts of individual officials, members or agents, *except upon clear proof of actual participation in, or actual authorization of, such actions, or the ratification* of such actions after actual knowledge thereof. [Emphasis added.]

However, this section of Norris LaGuardia has now been held to be inapplicable to actions against unions for breach of the no-strike provisions expressed or implied in labor agreements under Section 301.

---

[69]72 LA 1127 (Goodstein, 1979). Likewise, Arbitrator Stanley H. Sergent Jr. in *Westinghouse Transport Leasing Co.*, 69 LA 1210 (1977), did make the presumptive step to place financial responsibility directly on the union after a breach of the no-strike provision.

[70]*See also Philadelphia Newspapers, Inc.*, 68 LA 401 (Jaffee, 1977); *Almaden Vineyards, Inc.*, 56 LA 425 (Kagel, 1971); *ARO, Inc.*, 47 LA 1065 (Whyte, 1966).

Section 301 also provides that Union members are protected from liability, even if they are engaged in strike action in breach of the labor agreement, if the Union is liable for such breach:

(b) Any labor organization which represents employees in an industry affecting commerce as defined in this chapter, and any employer whose activities affect commerce as defined in this chapter *shall be bound by the acts of its agents* . . . .

. . .

(e) For the purposes of this section, in determining whether any person is acting as an "agent" of another person so as to make such other person responsible for his acts, the question of whether the specific acts performed were actually authorized or subsequently ratified shall not be controlling.[71] [Emphasis added.]

Presumption That Facts Reported in Unchallenged Prior Disciplinary Warnings Are Correct

Arbitrator McCoy advised the parties in an arbitration hearing that he would employ a presumption that the facts stated in warning notices previously given the employee were correct, to prevent a hearing on a discharge case from becoming a hearing on the merits of prior disciplinary warnings:

Some companies have a system of personnel reports on employees that go into their personnel file. For example, if a man does a negligent piece of work, for which he ought to receive a warning, do you make out a slip, and give him a copy, and send a copy to the labor relations office?

I have ruled in other arbitrations that where a company does have that system they cannot bring into evidence any previous offenses to help justify a subsequent disciplinary layoff or discharge unless a written record was made of the previous offense.

In addition, if under such a system a man has a chance to file a grievance to take such a reprimand off his record then the employee cannot claim that he did not engage in the conduct reported in the reprimand warning, unless he has filed such a grievance. In other words, if a man deserves a warning and is given it and is given a slip reporting the offense and doesn't protest it with a grievance, then at a subsequent hearing it must be taken as an admitted offense. In such a case, there is no need for testimony about the prior incident. . . .

This is the only way that I can see to keep a hearing concerning a discipline or discharge case from becoming a hearing about a thousand incidents.[72]

---

[71] 29 U.S.C.A. § 185(b) and (e) (1978).

[72] Quoted in LECTURES ON THE LAW AND LABOR MANAGEMENT RELATIONS, Michigan Univ. Law School, Summer Institute for International and Comparative Law (Ann Arbor: Univ. of Mich. Law School, 1951), pp. 216–17.

Presumption That Expert Medical Opinion Is Correct

Medical testimony which is not arbitrary or unreasonable and is given in good faith has been presumed to be correct by arbitrators. For example, in *Great Lakes Spring Corp.*[73] the company refused to reemploy an employee who had suffered a heart attack as a result of lifting a heavy object in the plant and who sought and was awarded compensation on the basis of total permanent disability. Arbitrator Charles Gregory upheld the employer's determination not to reemploy the grievant. Gregory based his decision on both the total permanent disability determination and testimony by the company's doctor. With extensive knowledge of the nature of the work in the plant, the doctor's judgment could not be shown to be arbitrary or unreasonable. In this regard, Arbitrator Gregory stated:

> Certainly an employer could hardly be said to be unreasonable or arbitrary following the advice of a physician whom it retains permanently to pass on matters of the sort involved here, especially when that physician, through years of familiarity with the plant's problems and available jobs, has acquired a fairly thorough working knowledge of what jobs are available and of the nature of such jobs. The only possible attack on the Company's position is that the doctor in question is himself arbitrary or unreasonable or is acting in bad faith. Concerning these possibilities, however, there is no evidence in the record.[74]

In *International Shoe Co.*[75] Arbitrator Saul Wallen said:

> The proper use of this power will be evident if the facts in a particular case show that management's action was taken in good faith, was based on reasonably adequate medical testimony and evidence, and was not taken against a background that would indicate a discriminatory purpose. If these facts exist, there is a presumption of validity that favors the plant physician's medical testimony. This presumption arises out of the fact that the plant physician has a knowledge of both the employee's health and the job conditions. On the other hand, if in a given case there is evidence that management's good faith is lacking, that its physician's conclusions are not well supported by the medical findings, or that there are circumstances surrounding the case tending to support a claim of discrimination, then there would be grounds to set management's action aside or at least cause the case to be submitted to impartial medical inquiry.

In a slightly different situation, Arbitrator Maurice Merrill in *Ideal Cement Co.*[76] held that a company could rely on the opinion of its own doctors even though contrary medical evidence was presented by the

---

[73] 11 LA 159 (Gregory, 1948).
[74] *Id.* at 160.
[75] 14 LA 253, 255 (Wallen, 1950).
[76] *Ideal Cement Co.*, 20 LA 480, 482 (Merrill, 1953).

grievant. The employer had discharged an employee because a brain tumor operation had changed his physical condition to such a degree that he was a danger to himself and others. Holding that the company was entitled to rely on the opinions of its own medical advisors so long as they were reasonable, he held:

> In view of the direct conflict in the medical testimony, with nothing to swing the balance preponderantly on one side or the other, I think that the Company is entitled to rely on the views of its own medical advisers, if it has given Mr. [S——] fair notice and opportunity to overcome those views before reaching a final decision. . . . I think that the Company has shown "good and legitimate reasons" for refusing to re-employ Mr. [S——] in the absence of available light work, provided it has observed the due process required by the contract in the separation procedure.

Title VII Presumptions Used in Arbitration

Many quite normal arbitration cases have become more difficult because in the grievance there is a Title VII discrimination charge. If the grievant is not satisfied with the award by the arbitrator, a skilled private attorney may attempt to start up *de novo* a Title VII complaint filed in a state or federal court. However, if the arbitrator puts into the arbitration record the necessary evidence and analyzes the Title VII aspects in a well-reasoned opinion, the judge, rather than hearing the evidence *de novo,* may treat the arbitration record and the award as the report of his own magistrate or master and issue the arbitration award as his or her decision.

Statistics are being used with increasing frequency in connection with court litigation under Title VII employment discrimination and the same types of statistics are creeping into arbitration cases because more grievances are coming before arbitrators that have a Title VII "edge." The arbitrators must be able to discuss the statistics presented in the arbitration hearing to prove or rebut improper discrimination claims in the award to avoid having the grievance moved to the district court as a full-blown Title VII case with full relitigation. (*See* Chapter XXII.) A former EEOC official has stated that arbitrators and representatives must learn to play the "numbers game"—*i.e.,* to use statistical data to prove or disprove charges of employment discrimination—because this, he said, is "the only game in town."

At first, statistical proof had loose rules, but now the rules have been tightened: *prima facie* claims can be set up with statistics and then rebutted with other statistics, etc. The "game" started in *Griggs v. Duke Power Co.*[77] in 1971. Later it was tightened up in *McDonnell*

---

[77]401 U.S. 424, 3 FEP Cases 175 (1971).

Douglas Corp. v. Green,[79] *Teamsters v. United States,*[79] and *Hazelwood School District v. United States.*[80] Isolated statistical proof (sometimes referred to as "statistical snapshots") would no longer be acceptable as proof.[81] Now adequate samples must be taken and the samples must be within the relevant time frame. These changes in the proof for a *prima facie* case are actually a shift of the burden from the defense to the plaintiff in a court case, which will shift the burden of proof in labor arbitration from the employer to the union (grievant). Because of this "tightening up" and shifting of the burden,[82] arbitrators should follow the game carefully and learn the meanings behind the statistical terms such as "random samples," "probability," "standard deviation," "expected values," "population data," "employer work force date," "geographic scope" and "labor market area." No effort to give meaning to these words will be attempted in this chapter. The purpose here is to set up an alert. Arbitrators and representatives must continue to "dig deeper to avoid the otherwise inevitable stumbles!"[83]

Arbitrator Gould in *Basic Vegetable Products Co.*[84] explained the care that has developed in analyzing statistics in the federal courts and the same care that must be used in labor arbitration cases:

> The Charging Party and the Union rely upon *McDonnell Douglas Corp. v. Green,* 411 U.S. 792, 802, 5 FEP Cases 965 (1973), and the Court's articulation of the test to be utilized under Title VII in connection with establishing a *prima facie* case of discrimination. The Arbitrator's attention is directed to the following portion of the Green opinion in which the Court stated:
>
> "The complainant in a Title VII trial must carry the initial burden under the statute of establishing a *prima facie* case of racial discrimination. This may be done by showing (i) that he belongs to a racial minority; (ii) that he applied and was qualified for a job for which the employer was seeking applicants; (iii) that, despite his qualifications, he was rejected; and (iv) that, after his rejection, the position remained open and the em-

---

[78]411 U.S. 792, 5 FEP Cases 965 (1973).

[79]431 U.S. 324, 14 FEP Cases 1514 (1977).

[80]433 U.S. 299, 15 FEP Cases 1 (1977).

[81]*Waters v. Furnco Construction,* 551 F.2d 1085, 14 FEP Cases 865 (7th Cir. 1977), *rev'd and remanded,* 438 U.S. 567, 17 FEP Cases 1062 (1978).

[82]Plaintiff's statistical proof was rejected because the sample was too small in *Harper v. Trans World Airlines,* 525 F.2d 409, 11 FEP Cases 1074 (8th Cir. 1975), and *Hester v. Southern Railway Co.,* 497 F.2d 1374, 8 FEP Cases 646 (5th Cir. 1974). *See also Employment Discrimination and Title VII of the Civil Rights Act of 1964,* 84 Harv. L. Rev. 1109, 1154 (1971).

[83]Morris, Current Trends in the Use (and Misuse) of Statistics in Employment Discrimination Litigation (Washington: Equal Employment Advisory Council, 1979).

[84]64 LA 620, 623 (Gould, 1975). For many years prohibitions against improper discrimination were set forth in labor agreements and many disputes were resolved by arbitrators under such provisions.

ployer continued to seek applicants from persons of complainant's qualifications."

. . .

It seems quite clear that the law enunciated by the United States
Supreme Court and all of the Circuit Courts of Appeals support the view
that the Union and Charging Party have made out a *prima facie* case of
discrimination in the instant proceeding. Under McDonnell, even where
rebuttal is provided by respondent, statistics are "helpful." In any event, a
statistical pattern makes out a *prima facie* case of discrimination, past or
present.

Employment statistics recording who has been hired compared with
who has applied but has not been hired are rarely involved in labor arbitration, since the labor agreement applies to employees who have
already been hired. However, the number of blacks, whites, His-
panics, females, and males in various classifications who bid for promotions and the number of those who do not, but could have, become
very important in labor arbitration when a bidder who is not chosen
files a grievance and claims a Title VII discrimination as well as a
labor agreement violation.[85]

When there is a question of discrimination based on race, statistics
may be used to find the percentage ratio of members of the minority,
their types of employment, and salaries in employment, together with
the number of members of that minority who reside in the community
and have sought employment. If the percentages do not correspond
appropriately, an attorney may seek to argue to the court that the statistics prove that the employer was guilty of racial discrimination. If a
claim of minority discrimination is built into a grievance, the statistics
must be collected and incorporated into the arbitration record to avoid
pushing the case into court.

If the union representative is arguing that racial discrimination was
operating against the grievant and statistics are presented to set up a

---

[85] So many females who are offered vacancies decline transfers that a term has been developed
for this phenomenon: "bidding disinclination." *Kerr Glass Mfg. Corp.*, 77 OFCCP 4 (1980).
The reason may be found in surveys that reveal that many women believe their work experience
will not be continuous and hence forego new employment experiences because the transfer requires them to accept training and enter a different and unfamiliar working situation. The
disparity between the average earnings of male and female employees who are working in a plant
comes not only from the "disinclination" to bid up but because the career choices made by
women have been different from those made by men and because as a group females do not acquire training for specific and more skilled work before seeking employment. *See* Kreps, SEX IN
THE MARKETPLACE: AMERICAN WOMEN AT WORK (Baltimore: Johns Hopkins Univ. Press,
1971), pp. 44-45; Polacheck, *Discontinuous Labor Force Participation and Its Effect on
Women's Market Earnings*, SEX, DISCRIMINATION AND THE DIVISION OF LABOR, C. Lloyd, ed.
(New York: Columbia Univ. Press, 1975), p. 111; Lloyd and Niemi, THE ECONOMICS OF SEX
DIFFERENTIALS (New York: Columbia Univ. Press, 1980), pp. 99-101, 152; and Reubens and
Reubens, *Women Workers, Nontraditional Occupations and Full Employment*, WOMEN IN THE
U.S. LABOR FORCE, A. Cahn, ed. (New York: Praeger Publications, 1979), pp. 121-33.

presumption adverse to the employer, the company representative should promptly analyze the statistical sample to determine if it is too small or if the employment decisions too infrequent.

For example, to rebut the presumption being built out of statistics, one district court explained:

> For example, suppose that there are ten persons in an employer's statistical population, all of whom are white. The comparable percentage of blacks in the community population might be 20%. Therefore, the inference could be drawn that in two employment decisions racial prejudice was the deciding factor. But considering the large number of possible factors in making the decision, the likelihood that race was determinative in two out of two or none out of two decisions is very small. The situation would give rise to a much stronger inference if there were 1,000 persons in the statistical group, 100 of which were black, with a general black population of 20%. While the percentages are greatly more disparate in the first example (0–100% as compared to 10–90%), the chance of random factors entering the decision is much less likely when 100 statistically improper decisions are made than when only two are made.[86]

In *Roman v. ESB*,[87] the court said about statistical presumptions:

> While some 63% of those laid off were black, in light of the small statistical sampling involved (83 persons), this figure does not prove a discriminatory layoff, especially considering the manner in which the layoff was effected. Only a small change (8) in the numbers of blacks and whites involved would yield a ratio the same as that of blacks to whites in the plant.

At what point statistical data cast a strong enough suspicion on an employment practice to cause a presumption is not clear even though the federal equal employment opportunity agencies have attempted to establish statistical presumption rules. In any event, the arbitrators need not be expert statisticians, but they should develop some background to absorb information into the record in an orderly way so that representatives can make the statistical arguments in their briefs.

Presumption That Writings Which Are Delivered Are Authorized, and Those Which Are Mailed Are Received

Arbitrators Arthur Stack and Robert Feinberg report that the following presumptions are most useful in labor arbitration:

1. When it can be shown that a letter has been mailed by U.S. mail, it shall be presumed to have been received.[88]

---

[86]*Johnson v. Shreveport Garment Co.*, 422 F. Supp. 526, 540, 13 FEP Cases 1677, 1687 (W.D. La., 1976).
[87](4th Cir. 1976). 550 F.2d 1343, 1352, 14 FEP Cases 235, 243
[88]*See* note 33 *supra*, at 297. *See also American Oil Co.*, 68-1 ARB ¶ 8211 (Bradley, 1967); *International Harvester Co.*, 21 LA 444 (Kelliher, 1953).

2. Any writing of the company or the union which is published or delivered by an official or authorized representative of the company or union shall be presumed to have been authorized.

3. Any writing which is published or delivered by an official or authorized representative of any other organization or third party shall similarly be presumed to have been authorized.

EXPERT TESTIMONY

The function of expert testimony in contested proceedings is to assist the trier of fact to draw proper inferences from the proven facts, inferences which the trier might be incompetent to draw on his or her own. Arbitrators appreciate good expert testimony presented by either side and, in some cases where such testimony is not proferred, arbitrators on their own motion have called in specialists to help them resolve disputed technical questions.[89] The Chicago Tripartite Committee said:

> The committee was of the opinion that it is improper for an arbitrator to seek expert advice without informing the parties. There are situations, however, where the arbitrator may suggest the use of an expert when the parties' experts are in conflict. This is particularly true in cases involving incentives or job evaluations. He should not, however, use such an expert without the consent of the parties, and should permit the parties to have access to whatever opinion is offered by the expert selected by him and to comment on the opinion before reaching his decision.[90]

It is not necessary to establish a formal procedure for qualifying a witness as an expert in a labor arbitration proceeding to the same extent that would be required in a court proceeding. The Pittsburgh Tripartite Committee said:

> The "expert" is allowed to draw inferences and conclusions because, in theory, his knowledge is superior to that of the person having to resolve the issue, be it judge, jury, or arbitrator.
>
>   Example #8—"Company Attorney: We will present Mr. Jones, a qualified Industrial Engineer, to testify as to the proper classification and rate for this job."
>
> *Ruling*: Clearly admissible evidence. One cornerstone of labor arbitration is the supposed expert knowledge of the arbitrator himself concerning the issues in dispute. Hence, the value of expert witnesses correspondingly diminishes, and the probability of substantial error involving misplaced

---

[89]*Chrysler Corp.*, 21 LA 573, 577 (Wolff, 1953) (engineer consulted to determine whether employer had control over power failure); *Container Co.*, 6 LA 218, 219–20 (Whiting, 1946) (incentive rates and an impartial study of plant operations by technical commissioners).

[90]*See* note 13 *supra*, at p. 108.

reliance on expert testimony is minimized. This logic does not apply where the expert is discussing medical or other non-industrial specialties.

Experts frequently are presented in cases involving job evaluation, incentive, and medical matters. Once the competence of the witness is established, there remain few valid objections to his testimony. If an arbitrator is not strong in this area of knowledge, he should question the witness for his own benefit.[91]

The Chicago Tripartite Committee said:

> Expert testimony should, of course, be received. There was general agreement that the strict court rules for establishing the qualifications of the expert need not be insisted upon, although, as a practical matter, most parties offering an expert witness will take pains to lay a detailed foundation for claiming that he is an expert. In weighing the testimony of an expert, attention should be given especially to the opportunity of the expert to have access to data which would give him a basis for expressing an opinion. Obviously an expert who testifies on the basis of what someone else has told him, in other words, on the basis of hearsay and not personal knowledge, is not entitled to have as much weight given to his testimony. Again primary reliance must be placed by the arbitrator on cross examination.[92]

In labor arbitration proceedings, since it is the arbitrator himself who is chosen for his expertise in constructing labor agreements, expert evidence concerning construction of the agreement would be out of place. The Chicago Tripartite Committee said:

> There is one area in which an arbitrator can justifiably refuse to receive opinion evidence. It occurs where the issue before the arbitrator is one of interpretation of an agreement and the opinion evidence offered goes to the witness' opinion as to what the contract means. But here again little harm will result from receiving the evidence. The arbitrator is not bound to give it any weight.[93]

DEMONSTRATIVE AND DOCUMENTARY EVIDENCE

The problems that arise when documentary evidence is offered usually involve the "best evidence" rule and authentication. The "best evidence" rule in this context is sometimes called the "original documents" rule and is the requirement that the original document rather than a copy of it should be the evidence submitted.[94]

---

[91]*Problems of Proof in the Arbitration Process: Report of the Pittsburgh Tripartite Committee,* PROBLEMS OF PROOF IN ARBITRATION, note 1 *supra*, at p. 253.

[92]*See* note 13 *supra*, at pp. 94–95. *See also* Chapter XIV.

[93]*Id.* at p. 94.

[94]4 J. Wigmore, EVIDENCE § 1232; 2 B. Jones, EVIDENCE § 560 (5th ed. 1958).

McCormick in his treatise on evidence has stated the rule as follows:

> [I]n proving the terms of a writing, where such terms are material, the original writing must be produced, unless it is shown to be unavailable for some reason other than the serious fault of the proponent.[95]

Behind every rule of evidence there is some reason justifying its existence. McCormick lists the three reasons basic to the original document rule:

> (1) that precision in presenting ... the exact words of the writing is of more than average importance, particularly as respect operative ... instruments, such as ... contracts, since a slight variation in words means a great difference in rights, (2) that there is a substantial hazard of inaccuracy in the human process of making a copy by handwriting or typewriting, and (3) as respects oral testimony purporting to give from memory the terms of a writing, there is a special risk of error, greater than in the case of attempts at describing other situations generally.[96]

The application of the rule in labor arbitration was stated as follows:

> Where objection is made to the introduction of evidence of a secondary nature on the ground that it is not the best evidence, the original document should be produced unless it is shown, for reasons satisfactory to the arbitrator, that it is not available. Reproductions of original documents shall be deemed the best evidence unless the authenticity of the purported original documents is significantly in question.[97]

The reasons that justify the introduction of secondary evidence in court hearings apply with equal validity in arbitrations:

> [L]oss, destruction, refusal to produce the original by an opponent, detention by a third person who will not surrender possession, physical or legal impossibility of removing the original, as for example, a notice which is pasted on a wall, the inconvenience of removing business records that are in constant use and may not be conveniently removed and voluminous documents the production of which would be wasteful time. Recollection testimony should be permitted where neither the original nor a copy is available if this testimony can give the substance of the document.[98]

The Pittsburgh Tripartite Committee made these comments about "best evidence" in labor arbitration:

> This rule, invented to prevent error, requires submission of the most

---

[95] C. McCormick, EVIDENCE § 196 (1954).
[96] *Id.* at § 197.
[97] *See* note 31 *supra*, at pp. 299–300. *See also* Updegraff, note 33 *supra*, at pp. 227–29.
[98] *See* note 13 *supra*, at p. 92.

authoritative source for the information sought to be introduced. Two phases are illustrated below:

Example #5—"Witness: The written agreement reached by the parties provides that double time is to be paid for all hours over eight (8) in a work day."

Ruling: Since the testimony concerns a written instrument and its contents, the evidence should not be admitted by oral testimony unless the written instrument cannot be obtained because of its destruction, etc.

Example #6—"Attorney: I offer into evidence this carbon copy of the agreement reached by the parties in connection with overtime rate."

Ruling: All carbon copies are really "duplicate originals." The mere fact that the original document is not introduced should not bar admission of the copy unless one of the parties expressly challenges the accuracy or correctness of the copy.[99]

The New York Tripartite Committee agreed that secondary evidence should be considered valid when it has been established that the original evidence cannot reasonably be presented at the arbitration proceeding.[100]

When documentary evidence is submitted, each document should be properly identified as to its source and authenticated.[101] Business records receive special considerations in courts. *Jones on Evidence* states:

In 1936 the National Conference of Commissioners on Uniform State Laws promulgated the Uniform Business Records as Evidence Act, which, after defining "business," provided: "A record of an act, condition or event, shall, in so far as relevant, be competent evidence if the custodian or other qualified witness testifies to its identity and the mode of its preparation, and if it was made in the regular course of business, at or near the time of the act, condition or event, and if, in the opinion of the court, the sources of information, method and time of preparation were such as to justify its admission.

This act eliminated the necessity for showing the unavailability of each person who was a party to the making of the record....[102] [Footnote omitted.]

This rule is particularly important in labor arbitration. It permits, for example, a supervisor in the payroll department to verify an employee's incentive production record even though the supervisor did not actually compile the record.

Some arbitration awards have distinguished between formal and informal business records. Both are generally admissible, but, in recog-

[99] *See* note 91 *supra*, at p. 252. *See also*, for less restrictive view, note 13 *supra*, at p. 92.
[100] *See* note 31 *supra*, at pp. 299–300.
[101] *See* note 95 *supra*, at §§ 304–12.
[102] 2 B. Jones, EVIDENCE § 12:11 (5th ed. 1958).

nition of the accuracy of the original business records, greater weight may be given to data taken from such business records than from informal records or estimates.[103] In this connection, it is of interest that evidence accumulated on a computer was admitted to prove that a grievant had falsified production reports.[104]

Demonstrative evidence consists of tangible things, such as machines, tools, finished products, models, blueprints, and photographs, submitted to the arbitrator to enable him to more easily understand the testimony of the witnesses. For example, in a job evaluation dispute, the arbitrator was furnished photographs of employees operating their machines.[105] The rules which regulate the use of such evidence in court hearings are applicable in labor arbitration.[106] Accordingly:

> [T]he demonstrative evidence must first be authenticated by testimony of a witness who testifies to facts showing that the object has some connection with the case which makes it relevant.[107]

Thus, if a company desires to show that a particular product is constructed in a certain manner, it may introduce into evidence a blueprint of the item, and place the foreman in charge of producing this item on the stand for the purpose of identifying the blueprint.

INSPECTION BY THE ARBITRATOR

Another form of demonstrative evidence consists of visits to the plant by the arbitrator.[108] The value of such visits was explained by Arbitrator William Simkin:

> The eye is better than the ear in many aspects of disputes, or at least is a valuable supplement to oral or written evidence. A plant visit is a simple device by which the arbitrator can secure a better understanding of the background of a case. In some instances a plant visit either before or during the hearing will serve to avoid voluminous testimony. The award may be more realistic and therefore acceptable because the plant visit fills part of the gap in the arbitrator's knowledge.[109]

In certain relationships, such visits to obtain familiarity with the set-

---

[103]*Jonco Aircraft Corp.*, 22 LA 819, 823 (Merrill, 1954).

[104]*American Chain & Cable Co.*, 68-2 ARB ¶ 8374 (Fitzgerald, 1968).

[105]*Brown & Sharpe Mfg. Co.*, 21 LA 461, 463-70 (Waite, 1953). *See also Westinghouse Elec. Corp.*, 26 LA 836, 842 (Simkin, 1956).

[106]*See* note 24 *supra,* at §§ 1150-69.

[107]*See* note 95 *supra,* at § 179.

[108]*Brown & Sharpe Mfg. Co.*, 21 LA 461, 463 (Waite, 1953).

[109]Simkin, *Acceptability as a Factor in Arbitration Under an Existing Agreement*, LABOR ARBITRATION SERIES, G. Taylor, ed. (Philadelphia: Univ. of Pa. Press, 1952), p. 24.

ting where the problem which caused the grievance arose are common-place. When an arbitrator makes an inspection he or she is visually ex-posed to evidence which does not find its way into the record of the proceeding, and when the arbitrator is accompanied by a representa-tive of one of the parties or even both, the arbitrator is often given lengthy explanations during the inspection which are in the nature of arguments. The following report contrasts views concerning the pro-priety of such inspections:

> [T]here is a general, and often incorrect, assumption by the parties that an arbitrator is familiar with the industry in which the case arose and the par-ticular operations involved in particular. Insistence upon a general tour of the employer's operation by the arbitrator, accompanied by a representa-tive of each party, with special attention given to the immediate area in-volved in the grievance, might prove valuable. It is possible that such a tour would reduce costs by eliminating certain testimony which might otherwise be essential to the arbitrator's grasp of the situation.
>
> . . .
>
> [There is a question] of visual inspection of the premises or the subject of the dispute. In most instances where inspections are requested, arbitrators do invest the time and effort to comply with the requests of either party. However, in a recent arbitration, the arbitrator upon company objection declined such inspection. In that proceeding, an inspection would have avoided the necessity of any formal hearings and the production of wit-nesses, documents, etc. I believe that where inspection is requested, it should be mandatory on the part of the arbitrator and the parties to in-spect the premises in the presence of the parties unless the request is frivolous.[110]

While inspection of the premises may be considered important by one or the other party, a refusal to make an inspection is not grounds for setting aside an arbitrator's award. The discretion of the individual arbitrator in this regard is protected by the courts even if the particular arbitrator had previously agreed to make inspections.[111]

JUDICIAL NOTICE

Arbitrators as well as courts take judicial notice of facts widely known or capable of irrefutable proof, such as dates, addresses, and statutes, as a means of expediting the proceeding. The use of judicial notice in labor arbitration was described by the New York Tripartite Committee:

---

[110]ABA Section of Labor Relations Law, PART II, 1963 PROCEEDINGS, OFFICERS, COMMIT-TEES, ROSTER 1963-1964, August 12-14, 1963 (Chicago: ABA, 1964), pp. 190-91.

[111]*Colasante v. Bridgehampton Road Races Corp.*, 16 Misc.2d 923, 185 N.Y.S.2d 203 (Sup. Ct. 1959).

1. Arbitrators should take judicial notice of any facts or law which the courts of law would generally notice. (These would include: (a) specific facts so notorious as not to be the subject of reasonable dispute; and (b) specific facts and propositions of generalized knowledge which are capable of immediate and accurate demonstration by resort to easily accessible sources of indisputable accuracy.)

2. Considerations of fairness would seem to require that: (a) the parties notify the arbitrator and each other of facts concerning which they desire the arbitrator to take notice; or (b) in the absence of such notification, the arbitrator advise the parties of facts concerning which he will take notice.[112]

In arbitration proceedings, however, some arbitrators go beyond such limited use of judicial notice and include certain propositions, particularly industrial practices, as matters that can be assumed to be true. For example, in *Duluth Restaurants*[113] the arbitrator said that he took "judicial notice" of the fact that the parties to labor agreements are generally in agreement that reopener clauses temporarily remove the bar against strikes and the use of other economic pressure.

EXCLUSION OF IMMATERIAL AND IRRELEVANT EVIDENCE

Arbitrators rarely deny a party the opportunity to present evidence on the basis that it is immaterial or irrelevant except where the presentation of such evidence is an imposition on the time and patience of both the other party and the arbitrator and could interfere with maintenance of an orderly hearing. Exclusions of such evidence occur only infrequently, because many arbitrators espouse the view that the freedom of the parties to present a full story has a therapeutic effect. Furthermore, where the parties are free to tell a full story, they may present helpful facts and, often, make helpful admissions. Arbitrator Harry Shulman said:

The more serious danger is not that the arbitrator will hear too much irrelevancy, but rather that he will not hear enough of the relevant. Indeed, one advantage frequently reaped from wide latitude to the parties to talk about their case is that the apparent rambling frequently discloses very helpful information which would otherwise not be brought out.[114]

The handling of objections to the materiality and relevancy of evi-

---

[112]*See* note 31 *supra*, at p. 297.

[113]20 LA 658, 662-63 (Lockhart, 1953). *See generally* Emerzian, *Standards in Labor Arbitration Awards*, 6 LAB. L.J. 743, 759 (1955):

Arbitrators are usually selected because of their special knowledge in connection with the matter in dispute. They may take notice of general practice in the area of industrial relations, even though no evidence or testimony was offered at the hearing.

[114]*See* note 29 *supra*.

dence is an individual matter and varies with each arbitrator to such a degree that documentation as to what arbitrators actually do would be of little value here. However, it should be noted that frequently arbitrators are chosen on the basis of their ability to quickly ascertain material facts in a case in order to guide the parties so they will produce evidence relevant to those material facts and not drag out the proceedings with irrelevant testimony.

As labor arbitration has evolved, certain exclusionary rules grounded not on materiality or relevancy considerations, but on policy considerations, have evolved and gained general acceptance. In addition to the exclusionary rules discussed in this chapter, certain exclusionary rules have evolved based on due process considerations. These are discussed in the next chapter.

EXCLUSION OF, AND REMAND AND ADJOURNMENT FOR, UNDISCLOSED EVIDENCE

Arbitrators take a flexible approach to the introduction of new evidence at the hearing in support of alleged contract violations which have been properly raised in the prior grievance procedure. Arbitrators take very seriously their duty to protect the grievance resolution process.[115] When either party has withheld evidence which might have produced a settlement in the lower steps of the process if it had been presented, arbitrators have refused to accept the evidence.[116] Arbitrator W. Willard Wirtz summarized the views of many arbitrators in this regard as follows:

---

[115]The failure of the company to reveal evidence that a disputed overtime assignment had been given to a probationary employee rather than to the grievant because the grievant was not qualified to perform the work caused Arbitrator J. P. Horlacher to grant the grievant monetary compensation for the lost overtime assignment despite his admitted inability to do the work on the ground that this odd result was justified by the "necessity to protect the integrity of the grievance procedure. . . . Both the company and the union have a duty to fully disclose all the facts in the processing of a grievance. Absent a showing—and there is none in the present instance—that it was not reasonably possible to discharge this duty to disclose, the party who has not met its obligation must be prepared to accept the appropriate consequences." *Chamberlain Corp.*, AAA Case No. 120-11 (Horlacher, 1968). *See also* Fleming, *Some Problems of Due Process and Fair Procedure in Labor Arbitration*, 13 STAN. L. REV. 235 (1961).

[116]*See* related discussion in Chapter VII concerning the remanding of cases to the grievance procedure to force disclosure and consideration of new evidence, a form of informal discovery procedure essential to a properly operating grievance procedure. *See also Bethlehem Steel Co.*, 18 LA 367 (Feinberg, 1951), where testimony of union's principal witness was rejected as evidence because it was withheld during the grievance meetings. For comments on the admissibility of new evidence, *see* Fleming, THE LABOR ARBITRATION PROCESS (Ann Arbor: Univ. of Mich. Press, 1965), pp. 144-51; Elkouri and Elkouri, HOW ARBITRATION WORKS, note 1 *supra*, at pp. 258-61, 272-73; various *Area Reports*, PROBLEMS OF PROOF IN ARBITRATION, note 1 *supra*.

There are obvious interests, from the standpoint of the parties' continuing relationship, in keeping such matters out. It is important to the efficient functioning of the grievance procedure that the company and the union representatives do their job below. The Industrial Relations Manager insists properly that he must, as a matter of operating efficiency, be in a position to rely on what the union committee has found out and decided at least by the third step meeting, and the committee has a commensurate interest in being fully informed by that time of what the basis is for the company's position. The grievance procedure will work better, furthermore, if any practice of saving the best ammunition for the hearing before the arbitrator is discouraged.

Arbitrators have responded to these considerations, to the extent that the "general rule" is usually stated as being that new evidence or argument will not be admitted at the arbitration hearing unless some special reason is shown for its not having been brought out before.[117]

The view of Umpire Gabriel Alexander is shared by many arbitrators:

[S]ound collective bargaining requires frank and candid disclosure at the earliest opportunity of all facts known to each party. There will undoubtedly be times when facts are not discovered, and therefore not disclosed, until after the grievance has been partially processed, and problem enough is created by those instances. There is not a scintilla of justification for the withholding of information by either party from and after the time it is discovered.[118]

Evidence not previously exchanged and discussed between the parties during the grievance steps prior to arbitration is classified under one of two headings. Evidence that one side had in its possession throughout the grievance resolution process is commonly referred to as "surprise evidence" held back for tactical purposes or harassment. As noted above, some arbitrators discourage this practice because the grievance procedure conferences are designed to resolve matters, not to frustrate the process until resolution is to be presented as a "win" or "lose" process before an arbitrator. Evidence that one side did not have in its possession until the in-depth investigation was completed prior to presentation to the arbitrator is referred to as "new evidence."

Some arbitrators, rather than exclude new and/or surprise evidence and remand the case, will accept the evidence and then grant an adjournment to permit the surprised party an opportunity to evaluate it and collect rebuttal evidence for presentation.

Arbitrator Earl Miller discussed the problems caused by surprise evidence in *Cadillac Gage Co.*:

---

[117]Wirtz, note 51 *supra*, at pp. 14–15.
[118]General Motors Umpire Decision No. F-97 (Alexander, 1950). *See also* note 13 *supra*, at pp. 104–05.

With regard to the Union objection that at the arbitration hearing the Company had brought in secret and surprise witnesses, it should be noted that when [S——] was first called as a witness by the Union, several hours before the Company called [Z——] and [W——], the Union was aware that they would be called and was aware of the statements they would make. . . .

In any event, there is nothing in the Agreement or in the law governing arbitration requiring either party to reveal all its evidence to the other party before coming to an arbitration hearing. Material submitted by the Union indicates that in the steel industry agreements have been reached to reveal all evidence before arbitration, but no understanding existed between the parties in this case. Absent such an agreement between the parties, the course open to either party is to request a continuance of the hearing in order to rebut surprise evidence. The Arbitrator believes that if there is merit in such a request, it should be granted.[119]

When, however, new evidence merely grows out of a deeper investigation prior to the arbitration hearing, the policy of encouraging a free exchange of facts in the lower steps of the procedure is not applicable and the arbitrator will not return the case to the parties unless the newly discovered evidence creates a surprise prejudicial to the opposing party.[120]

On the other hand, it has been said that many pre-arbitral grievance meetings are informal, and as Arbitrator W. Willard Wirtz has observed, the "company, for its part, may very reasonably not have made the thorough investigation it will properly consider warranted if the union ultimately decides to take the case seriously enough to go to arbitration."[121] For these reasons, arbitrators will often receive relevant evidence which one party claims should not be received because it is new evidence that should have been presented at the lower steps of the procedure.[122]

---

[119]66-3 ARB ¶ 8969 at 6380 (Miller, 1966).

[120]*Borg-Warner Corp.*, AAA Case No. 14-21 (Edes, 1959); *Bethlehem Steel Co.*, 18 LA 366 (Feinberg, 1951).

[121]*See* note 51 *supra*, at p. 15. Wirtz indicated:
[U]nless some deliberate attempt to mislead the other party is disclosed, and particularly if the "new" evidence or argument appears substantially material, most arbitrators will be disinclined to rule the matter out of the proceedings.
See also Pittsburgh Steel Co., 11 STEEL ARB. 8131 (McDermott, 1963).

[122]In *Zinsco Electrical Products*, 64 LA 107 (Caraway, 1975), the arbitrator found that evidence withheld by the union was admissible at the hearing because (1) the contract did not penalize either party for withholding facts and did not authorize exclusion of such facts, and (2) the employer knew the contents of the testimony as it was the outgrowth of an earlier arbitration case, and therefore had ample time to prepare rebuttal of testimony. *See also Standard Oil Co.*, 68-1 ARB ¶ 8305 (Anrod, 1968); *United Parcel Service, Inc.*, 66-2 ARB ¶ 8703 (Dolson, 1966); *C. V. Hill Co.*, AAA Case No. 23-10 (Rock, 1960); *North American Aviation, Inc.*, 17 LA 183 (Komaroff, 1951); *Texas Co.*, 7 LA 735 (Carmichael, 1947); *Bethlehem Steel Co.*, 6 LA 617 (Wychoff, 1947); *American Steel & Wire Co.*, 5 LA 193 (Blumer, 1946).

Where the evidence is neither presented during the processing of the grievance nor at the hearing itself, but appears for the first time in the post-hearing brief, it may be stricken by the arbitrator.[123]

EXCLUSION OF EVIDENCE JUSTIFYING BREACH OF AGREEMENT

Arbitrators typically will not accept evidence to prove the assertion that unresolved grievances justified wildcat strike activity. Arbitrators have pointed out that if employees can present such evidence (on the grounds that the breach of the no-strike clause can be justified), the grievance-arbitration mechanism for handling grievances will fall into disuse and the no-strike pledge will be rendered a nullity. As noted by Arbitrator Saul Wallen:

> The lesson to be drawn from this unfortunate case is that grievances real or fancied, must be handled through the orderly procedures of the contract and not by "hitting the bricks." Not only management but Union members are entitled to rely on the contract negotiated for the parties' joint benefit as an instrument that promotes stability and order. This is its purpose. The grievance procedure may appear to take longer than it should but its end result is justice through reason. The wildcat strike can lead only to frustration.[124]

Similarly, Arbitrator Bothwell has said:

> While the Company bears a considerable responsibility, therefore, for the development of the situation which led to the walkout, this is not a defense for the actions of those who took part in the work stoppage in violation of the contract. Grievance and bargaining procedures exist for this very purpose. These are part of the orderly processes of collective bargaining. Even if the Company takes an action which clearly violates the contract the remedy lies in the grievance procedure, not in mob action, or gangland techniques. This is what the Union, and the employees collectively and individually, contracted to do.[125]

The reason an employee was insubordinate, or engaged in a prohibited refusal to work, is typically not considered by the arbitrator to be material or relevant to the question of whether the employer had just cause to terminate the employee.[126] Thus, Arbitrator Schmidt, re-

---

[123]*H. H. Meyer Packing Co.*, 66 LA 357 (Mulhall, 1965).

[124]*Borden Chemical Co.*, 34 LA 325, 328 (Wallen, 1959).

[125]*Vickers, Inc.*, 33 LA 594, 602 (Bothwell, 1959). *See also American Potash & Chemical Co.*, 67-2 ARB ¶ 8606 (Meyers, 1967); *McGraw Edison Co.*, 62-3 ARB ¶ 8775 (Howlett, 1962). The exception to this rule—again, a substantive issue—is where employee safety is being imperiled. *See, e.g., Wilcolator Co.*, 44 LA 847 (Altieri, 1964). As pointed out in *Wilcolator*, however, the union must prove that the safety problem was acute and that normal dispute-resolution channels were ineffective.

[126]*Cf. Mastro Plastics Corp. v. NLRB*, 350 U.S. 270, 37 LRRM 2587 (1956) where the Court

sponding to a claim that a grievant's verbal attack on his supervisor was prompted by personal problems, held that evidence of personal problems should not be accepted since such evidence was not material.[127] The refusal to permit evidence of personal problems is based in part on the concept that management must be allowed to evaluate employee conduct by objective standards rather than becoming concerned with subjective considerations.[128]

EXCLUSION OF EVIDENCE OF PRIOR UNRELATED DISCIPLINARY INCIDENTS

Questions concerning relevancy often arise when management submits in evidence prior disciplinary records. Such records are relevant when the employee is disciplined for careless work when the prior offense was similar because a pattern of careless work is being demonstrated, whereas, if the single instance were viewed alone, management's action might seem trivial and unreasonable. Prior discipline, however, is considered irrelevant by some arbitrators where the former offense is unrelated to the matter in issue,[129] but has, by other arbitrators, been admitted over the objection from the union.

Arbitrator Louis S. Belkin discussed various aspects of the admissibility of evidence of prior discipline in *Harshaw Chemical Co.*[130] An employee had been discharged for insubordination and use of profane language to a supervisor. The Union's objection to the admissibility of the employee's past work record, on the ground that the employer was bound by the language of the termination notice which stated the cause of discharge, was overruled:

> The question of the use of the employee's past work record by the company in making its determination to discharge him is one which has several ramifications. In the opinion of the undersigned it would be inconceivable that the company do anything else. We have here a matter of equity and

---

held that, under the National Labor Relations Act, a contract waiver of the right to strike was unenforceable where an employer's unfair labor practices generated the strike action.

[127] *Ross Gear & Tool Co.*, 35 LA 293 (Schmidt, 1960).

[128] *See, e.g., Ohio Packing Co.*, 30 LA 1021, 1024 (Stouffer, 1958); *Aspinook Corp.*, 15 LA 593, 595 (Shapiro, 1950); *Goodyear Clearwater Mills No. 2*, 11 LA 419 (McCoy, 1948).

[129] *Grief Bros. Cooperage Corp.*, 42 LA 555, 558-59 (Daugherty, 1964); *Givaudan Corporation*, 62-3 ARB ¶ 8934 (Pierce, 1962); *but see United States Steel Corp.*, 62-1 ARB ¶ 8144 (Rock, 1962); *Cities Service Oil Co.*, 17 LA 335 (Larkin, 1951). Typically, the relevancy of such disciplinary records is restricted to the question of penalty and not the issue of cause. *Borg-Warner Corp.*, 22 LA 589 (Larkin, 1954). *See Chicago Newspaper Publishers Ass'n*, 38 LA 491 (Sembower, 1962); *Bird & Son, Inc.*, 30 LA 948 (Sembower, 1958); *Capital Airlines, Inc.*, 27 LA 358 (Guthrie, 1956).

[130] 32 LA 23 (Belkin, 1958). *See also National Malleable & Steel Casting Co.*, 12 LA 262 (Pedrick, 1949); *Lake Shore Tire & Rubber Co.*, 3 LA 455 (Gorder, Chm., 1946); *Mueller Brass Co.*, 3 LA 285 (Wolf, 1946).

fairness. In order to be fair and equitable the totality of an employee's record, good or bad, must be weighed. This would certainly be applicable where the record is good. It must also apply where the opposite is true. It must also apply insofar as an arbitrator is concerned.

I could not decide this matter if I had no knowledge of any employee's work performance and work record. This is a matter of discharge or reinstatement and thus transcends the realm of the ordinary grievance. I shall hold therefore that despite the wording of the notice the company may show evidence of the employee's record.

This does not mean nor is it intended to mean that the union is barred from asserting its claim that the notice shows that the company's use of the employee's work record is an afterthought. The union may offer proof, if it can, that when the employee was discharged the foreman did not know of his past record and thus only the immediate incident was in his mind. It may offer proof, if it can, that this is the first time an employee's record of absenteeism or tardiness was used in a discharge for insubordination.

These, however, are matters of evidence going to motivations. They are matters of proof and issues for argument. They do not and cannot obviate the requirements and necessity for viewing the whole record of performance.[131]

Some arbitrators in nondiscipline cases hold that evidence of prior discipline has no relevancy and should not be admitted. For example, when the question in issue is the ability of the grievant to perform a job requiring greater skill which the employee seeks as a promotion, weighing the employee's discipline record as part of the consideration of relative ability might cause a denial of the promotion to become a second penalty for the same offense.[132] On the other hand, other arbitrators have held that evidence of prior disciplinary action is at least one measure of fitness for promotion and hence is admissible.[133]

Arbitrators usually consider the entire disciplinary record relevant to an evaluation of the reasonableness of the determination by management of the amount of discipline to be imposed, particularly when the grievant has been discharged.[134] One case illustrating this point is *Lone Star Cement Corp.*,[135] where Arbitrator Leonard Oppenheim

---

[131]32 LA at 24-25.

[132]*St. Mary's Kraft Corp.*, 40 LA 365 (Duncan, 1963); *Waller Bros. Stone Co.*, 34 LA 852 (Dworkin, 1960).

[133]*Penn Controls, Inc.*, 45 LA 129 (Larkin, 1965); *International Smelting & Refining Co.*, 65-1 ARB ¶ 8052 (Justin, 1964).

[134]*Foremost Dairies, Inc.*, 44 LA 148 (Tatum, 1965); *American Forest Products Corp.*, 44 LA 20 (Lucas, 1965). Concerning the admissibility and significance of grievant's record after the disciplinary action but prior to the arbitration, *see Robertshaw-Fulton Controls Co.*, 36 LA 4 (Hilpert, 1961); *Westinghouse Electric Corp.*, 26 LA 836 (Simkin, 1956); *Southern Bell Telephone & Telegraph Co.*, 25 LA 270 (McCoy, 1955).

[135]39 LA 652 (Oppenheim, 1962). *See also Columbus Auto Parts Co.*, 49 LA 686, 688 (Seinsheimer, 1967); *Ebinger Baking Co.*, 47 LA 948 (Singer, 1966); *Foremost Dairies, Inc.*, 44 LA

found discharge an appropriate penalty for falsifying work records when evaluated in the light of the employee's past record:

> While all arbitrators have not agreed upon this matter of past work records, some consideration is generally given to the past record of any disciplined or discharged employee. Thus a good past record may result in the mitigation of an offense and a bad past record may aggravate it. An employee's past record may often be an important factor in the determination of a proper penalty for an offense.[136]

The reasons why the employee's entire record is material in considering the question of the amount of discipline was explained by Arbitrator John Seybold:

> Generally speaking, if the employee is guiltless, then his past record, good or bad, is irrelevant. But, if he did commit the offense which gave rise to the disciplinary action or discharge, it is entirely right and proper to look at his entire employment record.... To fail to look at this record would require that we judge each episode in a vacuum and would deprive an employee of the opportunity of capitalizing upon a past record of good performance and behavior which should be "cash in the bank" to him. But if we are to accept the good, in mitigation of an offense, we must also be prepared to examine that which is not so favorable.[137]

The union in this case contended that to permit consideration of prior offenses would put it in the position of having to file an excessive number of grievances. The arbitrator replied:

> It is this arbitrator's opinion that it is in fact incumbent upon the union to form a judgment in each case as to whether there is some basis for the warning slip or action. If no basis at all exists, it should contest it. If the basis is arguable it should establish that, while it does not concur it will not contest.[138]

EXCLUSION OF EVIDENCE OF MISCONDUCT DISCOVERED AFTER THE DISCHARGE

Where a discharge occurs, its propriety must be determined from an analysis of the cause for the discharge, and evidence of misconduct discovered after the discharge cannot be presented to justify the dis-

148 (Tatum, 1965); *Wheland Products Div.*, 43 LA 634, 636 (Volz, 1964); *Coast Pro-Seal & Mfg. Co.*, AAA Case No. 48-14 (Komaroff, 1962); *A. E. Staley Mfg. Co.*, AAA Case No. 24-24 (Dolnick, 1960).

[136] 39 LA at 653.

[137] *Treadwell Corp.*, AAA Case No. 86-3 (Seybold, 1965).

[138] *Id. See also* "Presumptions That Facts Reported in Unchallenged Prior Disciplinary Warnings Are Correct" in this chapter, *supra*.

charge action. Arbitrator William Loucks in *Surety Co.*[139] so ruled
even though he recognized that the employer might well discharge the
employee again immediately upon his reinstatment, stating that the
arbitrator's obligation is "to judge the merits of the discharge as of the
date the discharge took place, and on the basis of the specific charge
then brought by the company against the employee."

The members of the Canadian Arbitration Board reported the same
principle in *St. Joseph's Hospital, Hamilton and Ontario Nurses Association:*

> We find that the evidence sought to be introduced by the employer of in-
> cidents involving the grievor discovered following the grievor's discharge
> but which occurred prior to the discharge and which relate to the basis on
> which the employer's action was taken is admissible. The general rule is
> that employers are held by arbitrators to substantiating their cases on the
> basis of the grounds on which they originally took the disciplinary action,
> and they are not allowed to submit evidence in support of reasons different
> than the stated basis for the disciplinary action. Nor is the employer en-
> titled to submit evidence to justify the disciplinary action on new and unre-
> lated matters to the action which precipitated the discharge.[140]

This principle was not applied, however, when the evidence being
submitted involved successful rehabilitation of an employee from
alcoholism after his discharge. Arbitrator Aaron Horvitz said:

> If ... the case must be viewed and should be decided solely as to the facts
> as they existed as of the date of discharge, I would have no choice but to
> sustain the employer's action. But the company's position, it seems to me,
> is not sound under the circumstances and is in conflict with the weight of
> estimable arbitrable authority.... [M]edical authority ... agrees that al-
> coholism is a disease in the same sense as many other afflictions which are
> beyond the capacity of the individual to control except through outside
> help and treatment. If the grievant had been discharged for excessive
> absenteeism and poor work caused, let us say, by an aggravated ulcer con-
> dition, which condition had been cured or relieved by surgery between the
> time of discharge and the time of arbitration, it is clear to me that I would

---

[139] *Surety Co.*, AAA Case No. 50–15 (Loucks, 1962). *See also*, *Ready-Mix Concrete Co.*, 73–1
ARB ¶ 8082 (Mulhall, 1973), where the arbitrator stated the cause of discharge may not be
justified by subsequent developments. In *Becks Transfer, Inc.*, 71-2 ARB ¶ 8490 (Witney,
1971), the arbitrator held that although no hard and fast rule governs exclusion of evidence of
misconduct discovered after discharge, evidence of dishonesty discovered by the company after
discharge should be excluded because it was not previously disclosed to the union, and because
in connection with a discharge for reasons involving moral turpitude, an employer must be im-
peccable in discharge procedure. On the other hand, in *Amoco Oil Co.*, 61 LA 10 (Cushman,
1973), the arbitrator did admit evidence of an attempt to commit suicide after discharge,
holding that it was part of the grievant's total conduct. *See also Westinghouse Electric Corp.*, 26
LA 836 (Simkin, 1956); *Southern Bell Telephone & Telegraph Co.*, 25 LA 270 (McCoy, 1955).

[140] Canadian Labor News, LVI ARB. REV. 1195 (Brown, Sanderson, and McIntyre), June 12,
1978.

have the right to consider the prognosis as of the time of the arbitration in reaching a decision.[141]

Horvitz explained that if the arbitrator could not consider evidence of post-discharge conduct in such a case, "it would render rehabilitation, in many cases, a meaningless effort." Horvitz held that since the grievant had since his discharge "been making a strenuous effort to effect a cure," and had "apparently ... been successful," he should be reinstated without back pay "predicated on his ability to maintain this favorable record."[142]

Arbitrator Kates in *Cadillac Plastics & Chemical Co.*,[143] for his part, summarized a rule different from that in *Surety Co.*, *supra*, with respect to exclusion of evidence discovered after discharge, as follows:

> As a general rule, occurrences subsequent to a discharge may not properly be taken into account in an arbitration involving the propriety of that discharge. An exception arises, however, when subsequent occurences are so closely related to the event or events leading to the discharge, as, in substantial effect, to constitute an extension or continuation or integral part thereof. Another exception arises when misconduct preceding the discharge has been proved, and when the question to be decided by the arbitrator is as to the justice of the particular penalty imposed, and when the subsequent misconduct, in light of the dischargee's previous history, indicates that even if the dischargee were reinstated he could not reasonably be expected to be of reasonable value as an employee of the particular employer.

Along the same lines, in *Link-Belt Co.*[144] Arbitrator Clarence Updegraff refused to reinstate the grievant as a remedy in a discharge dispute because the grievant had engaged in interim conduct that would also justify discharge. The grievant's intervening conduct was, therefore, considered by the arbitrator and taken into account in upholding the discharge. A similar decision is *Robertshaw-Fulton Controls Co.*,[145] where the arbitrator considered that post-incident conduct negated mitigating factors urged as a reason for reducing the penalty.

In another area, in connection with back pay determination, an arbitrator has the right to consider conduct following the date that the

---

[141]*Hooker Chemical Corp.*, AAA Case No. 81-2 (Horvitz, 1965). *See also Sharon Steel Corp.*, 71 LA 737 (Klein, 1978).

[142]*Id.*

[143]58 LA 812, 814 (Kates, 1972); *cf. New York Telephone Company*, 66 LA 1037 (Markowitz, 1976) (while employer cannot enlarge reasons for disciplinary action beyond those provided at the time of its determination, it may continue its investigation after discharge to buttress its allegations).

[144]17 LA 224 (Updegraff, 1951).

[145]36 LA 4 (Hilpert, 1961).

incident causing the discipline occurred if it is relevant to the fashioning of the remedy.

EXCLUSION OF EVIDENCE OF SETTLEMENT OFFERS

As in court-litigated proceedings, arbitrators typically regard evidence of prehearing settlement discussions as being inadmissible. Thus, Arbitrator Alpheus Marshall held:

> [T]here may be many considerations in getting a grievance settled by negotiation rather than bringing it to arbitration. But more important than this is the fact that no agreement was reached at the time, and it would be very arbitrary for an arbitrator to decide a case by considering the offers and counter-offers of the parties in an attempt to reach a settlement.[146]

Arbitrator Clair Duff explained the basis for this assumption as to relevancy:

> Settlement offers made in a spirit of compromise do not bind the offering party as admitting that his arguments are weak or incorrect. Harmonious labor relations are encouraged by such compromises and it is understandable if a party makes an offer to compromise to attain better, or continued good, labor relations even though, in fact, he does not agree with the offeree's view of the Grievance. If offers of compromise and settlement may be used to determine the merits of Grievances, no exploratory offers of settlement would be made, negotiations will become more cautious, disputes will be prolonged and the number of cases that will ultimately reach arbitration will be increased. In our consideration of the dispute we have completely ignored any offers of settlement mentioned in the Arbitration Hearing.[147]

In *Fulton-Sylphon Co.*[148] Arbitrator Greene said:

> [I]t is clear that any offer made by either party during the course of conciliation cannot prejudice that party's case when the case comes to arbitration. It is the very essence of conciliation that compromise proposals will go further than a party may consider itself bound to go, on a strict interpretation of its rights.

Another reason for excluding evidence of settlement offers was noted by Arbitrator Jerome Klein:

> [I]t should be mentioned that the arbitrator excluded evidence offered by the union relative to an offer of settlement which was rejected by [the grievant]. It is common knowledge that a company or union may make an offer of settlement to avoid the cost and difficulty of processing a matter to arbi-

---

[146]*Stylon Southern Corp.*, 24 LA 430, 436 (Marshall, 1955).
[147]*Koppers Co.*, 61-1 ARB ¶ 8041 at 3193–94 (Duff, 1960). *See also* note 26 *supra*.
[148]8 LA 993, 996 (Greene, Chm., 1947).

tration even though the party making the offer may believe that the probability of its action being sustained by the arbitrator is excellent.[149]

The Pittsburgh Tripartite Committee strongly echoes the view that evidence of offers in compromise must be excluded:

> Most arbitrators and advocates agree that the exclusion rule should be absolute in arbitration cases. Successful solution of grievances short of arbitration is vital to the process. Anything which imperils this philosophy must be avoided. Additionally, parties normally have neither inclination nor skill sufficient to cloak their settlement offers protectively. There are many reasons why offers of settlement are made, and they do not necessarily imply that the offering party admits it was wrong.[150]

One flaw inherent in the general trend in favor of admissibility is in the possibility it would lead to allowing inclusion of offers of compromise as evidence. Despite the fact that there is no legal obstacle to revealing earlier compromise offers, an analysis of arbitration cases indicates almost complete uniformity in refusing to admit such evidence. All four of the National Academy of Arbitrators' committees on problems of proof in arbitration agreed that evidence of attempts to compromise must be excluded.

Arbitrators seem so universally committed to encouraging dispute settlement in the grievance machinery that they will not merely exclude compromise offers when timely objection is made but, without a request from either side, will take the initiative and halt attempts to introduce such offers.

Sometimes a representative on one side or the other in an arbitration hearing will desire to introduce settled grievances as evidence. The grievances may actually involve different facts and may have been settled by the company for different reasons; hence, grievance settlements are highly unreliable evidence as to the meaning of a particular provision in a labor agreement. Arbitrator Brandschain explained:

> ... previously processed grievances are often presented as evidence ... with the claim that they are controlling or have a bearing on the instant case.
>
> The introduction of such material places the burden upon counsel, and of course the arbitrator, to analyze each of these cases to determine the relevance of the fact situations and the dispositions of these grievances to the instant case. This may complicate the presentation of the case by expanding it to retry a large number of earlier grievances to determine their fact situations and relevance to the case at hand.[151]

---

[149]*Cleaners Hanger Co.*, AAA Case No. 51-8 (Klein, 1962).

[150]*See* note 91 *supra*, at p. 253.

[151]*See* note 3 *supra*, at 37.

PRIVILEGED MEDICAL EVIDENCE

The New York Tripartite Committee stated that an arbitrator should exclude evidence concerning the grievant's communications with his or her physician in any situation where the same claim for exclusion could properly be made in court, with these qualifications:

(2) An employee asserting a claim or defense based on a physical condition may assert the privilege. However, the consequences of nondisclosure are for the arbitrator to determine.

(3) The disclosure of the fact of a communication with a physician is not privileged, even though the content of a communication may be privileged.

(4) If an employee's employment or continued employment is, by contract, controlling practice, or company rule, conditioned on his physical condition, he may not claim the privilege.

(5) If an employee's employment or continued employment is not explicitly or implicitly, by contract, controlling practice, or a company rule, conditioned on his physical condition, he may claim the privilege.[152]

The Tripartite Committee also recommended a procedure which would bring necessary medical information before the arbitrator without making it public knowledge:

In the event that an employee desires, for some special reason, to avoid the general disclosure of his communication with his physician, the arbitrator may, at his discretion, limit such disclosure to selected representatives of the parties.[153]

The Chicago Tripartite Committee made a special comment concerning the admissibility of doctor's statements:

(b) *Doctor's Statements.* It was agreed that doctor's certificates should be admissible in recognition of the difficulty of a busy doctor taking time to come to a hearing. There are occasions where the medical issue may become the central point of the case and here the arbitrator must be quite careful in determining whether the statement should be admitted. In general, the committee would admit the certificate of the doctor with the qualification that, absent the opportunity for cross examination, such evidence is entitled to less weight than medical evidence given in person by a doctor.[154]

MISCELLANEOUS PRIVILEGES TO HAVE EVIDENCE EXCLUDED

The New York Tripartite Committee said that witnesses need not testify concerning certain privileged communications with parties other than physicians:

---

[152]*See* note 31 *supra*, at pp. 298-99.
[153]*Id.* at 299.
[154]*See* note 13 *supra*, at pp. 107-08.

b. *Husband-Wife*—A confidential communication between spouses is privileged where a witness is, at the time of testifying, one of the spouses.

c. *Grand Jury*—A witness is privileged to refuse to disclose a communication made to a grand jury by a complainant or witness unless the findings of the grand jury have been made public by virtue of having been filed in court or otherwise.

d. *Classified Information*—A witness who, in the course of his duties, acquired official information, such as classified information not open or disclosed to the public relating to the internal affairs of a government, is privileged to refuse to disclose such information. However, if the arbitrator has government clearance for access to such classified information, the privilege may not be claimed.

e. *Union and Employer Communications*—Intra-union and intra-employer communications are not privileged.

f. *Grievance Discussions*—Evidence concerning grievance discussions, other than offers of settlement or compromise, is not privileged unless the parties have explicitly agreed otherwise. (The labor members would limit such evidence to admissions and statements of position unless the contract provides for some type of reporting of grievance discussions.)

g. *Witness-Attorney*—Communications between a union member testifying on behalf of a union and a union's attorney, or between a company employee and a company's attorney, are privileged.[155]

As a general rule, exclusionary rules of evidence applicable in criminal proceedings are not automatically or uniformly applied in arbitration proceedings. Arbitrator Lawrence Doppelt notes that an arbitrator is chosen for presumed expertise in matters pertaining to labor-management relations rather than as an expert on rules of evidence in criminal cases. Accordingly, he explains why the rationale supporting the application of exclusionary rules of evidence in the courts cannot be automatically carried over to the arbitral forum:

There is a serious question whether the exclusionary rules of evidence applicable in criminal proceedings should ... be uniformly applied to labor arbitration. Aside from the difficulties inherent in having a labor arbitrator decide issues involving such,... different policies are involved in the two proceedings. Criminal law pertains to vindicating the rights of society against individuals who have broken society's laws. In vindicating such rights, the individual must be protected against certain possible governmental abuses, and exclusionary rules of evidence help afford that protection. Labor arbitration, on the other hand, adjudicates the rights and responsibilities of employers, unions, and employees under a labor contract. It involves private disputes without any spectre of governmental excesses. It is doubtful whether all various evidentiary rules necessary to protect individuals against possible governmental abuses should automatically be applied in employer-employee relations matters which involve private disputes.

---

[155]*See* note 31 *supra*, at p. 299.

Indeed, the main issue in many arbitration matters is whether the employer acted in a reasonable manner. And this cannot be determined unless the arbitrator is aware of all the evidence based on which an employer acted. To exclude certain evidence which motivated an employer's actions, and then to ignore such evidence in labelling an employer's activities unreasonable, could well work an injustice on the employer.[156]

Arbitrator McGury, in *Aldens, Inc.*,[157] in contrast to the decision of Arbitrator Doppelt referred to above, found the rationale which supports application of the exclusionary rule in judicial proceedings supported its application in the arbitral forum in a situation where the consequence to the grievant—discharge—was comparable to a criminal conviction and where a search was made off company premises outside of working hours and did not involve management personnel. Thus, Arbitrator McGury looked to the seriousness of the consequences to the grievant and to the fact that the search was conducted off company property by nonmanagement personnel, as justifying an exception to the general rule against application of criminal procedure to the arbitration proceeding. Arbitrators have granted witnesses the right to not reply to questions concerning views regarding the meaning of contract language expressed by mediators during negotiations. The other party has the corollary right to have objections to such questions sustained. The rule can be expressed as follows:

> *Communications With Mediators.* Offers of evidence concerning a conversation with a mediator to prove the meaning of an agreement clause or the views of the other party to an agreement are rejected by arbitrators. Arbitrators agree that the introduction of evidence obtained in this matter affects the confidentiality and privilege that should surround such conversations with mediators.[158]

Objections are often raised that evidence is irrelevant, immaterial, and incompetent. The majority of commentators, however, limit their discussions of these questions to the issues of relevancy and materiality, feeling that questions of competency have no place in the arbitration setting.

The Pittsburgh Tripartite Committee defined evidence as relevant "if it reasonably tends to prove or disprove the fact at issue or facts closely related to the point at issue." "Materiality" refers to issues of substantial importance or influence. Objections to evidence on the basis of immateriality are usually attempts to exclude matters too remote to be worth considering.[159]

---

[156]*Commodity Warehousing Corp.*, 60 LA 1260, 1262-63 (Doppelt, 1973); *see also Aldens, Inc.*, 61 LA 663 (Dolnick, 1973); *but see Aldens, Inc.*, 72-1 ARB ¶ 8275 (McGury, 1972).

[157]*See* note 156 *supra.*

[158]*See Management Services, Inc.*, 58 LA 552 (Nicholas, 1972); *Day Care Council*, 55 LA 1130 (Glushein, 1970); *Air Reduction Chemical & Carbide Co.*, 41 LA 24 (Warns, 1963).

[159]*See* note 91 *supra*, at pp. 250-51.

Generally, arbitrators react negatively to claims of irrelevancy or immateriality. As mentioned at the beginning of this chapter, arbitrators usually believe it is better to hear too much than too little; they believe in the cathartic value of arbitration, and they also recognize that failure to admit relevant or material evidence is a ground for vacating an arbitration award.

CHAPTER XIII

Due Process Considerations

Most arbitrators endeavor to give meaning and application to "due process" considerations in labor arbitration. Yet, while recognizing that "due process" arguments are not to be regarded lightly,[1] many find that the strictures which result from too free borrowing of "due process" principles from criminal law are out of place in the "shirt sleeves business of arbitration."[2] Abram Stockman, for example, has identified some of the problems of "loose borrowing":

"I think it would be generally agreed that in an arbitration proceeding something less than the ultimate in the protection afforded those accused of crime is apt to be the measure of the protection afforded employees for acts of misconduct committed during the employment relationship. For there is undeniably a fundamental distinction between a criminal prosecution and an arbitration proceeding. Because our society has seen fit to require that every possible protection be extended to those accused of crime in order to insure that no one will be deprived of his liberty unjustly, it does not follow that an employee is entitled to protection in the same degree for the purpose of determining whether he is to be subjected to job discipline or even deprived of his job. Notwithstanding frequent resort to the euphe-

---

[1]*Congoleum-Nairn, Inc.*, 63-2 ARB ¶ 8843 (Short, 1963). On searches without warnings set forth in *Miranda v. Arizona*, 384 U.S. 436 (1966), *see Anchor Hocking Corp.*, 66 LA 480 (Emerson, 1976). On searches without warrant by either plant or regular police, *see International Nickel Co.*, 68-1 ARB ¶ 8229 (Shister, 1967); *Hennis Freight Lines*, 44 LA 711 (McGury, 1964); *Lockheed Aircraft Corp.*, 27 LA 709 (Maggs, 1956); *Campbell Soup Co.*, 2 LA 27 (Lohman, 1946). On self-incrimination, *see Weirton Steel Co.*, 68-1 ARB ¶ 8249 (Kates, 1968); *United Parcel Service, Inc.*, 45 LA 1050 (Turkus, 1965); *Simoniz Co.*, 44 LA 658 (McGury, 1964); *Jones & Laughlin Steel Corp.*, 29 LA 778 (Cahn, 1957); *Republic Steel Corp.*, 6 STEEL ARB. 3945 (Platt, 1957); *Southern Bell Tel. & Tel. Co.*, 26 LA 742 (McCoy, 1956).

[2]Jones, *Evidentiary Concept in Labor Arbitration: Some Modern Variations on Ancient Legal Themes*, 13 U.C.L.A. L. REV. 1241, 1286–90 (1966); Fleming, THE LABOR ARBITRATION PROCESS (Ann Arbor: Univ. of Mich. Press, 1965), pp. 181–86; Fleming, *Some Problems of Due Process and Fair Procedure in Labor Arbitration*, 13 STAN. L. REV. 235 (1961); Wirtz, *Due Process of Arbitration*, and Stockman, related *Discussion*, THE ARBITRATOR AND THE PARTIES, Proceedings of the Eleventh Annual Meeting, National Academy of Arbitrators, J. McKelvey, ed. (Washington: BNA Books, 1958), pp. 1–36, 39–40; *Problems of Proof in the Arbitration Process: Report of the Pittsburgh Tripartite Committee*, PROBLEMS OF PROOF IN ARBITRATION, Proceedings of the Nineteenth Annual Meeting, National Academy of Arbitrators, D. Jones, ed., (Washington: BNA Books, 1967), pp. 273–79.

mism, "economic capital punishment," I submit that incarceration is punishment of greater severity than loss of work and its concomitant effects.[3]

It has been noted that in labor arbitration there are group rights as well as individual rights that need protection. Most of the rights which are basic to an employee's claim in arbitration are acquired for the group as well as for the individual via the collective bargaining process. The *group* has rights which must be protected by the union and the *individual* employee has separate rights which must be protected by the union but which may be found to be in conflict with the interests of the *group* and the employer, and the employee may have separate rights to be protected by the company representatives. Hence, "due process" in labor arbitration involves a balancing of the interests of the three—individual, employment group and employer—and hence the balancing is different from the balancing of two parties' interests—*i.e.*, the individual and the state—in criminal law.

The differences between criminal proceedings (two parties) and labor arbitration proceedings (three parties) was well noted in one commentary:

That the analogy between judicial and arbitral decisions breaks down at times should be neither surprising nor troubling. Due process of law in the judicial system involves a balancing of interests.... The defendant accused of the commission of a crime struggles against his accuser, the state, with its overwhelming powers and sanctions threatening his life and liberty. His survival or defeat primarily affects only him. He may well demand that society subordinate some of its powers and rights to the protection of those of his rights that "history, reason, [and] the past course of decisions" have recognized as immutable and fundamental. The subject matter and the necessities of the situation determine the balance of interest in his favor.

The grievant on the other hand is part of an industrial community. The group to which he belongs is not merely a vessel containing the sum total of the individual interests of its members. It has independent rights and interests of its own which may be deeply affected by his actions. Moreover, a large part of the "rights" claimed by the grievant owe their existence to the group. Nevertheless, he can demand that they be given recognition and protection. But the subject matter and the necessities of the situation strike a different balance, because they have to take into account those independent rights and interests of the group. Due process of law here has a different content than due process of law in the courts. Both require fairness, but "fairness is a relative, not an absolute concept," and in the overall scheme of the tripartite relationship greater subordination does not seem to violate that principle.[4]

---

[3]Stockman, note 2 *supra.*
[4]*Industrial Due Process and Just Cause for Discipline: A Comparative Analysis of the Arbitral and Judicial Decisional Processes,* 6 U.C.L.A. L. Rev. 603 (1958-59).

The difference in the relationship of an accused versus the state and the relationship of a grievant to the total work group and to his or her employer must be emphasized to discourage arbitrators from blindly adopting criminal law "due process" rules in arbitration. Thus, in discussing the Fourth Amendment (search and seizure), the Supreme Court in *Burdeau v. McDowell*[5] stated that its "origin and history clearly show that it was intended to be a restraint upon the activities of sovereign authority, and was not intended to be a limitation upon other than governmental agencies."[6] For these reasons, some arbitrators, but only some, have clearly said that constitutional rights can only be asserted against the government, not against an employer.[7]

Requiring an employer to follow the strict rules imposed on government prosecutors can produce a strained relationship between the employer, the employees, and the union. The employer's representatives should not assume that they are, in connection with grievances, prosecutors. Nor should the union representatives assume that they are criminal law defenders. There is a third large group of employees which is most significant to both—the employment group.

This chapter reports how arbitrators have reacted to assertions that "due process" rules associated with criminal law should be absorbed into labor arbitration.

ADMISSIONS AND CONFESSIONS

Under traditional views expressed in arbitral law, a confession or admission of wrongdoing by an employee to the employer is usually sufficient without anything more in the way of proof to establish the guilt of the employee.[8] Some union representatives have argued that an employee's admission can be invalidated if the employed can show he or she had been given reason to fear discipline by the action of company investigators or by the absence of union representation during the interrogation at which the admission occurred. Such a contention was made by Arbitrator Samuel Kates in *Weirton Steel Co.*[9] Following

---

[5]256 U.S. 465, 475 (1921).

[6]*Id.* at 475.

[7]*See, e.g., Smith's Food King,* 66 LA 619 (Ross, 1976); *Aldens, Inc.,* 61 LA 663 (Dolnick, 1973). *But see Anchor Hocking Corp.,* 66 LA 480 (Emerson, 1976); *Aldens, Inc.,* 58 LA 1213 (McGury, 1972); *Thrifty Drug Stores Co.,* 50 LA 1253 (Jones, 1968). In *Thrifty Drug Stores* the arbitrator was particularly impressed with the Supreme Court's sweeping dictum in *Miranda v. Arizona,* 384 U.S. 436, 467 (1966), wherein the Court said:

Today, then, there can be no doubt that the Fifth Amendment privilege is available outside of Criminal Court proceedings and serves to protect persons in all settings in which their freedom of action is curtailed in any significant way from being compelled to incriminate themselves.

[8]*Phelps Dodge Copper Products Corp.,* 66-1 ARB ¶ 8031 (Dworkin, 1965); *Western Electric Co.* (Kelliher, 1965) (unreported).

[9]68-1 ARB ¶ 8249 (Kates, 1968).

on an anonymous tip, company investigators had found stolen property at the grievant's home.[10] The company interrogated the grievant without a union representative present and told him that he could be arrested when, in fact, the statute of limitation for a criminal prosecution had run. When confronted with the evidence obtained through the search, the grievant admitted the theft. He later recanted his confession at the hearing, and the union representatives argued that the confession should not be admitted in the hearing on the propriety of the discharge. Arbitrator Samuel Kates accepted the evidence of the confession and discussed the union's contentions concerning it in his award:

> I do not subscribe to the doctrine that purity must always envelop those engaged in attempting to ascertain the truth, or that subterfuge or pretense is always improper in a truth-seeking endeavor. Each such case must, I believe, be judged upon its own facts.[11]

Concerning the union's contention that the threat of arrest made the admissions in the confession unreliable, Arbitrator Kates said:

> The evidence does not warrant any holding that the grievant's fear of possible arrest ... affected the truth of his express oral admission.[12]

On the other hand, circumstances can exist where testimony concerning an alleged confession is viewed by the arbitrator with greater caution. Arbitrator Ray in *Gardner-Denver Co.*[13] concluded that the grievant's discharge was the result of a supervisor's "search for some evidence on which to base a discharge," and therefore that the supervisor's testimony that the grievant confessed to him the wrongdoing was found to be wholly incredible. This case suggests that when a supervisor (who has authority to discipline the employee) testifies that an employee has "confessed" to the alleged act of misconduct and the employee denies it at the hearing, the resulting issue is really one of credibility rather than due process.

Criminal law due process rules were applied by Arbitrator Edgar A. Jones, Jr. in *Thrifty Drug Stores Co.*,[14] which involved theft of company merchandise. An employee confessed to his own wrongdoing and informed on two other employees. He then acted as a witness at the arbitration hearing and again identified the two fellow participants in the theft and was subjected to cross-examination. Arbitrator Jones became concerned about the setting in which the informer was

---

[10]*Cf. Lankford v. Gelston,* 364 F.2d 197 (4th Cir. 1967), in which it was ruled that an anonymous tip was not probable cause upon which to permit a search.

[11]68-1 ARB ¶ 8249 at 3861–62 (Kates, 1968).

[12]*Id.* at 3862.

[13]51 LA 1023 (Ray, 1969).

[14]50 LA 1253 (Jones, 1968).

originally interrogated—a small security cubicle without the benefit of union representation and under the threat of discipline. In this connection, he said:

> Therefore when interrogations occur in which discipline is a prospect and without the presence of a union representative, the statements then elicited must be regarded with skepticism and given weight only when other evidence corroborates their substance.[15]

The *Thrifty Drug* case also involves credibility issues, rather than problems of due process. The company was not attempting to prove the guilt of the grievants by written hearsay statements of an informer (called a confession), for the informer was called to testify at the arbitration hearing and was subject to cross-examination. The company did not rely on an allegedly coercive confession of an accused and, therefore, reliance on two Supreme Court cases—*Miranda v. State of Arizona*[16] and *Garrity v. State of New Jersey*[17]—which declare that in criminal cases involuntary or coerced confessions may not be used to establish the guilt of the confessor, was wholly misplaced. Furthermore, Arbitrator Jones misapplied the *Miranda* rule because he applied the right against self-incrimination to the informer, not to the accused.[18]

In *Armco Steel Corp.*[19] Arbitrator Sidney Cahn overturned the discharge of an employee for theft on the basis of the unreliable "confessions" given by his two alleged accomplices. He explained that the testimony of the informers was fraught with inconsistencies. If lack of credibility had been the only basis for the arbitrator's findings and his findings caused the reinstatement, the decision could not be challenged. The arbitrator, however, also relied on stringent criminal law rules to further justify his findings:

> Even were I to apply the criminal law of evidence in effect in the State of Texas, I would be compelled to find X innocent, for under the law of that State, in felony cases, the existence of a conspiracy concerning one defendant cannot be proved by the acts or declarations of another. In other words, a conviction cannot be had on the testimony of an accomplice alone, but there must be other evidence testimony to connect the accused

---

[15]*Id.* at 1262. (*See also S-J Iron & Steel Corp.*, 56 LA 430 (Roberts, 1971), where the arbitrator sustained an objection to admission of the grievant's alleged confession and alleged statement that he wished to withdraw a grievance he filed, *inter alia*, because the company threatened to lay off four employees if he did not.)

[16]384 U.S. 436 (1966).

[17]385 U.S. 493 (1967).

[18]*See Hoffa v. United States*, 385 U.S. 293 (1966) where the Supreme Court held that testimony by a witness of the accused's conversation with that witness did not violate the accused's Fifth Amendment right against self-incrimination.

[19]48 LA 132 (Cahn, 1967).

with the crime so that his conviction will not rest entirely upon the testimony of the accomplice.[20]

In contrast to *Thrifty Drug* and *Armco Steel* is the decision in *Eastern Air Lines*.[21] An airline pilot was discharged for drinking within 24 hours of his next flight. The co-pilot, who had also been drinking (and who was discovered by the security officer in a stewardess' hotel room late at night), gave a written confession "under the pressure of the circumstances"[22] which implicated the pilot. Arbitrator Jacob Seidenberg upheld the discharge of the pilot, primarily because he had been previously warned about drinking and because he admitted at the hearing that he had been drinking on the evening in question. To reach this result, the arbitrator reviewed "the procedural rights of due process of the Grievant." He ruled that (1) the interrogation of the grievant without union representation was not by itself undue pressure violative of due process, and (2) the co-pilot's statement, although given in a "compromising situation did not constitute the sort of duress and coercion which might under certain circumstances invalidate the proceedings."[23]

Thrifty Drug and *Armco Steel* should be contrasted in approach with the award by Arbitrator Rohman in *Braniff Airways, Inc.*[24] There, two airline mechanics were discharged for stealing liquor from an airplane; a mechanic gave a written confession implicating the grievant and, except for some circumstantial evidence, there was no other first-hand evidence against the grievant, who denied participation. The confession was admitted in evidence, but the informer was not called to testify and this caused Arbitrator Rohman to become troubled by the "due proces" considerations (no opportunity to cross-examine the confessor) and he reduced the penalty, saying:

> The question which disturbs me, however, is whether on the basis of this type of proof—a confession, without confrontation, by an alleged accomplice and some circumstantial evidence—discharge was the proper punishment? Of course, seldom is one who participates in a theft ever caught red-handed. Here, the evidence presented certainly does not come close to meeting the standard described as being beyond a reasonable doubt. Furthermore, it appears to be a travesty on justice to permit the one who instigated, planned and executed the theft to be completely exonerated because of a technicality; then draw the full measure of blood

---

[20]*Id.* at 135.
[21]46 LA 549 (Seidenberg, 1965).
[22]*Id.*
[23]*Id.* at 554-55. In *Sterling Optical Co., Inc.*, AAA Case No. 162-10 (McKelvey, 1972) the arbitrator found a confession was obtained by "coercion" bordering on "entrapment," and the discipline was modified.
[24]44 LA 417, 421 (Rohman, 1965).

from another individual who was duped into the crime and compel him to bear the entire brunt. Parenthetically, Y had been employed by the Company for approximately nine years without having been previously reprimanded or disciplined.

Although I am completely in accord with the right of management to discourage pilferage, I, nevertheless, believe that in this instance, discharge under all the circumstances prevalent herein, is too harsh a punishment. I am, therefore, sustaining the grievance to the extent that the discharge is reversed, and, instead, Y____shall receive a disciplinary suspension, without pay, through February 7, 1965.

SELF-INCRIMINATION VERSUS DUTY TO COOPERATE

An employee has a duty to cooperate with an employer's efforts to make investigations. Arbitrator Jones in *Thrifty Drug*[25] said:

> It is manifest that an employee has an obligation arising from operational necessity, to make reasonable disclosures to his employer of facts which are relevant to the employer's operations. If an employer is honestly seeking facts rather than really just probing for a confession, he is entitled to the cooperation of his employee in achieving reasonable disclosure of his activities or observations while on the job, and this is an incident of the employment relationship. For it unreasonably to be withheld by an employee would make him vulnerable to discipline....

In *Kammerer v. Board of Fire and Police Commissioners of the Village of Lombard,*[26] the Illinois Supreme Court held that if a public employee refuses to answer questions concerning a matter about which his employer is entitled to inquire, he may be discharged for insubordination. Although the decision involved a public employer, it is grounded on the view that an employer has the right to require an employee to answer questions relating to the employee's own fitness for further employment and that a failure to answer is a violation of the duty of the employee to cooperate with the employer in the investigation.

In at least one case an employer has granted employees "immunity" from discipline to avoid the self-incrimination issue, in an attempt to gain information on the activities of another employee. This practice was upheld in court. In *Cook Paint and Varnish Co.*[27] the NLRB was faced with a situation where the company's labor counsel, in preparation for an arbitration hearing on the discharge of an employee,

---

[25] 50 LA 1253, 1262-63 (Jones, 1968). *See Simoniz Co.,* 44 LA 658 (McGury, 1964) and *Allen Industries, Inc.,* 26 LA 363 (Klamon, 1956), both upholding discharge for refusal to cooperate. *Contra,* an arbitrator reinstated an employee who refused to say whether he was working for a competitor because the employer was then unable to prove the rule violation. *Exact Weight Scale Co.,* 50 LA 8 (McCoy, 1967).

[26] 44 Ill.2d 5000, 256 N.E.2d 12 (1970).

[27] 246 NLRB 646, 102 LRRM 1680 (1979).

sought to interview two other employees, one of whom was a union steward, concerning an incident which led to the discharge. The employees were told that they were not subjects of any investigation and would not be disciplined for truthful answers, but that they would be subject to discipline if they refused to answer the attorney's questions. The questions were "purely factual in nature" and neither employee was asked whether he would testify or had been asked to testify at the upcoming arbitration. Both employees answered the questions under protest.

The NLRB found that the company had engaged in improper coercion by threatening the employees with discipline if they refused to cooperate by providing information to the company and that statements by the company's labor counsel were a *per se* violation of Section 8(a)(1) of the NLRA. On review, Judge Edwards of the D.C. Circuit in *Cook Paint and Varnish Co. v. NLRB*[28] observed that pre-arbitration interviews are a matter of "routine practice" in industrial relations. As such, the Board's rule "unnecessarily and impermissibly interferes with the manner in which parties to a collective bargaining relationship structure the arbitration process." The court held that an interview in which the attorney obtains factual information from witnesses, observes their demeanor, and in general evaluates the merits of a dispute, is not *per se* coercive. Therefore, an employee does not have an automatic right to refuse to respond to questions concerning a matter which has been scheduled for arbitration.

Arbitrators have upheld discharges when the grievant invoked the Fifth Amendment in the case of editorial writers in newspapers,[29] where the employees were engaged in defense work,[30] and where there was unrest in the plant.[31]

That no man can be compelled to be a witness against himself is a fundamental principle in *criminal* law, and despite the language of the Fifth Amendment which purports to limit the privilege against self-incrimination to criminal cases, it has sometimes been extended to judicial or official hearings, investigations, or inquiries where persons are called upon formally to give testimony.[32] Self-incrimination has little application in labor arbitration. Some arbitrators have used criminal standards when the discipline offense also constitutes a crime. In such situations, the grievant has been discharged on evidence considered by the employer to be sufficient and the grievant must rebut the employer's "just cause" evidence to obtain reinstatement, and remaining mute

---

[28] 648 F.2d 712, 106 LRRM 3016 (D.C. Cir. 1981).
[29] *Los Angeles Daily News,* 19 LA 39 (Dodd, 1952).
[30] *Bethlehem Steel Co.,* 24 LA 852 (Desmond, 1955).
[31] *Burt Mfg. Co.,* 21 LA 532 (Morrison, 1953).
[32] McCormick, EVIDENCE ¶ 123 (1954).

will not be helpful to the dischargee.[33] Arbitrator Douglas B. Maggs in *Lockheed Aircraft Corp.*[34] has said that the privilege against self-incrimination is not applicable to grievance arbitrations:

> [T]he constitutional privilege against self-incrimination is available only against the Government. If, in a hotel, arsenic has been discovered in food served in the dining room and also in the bedroom shared by the chef and one of the hotel's private detectives, and the latter refuses to tell management something he admittedly knows about how the arsenic got into the room, surely management would have just cause for discharging him.

Arbitrator John P. McGury in *Simoniz Co.*[35] in a case where the employee was terminated for refusal to cooperate in the investigation of a theft because he "took the Fifth," pointed out:

> The grievant, out of confusion, or overzealous protective measure against criminal prosecution, or reluctance to involve co-workers, took a position which went beyond the need of his own security and unreasonably infringed upon the right of the Company to make a thorough investigation of the incident, to the substantial disadvantage of the Company.
>
> The grievant had a right to make himself 200 percent secure against criminal involvement, but he cannot simultaneously protect his rights to future employment when his position frustrated the legitimate right and interest of the Company.

Another kind of asserted "industrial surveillance" is related to the observations made by members of supervisory staff of production and maintenance operations observed in their normal course of work. It is only by personally circulating about his area of responsibility that a supervisor can effectively witness what is going on. Surveillance in this context is more frequently an allegation that the supervisor has taken wrongful action on the basis of his or her observations rather than a claim that the supervisor has no right to see what is going on.

Arbitrator Nathan Cayton in *ARO, Inc.*[36] said this in reply to the contention that a foreman was excessively supervising an employee:

> The basic position stated in the Union's brief is that the Company discriminated against [the grievant] by giving orders through [the foreman] to

---

[33]The New York Tripartite Committee stated:

A witness may invoke his constitutional privilege to refuse to disclose any matter or information which would tend to incriminate him. The term "incriminate," in this context, refers to a statutory crime.

Problems of Proof in the Arbitration Process: Report of the New York Tripartite Committee, PROBLEMS OF PROOF IN ARBITRATION, Proceedings of the Nineteenth Annual Meeting, National Academy of Arbitrators, D. Jones, ed. (Washington: BNA Books, 1967), p. 300.

[34]27 LA 709, 712–13 (Maggs, 1956).

[35]44 LA 659, 663–64 (McGury, 1964). *See also C & P Telephone Co.*, 51 LA 457 (Seibel, 1968).

[36]70-1 ARB ¶ 8278 at 3921 (Cayton, 1969).

observe [the grievant] and make notes on him, while no such orders had been given with reference to six or seven other men under the same supervisor. The short answer to this is that the other men had not given reason for criticism or complaint.

Arbitrator George H. Hildebrand in *Los Angeles Transit Lines*[37] discussed the admissibility as evidence of reports of a spotter in the case of a bus driver who was discharged for allegedly violating company rules governing collection of fares. He said that a spotter's report should meet the requirements of the California Uniform Business Records as Evidence Act and added that beyond this:

(1) It must be shown that the reports were prepared before the decision to discharge had been taken and the issue joined between the parties.... (2) There must be no tangible basis for believing that the company is biased against the employee and has set out to get him.

In *Colgate-Palmolive Co.*,[38] where the grievants were discharged for refusing to submit to a fingerprint test to verify or negate suspicion of theft, the union contended that a request to give fingerprints or be discharged was the same as a request to submit to a lie detector test.[39] Arbitrator Koren upheld the discharge, ruling that if there was a reasonable basis to suspect the grievants, management could require them to cooperate in investigative tests. In so ruling, the arbitrator rejected the view that the privilege against self-incrimination voided the grievants' obligation to cooperate with their employer.

A different consideration was involved in *Scott Paper Co.*,[40] where Arbitrator Williams ruled that "in the absence of a clear plant rule requiring it, an employee may not be required to give evidence against himself, or to submit to a search of his person, or to disclose the con-

[37]25 LA 740, 745 (Hildebrand, 1955).
[38]68-1 ARB ¶ 8357 (Koven, 1968).
[39]*See* Chapter XV, "The 'Duty' to Cooperate With Polygraph Testing Versus the Right to Refuse."
[40]69-2 ARB ¶ 8470 (Williams, 1969). *See also Congoleum-Nairn*, AAA Case No. 54-3 (Short, 1963); *Dow Chemical Co.*, 65 LA 1295, 1298 (Lipson, 1976) ("[W]hile constitutional limitations on unlawful searches are normally construed as restraints on government authorities, and are not usually applicable to contractual disputes between private parties, nevertheless *the rights to privacy and personal dignity* are so fundamentally a part of the American tradition that they should at least be given consideration by a labor arbitrator in passing on search problems in plants" [Emphasis added.]); *contra, International Nickel Co.*, 68-1 ARB ¶ 8229 (Shister, 1967) (employer did not violate personal rights of employee by searching part of company's property which had been designated to the employee for personal use); *Champion Spark Plug Co.*, 68 LA 702 (Casselman, 1977) (order to grievant to unbutton sweater with steward present proper where probable cause that serious breach of plant rule [use of alcohol] existed; inappropriate to attempt to establish exact parallel between rights of citizens on street and employees in plant); *Smith's Food King*, 66 LA 619 (Ross, 1976) (arbitrator believes that the constitutional protection against unreasonable searches and seizures does not apply against a private company to prevent their searching an employee at his place of employment under suspicious circumstances).

tents of his pockets." There it was held that a request by the grievant's supervisor that the grievant empty his pockets to verify or refute reports that he was carrying a gun was an improper request by the supervisor and its refusal was not insubordination. The ruling by the arbitrator was made in spite of a plant rule that employees could be searched as they entered and left the plant, if theft was suspected.

The *Scott Paper Co.* decision raises several questions. Should an employer be free to protect the members of its employment community from employees with guns or not? If an employer has information from a reliable source that an employee is carrying a gun, is it not the employee's duty to cooperate with the employer when asked to disclose the contents of his pockets or suffer discharge?

The opposite approach to the question was well explained by Arbitrator Bernard Meltzer in *Maremont Corp.*[41] A grievant, accused of being drunk, refused to take a breath analyzer test. The union representatives asserted that the privilege against self-incrimination means that no adverse inference can result from the refusal to take the test.

Arbitrator Markovitz in *New York Telephone Co.*[42] sustained the discharge of a grievant who drove a company truck into a utility pole. While he was unconscious, a blood test was administered at the hospital. The test indicated that the employee was intoxicated. Arbitrator Erwin Ellman, on the other hand, in *Capital Area Transit*[43] reinstated a garage mechanic discharged when he refused to have the same blood test as that administered in *New York Telephone Co.*[44] and proof of intoxication could not be established in the employer's *prima facie* case because of the non-consent of the grievant.

In *Southern Bell Telephone & Telegraph Co.*[45] Arbitrator McCoy said:

> I think that the inferences justifiable from such refusal cannot be extended to an inference of guilt of the very act with which the man is charged. . . . In other words, I think that the inferences to be drawn from a refusal to testify are limited to evidentiary facts, and do not extend to the ultimate conclusion of guilt or innocence which must be drawn from evidentiary facts. Inferences may be resorted to in aid of evidentiary facts; they cannot supply facts of which there is no evidence. Findings of fact must be based on credible evidence. The failure to deny or refute incredible evidence does not change the character of that evidence from incredible to credible.

---

[41]*Maremont Corp.*, (Meltzer, 1969) (unreported). This case is discussed at greater length under "Cases Supporting the Duty to Cooperate by Being Tested" in Chapter XV.

[42]76-2 ARB ¶ 8420 (Markovitz, 1976).

[43]741 GERR 13 (Ellmann, 1978).

[44]*See* discussion of the "Rights of Privacy" and how they are waived by consent, *infra*.

[45]25 LA 270, 273 (McCoy, 1955).

In *Brown Shoe Co.,*[46] Arbitrator Joseph M. Klamon commented thus on the failure of the grievants to come forward, appear, and testify:

> [I]t is the duty of the men involved to come forward and give the true explanation of what they were doing when they were where they had no right to be. The fact that they did not do so at the time of discharge and did not appear at the hearing coupled with the auditory evidence and the previous pattern of behavior abundantly sustains the Company's position and contention.

On the other hand, some arbitrators have said that no inferences can be drawn from such a refusal. Arbitrator John Sembower in *American International Aluminum Corp.*[47] said:

> The Arbitrator disregards any adverse inferences which might be drawn from the Grievant's not being present at the hearing. While this is in no sense a criminal matter, there is an inescapable analogy between the absence from an arbitration hearing of the Grievant in a disciplinary case and the rule of law that a defendant in court may not be required to take the stand if he chooses not to do so, and it shall not be held against him if he does not.

In spite of the two views, however, the failure of the grievant to testify is usually detrimental to his position because the grievant must then rebut remaining inferences. Arbitrators have upheld discharges when the grievant was acquitted of criminal charges for thievery (remaining mute). One arbitrator sustained a discharge for the grievant's refusal to cooperate with the employer in the elimination of thievery in the plant.[48] Discharges of grievants have been sustained on the same theory where grievants refused to be finger-printed,[49] to take a polygraph examination, or to negate or verify suspension for theft.[50]

---

[46] 16 LA 461, 466 (Klamon, 1951). *Accord, Pilot Freight Carrier, Inc.,* 22 LA 761 (Maggs, 1954). *See International Harvester Co.,* 23 LA 64 (Cole, 1954), where the arbitrator dismissed the grievance because the grievant did not appear:

The failure of a grievant to appear and testify at the hearing of his grievance may be one of the factors leading to the arbitrator's conclusion that the grievance is without merit.

[47] 68-2 ARB ¶ 8591 at 5045 (Sembower, 1968). *Accord, Milgrim Food Stores, Inc.,* 68-2 ARB ¶ 8622 (Murphy, 1968), and *United Parcel Service, Inc.,* 45 LA 1050 (Turkus, 1965) where a mere refusal to answer questions was said to be insufficient to discharge someone, as that would entail a presumption of guilt from silence. *See also Exact Weight Scale Co.,* 68-1 ARB ¶ 8128 (McCoy, 1967); *RCA Communications, Inc.,* 29 LA 567 (Harris, 1957); *Pratt & Whitney Co.,* 28 LA 668 (Dunlop, 1957); *J. H. Day Co.,* 22 LA 751 (Taft, 1954); *United Press Ass'n,* 22 LA 679 (Spiegelberg, 1954).

[48] *General Tire & Rubber Co.,* referred to in Wirtz, note 2 *supra*, at p. 20.

[49] *See Colgate-Palmolive Co.,* note 38 *supra*, and related discussion in text.

[50] *Bowman Transportation, Inc.,* 61 LA 549 (Laughlin, 1973); *see also Bowman Transportation, Inc.,* 64 LA 453 (Hon, 1975); *but see Chapman Harbor Convalescent Hospital,* 64 LA 27 (Neblett, 1975) (arbitrator held, *inter alia*, that, under the labor agreement, refusal to take a polygraph examination did not constitute "unbecoming conduct" which should warrant dis-

Arbitrator Burton B. Turkus in *United Parcel Service, Inc.*[51] had this to say concerning an employee who refused to cooperate based on a claimed privilege against self-incrimination:

> As broad and comprehensive as it so properly is in the protection of the inno-
> cent as well as the guilty when the privilege of self-incrimination is invoked,
> the Constitution, however, neither guarantees to a grievant, exercising the
> privilege, the right to his job nor his reinstatement to employment, when
> evidence sufficient to satisfy a reasonable mind of guilt of "proven
> dishonesty" is *independently* established.[Emphasis in original.]

Arbitrator Russell Smith analyzed the problem as follows:

> An arbitration proceeding is not a criminal proceeding; hence there is
> technically no basis for reliance upon the Fifth Amendment. But this is not
> dispositive of the issue. Some of the basic principles of our jurisprudence,
> notably the concept of due process, have been borrowed and applied in the
> negotiation of the grievance procedure and in its application, and the no-
> tion that an employee ought not to have to testify when a disciplinary pen-
> alty assessed against him is being reviewed has some appeal. The employee
> must, if called and if guilty of the act charged, either testify falsely or con-
> fess his guilt. Thus, if he is honest, he will convict himself out of his own
> mouth; if he is dishonest, he will have added to his dishonesty in testifying
> to the fact of his guilt if otherwise established. His dilemma will be acute.
> If an arbitrator regards the Fifth Amendment privilege as one of the really
> important constitutional guarantees, he may be inclined to think a like privi-
> lege should exist in the arbitral review of managerial action; if, however,
> he has some skepticism about the basic validity of the privilege in general,
> or if he thinks the employer-employee relationship has unique characteris-
> tics, he will take a different view.[52]

EVIDENCE OBTAINED THROUGH AN UNLAWFUL SEARCH

Some arbitrators have adopted the view that the Fourth Amendment's protection against illegal search and the use of evidence obtained thereby is not applicable in labor arbitration.[53] The U.S.
Supreme Court said in *Burdeau v. McDowell*[54] that the Fourth Amend-

---

charge); *Bowman Transportation Co.,* 60 LA 837 (Hardy, 1973). The admissibility of polygraph
examination results is discussed in Chapter XIV, "Polygraphy in Labor Arbitration."

[51]45 LA 1050, 1052 (Turkus, 1965).

[52]Smith, *The Search for Truth—The Whole Truth,* TRUTH, LIE DETECTORS, AND OTHER
PROBLEMS IN LABOR ARBITRATION, Proceedings of the Thirty-First Annual Meeting, National
Academy of Arbitrators, J. Stern and B. Dennis, eds. (Washington: BNA Books, 1979), pp.
54–55.

[53]*See, e.g., Smith's Food King,* 66 LA 619 (Ross, 1976); *Aldens, Inc.,* 61 LA 663 (Dolnick,
1973); *Hennis Freight Lines,* 44 LA 711 (McGury, 1964); *Simoniz Co.,* 44 LA 658 (McGury,
1964); *Lockheed Aircraft Corp.,* 27 LA 708 (Maggs, 1956); *but see Anchor Hocking Corp.,* 66
LA 480 (Emerson, 1976); *Aldens, Inc.,* 58 LA 1213 (McGury, 1972).

[54]256 U.S. 465 (1921).

ment's "origin and history clearly show that it was intended to be a restraint upon the activities of sovereign authority, and was not intended to be a limitation upon other than governmental agencies."[55] The restraint in the Amendment applies to criminal and quasi-criminal proceedings, and not to litigation in civil cases between individuals.[56]

Therefore, arbitrators have uniformly upheld disciplinary actions and discharges of employees who refused to permit a search of lunch boxes,[57] lockers,[58] and purses.[59] Similarly evidence obtained from searching an employee's person,[60] employee's hotel room,[61] an employee's automobile trunk,[62] and even an employee's garage[63] has been used in arbitration for supporting a discharge.

In *International Nickel Co.*[64] Arbitrator Shister set forth the typical rationale concerning personal rights of employees when improper search is asserted as a reason for excluding evidence (a foreman had a janitor open employee lockers in the search for missing company property):

> We are not here dealing with a sweeping, indiscriminate search lacking in reasonable and specific foundation. Quite the contrary. The lockers were unlocked in response to a definite problem—namely, missing clipboards (Company property). True, as the Union agrees, the Company could have asked the employees which of them had put the clipboards in their lockers. But that would have imposed administrative inconvenience and delay, which the Company was not contractually obliged to assume in the light of past practice already alluded to.

In *Aldens, Inc.*[65] Arbitrator Peter Kelliher held that two women were properly discharged when they refused to allow a female security

---

[55]*Id.* at 475.
[56]*People v. Johnson,* 153 Cal. App. 2d 870, 315 P.2d 468 (1957); *Walker v. Penner,* 190 Or. 542, 227 P.2d 316 (1951).
[57]*Fruehauf Corp.,* 49 LA 89 (Daugherty, 1967).
[58]*International Nickel Co.,* 50 LA 65 (Shister, 1967).
[59]*Alden's, Inc.,* 68-2 ARB ¶ 8814 (Kelliher, 1968).
[60]*Jones & Laughlin Steel Corp.,* 29 LA 778 (Cahn, 1957). *Cf. Smith's Food King* (Ross, 1976), *But see, contra, Orgill Brothers & Co.,* 66 LA 307 (Ross, 1976) (bulge at back of employee's left leg when leaving plant; refusal to submit to search cause for discharge); *Dow Chemical Co.,* 65 LA 1295 (Lipson, 1976) (employee had obligation to unzip bulky jacket). *See also Colgate-Palmolive Co.,* note 38 *supra,* and related discussion in text. It should be noted, however, some arbitrators have required a clear plant rule notifying employees that they are subject to search before a discharge will be upheld for refusal to submit to same. *See, e.g., Scott Paper Co.,* 69-2 ARB ¶ 8470 (Williams, 1969).
[61]*Eastern Airlines,* 46 LA 549 (Seidenberg, 1965).
[62]*Aldens, Inc.,* 61 LA 663 (Dolnick, 1973).
[63]*Weirton Steel Co.,* 68-1 ARB ¶ 8249 (Kates, 1968).
[64]68-1 ARB ¶ 8229 at 3787 (Shister, 1967).
[65]68-2 ARB ¶ 8814 (Kelliher, 1968). *But see Campbell Soup Co.,* 2 LA 27 (Lohman, 1946); *Imperial Glass Corp.,* 61 LA 1180 (Gibson, 1973); *Anchor Hocking Corp.,* 66 LA 480 (Emerson,

guard, pursuant to a company rule, to examine the contents of their oversized purses. In response to the union's argument that the search was an improper invasion of privacy and violated the employee's constitutional rights, Arbitrator Kelliher said:

> It was not disputed that the Company here has a serious problem with reference to thefts. The rule established by the Company is entirely reasonable. No Company could stay in business and continue to provide job opportunities for the membership of this Union unless it protected itself against loss by theft. The Company rule is directed at large purses which could be used to secrete Company merchandise. The Union, on the other hand, is properly concerned, as it stated here, with the protection of the privacy and dignity of employees under the circumstances of an inspection. The record, however, shows that the Company took all reasonable procedural precautions to assure this protection to the employees.
>
> . . .
>
> ... When an employee brings a large purse on to the premises, she must expect that she will be subject to such an inspection. It would be unreasonable and totally unrealistic for the Company to attempt to get a search warrant.[66]

The admissibility in arbitration of evidence obtained by a search of lockers, lunch boxes, or purses without the search warrant required in a criminal case presents problems related to those discussed above.[67] As Arbitrator Kelliher said in *Aldens, Inc.*, to require an employer to obtain a search warrant to examine an employee's purse or locker, or to ask the employee to disclose the contents of his or her pockets, could be an unrealistic restriction to impose on the employer. Moreover, fear of unrestricted use of such searches is unrealistic, for the employee is protected by the fact that the employer has many business

---

1976) (discharge improper where employer searched lunch boxes of 75 employees and discovered company-owned quart jars, lids, and rings worth $1.28, since employer failed to comply with *Miranda* requirements pertaining to right to counsel and also invaded employees' right to privacy).

[66]68-2 ARB ¶ 8814 at 5822.

[67]In *Air Line Pilots*, 97 NLRB 929, 29 LRRM 1155 (1951) (n. 1), *overruled on other grounds, Oregon Teamsters Security Plan Office*, 113 NLRB 987, 36 LRRM 1408 (1955), the Board said:
> It has been Board practice to admit allegedly purloined documents unless it is established that an agent of the government has been a party to their unlawful seizure.

See also General Engrg., Inc., 123 NLRB 586 (1959); *accord,* 8 J. Wigmore § 2184A(U) (*cf. Hoosier Cardinal*, 67 NLRB 49 (1946), where connivance of Board agent was found); *Lucky Stores, Inc.*, 53 LA 1274, 1276 (Eaton, 1969) (exclusionary rules of *Miranda* not applicable to private investigations where there is not an agent of state present); *International Nickel Co.*, 68-1 ARB ¶ 8229 (Shister, 1967) (no authority to consider constitutional implications of search of employee's lockers; arbitration board, which derived authority from contract, could only look to agreement in determining propriety of employer action); *United Packinghouse Workers of America*, 62-2 ARB ¶ 8544 (Kelliher, 1962) (federal substantive law not controlling in arbitration proceeding where arbitrator required to construe language of contract by application of recognized maxims of contract interpretation). *Cf. U.S. Postal Service*, 241 NLRB 141, 100 LRRM 1520 (1979).

reasons to be considerate of employees. Hence, the search of person, locker, or lunch box only occurs when a need for such a search exists.

There is a split among arbitrators concerning the issue of whether improperly obtained evidence should be admitted in an arbitration hearing. Arbitrator Joseph Lohman in *Campbell Soup Co.*,[68] in overturning a discharge, focused on the apparent invasion of the personal rights of the grievant:

> To the majority members of the arbitration committee, the adoption of the aforementioned procedure by the company guards represented a serious error in judgment and invaded the personal rights of the aggrieved. In certain respects the tactic bordered on that of entrapment since the aggrieved's innocence of the company's objective or of her own rights placed her honesty and good will at the disposal of the company and caused her to incriminate herself. Such self-incrimination has long been outlawed by the basic law of the United States, specifically, under the Fifth Amendment of the Constitution and the precedent-making Supreme Court decisions in the noted Search and Seizure cases....
>
> In the present case, the majority members of the arbitration committee are of the considered opinion that both the knowledge and possession of the knife by the company were brought about under highly questionable if not illegal procedures. Knowledge, even though incriminating, if acquired through such illegitimate procedures, is of questionable validity in bringing action against the individual....
>
> Under the circumstances, the majority members conclude that the evidence of the possession of the knife is inadmissible, and, consequently, the discharge of the aggrieved was unjustified.

A similar approach was taken by Arbitrator Rankin Gibson in *Imperial Glass Corp.*:[69]

> [T]he arbitrator finds that although all rights of a criminal defendant do not automatically extend to a grievant in every disciplinary case, e.g., absenteeism, incompetence, negligence, in those cases involving moral turpitude, such as theft, the privilege against self-incrimination and the protection against unreasonable search and seizure should be applied. Under these circumstances, the physical evidence obtained as a result of the unlawful search and seizure, as well as the testimony of the police officer who made the search and seizure, and the testimony of the Plant Manager who accompanied the policer officer in making the unlawful search and seizure, should be suppressed, such testimony being the fruit of the poisonous tree of the illegal search.

The policy considerations with regard to admissibility of evidence following an alleged unlawful search was explained by Arbitrator Lawrence Doppelt in *Commodity Warehousing Corp.*:[70]

---

[68]2 LA 27 (Lohman, 1946).
[69]61 LA 1180, 1183 (Gibson, 1973).
[70]60 LA 1260, 1263 (Doppelt, 1973).

Labor arbitration ... adjudicates the rights and responsibility of employers unions, and employees under a labor contract. It involves private disputes without any spectre of governmental excesses. It is doubtful whether all various evidentiary rules necessary to protect individuals against possible governmental abuses should automatically be applied in employer-employee relations matters which involve private disputes.

Indeed, the main issue in many arbitration matters is whether the employer acted in a reasonable manner. And this cannot be determined unless the arbitrator is aware of all the evidence based on which an employer acted. To exclude certain evidence which motivated an employer's actions, and then to ignore such evidence in labelling an employer's activities unreasonable, could well work an injustice on the employer.

. . .

... [The] rights accorded an employee are not necessarily those granted individuals under exclusionary rules of evidence in criminal matters.

. . .

... The employer must have leeway to take all reasonable action to protect itself against theft. When a theft is reasonably suspected, as it was here, the employer must be allowed reasonable action to detect and smother such. Calling in the police to apprehend an employee reasonably suspected of theft, and relying on the police action, is not unreasonable under circumstances such as are here present.

The difficulties of applying the rules of the criminal law to the employment situation, some of which were suggested by Arbitrator Kelliher in the *Aldens* case, *supra*, were also discussed by Arbitrator McGury in *Hennis Freight Lines*:[71]

It may be argued that the spirit of the Constitutional prohibition against unreasonable search and seizure is violated, when the fruits of what has been judicially determined to be an illegal arrest and, therefore, an unreasonable search and seizure, are nevertheless allowed to be considered by the Company or an arbitrator for discharge.

There is an essential difference between procedural and substantive rights of the parties. The constitutional principles may keep the grievants out of jail but do they guarantee them their jobs in the face of Company knowledge of extremely strong proof of dishonesty involving Company property?

Similarly, in *Weirton Steel Co.*,[72] company investigators searched the grievant's garage after they misrepresented to the grievant's fourteen-year-old son the reason for the search. Arbitrator Kates ruled that the investigators' testimony concerning the discovery of stolen

---

[71] 44 LA 711, 713 (McGury, 1964).

[72] *See* note 9 *supra*, at 3861-62, and related discussion of this case in text. *See also Sun Drug Co.*, 31 LA 191 (Marcus, 1958).

goods during the search was admissible evidence and distinguished the lack of admissibility of evidence obtained during searches in criminal investigations:

> In my opinion, the comments made by the Company's security officers and their police associates, for purpose of ascertaining the truth, and the occurrences leading to and resulting in the grievant's admission of guilt and the redelivery of the Company's property, did not fall to such levels as could truly be said to have wrongfully pierced the grievant's constitutional shield. I do not consider that the strict rules of vigorous practices under which the State or Federal constitution is applied to criminal investigations necessarily apply with equal force to private investigations by an employer into the conduct of an employee.

Another good explanation of the difference between the criminal law rules and those employed in labor arbitration was set forth by Arbitrator Short in *Congoleum-Nairn, Inc.*[73] There, an employee's discharge for possession of gambling slips was based on evidence gathered by police officers pursuant to a search warrant, subsequently quashed by the court. The arbitrator, over the union's objection, admitted into evidence the seized material and permitted the police officers to testify regarding the arrest of the grievant:

> Company counsel called the two police officers as witnesses. The Union attorney objected that any testimony by Patrolman [M——] or Sergeant [B——], as a result of an illegal search, would be improper and unconstitutional and deprive [P——] of a very valuable property right, since his job was at stake. Union counsel argued that since the Court had suppressed the seized evidence and quashed the search warrant, such evidence thereby became a nullity, as if it had never happened, and to permit testimony concerning the articles which had been seized would give life and vitality to what a Court had decreed has no vitality.
>
> The arbitrator overruled these objections to the extent of permitting testimony relating to the information and basis upon which Management acted in reaching the decision to terminate the employment of [P——].[74]

Arbitrator Short, however, had some grave misgivings about the use of the evidence in the arbitration, if it was illegally obtained under criminal law standards. His misgivings were enhanced by the peculiar factual development which he described:

> At the arbitration hearing on November 14th counsel for the Union served upon Patrolman [M——] and Sergeant [B——], who were present as witnesses for the Company, an order signed by the Honorable Clifton C. Bennett, Judge of the Superior Court of New Jersey [to quash the illegally obtained evidence]. . . .

---

[73]63-2 ARB ¶ 8843 (Short, 1963). *Contra,* 58 LA 1213 (McGury, 1972).
[74]63-2 ARB at 5723.

The officers asked for a recess to consider the Order. Upon returning from the recess, Sergeant [B——] announced that the officers would comply with the Court Order. Thereupon [the gambling slips] were turned over to [P——], who was asked if the articles were his. In the course of [P——]'s examination of the returned articles, the officers placed him under arrest for possession of numbers slips and took him to the Hamilton Township Police Station. [P——] was released on his own recognizance and returned to the arbitration hearing, which was then resumed.[75]

The grievant was placed in the following awkward position: if he refused to testify, he would let stand without contradiction the evidence put in by the employer; if he took the stand and attempted to explain away his possession of the gambling slips, whatever he said might be used against him in a subsequent criminal hearing. The Arbitrator noted:

> Notwithstanding the distinction between a criminal proceeding, as such, and an arbitration relating to the discharge of an employee, the present proceeding is somewhat novel in that some aspects of the public proceedings became intertwined with the arbitration proceeding.[76]

Arbitrator Short explained that the criminal case was closely related to the arbitration case:

> If equity is proper for the Arbitrator's consideration, the "clean hands" maxim requires consideration, for equity will never assist the harsh assertion of legal rights. Moreover, the constitutional protection against unlawful search and seizure is of little value if evidence ordered supressed may be recaptured by public authorities and used against an accused in a collateral arbitration proceeding without risking possible self-incrimination in a related judicial proceeding.[77]

Because of the unusual circumstances to the case, however, Arbitrator Short reinstated the employee without back pay.

The search issue usually arises when evidence for theft by a grievant is being presented to the arbitrator and the union representative attempts to block its introduction. Whether searching an employee can become a basis for a false imprisonment, assault, or slander charge if no company property is discovered in the search, became the central question in *General Motors Corp. v. Piskor*.[78] The company was sued when employee Piskor, as the employees were lining up to leave the plant, was directed to enter the guard house. According to Piskor, he "was grabbed" by a guard in front of a glass window, the guards evidently believing "they got him for stealing or something."[79]

---

[75]*Id.* at 5722–23.
[76]*Id.* at 5725.
[77]*Id.* at 5727.
[78]27 Md. App. 95, 340 A. 2d 767 (Ct. Spec. App. 1975).
[79]*General Motors Corp. v. Piskor*, 277 Md. 165, 352 A.2d 810 (Ct. App. 1976).

Piskor had been instructed to come into the guard house because the security office had received a telephone call from Piskor's foreman. The foreman had observed Piskor leave his work station and go to the area where radios and tape players were installed. Serious losses in the inventory of radios and tape players had been recently discovered in this department. Piskor, as he passed his foreman, had his army jacket pockets bulging so much that he walked "hunched over," according to the foreman. When Piskor was searched at the guard house, no company property was found in his possession.

Piskor filled a suit and a jury found General Motors liable for compensatory damages: $1,000 for slander, $300 for assault, $200 for false imprisonment, and $25,000 for punitive damages—a total of $26,500.[80] The Court of Appeals reversed in part and remanded.[81] A second award was affirmed.[82]

Some companies are attempting to adopt measures to avoid the *Piskor* search liability by posting notices on all bulletin boards stating that requesting an employee to go to the guard house for a search is a routine procedure which *does not* imply an accusation of theft (slander). Guards have also been instructed not to touch (assault) an employee. Many companies have routine lunch box and package inspections at each gate when the employees leave. Since they are announced as routine and apply to all, they cannot be attacked as containing elements of slander, assault and false imprisonment.

Somewhat related problems have arisen when an employer suspects that the employee has not answered all the medical history questions on an employment application form. One employee was discharged when he answered the questions incorrectly or imcompetently or refused to authorize release of all his medical records. Arbitrator William H. Coburn in *Bondtex Corp.*[83] reinstated the grievant on the ground that the request for the medical records was merely "a fishing expedition into private affairs and an abuse of managerial discretion."

EVIDENCE OBTAINED INTERROGATING EMPLOYEES
WITHOUT UNION REPRESENTATION

One of the conflicts between the views of arbitrators and the NLRB developed over the right of an employee to refuse to respond to a man-

[80]340 A.2d at 772 (Ct. Spec. App. 1975).
[81]277 Md. 165, 352 A.2d 810 (Ct. App. 1976).
[82]*General Motors Corp. v. Piskor,* 281 Md. 627, 381 A.2d 16 (Ct. App. 1977).
[83]68 LA 476 (Coburn, 1977); *see also Jamestown Telephone Corp.,* 61 LA 121 (France, 1973), where the arbitrator found that the employer did not have the right to require an employee to submit to a psychiatric examination before reinstating the employee after an absence possibly caused by emotional stress problems.

ager's request to report to the manager's office or to some other appropriate place for a conference when the employee believes the manager might ask questions about the employee's conduct that might lead to a disciplinary action, even though merely a stern warning.

In 1957, Arbitrator Charles O. Gregory in *E. I. du Pont de Nemours & Co.*[84] held that a refusal of an employee to report to his supervisor upon request was insubordination.

> [I]f [B——] had talked with [S——] as soon as he was asked to do so, ... he would *immediately thereafter* have been at liberty to file a grievance complaining of the fact that [S——] had at that time denied his request to have a steward present at the encounter....
>
> ... [A]ny other view would seem to entitle a unit man to have a Steward present at his request whenever a supervisor undertook to have any communication with him about anything to do with his work. Clearly this would result in an impossible situation.... [A] supervisor is entitled to question a unit man with a view to disciplining him and may go ahead and discipline him, without a steward present. [Emphasis added.]

In contrast to the award of Arbitrator Gregory, some arbitrators have decided that since a grievance procedure had been set up by union-management agreement, the parties must have concluded that if there would be any possibility that at a manager-employee conference any disciplinary action would occur (from a stern warning up to discharge), the union representation had the right to be present at the conference between the manager and the employee.[85]

In 1972 and 1973 an NLRB view, similar to that in this latter group of awards but emanating not from the labor agreement but from the National Labor Relations Act, was announced. Discharged employees were reinstated by the Board in *Quality Mfg. Co.*[86] and *J. Weingarten.*[87] Two circuit courts then reversed these reinstatement orders,[88] then later these decisions were reversed by the Supreme Court.[89]

The Supreme Court held that the two intermediate courts (Fourth

---

[84]29 LA 646, 650 (Gregory, 1957). To the same effect *see United Air Lines, Inc.*, 28 LA 179, 180 (Wenke, 1956).

[85]*John Lucas and Co.*, 19 LA 344, 346–47 (Reynolds, 1952); *Braniff Airways, Inc.*, 27 LA 892 (Williams, 1957); *Singer Mfg. Co.*, 28 LA 570 (Cahn, 1957); *Schlitz Brewing Co.*, 33 LA 57, 60 (Meyers, 1959); *Valley Iron Works*, 33 LA 769, 771 (Anderson, 1960); *The Arcrods Co.*, 39 LA 784, 788–89 (Teple, 1962); *Dallas Morning News*, 40 LA 619, 623–24 (Rohman, 1963); *Waste King Universal Products Co.*, 46 LA 283, 286 (Petree, 1966); *Thrifty Drug Stores Co., Inc.*, 50 LA 1253, 1262 (Jones, 1968); *Allied Paper Co.*, 53 LA 226 (Holly, 1969); *Universal Oil Products Co.*, 60 LA 832, 834 (Shieber, 1973); *Chevron Chemical Co.*, 60 LA 1066, 1071 (Merrill, 1973).

[86]195 NLRB 197, 79 LRRM 1269 (1972).

[87]202 NLRB 446, 82 LRRM 1559 (1973).

[88]*Quality Mfg. Co. v. NLRB*, 481 F.2d 1018, 83 LRRM 2817 (4th Cir. 1973); *J. Weingarten v. NLRB*, 485 F.2d 1135, 84 LRRM 2436 (5th Cir. 1973).

[89]*NLRB v. Weingarten, Inc.*, 420 U.S. 251, 88 LRRM 2689 (1975); *Garment Workers v. Quality Mfg. Co.*, 420 U.S. 276, 88 LRRM 2698 (1975).

and Fifth Circuits)[90] had not granted to employees the right to refuse to respond to a meeting with their supervisors unless the union steward accompanied them to the meeting though a " 'well established current of arbitral authority' sustains the right of union representation at investigatory interviews which the employee reasonably believes may result in disciplinary action...."[91] The Court said that by a margin of 12 awards to 2, arbitrators supported the right of employees to refuse to report,[92] and that "the well established current of arbitral authority" was in this direction even though such a right was *not explicitly provided in the agreement...."* [Emphasis added.] That the Supreme Court used arbitration awards intended to interpret labor agreements to interpret the congressional intention set out in the National Labor Relations Act is of interest. Possibly, however, it is more significant that the Supreme Court relied on arbitration awards that, as the Court acknowledged above, did not draw their "essence from the collective bargaining agreement"[93]—a longstanding principle of the Supreme Court for determining the legitimacy of arbitrators' awards.

Upon this analysis the Court in *Weingarten*[94] sustained the NLRB holding that Section 8(a)(1) of the National Labor Relations Act provided employees the right to union representation during investigatory interviews. In this specific regard, the Court stated:

> [T]he Board's recognition that § 7 guarantees an employee's right to the presence of a union representative at an investigatory interview in which the risk of discipline reasonably inheres is within the protective ambit of the section...."[95]

Further, if the employee is a union representative, the employee is entitled to request another union representative's presence at an investigatory interview.[96]

Arbitrator Lubow in *Commercial National Bank*[97] followed the Board view that the fact that the employee was the union president

---

[90]*See* note 88 *supra.*

[91]420 U.S. at 267, 88 LRRM at 2695 (1975), quoting from *Chevron Chemical Co.,* 60 LA 1066, 1071 (Merrill, 1973).

[92]The twelve arbitration awards cited by the Supreme Court to support the reversal of the circuit courts are cited in footnote 85 *supra,* and the *contra* two awards referred to by the court are cited in footnote 84 *supra.*

[93]*United Steelworkers v. Enterprise Wheel and Car Corp.,* 363 U.S. 593, 597, 46 LRRM 2423, 2425 (1960).

[94]420 U.S. 251, 88 LRRM 2689 (1975), *rev'g* 485 F.2d 1135, 84 LRRM 2436 (5th Cir. 1973).

[95]420 U.S. at 262, 88 LRRM at 2693 (1975); *see also ILGWU v. Quality Mfg. Co.,* 420 U.S. 276, 88 LRRM 2698 (1975).

[96]*Detroit Edison Co.,* 218 NLRB 61, 89 LRRM 1336 (1975); *Keystone Steel & Wire, Div. of Keystone Consol. Indus., Inc.,* 217 NLRB 995, 89 LRRM 1192 (1975); *Detroit Edison Co.,* 217 NLRB 622, 89 LRRM 1123 (1975).

[97]67 LA 163, 165, 166 (Lubow, 1976).

would not negate his need for a union representative when he was being disciplined. He explained that although the labor agreement did not specifically provide for a committeeman to be present during the imposition of discipline, "the general labor law provides that a union representative must be present during the imposition of discipline, if his presence is requested. Our notes do not reveal that such a request was made." In reference to the effect on the employer's failure to have a union representative at the disciplinary conference, the arbitrator said:

> We detect no harm done the Grievant here for failure of representation. Nothing he said at the time was of such a nature that it was used against him at the arbitration hearing. We therefore move past this issue to the primary one.

The *"Weingarten* rule" generated confusion for the Board after its invention and so the Board narrowed the rule's scope. It decided that (1) an employee cannot refuse to report to a supervisor without being accompanied by a union representative merely because the employee imagines that the meeting would be of an investigative nature and could lead to discipline, because it is difficult for the employee to prove after the refusal what would have transpired at a meeting that did not take place;[98] (2) the employee cannot refuse to be questioned or instructed about work performance without a union representative, even if such questioning inevitably carries with it the threat that if the employee could not or would not comply with a directive, discharge or discipline might follow (a latent threat);[99] (3) the right to assistance does not apply to "run-of-the-mill" shop floor conversations, such as when the foreman asks an employee about faulty parts and the need for their correction;[100] (4) the employee cannot refuse to attend a requested meeting after the employee is advised that there will be no interrogation at the meeting.[101]

Since the *Weingarten* right to have union representation assistance only arises in situations when the employer is actually conducting an investigatory interview in which disciplinary action may occur, it can be seen that it is frequently difficult for an arbitrator to distinguish the factual shadings that are involved when an employee is disciplined because he or she refuses to report to an interview that does not take place.

---

[98]*Exxon Co., USA,* 223 NLRB 203, 91 LRRM 1591 (1976).

[99]*Alfred M. Lewis, Inc.,* 229 NLRB 757, 95 LRRM 1216; *see also AAA Equipment Service Co.,* 238 NLRB 390, 99 LRRM 1262, 1330 (1978), *enforced in part, denied in part,* 598 F.2d 1142, 101 LRRM 2381 (8th Cir. 1979).

[100]*General Electric Co.,* 240 NLRB 479, 100 LRRM 1248 (1979). *Alfred M. Lewis, Inc.,* 229 NLRB 757, 95 LRRM 1216 (1977).

[101]*Roadway Express,* 246 NLRB 1127, 103 LRRM 1050 (1979).

A rather colorful decision by the Board with respect to the *Weingarten* rule occurred in *Roadway Express, Inc.*[102] and is worth reporting here to illustrate the due process problems that may face labor arbitrators after hearing the testimony surrounding a meeting at which a grievant's statements made out of the hearing of a union steward were being reported. The arbitrator will also have the same difficulty if the employer disciplined an employee for a failure to report. In this case, the employee was absent from his work station; the supervisor located him and directed him back to work; later the employee confronted the supervisor and threatened him with physical harm; the supervisor requested that the employee accompany him to an office; the purpose of that meeting was uncertain; the employee said he would only go to the office when his union steward arrived (approximately a four-hour delay); when the employee again refused the request when the supervisor made it later in the presence of another supervisor, the first supervisor instructed the employee to leave the terminal for flagrantly disobeying orders. The Board held that the employee's refusal to go to the office undermined the employer's right to maintain discipline and held that the employee should have gone to the office when requested by the supervisor. Once there, the Board said, the employee could have requested the presence of the steward and then if the request was refused *and* the employer conducted an *investigatory interview*, and was not merely giving the employee instructions, a *Weingarten* violation would have occurred. The Board stated: "Our interpretation of *Weingarten* must be tempered by a sense of industrial reality."[103]

In another case the NLRB ordered Montgomery Ward & Company to reinstate and give back pay to employees discharged after they admitted stealing merchandise from the company at the investigative interview, because the company representatives did not call in the union steward before discharging the thieves. The employees who were subsequently discharged had signed an interview consent form and also had signed statements admitting the thefts. The court overturned the NLRB order, saying that the Board lacked authority to order reinstatement of employees discharged for good cause.[104] The court found clear evidence that the firings were a result of the admitted thefts and not the result of the employees' insistence on the presence of a union steward. It concluded that "the employees effected their own discharge by stealing and the section 8 (a)(1) [*Weingarten*] violation was simply incidental to the investigation which preceded the firing."

Some arbitrators have expressed concern over the admission of evi-

---

[102]*Id.*
[103]*Id.* at 1052.
[104]*Montgomery Ward & Co. v. NLRB*, 109 LRRM 2005 (8th Cir. 1981).

dence obtained at an investigatory interview after the employee has asked for and has been denied the presence of his or her union steward or committeeman during the interview.[105] These arbitrators have concluded that an employee has a right to have a union representative present during such an interview by analogizing the situation of the employee to that of an individual arrested by the police. They have reasoned that since the latter has the right to have an attorney present when being questioned by the police concerning possible involvement in a crime, an employee also should be entitled to have a representative present.

Other arbitrators have espoused the views that whatever right to union representation exists to be enforced by an arbitrator must be found in the terms of the collective agreement. Unless the parties have agreed that an employee is to be entitled to union representation during an investigatory interview, they have reasoned, evidence obtained at such an interview without union representation is admissible because there is no other ground on which to base the claim for the right to union representation during such interrogation.

Unions have also argued that the right of representation can be implied from the recognition clause found in all labor agreements, but several arbitrators rejected such a contention. For example, in *International Harvester*,[106] Arbitrator Seward pointed out:

> The clear right of the Union, under Article IV, Section 1, to represent the employee in the bargaining unit "for the purpose of collective bargaining with respect to rates of pay, wages, hours of employment and other conditions of employment" does not carry with it a prohibition against any direct conversation between Management and its employees carried on without the participation or consent of Union officials.

A grievance, Arbitrator Gregory reasoned in *E. I. du Pont de Nemours & Co.*,[107] does not come into being until there is formal protest against a management action:

> And it is usually in connection with the first hearing on such a formal complaint or grievance, which takes place between the aggrieved employee and his foreman, that provision is made for the Employees' Steward to be present. But all of this depends on there first being in existence a formal grievance or complaint often required to be in writing to be processed at

---

[105]*See, e.g., City of Port Huron, Mich.*, 628 ARB ¶ 8788 (Keefe, 1968); *Dow Chemical Co.*, 68-2 ARB ¶ 8647 (Davis, 1968); *Thrifty Drug Stores Co.*, 50 LA 1253 (Jones, 1968); *American Enka Corp.*, 68-2 ARB ¶ 8558 (Pigors, 1967). *See also Humble Oil & Ref. Co. v. Ind. Indus. Workers Union*, 337 F.2d 321, 57 LRRM 2112 (5th Cir. 1964), *cert. denied*, 380 U.S. 952, 58 LRRM 2720 (1965), holding an employer's refusal to permit a union representative to attend the interrogation of an employee was a grievance subject to arbitration.

[106]14 LA 925, 928 (Seward, 1950).

[107]29 LA 646, 650 (Gregory, 1957). *See also American Can Co.*, 57 LA 1063 (Kerrison, 1972).

all, before any of the contract grievance procedure hearings or steps are appropriate.

A board of arbitration chaired by Arbitrator Peter Kelliher held in *Western Electric Co*:[108]

[T]he Company clearly does have a right under the Contract to conduct interviews or interrogations without according the employee a right to have a Union Representative present. Employees, however, are not to be subject to interrogations of an unreasonable length. The Union certainly has a right to advise its members that they should not sign written confessions where they have any reservations as to their being guilty of the offense charged.

Later, in another *Western Electric Co.*[109] case arising at the same plant, a board of arbitration, chaired by Arbitrator Dudley Whiting, held:

The Union contends that any employee is entitled to Union representation when interrogated in connection with suspected misconduct which might result in disciplinary action. A prior Board of Arbitration rejected that contention because the contract does not provide for such representation until the Company had decided to discipline an employee or terminate his employment. . . . The achievement of such an extension of the Union's right to represent employees can only be accomplished by negotiating a provision therefor into the contract.

Arbitrator Kates in *Weirton Steel Co.*[110] specifically rejected the view that the rules promulgated by the Supreme Court in its *Escobedo* and *Miranda* decisions had application in arbitration:

The Union has contended that the Company was obligated to provide the grievant with Union representation while questioning him.

Until contrary authority shall have been pointed out, whether contractual, statutory, judicial or logical, I feel constrained to hold that, in the absence of a specific request for Union representation, the *Escobedo* and *Miranda* doctrines do not obligate an employer to refrain from interrogating an employee about alleged misconduct except in the presence of a Union representative.

Arbitrator Jones, however, in *Thrifty Drug Stores Co.*[111] adopted the diametrically opposite view; relying on *Escobedo* and *Miranda*, he said:

Therefore when interrogations occur in which discipline is a prospect and without the presence of a union representative, the statements then

---

[108](Kelliher, 1965) (unpublished).
[109](Whiting, 1966) (unpublished).
[110]68-1 ARB ¶ 8249 at 3862 (Kates, 1968).
[111]50 LA 1253, 1262 (Jones, 1968). *See also American Enka Corp.*, 68-2 ARB ¶ 8558 (Pigors, 1967).

elicited must be regarded with skepticism and given weight only when other evidence corroborates their substance. Particularly is this so when the employee being interrogated requests union representation and is refused. It is not compatible with the Parties' contractual commitment to fair grievance procedures for the employer to bar union representation when the interrogation forseeably is aimed at securing disclosures which may result in the discipline of the employee being subject to it.

Thrifty Drug suggested that whenever an employee was being interrogated by a company representative to determine involvement or lack thereof in an alleged wrongful act, the employee was entitled to the presence of a shop steward or committeeman because the union is the bargaining agent for employees. But, it should be noted, shop stewards and committeemen are not trained in the law and, therefore, the best advice that they could offer would be to tell the employee to say nothing.[112] Such advice not only would frustrate the investigation process, but could lead to disciplining of the employee for refusing to cooperate in a management investigation.[113]

The view that *Escobedo* has application in an industrial setting has also been criticized on the ground that the presence of a union representative would soon be insisted upon at every discussion between an employee and a supervisor. Thus, Arbitrator Gregory rejected the view that there was a right to representation at investigatory discussions, observing that:

[A]ny other view would seem to entitle a unit man to have a Steward present at his request whenever a supervisor undertook to have any communication with him about anything to do with his work. Clearly this would result in an impossible situation, since it is the traditional function of the supervisor to transmit orders and criticisms to unit men. Indeed, the Impartial Arbitrator would go even further than this. He believes that under all grievance procedures he has seen, including that in the present contract, a supervisor is entitled to question a unit man with a view to disciplining him, and may go ahead and discipline him, without a Steward present.[114]

A similar result was announced by Arbitrator Wenke in *United Air Lines, Inc.*[115] There, a large scale investigation was initiated into the

---

[112]In one instance, the president of a union at an arbitration hearing wanted to have a union representative present at an investigation interview not to cause employees not to talk but to find out who did talk:

These employees should be named. We want to know who they are for the purpose of determining whether or not these employees are typical stool pigeons.... Now, this is something we must know.

Western Electric Co., (Kelliher, 1965) (unpublished).

[113]*See Colgate-Palmolive Co.*, note 38 *supra*, and related discussion in text.

[114]*E. I. du Pont de Nemours & Co.*, 29 LA 646, 650 (Gregory, 1957).

[115]28 LA 179 (Wenke, 1956).

disappearance of scrap from a maintenance base. All employees were scheduled for interviews and all but two cooperated. These two demanded union representation at the investigation and their request was denied. A grievance was filed stating that the company violated the contract by denying the employees the requested representation at the fact-finding interview. The arbitrator denied the grievance, holding that union representation was available only after the employee was disciplined. The arbitrator stated:

> We think the Company had a right to interrogate X, Y, or any other employee in an attempt to ascertain what was happening to its scrap metal and, while doing so, such employees were not, as a matter of right, entitled to have union representatives present.[116]

Certain arbitrators have taken the opportunity to consider and apply *Weingarten*, as well as construe appropriate contract provisions, when faced with alleged denials of union representation at grievance meetings. In *Ward LaFrance Truck Corp.*,[117] a case involving a discharge for theft, Arbitrator Levy discussed the employee's rights in the following (and somewhat exaggerated) manner:

> It is fundamental that B——— is entitled to basic due process rights as guaranteed by the U.S. Constitution. It must be determined whether his Constitutional rights had in any way been violated by the acts of the Company.
>
> Section 2 of Article IX of the Contract states that the provisions of the Agreement must be applied without discrimination, and that the Company's actions must be in compliance with Federal and State laws. Under Federal law, an employee threatened with criminal prosecution must be advised of and has the protection of his Constitutional rights. Both by law and under this Contract, B——— had the right to have a Union representative present at any Company investigatory meeting (Article XXIV of the Labor Contract). The U.S. Supreme Court has stated that there is a "well-established current of arbitral authority" upholding this principle of the right to have a Union representative present at an investigatory interview where there is reason to believe that discipline or discharge might result. B——— was not afforded the protections guaranteed to him by the U.S. Constitution and the Labor Contract.

The statements concerning "due process rights" and "protections" as guaranteed by the U.S. Constitution are simply *dicta* since no grievance meeting was actually held prior to the discharge. In fact, the company took the position that the grievant had resigned. Morever, the arbitrator at least suggests that the *Weingarten* decision had a

---

[116]*Id.* at 180. *See also North American Aviation, Inc.,* 19 LA 565 (Komaroff, 1952).
[117]69 LA 29, 33 (Levy, 1977).

constitutional basis, whereas it is based entirely upon the National Labor Relations Act.

Auburn Faith Community Hospital, Inc.[118] resulted from a deferral by the NLRB[119] to the arbitration procedure, and as a result, Arbitrator Killion considered the union representation issue in light of the labor agreement and *Weingarten.* In reference to the labor agreement, the arbitrator observed:

> When the contract provides that an employee may be assisted or represented by a representative of the Association "at any step in the Grievance procedure," the Arbitrator construes this language to mean that a Registered Nurse has the right to be represented at *any* time during the Grievance procedure if she so desires. She may bring in a union representative at any time, at any step, or *beyond.* This is so because, apart from specific contract language, an employee, by just being employed under a union contract, is accorded this right. Even prior to the landmark decision in *NLRB v. J. Weingarten, Inc.,* 420 U.S. 251, 88 LRRM 2689 (1975) labor Arbitrators, in cases from, at least, *John Lucas & Co.,* 19 LA 344, 346–347 (Reynolds, 1952) to *United States Postal Service,* 62 LA 293, 302; 73-2 ARB ¶ 8570 (Killion, 1974), had held it to be an arbitral right for an employee, upon request, to be provided with Union representation and assistance in serious disciplinary meetings with the Employer. And it, of course, follows that if an employee has this Union representation right in *pre*-grievance procedure-proceedings, he would have the same right at any time during a labor contract's actual grievance procedure. Accordingly, the Grievant was here operating within established contract procedures when she was being represented by CNA representatives at the meeting of February 18.[120] [Emphasis in original.]

The hospital had criticized the grievant for seeking (and obtaining) union representation for a meeting with management to discuss staffing problems. This, according to the arbitrator, ran afoul of the *Weingarten* holding:

> The Supreme Court in *NLRB v. J. Weingarten,* supra, settled the rule that a *single employee* voicing or presenting his grievance to his employer under the collective bargaining agreement is engaging in protected concerted activity....
>
> In our case, the Union entered the case after the Grievant had first presented her grievance to her Supervisor in oral form. The grievance had been put into written form and was about to be processed to the second step when the Union representatives met with the Director of Nurses. At this time, the Grievant had every right to have Union representation and

---

[118]66 LA 882 (Killion, 1976).

[119]Deferral was pursuant to the policy set forth in *Collyer Insulated Wire,* 192 NLRB 837, 77 LRRM 1931 (1971).

[120]66 LA at 895.

the Employer in criticizing her and punishing her for so having violated her Section 7 rights ... thus violated Section 8(a)(1) and (3) of the Act.[121] [Emphasis in original.]

ELECTRONICALLY OBTAINED EVIDENCE

The question of admissibility of evidence obtained by electronic surveillance, either by visual or oral recording, arose in the arbitration context when Attorney Lee M. Burkey wrote numerous articles asserting that the employee's right of privacy and dignity should cause arbitrators to refuse to admit evidence of wrongdoing which was obtained by an electronic device. Burkey has written:

I believe our constitutional safeguards, which I am well aware are largely designed to safeguard persons in criminal proceedings, should be carried over not only into civil matters pending before the courts, but should also be extended to industrial relations.[122]

Burkey's emphasis on due process considerations was challenged by Attorney Evan J. Spelfogel:

[T]here are many such as Mr. Burkey who sincerely believe in their cause as one of principle, yet, one wonders whether the intensity of union opposition to the lie detector, closed-circuit TV, and other scientific advances described above is not in direct proportion to the effectiveness of such devices in uncovering and preventing theft.[123]

There are reported cases dealing with the admissibility of evidence obtained through electronic surveillance.[124] In *Sun Drug Co.*[125] Arbi-

---

[121]*Id.* at 898.

[122]Burkey, *Employee Surveillance: Are There Civil Rights for the Man on the Job?* PROCEEDINGS OF NEW YORK UNIVERSITY TWENTY-FIRST ANNUAL CONFERENCE ON LABOR, T. Christensen, ed. (New York: Matthew Bender, 1967), p. 214; *see also* Burkey, *Privacy, Property and the Polygraph,* 18 LAB. L. J. 79 (1967); Burkey, *Lie Detectors in Labor Relations,* 19 ARB. L. J. 193 (1964).

[123]Spelfogel, *Surveillance and Interrogation in Plant Theft and Discipline Cases,* PROCEEDINGS OF NEW YORK UNIVERSITY TWENTY-FIRST ANNUAL CONFERENCE ON LABOR, note 108 *supra,* at pp. 183–84. In addition to those cases cited *infra, see* dictum in *Cooper Carton Corp.,* 61 LA 697, 700 (Kelliher, 1973).

[124]31 LA 191 (Marcus, 1958). *See also Walton Mfg. Co.,* 124 NLRB 1331, 45 LRRM 1007 (1959) (transcriptions of employer's anti-union speech from dictaphone tapes admissible as accurate reproductions of speeches); *Duro Fittings Co.,* 130 NLRB 653, 47 LRRM 1363 (1961) (trial examiner did not err in refusing to admit tape recordings of numerous bargaining conferences held between employer and union where tapes of two sessions were admittedly garbled).

[125]31 LA at 194. *See* Fleming. THE LABOR ARBITRATION PROCESS, note 2 *supra,* at p. 191. Fleming used the facts in the *Sun Drug* case as hypothetical question to poll arbitrators and reported:

[The arbitrators] were badly split in their responses. Many said that they would not admit evidence which had been illegally obtained; others said that they would follow the law of the particular state as to admissibility; and still others pointed out that illegal methods used in securing evidence did not impair its truth or relevancy....

trator Marcus admitted the recording of a telephone conversation between the grievant and a bookie during which the grievant placed bets. When the recorded conversation was played back to the employee in his supervisor's office, he admitted the placing of bets by telephone. The arbitrator considered the question of admissibility of the recording and, following the general view, distinguished arbitration hearings from a criminal trial, saying:

> Suffice it to say that while the legality of the means by which information has been gathered is for other authorities to determine, it is sufficient for the purpose of arbitration, based upon the uncontroverted facts in the instant case, for the Arbitrator to sustain the discharge.[126]

Arbitrator Marcus added that it was not for him to determine admissibility of such evidence and that "the legality of the means by which information has been gathered is for other authorities to determine."[127]

In some contrast, in *Needham Packing Co., Inc.*[128] Arbitrator Harold Davey refused to admit a tape recording of a telephone conversation between a company attorney and a union official. The case involved the disciplining of employees for engaging in a strike in violation of a no-strike clause. The recorded phone conversation was kept secret until the last day of the arbitration proceeding. The arbitrator excluded it on the ground that the union official had not consented to the recording of the conversation and that all of the parties to the conversation were present at the hearing and able to testify concerning what had transpired. In effect, the arbitrator based his decision concerning admissibility on concepts of best evidence, rather than on criminal "due process."

Several reported cases deal with visual surveillance, but do not involve the question of admissibility of evidence. They involved the right to install visual surveillance equipment without first obtaining the

---

See also Fontaine Truck Equip. Co., 195 NLRB 508, 79 LRRM 1527 (1972), *supplementing* 193 NLRB 190, 78 LRRM 1191 (1971), where the NLRB held that a tape recording made at the employee's discharge interview, unknown to the employee, should have been admitted in evidence. In *NLRB v. Plasterers, Local 90,* 606 F.2d 189, 102 LRRM 2482 (7th Cir. 1979), the Court of Appeals for the Seventh Circuit held that the NLRB did not err in admitting into evidence telephone conversations between a job applicant and a union official that were recorded by the applicant, notwithstanding the fact that use of recording devices during the telephone conversations was in violation of an Illinois statute and that Illinois courts would not admit these recordings as evidence at trial. Section 10(b) of the NLRA states that hearings "shall, so far as practicable, be considered in accordance with the rules of evidence applicable in the district courts." 606 F.2d at 192, 102 LRRM at 2484. The Seventh Circuit concluded that federal and not state law governs admission of evidence in federal proceedings.

[126]31 LA at 194 (Marcus, 1958).
[127]*Id.*
[128]44 LA 1057 (Davey, 1965).

agreement of the union. *Elco, Inc.* [129] involved the interpretation of an agreement which had no management rights clause, but did have a preservation of beneficial working conditions clause. The company had installed a television monitoring system in the plant. Arbitrator Delany held that the company had violated the agreement because the use of television destroyed a beneficial working condition.

But in *FMC Corp.* [130] Arbitrator Richard Mittenthal reached the opposite result. The company installed closed-circuit television to decrease pilferage and increase efficiency. The union grieved, arguing (1) that the company's nonuse of television in the past created a beneficial working condition, (2) that the company had not established sufficient need to warrant a change from nonuse to use of television, and (3) that being monitored by television created a serious burden on the employees. Arbitrator Mittenthal, discussing the assertion that lack of television monitoring was a beneficial working condition much more fully than did Arbitrator Delany, found no violation of the agreement when the television monitoring was introduced. He held that the prior nonuse of television did not establish a beneficial working condition unless there was an agreement concerning the prior nonuse practice. Mittenthal then held that, in the absence of a specific contract restriction, management can change its methods of supervision without mutual agreement, citing the reservation of powers clause in the agreement, and said:

> The right of privacy concerns an individual's right not to have his statements, actions, etc., made public without his consent. But this serves only to protect him against the publication of his private statements or private actions. It should be evident that an employee's actions during working hours are not private actions. Management is properly concerned with the employee's work performance, what he does on the job and whether he obeys the plant's rules and regulations. This and other information about employees is obtained through line supervisors.... For all the Company has done is to add a different method of supervision to the receiving room—an electronic eye (i.e., the television cameras) in addition to a human eye. Regardless of the type of supervision (a camera, a supervisor, or both) the employee works with the knowledge that supervision may be watching him at any time. [131]

---

[129] 44 LA 563 (Delany, 1965). *See also Colonial Baking Co.*, 62 LA 586 (Elson, 1974) (closed-circuit television in high crime area to improve security); *Ford Motor Co. of Canada*, note 118 *infra* and related discussion (closed-circuit television cameras at plant gates); *Hobart Manufacturing Co.*, 62 LA 1285 (Kabaker, 1974) (video tape equipment for time studies); *Cooper Carton Corp.*, note 121 *infra* and related discussion (employer permitted to install two television cameras to observe production operations where contract gives exclusive direction of working force).
[130] 46 LA 335 (Mittenthal, 1966).
[131] *Id.* at 338.

A similar result was reached by Arbitrator Weatherill in *Ford Motor Co. of Canada*,[132] where the arbitrator upheld the company's right to install closed circuit television cameras at the plant gates. Analogizing such cameras to the presence of plant guards, the arbitrator held:

> The company is entitled to know who comes into its plant, and to observe those who are approaching. It may observe them carefully or carelessly, and I see no reason to restrict it from taking advantage of whatever technological aids which may be available to it to assist in this regard. Whether such aids are effective or not is a matter for the company to determine.

Another pertinent decision related to this area is *Thomas v. General Electric Co.*,[133] where an employee objected on right-of-privacy grounds to an employer's continuing its longstanding practice of taking motion pictures of employees at work, by which it established work standards and improved production methods and safety procedures. The court in dismissing the employee's complaint did not base its decision on a lack of a right-of-privacy issue, but instead held that so long as the employer's purpose in taking the pictures was to improve efficiency and promote safety, it could take motion pictures at its discretion.

In *Caproco, Inc.*[134] the employer installed a closed-circuit television system to study the performance of incentive workers, and a grievance resulted. Arbitrator John Day Larkin denied the grievance. The employer, he said, has the responsibility to run an efficient operation, and the evidence showed that performance, and incentive earnings, had improved with the new system. Moreover, the union acknowledged that nothing in the agreement restricted the company's choice of instruments for making time studies.

Finally, in *Cooper Carton Corp.*[135] Arbitrator Kelliher sustained the company's right to install television cameras to allow senior management officers, both of whom had heart ailments, to watch plant operations. He did so because the contract contained a broad management rights clause, and because no provision specifically forbade installation of the cameras.

In 1968, Congress passed the Omnibus Crime Bill, which included a chapter entitled, "Wire Interception and Interception of Oral Communications."[136] This statute places broad restrictions upon electronic

---

[132]57 LA 914, 916 (Weatherill, 1971). *Cf. United States Steel Corp.*, 49 LA 101 (Dybeck, 1967), where a discharge for theft was upheld based on an observation from a concealed position in the plant adjacent to the locker room where the theft occurred.
[133]207 F. Supp. 792 (W.D. Ky. 1962).
[134]56 LA 65 (Larkin, 1971).
[135]61 LA 697 (Kelliher, 1973).
[136]82 Stat. 212, 18 U.S.C. § 2510-20 (1968). Prior to the passage of the Omnibus Crime Bill, the principal statute governing electronic surveillance was the Federal Communications Act, 48 Stat. 1104 (1934), 47 U.S.C. § 605 (1958), which prohibited the interception of certain communications. Evidence obtained from the illegal interception of communications is inadmissible

eavesdropping and provides that evidence obtained in violation of the statute is inadmissible "before any court, grand jury, department, officer, agency, regulatory body, legislative committee, or other authority of the United States, a State, or a political subdivision thereof." In addition to the federal statute, many states have adopted comprehensive legislation regulating electronic eavesdropping and restricting the admissibility of evidence obtained illegally.[137]

The federal and state statutes are concerned with the interception of oral communications.[138] They place no restrictions on the admissibility of evidence obtained through visual surveillance by television cameras or other equipment. Further, these statutes place no limitations upon the admissibility of intercepted oral evidence in an arbitration proceeding. Whether an arbitrator might exclude electronic evidence based on an analogy with the statutory rule undoubtedly will depend in part on what the issue is. If the employer intercepted a telephone call to a hard drug seller or a syndicate gambling agent working in the plant, the duty of the employer, and for that matter the union, to protect the group from exploitation would arguably override the due process considerations being urged by analogy with the state and federal statutes.

THE DEFENSE OF DOUBLE JEOPARDY

Another "due process" consideration which occasionally arises in the arbitration setting is the policy to protect grievants from "double

---

in criminal cases in both state and federal courts. Whether the prohibition extends to civil cases in state courts is an open question. *See generally Lee v. Florida*, 392 U.S. 378 (1968); *Mapp v. Ohio*, 367 U.S. 643 (1961).

[137]*See* Alaska Stat. §§ 4.60.290–11.60.350 (Supp. Sept. 1970); Ariz. Rev. Stat. Ann. §§ 13-1051–13-1059 (Supp. 1970); Cal. Pen. Code Ann. §§ 630-637-2 (West 1970); Colo. Rev. Stat. Ann. §§ 40-4-26, 40-4-30, 40-4-33 (Supp. 1969); Conn. Gen. Stat. Ann. § 52-184a (Supp. 1970) and §§ 189–91 (Pen. Code; West 1969); Fla. Stat. Ann. §§ 934.01–934.10 (Supp. 1970); Ga. Code Ann. §§ 26-3001–26-3010 (Supp. 1970); Hawaii Sess. Laws Act 209 (1967); Ill. Ann. Stat. ch. 38 §§ 14-1–14-7 (Smith-Hurd, 1964); Kan. Gen. Stat. Ann. §§ 21-4001–21-4002, 22-2513 (Supp. 1970); Md. Ann. Code Art. 35 §§ 92–99, Art. 27 §§ 125A–125D (1957); Mass. Gen. Laws Ann. ch. 272 § 99 (1970); Mich. Stat. Ann. §§ 28.807(1)–28.807(9) (Supp. 1970); Minn. Stat. Ann. §§ 626A.01–626A.23 (Supp. 1970); Neb. Rev. Stat. §§ 86-701–86-707 (Supp. 1969); Nev. Rev. Stat. §§ 200.610–200.690 (1969); N.H. Rev. Stat. Ann. §§ 570-A:1–570-A:11 (Supp. 1969); N.J. Stat. Ann. §§ 2A:156A-1–2A:156A-26 (Supp. 1970); N.Y. Pen. Law §§ 250 *et. seq.* (Supp. 1970) and N.Y. Civ. Prac. Law § 4506 (Supp. 1970); Ohio Code Ann. § 2933.58 (Page; Supp. 1970); Ore. Rev. Stat. §§ 41.910, 141.720–141.990, 165.535–165.545 (1969); S.D. Comp. Laws 1967 Ann. §§ 23-13A-1–23-13A-11 (Supp. 1970); Wash. Rev. Code Ann. §§ 9.73.030–9.73.100 (Supp. 1970); Wis. Stat. Ann. §§ 968.27–968.33 (Supp. 1970).

[138]The statues rejecting evidence collected by a wiretap usually apply to court proceedings, but in three states they apply to a "proceeding" and could be construed to reject such evidence in an arbitration proceeding. *See* Cal. Pen. Code Ann. §§ 631(c), 632(d) (West, 1970); Minn. Stat. Ann. § 626A.11(1) (Supp. 1970); Nev. Rev. Stat. § 200.680(1) (1969).

jeopardy." Arbitrators conclude that it is not "just" for a grievant to be disciplined by a double penalty under various circumstances. Where the employer seeks to punish the employee for the same alleged misconduct twice, double jeopardy comes into play. For example, in *Auburn Faith Community Hospital, Inc.,*[139] Arbitrator Killion held that the grievant had been placed in double jeopardy when, following an oral reprimand for an alleged wrongdoing, she was again reprimanded and then placed on probation for the same act.

Arbitrator Harry T. Dworkin in *Misco Precision Castings Co.*[140] explained the difference between "double jeopardy" and "suspension pending an investigation of the facts":

> A further facet of this case which requires appraisal is the form of the application of the disciplinary penalties. The Personnel Director upon discovering the infraction of the rule made an on-the-spot determination. The decision was that the card-playing employees "either put away your cards and go back to work, or go home!" The erring employees responded as requested; they promptly returned to their jobs. A little later, they received suspension notices. This procedure reasonably amounts to a disciplinary warning, followed by a suspension for the original offense. It constitutes a form of double jeopardy. The situation here presented is readily distinguishable from one in which an employee is suspended pending an investigation of the facts, and where the application of a penalty is deferred for legitimate reasons.

Even a "mix-up" between supervisors' instructions does not eliminate the "double jeopardy" rule, said Arbitrator Neil Gundermann in *Hub City Jobbing Co.*:[141]

> The grievant was suspended by [B——], sent back to work by [F——] and discharged by [C——] in connection with the same offense. While the Company argued that X—— was suspended in order to give [C——] time to investigate the case and that this was done as soon as [C——] returned from his trip, the undersigned rejects this argument. Although [C——] was out of town and could not investigate the circumstances surrounding the grievant's conduct until he returned, action was taken by a Company representative prior to [C——'s] return. [F——], a supervisor, having complete knowledge of the grievant's actions and the instructions given the grievant by [B——], instructed the grievant to return to work. Once the Company assesses a penalty the Company does not have the right, in the absence of additional facts, to increase the severity of the penalty. In a sense the grievant was placed in double jeopardy by the Company's actions.

---

[139] 66 LA 882 (Killion, 1976).
[140] 40 LA 87, 90 (Dworkin, 1962).
[141] 43 LA 907, 910 (Gundermann, 1964).

Arbitrator Herman in *Wolverine Worldwide, Inc.*[142] determined that unless a right to amplify a penalty had been reserved at the time of the oral reprimand, a discharge after a reprimand for the same offense is double jeopardy. Double jeopardy was also the rationale basic to a reinstatement by Arbitrator Getman in *Laidlaw Corp. of the West*[143] when the grievant, absent without excuse and with a forged doctor's note, initially received a three-day suspension with the assurance from local management that this was to be the final penalty, but the corporate management overruled its local management and directed a discharge.

Double jeopardy principles would rarely operate between a criminal punishment and a punishment by the employer although such claims have been presented in arbitration hearings. For example, in *Consolidated Badger Cooperative*[144] the grievant had been convicted of the crime of fornication and the union claimed that discipline by the employer for the same reason would amount to double punishment. After determining that the employee's conviction would hamper his effectiveness as an employee and resulted in detrimental publicity affecting not only the employee but the employer's business, Arbitrator Mueller discussed the double jeopardy defense, saying:

> The double jeopardy argument has been advanced in numerous cases before arbitrators and the undersigned is in accord with the majority of other arbitrators to the effect that while the law provides the civil or criminal punishment for any given case the resultant penalties which often result are many times more severe than the penalty itself.... The real criterion, however, in double jeopardy arguments is not the fact that two penalties may be assessed for the same cause but whether or not the act of said employee did in fact substantially affect his relationship with the Employer as an employee and if such is found to be the case any resultant discipline or even discharge which may follow therefrom is based upon his rights as derived from the contract. It must be remembered that without the contract the Employer could discipline or discharge the employee at will.[145]

For example, in *Westinghouse Electric Corp.*[146] Arbitrator Schmidt considered the defense that to discipline an employee for an act for which he could be criminally prosecuted violated the prohibition against double jeopardy. In that case the grievants were discharged for acts of violence during a strike. The arbitrator said:

---

[142]66 LA 796 (Herman, 1976).

[143]76-2 ARB ¶ 8564 (Getman, 1976).

[144]36 LA 965 (Mueller, 1961), *see* also cases cited therein.

[145]*Id.* at 968. *Cf. New York State Dept. of Correctional Service,* 69 LA 344 (Kornblum, 1977), where the arbitrator held that dismissal of criminal charges did not preclude discipline of emloyee by employer for act out of which arrest arose; principle of *res adjudicata* did not apply.

[146]40 LA 1169 (Schmidt, 1963).

I am unable to agree with the union's argument of double jeopardy which is based upon the claim that the discharges were for acts which were also violations of the criminal laws and for which grievants were or could be prosecuted. An employer is not precluded from imposing discipline upon employees for acts which are violations of the penal code and which take place in or about the plant premises or are connected with the employment relationship. Nor, conversely, is punishment by the employer, as authorized by the collective bargaining agreement, any defense to prosecution of the employee by state authorities for a criminal offense based upon the same act.[147]

Arbitrator Ralph Seward rejected a double jeopardy claim when the grievant argued that the specific discipline assigned should not be greater than that assigned for similar misconduct in the past by the same grievant:

As for the Union's "double jeopardy" claim, the Umpire does not believe the latter doctrine has any application herein. Obviously, an employee's past record may not be used by itself to justify the discharge penalty, where there has been no offense—i.e., no new disciplinary "event"—to warrant disciplinary action. But where a fresh offense has been committed, the magnitude of the penalty to be applied may certainly be determined not only be the new offense, alone, but in the perspective of the employee's record as a whole. Indeed, where the employee's record has been good, the Union would be the first to claim that it should be considered as a mitigating circumstance in setting a penalty.[148]

The arbitrator has authority in many labor agreements to adjust the penalty and in doing so may reexamine the penalties provided by the employer in prior cases. This evaluation of the fairness of the penalty is not related to the principle of double jeopardy.

CONSIDERATIONS RELATING TO THE "AGREED" AWARD

In the course of an arbitration proceeding the parties often decide to settle their dispute, and may ask the arbitrator, as part of the mechanism of settlement, to include the stipulated settlement in the award. This procedure has its counterpart in civil litigation where judgment may be entered upon stipulation of the parties, and comports with the *Code of Ethics and Procedural Standards for Labor-Management Arbitration* prepared by the American Arbitration Association and Na-

---

[147]*Id.* at 1173.

[148]*Bethlehem Steel Co.*, 41 LA 890, 892 (Seward, 1963). *See also Bi-State Development Agency*, 67 LA 231 (Dugan, 1976); *American Airlines, Inc.*, 46 LA 737 (Sembower, 1966); *Arden Farms Co.*, 45 LA 1124 (Tsukiyama, 1965).

tional Academy of Arbitrators.[149] For these reasons commentators have found no ethical problem in such procedure.[150]

A situation more difficult to evaluate in terms of due process can arise, however, when the parties have agreed beforehand that they want the arbitrator to decide a case in a certain way and the representatives of the two parties want to conceal their agreement from either the grievant, the union membership, or from other company officials.

In court proceedings the lawyers representing the two parties to the litigation often confer together with the judge in chambers on various matters and may upon such an occasion communicate to him a result that the lawyers for the two parties have agreed would satisfy each. In labor arbitration, so long as the representatives of both parties are present in a "chambers" conference with the arbitrator, a similar communication should not raise any more serious questions of ethical conduct than does the parallel chambers conference in a court proceeding,[151] except that there is possibly more uneasiness when an arbitration involves a discharge. One observer, however, believes any type of "agreed award" is harmful to the reputation of the arbitration process:

> The "sweetheart" arbitration—From time to time over the years there have been a few reports of instances where Union and management agreed upon the decision which the arbitrator should reach and then transmitted their decision to the arbitrator for effectuation by him. Such cases arise in many different settings. For example, the Union may agree that a discharged employee deserves to be fired but refuses to accept the responsibility of agreeing with the employer publicly or the issue involved may be one in which the parties agree but for which neither wants to take specific responsibility insofar as either the employee body or the general public are concerned. While such instances are rare, it is believed that such "agreed" or "sweetheart" arbitrations in which the result is pre-ordained by the par-

---

[149]THE PROFESSION OF LABOR ARBITRATION, Selected Papers from the First Seven Annual Meetings of the National Association of Arbitrators, 1948-1954, J. McKelvey, ed. (Washington: BNA Books, 1957), pp. 151-63.

[150]See generally Fleming, Some Problems of Due Process and Fair Procedure in Labor Arbitration, note 2 supra; Wirtz, Due Process of Arbitration, note 2 supra, at pp. 26-32; The Agreed Case: A Problem in Ethics, 20 ARB. J. 41-48 (1965). See, e.g., Holodnak v. Avco Corp., 381 F. Supp. 191, 87 LRRM 2337 (D. Conn. 1974), aff'd in part and rev'd in part, 514 F.2d 285, 88 LRRM 2950 (2d Cir.), cert. denied, 423 U.S. 892, 90 LRRM 2614 (1975) (employee published an article critical of company and union practices); Summers, The Individual Employee's Rights Under the Collective Agreement: What Constitutes Fair Representation, ARBITRATION— 1974, Proceedings of the Twenty-Seventh Annual Meeting of the National Academy of Arbitrators, B. Dennis and G. Somers, eds. (Washington: BNA Books, 1975), p. 24.

[151]Fleming, note 135 supra, at pp. 248-251, also published in ARBITRATION AND PUBLIC POLICY, Proceedings of the Fourteenth Annual Meeting of the National Academy of Arbitrators, S. Pollard, ed. (Washington: BNA Books, 1961), at pp. 87-90. For an earlier study, see Wirtz, note 135 supra, at pp. 26-32; but see to the contrary Hays, Labor Arbitration—A Dissenting View, 74 YALE L.J. 1019, 1033 (1965).

ties and the arbitrator acts merely as a rubber stamp are unwise and do serious harm to the integrity of the arbitration process. If the parties have reached agreement on a proposition, they should not seek to make it appear that the decision is not theirs but that of the arbitrator; nor should the arbitrator lend himself to such perversion of his functions.[152]

Because collusion is rarely, if ever, involved unless a grievance claim is an objection to discipline or discharge, many commentators see no objection to private joint communication by representatives of both parties in cases that do not involve discharge or discipline.[153] Where it becomes evident that there is unfair representation, the award would be set aside by a court on that ground. Arbitrator Herbert L. Sherman, Jr., reported:

> Where the Union representative does not ask the arbitrator to make a prior commitment on the decision that he will render but simply tells the arbitrator that a hearing must be held for "political" reasons even though the Union representative agrees with the Company's position, the prevailing view among arbitrators (except in the South) is that there is no duty of disclosure. Most Union and Company representatives also believe that there is no duty of disclosure in this situation in which the arbitrator has not been asked to make a commitment on how he will decide the case and in fact he has made no such commitment.
> . . . [T]he Union representative may hint, after the hearing, that he expects to lose the case. Most respondents to my questionnaire believe that an arbitrator has no duty to disclose that on a plant visit, after the hearing, the Union representative, who presented the Union's case, indicates that he has done his best in presenting the case but that he will understand if the arbitrator rules in favor of the Company under the contract.[154]

These views are consistent with the view of the Ninth Circuit. In *Local 13, ILWU v. Pacific Maritime Ass'n,*[155] that court said that an "agreed" award is not improper if not motivated by an improper hostility toward the individual member. The court explained that on occasion there are strong political reasons for union representatives to submit a grievance and yet want the award to be in favor of the employer. While such actions by the union could well be free of hostile motivation toward the individual, some observers have believed that the very fact that a representative "agreed" to an award would be *prima facie* evidence of hostility toward the individual. Implicitly, the Ninth Circuit rejected the view that evidence of an agreed award was *prima facie*

---

[152]Levitt, *Lawyers, Legalism, and Labor Arbitration, Symposium on Labor,* 6 NEW YORK LAW FORUM 398 (1960).

[153]*See* note 2 *supra.*

[154]Sherman, *Arbitrators' Duty to Disclose—A Sequel.* 32 U. PITT. L. REV. 167, 181 (1970).

[155]441 F.2d 1061, 77 LRRM 2160 (9th Cir. 1971).

evidence of hostility, and required the proponent of vacation to show additional evidence of hostility. The Court said:

> We agree with appellees that a breach of the duty of fair representation would not be established merely by proof that the International Union "swapped" a concession that section 17.81 applied to union officials for acceptance by the employers' association of the position that the contract limited the individual packing of sacks. In this practical world such issues, susceptible of no absolutely "right" solution, are often resolved by accommodation.... If the choice were motivated by a good-faith balancing of interests of different elements within the International Union, it might well fall within the "wide range of reasonableness ... allowed a statutory bargaining representative in serving the unit it represents." Ford Motor Co. v. Huffman ..., 345 U.S. at 338.[156]

FREEDOM OF SPEECH VERSUS EXCLUSION OF DEFAMATION

Although workers have a First Amendment right to publish a newspaper critical of their employer and union, Arbitrator Richard Mittenthal in *Great Lakes Steel Corporation*[157] held that an employer had a corresponding right to promulgate rules prohibiting the bringing in and distribution on plant property of "vicious and defamatory" material and to enforce these rules with discharge if necessary.

In March 1971, after an underground newspaper entitled the "GREAT LAKES STEAL" was first distributed at the plant, the employer issued a rule forbidding employees from bringing in or distributing "literature which is libelous, defamatory, scurrilous, abusive or insulting." About a year after this rule was posted, 115 copies of the newspaper were found in an employee's automobile, and management concluded that the owner of the automobile was one of the employees in the newspaper's distribution network and discharged him.

Even though the newspaper was an attack on Steelworkers Local 1299, the union filed a grievance; the union representative contended that the no-distribution rule abridged the employee's First Amendment rights and should have been protected on the same basis as the official union newspaper, which the company had made no attempt to suppress.

Arbitrator Mittenthal rejected the union's view, pointing out that the company's rule prohibited only in-plant circulation, not publication, and that in any event the First Amendment does not insulate "libels and slanders." The underground publication, he said, is essentially

---

[156]*Id.* at 1067, 77 LRRM at 2165.
[157]60 LA 860 (Mittenthal, 1973).

"hate literature" that the company had a right to bar to maintain order and discipline on its premises.

FAILURE TO COMPLY WITH CONTRACTUAL PROCEDURE

In certain labor agreements a procedure that will be followed before an employee will be discharged is described. For example, in the labor agreement between the United Steelworkers and the major steel producing companies and many fabricating companies, the employer is required to suspend the employee for five days and hold a hearing before any final determination that an employee will be discharged. In *Republic Steel Corp.,*[158] Arbitrator Stashower overturned a discharge for failure to provisionally discharge an employee prior to final termination. He said:

> While I agree that substantially [Z——] was afforded the protection intended by the clause when he asked for and was given a hearing within the time limits contained in the Contract, it must be concluded that the procedural requirement as to the provisional discharge was not complied with by the company. Its failure to do so constituted a violation of the Contract.
>
> In view of this finding, it is unnecessary to discuss the merits of the discharge and the grievance must therefore be upheld.

An employee who was arrested for taking indecent liberties with a nine-year-old girl and who subsequently pleaded guilty and was sent to a mental hospital for observation and then was sentenced to jail for a year, with six months of the sentence suspended, was reinstated by Arbitrator Kates in *Armco Steel Corporation*[159] because the grievant was notified of his discharge while in the hospital rather than being notified of a five-day suspension with the intention of discharge. This is an example of a reinstatement due to the company's use of the wrong words. Arbitrator Kates explained:

> The parties in their collective bargaining agreement have gone into considerable detail to assure bargaining unit members of so-called "due process" before being severed from their employment. Due process is often as important in the protection of a man's means of livelihood as with reference to his freedom from imprisonment.
>
> Any action taken by an employer to terminate a man's employment

---

[158]3 STEEL ARB. at 1834.

[159]*Armco Steel Corp.,* 43 LA 977, 979 (Kates, 1964). *See also Michigan Fleet Equipment,* 72-2 ARB ¶ 8381 (Belkin, 1972) where back pay was ordered for an employee suspended for refusal to wear safety glasses because the foreman neglected to offer a copy of the suspension notice to the employee before he left the plant.

status, if in violation of agreed contractual procedures which have not been waived, must ordinarily be deemed invalid.

. . .

In my opinion, the Company violated the "due process" specified by the contract in its actions in terminating the grievant's employment.

Thus, some arbitrators conclude that a failure by the employer to precisely follow a contractual procedure causes an ineffective discharge and hence requires a reinstatement.

To the contrary, however, other arbitrators take the position that a procedural defect by the employer, such as an oral notice rather than one in writing, or the use of the word "discharge" rather than "suspension with intention to discharge" in the notice, cannot wipe away the industrial misconduct engaged in by the grievant. These arbitrators do consider it their duty to provide the discharged grievant all of the protections that the procedural steps set forth in the agreement were designed to provide, but they do not treat these procedural matters as conditions precedent to an effective discharge, if the protection has been provided using different words or procedures.

Arbitrator John Day Larkin espoused this viewpoint in *Valley Mould & Iron Co.,* [160] where an employee participated in a strike in violation of the agreement and the grievant was told to return to work or he would be discharged. Upon his failure to return to work he was "indefinitely suspended" instead of receiving a preliminary suspension for five days, a requirement provided for in the agreement. In upholding the discharge, Arbitrator Larkin said:

This record shows that Mr. [G——] did not receive the usual "pink slip" or specific form used in discharge cases, wherein he was notified that he was suspended for "five (5) calendar days excluding Sundays and holidays . . .", after which his discharge was to take effect. . . . Instead he got a letter stating that his suspension was "indefinite" but that the termination would be in accordance with the provisions of the Agreement. Because of this disparity in form and language, it is now argued that Mr. [G——] is being denied his procedural rights. It is said that he was summarily discharged.

With this we cannot agree. Mr. [G——] was privileged to file a grievance. He was given a hearing locally, and the matter was taken up with union officials from the District Office. From these hearings, the matter was appealed to arbitration. Under the terms of the parties' agreement, no discharge is final until all steps in the grievance procedure have been exhausted. Therefore, Mr. [G——'s] case is not concluded until this arbitration award is released. In short, until this report is completed and in the

---

[160] *Valley Mold & Iron Co. and USWA Local 1058,* Grievance No. 8, 54–56 (Larkin, 1954) (unreported).

hands of the parties, Mr. [G——'s] discharge is still provisional. A discharge brought about in this way cannot be considered a preemptory discharge. Or, to use the language of Article VIII, Mr. [G——] has not been "preemptorily" discharged; he was only suspended, pending the process prescribed by the parties in their agreement. Therefore, any claim to his restoration under the provisions of Article VIII is simply without foundation.

Suffice it to say that both Mr. [G——'s] warning notice and his suspension notice assured him that he would be accorded his full rights under the Agreement. And in spite of some slight variation in form and language, we believe that he was given a proper procedural treatment under the circumstances then prevailing.[161]

Similarly, in *Frito-Lay, Inc.,*[162] Arbitrator Dykstra sustained the discharge of a grievant for an unsatisfactory course of conduct, even though the advance notice of discharge required in the labor agreement was not provided. After finding that the company had made out a *prima facie* case justifying discharge in substantive terms, the arbitrator held:

I have concluded in the instant case that the delay in the communication should not result in the reversal of the Company's action. As the facts reveal, efforts were made to inform the Union in advance of the discharge, and word was left at the Union's office to return the Company's call. While other means of communication could have been employed, the efforts made to [sic] reflect that the Company was not striving to circumvent the intent of the contract.... Furthermore, it is clear that the Company's decision was not made in haste or in anger. In such a setting it is difficult to conclude that notice to the Union in advance of the termination could have stayed the results. It is also significant that notice was conveyed very shortly after the discharge, and thus the delay constituted no hurdle to the investigation of facts or to the implementation of the grievance proceedings.[163]

In *Thompson Bros. Boat Mfg. Co.,*[164] Arbitrator Schurke sustained the discharge of a truck driver for serious misconduct during the course of his employment. The union sought his reinstatement because the company failed to provide the union a written notice of the discharge as required by the agreement. In sustaining the discharge, Arbitrator Schurke stated:

There is no evidence that either the Union or the grievant has been prejudiced or that the grievance settlement machinery created by the collective bargaining agreement has been obstructed by the lack of a separate letter to the Union, separately delivered. It is apparent that the grievant promptly

---

[161]*Id.*
[162]52 LA 1213 (Dykstra, 1969).
[163]*Id.* at 1216-17.
[164]56 LA 973 (Schurke, 1971).

transmitted the letter addressed to him to the Union. . . . Since there has been actual notice to the Union and since there is no evidence of prejudice requiring remedy, the undersigned will proceed to the merits of the case. . . .[165]

Likewise, Arbitrator George Carroll in *Minerals and Chemical Corp.*[166] held in a case where the company neglected to provide the union with a written notice of the reasons for discharge before it occurred, that this was a procedural defect but not sufficient reason for reinstatement. The employee had been discharged for striking another worker with a heavy metal object and when the case came to arbitration the grievant's only defense was that the company had neglected to give the union the required written notice. Arbitrator Carroll said that the purpose of the notice-of-discharge provision was to inform the employee of the reasons for the discharge, but that since there was "uncontroverted testimony" that both the employee and the union understood fully the reasons for the discharge, the lack of the notice was no detriment to the employee.

Arbitrator Hillard Kreimer in *Mead Corp.*[167] similarly refused to reinstate a dischargee where the company, contrary to the agreement, gave the employee only an oral rather than written notice of the reasons for his suspension prior to discharge. In reaching his conclusion the Arbitrator said:

> But Grievant knew, at all times, the precise reasons for the suspension. The oral notice in no way affected his substantive rights. Certainly, in the rush and pressure of attempting to settle the work stoppage, the Company can be forgiven a procedural oversight.
>
> . . .
>
> During the discussions to end the work stoppage, Grievant and the Union were both fully aware that the Company already felt Grievant was involved in it. The suspension was inflicted before the men returned to work, so that everyone had the opportunity to present the information on that issue. . . . Although the contract requires that the reasons for suspension or discharge be specified, it also indicates reinstatement should take place if further investigation proves an injustice had been done.[168]

In *Ranney Refrigerator Co.,*[169] the employer had failed to follow the contractual requirement that the union was to be notified of each dis-

---

[165]*Id.* at 977.

[166]*Minerals and Chemicals Corp.,* AAA Case No. 13-23 (Carroll, 1959). *See also Wilson & Company, Inc.,* 50 LA 807 (Eaton, 1968); *Neway Uniform and Towel Supply of Florida, Inc.,* 66-1 ARB ¶ 8126 (Kuvin, 1966); *United Engineering & Foundry Co.,* 37 LA 1095 (Kates, 1962).

[167]53 LA 342, 344 (Kreimer, 1969). *Contra, Huffman Mfg. Co.,* 38 LA 882 (Stouffer, 1962).

[168]53 LA at 344.

[169]5 LA 621 (Lappin, 1946).

charge. Arbitrator Lappin ordered back pay to the grievant up to the date of the grievant's employment elsewhere, less five days (he did not reinstate the grievant, at the grievant's request). Arbitrator Lappin did this not because the notice was a condition precedent necessary to make the discharge action effective, but for several other reasons, one of which was to encourage the employer to send notices to the union. Other arbitrators have sustained the discharges of employees when they concluded the termination was for just cause, but then have ordered the employer to pay the grievant a certain amount to encourage the employer to comply with the procedural steps provided in the labor agreement.[170]

The various positions that can be taken by arbitrators in discipline and discharge cases where the employer makes a procedural mistake were summarized by Arbitrator Fleming in these words:

> ... (1) that unless there is strict compliance with the procedural requirements the whole action will be nullified; (2) that the requirements are of significance only where the employee can show that he has been prejudiced by failure to comply therewith; or (3) that the requirements are important, and that any failure to comply will be penalized, but that the action taken is not thereby rendered null and void.[171]

Arbitrator Fleming was very critical of arbitrators who take position (1) above and permit form to control substance.

> The procedural irregularity may not have been prejudicial in any sense of the word, the emphasis upon technicalities would be inconsistent with the informal atmosphere of the arbitration process, and the end result could on many occasions be quite ludicrous. If, for instance, an employee gets drunk on the job and starts smashing valuable machinery with a sledge hammer, it would hardly seem appropriate to nullify his discharge on the sole ground that it was in violation of a contractual requirement that the union be given advance notice.[172]

---

[170]*National Lead Co.*, 13 LA 28 (Prasow, 1949); *Pittsburgh Plate Glass Co.*, 8 LA 317 (Blair, 1947); *Schreiber Trucking Co.*, 5 LA 430 (Blair, 1946); *Torrington Co.*, 1 LA 35 (Courshon, 1945).

[171]Fleming, THE LABOR ARBITRATION PROCESS (Urbana: Univ. of Ill. Press, 1965), p. 139.

[172]*Id.* at pp. 139-40.

CHAPTER XIV

Polygraphy in Labor Arbitration

The attitudes of labor arbitrators are in sharp conflict with respect to the acceptability of and—if accepted—the weight to be given to, the testimony of a polygrapher reporting his views as to the credibility of other witnesses. Some arbitrators accept such testimony, believing that polygraphy is in general use and that the views of a qualified polygrapher acting as an expert witness will provide additional information which will assist the arbitrator in resolving the credibility problems with which he or she is confronted. Other arbitrators refuse to listen to the polygrapher's views, believing that judges in criminal and civil courts do not listen to such views and hence, as a matter of policy, an arbitrator should also refuse to do so. (As explained in a subsequent section, the testimony of polygraphers has been accepted by both criminal and civil judges since 1934 when covered with a "stipulation," and beginning in 1972 some judges began to accept the testimony without "stipulation.") And some arbitrators accept the testimony but then straddle the conflicting views by announcing in their awards that they have given little weight to the testimony.

The first presentation of a polygrapher as an expert witness occurred in 1959[1] but now arbitrators are encountering them often. Arbitrator Edgar Jones, when he read a paper on polygraph evidence at the thirty-first annual meeting of the National Academy of Arbitrators in 1978, was astonished at the numbers of encounters. He said:

> There were about 1,000 persons present. Some 250 of them were arbitrators. To my—and their—astonishment, fully half of them indicated that they had had hearings in which polygraph evidence had been proffered, although there is a relative paucity of published cases. Of the persons present who indicated that they were representatives of the unions (about 200 or so), half of them, in turn, had encountered polygraphs. The 500 or so management representatives present also indicated that half of them, as well, had had contact with grievance situations involving the polygraph.[2]

---

[1]*Marathon Elec. Mfg. Co.*, 31 LA 1040 (Duff, 1959).
[2]Jones, *"Truth" When the Polygraph Operator Sits as Arbitrator (or Judge): The Deception of "Detection" in the Diagnosis of Truth and Deception,"* TRUTH, LIE DETECTORS, AND OTHER

357

Arbitrator Rimer in *Temtex Products Inc.*[3] reported the confusion
surrounding polygraphy in labor arbitration that still existed in 1980:
"Different arguments are expected to be derived from the same source
in adversary proceedings; however in this case they are as far apart as the
poles."

THE INSTRUMENT AND THE EXAMINER

Dr. William Marston, a criminal lawyer and psychology student,
undertook some research in 1913 at the Harvard Psychological Labora-
tory correlating lack of truthfulness in answers to changes in systolic
blood pressure. Later Marston was commissioned by the U.S. Army to
continue his research. The concept of the instrumental detection of
deception was not the invention of Dr. Marston because in 1895 Cesare
Lombroso had reported some success identifying lack of truthfulness in
answers to questions by the measurement of changes of blood pressure
and pulse rate, and in 1914, Vittorio Benussi reported the detection of
deception by changes in the rate of breathing.[4]

In 1923, Marston was requested to examine James Alphonzo Frye, an
accused murderer, and Marston reported that he was not guilty of that
crime. The court rejected Marston's testimony on the grounds that the
systolic blood pressure test for the detection of deception had not gained
acceptance by the scientific community.[5] Three years later, another individual confessed to the murder, and Frye, as well as Marston's opinion, was vindicated, stimulating interest in instrumental detection of
deception.[6]

Further research into instrumental detection of deception techniques
was conducted and the instruments were improved. During the late
1920s the process of simultaneously recording cardiac and respiratory
patterns of an examinee was developed, and shortly thereafter a device
to record galvanic skin response was added to the simultaneous recording. A district judge in Michigan explained in 1972 that "the machines
used are constantly improving and have improved markedly in the past
ten years."[7]

PROBLEMS IN LABOR ARBITRATION, Proceedings of the Thirty-First Annual Meeting, National
Academy of Arbitrators, J. Stern and B. Dennis, eds. (Washington: BNA Books, 1979), p. 97
n. 55.

[3] 75 LA 233, 236 (Rimer, 1980).

[4] Romig, A Survey of Polygraph Legislation as of January 1981 (paper presented at a meeting
of the Academy of Criminal Justice Sciences, Philadelphia, Pa., March 1981), p. 2.

[5] *United States v. Frye,* 293 F. 1013 (D. D.C. 1923).

[6] Wicker, *The Polygraphic Truth Test and the Law of Evidence,* 22 TENN. L. REV. 711, 715
(1953); *See also* Romig, note 4 *supra,* p. 2.

[7] *United States v. Ridling,* 350 F. Supp 90, 97, 99 (E.D. Mich. 1972).

When the instrument was developed to the point where it recorded several physiological reactions, it became known popularly as a "polygraph," a derivation of the Greek word for "many writings." This general use of the term "polygraph" helps avoid the misnomer "lie detector," because the instrument is not able to detect and report lies.[8]

Although the instrument has been continuously improved, the theory basic to it is quite simple. It merely measures and records on paper tape a composite of various physical changes: blood pressure, pulse rate, respiration rate and depth, electrical (galvanic) skin conductivity, skin temperature (perspiration), and muscular movements. The act of not telling the truth causes a psychological conflict, and such conflict causes subconscious strain which produces measurable physiological changes that cause the stylus to vibrate and to record the changes on the polygraph machine tape. When answers are given that the examinee knows to be true and others are given that the examinee knows to be false, different variations or lack thereof (heart rate, blood speed, respiration and perspiration) will be recorded on the tape. Most variations are said to be caused by a "deception" and a comparison of these with the question asked and the answers given is basic to the polygrapher's conclusion about the examinee's truthfulness.

One district judge explained that "several law enforcement agencies in California uniformly refuse to file complaints or information when no deception is shown in polygraph examination of suspects,"[9] a result some refer to as passing a "truth test." Most individuals who consent to be tested are not guilty and they answer truthfully because they want to be cleared and excused. Sometimes, however, suspects believe they can take the test and "pass" it even though they know they are guilty; they hope they can "beat the machine," and be excused. Suspects may dull their reactions with alcohol or drugs, but Cleve Backster, a prominent polygrapher in California, has said this ploy rarely works because under some stimuli subconscious reactions (respiration, heart rate, etc.) become stronger. Backster answered this question:

> [Q:] To what extent are there methods ... to deceive an examiner into thinking that there were no responses, when, in fact, deception was being attempted? Would drugs or any kind of conditioning operate to deceive an experienced and qualified examiner in your opinion?
>
> [A:] I might mention that there are a lot of rumors that are passed around as to how you can beat the polygraph.... [T]he person, in order to adequately fool a polygraph examiner would have to prevent an oncoming re-

---

[8]Romig, note 4 *supra* at p. 2.

[9]Tarlow, *Admissibility of Polygraph Evidence in 1975: An Aid in Determining Credibility in a Perjury-Plagued System,* 26 HASTINGS L.J. 917, 929 (1975), quoting *People v. Cutler,* No. A176965, 12 CrL 2133, 2134 (Super. Ct. Los Angeles County, Cal., Nov. 6, 1972).

action. And frankly I've been in this field . . . for well over 20 years and I, myself, could not "beat" the polygraph. . . . This has never been an actual problem.[10]

Some individuals have attempted to alter their reactions by other ploys—even by inflicting pain on themselves with sharp objects hidden in their shoes. Any abnormal reaction unrelated to critical questions will reveal such a ploy on the tape as an artificial reaction and if by chance the abnormal reaction coincides with the answer to a critical question, the reaction will report deception—hence being of no benefit to the one who attempted to so crudely "beat the machine."

In *Illinois Bell Telephone*[11] an employee decided to undergo a test hoping to save his job. He had denied that he was one of the employees who had installed telephone service to a gambling house. The test indicated he did not answer the questions truthfully. Arbitrator Ryder sustained the discharge of the employee, explaining that "the polygraph has been an effective instrument in indicating deception in the heavy preponderance of cases."

The polygrapher (examiner) prepares the test with critical questions. Evaluation of the reactions (variations, deceptions, etc.) requires experience. Arbitrator Bert Luskin recognized this as early as 1958:

> The machine and its component parts are only as good as the person performing the tests, and the value of the findings is the result of experience, qualifications or inexperience of the operator of the machine.[12]

Professor Fred Inbau of Northwestern University and John E. Reid, who co-authored the standard polygraph testing text, explained, just as Arbitrator Luskin did, that a polygraph test is "no better than the man who is making the diagnosis."[13] The role of the examiner is so important that John E. Reid urged slow acceptance of testimony of polygraphers in courts because examiners first had to be well-trained. A district judge in Florida in 1972 reported the changes in Reid's views:

> At one time, Reid was of the opinion that the results of such testing should not be admitted in a judicial proceeding. By 1966, however, he began advocating the acceptance of polygraph tests as reliable scientific evidence. Although the basic polygraph apparatus has not changed, Reid now suggests that the experience, competency, and reliability of the polygraph ex-

---

[10]Zimmerman, THE POLYGRAPH IN COURT (1972) at pp. 23-24.
[11]39 LA 470, 479 (Ryder, 1962).
[12]The statement of Arbitrator Luskin is found in Jones, note 2 *supra*, at p. 144.
[13]Reed and Inbau, TRUTH AND DECEPTION: THE POLYGRAPH (LIE-DETECTOR) TECHNIQUE, Second Edition (Baltimore: Williams & Wilkins, 1977); statement is quoted by Arbitrator Jones, who does not believe in polygraphy testing, or polygraphers (Jones, note 2 *supra* at p. 144).

aminers has so improved as to qualify them to administer examinations fully acceptable to the courts.[14]

And the reasons for the change in John Reid's views were explained as follows:

> Reid testified that he has personally conducted at least 25,000 polygraph examinations and has supervised the administration of another 75,000 exams. Of all cases studied, 10% are unintelligible, inconclusive, and impossible to interpret, 25% are obvious cases and can be easily interpreted, and the remaining 65% are the hard cases which can be properly interpreted only by a qualified examiner. Based on the documented performance of qualified examiners in this 65% group and other test cases, Reid can demonstrate examiner error in only one-tenth of 1% of all cases. However, to be on the safe side, he projects a maximum possible rate of error of 1%.[15]

Arbitrator Charles Laughlin in *Bowman Transportation, Inc.*[16] said:

> The reliability of polygraph testing has long been accepted by government agencies and by industries. An expert in the case of A. v. B. 72 Misc. 2d 719, 336 N.Y.S. 2d 839 (1972) was willing to concede only about 20 errors out of 15,000 tests. Even arbitrators who have not admitted, or are not influenced by the results of tests, concede that their use is very general.

Many expert witnesses other than polygraphers use machines to record heartbeats or analyze blood, breath, etc., and from this data they formulate conclusions that they report to a trier of fact (judge or arbitrator).[17] For example, the stylus marks on the polygraph tape are similar to the marks made by the stylus on an electrocardiogram. From these marks the cardiologist as an expert witness will report to the trier of fact conclusions about the examinee's heart condition. Such a trier of fact will of course place more confidence in a report from the cardiologist than he would in one by a doctor who reported conclusions after listening to heartbeats through a stethoscope or after pressing his ear to the examinee's chest. Psychologists and psychiatrists are often qualified as expert witnesses and reach their conclusions without the aid of any instrumentation, only personal interviews with the examinee.

---

[14]*United States v. Lanza,* 356 F. Supp. 27, 31 (M. D. Fla. 1973).

[15]*Id.*

[16]61 LA 549, 556 (Laughlin, 1973).

[17]Arbitrator Edgar Jones said that to use a polygraph rather than to use "the time-immemorial groping efforts of triers of fact to separate honest from dishonest accounts is to despair of the imperfections of the human situation, a dangerous state of mind to slip into our compulsively technological era" [Footnote omitted.] Jones, note 2 *supra*, at p. 130. Technological testing to more accurately determine facts is developing rapidly. The Syva Co. of Palo Alto, California has developed a urinalysis kit to test for marijuana, which is rapidly being adopted by many employers, The Wall Street Journal, June 1, 1982, at 1. A breathalizer machine is used to determine the extent of an employee's intoxication and record the facts and is an improvement over asking the foreman to recall his judgment when he "smelled the breath."

THE EVALUATION OF POLYGRAPHY TESTIMONY

In the chapter on rules of evidence (Chapter XII) it is reported that arbitrators generally assume that they need not become entangled in the technical rules of evidence that apply in federal or state courts. It is true, however, that in more recent times arbitrators often seem to be "looking over their shoulders," examining court rules in the belief that a failure to follow them might add complications if an award subsequently is submitted for review to the NLRB or to a federal district court.[18]

In spite of the trend toward more formalism, arbitrators accept evidence that is presented by either party if it is *relevant* and not barred by some established exclusionary rule. Arbitrator Shulman in his significant Harvard Law School lecture said, "the more serious danger is not that the arbitrator will hear too much irrelevancy, but rather that he will not hear enough of the relevant."[19] It is stated in the Federal Rules of Evidence that *"relevant evidence"* means "evidence having any tendency to make the existence of any fact that is of consequence to the determination of the action more probable or less probable than it would be without the evidence."[20] Accordingly, "if testimony or exhibits arguably have *any* tendency to make the existence of the fact more probable than not, the criterion of *relevancy* is established.[21] [Emphasis in original.]

Again, as discussed in Chapter XII, no vacation of an award occurs if the arbitrator admits evidence into the record which would be excluded in a courtroom, but under some arbitration statutes an award can be vacated if a party asserts that his or her rights "were substantially prejudiced by the refusal of the arbitrator to hear evidence material to the controversy."[22] Thus, there is not only a policy to admit relevant information, but a legal stimulus to do so.

If one party presents a witness and the expected testimony is challenged as irrelevant, the arbitrator will usually respond to the objection

---

[18]*See* Chapter XXI, "Vacation, Enforcement or Correction," and Chapter XXII, *"De Novo* Reviews in a Court."

[19]Shulman, *Reason, Contract, and Law in Labor Relations,* 68 Harv. L. Rev. 999, 1017 (1955); *see also* Smith, *The Search for Truth—The Whole Truth,* Truth, Lie Detectors And Other Problems In Labor Arbitration, Proceedings of the Thirty-First Annual Meeting, National Academy of Arbitrators, J. Stern and B. Dennis, eds. (Washington: BNA Books, 1979), p. 49.

[20]*See* Fed R. Evid. 401.

[21]Hill and Sinicropi, Evidence in Arbitration (Washington: BNA Books, 1980), p. 8.

[22]Cal. Code Civ. Proc. § 286 (e); *see also* the discussion in Chapter XXIII, "Fair Representation Obligations," of unfair representation charge that is generated if a grievant does not have relevant testimony presented or accepted in a labor arbitration hearing.

with "the arbitrator will accept the evidence for what it is worth."[23]
With this announcement, the parties are put on notice (1) that the arbitrator considers the testimony to be of some relevance but (2) that the
arbitrator will make his or her own evaluation as to the "weight" he or
she will give to the evidence and that it could well be given no weight.

In spite of the normal policy of accepting *relevant* testimony from a
witness unless it is barred by an exclusion rule, the acceptance of testimony from an expert witness is handled somewhat differently. The expert witness must first establish an "expertise" foundation before he or
she testifies as an expert, and is first exposed to *voir dire* cross-examination during which the "expertise" of the witness can be probed by the
other side and by the trier of fact (in this case the arbitrator). This probing step is especially important to an arbitrator because by definition an
expert witness is being presented to the arbitrator to assist the arbitrator, and probing the witness's expertise will help the arbitrator determine what weight to ascribe to it.[24] When the foundation of the expert
was probed in *Illinois Bell Telephone Co.*,[25] Arbitrator Ryder accepted
the testimony over the objection of the union representative while reserving his right to determine the "weight" he would give to it when he
evaluated it with the other evidence. In this case the testimony being accepted was by John Reid, a very well-known polygrapher:

> Chairman holds that the testimony of Mr. John E. Reid, polygraphic ex-
> pert, teacher and former president of the American Academy of Polygraph
> Examiners, and conceded by the Union as probably the best known man in
> the field in the country, where it relates to the results of the polygraphic
> testing he administered to V——, is admissible, over objection, as relevant
> and pertinent testimony.[26]

Arbitrator Charles Laughlin in *Bowman Transportation, Inc.*[27] explained that because a polygrapher is being presented as an expert witness, he or she must testify personally so the expertise foundation can
be probed. It is the polygrapher who is the witness, not the polygraph
machine.

> The union's argument is that a person subjected to a polygraph test is
> denied his right to confront the witnesses against him. It is stated, not only

---

[23]*See* Chapter XII, "Rules of Evidence"; *see also Temtex,* 75 LA 233 (Rimer, 1980), in which
Arbitrator Rimer said that the testimony of a qualified polygrapher is not admissible in arbitration cases because the weight of arbitral authority supports the inadmissability of polygraph test
results and "where rarely accepted in an arbitration proceeding it was 'for what it was worth.' "
[24]The rules of expert witness evidence in United States courts are found in FED R. EVID.
701–05.
[25]39 LA 470 (Ryder, 1962).
[26]*Id.* at 479.
[27]61 LA 549 (Laughlin, 1973).

in the Union's brief but also in decisions of some arbitrators, that a polygraph cannot be cross-examined. A corollary of that argument is that hearsay evidence is used.

The fallacy in the argument is that it is the operator who administered the test, and how he interprets it, and not the machine, that is cross-examined. In this regard, polygraph evidence is no different from any other kind of scientific demonstrative evidence. Many types of scientific evidence are known to our law. Examples are blood tests, fingerprint evidence, ballistic evidence, and handwriting analysis. In none of these instances is the blood, the fingerprints, the ballistic charts or the handwriting cross-examined. The person who administers the test and the person who interprets it are subject to cross-examination. Expert testimony is also known to our law. No type of scientific demonstrative evidence is of value unless interpreted by a competent person. The qualifications of the administrator and interpreter are always the proper subject matter for cross-examination. In this regard polygraph evidence is no different from any other type of scientific evidence. ... In Marathon Electric Mfg. Corp. 31 LA 1040 (1959) and McDonald Aircraft Corp., 66-1 A.R.B. § 8236, the arbitrators correctly refused to recognize polygraph tests because the operator did not appear as a witness. Only a certified copy of the result of the test was offered.[28]

Since the probing of the foundation is a preliminary step before the acceptance of the testimony of the polygrapher, the arbitrator stated that no report prepared by a polygrapher should be accepted unless it is presented as an exhibit by the polygrapher after having completed the *voir dire* examination. The report or exhibit is merely an extension of the polygrapher's testimony.

In *Wilkof Steel and Supply*[29] Arbitrator Edward Maxwell did not follow this normal practice. The employer testified that he had helped the grievant load an air compressor hose into a truck. The grievant responded that he had never seen the hose—thus a testimony conflict arose. The employer had been examined by a polygrapher who then submitted a report that the story was truthful. The arbitrator accepted the report of the polygrapher without having the polygrapher appear to be examined as an expert witness. In his award the arbitrator did, however, explain that he had given the polygrapher's report low weight because he had not been present at the hearing as an expert witness and subject to cross-examination on his expertise. The arbitrator explained:

The Arbitrator takes the broad view toward receipt of evidence and permits the introduction of evidence such as the polygraph examination. Receipt of such evidence is made to provide the Arbitrator with as much information as possible. After receipt, the amount of weight or authority to

---

[28]*Id.* at 553.
[29]39 LA 883 (Maxwell, 1962).

be given such evidence is within the Arbitrator's discretion. The parties were advised at the hearing and are again reminded that the weight given such evidence must be reduced by the inability of the party to cross-examine the affiant.[30]

During the normal *voir dire* examination one of the normal questions to be asked of the polygrapher is about his or her license. By 1981 the legislators in 27 states had enacted statutes requiring a practicing polygrapher to be licensed.[31] District Judge Thompson in his opinion in *United States* v. *De Betham*[32] pointed out that in 1972 there were eleven states that had such license statutes. This means that between 1972 and 1982 sixteen additional state polygraphy license statutes have been added.

Arbitrator Hon in the award in *Bowman Transportation, Inc.*[33] explained what licensing means:

> Polygraph examinations, in the State of Georgia, are administered under the statutory and administrative requirements designed to assure that tests will be given by qualified personnel.

So did Arbitrator Charles Laughlin in another *Bowman Transportation, Inc.*[34] award.

> The method by which polygraph tests are administered is controlled by law in the State of Georgia. Georgia Statutes, Chapter 84-50m Company's exhibit 2, supplemented by Rules 502-3-.01 and 502-4-.01 of the State Board of Polygraph Examiners, Company's exhibit 3. The statutory and

---

[30]*Id.* at 885.
[31]ALA. CODE tit. 46, ch. 13–1/2 §§ 297 (2200)-(22) (Supp. 1973); ARIZ. REV. STAT. ANN. tit. 32, ch. 27 (1976); ARK STATS. ANN. §§ 71-2201-25 (1927); FLA. STATS. ANN. § 493–40 (1967); GA. CODE ANN. §§ 84-501-16 (1968); ILL. REV. STAT. ch. 38 § 202-1-30 (1963); IOWA CODE, Public Safety, 680, Chapter 2, § 680-2. 100 (17A, 80A) (1979); KY. REV. STATS. § 329-010-990 (1962); LA. REV. STAT. ANN. § 2838-2854 (West Supp. 1982); ME. REV. STAT. ANN., Chapter 508, Public Law § 1, 32 MRSAC 54 (1977); MASS. GEN. LAWS ANN. ch. 147 §§ 22–30 (West, 1972); MICH. STATS. ANN. § 18-186 (1)-(29) 1973; MISS. CODE ANN. § 73-29-1-47 (1968); NEB. REV. STAT. § 81-1901 *et seq.* (Supp. 1980); NEV. REV. STATS. § 648-005-210 (1969); N.M. STATS. §§ 67-31-1-14 (1963); N.C. GEN. STATS. §§ 66-49.1-7 (1975); N.D. CENT. CODE ANN. 43-31-01-14 (1965); OKLA. STATS. ANN. tit. 59, §§ 1451-76 (Supp. 1975); OR. REV. STAT. ch. 608 (1975); S.C. CODE § 56-1543-51-.75 (Supp. 1974); TENN. CODE ANN. § 62-2701-2724 (Supp. 1981); TEX. STATS. ANN. § 4413(29cc) (1978); UTAH CODE ANN., "Detection of Deception Examiners' Act" (1973) (amended 1976); VT. STATS. ANN. tit. 26, §§ 2901-10 (Supp. 1975); VA. CODE §§ 54-729.01-018, 54917 (1975), and POR 22 (1975) (1968) (amended 1975). WIS. LAWS OF 1979, Chapt. 319, § 1.111, 31 (4) (1980). In twenty-six states a polygrapher must be licensed. In eight of the twenty-six states, law enforcement agents are exempt from the licensing requirement. In six states qualifying examinations for a license are not required; in six no special polygraph school is required; in four the polygraph machine to be employed is not described; Romig, note 4 *supra* at p. 7.
[32]347 F. Supp. 1377 (S.D. Cal. 1972), *aff'd,* 470 F.2d 1367 (9th Cir. 1972), *cert. denied,* 412 US 907 (1973).
[33]64 LA 453, 457 (Hon, 1975).
[34]61 LA 549, 556-57 (Laughlin, 1973).

administrative requirements assure that tests will be given by qualified personnel. Also, the pretest procedure specified in Rule 502-04-.01 is such as to put the examinee at ease so as to reduce the probability of inaccuracy from emotional reaction. The questions to be asked are made known to him and his answers taken before the polygraph test starts. This avoids the use of an emotional surprise question. The method prescribed for taking the test is similar to that approved by the New York Court in A.V.B., 72 Misc.2d 719, 336 N.Y.S. 2d 839 (1972).

Polygraph testing is not free from error, but neither is any other evidence. Certainty is unattainable in the field of adjudicatory fact finding. It cannot be said that polygraph testing is so unreliable as to make the Company's requirement unreasonable.

A state license law is a protection to the general public. In the various states there are variable requirements that must be met to obtain a license. Generally the law requires an individual to be trained as an intern or apprentice under a licensed polygrapher. Since some statutes are more stringent than others, reciprocity understandings that are provided for in 25 statutes are quite difficult to administer. Professor Inbau and John E. Reid suggested that a polygrapher should not be licensed unless he or she has (1) a college degree, (2) a special six-month training experience under experienced trainers, and (3) at least five years' experience working in polygraphy with an experienced specialist.[35] But requirements at this level are not required in the less stringent statutes. Beyond the license requirements, in the six-month training experience at one of the well-known training centers, for example, a trainee must spend three months receiving special instruction in interviewing techniques, behavior symptoms, question formulation, test procedures; instrument operation; and the physiological, psychological and legal aspects of the technique. The trainee then spends the second three months conducting examinations under supervision. This type of training could be probed during the *voir dire* examination.

If an arbitrator is holding a hearing in a state wherein there is no license requirement, the arbitrator can still question the polygrapher about the requirements of the state where he or she obtained the license. Arbitrator Jaffee reported in *Golden Pride*[36] that he set up no

---

[35]Arbitrator Edgar Jones speaks of the "despair" shown by the use of polygraphs (*see* note 17 *supra*); he also thinks little of polygraphers:

> [A]t least 80 percent of the polygraph operators are publicly declared by the elite among them in this simplistic business to be incompetent or charlatans (one operator gloomily asserting that there are no more than 50 who are competent out of all 3,000 in the country). Second it must also be said that however honest, well intentioned, or versed in the manipulation of the machine, even the elite polygraph operators are not competent. [Footnote omitted.]

Jones, note 2 *supra*, at p. 88.
[36]68 LA 1232 (Jaffee, 1977).

limitations because the polygrapher was licensed in a state different from that where the hearing took place.

> The Maryland polygraph operator in this case is employed by a private firm of investigators. He is "certified," is licensed in Virginia and Georgia; there is no licensing procedure for such operators in Maryland. He has, he said, examined about 2500 "subjects." He said on cross that he had never testified in any court on polygraph tests but did testify in "one or two" arbitration cases. He has done such work for 10 years.
>
> On the whole, I was not especially impressed with this witness.[37]

Arbitrator Edgar Jones, who does not favor polygraphy, said in his extensive paper that he would not accept testimony from a polygrapher in an arbitration hearing even when such testing was required in the labor agreement because such testing, he said, "so contravenes public policy as to make it unconscionable for me to become the parties' instrument of injustice. . . ."[38] One cannot reconcile this bold statement with the presence of polygraphy license statutes in 27 states. Quite obviously the legislators in these states would not provide for polygraphers licenses which upgrade their professional status if polygraphy "contravenes public policy."

During the *voir dire* examinations into the polygrapher's expertise the representative of either side may attempt to discredit the polygrapher. This discrediting can take place to such an extent that the arbitrator will excuse the polygrapher on the ground he or she does not have the necessary foundation to be an expert witness. The following is a report of a successful discrediting of a polygrapher by some adroit cross-examination. In *Spiegel, Inc.*[39] Lee Burkey, a union attorney, asked the polygrapher about his educational qualifications and then trapped him:

> Q. As an operator and as a supervisor [of operators], do you have any general acquaintance with the literature in this field on lie detectors and their uses?
>
> A. Yes, sir.
>
> Q. I suppose you have heard of John E. Reid, haven't you?
>
> A. Yes, sir.
>
> Q. Do you know a man by the name of Holcomb at the University of Iowa, or of him?
>
> A. Yes, sir.
>
> . . .
>
> Q. You are, however, acquainted with the work of Charles R. Judson at the California Institute of Technology on this subject, are you not?

---

[37]*Id.* at 1235.

[38]Jones, note 2 *supra*, at p. 108.

[39]44 LA 405 (Sembower, 1965).

A. Not fully, sir.

Q. But you know of him and have at least seen some of his work, haven't you?

A. Yes, sir.

ATTORNEY: I would like the record to show that I have a better lie detector than this witness. There is no such person. I have no further questions.[40]

On motion of Attorney Burkey, Arbitrator Sembower refused to admit the examiner's testimony.

THE ARBITRATOR CONTROLS THE AMOUNT OF THE WEIGHT

After the *voir dire* examination on the polygrapher's foundation has been completed, the polygrapher's testimony is presented. The polygrapher will explain the examination procedure and the reasons for conclusions concerning truthfulness or deceit. In arbitration the testimony of a polygrapher will sometimes be offered by the party proving up a *prima facie* case (which is not permitted in criminal trials), because the statements of the denials of the grievant may be impeached initially rather than as part of the rebuttal permitted in criminal trials. The testimony of the polygrapher may also be presented on behalf of the grievant, proving up his or her rebuttal to the *prima facie* case. Then after the polygrapher's testimony is concluded, the polygrapher again is subject to cross-examination to probe for weak points. The weight to be given to the polygrapher's testimony by the arbitrator will likely be reduced as weak points are identified.

The sequence and clarity of the critical questions are most important. If they are clear, the subject's affirmative and negative answers will produce sharper reactions if any answers are not completely truthful. If on the other hand the questions are obtuse, the subject's reactions will be clouded, making evaluations more difficult. Such an analysis was recorded by Arbitrator James C. Vadakin in *Coronet Phosphate Co.*:[41]

A number of the questions asked of Mr. [B——] during the test are of little value.

With reference to the latter criticism, Mr. [B——] was asked: "On May 17th did you give grievant permission to leave the plant to look for [H——]?" The reply was in the negative. As was pointed out above, there was genuine

---

[40]Jones, note 2 *supra* at p. 116, n. 89, quoting Burkey (excerpt from transcript of *Spiegel, Inc.*, 44 LA 405 (Sembower, 1965)).

[41]31 LA 515, 519 (Vadakin, 1958).

room for difference of opinion as to wheather [B——'s] statement to X——
constituted permission for X—— to leave. Mr. [B——] was also asked the
question: "When you were talking with X—— on the 25th, did he wave his
arms?" He replied in the affirmative. As was also explained above, this
arm-waving was undoubtedly in the nature of emphatic gestures. Even accepting the Foreman [B——'s] answers, nothing was proved by these answers which would show that the grievant's statements were untruthful.

Arbitrator Hon in *Bowman Transportation, Inc.*[42] reviewed the critical questions:

> "Did you hit that post?"
> "Did you hit that post during Friday night-Saturday morning?"
> S—— answered "No" to both questions on both the pre-test and the test.
> [The polygrapher] testified that deception was not only indicated in both
> answers but that the deception was obvious. This interpretation was veri-
> fied by other polygraph examiners, including W. A. Robinson, Chairman
> of the Board of Polygraph Examiners in the State of Georgia.

Arbitrator McIntosh in *Indianapolis Transit System*[43] explained
that an analysis of the critical questions was part of his determination
of the "weight" he would give to the polygrapher's conclusion; the examination had been arranged by the union:

> The lie detector test made at the Union's request is of some, but not great,
> value. . . . [A] test which took a short time and only involved one or two
> questions on which fear reaction could be recorded is not of such reliable
> nature as to be completely convincing. However, X——'s willingness, in
> fact, insistence on taking the test is not the conduct of a guilty man.[44]

Arbitrator Edward Pinkus in *Brink's, Inc.*[45] refused to accept the
testimony of a polygrapher retained by the FBI to assist with an investigation because he did not consider the polygrapher had a sufficiently
sound expertise foundation.

> The Arbitrator . . . did not find him to be a persuasive expert witness for
> four reasons. First, when asked on cross-examination how much his com-
> pany was paid for its services, he stated that he had no idea. The arbitrator
> does not believe that was a wholly truthful answer. Second, he testified
> that Grievant had no difficulty with the English language, but the Arbitra-
> tor had a distinctly contrary impression after hearing Grievant's testi-
> mony. Third, during direct examination the examiner changed his testi-
> mony significantly to state a conclusion more unfavorable to Grievant than

---

[42] 64 LA 453, 457 (Hon, 1975).
[43] 31 LA 433 (McIntosh, 1957).
[44] *Id.* at 436.
[45] 70 LA 909 (Pinkus, 1957).

his initial, carefully phrased answers. That he did so in response to further questions from the Company's attorney does not lessen the effect on his own posture as an expert witness. Finally, his reliance exclusively upon an intra-industry journal article as the only scientific support for the reliability of the polygraph tests does not in the view of the Arbitrator measure up to the standards appropriate for an expert witness in a controversial and unsettled field.[46]

Because the instrument was not functioning properly, the testimony of a polygrapher was given no weight by Arbitrator Taylor in *Service Supply;*[47] among other things, the "sweat gland" indicator on the machine was inoperative. The arbitrator then reinstated the grievant even though the polygrapher had testified that he had failed the polygraph test.

> The Arbitrator could not help but wonder (since the machine is designed to register several types of reactions, including those of the sweat glands) how an examiner could omit any of the indicators by calling one of them insignificant.[48]

In addition, a police officer who was also a polygrapher said the questions were not clear and hence that the reactions to the answers were not sharp enough for him to conclude that the grievant had failed the test.

> Company witness, Sgt. Baker of the police department, testified that the lie detector results did not represent sufficient evidence against D—— for them to charge him and that, in fact, the Company requested no charges be filed.[49]

After giving the polygraph evidence low weight, the arbitrator concluded that the company had not proved that the discharge was for "just cause."

Arbitrator Charles V. Laughlin in *Daystrom Furniture Company, Inc.*[50] said that the weight that he gives polygraph testimony varies with the conclusions: if the examiner says the story is "true" he gives the testimony great weight, but if the examiner says the story is "false" he gives it little weight. He explained his reasons.

> It has long been the view of this arbitrator that polygraph tests are more useful in verifying the truthfulness of testimony that in detecting its unreliability. From that point of view the term *truth verifier* would be more apt than lie detector. This distinction is forcefully made in a book by F. Lee

---

[46]*Id.* at 911.
[47]59 LA 1280 (Taylor, 1972).
[48]*Id.* at 1284.
[49]*Id.*
[50]65 LA 1157 (Laughlin, 1975).

Bailey and Harvey Aronson entitled The Defense Never Rests, on page 17 as follows:

> "Finally, it is up to the examiner to interpret the finished chart correctly. The term 'lie detector' is a misnomer; 'truth verifier' would be more accurate. Essentially, the polygraph has a single function—it separates those who have told the truth from those who have not. This is all it can do. Anyone can pass a polygraph test—all he has to do is tell the *whole* truth. A person can tell the *literal* truth and still show deceptive responses." (Italics in the original)

If the results of the polygraph test had verified the Grievant, great weight would have been given thereto. As is, the arbitrator places little, if any, weight upon the results of the polygraph test.

For the reasons heretofore expressed, the Union's objection to the admission of the results of the polygraph test is hereby overruled. The results of said test, however, play little if any part in the conclusions of the arbitrator.[51]

In another case (*Bowman Transportation, Inc.*[52]), Arbitrator Laughlin added more discussion about the "weight" he gives to the testimony of a polygrapher.

> Two generalizations occur to this arbitrator. First, that polygraph evidence is more reliable when offered to prove the truth of statements made than when offered to prove untruth. The reason suggested is that an emotional reaction may cause a true statement to look like a lie. Second, in a case tried by a fact finder, such as an arbitrator, without a jury, questions of admissibility merge into questions of weight. Without a jury, the test may be admitted but with a variable amount of weight attached, depending upon the rest of the evidence.

Arbitrator Marshall T. Seidman in *Trans-City Terminal Warehouse*[53] reinstated a grievant because the discharge was based on evidence of deceit while answering questions about matters not relevant to the theft of some television equipment and cash that was involved in the investigation. The polygrapher had asked questions about "some nuts, bolts and a lock and key" and answers to these irrelevant questions produced some deceptive reactions. The arbitrator ignored these findings of deception. He was either giving them no weight (1) because the deception did not prove a stealing that justified a discharge or (2) because the polygrapher had "fished" into matters irrelevant to the investigation or (3) because the grievant had cooperated in taking the test and his denials with any involvement with the particular theft had been corroborated by the examiner.

In the same vein, Arbitrator David Dolnick in *Purolator Armored,*

[51]*Id.* at 1162.
[52]61 LA 549, 556 (Laughlin, 1973).
[53]77 LA 11 (Seidman, 1981).

Inc.[54] dealt with an employee who would have been recalled from a lay-off if he had passed a polygraph test. The employee had been asked questions about activity during the lay-off period and the examiner reported that the grievant gave some false answers to certain such questions. Since the questions were not relevant to any theft or misconduct that affected the employer, the reported deceptions were irrelevant and did not constitute a "just cause" to support a failure to recall, the arbitrator said.

> [I]f the Company had the unrestricted right to require that recalled employees take polygraph examinations, that right would not only have to be reasonably exercised, but the circumstances would need to show that the employee in question had committed some act of moral turpitude . . . .
>
>   . . .
>
>   . . . The Company has not shown by good and substantial evidence that there is just and proper cause for denying recall rights to the grievant.[55]

Deception *per se* is not a misconduct that justifies discipline. However, when the deception impeaches a denial of theft or misconduct, it may cause the arbitrator to confirm the discipline. Arbitrator Charles Laughlin in *Bowman Transportation, Inc.*[56] struggled with the "weight" he should give some testimony that made it clear the polygrapher had probed some private matters that were unrelated to the company's business, and concluded the investigation had gone too far.

> Since the Company's requirement that the test be taken is not forbidden by positive law, the Company need not justify to the arbitrator what it intends to do with the result of the test. It is not the function of the arbitrator to tell the Company how to run its business. But when the requirement that the test be taken gets dangerously near the employee's interest in his privacy, the Company should have a reasonable basis for desiring to have the test to make its requirement reasonable.

The authority of arbitrators to reduce the "weight" of the polygrapher's testimony permits them to blend that evidence with other evidence that has been presented as they resolve the corroboration problems. Arbitrator James C. Vadakin in *Bowman Transportation, Inc.*[57] stated:

> As a practical matter, arbitrators do sometimes permit compulsory polygraph testing, admit the test results as evidence, and place probative weight thereon.

---

[54] 80-2 ARB § 8409 (Dolnick, 1980).

[55] *Id.* at 4830, 4831.

[56] 61 LA 549, 557 (Laughlin, 1973).

[57] Award of August 28, 1974 (Vadakin), unreported, cited and quoted in *Bowman Transportation, Inc.*, 64 LA 453 (Hon, 1975).

A careful reading of reported decisions would indicate that arbitrators uniformly regard the results of a polygraph examination, standing alone, as not being of sufficient weight to result in a finding of guilty. But these same decisions, either by inference or direct language, also affirm that, in conjunction with other evidence, polygraph tests results may be accorded probative value, as determined by the arbitrator.

From this section's discussion of what arbitrators do with the testimony of a polygrapher after they have accepted the testimony, it should be clear that such testimony is only one factor that is evaluated by the arbitrator.[58]

IS ACCEPTANCE OF POLYGRAPH EVIDENCE BENEFICIAL OR DETRIMENTAL TO THE TRIER OF FACT?

Some arbitrators have said that making credibility determinations simply by observing the attitude or the demeanor of the witness (sometimes called "eyeball" contact) is a process that is quite shaky. Arbitrator Samuel H. Jaffee in *Golden Pride, Inc.*[59] aptly explained:

I have in 55 years presented or heard (mostly heard) evidence in some 3,000 or more disputes, during which many thousands of witnesses testified. I have long been of the opinion that the "attitude and demeanor" of witnesses is almost always a shaky foundation on which to rest conclusions. I have seen witnesses whose nervousness or other physical manifestations while testifying (or listening to testimony) seemed more conducive to lying, and others who spoke "forthrightly" and made "eyeball contact" with their opponents, and yet the former told the truth while the latter did not.

Arbitrator Edgar Jones would judge it differently. In his lengthy paper wherein he recommends against the acceptance of a polygrapher's testimony in arbitration, he states that arbitrators should not hear such testimony because they do not need it or because they would be confused by it. He said:

---

[58]Arbitration cases in which arbitrators have accepted the testimony of the polygrapher but have given it weight at their discretion include the following: *B. F. Goodrich Tire Co.*, 36 LA 552 (Ryder, 1961); *Lag Drug Co.*, 39 LA 1121 (Kelliher, 1962); *Wilkof Steel & Supply*, 39 LA 883 (Maxwell, 1962); *Illinois Bell Telephone Co.*, 39 LA 470 (Ryder, 1962); *Dayton Steel Foundry Co.*, 39 LA 745, 746–47 (Porter, 1962); *Westinghouse Electric Corp.*, 43 LA 450 (Singletary, 1964); *McDonnell Aircraft Corp.*, 66-1 ARB 8236 (McKenna, 1965); *Saveway Inwood Service Station*, 44 LA 709 (Kornblum, 1965); *Koppers Co. Inc.*, 68-1 ARB 8084 (Kates, 1967); *Owens-Corning Fiberglass Corp.*, 48 LA 1089 (Doyle, 1967); *American-Maize Products Co.*, 56 LA 421 (Larkin, 1971); *Grocers Supply Co., Inc.*, 59 LA 1280 (Taylor, 1972); *Southern Biscuit Co.*, 74-2 ARB 8385 (Brewer, 1974); *Bowman Transportation, Inc.*, 64 LA 453 (Hon, 1975); *Daystrom Furniture Co., Inc.*, 65 LA 1157 (Laughlin, 1975); *Golden Pride, Inc.*, 68 LA 1232, 1235 (Jaffee, 1977); *Distribution Center of Atlanta*, 80-1 ARB 8131 (Amis, 1980); *Purolator Armored, Inc.*, 80-2 ARB ¶ 8409 (Dolnick, 1980); *Trans-City Terminal Warehouse*, 77 LA 11 (Seidman, 1981).

[59]68 LA 1232, 1235 (Jaffee, 1977).

When I remarked some time ago to my friend and fellow arbitrator, one of the real pros, Pat Fisher, on the difficulties, even the impossibility, of determining with assurance who is and who is not telling the truth under oath, he grinned characteristically and said, "Well, I may not know who is telling the truth, but I know whom I believe." That is a piece of arbitral wisdom that is worth some reflection relative to the crucial distinction between the making of findings of fact and the "ascertainment of the truth."[60]

He stated that arbitrators could make decisions on credibility more accurately by simply observing the witnesses' attitude and demeanor than by also having polygraph test information.

We have recently been told that persons unconsciously use their eyes, their arms and legs, their voices, even their bodily attitudes in non-verbal, even unrealized ways of communicative significance. It may be, it is even suggested, that each of us radiates a constantly active and changing personal "aura" composed of electrical and "auroral" fields that are somehow communicative in nature. . . .

Now . . . who needs a polygraph? We've got Pat Fisher and his peers! The informed-hunch judgments of the arbitrator and the trial judge . . . would be vindicated! . . .

The problems of credibility are assuredly real. But I fear that the willingness of my colleague, Professor Charles Craver of U. C. Davis, to substitute the polygraph, itself an imperfect and subjectively operated instrument, for the time-immemorial groping efforts of triers of fact to separate honest from dishonest accounts is to despair of the imperfections of the human situation, a dangerous state of mind to slip into our compulsively technological era."[61] [Footnotes omitted.]

Since arbitrators can listen to a polygrapher's testimony in addition to making their own observations, and then conclude what "weight" they will give the test results after blending in their intuitions ("attitude and demeanor" reactions), the testimony of a qualified polygrapher should, on balance, be an aid to arbitrators rather than confusing them. The blending of such testimony with the other evidence was explained by Arbitrator Samuel S. Kates in *Koppers Co., Inc:*[62]

Mere number of witnesses on one side or the other does not determine the truth when conflicting stories are told. The arbitrator, as trier of the facts, must seek to find the truth from the credible evidence. The personal interest of the witnesses is a factor to be taken into account, as also must the nature of their testimony, their demeanor on the witness stand, whether the attendant circumstances support or impeach their testimony, and all the other factors appearing in evidence which have the effect of persuading the trier of the facts as to just what did happen.

---

[60]Jones, note 2 *supra* at pp. 128–129.
[61]*Id*. at pp. 129–130.
[62]68-1 ARB ¶ 8084 at 3307 (Kates, 1967).

With respect to the polygraph (lie detector) test given to supervisor [H.], I consider the results of that test to be one element tending to support [H.'s] story.

This explanation by Arbitrator Kates also reveals the fact that arbitrators are not awed or dominated by the testimony of a polygrapher. Another trier-of-fact who was not overawed was the judge in *United States v. Lanza*.[63] John E. Reid was the polygrapher appearing as an expert witness. He concluded the witness had told the truth, but the judge said "no." The defendant had been charged with improper gambling loans; John Reid had read the indictment and based thereon set up a series of critical questions; but the judge said this series had not been well designed. The judge said when the word "illegal," (a word that mixes law and fact concepts), is in a critical question, and when the word "gave" money rather than the word "loaned" was used in critical questions, the testee finds it difficult to answer without qualification.

I did loan the money to him, but I didn't do it for gambling purposes or illegal purposes.[64]

The Judge concluded that these responses were "clouded," and the reaction to these answers could have meant that the defendant was apprehensive about the question or simply did not understand it. Reid concluded the defendant told the truth but the judge decided he had not.

On cross-examination Reid admitted that in his book, Truth and Deception, it is stated that an examiner ought to have all the available facts and circumstances giving rise to the charge against his subject before administering a lie detector test.[65]

The accuracy of the conclusions of polygraphers in percentage terms has often been averaged and reported.[66] Average percentages may mean little in a particular case because no expert witness can prove in advance that his or her conclusions are always 100 percent accurate. If 100 percent accuracy were the rule, no expert witness could

---

[63] 356 F. Supp. 27 (M.D. Fla. 1973).

[64] *Id.* at 32.

[65] *Id.* at 31.

[66] Both empirical and experimental research have been conducted concerning the accuracy of the conclusions of examiners using polygraph detection of deception techniques. Reported by Larson, Trovillo, Cureton, Horvath and Reid, Slowik and Buckley, and Raskin, Barland and Podlesny to name a few. In essence, the reported research was effective in the detection of deception ranging from 64% to 100% and was influenced by the research methodology, number of subjects, field or clinical settings, and sophistication of the researchers." [Footnotes omitted.] Romig, note 4 *supra* at p. 3.

ever testify.[67] The accuracy in a polygrapher's conclusions will vary depending on his or her training and experience and depending on the clarity of the critical questions that he or she has prepared in the particular case. The most significant fact, however, is that the arbitrator is still not bound to accept the polygrapher's conclusions because this expert witness testimony is to assist the arbitrator to make a credibility determination, and the arbitrator weighs all the evidence as he or she decides. The arbitrator can give the conclusions of the polygrapher full weight, small weight, or simply ignore them.

Possibly, a discussion about tight hearsay limitations by Arbitrator Ernst E. Marlatt in *Baker Marine Corp.*[68] belongs in Chapter XII, "Rules of Evidence."[69] However, it is reported here to point up the difference between hearsay limitations in a jury trial in a criminal case and in labor arbitration; in the latter, the arbitrator believes he or she has the right to "weigh" evidence (*exclude* all or accept *some* or *all*), just as other arbitrators have said they should accept and then "weigh" the testimony of a polygrapher. In this case, written reports had been submitted by an investigator about the use of marijuana in the plant, but after the professional investigator had been discovered to be the "informer," he felt impelled to quit for reasons of personal safety. The company could not locate him and hence was unable to ask him to be a witness. The arbitrator accepted the investigator's written reports and explained his reasons:

> The Company offered evidence of having made a good faith effort to secure the presence of Mr. [M——] as a witness in this arbitration, but found that he had since left his employment with the Security Service and had moved away from the area to points unknown. The Company thereby offered in evidence a report made by [M——] to the Company on May 13, 1980, which formed the basis of the Company's decision to discharge the Grievant. The union vigorously objected to the admission of this document in evidence on the grounds of hearsay.[70]

The arbitrator then discussed the application of formal rules of evidence in arbitration proceedings:

> Therefore, if this evidence had been offered in a court of law, the judge would have no choice but to exclude it upon proper objection. The question to be decided is whether, or perhaps to what extent, an arbitrator is bound by the rules of evidence which prevail in the courts. The profession

---

[67]In *United States v. De Betham*, 348 F. Supp. 1377, 1387 (D.C. Cal. 1972), the court said that 90 percent of the conclusions of a qualified polygrapher are considered accurate and that infallability by an expert witness is not a requirement for general admissibility.

[68]77 LA 721 (Marlatt, 1981).

[69]*See* discussion in text associated with nn. 36–39 in Chapter XII.

[70]77 LA at 722.

of arbitration is dominated by lawyers who, like myself, tend to think in terms of the familiar, and who find the formal rules of evidence a comfortable backstop when called upon to rule on objections. Edgar A. Jones, Jr., the president of the National Academy of Arbitrators, expressed the general opinion of arbitrators everywhere when he said of hearsay evidence, "Unless corroborated by truth-tending circumstances in the environment in which it was uttered, it is unreliable evidence and should be received with mounting skepticism of its probative value the more remote and filtered it appears to be." (Quoted from Jones, "Evidentiary Concepts in Labor Arbitration," UCLA Law Review 13 (1966) at p. 1278.)[71]

A subsequent comment by Arbitrator Marlatt appears to be a criticism of the view that exclusion of evidence is being recommended by Arbitrator Edgar A. Jones, Jr. because the arbitrator does not have the skill to sort out the different material evidence he may receive (see prior comment in contrast to the following):

> I think, however, that the arbitrator who tries to fit the hearing within the concepts designed for the law courts does a disservice to the parties. Rules of evidence were developed over the years on the implied assumption that the jury in a court consists of people who are not particularly bright. . . . Arbitrators, by training, are presumably better qualified to evaluate the weight of hearsay evidence and put it somewhere on the spectrum between "strongly persuasive" and "vicious gossip." It stands to reason that the more the arbitrator can learn about the facts, the more likely his award will result in a fair and just decision. For this reason, the arbitrator ought not totally to exclude any offered evidence unless it is clearly irrelevant or immaterial to any genuine issue in the case. . . .
>
> I am very conscious of the fact, which the Union stresses in its brief, that it has been deprived of the opportunity to cross-examine Mr. [M——] (the investigator who submitted the written reports) and thereby perhaps to impeach his very serious accusations against the Grievant. All that a fair and conscientious arbitrator can do under these circumstances is to scrutinize the hearsay evidence very closely, *and to give it little or no weight if there is any indication that the evidence is untruthful, misleading, or biased.*[72] [Emphasis added.]

Hence, Arbitrator Marlatt subscribes to the view of those arbitrators who conclude that total exclusion of evidence in labor arbitration is unwise because exclusion may eliminate *all* illumination, and that since arbitrators have the right to determine the "weight" they will give to the evidence they will accept, they may obtain some needed illumination and have the skill to sort out evidence without becoming confused as might an unskilled jury. This is the same view of those arbitrators who accept the testimony of a qualified polygrapher, believ-

---

[71]*Id.* at 722–23.
[72]*Id.* at 723.

ing they can sort out the evidence without becoming confused as might a jury, and that exclusion may injure a grievant's ability to rebut a *prima facie* case and possibly deny to the arbitrators themselves the needed "illumination."

Arbitrator Hon in *Bowman Transportation, Inc.*[73] quoted a judge's explanation that collateral evidence presented to the trier of fact to assist in resolving conflicts in testimony is often of dubious value. This judge said he wanted assistance from a neutral third party—a trained polygrapher.

"Every day courts are filled with witnesses who color the facts everywhere from exaggeration to perjury. Any experienced trial judge or courtroom attorney will privately admit that perjury is the best defense there is.

"So, historically, Courts have admitted a variety of collateral issues in evidence on the theory that they have a bearing on credibility. Unchastity of a rape victim, conviction for a prior crime, any degrading or unfavorable act from the witness' past, even one's reputation in the community for truthfulness, all of these have been allowed in evidence as guides to the believability of the one testifying. We allow these collateral matters in evidence on the questions of credibility, know that they are of dubious value, because they are the only things the courts have to go on in this field.

"Compare these with lie detector evidence. Here we have a scientific test of proven value, administered by a trained examiner who is, like the court, a neutral third party. His aim, like that of the Court, is the same—a search for the truth."[74]

Another observer summarized:

If the judicial system is to fulfill its duty of searching for truth and maintaining integrity, it must commence a war against perjury. The war cannot be won with weapons restricted to cross-examination, inferences from demeanor, and other relics from the crossbow era of Henry II.[75] [Footnote omitted.]

There are many examples of cases where the trier of fact improperly convicted a defendant because of perjured evidence he or she could not detect; the subsequent confessions show how unexpert the credibility resolution had been.[76]

---

[73]64 LA 453 (Hon, 1975).

[74]*Id.* at 457, quoting from a family court case, *A.v.B.,* 72 Misc. 2d 719, 336 N.Y.S. 2d 839 (1972).

[75]Tarlow, *Admissibility of Polygraph Evidence in 1975; An Aid in Determining Credibility in a Perjury-Plagued System,* 26 HASTINGS L. J. 920 (1975).

[76]To illustrate the difficulty of making credibility determination, the following reversals have occurred when an error in the determination came to light: *Napue v. Illinois,* 360 U.S. 264 (1959) (murder conviction reversed, principal prosecution witness committed perjury); *Mesarosh v. United States,* 352 U.S. 1 (1952) (conviction reversed, principal witness committed per-

POLYGRAPHER TESTIMONY TO
CORROBORATE OR IMPEACH TESTIMONY

It is well established that an arbitrator should not rely on a polygrapher's testimony as proof that the grievant is guilty or innocent, but that such testimony should be used to corroborate or impeach the testimony of the grievant or other witnesses.

Arbitrator Ralph T. Seward in *Bethlehem Steel Corp., Burns Harbor Plant*,[77] would not accept the testimony of a polygrapher when he testified that the grievant had assaulted a fellow employee; the polygrapher was testifying because he had tested the fellow employee and found her story to be true. The polygrapher had not testified to corroborate the story of the witness because she was not there. Polygraphers cannot testify as some type of *alter ego* to the absent witness. The company had discharged the grievant on the grounds she had assaulted the fellow employee in the women's locker room but under a long-standing company policy one unit employee could not be asked by the company to testify "against" another. For this reason the company attempted to have the polygrapher tell the story.

The arbitrator said that the failure of the fellow employee to testify about the attack meant that no *prima face* case had been established. Testimony by an examiner did not set up the needed facts. The grievant testified she had not assaulted anyone.

Arbitrator Charles Laughlin in *Bowman Transportation, Inc.*[78] supported Arbitrator Seward's view that the testimony of a polygrapher is presented merely to assist the arbitrator with credibility problems:

Notwithstanding the greater reliability of polygraphs to establish truth than to establish falsity, they have been recently accepted for both pur-

---

jury in several instances); *Hysler v. Florida*, 315 U.S. 411 (1942) (denial of rehearing on writ of error *corum nobis, affirmed*, where proof of perjury inconclusive); *United States v. Basurto*, 497 F.2d 781 (9th Cir. 1974) (conviction reversed, government's chief witness committed perjury before grand jury); *United States v. Chisum*, 436 F.2d 645 (9th Cir. 1971) (narcotics conviction reversed when narcotics agents, who were principal witnesses, were convicted of perjury); *United States v. Polisi*, 416 F.2d 573 (2d Cir. 1969) (robbery conviction reversed, principal government witness committed perjury); *Curran v. Delaware*, 259 F.2d 707 (3rd Cir. 1958) (habeas corpus granted as to murder conviction when officers destroyed defendant's statements and perjured themselves by claiming that no such exculpatory statements had been made); *Gondron v. United States*, 242 F.2d 149 (5th Cir. 1957) (conviction reversed, government agreed that key witness testified falsely. The court in *Commonwealth v. Vitello*, 376 Mass. 426, 381 N.E. 2d 582 (1978), reported in the decision a statement on polygraph testing reported in a previous decision of the same court, *Commonwealth v. A Juvenile*, 365 Mass. 421, 313 NE.2d 120 (1974). In *Vitello* the court stated "a majority of the court recognized that a properly conducted test had potential value 'as an aid to determining whether an individual is telling the truth.' " *Commonwealth v. Vitello*, 381 N.E.2d at 585, quoting *Commonwealth v. A Juvenile*, 365 Mass. at 429, 313 N.E.2d at 126.

[77]68 LA 581 (Seward, 1977).
[78]61 LA 549 (Laughlin, 1973).

poses. Walther v. O'Connell, 72 Misc. 2d 316, 339 N.Y.S. 2d 386 (1972) was a suit for money loaned. The case turned out to be a one against one question of belief. Plaintiff testified he loaned the money, defendant denied it. To solve said impasse the Judge ordered both parties to take a polygraph test. The power of the Judge to make the order was not adjudicated because after the order was entered the parties agreed to the tests. The tests both sustained the plaintiff and refuted the defendant. The case was decided accordingly. In United States v. Hart, 344 F. Supp. 522 (E. Dist., N.Y., 1971), the principle witness for the prosecution inadvertently admitted having taken a polygraph test. The court required the prosecution to reveal the results of the test which were unfavorable to the witness.[79]

Arbitrator Laughlin also explained why the testimony of a polygrapher should only be used to corroborate or impeach the testimony of other witnesses:

So far as the union's hearsay argument is concerned, it makes a difference how the test is used. If the test is used in favor of the person tested a hearsay problem would be involved only if the tested person did not appear as a witness. If a transcript of the answers given while under examination should be offered, a true hearsay problem would be involved. If, as would be the proper procedure, the tested person appears as a witness, it is his testimony, which is not hearsay, which is considered. The polygraph test is used merely as corroboration.

The union hearsay objection to compelling a person to take the test is likely based upon the possibility that there is danger of the results being used against the examinee. A hypothetical situation will illustrate this point. An employee is suspected of theft. He denies the theft but the results of a polygraph test cast doubt upon the veracity of his denial. If he is discharged and a grievance proceeding follows and the employer offers the answers given in the test and the operator's interpretation of the machine's recordings relative to those answers, a problem of relevancy (circumstantial evidence and reliability) is presented but not a problem of either hearsay or confrontation. The record of statements made by the person while being examined are not offered to prove the truth of the matters asserted in those statements, quite the contrary. The fact that the statements were made is the significant thing. Thus there is no hearsay problem. Neither is there a problem of confrontation because the person examined may cross examine the operator who conducted the test and the witness who now offers to interpret the results. The question is whether the employee's assertion of innocence, combined with the results of the test which tend to question his veracity, is proper evidence of guilt. This is a question of relevancy.[80]

[79]Id. at 553.
[80]Id.

Corroboration of a Supervisor's Story

Arbitrator Larkin in *American Maize Products Co.*[81] reported that the company had the foreman take a polygraph examination given by a qualified examiner because, during the grievance procedure meetings, the grievant had flatly contradicted the foreman. The company representative had the foreman tested because he wanted to be certain that the foreman was not overstating the truth; the representative also asked the grievant to agree to be examined, but on advice of the union representative he declined. Arbitrator Larkin wrote:

> When the accuser and the accused are each telling a story which flatly contradicts the other, it is not always easy to determine which one is telling the truth. At times it is possible to find circumstantial evidence which corroborates one or the other, or lends credence to one of the conflicting stories. In the instant case, the Company decided to rely on polygraph examinations which, on the advice of the Union, the grievant declined to take. Since it is clear from the record that the decision to change the grievant's suspension to a discharge was predicated solely upon the report of the polygraph examiner, the arbitrator deemed it necessary to make this "Laboratory Report" a part of this record, even though the Union has entered strong objections.[82]

The grievant had no evidence to rebut the presumption supporting the foreman's story that was confirmed by the testing, and Arbitrator Larkin supported the discharge.

Arbitrator Samuel S. Kates in *Koppers Co., Inc.*[83] discussed the polygraph evidence in a case involving an assault of two grievants on the foreman.

> The Company proposed to the Union that lie detector tests be taken by [H.] [the foreman], [M.] and [D.] [the two employees the foreman said attacked him]. The Union left the decision on this to the individuals involved. [H.] took such a test conducted by the polygraph expert of the Allegheny County District Attorney's office. [M.] and [D.] refused to take the test on advice of counsel.[84]

The arbitrator explained the positions of the examiner and the parties:

> The polygraph expert, whose qualifications were conceded, testified in detail as to the results of the lie detector test given [H.]. The results of the

---

[81]56 LA 421 (Larkin, 1971).
[82]*Id.* at 423.
[83]68-1 ARB ¶ 8084 (Kates, 1967).
[84]*Id.* at p. 3307.

test showed that [H.] sincerely believed the truth of his identification of [M.] and [D.] as the two who had attacked him.

. . .

The Union contends in effect that the Company has not carried its burden of proving that [M.] and [D.] were the two men who attacked [H.]; that, in fact, [G.'s] testimony and the testimony of the grievants and Mrs. [M.] and [C.'s] affidavit affirmatively show that they were not the guilty persons.

The Company contends in effect that the credible evidence clearly established the guilt of the two grievants.[85]

The Arbitrator then said with regard to the polygrapher's testimony:

With respect to the polygraph (lie detector) test given to supervisor [H.], I consider the results of the test to be one element tending to support [H.'s] story.[86]

Arbitrator Reynold C. Seitz in *Johnson & Johnson*[87] sustained the discharge of employee V—— because he had become involved in a kickback scheme with Foreman B——. B—— would credit eight employees with overtime hours they did not work and then would receive regular kickbacks out of excess payments. B—— and six employees quickly resigned; two others were discharged and became grievants. Before the arbitration hearing one grievant withdrew, leaving only Grievant V——.

Prior to the arbitration hearing, B—— (the foreman) was asked by the company representation to have his statements concerning the kickback scheme in which he was involved tested with a polygraph examination. The examiner reported that B——'s story was truthful. There was substantial evidence that Employee V—— was also involved and hence Arbitrator Seitz explained the polygraph corroboration of Foreman B——'s admission and the foreman's testimony about the Grievant to the effect that V—— had participated in the kickback plan. He explained:

The company attempted to corroborate the testimony of [B——] which implicated [V——] by submitting the testimony at the hearing of an expert who had administered a lie detector test to [B——] shortly before the arbitration hearing. The test did indicate that [B——] was telling the truth. It was clear that the man who administered the test was truly very well qualified by training and experience as a polygraph expert. . . . I find it unnecessary to rely on the test . . . except to note that the company seemed con-

---

[85]*Id.*
[86]*Id.*
[87]AAA Case No. 51, 30-001 69 (Seitz, 1969).

vinced enough of the truth of [B——'s] story to take the risk of subjecting him to a lie detector test.[88]

Because the Company asked the ex-foreman to take a test, Arbitrator Seitz said his confidence in his finding of V——'s guilt increased because it was clear the company representatives were concerned about the accuracy of the ex-foreman's testimony.

Another use of polygraph testing of a foreman occurred in *Coronet Phosphate Co.*[89] Arbitrator James C. Vadakin explained in his award:

> The Company introduced the results of a lie detector test administered to Foreman Brown in corroboration of his testimony concerning the incidents of both May 17th and May 25th. . . . The arbitrator, in his discretion, allowed this to be entered.[90]

Corroborating Testimony of Employees

Arbitrator Arthur R. Porter in *Dayton Steel & Foundry Co.*[91] sustained a discharge of a grievant because he was the aggressor in a fight with another employee in the washroom. No one observed the fight. The company offered both individuals the opportunity of taking a polygraph test; the dischargee—the grievant—refused to take the test, whereas his adversary agreed to take it. Arbitrator Porter reported:

> [S——] voluntarily took a polygraph test covering the incidents of the fight. The testimony of the expert ". . . revealed that [S——] . . . was telling the truth . . . ." The Examiner was Captain R. C. Grundish of the City of Dayton Police Detective Bureau, who is qualified to use the polygraph machine. N—— C—— refused to take the test.
>
> . . .
>
> There is no evidence from a witness who saw the fight. No one observed the two men in the shower room; the evidence supporting the story of [S——] is indirect. Impressions from the hearing and the results of the polygraph examination may have played a role in the decision of the arbitrator, although an effort has been made to rule only on the basis of the factors that have been described and analyzed.[92]

Arbitrator James P. Whyte handled the *Bowman Transportation, Inc.*[93] case involving a polygraph examination which had been given to Assistant Driver P—— to determine whether P——'s statements that

---

[88]*Id.*

[89]31 LA 515 (Vadakin, 1958).

[90]*Id.* at 519.

[91]39 LA 745 (Porter, 1962).

[92]*Id.* at 746–47.

[93]Award of September 11, 1974 (Whyte), unreported, cited and quoted in 64 LA 453 (Hon, 1975).

Driver B—— had been drinking while driving a truck were truthful. When the safety supervisor asked B—— to take a polygraph test as well, he refused, saying that such tests "were for hoodlums and murderers" and that by asking him to take such a test, "the company was impugning his integrity." P——, on the other hand, cooperated by taking the test, and passed. Arbitrator Whyte said he accepted the testimony of the assistant driver because the examiner concluded he was truthful.

> As to the weight to be given the polygraph examination insofar as it tended to collaborate [P——'s] testimony, it may be briefly stated that it is fully credited. But this may be as much due to the intrinsic merit of [P——'s] testimony as to anything else.[94]

Rebutting Theft Presumptions

Arbitrator Doyle in *Owens-Corning Fiberglass Corp.*[95] reinstated a grievant who had been discharged when some company goods were found in his automobile. The guards had "looked in" after receiving a telephone tip. The normal presumption operated against the grievant (without some rebuttal his discharge would undoubtedly have been sustained), but he took a polygraph test and the polygraph examiner reported that the grievant's denial that he was not involved with the theft was truthful. Arbitrator Doyle said that after the examiner testified that the grievant had passed the truth test, the rebuttable presumption was rebutted. He said the facts in the record were then "as consistent with innocence as with guilt" and the grievant was reinstated.

Without strong alibi witnesses available, an innocent grievant may find his or her discharge sustained by an arbitrator because of a presumption arising out of possession of stolen property. The grievant may have no defensive testimony except his or her own denial with which to rebut the presumption and to shift the burden back to the company. Taking a "truth test" conducted by a qualified examiner may well be the grievant's only way to rebut such a presumption.

In a case handled by Arbitrator Theodore K. High, *Nettle Creek Industries,*[96] the grievant took the polygraph test hoping that her story would stand up and she could thus rebut a presumption of theft based on her having company property in her purse. But her story did not stand up under testing. A union steward had come to the supervisor and reported that another employee had said that the grievant had

---

[94]*Id.*, quoted, by Arbitrator Hon, 64 LA at 456.
[95]48 LA 1089 (Doyle, 1967).
[96]70 LA 100 (High, 1978).

taken two spools of thread, had placed them in her purse, and was leaving the plant. The supervisor telephoned the personnel manager, who then pursued the grievant towards the door of the parking lot. She was asked to step back to the lounge area and open her purse. Two spools of thread were found in her purse. The Grievant denied any knowledge of how the spools got there. The following Monday the Supervisor advised her to attend a meeting with the Personnel Manager and there she was asked if she would take a lie detector test. She agreed. The following morning the personnel manager, the grievant and the local union president drove to Indianapolis, where the head of the Indiana Research Association administered the test. The grievant did not pass the test, and based on the examiner's report and the presence of the spools of thread in the grievant's purse she was terminated.

At the arbitration hearing, the grievant took the stand and testified that at the time in question she heard the first bell prior to the end of the shift, reached down for some money and discovered that her wallet was in the bin under the table, next to her purse. She testified that she picked up the wallet, took out the money she needed for a phone call and dropped the wallet into her purse without looking into the purse. She testified that she was surprised later to find the two spools of thread in her purse and that she had no idea how they got there, saying that when she looked in her purse she had told the supervisor, "I ain't going to lie; I don't know how it got there."

The grievant made no claim that someone might have attempted to plant the spools of thread in her purse but did say that some girls were jealous because of her seniority. The grievant did admit that she used the same type of thread on a machine in her home.

The polygraph operator was called as an expert witness. He described his professional qualifications, the manner in which he conducted tests generally and the manner in which he conducted the specific test given the grievant. The polygrapher testified that the grievant's explanation that she did not know how the spools got in her purse was not truthful. Arbitrator High stated that he added the polygraph evidence to the other evidence, testimony of the eyewitness, who came forward at the hearing, and it assisted him to conclude that the grievant's statement was not truthful.

> The Union does not challenge the qualifications of the polygraph operator who administered the test. To the contrary, it accepts the qualifications, but objects to receiving the evidence of the polygraph operator. The objection to the evidence was overruled until such time as the parties had had an opportunity to brief the issue.
> Generally, arbitrators have held that the results of polygraph tests should be given little weight. This is particularly true where the polygraph test is the primary evidence relied upon in the discharge of an employee.

Some arbitrators, however, have considered the results of lie detector tests where those results corroborate direct evidence of innocence or guilt of the Grievant. It should be emphasized that this consideration of such evidence is given where the evidence corroborates other evidence. As the Union points out in this case, the Company's decision to discharge the Grievant was based primarily upon the results of the polygraph test and finding the spools in Grievant's purse.[97] [Citations and footnote omitted.]

Rebutting Eyewitness Testimony

If a foreman testified that he saw one of the employees under his supervision engage in misconduct—to illustrate, place some valuable company property in a box subsequently taken to the parking lot—but the employee denied the misconduct, the problem for the arbitrator is whether the eyewitness should or should not be believed. If a polygrapher tested the foreman and then the employee, both could conceivably pass the test: the foreman may believe he saw the particular employee engage in the misconduct, while the employee could respond truthfully that he did not do what the foreman said he did. He also could pass the test.

The observations of eyewitnesses are not infallible. Arbitrator Murphy in *Bowman Transportation, Inc.*[98] pointed this out by incorporating in an award some comments from F. Lee Bailey's *The Defense Never Rests,*[99] about a man accused of rape who had been "identified" by the girl and the boy companion. The only way to avoid imprisonment was to prove that the identification by the two eyewitnesses was erroneous, and this rebuttal could be done only by a polygraph examination. The accused agreed with the police to take a polygraph test, but no such test was taken. A "highly experienced examiner," arranged for by Bailey, reported that the accused "doesn't know anything about the affair."[100] The trial proceeded and the defendant's examiner was not permitted to testify. Arbitrator Murphy reported that among the polygraph authorities Mr. Bailey used in the case was an army polygraph examiner who had protected many GIs from arrest and court-martial by giving "polygraph tests all over the world."[101] In more than twenty years, the army examiner said, he could not recall a single case in which a suspect, cleared by a test, had subsequently been prosecuted in a military court. Arbitrator Murphy then incor-

---

[97]*Id.* at 102.

[98]59 LA 283 (Murphy, 1972).

[99]F. Lee Bailey with Harvey Aronson, (New York: Stein and Day, 1971).

[100]59 LA at 291, quoting from Bailey, note 99 *supra,* at p. 37.

[101]*Id.,* quoting from Bailey, note 99 *supra,* at p. 43.

porated Bailey's subsequent comment of frustration on the exclusion of polygraph testing when it is not agreed upon by the prosecutor:

> "I looked from one to the other and thought about what that moment meant. If the testimony of these men couldn't win the polygraph its rightful place in our system of jurisprudence, whose could? And failure could mean that Willard Page and others like him—men who should never have been brought to trial in the first place—might spend years locked away from the world. And where, then, on God's green earth was justice?"[102]

In addition, Arbitrator Murphy explained that the district attorney's office in Orange County, California, has a standing policy—any defendant who takes and passes a polygraph test will be excused, regardless of whether an eyewitness claims to have seen the defendant engage in the crime. One defendant, accused of robbery after identification by eyewitnesses, was dismissed after the examiner stated that his denial was true.[103] What happens in the district attorney's office in Orange County is not so different from what happens when an employee is summoned into an industrial relations office and shown statements and documentary evidence that leads to charges of being a thief, of involvement with a theft, or of misconduct. In these cases the employee will deny the charge. However, if the company representatives have collected statements from one or more "eyewitnesses" (often the foreman), the employee's denial will rarely be believed and the company's belief will tend to harden once a grievance has been filed and the case moves up step by step to arbitration. Arbitrator Charles Laughlin in another *Bowman Transportation, Inc.*[104] case pointed out that a grievant may be exonerated if the polygrapher corroborates his story.

> There are several legitimate reasons why the Company may want the polygraph test to be taken. First, there is always the chance that the test may exonerate the grievant. Although that is principally a concern of the grievant, the Company has a legitimate interest in establishing the honesty of its employees. Allen Industries, 26 LA 363 (1956). A sizeable theft occurred of an especially sensitive type of cargo. Not only the Company but the general public has an interest in determining who was guilty.

---

[102]*Id.* In *United States v. De Betham*, 348 F. Supp. 1377, 1385 (S.D. Cal. 1972) it was stated that the accuracy of polygraph testing was "substantial," and that the percentage of accuracy may be higher than that for eyewitness observations.

[103]*People v. Cutler,* No. A-176965, 12 CrL 2133 (Sup. Ct. Los Angeles County, Cal., Nov. 6, 1972); testimony of Fred Martin, former chief polygrapher of the Orange County District Attorney's office. Polygraph testing is also used in district attorneys' offices in New York City and in more than 30 other cities. Jones, note 2 *supra,* at p. 82, n. 9.

[104]61 LA 549, 557 (Laughlin, 1973).

The Unfair Representation Risk: A *Caveat*

Union representatives often object to the use of polygraphers' testimony in labor arbitration because such use is contrary to union policy. However, *caveat emptor* (buyer beware) or more accurately *caveat veotor* (watch out for defects in policy). If a grievant asks the union representative to arrange for a truth test to rebut (1) inaccurate eyewitness evidence from a supervisor or (2) a theft "presumption" growing out of possession of company property or (3) some significant conflict in statements, and the union representative does not arrange for the test the grievant could quite properly file an unfair representation charge if the grievance is not upheld,[105] and the judge or the jury in such a case would undoubtedly conclude that the failure to have the test made to corroborate the grievant's denial was an "unfair representation," and the court would then order a polygraph examination to be administered.

In various cases discussed in this chapter, union representatives have encouraged employees to take a polygraph test. However, at least by reputation, unions do not favor polygraph testing in labor arbitration cases. District Judge Gordon Thompson, Jr., in *United States v. De Betham*[106] explained:

> Probably the largest active lobby against the use of the polygraph consists of organized labor, which has succeeded in its sponsorship of legislation in at least twelve states restricting or prohibiting mandatory polygraph examinations of job applicants or employees. The unions allege that such legislation is necessary to prevent the invasion of the employees' privacy. [Footnotes omitted.]

Duane Beeler, a union representative who wrote a book entitled *Discipline and Discharge*,[107] became supportive of Arbitrator Edgar

---

[105]*See* Chapter XXIII, "Fair Representation Obligations."

[106]348 F. Supp. 1377, 1390 (S.D. Cal. 1972), *aff'd,* 470 F.2d 1367, 1389 (9th Cir. 1972), cert. *denied* 412 U.S. 907 (1973).

[107]Cited in *Bunker Ramo Corp.,* 76 LA 857 (Hon, 1981). Clarence H. A. Romig wrote: "The increased use of the polygraph by the police and also in the business field drew the attention of the trade unions . . . . By the start of the 1970's, the AFL-CIO Maritime Trades Department published a series of reports on The Invasion of Privacy in America, with its first report entitled 'The Lie Detector, Guilty Until Proven Innocent.' " [Footnote omitted.] Romig, note 4 *supra,* at p. 4. The AFL-CIO Executive Council in 1965 mobilized against use of polygraphy. Arbitrator Charles Laughlin in *Bowman Transportation, Inc.* (61 LA 549, 554) quoted from the text of the AFL-CIO 1965 policy: " 'the use of lie detectors violates the basic consideration of human dignity in that they involve the invasion of privacy, self-incrimination, and the concept of guilt until proven innocent.' This report was adopted by the Executive Council is [sic] a resolution which states, 'We object to the use of these devices, not only because they infringe on the fundamental rights of American citizens to personal privacy.' " Arbitrator Edgar Jones wrote that unions uniformly object to admission of polygrapher testimony in labor arbitration hearings but that various labor unions have used polygraph testing in connection with internal investigations. Five

A. Jones' attack on the use of polygraphs. He applauded the paper with the comment that "Ted Jones' scintillating performance . . . personified—to me—*the last nail being driven in the coffin of the polygraph.*"[108] [Emphasis in original.] Arbitrator Hon, however, made this retort: "Beeler's conclusion may reflect an element of wishful thinking. . . ."[109]

ADMISSIBILITY OF POLYGRAPHER'S TESTIMONY IN CRIMINAL AND CIVIL COURTS

An arbitrator can accept the testimony of a polygrapher as an expert witness under the normal evidence rules applicable to such witnesses. Some arbitrators do[110] and some do not.[111] Those who do not have adopted a nonacceptability policy because they believe that such testimony is not accepted in courts, and hence should not be accepted in their arbitration hearings. Some of the arbitrators adopted this policy because other arbitrators have done so; whereas other arbitrators have probed into the criminal decisions and have read the *Frye v. United States* decision announced by the appellate court of the District of Columbia in 1923.[112]

As noted earlier, at the trial court level in this case Dr. William Marston, an early polygrapher, was asked to examine the defendant Frye, who was being tried for murder. Marston reported that from his

polygraphers conducted thirty-two separate lie-detector investigations for individuals working in or with local unions between 1960 and 1971. Jones, note 2 *supra* at p. 77, n. 2.

[108]Quoted in *Bunker Ramo Corp.*, 76 LA 857, 862 (Hon, 1981) in regard to Jones, note 2 *supra*.

[109]*Bunker Ramo Corp.*, 76 LA 857, 862 (Hon, 1981).

[110]*See* list of arbitrators in note 58 *supra*.

[111]In the awards set forth below the arbitrator denied admission of testimony of polygraphers as a matter of policy because they believed that such testimony would not be accepted in a criminal or civil trial. *Marathon Elec. Mfg. Co.*, 31 LA 1040 (Duff, 1959); *Publishers' Assn. of New York City*, 32 LA 44 (Simkin, 1959); *B.F. Goodrich Co.*, 36 LA 552 (Ryder, 1961); *Brass-Craft Mfg. Co.*, 36 LA 117 (Kahn, 1961); *Continental Air Transport Co.*, 39 LA 778 (Eiger, 1962); *Town & Country Food Co., Inc.*, 72-3 ARB ¶ 9054 (Lewis, 1962); *Skaggs-Stone, Inc.*, 40 LA 1273 (Koven, 1963); *United Mills, Inc.*, 63-1 ARB ¶ 8179 (Miller, 1963); *Sanna Daires, Inc.*, 43 LA 16 (Rice, 1964); *American Maize-Products Co.*, 45 LA 115 (Epstein, 1965); *McDonnell Aircraft*, 66-1 ARB ¶ 8236 (McKenna, 1965); *Spiegel, Inc.*, 44 LA 405 (Sembower, 1965); *Ramsey Steel Co.*, 66-1 ARB ¶ 8310 (Carmichael, 1966); *Kwik Kafeteria Inc.*, 66-1 ARB ¶ 8359 (Eiger, 1966); *Saveway Inwood Service Station*, 44 LA 709, 710–711 (Kornblum, 1967); *Art Carved, Inc.*, 70 LA 869 (Kramer, 1977); *Mount Sinai Hospital Medical Center*, 73 LA 297 (Dolnick, 1979); *Temtex Products, Inc.*, 75 LA 233 (Rimer, 1980); *Buy-Low*, 77 LA 380 (Dolnick, 1981). Other arbitrators have denied admission of the testimony of a polygrapher because they borrowed the stipulation agreement standard for acceptability in criminal courts. This rule developed after 1935 is discussed in the text associated with note 115. *See, e.g., Coronet Phosphate Co., Inc.*, 31 LA 515 (Vadakin, 1958); *Bethlehem Steel*, 68 LA 581 (Seward, 1977); *Golden Pride, Inc.*, 68 LA 1232 (Jaffee, 1977).

[112]293 F. 1013 (D.C. Cir. 1923).

tests Frye's denial of the murder was truthful.[113] The trial judge did not accept testimony from Marston, and the appellate court held that the judge's nonacceptance of this testimony was not error because Marston's polygraphic procedure was still within the experimental period of development. Frye was convicted, but unjustly, because three years later another individual confessed to the murder of which he had been convicted. Frye was vindicated and so were Marston's conclusions based on this early polygraph model.[114]

The articulation set forth by the appellate court in 1923 became known as the *Frye* standard for the acceptability of the testimony of a polygrapher as an expert witness in a court:

> Just when a scientific principle or discovery crosses the line between the *experimental* and *demonstrable states* is difficult to define. Somewhere in this twilight zone the evidential force of the principle must be recognized and while courts will go a long way in admitting expert testimony deduced from a well-organized scientific principle or discovery, the thing from which the deduction is made must be sufficiently established to have gained *general acceptance in the field* in which it belongs.[115] [Emphasis added.]

The *Frye* standard was then adopted by other courts including the Supreme Court of Massachusetts. In *Commonwealth v. Fatalo*[116] this court stated a similar articulation:

> Judicial acceptance of a scientific theory or instrument can occur only when it follows a general acceptance by the community or scientists involved.

These two articulations have sometimes been referred to as the *Frye-Fatalo* standard of acceptability. It appeared to be a simple test: A trial court should not accept the testimony of a polygrapher into the trial as an expert witness until polygraphy ceased to be an experimental procedure, i.e., ceased to be within the *twilight zone,* which meant that it would have gained general acceptance in the field in which polygraphy belongs. It was assumed that under this articulation there would be a "point in time" when the *twilight zone* would end and the *general acceptance* period would start. One also would assume that attorneys for defendants would want to have qualified polygraphers corroborate the defendants' denials in the trials just as the attorney for Frye wanted to have Marston corroborate Frye's denial at his trial.[117] As noted in *State v. Stanislawski,* [118] polygraphy was being used by the U.S. Army, U.S. Navy, police departments, prosecutors' offices, gov-

---

[113]*See* Romig, note 4 *supra*, at p. 2. *See also State v. Sims*, 52 Ohio Misc. 31, 369 N.E. 2d 24 (c.p. 1977).

[114]*Id.* at p. 2.

[115]293 F. 1013, 1014 (D.C. Cir. 1923).

[116]346 Mass. 266, 269-270; 191 N.E.2d 479, 481 (1963).

[117]*See* note 113 *supra*.

[118]62 Wis.2d 730, 216 N.W.2d 8 (1974).

ernmental agencies, financial institutions, life insurance companies and banks, stores and restaurants, and finally by general manufacturers and merchandisers, etc. More and more and one would assume that pressure would be developing on the courts generally to state that the "twilight zone" has ended.

In spite of the apparent simplicity of the *Frye-Fatalo* articulation, no effort was made to effectively test it until 1972. This delay was because, starting in 1934,[119] the defendant attorneys, prosecutors, and the judges found another route to acceptability, which was much more satisfactory to the judges. This was the acceptance of the testimony after the defendant attorneys and the prosecutors agreed, called a "stipulation."[120] This practice spread rapidly into many other jurisdictions and, by the time the Supreme Court of Ohio in *State v. Souel*[121] approved the stipulation procedure in 1978, trial courts were accepting the testimony of polygraphers when it was covered with a "stipulation" in twenty jurisdictions.[122]

Without a "stipulation" agreement between the parties, the polygrapher's evidence can be challenged on the ground that polygraphic evidence does not yet enjoy "general acceptability." In such cases the judge might then be forced to resolve the test articulated in *Frye*, a task the judge might not relish because he or she would have to accept a mass of general polygraph use information, statistics, etc., and if he or she held the *Frye* test was satisfied, the long trial would end in an appeal.[123] If the two sides agreed they would not raise such a challenge, the testimony would be accepted without the inevitable debate.

There were other serious collateral issues that were also resolved by stipulations. The two sides agreed neither would challenge the expertise of the polygrapher,[124] or the procedures used during the examination,[125] or object either that the jury had been so confused by the

---

[119]McCormick, LAW OF EVIDENCE, 203 at 491 (Cleary Rev. Ed., 1972).

[120]One court in 1938 accepted the testimony of a polygrapher without a stipulation from the prosecutor (*People v. Kenny*, 167 Misc. 51, 3 N.Y.S.2d 348 (1938)). This was the only instance when a stipulation agreement was not basic to the acceptability of a polygrapher's testimony until *United States v. Ridling*, 350 F. Supp. 90 (E.D. Mich. 1972).

[121]53 Ohio St. 2d 1923, 372 N.E.2d 1318 (1978).

[122]*See* Comment, 14 AKRON L. REV. 1 (1980).

[123]*See People v. Leone*, 25 N.Y.2d 511, 255 N.E.2d 696 (1969). Since "generally accepted as reliable" is left undefined, it is likely to be discovered that the phrase means different things to the courts which invented the phrase and to scientists. *See, e.g.*, Kirk, *The Interrelationship of Science and Law*, 13 BUFFALO L. REV. 393 (1964); Fong, *Criminalistics and the Prosecutor*, THE PROSECUTOR'S SOURCEBOOK, George and Cohen, eds. (New York: Practising Law Institute, 1969) ¶¶ 14.1–14.19.

[124]*Henderson v. State*, 94 Okla. Crim. 45, 230 P.2d 495 (1951), *cert. denied*, 342 U.S. 898 (1951). *See also* Wicker, *The Polygraph Truth Test and the Law of Evidence*, 22 TENN. L. REV. 711, 723 (1953).

[125]*People v. Davis*, 343 Mich. 348, 72 N.W.2d 269 (1955).

testimony that the testimony was in error[126] or—another quite basic matter—that the testimony about the defendant's examination violated the defendant's Fifth Amendment rights.[127]

The testimony of the polygrapher under a stipulation was almost automatically accepted as the practice spread from court to court,[128] and the *contra* rule hardened—nonacceptance of the polygrapher's testimony if a "stipulation" agreement was not tendered to the trial judge.[129]

The Eighth Circuit Court adamantly opposes admission of unstipulated polygraph results (*United States v. Alexander*),[130] but admits stipulated evidence (*United States v. Oliver*).[131] The court in *United States v. Urguidez*[132] explained that polygraph debate would consume too much time; debate is eliminated when both parties stipulate. Some courts have said that when the testimony is under a stipulation,

---

[126]*People v. Leone*, 25 N.Y.2d 511, 255 N.E.2d 696 (1969); *People v. Davis*, 343 Mich. 348, 72 N.W.2d 269 (1955); *United States v. Stromberg*, 179 F. Supp. 278 (S.D. N.Y. 1959).

[127]*Schmerber v. California*, 384 U.S. 757, 764 (1966); *Bowen v. Eyman*, 324 F. Supp. 339, 341 (D. Ariz. 1970); *People v. Simms*, 395 Ill. 69, 71, 69 N.E.2d 336, 338 (1946).

[128]Since the trial judges were no longer concerned about the "expertise" of these expert witnesses, few judges would even require a *voir dire* examination on the competency of the polygrapher. *Voir dire* examinations were only emphasized by the appellate court after the shift against stipulations (*see* discussion in text, *infra*) started. *Commonwealth v. Vitello*, 376 Mass. 426, 381 N.E.2d 582 (1972). Examples of acceptance with stipulation are: *People v. Houser*, 85 Cal. App.2d 686, 193 P.2d 937 (1948); *State v. McNamara*, 252 Iowa 19, 104 N.W.2d 568 (1960); *State v. Valdez*, 91 Ariz. 274, 371 P.2d 894 (1962); *State v. Freeland*, 255 Iowa 1334, 125 N.W.2d 825 (1964); *State v. Brown*, 177 So.2d 532 (Fla. Dist. Ct. App. 1965); *Herman v. Eagle Star Ins. Co.*, 283 F. Supp. 33, *aff'd*, 396 F.2d 427 (9th Cir. 1968); *State v. Fields*, 434 S.W.2d 507 (Mo. 1968); *State v. McDavitt* 62 N.J. 36, 297 A.2d 849 (1972); *State v. Ross*, 7 Wash. App. 62, 497 P.2d 1343 (1972); *Walter v. O'Connell*, 339 N.Y.S.2d 386 (1972); *State v. Bennett*, 17 Or. App. 197, 521 P.2d 31 (1974); *State v. Jones*, 110 Ariz. 546, 552, 521 P.2d 978 (1974); *State v. Jenkins*, 523 P.2d 1232 (Utah 1974); *Robinson v. Wilson*, 44 Cal. App.3d 92, 118 Cal. Rptr. 569 (1974); *State v. Stanislawski*, 62 Wis.2d 730, 216 N.W.2d 8 (1974); *Codie v. State*, 313 So.2d 754 (Fla. 1975); *State v. South*, 136 N.J. Super. 402, 346 A.2d 437 (1975); *United States v. Oliver*, 525 F.2d 731 (8th Cir. 1975), *cert. denied*, 434 U.S. 973 (1976); *Chambers v. State*, 240 Ga. 76, 239 S.E.2d 324 (1977); *Cullin v. State*, 565 P.2d 445 (Wyo. 1977); *State v. Roach*, 223 Kan. 732, 567 P.2d 1082 (1978); *State v. Alexis*, 21 Wash. App. 161, 584 P.2d 963 (1978); *State v. Malino*, 297 N.C. 485, 256 S.E.2d 154 (1979). No effort has been made to estimate the number of times polygraphers have testified in courts. Trial courts often write no formal decision and sometimes a typed decision will not be printed. Whether a polygrapher testified under a stipulation would hardly be significant to record in a decision unless the case had unique aspects and an appeal could be expected.

[129]The court in *United States v. De Betham*, 348 F. Supp. 1377, 1379 (S.D. Cal. 1972) reported that the nonacceptance of polygraph testimony became essentially automatic if no "stipulation" was tendered to the trial judge:
"The result has been almost universal rejection of unstipulated polygraph evidence, occasionally without any stated reason therefor."
See, e.g., *People v. Oswalt*, 26 Ill. App.3d 224, 324 N.E.2d 666 (1975); *State v. Christopher*, 134 N.J. Super. 263, 339 A.2d 239 (1975); *State v. Bell*, 90 N.M. 134, 560 P.2d 925 (1977); *Williams v. State*, 378 A.2d 11 (Del.), *cert. denied*, 436 U.S. 908 (1978); *Owens v. State*, 373 N.E.2d 913 (Ind. Ct. App. 1978).

[130]526 F.2d 161 (8th Cir. 1975).

[131]525 F.2d 731 (8th Cir. 1975).

[132]356 F. Supp. 1363, 1367 (C.D. Cal. 1973).

"doubts about reliability" are removed.[133] Doubts about reliability cannot be the reason for "acceptability with stipulation," because if the lie detector results are unreliable, this defect is not cured by a stipulation.[134] Thus, removal of the collateral issues which, if debated, would stretch out the trial's length and expense is the fundamental. The removal of the collateral issues causes some courts to require a formal written stipulation prepared and filed in advance with the trial judge,[135] whereas in other courts oral stipulations "on the record" are satisfactory. In still others the stipulation agreement is implied when the prosecutor raises no objection; this is sometimes called "lack of prosecutorial objection."[136]

In these cases the defendant's attorney would usually make the request for a "stipulation" in the hope that the polygrapher would corroborate the defendant's denial, and the prosecutor usually would agree because he or she did not desire to struggle through a trial if the defendant could "pass" the polygraph examination. In some jurisdictions a defendant who did not "pass" the polygrapher's test could still be presented in court. In *United States v. Oliver*[137] the Eighth Circuit explained:

> We are satisfied that the appellant voluntarily, knowingly and intelligently chose to waive his rights to object to the admission of the test results in evidence. It is obvious that Oliver calculated that he could pass the test even though he did not ultimately do so. His agreement as to the admissibility of the test, therefore, could be looked upon as a "deliberate bypass" of his constitutional rights based on an exercise of trial strategy.[138]

In other jurisdictions the defendant can take the test and if he "does not pass" he can block the polygrapher's testimony by remaining mute during the trial because of the limitation in the use of such testimony, which is only usable to "impeach or corroborate" a witness; if the defendant does not testify the polygrapher's testimony is not acceptable.

In *Oliver* the Eighth Circuit explained that with a "stipulation" covering it the testimony is acceptable even though the *Frye* articulation is not resolved. The Eighth Circuit said it might have had enough evidence to accept the polygrapher's testimony presented unilaterally under the *Frye* test rather than to accept it simply because it was covered by a stipulation. The court reported that the polygrapher involved had conducted more than 50,000 polygraph examinations with an estimated accuracy in excess of 90 percent, that he was the president of the Polygraph Institute, had taught polygraphy to students,

---

[133]*United States v. Alexander*, 526 F.2d 161 (8th Cir. 1975).

[134]Annot., 53 A.L.R.3d 1005, 1008 (1973 & Supp. 1979).

[135]*State v. Souel*, 53 Ohio St. 2d 123, 372 N.E.2d 1318 (1978).

[136]Downs, *Admission of Polygraph Results: A Due Process Perspective*, 55 IND. L. J. 157, 168 (1978-80).

[137]525 F.2d 731 (1975).

[138]*Id.* at 736.

and performed examinations regularly. In spite of all this general acceptability the Eighth Circuit did not follow the *Frye* route but followed the *stipulation* route:

> We cannot conclude that the stipulated or consented to polygraph is so
> unreliable as to be inadmissible in this particular case. We deem it un-
> necessary to determine whether the polygraph had attained sufficient
> "general scientific acceptance" to justify the admission of polygraph re-
> sults absent waiver or stipulation.[139]

But the "stipulation" requirement, basic to acceptability insisted
upon by many courts, may be on the way out—being replaced by other
requirements and limitations. The first step in this change occurred
when the Supreme Court of New Mexico in *State v. Valdez*[140] stated
that a trial judge (1) could not skip over the *voir dire* cross-
examination probing the polygrapher's expertise foundation even if a
stipulation was tendered, (2) should limit the testimony to the impeachment or corroboration of a witness's testimony, and (3) should
make careful instruction to the jury to reduce the risk of confusion.
These requirements were added to the "stipulations" requirement and
these additions spread into other jurisdictions and became known as
the *"Valdez* formulations."[141]

The Supreme Court of New Mexico had specifically adopted the
Valdez formulations in addition to a "stipulation" in *State v.
Lucero.*[142] Then two years later this court in *State v. Dorsey*[143] removed the "stipulation" requirement yet retained the other formulations. This sharp break from tradition occurred because the court
recognized that a "due process" problem arises when a prosecutor
does not stipulate at the request of the defendant's attorney and the
evidence considered essential to a defendant is blocked by the prosecutor's refusal. This "due process" concern arose in part out of the
U.S. Supreme Court decision in *Chambers v. Mississippi.*[144]

In that case the Supreme Court removed a blockage on evidence
considered essential to the defendant's case, a blockage caused by a
prosecutor's refusal to stipulate. The attorney representing defendant
Chambers wanted to call Gable McDonald as a witness because he

---

[139]*Id.* at 737.

[140]91 Ariz. 274, 371 P.2d 894 (1962).

[141]The *"Valdez* formulation" has been adopted in a number of other jurisdictions. *See, e.g.,*
State v. Galloway, 167 N.W.2d 89 (Iowa 1969); *State v. McDavitt,* 62 N.J. 36, 44–47, 297 A.2d
849 (1972); *State v. Lassley,* 218 Kan. 758, 760, 545 P.2d 383 (1976); *State v. Souel,* 53 Ohio St.
2d 123, 133, 372 N.E.2d 1318 (1978).

[142]86 N.M. 686, 526 P.2d 1091 (1974).

[143]88 N.M. 184, 539 P.2d 204 (1975); also *see State v. Bell,* 90 N.M. 134; 560 P.2d 925 (1977).

[144]410 U.S. 284 (1973).

believed McDonald had confessed to the murder for which Chambers was being tried. In addition, Chambers' attorney also planned to call three more witnesses, believing that each of them would swear that they heard McDonald at separate times confess to the murder. The Mississippi trial judge had refused to accept the testimony of the witnesses under an old technical "voucher rule." The "voucher rule" is a reverse of the constitutional right of a defendant to confront his or her accuser;[145] but since McDonald was not Chambers' accuser, the judge held the defendant could not call these witnesses. The "voucher" rule applied by the trial judge may well be some type of *non sequitur*, but regardless of its history Justice Powell removed it as a block on this evidence, considered by the defendant to be essential:

> It can hardly be disputed that McDonald's testimony was in fact seriously adverse to Chambers.... We reject the notion that a right of such substance in the criminal process may be governed by [a] technicality.... The "voucher" rule, as applied in this case, plainly interfered with Chambers' right to defend against the State's charges.[146]

The nonacceptance of the testimony because of a technical "voucher" rule is essentially the nonacceptance of the testimony of a polygrapher desired by the defendant because the prosecutor refuses to "stipulate." The Supreme Court and Court of Appeals of New Mexico recognized the "due process" problem similarity in such a rule because the prosecutor can block evidence considered essential to the defendant. The court removed the "stipulation" requirement but left intact all of the other parts of the *"Valdez* Formulations."[147]

---

[145]*Chambers v. State,* 252 So. 2d 217, 220 (Miss. 1971).

[146]410 U.S. at 297–8.

[147]*State v. Dorsey,* 88 N.M. 184, 185, 539 P.2d 204, 205 (1975). Thomas K. Downs in *Admission of Polygraph Results: A Due Process Perspective,* 55 IND. L. J. 157, 166–170 (1979-80) explained:

"Extrapolation from this *Chambers* line of cases to polygraph exclusions suggests that when polygraph results are found to be reliable and to occupy a critical position in the accused's defense, he has a due process right to present those results absent a valid and sufficiently compelling state justification for exclusion . . . " In *State v. Dorsey* [88 N.M. 184, 539 P.2d 204 (1975)] the New Mexico Supreme Court found that its prior requirement of stipulation . . . was, among other infirmities, '[I]nconsistent *with the concept of due process.'* [*Id.* at 166, 539 P.2d at 205]. [Emphasis in original.]

. . .

The New Mexico Court of Appeals did consider *Chambers,* however, in its *Dorsey* opinion [87 N.M. 323, 532 P.2d 912 (Ct. App. 1975)].

. . .

[T]he court hinted that exclusion absent stipulation or . . . prosecutorial objection was unreasonable because it denied the fact finding process useful information, "thereby inhibiting the growth and development of the law of evidence" [88 N.M. 184, 185, 539 P.2d 204, 205 (1975)].

. . .

If a criminal defendant offers such evidence [polygrapher testimony] which appears to be critical to his defense, a *Chambers* due process analysis requires the trial court to evaluate that

The "due process" concerns that arise when the defendant desires the testimony of a qualified polygrapher but this is blocked by the prosecutor are reflected in *United States v. Hart.*[148] In that case the prosecutor's principal witness was tested by an examiner and his story was found not to be truthful. The defendants' attorney asked for a report by the examiner and the prosecutor refused to deliver it, claiming that the report remained private until the parties "stipulated," and that he (the prosecutor) would not do so. The district court, however, ordered the prosecutor "to make available as witnesses on the trial all persons who participated in directing that polygraph tests be given to Leslie Alkinson (the prosecutor's principal witness) or in the taking of the tests or in the decision that the results of the test did not impair his credibility as a witness."[149] Thus the nonstipulation blockage was removed on the polygraph testing information for reasons similar to the "due process" concerns in *Chambers v. Mississippi.*[150]

The Supreme Court of Massachusetts in *Commonwealth v. Vitello*[151] added its emphasis to this change by stating that a proper *voir dire* examination should be substituted for the "stipulation" requirement. During this examination the prosecutor can tell the judge any reasons why the polygrapher should not be accepted as an expert witness if he or she has such concerns. This court emphasized that such testimony should be limited to "impeachment or corroboration" of the testimony of a witness. It explained its rationale.

> One of the accepted methods of impeaching the credibility of a witness in this Commonwealth is by attacking his reputation for truthfulness and veracity. Evidence to rehabilitate the witness is then admissible. Use of this type of "character" evidence is analogous, but not perfectly so, to the admission of polygraph evidence for the purpose of impeaching or corroborating the defendant's testimony. Indeed, we think it accurate, based on our analysis of the role of the polygraph examiner, ... to describe an examiner as a potential "expert character witness." This is so because the polygraph examiner has no special knowledge of the acts or circumstances surrounding the criminal event; at most he can claim special knowledge of the truthfulness of the subject at the time of the examination.[152] [Citations and footnotes omitted.]

---

offer, and precludes either a "mechanistic" application of the *Frye* principle—which is as out of date as many voucher and hearsay rules—or exclusion based on non-reliability grounds similar to the *Lucero* requirements rejected in *Dorsey.*

[148]344 F. Supp. 522 (E.D. N.Y. 1971).

[149]*Id.* at 524.

[150]410 U.S. 284 (1973).

[151]381 N.E.2d 582 (Mass. 1978). The usefulness of polygraph tests to a court or a jury, "remains the same regardless if they are admitted by stipulation or not." *Id.* at 595.

[152]*Id.* at 597-98. Thomas Downs explained that when a prosecutor is unwilling to stipulate, the refusal is not because the polygrapher is not competent but for other reasons. A defense at-

Even though the "stipulation" practice is not now respected by important courts such as those which decided *Vitello, Dorsey,* and *Hart,* the "stipulation" rule still determines acceptability in many courts. Ohio clearly adopted the "stipulation" for acceptance rule as late as 1978, and even in civil cases where the collateral issues are less troublesome (e.g., no Fifth Amendment risks and proof standards lowered from "beyond reasonable doubt" to "preponderance of the evidence") a stipulation between the attorneys on both sides produced acceptance in *Herman v. Eagle Star Life Insurance Co.* [153] In that case, the district court admitted the testimony without any *voir dire* examination as to the capability of the polygrapher.

The rule that the acceptance of such testimony must be by "stipulations" (which started in 1934) was breached by two district judges and some judges in state courts in 1972 when the prosecutors involved refused to "stipulate." This breakaway from the stipulation refinement occurred after 50 years of requiring stipulations. These courts reexamined the *Frye* articulation to determine whether polygraphy "without a stipulation" had emerged from the "twilight zone."

In *United States v. Ridling*[154] the defendant's attorney wanted the denial by his client to be corroborated by a polygrapher but the prosecutor would not stipulate. The court assumed that the qualifications of the polygrapher would be attacked, substantial facts about leaving the "twilight zone" were accepted into the record, and then—because the judge would be accepting the testimony over the objections of the prosecutor and he did not consider himself fully qualified to determine the qualifications of the defendant's polygrapher—the judge, under the Federal Rules of Criminal Procedure, Rule 28, appointed *his* own polygrapher as *his* expert to also examine the defendant and then advise him about the competency of the defendant's polygrapher. This judge also added the significant limitation on the use of polygraph testimony that it should be used only to corroborate or impeach testimony of a witness. Even after *Ridling* various judges in various courts, in cases such as *United States v. Trogge,* [155] *United States v. Alexander,* [156] *United States v. Wilson,* [157] and *United States v. Urquider,* [158]

---

torney who wants to have a polygrapher testify to protect his or her client will always ask the prosecutor to stipulate with a polygrapher who is well respected in the legal community and, if possible, a polygrapher that the prosecutor has used in an investigation or in a prior stipulation agreement. Downs, *Admission of Polygraph Results: A Due Process Perspective,* 55 Ind. L. J. 157-90 (1979-80).

[153] 396 F.2d 427 (9th Cir. 1969), aff'g 283 F. Supp 33 (C.D. Cal. 1966).
[154] 350 F. Supp 90 (E.D. Mich. 1972).
[155] 476 F.2d 969, 970 (5th Cir. 1973).
[156] 526 F.2d 161 (8th Cir 1975).
[157] 361 F. Supp. 510 (D. Md. 1973).
[158] 356 F. Supp. 1363 (C.D. Cal. 1973).

continued to follow the well-established rule in criminal cases that a polygrapher's testimony is accepted only with a "stipulation."

In *United States v. Zeiger*[159] the defendant was charged with assault with intent to kill. The defendant's attorney wanted the judge to accept the testimony of a police polygrapher to corroborate the defendant's denial even though the prosecutor had refused to stipulate. The judge accepted the testimony because he believed that "an adequate and sufficient foundation has been established in *this* case to meet the standard promulgated by *Frye.*" The court stated:

> Today, polygraphy has emerged from that *twilight zone* into an established field of science and technology. The polygraph has been and continues to be the subject of scientific study and investigation, and although the precise limitations of the device and the intricacies which affect its performance may not be understood to the complete satisfaction of the scientific community, enough is known about it to confirm that it is a useful tool for detecting deception.[160] [Footnotes omitted. Emphasis added.]

In spite of the criticism of some judges for breaking the "stipulation" requirement for acceptability, the judge in *People v. Cutter,*[161] a California court, in 1972, citing both *Ridling* and *Zeiger,* accepted the testimony of a polygrapher even though no stipulation had been tendered. The judge added this comment:

> It is the experience of this court during his ten years of presiding at criminal trials that the great majority of trials on [the] credibility of witnesses that perjury is prevalent and the oath taken by witnesses has little effect to deter false testimony. The principal role of a trier of fact is the search for *truth and any reasonable procedure or method to assist the court in this search should be employed.*[162] [Emphasis added.]

Then the Wisconsin Supreme Court in *State v. Stanislawski*[163] said:

> Under the test of general acceptance or scientific standing in the field in which it belongs, there had been a marked change in acceptance of polygraph testing ... by industries, banks, insurance companies, police departments, and governments, including the armed forces. The business of private polygraph examiners increased eight to ten times in the decade 1950–1960. This increased use and acceptance reflects the establishing of polygraph tests, conducted by a competent examiner.... Polygraph test accuracy is viewed as comparing favorably with other types of expert testimony such as that given by psychiatrists, document examiners, and physicians.

---

[159]350 F. Supp. 685 (D.C. Cir. 1972).
[160]*Id.* at 688.
[161]No. A-176965, 12 CrL 2133 (Super. Ct. Los Angeles County, Cal., Nov. 6, 1972).
[162]*Id.*
[163]62 Wis.2d 730, 216 N.W.2d 8, 11–12 (1974).

The judge explained that acceptability of polygraph evidence had been moved out of the "twilight zone."

> We find it clear that ... polygraph tests have moved from the "twilight zone" ... to such degree of standing and scientific recognition that unconditional rejection of expert testimony based on polygraph testing is no longer indicated.[164]

This court set up four standards: (1) admission only on stipulation, (2) a hearing *sua sponte* to determine the qualifications of the examiner, whether the defendant was a suitable subject, and whether the methods used were sound, (3) cross-examination of the examiner, and (4) proper instructions to the jury on the limited function of the examiner's testimony. Seven years after *Stanislawski*, the Wisconsin Supreme Court questioned these principles in *State v. Dean.*[165] It pointed out that when the parties entered into a *"Stanislawski* stipulation" on the admission of the polygrapher's testimony, the parties have agreed in advance they would forego their usual opportunity to impeach expert opinion by calling other expert witnesses and the stipulation also neutralized the second and much of the third standard. Since the stipulation limits cross-examination, the court said, it may not provide a sufficient basis for the jury to assess the competence of, and the merits of, the test. The court's concern in regard to the final condition was that the jury instructions will not overcome the jury's inclination to accept the seemingly objective evidence and place the polygraph evidence in its proper perspective.

The court said in *Dean* that in the seven years since the *Stanislawski* rule, adequate standards had not been developed to guide the trial courts. The court therefore overruled the *State v. Stanislawski* decisions, stating in part that an admit-on-stipulation approach "does little, if anything, to enhance the reliability of the polygraph evidence" when it eliminates cross-examination testing and, in addition, "we are also concerned, as was the Seventh Circuit Court of Appeals as well as other courts, with the validity of allowing the prosecutor to veto the defendant's wish to introduce polygraph evidence by refusing to execute a stipulation."[166] A careful reading of this and other decisions reports the concern of the judges about the "due process" aspects of a rule that permits an adversary (the prosecutor) to block evidence that the defendant considers essential to obtain a "not guilty" result. *State*

---

[164]216 N.W.2d at 13.
[165]103 Wis.2d 228, 307 N.W.2d 628 (1981).
[166]307 N.W.2d at 648.

v. Dorsey[167] and *United States v. Hart*[168] spoke out clearly on the "due process" concerns inherent in the "stipulation" practice.

This section about acceptance of polygrapher testimony in court has been included in this chapter for two reasons. The first is to help strip away the confusion that results when an arbitrator asserts that the *Frye* and *Fatalo* articulations are still blocking the admission of such testimony into courts. If arbitrators are still asserting this they must be viewing *Frye* and *Fatalo* as two gladiators standing on a bridge ready to battle anyone who dared to try to squeeze a polygrapher across the bridge and into a courtroom. Since their attention was so attached they failed to see hundreds of polygraphers riding on "stipulations" under the bridge and into the courts, there to be accepted as expert witnesses.

Arbitrator Edgar Jones says that *Frye* still says polygraphy has no scientific status in courts. He said:

> The leading court case rejecting the claim to scientific status for lie detection by polygraph administration remains the 1923 federal court of appeals decision in *Frye v. United States*.[169]

And then he says courts reject the testimony of polygraphers:

> Although there have been instances of trial courts improperly deviating from the declared law of their jurisdictions, and of arbitrators curiously crediting them as if they were valid statements of law, it remains true in 1978 that the substantial weight of legal authority rejects the admissibility of polygraph evidence.[170] [Footnotes omitted.]

He overlooks, or barely mentions, the hundreds of polygraphers who have testified in courts under stipulations. The judges insisted on these stipulations to resolve collateral issues that might stretch out a trial and ensure an appeal. As noted earlier, the "scientific status" or "reliability" concerns of some are not eliminated when the two litigants sign stipulations. Saying it another way, "if lie detector results are unreliable [the thesis of Arbitrator Jones], this defect is not corrected by a stipulation." If Arbitrator Jones' thesis were correct, the sides would not have permitted testimony to be accepted using the stipulation route in federal and state courts throughout this country for at least fifty-eight years.

The statements by some judges in and after 1972 when reexamination of *Frye* and *Fatalo* began is not the point in time when polygrapher testimony entered the courts. The reexamination is merely illustrative of

---

[167]88 N.M. 184, 548 P.2d 204 (1975).
[168]344 F. Supp. 522 (E.D. N.Y. 1971).
[169]Jones, note 2 *supra* at p. 86.
[170]*Id.* at p. 93.

the desire of some judges to have an alternate route to the acceptability of the testimony of polygraphers available when the prosecution does not agree to a stipulation.

The second and possibly more important reason for this section is to record that those labor arbitrators who have accepted the testimony of polygraphers into labor arbitration hearings have quite generally limited the use of that testimony to "corroboration and impeachment" and have given low weight or no weight to the results when the testimony starts "dredging up" facts which involve matters irrelevant to the grievance inquiry. These arbitrators also quite uniformly require the polygrapher to be presented to the arbitrator for a *voir dire* examination to test his or her expertise as an expert witness, a practice now again being insisted upon by leading courts. These arbitrators are busy. It may be assumed they have not had time to dig deeply into the criminal law procedures, yet without slavishly borrowing them they have generally followed a similar path.

THE EFFECT OF PREHIRE AND WORKING CONDITION AGREEMENTS ON ADMISSIBILITY OF TESTIMONY IN ARBITRATION

Arbitrator Britton in *Pearl Beer Distributing Co.*[171] discussed the admission of polygraph evidence when it was obtained pursuant to a request of an employer pursuant to an agreement signed by the employee at the time of hire. It was explained:

> The evidence shows that in 1963 the Employer adopted a rule which required all employment applicants to take physical and polygraph examinations subsequent to their filling out application forms.
> ... In a number of instances the employer has discovered through the use of polygraph that injuries were not admitted by the employee and undiscovered by the employer's physicians, and secondly, that utilization almost entirely eliminated the need for verifying the answers on the employment application forms with former employers.
> Employees returning from sickness or injury are not required by the employer to take polygraph tests because the reason that these employees have been off work is known, i.e., if an employee is off work because of injury or illness he is usually unable to work for any other employer so as to be susceptible to another injury.[172]

Many employers have asked prospective employees to take such a test to help the employer make judgments in connection with the

[171]59 LA 820 (Britton, 1972).
[172]*Id.* at 821.

employment of the prospect. Sometimes these questions have drifted into matters that are considered quite private. In various states prehire examination on behalf of an employer is considered a misdemeanor subjecting the employer to a fine. These statutes also make the employer subject to a fine if the employer requires as a condition of employment that the prospect agree to take polygraph tests in the future upon request by the employer.[173] No such limitations are placed on governmental agencies such as the police.

Prehire testing of police candidates produced in one group of 130, 35 candidates that admitted they had committed burglaries, 3 that they had committed robberies, 13 that they used narcotics, 31 that they paid bribes to police officers, and others that admitted having had their drivers licenses revoked for past periods. In another group of 225, 80 admitted that they had committed burglaries, 7 admitted that they were selling narcotics, 32 that they had used narcotics, 38 that they paid bribes to police officers, 30 that they bought and sold stolen merchandise, and 6 that they either stole automobiles or had been involved in hit-and-run accidents.[174]

Some union representatives have asserted that these statutory restraints would also apply to testing in connection with a grievance and have urged the arbitrator to construe the state statute and then, if he detects a violation, help enforce the state statutes by refusing to accept a polygrapher's testimony at the arbitration hearing. In *Daystrom Furniture Co.*[175] Arbitrator Charles Laughlin discussed this argument and concluded that enforcement of the state statutes of this type are not an arbitrator's duty. The Code of Virginia[176] was involved in this case and provided that the "record of polygraphic examination" must be furnished to an employee who had been tested and "if this record is

---

[173]Twenty-two states and the District of Columbia have statutes that restrict employers from polygraph testing of prospective employees and from requiring such prospective employees to sign an agreement that polygraph testing is a condition of continued employment. The words in the statute vary the restriction to some degree and the penalty against the employer varies. For convenience, these statutes are listed with the page number of text in the *Fair Employment Practices Manual* of BNA's LABOR RELATIONS REPORTER: Alaska, 453 FEP Manual 225; California, 453 FEP Manual 843; Connecticut, 453 FEP Manual 1236, Delaware, 453 FEP Manual 1445; District of Columbia, 453 FEP Manual 1685; Hawaii, 453 FEP Manual 2215; Idaho, 453 FEP Manual 2446; Maine, 455 FEP Manual 437; Maryland, 455 FEP Manual 635; Massachusetts, 455 FEP Manual 865; Michigan, 455 FEP Manual 1007, 1013; Minnesota, 455 FEP Manual 1236; Montana, 455 FEP Manual 1826; Nebraska, 455 FEP Manual 2051; Nevada, 455 FEP Manual 2235; New Jersey, 455 FEP Manual 2626; New York, 455 FEP Manual 3045; Oregon, 457 FEP Manual 616; Pennsylvania, 457 FEP Manual 823; Rhode Island, 457 FEP Manual 1236; Virginia, 457 FEP Manual 2626; Washington, 457 FEP Manual 2841; Wisconsin, 457 FEP Manual 3210.

[174]Reid and Inbau, note 13 *supra*, at p. 59.

[175]65 LA 1157 (Laughlin, 1975).

[176]Code of Virginia § 54-729.01 6:1

not provided the employer is subject to a fine." The union representative contended that the employer had failed to deliver the test "record" to the grievant and, for this reason, the polygrapher should not testify. Arbitrator Laughlin concluded that he would not resolve such a claim because if a fine should be assessed it was the concern of the state officials, not a labor arbitrator. However, Arbitrator Laughlin did say very clearly that if the union representative had made a clear demand for polygraph information before the arbitration hearing, the information should have been delivered to the union representative to permit him to make a proper investigation and analysis. This exchange of information is proper and discussed in Chapter VII *supra.* Arbitrator Laughlin stated that in this situation the union had failed to make the request in advance:

> At the first hearing the Union knew that the Company planned to call the polygraph examiner and introduce evidence as to the results of the examination. In fact, the inability of the polygraph examiner to attend the first hearing is the reason the second hearing was held. The arbitrator has no doubt but that if the Union's demand had been renewed at that time the Company would have furnished the Union all of the items demanded. Therefore, the second basis for the Union's objection is rejected.[177]

Arbitrator Edward Pinkus in *Brink's, Inc.*[178] was not so secure about the acceptance of polygraph evidence if the employer had obtained the test under a pre-hire condition-of-employment agreement.[179] Brink's, Inc. was operating armored cars to transport money and other valuables from one place to a bank. One grievant had been employed for over six years in various capacities (driver, guard, and messenger), and one December was working as the driver of a three-man crew operating an armored car over Route 15. At each stop the driver remained locked into the front section of the vehicle when the guard and messenger went to various buildings to pick up bags of currency and coins. At the end of Route 15, when the vehicle was returned to the company's garage and the bags were removed and taken to the counting facility, it was discovered that one bag containing $135,000 was missing. The company immediately commenced an investigation. All four employees were asked to take a test and all did so but the grievant "had exhibited specific reactions (indicative of deception) when all relevant questions were asked." The company later discharged him and a grievance was filed that reached arbitration. In the company's post-hearing brief it stated:

[177]65 LA 1157 (Laughlin, 1975).
[178]70 LA 909, 911 (Pinkus, 1978).
[179]Massachusetts statute, 455 FEP Manual 865.

"Now, to be clear on the point, Brink's is not accusing [Grievant] of stealing the item. The criminal investigation is proceeding on its own.... The company does not know and the Company does not accuse.... If the case to be proven against [Grievant] was theft, it would fail. But the issue with [Grievant] was—was he lying—was he telling the truth."[180]

Arbitrator Pinkus then accepted this position: "the discharge of Grievant must therefore stand or fail with the ... polygraph results as evidence of dishonesty, not merely as evidence tending to corroborate other testimony." The arbitrator then stated that the polygraph testimony *per se* will not establish a "discharge for good cause":

Generally arbitrators as well as courts have been reluctant to place much if any weight on polygraph results as proof of lying, although there is more acceptance of them as proof of truthfulness.[181]

In addition he did not find the polygrapher to be a persuasive expert (1) because he did not know how much *his* company had been paid for his services; (2) because he thought the grievant had no difficulty with the English language whereas the arbitrator thought otherwise; (3) because he changed his testimony to make a conclusion more unfavorable to the grievant; and (4) because his scientific support for the reliability of the test was an intra-industry journal article.

Arbitrator Pinkus then evaluated the effect of any inconsistency between the provision of the Massachusetts statute and the testing of the grievant.[182] The company representatives explained to the arbitrator that the statutory remedy is a fine and not evidentiary exclusion of the polygrapher's testimony in labor arbitration, yet Arbitrator Pinkus said, "the statute can hardly be said to favor the Company's position.[183]

The arbitrator in *A.P.A. Transport*[184] did not view any statutory restraint on the employer's pre-hire testing or agreement-making ability to be a reason for excluding the testimony of a polygrapher in an arbitration hearing. The arbitrator reacted as did Arbitrator Charles V. Laughlin in *Daystrom Furniture Company, Inc.*[185] A.P.A. Transport had been experiencing thefts of electronic equipment from its terminal, and examining the records an investigator concluded that the thefts were taking place when switchers were handling items in the terminal. All switchers were asked to submit voluntarily to a polygraph test. The grievant agreed to submit to the polygraph because he

---

[180]70 LA 909, 910 (Pinkus, 1978).

[181]*Id.* at 910.

[182]*Id.* at 910–11.

[183]*Id.*

[184]Award of April 20, 1982, unreported, subjected to de novo review in *Simpson v. APA Transport Corp.*, 108 LRRM 2754 (D. N.J. 1981).

[185]65 LA 1157 (Laughlin, 1975).

"wanted to exonerate himself from any complicity" and because the FBI agents asked him to do so.

At the conclusion of the examination, and before the apparatus was removed, the polygraph operator questioned the grievant as to the reason for his nervousness, and he then admitted to several thefts of company property committed some years earlier. On the basis of these admissions, the grievant was discharged; the discharge was contested and a grievance claiming reinstatement was filed by the union, and the case went on to arbitration.

The arbitrator found that the grievant had admitted the thefts without intimidation and sustained the discharge. The grievant then became a plaintiff in a suit filed in the New Jersey District Court for a *de novo* review, and the plaintiff contended that the polygraph evidence could not properly be accepted under the New Jersey statute that:

> Any person who as an employer shall influence, request or require an employee to take or submit to a lie detector test as a condition of employment or continued employment, is a disorderly person.[186]

Judge Sarokin rejected the claim that the polygraph evidence should not be accepted because of the New Jersey statute under two headings: *first*, that the interpretation of the "just cause" provision is an issue of contract interpretation and that the arbitration award drew its essence from the collective bargaining agreement and *second*, that concerns of statutory construction of the state statute and assisting with its enforcement are of no concern to the arbitrator. Such concerns would cause him to go beyond the interpretation of the labor agreement. State statutes do not provide the legal rules in labor arbitrations; these are the laws developed out of Section 301 of the National Labor Relations Act.[187]

Judge Sarokin said any statutory violation on the part of the employer should be remedied by the fine and that this statute does not limit "the use of information gathered [by a polygraph examination]" and the judge said it is doubtful that the public policy of New Jersey "would extend so far as to require an employer to retain an employee who has admitted thefts [of property] from such employer."[188]

---

[186]New Jersey statute, 455 FEP Manual 2626.
[187]*See* Chapter I, "Source of Law in Labor Arbitration."
[188]*Simpson v. APA Transport Corp.*, 108 LRRM 2754, 2758 (D. N.J. 1981).

CHAPTER XV

The "Duty" to Cooperate With Polygraph Testing
Versus the Right to Refuse

This chapter is not involved with the acceptance and use of the testimony of a polygrapher in labor arbitration but rather discusses what arbitrators do when an employee refuses to be tested following a request of the employer and then is disciplined.[1] Such requests for a polygraph test usually occur after a theft of company property. The testing request is part of an investigation initiated to discover who has information about the theft or who the thief is. The employee is not being asked to take a test because the employee is suspected of being the thief or of knowing anything about the theft. Even if the test establishes that the employee knows nothing it may be helpful to the investigation.

The first group of awards discussed in this chapter starts with Arbitrator Joseph Klamon's award in *Allen Industries, Inc.*[2] in 1956, the first one that involved polygraphy in any way. The arbitrators in this group believe that discipline is justified if the employee refuses to be tested because employees have a duty (1) to comply with reasonable instructions of an employer, and (2) to cooperate with the employer in protecting company property—a duty that grows out of the employment relationship.

The arbitrators in the second group support the view that an employee can refuse to take a test for various reasons. This second group starts with the award of Arbitrator Sembower in *General American Transportation*,[3] which appears to be the second award that involves polygraphy in any way. Because these two early awards are clearly opposite, they and their progeny are discussed herein.[4]

---

[1]The decisions of various arbitrators relating to the disciplining of employees who have not cooperated with their employer in investigations in situations unrelated to polygraph testing are discussed under "Self-Incrimination Versus Duty to Cooperate" in Chapter XIII.

[2]26 LA 363 (Klamon, 1956).

[3]31 LA 355 (Sembower, 1958).

[4]"Arbitrator Sembower's decision 20 years ago in *General American Transportation Corp.* . . . has been cited as a leading case ever since." Jones, *"Truth" When the Polygraph Operator Sits*

406

CASES SUPPORTING THE DUTY TO COOPERATE
BY BEING TESTED

In *Allen Industries, Inc.*[5] stolen company property was found in the grievant's automobile. This caused the normal presumption that the grievant was somehow involved with the theft. The company asked the employee who owned the automobile to have his denial of the theft tested by a polygrapher and he refused. He was discharged; a grievance was filed and presented to Arbitrator Klamon, who discussed in his award why the discharge of the employee should be sustained:

> X himself said that the Company had every right to be suspicious since valuable material admittedly the property of the Company was found in two cars, one of which was his car, and up to the present time there is no satisfactory explanation as to how the material got there. This clearly does not mean that X is guilty of anything. He testified that he had no enemies in the plant and no one who might be interested in "framing" him. Conceivably whoever was the thief may have had a car parked close by the lot and may have intended to effect a quick transfer to his own car to accomplish the theft. If this were so, then perhaps all the more reason why X who may be entirely innocent of any wrongdoing, and who also may have no knowledge at all of who may have engineered the theft, should be more than eager to take a lie detector test, in order to clear himself emphatically of the suspicious circumstance of having this material found in his car.

Arbitrator Klamon explained more:

> While a lie detector test is far from perfect and while it may have many shortcomings, it is very difficult to see how the taking of such a test by X could in any way adversely affect his interest if he has no knowledge at all that might be helpful to the Company in ascertaining whether or not he was an accessory or whether or not X has any knowledge of who may have placed this Company material in X's car.[6]

Arbitrator Klamon offered the grievant an additional ten days after the hearing to have his alibi tested by a polygrapher and he again refused. The arbitrator explained that "as the record shows, with the consent of the Company [the arbitrator] afforded X and the Union another opportunity to take a lie detector test by X, with the following difference from the previous agreement: 1. Although the Company would pay all of the expense, it would at no time be present in any way when the test was to be taken by X. 2. The results of such test if taken

as *Arbitrator (or Judge): The Deception of "Detection" in the "Diagnosis of Truth and Deception,"* TRUTH, LIE DETECTORS, AND OTHER PROBLEMS IN LABOR ARBITRATION, Proceedings of the Thirty-First Annual Meeting, National Academy of Arbitrators, J. Stern and B. Dennis, eds. (Washington: BNA Books, 1979), p. 100 n. 61.
[5]26 LA 363 (Klamon, 1956).
[6]*Id.* at 369.

were to be made known confidentially by the Company giving the test, to the Arbitrator and under no circumstances to any one else."

X was given time "in which to notify the Company of assent to the foregoing so that the Company might make the necessary arrangements; such notification was also to be made known to the Arbitrator. The record shows that the Union said it would take under consideration this opportunity. The Union and X, however, did not avail themselves of the opportunity thus afforded."[7]

Arbitrator Klamon did not support the discharge of the grievant on the ground that he was presumed to be involved in the theft of company property found in his automobile (a rather general presumption)[8] but because he had not cooperated with the employer in a theft investigation, having refused to take the test:

> At no time has the Company accused any employee of anything other than as in this case the failure to cooperate in attempting to stop possible thefts and the failure of an employee to cooperate in completely clearing himself of any suspicious circumstantial evidence relative to Company material that was found in the car of Mr. X.[9]

Arbitrator Klamon went on:

> The Arbitrator is not directly interested in the innocence or guilt of X in this matter. He is, however, very much interested in whether or not X and the Union are willing to cooperate to the fullest extent with the Company in its endeavor to find out who may have been involved in this theft and whether or not the circumstantial evidence pointing in a *prima facie* way to X is wholly without foundation.[10]

He also said:

> As indicated, the guilt or the complete innocence of the aggrieved is not an issue in this case since there are no criminal proceedings of any nature pending. . . .
>
> The refusal on the part of X to take a lie detector test even after the Arbitrator has afforded an opportunity to take such a test at any time within ten days of the hearing does not indicate guilt or innocence in any way; it does indicate a complete failure to respond affirmatively to requests that appear to us to be reasonable to cooperate with the Company in its effort to find out who was responsible for what happened.[11]

---

[7]*Id.* at 368

[8]Convictions in criminal cases have been upheld entirely upon presumptions resulting from possession of stolen property. *Lawrence v. State,* 244 Ind. 305, 192 N.E.2d 629 (1963); *Seift v. State,* 255 Ind. 337, 264 N.E. 317 (1970); and *Getty v. State,* 227 Ind. 699, 88 N.E.2d 759 (1949) *See also* 52 C.J.S. *Larceny* § 593 (1968). The same presumption is discussed in Chapter XII, "Rules of Evidence," and in Chapter XIII, "Due Process Considerations."

[9]26 LA at 363.

[10]*Id.* at 368.

[11]*Id.* at 369.

The general duty to cooperate was set forth by Arbitrator Klamon:

> While the Company may not require any employee at random or selec-
> ted in a capricious manner to serve as an informer upon other employees,
> under pain of discharge, nevertheless it is the duty of every employee to as-
> sist the Company in every way to prevent theft of its property or material
> used in manufacture.
>
> In view of all of the facts and circumstances in this case, we must find
> and hold that the Company in no way violated the contract and had every
> right to discharge the aggrieved, X, for his failure to cooperate with the
> Company in its efforts to ascertain who was responsible for what happened,
> who had knowledge of it beforehand, and who may have been guilty of the
> theft of its property or of having acted as an accessory before or after the
> fact in such theft; or who may have had any information helpful to the
> Company in its efforts to stop such activities.[12]

Arbitrator Whyte in *Bowman Transportation, Inc.*[13] followed Arbitrator Klamon's view. He explained that employees have a *duty to cooperate* with their employer in theft investigations and this duty includes taking a polygraph test:

> While the issue involves only Company's right to use polygraph tests in
> investigations, in contrast to admissibility of test results as evidence, the
> polygraph in many instances is recognized as an established mechanism of
> adjunct utility in personnel administration and is finding admissibility in
> courts.... The right of an employer to discharge employees for refusing
> to cooperate in investigations has been recognized. And the polygraph has
> been recognized as a legitimate investigative instrument.

Arbitrator Whyte based the duty of employees to take the test on
the "managerial right" to employ accepted investigation techniques to
protect company property:

> If the Company has the right to investigate property losses, it has the
> right to use investigative techniques which are not illegal and not prohib-
> ited by the labor agreement. No evidence was introduced to show that the
> use of the polygraph is contrary to law and the contract does not pro-
> hibit its use.
>
> Such tests are extensively used.... In view of these considerations, this
> arbitrator does not see how he can say that a suspension for refusal to take
> the test is not based upon reasonable cause.[14]

Awards in two unreported cases involving Bowman Transportation,
Inc.[15] and dealing with polygraph testing were related. The first was

---

[12]*Id.* at 370.

[13]Award of September 11, 1974 (Whyte), unreported, cited and quoted in *Bowman Transportation, Inc.*, 64 LA 453, 456 (Hon, 1975).

[14]*Id.*

[15]Awards of August 28, 1974 (Whyte) and September 11, 1974 (Vadakin), unreported, cited
and quoted in *Bowman Transportation, Inc.*, 64 LA 453, 456 (Hon, 1975).

by Arbitrator James C. Vadakin and the second by Arbitrator James P. Whyte. They dealt with the suspension and subsequent discharge of C—— B——, who had been a co-driver with D—— P——, a trainee. The latter submitted a written statement explaining why he desired to be assigned to work with a different driver. He charged B—— with various rule violations, including the drinking of beer while on duty. In view of the seriousness of these charges, the safety supervisor requested that P—— take a polygraph test, which he did. The polygrapher reported that the charges were truthful. B—— denied the charges but refused to take a test, "asserting that such tests were for hoodlums and murderers, that the Company was impugning his integrity and that he would stand on his twelve years of loyal service to the Company."[16] He was then suspended until he took the test.

Arbitrator Vadakin, in the first opinion, said the "suspension is indefinite, the grievant, figuratively speaking, is left 'dangling in the wind.' A sort of cat and mouse situation exists," he said, stating that it was unreasonable to keep B—— on suspension. He directed that the company should determine a final penalty "based on [B——'s] refusal to cooperate."[17] Then, if a final penalty was imposed, he stated, a prompt hearing should take place before another arbitrator selected by the parties. B—— was discharged and the next arbitration on the discharge was assigned to Arbitrator James P. Whyte. He denied the grievance.[18]

Arbitrator Daugherty in *Warwick Electronics, Inc.*[19] was asked to decide whether written warnings to six plant guards, who refused to take polygraph examinations to test their denials of any knowledge of the theft of television units, should be rescinded and removed from their records. There was no reason to conclude that the guards were involved in the theft. The labor agreement covering the guards stated that employees would cooperate in investigations of theft but it did not specifically require that the guards take polygraph tests upon request. However, Arbitrator Daugherty concluded that the failure of the guards to take the test constituted sufficient lack of cooperation in the investigation to support the discipline given by the employer (warning notices including a statement that severe disciplinary action could follow any future refusals). Since the employees being asked to take the test were not under any "presumption" of involvement, the discipline was simply for the failure to cooperate by not taking the polygraph

---

[16] Award of August 28, 1974 (Vadakin), unreported, cited and quoted in *Bowman Transportation, Inc.*, 64 LA 453, 456 (Hon, 1975).

[17] *Id.*

[18] Award of September 11, 1974 (Whyte), unreported, cited and quoted in *Bowman Transportation, Inc.*, 64 LA 453, 456 (Hon, 1975).

[19] 46 LA 95 (Daugherty, 1966).

tests. Arbitrator Jones stated in his paper on polygraph testing that Arbitrator Daugherty's decision was a "bad" one.[20] He suggested that Arbitrator Daugherty should have ordered the warning notices rescinded and that he would have done so if he (Arbitrator Daugherty) had "been more informed, or more convinced, of the essential irrationality of polygraph testing, of its capricious and untutored capacity for harm to innocent workers...."[21]

Arbitrator Thomas J. McDermott in *Monarch Rubber Co.*[22] was asked to evaluate a series of grievances asking him to reinstate ten employees who had been suspended because they had refused to cooperate by taking a polygraph test in an investigation of a series of sabotage events that almost caused a plant to be closed. The plant was located in a West Virginia community where some 200 employees worked producing sheets of plastic material used to make heels and soles for shoes. Some person or persons unknown had thrown pieces of metal (small nuts, bolts, parts of hacksaw blades, small washers, and even broken knives) into the plastic compounds before they were hardened into shape, and the metal became embedded therein, making the sheets of material nonsaleable. The perpetrator or perpetrators could not be discovered through questioning or by covert observation by supervisors.

After another fouled batch, the plant was shut down for several days for cleaning and then, when the employees returned, another fouled batch occurred and the plant was again shut down.

Union officials met with the chairman of the board of directors and the other corporate officers. The chairman declared his intention to close the plant. The company's attorney then, in an effort to save the plant and the jobs of many innocent employees, proposed to the union officials that polygraph tests be taken by all employees who worked near the area where the sabotage occurred. The union official stated that "he did not like lie detector tests, that the international did not endorse the use of such tests but that the situation was grave and the life of the bargaining unit was at stake so that he could understand."[23]

The day after another meeting occurred between union and management representatives to complete the final plan for the polygraph testing, another act of sabotage occurred. The plant was closed down five days for cleaning. During this period the polygraph testing started, handled by examiners employed by a detective agency. Thirty employees (including some supervisors, at the request of union repre-

---

[20]Jones, note 4 *supra*, at pp. 103–04.

[21]*Id.* at p. 104

[22]Award of October 23, 1975 (McDermott), unreported, cited and discussed in Jones, note 4 *supra*, at pp. 110–14.

[23]*Id.* at p. 111.

sentatives) were scheduled for testing. Out of the thirty, ten refused to take the test and were suspended.

Grievances were subsequently filed on behalf of the ten, and these cases moved step by step up to Arbitrator McDermott. In addition to the filing of the grievances, the union filed an unfair practice charge with the NLRB against the company. The charge stated:

> The Employer, without just cause and in violation of the terms and provisions of the contract, discharged from their employment on September 12, 1974, the following named employees because of their failure to submit to a polygraph (lie-detector examination) in connection with an investigation being conducted regarding damage to certain company property. The Company acted in a discriminatory nature in the choice of persons to submit to said examination.[24]

The NLRB regional office investigated the charge and notified the union and the company that a complaint would not be issued, with this advice:

> The evidence revealed that the Employer's request that certain employees submit to a lie detector test to determine who was responsible for sabotage of the Employer's production process, and the subsequent suspension of employees who refused to submit to such test, was not in violation of the [National Labor Relations] Act. Where the Employer requires, as here, employees to submit to a lie detector test for legitimate business considerations, [an] individual employee's refusal to submit to the lie detector test does not constitute protected activity.[25]

During the sabotage period (over three months) more than 36,000 pounds of plastic compound mix had been destroyed. Over 60 shipments of material were sent back by customers. The measurable damage exceeded $300,000.

At the hearing two of ten grievants told Arbitrator McDermott that they had refused to take the test "because of the principle of the thing" and because "if they could not take my word, I would not take the test."[26] Others refused for other reasons. Arbitrator McDermott approved the suspension of the ten employees who refused to take the test. No further acts of sabotage occurred after the ten employees were suspended.

Arbitrator Edgar Jones in his paper said about this award: "Hard cases make bad law, Justice Holmes once observed."[27] Twenty employees took the test, ten refused; the sabotage ended. In spite of his general view opposing polygraph testing, Arbitrator Jones concluded

---

[24]*Id.* at p. 113.
[25]*Id.*
[26]*Id.*
[27]*Id.* at p. 114.

that the suspension of the ten grievants in this case should be considered an *exception:*

> It is difficult to fault Arbitrator McDermott's decision. This was subversive warfare. Substantial harm was being inflicted on the employer and on the community of workers and their families by some mentally unbalanced person or persons which was destroying this common enterprise.
>
> . . .
> ...The employees were being compelled on the threat of loss of livelihood to surrender a certain measure of dignity, in the sense of self-worth and of pride in personal integrity. It is those compelled surrenders—even aside from its inherent unreliability—which render the polygraph unacceptable as a tactic of investigation, ... *except,* the circumstances of *Monarch Rubber* now compel us to concede, when the dilemma confronting the employer is of such a harmful magnitude....[28] [Emphasis in original.]

Arbitrator Jones did, however, state that if employees were required by terms of a labor agreement to take a polygraph test in connection with an investigation of a theft, he as arbitrator would not sustain the discharge or suspension of any employee who refused to take a test because polygraph testing "contravenes public policy." He said:

> "What if the parties make [polygraph testing] subject to a term of their agreement...?" I must answer that I cannot as an arbitrator effectuate an express term which so contravenes public policy as to make it unconscionable for me to become the parties' instrument of injustice, as an accessory, as it were, to their wrongdoing.
>
> . . .
> ...[T]he uses of polygraphs are so contrary to accepted tenets of public policy that contract terms authorizing or requiring the subjecting of employees to them may not be effectuated by me as an arbitrator.[29]

Arbitrator Charles V. Laughlin sustained the suspension of a grievant in *Bowman Transportation, Inc.*[30] because he did not take a polygraph test. He had agreed to take one but finally refused on advice of his lawyer:

> In March, 1973, and prior thereto, grievant was a city driver for Bowman Transportation, Incorporated....
> In March, 1973, four cartons of revolvers were checked to the Atlanta terminal and placed in the dock office, a procedure followed because of the sensitive nature of firearms. Two dock employees, by the names of [M—— M——] and [W—— B. C——] loaded the four cartons on the city truck for delivery. The grievant was the driver of that truck....

[28]*Id.* at pp. 114–15.
[29]*Id.* at pp. 108–09.
[30]61 LA 549 (Laughlin, 1973).

Later in the day grievant called [L—— L——], terminal manager for the Company, and reported that when it came time to deliver the four cartons of revolvers only three cartons were on the truck. The missing carton contained 32 revolvers, valued at $904.48.

Upon being notified of the loss, the Company immediately notified the F.B.I. and the Atlanta police. Those agencies were given the serial numbers of the missing revolvers. The freight bill is in evidence as Company's exhibit one and shows all four cartons to be on the truck. [L——] questioned [M——] and [C——] as to whether the four cartons had been placed on the truck, as shown by the freight bill and manifest. They asserted that the four cartons were placed on the truck. They claimed to specifically remember because the cartons were carried from the dock office. These two loaders were asked to submit to a polygraph test, to which request they acquiesced. The tests were administered and the results were interpreted by the examiner as confirming the truthfulness of their assertions that they placed all four cartons on the truck.

Grievant was interviewed by [L——] and denied knowledge as to what could have become of the fourth carton. When asked if he would submit to a polygraph test he consented to take the test. Later that evening grievant called [L——] and stated that he had consulted a lawyer, and that, pursuant to his advice, grievant would not submit to the polygraph test. Shortly thereafter grievant was injured in an accident and was out of work for a month.

Upon his return to work grievant was again asked to submit to a polygraph test. He agreed, provided his lawyer could be present when the test was administered. To this condition [L——], for the Company, consented. All tests taken for the Company were administered by W. A. Robinson Associates, polygraph examiners licensed by the State of Georgia. . . .

Pursuant to the requirements of Georgia law the examiner prepared and submitted to grievant and his counsel the questions which would be propounded. . . . Pursuant to advice by his counsel, grievant refused to submit to the test unless it be limited to one or two questions limited to the specific issue of whether or not grievant took the carton of revolvers. The examiner refused to give a test so limited upon the ground that it could not be validly interpreted. The test, therefore, did not proceed.

[L——] testified that in recent times the Company had had a goodly number of thefts, and that it has become a standard Company policy and practice to require polygraph tests from those under suspicion. Upon cross examination by the Union representative, [L——] admitted that he was aware that the Union opposed the policy of requiring said tests. Grievant was informed that either he should take the test, as administered by W. A. Robinson and Associates, or he would be suspended until he did. Grievant still refused "as a matter of principle" and on May 16th a letter of suspension (joint exhibit two) was delivered to him.[31]

The arbitrator, after writing a substantial analysis, sustained the suspension on the ground the grievant had failed to cooperate.

---

[31]*Id.* at 549–50.

Arbitrator Ralph Roger Williams in *Grocers Supply Co.*[32] also sustained the discharge of an employee for refusing to take a polygraph test in violation of his agreement to do so if and when requested by the employer. Some $5,000 worth of company merchandise had been found by the police in a motor vehicle registered in the name of the grievant. The promise of the grievant to submit to a test, signed by him, read as follows:

I, K——, do hereby agree to submit to a Polygraph Test during my employment for Grocers Supply Company at any time the company may request. I fully understand that refusal to do so will be sufficient cause for dismissal.[33]

Arbitrator Williams stated his reasons for sustaining the discharge:

Employees may be required by their employer to undergo polygraph tests as a part of an investigation, and may be disciplined or discharged for refusal to submit to such a test. This is especially true when the employees sign a statement at the time they are hired agreeing to submit to a polygraph test during their employment at any time the employer may request.

The Grievant refused to follow instructions, and failed to do what he had agreed to do when he was hired. The guilt or innocence of the Grievant, with respect to the merchandise found by the police in a motor vehicle registered in the Grievant's name, is not at issue and is immaterial. The issue concerns whether or not the Company may require an employee to honor a written promise—made at the time of employment—to submit to a polygraph test if requested to do so by the Company at any time during the term of employment.[34]

Arbitrator Bernard Meltzer in *Maremont Corporation*[35] sustained the discharge of an employee who refused to cooperate, refusing to take a slightly different test requested by the employer. Arbitrator Meltzer explained:

A grievant, accused of being drunk, refused to take a breath analyzer test. . . .

. . .

. . . [T]he Union's contention raises the question of whether the privilege operates in an arbitration proceedings to bar evidence of a grievant's refusal to take an intoxication test when the only purpose and effect of that evidence relates to the propriety of Company discipline. . . .

. . .

The privilege against self-incrimination operates to protect individuals in their relations with government, and specifically, is designed to provide protection against the risk of criminal penalties arising from compulsion

---

[32]75 LA 27 (Williams, 1980).
[33]*Id.* at 28.
[34]*Id.* at 29.
[35](Meltzer, 1969), unreported.

of government... The relationship between an employer and his employees is significantly different from the relationship between a state and its citizens.... The penalties imposed by the state for criminal offenses are also materially different from discharge in some situations.

. . .

There is plainly no basis for distinguishing between a grievant's refusal to answer and this grievant's refusal to take a test under the circumstances here involved.[36]

Arbitrator Ryder in *B. F. Goodrich Tire Co.*[37] discussed the "just cause" *difference* between the discharge of a grievant who refused to cooperate by refusing to take the test and one who takes the test but does not "pass" it:

Next, standing alone and unconnected and uncoupled with evidence of some relationship to the robberies, can the failure of all three employees to satisfactorily pass the polygraphic testing, or even the affirmative refusal of two of them at the time to continue being tested so that they stand as having failed, be that kind of behavior reasonably defined as uncooperative on the part of an employee under the circumstances? In addition to what already has been stated the following reasoning requires the perforce answering of this question in the negative.

In essence, the Company's position here is that the employees did not cooperate because they denied untruthfully knowledge they had about the robberies or their participation therein. The Company invests them with such knowledge purely on the results of the tests. The charge of not cooperating was premised on the basis that the grievants did not clear themselves of falsehoods connected with the sparkplug thefts and until they told the truth they remained uncooperative. The mere refusal of B—— and Z—— at the time to take a second series of testings is not the real grievance of the Company's charge of lack of cooperation with respect to them. The charge is founded on the conclusion that all the men have deceived and until they remove their deception by telling the truth of what they know about the sparkplug thefts they remain uncooperative and should not continue in their employ.[38]

Arbitrator Ralph C. Hon in *Bunker Ramo Corp.*[39] also discussed the issue of "cooperation" that arises when an employee takes the test but does not pass (*i.e.*, deception is reported) and came to the same conclusion as Arbitrator Ryder. Eighteen thousand dollars' worth of silver bars which had been hanging in the plating tanks were stolen. An investigator working with the Chicago police recovered the bars from a Chicago coin dealer and learned that T—— R——, a former

---

[36]*Id.*
[37]36 LA 552 (Ryder, 1961).
[38]*Id.* at 556-57.
[39]76 LA 857 (Hon, 1981).

Bunker Ramo employee terminated about seven weeks before the theft was discovered, sold the bars to the coin dealer. T—— R—— then admitted his involvement (the sale of the bars) in the theft and was convicted. He refused, however, to reveal the name or names of Bunker Ramo Corporation employees who had access to the plating tanks area and who took the bars out of the tank. The investigation was then directed toward the group of employees "who might have knowledge concerning the disappearance of the silver" from the plating tanks; these employees were asked to take a polygraph test.

Of the twenty-eight employees in the group, twenty-four were removed from the group under investigation because they "passed" the test when they said they had no information related to the theft. Their answers were considered to be truthful. The remaining four were suspended and later discharged for "failing to cooperate in a legitimate company investigation." Grievances were filed and consolidated and presented to Arbitrator Hon.

At the hearing the four grievants said they took the test because the employer asked them to do so but that they cooperated only because, Arbitrator Hon reported, "they felt they had no realistic choice." One of the four said, the arbitrator noted, "if they did not take the tests they would not be cooperating and if they did not cooperate they would be subject to discipline."[40]

The polygrapher testified at the hearing that the four had not answered truthfully, explaining: (1) Grievant R—— H—— denied having any knowledge of the missing bars and how they were removed from the plant but deceptive reaction was reported on these denials. He admitted he knew T—— R——. (2) Grievant K—— did not answer the question as to whether or not he was directly involved in the disappearance of the bars and hence no deception on answer to that question was measured. The examiner "found deception in K——'s answers as to participation in thefts of precious metals from the company and withholding knowledge about the theft and who wrote a letter to the company naming a person who was involved." K—— stressed that the stealing of the silver "just had to be an inside job." (3) Grievant J. R—— withheld "information concerning the bars," "knowledge as to who is involved," "information pertinent to the investigation," knowledge as to who wrote the letter. R—— said he was a good friend of T—— R——. (4) Grievant R—— S—— denied being "directly or indirectly involved" in the removal of bars from the plant and her denial indicated a "deception" and another "deception" when she denied she saw someone "take the silver from the tank, and further, assisting or

---

[40]*Id.* at 866.

helping someone in the theft of the silver." She admitted that she "knew T——."[41]

Arbitrator Hon concluded that once the grievant took the test, the "duty to cooperate" threshold had been crossed. Thereafter deception alone would not support a discharge. The company would have to then prove that the grievant was involved in the theft. Since the company had not made such a claim but merely discharged the grievants for deception, he reinstated the grievants. Lack of candor *per se* is not "just cause" for a discharge.[42]

Arbitrator Lawrence E. Seibel in *C & P Telephone Co.*[43] has a somewhat different view of the degree to which there is a duty to cooperate. In a case not involving polygraph testing, he sustained the discharge of a storekeeper because he had withheld information about a theft of 2,000 pounds of wiping solder. After the solder had been found in the possession of a junk dealer, with the words "Bell System" stamped in the pigs, the service center at the plant had been placed under surveillance on those nights when wiping solder was being delivered. Approximately five weeks later, two of the employees in the "supply group" were apprehended and indicted for stealing company property. The arbitrator sustained the discharge of the storekeeper:

> The Grievant admitted that at least from September 1967 he knew what was transpiring but did not divulge his information to his supervisor.... The Grievant was discharged for knowing about the situation and not telling management about it and further, for continuing to order solder in excessive quantities during the period in question, when he knew or should have known it was being stolen.
>
> . . .
>
> ...[T]here is no evidence that the Grievant was in the company of the employees who were stealing Company material or that he participated in the theft. Admittedly, the Union concedes, the Grievant knew what was going on but did not pursue the matter as diligently as, he now realizes, he should have....
>
> The Union concedes that perhaps the Grievant was trying to be "too much of a buddy to his co-workers" in not being a "stool pigeon" but, it argues, much has been done in the way of friendship which objectively should not have been done....
>
> . . .
>
> To sum up, the Grievant was fully aware, or at the very least should have known, that extensive thefts were occurring, that despite his obligation to inform the Company he failed to do so under a misguided sense of loyalty to fellow-employees, and that as a consequence, the period during

---

[41]*Id.* at 858–60.
[42]*Id.* at 867.
[43]51 LA 457 (Seibel, 1968).

which stealing occurred was extended. Under such circumstances it cannot be concluded that the Company's discharge action was not justified.[44]

In the *Bowman Transportation, Inc.* case[45] discussed *supra* involving the theft of a number of revolvers, when the issue submitted was "whether grievant's refusal to submit to a polygraph test is 'reasonable cause' for suspension," Arbitrator Charles V. Laughlin denied the grievance:

> At the hearing both parties clearly emphasized that grievant has not been accused of the theft of the revolvers. He was not suspended either for theft or for suspicion of theft. At the hearing the Union representative asked the witness [L——], the Company's terminal manager, what the Company would do if grievant would take the test and "flunk" it. [L——] frankly answered "I do not know." We are not confronted with either the question of whether, had grievant been disciplined for alleged theft, his refusal to take the test could be used as circumstantial evidence of guilt, or the question of whether had he taken the test, the result thereof could be used as evidence.[46]

Arbitrator John P. McGury in *Simoniz Co.*[47] sustained the discharge of an employee who refused to cooperate in a theft investigation:

> Employers properly have a higher criteria of employee qualifications than the mere freedom from a criminal conviction. Employers have a right to absolute honesty, as well as a reasonable amount of cooperation, from their employees.
>
> . . .
>
> The background fact stipulated to, or amply-proven, that the grievant occupied a position in the plant which made it logical for the Company to seek his full cooperation in establishing the anatomy of the crime.
>
> . . .
>
> An employee is in a position of trust while in the scope of his employment when he has custody of, or access to, Company property.
>
> None of these reasons assume, or even suggest, the personal guilt of the grievant, but they clearly establish that the Company had ample reason to be concerned over the large theft, to be thorough in their investigation thereof, and to be suspicious of the grievant's lack of cooperation in said investigation.[48]

It is quite understandable why tellers in banks, cashiers in stores, or other employees who handle thousands of dollars each day can be asked to be tested often, either on a regular or irregular basis. Employees

---

[44]*Id.* at 457-60.
[45]61 LA 549 (Laughlin, 1973).
[46]*Id.* at 550.
[47]44 LA 658 (McGury, 1964).
[48]*Id.* at 663.

working directly with money know they will be asked to take tests. Losses due to employee theft now total millions of dollars each year[49] and since the managers are obligated to take all reasonable steps to protect the company's property to reduce losses, more polygraph testing will undoubtedly be introduced.

There may be more requests for testing, and the limits on the duty to cooperate should be defined. The arbitrator in *Neuhoff Bros. Packers*[50] reinstated an employee who had been discharged for failing to cooperate by refusing to take a *second* polygraph test in connection with the same theft. The district court vacated the reinstatement order, holding that the employee's duty to cooperate included the taking of a second test, but the Fifth Circuit in *Meat Cutters v. Neuhoff Bros. Packers*[51] reversed, concluding that the district court was in error in vacating the arbitrator's reinstatement order.

Somewhat related to the problem of the limit on the number of times an employee can be asked to be tested concerning the same event is the problem of the limit on the scope of the questions that may be asked in a specific investigation by a polygrapher. The willingness to "cooperate" by taking the test is related to a willingness to be questioned about a particular theft, and if the questions drift into other areas, the questioning might be considered "fishing." Arbitrator Charles Laughlin in *Bowman Transportation, Inc.*[52] said the questioning should be related to the investigation:

> This arbitrator proceeds upon premise that an employer may compel an employee to take a polygraph test if, without said test, there is a plausible showing that the employee is guilty of seriously dishonest acts. In at least two of the cases in which polygraph testing was not looked upon with favor by the arbitrators, there was no other evidence against the grievant. The employer sought to use the polygraph test as a "fishing expedition."
>
> . . .
>
> In this case the circumstantial evidence against the grievant was sufficient to justify further investigation. Grievant was one of three persons who might be normally suspect. The other two took the polygraph test and were exonerated. It is not here determined that grievant was guilty of the theft. That is not the issue. The issue is whether, under the circumstances, the employer acted reasonably in requiring grievant to take the test.
>
> The Arbitrator is not passing upon any question except that narrowly involved here. He does not pass upon whether an employer could require a test of an employee against whom there is no other evidence of guilt.

[49]Jones, note 4 *supra*, at p. 92, n. 36; *See also Business Buys the Lie Detector*, Business Week, February 6, 1978, 100–104.
[50]Award discussed in the court decision, note 51 *infra*.
[51]481 F.2d 817, 83 LRRM 2652 (5th Cir. 1973).
[52]61 LA 549 (Laughlin, 1973).

Neither is the arbitrator passing upon the admissibility, or probative value, of the results of tests voluntarily taken by a small or large number of employees.[53]

THE RIGHT TO REFUSE TO COOPERATE AND
NOT TAKE A TEST

The sharply *contra* view to that discussed *supra*, held by some arbitrators, is that employees have no duty to cooperate with their employer and can refuse to take a polygraph test in a theft investigation after being requested to do so by their employer. As mentioned earlier in this chapter, this view was announced by Arbitrator Sembower in *General American Transportation Corporation*[54] in 1958. Thirty-four welders at the General American Transportation plant located in South Chicago had been welding railroad car roofs for a 500-car order. As each roof was welded, it was lifted by a crane to the erection track and there welded onto the car frame. Each day the welders turned in a report of the numbers of roofs they had welded and each week they were paid an incentive payment based on the number of roofs welded that week. It was not until the costs were examined about two months after the order was completed that it was discovered that an excess of $3,300 had been paid to welders for welding roofs. Obviously, some of the 35 welders who welded roofs had falsely reported the number they had worked on, thus stealing incentive money from the company.[55]

The General American Transportation manager decided to deduct the excess payment from each welder's pay by dividing the total excess by the hours spent welding roofs and multiplying the result by the hours spent by a particular welder welding roofs during the two-month period. The union representatives challenged this deduction procedure on the ground that there was *no* evidence that *all* of the welders had turned in false counts. The manager then offered a more equitable plan: Each employee who had worked one or more hours welding roofs would take a polygraph test and those who *denied* false counting and *passed* the test (no deception) would have no deduction. This would mean that the $3,300 stolen from the company would be spread over the hours worked by those welders who (1) did not pass the test or (2) refused to take one. Under this plan it was specifically stated that no discipline would be imposed for failure to pass or refusal to be tested. This second plan was offered to improve the equity in the deduction plan. The union representative said that some plan of deduction

[53]*Id.* at 555–56.
[54]31 LA 355 (Sembower, 1958).
[55]*Id.* at 356.

should be developed but he would not approve the plan suggested by the company because polygraph testing was inconsistent with union policy.[56]

The dispute over (1) the original deduction plan and (2) the alternative deduction plan was submitted to Arbitrator Sembower. Fred E. Inbau, of the Northwestern University School of Law, was made available as an expert witness and he explained that the testing would be direct and uncomplicated. A "no pass" would report accurately whether the welders had overcharged by reporting an excess number of roofs welded.[57]

The Right to Refuse Because the Investigation Was "Wholesale"

Arbitrator Sembower discussed Arbitrator Klamon's *Allen Industries* decision,[58] issued two years earlier, and said that the discipline of a single employee who refused to take a polygraph test might be proper, but in this case the company's proposal to distribute deductions for the overcharging was a "wholesale" polygraph investigation:

> In the instant case no formal accusations were proffered against the individual employees and therefore a *wholesale* application of a lie detector test ought not be imposed as a condition precedent to the reinstatement of the blanket across-the-board pro rata deductions from the incentive paychecks. . . .[59] [Emphasis added.]

Arbitrator Sembower attempted to explain the difference between his award and the one by Arbitrator Klamon:

> That appears to give us the test as to when it is reasonable for the lie detector to be used: when the individual is, at least, the subject of a formal accusation. It will be noted that in the *Allen Industries* arbitration, the employees indeed were formally accused. By this is not meant that they must be indicted for a crime, but that, at least, the employer shall have made sufficient investigation to equip him with facts warranting an accusation of the employee, and not merely be on a fishing expedition that will [seine] up the fish simply because a predatory fish or two is known to be at large in the pond.[60] [Emphasis omitted.]

---

[56]*Id.* at 360.

[57]*Id.* at 361. Arbitrator Sembower was not concerned with the lack of accuracy in the distribution formula. He reported in his award at 31 LA 361:

The arbitration had the advantage of testimony in detail from Prof. Inbau, whose writings are almost an oracle on the modern version of the lie detector, the polygraph, which is regarded by some criminologists as an invaluable if not indispensable adjunct to criminal detection. Although he was called by the Company, his testimony was objective and scientific. In his expert opinion, the device would be 95 per cent accurate in screening the truth from the employees involved here, and the rest of the five percent would include four that were inconclusive and one potential error.

[58]26 LA 363 (Klamon, 1956), discussed at 31 LA 362.

[59]31 LA at 364.

[60]*Id.* at 363.

The fact that thirty-five welders were in the investigation group in *General American* and one in *Allen Industries* does not seem to make the former investigation wrong and the latter right. The Department of Justice used polygraph testing procedures to investigate 200 FBI employees to seek to discover who had leaked information to the press which caused the investigation of the bribing of members of Congress, referred to as the FBI ABSCAM program, to end.[61] Attorney Michael Abbell of the Department of Justice said he saw "no paradox in having a policy against admitting polygraph evidence at a criminal trial while using polygraph tests in investigating the leaks of information about the ABSCAM Congressional bribery probe. We find the polygraph to be a valuable investigative tool."[62]

The Right to Refuse to Cooperate to Protect Against Self-Incrimination

Arbitrator Sembower objected to the General American Transportation plan not merely because it was "wholesale" but because polygraph testing "is a violation of the privilege against self-incrimination."[63] On the other hand, Arbitrator Charles V. Laughlin in *Bowman Transportation, Inc.* [64] explained why the privilege against self-incrimination does not support an employee's refusal to cooperate with the employer when he or she refuses to take a test:

> There are two reasons why grievant cannot refuse the polygraph test for any reason analogous to the Fifth Amendment's privilege against self incrimination.
>
> First, even a governmental agency may dismiss an employee who refuses to answer questions which relate to his competence to hold his position, even though the answers to said questions might tend to incriminate him. True, a governmental agency may not use a threat of discharge as an instrument for forcing an employee to abandon his privilege, if law enforcement rather than job competence is the reason for the threatened discharge. But a different result obtains when there is a connection between the interrogation and competence to do the work. Gardner v. Broderick, 392 U.S. 273, 278 (1967). Although the Company, in this case, is interested in helping the law enforcement agencies solve this unfortunate theft, the honesty of an employee is definitely an appropriate interest of the employer. The arbitration in Simoniz Co. 44 LA 659 (1944) reached the conclusion that an employer may discharge an employee who refuses to testify about alleged thefts, not withstanding the protection of the Fifth Amendment.

---

[61]LEGAL TIMES OF WASHINGTON No. 10 (August 11, 1980), at 13.
[62]*Id.*
[63]31 LA at 364.
[64]61 LA 549 (Laughlin, 1973).

There is an even stronger reason why the privilege against self incrimination is not involved in this case. There is no threat of the privilege being
violated. The privilege is against being required to answer questions which
are susceptible to incriminatory answers. It is not a privilege to lie. It does
not protect a person who willingly answers a question susceptible to an incriminatory answer from having the veracity of his answer checked. For example, a person who answers incriminatory questions may be subject to
having his answers checked by cross-examination. The polygraph test is
similar. It neither adds nor detracts so far as the privilege is concerned.
Here, the only question grievant is willing to answer is one of an incriminatory nature. Since he is willing to answer, the only objection grievant legitimately has, based upon self incrimination, to having his answers
checked by a polygraph is the reliability of the test.[65]

Arbitrator Ryder in *Illinois Bell Telephone Co.*[66] supported Arbitrator Sembower's view. He said that a requested polygraph test in a
theft investigation was inconsistent with an employee's privilege
against self-incrimination and hence was "a proposition repugnant to
Anglo-Saxon legal codes." A reference to an Anglo-Saxon legal code is
quite out of place in labor arbitration because that code was signed by
King John of England in 1215 to ensure that the kings could no longer
torture or imprison royal subjects to force them to incriminate
themselves.[67] The protection against self-incrimination set forth in this
important charter was incorporated as the Fifth Amendment of the
United States Constitution. Arbitrator Douglas B. Maggs in *Lockheed
Aircraft Corp.*[68] explained that the privilege to stand mute (called
"taking the Fifth") is effective only in criminal interrogations by police
officers or prosecutors in a criminal trial. No legal "privilege" permits
an employee to refuse to answer an employer's questions about his or
her misconduct.[69] Arbitrator John R. McGury in *Simoniz Co.*[70] said
that an employee cannot avoid discipline by the employer by "taking
the Fifth":

> If a trusted Union official, who had custody of a substantial amount of
> Union funds, was suddenly unable to account for such funds, and invoked

[65]*Id.* at 554.
[66]39 LA 470, 479 (Ryder, 1962).
[67]The origin of this privilege was well explained in *Burdeau v. McDowell,* 256 U.S. 465, 475
(1921) and *Schmerber v. California,* 384 U.S. 757, 764 (1966). For a thorough discussion of the
application of Fifth Amendment principles to polygraphy examination, *see* Note, *Problems Remaining for "Generally Accepted Polygraph,"* 53 B.U.L. REV. 375, 390-400 (1973). *See also
United States v. Ridling,* 350 F. Supp. 90, 97-98 (E.D. Mich. 1972); *Bowen v. Eyman,* 324 F.
Supp. 339, 341 (D. Ariz. 1970); *Griffin v. California,* 380 U.S. 609 (1965).
[68]27 LA 709, 713 (Maggs, 1956).
[69]"Taking the Fifth" (i.e., remaining mute) would mean the grievant would give up his or her
opportunity to rebut the employer's *prima facie* case, usually causing the arbitrator to sustain
the discharge when the grievant does not respond and rebut.
[70]44 LA 658 (McGury, 1964).

his Fifth Amendment privilege in a subsequent criminal proceeding, and was, through the complexities of the criminal law, acquitted, could he reasonably be guaranteed his high Union post on the grounds that his dismissal therefrom would be in consequence of his taking the Fifth Amendment, and thereby, a violation of the spirit of the said Amendment?

. . .

The Fifth Amendment does not guarantee that a person who invokes it will not be subject to any unfavorable inference and does not guarantee that a person who invokes it shall be continued in employment.

The responsible Company official who ignored this would be hard put to explain to his superiors, or to the bonding company, why he retained an employee who took the Fifth Amendment in a case involving substantial theft from the Company.[71]

In contrast, Arbitrator Seth Brewer in *Southern Biscuit Co.,*[72] like Arbitrator Sembower, believes that an employee should be able to refuse to comply with the employer's request to take a test in a theft investigation. In *Southern Biscuit Co.* he went even further, borrowing criminal law principles. He said when an employer makes a request of an employee to take a test the employer must add a *Miranda*-type warning[73] so the employee would know that the employer would not discipline or even criticize that employee if the employee refuses to cooperate. A police officer must tell a suspect that he or she may refuse to answer questions without adverse effect. Requiring the employer to give this warning places the employer in the role of a police officer.

In this case the grievant had been discharged for breaking the lock on the milk dispensing machine during a night shift. The guard testified that he saw the grievant standing outside the building for about two or three minutes and then saw him enter the building and start up the stairs. The guard followed the grievant because he had been asked to keep "a close eye" on the food machine because "there had been several break-ins in the last few months." The guard said that after reaching the third floor landing "he heard a crack like a lock on a food machine being broken" and he immediately went into the lunch room. There he saw the grievant "walking toward the northernmost door" and after inspecting the food machine he found the lock had been broken.[74]

The grievant agreed to take a polygraph test but the arbitrator ignored the results reported by the polygrapher because the grievant "was not only not advised of his right not to take the test, but he was

---

[71]*Id.* at 663.
[72]74-2 ARB ¶ 8386 (Brewer, 1974).
[73]*Id.* at 4462.
[74]*Id.* at 4461.

obviously coerced into taking it when he was first informed of his discharge and then offered a chance to redeem himself by submitting to the test."[75] Arbitrator Brewer said that because the employer did not give the employee the *Miranda*-type warning and asked him to take the test *after* rather than *before* his discharge, "I can give no effect to the results of the test" and stated:

> This boils the case against [D.] down to the evidence and testimony of Guard [S.] concerning hearing a noise that could have been the breaking of a lock on an automatic food machine as he approached the cafeteria area and getting a glance of [D.] leaving the area, some 70–80 feet . . . away when the guard entered the area.
>
> . . .
>
> However the Company failed to establish a case against [D.] beyond a reasonable doubt and I do not insist upon "seeing the smoking gun."[76]

The Right to Refuse to Cooperate to Protect Privacy

Arbitrator Sembower in *General American Transportation*[77] also added that an employer cannot properly ask an employee to take a polygraph test because "its use constitutes an unwarranted invasion of the subject's privacy." The phrase "right of privacy" was first initiated in a famous *Harvard Law Review* article[78] written by Samuel Warren and Louis Brandeis in which it was explained that the "right to privacy" has four general types: *appropriation* (*e.g.,* using a plaintiff's photograph in an advertisement *without consent*);[79] *intrusion* (for example, having a private conversation monitored by an eavesdropper through wiretapping *without consent*);[80] *public disclosure of private facts* (for example, giving publicity to private information *without consent*);[81] and *false light in the public eye* (*e.g.,* placing the plaintiff's name or photograph in association with persons considered to be disreputable *without consent*).[82] Since no polygraph examination can

---

[75]*Id.* at 4462.

[76]*Id.*

[77]31 LA 355 (Sembower, 1958). *See also Town & Country Food Co.,* 39 LA 332 (Lewis, 1962) (polygraph tests were viewed to be "an invasion of privacy").

[78]Warren and Brandeis, *The Right of Privacy,* 4 HARV. L. REV. 193 (1890). *See also* Prosser, LAW OF TORTS (St. Paul: West Pub. Co., 1972), pp. 802–18.

[79]In an early case a claim was made against a woman because her picture was printed on a flour sack *without her consent. Roberson v. Rochester Folding Box Company,* 171 N.Y. 538, 64 N.E. 442 (1902).

[80]Prosser, note 78 *supra,* at p. 807. *Rhodes v. Graham,* 238 Ky. 225, 37 S.W.2d 461 (1931).

[81]Prosser, note 78 *supra,* at p. 809. The defendant placed a notice in a window of his garage to the effect that the plaintiff owed him money and would not pay him. *Brents v. Morgan,* 221 Ky. 765, 299 S.W. 867 (1927).

[82]Prosser, note 78 *supra,* at p. 811.

be taken *without the consent* of the employee, the basic lack of consent element needed to prove an invasion of the employee's privacy cannot be found in the *General American Transportation* plan to redistribute a deduction of the stolen money. Arbitrator Charles V. Laughlin in *Bowman Transportation, Inc.*[83] discussed Arbitrator Sembower's invasion of privacy view:

> The most forceful objection to requiring polygraph testing, made by the Union, may best be stated by quoting from the union brief:
> Polygraph testing has nothing to do with the dubious accuracy of the polygraph technique but is addressed to its effect on the privacy and liberty of an individual. Few Labor Boards and other regulatory agencies and courts who have criticized and rejected the use of these machines in a variety of contexts have based their criticism on this argument. Professor Gerhard Mueller of New York Law School has suggested the courts and critics seem to be merely using a scientific imperfection argument to avoid the issue of ethical justification for probing a man's mind.[84]

In another situation Arbitrator Ray reinstated an airline stewardess in *Braniff Airways, Inc.*[85] who had been discharged because contraband drugs had been found in her purse; this set up the normal presumption that she was involved in moving the illegal drugs, because they were in her possession. She testified that her husband had put the marijuana in her purse before she left the mainland on a flight to Hawaii and back, and that she did not notice it in her folio throughout this period. The stewardess refused to take a polygraph test because she was apprehensive that the test might report that she knew the drug was in her possession because she discovered it in her folio after she returned. Arbitrator Ray said:

> Assuming that the drug was in Grievant's folio when she picked it up at her husband's home on September 15 it seems unlikely that she would not have discovered it during the trip to and from Honolulu since she admittedly opened the folio two or more times to check her paperwork. But it is entirely possible that the drug could have been overlooked.... Under the circumstances I have a nagging doubt and I think a reasonable one as to whether Grievant knew the marijuana was in her possession. In this situation I could not in good conscience uphold the extreme penalty of discharge.[86]

Arbitrator Ray did not consider the grievant's refusal to take the test a breach of cooperation. Likewise, Arbitrator Thomas Fair Neblett in

---

[83]61 LA 549 (Laughlin, 1973).
[84]*Id.* at 554.
[85]73 LA 304 (Ray, 1979).
[86]*Id.* at 310.

Chapman Harbor Convalescent Hospital[87] said a grievant who agreed to take a test and then changed her mind had the right to do so.

The Right to Refuse to Cooperate Because "The Weight of Arbitral Authority Is Against Polygraphy"

Arbitrator Paul Hardy in *Bowman Transportation, Inc.*[88] based his reinstatement on the "great weight of both arbitration and legal authority" that a grievant can refuse to cooperate with the employer after being asked to take a test:

> Relative to the charge that the Grievant refused to cooperate by not agreeing to take a polygraph test, it is the opinion of the Arbitrator that no individual's refusal to submit to a polygraph test should prejudice him in any way. I find that the great weight of both arbitration and legal authority is opposed to the use of polygraph results as competent evidence.[89]

In *Temtex Products, Inc.*[90] the grievant had been discharged because she refused to take a polygraph test even after nineteen employees in the group had been tested when it was discovered after an inventory was completed that 300 to 400 copper discs used in manufacturing artillery shells had been stolen. The twenty employees selected as the investigation group were told they would be dismissed if they refused to take the test. Nineteen took the test and were cleared; the grievant refused and was discharged. During various grievance meetings she was offered reinstatement if she took a test but she "continued to refuse." Arbitrator Thomas Rimer read Arbitrator Edgar Jones' paper[91] and explained:

> The clear weight of arbitral and judicial authority holds that lie detector evidence is inadmissible and that an individual's refusal to submit to such a test should not prejudice him in any way. An analysis of this principle is found in a paper presented to the National Academy of Arbitrators in the proceedings of its Thirty-First Annual Meeting (1979) by Edgar A. Jones, Jr., Professor of Law at the University of California at Los Angeles. His lengthy evaluation of the polygraph device includes this statement, "In summary, the conclusion is compelling that no matter how well qualified educationally or experientially may be the polygraphist, the results of the lie-detector tests should routinely be ruled inadmissible."[92]

---

[87]64 LA 27 (Neblett, 1975); *see also to the same effect Skaggs-Stone, Inc.*, 40 LA 1273 (Koven, 1963); *Sanna Dairies, Inc.*, 43 LA 16 (Rice, 1964); *Continental Air Transport Co.*, 38 LA 779 (Eiger, 1962).

[88]60 LA 837 (Hardy,1973).

[89]*Id.* at 838; *see* "Admissibility of Polygrapher's Testimony in Criminal and Civil Courts" in Chapter XIV.

[90]75 LA 233 (Rimer, 1980).

[91]Jones, note 4 *supra*.

[92]75 LA at 233.

The discipline for "refusing to cooperate" by refusing to take a polygraph test in a theft investigation is not directly related to the admissibility or nonadmissibility of a polygrapher's testimony in an arbitration hearing (discussed in the chapter XIV). Those arbitrators who do not in this situation support discipline for refusal to cooperate with the employer reason that if the test had been taken and the test results could not be presented to the arbitrator, the arbitrator should not support discipline for the employee's refusal to do something the results of which the arbitrator would refuse to hear. It does not follow, of course, that after such an investigation a grievance will always be filed and that an arbitration will take place and that one party will then submit a polygrapher to the arbitrator as an expert witness.

Arbitrator Charles Laughlin in *Bowman Transportation, Inc.*[93] explained that during testing an individual who produces a "deception" reaction on the tape to a critical question will often confess:

[I]f the result of the test should be adverse to grievant it might induce him to confess. It has been recognized that one of the values of polygraph testing is the inducing of confessions. A. v. B., 72 Misc.2d 719, 336 N.Y.S.2d 839 (1972), Marathon Electric Mfg. Corp., 31 LA 1040 (1959). If that result should occur a serious problem would be solved.

Arbitrator M. S. Ryder in *Ilinois Bell Telephone Co.*[94] accepted the testimony of Mr. John E. Reid, a well-known polygrapher at the hearing, over the objection of the union:

Next, the Chairman holds that the testimony of Mr. John E. Reid, polygraphic expert, teacher and former president of the American Academy of Polygraph Examiners and conceded by the Union as probably the best known man in the field in the country, where it relates to the results of the polygraphic testing he administered to V——, is admissible over objection, as relevant and pertinent testimony. V——freely consented to the testing. The test results are coupled with much other independent and significant evidenciary material leading to and causing the Company to discharge V——. These will be set forth later in this Opinion.[95]

In spite of the fact that he disagrees with the general nonacceptability thesis expressed by Arbitrator Thomas Rimer, Arbitrator Ryder does agree with him that discipline of an employee who refused to take a test in an investigation would be improper:

It appears that the polygraph has been an effective instrument in indicating deception in the heavy preponderance of cases. However, where there is employee refusal to give consent to such testing, the refusal, stand-

[93]61 LA 549, 557 (Laughlin, 1973).
[94]39 LA 470 (Ryder, 1962).
[95]*Id.* at 479.

ing by itself and coupled or not coupled with the presence of factual material giving reasonable suspicion of culpability, is not that kind of behavior that should be an offense in and of itself.[96]

Arbitrator David Dolnick in *Mount Sinai Hospital Center*[97] said that *"a refusal to submit* to a lie detector is not evidence of guilt nor is it an act of *insubordination* justifying disciplinary action.... This *principle* is generally accepted by arbitrators *and by courts."* (Emphasis added.) Courts quite obviously do not announce *principles* over the discipline of employees who refuse to cooperate with the employer by refusing to take tests in a theft investigation, nor have courts announced legal *principles* over the act of *insubordination* by an employee. Insubordination in the form of refusal to cooperate is a personnel concern and Arbitrator Dolnick's assertion that courts have announced principles in this area is obviously overstated.

Arbitrator Dolnick also stated in *Purolator Armored*[98] his view that: "There is even no unanimity among arbitrators that polygraph results were admissible in evidence even when the subject voluntarily takes the examination."[99] He explained in his award that Arbitrator Edgar H. Jones reported in his paper that the concerns over nonacceptability of the testimony of a polygrapher "would be wholly dissipated if an employee were to 'consent' to be tested."[100] He stated in the award:

> Edgar A. Jones, Jr., Professor of Law at the University of California in Los Angeles ... discussing the admissibility of polygraph evidence wrote as follows:
> "Oddly, my research disclosed that there are arbitrators who reason to exclusion or no weight conclusions based on 'unreliability,' yet whose concerns in this regard would be wholly dissipated if an employee were to 'consent' to be tested. But that is surely an unwordly view on at least two grounds. First, and obviously, unreliability is not altered simply because some workers succumbing to employer appeals to motivations of fear or favor express or implicit in the situation, have been conned into submitting to it. Second, and less obviously but no less realistically, the 'consent' of an innocent employee, fearful of the loss of livelihood or reputation, over whom looms the possibility of criminal proceedings brought by a presumed influential employer in the community who is angered by the refusal of a suspected employee to 'cooperate,' is no real consent."[101] [Footnotes omitted.]

It is quite obvious that any grievant who has been tested has consented to be tested—no one can force a grievant into an examining

[96]*Id.*
[97]73 LA 297, 303 (Dolnick, 1979).
[98]80-2 ARB ¶ 8409 (Dolnick, 1980).
[99]*Id.* at 4831.
[100]*Id.* at 4831, quoting Jones, note 4 *supra*, at pp. 102–103.
[101]*Id.*

room, tie him or her down, and ask questions. A grievant's answering of questions can only occur if he or she has consented. Of course, the willingness to consent may well be because the individual wants to cooperate with his or her employer or because the individual believes that it is wise for him or her to do so.

The Right to Refuse to Cooperate Because Testing Contravenes Public Policy

Arbitrator Jones said in his paper that even if employees were required by the terms of the labor agreement to take a polygraph test upon the request of the employer, and the employee violated the agreement by refusing to take the test, he (Jones) would not sustain a discipline for the employee's breach of the agreement.

He said that he could not, "as an arbitrator, effectuate an express term which so contravenes public policy as to make it unconscionable for me to become the parties' instrument of injustice, as an accessory, as it were, to their wrongdoing."[102] And he added:

> [T]he uses of polygraphs are so *contrary to accepted tenets of public policy* that contract terms authorizing or requiring the subjecting of employees to them may not be effectuated by me as an arbitrator.[103] [Emphasis added.]

As pointed out, *supra*, polygraphy cannot be contrary to public policy because legislators have provided for licensing of polygraphers to operate in twenty-three states, making polygraphy a licensed profession. The legislators in these states could not be enacting statutes that are contrary to public policy.

At the time Arbitrator Jones stated his refusal to enforce a provision of a labor agreement, he had not actually faced such a case. He merely said he *would* refuse to enforce the agreement between the parties if he personally faced such a case. The Supreme Court has clearly stated that an arbitrator should not ignore the commitment of the parties because some commitment of the parties was contrary to *his* brand of industrial justice:

> [H]e [the arbitrator] does not sit to dispense his own brand of industrial justice. . . . When the arbitrator's words manifest an infidelity to the obligation, courts have no choice but to refuse enforcement of the award.[104]

---

[102]Jones, note 4 *supra*, at p. 108.
[103]*Id.* at p. 109.
[104]*United Steelworkers of America v. Enterprise Wheel and Car Corp.*, 363 U.S. 593, 597, 46 LRRM 2423, 2425 (1960).

In contrast, however, Arbitrator David Dolnick, in *Buy-Low, Inc.* [105] *did* face the situation speculated upon by Arbitrator Jones. The company was a signatory to an industry-wide labor agreement negotiated with the United Food and Commercial Workers International Union. The parties agreed that all employees would be required to submit to polygraph tests whenever requested by the employer.[106] Buy-Low, Inc. also negotiated a supplemental agreement with that union which included a "management rights" provision, and negotiated individual agreements to be signed by the employees. The latter individual agreements were consistent with the two labor agreements with the union (one industry-wide and one local). One specifically required the employee-signer to take tests upon request.[107] This agreement provided the following:

> I, _____, hereby agree that at any time or from time to time at the request of my employer to submit to a polygraph (lie detector) examination to be given by Personnel Screening Service to determine my honesty, integrity and general reliability or for any other reasonable purpose. I further agree that should I ever unreasonably refuse to submit to such an examination my employer may take such disciplinary action as he may.

These agreements had been signed because several stores had experienced serious "shrinkage" (theft). A severe "shrinkage" subsequently showed up at one store. The company management issued a letter to the employees working at that store stating that they were to take polygraph tests administered by a qualified examiner.[108]

Out of the total complement of employees at that store only two refused; one was Employee [A] who had been tested five or six times during her twenty years of employment and always passed, and the other was Employee [B] who had been tested six to eight times during her sixteen years. Hence, neither was frightened by the request. In spite of their experience with testing, both refused because a local union representative told them they could not be "compelled to submit to a polygraph test" and that the union would support "anyone who refused." The two who refused were suspended for one week. These modest suspensions were then appealed to Arbitrator Dolnick.

With respect to the commitment in the industry-wide agreement that required employees to take polygraph examinations upon request, Arbitrator Dolnick said:

> True, the Union's Agreement with Employer is part of an industry and area wide contractual relationship. And it may also very well be that

---

[105]77 LA 380 (Dolnick, 1981).
[106]*Id.* at 382.
[107]*Id.* at 381.
[108]*Id.*

employees of other supermarkets, under contract with this Union, have from time to time taken polygraph tests when requested by their employers. But that does not establish an accepted past practice sufficient to legalize grievant's individual agreements. . . .[109]

With respect to the individual agreements requiring the employee signing one to take a polygraph test upon request, Arbitrator Dolnick said they were "invalid and unenforceable when each grievant continued to work for the employer beyond the probationary period" because such agreements were contrary to "established legal and arbitral interpretations."[110]

With respect to the commitments in the *local* agreement, Arbitrator Dolnick restated the view previously announced by Arbitrator Thomas Rimer that "we do not agree that the requirement that employees submit to lie detector tests is a right retained by the management"[111] and cited Arbitrator Jones' paper as the authority that polygraph testing was "contrary to public policy" in spite of the fact that legislators in twenty-three states have enacted licensing statutes.[112] In the author's opinion, when Arbitrator Dolnick refused to enforce the specific provisions of the labor agreement because he did not like polygraphy, he was dispensing "his own brand of industrial justice," which is "an infidelity to the obligation" of a labor arbitrator set forth by the U.S. Supreme Court.[113]

Since different arbitrators deciding grievances over the disciplining of employees who have refused to cooperate by taking a polygraph test take diametrically opposite views, it is appropriate to close this chapter with Arbitrator Charles V. Laughlin's "score" analysis in *Bowman Transportation, Inc.*[114] under this definition:

> The narrow issue submitted to the arbitrator is whether grievant's refusal to submit to a polygraph test is "reasonable cause" for suspension within the provisions of Article XIV of the contract between the Company and the Union which provides:
> "Employees shall be discharged, suspended or disciplined only for reasonable cause."[115]

Then he was asked at his hearing:

---

[109]*Id.* at 382–83, 385.

[110]*Id.* at 383, 385.

[111]*See Temtex Products, Inc.*, 75 LA 233, 236 (Rimer, 1980).

[112]*See* "Admissibility of Polygrapher's Testimony in Criminal and Civil Courts" in Chapter XIV.

[113]*Steelworkers v. Enterprise Wheel and Car Corp.*, 363 U.S. 593, 597, 46 LRRM 2423, 2425 (1960).

[114]61 LA 549 (Laughlin, 1973).

[115]*Id.* at 550.

At the hearing this arbitrator was questioned as to what extent he would be influenced by decisions of other arbitrators. He indicated that he would be more influenced by the reasoning used by other arbitrators than by the fact that they did decide a particular way. Certainly a manifest trend in arbitrator decisions would not be ignored. No such manifest trend exists in this case.[116]

Then he reported the score that then existed:

As indicated in the preceding paragraph, there are few arbitrator decisions on the specific issue to be decided in this case. Two arbitrators have held that a company may not suspend an employee who refuses to take a polygraph test. Three arbitrators have reached the other conclusion.

One case on each side involves the same company and the same union as are involved in this arbitration proceeding. Neither case involves the same incident as is here involved. Apparently, neither decision has been officially published as of now. The opinion favorable to the Union accompanied the Union brief, that favorable to the Company accompanied the Company brief. The case favorable to the Company was not decided until after the hearing in this proceeding.

Neither opinion presents any extensive reasoning or is very helpful to this arbitrator in reading [sic] a conclusion. The decision favorable to the Union did cite a number of decisions of other arbitrators. They have all been considered. So far as their two cases are concerned, the score stands even.

In addition to the case referred to as favorable to the grievant, B. F. Goodrich Co. 36 LA 552 (1961) upholds the Union's position. Also, in addition to the case referred to as rejecting the grievance Warmick Electronics Inc., 26 LA 363 (1966) and Allen Industries, 26 LA 363 (1956) upheld the Company. These three cases, where the reasoning is pertinent, are discussed elsewhere in this decision. In addition to the three arbitrator decisions favorable to the Company is one case decided by the National Labor Relations Board. American Oil Co., 189 NLRB #2, 76 LRRM 1506 (1971). Said case is not strictly in point because it involved the issue as to whether discharges for refusals to submit to a polygraph test, when there was evidence that the employees involved were very pro-union, would violate section 8(a)(3) of the National Labor Relations Act. The Board held not so as far as the evidence in the case was concerned. Pertinent to the case here considered the Board did say: (76 LRRM 1507):

"Although a requirement that employees take polygraph tests may in certain circumstances be unreasonable, the circumstances here, ... persuade us that, ... respondent required Williams and Carter to take the lie detector test as an understandable and permissible measure to learn whether either of the two or both had been involved in the burglary...."

In addition to the two cases cited as upholding the Union may be added three others, by inference. Illinois Bell Telephone Co., 39 LA 471 (1962),

---

[116]*Id.* at 551.

Simoniz Co., 44 LA 659 (1964), and Publishers Assn. of New York City, 32 LA 44 (1959). In these three cases the grievants had been discharged for other reasons. In deciding whether the discharges were reasonable the arbitrators declined to consider against grievants evidence that they had refused to submit to polygraph tests. In all three cases the arbitrator decided against the grievants based upon other evidence. The use of evidence of refusal to take a test may be regarded as a type of sanction. Thus, these three cases support the Union in rejecting the sanction. However, they do not involve the type of disciplinary action used in this case. So, they are not squarely in point. In addition to the policy and reliability arguments involved in ... requiring polygraph tests, evidence of a refusal to take such tests may be rejected upon the grounds that guilt cannot be inferred from a refusal to take the test. This does seem to be the reasoning of the arbitrator, at least in part, in Illinois Bell Telephone Co.[117]

Arbitrator Laughlin did not base his conclusion on a score. His award contains an extensive analysis. He denied the grievance.[118]

---

[117]*Id.*
[118]*Id.* at 558.

CHAPTER XVI

The Impact of "External Law" on Arbitration

"External law" is now part of the jargon of labor arbitration.[1] Among other things, these words now mean the friction that is generated when one party says to the arbitrator, "You have been authorized only to look at and interpret the provisions of the labor agreement"; and the other party replies, "It is your duty to examine the surrounding law because your award must be compatible with the law." The sides of these arguments often shift, depending upon a party's desired result.

Labor arbitration essentially sprang up when the War Labor Board introduced arbitration procedures during World War II. The Board said in effect: "If the union cannot strike because of the no-strike commitment during the war, disagreement arising during the life of the labor agreement should be resolved by arbitration." The roots of the arbitration for no-strike exchange were widely planted. They grew slowly into a large and complicated tree. The courts recognized the important role of labor arbitration and followed up with the addition of the injunction against strikes, if there existed in the labor agreement a "no-strike" commitment and an arbitration procedure. The courts then made another jump, inferring that the parties accepted arbitration as the exchange for a no-strike commitment even if this was not set forth in specific terms in the labor agreement.[2]

Some in the arbitration field would assert that arbitrators should ignore the external law when it impacts on a labor agreement provision. Arbitrator Seward in 1954 in *Allegheny Ludlum Steel Corp.*[3] refused to award a monetary benefit for an election absence as set out in the state law.[4] Others, on the other hand, asserted that it was the ar-

---

[1]*See* Bloch, *Labor Arbitration's Crossroads Revised: The Role of the Arbitrator and the Response of the Courts,* 47 CIN. L. REV. 363 (1978); Edwards, *Labor Arbitration at the Crossroads: The "Common Law of the Shop" v. External Law,* 32 ARB. J. 65 (1977).

[2]An injunction will issue against threats of strikes even when there is no specific language in the labor agreement exchanging arbitration to resolve the dispute for the no-strike commitment. *See Boys Markets, Inc. v. Retail Clerks, Local 770,* 398 U.S. 235, 74 LRRM 2257 (1970).

[3]23 LA 606 (Seward, 1954).

[4]*Id.* at 607.

bitrators' duty to produce compatibility. The academic debate started as a low rumble in 1950. Arbitrator Archibald Cox, one of the most articulate speakers on the pragmatic side, said in 1952:

> There is considerable temptation to say of such cases that the arbitrator should not concern himself with the law because he is the creature of the parties given the sole duty to apply their agreement. A rule of this kind would comfort those who worry—and wisely so—about encumbering with knotty legal questions what should be an informal method of adjusting laymen's differences....
>
> On reflection, however, the opposing considerations seem stronger. The parties to collective bargaining cannot avoid negotiating and carrying out their agreements within the existing legal framework. It is either futile or grossly unjust to make an award directing an employer to take action which the law forbids—futile because if the employer challenges the award, the union cannot enforce it; unjust because if the employer complies he subjects himself to punishment by civil authority.
>
> Furthermore, if arbitrators are unable or unwilling to determine whether a grievant is seeking to bring about an unlawful consequence, the courts and administrative agencies are bound to intervene at least to the point of deciding that question.... The attitude of both courts and agencies toward the growing jurisprudence of labor arbitration will be deeply influenced by the attitude of arbitrators toward the law.[5] [Footnote omitted.]

Cox pointed out that the labor agreement was the arbitrator's source of the private law and when this private law begins to touch the new public statutory law, arbitrators can usually find a theory that permits them to write a compatible award, knowing that if they do not the courts will move in and vacate the award and produce compatibility by court order.[6]

---

[5]Cox, *The Place of Law in Labor Arbitration*, THE PROFESSION OF LABOR ARBITRATION, Selected Papers from the First Seven Annual Meetings, National Academy of Arbitrators, J. McKelvey, ed. (Washington: BNA Books, 1957), pp. 77–78. Two years earlier an article to the same effect appeared: Scoles, *Judicial Review of Labor Arbitration Awards*, 197 U. CHI. L. REV. 616 (1950).

[6]However, the courts have had to consider the impact of a wide variety of federal and state laws on arbitration awards where the law was not taken into account by the arbitrator (Sherman Act), *Steelworkers v. United States Gypsum Co.*, 492 F.2d 713, 85 LRRM 2962 (5th Cir. 1974), *cert. denied*, 419 U.S. 998, 87 LRRM 2658 (1974) (state protective legislation); *Associated Milk Dealers, Inc. v. Teamsters, Local 753*, 422 F.2d 546, 73 LRRM 2435 (7th Cir. 1970); *Robb v. Clothing Workers, New York Joint Board, vacated on other grounds*, 506 F.2d 1246, 87 LRRM 3227 (2d Cir. 1974); *Newspaper Guild, Local 35 v. Washington Post Co.*, 442 F.2d 1234, 76 LRRM 2274 (D.C. Cir. 1971); *Glendale Mfg. Co. v. Garment Workers, ILGWU, Local 520*, 283 F.2d 936, 47 LRRM 2152 (4th Cir. 1960), *cert. denied*, 366 U.S. 950, 48 LRRM 2323 (1961); *Local 453, Electrical Workers, IUE v. Otis Elevator Co.*, 314 F.2d 25, 52 LRRM 2543 (2d Cir. 1963), *cert. denied*, 373 U.S. 949, 53 LRRM 2394 (1963); *Torrington Co. v. Metal Products Workers, Local 1645*, 362 F.2d 677, 62 LRRM 2495 (2d Cir. 1966); *Machinists, District 8 v. Campbell Soup Co.*, 406 F.2d 1223, 70 LRRM 2569 (7th Cir. 1969), *cert. denied*, 396 U.S. 820, 72 LRRM 2431 (1969); *Ludwig Honold Mfg. Co. v. Fletcher*, 405 F.2d 1123, 70 LRRM 2368 (3d

The comments by Cox occurred roughly twelve years before the various public laws that interact with labor arbitration in addition to the National Labor Relations Act[7] and the Labor Management Relations Act[8] were enacted. These were the Occupational Safety and Health Act,[9] the Employee Retirement Income Security Act,[10] the Civil Rights Act,[11] the Equal Pay Act,[12] the Economic Stabilization Act,[13] the Fair Labor Standards Act,[14] and the Vocational Rehabilitation Act.[15] The early rumble of academic debate over the degree, if any, to which an arbitrator should go outside the four corners of the labor agreement and examine statutory law began to become a roar. Arbitrator-theorists began to take sides: Should the arbitrator explore into the area of statutory law seeking to render an award that is compatible, or should the arbitrator stay within the labor agreement provisions and "ignore the law" unless he or she is given specific authority to "roam" the law.[16]

Because there is now so much external law touching grievance matters, one court wisely pointed out that if the arbitrator would have to touch the external law to resolve the grievance, the arbitrator would then essentially lose jurisdiction and the defendants would begin to

---

Cir. 1969); *Holodnak v. Avco Corp.*, 387 F. Supp. 191, 88 LRRM 2950 (2d Cir. 1975) (setting aside award of Arbitrator Turkus who found just cause for discharge for leafletting fellow employees, on the ground the discharge was inconsistent with freedom-of-speech guarantees); *Longshoremen, ILA, Local 1852 v. Amstar Corp.*, 363 F. Supp. 1026, 1033, 84 LRRM 2815 (D. Md. 1973); *Gulf States Telephone Co. v. Electrical Workers, IBEW, Local 1692*, 416 F.2d 198, 201, 72 LRRM 2026 (5th Cir. 1969); *Automobile Workers, Local 985 v. Chace Co.*, 262 F. Supp. 114, 64 LRRM 2098 (E.D. Mich. 1966) (court refused to enforce award which required violation of state law).

[7]29 U.S.C. § 151 *et seq.* (1976).
[8]29 U.S.C. § 141 *et seq.* (1976), LRX 3751.
[9]29 U.S.C. § 654 (1976), LRX 6201.
[10]29 U.S.C. § 1001 (1976).
[11]42 U.S.C. § 200 *et seq.* (1976), 401 FEP Manual 1.
[12]29 U.S.C. § 206 (1976), 401 FEP Manual 451.
[13]12 U.S.C. § 1904 (1976).
[14]29 U.S.C. § 201 (1976), LRX 8101.
[15]29 U.S.C. § 701 *et seq.* (1976), 401 FEP Manual 501.
[16]Edwards, *Labor Arbitration at the Crossroads: The Common Law of the Shop v. External Law*, note 1 *supra;* Meltzer, *Ruminations About Ideology, Law and Labor Arbitration*, The Arbitrator, The NLRB, and the Courts, Proceedings of the Twentieth Annual Meeting, National Academy of Arbitrators, D. Jones, ed. (Washington: BNA Books, 1967), p. 16; Bloch, *Some Far-Sighted Views of Myopia*, Arbitration—1977, Proceedings of the Thirtieth Annual Meeting, National Academy of Arbitrators, B. Dennis and G. Somers, eds. (Washington: BNA Books, 1977), p. 233; Feller, *The Coming End of Arbitration's Golden Age*, Arbitration—1976, Proceedings of the Twenty-Ninth Annual Meeting, National Academy of Arbitrators, B. Dennis and G. Somers, eds. (Washington: BNA Books, 1976), p. 97; Feller, *The Impact of External Law Upon Labor Arbitration*. The Future of Labor Arbitration in America (New York: American Arbitration Association, 1976), pp. 83–112.

march back into court seeking the stays that were essentially eliminated in 1968 by the *Steelworkers Trilogy*.[17]

The union challenged an award in *Cott Corp.*,[18] believing that Arbitrator Kupsinel should have "looked only within the four corners of the labor agreement" and, hence, should have ignored the law. Arbitrator Kupsinel said he believed he should provide a "compatible" award if his alternative was to produce an illegal result, and he explained the different views of various arbitrators:

> There has been much debate in arbitral circles concerning the application of "external law" to the construction and interpretation of collective bargaining agreements. Simply put, one school of thought states that the arbitrator is limited by the four corners of the collective bargaining agreement and once he steps beyond those boundaries, he is in essence acting as a court or an agency and either is incompetent in these other roles or has no "jurisdiction" to consider outside "laws" which would change a decision based on the collective bargaining agreement, if the agreement were viewed in isolation.
>
> My "philosophy" is, basically, that the arbitrator is a creature of the collective bargaining agreement and his award should be based on the collective bargaining agreement. Some collective bargaining agreements contain provisions which specifically refer to matters which are also the subject of federal, state, or governmental agency regulation. Thus, if an agreement states that the employer shall not discriminate against an employee because of his union activities, and barring other limiting provisions in the agreement, the arbitrator *is* authorized by the parties to determine whether an employee has been discriminated against because of his union activities, even though the National Labor Relations Board or a similar state agency might entertain the same issue.[19] [Emphasis in original.]

These debates started with opposing views in law review articles and then became face-to-face discussions at conferences. The sharp differences of view crept into federal court opinions. For example, Judge Weber in *General Telephone Co. of Pennsylvania v. Locals 1635, 1636, 1637*,[20] vacated an award because the arbitrator had not enforced a provision of the labor agreement on the ground that enforcement would be contrary to the statutory law, as well as because the Supreme Court had ruled in the meantime that the application of

---

[17]*Steelworkers v. Warrior & Gulf Navigation Co.*, 363 U.S. 574, 46 LRRM 2416 (1960); *Steelworkers v. Enterprise Wheel & Car Corp.*, 363 U.S. 593, 46 LRRM 2423 (1960); *Steelworkers v. American Mfg. Co.*, 363 U.S. 564, 46 LRRM 2414 (1960); *see also Carey v. General Electric Co.*, 315 F.2d 499, 52 LRRM 2662 (2d Cir. 1963), *cert. denied*, 377 U.S. 908, 55 LRRM 3023 (1964).

[18]AAA Case No. 12-30-1058-78 (Kupsinel, 1978).

[19]*Id.*

[20]427 F. Supp. 398, 95 LRRM 2899 (W.D. Pa. 1977).

the external law was other than the arbitrator had supposed. In the course of the opinion vacating the award, Judge Weber quoted from Arbitrator Bernard Meltzer's paper in a law review:

> [T]he arbitrator should respect the agreement and ignore the law. There is no reason to credit arbitrators as a class with any special competence with respect to the law.[21]

And then the judge added:

> This is an interesting observation inasmuch as the court has noted in the past that a substantial number of arbitrators are drawn from the faculties of law schools.[22]

Judge Weber nonetheless concluded with the Supreme Court standard:

> "The arbitrator, however, has no general authority to invoke public laws that conflict with the bargain between the parties.... If an arbitral decision is based 'solely on the arbitrator's view of the requirements of enacted legislation' rather than on an interpretation of the collective bargaining agreement, the arbitrator has 'exceeded the scope of his submission,' and the award will not be enforced."[23]

Arbitrator Milton T. Edelman in *Hollander & Co.*[24] recorded how various arbitrators view their authority to examine the statutory law that touched a grievance:

> Arbitration is a private forum in which the arbitrator receives his authority from the parties to the collective bargaining agreement and is charged with interpretation of that agreement. Although he may not be hired to apply and interpret federal and state law the arbitrator cannot escape the legal framework that surrounds the employment relationship and helps shape the collective bargaining agreement. It is necessary to review the approaches taken by arbitrators to the question raised by this case; where a conflict exists between the law (particularly federal law) and the collective bargaining agreement, from which should the arbitrator draw his authority?
>
> Arbitrator Bernard Meltzer has become the most often cited and leading proponent of the view that where a direct conflict exists between the collective bargaining agreement and the law, the arbitrator must ignore the law and follow the agreement....

---

[21]*Id.* at 399, 95 LRRM at 2899, citing Meltzer, *Labor Arbitration and Overlapping and Conflicting Remedies for Employment Discrimination,* 39 U. CHI. L. REV. 30, 33 (1971).

[22]*Id.* at 399, 95 LRRM at 2899.

[23]*Id.,* 95 LRRM at 2900, quoting from *Alexander v. Gardner-Denver Co.,* 415 U.S. 36, 7 FEP Cases 81 (1974).

[24]64 LA 816 (Edelman, 1975).

The opposite position has been supported by Robert G. Howlett ... who argues that arbitrators should render decision "based on both contract interpretation and law," and that "each contract includes all applicable law".... Arbitrator Richard Mittenthal ... argued that the arbitrator may permit conduct forbidden by law but sanctioned by contract, but should not require conduct forbidden by law even though it may be sanctioned by contract.... Dean Michael I. Sovern argued two years later that the arbitrator may follow federal law rather than the agreement when 1) the arbitrator is qualified; 2) the question of law is implicated in the dispute; 3) the law may immunize or even require certain conduct that violates the agreement; and 4) the court lacks primary jurisdiction.

. . .

In the final analysis an arbitrator's position on this matter of law versus agreement must rest on his conception of the arbitration process, the clarity of the law, and the role ascribed to arbitration by the legislature and the courts. Neither arbitrators nor legal scholars speak with a single voice on this matter, in fact, the voices are particularly divided.[25]

Then Arbitrator Edelman expressed his view:

The arbitrator regards the institutional role of arbitration to be that of a private forum endowed by employers and unions with the authority to interpret and apply the collective bargaining agreement. The first loyalty of the arbitrator is to the agreement. It is that document which he must follow. But he works within a framework of national policy created by legislatures and the courts. The assumption behind the Supreme Court decisions in the Steelworker Trilogy decisions was that such national policy favors the use of arbitration to settle issues arising from alleged violations of the collective bargaining agreement, that such a policy stems from the emphasis on voluntary settlement contained in the Taft-Hartley Act and other statutes of Congress and that, therefore, the arbitrator is following national policy when he performs his usual task. Most important, the Supreme Court, in the Trilogy cases, interpreted national policy and clarified it in a way that allowed arbitrators to use it as a guide, so that, in fact, every arbitration decision takes place under a national policy umbrella.[26]

This book reports the practice and procedure of arbitrators producing awards—not what it should be, but what it is. Hence, it is hoped that this chapter does not rekindle the debate—should the arbitrator examine the public law and attempt to produce an award compatible with the external law, or should the compatibility occur when the award is reviewed and changed by a federal court or by the National Labor Relations Board?

---

[25]*Id.* at 818–19.
[26]*Id.* at 819.

THE ABSORPTION OF LEGAL PROCEDURE

As the number of labor agreements began to grow, the number of procedural rules affecting arbitration, borrowed from federal court procedure with or without some modification, also grew. Because the representatives of the two sides in arbitration rarely objected to the procedural rule announced by the arbitrator to solve some procedural need, the rule became a practice that was often followed in future cases. Courts would often say that an arbitrator has exclusive control over procedure. Now that awards can be reviewed by federal courts and by the NLRB, the legal procedures in both forums have become the model followed by arbitrators. They want their awards to be approved rather than serving as a starting point for a *de novo* retrial. These aspects of the introduction of legal procedure into arbitration are discussed in Chapter XXI, "Vacation, Enforcement or Correction" and Chapter XXII, *"De Novo* Reviews in a Court."

"Just Cause" Is Easily Shifted by Legal Change

Unless an employee engages in conduct that constitutes "just cause" or "proper cause" for discharge, the employment relationship is not considered terminated. Under the labor agreement, termination of employment can only occur if the discharge is for "just cause" or "proper cause," and hence "reinstatement" by an arbitrator is simply a finding that under the labor agreement the employment contractual rights have remained connected, *i.e.,* no effective severance by discharge had occurred.

One simple illustration of how the "just cause" or "proper cause" standard will shift when a statutory law sets up a restraint on employment severance—*i.e.,* discharge—is the statutory prohibition against discharge of an employee when the employee's wages are garnished to collect against a single indebtedness, even though a series of garnishments occurred on the wages of the employee as a result of that single indebtedness.[27] Prior to this insulation of an employee from discharge, the employer could set up its own rule and would often discharge an employee if more than one garnishment occurred within a specified time, requiring the employee to pay off his or her remaining debt when the first garnishment occurred. Discharge for such repetition of garnishment was considered to be for "just cause" because the employer could establish such rules to reduce the cost in-

---

[27]Consumer Credit Protection Act (1970), 15 U.S.C. § 1673, which provides that the Secretary of Labor can substitute a state law provision if it is essentially the same in effect as the federal law.

volved in processing wage attachments, so long as the rules were uniformly applied. The statutory insulation was a simple and direct external law impact which shifted the construction of the words "just cause for discharge" found in the labor agreement.

In *Farmer Brothers Co.*[28] the grievant who was the shop steward was discharged because he refused to change his scheduled working days, a right the company clearly had under the labor agreement. Arbitrator Edgar Jones speculated that under the circumstances the NLRB might well regard the discharge to be an 8(a)(3) violation because at least one of the dischargees was considered by the employer to be a "hyperactive" as a steward. The arbitrator said:

> In this case, therefore, the reasoning of decision proceeds from the contract, not the statute. While the findings of fact reflect statutorily significant events, it suffices in this instance to base the arbitral conclusions upon the contract. This by no means slights the import of the relevant statutory provisions. As in many labor-management situations, this contract and the statute are almost wholly duplicative. By necessary implication, if not expressly, collective agreements, every bit as much as the statute, typically proscribe antiunion disciplinary actions discriminating against employees because of their union acts or views.[29]

Although Arbitrator Jones recognized that a Section 8(a)(3) charge could be litigated up to the NLRB or that he could absorb the Board policies and render his award on an unfair labor practice theory and then have the award reviewed under *Collyer Insulated Wire*[30] and administratively deferred to by the Board, he chose to render his award within the "four corners" of the labor agreement. Two grievants had been discharged because they refused to follow instructions from their employer to comply with new working schedules that they believed were in violation of the labor agreement. Both subsequently agreed to comply with the schedule changes. A higher-ranking union representative asked Grievant F—— to comply, as the other grievant did, and then file a grievance so an arbitrator could determine whether the change in the working schedule was a violation in the labor agreement. Once the grievants complied with the new schedule and filed a grievance, Arbitrator Jones said, the "just cause" reasons for the discharge dissolved and the grievants should have been reinstated. Since the employer had not reinstated them, Arbitrator Jones ordered reinstatement. A reinstatement might have been the order from the NLRB or by an arbitrator deciding his or her award under Board

---

[28]64 LA 901 (Jones, 1975).
[29]*Id.* at 904–05.
[30]192 NLRB 837, 77 LRRM 1931 (1971).

policies. Arbitrator Jones said his decision was based only on the labor agreement and uninfluenced by NLRB policies:

> There was an unequivocal offer by the Union on behalf of the Grievants to retract the refusals and accept the disputed work assignments without any condition other than the pursuit of the claim through the grievance procedure, itself wholly proper and what they should have done in the first place. There is no "principle" justifying the Employer's own refusal to reinstate simply because of an earlier discharge. To the contrary, the agreement itself contemplates in Article III the prospect of reinstatement without back pay.... [T]he Employer was obliged to reinstate them on October 4 and to allow them to perform their work while processing a grievance charging contractual impropriety of the unilateral shift change.[31]

Arbitrator Jones discussed at length the problems involved when a statutory and a contract problem become involved and explained that if both problems can be resolved only under the labor agreement, the arbitrator's resolution should stay under the labor agreement:

> There is little doubt that the Employer welcomed this chance to cure the pain in its neck caused by Grievant F——'s conduct as an employee and as a shop steward, but most particularly the latter.... The NLRB might well regard the Employer's response to his conduct, however, to be an 8(a)(3) violation, objectively viewed. What caused its pain was concededly attributable to his acts as steward which it regarded as contentiously hyperactive and needlessly disruptive.
>
> It is unnecessary, however, to couch this arbitral decision in a statutory mold. It suffices that the decision here be made on the basis of the terms of the collective agreement rather than those of the statute as read by the NLRB and the federal courts of appeal.
>
> It is as yet unresolved what will be the fate, upon federal judicial review, of arbitral decisions that purportedly are based on statutory rather than, or in addition to, contractual grounds. How will the Supreme Court ultimately apply its 1960 Steelworkers doctrine of arbitral insulation to cases in which, on initial deferral by the Board under Collyer Insulated Wire, arbitrators rule directly on charged violations of the National Labor Relations Act? Will "Collyerized" arbitral decisions, later accepted for post-award deferral by the Board under its Spielberg rationale, be found vulnerable to the intrusive wisdom of federal courts remote from industrial realities in the even more remote span of time that normally characterizes the interaction between the Board and the reviewing courts? ... More precisely, if an arbitrator brackets a statutory issue within his decision, instead of sticking to the contract, will he thereby open his award to the searching scrutiny of courts to which NLRB orders are routinely subjected? Or will the Supreme Court instead adhere to its often repeated view

---

[31] 64 LA at 906.

of judicially unhindered grievance arbitration as central to national labor policy even though arbitral rulings expressly interpret statutory as well as, or in preemption of, contractual mandates?

If there is an available contractual ground for resolving a grievance, why should an arbitrator be expected to reach for the statute as well? The Supreme Court's historical approach has usually been to seize the low ground rather than the high to position its decisions, preferring dispositive statutory intent—frequently "interpreted" with considerable creativity—in place of constitutional application. Why should not the lesser mandate, but the mandate nonetheless, also be the one applied by an arbitrator? The parties are governed by the statute, assuredly, and their contracts are subordinate to it. But the office of arbitrator is not a statutory creation even though it is statutorily encouraged and judicially nourished—at least at the level of the Supreme Court.

It seems the course of prudence at least, if not wisdom, that arbitrators should protect their awards by rooting them in the contract whenever that is possible, even though there undoubtedly will be cases in which the parties expressly submit issues for arbitral decision framed in and requiring answers from statutory terms. Even in that latter context, however, it seems vital to bear in mind that arbitration remains consensual in nature, not statutory, and that the arbitrator's decisional life is tied, not to Congress or the Labor Board, but to the contracting parties.

Of course, to the extent that an arbitrator makes explicit the facts, and his contractual views of them, from which emerges his decision, the NLRB is enabled to make its own judgment of the statutory significance of the arbitral decision, leaving the arbitral award itself unencumbered by judicial review, at least on the contractual merits. And in no event is the arbitrator statutorily empowered to make the legal conclusion that an unfair labor practice does or does not exist. That is solely the NLRB's prerogative (one which it does not purport in Collyer to delegate to arbitrators, it is important to note).[32]

Arbitrator Jones stated that his decision to reinstate two employees (one the "hyperactive" steward) was simply an interpretation of the "just cause" provision in the labor agreement. The two employees had properly been discharged because they refused to follow the work schedule set out by the employer; however, when they changed their minds twenty-four hours after the discharge, Arbitrator Jones held, the employer had obtained compliance and should have reinstated the dischargees. No one will know how much the external law built up pressure upon Arbitrator Jones to cause him to order reinstatement and thereby produce compatability with a reinstatement order that quite likely would have been the NLRB's decision.[33]

---

[32]*Id.* at 904.

[33]The vacation of an award that involves NLRB policies is discussed in Chapter XXI, "Vacation, Enforcement, or Correction."

The Meaning of "Discrimination" Is Easily Shifted

In most labor agreements there is a provision that the company shall not discriminate against an employee because of race, sex, national origin, etc. The General Motors "no discrimination" provision is as follows:

> It is the policy of General Motors and the UAW-AFL-CIO that the provisions of this Agreement be applied to all employees covered by this Agreement without regard to race, color, creed or national origin. Any claims of violation of this policy may be taken up as a grievance.
>
> . . .
>
> The right to hire; promote; discharge or discipline *for cause*; and to maintain discipline and efficiency of employees, is the sole responsibility of the Corporation *except that Union members shall not be discriminated against as such.*[34] [Emphasis added.]

Since these words are essentially a restatement of Title VII of the Civil Rights Act of 1964, the determination by courts that certain actions of employers are discriminatory under that statute (Title VII) will be urged upon arbitrators as indicating such actions should be considered discrimination under the similar provision of the labor agreement.[35] In defense, the employer will explain to the arbitrator that the facts presented on behalf of the grievant would not prove discrimination under Title VII in court and hence the presented facts should not be considered discriminatory under the labor agreement provisions.

When a discrimination claim is included in the grievance, the employee must present facts that set up a *prima facie* case of employment discrimination and then the employer seeks to rebut it.[36] This process is the reverse of discharge cases, wherein the employer will submit facts that set up a *prima facie* case and the employee then seeks to rebut it. When the employer does present facts that would rebut the *prima facie* discrimination case, the Supreme Court concluded in *Texas Dept. of Community Affairs v. Burdine,* the employer does not need to prove its actual motivations nor must it prove by objective evidence that the person hired or promoted was more qualified than the employee who was rejected.[37] The circuit court had found the

---

[34]Agreement between General Motors Corporation and the UAW-AFL-CIO, September 14, 1979, pp. 11-12.

[35]There usually is an anti-discrimination clause in the agreement, and arbitrators can broaden the meaning of the labor agreement words as the scope of the word "discrimination" in the statute broadens. *See Howmet Corp.,* 63 LA 179 (Forsythe, 1974); *Spencer Foods, Inc.,* 64 LA 1 (Smith, 1974); *Farmer Bros. Co.,* 64 LA 901 (Jones, 1975).

[36]*Texas Dept. of Community Affairs v. Burdine,* 450 U.S. 248, 25 FEP Cases 113 (1981).

[37]*Id.* at 259-60, 25 FEP Cases at 118.

employer guilty because the employer was unable to prove the discharge was not nondiscriminatory by a preponderance of the evidence, and the Supreme Court reversed.[38] This reversal will probably slow down discrimination activity in courts and arbitration. Once the employer produces admissible evidence that the decision was made for a legitimate, nondiscriminatory reason, the Supreme Court said, then the employee must set out to show that the employer's evidence is "unworthy of credence." Arbitrators probably will follow this procedure.

The only discrimination area that cannot be handled easily is that involving Title VII determinations when a seniority provision in the labor agreement sets up a discrimination barrier claim, when the seniority grievance reaches the arbitrator. If the labor agreement provision is clearly illegal, most arbitrators will consider it nonoperative under the view that the parties desire a legal award, *infra*. Where, however, the seniority provision does not cause an illegal discrimination but an agency under Executive Order 11246 directs a change in the seniority rules in the labor agreement under penalty of loss of government purchases, some arbitrators have attempted to continue to comply with the labor agreement provision and yet accommodate the change directed by the agency. These accommodation efforts produce some odd awards (*see* "Effect of Regulations," *infra*).

THE ARBITRATOR'S AUTHORITY TO PRODUCE COMPATIBILITY BETWEEN THE STATUTE AND THE AGREEMENT

Various arbitrators have found authority in the words in the labor agreement or, by implication, to examine the statutory law. Some arbitrators are more unwilling to imply the right to blend the statutory and contract words.[39]

Authority to Absorb the Law Is Found in Many Agreements

Some agreements set forth the authority of the arbitrator to examine "external law" and construe the provisions in the labor agreement so the award will be compatible with public law. Often there are "savings clauses" and "legal supremacy clauses" in labor agreements. These clauses permit external public law to be absorbed into the labor agreement and permit the arbitrator to produce awards that are compatible with the external law.

---

[38]*Id.* at 251, 25 FEP Cases at 115.

[39]*Western Airlines, Inc.*, 71-1 ARB ¶ 8115 (Meiners, 1970); *Western Airlines, Inc.*, 70-1 ARB ¶ 8367 (Wyckoff, 1970); *Pitman-Moore Div.*, 49 LA 709 (Seinsheimer, 1967).

448 PRACTICE AND PROCEDURE IN LABOR ARBITRATION

In *W. R. Grace & Co. v. Rubber Workers, Local 759,*[40] the court explained that a rather typical savings or legal supremacy clause was included:

> Within the terms of the contract itself, the company relies upon Article XIV, Section 7, which provides:
>> In the event that any provision of this Agreement is found to be in conflict with any State or Federal Laws now existing or hereinafter enacted, it is agreed that such laws shall supersede the conflicting provisions without affecting the remainder of these provisions.[41]

The court then explained the law that governs the arbitrator:

> In answering this question the starting point must be that in general the law is now but also has in the past been what the highest tribunal which considers the issue decides is the law. It is in the essential nature of judicial decisions that they normally do not enact law but declare the law which already exists.[42]

Sometimes such provisions of the labor agreement might seem to be in conflict. For example, in *American Air Filter Co.*[43] Arbitrator William F. Dolson pointed out that one sentence in the labor agreement did not permit him to "modify any of the terms and conditions of this Agreement," but in another sentence he was required to interpret the agreement "in the light of valid and applicable laws and regulations."

When there is no "savings clause" or "legal supremacy clause" in a labor agreement, arbitrators may examine carefully the nondiscrimination provisions and then rationalize that they have the authority to explore the external law so as to produce an award that will not discriminate between groups of employees. The arbitrator will hold that the nondiscrimination clause is so broad that an employee will be improperly discriminated against when the labor agreement appears to require that a federal or state law be ignored, and under this nondiscrimination mandate, the statutory law is absorbed and the necessary adjustment accomplished.[44] For example, Arbitrator Draznin said that when an antidiscrimination provision is found in a labor agreement, applicable provisions in state and federal law are im-

---

[40]652 F.2d 1248, 107 LRRM 3251 (5th Cir. 1981), *cert. granted*, 50 USLW 3998.18 (U.S. June 28, 1982) (No. 81-1314).

[41]652 F.2d at 1225, 107 LRRM at 3256.

[42]*Id.*

[43]57 LA 549 (Dolson, 1971).

[44]*Kaiser-Permanente Medical Care Program*, 64 LA 245 (Dykstra, 1975); *McCall Printing Co.*, 57 LA 933 (Draper, 1971); *Brown-Jordan Co.*, 64 LA 972 (Woodward, 1975); *Jesco Lubricants Co.*, 62 LA 1294 (Allen, 1974); *Basic Vegetable Products, Inc.*, 64 LA 620 (Gould, 1975); *Community Unit School District 205*, 55 LA 895 (Seitz, 1970); *Wausau District Public Schools*, 64 LA 187 (Marshall, 1975).

pressed upon the labor agreement and he must give the law consideration in preparing his award. He used this rationale in *California-
Sample Service Co., Inc.*[45] to protect the employer. Reinstatement,
under an "antidiscrimination provision" in the labor agreement, of
workers who were picked up in an Immigration and Naturalization
Service raid and who did not return with an INS letter stating they
were not illegal aliens would have caused the employer to violate a
criminal statute because the reinstated employees would be employed
without proper work permits.

Other arbitrators, however, have been less free with specific "savings clauses" or "antidiscrimination provisions" in labor agreements.
For example, Arbitrator Kleinsorge in *General Electric Co.*[46] held he
could not interpret the law regulating the docking of pay checks under
a "savings clause," commenting that "even though the contract has
been made subject to applicable Federal and State laws, [he] has no
authority to interpret these laws. If a law has been violated, redress
should be sought through the proper courts."

Arbitrators Infer That the Parties Desire a Legal Award

It is clearly the law that a contract that requires a party to violate
the law cannot be enforced.[47] This principle applies to a labor agreement because it is simply another contract. If the arbitrator's award
were to be enforced in such a situation it would be a direction of an illegal act, and the court will vacate the award because the court is
always "concerned with the lawfulness of its enforcing the award and
not with the correctness of the arbitrator's decision."[48] One court
referred an award that required illegal action back to the arbitrator
with instructions concerning the law. In *Glendale Mfg. Co. v. Local
520,*[49] the union had been decertified after the award had been released and the instructions from the court were in no sense a direction
that the arbitrator should have looked at the external law and produced an award that was compatible with the law. The decertification
occurred after the fact but made the award unenforceable, and the
court permitted a revision, rather than a mere vacation.

---

[45]70 LA 338 (Draznin, 1978). *Contra, Farmer Bros. Co.*, 64 LA 901 (Jones, 1975).

[46]32 LA 769, 772 (Kleinsorge, 1959). *Accord, Aero Supply Mfg. Co.*, 24 LA 786 (Shister,
1955).

[47]17 C.J.S. *Contracts* § 189 (1963).

[48]*Botany Industries, Inc. v. New York Joint Bd.*, 375 F. Supp. 485, 490, 86 LRRM 2046, 2049
(S.D. N.Y. 1974), quoting *Local 985, Auto Workers v. W.M. Chace Co.*, 262 F. Supp. 114, 117,
64 LRRM 2098, 2100 (E.D. Mich. 1966) [Emphasis omitted.]; *Postal Workers v. U.S. Postal
Service*, 682 F.2d 1280, 110 LRRM 2764 (9th Cir. 1982).

[49]283 F.2d 936, 47 LRRM 2152 (4th Cir. 1960), *cert. denied*, 366 U.S. 950, 48 LRRM 2323
(1961).

[We] have the simple case of a minority union seeking to act as the exclusive representative of the employees with respect to their wages for this limited period. If we compel the employer to bargain with this union under these circumstances, we compel the employer and permit the union to commit an unfair labor practice in violation of the rights guaranteed to the employees under § 7.

The courts have been extremely careful to protect the rights of employees under the act and to avoid ordering an employer to bargain with a union if there was even so much as doubt about the majority status of the union.[50]

Arbitrator Richard Mittenthal said it is reasonable to assume that parties "do not wish to be bound by an invalid provision." He stated:

Consider some of the language in the typical contract. First, it is not unusual to find a *"separability"* or *"saving"* clause. Such a clause says that if any contract provision "shall be or become invalid or unenforceable" by reason of the law, "such invalidity or unenforceability shall not affect" the rest of the contract. The parties thus intend to isolate any invalidity so as to preserve the overall integrity of the contract. *But they also recognize the fact that a contract provision can be held "invalid" or "unenforceable" because of a state or federal statute. They do not wish to be bound by an invalid provision.* The implication seems clear that the arbitrator should not enforce a provision which is clearly unenforceable under the law.[51] [Footnote omitted. Emphasis added.]

And Arbitrator Robert G. Howlett said:

There are arbitrators to [sic] take the position that arbitrators may not, or should not, be concerned with constitutional or statutory issues. In my opinion, however, every contract includes all applicable provisions of the law and arbitrators, as well as all other decision making entities, are bound by the law applicable to the contract being construed.[52] [Footnotes omitted.]

Judge Jerre S. Williams, in *W. R. Grace & Company v. Rubber Workers, Local 759,*[53] also questioned the reality of not looking outside the actual working of the labor agreement:

For many years there has been a philosophical and jurisprudential dispute among labor arbitrators as to whether they are entitled to and whether they should look outside the actual wording of the contract to laws which may require the parties to act in ways different from those provided

---

[50]*Id.* at 940, 47 LRRM at 2155.

[51]Mittenthal, *The Role of Law in Arbitration,* DEVELOPMENTS IN AMERICAN AND FOREIGN ARBITRATION, Proceedings of the Twenty-First Annual Meeting, National Academy of Arbitrators, C. Rehmus, ed. (Washington: BNA Books, 1968), p. 49.

[52]*Warren Consolidated Schools,* 67-1 ARB ¶ 8228 at 3800 (Howlett, 1967).

[53]652 F.2d 1248, 107 LRRM 3251 (5th Cir. 1981), *cert granted,* 50 USLW 3998.18 (U.S. June 28, 1982) (No. 81-1314).

for in the agreement itself. *See* Gorman, Basic Text on Labor Law, p. 534. The discussion, however, becomes unrealistic when the wording of the collective agreement is clearly in conflict with law. It is elementary that a contract provision contrary to law is unenforceable and does not bind the parties. 6A Corbin, Contracts §§ 1373-5; Fairweather, Practice and Procedure in Labor Arbitration [1973], p. 117.[54]

Arbitrators Infer That the Parties Do Not Want a Vacuum

It is one thing for an arbitrator to conclude that a provision in the labor agreement cannot be enforced because to do so would require a legal violation; but it is something else for the parties to the agreement to conclude that the provisions of the labor agreement should not be enforced and then request the arbitrator to make a slight revision in the provision of the labor agreement so that the revised provision can be enforced without entailing a violation of the law.

A classic example of such a situation occurred when various arbitrators declared that the seniority provisions in the labor agreement were illegal when the Selective Service Act of 1940, Section 8(b)—issued after the end of World War II—provided that veterans were granted a seniority preference during their first year in active employment with an employer. It was not possible to make this statutory rule compatible with the labor agreement seniority provisions by merely construing words, and arbitrators produced awards compatible with the Selective Service Act. For example, Arbitrator Emery in *Vanette Hosiery Mills*[55] explained three options, saying he either had to (1) hold that the preference order for layoff for veterans had to be added to the seniority provision in the labor agreement, or (2) make the seniority provisions illegal, or (3) make the seniority provisions not enforceable, thereby setting up a vacuum in the labor agreement. The arbitrator set up a new layoff plan and enforced it so the agreement, as amended, would be compatible with the new Selective Service Act amendment. Arbitrator Emery explained the reasons for his choice:

> Before deciding finally about the two Union contentions, let us examine the federal statute with which the Company had to comply when Mr. [D——] returned from the service. It is the Selective Service Act of 1940, Section 8(b)(B): "if such position was in the employ of a private employer, such employer shall restore such person to such position or to a *position of like seniority, status and pay* ..." (emphasis added)... [The] veteran's seniority was clearly the same as if he had worked all the time in the mill;

---

[54]652 F.2d at 1253, 107 LRRM at 3255-56. The impact of an illegal result is discussed under "Vacation for Error in Law" in Chapter XXI.

[55]17 LA 349 (Emery, 1951).

and as to status, he was still a knitter. The crucial requirement, therefore, was "a position of like pay," if that was possible and reasonable.

The Agreement is of course subject to federal and state law, as fully as if such provisions were copied into the contract. Therefore if the Company places the returning veteran on a machine which pays approximately the same as the machine he had before drafted, he is entitled to it. In other words, there is some doubt as to the Union's two contentions about seniority, discussed above; but assuming that both are entirely right, they would be overridden by the federal statute if what the Company did was merely to place the veteran on an equal-paying job.[56]

Arbitrator Larkin in *Gary-Hobart Water Corp.*[57] started with the view that the parties want an award that will resolve the dispute rather than one that will produce simply a vacuum award and no more.

> In fact, it is our candid opinion that if this Board should deny this grievance, the Union would have very good grounds for going to court and having the award set aside.

Arbitrator Draznin's award in *California-Sample Service Co., Inc.*[58] is worth a second mention. A labor agreement "does not exist in a vacuum" and hence the U.S. Immigration and Naturalization Service rules had to be blended in to prevent eighty illegal aliens from being reinstated (if the rules of the labor agreement were followed) and then promptly arrested because they did not possess valid work permits.

The Arbitrator Has an Obligation to Provide a Final Resolution to the Dispute

In Section 173(d) of the Labor Management Relations Act[59] there is this statement:

> *Final* adjustment by a method agreed upon by the parties [arbitration] is declared to be the desirable method for settlement of grievance disputes arising over the application or interpretation of an existing collective-bargaining agreement. [Emphasis added.]

The Supreme Court said in *Local 174, Teamsters v. Lucas Flour Co.*[60] that arbitrators have the statutory task of "adjusting competing" interests. Competing interests arose in *Hospital for Joint Diseases and Medical Center v. Davis*[61] when the hospital's laundry equipment no longer met the statutory standards and the washing of the patient's

---

[56]*Id.* at 351.
[57]53 LA 1311, 1313 (Larkin, 1969).
[58]70 LA 338 (Draznin, 1978).
[59]29 U.S.C. § 173(d) (1976).
[60]369 U.S. 95, 49 LRRM 2717 (1962).
[61]442 F. Supp. 1030, 97 LRRM 2330 (S.D. N.Y. 1977).

bedding had to be subcontracted to a large laundry even though the labor agreement provided that the hospital could not subcontract out work. The hospital filed a petition with a state court to stay arbitration because the laundry facility would violate health codes if the labor agreement no-subcontracting provision was enforced. The federal court granted the union's cross petition and sent a grievance back to the arbitrator, explaining that "[t]his court cannot assume that an arbitrator will totally disregard the laws applicable to the Hospital's laundry situation and deliberately order the Hospital to violate such laws. . . . Furthermore, should an arbitrator render an award compelling the Hospital to violate any law, such award is subject to challenge in an action to vacate."[62]

In the contrary situation, Arbitrator Katz in *Alexander's Personnel Providers, Inc.,*[63] changed the labor agreement provision agreed upon in 1974 to eliminate the requirement that double-time wages were to be paid on Sunday. He did this because the Sunday Blue Laws restricting work on Sunday were determined in 1976 to be unconstitutional in New York State. The stores competing with Alexander began to operate on Sunday, but when Alexander followed suit, a grievance was filed.

Arbitrator Katz traced the source of the "double time on Sunday" language in the prior labor agreements that covered 35 engineers and mechanics who worked in 13 Alexander stores where 10,000 employees were at work. The engineers and mechanics were scheduled in the different stores for 7-1/2 hours on five days. Some started work on Monday and others on Tuesday. If they worked more than 7-1/2 hours a day, they were paid time and one-half. In the 1972 agreement, the language about double time being paid on Sunday included words specifying double-time rates for engineers and mechanics if Sunday was "their sixth day worked in a work week."[64] When the 1974 labor agreement was submitted for ratification, no reference to double time on Sunday was included and because of this change in language, the members did not ratify. Then language specifying "double time on Sunday," without reference to the sixth day worked, was included and the agreement was ratified.

When these additional words were reincluded, the company negotiator informed the union negotiator that the "double time provision was meaningless and Alexander's did not intend to open its stores on Sunday."[65]

---

[62]*Id.* at 1033–34, 97 LRRM at 2332.
[63]68 LA 249 (Katz, 1977).
[64]*Id.* at 250.
[65]*Id.* at 252.

The company representation argued to Arbitrator Katz at the hearing that "[a]t the time the contract was signed, no one anticipated that within two years, the Court of Appeals would nullify the Sunday Blue Laws and thereafter the various stores would be open for work on Sunday."[66] The union representative argued that "[t]he contract is clear, explicit and unequivocal. It means exactly what it says, the men are to be paid double time for working on Sunday. It does not mean anything more or less."[67]

Arbitrator Katz then made this legal finding in his award:

> In questions involving the interpretation of a contract, the Courts have universally adhered to the principle that effect is to be given to the mutual intent and understanding of the parties in the light of all the surrounding facts and circumstances existing as of the time the contract was signed, Williston On Contracts, Third Edition, Volume IV, Chapter 22, Construction and Interpretation of Contracts.[68]

Arbitrator Katz changed the language in the labor agreement (removed the obligation to pay double time on Sunday), using an "external law change—and a burden of proof" articulation.

> The Union has the burden of establishing by credible evidence that it inserted the double pay provision in the contract with the mutual intent and understanding of both parties that this provision was intended to apply in the event the Alexander's stores opened for regular business on Sundays. Having considered all the evidence, the testimony and the briefs submitted by the Parties, the Arbitrator finds that the Union has failed to sustain its burden of proof. The Issue will be answered in the negative.[69]

By this construction process, the arbitrator changed the words in a provision of the labor agreement when the state law was changed to produce a competitive result and, quite likely, an equitable result in view of the new normal store hour schedules of other stores.

Some Arbitrators Obtain Specific Authority at the Hearing

Since employers and unions generally desire an award that produces a complete and legal answer to the dispute, some arbitrators obtain their authority to produce such an award not by going through the series of inferences discussed in the three prior subsections but merely by asking the parties at the hearing whether they want the arbitrator to have the authority to examine external law and absorb it into the labor agreement if a conflict between the statutory law and the labor

---

[66]*Id.*
[67]*Id.* at 251.
[68]*Id.* at 252.
[69]*Id.* at 253.

agreement occurs. It is considered very difficult for either party at an arbitration to say to the arbitrator and to the other party that that party does not want the arbitrator to render a legally sound and final resolution to the dispute.

The wisdom of the arbitrator in asking the parties to stipulate on the record his or her authority if a legal rule comes into conflict with a labor agreement rule resembles the wisdom of asking the parties whether the arbitrator (1) has authority to convert a discharge to disciplinary suspension (*see* "Remedies in Disciplinary Cases," Chapter XVIII *infra*) or (2) is obligated to reinstate with full back pay if the arbitrator concludes that the discharge is not supported by a "sufficient cause," even though the arbitrator would have concluded that there was "sufficient cause" to support a disciplinary suspension.

If the employer takes the position at the hearing and on the transcript that the grievance before the arbitrator cannot be properly resolved by arbitration because the external law would obviously be involved, the employer would be stating that the arbitrator has no jurisdiction to resolve the dispute. When arbitration ceases to be a method of resolving the dispute and a strike breaks out, no court can issue a *Boys Markets*-type of injunction against the strike since the *quid pro quo* (arbitration resolution rather than striking) is not available.[70] Since the employer stands to lose the *Boys Markets* injunction protection by asserting an arbitrator loses jurisdiction if interpreting external law because the labor agreement does not permit such absorption, the employer will grant such absorption on the transcript to permit the arbitrator to have the necessary jurisdiction to resolve the dispute.

Arbitrator Brown in *UMC Industries*[71] had to resolve a conflict between the labor agreement, the federal civil rights law, and the state law barring employment of female employees in excess of nine hours in any one day or fifty-four hours in any one week. One female employee had lodged a complaint with the Equal Employment Opportunity Commission that she was being discriminated against because she was denied the opportunity to work as much overtime as the male employees, and the company agreed with the EEOC to offer men and women equal overtime opportunities. Other female employees would refuse to work more than nine hours, relying on the state statute limiting hours for females to nine. Some females obtained certificates from a doctor to the effect that they were physically unable to work the scheduled overtime in excess of the state law limits. The company took the position that any female who refused to work the scheduled hours

---

[70]*Boys Markets, Inc. v. Retail Clerks, Local 770*, 398 U.S. 235, 74 LRRM 2257 (1970).
[71]58 LA 789 (Brown, 1972).

was subject to discipline. It ignored the medical certificates because "people who want such certificates can, by a judicious choice of doctors, readily get them."[72]

Arbitrator Brown explained that "when the Company schedules overtime it must schedule it for balanced crews. It can't have one part of the assembly line working ten hours and another part working nine hours."[73] He went on to explain that "[t]he employees whose grievances we are considering in these proceedings tell us that they have doubts ... about the Company's legal right to work them ... more than 9 hours in any day or 54 hours in any one week"[74] and rather than filing a grievance and have the difference in state law, federal law, and labor agreement conflicts resolved by arbitration they "resorted to self-help; they simply refused to work scheduled overtime."[75] Arbitrator Brown commented:

> When the grievants took that action, they left the employer no choice.... The employer's hand was forced. He had to discipline the grievants.
> The resort to the doctor's certificates as a device for evading the obligation to work overtime cannot be tolerated. If some employees choose that route, the employer will have no choice but to place them on leave until they can bring in doctor's statements certifying them as able to work the scheduled hours....[76]

The overtime schedules in question for both male and female employees were those in August and September, 1971. The confusion about the Missouri statute that set up limits on female working hours continued until the Missouri attorney general issued a ruling in November 1971, that the federal Civil Rights Act superceded the Missouri statute. Arbitrator Brown concluded that the suspensions of females who had refused to work overtime above nine hours a day prior to November (*i.e.,* during August and September) should be revoked and compensation granted during any disciplinary suspension prior to November. However, oral warnings effective subsequent to November were to remain in effect. Any female who presented a doctor's certificate stating that she was physically unable to work overtime, the arbitrator ruled, could be required by the employer to take a leave of absence until she presented a doctor's certificate stating that she was able to work the overtime schedule established on her job.

An example from another area of the effect an agreed stipulation may have when it creates in the arbitrator authority that could other-

---

[72]*Id.* at 790.
[73]*Id.* at 791.
[74]*Id.*
[75]*Id.*
[76]*Id. See also IMC Chemical Group,* 73 LA 215, 217 (Owen, 1979).

wise be questioned occurred during a hearing before Arbitrator Jerome Smith in *Howard P. Foley Co.* [77] It also is an illustration that pitfalls can arise for the unwary if stipulations are not clearly phrased. During the first hearing in July, Arbitrator Smith held that three employees should be paid for a one-half hour absence from work on March 6, 1979, because they had been directed by their foreman to leave work and go to a holding area because of a bomb scare. At the commencement of this hearing, the parties stipulated that the disposition of the grievances of the three employees would "be applicable to all workmen who were similarly affected by the company action from March 6, 1979 forward." Later the union asked for the half-hour payment for 134 other employees who had been directed by their foreman to go to the holding area. The company disagreed and a second hearing before Arbitrator Smith took place, and he held that the stipulation entered into earlier applied to the 134 other employees and no separate award was therefore needed to require the company to pay the 134 others.

Arbitrator Gould in *Basic Vegetable Products, Inc.* [78] worked out with the parties, including grievant's counsel of her own choosing, a careful stipulation to allow him to resolve the issue under both a conciliation and settlement agreement and the labor agreement. The arbitrator reported that he found "stipulations" to be rare:

> To my knowledge, this is the first arbitration procedure negotiated in the United States in which the parties have specifically attempted to provide the Arbitrator with all the authority which is accorded a Federal District Court operating under Title VII of the Civil Rights Act of 1964. In so doing, the parties apparently attempt to obtain the equivalent of whatever deference the Supreme Court may have accorded arbitration in *Alexander v. Gardner-Denver Co.*
>
> . . .
>
> I commend the parties for entering into this novel and important agreement. . . . [T]raditional arbitration procedures are no answer to this problem. It is axiomatic that the parties provide the arbitrator with the authority to act as a Federal District Court as was done in this case. [79]

Because the stipulation technique is available, there should be few disputes about whether an arbitrator has applied external law rather than working simply within the "four corners" of the labor agreement. *Since Boys Markets* injunctions are available only when the arbitrator has authority to rule on the dispute, employers should want to enter into stipulations if the union questions the arbitrator's authority.

---

[77] 73 LA 1205 (Smith, 1979).
[78] 64 LA 620 (Gould, 1975).
[79] *Id.* at 624–25.

However, employers may not suggest a stipulation at the hearing for fear that the union representatives might respond with a proposal to negotiate some change into the labor agreement; employers have strong "anti" feelings about renegotiating provisions of the labor agreement during its term. In addition, both parties could be afraid that the arbitrator might start an extensive "renegotiation" if he has clear authority to blend into the labor agreement interpretations based on his view of the external law.

TO WHAT SHOULD AN ARBITRATOR REACT?

If the arbitrator believes he or she should examine the external law when a representative of one or the other parties asserts that conflicts between the labor agreement and the external law could cause the award to be upset by either the court or the NLRB, the arbitrator should examine not only the authority to react to the external law, but also the following: (1) whether the external law being urged upon the arbitrator as in conflict with the labor agreement is sufficiently stabilized to permit the arbitrator to clearly determine what the law is and (2) whether the law being urged upon the arbitrator is actual law or has its origin in regulation.

Effect of Unstable Law

It is often difficult for an arbitrator to select from conflicting views of a given law (sometimes prepared by the staff of commissions or by writers in legal periodicals) which view the U.S. Supreme Court or a state supreme court will subsequently adopt.[80] Arbitrator Samuel Kates, confronting such a confusion in *Dayton Tire and Rubber Co.*,[81] denied the grievance of a female employee who claimed that her employer should have paid her double time on the seventh day of a calendar week in compliance with an Ohio state statute. The arbitrator ruled that the double time for women was discrimination on the basis of sex and hence the state statute was ineffective in light of federal law in this area. However, Arbitrator Paul Lehoczky in *Goodyear Aerospace Corp.*[82] denied a grievance by some females claiming that they should be assigned jobs that under the state law would be improper for females because of the weight of objects that had to be lifted, holding that the weight rules remained in effect until the law was declared void by a court or was modified by the legislature; until either one of these

---

[80]*See, e.g., Griggs v. Duke Power Co.*, 401 U.S. 424, 3 FEP Cases 175 (1971).
[81]55 LA 357 (Kates, 1970).
[82]60 LA 1011 (Lehoczky, 1973).

happened, he said, no individual arbitrator could substitute his or her discretion or judgment for the judgment of the Ohio legislature.

The classic example of arbitrators absorbing the law too quickly into the labor agreement involved the law that developed around pregnancy. Arbitrator Edwin R. Teple in *Goodyear Tire & Rubber Co.*[83] held that a six-week limitation to weekly benefits for absences from work due to pregnancy was an illegal discrimination under Title VII because weekly benefits for absences due to sickness or accident did not stop until the absence exceeded 52 weeks. Arbitrator Teple assumed that pregnancy was a sickness and that if the company limited the benefit periods to six weeks, the females involved were being treated in a discriminatory manner. When Arbitrator Teple concluded that under the statutory law absences due to pregnancy and sickness had to be treated the same way, he modified the labor agreement, believing he had the authority to do so. The company filed a suit[84] in Ohio and there the case was held in limbo until the Supreme Court released *General Electric Co. v. Gilbert.*[85] The regulation issued by the EEOC and relied upon by Arbitrator Teple was found to be incorrect and hence the award by Arbitrator Teple was incorrect. Then when the Pregnancy Discrimination Act[86] became effective on April 29, 1979, the premature Teple award became compatible with the new law. This "on and off" experience by Arbitrator Teple should cause arbitrators to resist the temptation to plunge into the evaluation of the statutory law until the statutory law is fully stabilized.

Effect of Regulations

The question of what arbitrators do when a law has some bearing on the labor agreement rules has been discussed *supra,* with examples of situations where the arbitrator responds to a legal rule that can be forced upon the parties by legal sanctions. However, a new type of regulatory law developed when President Johnson issued Executive Order 11246[87] in 1965. He directed the Secretary of Labor to set up an Office of Federal Contract Compliance (OFCC) to encourage formation of, and then supervise, affirmative action plans through the various purchasing agencies of the government. These plans were designed to

---

[83]*Goodyear Tire & Rubber Co.* (Teple, 1974)) (private award); *see also General Telephone Co. of Pa. v. Locals 1635, 1636, 1637,* 427 F. Supp. 398, 95 LRRM 2899 (W.D. Pa. 1977).

[84]No. 73-74 (C.P. Auglize County, Ohio) (unpublished).

[85]429 U.S. 125, 13 FEP Cases 1657 (1976).

[86]42 U.S.C. § 2000e *et seq.* (Supp. III 1979).

[87]3 C.F.R., 1964-65 Comp., pp. 339-48, as amended by Executive Order 11375, 3 C.F.R. 1966-1970 Comp., pp. 684-86 (banning sex discrimination), and by Executive Order 12086, 3 C.F.R., 1978 Comp., pp. 230-34 (transferring compliance functions of various agencies to the OFCC), 401 FEP Manual 601.

cause contractors selling goods to the government to employ more women and members of minority groups.

The Department of Defense was one of the government purchasing agencies (called contracting agencies), and the Defense Supply Agency (DSA) was the subagency that set up and enforced the affirmative action plans for defense contractors—*i.e.*, contractors selling goods to the Department of Defense. Under Executive Order 11246, the DSA asserted, it could require each defense contractor that held purchase contracts valued at $50,000 or more and employing 50 or more employees to file an annual EEO-1 report (1) describing the ethnic composition of the contractor's work force and (2) attaching an affirmative action plan to cause more women and members of minority groups to be hired and to move them within the work force to more responsible positions. Under this executive order, the DSA in 1975 directed the Farrel Division of the United Shoe Machine Company to follow a seniority plan different from the one incorporated as part of the company's labor agreement with the United Steelworkers Union.

The seniority system in the labor agreement did not block women or members of a minority from bidding into different departments but did provide that the bid across the department line was to the vacancy that resulted after the employee with the highest seniority in the department desiring the vacancy was promoted, leaving a resulting lower-level vacancy open for the bidder from the foreign department. This two-step bidding feature did not create any illegal discrimination but the DSA representative attempted to force, through the threat of loss of business, a change in the seniority plan because undoubtedly more women and members of minorities could transfer to higher-paid jobs if they could bid on the original vacancy. The DSA representative issued an order to Farrel Division to make the change or the orders for military shoes would be cancelled.

In an effort to renegotiate the seniority plan to meet the demand of the DSA representative the Union and management representatives participated in 13 meetings, and in some of these the DSA representative was present. In spite of this pressure, the Union representatives refused to agree to a different sequence of vacancy filling because (1) they were under no legal obligation to do so and (2) their members in the department who were entitled to bid on the original vacancy had usually been patiently waiting for a promotional opportunity in the department and would consider it unfair that someone from a foreign department could bid over their heads on a higher-rated vacancy, thereby denying them their anticipated opportunity for advancement.

However, the risk of economic loss if the military shoe orders were cancelled became so real that the company representatives followed the DSA plan, violating the seniority plan set out in the labor agreement.

When an employee from a different department was transferred to the primary vacancy in a "learner grinder operator" position, the employee in the original department who desired to be promoted to the vacancy and who had the greatest length of service of any employee bidding from within the department to the vacancy became the grievant in *United Shoe Machine, Farrell Division*.[88] The grievance was submitted to Arbitrator Charles Gregory (who had been a university law professor and a busy arbitrator for many years). Both the union and company representatives explained to him that the grievant would have been awarded the vacancy if the company had followed the seniority rules incorporated in the labor agreement; the union representative explained that the company was not privileged to violate the provisions of the labor agreement in spite of the threat of economic loss to force the change. Arbitrator Gregory upheld the grievance and directed that the grievant (the disappointed bidder in the department) be transferred to the "learner grinder operator" position that he desired without displacing the employee transferred into that position from the "foreign" department, and that if the grievant could not be absorbed into that job classification he must be absorbed into a classification with the same rate of pay and with the payment of "back pay" for his loss from the date of his bid. He explained:

> A reading of the voluminous record in this case shows what an appalling burden federal bureaucracy has imposed on employers doing business with the government. Both the Company and the Union have maintained right along that there is nothing discriminatory in the terms of their collective agreement....[89]

Arbitrator Gregory recognized the extreme economic pressures that had been placed on the company by the threat of shoe manufacturing order cancellations by the Defense Supply Agency:

> The Company says that it was *forced* to comply with the federal mandate requiring it to displace the provisions of the agreement between the parties with the terms dictated by the DSA/OFCC.... The Company declares that if it refused to comply with such directive, it risked cancellation of existing contracts with the Department of Defense and debarment from further defense contracts.[90] [Emphasis in original.]

In spite of the union's understanding of the economic threat, the union had argued against changing the labor agreement, the arbitrator noted:

---

[88] 69 LA 1051 (Gregory, 1977).
[89] *Id*. at 1055.
[90] *Id*.

The Union's position, on the other hand, is that my authority to act as arbitrator arises from the collective agreement between the parties and is confined to construing and applying its terms, with the expressed limitation that "... he [the arbitrator] shall, however, have no authority to add to, subtract from or in any way modify the terms of this Agreement." Therefore, it contends, this grievance is arbitrable and my only legitimate task is made simple by the Company's admission that *under the terms of the agreement* [N——] instead of [H——] should have been awarded the job opening in question, thus even saving me the effort of construing Articles VI and VII and applying them to the instant case. The Union's attorney argues that the Company's proffered defense—that the contract seniority provisions were superseded by a subsequent agreement the Company made with the procurement branch of the Department of Defense or with the DSA/OFCC to remedy an "affected class" situation—must be rejected by me because I have no power to nullify a specific provision of the collective agreement even if it does conflict with the directives of federal agencies. But, the Union's attorney continues, even if I decide that I do have the authority to resolve conflicts between the collective agreement and the law, the remedial agreement made by the Company with DSA/OFCC for the Department of Defense does not have the force of law and does not supersede the terms of the collective bargaining agreement.[91] [Emphasis in original.]

The arbitrator concluded that it was his obligation to apply the labor agreement rather than the Department of Defense plan backed up with orders:

After extensive reading and reflection I have concluded that the grievance herein is arbitrable and that I had best fulfill my responsibility as an arbitrator acting under the agreement, in accord with the terms of that agreement, leaving to the courts the interpretation and appropriateness of the various federal anti-discrimination laws, rulings and sanctions. I feel especially justified in this course of action, as applied to this particular case, since I think it is pretty obvious that there was nothing discriminatory in Articles VI and VII of the collective agreement here involved or in the employment situation prevailing in the Foundry and Welding departments at the Company's plant.[92]

The company filed a suit in the Federal District Court for the District of Connecticut seeking an enforcement order from the court to reduce the risk that the Defense Supply Agency would cancel the military shoe orders in retribution for Arbitrator Gregory's order to comply with the seniority plan contained in the labor agreement.

Arbitrator John P. Owen in *IMC Chemical Group*[93] did not follow Arbitrator Gregory's path, concluding he should not approve some

---

[91]*Id.* at 1056.
[92]*Id.*
[93]73 LA 215 (Owen, 1979).

grievances protesting deviations from the seniority plan set up in the labor agreement. The deviations occurred because some members of the Department of Energy had threatened, under Executive Order 11246, to cancel purchases by the Department of Energy unless the deviations were made. Grievances were filed because five employees were given seniority rights out of line with the seniority plan set forth in the labor agreement, and Arbitrator Owen did not grant the grievances saying that "to rule in favor of the Union and to provide the remedy it has requested would lead very possibly to an illegal award running counter to national policy."[94]

Similarly, Arbitrator F. J. Taylor in *International Paper Company*[95] did not follow arbitrator Gregory's path and enforce the seniority arrangements incorporated in the labor agreement. The company selected a black applicant over the grievant who had two years more seniority, because the Office of Federal Contract Compliance investigator threatened to cancel government contracts unless the preference was given to the selectee. Arbitrator Taylor conceded that the selection of the black applicant was a "leapfrogging" violation of the labor agreement but he did not grant the grievance because of the economic pressure generated upon the company by the government agency. Arbitrator Taylor explained:

> Not to [approve the deviations from the promotional sequences, using an Affirmative Action Program] places the Company in an impossible position. The Company has no alternative but to comply with the directives of the Office of Contract Compliance. Failure to do so would be a violation of Executive Order 11246 and would jeopardize the economic well being, even survival, of the International Paper Company.... Those [contractors] not found in compliance would suffer potential loss of government contracts and subcontracts.... Thus, the Company faced drastic consequences if it failed to follow the directions of Federal enforcement authority.[96]

In the award Arbitrator Taylor attempted to placate the Union:

> I am sympathetic to the frustrations which the Union must feel in an issue such as this. The Contract is clear and unequivocal.... The Union simply believed that it had, in good faith, negotiated an agreement on questions of transfers and seniority, and now it finds this agreement altered by a Federally mandated remedial action program. Nevertheless, such sympathy did not alter my conclusions. I shall sign an AWARD denying the grievance.[97]

---

[94]*Id.* at 223.

[95]69 LA 857 (Taylor, 1977); in *International Paper Co.*, 68 LA 155 (1977), Arbitrator Taylor followed the same theory, i.e., that an EEOC order should modify a nondiscriminatory seniority provision, and granted the grievance in this case due to certain unique reasons.

[96]*Id.* at 861.

[97]*Id.* at 862.

In contrast, Arbitrator Milton T. Edelman in *Hollander & Co.*[98] did follow the path of Arbitrator Gregory rather than the path of Arbitrators Owen and Taylor. Arbitrator Edelman took the position that arbitrators should not order deviations from the seniority plans in labor agreements unless they are clearly illegal—which means clearly illegal determined by either a Supreme Court pronouncement or clear Congressional edict:

> One of the branches of government will ultimately have to decide whether Title VII takes precedence over collective bargaining agreements and under what conditions. One or both may have to lay down guidelines or authorize EEOC to lay down guidelines for arbitrators to follow.... Such guidelines, after receiving court approval, could provide the kind of specific rules arbitrators would need in order to consider both Title VII and the collective bargaining agreement.
> ...[I]n the present case we have no such guidance.[99]

Two arbitrators rendered awards for W. R. Grace & Co., and the awards went in opposite directions. Arbitrator Anthony J. Sabella did not enforce the seniority provisions of the labor agreement because the Equal Employment Opportunity Commission requested changes (thus following the path of Arbitrators Owen and Taylor), whereas Arbitrator Gerald A. Barrett enforced the labor agreement in spite of the deviations insisted upon by the EEOC, thus following the path of Arbitrators Gregory and Edelman.[100] The Fifth Circuit[101] set out to unscramble the contrasting awards that caused some confusion, referred to as an "industrial relations imbroglio." Not only did the Court clearly determine the path that arbitrators should tread when nondiscriminatory seniority provisions of the labor agreement and an EEOC order come into conflict, but the court also announced a series of legal rules which will add more of the judicial supervision of arbitrators that is so rapidly developing as arbitration awards are being reviewed.

In this case the EEOC had started an investigation in 1972, and concluded that, prior to the enactment of the Civil Rights Act in 1964, women who performed office work had not been given the opportunity to transfer to jobs in the production operating departments. Even though the seniority arrangement negotiated with the union as part of the labor agreement generated no current discrimination, the commis-

---

[98]64 LA 816, 820 (Edelman, 1975).

[99]*Id.*

[100]Awards by Arbitrators Sabella and Barrett are discussed in *W. R. Grace & Co. v. Rubber Workers, Local 759*, 652 F.2d 1248, 1252, 107 LRRM 3251, 3253 (5th Cir. 1981).

[101]*W. R. Grace & Co. v. Rubber Workers, Local 759*, 652 F.2d 1248, 107 LRRM 3251 (5th Cir. 1981), *cert. granted*, 50 USLW 3998.18 (U.S. June 28, 1982) (No. 81-1314).

sion insisted that the company grant some seniority preferences to females to rectify the prior "discrimination."[102]

Shortly after a conciliation agreement was signed in 1974, the union instituted grievances on behalf of certain male employees who had been laid off while female employees, junior to them, had been retained in production operating jobs. The company brought a Section 301 suit in a district court to enjoin the arbitration of the grievances if they were in conflict with EEOC agreement even though consistent with seniority provisions of the labor agreement. In 1975 the district court issued the desired injunction blocking the arbitration, concluding that the EEOC agreement had superseded the labor agreement.[103]

The union appealed to the Fifth Circuit based on a Supreme Court decision giving nondiscriminatory seniority provisions in labor agreement precedence over inconsistent EEOC orders.[104] The court in 1978 reversed the district court and directed that the still pending grievance cases should proceed to arbitration.[105]

The company immediately changed its policy and applied the seniority rules in the labor agreement rather than those in the EEOC order and the grievance of a male operator who had been reduced in grade and later laid off while a junior female had been retained was submitted to Arbitrator Sabella. He refused to enforce the applicable provisions in the labor agreement because the delay in the processing of the grievances due to the time involved while the case was going up to and through the district and circuit courts would place an unfair back pay award penalty on the employer. Arbitrator Sabella explained:

> Unquestionably in the period of the violation the Employer was acting in concurrence with the District Court's order, as it was required to do. There is no evidence that the Employer was not acting in good faith in accordance with a legal court order. The Employer could not anticipate nor was it required to anticipate the Circuit's reversal. It would be inequitable and manifestly unfair to penalize the Employer under these circumstances.[106]

In the court case that ensued, the circuit court commented on the reasoning of Arbitrator Sabella:

> ... Arbitrator Sabella did not even refer to the collective bargaining agreement in his award but referred only to the fact that "it would be unequitable and manifestly unfair" to hold against the employer. There is

---

[102]652 F.2d at 1251, 107 LRRM at 3252.

[103]*Southbridge Plastics Div. v. Rubber Workers, Local 759*, 403 F. Supp. 1183 (N.D. Miss. 1975).

[104]*Teamsters v. United States*, 431 U.S. 324 (1977).

[105]*Southbridge Plastics Div. v. Rubber Workers, Local 759*, 565 F.2d 913 (5th Cir. 1978).

[106]*W. R. Grace & Co. v. Rubber Workers, Local 759*, 652 F.2d 1248, 1251, 107 LRRM 3251, 3253 (5th Cir. 1981). (This portion of arbitration award quoted in the opinion.)

nothing in the contract about the arbitrator balancing the equities or deciding whether something is unfair or not. Literally, the Sabella decision departed from the terms of the collective bargaining agreement.[107]

And again the court said:

> He was given no authority to ignore the seniority provisions of the contract and to decide the case on the basis of equity and fairness. His award clearly exceeded his jurisdiction and authority.[108]

The union then presented some other still pending grievances to Arbitrator Gerald A. Barrett and obtained precisely the opposite results. He enforced the labor agreement, which caused the company to pay back pay to the grievants who had been downgraded and/or laid off while junior females had been retained in their operating jobs.

The company filed the second Section 301 suit in the district court seeking a vacation of Arbitrator Barrett's award and an injunction to block further similar grievances.[109] The district court vacated Arbitrator Barrett's award and issued the requested injunctive order. Again the Fifth Circuit reversed, this time vacating the award by Arbitrator Sabella and approving the one by Arbitrator Barrett.[110] The Court explained again that on the basis of Supreme Court decisions a nondiscriminatory seniority provision in a labor agreement takes precedent over an inconsistent EEOC order.

The seven years of struggle over these grievances have not settled them; the Supreme Court granted *certiorari* in June 1982.[111] During this struggle the Fifth Circuit made some significant legal pronouncements about the conflicting awards and about arbitration in general, pronouncements which lead to more legal supervision over the labor arbitration process. First, the court said:

> In general, it is established that an arbitrator will follow a prior award on controlling facts under the same contract....
>
> ... But it is also established that if an award exceeds the arbitrator's jurisdiction or authority, does not draw its essence from the collective agreement, it cannot be considered to be binding.[112]

And then the Fifth Circuit wrote quite clearly that the court determines the law for the arbitrator and that when it sends the grievance back to an arbitrator it can withdraw from the arbitrator decisional

---

[107]*Id*. at 1255, 107 LRRM at 3255.
[108]*Id*. at 1257, 107 LRRM at 3257.
[109]*Id*. at 1252, 107 LRRM at 3254.
[110]*Id*.
[111]*W. R. Grace & Co. v. Rubber Workers, Local 759*, 50 USLW 3998.18 (U.S. June 28, 1982) (No. 81-1314).
[112]652 F.2d at 1257-58, 107 LRRM at 3254.

authority just as the court can withdraw decisional authority from a district court when it remands a case back to that lower court:

> In the last paragraph of Judge Morgan's [*Southbridge Plastics*] opinion, quoted above, we withdrew from the authority of the arbitrator any right to decide that the employer had not breached the contract and, therefore, was not liable to the employees for having followed the conciliation agreement. It was determined by the specific holding that the employer had breached the contract. Our interpretation of the contract is res judicata and is binding. Arbitrator Sabella's decision is directly contrary to our holding. He specifically found no breach. This Court's binding decision left as the only issues before the arbitrator which employees had been victims of the breach and damages for the breach. Our holding meant the arbitrator was no longer free to decide whether the employer should be liable for a breach or not.
>
> In summary, the working of the contract itself is restrictive enough to reveal that arbitrator Sabella exceeded his jurisdiction and authority, but also he exceeded the authority defined for him specifically by the holding of this Court in the Southbridge Plastics decision. Further, this same analysis reveals that arbitrator Barrett's decision is correct under the collective bargaining agreement and under our Southbridge Plastics mandate. He applied the seniority provisions of the contract, recognized that the employer had breached them, and he awarded damages to the employees who had been injured by the employer's breach. In doing so he properly refused to follow the earlier Sabella award.[113]

The direction by the court to an arbitrator and the subsequent review and vacation of the award by the same court is an illustration of the movement of labor arbitration onto the lowest rung of the judicial ladder, and those courts or agencies located on the higher rungs are the supervisors. Considerable detail on this shift from authority of the labor arbitrators to the courts is discussed in Chapter XXI, "Vacation, Enforcement, or Correction," Chapter XXII, "*De Novo* Review in a Court," and Chapter XXIII, "Fair Representation Obligations."

However, some courts still give a tolerance to the arbitrators' interpretation of the law. In *S & W Fine Foods, Inc.*[114] an arbitrator examined the law as he developed his award and interpreted the law. His award was then moved up to the state court because the employer sought a vacation on the ground that the arbitrator had not interpreted the law accurately. The court vacated the award and then on appeal the higher court reversed and reestablished the award. Even though the court's interpretation of the law might be different from the interpretation by the arbitrator, the higher court found, finality of

---

[113]*Id*. at 1257–58, 107 LRRM at 3257–58.

[114]*In re S & W Fine Foods, Inc.*, 30 LA 346 (N.Y. App. Div., April 24, 1958), *rev'd*, 185 N.Y.S.2d 1021, 8 A.D.2d 130, 32 LA 660 (1959), *aff'd*, 7 N.Y.S.2d 1018, 35 LA 649 (1960).

arbitration awards is an important principle because it decreases litigation and generates industrial peace. Substantial tolerance of the difference between an arbitrator's interpretation of the law and a court's interpretation is proper before a vacation should occur. The court explained its reasons:

> [T]he perverse misconstruction must be more than an egregious error of law before it satisfies the statute; it must be one which is so divorced from rationality that it can be accounted for only by one of the kinds of misbehavior recited in the statute. In that event, the [vacation] is granted not for error of law or misconstruction of documents but for misconduct under one or more of the permitted categories, which misconduct has been established. Nothing like that was established in this case.[115]

A discussion of the vacation of an award when a court believes the arbitrator has not interpreted the law properly is found under "Vacation for Error in Law" in Chapter XXI.

---

[115]8 A.D.2d at 132, 32 LA at 660.

CHAPTER XVII

Subcontracting

A "make or buy" analysis is made by a management to determine whether purchasing a part, product, or a service, instead of making or providing it, reduces costs, thereby increasing profits or decreasing prices. Often the lower cost results from the fact that the specialist has more efficient manufacturing procedures or has lower transportation costs due to location. The comparison of purchase price to manufacturing cost is simply the competition process at work. If purchasing bolts, pulleys or anything else from a specialist (in this chapter called the "subcontractor")[1] reduces costs, most economists would believe the work involved should move toward the specialist.

When similar products are produced in different plants operated by the same company, the management may have the production centralized at the plant where production and transportation costs are the lowest. This movement of work is sometimes called "subcontracting" of the product from one plant to another within the same company.[2] Sometimes the work is "moved" not by central management decision, but as a result of the submission of "bid" prices from the different plants to customers; the customer, rather than the management, orders from the different plants because of different bids or transportation costs. In this practice, no work is "moved" by central management decision; work is "moved" rather by customer orders.

Specific limitations on subcontracting have been negotiated into some labor agreements. These limitations now usually are called "work preservation agreements," to distinguish them from "secondary boycotts," which are now clearly illegal.[3] This chapter does not discuss such specific agreements, but rather the restrictions on sub-

---

[1]*Standard Oil v. FTC,* 340 U.S. 231, 248 (1951). The competitive process was first given statutory protection in 1890 by the Sherman Act, 15 U.S.C.A. §§ 1-7. The Supreme Court explained that this law meant that "all combinations and conspiracies which restrain the free and natural flow of trade" to the lower cost and lower price producer are detrimental to the consumer. *Eastern States Retail Lumber Dealers Ass'n v. United States,* 234 U.S. 600, 609 (1914).

[2]*International Harvester Co.,* 24 LA 32 (Cole, 1955).

[3]*See* "The Impact of Section 8(e) on Implied Restrictions on Subcontracting" in this chapter, *infra.*

contracting set forth in the awards of some arbitrators who have implied restrictions from non-specific general language in the labor agreement. Other arbitrators have rejected such implied restrictions. The discussion of the pros and cons of finding subcontracting restrictions by implication has been referred to as the arbitration "battleground."[4]

The different rationalizations of various arbitrators have been tabulated by some arbitrators. In 1958, Arbitrator Ralph Seward made such an analysis and then announced, with quotations from Omar Khayyam, that the variety he found revealed a confusion.[5] Arbitrator G. Allan Dash in 1959, Arbitrator D. A. Crawford in 1960, and Arbitrator John G. Sembower in 1961 attempted the same exercise.[6] Finally, in 1979, Arbitrator Anthony V. Sinicropi, twenty-one years after Arbitrator Seward, made a similar tabulation, and reported that the variety still remains an "old battleground" in arbitration. He emphasized the current confusion by repeating the same quotation by Omar Khayyam[7] first introduced by Arbitrator Seward.

The reasoning of arbitrators who set up limitations on the purchasing of parts, products, and services, working with a labor agreement that did not contain any specific provision restricting subcontracting, are discussed below.

LIMITING SUBCONTRACTING BY "GOOD-BAD FAITH" DETERMINATIONS

Some arbitrators have developed personal tests to determine whether they will approve or not approve the purchasing of parts, products, and services from a contractor. Some arbitrators hold that

---

[4]Sinicropi, *Revisiting an Old Battleground: The Subcontracting Dispute,* ARBITRATION OF SUBCONTRACTING AND WAGE INCENTIVE DISPUTES, Proceedings of the Thirty-Second Annual Meeting, National Academy of Arbitrators, J. Stern and B. Dennis, eds. (Washington: BNA Books, 1980), p. 125.

[5]*Bethlehem Steel Co.,* 30 LA 678, 682 (Seward, 1958). After Arbitrator Seward in a note had analyzed twenty-three awards by different arbitrators involving subcontracting, he found they had "little uniformity of either theoretical argument or ultimate decision.... [M]oreover there are conflicts of principle and approach." He said he returned from his exploration of the cases a sadder, if not a wiser, man and echoed the plaint of Omar Khayyam: "'Myself when young did/ eagerly frequent/ Doctor and Saint and/ heard great argument/ About it and about but/ evermore came out by the same door/ wherein I went.'" 30 LA at 862.

[6]*Celanese Corp. of America,* 33 LA 925 (Dash, 1959); Crawford, *The Arbitration of Disputes Over Subcontracting,* CHALLENGES TO ARBITRATION, Proceedings of the Thirteenth Annual Meeting of the National Academy of Arbitrators, J. McKelvey, ed. (Washington: BNA Books, 1960), p. 51; *Central Soya Co.,* 36 LA 1173, 1176 (Sembower, 1961).

[7]Sinicropi, note 4 *supra,* at p. 156. When Arbitrator Sinicropi made his analysis of awards by different arbitrators involving subcontracting, he reported, "[w]hen I first began delving into the topic of subcontracting, I was impressed with Ralph Seward's now famous footnote.... He quoted Omar Khayyam [*see* note 2 *supra*].... After considering the material gathered for this paper, Seward's choice of words appears to be more appropriate than ever." This comment

when the employees in the units covered by labor agreements are not adversely affected by such purchasing, it is "good faith" subcontracting, and approved; but if the employees are adversely affected, it is "bad faith" subcontracting, and the purchasing is not approved. No words are found in the labor agreements to support these distinctions. Arbitrator Russell Smith in *Allis Chalmers Mfg. Co.*[8] set out his rationalization for this under the two headings "good faith" and "bad faith." He identified four situations in which an employer would be acting in bad faith by purchasing parts, products, or services from a subcontractor:

> (1) To negotiate a collective agreement with the Union representative covering classifications of work while withholding from the Union the fact that the employer contemplates, in the immediate future, a major change in operations which will eliminate such work; (2) entering into a "subcontracting" arrangement which is subterfuge, in the sense that the "employees" of the ostensible "subcontractor" become in substance the employees of the employer; (3) the commingling of employees of a subcontractor, working under a different set of wages or other working conditions, regularly and continuously with employees of the employer performing the same kinds of work; (4) contracting out work for the specific purpose of undermining or weakening the Union or depriving employees of employment opportunities.

His four "bad faith" standards relate somewhat to the standards announced in decisions by the NLRB and courts; hence, the standards he uses may come into arbitration from the "external law." Arbitrator Smith's first bad faith test (1) is a direct borrowing from the NLRB's view enunciated in the *Town & Country* decision[9] that requires an

---

about the conflicting theories of arbitrators in this area and his confusion was written twenty-one years after Arbitrator Seward's similar comment.

[8] 39 LA 1213, 1219 (Smith, 1962).

[9] *Town & Country Mfg. Co.*, 136 NLRB 1022, 49 LRRM 1918 (1962). The Board said that subcontracting of work without advance notice to the union to provide it the opportunity to negotiate with the employer was evidence, when evaluated as part of a pattern of conduct, of a refusal to bargain in good faith required by section 8(a)(5) of the Act. The Fifth Circuit affirmed in *Town & Country Mfg. Co. v. NLRB*, 316 F.2d 846, 53 LRRM 2054 (5th Cir. 1963). The *Town & Country* principle had been rejected earlier by the Board in *Fibreboard Paper Products Corp.*, 130 NLRB 1558, 47 LRRM 1547 (1961) and then, in a highly unusual reconsideration, the Board reversed itself in *Town & Country, supra.* This second opinion was then affirmed by the Supreme Court in *Fibreboard Paper Products Corp. v. NLRB*, 379 U.S. 203, 57 LRRM 2609 (1964). Where a plant shuts down without notice, the Board's view was initially the same (*Darlington Mfg. Co.*, 139 NLRB 241, 51 LRRM 1278 (1962)). Enforcement was denied by the Fourth Circuit (325 F.2d 682, 54 LRRM 2499 (4th Cir. 1963)) and then the Supreme Court reversed this court, approving the Board's decision in *Textile Workers v. Darlington*, 380 U.S. 263, 58 LRRM 2657 (1965). In *First National Maintenance Corp.*, 242 NLRB No. 72, 101 LRRM 1177 (1979), the NLRB held that an employer must bargain with the union over the closing of part of its business. The Supreme Court decision in *First National Maintenance Corp. v. NLRB*, 449 U.S. 1076, 107 LRRM 2705 (1981), reversed the Board decision, modifying the earlier trend of holdings that a union has the right to bargain over management decisions regarding reductions in work.

employer to notify the union representatives before purchasing parts from an outsider if such purchasing could reduce employment. His "bad faith" tests (2) and (3) are a borrowing from the legal doctrine that a "sham" avoidance of a contractual obligation is improper.[10] His test (4) is related to the "good faith" tests used by the NLRB in "runaway shop" cases.[11]

Arbitrator Alexander Cocalis, in *Continental Tennessee Lines, Inc.,*[12] with apologies to his fellow arbitrators, rejected such an importation of the "bad faith" and "good faith" standards.

> The line of cases cited by the company generally holds that, in the absence of a specific limitation on contracting out bargaining unit work, the Company is free to do so if it is done in "good faith" to meet a legitimate business exigency and if the effect upon the bargaining unit is "minimal."
>
> With apologies to my fellow arbitrators, I find both the "good faith" and "minimal effect" tests fallacious. In a case like this, the function of an arbitrator is to interpret and construe the contract to determine the rights and obligations, if any, granted by the agreement. To do so, the arbitrators must ascertain the intent of the parties as expressed in the language used, taking into consideration subject matter, nature and purpose of the agreement. The intention which controls is the intention of the parties when the contract was made, irrespective of subsequent events.[13]

He said that labeling the purchasing of products from outsiders as "good faith" when the effect is "minimal" is insidious:

> If the good faith–minimal effect test is inappropriate, how does one determine the parties' intent regarding subcontracting when the agreement is silent on the subject and when the subject was not even discussed during negotiations?[14]

Even though Arbitrator Cocalis rejected the "good faith-minimal effect" test, he did absorb the standards developed by the NLRB in this *particular* case. Continental Tennessee had released from employment many employees who operated bus terminals and these ex-employees were then employed by contractors who were to operate the terminals at lower wage rates.

---

[10]*Rutherford Food Corp. v. McComb,* 331 U.S. 722 (1947); *United States v. Silk,* 331 U.S. 704 (1947); *Superior Dairy, Inc.,* 77-1 ARB ¶ 8281 (Chattam, 1977); *Virginia Stage Lines, Inc. v. Amalgamated Transit Union, Local 1544,* 87 LC ¶ 11,689 (D. D.C. 1979).

[11]*Pet Milk Co.,* 33 LA 278 (McCoy, 1959); *NLRB v. U.S. Air Conditioning Corp.,* 302 F.2d 280, 50 LRRM 2151 (1st Cir. 1962); *NLRB v. Brown-Dunkin Co., Inc.,* 287 F.2d 17, 47 LRRM 2551 (10th Cir. 1961); *Town & Country Mfg. Co.,* 136 NLRB 1022, 49 LRRM 1918 (1962); *Sidele Fashions, Inc.,* 133 NLRB 547, 48 LRRM 1679 (1961), enf'd sub nom. *Philadelphia Dress Joint Board v. NLRB,* 305 F.2d 825 (*mem.*), 50 LRRM 2957 (3d Cir. 1962).

[12]72 LA 619 (Cocalis, 1979).

[13]*Id.* at 620–21.

[14]*Id.* at 621.

He concluded that the employer (Continental Tennessee) did not have the right under the National Labor Relations Act to hire subcontractors simply to reduce the wages of the ex-employees as negotiated between Continental Tennessee and the union. The furlough of one employee in favor of another who will do the same work at less pay is not reasonable, he said. Applying this principle to this situation, his question and answer became:

> "When a three-year employment contract specifies hours, wages and other benefits, reserves the employer's right to abolish the job and otherwise operate and conduct its business, would a reasonable man about to enter into that agreement understand that the Company, for economic reasons, can furlough him in favor of another who will do the same work at less pay?"
>
> I think not. Any other conclusion would not only be unreasonable but frustrate the object and spirit of the agreement itself. The grievance, accordingly, is sustained.[15]

Arbitrator J. A. Hogan, in *White Bros.,*[16] said that to protect the employees he was impelled to restrain the employer from purchasing products from a subcontractor who pays low wages, but that he would not restrain the purchasing if the subcontractor charged low prices simply because it was more efficient. Because of his concerns, he could not decide whether he should restrain the purchasing of the product until he received information on (1) the relative efficiency of the subcontractor and (2) the relative wage and fringe costs paid by the subcontractor. He wanted these two factors probed carefully because he believed them to be determinative. This rationalization was set forth eighteen years before Section 8(e)[17] and Section 8(b)(4)(B) when secondary boycotts became clearly illegal, and it is mentioned here to sharpen the effect of the discussion, *infra*, of the subsequent legal change.

A balancing "good faith" test is used by some arbitrators to approve "subcontracting" if (1) job security is minimally affected, (2) strong economies are accomplished, and (3) no express contractual limitations are contained in the labor agreement.[18] When the labor agreement does not describe specific restraints on subcontracting, most arbitrators that have used the "good faith-bad faith" test are attempting

---

[15]*Id.*

[16]32 LA 965 (Hogan, 1958). *Continental Tennessee Lines, Inc.,* 72 LA 619 (Cocalis, 1979); *City of Hamtramck,* 71 LA 822 (Roumell, 1978); *Rochester Methodist Hospital,* 67 LA 927 (Conway, 1976); *Allis-Chalmers Mfg. Co.,* 39 LA 1213 (Smith, 1962); *Black-Clawson Co.,* 34 LA 215 (Teple, 1960).

[17]*See* "The Impact of Section 8(e) on Implied Restrictions on Subcontracting" in this chapter, *infra*.

[18]*See Hobart Mfg. Co.,* 73 LA 29 (Turkus, 1979); *City of Hamtramck,* 71 LA 822 (Roumell, 1978); *Allis-Chalmers Mfg., Co.,* 39 LA 1213 (Smith, 1962); *Black-Clawson Co.,* 34 LA 215 (Teple, 1960); *but see Continental Tennessee Lines, Inc.,* 72 LA 619 (Cocalis, 1979).

to protect the employment of employees in one unit from competition by employees in another.

Arbitrator Elmer E. Hilpert, in an *Allis-Chalmers* award,[19] said the cleavage between "schools of arbitrators" in the subcontracting area is very "sharp." He summarized his view of the situation by stating that the "good faith" tests used by arbitrators to determine violations by the employer, when there is no specific subcontracting prohibition language in the labor agreement, results from the assumption that some "unfair labor practice" has occurred and that the arbitrator has the duty to make a correction. He said:

> One may question whether doctrines of (1) "bad faith" and of (2) "past practice" are not associated with the presence or absence of an *interim* "unfair labor practice," over which arbitrators have no jurisdiction, rather than with the contractual scope of a company's *residual* "managerial powers," to which their jurisdiction is confined.[20] [Emphasis added.]

Some arbitrators, on the other hand, use the words "good faith" to reach an opposite conclusion. Arbitrator A. R. Marshall in *International Papers*[21] said that there was evidence that the company did act in "good faith" because it contracted out work to outsiders in "an attempt to operate the mill in an efficient manner"; Arbitrator R. Seward in *Bethlehem Steel Co.*[22] cited with approval the principle that the employer's action was in "good faith" because its action was a normal and reasonable management action; and Arbitrator S. Garrett in *National Tube Co.*[23] said a "subcontracting" is in "good faith" when the employer's action is a "normal and reasonable management ac-

---

[19]Case Nos. 13-14, 1959–1961 Agreement, Terre Haute (Hilpert, 1963), unreported.

[20]*Id.*

[21]35 LA 403 (Marshall, 1960).

[22]35 LA 943 (Seward, 1960).

[23]17 LA 790, 794 (Garrett, 1951). Other cases involving arbitrators who followed the view that effective lower cost purchasing is considered to be in "good faith": *Pure Oil Co.*, 38 LA 1042 (Larkin, 1962); *Reynolds Metals Co.*, 37 LA 599 (Caraway, 1961); *Weyerhaeuser Co.*, 37 LA 308 (Sembower, 1961); *Central Soya Co.*, 36 LA 1173 (Sembower, 1961); *Allegheny Ludlum Steel Corp.*, 36 LA 912 (Ryder, 1961); *American Sugar Refining Co.*, 36 LA 409 (Crawford, 1960) (". . . must demonstrate the existence of compelling logic or economies of operation and the consideration of Union status and integrity of the bargaining unit." *Id.* at 414); *Holub Iron & Steel Co.*, 36 LA 106 (Dworkin, 1961); *International Paper Co.*, 35 LA 403 (Marshall, Haynes, Wissner, 1960); *Black-Clawson Co.*, 34 LA 215 (Teple, 1960); *United States Steel Corp.*, 33 LA 282 (Garrett, 1959); *Reynolds Metals Co.*, 32 LA 815 (Anrod, 1959); *Republic Steel Corp.*, 32 LA 799 (Platt, 1959); *Haven Busch Co.*, 32 LA 781 (Piercey, 1959); *White Brothers*, 32 LA 965 (Hogan, 1958); *Weatherhead Co.*, 30 LA 1066 (Dworkin, 1958); *Texas Gas Transmission Corp.*, 27 LA 413 (Herbert, 1956); *Temco Aircraft Corp.*, 27 LA 233 (Larson, 1956); *Cannon Electric Co.*, 26 LA 870 (Aaron, 1956); *International Harvester Co.*, 25 LA 1 (Smith, 1955); *Devoe & Reynolds*, 22 LA 608 (Porter, 1954); *Koppers Co., Inc.*, 22 LA 124 (Reid, 1954). Cases in which arbitrators disapproved management action: *Gulf Oil Corp.*, 33 LA 852 (Crawford, 1959); *General Metals Corp.*, 25 LA 118 (Lennard, 1955); *Niagara Weldments, Inc.*, 63-1 ARB ¶ 8062 (Shister, 1962).

tion." Therefore, the words "good faith" in contrast to "bad faith" mean different things to different arbitrators.[24]

In *Iowa Mfg. Co.*[25] the labor agreement contained a commitment by the employer that "during the period of layoff the company will not have any work that is normally done by Iowa Manufacturing performed by any outside source."[26] The company stopped manufacturing pulleys and purchased them from an outsider at a savings of from 30 to 59 percent. Arbitrator John Sembower held that the purchasing of pulleys of the type that had been manufactured in the plant when employees were on layoff did not violate the employer's commitment because the pulleys were ordered from a catalogue and hence they were not manufactured especially for the company by an outsider. He explained that the purchase of the pulleys was a mere sales transaction and not the "subcontracting of work."[27] A difference between "contracting out work" and "purchasing parts" from a supplier has no substance—it is merely semantics. In contrast, in *Vulcan Rivet & Bolt Corp.*,[28] Arbitrator R. R. Williams became involved with the "good faith" versus "bad faith" balance, and called it "bad faith" when T-head bolts were purchased from a catalogue. He directed the employer to stop purchasing the bolts from such a supplier and produce them in the plant using the employees in the unit, at a cost higher than the purchase price.

In *Pet Milk Co.*,[29] Arbitrator McCoy required the employer to cease shipping ice cream mix by railroad and to hire back drivers so the ice cream mix could be shipped in company-owned trucks, even though shipment by railroad was found to be a less expensive method of transportation. In *Bridgeport Brass Co.*,[30] the arbitrators required the company to repurchase a railroad locomotive and rehire the crew. The locomotive had been sold after it was discovered that the servicing railroad would switch railroad cars at no cost. In *International Harvester Co.*,[31] Arbitrator Cole directed the company to have

---

[24] "When *I* use a word," Humpty Dumpty said, in rather a scornful tone, "it means just what I choose it to mean—neither more nor less."

"The question is," said Alice, "Whether you can make words mean so many different things."

"The question is," said Humpty Dumpty, "which is to be master—that's all." [Emphasis in original.]

Carroll, ALICE IN WONDERLAND AND THROUGH THE LOOKING GLASS (New York: Grosset & Dunlap, 1946), p. 238.

[25] 68 LA 599 (Sembower, 1977).

[26] *Id.*

[27] *Id.*

[28] 36 LA 871 (Williams, 1961). *See also A.D. Juilliard Co., Inc.*, 21 LA 713 (Hogan, 1953).

[29] 33 LA 278 (McCoy, 1959).

[30] 25 LA 151 (Donnelly, Curry with Mottram dissenting, 1955).

[31] 24 LA 32 (Cole, 1955).

manufacturing work performed by the company in the plant where the work previously had been performed instead of at a new Harvester plant where the operating and transportation costs would be lower.

The words "contracting in" are used in contrast to "contracting out." The former words are used when nonemployees come into the plant or location to perform work previously performed by employees in the unit. Arbitrator Charles P. Chapman, in *Transit Authority of River City*,[32] heard arguments about a grievance that was filed by the union when a janitorial service was hired by a public utility to clean areas in the plant between 12:01 a.m. and 5 a.m. on weekends. The four employed janitors were no longer scheduled on rotation on weekends. The company manager explained that the subcontracting of the cleaning work over the weekend from a service was undertaken for economy, and pointed out that the rescheduling of the four janitors did not cause any of them to be laid off. The union, however, argued that the "recognition," "wage rate," and "seniority" clauses, plus a provision in the labor agreement granting employees the right to "claim the opportunity for any job covered by this Agreement then available in any branch or department,"[33] prevented the subcontracting-in of work "belonging to the bargaining-unit employees during the term of the agreement."[34] Arbitrator Chapman approved the subcontracting because (1) the company acted in good faith; (2) the subcontracting caused no serious impact on the employees in the bargaining unit; and (3) the subcontracting produced savings of substantial size ($80,000 per year).

Another "contracting in" situation involved a grievance over the hiring of a foreman as the subcontractor for the painting of the warehouse on a Saturday. The foreman operated a small painting contracting business. The grievance alleged that the employer had violated the labor agreement prohibition against supervisors performing bargaining unit work. After determining that the painting was bargaining unit work, Arbitrator Edward L. Harrison in *Ralston Purina Co.*[35] found that the foreman was a painting contractor during his off-duty time and, hence, this work did not violate the prohibition against supervisors working in the labor agreement. He pointed out that the foreman performed the work on his own time and for a predetermined contract fee.

---

[32]74 LA 616 (Chapman, 1980).
[33]*Id.* at 617.
[34]*Id.* at 618.
[35]78 LA 35 (Harrison, 1982).

SUBCONTRACTING LIMITATIONS IMPLIED
FROM GENERAL LANGUAGE

Some arbitrators, rather than using the "good faith" or "bad faith" tests to approve or deny subcontracting, imply restrictions on subcontracting from certain typical general provisions found in almost all labor agreements. The three typical provisions involved are: (1) the mandatory recognition provision in the agreement that also describes the unit; (2) the typical seniority provision; and (3) the list of job classification wage rates. Some arbitrators say that the "totality" of these three provisions permits the inference that the employer has agreed not to engage in subcontracting activity.[36] Sometimes arbitrators refer to this "totality" inference as the "implied covenant of fair dealing." The use of these three bases for implying a restriction upon the purchasing of parts, products or services from subcontractors by some arbitrators has been strongly rejected by others. The contrasting views of various arbitrators are reported below.

Limitations From the Recognition Clause

A recognition clause is found in all labor agreements. It consists of a statement that the employer recognizes a particular union as the exclusive bargaining agent of the employees in the described appropriate unit. The inclusion of such a provision in all labor agreements is mandatory. If the employer refused to recognize the union in writing, the employer would be refusing to bargain in good faith, causing an unfair labor practice. In spite of the fact that this provision is the most non-volitional in the agreement, some arbitrators have reasoned that the employer's agreement to this provision is an agreement *not* to engage in subcontracting activity that might reduce the work provided to the employees.[37] They assert that to do anything that might reduce

[36]*Campbell Truck Co.*, 73 LA 1036 (Ross, 1979).

[37]Cases with the recognition clause as a basis for the restriction: *U.S. Potash Co.*, 37 LA 442 (Schedler, 1961); *Mead Paper Corp.*, 37 LA 342 (Hawley, 1961); *Container Corp. of America*, 37 LA 252 (Dworet, 1961); *Vulcan Rivet & Bolt Corp.*, 36 LA 871 (Williams, 1961); *Socony Mobil Oil Co.*, 36 LA 631 (McIntosh, 1960); *Gulf Oil Corp.*, 33 LA 852 (Crawford, 1959); *Continental Can Co.*, 7 BASIC STEEL ARB. 4975 (Schmidt, 1959); *Pet Milk Co.*, 33 LA 278 (McCoy, 1959); *Electric Auto-Lite Co.*, 30 LA 449 (Marshall, 1958); *Arkansas-Best Freight System, Inc.*, 30 LA 26 (Hoel, 1957) (*dictum*); *Continental Can Co., Inc.*, 29 LA 67 (Sembower, 1956); *Thompson Grinder Co.*, 27 LA 671 (McCoy, 1956); *Temco Aircraft Corp.*, 27 LA 233 (Larson, 1956); *Bridgeport Brass Co.*, 25 LA 151 (Donnelly, Curry with Mottram dissenting, 1955); *General Metals Corp.*, 25 LA 118 (Lennard, 1955); *Weber Aircraft Corp.*, 24 LA 821 (Jones, 1955); *Devoe & Reynolds*, 22 LA 608 (Porter, 1954); *Koppers Co., Inc.*, 22 LA 124 (Reid, 1954); *Journal Publishing Co.*, 22 LA 108 (Seering, Chmn., Wykoff, Abramson with Knight and Rodbury dissenting, 1954); *A.D. Juilliard Co., Inc.*, 21 LA 713 (Hogan, 1953); *Yale & Towne Mfg.*

employment would violate "the spirit, intent and purpose of such collective agreement,"[38] that "the unit could be emasculated,"[39] or "shrunk"[40] and that the "entire agreement could be nullified."[41] Arbitrator C. R. Schedler, in *U.S. Potash Co.*,[42] explained the rationale:

> [T]here is no express language either prohibiting or authorizing contracting out. What is more significant is that the contract contains a clause recognizing the Union.... The infraction here is in the unavoidable effect on these rights. To me it is clear that the work belonged to the unit, which contained employees fully capable of executing it.... [T]he contracting out had the inevitable impact of derogating the Union's status as recognized exclusive representative.[43]

In sharp contrast, Arbitrator M. Beatty, in *American Sugar Refining Co.*,[44] explained why the recognition provision could not properly support an inference that the employer had agreed not to subcontract:

> The purpose of this clause is to assure fulfillment of the Company's legal obligation to bargain with this Union and assures that this particular Union may represent all hourly paid employees in this plant. It is stretching the point, I believe, to argue that it also means that the Union has jurisdiction over all work which this employer has or which is customarily done by these employees, or that all such work will remain with these employees. The contract does not provide jurisdiction over work or detract substantially from management's customary right to direct the working force, or to determine what work will be done and how.[45]

Co., 19 LA 882 (Cahn, 1953); *Stockholders Publishing Co., Inc.*, 16 LA 644 (Aaron, 1951); *Tin Processing Corp.*, 17 LA 493 (Meyers, 1951); *Parke, Davis & Co.*, 15 LA 111 (Scheiber, 1950); *Celanese Corp. of America*, 14 LA 31 (Wolff, 1950); *Sinclair Prairie Oil Co.*, 6 LA 855 (Dwyer, 1947).

[38] *Parke, Davis & Co.*, 15 LA 111, 115 (Scheiber, 1950).

[39] *Gulf Oil Corp.*, 33 LA 852, 855 (Crawford, 1959).

[40] *Electric Auto-Lite Co.*, 30 LA 449, 454 (Marshall, 1958). The contrary view was espoused in one of the earliest reported arbitration cases concerning subcontracting, by Arbitrator Emanuel Stein in *Cords, Ltd., Inc.*, 7 LA 748 (Stein, 1947). He rejected a union claim that the recognition clause prevented the employer from abolishing the jobs of its guards when an outside property protection service was hired, a subcontracting action. He brushed aside as irrelevant the claim that the employer's action was vulnerable because it would "shrink or alter the bargaining unit."

[41] *Thompson Grinder Co., Inc.*, 27 LA 671, 674 (McCoy, 1956).

[42] 37 LA 442 (Schedler, 1961).

[43] *Id.* at 447–48.

[44] 37 LA 334 (Beatty, 1961).

[45] *Id.* at 336. To the same effect is the discussion by Arbitrator Herman A. Gray in *Hearst Consolidated Publications, Inc.*, 26 LA 723, 725 (1956), and Arbitrator Saul Wallen in *Hershey Chocolate Corp.*, 28 LA 491 (1957). The recognition clause was specifically rejected as a basis for restricting work movement in the following cases: *Allis-Chalmers Co.*, Case Nos. 13–14, 1959–1962 Agreement, Terre Haute (Hilpert, 1963), unreported; *Olin Mathieson Chemical Corp.*, 36 LA 1147 (McDermott, 1961); *American Sugar Refining Co.*, 36 LA 409 (Crawford, 1960); *Columbus Bolt & Forging Co.*, 35 LA 397 (Stouffer, 1960); *Black-Clawson Co.*, 34 LA 215 (Teple, 1960); *Minneapolis-Moline Co.*, 33 LA 893 (Kelliher, 1960); *Lukens Steel Co.*, 33 LA 228 (Crawford, 1959); *Reynolds Metals Co.*, 32 LA 815 (Anrod, 1959); *Cooperative Farm Chemicals Ass'n*,

Arbitrator Elmer Hilpert, in *Allis-Chalmers Mfg. Co.*,[46] also rejected the use of the recognition clause to infer a restriction on subcontracting. He said that "it is asking too much to ask one to assume that in one swell [sic] swoop," nearly thirty years after the law required the clause, it really was an agreement by the management of a unionized plant to surrender the right to subcontract work or move work to lower-cost plants, which rights had traditionally been "an all important and widely used managerial power."[47]

Even the NLRB echoed the view that no inferences of unexpressed agreement between the parties could be made from a recognition provision in a labor agreement. In *Plumbing Contractors Ass'n*[48] the Board said:

As the Board has heretofore held, and as we here reiterate, a Board certification in a representation proceeding is not a jurisdictional award; it is merely a determination that a majority of the employees in an appropriate unit have selected a particular labor organization as their representative for purposes of collective bargaining.... [T]his determination by the Board does not freeze the duties or work tasks of the employees in the unit found appropriate. [Footnotes omitted.]

Judge Aldrich said in *Street, Electric Ry. & Motor Coach Employees, Div. 1509 v. Eastern Massachusetts Street Ry. Co.*[49] that a recognition clause cannot be used to assert a restriction on subcontracting work:

I hold that the union recognition clause and the classification clause do not even raise an arbitrable question as to the defendant's obligation not to contract out fare box work.

Limitations From the Seniority Clause

The typical seniority clause has also been used to block the purchasing of lower-priced parts. In 1947, in *New Britain Machine Co.*,[50] Arbitrator S. Wallen said, "If wages are the heart of the labor agreement, job security may be considered its soul." With these words, he said subcontracting violated the seniority clause, and arbitrators

---

31 LA 482 (Coffey, 1958); *Richmond Baking Co.*, 30 LA 493 (Warns, 1957); *Dairy Workers v. Detroit Creamery Co.*, No. 541758, 26 LA 677 (Mich. Cir. Ct., Wayne Co., April 18, 1956); *Jones & Laughlin Steel Co.*, 26 LA 568 (Cahn, 1956); *Carbide & Carbon Chemicals Co.*, 24 LA 158 (Kelliher, 1955); *Vickers, Inc.*, 24 LA 121 (Haughton, 1955); *Dalmo Victor Co.*, 24 LA 33 (Kagel, 1954); *National Sugar Refining Co.*, 13 LA 991 (Feinberg, 1949).

[46]Case Nos. 13-14, 1959-1962 Agreement, Terre Haute (Hilpert, 1963), unreported.
[47]*Id.*
[48]93 NLRB 1081, 27 LRRM 1514, 1518 (1951).
[49]162 F. Supp. 942, 944, 30 LA 851, 852 (D. Mass. 1958). *See also Street, Electric Ry. & Motor Coach Employees v. Greyhound Corp.*, 231 F.2d 585, 37 LRRM 2834 (5th Cir. 1956).
[50]8 LA 720, 722 (Wallen, 1947).

began to imply a "subcontracting" restriction from that clause.[51] Ten years later, Wallen changed his earlier view. In *Hershey Chocolate Corp.*[52] he said:

> [T]he seniority provisions guarantee, not a constant employment opportunity for each category of employees covered by the contract, but a set of rules for the parcelling out of employment opportunities, the availability of which can be affected by diminution of work volume due to changes in the market, due to changes in technology, or due to changes in the realm of good faith managerial decision-making.

Likewise, in *American Sugar Refining Co.*,[53] Arbitrator Beatty stated clearly that a seniority clause only establishes relative rights to available work and could not properly be used to prevent competition from lower-priced parts:

> The seniority provisions of a working agreement are for the purpose of determining relative status of employees, which status entitles senior employees to certain preferences for purposes of promotion, layoff, recall, etc. Seniority carries no guarantee that jobs will always be provided even for the most senior employees.... It is likely that neither party, the Company nor the Union, contemplated seniority as having any relevancy to contracting-out at the time they wrote the contract. In my opinion the seniority provisions are not relevant to this issue.

Many arbitrators have rejected the argument that the "seniority clause" was a hidden restriction on subcontracting.[54]

Limitations From the Job Classification List

The third basis used by some arbitrators to restrain subcontracting activity (*i.e.*, purchasing lower-cost parts, products, or services from a specialist) is the list of job classifications that is attached to the labor agreement or referred to in the agreement. This list establishes the hourly rates to be paid employees performing the described work.

---

[51]Cases with the seniority clause as a basis for the restriction; *Zdanok v. Glidden Co.*, 288 F.2d 99, 47 LRRM 2865 (2d Cir. 1961), *cert. denied*, 368 U.S. 814, 48 LRRM 3111 (1961); *Selb Mfg. Co.*, 37 LA 834 (Klamon, Barken, Bingamon, 1961); *U.S. Potash Co.*, 37 LA 442 (Schedler, 1961); *Mead Paper Corp.*, 37 LA 342 (Hawley, 1961); *Metropolitan Brick Co.*, 34 LA 394 (Teple, 1960) (displaced employee cannot be paid lower rate because of specific provisions); *A.D. Juilliard Co., Inc.*, 21 LA 713 (Hogan, 1953); *New Britain Machine Co.*, 8 LA 720 (Wallen, Knauss, and Kosinski, 1947).

[52]28 LA 491, 493 (Wallen, 1957).

[53]37 LA 334, 336 (Beatty, 1961).

[54]The view that a typical seniority clause supports an implied restriction on subcontracting was specifically rejected in *Allis-Chalmers Mfg. Co.*, 39 LA 1213 (Smith, 1962); *Reactive Metals, Inc.*, 62-2 ARB ¶ 8495 (Begley, 1962); *American Sugar Refining Co.*, 36 LA 409 (Crawford, 1960); *Carbide and Carbon Chemicals Co.*, 34 LA 158 (Kelliher, 1955); *Phillips Pipe Line Co.*, 20 LA 432 (Coffey, 1953); *Tungsten Mining Corp.*, 19 LA 503 (Maggs, 1952).

However, some arbitrators have gone farther and said that, where such classifications are listed, there is the "assumption that ... work in these categories ... would be performed by those ... covered by the agreement,"[55] and thus there is an implied agreement not to purchase parts from a contractor or to have units produced in other plants if such action would reduce the work of the employees who are then being paid the hourly rate applicable to the particular work.

Arbitrator John F. Sembower in his *Continental Can Co.* award[56] implied from the job classification wage rate list a restriction on the purchase of parts from a subcontractor:

> [T]he agreement is not silent on the matter of subcontracting. If it does not speak out on it, it at least whispers when it spells out in Appendix A that janitors are included in the bargaining unit....
> ... [W]hen the Company specifies job classifications in the recognition of the bargaining unit, it in effect gives up its right to subcontract in that field unless something is added in the way of a contract provision giving the right to subcontract....

In sharp contrast, Arbitrator V. L. Stouffer rejected such a basis for implying a restriction on subcontracting in *Columbus Bolt & Forging Co.*,[57] saying:

> [T]he list of job classifications contains nothing to indicate that any particular number of jobs will be maintained or that all work described in any particular classification will be done exclusively by Employees of the Company.

Despite the sharp and somewhat critical comments by some arbitrators about the use by other arbitrators of "wage rate schedules" or "job classification lists" to block the purchasing of lower-priced parts and other types of cost-reducing subcontracting, these are still used as a basis for the inference. For example, in *Mead Corporation*,[58] Arbitrator Wilber Bothwell explained that the "schedule of wage rates" set up a restraint on subcontracting:

> A review of arbitration awards indicates that arbitrators have almost invariably held subcontracting to be improper when it results in the layoff of

[55]*Parke, Davis & Co.*, 15 LA 111, 115 (Scheiber, 1950).

[56]29 LA 67, 73 (Sembower, 1956). Other cases with the list of job classifications as a basis for the restriction are: *Container Corp. of America*, 37 LA 252 (Dworet, 1961); *Meade Paper Corp.*, 37 LA 342 (Hawley, 1961); *U.S. Potash Co.*, 37 LA 442 (Schedler, 1961); *Krey Packing Co.*, 32 LA 68 (Klamon, 1959); *Thompson Grinder Co.*, 27 LA 671 (McCoy, 1956); *East Texas Salt Water Disposal Co.*, 22 LA 484 (Emery, 1953); *Celanese Corp. of America*, 14 LA 31 (Wolff, 1950); *American Cyanamid Co.*, 13 LA 653 (Copelof, 1949).

[57]35 LA 397, 402 (Stouffer, 1960). To the same effect *see Square D. Co.*, 37 LA 892 (Teple, 1961); *American Sugar Refining Co.*, 37 LA 334 (Beatty, 1961); *Black-Clawson Co.*, 34 LA 215 (Teple, 1960); *Hertner Electric Co.*, 25 LA 281 (Kates, 1955).

[58]62 LA 1000, 1006–1007 (Bothwell, 1973).

employees, if the work contracted out is done by the same methods at wage rates which are substantially less than those negotiated by the Union. In the present instance, the work on the corner posts was contracted out to be performed not only by the same methods but on the same equipment as used in the Company's plant, the machinery being sold to the subcontractor. The work is being performed at wage rates which are approximately one-third less than those currently in effect for the bargaining unit employees who did perform the work. The employer cannot negotiate wage rates for certain work and then subcontract the identical work to be performed at wage rates substantially below those negotiated, at least not without bargaining with the Union. *This is a violation of the wage provisions of the Agreement.* [Emphasis added.]

THE REJECTION OF IMPLIED RESTRICTIONS ON SUBCONTRACTING

The criticism by some arbitrators of their fellows who have constructed restrictions on the purchasing of parts, products, and services are often quite "pithy." Arbitrator M. Beatty in *American Sugar Refining Co.*[59] said:

Arbitrators are not soothsayers and "wisemen" employed to dispense equity and good will according to their own notions of what is best for the parties, nor are they kings like Solomon with unlimited wisdom or courts of unlimited jurisdiction. Arbitrators are employed to interpret the working agreement as the parties themselves wrote it.[60]

Arbitrator Beatty went on to explain his criticism of the thinking of arbitrators on the other side of the fence on this issue:

When an arbitrator finds that the parties have not dealt with the subject of contracting-out in their working agreement, but that the employer is nevertheless prohibited from contracting-out (a) unless he acts in good faith; (b) unless he acts in conformance with past practice; (c) unless he acts reasonably; (d) unless his act does not deprive a substantial number of employees of employment; (e) unless his acts were dictated by the requirements of the business; (f) if his act is barred by the recognition clause; (g) if his act is barred by the seniority provisions of the working agreement; or (h) if his act violates the spirit of the agreement, *the arbitrator may be in outer space and reading the stars instead of the contract.*[61] [Emphasis added.]

Those arbitrators who refuse to find implied restrictions upon subcontracting actions when the purchasing is not limited by specific pro-

---

[59]37 LA 334, 337.
[60]*Id.* at 337.
[61]*Id.*

visions set out in the labor agreement are following a simple, straightforward view of the labor agreement. They say that the management reserves the right to purchase parts instead of producing them if it costs less to do so.[62] They refer to the typical "management clause" in the labor agreement which states that management has reserved all managerial rights not specifically bargained away. Where no management rights clause is included in the labor agreement, the view is the same: management retains all rights to manage that have not been specifically limited by some clear provision of the agreement. Arbitrator P. M. Kelliher, in *Carbide and Carbon Chemicals Co.*,[63] noted:

> It is a fundamental principle in the construction of Collective Bargaining Agreements that Management continues to retain those rights that it had prior to entrance into an effective Collective Bargaining Contract. A careful analysis of the current Collective Bargaining Agreement fails to disclose any language that can be reasonably interpreted as indicating an intention of the Parties that this Management thereby surrendered or limited its right to contract out maintenance work.... This Arbitration Board simply lacks the authority to, in effect, add an amendment to this Agreement placing such a restriction upon the Company's rights.

Arbitrator Elmer E. Hilpert in *Allis-Chalmers Mfg. Co.*[64] forthrightly stated the same view:

> Admittedly, there is no provision in the agreement of these parties (as there are provisions in the agreements of some *other* parties) which *expressly* prohibits the Company from "contracting out" so-called "unit" work; *i.e.*, work which has been, traditionally, historically, or characteristically, done by "unit" employees; and, hence, the Union is compelled to contend that there is such an *implied* prohibition on the Company's "contracting out" for such work.
>
> But it is axiomatic that, before a company enters into a collective bargaining agreement, it possesses, as a mere incident of its ownership of

---

[62]*ACF Industries,* 38 LA 14 (J.S. Williams, 1962); *Allis-Chalmers Mfg. Co.,* 37 LA 944 (D. J. White, 1961); *Los Angeles Standard Rubber Co.,* 37 LA 784 (LeBaron, 1961); *Harnishfeger Corp.,* 37 LA 685 (Young, 1961); *Beaunit Mills, Inc.,* 37 LA 366 (H.T. Dworet, 1961); *American Sugar Refining Co.,* 37 LA 334 (Beatty, 1961); *Rockwell-Standard Corp.,* 36 LA 1447 (Bradley, 1961); *Edward Balf Co.,* 36 LA 1396 (Donnelly, 1961); *Reynolds Metals Co.,* 36 LA 1341 (Wycoff, 1961); *Allegheny Ludlum Steel Corp.,* 36 LA 912 (Ryder, 1961); *Volunteer Electric Cooperative,* 36 LA 787 (Redden, 1961); *Snyder Mining Co.,* 36 LA 861 (Graff, 1961); *West Virginia Pulp and Paper Co.,* 36 LA 137 (Roberts, 1960); *Columbus Bolt & Forging Co.,* 35 LA 397 (Stouffer, 1960); *Richmond Baking Co.,* 30 LA 493 (Warns, Jr., 1957); *American Airlines, Inc.,* 29 LA 594 (Wolff, 1957); *Waller Bros. Stone Co.,* 27 LA 704 (Dworkin, 1956); *Mallinckrodt Chemical Works,* 27 LA 530 (Klamon, 1956); *American Airlines, Inc.,* 27 LA 174 (Wolff, 1956); *Stix, Baer & Fuller Co.,* 27 LA 57 (Klamon, 1956); *Parke, Davis & Co.,* 26 LA 438 (Haughton, 1956).
[63]24 LA 158, 159 (Kelliher, 1955).
[64]Case Nos. 13–14, 1959–1962 Agreement, Terre Haute (Hilpert, 1963), unreported.

the business enterprise, inherent, plenary "managerial powers," which include the power so to "contract out," and that, after a company enters into
a collective bargaining agreement, it still retains all such of its formerly-
existent, inherent, plenary managerial powers as were not proscribed, or
restricted, in such agreement. When it enters into a collective bargaining
agreement, a company, of course, "loses" such of its formerly-existent
powers as were *expressly* proscribed, or restricted, in such agreement; but
because it was the possessor of "inherent and plenary" powers, to begin
with, a company "loses" additional powers by *implication* only if such implication is a "necessary"—in the sense of being an "inescapable"—one.
In sum, although there may be *implied*, as well as *express*, limitations on a
company's managerial powers in a collective bargaining agreement, a rule
of "strict construction"—in "finding" such *implied* limitations—is to
be applied.

No such *implied* limitation on the Company's power to "contract out"
may be derived from the "recognition" clause in the parties' agreement ... on which the Union herein principally relies.[65] [Emphasis in
original.]

The reserved rights of the management concept described above are
deeply impressed on arbitration analysis. Under this view the management has the ability to purchase parts, products, and services from
outsiders if it believes it is economically sound to do so and the
management has not clearly agreed not to do so in the labor agreement. Arbitrator R. R. Williams, in *Hercules Powder Co., Ltd.*,[66]
cited the reserved rights concept:

Nowhere in the agreement is there to be found either expressly or by implication, any restriction upon the right of the Company to have work
covered by the job classifications performed by persons who are not its
employees.... A Company's right to make decisions affecting the
management of its plant is founded in basic and fully accepted tenets of
the common law; while this right may be contracted away or modified by
agreement, it is not removed by inference. The federal courts have
recognized the law to be that, where the agreement contains no ban upon
such action, and where the Company's action is not discriminatory, contracting out is a proper practice and right of management. *Timken Roller
Bearing Co. v. NLRB*, 161 F.2d 949, 6th Circuit, 1947.

This simple reserved right construction has been announced by
various other experienced arbitrators[67] and by federal courts. For ex-

---

[65]*Id.*

[66]21 LA 330, 334 (Williams, 1953).

[67]*E.g.*, in *Los Angeles Standard Rubber Co.*, 37 LA 784, 786 (1961), Arbitrator H. LeBaron
said:

The undersigned agrees with what appears to be the general holding of arbitrators on this subject and that is that absent a specific prohibition against subcontracting, management retains
this right.

ample, in *Automobile Workers, Local 600 v. Ford Motor Co.*,[68] a federal district court in Michigan refused to imply a restriction on work movement, saying:

> The Court has before it, as a part of the pleadings, a copy of the labor agreement which is the subject of this controversy. It is obvious that it was a carefully and laboriously prepared document, and that both the UAW-CIO and the Ford Motor Company had the benefit of competent counsel and representatives in the negotiations....
>
> A reading of all the terms and conditions of this agreement leaves one with the unshakable impression that its framers fully intended to state clearly therein every point of importance in the minds of the contracting parties, yet the plaintiffs [the union] wish us to believe that there was a major area of understanding on a specific point, easily includable in the written contract, but not so included....
>
> ...It is difficult to conceive of parties to a contract, who were as diligent in its preparation as these parties, purposely omitting a vital condition. The only possible conclusion that can be drawn is that such condition did not in fact exist.[69]

A federal district court, in *Automobile Workers, Local 586 v. Federal Pacific Electric Co.*,[70] expressed the same view:

> Since the contracts created no duty to continue operations, damage to the employees and union from their termination was not the result of illegal or tortious conduct by defendant, and no right of action exists founded either in tort or contract for the consequences of the closing.
>
> The only possible basis for relief of the employees or union would appear to be on a showing that the closing was without economic cause or justification or other cause except a purpose to break the union, in some way prohibited as an unfair labor practice under the Taft-Hartley Act. If the Act has created such rights in plaintiffs, however, their vindication can be only through the exclusive machinery set up by the Act....

Arbitrator H. J. Dworkin in *Holub Iron & Steel Co.*[71] reached into a summary in the *American Law Report* to find a pertinent statement from the "external law":

> As a matter of law, the right of the company to subcontract is clear. In recent years many courts have had occasion to pass upon the question of the right of companies to subcontract work, where a collective bargaining

---

And Arbitrator T. G. Begley said in *Reactive Metals, Inc.*, 62-2 ARB ¶ 8495 at 8495-96 (1962): The Arbitrator has read the arbitration decision given to him by the Union and the Company, and he finds that the weight of the decisions as to subcontracting work is in favor of this Company due to the fact that the contract does not contain a specific provision prohibiting the Company from contracting out unit work.
[68] 113 F. Supp. 834, 32 LRRM 2344 (E.D. Mich. 1953).
[69] *Id.* at 841-42, 32 LRRM at 2350-51.
[70] 36 LRRM 2357, 2358 (D. Conn. 1955).
[71] 36 LA 106, 111 (Dworkin, 1961).

agreement exists. The decisions of these courts are cited in an annotation on this subject appearing in 57 A.L.R.2d 1399 (1958). On the basis of court decisions on this subject, the general rule is stated in that annotation, at page 1400, as follows:

"It has been generally held, that, at least in the absence of bad faith on the part of the employer, a collective labor contract which contains no express prohibition against an employer's hiring an independent contractor for the performance of work formerly done by employees covered by the contract does not preclude the employer from hiring an independent contractor to do such work."

The Impact of Section 8(e) on Implied Restrictions on Subcontracting

Section 8(e) of the National Labor Relations Act states in part:

It shall be an unfair labor practice for any labor organization and any employer to enter into any contract or agreement, express or implied, whereby such employer ceases or refrains or agrees to cease or refrain from handling, using, selling, transporting or otherwise dealing in any of the products of any other employer, or to cease doing business with any person, and any contract or agreement entered into heretofore or hereafter continuing any agreement shall be to such extent unenforceable and void.[72]

The provisos attached to Section 8(e) expressly permit the labor agreements between employers and the unions in the construction and clothing industry to contain provisions that restrict the purchasing of parts, products, or services of the employer from "subcontractors."[73] These provisos support the view that without being protected by language of a specific proviso, an agreement *not* to subcontract parts, products, or services would be made an unfair labor practice by Section 8(e).

---

[72] National Labor Relations Act § 8(e), 29 U.S.C. § 158(e) (1976). Dannett, *The Legality of Subcontracting Provisions Under Section 8(e)*, SYMPOSIUM ON LABOR-MANAGEMENT REPORTING AND DISCLOSURE ACT OF 1959, R. Slovenko, ed. (Baton Rouge: Claitoris, 1961), p. 905. Section 8(e) was disregarded in an award by Arbitrator James J. Healy in *Narragansett Brewing Co.*, 61-2 ARB ¶ 8495 (1961). The labor agreement included the following provision:

Only union-made malt shall be used if the same is obtainable. All other union-made material and supplies shall be given preference provided price, quality, and general conditions are equal.

Id. at 5340. To meet competition, the company had changed beer carton sizes and a rush order was sent to an outside supplier. Upon discovering that the cartons were not union-made, the union filed a grievance alleging violation of the contract. Without considering the legality of the clause, Arbitrator Healy directed the company to make reasonable investigation in the future to insure that goods purchased were union-made.

[73] *Marsh & McLennan, Inc., Ackerman-Chillingworth Div. v. Pacific Electrical Contractors Ass'n*, 579 F.2d 484, 502–505, 98 LRRM 2415, 2428–2431 (9th Cir. 1978), *cert. denied*, 439 U.S. 1089, 100 LRRM 2268 (1979); 73 STAT 544 (1959), 29 U.S.C. § 158(e) (1958); *see also Brown v. Local 17, Lithographers*, 180 F. Supp. 294, 45 LRRM 2577 (N.D. Cal. 1960).

However, a careful reading of the Supreme Court's decision in *NLRB v. Longshoremen*[74] reveals that the words set out in Section 8(e) do not mean what one might believe they meant. The Court said Congress must have intended the prohibition on restraints on subcontracting to be limited to restraints that were some type of secondary boycott.

> Section 8(b)(4)(B) of the Act prohibits unions and their agents from engaging in secondary activities whose object is to force one employer to cease doing business with another. Section 8(e) makes unlawful those collective-bargaining agreements in which the employer agrees to cease doing business with any other person. Although § 8(e) does not in terms distinguish between primary and secondary activity, we have held that, as in § 8(b)(4)(B), Congress intended to reach only agreements with secondary objectives.[75] [Footnotes omitted.]

The legal impact on an arbitrator who implies a restriction on subcontracting from a general nonspecific provision or provisions in a labor agreement is found in the words in Section 8(b)(4)(B) rather than those in Section 8(e). These words must be examined carefully:

§ 158. Unfair labor practices
. . .
(b) Unfair labor practices by labor organization
"It shall be an unfair labor practice for a labor organization or its agents—
. . .
4 . . . (ii) to threaten, coerce, or restrain any person engaged in commerce or in an industry affecting commerce, where . . . an object thereof is:
. . .
(B) forcing or requiring any person to cease using, selling, handling, transporting, or otherwise dealing in the products of any other producer, processor, or manufacturer, or to cease doing business with any other person . . . : *Provided,* That nothing contained in this clause (B) shall be construed to make unlawful any primary strike or primary picketing[.][76] [Emphasis in original.]

The Court explained the legality of agreements between employers and unions:

> Whether an agreement is a lawful work preservation agreement depends on "whether, under all the surrounding circumstances, the Union's objective was preservation of work for [bargaining unit] employees, or whether the agreement [] . . . [was] tactically calculated to satisfy union objectives elsewhere. . . . The touchstone is whether the agreement or its mainte-

---

[74]447 U.S. 490, 104 LRRM 2552 (1980). *See* as background *NLRB v. Enterprise Ass'n of Pipefitters,* 429 U.S. 507, 517, 94 LRRM 2628, 2632 (1977); *National Woodwork Manufacturers Ass'n v. NLRB,* 386 U.S. 612, 620, 635, 64 LRRM 2801, 2803 (1967).
[75]447 U.S. at 503–04, 104 LRRM at 2557.
[76]29 U.S.C. § 158(b).

nance is addressed to the labor relations of the contracting employer *vis-a-vis* his own employees." ... Under this approach, a lawful work preservation agreement must pass two tests: First, it must have as its objective the preservation of work traditionally performed by employees represented by the union. Second, the contracting employer must have the power to give the employees the work in question—the so-called "right of control" test of Pipefitters, supra. The rationale of the second test is that if the contracting employer has no power to assign the work, it is reasonable to infer that the agreement has a secondary objective, that is, to influence whoever does have such power over the work.[77]

In both of these two tests the word "work" is basic. The court went on to say:

In applying the work preservation doctrine, the first and most basic question is, what is the 'work' that the agreement allegedly seeks to preserve? Sometimes the process of identifying the work at issue will require no subtle analysis....

But in many cases it is not so easy to find the starting point of the analysis. Work preservation agreements typically come into being when employees' traditional work is displaced, or threatened with displacement, by technological innovation.[78]

Whether the "restriction agreement" was designed to *preserve* the "work" of the longshoremen or to acquire "work" from the Teamster members working in land-based transportation was difficult to determine. Chief Justice Burger wrote a dissent in which Justices Stewart, Rehnquist, and Stevens joined, making the dissenters four out of nine. The dissent stated in part:

This case turns on the definition of the work in controversy. If viewed exclusively from the perspective of the ILA, without regard to other aspects of the transportation industry or to the evolutionary changes in methods of doing business, the work can be characterized broadly as the loading and unloading of vessels; that gives the contract Rules on Containers a plausible work preservation objective sufficient to escape what would otherwise be a violation of § 8(e) of the National Labor Relations Act. If viewed from the perspective of the consolidators and motor carriers—many of whose employees are also union members—the objective is not preservation of traditional longshoremen's work but a claim to work historically and traditionally performed by teamsters, truckers, and similar inland laborers. Which of these perspectives is chosen in turn depends on the view taken of the nature and function of a "container."

This is where the Court's analysis runs astray.[79]

---

[77]447 U.S. at 504–05, 104 LRRM at 2557.
[78]*Id.* at 505, 104 LRRM at 2557.
[79]*Id.* at 522–23, 104 LRRM at 2564.

If four out of the nine Justices could not agree on the scope of the carefully drafted Rules on Containers, it clearly means that labor arbitrators should not imply restrictions on subcontracting from general nonspecific language. It is quite clear in the Supreme Court's opinion that in order for a work preservation provision to be legally permissible it must be in writing and produced from active collective bargaining:

> Thus, in judging the legality of a *thoroughly bargained* and apparently reasonable accommodation to technological change, the question is not whether the Rules represent the most rational or efficient response to innovation, but whether they are a legally permissible effort to preserve jobs.[80]

The Court also said:

> Identification of the work at issue in a complex case of technological displacement requires a careful analysis of the traditional work patterns that the parties are allegedly seeking to preserve, and *of how the agreement seeks to accomplish that result* under the changed circumstances created by the technological advance.[81] [Emphasis added.]

And again the Court said:

> The *legality of the agreement* turns, as an initial matter, on whether the historical and functional relationship between this retained work and traditional longshore work can support the conclusion that the objective of the agreement was work preservation rather than the satisfaction of union goals elsewhere.[82] [Emphasis added.]

Chief Justice Burger and his three colleagues in the dissent studied the *written rules* in the labor agreement and then concluded that these words provided for nothing less than an invidious form of "featherbedding" to block implementation of modern technological progress.[83]

If a work preservation agreement should be incorporated in clear words in the agreement to restrict subcontracting as a work preservation measure, the next question is: how clear must the words be? In *Mine Workers, UMW, District No. 5 v. Consolidated Coal Co.*[84] the union sought an injunction to block some subcontracting desired by the employer, under a work prevention clause in the agreement and separate implementing agreement. In the National Bituminous Coal Wage Agreement in 1978 there was a provision protecting the work of employees classified as "maintenance and repair," and in January

---

[80]*Id.* at 511, 104 LRRM at 2560.
[81]*Id.* at 507, 104 LRRM at 2558.
[82]*Id.* at 510, 104 LRRM at 2559.
[83]*Id.* at 527, 104 LRRM at 2566.
[84]109 LRRM 2001 (3d Cir. 1981).

1981 the union filed a grievance under the grievance-arbitration procedure, alleging that a subcontractor had been hired to perform routine maintenance and repair work (a "contracting in" example) in violation of the agreement.

That grievance was resolved by a written settlement agreement. Two months later, the company informed the union that a subcontractor was to be retained to perform some repair work on deister tables. The union objected on the grounds that employees in the maintenance and repair classifications had repaired such tables in the past and hence the subcontracting would violate the agreement. The company disputed this assertion.

The union then filed a suit under Section 301, seeking an injunctive order to block the subcontracting. The district court agreed with the union and ordered the company to refrain from subcontracting the work, but on appeal the Third Circuit reversed.[85] It ruled that the words in the settlement agreement and the work preservation clause in the labor agreement were not specific enough to support an injunctive order to block the subcontracting. To issue an injunctive order blocking a subcontracting "the court must be able to say with 'positive assurance'" that the agreement intended to block the subcontracting of repair or maintenance on deister tables and absent such "positive assurance," the court should deny enforcement, the Third Circuit stated.[86]

This decision acts as a follow-up to the clear language requirement set out in *NLRB v. Longshoremen, supra.* Together they may well signal the end of awards by arbitrators creating restrictions on subcontracting based on implications of loose and general nonspecific language in the labor agreement.

The Impact of the Antitrust Acts on Implied Restrictions on Subcontracting

Section 8(e) of the NLRA has an impact on an arbitrator's ability to imply from various general provisions in a labor agreement a restriction on subcontracting for another reason—a risk of violation of the Sherman Act.[87] Since 1976 it has been illegal for a union to engage in a secondary boycott, *i.e.,* an attack on a subcontractor by a restriction in a labor agreement providing that the employer may not purchase parts, products, or services from a subcontractor who does not pay compatible wages or does not manufacture the parts or products in a

---

[85]*Id.*
[86]*Id.* at 2004.
[87]15 U.S.C.A. §§ 1–7 (effective in 1890).

"union shop," because the employees of the subcontractor are not members of the union, and so on. A restraint on the use of a subcontractor that can be construed as a union attack against the subcontractor was dissolved by Section 8(e) and is a violation of the Sherman Act[88] because of Section 8(e)'s alteration of the shield against such a violation, a shield which was interpolated from the Clayton Act and the Norris-LaGuardia Act and set forth in the significant opinion of Justice Frankfurter in *U.S. v. Hutcheson*[89] in 1941.

As soon as Section 8(e) became effective, an attack on the subcontractor became illegal,[90] and the noninjunction part of the Norris-LaGuardia Act could not be asserted because the secondary boycott became illegal.[91] The "legitimate objection" requirement in the Clayton Act needed as part of the shield could no longer apply.[92] Hence, if any agreement *expressed* or *implied* a restraint on a subcontractor that in any way could be considered a union effort against the subcontractor, the restraint would be a violation of the Sherman Act imposing its expensive penalties on the union.

There were various agreements between employers and unions that were found to be violations of the Sherman Act as "restraints of trade"

---

[88]*United States v. Hutcheson,* 312 U.S. 219, 7 LRRM 267 (1941).

[89]The protection shield was forged from the Clayton Act, 38 STAT 731 (1914), 15 U.S.C. § 12 *et seq.* (1973) and the Norris LaGuardia Act, 47 STAT 73 (1932), 29 U.S.C. § 101 (1973) so labor unions could restrain commerce if the restraint was in connection with a legal labor dispute. Justice Frankfurter explained:
[W]hether trade union conduct constitutes a violation of the Sherman Law is to be determined only by reading the Sherman Law and § 20 of the Clayton Act and the Norris-LaGuardia Act as a harmonizing text of outlawry of labor conduct.
United States v. Hutcheson, 312 U.S. 219, 231, 7 LRRM 267, 269 (1941).

[90]Cox, *The Landrum-Griffin Amendments to the National Labor Relations Act,* 44 MINN. L. REV. 257, 272 (1959). Solicitor General Archibald Cox wrote:
Apart from the participation of the labor union, [hot cargo] agreements would violate the Sherman Act. [Fashion Originators Guild v. FTC, 312 U.S. 457 (1941)]. This was the theory upon which the Senate voted to outlaw "hot cargo" contracts in the trucking industry. In the House, the prohibition was expanded to all agreements by which an employer agrees with a labor organization not to handle *or use the goods of another person*.... [Emphasis added.]
See also Report of the Attorney General's National Committee to Study the Antitrust Laws (Oppenheim Report) (Washington: U.S. Govt. Print. Off., 1955), pp. 299-330.

[91]Norris-LaGuardia Act § 13(c), 47 STAT 73 (1932), 29 U.S.C. § 113(c) (1958) provides:
The term "labor dispute" includes any controversy concerning terms or conditions of employment, or concerning the association or representation of persons in negotiating, fixing, maintaining, changing, or seeking to arrange terms or conditions of employment, regardless of whether or not the disputants stand in the proximate relation of employer and employee.

[92]Clayton Act § 6, 38 STAT 731 (1914), 15 U.S.C. § 17 (1958) provides:
The labor of a human being is not a commodity or article of commerce. Nothing contained in the antitrust laws shall be construed to forbid the existence and operation of labor, agricultural, or horticultural organizations, instituted for the purposes of mutual help, and not having capital stock or conducted for profit, or to forbid or restrain individual members of such organizations from lawfully carrying out the *legitimate objects* thereof; nor shall such organizations, or the members thereof, be held or construed to be illegal combinations or conspiracies in restraint of trade, under the antitrust laws. [Emphasis added.]

before Section 8(e) became effective.[93] But when that provision became effective, the violation of the Sherman Act was easier to establish.

In *Connell Construction Co., Inc. v. Plumbers, Local 100*,[94] a company successfully sued a union and recovered damages after the union had set up a picket line because the company had purchased some parts from a subcontractor who had not "signed up" with the union. In *Larry V. Muko, Inc. v. Building & Const. Trades Council (Southwester Pennsylvania)*,[95] a subcontractor successfully sued the union because his building contracts were no longer accepted by a company, even though he had filed the lowest bids.

A suit by a subcontractor against a union could be successful in spite of a statement by the arbitrator, after he or she found a restriction on purchasing from the subcontractor was implied, that the restriction was not intended to be directed toward the contractor, *i.e.,* a secondary boycott. The suit by the subcontractor would not be blocked by such finding any more, or by a finding by the NLRB that the restrictions on the purchases from the contractor were not an unfair labor practice (*i.e.,* a secondary boycott). The Fifth Circuit explained this in *W. R. Grace & Co. v. Rubber Workers, Local 759:*[96]

> One of the clearest examples in the law of the situation where persons may in good faith believe they are acting properly but nevertheless be found to be responsible in damages for improper conduct is in the secondary boycott provisions of the National Labor Relations Act, 29 U.S.C. § 158(b)(4) (unfair labor practice), and 29 U.S.C. § 187 (creating civil liability for exactly the same conduct). It is well established that a NLRB determination not to prosecute a union for violation of § 8(b)(4) is not res judicata and does not bar a suit for damages under § 187 for the same episode. In other words, the union may not only be in good faith before charges are filed that it is not violating the secondary boycott provisions, it may be further convinced by the Board considering its actions but deciding not to

---

[93]*Allen Bradley Co. v. Electrical Workers, IBEW, Local 3*, 325 U.S. 797, 16 LRRM 798 (1945); *Los Angeles Meat and Provision Drivers, Local 626 v. United States*, 371 U.S. 94, 51 LRRM 2448 (1962); *Westlab, Inc. v. Freedom, Inc.*, 198 F. Supp. 701, 48 LRRM 2773 (S.D. N.Y. 1961); *U.S. v. Fish Smokers Trade Council, Inc.*, 183 F. Supp. 227, 232, 229, 46 LRRM 2144, 2148, 2145 (S.D. N.Y. 1960); *Columbia River Packers Ass'n v. Hinton*, 315 U.S. 143, 9 LRRM 403 (1942); *Mineworkers v. Pennington*, 381 U.S. 657, 59 LRRM 2369 (1965). *Compare Meatcutters, Local 189 v. Jewel Tea Co.*, 381 U.S. 676, 59 LRRM 2376 (1965).

[94]421 U.S. 616, 89 LRRM 2401 (1973), *rehearing denied*, 423 U.S. 884 (1975).

[95]*Larry v. Muko, Inc. v. Building & Const. Trades Council (S.W. Pa.)*, 609 F.2d 1368, 99 LRRM 2001 (3d Cir. 1979), *on rehearing*, 101 LRRM 2875; *see also California Dump Truck Owners Ass'n, Inc. v. Associated General Contractors of America, San Diego Chapter, Inc.*, 562 F.2d 607, 612–613, 96 LRRM 2988 (9th Cir. 1979); *In re Bullard Contracting Corp.*, 464 F. Supp. 312, 100 LRRM 2959 (W.D. N.Y. 1979).

[96]652 F.2d 1248, 1258, 107 LRRM 3251, 3256 (5th Cir. 1981), *cert. granted*, 50 USLW 3998.18 (U.S. June 28, 1982) (No. 81-1314).

prosecute a complaint under § 8(b)(4) but still be found liable for damages under § 187.[97]

These cases should alert union representatives as well as labor arbitrators when the union side is arguing to the arbitrator that purchases of parts, products, or services from a subcontractor should be blocked by implied restrictions built up from a general labor agreement provision. Specific words must be found in the labor agreement before a restriction on subcontracting can be awarded and tested as a "work preservation" agreement. The work preservation words in the agreement must "sparkle" before the restriction should be enforced by the arbitrator.[98]

---

[97] Citations to the following cases were set out in the court's decision at 652 F.2d 1256: *Teamsters, Local 290 v. Oolite Concrete Co.*, 341 F.2d 210, 58 LRRM 2336 (5th Cir. 1965), *cert. denied*, 382 U.S. 972, 61 LRRM 2147 (1966). *Accord, Clark Engineering & Construction Co. v. Carpenters, Four Rivers District Council*, 510 F.2d 1075, 88 LRRM 2865 (6th Cir. 1975). *See also Painters, District Council 38 v. Edgewood Contracting Co.*, 416 F.2d 1081, 1085, 72 LRRM 2524 (5th Cir. 1969).

[98] *See* discussion under "The Impact of Section 8(e) on Implied Restrictions on Subcontracting" in this chapter, *supra*.

CHAPTER XVIII

Remedies

An arbitrator's award normally is accompanied by an opinion setting forth the basis for the decision and the remedy considered necessary to rectify the violation if one is found to exist.[1] Arbitrators have sometimes been asked by one party to issue an award without a remedy, but generally refuse to do so absent an express agreement between the parties.[2]

BASIS OF THE ARBITRATOR'S REMEDIAL AUTHORITY

Generally speaking, arbitrators rule that their appointment carries with it an implicit power to specify the appropriate remedy.[3] This position was given court approval in the New York case of *Utility Laundry Service, Inc. v. Sklar:*[4]

> An agreement to arbitrate "any and all controversies" arising under a contract will be construed as affording "authority to assess damages against the party in default." ... The issue must turn upon the intent of the parties as expressed in their agreement, and the general submission of "any dispute" has been held to confer power to award damages.[5]

The view that a union could not in an arbitration proceeding obtain wages due the employees because the labor agreement did not provide

---

[1]*See generally* Stein, *Remedies in Labor Arbitration,* CHALLENGES TO ARBITRATION, Proceedings of the Thirteenth Annual Meeting, National Academy of Arbitrators, J. McKelvey, ed. (Washington: BNA Books, 1960), p. 39. *But see* Freidin, Discussion, "Remedies in Arbitration," LABOR ARBITRATION—PERSPECTIVES AND PROBLEMS, Proceedings of the Seventeenth Annual Meeting, National Academy of Arbitrators, M. Kahn, ed. (Washington: BNA Books, 1964), p. 201.

[2]*See, e.g., City of Dearborn, Mich.*, 69-2 ARB ¶ 8442 (Keefe, 1969); *U.S. Steel Corp.*, 35 LA 453 (Crawford, 1960).

[3]*See, e.g., Lucky Stores, Inc.*, 70-1 ARB ¶ 8271 (Feller, 1969); *Vannette Hosiery Mills*, 17 LA 349 (Emery, 1961); *International Harvester Co.*, 9 LA 894 (Wirtz, 1947); *Warren City Mfg. Co.*, 7 LA 202 (Abernethy, 1947); *Glen L. Martin Co.*, 6 LA 500 (Brecht, 1947).

[4]300 N.Y. 255, 90 N.E.2d 178 (1949).

[5]90 N.E.2d at 180. *See also Texas Gas Transmission Corp. v. Chemical Workers, Local 187,* 200 F.Supp. 521, 49 LRRM 2409 (W.D. La. 1961).

for money awards was rejected by a federal court shortly after *Lincoln Mills*.[6] The court viewed *Lincoln Mills* as "a retreat" from the prior line of cases finding that, since a union could not sue to recover unpaid wages owed to individual employees, it could not, under Section 301 of the Taft-Hartley Act, obtain enforcement of an arbitration award directing a company to pay unpaid wages to employees.[7] This, of course, is a proper view of the remedial scope available under *Lincoln Mills*. Writing in *Lincoln Mills* on the remedial authority of courts under Section 301 (which would include the authority to enforce arbitration awards), Justice Douglas emphasized that courts should resolve the problems presented by "looking at the policy of the legislature and fashioning a remedy that will effectuate that policy. The range of judicial inventiveness will be determined by the nature of the problem."[8]

In striking contrast, however, the Eighth Circuit in *Kansas City Luggage & Novelty Workers, Local 66 v. Neevel Luggage Mfg. Co., Inc.*,[9] affirmed a trial court's denial of enforcement of an award where the arbitrator granted back pay to an employee he found had been laid off improperly, because the remedy of back pay had not been requested in the submission.

The view that the remedial power of the arbitrator is limited to the remedies requested in the submission appears to be inconsistent with the much broader power which the Supreme Court has said resides in the arbitrator.[10] The Supreme Court held in *Steelworkers v. Enterprise*

---

[6]*Textile Workers, TWUA v. Lincoln Mills of Ala.*, 353 U.S. 448, 40 LRRM 2113 (1957).

[7]*See, e.g., Electrical Workers, IBEW, Local 130 v. Mississippi Valley Electric Co.*, 175 F.Supp. 312, 44 LRRM 2674 (E.D. La. 1959).

[8]353 U.S. at 457, 40 LRRM at 2116.

[9]325 F.2d 992, 55 LRRM 2153 (8th Cir. 1964), distinguished in *American Bosch Arma Corp. v. Electrical Workers, IUE, Local 794*, 243 F.Supp. 493, 59 LRRM 2798 (N.D. Miss. 1965). *See also Retail Clerks, Local 782 v. Sav-On Groceries*, 508 F.2d 500, 88 LRRM 3205 (10th Cir. 1975) where the court cited the *Neevel* case with approval, and *Staklinski v. Pyramid Electric Co.*, 6 N.Y.2d 159, 160 N.E.2d 78 (1959), where the court said the agreement to arbitrate under the American Arbitration Association Rules empowered the arbitrator to grant specific performance of a personal service contract. Rule 1 of the American Arbitration Association *Voluntary Labor Rules* (1979) provides in part that:

The parties shall be deemed to have made these Rules a part of their arbitration agreement whenever, in a collective bargaining agreement or submission, they have provided for arbitration by the American Arbitration Association ... or under its rules.

[10]   It is apparent that in order to carry out the Congressional policy in favor of the arbitrability of labor disputes, arbitrators must be vested with broad power to fashion appropriate remedies in the cases before them. The need for such broad power has generally been recognized by the federal courts which have usually held that in the absence of restrictive language in a collective bargaining agreement the arbitrator has power to fashion a remedy appropriate to the case before him.

E. Dannelle, *Norris-LaGuardia and Injunctions in Labor Arbitration Cases*, REPORT OF THE SIXTEENTH ANNUAL NEW YORK UNIVERSITY CONFERENCE ON LABOR, M. Christenson, ed.

Wheel & Car Corp.[11] that under Section 301 courts should recognize that the arbitrator has powers to formulate remedies that are compatible with national labor policy.

When an arbitrator is commissioned to interpret and apply the collective bargaining agreement, he is to bring his informed judgment to bear in order to reach a fair solution of a problem. *This is especially true when it comes to formulating remedies.* There the need is for flexibility in meeting a wide variety of situations. The draftsmen may never have thought of what specific remedy should be awarded to meet a particular contingency.[12] [Emphasis added.]

Indeed, to underscore the broad remedial powers of an arbitrator, the Court in *Enterprise Wheel* enforced an arbitrator's award which granted back pay to discharged employees beyond the expiration date of the contract.

Taking a cue from this case, courts have enforced broad remedies fashioned by arbitrators. For example, in *Selb Mfg. v. Machinists*,[13] the Eighth Circuit upheld an award ordering a company:

(1) to return to their plants in St. Louis machinery, equipment and work they had transferred to the plants in Arkansas and Colorado, and (2) to recall all their St. Louis employees laid off since September 23, 1960, and to reinstate them without loss of seniority or loss of pay.[14]

Likewise, in *Machinists v. Cameron Iron Works, Inc.*,[15] the Fifth Circuit, also taking its cue from the Supreme Court, reversed its prior position[16] that, absent express contractual authority, an arbitrator was not authorized to award damages. The court explained the abruptness of its reversal:

Likewise, whether it is thought to be a part of the substantive right or more a part of the grievance procedure, in the absence of clearly restrictive

---

(New York: Matthew Bender, 1963), pp. 275–76. *See generally* Comment, *Labor Law: Authority of Arbitrator to Determine Remedy for Violation of Collective Bargaining Agreement,* 43 MARQ. L. REV. 260 (1959); Cornfield, *Developing Standards for Determining Arbitrability of Labor Disputes by Federal Courts,* 14 LAB. L.J. 564, 573 (1963); Fleming, *Arbitrators and the Remedy Power,* 48 VA. L. REV. 1199 (1962); *Labor Arbitration in the Federal Courts: Excerpts From a Report of the Subcommittee on Labor Arbitration Law of the Section on Labor Relations Law, American Bar Association,* 15 ARB. J. 113 (1960).

[11]363 U.S. 593, 46 LRRM 2423 (1960).

[12]*Id.* at 597, 46 LRRM 2425. *See also Alexander v. Gardner-Denver Co.,* 415 U.S. 36, 53, 7 FEP Cases 81 (1974).

[13]305 F.2d 177, 50 LRRM 2671 (8th Cir. 1962).

[14]*Id.* at 179, 50 LRRM at 2672.

[15]292 F.2d 112, 48 LRRM 2516 (5th Cir. 1961), *cert. denied,* 368 U.S. 926, 49 LRRM 2173 (1961). *See also Texas Gas Transmission Corp. v. Chemical Workers, Local 187,* 200 F. Supp. 521, 49 LRRM 2409 (W.D. La. 1961).

[16]*See, e.g., Refinery Employees of Lake Charles Area v. Continental Oil Co.,* 268 F.2d 447, 44 LRRM 2388 (5th Cir. 1959), *cert. denied,* 361 U.S. 896, 45 LRRM 2131 (1959).

language, great latitude must be allowed in fashioning the appropriate remedy constituting the arbitrator's "decision."

...[W]e find no such positive declaration as would exclude from the arbitrators the power to determine whether the award of back pay is or is not within the terms of the agreement, and if so, whether it is or is not an appropriate remedy.[17]

Similarly, in *Steelworkers v. United States Gypsum Co.*,[18] the court enforced an award of Arbitrator Rolf Valtin's[19] which required the company—under the labor agreement executed with a predecessor—to pay retroactive increases to its employees. Although the agreement contained a wage reopener clause, the successor had refused to negotiate with the union. After determining that because five years had elapsed it would be futile to order negotiations, the arbitrator calculated an increase which he found would have been granted had the negotiations been held, and the Company was ordered to pay that amount to its employees. The Union filed suit in federal court to enforce the award and the district court[20] held that the arbitrator had exceeded his authority by ordering the retroactive increases. The 5th Circuit disagreed and ordered enforcement of the award, noting that the rationale of *H. K. Porter Co. v. NLRB*[21] was inapplicable.

REMEDIES IN DISCIPLINARY CASES

When considering discipline or discharge cases, the arbitrators will ask themselves some very important questions. Many of these were summarized by Arbitrator Harry Shulman in 1955:

The agreement may be quite clear that the employer has the power to discharge or discipline for cause. It may be quite clear in empowering the arbitrator to pass on grievances protesting the employer's action and even to reduce or modify penalties. But what and where are the guides for his

---

[17]292 F.2d 112, 119, 48 LRRM 2516, 2520 (5th Cir. 1961). The wide range of remedies available to the arbitrator is further evidenced by the Uniform Arbitration Act, which provides in Section 12(a)(5):
[T]he fact that the relief was such that it could or would not be granted by a court of law or equity is not ground for vacating or refusing the affirm the award.
Act Relating to Arbitration and to Make Uniform the Law With Reference Thereto, 7 Uniform Laws Annotated, BUSINESS AND FINANCIAL LAWS (St. Paul: West Pub. Co., 1978), p. 55.

[18]492 F.2d 713, 85 LRRM 2962 (5th Cir. 1974), *rehearing denied*, 498 F.2d 334, 85 LRRM 2962 (5th Cir. 1974), *cert. denied*, 419 U.S. 998, 87 LRRM 2658 (1974).

[19]*United States Gypsum Co.*, 56 LA 363 (Valtin, 1971).

[20]339 F. Supp. 302, 79 LRRM 2833 (N.D. Ala. 1972).

[21]397 U.S. 99, 73 LRRM 2561 (1970). *See also Auto Workers v. NLRB*, 449 F.2d 1058, 76 LRRM 3055 (D.C. Cir. 1971); *Braswell Motor Freight Lines*, 196 NLRB 76, 80 LRRM 1150, *enforced*, 486 F.2d 743, 84 LRRM 2433 (7th Cir. 1973).

decision? With the advent of grievance procedures in arbitration, discharge has ceased to be regarded as the only available disciplinary measure. Layoffs for various periods are now in general use; and suggestion is made of disciplinary demotions, transfers, reduction-in-seniority, and the like. What is proper cause of disciplinary action, and more particularly, for discharges, rather than for some other penalty? May such measures as demotions or reduction in seniority be properly used for disciplinary purposes? How much weight is to be attached in each case to the employer's judgment, particularly in view of the fact that it is precisely that judgment which is sought to be curbed by the grievance procedure? What significance is to be attached to personality of the individual employee, his age, his seniority, his prior record, his promise? What consideration, if any, is to be given to probable effects on plant "morale," the morale of supervisors as well as of the workers, and the effect at the time the decision is to be made, as well as the time the penalty is imposed? The frequent instances of stoppage of work in a department or a whole plant because of a disciplinary penalty imposed on a single employee indicates that what is involved is not merely the case of an individual but a group dispute. Factors of this kind should be and doubtless are considered by the parties in other stages of the grievance procedure. Do they become irrelevant when the case is appealed to arbitration?[22]

In answering these and other questions, the parties may find that the arbitrator is reaching a conclusion that varies considerably from one or both of the parties' expectations. As a general rule, arbitrators are warned against substituting their own judgment for that of management. Arbitrator Ross explained the tests used by arbitrators to evaluate the amount of cause:

> As arbitrators we are frequently criticized on the ground that we substitute our judgment for that of the employer. In the whole lexicon of arbitration cliches, that one is the most overworked. If our task is officially to review the employer's judgment, obviously we must be ready to substitute our own if we find that his was unreasonable. What else are we there for? It is no answer to say that we should uphold the termination unless it was arbitrary and capricious. Let us face it, in most discharge cases the grievants are not model employees. There is generally some cause for discharge; the real problem is whether it was sufficient cause. We are not brought in to try the facts, but to review the employer's judgment.[23]

Disciplinary cases constitute the largest single group of cases which are brought to arbitration, and a wide variety of special remedies in such cases have been fashioned by arbitrators. Arbitrators have noted

[22]Shulman, *Reason, Contract, and Law in Labor Relations,* 68 Harv. L. Rev. 68 (1955).

[23]Ross, Discussion of Kadish, *The Criminal Law and Industrial Discipline as Sanctioning Systems: Some Comparative Observations,* Labor Arbitration—Perspectives and Problems, Proceedings of the Seventeenth Annual Meeting, National Academy of Arbitrators, M. Kahn, ed. (Washington: BNA Books, 1964), p. 144.

that the contractual right of the employer to discipline and discharge employees for "just cause" requires the arbitrators to make two determinations in considering cases: (i) whether a cause for discipline exists and (ii) whether the amount of discipline was proper under the circumstances. For example, in *Great Atlantic & Pacific Tea Co.,*[24] Arbitrator Burton Turkus explained:

> In applying the test of "just cause" the arbitrator is generally required to determine two factors: (a) has the commission of the misconduct, offense or dereliction of duty, upon which the discipline administered was grounded, been adequately established by the proof; and (b) if proven or admitted, the reasonableness of the disciplinary penalty imposed in the light of the nature, character and gravity thereof—for as frequently as not the reasonableness of the penalty (as well as the actual commission of the misconduct itself) is questioned or challenged in arbitration.
>
> In the absence of contract language expressly prohibiting the exercise of such power, the arbitrator, by virtue of his authority and duty to fairly and finally settle and adjust (decide) the dispute before him, has the inherent power to determine the sufficiency of the cause and the reasonableness of the penalty imposed.[25]

As Arbitrator Turkus noted, some labor agreements deny the arbitrator the power to modify the penalty if "just cause" for the discipline is established, and this limitation on an arbitrator's remedial power is considered below.

Reinstatement

Where an arbitrator finds that a discharge was not for "just cause," an essential part of the remedy is reinstatement.[26] It is, however, a matter of historical interest that as late as 1936 courts held that an order of reinstatement was unenforceable since the common law forbids the specific performances of an employment contract, *i.e.*, forcing an employee by court order to work for a particular employer, or forcing an employer to continue in employment a particular employee.[27] The employee's right to employment (seniority rights) unless he or she is guilty of misconduct constituting "just cause" for termination by discharge is the employment right found in the labor agreement. This employment right in the labor agreement became more important than the employment rights in the individual contract

---

[24]63-1 ARB ¶ 8027 (Turkus, 1962).

[25]*Id.* at 3090. *See also* Davey, *The Arbitrator Speaks on Discharge and Discipline*, 17 ARB. J. 98 (1962).

[26]*See Retail Clerks, Local 57 (Great Falls) v. Western Drug of Great Falls*, 409 F. Supp. 1052, 93 LRRM 2060 (D. Mont. 1976); *Reece v. Westmoreland Coal Co.*, 340 F. Supp. 695, 80 LRRM 2032 (W.D. Va. 1972).

[27]*Louisville & Nashville R.R. v. Bryant*, 263 Ky. 578, 92 S.W.2d 749 (1936).

of employment, which at one time were considered paramount.[28] With this shift, reinstatement by order of an arbitrator became a fundamental difference between the labor relations system in the United States and that in European countries. In European countries the individual contract of employment has remained legally paramount over labor agreements negotiated between unions and employers.[29]

In the United States labor agreements enforced by arbitration became an almost universal part of the employer-union relationship under the stimulus of the War Labor Board established in World War II, and labor agreements negotiated with unions usually have provided that employees may be discharged *only* for just cause. It is this provision which generates reinstatement as the remedy for a discharge when an arbitrator finds that the discharge was *not* for just cause. Under this system, it is technically more accurate to say that an employee who was discharged *not* for just cause was not in fact discharged, and hence the employment relationship set out in the seniority provisions in the labor agreement was not broken. Such an arbitration award is enforceable in the courts like any other, notwithstanding the old common-law doctrine that a court may not enforce performance of a contract of personal service: in the case of a contract of personal service, such an enforcement would be an order to *reestablish* an employment relationship, whereas the enforcement of an arbitration award of reinstatement, under the technical explanation offered above, is an order that the employment relationship *was not broken* by a discharge for just cause.

Conditional Reinstatement

Arbitrator Peter M. Kelliher in *Del Monte Corp., Midwest Div.*,[30] concluded the discharge of the grievant was not for just cause and would reinstate her if she met two conditions. The grievant had been attending a retirement party of about 100 employees at a restaurant about five miles from the plant in honor of three Del Monte employees who were retiring. The party commenced at 6 p.m., with dinner at 7, but since the grievant planned to have dinner with her sister, she did not purchase a dinner ticket. At 9:30 p.m., after she had consumed at least six drinks, she noticed the assistant manager of the plant standing near the bar and "for some reason" she "grabbed a partially filled bottle of beer" and poured some beer on the coat sleeve of Mr.

---

[28]*J. I. Case Co. v. NLRB*, 321 U.S. 332, 14 LRRM 501 (1944).

[29]Seyfarth, Shaw, Fairweather & Geraldson, Labor Relations and the Law in the United Kingdom and the United States (Ann Arbor: Univ. of Mich. Press, 1968), p. 114.

[30]*Del Monte Corp., Midwest Division [Retail, Wholesale & Department Store Union, Local No. 17]* (discharge of Paula Phipps) (Kelliher, November 19, 1980) (unpublished).

K——. This action was noticed by only one other person. Without making any abusive or threatening statements, the grievant promptly left the party.

The two conditions set up by Arbitrator Kelliher were that the grievant (1) write a letter of apology to the assistant manager and (2) authorize the company to have $15 deducted from her first week's wages to compensate him for the expense he incurred in having his jacket cleaned.

Where an award reinstated a union steward discharged for alleged insubordination with the condition that "upon his return to work he will resign his position as shop steward and will not act in any capacity as a union representative in the plant for a period of one year," a California court modified the award to remove the condition on the ground that it was a remedy beyond the arbitrator's authority.[31] However, to the contrary, a New York court reviewed an award reinstating a steward with a proviso that he could not hold a union office for three years and held that the condition was within the authority of the arbitrator.[32]

In another case a complaint was filed with the NLRB asking that an arbitration award be upset because the reinstatement of the dischargee was conditioned on the taking of a proficiency test that he failed, making the discharge final.[33] The Board dismissed the complaint. Arbitrator McLeod, in *Ionac Chemical Co.*,[34] reinstated two employees discharged for loitering, on the condition that if they were found guilty of violating any plant rule during the first two years after reinstatement they would be discharged summarily.

The Authority to Reduce the Discipline

Often the language of the labor agreement gives the arbitrator the authority to change the amount of disciplinary penalty imposed by the management once "just cause" for discipline has been established. In other agreements, this authority is not clear and the arbitrator's authority to change the amount of the discipline once "just cause" is determined is often a hotly contested issue. This debate often involves

---

[31]*Arterberry of Lodge 120, IAM v. Lockheed Aircraft Service*, 33 LA 292 (Cal. Sup. Ct. 1959).

[32]*Consolidated Edison Co. v. Rigley*, 73 LRRM 2220 (N.Y. Sup. Ct. 1970). Arbitrators have occasionally penalized employees in discipline cases with a stated loss of seniority. *University of California*, 63 LA 314 (Jacobs, 1974); *Butler Mfg. Co.*, 55 LA 451 and 55 LA 1214 (Purdom, 1970); *Sam Shainberg Co.*, 54 LA 135 (Caraway, 1970).

[33]*Terminal Transport Co.*, 185 NLRB 672, 75 LRRM 1130 (1970) *See also Spielberg Mfg. Co.*, 112 NLRB 1080, 1082, 36 LRRM 1152 (1955), wherein the Board held it would give binding effect to arbitral decisions made in proceedings to which all parties have acquiesced where the proceedings are fair and regular on their face and where the results are not repugnant to the purposes and policies of the National Labor Relations Act.

[34]63 LA 1135 (McLeod, 1974).

the question of whether the agreement (i) limits the arbitrator to either upholding the discipline imposed by the management or making the employee whole by reinstating the employee with full back pay even though cause for some discipline exists, where in the arbitrator's opinion this is insufficient to support a discharge, or (ii) grants the arbitrator the remedial power to direct some intermediate form of penalty.

Some employers believe that granting an arbitrator the power to convert a discharge to a disciplinary suspension would cause some arbitrators to reinstate discharges without back pay where they would not do so if they only were given the power to reinstate with full back pay, since the arbitrators often might conclude the employee concerned deserved at least some discipline. These employers negotiate labor agreements clearly denying the arbitrator the power to convert discipline. Even where the agreement language would seem to prevent the arbitrator from converting a discharge to a disciplinary layoff, however, some strange and inconsistent awards have occurred.

The Michigan Supreme Court held that a discharged employee who was reinstated without back pay could sue the employer for back pay since the labor agreement expressly provided that in the event the discharge was found to be without "just cause" the employee would be reinstated with "full seniority and shall receive pay for all time lost from work."[35]

In contrast, the Fourth Circuit has held that an arbitrator did not exceed the scope of his authority when he reinstated a dischargee without back pay under an agreement which stated:

> "In the event it should be decided [by the arbitrator] that an injustice has been dealt the discharged employee, the Company shall reinstate such employee to his former position and pay full compensation for time lost."[36]

In reaching its conclusion, the court stated that it felt that the terms of the labor agreement could be construed to allow the arbitrator the discretion to find that the employee had engaged in "culpable conduct" warranting some "disciplinary sanction" but that discharge was an "excessive" penalty and therefore unjust.

In another case an arbitrator reduced a penalty for the violation of a management rule that carried with it a penalty of a one-week suspension even though the labor agreement specifically reserved to the

---

[35]*Carr v. Kalamazoo Vegetable Parchment Co.*, 354 Mich. 327, 92 N.W.2d 295 (1958). *Accord, Nuest v. Westinghouse Air Brake Co.*, 313 F. Supp. 1228, 74 LRRM 2564 (S.D. Ill. 1970); *Gulf States Telephone Co. v. Electrical Workers, IBEW, Local 1692*, 416 F.2d 198, 72 LRRM 2026 (5th Cir. 1969); *Electrical Workers, IBEW, Local 2130 v. Bally Case & Cooler, Inc.*, 232 F. Supp. 394, 56 LRRM 2831 (E.D. Pa. 1964).

[36]*Woodward Iron Co., Lynchburg Foundry Co. Div. v. Steelworkers, Local 2556*, 404 F.2d 259, 260, 60 LRRM 2878 (4th Cir. 1968). *See also Reece v. Westmoreland Coal Company*, 340 F. Supp. 695, 80 LRRM 2032 (W.D. Va. 1972).

management the right to promulgate disciplinary rules. The court on a motion to vacate the award ruled that the arbitrator was precluded from modifying the penalty prescribed by management for violating the rule despite clear mitigating circumstances.[37]

A Pennsylvania court and an arbitrator had a unique collision over a discharge. The court ordered that the dischargee was "to be continued on the payroll but removed off the premises," until an arbitrator could determine the issue of wrongful discharge. The arbitrator reinstated the dischargee but directed him to repay the company the money paid him from the day of his discharge to the date of his reinstatement "during which time he did nothing to earn it." On a motion to confirm the award, the court struck from the award the repayment order. The court held that the previous court order, directing arbitration and specifically stating that the employee was to remain on the payroll, constituted a restriction on the arbitrator's remedial authority.[38]

In another case, the Sixth Circuit held that an arbitrator had exceeded his authority in finding that an employee had quit when the employee failed to report to work because he was imprisoned for a traffic offense. The court held that such a finding was discriminatory and vacated the award. The court noted that an arbitrator is limited to the interpretation and application of the agreement and that the absence, in jail, could not be construed to mean that the employee had voluntarily quit.[39]

Remedies Where the Employee Breaches the Agreement

The typical labor agreement provides that employees may be discharged only for "just cause." The type of misconduct which constitutes "just cause" for discharge may vary from plant to plant. Arbitrators generally conclude that unless an employer is "even-handed" in his disciplinary determinations, the discharge is capricious and is subject to modification.

To determine whether the employer's disciplinary determination is "even-handed," arbitrators typically examine the type of misconduct for which employees have been discharged in the past. If the misconduct, basic to a discharge action, is completely out of pattern with the misconduct of other employees previously discharged, or is not greater than the misconduct of others not discharged, arbitrators, unless

---

[37]*Electrical Workers, IUE, Local 217 v. Holtzer-Cabot Corp.*, 277 F. Supp. 704, 67 LRRM 2244 (D. Mass. 1967).

[38]*Sley System Garages v. Transport Workers, Local 700*, 406 Pa. 370, 178 A.2d 560, 49 LRRM 2407 (1962).

[39]*Timken Co. v. Steelworkers, Local 1123*, 482 F.2d 1012, 1015, 83 LRRM 2814 (6th Cir. 1973).

there are other important considerations, will often reinstate and reduce the discharge to a suspension.

The authority for such a remedy is found in the simple fact that the discharge action taken by the employer is not effective in severing the employment relationship because, when tested against the "just cause" standard established in the agreement, there is insufficient cause to support the discharge action. For this reason, arbitrators have held that the employment relationship has not been terminated. The appropriate remedy is then reinstatement.

When, however, the employee engages in conduct which is described in the labor agreement as conduct which will automatically terminate the employment relationship, arbitrators can no longer evaluate an action initiated by the employer to determine whether the conduct constitutes "just cause" for discharge.

A quit, an absence for three working days without notification to the employer, accepting employment elsewhere when on leave of absence, failing to report on the first working day after the expiration of a leave of absence or vacation, or failing to return within a specified time when recalled from a layoff are often listed in labor agreements as conduct that constitutes a "quit" which terminates employment.[40] Arbitrator Harry Dworkin in *Brush Beryllium Co.*[41] pointed out the distinction between termination for being absent for three days without notice to the employer and termination by discharge for a standard described as "just cause":

> There is no evidence in the instant case that the grievant was disciplined through application of either "a suspension, layoff or discharge" for any specific act of misconduct or infraction which would warrant disciplinary action. There is not here involved an incident of discipline for just cause in accordance with the accepted principles of disciplinary procedure. The grievant was terminated and his seniority ceased pursuant to the notice of January 23, 1969, due to his absence for three consecutive days without notifying the company of a reason to justify such absence. The situation is distinguished from one of discharge or suspension for misconduct. Article XV, is a comprehensive provision dealing with application of length of service in a variety of situations. As regards its application to the instant case, Section 3 specifically provides for a number of situations that may result in termination of seniority.

When employment is broken by an act of the employee constituting a breach of the agreement, an arbitrator would have no authority to

---

[40]*Midland-Ross*, 49 LA 283 (Larkin, 1967); *U.S. Corrugated-Fiber Box Co.*, 41 LA 804 (Shister, 1963); *Bassick Co.*, 38 LA 279 (Seitz, 1962). *See also City of Warren, Mich.*, 68 LA 1195 (Rehmus, 1977).

[41]55 LA 709, 714-15 (Dworkin, 1970). (This case is of interest in connection with the contract breach discussion because the employee was absent on a "one-man strike.")

reinstate the employee. The remedy of reinstatement is reserved for those situations in which an employer discharged an employee but it was not for *"just cause."* Where an arbitrator is being asked to reinstate employees who participated in a strike in violation of a no-strike clause, the arbitrator's remedial authority is more closely related to the remedial authority granted in cases where the termination occurs by an action of the employee (*i.e.*, a quit) than that granted in cases where the termination occurs by an action of the employer (discharge).

Many labor agreements define the arbitrator's remedial power where there has been a termination of employment because of participation in a strike which breaches the contract. For example, an arbitrator concluded he had no authority to reinstate twenty-one strikers who were not permitted to return to work even though several hundred other participants were permitted to do so. The agreement in express language limited any grievances arising out of violations of the no-strike provision to the question of whether the employee "did or did not ... participate" in the action charged, and prohibited the arbitrator from substituting "his judgment or discretion for that of management."[42]

In another case, the Sixth Circuit set aside an award of an arbitrator who had reinstated twenty-eight employees who had violated the no-strike clause of the agreement. The court held that the award was contrary to the express terms of the agreement and as such was beyond the scope of the arbitrator's authority.[43]

Where there is no special language limiting the arbitrator's remedial authority, arbitrators have taken differing positions when employees breach the labor agreement by striking. Some equate a termination of employment for participation in a strike in violation of the agreement to a discharge for "just cause." In these cases, the arbitrators employ the same standards as those used in other discharge cases; other arbitrators consider the termination of employment to be the result of the employee's breach of the agreement and analogous to a quit.

When arbitrators treat participation in a contract-breach strike simply as grounds for discharge by the employer, the "even-handed"

[42]*Magnavox Co.*, AAA Case No. 111-8 (Oppenheim, 1967). *See also Hal Art Automotive Warehouse, Inc.*, 73-1 ARB ¶ 8123 (Wilmoth, 1973); *Masonite Corp.*, 54 LA 633 (Stouffer, 1970); *Randall Co.*, 66-2 ARB ¶ 8692 (Wissner, 1966); *Philips Industries, Inc.*, 66-1 ARB ¶ 8042 (Stouffer, 1965); *Yale & Towne Mfg. Co.*, 41 LA 1100 (Wallen, 1963); *Chrysler Corp.*, 9 LA 789 (Wolff, 1947); *Borg-Warner Corp.*, 4 LA 4 (Updegraff, 1945).

[43]*Amanda Bent Bolt Co. v. Automobile Workers, Local 1549*, 451 F.2d 1277, 79 LRRM 2023 (6th Cir. 1971).

discipline principle that is involved creates a quandary. Arbitrator Ralph T. Seward in *General Motors Corp.* [44] stated:

> The union is right in its contention that employees with a similar degree of guilt should be similarly penalized and that a few should not be arbitrarily chosen to serve as examples for the many.

Some arbitrators who subscribe to the "even-handed" discipline principle in the cases in which an employee has breached the no-strike provision almost uniformly hold that an employer may employ selective discharges in such cases because an employer can hardly be required to discharge all of the employees in an attempt to satisfy the "even-handed" discipline mandate. In a conceptually unsatisfying attempt to cling to the notion that employees who breach the labor agreement by participating in a wildcat strike are actually being discharged, these arbitrators state that the selective process employed by employers must not be capricious or discriminatory. For example, arbitrators have upheld employers in "discharging" employees who led, instigated, or most actively participated in the wildcat strike. Even this standard can lead to an unsatisfactory result, however. In many instances, the employer will not know which employees were not at fault for an illegal work stoppage, or will make errors when selecting those thought to be the most active. Arbitrator Leonard Oppenheim, in *Magnavox Co.*, [45] noted the absurd result that could occur if the "capricious" test were carried to its logical extreme in a wildcat strike situation, and indicated that a wise tolerance must be allowed because the employer may not know who the leaders were:

> In passing on disciplinary action after a strike in breach of the labor agreement and which has subverted the no-strike commitment of the Union, Arbitrators have held that in these situations the Employer may properly engage in selective discipline. Thus, an employer who is the victim of such a strike is not required to deprive itself of all employees participating in the strike and it may select those for punishment for the offense as it sees fit, provided such selection is not capricious.

Arbitrator John P. Horlacher, in *Kaye-Tex Mfg. Co.*, [46] recognized that the "even-handed" principle can create a trap that could well make the prohibitions in the "no-strike clause" unenforceable by employee discipline, if an employer is required to identify *all* the in-

---

[44]*General Motors Corp.* (Seward) quoted in *Stockham Pipe Fittings Co.*, 4 LA 744, 746 (McCoy, 1946). *See also Kaye-Tex Mfg. Co.*, 36 LA 660 (Horlacher, 1960); *South Side Dye House, Inc.*, 10 LA 533 (Myers, 1948); *Brewer Dry Rock Co.*, 9 LA 845 (Copelof, 1948); *Art Metal Works, Inc.*, 8 LA 340 (Kirsh, 1947); *Simplicity Pattern Co.*, 7 LA 180 (Wolff, 1947); *Stockham Pipe Fittings Co.*, 4 LA 744 (McCoy, 1946); *Argonne Worsted Co.*, 4 LA 81 (Copelof, 1946).

[45]AAA Case No. 111-8 (Oppenheim, 1967).

[46]36 LA 660, 663–664 (Horlacher, 1960).

stigators or *all* those who were active in the strike, etc. He proposed the following standard in this regard:

> 3. An interpretation making the no-strike clauses of the Agreement a nullity must be rejected. Something short of a universal flat penalty is permissible provided *the basis of selection makes sense and is not patently and avoidably unfair.* [Emphasis added.]

Arbitrator Horlacher then explained the reasons for the wide tolerance in the selection standard:

> 2. Adoption of the Union view that the Company must equally penalize everyone who participated in the walkout—using participation in its simplist sense as failure to report for work during the two days of the stoppage—would convert the no-strike provisions of the contract into a nullity. The entire work force participated, in the sense indicated. A three-day suspension for the whole group would mean a three-day loss of production on top of the two days of the wildcat. This would be so grievous for the Company it would decline to apply such a penalty.[47]

Arbitrator Harry P. Shulman, in *Ford Motor Co.*,[48] recognized these discipline problems in wildcat strikes years ago:

> It will serve no useful purpose to relate in detail the evidence with respect to the nineteen employees against whom the company took action as a result of this stoppage. It is loudly whispered—and doubtless truly—that the real instigators of the stoppage, or at least some of them, have not been penalized. But if this is so, it is because the Company lacked knowledge of the alleged real instigators. The employees upon whom it imposed penalties are those against whom it had evidence of active participation which it believed would support its judgment in the ultimate proceedings before the Umpire. If the real instigators have been omitted, they are still subject to the Union's own powers of discipline. And perhaps more accurate findings of guilt could have been made in the first place if the Union had fully assumed responsibility for investigating the stoppage and taking action against the violators.

Arbitrator Horlacher explained in *Kaye-Tex Mfg. Co., supra*, that he would not approve discipline of employees in wildcat strike situations on a capricious basis such as disciplining participants who have names starting with K, L or M, or only those who are six feet tall, but that he would approve a selection of participants that is the "most reasonable that can be devised under the circumstances." In its selection, "the Company is not under a duty to be absolutely just regardless of how feasible this is. It is only under a duty to be as just as is

---

[47]*Id.* at 663. *See also Schult Homes Corp.*, 76-1 ARB ¶ 8062 (Boals, 1975).
[48]*Ford Motor Co.*, 1 ALAA ¶ 67 at 278 (Shulman, 1945).

reasonably possible under the circumstances."[49] In attempting to explain what he meant, Arbitrator Horlacher pointed to Arbitrator Lehoczky's approval in another case of the discharge of "the first major group who walked off" even though this was the "sole difference between them and the rest of the three hundred [who participated in the strike]."[50]

The requirement that there be some logic to the selection from within the larger group of participants to be discharged has often caused employers to discharge union stewards and officers if they participate in the strike. This is not because the employer can prove that each steward and officer individually instigated the strike, but because, as union officers, they are presumed to be the leaders and are presumed to be cognizant of the obligations created by the labor agreement, making their participation a more serious industrial offense.[51]

A union committeeman in the welding department of Bethlehem Steel Corporation participated with other employees in a wildcat strike (a violation of the labor agreement). For his participation, the company suspended him for ten days whereas the rank-and-file strikers were suspended for only five days.

The union committeeman filed a charge with the NLRB and the Board decided that the distinction between the union official and the rank-and-file strikers was an unfair labor practice and the committeeman should be given back pay for five days.[52] On appeal to the circuit court the Board's decision was reversed; in *Fournelle v. NLRB*[53] the court explained that a difference in the discipline of union officials and rank-and-file strikers was lawful because "the collective bargaining process has imposed a higher duty on union officials to comply with the provisions in the labor agreement."[54]

Judge Harry Edwards, who before his appointment to the bench had been a labor law teacher in two universities and a busy labor arbitrator, prepared the opinion in *Fournelle*, and what he wrote is significant: the construction of a contract clause by a labor arbitrator now takes a primary status over a different construction by the panel of the National Labor Relations Board.

---

[49]36 LA at 665.

[50]*Goodyear Atomic Corp.*, 27 LA 321, 324 (Lehoczky, 1956).

[51]*General American Transportation Corp.*, 42 LA 142 (Pollock, 1964). *See also Amanda Bent Bolt Co. v. Automobile Workers, Local 1549*, 451 F.2d 1277, 79–80, 79 LRRM 2023 (6th Cir. 1971); *Phillip Morris, USA*, 66 LA 626 (Beckman, 1976).

[52]*Bethlehem Steel Corp.*, 252 NLRB No. 138, 105 LRRM 1441 (1980). Violations of §§ 8(a) (1) and 8(a) (3) of the National Labor Relations Act were found.

[53]670 F.2d 331, 109 LRRM 2441 (D.C. Cir. 1982).

[54]*Id.*, 109 LRRM at 2449.

Arbitrator Lawrence E. Seibel acting as a regular umpire had explained in an earlier arbitration award[55] that a union official *does* have a higher duty than a rank-and-file member to comply with the no-strike clause of the labor agreement between Bethlehem Steel Corporation and the union, and Judge Edwards said this construction determined the meaning rather than that of the Board, in spite of the fact that a construction by a labor arbitrator is not binding on other labor arbitrators in later cases. He explained:

> We need not engage in an unaided examination of the contract to determine whether Bethlehem and the IUMSW agreed that union officials could be more harshly punished. All we need decide is whether to give effect to an arbitration decision, construing the same no-strike clause at issue here but involving a different grievance claim. This arbitration decision explicitly held that union officials working under the Bethlehem-IUMSW agreement have higher duties during strikes than rank-and-file employees, and that breach of those duties may subject union officials to more severe discipline.[56]

Judge Edwards also explained that the arbitrator had rendered a binding arbitration decision "based on facts virtually indistinguishable from those in the present case." In that case the union official in another department had also been suspended for ten days when the rank-and-file strikers had been suspended for only five days.

Judge Edwards' quoting of the words written by Arbitrator Seibel in the award make the decision even more significant. The arbitrator wrote:

> [T]here is no evidence that [G——], as a Shop Steward, took any action whatsoever to discourage the men from leaving and while he may well have not been the instigator nevertheless his inactivity could well be viewed as an encouragement or at least as representing tacit approval of what was happening. As Shop Steward he was under an obligation to seek to dissuade the employees in the shop under his jurisdiction from taking any illegal work stoppage action and evidence in this regard that he did so is completely lacking. In my opinion, Grievant [G——'s] action or lack of actions cannot be regarded in the same vein as that of other employees. He had a greater obligation than they to make an effort to preclude violation of the Agreement and in this respect he failed to meet such obligation. Accordingly, the imposition of an additional five day suspension does not appear to me to be unwarr[a]nted.[57] [Emphasis in decision omitted.]

---

[55]*Sparrows Point Shipyard, Bethlehem Steel Corp.* (Seibel, 1977), cited and quoted, 670 F.2d at 342, 109 LRRM 2449.

[56]670 F.2d at 341–42, 109 LRRM at 2449.

[57]*Id.*

Judge Edwards explained in a footnote:

> It is irrelevant that Umpire Seibel did not undertake a chapter-and-verse exegesis of the contractual document in rendering his decision. As the Supreme Court has stated, the arbitrator may fill "[g]aps" in the agreement" by reference to the practices of the particular industry and of the various shops covered by the agreement." Steelworkers v. Warrior & Gulf Navigation Co., 363 U.S. 574, 580, 46 LRRM 2416 (1960). In proceedings to enforce arbitration awards, the Court has held, even though "an arbitrator is confined to interpretation and application of the collective bargaining agreement," and "does not sit to dispense his own brand of industrial justice," courts should enforce an award "so long as it draws its essence from the collective bargaining agreement." Steelworkers v. Enterprise Wheel & Car Corp., 363 U.S. 593, 597, 46 LRRM 2423 (1960).[58]

Various arbitrator awards have been vacated by the NLRB after the disappointed grievant files a charge merely by the Board's not deferring to the award.[59]

Judge Edwards went on to say that the construction given provisions in labor agreements has a *stare decisis* effect binding on the Board:

> The parties to the collective bargaining agreement in the present case would no doubt be highly displeased if arbitral *stare decisis* were as inconstant a doctrine as Fournelle and the Board would have us believe. The whole function of arbitration as a "vehicle by which meaning and content are given to the collective bargaining agreement" would be impaired if the parties could not rely on a settled construction of their agreement. It is instructive to note that neither of the *parties* to this agreement—Bethlehem and the IUMSW—has challenged Umpire Seibel's construction of the no-strike clause.[60]

To avoid the problems that flow from the view that all participants should be given an equal penalty, one employer discharged all participants and then re-employed those individuals he wished to.[61] Such an action, taken to establish identical discipline for all participants, results in the loss of seniority for all re-employed workers because they re-enter as new hires.

Some courts and arbitrators avoid the confusion arising from the equality-of-discipline principle in contract-breach strike situations by holding that participation in the strike severs the employment relationship. The Supreme Court is in accord with this second view. In *NLRB v. Sands Mfg. Co.*[62] the Court said:

---

[58]*Id.* n. 20.
[59] See discussion under "Vacation by Nondeferral by the NLRB" in Chapter XXI.
[60] 670 F.2d at 345, 109 LRRM at 2451.
[61]*National Lock Co.,* Grievance Nos. 195, 196 (Rader, Aug. 3, 1949) (unpublished).
[62] 306 U.S. 332, 344, 4 LRRM 530 (1939).

Respondent rightly understood that the men were irrevocably committed not to work in accordance with their contract. It was at liberty to treat them as having severed their relations with the company because of their breach....

Likewise, the Seventh Circuit, in *NLRB v. Columbian Enameling & Stamping Company*,[63] explained that employees who strike in violation of their contract engage in an act that breaks the employment relationship:

What is the status of a group of employees who in the face of such a definite agreement left their employment?...

...

...[T]hey went on strike ... in the face of their agreement— "There shall be no stoppage of work by either party to the contract, pending decision by the Committee of Arbitration."

In the face of such an agreement, were they strikers, that is, was there an employer-employee relationship existing, when they quit work? Did the status of employer-employee continue as to them after they quit?

We must answer this question in the negative.[64]

In another case the D.C. Circuit court said:

In our view the strike of April 25 was a breach of the 1946 contract which was still in force on that date....

...[T]he Company was at liberty to treat the employees as having severed their relations with the Company because of their breach of contract....[65]

And in still another case the Sixth Circuit court said:

If the strike was one in violation of the Union's contract with the Respondent... there was no duty on the part of the Respondent to consider the strikers as employees....[66]

Under the law, as promulgated by the Supreme Court and other courts, a contract-breach striker acquires the same status as an individual who is recorded as a *quit*. The doctrine of equality of penalty applied by arbitrators in discharge cases is not a doctrine that would be applied if the legal principles discussed *supra* were employed. Arbitrator Francis Hauser, following the principles evaluated in the courts, said in *Interstate Plating Co.*:[67]

[C——] and [M——] by participating in an unauthorized strike terminated their employee relations with the Company, and so did the other

---

[63] 96 F.2d 948, 2 LRRM 727 (7th Cir. 1938), *aff'd.*, 306 U.S. 292, 4 LRRM 524 (1939).
[64] 96 F.2d at 953, 2 LRRM at 730-731.
[65] *Boeing Airplane Co. v. NLRB*, 174 F.2d 988, 991, 24 LRRM 2101, 2104 (D.C. Cir. 1949).
[66] *NLRB v. Deena Artware*, 198 F.2d 645, 651, 30 LRRM 2479, 2483 (6th Cir. 1952), *cert. denied*, 345 U.S. 906, 31 LRRM 2444 (1953).
[67] 7 LA 583, 585 (Hauser, 1947). *See also Stone and Webster Engineering Corp.*, 77-1 ARB ¶ 8117 (McCoy, 1977).

participants. Management's discretion with respect to rehiring the strikers was not restricted by the terms of the collective agreement; it could rehire none, or all, or—as has been the case—reemploy those who reported for work up to a certain date, while refusing to hire latecomers.

Arbitrator Herbert Blumer in *Carnegie-Illinois Steel Corp.*[68] explained that the fact that other employees who participated in a contract-breach strike were permitted to return to employment after the strike does not create a reemployment right for other participants who were not permitted to return:

[T]he participation of other employees in the work stoppage and strike lessen in no way the fact that the aggrieved employee committed an unquestioned violation of the agreement.

Arbitrator James J. Healy, in *U.S. Rubber Co.*,[69] refused to reinstate grievants who violated a no-strike clause:

The arbitrator has no way of knowing what type of thinking motivates the members of a bargaining unit to walk off their jobs whenever they feel like it. But the time has certainly arrived when they should be apprised in the most forceful manner possible that they have entered into a contract with a Company, one of the specific provisions of which denies them the privilege of such individual action.... In the instant case, employees who consider themselves aggrieved seek relief when they themselves have violated the contract.

Back Pay Awards

Arbitrators hold that the power to decide that there is insufficient cause to support the discipline imposed includes the power to award back pay to remedy the wrong.[70] Arbitrator Fred Witney in *Cincinnati Cleaning & Finishing Machinery Co.*[71] rejected a company argument that he did not have authority to award back pay to an employee he found to have been discharged without proper cause because the labor agreement did not contain a provision granting him authority to award retroactive pay:

In this case, the Company violated Section 6 of the Labor Agreement when it discharged the grievant without proper cause. Under these cir-

---

[68]5 LA 363, 368 (Blumer, 1946).

[69]8 LA 44, 48 (Healy, 1947).

[70]*See generally* Wolff, *The Power of the Arbitrator to Make Monetary Awards*, Labor Arbitration—Perspectives And Problems, Proceedings of the Seventeenth Annual Meeting, National Academy of Arbitrators, M. Kahn, ed. (Washington: BNA Books, 1964), pp. 176, 178–80.

[71]66-3 ARB ¶ 8876 (Witney, 1966); *see also Minute Maid Co. v. Citrus, Cannery, Food Processing, & Allied Workers, Local 444*, 331 F.2d 280, 56 LRRM 2095 (5th Cir. 1964).

cumstances, the grievant deserves a meaningful remedy which is reinstate-ment on the job and with back pay. Indeed, if the parties actually intended that employees discharged without proper cause are only to be reinstated to the job, but without back pay, they would have adopted unambiguous language to accomplish this objective. Language such as the following would be required:

...."[I]f an arbitrator finds that an employee is discharged without pro-per cause, the arbitrator shall reinstate such employee to his job, but with-out back pay."

...

No such restrictive language, of course, appears in either Section 6 or in Section 20 of the Labor Agreement. Therefore, the Arbitrator finds that he has the authority to award back pay under the circumstances of this case. To hold otherwise would fly in the face of a most settled principle of the arbitration process. It would be as if in a civil proceeding a court would find for the plaintiff, but refuse to award monetary damages so as to make the plaintiff financially whole for an injury caused by the defendant.[72]

Arbitrator Archibald Cox observed in *Electric Storage Battery Co.*[73] that back pay awards, when a dischargee is reinstated, are punitive for the company as well as compensatory for the employee because:

[T]he company pays twice when it improperly discharges a man or violates his seniority. It pays back wages and also pays the person who took the grievant's place. And the "only justification for an award of back pay is that there is no method of doing perfect justice." Thus the dilemma lies in being forced to choose between denying the employee an adequate remedy or forcing the employer to pay twice for the same work. When the em-ployer causes the loss, however innocently, it is more just that he should bear the cost of making the employee whole than that the employee should be forced to suffer a denial of contract rights without a remedy.

Reductions in the Amount of Back Pay

Arbitrators have reduced the amount of back pay even though the discharge is found to be without just cause where (i) the grievant or the union was guilty of unusual delay in seeking arbitration or in selecting

[72]66-3 ARB at 6045. *See also American Oil Co.*, 37 LA 487 (Edelman, 1961); *Jeffrey Mfg. Co.*, 34 LA 814 (Kuhn, 1960); *Elberta Crate & Box Co.*, 32 LA 228 (Murphy, 1959). The princi-ple of these decisions has been sustained in several court cases. *See, e.g., Minute Maid Co. v. Citrus, Cannery, Food Processing, & Allied Workers, Local 444*, 331 F.2d 280, 56 LRRM 2095 (5th Cir. 1964); *Machinists, Lodge 12 v. Cameron Iron Works, Inc.*, 292 F.2d 112, 48 LRRM 2516 (5th Cir. 1961), *cert. denied*, 368 U.S. 926, 49 LRRM 2173 (1961).
[73]AAA Case No. 19-22 (Cox, 1960). *See also Charles Taylor & Sons Co.*, AAA Case No. 35-16 (Sanders, 1961).

the arbitrator,[74] (ii) the grievant had outside wage earnings which should be deducted,[75] (iii) the dischargee "failed to seek other employment which would have mitigated the amount of back pay,"[76] and (iv) the grievant had a poor attendance record.[77]

In reducing back pay awards by the amount of an employee's interim earnings, arbitrators have disagreed, however, as to how much outside pay should be deducted. It has been held that the deduction should not include overtime earnings which the dischargee earned from another employer.[78] Where an employee worked part-time at another company prior to his discharge and then began working full time at that company, only those hours worked in excess of his regular working hours could be used to mitigate damages, an arbitrator held.[79] Arbitrator Abernethy wrote in *A. H. Bello Corp.*[80] that the calculation of back pay, if it is awarded, will normally include overtime and shift premiums which would have been earned.[81]

---

[74]*Koppers Co.*, 65-1 ARB ¶ 8013 (Loucks, 1964); *U.S. Industrial Chemical Co.*, 62-2 ARB ¶ 8666 (Nichols, 1962); *Gulf States Utilities*, 62-2 ARB ¶ 8548 (Autrey, 1962); *Valve Corp. of America*, 61-2 ARB ¶ 8591 (Stutz, 1961); *Hale Bros. Stores*, 32 LA 713 (Ross, 1959). *But see Thorsen Mfg. Co.*, 55 LA 581 (Koven, 1970); *W. Va. Pulp & Paper Co.*, 62-3 ARB ¶ 8753 (Stark, 1962).

[75]*See, e.g., Commercial Warehouse Co.*, 62 LA 1015 (Sater, 1974); *Keystone Steel & Wire Co.*, 65-2 ARB ¶ 8786 (Dougherty, 1965); *Gulfport Shipbuilding Corp.*, 64-3 ARB ¶ 9233 (Ray, 1964); *Bethlehem Fabricators, Inc.*, 63-2 ARB ¶ 8728 (Schedler, 1962). *But see United States Steel Corp.*, 40 LA 1036 (McDermott, 1963). In *Steelworkers v. Enterprise Wheel & Car Corp.*, 363 U.S. 593, 46 LRRM 2423 (1960), the court held that the grievant should be reinstated with back pay for the time lost but with a deduction for amounts received by the grievant from other employment. The duty of an employee unlawfully discharged under the National Labor Relations Act to mitigate his damages in a back pay award was affirmed in *Phelps Dodge Corp. v. NLRB*, 313 U.S. 177, 8 LRRM 439 (1941). *See also* Teele, *But No Back Pay is Awarded* ..., 19 Arb. J. 103, 107 (1964); Gorske, *Arbitration of Back-Pay Awards*, 10 Lab. L.J. 18 (1959).

[76]*See, e.g., Master Carbide Co.*, AAA Case No. 140-5 (Cole, 1970); *Allegheny Airlines, Inc.*, 67-1 ARB ¶ 8244 (Kelliher, 1967); Flintkote Co., 66-3 ARB ¶ 8895 (Merrill, 1966); *E. F. Hauserman Co.*, 66-3 ARB ¶ 8887 (Gibson, 1966); *Hall-Omar Baking Co.*, 62-3 ARB ¶ 8926 (Hampton, 1962); *General Tel. Co. of Ind.*, AAA Case No. 50-1 (Chalfie, 1962); *but see Crowell-Collier Broadcasting Corp.*, 65-2 ARB ¶ 8739 (Jones, 1965). The NLRB, with the affirmance of the courts, has also held that an employee should not be entitled to full back pay where there is a willfully incurred loss. *NLRB v. Mastro Plastics Corp.*, 354 F.2d 170, 60 LRRM 2578 (2d Cir. 1965), *cert. denied*, 384 U.S. 972, 62 LRRM 2292 (1966).

[77]*Alliance Mfg. Co.*, 61 LA 101 (Gibson, 1973); *but see McCreary Tire and Rubber Co.*, 77-1 ARB ¶ 8218 (Lewinter, 1977).

[78]*Foote Bros. Gear & Machine Corp.*, 1 LA 561 (Courshon, 1945).

[79]*American Iron & Machine Works Co.*, 19 LA 417 (Merrill, 1952).

[80]65-2 ARB ¶ 8711 (Abernethy, 1965).

[81]*See, e.g., McCreary Tire & Rubber Co.*, 77-1 ARB ¶ 8218 (LeWinter, 1977) (overtime, shift preferential and incentive pay premiums); *Towmotor Corp.*, 66-3 ARB ¶ 9028 (Kates, 1966) (shift premium); *Allen Warehouse Co.*, 63-2 ARB ¶ 8623 (Koven, 1963) (overtime would regularly have been worked); *Brass-Craft Mfg. Co.*, 61-3 ARB ¶ 8743 (Kahn, 1961) (bonus payments). *But cf. Alliance Mfg. Co.*, 61 LA 101 (Gibson, 1973) (overtime too speculative); *Standard Brands, Inc.*, 57 LA 449 (Nicholas, 1971) (no showing of expected overtime); *Shenango, Inc.*, 66-3 ARB ¶ 8748 (McDermott, 1966) (regular rate, not rate of probable assignments).

Arbitrators have struggled over the question of whether unemployment compensation during the period of layoff or suspension should be deducted from a back pay award.[82] Under one view, unemployment compensation is a financial benefit and should be deducted. The view was aptly stated by Arbitrator Ted T. Tsukiyama in *Hawaiian Telephone Co.*:[83]

> Under the Hawaii Employment Security Law, benefits are paid out of a fund contributed to only by the employer and not the employees, hence the benefits are not as "collateral" or indirect as may appear at first blush.... From the standpoint of the employee involved, payment received, whether by way of paycheck or by employment compensation, represents good, sound American dollar values in the pocket, either way. Thus, the classification of unemployment compensation payment as being "collateral" rather than a direct benefit appears too fine and esoteric a distinction to make in deciding this controversy, particularly when the controlling test or criteria in attempting to make an employee "whole" is to make him "FINANCIALLY WHOLE"....

Other arbitrators have treated unemployment compensation as a collateral benefit which is not deductible from back pay for time lost. Thus, Arbitrator Wagner, in *National Rejectors, Inc.*,[84] said:

> To the employee who receives them, the benefits are income. To the employer of the employee, they represent costs since the fund [sic] from which they are paid are built up by employer contributions. Yet the payments are made by a public agency to carry out a public policy. In this sense, they are not payments made by the employer for work performed by an employee. They are collateral benefits and not earnings and therefore should be disregarded in a situation in which an employee is to be made whole by the employer just as collateral costs are disregarded for the same purpose.

---

[82]*See generally Back Pay Awards and Unemployment Insurance Benefits*, 4 ARB. J. 268 (1949); Gorske, note 75 *supra*, at 26-27. In the 1971 can industry and aluminum industry settlements with the United Steelworkers, the parties agreed that "earnings or money" received by the employee between his discharge or suspension and reinstatement are not deductions if back pay is awarded. *Agreement Between Reynolds Metals Co. and United Steelworkers*, June 1, 1971, Article XI, Section 4; *Agreement Between American Can Company and United Steelworkers*, February 15, 1971, Article 15.5.

[83]65-2 ARB ¶ 8695 (Tsukiyama, 1965) at 5559. See also *Mueller Industries, Inc., Love Bros. Div.*, 45 LA 751 (Solomon, 1965); *Gusdorf & Sons*, 64-1 ARB ¶ 8043 (Stix, 1963); *American Chain & Cable Co.*, 40 LA 312 (McDermott, 1963); *Continental Can Co.*, 39 LA 821 (Sembower, 1962); *Pittsburgh-Des Moines Steel Co.*, 38 LA 148 (Wood, 1962); *Kroger Co.*, 12 LA 1065 (Blair, 1949).

[84]38 LA 1091, 1092 (Wagner, 1962). *See also Littleford Bros.*, 62-3 ARB ¶ 8840 (Warns, 1962); *International Harvester Co.*, 16 LA 376 (Seward, 1951). These cases rely on *NLRB v. Gullett Gin Co.*, 340 U.S. 361, 27 LRRM 2230 (1951), which held unemployment compensation payments were "collateral benefits" and hence not deductible from an NLRB back pay order. *See also Machinists, Local Lodge 790 v. Champion Carrier, Inc.*, 470 F.2d 744, 82 LRRM 2160 (10th Cir. 1972); *Union Carbide Corp.*, 56 LA 707 (Williams, 1971).

Certainly, in the author's opinion, if the intent of back pay is to make the grievant financially whole, unemployment compensation payments should be deducted. This seems reasonable given the fact that these payments are indirectly based on employer contributions. Some arbitrators determine the subtraction issue by applying the method of calculating used in state refunding statutes. For example, the Pennsylvania statute provides:

> [I]n the absence of misrepresentation or nondisclosure of a material fact, no recoupment shall be had if such overpayment is created by reason of... (2) a retroactive allocation of wages pursuant to an award of a labor relations board arbitrator or the like, unless such award provides for the repayment of unemployment compensation benefits received during the period to which such payments are allocated.[85]

Full back pay was not awarded to a grievant discharged following a report by the company doctor that he was suffering from a disabling heart condition, a report subsequently proven to be incorrect. The arbitrator held that the back pay should start from the date the company received the report of the employee's personal doctor challenging the validity of the diagnosis. After that date, there was a "strong preponderance of medical evidence" against the company doctor's finding that a disability did exist.

Arbitrator Hogan in *Shahmoon Industries*[86] rejected the union's contention that back pay should start at the time the grievant was being recalled from layoff but was not reinstated because the company's doctor found the grievant not medically fit for reinstatement, which finding was not established at the hearing. A provision for back pay in cases where a discharge is found to be unjust was applied when the failure to reinstate was found to be unjust:

> The injustice to the employee from the standpoint of back pay occurred when he was kept from working after the Company was told of his doctors' reports; after the Company was aware that the doctors disagreed and after the Company had had a chance to consider the Union's proposal to settle the disagreement by an impartial examination by a specialist.

Similarly, in a case where an employee was discharged because of a fainting spell at his home which revealed a cardiovascular condition, but with insubstantial evidence of the probability of death or permanent injury if the employee resumed his duties, the employee was rein-

---

[85]Pa. Cons. Stat. tit. 43, § 874 (1964); *see* Wolff, note 70 *supra*, at p. 185. *See also Universal Producing Co.*, 57 LA 1072 (Sembower, 1971).

[86]AAA Case No. 19-8 (Hogan, 1960).

stated, but without back pay. Arbitrator Millard L. Midonick, in *Carborundrum Co.*,[87] explained why back pay was not ordered:

> The medical evidence favoring the employee's contentions as presented at the hearing in this arbitration are much more impressive than the earlier presentations of expert opinion evidence made by the Union to the Company at any time prior to these hearings.... The Company... had a right to rely upon the only substantial scientific medical opinion available to it at the time of discharge.

Arbitrator Naehring in *Air Carrier Engine Services*[88] awarded only one-half the amount of accrued back wages where neither the union nor the employer had complied with the labor agreement procedure that required, if there was a dispute, that a third physician prepare an opinion to determine the employee's fitness or lack thereof to return to work.

Arbitrator John F. Sembower in *Cleveland Cliffs Iron Co.*[89] held that no back pay was due an employee sent home by a supervisor who, in good faith, concluded the employee was intoxicated, even though the arbitrator concluded that other evidence did not support the supervisor's judgment. Arbitrator Sembower analogized his refusal to award back pay to the law's refusal to allow an employee-driver who was arrested by a police officer for driving after drinking to sue for false arrest even though it was later legally established that the employee-driver had not been drinking. The company, Sembower said, cannot be penalized when a supervisor in his best judgment believes an employee has been drinking; the loss of income is an "unfortunate consequence" of an incident for which no one is technically to blame. In a similar set of facts, Arbitrator Rayson in *Memphis Light, Gas & Water Div.*[90] awarded less than the full amount of back pay because the employer had "probable cause" to believe that the grievant had violated the rule that no employee can report to work under the influence of alcohol, where the penalty for this transgression was termination.

The Amount Due

The arbitrator need not compute the back pay of each grievant in the award, it being sufficient to supply a specific formula. One court said the arbitrator need not have

> gone through the accounting process of computing precisely how much back pay each aggrieved employee is entitled to receive, or how much

---

[87]AAA Case No. 35-11 (Midonick, 1961).
[88]65 LA 666 (Naehring, 1975).
[89]52 LA 435 (Sembower, 1969).
[90]66 LA 948 (Rayson, 1976).

must be deducted by reason of wages earned elsewhere during the period these employees were wrongfully deprived of employment. A good faith compliance with the award by both parties eliminates the necessity of the arbitrator considering such petty, ministerial computations.[91]

In *Pelletier v. Auclair Transportation, Inc.*,[92] an arbitration board ordered the company to reinstate two employees and pay them the earnings that would have been paid if they had not been discharged. No settlement was reached and the arbitration board resumed jurisdiction and awarded each employee $1,000. The employees then sought to set aside the award on the ground that the amounts were merely a compromise rather than a determination of actual amounts due and that their evidence showed that they were due $9,209.24 and $7,683.25, respectively, and that the employer's own evidence showed that they were entitled to more than $1,000 each. The court sustained the awards because the arbitration board had the authority to decide the amounts due upon "principles of equity and good conscience" and hence the board did not exceed its power.

Interest on Back Pay (and on Other Payments)

Another area of disagreement involves awarding interest on back pay and on other payments. In *Allied Chemical Corp.*[93] Arbitrator Hilpert ordered that interest be paid on back pay because:

> Although interest on the monetary relief, due to a wrongfully suspended, or wrongfully discharged, employee has seldom been awarded, it has also seldom been requested; but it is a part of the "common law" damages for wrongful suspensions or discharge; and, in the absence of language in a collective bargaining agreement to the contrary (as there may be, here, respecting a wrongfully discharged employee), the arbitration process should, and does, recognize the "common law" relief.
>
> Hence, the Chairman concludes that the Arbitration Board may award [H——] interest, on his monetary award, at the rate of 6% per annum, computed from the day the involved wages would otherwise have been paid to the day the check to him is issued.

---

[91]*Steelworkers v. Enterprise Wheel & Car Corp.*, 168 F. Supp. 308, 43 LRRM 2291 (S.D. W. Va. 1958). *See also Reynolds Metals Co.*, 54 LA 1187 (Purdom, 1970); *All States Trailer Co.*, 44 LA 104 (Leflar, 1965); *General Electric Co.*, 39 LA 897 (Hilpert, 1962). *See generally* remarks of David Feller, former Steelworkers general counsel, who rejects the view that back pay is an award of money damages: Feller, Discussion of Wolff, *The Power of the Arbitrator to Make Monetary Awards*, note 70 *supra*, at p. 193; Youngdahl, *Awarding Interest in Labor Arbitration Cases*, 54 KY. L.J. 717 (Summer, 1966).
[92]250 A.2d 834, 70 LRRM 3261 (N.H. Sup. Ct. 1969).
[93]66-3 ARB ¶ 9022 (Hilpert, 1966) at 6650.

The opposite position was taken by Arbitrator Sanford H. Kadish in *Intermountain Operators League:*[94]

> The important point is that it is not customary in arbitrations for the arbitrator to grant interest on claims which he finds owing. If the contract or submission agreement had expressly authorized the arbitrator to grant interest, the matter would be different. In view, however, of the almost unanimous practice on the part of arbitrators not to grant interest, and the failure of the parties to authorize the arbitrator to do so here, I would think it highly inappropriate to do so. Certainly the Union has presented no reason for awarding interest in this case which can not be said to apply equally in any arbitration where a sum of money is involved.

As noted earlier, Arbitrator Archibald Cox in *Electric Storage Battery Co.*[95] explained that an award of back pay to an employee who has been discharged is a double payment by the employer, since the dischargee performed no work and another employee was paid to perform the work in his or her stead. An order of back pay to the reinstated dischargee requires the employer to pay twice for the same work. Hence, adding interest on the back pay merely increases the effect beyond double payment. Arbitrators usually add interest not as a right but as a type of additional penalty. For example, Arbitrator Thomas J. McDermott in *American Chain & Cable Co.*[96] assessed interest because there was evidence of employer arbitrariness:

> The demand for payment of interest on the monies due is one that is only occasionally raised in arbitration cases, which involve damages. It is, however, a demand that can only be granted under very special circumstances. As an example, if it can be shown that a Company acted in a very arbitrary fashion in its handling of a case, so that the logical conclusion could be drawn that the Company was deliberately trying to injure the affected employees, an arbitrator might find cause for inclusion of interest as a part of damages. In the instant case I can find no evidence of a lack of good faith. The delay in the resolution of the case has resulted from a failure of the parties to agree, and not for any other motive.
>
> . . .
>
> Also, while the workers being recompensed in this case are receiving at the most only what they would have gotton had the cut-back not taken place, they still are obtaining a monetary return for which they did not actually work. Therefore, while these workers have had to suffer a delay in

---

[94]26 LA 149, 154–55 (Kadish, 1956). *See also Berg Mfg. & Sales Co., Inc.*, 71-1 ARB ¶ 8294 (Anrod, 1971).

[95]AAA Case No. 19-22 (Cox, 1960).

[96]40 LA 312, 315 (McDermott, 1963). In *Isis Plumbing & Heating Co.*, 138 NLRB No. 97 (1962), *rev'd on other grounds*, 322 F.2d 913 (9th Cir. 1963), the NLRB reversed its longstanding policy by awarding interest.

the receipt of their compensation, this loss of time is offset by the above gain.

Arbitrator Sandler in *Smithtown Nursing Home*[97] awarded interest on contributions to employee benefit and pension funds when he found they were wrongly withheld. This seems to suggest that the granting of the grievance is proof that the employer was acting "wrongfully."

Finding that an employer violated the contractual seniority provisions when it laid off senior white employees rather than junior black employees, Arbitrator Milton T. Edelman, in *Hollander & Co.*,[98] ordered recall of the laid-off employees and awarded interest of six percent per annum on back pay from the date of layoff to the date of recall. Other arbitrators have awarded interest in what they considered extraordinary situations. Ten percent interest was awarded on back pay where the arbitrator found the employer had engaged in "dilatory tactics" in reinstating improperly discharged employees.[99] Interest from the date of discharge was awarded by another arbitrator to "fully compensate" an improperly discharged employee who alleged her supervisor had made sexual advances to her.[100] However, in *Nevada Resort Association*,[101] Arbitrator Sanford Cohen denied a claim for interest on back pay awarded to performers under a "play or pay" provision (requiring payment to entertainers upon cancellation of a performance), since the interest claim was first made *after the hearing*.

MAKE-WHOLE LIMITATIONS IN NONDISCIPLINARY CASES

Money awards (damages) have been imposed by arbitrators in nondisciplinary cases when a grievant has been financially injured as a result of a breach of the labor agreement.[102] Arbitrator Thomas T. Roberts, in *California Brewers Ass'n,*[103] has noted:

[97]65 LA 363 (Sandler, 1975).

[98]64 LA 816 (Edelman, 1975).

[99]*Farmer Bros. Co.*, 66 LA 354 (Jones, 1976).

[100]*Osborn and Ulland, Inc.*, 68 LA 1146 (Beck, 1977).

[101](Cohen, 1972) (private award).

[102]*See generally* Wolff, note 70 *supra*, at p. 176; Fleming, *Arbitrators and the Remedy Power*, 48 Va. L. Rev. 1199 (1962); Smith and Jones, *The Impact of the Emerging Federal Law of Grievance Arbitration on Judges, Arbitrators, and Parties*, 52 Va. L. Rev. 831 (1966).

[103]65-2 ARB ¶ 8603 (Roberts, 1965) at 5247. For a few of the many cases where money awards were made in nondisciplinary cases, *see Kimberly-Clark Corp.*, 61 LA 1094 (Fellman, 1973); *PPG Industries, Inc.*, 68-2 ARB ¶ 8807 (Vadakin, 1968); *Sears, Roebuck & Co.*, 39 LA 567 (Gillingham, 1962); *Standard Oil Co.*, 61-1 ARB ¶ 8013 (Karlins, 1960); *Jeffrey Mfg. Co.*, 34 LA 815 (Kuhn, 1960); *Oregonian Publishing Co.*, 33 LA 574 (Kleinsorge, 1959). This view has generally been supported by the courts. *See, e.g., Hiller v. Liquor Salesmen, Local 2*, 226 F. Supp. 161, 55 LRRM 2310 (S.D. N.Y. 1964), *rev'd on other grounds*, 338 F.2d 778, 57 LRRM 2629 (2d Cir. 1964); *Texas Gas Transmission Corp. v. Chemical Workers, Local 187*, 200 F.

[I]t is almost universally accepted that Arbitrators have the power (the Courts would say jurisdiction) to fashion remedies where a violation of the Collective Bargaining Agreement submitted to their consideration is found to exist. This remedial power includes the assessment of compensatory damages, or to use a phrase more commonly invoked, "the power to make the wronged party whole."

Arbitrator Ralph T. Seward, in *International Harvester Co.*,[104] has likewise stated:

The ordinary rule at common law and in the developing law of labor relations is that an award of damages should be limited to the amount necessary to make the injured party "whole." Unless an agreement provides that some other rule should be followed, this rule must apply.

One of the keys to affirmative relief is proof of loss. On this point, Arbitrator John R. Abersold, in *Bearing Co.*,[105] has said:

[U]nless it can be shown that the employees suffered some *actual* loss, which the Company was not justified under another provision of the Labor Agreement in requiring them to take, they have no recourse. [Emphasis in original.]

And, Arbitrator Philip G. Marshall, in *National Lead Co.*,[106] has held:

It is equally clear that no one was hurt or damaged by the misassignment made; no one was laid off; no one lost any time; and no one was deprived of overtime opportunities.

However, a request for a money award to make a party whole has been denied by arbitrators where the proof of loss is considered too speculative.[107]

CLAIMS CONSIDERED *DE MINIMIS*

The *de minimis* doctrine is a principle used by some arbitrators when they fashion a remedy. Various arbitrators have stated that the

Supp. 521, 49 LRRM 2409 (W.D. La. 1962). *But see Railroad Trainmen v. Denver & Rio Grande R.R. Co.*, 338 F.2d 407, 57 LRRM 2502 (10th Cir. 1964), *cert. denied*, 380 U.S. 972, 59 LRRM 2063, 2064 (1965), which held an employee could only recover nominal damages in the absence of proof of an actual loss.
[104] 15 LA 1 (Seward, 1950). The computation of damages is often left to the parties. *See Mallinckrodt Chemical Works*, 69-1 ARB ¶ 8352 (Goldberg, 1968); *Five Star Hardware & Electric Corp.*, 44 LA 944 (Wolff, 1965).
[105] 35 LA 569, 573 (Abersold, 1960).
[106] 36 LA 962, 964 (Marshall, 1961). *See also Harley-Davidson Motor Co.*, 63 LA 1149 (Kossoff, 1974).
[107] *See, e.g., Walker Mfg. Co.*, 42 LA 632 (Anderson, 1964); *Sylvania Electric Products, Inc.*, 37 LA 458 (Jaffee, 1961); *Sears, Roebuck & Co.*, 35 LA 757 (Miller, 1960); *Permutit Co.*, 19 LA 599 (Trotta, 1952). *But see Mallinckrodt Chemical Works*, 69-1 ARB ¶ 8352 (Goldberg, 1968). *See also Schneider v. Electric Auto-Lite*, 456 F.2d 366, 79 LRRM 2825 (6th Cir. 1972).

asserted violation did occur but have declined to grant damages because the violation was so trivial. The scope of violations that have been excused under this doctrine has been examined in a search for some consensus on the permissible amount. There is no simple answer.

In *Maui Pineapple Co.*[108] the union filed a payment claim on behalf of the pineapple trimmers and packers because they twice daily donned hairnets, powdered their hands, and slipped them into rubber gloves. The arbitrator observed that the practice had been followed for ten years and the claim for payment had never been raised before. Dismissing the claim as trivial, Arbitrator Harold Burr relied upon the Supreme Court opinion in *Anderson v. Mt. Clemens Pottery Co.*,[109] which pointed out that a wage claim under the Fair Labor Standards Act for the time required to walk from the time clock to a work station should be considered a *de minimis* claim:

> We do not, of course, preclude the application of a *de minimis* rule where the minimum walking time is such as to be negligible. The workweek contemplated by [the Act] must be computed in light of the realities of the industrial world. When the matter in issue concerns only a few seconds or minutes of work beyond the scheduled working hours, such trifles may be disregarded.

On the other hand, Arbitrator Sam Tatum in *Wheland Co.*[110] held that supervisory performance of production work for a ten-second period each day was sufficient to violate the agreement. In that case, the work involved pressing three electric buttons to start up a compressor at the beginning of a shift. Management argued that such work was patently inconsequential, but the arbitrator pointed out that the agreement provided that no supervisor at any time, other than for emergency or instructional proposes, could perform bargaining unit work, and in the face of that decision he could not consider the violation *de minimis*.

The effect of contract language upon the application of *de minimis* was pointed out by Arbitrator Eli Rock in *Air Mod, Division of Cook Electric Co.*:[111]

> It seems clear that the amount of work done by the foreman here was so small and *de minimis* in nature as to make extremely difficult any meaningful remedy to the union, absent a clause which strongly outlaws bargaining work by supervisors.

---

[108]31 LA 442 (Burr, 1958). *See also Foote Mineral Co.*, AAA Case No. 12-26 (Seibel, 1960).

[109]328 U.S. 680, 682 (1946).

[110]34 LA 904 (Tatum, 1960). *See also Imco Container Co.*, AAA Case No. 100-11 (Schmertz, 1967).

[111]AAA Case No. 24-9 (Rock, 1960). *See also Atlantic Richfield Co.*, 53 LA 958 (Duff, 1969); *Superior Fiber Products, Inc.*, 58 LA 582 (Johnson, 1972).

Similarly, in *Acheson Dispersed Pigments Co.*,[112] Arbitrator E. E. Hale said:

> Even should it be assumed this was Mechanic's work, the senior qualified Operator ... would have lost so little pay as a result of [a supervisor] doing it as to be inconsequential. *De minimis non curat lex.*

And Arbitrator James J. Healy in *New York & Pennsylvania Co.*[113] said:

> [I]t seems absurd to have some men idle and to be unable to use them for a few minutes on work other than their own, but which nevertheless they are entirely competent to do. But the union in this case is more preoccupied with principle, and technically, the union is correct and must be sustained in the basic complaint. However, the undersigned cannot bring himself to award any damages because of the *de minimis* nature of the violation.

One arbitrator explained that *de minimis* means a monetary award that would become a "trifle" that is so small that it is not "tangible."[114] Arbitrators also explain that a money award requires a "provable monetary loss." Arbitrator Lewis Amis, in *Allis-Chalmers Corp.*,[115] applied the *de minimis* principle to dismiss a grievance over work done by one foreman and to grant a grievance over work done by another foreman:

> Foreman [E——] ... operated the jib crane controls once briefly to try to assess and rectify the problem with the pinched saw blade, but he did not do more than he had a right to do in attempting to size up the situation. His *assisting the saw operator in carrying the jack* was inconsequential and does fall under the *de minimis* doctrine.
>
> Foreman [S——'s] activities, however, were of a much broader and more significant kind. He stepped in and performed work along with the rigger, [P——], and ... that was clearly of a kind normally reserved to the bargaining unit. [S——] spent about two hours at the saw actively engaged in assisting ... [P——] in turning the ring....
>
> [S——] testified that he was actually working only 20 minutes during the time he was at the saw, but if one counts waiting time, planning time, etc., the 20 minutes of actual rigging and crane operation could amount to fairly steady work over the two hour period and would explain the testimony of Union witness that he appeared to be busy most of the time.... The work in question was of a kind that should not have been assigned to a helper or the saw operator, to be sure, but it was not work that could not

[112]36 LA 578, 583-84 (Hale, 1960). *See also Consolidation Coal Co.*, 65 LA 892 (Stokes, 1975).
[113]AAA Case No. 33-16 (Healy, 1961).
[114]*DeAtley Paving & Crushing, Inc.*, 37 LA 496 (Derk, 1961).
[115]Referee Case No. 9 (Amis, Feb. 11, 1978) (unpublished).

safely have been assigned to a qualified rigger. There was no showing that anyone tried to call any additional riggers, nor was there any showing that there was any reason why riggers would not have been available if they had been called. Thus, I must rule that in working at the saw, [S——] did cross the line between what is permissible and what is not when it comes to supervisors doing bargaining unit work.

. . .

. . .[T]he Company believes the doctrine of *de minimis* applies, especially in the case of Foreman [S——'s] activities in the afternoon while he was disposing of unwanted materials and sweeping up.

. . .

. . .[G]iven the small amount of sweeping that is likely to be done by anyone but a janitor, fifteen minutes of such activity cannot be passed off as *de minimis*. Again, [S——] exceeded the bounds of his supervisory duties and invaded the area of bargaining unit prerogative. Here, the Union is quite right in identifying the work involved as something that should have been done by the helper.

Likewise relevant is the following excerpt from Arbitrator Cheney's opinion in *Continental Can Co.*:[116]

In addition he spent a total of two (2) hours during seventy-two (72) man hours worked by others, on manual production duties. Such a situation manifestly calls for the application of the familiar legal maxim *De Minimis Non Curat Lex*. Broken down into "Baseball English," and apparently the National Labor Relations Board and arbitrators as well have held, that generally they will not take trifling or immaterial matters into account, except under peculiar circumstances. The sense and connotation attributable to the arbitration decisions cited . . . is, that where trifling irregularities or infractions of the strict letter of a Collective Bargaining Agreement are brought to the attention of the Arbitrator, the maxim *De Minimis Non Curat Lex* will be applied.

But Arbitrator A. August Lanna in *Gulf States Paper Corp.*[117] rejected reliance on the *de minimis* doctrine in a case involving a supervisor performing bargaining unit work:

It was argued that the work took only a few minutes and that because the time was so miniscule and that the skills required were minimal that the supervisor therefore was not taking away from the covered employees' work which they normally enjoyed. Under different circumstances the *de minimis* theory might apply. The Arbitrator, however, could not hold to this because there was adequate time for the work to be performed.

---

[116]*Continental Can Co.*, 12 LA 422, 426–27 (Cheney, 1948).
[117]AAA Case No. 34-2 (Lanna, 1961). *See also Consolidation Coal Co.*, 65 LA 848 (Stokes, 1975); *Marion Power Shovel Co.*, 34 LA 709 (Stouffer, 1960); *Kroger Co.*, 33 LA 188 (Howlett, 1959); *Electric Auto-Lite Co.*, 30 LA 449 (Marshall, 1958).

The doctrine of *de minimis* is held not to apply when there have been repeated violations. Thus, in *Foote Mineral Co.*[118] Arbitrator Samuel Jaffee said:

> Even if the fifteen or twenty minutes involved may be considered *de minimis* I do not think that the principle has application where, as here, violations of this character (presumably also *de minimis*) have occurred repeatedly, and especially when an award to that effect has previously been issued.... The little *de minimis* "acorns" have by this time grown into an "oak" of some size.

PUNITIVE DAMAGES AND PENALTIES

Arbitrators have generally been unwilling to award punitive or exemplary damages.[119] Arbitrator J. Earl Williams in *ACF Industries, Inc.*[120] said:

> [O]ne thing that is clear in the developing body of arbitration and labor relations law is that arbitrators almost universally will refuse to award any damages which appear to be punitive.

This view is premised on the theory that punishment and retribution, which are inherent in the punitive damage concept, are foreign to the need for amicable and continuing settlement of disputes via the grievance procedure and arbitration process.[121]

A few arbitrators have awarded punitive damages in certain limited situations when an the employer was found guilty of a willful violation

---

[118]AAA Case No. 36-6 (Jaffee, 1961). *See also Foote Mineral Co.*, AAA Case No. 19-26 (Seibel, 1960); *Budd Co.*, AAA Case No. 10-8 (Gill, 1959); *Minneapolis-Honeywell Regulator Co.*, 31 LA 213 (McCormick, 1958).

[119]*See generally* Bernstein, PRIVATE DISPUTE SETTLEMENT, (New York: Free Press, 1969), pp. 584–91; Note, *Mandatory Default Provision in Arbitration Contract Held Not a Penalty*, 5 SYRACUSE L. REV. 111 (1953); Note, *Arbitration—Confirmation of Penal Awards for Breach of Contract*, 27 ST. JOHN'S L. REV. 346 (1953); Note, *Arbitration and Award*, 66 HARV. L. REV. 525 (1953).

[120]62 LA 364, 365 (Williams, 1974). *See also Consolidation Coal Co.*, 65 LA 1167, 1175 (Dworkin, 1975); *Sunstrand Corp.* 47 LA 284, 286 (Kelliher, 1966); *Pittsburgh Steel Co.*, 42 LA 1002, 1008 (McDermott, 1964); *Walker Mfg. Co.*, 42 LA 632, 637 (Anderson, 1964); *Green River Steel Corp.*, 41 LA 132, 137 (Stouffer, 1963).

[121]For a few of the many cases in which arbitrators have refused to issue an award of punitive damages, *see Corn Products Co.*, 46 LA 1073 (Rezler, 1966); *Weyerhaeuser Co.*, 46 LA 707 (Kelliher, 1966); *Walker Mfg. Co.*, 64-2 ARB ¶ 8634 (Anderson, 1964); *Celanese Fibers Co.*, 64-2 ARB ¶ 8585 (Howard, 1963); *Philip Carey Mfg. Co.*, 37 LA 134 (Gill, 1961); *A. O. Smith Corp.*, 33 LA 365 (Updegraff, 1959). Punitive damages were denied on the ground that violation was not willful, malicious, fraudulent, or in bad faith in *Ace Industries, Inc., WKM Valve Division*, 73-2 ARB ¶ 8612 (Williams, 1974); *Day and Zimmerman, Inc., Lone Star Division*, 70-2 ARB ¶ 8624 (Caraway, 1970) (relying on prior award which was not clearly erroneous); *WFMJ Broadcasting Co.*, 69-2 ARB ¶ 8612 (Belkin, 1969); *Timken-Detroit Axle Co.*, 6 LA 926 (Marshall, 1947).

of the contract.[122] An interesting example of punitive damages occurred in the second of two Bethlehem Steel arbitrations. In the first, the company had changed the dates normally set for vacations. The union demanded additional vacation pay for those employees affected. The Company argued that, inasmuch as the employees did get their vacation, albeit at an earlier date, the shift in time did not affect their total earnings. Arbitrator Ralph T. Seward, in *Bethlehem Steel Co. I*,[123] denied the grievance, explaining that he could not establish a monetary value for grievants' "mental discomfort," even though he sympathized with the employees affected. But he did issue a warning:

> And the Umpire would see nothing unreasonable or unfair in a holding that if the Company deliberately forced an employee to take an accelerated vacation in order to avoid layoffs, *knowing* that its action violated the Agreement, it would not thereby have discharged its obligations to the employees ... and could properly be required to give the employee either a further vacation on the proper dates or pay-in-lieu thereof. [Emphasis in original.]

There was a sequel to this award. The employer again rescheduled vacations. Another grievance was filed and this time Arbitrator Rolf Valtin, in *Bethlehem Steel Co. II*,[124] granted double vacation pay, holding that since Seward had issued a warning, "all concerned have known—or should have known" that forced earlier vacations were violations.

Punitive damages by the few arbitrators who have issued them have been approved by a court. A federal district court in *Sidney Wanzer & Sons v. Teamsters, Local 753*[125] refused to dismiss an award for punitive or exemplary damages, although it explained that normally excessive sanctions are prohibited as being punitive rather than remedial:

> [W]here the award is a uniquely effective device for changing a specific pattern of illegal conduct by a party before the court, it comes within the remedial purpose of the labor laws, even though the defendant may suffer as if he had been "punished" for other reasons.

---

[122]*See, e.g., Yale & Towne, Inc.*, 46 LA 4 (Duff, 1965).

[123]31 LA 857, 858 (Seward, 1958).

[124]37 LA 821, 824 (Valtin, 1961).

[125]249 F. Supp. 664, 671, 61 LRRM 2376, 2381 (N.D. Ill. 1966); *see also Patrick v. I. D. Packing Co.*, 308 F. Supp. 824, 74 LRRM 2060 (S.D. Iowa 1969). *But see Local 127, United Shoe Workers v. Brooks Shoe Mfg. Co.*, 298 F.2d 277, 49 LRRM 2346 (3d Cir. 1962); *Texas Gas Transmission Corp. v. Chemical Workers, Local 187*, 200 F. Supp. 521, 49 LRRM 2409 (W.D. La. 1961). *See generally* Bernstein, PRIVATE DISPUTE SETTLEMENT, note 119 *supra*, at p. 591; Note, *Damages—Punitive Damages for Breach of Collective Bargaining Agreement May Be Awarded Under Section 301 of Taft-Hartley Act*, 52 VA. L. REV. 1377 (1966).

The court cautioned, however:

> Such an award is extraordinary and should be reserved for those labor-management situations which cannot be pacified by other remedies.[126]

A "make whole" money remedy rather than a "punitive damages" generally has been awarded when a company violates the requirement in the agreement to distribute overtime "equally" among employees in a classification or in other groups. Where employees are not scheduled for overtime in regular rotation and a grievance is filed, the employer usually will say that the injury to the employee's earnings can be corrected by scheduling the passed-over employee for overtime work at a later date to bring the employee's amount of overtime back into balance. The union representative will reply that such a remedy means that the employer can fail to comply with a clear commitment in the agreement with impunity. In spite of this argument, most arbitrators have held that if the employer can restore equality of distribution within a reasonable time, no further remedy is necessary.[127]

The reason arbitrators do not award pay when overtime has been distributed unequally, thereby technically violating the labor agreement, was explained by Arbitrator Clarence Updegraff in *A. O. Smith Corp.*:[128]

> [O]rdinarily the assessment of damages by a court or by an arbitrator requires clear proof that the person to benefit from the payment of damages has actually suffered by the amount to be reimbursed. In the present case, there would normally be many instances where the person who was not called in his turn might first collect for the shift which he failed to work as is claimed here, and subsequently obtain his full share of the overtime of the month or quarter or year, as also was the case here.
>
> It is of course possible for parties to draft a contract authorizing an arbitrator to assess penalty payments, but since, as has very often been stated, the law abhors penalties, the language should be clear, definite and positive or the award of the arbitrator granting a penalty rather than damages would quite likely be set aside by a court reviewing the same. It is

---

[126]249 F. Supp. at 671.

[127]*See, e.g., Beryllium Corp.*, 68-2 ARB ¶ 8641 (Hardy, 1968); *Butler Mfg. Co.*, 42 LA 304 (Johnson, 1964); *Morton Salt Co.*, 42 LA 525 (Hebert, 1964); *Kimberly-Clark Corp.*, 35 LA 792 (Hawley, 1960); *Singer Mfg. Co.*, 35 LA 526 (Cahn, 1960); *Reed Roller Bit Co.*, 30 LA 437 (Hebert, 1958); *Fruehauf Trailer Co.*, 27 LA 834 (Seligson, 1957); *Goodyear Atomic Corp.*, 27 LA 634 (Shister, 1956); *Celanese Corp. of America*, 24 LA 168 (Justin, 1954); *Goodyear Tire & Rubber Co. of Ala.*, 5 LA 30 (McCoy, 1946). Sometimes restoring equality of overtime distribution is the remedy specified in the agreement, as in *Olin Mathieson Chemical Corp.*, 62-2 ARB ¶ 8566 (McGury, 1962). *But see U.S. Industrial Chemicals Co.*, 33 LA 335 (Sullivan, 1959); *Pittsburgh Plate Glass Co.*, 32 LA 622 (Sembower, 1958), to name but two cases in which arbitrators have granted monetary damages for breach of an equal distribution of overtime provision.

[128]33 LA 365, 366 (Updegraff, 1959).

to be noted that one of the positions taken by management in this case was the positive one that there is no authorization in the contract between the parties providing for the awarding of a penalty against the Company in situations like the present, or in any other.

This same principle was stated by Arbitrator George Cheney in *Mode O'Day Corp.*:[129]

> A party claiming a forfeiture or penalty under a written instrument has the burden of proving that such is the unmistakable intention of the parties to the document. In addition, the courts have ruled that a contract is not to be construed to provide a forfeiture or penalty unless no other construction or interpretation is reasonably possible. Since forfeitures are not favored either in law or in equity, courts are reluctant to declare and enforce a forfeiture if by reasonable interpretation it can be avoided.

Arbitrator Howard in *Celanese Fibers Co.*[130] said that punitive damages were only justified in an overtime distribution violation case where the action is a willful attempt to injure the employee:

> Although the Union, in effect, asks for punitive damages for violation of the cited provision, in the opinion of the undersigned arbitrator, punitive damages are out of place in the arbitration process absent a showing of a willful attempt to injure the other party by violating the Agreement. In the case at issue, the question of violation of Article 12(A) was at worst an honest difference of opinion over the Company's responsibility in this regard.

That the law abhors penalties is an important guide in fashioning remedies in arbitration. Arbitrator Klamon explained in *Gas Service Co.*[131] that even a past practice of paying penalties was insufficient to justify a penalty award:

> The Company is not required to pay anyone a penalty for time not worked. A past practice in which the Company has sometimes done so and then very often has refused to do so, can in no way be relied upon to modify the Contract. There is nothing in the Contract, as we have said, that permits the Union to claim pay for time not worked, in an emergency overtime situation such as this.

The principle of construction—that an agreement should not be construed to require a penalty if any other construction is possible—was applied by Arbitrator Peter M. Kelliher in *Alpha Cellulose Corp.*,[132] in words that in part echoed those of Arbitrator Cheney, *supra*, to reject a construction urged by an employer:

---

[129]1 LA 490. 494 (Cheney, 1946).
[130]64-2 ARB ¶ 8585 (Howard, 1963) at 5062-63.
[131]43 LA 982, 995 (Klamon, 1964).
[132]27 LA 798, 800 (Kelliher, 1956).

In essence the Company is attempting to declare a forfeiture of this "double time" premium as a penalty where the employees fail to meet the conditions of Section 1. As Courts and Arbitrators have frequently stated, if an Agreement is susceptible of two constructions, one which would work a forfeiture and one which would not, the [NLRB] must adopt the interpretation which will prevent the forfeiture.

The party urging a forfeiture or a penalty under a written instrument has the burden of proving that such was the unmistakable intention of the parties to the document. A Contract is not to be construed to provide a forfeiture or penalty unless no other construction or interpretation is reasonably possible. Forfeitures are not favored either in law or in equity and Courts as well as Arbitrators are reluctant to declare and enforce a forfeiture if by reasonable interpretation it can be avoided.

A deduction penalty applied weekly by a company to a worker's salary was approved by Arbitrator Mintzer in *Hearst Corp*.[133] The deduction was proportional to the amount of time by which the employee was late after the employee was guilty of "repeated and unjustified lateness" after frequent warnings. The union contended that the deductions constituted a wage cut penalty in violation of the labor agreement. This contention was rejected:

Repeated and unjustified lateness may be good and sufficient cause for dismissal. The [employer] has the right to discharge for good and sufficient cause. Discharge is the maximum penalty an employer might invoke. A pro rata deduction from an employee's salary for repeated and unjustified lateness is a lesser penalty and may be invoked by the employer rather than the extreme penalty of dismissal.

Other decisions have awarded unusual remedies which have overtones of punitive damages. Arbitrator Koven, in *Thorsen Mfg. Co.*,[134] awarded four months' back pay to a dischargee, even though the employee had been discharged on the assertion that his job application failed to report the fact that he had been fired by two previous employers—once for insubordination and once for unsatisfactory work. The four months of back pay was awarded because the company had left the grievant's status in doubt for a significant period of time and, finally, could not prove its charges at the hearing:

What I have said above amply demonstrates that the grievant deserved to be discharged because of the false statements contained in his employment application. However, there are some unusual aspects about this case. The Company presented two other grounds for discharge at the hearing which they were unable to sustain. Furthermore, the Company

---

[133]AAA Case No. 23-12 (Mintzer, 1960).
[134]55 LA 581, 585 (Koven, 1970). *See also Magnavox Co. of Tenn. v. Electrical Workers, IUE*, 410 F.2d 388, 389, 71 LRRM 2049 (6th Cir. 1969).

also charged the grievant with stealing and that charge was dropped at the Arbitration hearing. Because of the multi-charges and a very complicated record, an inordinate amount of time has passed from the date of discharge to the time of this decision, and this time lapse was not the fault of the grievant or his Union. The passage of time has left the grievant in doubt of his status for a substantial period. To compensate for this uncertainty and possible hardship, the grievant is awarded four months' straight-time pay at his normal wage rate.

Arbitrator Hardbeck in *Rohr Industries*[135] awarded back pay for a full seven-month period to equalize a contractual pay differential, notwithstanding contractual language barring retroactive adjustments for time periods longer than thirty days prior to the filing of a grievance. The arbitrator reasoned that the Company was obligated to make the payment despite the contractual language, since the employer had sole control of the relevant wage information.

Arbitrator Peter Seitz in *Publishers' Ass'n of New York City*[136] rejected a request for punitive damages when a union refused to direct the employees to operate printing presses at speeds directed by the employer:

> When and where punitive damages are awarded, I assume that the award would be based on the theory (a) of pure punishment (of the eye for an eye and a tooth for a tooth variety) or (b) of providing a deterrent to future similar insupportable conduct. I have never considered previously that *lex talionis* was part of the arsenal of remedies normally available to an arbitrator and am unprepared, at this time, to grasp in my hand and to wield unflinchingly, the avenging sword. It seems to me (although I am open to conviction to the contrary) that such blood-letting and sword-wielding might better be done in other tribunals and authorities than by arbitrators.

In a 1952 New York case[137] involving the same association as in the later Seitz arbitration, the court refused to enforce an award for punitive damages even though the labor agreement provided for such. The New York court held that it could not enforce punitive damages because the court itself would be unable under state law to make such an award if the case had come initially before it.[138]

Arbitrator Goldberg in *Mallenckrodt Chemical Works*[139] included in his award a significant monetary penalty if the employer assigned

---

[135]65 LA 779 (Hardbeck, 1975).

[136]37 LA 509, 519–20 (Seitz, 1961).

[137]*Publishers' Ass'n of New York v. Newspaper & Mail Deliverers*, 280 App. Div. 500, 114 N.Y.S.2d 401, 18 LA 855 (1952).

[138]*See Wilko v. Swan*, 346 U.S. 427 (1953) (*dictum*). *But see East India Trading Co., Dada Haji Ebrahim Halari*, 280 App. Div. 420, 114 N.Y.S.2d 93 (1952).

[139]50 LA 933 (Goldberg, 1968).

work to nonbargaining unit employees at a time when all unit employees were fully employed. This meant that the unit should be paid the overtime pay its members had not been paid, for work they had not performed. Arbitrator Goldberg said that a financial penalty should be assessed on the company to force assignment of overtime opportunities:

> [T]he Company asserts there is nothing in the Agreement that authorizes the Arbitrator to award damages absent a showing of monetary loss. This argument is not convincing. It is equally true that there is nothing in the collective agreement authorizing the Arbitrator to award damages where there *is* a showing of monetary loss, yet the Company concedes the arbitrator's power to do so.
>
> . . .
>
> ... When a particular situation calls for a certain remedy, it is not at all clear to me that the parties can be said to have a reasonable expectation that the arbitrator will not utilize that remedy, however novel. To the contrary, absent contract language directed to the question of remedies for a breach of contract, I would think that the reasonable expectation of the parties would be that the arbitrator would order a remedy appropriate to the case. Normally this can be expected to be a familiar remedy, but where the familiar remedies are inadequate, the arbitrator (or at least some arbitrators) can surely be expected to acquiesce in a more satisfactory remedy requested by one of the parties.[140]

Arbitrator Goldberg went on to say:

> I reject ... the argument that the only appropriate award which an arbitrator may provide for knowing or repeated breaches ... is an order directing the offending party to cease and desist from the breach involved. An arbitral cease and desist order is meaningless absent judicial enforcement.[141]

Arbitrator C. Allen Foster in *Celanese Fibers Co.*[142] found that no employee had suffered a loss of overtime or a reduction in regular hours, but because the company's behavior lacked "even a colorable excuse," he awarded the union $400. A similar "pay twice" penalty was awarded by Arbitrator Charles A. Atwood in *Lockheed Aircraft Corp.*[143] He awarded pay to employees in one craft who did not perform any work because employees in another craft performed it. In both of these awards, the company had to pay twice for performance of the same work.

In *United Shoe Workers v. Brooks Shoe Mfg. Co.*,[144] the district court awarded the union $50,000 in punitive damages from an

---

[140]*Id.* at 938-39.
[141]*Id.* at 940.
[142]72 LA 271 (Foster, 1979).
[143]55 LA 964 (Atwood, 1970).
[144]187 F. Supp. 509, 512-13, 46 LRRM 3003 (D.C. Pa. 1960).

employer who moved his plant in violation of his labor agreement with the union. The Third Circuit reversed the lower court's decision,[145] noting that there is no provision for punitive damages in Section 301 and reasoning that the statute is generally remedial rather than punitive.[146]

Most often no financial penalty is added when the asserted breach of the labor agreement does not cause any employee financial injury. Some have referred to such an award as "remedy by pronouncement." Arbitrator Charles F. Ipavec discussed this type of remedy problem in *Valley Camp Coal Co.*[147] A grievance had been filed because the employer had not provided sufficient hot water for showers. The arbitrator pronounced that the failure to provide hot water was "inexcusable" and that after management had received a "plethora of complaints," its attempt to fix the showers had been "inadequate." Since the affected employees had "suffered no loss in wages in the lack of hot water," no award for monetary damages was provided.

MONEY DAMAGES FOR VIOLATION OF NO-STRIKE AGREEMENTS

Quite often the labor agreement does not provide for the arbitration of grievances filed against the union by the employer. Sometimes in the labor agreement there is a special exception that allows for the filing of grievances against unions when there is a strike, picket line interference, or an overtime ban. All of these are considered strikes in breach of the labor agreement, if they occur during the term of the labor agreement. When the arbitrator does have the jurisdiction to determine such employer's grievance, the remedy would involve the determination of monetary damages against the union. In regard to employer grievances, Arbitrator Sidney Wolff stated:

> If we justify an award of damages to an employee for a contract breach on the theory of implied power to formulate a remedy, why must we insist

---

[145]298 F.2d 277, 49 LRRM 2346 (2d Cir. 1962).

[146]*Id.* at 283-86, 49 LRRM at 2350-51. Cases that approve punitive damages: *Garment Workers, ILGWU, Joint Board of Cloak, Skirt & Dressmakers v. Senco, Inc.*, 289 F. Supp. 513, 69 LRRM 2142 (D. Mass. 1968), citing *Sidney Wanzer & Sons, Inc. v. Milk Drivers Union*, 249 F. Supp. 664, 61 LRRM 2376 (N.D. Ill. 1966). Cases that do not: *Local 127, United Shoe Workers v. Brooks Shoe Mfg. Co.*, 298 F.2d 277, 49 LRRM 2346 (3d Cir. 1962); *Hall v. Pacific Maritime Ass'n*, 281 F. Supp. 54, 67 LRRM 2756 (N.D. Cal. 1968).

[147]66 LA 930, 932 (Ipavec, 1976); *see also Grower-Shipper Vegetable Ass'n*, 70 LA 350 (Ross, 1978); *Day and Zimmerman, Inc.*, 54 LA 1080 (Caraway, 1970); *Modecraft Co.*, 44 LA 1045 (Jaffee, 1965); *Green River Steel Corp.*, 41 LA 132, 136 (Stouffer, 1963); *Philip Carey Mfg. Co.*, 37 LA 134, 136 (Gill, 1961); *National Lead Co.*, 36 LA 962 (Marshall, chm., 1961).

upon a specific grant of authority to award damages for violation of the no-strike covenant?[148]

Arbitrator James C. Vadakin in *PPG Industries*[149] rejected the union's argument that damages in a wildcat strike should be denied because there was no provision in the agreement granting the arbitrator authority to assess damages:

> When parties enter into a collective bargaining contract, each is assured of specified rights and each, in turn, assumes definite responsibilities. Unless the machinery for enforcement of the contract includes damages or other affirmative remedies for the benefit of an injured party, said remedies designed to make him whole in the face of the breach by the other party, the contract becomes a nullity.

Arbitrator H. H. Rains in *Brynmore Press*[150] imposed liability upon the union treasury when the employee members breached their agreement by engaging in strike action, stating:

> The crux of the issue before the Arbitrator is that a breach of the contract between the Company and Union took place and that the Company claims appropriate remedies for that wrongful breach. The responsibility of the Union ... for such wrongful breach is clear and a failure to apply proper effective remedies in form of prohibition orders, assessment of penalties, and award of damages claimed by the aggrieved party would have the effect of freeing the union and its members from liability for their actions. Such failure could only militate against the desirable ideal of "union responsibility." Assessment of penalties and award of damages payable to the aggrieved party is a step in direction of preserving "Union responsibility" and its integrity as the "responsible party" to the collective bargaining agreement.

In contrast, one district court judge in New Jersey said:

> I find that the contract between the parties did not expressly contemplate that such issue of damages was a dispute or controversy to be settled by grievance and arbitration procedures. Further, since this strike concerns a

---

[148]Wolff, note 70 *supra*, at pp. 178–80; *but see Baldwin-Lima-Hamilton Corp.*, 30 LA 1061 (Crawford, 1958). *See generally* Fleming, *Arbitrators and the Remedy Power*, 48 VA. L. REV. 1220; Smith, *Arbitrators & Arbitrability*. LABOR ARBITRATION AND INDUSTRIAL CHANGE, Proceedings of the Sixteenth Annual Meeting, National Academy of Arbitrators, M. Kahn, ed. (Washington: BNA Books, 1963), p. 75.

[149]68-2 ARB ¶ 8807 (Vadakin, 1968) at 5795. *See also Master Builders Ass'n of Western Pa., Inc.*, 68-2 ARB ¶ 8561 (McDermott, 1968); *American Pipe & Construction Co.*, 43 LA 1126 (Ladar, 1964); *Publishers' Ass'n of New York City*, 42 LA 95 (Berkowitz, 1964); *Publishers' Ass'n of New York City*, 39 LA 564 (Moskowitz, 1962); *Regent Quality Furniture, Inc.*, 32 LA 553 (Turkus, 1959).

[150]7 LA 648, 658 (Rains, 1947). *See also Fortex Mfg. Co.*, 67 LA 935 (Bryan, 1976); *Publishers' Ass'n of New York City*, 39 LA 564 (Moskowitz, 1962); *Oregonian Publishing Co.*, 33 LA 574 (Kleinsorge, 1959); *Regent Quality Furniture, Inc.*, 32 LA 553 (Turkus, 1959); *Canadian General Electric Co., Ltd.*, 18 LA 925 (Laskin, 1952).

violation of the no-strike clause it is not a grievance referable to arbitration. . . .

As I have found that the Union breached the contract when it induced the work stoppage, as the trier of the fact I shall determine the amount of damages to which the company is entitled.[151]

However, another branch of the same court in New Jersey held that the damages arising from a violation of a no-strike clause were a matter to be determined by the arbitrator.[152]

Arbitrator Joseph F. Gentile examined his authority as an arbitrator to determine damages in *Dan J. Peterson*,[153] where the contractor initially requested that the union pay him $45,057 for a two-day strike; and awarded the contractor $11,300, explaining that the calculation of damages against unions that violate a no-strike commitment is not simple under the variety of formulae that have been used by arbitrators:

In regard to the remedial aspects of damages, the Contractor cited . . . various arbitral decisions on this subject; these were duly reviewed and evaluated. . . . [T]he Chairman reviewed in depth the entire spectrum of damages in this and parallel situations. The case [authorities], both court and arbitral, were evaluated. . . .

The formulas utilized by arbitrators . . . , tend to be arbitrary (apparently utilizing the broad discretionary authority granted), fail to calculate the damages along precise lines probably because of the inability to have raw and sufficient supporting documentation to support the mere enumeration of damages, vary as to the role and impact of court decisions . . . , [and] base the amount of damages on reasonable estimates from the presence of certain compensable factors.

The Eleventh Circuit affirmed a damage award of more than $140,000 against a local of the United Mine Workers for a strike called by its members in violation of a no-strike clause.[154] The court discussed the various theories of union liability for damages caused by wildcat strikes and concluded that when a union meeting took place on the first day of the strike, the wildcat walkout became a breach for which the union was liable even though the local president directed the strikers to return to work and no vote was taken on the controversy at the meeting. A telegram sent by the local president to the company, stating his belief that the strike was not over an arbitrable matter, con-

---

[151]*Structural Steel & Ornamental Iron Ass'n v. Shopmen's Local 545, Iron Workers,* 172 F. Supp. 354, 360, 43 LRRM 2868, 2873 (D. N.J. 1959).

[152]*Tenney Engineering, Inc. v. Electrical Workers, UE,* Local 437, 174 F. Supp. 878, 44 LRRM 2422 (D. N.J. 1959).

[153]66 LA 388 (Gentile, 1976).

[154]*North River Energy Corp. v. Mine Workers, UMW,* 664 F.2d 1184, 109 LRRM 2335 (11th Cir. 1981).

stituted a union ratification of the strike since it was read to the union membership and paid for with union funds.

In a similar ruling, the Ninth Circuit held that the typical no-strike clause is violated by a slowdown, and affirmed a damage award of more than $26,000 against a union for a wildcat strike called by its members.[155] The court found that while the slowdown was not initiated by the union, the union was nonetheless liable under the agency theory since various statements and actions indicated its support for the slowdown.

The Overhead Formula

The Eighth Circuit set up a direct formula based on "overhead" expenses during a strike, reduced by the percentage by which production was reduced during the strike.[156] This formula has become basic to most determinations of damages by arbitrators. Overhead is the expense of maintaining the plant—salaries of supervisory and professional employees and essential employees necessarily retained by the company while the strike was in progress; property insurance; property taxes; compensation and group insurance; and social security taxes and employees' pension liability. The court explained:

> Overhead expense is the necessary cost incurred by a company in its operations which can not be easily identified with any individual product and which by accepted cost accounting procedure is spread over or allocated to the productive labor, which is labor performed in the processing of the company's products. Such expenses do not fluctuate directly with plant operations. They are expenses necessary to keep the company on a going concern basis and are based upon the company's production which is planned for a year in advance. They are constant regardless of fluctuations in plant operations. When productive labor in a plant is reduced for any period to less than the normal, the company sustains a loss in the expenditure of necessary overhead for which it receives no production.[157]

The overhead formula explained by the Eighth Circuit has been used with exclusions and "rough justice" adjustments by various ar-

---

[155]*Seattle Times Co. v. Mailer's Union, No. 32,* 644 F.2d 1366, 109 LRRM 2353 (9th Cir. 1982).

[156]*Electrical Workers, UE v. Oliver Corp.,* 205 F.2d 376, 32 LRRM 2270 (8th Cir. 1953). *See also Sheet Metal Workers, Local 223 v. Atlas Sheet Metal Co. of Jacksonville,* 384 F.2d 101, 65 LRRM 3115 (5th Cir. 1967); *W.L. Mead, Inc. v. Teamsters,* 129 F. Supp. 313, 35 LRRM 2700 (D. Mass. 1955), *aff'd,* 230 F.2d 576, 37 LRRM 2679 (1st Cir. 1956), *cert. dismissed,* 352 U.S. 802 (1956); *Overnite Transportation Co. v. Teamsters, Local 728,* 257 N.C. 18, 125 S.E.2d 277, 50 LRRM 2377 (1962), *cert. denied,* 371 U.S. 862, 51 LRRM 2267 (1962), *reh'g denied,* 371 U.S. 899; *Metropolitan Paving Co. v. Operating Engineers,* 439 F.2d 300, 76 LRRM 2744 (10th Cir. 1971), *cert. denied,* 404 U.S. 829, 78 LRRM 2464 (1971); *Steelworkers v. CCI Corp.,* 395 F.2d 529, 68 LRRM 2059 (10th Cir. 1968), *cert. denied,* 393 U.S. 1019, 70 LRRM 2225 (1969).

[157]205 F.2d at 387, 32 LRRM at 2278.

bitrators. For example, Arbitrator Bora Laskin in *Canadian General Electric Co.* [158] allowed the company to calculate its overhead cost during the strike period:

> The items of continuing expense so apportioned included: (1) depreciation on fixed assets; (2) insurance premiums, mainly for fire insurance; (3) rent of outside property used for storage; (4) salaries of office and managerial staff; (5) local taxes; (6) telephone and telegraph service; (7) travelling expenses; and (8) heat. [159]

Arbitrator Kates in *Vulcan Mould & Iron Co.* [160] accepted the view that a percentage reduction of production times the overhead was a proper formula—with some reduction in overhead because, among other considerations, utilities were used less during the strike and the foremen performed bargaining unit work. The arbitrator used these "rough justice" estimates:

> However, the compensation of salaried office people who worked on production in the strike period presumably is included in the claimed administrative expense figure. Unfortunately, no breakdown of this figure was presented in evidence to show what elements were to make up this lump sum figure. . . . Under the circumstances, I believe that I should consider not more than 1/6 of the claimed administrative figure. . . .
>
> . . .
>
> I recognize that professional accountants and others might consider that I have been inconsistent in my treatment of some of the classes of expense items discussed above. Nevertheless, I feel that I should not sacrifice my own concept of what is fair and just . . . to abstract theories of cost accounting. [161]

Arbitrator William Eaton in *Mercer, Fraser Co.* [162] reduced the company's claim for damages to approximately one-third of the original figure because the amount was not fully verified and because the company prolonged the strike. Arbitrator Thomas J. McDermott in *Master Builders' Ass'n* [163] evaluated a company claim that an overhead and administrative cost of 6 percent on income was an industry average percentage. The arbitrator reduced the amount to 5 percent to "adjust for variation."

Arbitrator Joseph Gentile made an extensive study of arbitration awards and court decisions (reported in *Dan J. Peterson Co.*) [164] and therein identified the many items of overhead cost that have been ac-

---

[158] 18 LA 925 (Laskin, 1952).
[159] *Id.* at 928.
[160] 70-1 ARB ¶ 8080 (Kates, 1969).
[161] *Id.* at 3289.
[162] 70-2 ARB ¶ 8615 (Eaton, 1971).
[163] 50 LA 1018 (McDermott, 1968).
[164] 66 LA 388 (Gentile, 1976).

cepted or rejected by courts and arbitrators. This information (reported up to 1976) may be helpful to arbitrators and representatives. In various cases, consultant fees expended as a result of the strike were claimed but not included because of no proof of the amount and payment;[165] attorney fees expended during and immediately after the strike were allowed;[166] charitable contributions included in overhead expense were disallowed;[167] cost of extra signs during the strike was included;[168] loss of profit involved in obtaining goods elsewhere to sell to customers during the strike and cost of the goods obtained were included;[169] depreciation on the fixed assets during the strike was included;[170] depreciation was disallowed on "the tools and equipment [that] were not in actual use during the strike";[171] damage for permanent loss of business was included;[172] entertainment expense was excluded from general and administrative expenses allowed.[173]

Since the effect of loss of profit due to lack of use of equipment owned by the company is difficult to measure, in various cases the fair rental value of the idled equipment due to strike was included;[174] and reasonable rental value for idled equipment was allowed for normal working days only;[175] and the rental value of idled equipment was taken from the 18th edition of *Monthly Rental Rates* by Association

[165]*Master Builders' Ass'n of W. Pa.*, 50 LA 1018 (McDermott, 1968).

[166]*Tedford v. Peabody Coal Co.*, 383 F. Supp. 787, 796, 87 LRRM 2565 (N.D. Ala. 1974); *Gruber v. Building & Const. Trades Council, San Diego County*, 83 LRRM 2351 (S.D. Cal. 1973); *Electrical Workers, IBEW, Local 4 v. Radio Thirteen Eighty, Inc.*, 469 F.2d 610, 615, 81 LRRM 2829 (8th Cir. 1972); *Steelworkers of W. Pa. v. Butler Mfg. Co.*, 439 F.2d 1110, 77 LRRM 2057 (8th Cir. 1971); *Mine Workers, UMW, District 50 v. Bowman Transportation, Inc.*, 421 F.2d 934, 73 LRRM 2317 (5th Cir. 1970); *Sheet Metal Workers, Local 223 v. Atlas Sheet Metal Co. of Jacksonville*, 384 F.2d 101, 65 LRRM 3115 (5th Cir. 1967). *See also Teamsters, Local 94 v. Humko Co.*, 287 F.2d 231, 47 LRRM 2651, 243–44, *cert. denied*, 366 U.S. 962, 48 LRRM 2430 (1961). *Cf. Mason-Rust v. Laborers, Local 42*, 435 F.2d 939, 76 LRRM 2090 (8th Cir. 1970); *H. L. Robertson & Assoc., Inc. v. Plumbers, Local 519*, 429 F.2d 520, 74 LRRM 2872 (5th Cir. 1970).

[167]*Structural Steel and Ornamental Iron Ass'n of New Jersey, Inc. v. Shopmen's Local 545, Iron Workers*, 172 F. Supp. 354, 43, LRRM 2868 (D. N.J. 1959).

[168]*Abbott v. Plumbers, Local 142*, 429 F.2d 786, 74 LRRM 2879 (5th Cir. 1970).

[169]*Mercer, Fraser Co.*, 70-2 ARB ¶ 8615 (Dworkin, 1970).

[170]*Vulcan Mold and Iron Co.*, 70-1 ARB ¶ 8080 (Kates, 1969); *Canadian General Electric Co.*, 18 LA 925 (Laskin, 1952).

[171]*Master Builders' Ass'n of W. Pa.*, 67-1 ARB ¶ 8243 (Kates, 1967); *Master Builders' Ass'n of W. Pa.*, 50 LA 1018 (McDermott, 1968).

[172]*Plumbers and Pipefitters v. Stine*, 76 Nev. 189, 351 P.2d 965, 46 LRRM 2239 (1960).

[173]*Structural Steel and Ornamental Iron Ass'n of New Jersey, Inc. v. Shopmen's Local 45, Iron Workers*, 172 F. Supp. 354, 43 LRRM 2868 (D. N.J. 1959).

[174]*Denver Building & Construction Trades Council v. Shore*, 287 P.2d 267, 36 LRRM 2578 (Colo. Sup. Ct. 1955); *Williams v. International Harvester Co.*, 172 Ore. 270, 141 P.2d 837 (1943); *Terrill Co. v. Davis*, 77 Okla. 302, 188 P. 676 (1920); *Elzy v. Adams Express Co.*, 141 Iowa 407, 119 N.W. 705 (1909).

[175]*Foster Grading Co.*, 52 LA 197 (Jarvis, 1968). *Wells v. Operating Engineers, Local 181*, 206 F. Supp. 414 (W.D. Ky. 1962), *aff'd*, 303 F.2d 73, 50 LRRM 2198 (6th Cir. 1962).

Equipment Distributors;[176] but rental value on office furniture and telephones during the strike was excluded because this rental was unnecessary during the strike.[177] One arbitrator reduced the company's estimate of loss by $2.00 per day.[178] In other cases, cost for loss of, and damage to, freight and loss due to inability to receive freight during the strike was allowed;[179] demurrage charges for railroad cars not unloaded and returned in time and cost of guards needed to protect freight were allowed;[180] the cost of plastic sheeting to protect wood components was allowed;[181] and amounts paid for warehouse rental to store material were accepted.[182]

In other cases, the *pro rata* cost of fire and other insurance during the strike period was included;[183] but a claim for expenses incurred for workmen's compensation and group insurance for supervisory personnel during the strike was not allowed because the company did not have to make these contributions during that time;[184] however amounts paid for builder's risk insurance were allowed.[185] Interest on the damages awarded was not added unless provided by statute.[186] Also allowed were the cost for show-up time for employees who were willing but unable to work;[187] the increased wage cost required to complete work after the strike ended and after a wage increase;[188] and the cost of overtime premium needed to produce work closer to customer schedule[189] and for any additional loss of good will caused by not delivering orders on time and not accepting new orders after the strike

[176]*Metropolitan Paving Co. v. Operating Engineers*, 439 F.2d 300, 76 LRRM 2744 (10th Cir. 1971), *cert. denied*, 404 U.S. 829, 78 LRRM 2464 (1971). *Foster Grading Co.*, 52 LA 197, 200 (Jarvis, 1968).

[177]*Mason-Rust v. Laborers, Local 42*, 306 F. Supp. 934 (E.D. Mo. 1969), *aff'd*, 435 F.2d 939, 76 LRRM 2090 (8th Cir. 1970); *Master Builders' Ass'n of W. Pa.*, 67-1 ARB ¶ 8243 (Kates, 1967).

[178]*Motor Haulage Co., Inc.*, 6 LA 720 (Sheridan, 1947).

[179]*Vulcan Mold & Iron Co.*, 70-1 ARB ¶ 8080 (Kates, 1969).

[180]*Overnite Transportation Co. v. Teamsters, Local 728*, 257 N.C. 18, 125 S.E.2d 277, 50 LRRM 2377 (1962), *cert. denied*, 371 U.S. 862, 51 LRRM 2267 (1962) *reh'g denied*, 371 U.S. 899 (1962).

[181]*Master Builders' Ass'n of W. Pa.*, 50 LA 1018 (McDermott, 1968).

[182]*Id.*

[183]*Vulcan Mold & Iron Co.*, 70-1 ARB ¶ 8080 (Kates, 1969).

[184]*Master Builders' Ass'n of W. Pa.*, 50 LA 1018 (McDermott, 1968).

[185]*A. I. Gage Plumbing & Supply Co. v. Local 300, Hod Carriers*, 202 Cal. App. 2d 197, 20 Cal. Rptr. 860, 50 LRRM 2114 (1962); *Canadian General Electric Co.*, 18 LA 925 (Laskin, 1952).

[186]*Denver Building & Construction Trades Council v. Shore*, 287 P.2d 267, 36 LRRM 2578 (Colo. Sup. Ct. 1955).

[187]*Mason-Rust v. Laborers, Local 42*, 306 F. Supp. 934 (E.D. Mo. 1969), *aff'd*, 435 F.2d 939, 76 LRRM 2090 (8th Cir. 1970), *Sheet Metal Workers, Local 223 v. Atlas Sheet Metal Co. of Jacksonville*, 384 F.2d 101, 65 LRRM 3115 (5th Cir. 1967); *A.I. Gage Plumbing and Supply Co. v. Local 300, Hod Carriers*, Cal. App.2d 197, 20 Cal. Rptr. 860, 50 LRRM 2114 (1962).

[188]*Master Builders' Ass'n of W. Pa.*, 50 LA 1018 (McDermott, 1968).

[189]*Mason-Rust v. Laborers, Local No. 42*, 306 F. Supp. 934, 72 LRRM 2743 (E.D. Mo. 1969), *aff'd*, 435 F.2d 939, 76 LRRM 2090 (8th Cir. 1970); *A. I. Gage Plumbing & Supply Co. v. Local 300, Hod Carriers*, 202 Cal. App. 197, 20 Cal. Rptr. 860, 50 LRRM 2114 (1962); *Overnite Trans-*

commenced.[190] Penalties for late completion were included where the plaintiff company suffered a penalty of $35 per day for thirty-five days.[191] Loss due to reduced efficiency of employees during a strike was not included in one case because figures were too speculative,[192] but in another case the cost was estimated and included.[193] In other cases a *pro rata* portion of fringe benefits including pension costs was allowed as overhead.[194] Salaries of nonbargaining unit personnel (supervisory and professional) retained by companies during strikes sometimes were included,[195] sometimes not.[196] *Pro rata* local, state, and federal taxes have been included,[197] telephone and telegraph service expenses have been both included[198] and not included,[199] and travel costs of company officials connected with strike violations have been allowed.[200]

The Loss-of-Profit Formula

The other theory on which requests for strike damages are based, paralleling the theory of percentage of overhead costs, is loss of profits. However, the latter approach has not been acceptable to various

---

portation Co. v. Teamsters, Local 278, 257 N.C. 18, 125 S.E.2d 277, 50 LRRM 2377 (1962), *cert. denied*, 371 U.S. 862, 51 LRRM 2267, *reh'g denied*, 371 U.S. 899 (1962).

[190]*Belmont Smelting and Refining Works, Inc.*, 68-1 ARB ¶ 8342 (Turkus, 1968).

[191]*Wells v. Operating Engineers, Local 181*, 303 F.2d 73, 50 LRRM 2198 (6th Cir. 1962).

[192]*Mason-Rust v. Laborers, Local No. 42*, 306 F. Supp. 934, 72 LRRM 2743 (E.D. Mo. 1969), *aff'd*, 435 F.2d 939, 76 LRRM 2090 (8th Cir. 1970).

[193]*A. I. Gage Plumbing and Supply Co. v. Local 300, Hod Carriers*, 202 Cal. App.2d 197, 20 Cal. Rptr. 860, 50 LRRM 2114 (1962); *Riverside Coal Co. v. Mine Workers, UMW*, 410 F.2d 267, 70 LRRM 3214 (6th Cir. 1969), *cert. denied*, 396 U.S. 846, 72 LRRM 2432 (1969).

[194]*Master Builders' Ass'n of W. Pa.*, 67-1 ARB ¶ 8243 (Kates, 1967); *A. I. Gage Plumbing and Supply Co. v. Local 300, Hod Carriers*, 202 Cal. App.2d 197, 20 Cal. Rptr. 860, 50 LRRM 2114 (1962); *Mason-Rust v. Laborers, Local No. 42*, 306 F. Supp. 934, 72 LRRM 2743 (E.D. Mo. 1969). *Contra, Vulcan Mold and Iron Co.*, 70-1 ARB ¶ 8080 (Kates, 1969).

[195]*Electrical Workers, UE v. Oliver Corp.*, 205 F.2d 376, 32 LRRM 2270 (8th Cir. 1953); *Canadian General Electric Co.*, 18 LA 925 (Laskin, 1952); *Foster Grading Co.*, 52 LA 197 (Jarvis, 1968); *Wells v. Operating Engineers*, 303 F.2d 73, 50 LRRM 2198 (6th Cir. 1962); *A. I. Gage Plumbing and Supply Co. v. Local 300, Hod Carriers*, 202 Cal. App.2d 197, 20 Cal. Rptr. 860, 50 LRRM 2114 (1962); *Metropolitan Paving Co. v. Operating Engineers*, 439 F.2d 300, 76 LRRM 2744 (10th Cir. 1971), *cert. denied*, 44 U.S. 829, 78 LRRM 2464 (1971).

[196]*Vulcan Mold & Iron Co.*, 70-1 ARB ¶ 8080 (Kates, 1969). *Masters Builders' Ass'n of W. Pa.*, 50 LA 1018 (McDermott, 1968); *see Master Builders' Ass'n of W. Pa.*, 67-1 ARB ¶ 8243 (Kates, 1967).

[197]*Vulcan Mold & Iron Co.*, 70-1 ARB ¶ 8080 (Kates, 1969); *Canadian General Electric Co.*, 18 LA 925 (Laskin, 1952).

[198]*Canadian General Electric Co.*, 18 LA 925 (Laskin, 1952); *Overnite Transportation Co. v. Teamsters, Local 728*, 257 N.C. 18, 125 S.E.2d 277, 50 LRRM 2377 (1962); *cert. denied*, 371 U.S. 862, 51 LRRM 2267 (1962), *reh'g denied*, 371 U.S. 899 (1962); *Sheet Metal Workers, Local 223 v. Atlas Sheet Metal Co. of Jacksonville*, 384 F.2d 101, 65 LRRM 3115 (5th Cir. 1967).

[199]*PPG Industries, Inc.*, 51 LA 500 (Vadakin, 1968).

[200]*PPG Industries, Inc.*, 51 LA 500 (Vadakin, 1968); *Abbott v. Plumbers, Local 142*, 429 F.2d 786, 74 LRRM 2879 (5th Cir. 1970); *Canadian General Electric Co.*, 18 LA 925 (Laskin, 1952).

arbitrators. Even if all the statistical information is available, the reduction in profit necessarily becomes a comparison between the profits during some period in the past and the profits during and after the strike. The problem is that such a comparison may reflect many factors other than the effect of the strike: customers may have been lost for reasons other than the strike; sales may have been demonstrably more favorable during the comparison period; the business may rush back after the strike and hence profit loss during the strike is recaptured.[201] Only one-half of the lost profit during the strike, plus continuing expenses during that period, was allowed in one case.[202] The Supreme Court of North Carolina approved damages not only for additional expenses during a strike (excess labor costs, guards, loss and damage to freight, extra telephone and communication expense, cost of operating additional tractor-trailers), but also for loss of profits during the strike, based on testimony that during the first four months of 1959 business had increased 22 percent but after the strike the rate of increase dropped to 16 percent.[203] On the basis of this statement, the jury approved a sum of $59,819 for lost profits plus $303,374 for excess expenses.

Offsets for Recovery of Strike-Related Losses

In various European countries, recovery against a local union for a strike loss is obtained by retaining the dues payable by the employer.[204] This recovery is almost automatic. No case has been found where an attempt was made to secure an offset against dues to pay for strike damage in the United States. An attempt was made to secure a strike damage offset against welfare fund payments, but this plan was declared improper by the Supreme Court in *Lewis v. Benedict Coal Corp.*[205] The Court said that such an offset would have been allowed except for the congressional intention expressed in Section 301 not to impose liability on the striking employee if the union, as an entity, is liable. Taking an offset against welfare contributions, the Court said, might well impose a loss upon an individual member. However, the Court did say that if there was express offset language in the labor agreement, it would be allowed:

---

[201]*Vulcan Mold & Iron Co.*, 70-1 ARB ¶ 8030 (Kates, 1969); *Canadian General Electric Co.*, 18 LA 925 (Laskin, 1952).

[202]*Canadian General Electric Co.*, 18 LA 925 (Laskin, 1952).

[203]*Overnite Transportation Co. v. Teamsters, Local 728*, 256 N.C. 18, 125 S.E.2d 277, 50 LRRM 2377 (1962); *cert. denied*, 371 U.S. 862, 51 LRRM 2267 (1962), *reh'g denied*, 371 U.S. 899 (1962).

[204]Seyfarth, Shaw, Fairweather & Geraldson, LABOR RELATIONS AND THE LAW IN BELGIUM AND THE UNITED STATES (Ann Arbor: Univ. of Mich. Bus. Div. Res., 1969), p. 137.

[205]259 F.2d 346, 43 LRRM 2237 (6th Cir. 1958); *modif'd and aff'd*, 361 U.S. 459, 45 LRRM 2719 (1960).

[W]e hold that the parties to a collective bargaining agreement must express their meaning in unequivocal words before they can be said to have agreed that the union's breaches of its promises should give rise to a defense against the duty assumed by an employer to contribute to a welfare fund meeting the requirements of Section 302(c)(5).[206]

Company Obligation to Mitigate Strike Damage

The obligation of the employer to mitigate the damages in a strike situation was discussed by Arbitrator Kates in *Vulcan Iron and Mould Co.*:[207]

> The evidence persuades me that the Company did all that could reasonably be expected, or more, in attempting to minimize its damages during the strike period insofar as maintaining production was concerned.
>
> The question nevertheless remains as to whether the Company's discharge of Local Union officials, and the Company's refusal to accept the Union's proposal to end the strike on condition that those officials be reinstated, warrant a finding that the Company itself provoked or caused a prolongation of the strike so as to require a reduction in the amount of damage shown.
>
> My hesitant opinion is that this question should be decided in the negative.... [I]n my opinion the Company, under the circumstances shown, was under no duty to give in to the pressure of the wrongful strike, although it had reason to believe that such refusal would prolong the strike.

Arbitrator Martin Conway in *Smitty's Glass & Lock Service, Inc.*,[208] by some odd logic essentially denied damages for a strike in violation of the labor agreement. He reasoned (1) that the labor agreement required the employer to increase wages for the glaziers on a particular date, (2) that the employer did not do so "because he had not received notice from the Construction Industry Stabilization Committee that the increase would be proper under the Wage Stabilization Act,"[209] (3) that the glaziers went on strike to force the wage increase rather than filing a grievance, and (4) since the employer violated the agreement the union strike was excusable. Arbitrator Conway awarded only one dollar against the union, in spite of the employer's claimed damages of $20,575. Arbitrator Conway explained his concept of mitigation:

> [The] Employer admits that he does have the duty to mitigate damages. However, he takes the position that he fully extinguished his duty to

---

[206]361 U.S. at 470–71, 45 LRRM at 2724.
[207]70-1 ARB ¶ 8080 (Kates, 1969) at 3290.
[208]77-1 ARB ¶ 8300 (Conway, 1977).
[209]*Id.* at 4301.

PRACTICE AND PROCEDURE IN LABOR ARBITRATION

mitigate damages.... Unfortunately, the Employer has omitted the most obvious obligation, which is to pay the wage increases he agreed to pay....

The Employer knew that he was obligated to pay the wage increase. The Employer knew also that it was very unlikely that the men would walk off the job if they were paid according to the collective bargaining agreement.

I think Labor Arbitration must be viewed fundamentally as an equitable proceeding. The various maxims are appropriate in finding a resolution of grievance disputes. He who asks equity must do equity, and he must have essentially "clean hands."

In spite of my predilection to resolve grievance matters by applying equitable measures and standards, I nevertheless recognize the real and necessary rules of law....

Award

My decision is that the Employer is entitled only to nominal damages of $1.00 against the Union.[210]

Some arbitrators reduce the damages in strikes when union officers attempt to bring employees back to work. In *Publishers' Ass'n of New York City*,[211] Arbitrator Berkowitz noted that the union officials had attempted to end an unlawful work stoppage and reduced the damages, but stated as follows:

The evidence indicates that the January 27 stoppage was truly an unauthorized stoppage and the union officials exerted sincere efforts to persuade the men to return to work. The Union, however, is the responsible party and a substantial amount of money damages must be assessed against it. However, in light of the efforts of the officials of the Union this amount will be less than the direct damages suffered by the Publisher.[212]

THIRD PARTY DAMAGES FOR A PICKET LINE

The right of action against an individual who induces a breach of contract between an employer and an employee was established in the famous 1853 English case, *Lumley v. Gye*.[213] A rival theater manager, Mr. Gye, had persuaded an opera singer not to honor her contract to sing in Mr. Lumley's theater. For doing so, Gye had to pay damages to Lumley. The same principle has been absorbed into the United States common law and has been applied in labor relations litigation. An Ohio court said:

It is unlawful to pursue any course of conduct, the sole purpose of which is to induce a breach of contract. This principle of law is equally applicable

---

[210]*Id.* at 4301-02.
[211](Berkowitz) (unpublished).
[212]*Id.*
[213]2 El. & Bl. 216, 118 Eng. Rep. 749 (1853).

to contracts covering labor relations. Hence, it is unlawful for one union or its members to engage in picketing activities which would otherwise be lawful for the sole purpose of inducing other unions and their members to breach their existing contracts with their employer.

. . .

The third person who with either a bad motive or a good motive induces a breach of contract . . . is guilty of a tort and becomes a subject to an action for damages or subject to the orders that a court of equity can and must impose.

. . .

We have no difficulty in finding that defendants should be enjoined from attempting to persuade the employees under contract with the plaintiff to breach their contracts. The holdings of our courts are uniform that injunctions should be granted to prevent such action.[214]

This principle has also been absorbed into arbitration. Arbitrator Stanley Sergent, Jr. in *Westinghouse Transport Leasing Corporation*[215] held that when one group of employees formed a picket line in front of the building where another group of employees from the same union was legally obligated to report to work (no-strike commitment by the Teamsters Union), the refusal to go to work was an illegal breach by the strikers. Arbitrator Sergent then imposed a financial damage penalty on the Teamsters Union for inducing the strike. By so doing, the arbitrator freed the employees from penalty, even though they set up the picket line causing members not to report to work.[216] In this case the arbitrator had jurisdiction over the one union that represented both the employees in one unit who induced the breach and the employees in another who did not cross. If two unions are involved, a trilateral arbitration could be set up[217] so the damages could properly be assessed.

Generally unions do not struggle in an arbitration hearing to deny responsibility for their involvement in the strike action because if they do and prove no involvement, the employees lose. Only if the union accepts the liability for the strike action are the employees who actually cause the breach insulated from personal financial liability.[218]

INJUNCTIVE RELIEF TO HALT VIOLATION OF THE NO-STRIKE CLAUSE

Arbitrators have issued injunctive orders directing employees to cease breaching the no-strike commitment contained in the labor

---

[214]*Sterling & Welch Co. v. Duke*, 33 Ohio App. 428, 67 N.E.2d 24 (1946).

[215]69 LA 1210 (Sergent, 1977).

[216]*Id.* at 1214.

[217]*See* discussion under "Securing Participation of All Interested Parties" in Chapter II.

[218]29 U.S.C. § 185(a) n. 1181 (1978).

agreement.[219] In the event that the strike action continues, the employer may petition a court for enforcement of the award (1) pursuant to the provisions of the state arbitration act if that act contains a provision for confirmation of the award, making it a decree by the court[220] and (2) pursuant to a Section 301 suit in a federal court to obtain an injunctive-type order. Even before the Supreme Court's decision in *Boys Markets, Inc. v. Retail Clerks, Local 770*,[221] suits to enforce injunctive relief issued by an arbitrator were generally successful in lower federal courts against the claim that the same injunctive relief could not be issued initially by a court because of the restrictions of the Norris-LaGuardia Act.[222]

An injunctive award enforced by a state court is of special interest because the confirmation of the award required the same court to reverse its prior decree. A picket line had been set up in front of the gate of a large manufacturing plant in Ohio in an attempt to force the management not to transfer some carpenters from one location to another within the plant. The employees who were coming to work observed the picket line and did not cross, and a plantwide work stoppage took place. Telegrams were sent by the management to the participating employees and to the union leaders asking that the picket line be dissolved. The union leaders then instructed the members to terminate their picketing and, when the picketing did not stop, telegrams signed by the president of the union were sent to the members instructing them to cease their breach. The picketing continued.

In an effort to have the picket line removed, a complaint was filed in the Court of Common Pleas for Trumbull County, Ohio, advising the court of the breach. The court refused to order the members to ter-

---

[219]*Ford Motor Co.*, 62-2 ARB ¶ 8491 (Platt, 1963) at 4622 (award enforced in Circuit Court of Cook County, Ill.); *General American Transportation Corp.*, 41 LA 214 (Abrahams, 1963); *In re Ruppert*, 3 N.Y.2d 576, 148 N.E.2d 129, 29 LA 775 (1958); *Cloak Suit & Shirt Mfrs., Inc.*, 5 LA 352 (Polette, 1946); *General Dynamics Corp. v. Local 5, Marine & Shipbuilding Workers*, 469 F.2d 848, 81 LRRM 2746 (1st Cir. 1972); *Pacific Maritime Ass'n v. Longshoremen & Warehousemen*, 454 F.2d 262, 79 LRRM 2116 (9th Cir. 1971).

[220]ILL. REV. STAT. ch. 10 § 101-23 (1963); OHIO REV. CODE ANN. ch. 4129. *See, e.g.,* FLA. STAT. ANN. § 682.12 (Supp. 1970); ME. REV. STAT. ANN. tit. 26, § 957 (1964); MONT. REV. CODES ANN. § 93-201 (1964); NEB. REV. STAT. § 25.2116 (1965); NEV. REV. STAT. § 614.040 (1964); N.D. CENT. CODE § 32-29-07 (1960); R. I. GEN. LAWS ANN. § 28-9-71 (1969); TENN. CODE ANN. § 23-513 (1955); W. VA. CODE ANN. § 55-10-3 (1966); WYO. STAT. ANN. § 1-1048.13 (Supp. 1969).

[221]398 U.S. 235 74 LRRM 2257 (1970).

[222]*See, e.g., Pacific Maritime Ass'n v. Longshoremen & Warehousemen*, 304 F. Supp. 1315, 71 LRRM 3117 (N.D. Cal. 1969), *aff'd*, 454 F.2d 262, 79 LRRM 2116 (9th Cir. 1971); *New Orleans Steamship Ass'n v. Longshoremen, ILA, Local 1418*, 389 F.2d 369, 67 LRRM 2430 (5th Cir. 1968), *cert. denied*, 383 U.S. 828, 69 LRRM 2434 (1968); *In re Ruppert*, 3 N.Y.2d 576, 148 N.E.2d 129, 29 LA 875 (1958). *But see Tanker Service Committee, Inc. v. Masters, Mates & Pilots*, 269 F. Supp. 551, 65 LRRM 2848 (E.D. Pa. 1967).

minate the picketing and actually approved it by ordering that the number of pickets at the gate should be no more than "three at any time."[223] The district director of the union recognized that the court's order limiting the pickets to three at a gate was simply a fluke, and he was willing to cooperate with the company management and sign a stipulation so an arbitrator with special powers could promptly hear a special company grievance. Arbitrator Harry Abrahams heard the grievance under the stipulation and he awarded the following injunctive order in *General American Transportation Corp.*:[224]

> I find that the employees ... who are represented by United Steelworkers of America are violating Article III of the Collective Bargaining Agreement....
>
> . . .
>
> I find that members and officers of ... United Steelworkers of America, by engaging in picketing at the North Gate, are in clear violation of Article III of the Collective Bargaining Agreement.
>
> In accordance with the authority given to me by the Submission Agreement dated September 16, 1963, and signed by the General American Transportation Corporation and the United Steelworkers of America, I make the following Order and Award.
>
> ORDER AND AWARD
>
> I hereby order and award that the United Steelworkers of America, ... and members, forthwith cease and desist from engaging in such strike ... and that they cease ... picketing at any plant gate.

Under the Ohio statute,[225] confirmation of an arbitration award is mandatory and, once confirmed by the court, the award becomes the court's decree. Under this statute, confirmation is mandatory if (1) the award was in writing, (2) it was made in county where the court geographically has jurisdiction, (3) it was signed by the arbitrator, and (4) each party in interest has received a copy. Since Judge Berel of the Ohio court became obligated to enter the award as soon as it was received, the Trumbull County court order that had limited the pickets to three at the gate and by doing so had approved the picketing was withdrawn, and the same court then confirmed the injunctive award by Arbitrator Abrahams (causing a replacement of the court's prior judgment):

> This day this cause came on to be heard upon the Application of the GENERAL AMERICAN TRANSPORTATION CORPORATION for confirmation of an award entered under the provisions of Ohio Revised Code Section 2711.09, being an award entered as a result and upon the

---

[223]*General American Transportation Corp. v. Steelworkers*, No. 73488 (C.P. Trumbull County, Ohio, Sept. 17, 1963).
[224]41 LA 214, 215 (Abrahams, 1963).
[225]OHIO CODE § 2711.12.

conclusion of an Arbitration Hearing held in Trumbull County, Ohio, on September 17, 1963, before HARRY ABRAHAMS, Arbitrator, and for the entry of a Decree in conformance with said award, and it appearing to the Court that said award being in conformity with law in all respects.

IT IS HEREBY ORDERED, ADJUDGED, and DECREED that said award be, and it is hereby confirmed.

IT IS FURTHER HEREBY ORDERED AND DECREED, in conformance with said award as follows:

THAT THE UNITED STEELWORKERS OF AMERICA AND LOCAL 1534 and LOCAL 2318 thereof, and their officers and members, forthwith cease and desist from engaging in such strike and other strikes in violation of the Collective Bargaining Agreement; and that they cease ... picketing at any plant gate ... and that said officers use their best efforts to secure the return of the striking employees to their jobs.[226]

A writ was then served by the sheriff on the pickets and the sheriff posted copies at the gate of the plant where the picketing had been occurring.

No special stipulation by the company and union representatives would have been required if there had been a special provision in the labor agreement that permitted a grievance by the employer to be filed against the union when there was a violation of the no-strike provision, giving the arbitrator authority to hear the case expeditiously and issue an injunctive award. An example of such a special provision, sometimes referred to as a "quickie" arbitration clause, is:

During the term of this Agreement the Union agrees that there shall be no strikes, work stoppages, slowdowns, or interferences with work on the part of the Union, any of its agents or any of its members. Any employee participating in such activity shall be subject to discipline including discharge. The parties further agree that in the event of an alleged violation of this Section, the issue arising therefrom may be submitted immediately by the Company to the permanent arbitrator to be heard by said arbitrator as soon as possible after such submission. If the arbitrator finds that the Agreement has been violated, he shall order that the party or parties in violation cease and desist from such conduct and any other conduct inducing said breach or causing it to continue and shall have authority to grant any further relief he deems proper. Said order by the arbitrator shall be in writing and shall issue at the conclusion of the arbitration hearing. The arbitrator shall have authority to retain jurisdiction in such a case to assess damages but the hearing on the question of damages shall occur after the contract violation has terminated.

Arbitrators became less involved with strikes in violation of labor agreements after injunctive orders could be issued by the federal

---

[226]*General American Transportation Corp. v. Steelworkers*, No. 73516 (C.P. Trumbull County, Ohio, September 17, 1963).

district courts following the Supreme Court decision in *Boys Markets, Inc. v. Retail Clerks, Local 770.*[227] However, it was still necessary for the company to prove to the satisfaction of the court that the dispute basic to the strike was one that could be resolved by arbitration before the strike would be enjoined. One type of strike that cannot be terminated by an injunction by the federal court under *Boys Markets* is a *sympathy* strike.[228] When employees do not cross a picket line and these employees have no dispute with their employer, the needed ingredient for a *Boys Markets* injunction is not present.[229]

A sympathy strike was, however, terminated by an arbitrator in conjunction with a federal district court in Pennsylvania. The salaried office and technical employees of General American Transportation Corporation had set up a picket line to generate pressure on the company to obtain for the group picketing a better labor agreement. The hourly paid production and maintenance employees "did not cross" the picket line, and this generated a strike which could not be terminated by a *Boys Markets*-type injunction because those who were on strike had no dispute with the employer that could be resolved by an arbitrator. This time the same union representatives would not sign the special stipulation that the district director of the same union signed fifteen years before, discussed *supra*. The company then sought a different route.

---

[227]398 U.S. 235, 74 LRRM 2257 (1969).

[228]*Buffalo Forge Co. v. Steelworkers*, 428 U.S. 397, 92 LRRM 3032 (1976). In *Buffalo Forge* the injunction requested was not granted because a sympathy strike does not revolve around a dispute that can be resolved by arbitration.

[229]*Id.* The Supreme Court expressly limited the scope of *Boys Markets* in this case (*Buffalo Forge*), holding that injunctive relief is plainly inappropriate in sympathy strike situations under a general no-strike clause because of the express prohibitions of the Norris-LaGuardia Act. *American Brake Shoe Co. v. Local 149, Automobile Workers*, 285 F.2d 869, 47 LRRM 2466 (4th Cir. 1961). The rules governing direct injunction action against a strike in a district court were first explained in *Boys Markets*, 398 U.S. at 253, 74 LRRM at 2263-64:

> We conclude, therefore, that the unavailability of equitable relief in the arbitration context presents a serious impediment to the congressional policy favoring the voluntary establishment of a mechanism for the peaceful resolution of labor disputes, that the core purpose of the Norris-LaGuardia Act is not sacrificed by the limited use of equitable remedies to further this important policy, and consequently that the Norris-LaGuardia Act does not bar the granting of injunctive relief in the circumstances of the instant case.

The subject of injunctive relief is discussed at 28 U.S.C.A. § 65. Courts have had difficulty locating the limit set by the Supreme Court on their authority to enjoin strikes in violation of agreements. In *General Cable Corp. v. Electrical Workers, IBEW, Local 1644*, 331 F. Supp. 478, 77 LRRM 3053 (D. Md. 1971), the court denied injunctive relief because the cause of the strike was picketing by a sister local and the court concluded this was not an arbitral issue, whereas in *General Cable Corp. v. Electrical Workers, IBEW, Local 1798*, 333 F. Supp. 331, 77 LRRM 3123 (W.D. Tenn. 1971), another district court came to exactly the opposite conclusion. The search of other courts for the limits set by *Boys Markets* is reported in *Ourisman Chevrolet Co., Inc. v. Machinists, Automotive Lodge 1486, District Lodge 67*, 77 LRRM 2084 (D. D.C. 1971); *Simplex Wire & Cable Co. v. Electrical Workers, IBEW, Local 2208*, 314 F. Supp. 885, 75 LRRM 2475 (D. N.H. 1970).

A Section 301 suit was filed in the District Court for the Western District of Pennsylvania (the picket line this time was in that state). The complaint did not seek an injunction to stop the sympathy strike activity, because the complaint would be dismissed under *Buffalo Forge Co. v. Steelworkers.*[230] The company only asked the court to order an arbitration of the breach of the no-strike provision. The district court did not grant the company's motion. It did, however, order Arbitrator Edwin Teple to determine whether he, as an arbitrator, had the jurisdiction to arbitrate the breach of the no-strike provision.[231]

The first hearing before Arbitrator Teple took place on July 10 and a decision was issued under the caption "Umpire's Opinion on Issue of Arbitrability."[232] The arbitrator accepted extensive testimony about the provisions of the labor agreement to determine whether, without the same special stipulation signed fifteen years previously, the employer could file with the umpire a grievance over the breach caused by the strike action and whether the umpire had the authority to issue an award. He concluded that under the labor agreement he could accept the company grievance and issue an award.

A second award was issued August 18 under the caption "Decision on Applicability of No-Strike Provision."[233] Since the labor agreement in Article III, Section 3, contained a commitment that "there shall be no strikes, work stoppages or interruption or impeding of work" the arbitrator said:

> The record clearly indicates that a work stoppage did occur in the production and maintenance sections of the plant on the dates outlined above. The rank and file, members of both Locals, did not report for their work as scheduled on these dates....
>
> The first sentence of Section 3 refers first to strikes, then to work stoppages. The parties may not be assumed to have engaged in redundancy, so the Umpire finds that the term "work stoppages," as used in this provision, was intended to mean something beyond the normal strike situation....
>
> ... On the basis of the record made, the Umpire determines that the work stoppage in which they engaged did breach Section 3 of Article III, referred to by the Court as the Union's no-strike obligation....
>
> The balance of the Court's order directs compliance with this decision....
>
> Umpire requested that the proceeding before him be limited to the immediate question of contract compliance.[234]

[230]428 U.S. 397, 92 LRRM 3032 (1976).
[231]*General American Transportation v. Steelworkers, Locals 1434, 2318*, CA 78-691 (W.D. Pa., August 18, 1978).
[232]*General American Transportation Corp.* (Teple, July 14, 1978) (unpublished).
[233]*General American Transportation Corp.* (Teple, Aug. 18, 1978) (unpublished).
[234]*Id. See Shop Rite Foods, Inc.*, 58 LA 965 (Ray, 1972); *Schofield Mfg. Co.*, 45 LA 225 (Duff, 1965); *Meletron Corp.*, 36 LA 315 (Jones, 1961).

The award by the arbitrator was not confirmed by the court because as soon as it was issued the picket line was dismantled. The union representatives knew (possibly because of the experience of fifteen years before) that a confirmation would produce a court order enforceable with contempt powers.

It is significant in this case that arbitrators, even after *Boys Markets, supra*, have more injunctive power than federal judges to stop some strike action that violates the labor agreement. A federal judge can only order a termination of a strike if it grows out of a dispute that can be resolved by arbitration. An arbitrator can generate an injunction when a sympathy strike breaches the labor agreement which, by definition, has no core dispute that can be resolved by arbitration.[235] The court can, however, convert an arbitrator's injunctive order into a court decree when the award is confirmed.

REMEDIES WHEN A LEGAL STRIKER IS REPLACED DURING THE STRIKE

As discussed above, the Supreme Court in *NLRB v. Sands Mfg. Co.*[236] explained that an employee who engages in, or supports, an *illegal* strike (in violation of a "no-strike" clause in the labor agreement) may be considered a quit. This risk of losing employment status when the employee engages in a wildcat strike deters such activity. A related problem also arises when an employee engages in a *legal* strike (a strike not a breach of the labor agreement) but is replaced by a new employee hired during the strike so the employer can maintain full or partial production activities during the strike. This new hire replacement gains a *permanent replacement* status and need not be laid off by the employer to make place for the striker who now is ready to return to work. This rather anomalous status was set up by the Supreme Court in *NLRB v. Mackay Radio & Telegraph Co.*[237] The Supreme Court said that the replacement becomes *permanent* as against the returning striker because otherwise replacements would not accept replacement employment.[238]

This *permanent replacement* status was challenged by the NLRB when it held that about 323 replacements hired by Giddings & Lewis Company should be laid off and 323 strikers who wanted to return

---

[235]*See, e.g., Atomic Uniform Corp. v. Garment Workers, ILGWU*, 86 LRRM 2331 (S.D. N.Y. 1973); *Jack Meilman*, 34 LA 771 (Gray, 1960); *cf. Selb Mfg. Co. v. Machinists, District 9*, 305 F.2d 177, 50 LRRM 2671 (8th Cir. 1962).

[236]306 U.S. 332, 4 LRRM 530 (1939).

[237]304 U.S. 333, 2 LRRM 610 (1938).

[238]*Id.* at 345–46, 2 LRRM at 614.

should be recalled.[239] Such a large number of ex-strikers could not have been absorbed at the end of the strike even if the company had complied with the Board's order. (The work force at Giddings & Lewis had been reduced from 980 to 487 as a result of the strike.) The company therefore filed suit to have the Board's order overturned.[240]

Arbitrators have been interpreting seniority causes for years. It would be assumed that a new hire replacing a striker would have less length of service than an ex-striker who had a hiring date possibly years before the strike commenced and the replacement was hired, and that under the seniority rules in the labor agreement, the new hires would have less seniority and should be laid off to create room for the ex-strikers. If the 323 ex-strikers who had not been reinstated at Giddings & Lewis Company had filed grievances rather than filing charges with the NLRB, the arbitrator would have been asked to construe the seniority rules in the labor agreement and then determine whether to apply another *legal* rule, developed by the Supreme Court—*i.e., permanent replacement* status that gives replacement hires a preference to the available work over more senior employees. Should the arbitrator *blend* the legal rule into the labor agreement and change the seniority rankings, or not?

The Seventh Circuit Court approved a change in the seniority rankings of the ex-strikers, following the Supreme Court's legal rule, that left the unreinstated strikers as employees but only with "priority consideration for any vacancies that were available."[241] The Court explained the legal rationale that permitted the seniority rules to be changed:

> One such justification for refusing to reinstate is that an employer may hire permanent replacements to perform the strikers' tasks.... The rationale for this exception to the general rule is that the employer's interest in continuing his business during a strike and the needed inducement of permanent employment to obtain replacements is a sufficient business justification overcoming protection for economic strikers.[242]

Some arbitrators believe they should limit their task strictly to the interpretation of the words in the labor agreement.[243] If arbitrators who advocate this approach had been involved in this case and had felt themselves so constrained, the 323 ex-strikers would have been rein-

---

[239]*Giddings & Lewis,* 255 NLRB No. 93, 106 LRRM 1391 (1981).

[240]*Giddings & Lewis v. NLRB*, 675 F.2d 926, 110 LRRM 2121 (7th Cir. 1982); *see* enforcement of NLRB order displacing replacements for ex-strikers in *George Banta Co. v. NLRB*, 686 F.2d 210, 110 LRRM 3351 (D.C. Cir. 1982).

[241]*Id*. at 929, 110 LRRM at 2123.

[242]*Id*. at 926, 110 LRRM at 2123, quoting *NLRB v. Mars Sales & Equipment Co.*, 626 F.2d 567, 572, 105 LRRM 2138, 2142 (7th Cir. 1980).

[243]The debate between arbitrators on opposite sides of this issue is reported in the text associated with notes 3-26 in Chapter XVI, "The Impact of 'External Law' on Arbitration."

stated and the 323 new hires would have been displaced onto layoff lists. Then the company would have sought to have the award vacated (seeking the same net effect requested in the petition for reversal of the Board's order) and the court likely would have vacated the award. Some arbitrators believe they should not render awards that will be vacated and, hence, should *blend* in the legal rule to produce a compatible result to avoid vacation through a Section 301 suit.[244]

INJUNCTIVE RELIEF IN GENERAL

Arbitrators are often called upon to issue injunctive relief in disputes involving issues other than breach of no-strike provisions and improper discharge of employees. For example, arbitrators have ordered employers to reopen plants and return machinery to plants,[245] to establish a new system for filling job vacancies,[246] to reclassify employees,[247] and to engage in bargaining.[248] And an arbitrator has ordered a union to undertake immediately to bring into its membership 100 new journeymen and take other steps to meet a critical manpower shortage.[249]

Where the request for specific relief is not the enforcement of the agreement but a request for an addition to or modification of it, the remedy has been ruled beyond the arbitrator's authority. Examples are grievances asking for an extra week of vacation,[250] a modification of an existing wage rate schedule,[251] a change in the existing fringe benefits,[252] a modification of the grievance procedure,[253] and the

---

[244]Variations in awards rendered to produce results compatible with law and public policy are discussed under "Vacation for Error in Law" and "Vacations Based on Public Policy Considerations" in Chapter XXI.

[245]*See, e.g., Ohio Edison Co.*, 46 LA 801 (Alexander, 1966); *W. Va. Pulp & Paper Co.*, 48 LA 657 (Rubin, 1966); *Sohio Chemical Co.*, 44 LA 624 (Witney, 1965).

[246]*American Brake Shoe Co. v. Local 149, Automobile Workers*, 285 F.2d 869, 47 LRRM 2466 (4th Cir. 1961). In *Hotel Employers Ass'n*, 47 LA 873 (Baines, 1966), Arbitrator Robert Baines ordered an employer to cease giving effect to a contract the employer had negotiated with a civil rights group following numerous demonstrations, sit-ins, and threatened violence, on the ground that a union had the exclusive representational rights.

[247]*See, e.g., American Bakeries, Inc.*, 46 LA 769 (Hon, 1966).

[248]*Park-Pitt Building Co.*, 47 LA 234 (Duff, 1966). *But see Magnavox Co.*, 35 LA 237 (Dworkin, 1960).

[249]The award was reviewed by the court and confirmed. *Sheet Metal Contractors Ass'n of New York v. Sheet Metal Workers, Local 28*, 301 F. Supp. 553, 71 LRRM 2836 (S.D. N.Y. 1969).

[250]*Board of Education, City of New York*, 44 LA 929 (Scheiber, 1965).

[251]*See, e.g., United States Steel Corp.*, 44 LA 774 (McDermott, 1965); *Pittsburgh-Des Moines Steel Co.*, 40 LA 577 (Koven, 1963); *Sparta Ceramics Co.*, 62-1 ARB ¶ 8034 (Nichols, 1961); *Waukesha Bearings Corp.* 33 LA 831 (Slavney, 1959). *But see St. Regis Paper Co.*, 66-3 ARB ¶ 8839 (Peck, 1966).

[252]*Marathon City Brewing Co.*, 45 LA 453 (McCormick, 1965).

[253]*Northwest Natural Gas Co.*, 46 LA 606 (Merrick, 1966).

maintenance of certain incentive payment records.[254] They were denied as beyond the arbitrator's remedial authority.

In the same area as injunctive remedies issued by arbitrators is a case involving an injunction issued by a court to enjoin the sale of a company before an arbitrator had an opportunity to rule on the union's contention that the sale violated the labor agreement. The judge concurred with the union, saying that if the sale had occurred before the arbitrator could issue his award the arbitrator would have been presented with a *fait accompli* leaving him without any adequate remedy in the event the union's claim were sustained. On appeal the Seventh Circuit approved the injunctive order.[255]

DECLARATORY JUDGMENTS

Whether a request for declaratory judgment is arbitrable depends largely on the contractual definition of a grievance.[256] One court has said that a request that an arbitrator render a declaratory judgment "is just as desirable here as in any other legal proceedings, inasmuch as it may avert constant bickering over specific grievances,"[257] and an arbitrator has noted that a grievance requesting a "declaration of rights" or "declaratory judgments" concerning certain work assignments raised an arbitrable issue.[258]

AWARDING ARBITRATION COSTS

Arbitrator Robben Fleming noted the danger of adding arbitration costs as damages in an arbitration award:

> For a number of reasons strong policy considerations militate against an award of costs in the above type of case. In the first place, it is well known that there are contracts which provide that the losing party shall pay the costs of the arbitration. A clause of that kind would have taken care of the problem, but it was not included and, on the contrary, the usual clause providing for the division of costs was included. Secondly, the legal question of the arbitrator's power to award a remedy assigning all costs of the arbitration to the company is sufficiently questionable as to almost certainly bring forth a court test which would be both costly and time consuming.

---

[254]*McLouth Steel Corp.*, 47 LA 1150 (Ryder, 1966).

[255]*Machinists (IAM), Local Lodge 1266 v. Panoramic Corp.*, 668 F.2d 276, 109 LRRM 2169 (7th Cir. 1981).

[256]See discussion under "Stays Granted for Lack of a Grievance" in Chapter IV and under "Lack of an Aggrieved" and "Lack of Jurisdiction Because the Claim is Settled" in Chapter VI.

[257]*In re Columbia Broadcasting System, Inc.*, 26 Misc.2d 972, 205 N.Y.S.2d 85, 46 LRRM 2408 (1960).

[258]*United States Pipe & Foundry Co.*, AAA Case No. 67-20 (Koven, 1964).

Thirdly, there is Harry Shulman's famed question as to whether, when their autonomous system breaks down, the parties might not better be left to the usual methods for adjustment of labor disputes rather than to court actions on the contract or on the arbitration award.[259]

Assessment of arbitration costs may well be beyond the arbitrator's authority. In *Brunswick Corp.*,[260] the union representative requested Arbitrator Jacob Seidenberg to assess the entire cost of the arbitration, including witnesses' expenses and counsels' fees, against the company on the ground that the company was "motivated by malice and indifference" in prosecuting the matter. But Arbitrator Seidenberg denied the claim on the ground that such a claim was "outside the authority" of the arbitrator because in the labor agreement or stipulation the parties had agreed to share arbitration costs equally. To change the equal share of costs would be "to change this provision..., a clear and deliberate rewriting of an important part of the contract."[261] He further noted that there are labor agreements which provide that the losing party is to pay the costs of the arbitration but "to introduce [such provisions] by construction into an agreement where there is not the slightest suggestion that either party desired or intended them is to distort the canons of construction and to subvert the underlying principle of voluntary arbitration."[262]

AWARDING ATTORNEYS' FEES

The general rule in arbitration is that attorneys' fees are not recoverable in the absence of specific statutory authorization. This may account for the rarity of awards of attorneys' fees. Arbitrator William Eaton in *Mercer, Fraser Co.*[263] denied the employer's claim that the union should pay him his attorney fees when his attorney obtained injunctive relief after the no-strike clause was violated. Similarly, Arbitrator Helbling in *Yellow Cab Co.*[264] denied attorney fees claimed by a grievant he reinstated. The employer had discharged the cab driver-grievant because he assaulted a passenger. The driver was charged with a felony, later reduced to a misdemeanor; the charge then was dismissed on the basis that the assault was in self-defense. The passenger did not appear for the criminal trial. The arbitrator reinstated the driver but without back pay, and denied his claim for attorney's fees.

---

[259]Fleming, *Arbitrators & Arbitrability and the Remedy Power*, 48 VA. L. REV. 1199, 1218.
[260]AAA Case No. 74-14 (Seidenberg, 1964).
[261]*Id.*
[262]*Id.*
[263]54 LA 1125 (Eaton, 1970). *See also Smithtown Nursing Home*, 65 LA 363 (Sandler, 1975).
[264]55 LA 590 (Helbling, 1970).

A court said that an attorney that won in arbitration could not recover attorney's fees unless the employer's position was totally unjustified.[265] However, a union was entitled to recover costs and attorneys' fees incurred opposing a suit to compel arbitration that had resulted in the erroneous issuance of an injunction.[266]

The fees due attorneys who have been retained by the union or by the grievant to process a grievance that involves a discrimination that could have been a Title VII claim processed through the district court may well be chargeable against the employer under the same limitations. The Supreme Court in *New York Gaslight Club v. Carey*[267] held that legal fees involved with a satisfactory settlement of a discrimination claim before Title VII litigation started can be considered costs chargeable to the individual who would have been the defendant, or settlements would not occur before litigation commenced. In another case a district court in New York decided that the legal fees were transferable to the employer when the legal service rendered was entering into a settlement procedure that involved resolution by arbitration.[268]

The complication that can be introduced in a grievance case when no factual record has been maintained and substantial attorneys' fees are claimed is well illustrated in *Electrical Workers, IBEW v. Cecil B. Wood, Inc.*[269] The labor agreement provided that if employees drove their own automobile to a work site, they would not be paid mileage unless the contractor specifically had instructed the employees to use their own automobiles. Contractor Wood transported all his employees from his shop in Rockford, Illinois to each job site, from job site to job site, and from the last job site back to the shop. On December 12, 1974, after Employee Ainsworth had completed his work, Contractor Wood arrived with his truck to transport Ainsworth and his tools to another job site six miles distant. Ainsworth elected, however, to drive his own automobile and Wood acquiesced, believing it would be more convenient for Ainsworth if he drove his own car. Ainsworth then claimed that Wood should pay him ninety cents (fifteen cents per mile). Contractor Wood refused to do so, explaining that the claim was inconsistent with the labor agreement. The biparty contractor committee awarded Employee Ainsworth the ninety cents, and the contractor refused to comply. The union's attorney then filed an enforcement action in the federal district court.[270] Even though the con-

[265]*Retail Clerks v. Lane County Independent Grocery Employers Committee*, 81 LRRM 2671 (D. Ore. 1972).
[266]*United States Steel Corp. v. Mine Workers, UMW*, 456 F.2d 483, 79 LRRM 2518 (3d Cir. 1972), *cert. denied*, 408 U.S. 923, 80 LRRM 2855 (1972).
[267]447 U.S. 54, 22 FEP Cases 1642 (1980).
[268]*Smith v. LaCote Basque*, 519 F. Supp. 663 (S.D. N.Y. 1981).
[269]No. 75 C 1191 (N.D. Ill. 1975).
[270]*Id.*, Complaint p. 5, Prayer for Relief para. (b).

tractor claimed that the ninety-cent award was clearly inconsistent with the language of the labor agreement, his attorney tendered at the hearing $1.00 *nolo contendere* to resolve the dispute.

Then a long difficult argument over the union's attorney's fees commenced; briefs were filed. The union attorney claimed that 36¾ hours had been expended in the prosecution of the claim and that, assuming a rate of $25 per hour, the claim for the attorney's fees would amount to $668.75 "or 714 times the total amount of the judgment sought."[271] Judge Frank J. McGan issued a full memorandum opinion dated September 17, 1975, which stated in part that "This case involving a dispute over 90¢ comes before the court on cross motions for summary judgment and the petition of plaintiff, International Brotherhood of Electrical Workers Local Union 364, for attorney's fees" and that the claim was not justified because "we do not find sufficient evidence of bad faith in the present case."[272]

REMEDY FOR THE NON-GRIEVANT

Difficult questions of remedial relief are posed when a provision in the labor agreement is breached but the employees who are actually hurt by the breach do not grieve. Arbitrators' awards in such cases have been diverse. For example, where the union steward and only four of the five employees involved in the identical distribution-of-overtime grievance signed the grievance, and where there was no evidence that the fifth employee who did not become a grievant was acknowledging the propriety of the company's action (he may not have known about the grievance signed by the four), Arbitrator Brecht in *National Vulcanized Fibre*[273] ruled that the award should apply to the fifth employee as well as to the four grievants. In *Jamestown Malleable Iron Div.*,[274] where management admitted that it had erred in assigning an office employee to do bargaining unit painting for one week of the two-week plant vacation shutdown, Arbitrator Kates awarded the grievant—who had signed up for vacation shutdown work but had not been assigned any—one week's pay, notwithstanding the fact that another bargaining unit employee who had not grieved might have had more of a right to the work.

In *Shahmoon Industries v. Steelworkers*[275] an arbitrator ruled that the employer had violated the labor agreement by not using the results of physical examinations to restrict the job assignments of certain em-

---

[271]*Id.*
[272]*Id.*
[273]AAA Case No. 83-6 (Brecht, 1965).
[274]AAA Case No. 140-3 (Kates, 1970).
[275]263 F. Supp. 10, 64 LRRM 2247 (D. N.J. 1966).

ployees. He granted back pay to the affected employees, even though only one had actually grieved. The employer moved to set aside the award on the basis that the arbitrator had no power to award back pay to employees other than those who had signed the original grievance. The court, however, found that the grievance had raised a challenge to the employer's practice relating to the grievant and also to other employees similarly involved, and it confirmed the back pay award. It should be emphasized, however, that arbitrators generally have no jurisdiction to grant relief to a nongrievant.[276]

REMEDIAL ORDERS SHOULD BE COMPLETE

Awards have been vacated when the remedial order was not self-executing and hence incomplete. In vacating such an order, a court said:

> By its terms the decision reserves to the parties the practical application of the general rules which it states. Thus, the decision constitutes an interpretation of the Contract, which becomes a part of the Contract, and if the parties cannot agree upon the application of that interpretation there would seem to be a basis for a new grievance and fresh invocation of the grievance machinery.[277]

Similarly, where claims of violations during a definite period were presented to an arbitrator who then rendered a "partial award without prejudice to the union proceeding ... as to violations ... during this period other than those herein presented," the award was vacated for lack of finality.[278] However, in another case where the arbitrator said that further proceedings might be necessary before the dispute could be finally resolved, the award was not vacated.[279] Similarly, a court enforced an arbitration award despite the arbitrator's recognition of the possibility that later experience with certain production standards might prove a portion of the award was erroneous.[280] No award was issued with respect to other standards covered in the grievance because of insufficient evidence. The arbitrator held that if experience under an approved standard demonstrated that the award was in error, a subsequent grievance could be filed. The court on review held the award was within the arbitrator's remedial powers.

[276]See "Enforcement by Third Parties" in Chapter III, where attempts of persons not party to the grievance filed to obtain relief through arbitration are discussed.

[277]District 50, Mine Workers, UMW, v. Revere Copper & Brass, Inc., 204 F. Supp. 349, 352, 51 LRRM 2033, 2034 (D. Md. 1962). See also Machinists v. Aerojet-General Corporation, 263 F. Supp. 343, 65 LRRM 2421 (C.D. Cal. 1966).

[278]In re Rosenblum, 15 Misc.2d 445, 182 N.Y.S.2d 641, 31 LA 822, 823 (1958).

[279]Quill v. Fifth Ave. Coach Lines, Inc., N.Y. Times, June 10, 1963 at 16, col. 6.

[280]Bakery & Confectionary Workers, Local 719 v. National Biscuit Co., 378 F.2d 918, 65 LRRM 2482 (3d Cir. 1967).

CHAPTER XIX

Post-Hearing Procedures

RECEIPT OF EVIDENCE AFTER THE HEARING

Under Rule 32 of the Voluntary Labor Arbitration Rules of the American Arbitration Association and pursuant to general arbitral practice, a hearing may be reopened[1] "by the arbitrator on his own motion, or on the motion of either party for good cause shown, at any time before the award is made."[2] The most common reason for reopening the hearing is a request of a party to introduce new evidence.

A federal district court has ruled that an arbitrator has the power to reopen a case so that evidence can be added to the record where the record was closed inadvertently by the arbitrator before the new evidence was received.[3] The arbitrator mistakenly closed the hearing before acting on the union's request for a subpoena *duces tecum*. Recognizing his mistake, the arbitrator reopened the hearing and granted the union's request for the subpoena. In upholding the award, the court noted:

> As soon as the arbitrator's error was discovered, the petitioner's motion to reopen was made and the adversary party notified.... [T]he Company's

---

[1] American Arbitration Association, *Voluntary Labor Arbitration Rules,* Rule 32 (1979):

Reopening of hearings—The hearings may be reopened by the Arbitrator on his own motion, or on the motion of either party, for good cause shown at any time before the award is made, but if the reopening of the hearings would prevent the making of the award within the specific time agreed upon by the parties in the contract out of which the controversy has arisen, the matter may not be reopened, unless both parties agree upon the extension of such time limit. When no specific date is fixed in the contract, the Arbitrator may reopen the hearings, and the Arbitrator shall have 30 days from the closing of the reopened hearings within which to make an award.

[2] In *Gateway Products Corp.*, 61-3 ARB ¶ 8639 (Marshall, 1961) at 5925, the arbitrator granted a motion for rehearing that was requested "[a]fter the hearing had been concluded and before the time of filing post-hearing briefs had expired...."

[3] *Machinists, Local Lodge 1746 v. United Aircraft Corp., Pratt & Whitney Div.*, 329 F. Supp 283, 77 LRRM 2596 (D. Conn. 1971). *See Full-Fashioned Hosiery Manufacturers*, 15 LA 452 (Taylor, 1950), where the arbitrator reopened the hearing on his own motion because he concluded that he needed additional evidence before he could render a proper award.

posture was not prejudiced and no hardship was imposed. Under such circumstances, the arbitrator acting pursuant to his own discretion had the
right, as well as the obligation, to reopen the hearing *sua sponte* to receive
any evidence, which he deemed necessary and relevant to a fair, just, and
knowledgeable disposition of the issues.

. . .

The arbitrator's reopening of the hearing and his subsequent issuance
of the subpoena corrected his prior oversight and procedural mistake, in
prematurely closing the evidentiary hearing. An arbitration hearing closed
under a mutual mistake of fact of the arbitrator and the parties, is not
closed at all and the arbitrator's subsequent actions to correct the error
were well within his jurisdiction. The employer's objection to the production of its investigation file because the arbitrator was without jurisdiction
when he issued the subpoena is without merit.[4]

Arbitrators have varied greatly in their willingness to admit evidence
into the record after the hearing has been concluded.[5] They do agree,
however, that no new evidence should be admitted subsequent to the
hearing without affording the other party an opportunity to agree to
the reopening or to explain its objections.[6]

Unless there is a joint agreement admitting evidence into the record
subsequent to the close of the hearing, or the hearing has been formally
reopened by the arbitrator, new evidence should not be received. Arbitrator Harry Dworkin in *Ohio Steel Foundry Co.*[7] explained why he
was required to ignore evidence submitted by a union in its post-hearing brief:

It is a fundamental principle which governs arbitration proceedings
that evidence may only be presented in the presence of both parties. It is
essential that the arbitrator hear testimony from the witnesses themselves,
wherever possible. The opposing side is entitled to the opportunity of
cross-examining the witnesses and to submit responsive evidence. Arbitrators consistently adhere to the principle that no new evidence may be offered or considered after the close of the hearing. It is therefore improper
to inject evidentiary matter in a post-hearing brief. Where such "evidence"
appears in the brief, inadvertently or otherwise, the arbitrator is required
to disregard such, and this must necessarily be the course which the arbitrator will follow in the instant case.[8]

---

[4]329 F. Supp. at 286, 77 LRRM at 2598.

[5]New evidence often is submitted by separate letter or, occasionally, is included in the post-
hearing brief. New evidence is not permitted in post-hearing briefs under international arbitral
procedures. Carlston, *Codification of International Arbitral Procedure*, 47 Am. J. Int'l. Law
203, 245 (1953).

[6]*Problems of Proof in the Arbitration Process: Report of the Pittsburgh Tripartite Committee,*
Problems of Proof in Arbitration, Proceedings of the Nineteenth Annual Meeting, National Academy of Arbitrators, D. Jones, ed. (Washington: BNA Books, 1967), p. 261.

[7]61-2 ARB ¶ 8429 (Dworkin, 1961).

[8]*Id.* at 5038. *See also Bendix-Westinghouse Automotive Air Brake Co.*, 36 LA 724 (Schmidt,
1961).

Similarly, Arbitrator John Sembower refused to accept a new medical statement after the hearing had been closed, and stated:

> The arbitrator really has no choice in this matter, for it is entirely clear that once a record is closed, new matter may not be introduced by either side in the absence of agreement to that effect.[9]

In *H. H. Meyer Packing Co.*,[10] Arbitrator Mulhall ruled nonadmissible as evidence pages from a manufacturer's catalogue which had been included in the employer's post-hearing brief, but which had not been admitted into evidence during the hearing. The catalogue pages had a bearing on the exact meaning of the word "frock" as used in the labor agreement. In ruling the pages inadmissible, the arbitrator rejected the employer's contentions that the catalogue pages were a matter of public reference and thus were properly included in the post-hearing brief as an exception to the general rule that new evidence cannot be submitted in a post-hearing brief.[11]

A modified version of the Sembower position, *supra*, was adopted by Arbitrator Harold Davey in *Geo. A. Hormel Co.*[12] There, newly discovered evidence was admitted where the existing record was defective or incomplete. In emphasizing the need for "compelling" reason to reopen the record and the hearing, Davey stated:

> It is ... well established that if one of the parties does introduce new material in his post-hearing brief, a formal objection by the other party to its consideration should be honored by the arbitrator unless he finds compelling circumstances causing him to conclude that the hearing should be re-opened, *e.g.*, a finding that the hearing record was incomplete or defective in some fashion.[13]

Arbitrator Marshall, relying on the rules of the American Arbitration Association, concluded that pertinent evidence should be accepted after the hearing, whether or not it was available at the time of the hearing. He concluded that the stricter rules relating to newly discovered evidence applied in court cases are not *per se* binding upon an arbitrator:

---

[9]*North Shore Gas Co.*, 40 LA 37, 43 (Sembower, 1963); *see also Printing Industry of Washington, D.C.*, 40 LA 727 (McCoy, 1963). In *Continental Can Co.*, 29 LA 67, 73 (Sembower, 1956), the arbitrator stated:
Matters of fact should properly be confined to the hearing stage, with post-hearing briefs reserved for argument, interpretation, and evaluation.
[10]66 LA 357, 362–364 (Mulhall, 1975).
[11]A prior arbitration award between the parties may properly be included in a post-hearing brief though not admitted into evidence at the hearing. *Lewin-Mathes Co.*, 37 LA 119, 121 (Moore, 1961).
[12]63-2 ARB ¶ 8462 (Davey, 1963). *See also Borden Co.*, 33 LA 302 (Morvant, 1959); *Madison Institute*, 18 LA 78 (Levy, 1952).
[13]63-2 ARB ¶ 8462 (Davey, 1963) at 8462.

While it is true that in an ordinary case of law it is exceedingly dubious as to whether the Company would be granted a motion to reopen the trial of a law suit on the basis of newly discovered evidence within the framework of the fact situation herein involved, the arbitrator nonetheless rules that the affidavit together with the accompanying documentary evidence are admissible and allows them as a part of the record of these proceedings. There is little need to belabor the differences which surround an arbitration proceeding as against an ordinary court action. The arbitrator is not bound by technical rules ¶ evidence and the sole object of an arbitration proceeding is to secure a fair and equitable resolution of differences which arise in the administration of the collective bargaining agreement. While rules of evidence are suggestive of what constitutes a fair hearing and a fair appraisal of the evidence, to follow them slavishly could only result in a distortion of the collective bargaining relationship not only because of the essential difference between a labor contract and an ordinary commercial contract but also because of the completely different climate in which the contract is given effect and the further fact that quite commonly cases are not only presented by non-lawyers but in many instances heard by non-lawyers as well.[14]

In support for this view, the arbitrator cited two rules of the American Arbitration Association: Rule 32, "Reopening of the Hearing,"[15] and Rule 29, "Evidence by Affidavit and Filing of Documents."[16] Arbitrator Marshall, reading these rules together, noted that they envision:

> [T]he possibility of not only the submission of affidavits and controverting affidavits during the hearing, but after the hearing as well where good cause is shown.[17]

Although Arbitrator Marshall made no attempt to explain what is "good cause," it is apparent that he gave the term a liberal interpretation. The evidence he received was a timecard that was available at the time of the hearing but had not been introduced because it was not known in advance that a certain witness was to testify. The timecard proved that a witness was not in the plant at the time he testified he had received a telephone call there.

---

[14]*Gateway Products Corp.*, 61-3 ARB ¶ 8629 (Marshall, 1961) at 5927.

[15]For full text, *see* note 1 *supra*.

[16]American Arbitration Association, *Voluntary Labor Arbitration Rules*, Rule 29 (1979):

Evidence by Affidavit and Filing of Documents—The Arbitrator may receive and consider the evidence of witnesses by affidavit, but shall give it only such weight as he deems proper after consideration of any objections made to its admission.

All documents not filed with the Arbitrator at the hearings but which are arranged at the hearings or subsequently by agreement of the parties to be submitted, shall be filed with the AAA for transmission to the Arbitrator. All parties shall be afforded opportunity to examine documents.

[17]*Gateway Products Corp.*, 61-3 ARB ¶ 8639 (Marshall, 1961) at 5926.

Arbitrator Byron Abernethy adopted a middle view which allows for the admission of newly discovered evidence if it can be shown that the evidence could significantly affect the outcome of the case and that it was not available at the time of the hearing. He explained his test in *United States Potash Co.*:[18]

> But once a hearing has been closed, after both parties have been afforded a full opportunity to present all their evidence and argument, and where one of the parties opposes the reopening of the case, as the Company does here, the interest in an expeditious settlement of disputed matters such as are involved in this case, dictates that an Arbitrator should grant a petition to reopen only upon a very substantial showing of the pertinence of the additional information to be adduced, a showing that the party filing the petition could not with reasonable diligence have produced the evidence at the time of the hearing, or that the party has been prevented, without fault on his part, by fraud, accident, etc., from making out his case. Such substantial showing of relevance or pertinence has not been made. There is no claim that through any accident, mistake or fraud, the petitioner was prevented from making his case at the hearing. It is true that the Union could not have produced this evidence with reasonable diligence. But the reason it could not have done so was that the evidence simply did not exist, not only at the time of the incident under consideration, but not even at the time of the hearing several months later. The very reason why the evidence could not be produced at the hearing goes far toward establishing its irrelevancy.

In *General Foods Corp., Maxwell House Division*,[19] Arbitrator Abernethy denied the union's motion to reopen the hearing to receive newly discovered evidence. The purpose of the new evidence was to impeach the uncorroborated testimony of a witness at the hearing, and it could not have affected the outcome of the case involving the discharge of the grievant. Arbitrator Abernethy stated, however, in accord with his ruling in *United States Potash Co.*,[20] that a motion to reopen the hearing to receive newly discovered evidence would be granted if the motion demonstrated: "(1) that the evidence to be adduced would be relevant; (2) that the evidence would be significant; (3) that the evidence could affect the outcome of the case; and (4) that with proper diligence the new evidence was not available to the petitioner at the time of the hearing."[21]

---

[18]30 LA 1039 at 1042-43 (Abernethy, 1958). The admission of new evidence after the close of an arbitration hearing has been approved in *District Lodge 71, Machinists v. Bendix Corp.*, 281 F. Supp. 742, 53 LRRM 2854 (W. D. Mo. 1963). *See also In re Zuckerman*, 30 LA 1009 (N.Y. Sup. Ct. 1958), allowing for reopening of the hearing where the employer failed to appear at the first hearing.
[19]65-1 ARB ¶ 8051 (Abernethy, 1964).
[20]30 LA 1039 (Abernethy, 1959).
[21]65-1 ARB ¶ 8051 at 3203.

In *Food Employers Council, Inc.*,[22] Arbitrator Gentile similarly denied the union's motion for a reopening of the hearing to receive newly discovered evidence, based upon the facts that 1) according to analogous NLRB precedent, an evidentiary hearing need not be reopened where the new evidence to be offered bears solely upon the credibility of a prior witness, and 2) the new evidence was, in fact, reasonably available at the time of the original hearing.

In *Madison Institute*[23] Arbitrator Edward A. Levy granted a request made "after the hearing was concluded" to reopen the hearing and introduce new pertinent evidence. He stated:

> Ordinarily where a hearing has been had in which all parties have participated, and have presented all evidence, and have stated on the record that they have nothing further to offer, the matter is deemed to be officially closed for the taking of evidence. However, where certain evidence is evidentiary and of material import and the admission thereof will probably affect the outcome of a cause, [if the evidence] is unavailable at the time of the hearing, and if the same is produced subsequently without seriously affecting any substantial right, and it is shown that reasonable grounds existed for its non-production at the time of the hearing, the arbitrator may, in his discretion, reopen the arbitration for the introduction of such evidence only. The reason for this rule is to afford to each of the parties full opportunity to present such material evidence as will assist the arbitrator in ascertaining the truth of all matters in controversy.[24]

Similarly, in *Borden Co.*[25] the union continued to investigate the facts after the hearing had been closed, and in its post-hearing brief discussed certain new findings and asked that the hearing be reopened. Arbitrator R. H. Morvant stated that the arbitration process was less formal than court procedure and that new evidence could be submitted if pertinent:

> Generally new evidence submitted by one of the parties after the hearing has been closed should be ignored, or stricken from the record, because the other party is unable to refute it, or have his day in court. Still, even in courts of law, new trials are ordered when it is discovered that new evidence has been uncovered which has a bearing on the case and which might result in a different result or decision. This same privilege should exist for arbitration cases as well. Perhaps even more leniency should be shown in arbitration cases than in courts of law, because the parties are not always versed in the law nor are they always astute in case preparation. To close the door of justice on such individuals would not serve the purpose for which the arbitration procedure was established and intended.

---

[22]67 LA 328, 329 (Gentile, 1976).
[23]18 LA 78 (Levy, 1952).
[24]*Id.* at 81.
[25]33 LA 302 (Morvant, 1969).

Consequently, allowances should be made which would protect the less astute and permit him to present his case to the best of his ability and leave him with the feeling that he has had his full day in court.[26]

His decision held that the additional evidence submitted was not pertinent and would not "necessitate further hearings or briefs."[27]

The rulings of most arbitrators are similar to the Regulations of the NLRB, which provide, in part:

A party to a proceeding before the Board may, because of extraordinary circumstances, move for reconsideration, rehearing, or reopening of the record after the Board decision or order. A motion for reconsideration shall state with particularity the material error claimed and with respect to any finding of material fact shall specify the page of the record relied on. A motion for rehearing shall specify the error alleged to require a hearing *de novo* and the prejudice to the movant alleged to result from such error. A motion to reopen the record shall state briefly the additional evidence sought to be adduced, why it was not presented previously, and that, if adduced and credited, it would require a different result. Only newly discovered evidence, evidence which has become available only since the close of the hearing, or evidence which the Board believes should have been taken at the hearing will be taken at any further hearing.[28]

The refusal of the arbitrator to reopen a hearing and receive "newly discovered" evidence, however, will not support a court order directing the arbitrator to do so. One court has said that such an order would undercut the finality and, therefore, the usefulness of arbitration as an expeditious and generally fair method of settling disputes.[29] Moreover, the court added, "[a]rbitrators are not and never were intended to be amenable to the 'remand' of a case for 'retrial' in the same way as a trial judge."[30]

POST-HEARING BRIEFS

It is well established in arbitration that either or both parties may file a post-hearing brief.[31] In a case where a union made a specific objection to the filing of a post-hearing brief, an arbitrator said that "either party had a right to file a post-hearing brief and that the other

---

[26]*Id.* at 307.

[27]*Id.*

[28]NLRB Rules and Regulations and Statements of Procedure, Series 8, as amended (1969), 29 C.F.R. Chapter 1, § 102.48(d) (1), LRX 4098.

[29]*Newspaper Guild, Local 35 v. Washington Post Co.*, 442 F.2d 1234, 76 LRRM 2274 (D.C. Cir. 1971).

[30]*Id.* at 1283, 76 LRRM at 2277.

[31]Horton, *The Arbitration of Discharge Cases,* 9 Sw. L. J. 332, 337 (1955).

party could file a brief also, or waive [its] right to file...."[32] In so ruling, the arbitrator distinguished between "evidence," which, under the contract, must be presented at the hearing, and "arguments" as to the meaning of evidence, which may be presented in a post-hearing brief. However, it is an accepted principle in labor arbitration that post-hearing briefs should be limited to argument and should refer only to testimony and evidence adduced at the hearing itself.[33] The general practice is for the arbitrator to conduct the exchange of the parties' briefs when he has received both, rather than for one party to serve a brief on the other. Unlike court litigation, where briefs are generally filed sequentially, arbitration briefs are generally filed simultaneously. An exchange of briefs carried out through the arbitrator prevents one party from having the advantage of seeing the opposing brief if it is filed early.[34]

Most arbitrators, including Benjamin Aaron, believe that post-hearing briefs are helpful and possibly necessary; opposition to them on cost or delay grounds is "unwise." He explained his position as follows:

> Oral summation at the conclusion of the hearing is not—save in the simple cases—an adequate substitute; the parties have not had sufficient time for reflection and for organization of their arguments and the arbitrator may be too tired to derive much benefit from what is being said. One must sympathize with complaints against over-written briefs and against tedious and time-consuming procedures of rebuttals and surrebuttals, but a single, concise, written summary of position, submitted shortly after the conclusion of the hearing, is worth its weight in gold. As a matter of fact, disputes over the interpretation of specific provisions of collective agreements which do not raise issues of fact can often be resolved speedily and economically on the basis of briefs alone.[35]

A contrary view has been expressed by Arbitrator Maurice Merrill, who believes that many post-hearing briefs are merely summaries of the evidence. He does acknowledge, however, that such a brief can be helpful if the arbitration involves a difficult question of contractual interpretation or an issue around which a body of arbitral doctrine has built up.[36]

---

[32]*Borg-Warner Corp.*, AAA Case 62-5 (McGury, 1964); *see also H. H. Meyer Packing Co.*, 66 LA 357 (Mulhall, 1975).

[33]*Geo. A. Hormel Co.*, 63-2 ARB ¶ 8462 (Davey, 1963).

[34]"Usually the company and union file their briefs simultaneously with the arbitrator, together with extra copies that he will interchange between them. There is generally no provision for reply briefs, although sometimes such briefs are filed." Brandschain, *Preparation and Trial of a Labor Arbitration Case*, THE PRACTICAL LAWYER, Vol. 18, No. 7 (Nov. 1972), p. 37.

[35]Aaron, *Labor Arbitration and Its Critics*, 10 LAB. L.J. 605, 608 (1959).

[36]Merrill, *A Labor Arbitrator Views His Work*, 10 VAND. L. REV. 789, 796-97 (1957).

Arbitrators must occasionally decide what consideration, if any, should be given to new arguments, as opposed to new evidence presented for the first time in a brief of one of the parties.[37] Arbitrator Robben Fleming reported the diversity of opinion among arbitrators on this matter:

> Some arbitrators take the view that there is nothing wrong with a new argument advanced in the brief, and that as long as the other side receives a copy the arbitrator is not even under any obligation to ask the second party to comment. Other arbitrators feel that any time a substantial new argument is advanced in the brief, comment from the other party should be requested even if it has previously received a copy of the brief and made no comment. Some arbitrators qualify either view by saying that it "depends on the kind of case and the kind of argument which is made."[38]

Arbitrator John Sembower has said that the failure of the company to mention at the hearing an argument later discussed in its post-hearing brief is significant because the union will not be afforded an opportunity to meet the argument.[39] In order to avoid the problem of new arguments, one arbitrator "asks the parties at the end of the hearing to state the grounds on which they will rely in their briefs so that there can be no surprise."[40] Another arbitrator "suggests to the parties that they indicate before the conclusion of the hearing what reported cases they will rely upon in their briefs so that the other side may respond."[41]

These positions seem quite rigid. There is no reason why all arguments must be placed before the arbitrator before the hearing closes. Some parties to an arbitration proceeding will waive closing arguments, preferring to present them in a brief. No surprise, consequently, can result from a procedure agreed upon in advance.

---

[37]Where a party in its post-hearing brief concedes the error of its grievances as filed and attempts to raise a new grievance, the arbitrator may dismiss the original grievance and refuse to hear the new grievance. *National Cash Register Co.*, 68-1 ARB ¶ 8359 (Rauch, 1968).

[38]Fleming, *Problems of Procedural Regularity in Labor Arbitration*, Wash. U.L.Q. 221, 242 (1961).

[39]*Pittsburgh Railways Co.*, 33 LA 862, 867 (Sembower, 1959).

[40]Fleming, note 38 *supra*, at 242 (arbitrator not named by the author).

[41]*Id.*

CHAPTER XX

The Award

Today labor arbitration awards usually are written and signed. At common law, they could be either written or oral, but statutes in most states require that awards be written.[1] Labor arbitration awards must follow a general pattern, influenced to some extent by the requirements of state statutes and by what courts have said when awards were reviewed. The Supreme Court has said that an award must be clear and contain an "operative command capable of enforcement" or it will be vacated.[2]

Arbitration cases are sometimes decided by a board of arbitrators consisting of one management representative, one union representative, and one impartial member who acts as the chairperson. The impartial member is usually a professional arbitrator. At common law, unless the submission agreement expressly or by implication authorized the board to decide by majority vote, all members of the arbitration tribunal were required to concur before a valid award could be rendered.[3] Today, statutes, arbitration submissions, and labor agreements provide that an award agreed upon by a majority of the board is valid and enforceable.[4] Absent an agreement or a statute to the contrary, an award concurred in by a majority of the board is enforceable under Section 301 of the Labor Management Relations Act.

Usually the impartial chairman prepares a "suggested" award and opinion. They are then concurred in by the satisfied party and dis-

---

[1]*See, e.g., Kenney v. McLean Trucking Co.*, 32 LA 323 (N.J. Sup. Ct. 1959), N.J. STAT. 2A:24-7(1952); Feldman, *Arbitration Modernized—The New California Arbitration Act*, 34 S. CAL. L. REV. 413, 429 (1961); Weinstein, *Notes on Proposed Revision of the New York Arbitration Law*, 16 ARB. J. 61, 75-76 (1961); *Commercial Arbitration Under the Utah Arbitration Act*, 4 UTAH L. REV. 174, 188 (1954); Kellor, *Standards of Practice for Arbitration*, 4 ARB. J. 46, 50 (1949); American Arbitration Association, *Voluntary Labor Arbitration Rules*, Rule 38, as amended, 1979 ("The award shall be in writing and shall be signed either by the neutral Arbitrator or by a concurring majority if there be more than one Arbitrator....").

[2]*Longshoremen, ILA, Local 1291 v. Philadelphia Marine Trade Ass'n*, 389 U.S. 64, 66 LRRM 2433 (1967).

[3]See 6 S. Williston, A TREATISE ON THE LAW OF CONTRACTS, § 1929 (rev. ed. 1938); *Creter v. Davis*, 30 N.J. Super. 60, 103 A.2d 392 (Ch. Div. 1954), aff'd, 31 N.J. Super. 402, 107 A.2d 17 (App. Div. 1954). Unanimity is required in Soviet arbitration procedure. Zawodney, *Grievance Procedures in Soviet Factories*, 10 IND. & LAB. REL. REV. 532, 545 (1957).

[4]*See, e.g.*, PA. CONS. STAT. ANN. §§ 7301-7320 (Purdon Supp. 1982).

sented to by the dissatisfied party; the latter may then prepare a dissenting opinion. However, if the two board members dissent, it would appear that the award of the chairman alone would not be effective unless the parties decide to treat the chairman's decision as the decision of a single arbitrator. However, no case has been found that discusses the effect of dissents by the two partial members of a three-member arbitration board to the award prepared by the impartial chairman.[5]

SUPPORTING OPINIONS BY THE ARBITRATOR

Although most awards are written, statutory requirements for reasoned elaborations are uncommon.[6] In the same tradition, the Supreme Court said in *Steelworkers v. Enterprise Wheel & Car Corp.*:[7]

> Arbitrators have no obligation to the court to give their reasons for an award. To require opinions free of ambiguity may lead arbitrators to play it safe by writing no supporting opinions. This would be undesirable for a well-reasoned opinion tends to engender confidence in the integrity of the process and aids in clarifying the underlying agreement.[8]

Where the arbitrator is selected under the Voluntary Labor Arbitration Rules of the American Arbitration Association, there is no need for the arbitrator to make findings of fact in the award even where the state law requires them, since Rule 38 does not require them.[9]

---

[5]*See* enforcement of an award where the arbitration board did not have a chairman and the employer's representative did not sign because of illness. *Carpenters & Joiners, Local 642 v. De Mello*, 67 L.C. ¶ 12,447 (Cal. Ct. App. 1972).

[6]*See Code of Professional Responsibility for Arbitrators of Labor-Management Disputes*, AR-BITRATION—1975, Proceedings of the Twenty-Eighth Annual Meeting, National Academy of Arbitrators, B. Dennis and G. Somers, eds. (Washington: BNA Books, 1976), p. 216; 64 LA 1317 (1975). Approved by the American Arbitration Association, Federal Mediation and Conciliation Service, and National Academy of Arbitrators, the Code contains no requirement that an arbitrator's award be accompanied by an opinion. *See Intext, Haddon Craftsmen, Inc. Div. v. Bookbinders, Local 97*, 229 Pa. Super. 206, 281 A.2d 713, 78 LRRM 2525 (1971) (award in which arbitrator had given no reasons could not be overturned in absence of fraud, corruption, or duress since arbitrators have no obligation to give reasons for their awards); *John Gibbs Agency, Inc. v. Beatty*, 31 Misc.2d 876, 217 N.Y.S.2d 788 (N.Y. Sup. Ct. 1961) ("There is no requirement that the award state the reasoning upon which it was based."); *In re Harris*, 169 Cal.2d 531, 337 P.2d 832 (Cal. Ct. App. 1959); *Pacific Vegetable Oil Corp. v. C.S.T., Ltd.*, 29 Cal.2d 228, 232, 174 P.2d 441 (1946); *Interinsurance Exchange of the Automobile Club of Southern California v. Bailes*, 219 Cal.2d 830, 33 Cal. Rptr. 533 (Cal Ct. App. 1963); *Willow Fabrics v. Carolina Freight Carriers Corp.*, 20 A.D.2d 864, 248 N.Y.S.2d 509 (1964), *aff'd*, 16 A.D.2d 929, 264 N.Y.S.2d 919, 212 N.E.2d 435 (1965); *Colletti v. Mesh*, 23 A.D.2d 245, 260 N.Y.S.2d 814; 213 N.E.2d 894 (1965); *Linwood v. Sherry*, 178 N.Y.S.2d 492 (Sup. Ct.) *aff'd*, 181 N.Y.S.2d 772 (N.Y. App. Div. 1958).

[7]363 U.S. 593 (1960).

[8]*Id.* at 598.

[9]*Fazio v. Employers' Liability Assurance Corp.*, 347 Mass. 254, 197 N.E.2d 598 (1964); *General Construction Co. v. Hering Realty Co.*, 201 F. Supp. 487 (E.D. S.C. 1962); *Hale v. Friedman*, 281 F.2d 635 (D.C. Cir. 1960).

The efforts of some unions and the American Arbitration Association to foster a faster arbitration process by dispensing with a written opinion has not been generally accepted by employers. Now these non-opinion awards are becoming very questionable, because grievance claims could well involve, lurking in the backround, a discrimination aspect developed under Title VII of the Civil Rights Act, or a wage or overtime matter developed under the Fair Labor Standards Act (discussed in Chapters XXII and XXIII), or an unfair labor practice matter developed under Section 8(a) (3) (discussed under "Vacation by Nondeferral by the NLRB" in Chapter XXI), and in such cases neither a federal district judge nor the NLRB could avoid relitigation unless the arbitrator sets forth the findings of fact (sometimes negative as well as positive findings) in a written opinion.

In the vast majority of arbitration cases the award is accompanied by a reasoned opinion. Most management and union representatives contend that opinions are desirable. In those isolated instances where a delay in the issuance of the award is undesirable, the opinion can be sent in after the award has been rendered.

Arbitrator Harry Shulman had this to say about the value of a written opinion:

> It has been urged by some that an arbitrator's award should be made without opinion or explanation in order to avoid the dangers of accumulating precedents and subjecting arbitration to the rigidities of *stare decisis* in the law. Perhaps this view has merit when the particular arbitration is regarded as solely a means of resolving the particular stalemate and nothing else. It is an erroneous view for the arbitration which is an integral part of the system of self-government and rule of law that the parties establish for their continuing relationship.
>
> ... In this system opinions are necessary, first, to assure the parties that the awards are based on reason applied to the agreement.[10]

It is good policy that awards should have supporting opinions for the reasons discussed herein and in the three following chapters. However, the Third Circuit said that, in the absence of a specific statutory requirement or provision in a collective bargaining agreement, an arbitrator was not required to provide written findings of fact or a written opinion with his award if the award is unambiguous and complete.[11] The Virgin Islands Nurses Association had sought to overturn an arbitrator's one-sentence award upholding the refusal of the Virgin Islands Department of Health to post a job vacancy. The court

---

[10]Shulman, *Reason, Contract, and Law in Labor Relations,* 68 Harv. L. Rev. 999, 1020 (1955).

[11]*Virgin Islands Nursing Ass'n's Bargaining Unit v. Schneider,* 668 F.2d 221, 109 LRRM 2323 (3rd Cir. 1981).

refused to overturn the award. The parties were free to negotiate more formal arbitration decision making for their next collective bargaining agreement if they so desired, the court said, stating:

> In light of the paramount principle of labor law that the relationship between employer and employees is best left to negotiation by the parties, we believe that principle would best be served if we decline to impose a requirement of arbitral opinions as a matter of las.[12] [Citation omitted.]

TIME LIMITS ON SUBMISSION OF AWARD

It is a well-settled common-law doctrine that an express time limitation contained in an arbitration agreement or statute must be complied with. Under this doctrine the arbitrator's authority terminates upon the expiration of the specified time limitation and, accordingly, an award rendered after the termination of such authority is null and void.[13]

Only relatively recently has a gradual process of erosion of this common-law doctrine begun.[14] Some courts draw a distinction between a time limitation set forth in the parties' arbitration agreement and time limitation imposed by law. These courts hold that the latter, as distinguished from the former, are directory only and, absent an express provision to that effect, do not require the automatic setting aside of a late award.[15] This line of authority still acknowledges the historical view that where the parties by contract make a grant of authority to an arbitrator for a limited period of time, the arbitrator's authority should be clearly limited by the grant.[16] However, various courts use practical public policy considerations to carve out in labor arbitration situations an exception to the general common law rule.[17] The Third Circuit in *Teamsters, Local 560 v. Anchor Motor Freight, Inc.*,[18] said

---

[12]*Id.* at 2326.

[13]*Goble v. Central Security Mutual Insurance Company*, 125 Ill. App.2d 298, 260 N.E.2d 860 (1970); *Librascope, Inc. v. Wymer*, 189 Cal. App.2d 71, 10 Cal. Rptr. 795, 36 LA 878 (1961); *Railway & Steamship Clerks v. Norfolk Southern Ry. Co.*, 143 F.2d 1015, 14 LRRM 905 (4th Cir. 1944).

[14]*See, e.g., Tomczak v. Erie Insurance Exchange*, 268 F. Supp. 185 (W.D. Pa. 1967).

[15]*See, e.g., Fagnani v. Integrity Finance Corp.* 53 Del. 193, 167 A.2d 67 (1960); *Teamsters v. Shapiro*, 138 Conn. 57, 82 A.2d 345 (1950), *aff'd*, 16 LA 671 (Conn. Sup. Ct. Err. 1951).

[16]*Goble v. Central Security Mutual Insurance Company*, 125 Ill. App.2d 298, 260 N.E.2d 860 (1970); *Librascope, Inc. v. Wymer*, 189 Cal. App.2d 71, 10 Cal. Rptr. 795, 36 LA 878 (1961); *Railway & Steamship Clerks v. Norfolk Southern Ry. Co.*, 143 F.2d 1015, 14 LRRM 905 (4th Cir. 1944).

[17]The Supreme Court, in *Steelworkers v. Warrior & Gulf Navigation Co.*, 363 U.S. 574, 46 LRRM 2416 (1960), approved the distinction between labor and commercial arbitration. The Court noted that commercial arbitration is a substitute for litigation, while labor arbitration, on the other hand, is the substitute for industrial strife.

[18]415 F.2d 220, 71 LRRM 3205 (3d Cir. 1969).

that the public interest in peaceful resolution of labor disputes has shifted the common law rule so that a late award may still be enforced. In this case, the arbitrator's award was rendered nearly seven months after the expressed thirty-day time limit had expired. The court took the position that the requirements of federal labor policy are best served by construing the expressed time limits as directive rather than jurisdictional. The court held that if the parties fail to include mandatory jurisdiction termination language in their agreement, the arbitrator retains authority to complete the award for a reasonable time beyond the period expressed in the labor agreement or stipulation.

However, long before the erosion of the common-law doctrine began, courts regularly enforced late awards where some fact could be found that could be considered a time limitation waiver by the objecting party. Today, courts regularly apply the waiver doctrine, except in situations where the time limitation is made mandatory by statute.[19]

As a practical matter, time limits for arbitration awards are waived by the parties when the arbitrator advises the parties that he or she is pressed for time, and cannot render the award within the "directed" limit. The only economic substance to award time limits appears to be in cases where back pay or similar liability continues to run. Failure to adhere to such time limits arguably permits the losing party to request that liability be tolled by the amount of the delay.

AWARDS AS *STARE DECISIS*

Arbitration awards involving different parties but similar issues are not considered to have the precedential value that judicial decisions have when they involve different parties but similar facts.[20] Many rules

---

[19]*Machinists, Lodge 725, v. Mooney Aircraft, Inc.*, 410 F.2d 681, 71 LRRM 2121 (5th Cir. 1969); *Teamsters, Local 560 v. Anchor Motor Freight, Inc.*, 415 F.2d 220, 71 LRRM 3205 (3d Cir. 1969); *Machinists, West Rock Lodge 2120 v. United-Greenfield Corp., Geometric Tool Co. Div.*, 406 F.2d 284, 70 LRRM 2228 (2d Cir. 1968).

[20]Manson, *Substantive Principles Emerging From Grievance Arbitration: Some Observations*, PROCEEDINGS OF INDUSTRIAL RELATIONS RESEARCH ASS'N (Washington: Industrial Relations Research Association, 1954), pp. 136–49; Davey, *Labor Arbitration: A Current Appraisal*, 9 IND. & LAB. REL. REV. 85, 88–89 (1955); Syme, *Opinions and Awards*, 15 LAB. ARB. 953, 959–61 (1950). *See also Timken Roller Bearing Co.*, 32 LA 595, 598 (Boehm, 1958); *Pan American Refining Co.*, 9 LA 731, 732 (McCoy, 1948). Of course, questions of *stare decisis* would be rather moot in the absence of published awards. The publication of arbitration awards is not required by statute, as is the case with appellate judicial decisions, but they are published in substantial number nonetheless because the award is sent in for publication by one of the parties or by the arbitrator. When sent in by the latter, it is with consent of the parties. Section 11.C.1.(c) of *The Code of Professional Responsibility for Arbitrators of Labor-Management Disputes* provides:

It is a violation of professional responsibility for an arbitrator to make public an award without the consent of the parties.

An arbitrator may request but must not press the parties for consent to publish an opinion.

and principles have evolved from labor arbitration awards involving this issue.[21] Arbitrator Merrill put it very candidly:

> As to arbitral decisions rendered under other contracts between parties not related to those in the case at hand, usefulness depends upon similarity of the terms and of the situations to which they are to be applied. They must be weighed and appraised, not only in respect to these characteristics, but also with regard to the soundness of the principles upon which they proceed. Certainly, an arbitrator may be aided in formulating his own conclusions by knowledge of how other men have solved similar problems. He ought not to arrogate as his own special virtues the wisdom and justice essential to sound decision. In at least two instances in recent months I have found by investigation that a strong current of arbitral decisions had overborne my first impression of the implications of particular language. To yield to this "common sense of most," especially as, on examination, the reasoning on which it was based carried plausibility, was neither to evade my responsibility nor to sacrifice my intellectual integrity....
>
> ... This resort to precedent in aid of interpretation and application does not deserve the scornful appellation of "playing follow-the-leader."[22]

Arbitrator Arthur Ross in *S. H. Kress & Co.*[23] analyzed past awards extensively in supporting his decision involving a company's right to retire employees at a certain age. He explained that "published awards are not binding on another arbitrator, but the thinking of experienced men is often helpful to him.[24] Arbitrator Carl Warns in *Cochron Foil Co.*,[25] a case involving an employer's right to unilaterally eliminate a job classification, reviewed awards by others and sa͟͟

ARBITRATION—1975, note 6 *supra*, at p. 224; 64 LA at 1322 (1975).
A similar policy has been set by the Federal Mediation and Conciliation Service:
    While the Service encourages the publication of arbitration awards, it is the policy of the Service not to release arbitration decisions for publication without the consent of both parties. Furthermore, the Service expects the arbitrators it has nominated or appointed not to give publicity to awards they issue if objected to by one of the parties.
29 C.F.R. § 1404.15(d) (1981). *See generally* Cherne, *Should Arbitration Awards Be Published?*, 1 ARB. J. (n.s.) 75 (1946); Taylor, *Reporting of Labor Arbitration: Pro and Con*, 1 ARB. J. (n.s.) 420, 422 (1946); Levenstein, *Some Obstacles to Reporting Labor Arbitration*, 1 ARB. J. (n.s.) 425 (1946). *See also* McPherson, *Should Labor Arbitrators Play Follow-the-Leader?*, 4 ARB. J. (n.s.) 163 (1949). Management and union representatives generally believe awards should be published. Warren & Bernstein, *A Profile of Labor Arbitration*, 4 IND. & LAB. REL. REV. 200, 217 (1951).
[21]Tobias, *In Defense of Creeping Legalism in Arbitration*, 4 IND. & LAB. REL. REV. 596, 602 (1960). *See Holland Suco Color Co.*, 43 LA 1022 (Geissinger, 1964); *Butler Mfg.*, 42 LA 304 (Johnston, 1964). *Cf. Union Carbide Corp.*, 46 LA 517 (Cahn, 1966) and *Allegheny Ludlum Steel Corp.*, 43 LA 1041 (Wallen, 1964).
[22]Merrill, *A Labor Arbitrator Views His Work*, 10 VAND. L. REV. 789, 797-98 (1957).
[23]25 LA 77 (Ross, 1955).
[24]*Id.* at 79.
[25]26 LA 155 (Warns, 1956).

Of course, other arbitration decisions are not binding on me, but it is obvious that in arbitration as in other fields, respect must be paid to accumulated wisdom and experience.[26]

A similar view was expressed by Arbitrator M. David Keefe in *Hydromation Engineering Company*:[27]

The responsibility of the arbitrator, in each case, is to exercise independent and impartial judgment on the issues before him. He has an obligation to consider the reasoning and basis which led to conclusions reached in cited awards. But, nevertheless, his fundamental duty is to make a decision which squares up with his own convictions as to where equity lies in the case which he is to decide.

Arbitrator Harry H. Platt in *Braniff Airways, Inc.*[28] noted that the principle of *stare decisis* has become integrated into labor arbitration, requiring that where a principle has become settled in a series of well-reasoned decisions, it should be followed in a similar case.

Arbitrator Sanford H. Kadish in *Thermoid Western Co.*[29] made the following statement:

While I am moved by the foregoing reasons and not precedent, it is nonetheless reassuring to observe that the overwhelming majority, indeed if not the unanimity, of arbitrators who have faced this very issue ... have reached this same conclusion.

However, Arbitrator Steven Carter in *The Coleman Co., Inc.*,[30] reported his freedom from precedent even when another arbitrator's

---

[26]*Id.* at 157. Accord, *Marathon Electric Mfg. Co.*, 29 LA 518 (Thompson, 1957); *National Lead Co.*, 28 LA 470 (Roberts, 1957); *Western Gear Corp. of Texas*, 26 LA 84 (Boles, 1956); *Philadelphia Transportation Co.*, 25 LA 379, 381–83 (Scheiber, 1955); *Cooper-Bessemer Corp.*, 25 LA 146, 149 (Reid, 1955); *Bethlehem Steel Co.*, 20 LA 91 (Seward, 1953); *Safe Bus Co.*, 21 LA 456, 460 (Livengood, 1953); *Great Lakes Carbon Corp.*, 19 LA 797, 799 (Wettach, 1953); *Coca-Cola Bottling Works Co.*, 19 LA 432, 434 (Schmidt, 1952). See Justin, *Arbitration: Precedent Value of Reported Awards*, 21 LRRM 8 (1947).

[27]67-1 ARB ¶ 8037 at 3130 (Keefe, 1966).

[28]70-1 ARB ¶ 8214 (Platt, 1969). See also *Sterling Brewers, Inc.*, 53 LA 1078 (Whitney, 1969); *Velsicol Chemical Corp.*, 52 LA 1164 (Oppenheim, 1969); *Blaw-Know Co.*, 52 LA 773 (Bradley, 1969); *Princeton Co.*, 49 LA 468 (Seinsheimer, 1967); *Muskogee Iron Works*, 29 LA 504, 507 (Singletary, 1957); *Sun Rubber Co.*, 28 LA 362, 369 (Dworkin, 1957); *Virginia-Carolina Chemical Corp.*, 23 LA 228, 233 (Marshall, 1954); *Jonco Aircraft Corp.*, 22 LA 706, 707 (Merrill, 1954); *St. Louis Terminal Warehouse Co.*, 19 LA 807, 808 (Treiman, 1952); *Coca-Cola Bottling Works Co.*, 19 LA 432, 434 (Schmidt, 1952).

[29]29 LA 424, 427 (Kadish, 1952). See also *Mississippi Lime Co.*, 29 LA 559, 562 (Updegraff, 1957); *Stockton Automotive Corp.*, 25 LA 687, 690–91 (Whitton, 1955); *American Smelting & Refining Co.*, 24 LA 857, 860–61 (Ross, 1955); *Carson Electric Co.*, 24 LA 667, 672 (Howard, 1955); *Cherry Growers, Inc.*, 24 LA 232, 237 (Howlett, 1955); *National Fireworks Ordnance Corp.*, 23 LA 349, 352–53 (Larson, 1954); *Bachman Uxbridge Worsted Corp.*, 23 LA 596, 602 (Hogan, 1954); *Allied Arts Corp.*, 23 LA 338, 340 (Smith, 1954); *American Wood Products Corp.*, 17 LA 419, 423 (Livengood, 1951); *International Harvester Co.*, 16 LA 307, 311 (McCoy, 1951); *Bethlehem Steel Co.*, 16 LA 111, 113 (Killingworth, 1951); *Struthers-Wells Corp.*, 17 LA 483, 485 (Stashower, 1951); *Grand Sheet Metal Products Co.*, 17 LA 388, 390 (Kelliher, 1951).

[30]52 LA 357 (Carter, 1969). (*See* text relating to note 51, *infra*.)

award was on an identical premium pay issue and interpreted the same labor agreement. Although agreeing that earlier awards, though not technically binding, should be followed whenever possible to promote stable industrial relations, Arbitrator Carter holds that this rule need not bind another arbitrator when the prior award was "clearly erroneous."

AWARDS AS *RES JUDICATA*

In spite of what Arbitrator Carter wrote above, when a prior arbitrator has rendered an award in a dispute between the *same* employer and the *same* union, the precedential effect of the prior award tends to move from that of *stare decisis* to that of *res judicata*. When the same parties are involved, arbitrators are willing to follow prior awards even though they would not have rendered the same award if they had heard the prior case.[31] In such cases, it is often held that adherence to precedent is desirable in order to maintain stable labor-management relations.[32]

For example, in *Union Pacific Railroad Co.*,[33] the chairman of the special board of adjustment admitted that the grievance under consideration logically dictated an award in favor of the union but the board, nevertheless, was required to abide by prior awards where the same issue had been arbitrated under the same labor agreement. Arbitrator McDermott faced such a case in *Magnavox Co.*:[34]

> If this had been a matter of first impression, the Arbitrator is not entirely sure how he would have answered the problem. The only certainty he feels is that the answer would not have been an easy one. He is certainly not prepared to conclude that the determination made by the previous arbitrator is clearly erroneous.
>
> ... In the Arbitrator's opinion, the only correct answer lies in the rule that once an identical issue between the same parties has been settled through arbitration, the former determination should not be lightly set aside.

---

[31]*Cf. Paramount Transport Systems v. Teamsters, Local 150*, 76 LRRM 2424 (E.D. Cal. 1970), *aff'd*, 436 F.2d 1064, 76 LRRM 2427 (9th Cir. 1971), where, in a suit by an employer for damages allegedly suffered as a result of an unlawful secondary boycott engaged in by two unions, the determination of the NLRB that such an unfair practice had occurred was considered *res judicata* and therefore binding on a federal district court. *Contra*, an employer was not required to honor a prior arbitration award with regard to a discharged employee's entitlement to accrued vacation benefits, since the prior award did not involve this grievant. *Chemical Workers, Local 189 v. Purex Corp.*, 427 F. Supp. 338, 95 LRRM 2271 (D. Neb. 1977, *aff'd*, 566 F.2d 48, 96 LRRM 3371 (8th Cir. 1977).

[32]*Brewers Board of Trade, Inc.*, 38 LA 679 (Turkus, 1962); *City Service Oil Company*, AAA Case No. 13-13 (Wirtz, 1959).

[33]62-3 ARB ¶ 8946 (Seidenburg, 1962).

[34]70-1 ARB ¶ 8002 at 3009 (Teple, 1969).

The arbitrator's dilemma here is clear: his thinking may be taking him in a direction other than that followed by his predecessor, but if his choice is just that—personal opinion of the best interpretation— then he should follow the prior award in the interest of continuity of interpretation. As Arbitrator Roy Ray succinctly put it in *General Portland Cement Co.*:[35]

> If one Board says no and another says yes, what will a third Board say sometime in the future when the same dispute arises once more? The parties will be right back where they started.

The necessity for finality was emphasized by Arbitrator Langston Hawley in *Mead Corp.*,[36] where he held that answers to questions obtained through arbitration should "not be overturned by subsequent proceedings unless there are powerful and compelling reasons for doing so."

The corollary of this necessity for finality is the need for consistency in contractual interpretation stressed by many arbitrators in upholding prior awards.[37] Arbitrator Saul Wallen, in *Allegheny Ludlum Steel Corp.*,[38] stated:

> I am constrained, both by the parties' essential agreement on the point and by my own recognition of the need for consistency in the interpretation of agreements, to regard the [prior] decision as the settled law of the case and to apply it to the extent it is applicable to the facts at hand.

Arbitrator Whitley McCoy set the guidelines for many arbitrators in *Pan American Refining Company*:[39]

> But where, as here, the prior decision involves the interpretation of the identical contract provision, between the same company and union, every principle of common sense, policy, and labor relations demands that it stand until the parties annul it by a newly worded contract provision.

The need for consistency has caused a decision rendered under a multi-employer agreement at one company to be extended to an identical situation at another company covered by the same provisions.[40] Also stressed has been the need for consistency in the mutual application of contractual interpretations rendered at different plants of the

---

[35]62-2 ARB ¶ 8611 at 5273 (Ray, 1962).

[36]43 LA 391, 394 (Hawley, 1964). *Accord, Owens-Illinois Glass Co.*, 43 LA 715 (Dworkin, 1964). *See also Lawson Milk Co.*, 46 LA 709, 710 (Gibson, 1966); *Hi-Torc Motor Corp.*, 40 LA 929, 930 (Kerrison, 1963); *Atlas Foundry, Inc.*, 69-2 ARB ¶ 8774 (Bradley, 1969); *Lewin-Mathes Co.*, 37 LA 119 (Moore, 1961); *Kennecott Copper Corp.*, 32 LA 646 (Ross, 1959).

[37]*See, e.g., Board of Education, City of New York*, 45 LA 43 (Rock, 1965).

[38]43 LA 1041, 1042 (Wallen, 1964).

[39]9 LA 731, 732 (McCoy, 1948).

[40]*American-Saint Gobain Corp.*, 62-3 ARB ¶ 8882 (McCoy, 1962).

same employer who has contracts with several locals unions containing identical language.[41] However, at least one arbitrator has refused to find a subsidiary bound by the interpretation of an applicable master contract provision rendered in a dispute involving the parent company,[42] holding that the required identity of parties and facts was not sufficiently established.

The policy of finality and consistency was combined by Arbitrator Ray in *General Portland Cement Company*.[43] He determined that although he was not legally bound to follow an earlier award involving the same parties and contractual provisions, a proper regard for the arbitral process required application of the prior decision since no clear error was perceived,[44] and refusal to do so would leave unresolved and unsettled the problem covered by the prior decision.[45] Preservation of the integrity of the prior decision is frequently the determining factor in choosing to follow a prior award, even though the new arbitrator may indicate he or she might have reached a different decision in the initial case. The criterion used to justify upsetting the prior award has been variously stated as requiring a finding that the previous award was "clearly wrong,"[46] "clearly and significantly wrong,"[47] and "so plainly and palpably erroneous as to be upset."[48]

The language of the collective bargaining agreement is basic to many decisions regarding the effect of prior awards. This is because many agreements provide that the arbitrator's award shall be "final and binding."[49] In *Mead Corp.*,[50] this language caused Arbitrator Hawley to state:

> Thus, unless the facts, the contract, and/or the relevant conditions upon which the prior decisions were reached have materially changed, it is the view of this arbitrator that he is bound by the awards which have been previously rendered.

---

[41]*National Lead Co.*, 28 LA 470 (Roberts, 1957).

[42]*Wallingford Steel Co.*, 34 LA 385 (Healy, 1960).

[43]62-2 ARB ¶ 8611 (Ray, 1962). Another arbitrator said that he did not adopt a strict *res judicata* rule which would prevent the union from re-arguing bargaining history before him, but that the union would have to show by a "preponderance of credible evidence" that the labor agreement should be construed differently than it was by the prior arbitrator. *Board of Education, City of New York*, AAA Case No. 78-8 (Horvitz, 1965).

[44]62-2 ARB ¶ 8611 at 5273, citing *O & S Bearing Co.*, 12 LA 132 (Smith, 1949).

[45]62-2 ARB ¶ 8611 at 5273, citing *Inland Steel Co.*, 1 ALAA ¶ 67, 121 (Blumer, 1944).

[46]*Neches Butane Products Co.*, 68-1 ARB ¶ 8361 at 4251 (Merrill, 1968); *Flintkote Co.*, 41 LA 268 (Merrill, 1963); *The Coleman Co., Inc.*, 52 LA 357 (Carter, 1969).

[47]*Brewers Board of Trade*, 38 LA 679, 680 (Turkus, 1962).

[48]*Lawson Milk Co.*, 46 LA 709, 711 (Gibson, 1966).

[49]*See, e.g., Atlas Foundry Inc.*, 69-2 ARB ¶ 8774 (Bradley, 1969); *Union Carbide Corp.*, 46 LA 517 (Cahn, 1966); *Hi-Torc Motor Corp.*, 40 LA 929 (Kerrison, 1963); *U.S. Industrial Chemicals Co.*, 41 LA 348 (Geissinger, 1953).

[50]43 LA 391, 394 (Hawley, 1964).

Similarly, in *Holland Suco Color Co.*[51] Arbitrator Geissinger held:

> The final sentence of Article X, Step 4, provides: "The award of the arbitrator shall be final and binding." In other words, the [prior] decision is *"res judicata"* meaning that the point, question, or subject matter which was in controversy or dispute has been authoritatively and finally settled by that decision.

Other arbitrators invoke the premise that the past award interpreting the contract's terms has become a part of the terms, and is therefore binding until the parties themselves amend the language.[52] This approach has gained such wide acceptance as to allow Arbitrator Uible in *Stewart-Warner Corp.*[53] to state:

> It is a well established principle in arbitration processes that arbitration opinions are not precedents; that each case stands upon its own feet. However, it also appears to be a well established principle that the interpretation of contract language embodied in an award becomes a part of that contract language.

The incorporation theory is strengthened where the parties to an award subsequently readopt the same language.[54] Arbitrator Rolf Valtin stated this proposition succinctly in *Allegheny Ludlum Steel Corp.*:[55]

> It is a generally recognized principle that the interpretation of contract language embodied in an award becomes a part of that contract language. If the parties fail to negotiate a change of the language in future contracts, but readopt the same language, that language having received an interpretation is presumed to be readopted with that interpretation.

Similarly, the failure of the adversely affected party even to raise the issue of change in subsequent negotiations has been held to constitute a presumption of acquiescence.[56] This presumption of contractual as-

---

[51]43 LA 1022, 1024 (Geissinger, 1964).

[52]*See, e.g., Pan American Refining Co.*, 9 LA 731 (McCoy, 1948). *See generally* Elkouri and Elkouri, How ARBITRATION WORKS (Washington: BNA Books, 1973), pp. 377–379.

[53]33 LA 816, 818–819 (Uible, 1960).

[54]*Todd Shipyards Corp.*, 69 LA 27 (Jones, 1977); *Magnavox Co.*, 70-1 ARB ¶ 8002 (Teple, 1969); *Gorton-Pew Fisheries*, 16 LA 365 (Wallen, 1951); *Pan American Refining Corp.*, 9 LA 731 (McCoy, 1948). The circuit court in *Westinghouse Elevators of Puerto Rico Inc. v. S.I.U. de Puerto Rico*, 583 F.2d 1184, 99 LRRM 2651 (1st Cir. 1978), held that a court cannot review an award on the grounds that it was inconsistent with a prior award which interpreted an expense reimbursement provision and which was then readopted into the labor agreement. The company explained that the first award became a part of the labor agreement and the second arbitrator had no authority to change this term of the agreement. The court concluded that the award was not *res judicata*.

[55]30 LA 1011, 1013 (Valtin, 1958); *see also Day and Zimmerman, Inc., Lone Star Div.*, 70-2 ARB ¶ 8624 (Caraway, 1970); *Ford Motor Co.*, 30 LA 46 (Platt, 1958); *Federal Bearings Co., Inc.*, 22 LA 721 (Justin, 1954).

[56]*U.S. Industrial Chemicals Co.*, 41 LA 348 (Geissinger, 1963). *See Magnavox Co.*, 70-1 ARB ¶ 8002 (Teple, 1969) and cases cited therein. *See also Tennessee River Pulp & Paper Co.*, 68 LA

similation could quite properly be considered a form of estoppel whereby the parties are entitled to rely upon the continued efficacy of the prior decision.

Thus, while the strict classical judicial formulations of *res judicata*—that is, that parties should be bound by prior determinations to avoid repetitive litigation—may be somewhat out of place in the less formalistic process of industrial arbitration, there is adequate evidence that arbitrators using various guises have permitted the ideas basic to that doctrine to thrive.[57]

Since the effects of an application of *res judicata* are so conclusive, encompassing matters that were, or could have been, raised, the rule necessarily operates upon a narrow basis of exact identity of parties, issues, and causes of action.[58] Thus, the relitigation situation most frequently encountered by arbitrators is one where the subsequent case arises from somewhat different circumstances between the same parties[59] and is sufficiently distinguishable to preclude the strict invocation of *res judicata*.[60]

---

421 (Simon, 1976); *Jackson Public Schools*, 67 LA 315 (Roumell, 1976); *Reynolds & Reynolds, Co.*, 63 LA 157 (High, 1974); *Tribune Publishing Co.*, 61 LA 1309 (Koven, 1974); *Red Wing Shoe Co.*, 53 LA 689 (Jacobowski, 1969); *Butler Mfg. Co.*, 42 LA 304 (Johnston, 1964); *Armstrong Cork*, 34 LA 890 (Morvant, 1960).

[57]In *Clover v. Columbus Retail Merchants Delivery, Inc.*, 115 Ohio App. 467, 185 N.E.2d 658, 51 LRRM 2387 (1962), the court quoted with approval the following statement from 4 OHIO JURISPRUDENCE 2d 697:

The decision of the arbitrators on all matters of fact and law is conclusive, and all matters in the award are thenceforth *res judicata*, on the theory that the matter has been adjudged by a tribunal which the parties have agreed to make final, a tribunal of last resort for that controversy.

In *Blumenthal Print Works, Inc. v. Johnson*, 173 N.E.2d 698 (Ohio Ct. App. 1960), the Ohio court held that an arbitration award rendered in New York prevented a relitigation of the same issue in Ohio.

[58]*Drake Motor Lines, Inc. v. Teamsters, Local 107*, 343 F. Supp. 1130, 80 LRRM 3003 (D. Pa. 1972); *Clemens v. Central R.R. Co. of New Jersey*, 399 F.2d 825, 68 LRRM 3054 (3d Cir. 1968), *cert. denied*, 393 U.S. 1023, 70 LRRM 2226 (1969); *Goldblatt v. Board of Education, City of New York*, 52 Misc.2d 238, 275 N.Y.S.2d 550 (1966), *aff'd*, 57 Misc.2d 1089, 294 N.Y.S.2d 272 (Super. Ct. 1968); *Todd Shipyards Corp v. Marine and Shipbuilding Workers, Local 15*, 242 F. Supp. 606, 59 LRRM 2613 (D. N.J. 1965); *Automobile Workers v. The Weatherhead Co.*, 203 F. Supp. 612, 49 LRRM 3036 (N.D. Ohio 1962), *aff'd*, 316 F.2d 239, 53 LRRM 2092 (6th Cir. 1963); *In re Frank Chevrolet Corp.*, 32 Misc.2d 1057, 224 N.Y.S.2d 928, 36 LA 19 (Sup. Ct. 1961).

[59]In *Nix v. Spector Freight Systems, Inc.*, 264 F.2d 875, 43 LRRM 2551, *reh'g denied*, 43 LRRM 2788 (3d Cir. 1959), the court dismissed an attempt by employees not party to an arbitration to attack the award, which determined seniority rights. The majority opinion characterized the plaintiff(s) as "[o]ne who was not even a party to the arbitration proceedings [and who] seeks relief which requires the invalidation of the award in a suit in which the beneficiaries of the award are not present or in any way represented." *Id.* at 877, 43 LRRM at 2552.

[60]*Pittsburgh Rys. Co. v. Street, Electric Ry. & Motor Coach Employees*, 176 F. Supp. 16, 44 LRRM 2790 (W.D. Pa. 1959); *Armak Co.*, 63 LA 997 (Shanker, 1974); *Armstrong Cork Co.*, 63 LA 517 (McKelvey, 1974); *Allison Steel Mfg. Co.*, 54 LA 1200 (Roberts, 1970).

For example, where a prior arbitrator dismissed a grievance because the union had filed it without having the grievant sign it, as required by the labor agreement, and a subsequent arbitrator granted the grievance after it was signed by the grievant and reprocessed, the Third Circuit held the dismissal of the grievance by the first arbitrator was for a procedural reason and was not *res judicata* on the merits of the claim.[61]

On the other hand, the First Circuit held that an award was *res judicata* on the issues decided in the arbitration even though an employee was not contractually bound to arbitrate the dispute.[62] Similarly, the Sixth Circuit upheld an employer's plea of *res judicata* against an attempt by a union to rearbitrate a case where an earlier award over the same issues had resulted in a favorable award for the company, but a part of the award not dealing with the issues at bar had been vacated because the arbitrator had exceeded his authority.[63]

Granting that most arbitrators will give great, and sometimes controlling, weight to prior awards involving the same issue between the same parties, there are situations where arbitrators feel compelled to refuse to apply a prior award. Arbitrator Ray, in *General Portland Cement Co.*,[64] enumerated these situations as follows:

(1) The previous award was clearly an instance of bad judgment; (2) the decision was made without benefit of some important and relevant facts; (3) the decision was based upon an obvious and substantial error of fact or law; (4) a full and fair hearing was not afforded in the prior case.

The Fifth Circuit held that the second arbitrator was not required under a *res judicata* rule to follow the first arbitrator when the second arbitrator and the court held that the first arbitrator had exceeded his jurisdiction and authority and the award did not draw its essence from the labor agreement.

The precise issue before this Court is whether the second arbitration involving the same factual situation, the Barrett award, should be set aside as invalid. This question, however, turns in large measure on whether the earlier Sabella award which yielded a contrary result was itself valid. In

[61]*Electrical Workers, IUE, Local 616 v. Byrd Plastics, Inc.*, 428 F.2d 23, 74 LRRM 2550 (3d Cir. 1970).
[62]*Reeves v. Tarvizian*, 351 F.2d 889, 60 LRRM 2339 (1st Cir. 1965).
[63]*Machinists v. Jeffrey Galion Mfg. Co.*, 350 F.2d 512, 60 LRRM 2108 (6th Cir. 1965), *cert. denied*, 383 U.S. 927, 61 LRRM 2419 (1966). *Accord, Edwards v. North American Rockwell Corp.*, 291 F. Supp. 199 (C.D. Cal. 1968); *Washington v. Aerojet-General Corp.*, 282 F. Supp. 517 (C.D. Cal. 1968).
[64]62-2 ARB ¶ 8611 at 5273 (Ray, 1962).

general, it is established that an arbitrator will follow a prior award on controlling facts under the same contract.[65]

Arbitrator Barrett in his award recognized this principle. But it is also established that if an award exceeds the arbitrator's jurisdiction or authority, does not draw its essence from the collective agreement, it cannot be considered to be binding.[66]

The awards of arbitrators go further. There is a substantial body of jurisprudence reflected in arbitration awards which holds that the second arbitrator need not follow the earlier arbitration if it is found to be "plainly erroneous."[67] [Citations omitted.]

MODIFICATION AND CORRECTION OF
AN AWARD BY THE ARBITRATOR

At common law, an arbitrator did not have authority to modify or correct an award once it had been rendered, because of the doctrine of *functus officio*; *i.e.*, having rendered the award, the arbitrator's task has been fulfilled.[68] Similarly, an arbitrator had no authority to com-

---

[65]*W.R. Grace & Co. v. Rubber Workers, Local 759*, 652 F.2d 1248, 1252, 107 LRRM 3251, 3254 (5th Cir. 1981), *cert. granted*, 50 USLW 3998.18 (U.S. June 28, 1982) (No. 81-1314), with citations and comment in the decision as follows:
Local 103, Int'l U. of Electrical, Radio and Machine Workers, AFL-CIO v. RCA Corp., 516 F.2d 1336 [89 LRRM 2487] (3rd Cir.1975); *Westinghouse Electric*, 45 L.A. 899 (1965); *Sears, Roebuck & Co., Inc.*, 39 L.A. 567 (1962). *But compare Westinghouse Elevator of Puerto Rico v. SIU de Puerto Rico*, 583 F.2d 1184 (1st Cir.1978), reviewing a second arbitration award on the established narrow grounds without regard to the fact that it was contrary to a prior award between the same parties.
[66]*Id.* at 1253, 107 LRRM at 3254, with citations and comment in the decision as follows:
Torrington v. Metal Products Workers, 362 F.2d 677 [62 LRRM 2495] (2nd Cir.1966) (setting aside such an award). *See also Amalgamated Meat Cutters and Butcher Workmen of North America, Dist. Local No. 540 v. Neuhoff Bros. Packers, Inc.*, 481 F.2d 817 [83 LRRM 2652] (5th Cir. 1973), recognizing the principle but in the particular case upholding the award. In *San Antonio Newspaper Guild, Local No. 25 v. San Antonio Light Div.*, 481 F.2d 821 [83 LRRM 2728] (5th Cir.1973), this Court granted enforcement of a second arbitrator's award when the first award was imperfect and inconclusive.
[67]*Id.*, with citations and comment in the decision as follows:
For a discussion of this principle see arbitrator Goldberg's opinion in *Mallinckrodt Chemical Works*, 50 L.A. 933, 935 (1968). For other similar arbitration awards see *Carbon Fuel Co.*, 67 L.A. 1038 (1976); *American Smelting & Refining Co.*, 59 L.A. 340 (1972); *Coleman Co., Inc.*, 52 L.A. 357 (1969); *American Cyanimid Co.*, 49 L.A. 314 (1967); *American Steel Foundries*, 19 L.A. 779 (1952). For an even more extreme statement see arbitrator Justin's opinion in *Federal Bearings Co., Inc.*, 22 L.A. 721, 725-6 (1954), "The arbitrator may consider prior awards between the parties . . . but he is not bound to follow them." As long as the arbitrator keeps within his jurisdiction, he can decide the issues submitted to him, notwithstanding any prior awards between the parties, unless the parties have agreed otherwise.
[68]*See* Seitz, *Problems of the Finality of Awards or* Functus Officio *and All That*, LABOR ARBITRATION—PERSPECTIVES AND PROBLEMS, Proceedings of the Seventeenth Annual Meeting, National Academy of Arbitrators, M. Kahn, ed. (Washington: BNA Books, 1964), p. 165.

mence a subsequent hearing. For example, the court stated in *Mercury Oil Refining Co. v. Oil Workers*:[69]

> It is a general rule in common law arbitration that when arbitrators have executed their award and declared their decision they are *functus officio* and have no power or authority to proceed further.

Arbitrator Adolph Koven in *Uarco, Inc.*[70] applied this rule when a company requested him to determine whether the company had fulfilled its obligations under the prior award he had rendered. He said that such a request "amounts to asking him to enforce his original award, thereby going beyond his authority in this case."

The common law rule was revised by the Uniform Arbitration Act.[71] That Act provides in Section 9 that the arbitrator can modify or correct his or her award upon the application of one of the parties:

> On application of a party or, if an application to the court is pending under Sections 11, 12 or 13, on submission to the arbitrators by the court under such conditions as the court may order, the arbitrators may modify or correct the award upon the grounds stated in paragraphs (1) and (3) of subdivision (a) of Section 13, or for the purpose of clarifying the award. The application shall be made within twenty days after delivery of the award to the applicant. Written notice thereof shall be given forthwith to the opposing party, stating he must serve his objections thereto, if any, within ten days from the notice. The award so modified or corrected is subject to the provisions of Sections 11, 12, and 13.[72]

[69]187 F.2d 980, 983, 16 LA 129 (10th Cir. 1951). *Accord, Indigo Springs, Inc. v. N.Y. Hotel Trades Council*, 59 LRRM 3024 (N.Y. Sup. Ct. 1965); *Shippers Express Co. v. Teamsters*, 59 LRRM 2744 (Cal. Sup. Ct. 1965); *Mole v. Queen Insurance Co.*, 14 A.D.2d 1, 217 N.Y.S.2d 330 (1961). Fleming, *Problems of Procedural Regularity in Labor Arbitration*, Wash. U. L.Q. 221, 247 (1961). *See generally* Justin, *Arbitrability and the Arbitrator's Jurisdiction*, Management Rights and the Arbitration Process, Proceedings of the Ninth Annual Meeting, National Academy of Arbitrators, J. McKelvey, ed. (Washington: BNA Books, 1956), p. 17.
[70]*Uarco, Inc.*, 43 LA 1060, 1063 (Koven, 1964).
[71]Alaska Stat. §§ 09.43.010 to 09.43.180 (1973); Ariz. Rev. Stat. Ann. §§ 12-1501 to 12-1518 (1982); Ark. Stat. Ann. §§ 34-511 to 34-532 (Supp. 1981); Col. Rev. Stat. §§ 13-22-201 to 13-22-223 (Supp. 1981); Del. Code Ann. tit. 10, §§ 5701 to 5725 (1974); D.C. Code Ann. §§ 16-4301 to 16-4319 (1981); Idaho Code §§ 7-901 to 7-922 (1979); Ill. Ann. Stat. ch. 10, §§ 101 to 123 (Smith-Hurd 1975); Ind. Code Ann. §§ 34-4-2-1 to 34-4-2-22 (Burns 1975); Kan. Stat. Ann. §§ 5-401 to 5-422 (1975); Me. Rev. Stat. Ann. tit. 14, §§ 5927 to 5949 (1964); Md. Cts. & Jud. Proc. Code Ann. §§ 3-201 to 3-234 (1980); Mass. Gen. Law Ann. ch. 251 §§ 1 to 19 (1959); Mich. Comp. Laws Ann. §§ 600.5001 to 600.5035 (1968); Minn. Stat. Ann. §§ 572.08 to 572.30 (West Supp. 1982); Mo. Ann. Stat. §§ 435.350 to 435.470 (Vernon Supp. 1982); Nev. Rev. Stat. §§ 38.015 to 38.205 (1973); N.M. Stat. Ann. §§ 44-7-1 to 44-7-22 (1978); N.C. Gen. Stat. §§ 1-567.1 to 1-567.20 (Supp. 1977); Okla. Stat. Ann. tit. 15, §§ 801 to 818 (West 1981-82); Pa. Cons. Stat. Ann. §§ 7301 to 7320 (Purdon Supp. 1982); S.C. Code Ann. §§ 15-48-10 to 15-48-240 (Law. Co-op. Supp. 1981); S.D. Codified Laws Ann. §§ 21-25A-1 to 21-25A-38 (1979); Tex. Rev. Civ. Stat. Ann. arts. 224 to 238-6 (Vernon 1973); Wyo. Stat. §§ 1-36-101 to 1-36-119 (1977).
[72]24 LA 886, 887 (Koven, 1955).

The grounds for such modification or correction do not involve objections to the merits of the award, but correction of miscalculation of figures, mistakes in descriptions, removal of portions of the award exceeding submissions, and corrections of form.

In several states where the Uniform Arbitration Act has not been enacted, a statute allows an arbitrator to modify or correct an award upon application of a party.[73] Such provisions are similar to the Uniform Arbitration Act as they only permit arbitrators "to correct formal errors or clarify their intent but not to ... alter the [merits of the] decision."[74]

The theory that an arbitrator's function is exhausted and that he or she becomes *functus officio* after submitting an award was specifically rejected by the Fourth Circuit in *Enterprise Wheel & Car Corp. v. Steelworkers*:[75]

> [T]he award directed the Corporation to reinstate the grievants and compensate them for the time lost less the ten-day suspension period and less such amounts as they may have received from other employment; but the arbitrator failed to include in the award the amounts which had actually been earned or, by the exercise of due diligence, could have been earned by the grievants in other employment. It has generally been held that a final award must be certain in its terms or provide means and data by which it may be made certain by mathematical calculation, and that if it is deficient in this respect it must be vacated since the powers of the arbitrator are exhausted and the award cannot be resubmitted to him for correction or amendment....
>
> ... If this rule were given effect in the pending case the award would be set aside, for it is obviously so incomplete that disputes may well arise as to the amounts of back pay which the employer is obliged to make to the discharged workers. We think, however, that the rule forbidding the submission of a final award, which was developed when the courts looked with disfavor upon arbitration proceedings, should not be applied today in the settlement of employer-employee disputes. As pointed out in *Textile Workers Union of America v. Lincoln Mills*, 353 U.S. 448, Congress has clearly indicated that the arbitration of grievance disputes for the preser-

---

[73]CAL. DIV. PRO. CODE § 1284 (West Supp. 1968-69). (For a detailed discussion of the California statute, *see* Comment, *Some Problems Relating to Enforcement of Arbitration Awards Under the New California Arbitration Act*, 9 U.C.L.A. L. REV. 422 (1962)); FLA. STAT. ANN. § 682.10 (Supp. 1969) (statute applies to all agreements unless the parties specifically provide otherwise); N.Y. CIV. PRAC. LAW § 7509 (McKinney, 1963) (*see also* Weinstein, *Notes on Proposed Revision of the New York Arbitration Law*,16 ARB. J. (n.s.) 61, 76 (1961)); WASH. REV. CODE ANN. § 7.04.170 (1961) (Act does not apply to labor agreements).

[74]*Legis. Studies & Rep.*, N.Y. CIV. PRAC. LAW § 7509 at 587 (McKinney 1963); *Historical and Practice Notes*, ILL. ANN. STATE. ch. 10, § 109 at 694 (Smith-Hurd, 1966).

[75]269 F.2d 327, 331-332, 44 LRRM 2349, 2352-53 (4th Cir. 1959). *See generally* Busch, *Does the Arbitrator's Function Survive His Award?* 16 ARB. J. 31 (1961); Jones, *Arbitration and the Dilemma of Possible Error*, 11 LABOR L.J. 1023 (1960).

vation of industrial peace is to be encouraged and the Supreme Court has directed the federal courts to fashion a federal substantive law in accordance with this policy. This may readily be done in the pending case by requiring the parties to take steps to complete the arbitration so that the amounts due the grievants for loss of time will be definitely ascertained.

The Supreme Court reversed that part of the court of appeals' ruling in *Enterprise* which had held that back pay could not be awarded for discharge in breach of the labor agreement for a period after the expiration of the agreement.[76] It sustained the ruling quoted above, stating: "We agree with the Court of Appeals that the judgment of the District Court should be modified so that the amounts due the employees may be definitely determined by arbitration."[77]

Even before the decision in *Enterprise*, a court pointed out that the *functus officio* doctrine could have no application to a permanent arbitrator for the reason that "he [is] not merely an arbitrator for the specific controversy."[78] In that case, the court held that the question of the amount of back pay due an employee who the permanent umpire earlier had held was wrongfully discharged could be resubmitted to the same permanent arbitrator as a new arbitration dispute. The arbitrator would hear the dispute over the back pay calculation if it became a new grievance and progressed through the various steps of the arbitration procedure.

A California court rationalized the common law rule that a permanent arbitration board does not lose jurisdiction after rendering an award when the award is submitted for rehearing.[79] The lower court had vacated an award which a permanent arbitration board had issued on the ground that the board had no power to entertain a rehearing to clarify its award. The appellate court ordered the rehearing, not because the Board was a permanent arbitration board, but because the California arbitration statute did not bar a court from ordering a rehearing when the labor agreement did not fix a time period for the rendering of the award.

Prior to the *Enterprise* decision, some arbitrators maintained at least part of the *functus officio* doctrine, stating that they would honor a request for modification or correction of an award if both parties to the case involved joined in the request.[80] Arbitrator Whitley McCoy, in

---

[76]363 U.S. 593, 597-98, 46 LRRM 2423, 2425-26 (1960).

[77]*Id.* at 599, 46 LRRM at 2426.

[78]*In re Wagner*, 11 LA 1173 (N.Y. Sup. Ct. 1948).

[79]*Union Local 679 v. Richmond-Chase Corp.*, 191 Cal. App.2d 841, 13 Cal. Rptr. 341, 36 LA 881 (1961).

[80]Kellor, *Standards of Practice for Arbitration*, 4 ARB. J. (n.s.) 46 (1949). By appearing at a hearing on a petition to clarify an arbitration award, a union was held to have waived its right to

Twin City Rapid Transit Co. [81] a number of years ago, noted the inadequacy of the *functus officio* doctrine. Although he said in his acceptance of a rehearing that he based his action on the "presumed intent of the parties"[82] and "upon the public policy which dictates that there be a definite point where litigation shall end and the rights and obligations of disputants be definitely and for all times settled,"[83] he also said that the *functus officio* doctrine is subject to an exception:

> The parties to an arbitration cannot be presumed to have intended that an award that contains on its face, or on the face of the record, fundamental mistakes of fact, as distinguished from errors of judgment, causing a miscarriage of justice, should be irremediable. Nor is public policy subserved by a principle that would perpetuate a miscarriage of justice in an arbitration award any more than in a judgment.[84]

In accordance with his opinion, Arbitrator McCoy amended the award based on corrections of certain errors that were in the record. The company's arbitration board member strongly objected, stating that the neutral arbitrator had no authority to amend the award and that the assumption of such power was "mischievous" and "calculated to do irreparable harm to arbitration."[85] McCoy answered:

> [I]t is far more in the interest of arbitration, and of peaceful labor relations, that arbitrators have the power to correct impeachable awards, than that it be necessary for a Company to apply to the courts, and thus precipitate a strike, as happened recently in Springfield, Ill., or that a union, in protest of an award go on strike, as happened even more recently in St. Louis.[86]

Where an award is unclear and the parties cannot agree on how to apply it, one court said the remedy is not vacation on the grounds that the award is indefinite, or reformation by the court, but resubmission to the arbitrator by the parties.[87] It is pointed out in the next chapter that more and more courts, rather than reform awards where error or ambiguity is shown, are ordering the case to be resubmitted to the arbitrator for clarification of the award.

---

object to any clarification ruling, even though its position was that the original award was not ambiguous and needed no clarification. *Textile Workers v. Courtaulds North America, Inc.*, 80 LRRM 2823 (S.D. Ala. 1972).

[81] 7 LA 845 (McCoy, 1947).
[82] *Id.* at 866.
[83] *Id.*
[84] *Id.*
[85] *Id.* at 869.
[86] *Id.*
[87] *Packinghouse Workers, Local 52 v. Western Iowa Pork Co.*, 247 F. Supp. 663, 62 LRRM 2800 (S.D. Iowa 1965), *aff'd*, 366 F.2d 275, 63 LRRM 2187 (8th Cir. 1966).

CHAPTER XXI

Vacation, Enforcement, or Correction

This chapter reports the vacation, enforcement, or correction of awards and is related to the next two chapters entitled "*De Novo* Reviews in a Court" and "Fair Representation Obligations." These three chapters involve various types of Section 301 suits that are used by a dissatisfied grievant to upset or modify labor arbitration awards.

A vacation, enforcement or correction of an award starts with the filing of a Section 301 suit in a federal or state court.[1] When such a suit is filed in a state court it is removable to a federal court.[2] Neither the arbitrator[3] nor the individual employee involved in the grievance[4] is an indispensable party, and the actions to enforce, vacate or correct generally are brought by the employer or the union. However, a grievant may seek to vacate an award if he or she alleges that the union and the employer breached their duty under the labor agreement,[5] or the award *touches* the public law.[6]

---

[1]29 U.S.C. § 185 (1964); *Charles Dowd Box Co. v. Courtney*, 368 U.S. 502, 49 LRRM 2619 (1962). *See also Avco Corp. v. Machinists, Lodge 735*, 390 U.S. 557, 67 LRRM 2881 (1968); *Espino v. Volkswagen de Puerto Rico, Inc.*, 289 F. Supp. 979, 69 LRRM 2364 (D. P.R. 1968); *Machinists, Lodge 2120 v. Geometric Tool Co.*, 406 F.2d 284, 70 LRRM 2228 (2d Cir. 1968); *Steelworkers v. Enterprise Wheel & Car Corp.*, 363 U.S. 593, 599, 46 LRRM 2423 (1960). *Textile Workers, TWUA v. Cone Mills Corp.*, 268 F.2d 920, 44 LRRM 2345 (4th Cir. 1958), *cert. denied*, 361 U.S. 889, 45 LRRM 2085 (1959).

[2]*Keystone Printed Specialties Co., Inc. v. Scranton Printing Pressmen, Local 119*, 386 F.Supp. 416, 87 LRRM 3191 (M.D. Pa. 1974), *aff'd* 517 F.2d 1398, 90 LRRM 2889 (3d Cir. 1975); *Bakery & Confectionery Workers, Local 719 v. National Biscuit Co.*, 252 F. Supp. 768, 62 LRRM 2182 (D. N.J. 1966), *aff'd*, 378 F.2d 918, 65 LRRM 2482 (3d Cir. 1967); *Kracoff v. Retail Clerks, Local 1357*, 244 F. Supp. 38, 59 LRRM 2942 (E.D. Pa. 1965); *Central Metal Products, Inc. v. Automobile Workers, Local 1249*, 159 F. Supp. 70, 48 LRRM 2452 (E.D. Ark. 1961).

[3]*Honeywell, Inc. v. Electrical Workers, IUE, Local 116*, 307 F. Supp. 1126, 73 LRRM 2210 (E.D. Pa. 1970).

[4]*Railway, Airline & Steamship Clerks, Local 1902 v. Safety Cabs, Inc.*, 414 F. Supp. 64, 93 LRRM 2520 (M.D. Fla. 1976); *see also Red Ball Motor Freight, Inc. v. Teamsters, Local 961*, 202 F. Supp. 904, 49 LRRM 2816 (D. Colo. 1962), although to the extent the court held that individuals cannot bring § 301 suits under any circumstances (*Id.* at 905, 49 LRRM at 2817), it erred. *See, e.g., Vaca v. Sipes*, 386 U.S. 171, 64 LRRM 2369 (1967); *Humphrey v. Moore*, 375 U.S. 335, 55 LRRM 2031 (1964); *Smith v. Evening News Ass'n*, 371 U.S. 195, 51 LRRM 2646 (1962).

[5]Discussed in Chapter XXIII, "Fair Representation Obligations."

[6]Discussed in Chapter XXII, " *De Novo* Reviews in a Court."

As explained in Chapter I, a procedural law has developed around Section 301. The limitation that will bar such a suit is the statute of limitations set out in the state statutes, but which time limitation in the various state statutes is to be applied to the various types of Section 301 suits is not yet clear.[7] The Second Circuit believed that the limitation on a suit to vacate an award is that applicable to breach-of-labor agreement suits, i.e., six years,[8] whereas the Supreme Court in *United Parcel Service v. Mitchell*[9] reasoned that since such a suit seeks a vacation of the award, a ninety-day limitation was appropriate. Justice Stewart, in his dissent, said the derivation of limitation rule should be shifted from the various state statutes to the six-month limitation set out in Section 10(b) of the National Labor Relations Act[10] so a standard limitation would apply in cases of this type. As mentioned in Chapter I, limitation rules may still be in flux and hence, *caveat*: a litigant should not assume that he or she can read a state statute of limitations rule and determine what limitation is applicable to each type of Section 301 suit. To illustrate, the Supreme Court has shortened "retroactively" the state limitation period to the NLRB six-month limitation in certain cases.[11]

VACATING AN AWARD

Under this heading only illustrative reasons why courts have vacated awards or have refused to vacate them will be discussed. Throughout this volume there are other citations to cases where *vacatur* has been granted or denied, and these will not be rediscussed in this chapter. For example, suits for the vacation of awards because the arbitrator failed to hear material evidence or relied on evidence not in the record is treated in Chapter XII, "Rules of Evidence."

As late as 1972 an experienced arbitrator reported that most "losing" parties did not attempt to have awards vacated:

---

[7]*Automobile Workers v. Hoosier Cardinal Corp.*, 383 U.S. 696, 61 LRRM 2545 (1966).

[8]*United Parcel Service v. Mitchell*, 624 F.2d 394, 105 LRRM 2301 (2d Cir. 1980).

[9]451 U.S. 56, 107 LRRM 2001 (1981).

[10]*Id.* at 65, 107 LRRM at 2004–2006. The Ninth Circuit in *Carpenters, San Diego County District Council v. G.L. Cory, Inc.*, 685 F.2d 1137, 111 LRRM 2222 (9th Cir. 1982), reversed the district court that had barred a suit to vacate because it was not filed within the 3-month deadline. This limitation rule was set out in the United States Arbitration Act. The circuit court permitted the suit to go forward because it had been filed within the California 100-day time limit. The court cited the Supreme Court's 1981 decision, *United Parcel Service, Inc. v. Mitchell*, 451 U.S. 56, 107 LRRM 2001 (1981), in support but conceded that a "uniform federal limitation period might be desirable." 685 F.2d at 1140, 111 LRRM at 2224. *See also* the First Circuit decision in *McNutt v. Airco Industrial Gases Division*, 687 F.2d 539, 111 LRRM 2212 (1st Cir. 1982) that barred a suit to vacate an award because it had not been filed within the 30-day Massachusetts rule time limit.

[11]*See* Chapter I.

[N]early all labor arbitration is conducted with the understanding that the decision of the arbitrator will be "final and binding."

. . .

This situation is undoubtedly what the parties desire in the vast majority of cases. They do not expect the arbitration to be merely a way station on the road to further and protracted litigation. The imperatives of the continuance of a harmonious collective bargaining relationship encourage this approach.[12]

But ten years later, the rush to set up Section 301 suits to vacate, modify, enforce, or revise awards had so increased that Chief Justice Warren Burger became concerned because these suits were clogging up the trial courts. He said that "remedies for personal wrongs, that once were considered the responsibility of institutions other than the courts, are now boldly asserted as legal entitlements."[13] In this chapter and the two that follow, the old and new reasons for the bringing of Section 301 suits involving labor arbitrators' awards are catalogued, and the newest holes that have been punched into the principle of finality in labor arbitration are described.

Vacation of an Award That Does Not Draw Its Essence From the Labor Agreement

The Supreme Court has held that courts have the power to vacate an award where the arbitrator exceeds the authority granted by the labor agreement. The Court stated in *Steelworkers v. Enterprise Wheel & Car Corp.*:[14]

[A]n arbitrator is confined to interpretation and application of the collective bargaining agreement; he does not sit to dispense his own brand of industrial justice. He may of course look for guidance from many sources, yet his award is legitimate only so long as it draws its essence from the collective bargaining agreement. When the arbitrator's words manifest an infidelity to this obligation, courts have no choice but to refuse enforcement of the award.

However, in the same decision the Supreme Court declared that "[t]he federal policy of settling labor disputes by arbitration would be undermined if courts had the final say on the merits of the awards," and that "the refusal of courts to review the merits of an arbitration

---

[12]Brandschain, *Preparation and Trial of a Labor Arbitration Case*, The Practical Lawyer, Vol. 18, No. 7 (Nov. 1972), p. 40.

[13]Burger, *Isn't There a Better Way?* (1982 report on the state of the judiciary), 68 A.B.A. J. 274. Also, *see* the discussion in the Foreword.

[14]363 U.S. 593, 597, 46 LRRM 2423, 2425 (1960).

award is the proper approach to arbitration under collective bargaining agreements."[15] Giving substance to this Supreme Court directive, the Third Circuit said in *Ludwig Honold Mfg. Co. v. Fletcher.*[16]

[A] labor arbitrator's award does "draw its essence from the collective bargaining agreement" if the interpretation can in any rational way be derived from the agreement, viewed in the light of its language, its context, and any other indicia of the parties' intention; only where there is a manifest disregard of the agreement, totally unsupported by principles of contract construction and the law of the shop, may a reviewing court disturb the award.

In H. K. Porter Co. v. Saw, File & Steel Products Workers,[17] the grievance raised the issue of the eligibility of employees to pension rights when they were terminated in a plant removal situation rather than merely in a reduction in work force. The arbitrator, notwithstanding the express eligibility requirement for a pension (age sixty-five and at least twenty-five years of service), held that employees *under* age sixty-five with twenty-five or *more* years of service *when terminated as a result of a plant removal* were entitled to a full pension, and employees over sixty-five with *less* than twenty-five years of service were entitled to a prorated pension. Because the arbitrator set forth in his record that the written age eligibility requirement had not been strictly applied in the past, the court upheld and enforced the first portion of the arbitrator's award, but it vacated the second portion because there was no evidence in the arbitrator's record that the written years-of-service eligibility requirement had ever been relaxed. The court criticized the arbitrator for attempting to administer "his own brand of industrial justice."[18] The court, rather than vacating the award and referring it back to the arbitrator for revision, simply revised the award.

Another district court in St. Louis set aside an arbitration award involving the Olin Mathieson Chemical Corporation arbitration award that required certain employees to wear metatarsal shoes for safety reasons. The union sought an order to enforce the arbitrator's decision, but the court disagreed, saying that the arbitrator had disregarded the clear provisions of the labor agreement when he set up his

---

[15]*Id*. at 596, 46 LRRM at 2425.

[16]405 F.2d 1123, 1128, 70 LRRM 2368, 2371 (3d Cir. 1969).

[17]333 F.2d 596, 56 LRRM 2534 (3d Cir. 1964). This decision has been criticized in Aaron, *Judicial Intervention in Labor Arbitration*, 20 STAN. L. REV. 41, 47 (1967) and in Note, 65 MICH. L. REV. 1647, 1659 (1967), but approved in Christensen, *Labor Arbitration and Judicial Oversight*, 19 STAN. L. REV. 671, 693 (1967).

[18]*Id*. at 600, 56 LRRM at 2537 as quoted from *Steelworkers v. Enterprise Wheel & Car Corp.*, 363 U.S. 593, 597, 46 LRRM 2423, 2425 (1960).

remedial order.[19] Looking back to *Enterprise*, District Judge James H. Meredith recited the guidelines the Supreme Court laid down in that decision, and stated that the arbitrator had not confined himself to interpretation and application of the labor agreement but had administered "his own brand of industrial justice."

In *Torrington Co. v. Automobile Workers, Metal Products Workers, Local 1645*,[20] the Second Circuit affirmed the lower court's vacation of an arbitration award directing the employer to pay employees for time lost while voting in national elections because of an alleged past practice of paying for such lost time. The labor agreement made no reference to past practice and was silent on the payment for time lost for voting, and the court below concluded that the award did not draw its essence from the labor agreement and should be vacated.

In partially enforcing and partially vacating an arbitration award, the District Court of Rhode Island decided in *Master Sheet Metal Workers & Composition Roofers Ass'n v. Local 17*[21] that the award was unenforceable since there was *no* effective labor agreement from which the award could derive its "essence," since the parties had never executed the labor agreement. In contrast to this decision, many courts have denied a request in a Section 301 suit to vacate an award,

---

[19]*Machinists, District 9 v. Olin Mathieson Chem. Corp.*, 335 F. Supp. 212, 78 LRRM 2949 (D. Mo. 1971). *See also Chromalloy American Corp., Kewanee Machinery Div. v. Teamsters, Local 21*, 450 F. Supp. 1074, 98 LRRM 2550 (D. Mo. 1978) (the court said the arbitrator exceeded his authority when he reinstated a grievant who had been terminated pursuant to the labor agreement rule that two absent occasions in a month cause termination because the absences were due to illness); *Piggly Wiggly Operators' Warehouse, Inc. v. Teamsters, Local 1*, 434 F. Supp. 83, 95 LRRM 3351 (W.D. La. 1977), *motion for reh'g*, 438 F. Supp. 164, 96 LRRM 2249 (W.D. La. 1977), *aff'd sub nom. v. Piggly Wiggly Operators' Warehouse Independent Truck Drivers*, 602 F.2d 134, 103 LRRM 2646 (5th Cir. 1980). The court vacated an award because the arbitrator exceeded his authority because he reinstated a truck driver that had been terminated under a labor agreement rule providing for discharge of a driver who became uninsurable. Awards were vacated when the arbitrator ignored the clear and unambiguous language in the labor agreement in *Teamsters, Local 205 v. Carl Colteryahn Dairy, Inc.*, 436 F. Supp. 341, 96 LRRM 3158 (W.D. Pa. 1977); *Signal Delivery Service. v. Teamsters, Local 249*, 432 F. Supp. 1233, 95 LRRM 2774 (W.D. Pa. 1977); *General Telephone Co. v. Electrical Workers, IBEW, Local 89*, 554 F.2d 985, 95 LRRM 2810 (9th Cir. 1977). Courts vacated awards because they were beyond the scope of the labor agreement in *Minnesota v. Berthiaume*, 96 LRRM 3240 (Minn. Sup. Ct. 1977); *Delta Lines, Inc. v. Teamsters, Local 85*, 409 F. Supp. 873, 93 LRRM 2037 (N.D. Cal. 1976); *Retail Clerks, Local 57 v. Western Drug*, 409 F. Supp. 1052, 93 LRRM 2060 (D. Mont. 1976); *Painters, Local 1179 v. Welco Mfg. Co.*, 542 F.2d 1029, 93 LRRM 2589 (8th Cir. 1976); *Garment Workers, ILGWU, Local 32 v. Melody Brassiere Co.*, 92 LRRM 2659 (S.D. N.Y. 1976); *Ferndale Education Ass'n v. School District*, 67 Mich. App. 637, 242 N.W.2d 478, 92 LRRM 3543 (1976).

[20]362 F.2d 677, 62 LRRM 2495 (2d Cir. 1966). *See also* criticism of *Torrington* in Griffin, *Judicial Review of Labor Arbitration Awards*, 4 Suffold L. Rev. 39, 59 (1969) and in Aaron, note 17 *supra* at 49–51. *See also Painters, Local 1179 v. Welco Mfg Co.*, 542 F.2d 1029, 93 LRRM 2589 (8th Cir. 1976); *Safeway Stores v. Bakery & Confectionery Workers, Local 111*, 390 F.2d 79, 82, 67 LRRM 2646 (5th Cir. 1968) (*dictum*); *H.K. Porter Co. v. Saw, File & Steel Products Workers*, 333 F.2d 596, 602, 56 LRRM 2534 (3d Cir. 1964).

[21]397 F. Supp. 1372 (D. R.I. 1975).

saying that the arbitrator had been given the authority to interpret the
labor agreement,[22] and the award would not be upset absent an express provision excluding the subject matter from arbitration or evidence that the arbitrator lacked jurisdiction to render the award. An
illustration of the support of an award by a court is found in *Musicians, Local 77 v. Philadelphia Orchestra Ass'n.*[23] The arbitrator had
been asked "whether under the labor agreement the musicians may be
required to fly"[24] and he held that the association could require orchestra members to travel by airplane to maintain the schedule on a
South American tour that the association considered important. Although the labor agreement made no mention of intercontinental travel,
the court refused to vacate the award, holding that its "essence" could
be found in the labor agreement.[25] Since there was nothing in the
agreement that concerned travel, the court's decision strongly suggests
that the award found its "essence" from the lack in the labor agreement of any restraints on managerial prerogatives.[26]

---

[22]*See, e.g., Teamsters, Local 251 v. Narragansett Improvement Co.*, 503 F.2d 309, 87 LRRM
2279 (1st Cir. 1974); *Keystone Printed Specialties Co., Inc. v. Printing Pressmen, Local 119*, 386
F. Supp. 416, 87 LRRM 3191 (M.D. Pa. 1974), *aff'd*, 517 F.2d 1398, 90 LRRM 2889 (3d Cir.
1975); *Procter & Gamble Mfg. Co. v. Indep. Oil & Chem. Workers*, 386 F. Supp. 213, 87
LRRM 3179 (D. Md. 1974); *Crigger v. Allied Chem. Corp.*, 367 F. Supp. 1133, 86 LRRM 3156
(S.D. W. Va. 1973), *aff'd*, 500 F.2d 1218, 86 LRRM 3162 (4th Cir. 1974); *Electrical Workers,
IUE v. Peerless Pressed Metal Corp.*, 489 F.2d 768, 82 LRRM 3089 (1st Cir. 1973); *Bell
Aerospace Co., Div. of Textron, Inc. v. Automobile Workers, Local 516*, 356 F. Supp. 354, 82
LRRM 2970 (W.D. N.Y. 1973), *aff'd in pertinent part, rev'd in part, remanded in part*, 500
F.2d 921, 86 LRRM 3240 (2d Cir. 1974); *Newark Wire Cloth Co. v. Steelworkers*, 339 F. Supp.
1207, 80 LRRM 2094 (D. N.J. 1972); *Mogge v. Machinists*, 454 F.2d 510, 78 LRRM 2939 (7th
Cir. 1971); *Washington-Baltimore Newspaper Guild, Local 35 v. Washington Post Co.*, 442
F.2d 1234, 76 LRRM 2274 (D.C. Cir. 1971); *Meat Cutters, Local 641 v. Capitol Packing Co.*,
413 F.2d 668, 71 LRRM 2950 (10th Cir. 1969); *San Francisco-Oakland Tribune Newspaper
Guild v. Tribune Publishing Co.*, 407 F.2d 1327, 70 LRRM 3184 (9th Cir. 1969); *Machinists,
District 8 v. Campbell Soup Co.*, 406 F.2d 1223, 70 LRRM 2569 (7th Cir. 1969); *Ludwig Honold
Mfg. Co. v. Fletcher*, 405 F.2d 1123, 70 LRRM 2368 (3d Cir. 1969); *Palacios v. Texaco Puerto
Rico, Inc.*, 305 F. Supp. 1076, 72 LRRM 2729 (D. P.R. 1969); *Sheet Metal Contractors Ass'n v.
Sheet Metal Workers, Local 28*, 301 F. Supp. 553, 71 LRRM 2836 (S.D. N.Y. 1969); *Graham v.
Acme Markets, Inc.*, 299 F. Supp. 1304, 71 LRRM 2155 (E.D. Pa. 1969); *Federal Labor Union
No. 18887 v. Midvale-Heppenstall Co.*, 298 F. Supp. 574, 71 LRRM 2876 (E.D. Pa. 1969); *Mine
Workers, UMW, District 50 v. Tenn Clad Industries*, 297 F. Supp. 52, 70 LRRM 3082 (E.D.
Tenn. 1969); *Teamsters, Local 75 v. Verifine Dairy Products Corp.*, 70 LRRM 3323 (E.D. Wis.
1969); *Anaconda Co. v. Great Falls Mill & Smeltermen's Union*, 402 F.2d 749, 69 LRRM 2597
(9th Cir. 1968); *Safeway Stores v. Bakery & Confectionery Workers, Local 111*, 390 F.2d 79, 67
LRRM 2646 (5th Cir. 1968); *Medo Photo Supply Corp. v. Livingston*, 274 F. Supp. 209, 66
LRRM 2016 (S.D. N.Y. 1967), *aff'd*, 386 F.2d 451, 67 LRRM 2032 (2d Cir. 1967); *Pulp,
Sulphite & Paper Mill Workers, Local 874 v. St. Regis Paper Co.*, 362 F.2d 711, 62 LRRM 2483
(5th Cir. 1966); *Textile Workers, TWUA v. Cone Mills Corp.*, 188 F. Supp. 728, 47 LRRM 2111
(M.D. N.C. 1960), *aff'd*, 48 LRRM 2544 (4th Cir. 1961).
[23]252 F. Supp. 787, 62 LRRM 2102 (E.D. Pa. 1966).
[24]*Id.* at 792, 62 LRRM at 2103.
[25]*Id.*, 62 LRRM at 2105.
[26]See Chapter X, " 'Parol Evidence,' 'Residual Management Rights,' and 'Just Cause.' "

One company attempted to challenge an award by a labor arbitrator on the ground that he had not "drawn the essence" from the labor agreement because his construction of the agreement provisions was different from that of another arbitrator in a prior award. The court in *Graphic Arts Union, Local 97-B v. Haddon Craftsmen, Inc.* [27] refused to set the second award aside on the ground that the first award was in conflict, explaining that "both awards must be sustained. This court is simply not free to vacate one award and uphold the other where both draw their essence from the collective bargaining agreement."

Vacation of an Award When a Grievant Is Reinstated But Without Back Pay

As discussed above the courts have often said that an award should not be upset if it "draws its essence from the labor agreement" and if the arbitrator was not exercising his "own brand of industrial justice." Using these two obscure standards, courts have vacated awards when they have determined (a) the arbitrator found that the grievant was guilty of misconduct that would support a "just cause" for discharge but (b) the arbitrator exercised his "own brand of industrial justice" when he reinstated the grievant because he believed discharge to be too harsh a penalty. Similarly, in 1964, the Eighth Circuit in *Teamsters, Local 784 v. Ulry-Talbert Co.* [28] decided that once the arbitrator found that the grievant was guilty of the misconduct for which he or she had been discharged, the arbitrator could not then decide that the discipline was too severe without substituting his or her judgment for that of the management. [29] And in 1980, the Sixth Circuit in *Firemen & Oilers v. The Nestle Co., Inc.* [30] vacated an award when the arbitrator converted the discharge to a long suspension on the ground the former discipline was too harsh. The Court said:

> Following his discharge, the employee filed a grievance for the alleged unjust termination of his employment which grievance was submitted to arbitration. The arbitrator made the following findings of fact:

---

[27] 489 F. Supp. 1088, 1098 (M.D. Pa. 1979). In contrast, the first of two conflicting arbitration awards was vacated in *W.R. Grace & Co. v. Rubber Workers, Local 759*, 652 F.2d 248, 107 LRRM 3251 (1981), *cert. granted*, 50 USLW 3998.18 (U.S. June 28, 1982) (No. 81-1314), discussed in Chapter XVI, "The Impact of External Law on Arbitration," in text associated with note 53 and note 101, and in Chapter XX, "The Award," in text associated with note 65.

[28] 330 F.2d 562, 564, 55 LRRM 2979, 2981 (8th Cir. 1964). The award, which reinstated twenty-eight employees striking in violation of the labor agreement because discharge was too harsh a penalty, was vacated because the employer should be able to determine the penalty. *Compare Kansas City Luggage Workers v. Neevel Luggage Mfg. Co.*, 325 F.2d 992, 55 LRRM 2153 (8th Cir. 1964) (back-pay award vacated because issue of back pay was not specifically submitted to arbitrator).

[29] *See* discussion under "The Authority to Reduce the Discipline" in Chapter XVIII.

[30] 630 F.2d 474, 105 LRRM 2715 (6th Cir. 1980).

1. The grievant "refused a direct order (of his foreman) two or three times, for reasons known only to the grievant." (Arb. Award p. 16).

2. The grievant fabricated the existence of a safety hazard as an excuse for his failure to obey the specific orders of his foreman. . . .

3. Grievant further disobeyed the foreman's orders by calling a maintenance man to look over the equipment. (Arb. Award p. 12).

4. The grievant called his foreman a "son-of-a-bitch" in the presence of the Division Manager of the Company and other employees. (Arb. Award p. 14).

The foreman further testified that the grievant was hostile, disrespectful, threatened him with violence and called him other obscene names. The arbitrator did not give credence to this additional testimony of the foreman because it was not corroborated.

The express finding of fabrication of his defense by the grievant is clear indication that grievant's disobedience of the three orders was without any justifiable reason or excuse.[31]

After reporting the arbitrator's finding, the court discussed the reasons the arbitrator gave for reinstating the grievant.

In the closing paragraph of his award, the arbitrator makes the following incredible statement:

Because of the seniority of the grievant and because of lack of proof of threats or swearing above and beyond the name-calling of "a son-of-a-bitch" there is insufficient proof in the record to make me believe that the grievant was, in fact, guilty of the vulgarities and threats as alluded to by the Company. For that reason I am going to give the grievant some relief.

IV. AWARD

The grievant shall be reinstated to his employment but without any back pay whatsoever and without loss of his seniority or contractual benefits.

Thus the arbitrator ignored his previous specific findings of insubordination by the grievant in his refusal to obey three orders of his foreman and the grievant's fabrication of his real defense, and then because the Company did not corroborate additional items of swearing, vile language and threats of violence, the arbitrator excuses the grievant's insubordination by declining to enforce the discharge provisions in the collective bargaining agreement.

But this is an arbitrator's own brand of industrial justice and is in violation of the provisions of the collective bargaining agreement which mandates and provides that insubordination "shall" be grounds for discharge. It is not for the arbitrator to decide that discharge is too severe a penalty for the insubordination which he found because the penalty, namely, discharge is contractual.[32]

---

[31]*Id.* at 476, 105 LRRM at 2716.
[32]*Id.*

The court concluded that the arbitrator had indulged in his "own brand of industrial justice" when he reinstated the grievant *but without back pay,* and cited other decisions supporting the vacation of awards for the same reason:

> In *Amanda Bent Bolt Co. v. International U., U.A., A., A. I. W.,* 451 F.2d 1277, 79 LRRM 2023, 6th Cir. 1971, we reversed the same District Judge who decided the present case, for affirming an arbitrator's award reinstating strikers who violated their contract by striking and were subjected to discharge. In our view, *Amanda* requires reversal in the present case.
>
> In *Detroit Coil v. Intern. Assn. of M. & A. Workers, Etc.,* 594 F.2d 575, 100 LRRM 3138 (6th Cir. 1979), we held again that an arbitrator is confined to interpretation and application of a collective bargaining agreement, and does not sit to dispense with his own brand of industrial justice citing *Amanda* and other cases.
>
> To the same effect is *Storer Broadcasting Co. v. [AFTRA], Cleveland Local,* 600 F.2d 45, 101 LRRM 2497 (6th Cir. 1979).[33]

The court clearly stated that only if the agreement grants to the arbitrator the authority to "convert" discipline from a discharge to a suspension can the arbitrator do it without exercising "his own brand of industrial justice"; only in this situation can the arbitrator be considered as having drawn "the essence" of the award from the labor agreement. The court said:

> In our case, the collective bargaining agreement expressly provided that insubordination shall be grounds for discharge. It is clear and unambiguous. It needs no interpretation and we find no provision in it giving the arbitrator power to prescribe the penalty for violation of the collective bargaining agreement or to control the exercise of it by the employer. This power was vested solely in the employer.[34]

Arbitrator Marvin J. Feldman in *Felters Co.*[35] reinstated a grievant who had been discharged after failing to return to work following six weeks of leave during which she had had to have surgery from which she was still recovering. She had been terminated by the employer under the labor agreement provision that provided that "Seniority rights shall be terminated when an employee ... [i]s absent for three (3) working days without notifying the Company of proper reason for

---

[33]*Id.* at 477, 105 LRRM at 2717.
[34]*Id. Compare Lynchburg Foundry Co. v. Steelworkers, Local 2556,* 404 F.2d 259, 69 LRRM 2878 (4th Cir. 1968) (arbitrator's reduction in discipline upheld); *Minute Maid Co. v. Citrus Workers,* 331 F.2d 280, 56 LRRM 2095 (5th Cir. 1964) (back-pay award held proper, although labor agreement was silent on back-pay remedy).
[35]AAA Case No. 5430-1426-78.

absence...."[36] The reinstatement was without back pay. The arbitrator said that, even in light of the mandatory word "shall" appearing in the provision, the employer knew that the absence was for "good and sufficient cause."

> [The grievant] fractured her finger while working. Because the fracture did not heal, she was given six weeks of leave commencing July 7, 1979, during which she had the tip of her finger amputated. When [the grievant] did not return to work on August 25, 1979, she was discharged by Felters.[37]

The arbitrator decided that the mandatory termination did not operate when the four-day absence passed without notice because the reason for the absence already was known to the employer. It had resulted from an injury that occurred during the course of employment.

In spite of the arbitrator's determination, the employer filed a motion for summary judgment to vacate the award in the Jackson County Circuit Court in Michigan asserting that the arbitrator was compelled to sustain the discharge once he found that the grievant was late in reporting within the time limit since the labor agreement included the mandatory words "*shall* be subject to discharge."[38] [Emphasis added.]

Judge Fleming, the circuit judge, granted the summary judgment, finding "that the arbitrator was without authority to return Defendant, W ——, to work after it was determined that W —— failed to notify the Company for five (5) days" and then remanded the "matter to the Arbitrator for entry of an award, within his authority, consistent with his finding that the contract was violated by Defendant, W ——."[39]

Arbitrator Feldman wrote a second award, known as *Felters Co. (No. 2)*[40] and it became an interesting variation because he did not follow the instructions of Judge Fleming. Since the arbitrator believed his first award was proper because it was drawn from the essence of the labor agreement, he refused to change his award and in support of his refusal cited the following words written by Justice Douglas in *Steelworkers v. American Manufacturing Co*:[41]

> The courts therefore have no business weighing the merits of the grievance, considering whether there is equity in a particular claim, or determining whether there is particular language ... which will support the claim.

---

[36]Quoted in *Felters Co. v. Clothing & Textile Workers, Local 318*, 108 Mich. App. 33, 310 N.W.2d 233, 108 LRRM 2500 (1981).

[37]*Id.*

[38]*Felters Co. (No. 2)*, 73 LA 363, 365 (Feldman, 1979).

[39]*Id.* at 364. *See* other examples of cases in which a judge remanded the award back to an arbitrator with instructions to revise his award in text associated with notes 252-57 *infra*.

[40]*Id.*

[41]363 U.S. 564, 568, 46 LRRM 2414, 2415-16 (1960).

Since Arbitrator Feldman had simply slapped the Michigan Circuit Court Judge's wrist when he did not change his prior award, even after having been directed to do so, the Felters Company went back to Judge Fleming in the Jackson County Circuit Court and moved to have the award vacated the second time. The judge again vacated the award, but this time did not return it to Arbitrator Feldman.[42] The defendant then appealed that decision to the Michigan Court of Appeals and the court reversed, enforcing the award. The Michigan Court of Appeals explained:

> Questions concerning the scope of judicial review of arbitrability and the awards made by arbitrators in labor disputes have been almost a plague on both state and Federal courts for years, but the eminently proper attitude that we have taken is one of "hands off." The party that ends up holding the short end of an arbitrator's award may try desperately to fit the facts within the narrow doorway to the courts, but the judicial policy is clear. In the Steelworkers trilogy, the United States Supreme Court held that the merits of either the grievance or the arbitration award are irrelevant when a Federal court is asked to enforce an arbitration agreement or award thereunder. Judicial review is limited to whether the award "draws its essence" from the contract, whether the award was within the authority conferred upon the arbitrator by the collective bargaining agreement. Once substantive arbitrability is determined (as it was in the court below) judicial review effectively ceases. The fact that an arbitrator's interpretation of a contract is wrong is irrelevant.[43]

The appellate court then explained the award by Arbitrator Feldman:

> In his arbitration award, Arbitrator Feldman recognized that the word "shall" was mandatory in nature. He also recognized that [the grievant] failed to give notice to Felters within the required time. However, he ruled that section 7H(4) was not meant to apply to cases where the work-injured employee failed to give notice, but the company knew that the employee had been seriously injured. Furthermore, Feldman found that Felters knew [the grievant] would not be returning on August 25, 1978. He therefore ordered her reinstatement.[44]

The appellate court reversed, saying:

> While the arbitrator's interpretation of the contract might be erroneous, it was his interpretation that the parties bargained for and the courts may

---

[42]Discussed in *Felters Co. v. Clothing & Textile Workers, Local 318*, 108 Mich. App. 333, 310 N.W.2d 233, 108 LRRM 2500 (1981).

[43]310 N.W.2d at 234, 108 LRRM at 2501, quoting *Ferndale Education Ass'n v. School District*, 67 Mich. App. 637, 642–43, 92 LRRM 3543 (1976).

[44]310 N.W.2d at 234–35, 108 LRRM at 2501.

not reverse his award. Therefore, the circuit court erred when it vacated the arbitrator's award.[45]

Another award in which the facts were very similar and the labor agreement provision was almost identical, including the mandatory word "shall," was reviewed by a federal district court in Pennsylvania when a Section 301 suit for vacation had been filed. The arbitrator had reinstated a grievant who had been absent for more than four consecutive days without notifying the company with a proper reason as specified in the agreement. (*Arco Polymers, Inc. v. Oil, Chemical & Atomic Workers, Local 8-74.*)[46] District Judge Diamond adopted a view essentially the same as State Circuit Judge Fleming's and vacated the award. He wrote:

> The arbitrator ... was clearly in excess of his authority under ... the agreement when he proceeded to modify it by nullifying the specific, unambiguous, contractual right of the plaintiff to discharge an employee who had been absent for more than four days without "good and sufficient cause."
> ...
> Under the collective bargaining agreement, the plaintiff had the express right to discharge an employee who was absent from work without good and sufficient cause for more than four consecutive days. Once the arbitrator made the finding of the fact, as he did at page 9 of his opinion, that [the grievant] failed to show good and sufficient cause for his nineteen-day absence, the arbitrator was bound to affirm the discharge unless there was a basis in the record to modify or nullify that express contractual right.... There was no such basis, and it was not the function of the arbitrator to substitute his discretion for that of the employer.[47]

This vacation decision was then appealed to the Third Circuit Court and reversed for reasons similar to those given by the Michigan Appellate Court:

> "[T]he interpretation of labor arbitrators must not be disturbed so long as they are not in 'manifest disregard' of the law, and that 'whether the arbitrators misconstrued a contract' does not open the award to judicial review...."[48]

The Third Circuit went on to say:

> Thus, the scope of our inquiry is narrow. While the arbitrator's task is to interpret the clauses of the agreement, a reviewing court may only deter-

---

[45]310 N.W.2d at 235, 108 LRRM at 2501.

[46]517 F. Supp. 681, 107 LRRM 3200 (W.D. Pa. 1981).

[47]*Id.* at 684, 685, 107 LRRM at 3202, 3203 (1982).

[48]*Arco Polymers, Inc. v. Oil, Chemical & Atomic Workers, Local 8-74,* 671 F.2d 752, 756, 109 LRRM 3157, 3160 (3d Cir. 1982), quoting *Ludwig Honold Mfg. Co. v. Fletcher,* 405 F.2d 1123, 1128, 70 LRRM 2368 (3d Cir. 1969).

mine whether the arbitrator's award was "totally unsupported by princi-ples of contract construction."[49]

It is irrelevant whether the courts agree with the arbitrator's ap-plication and interpretation of the agreement:

> The fact that the arbitrator wrote an opinion, albeit one that might be viewed as confusing and subject to various interpretations, should not cause the award to be vacated. A court should not substitute its interpreta-tion of a contract for that of the arbitrator simply because the arbitrator's analysis is opaque.[50]

The Award Must Not Exceed the Scope of the Question

Courts reviewing arbitration awards have held that the award is unenforceable when it goes "beyond the scope of the submission."[51] An award that reinstated a grievant without back pay was challenged in a vacation suit on the ground that the award went beyond the scope of the submission which had been limited to: "Was employee disci-plined for just cause ... ?"[52] The judge agreed with the challenge and vacated the award because a reinstatement *without back pay* estab-lished that there was "just cause" for discipline and that the award should simply have been "yes."[53] The decision by the Tenth Circuit in *Retail Clerks, Local 782 v. Sav-On Groceries*[54] involved a more techni-cal vacation problem. The arbitrator had awarded back pay but, since the submission did not include any question of the remedy, the district court vacated the award, and that action was approved by the majority of the Tenth Circuit, with Judge Doyle dissenting.[55]

One court took a somewhat less technical view of the scope of the submission. It approved an award that granted pay for one unworked day when the grievance had requested pay for another unworked day.

> It has never been the proper function of courts in cases such as this to look over the shoulder of an arbitrator and relitigate in detail all or any of the issues properly submitted to him for his decision.[56]

---

[49]671 F.2d at 756, 109 LRRM at 3160.

[50]*Id.* at 757, 109 LRRM at 3161.

[51]*See* note 22 *supra*.

[52]*Kansas City Luggage Workers v. Neevel Luggage Mfg. Co.*, 325 F.2d 992, 55 LRRM 2153 (8th Cir. 1964).

[53]*Id. See* discussion in Chapter X, " 'Parol Evidence,' 'Residual Management Rights,' and 'Just Cause.' " Reinstatement with *full* back pay is the remedy if there is not "just cause" to sup-port a discharge, unless the parties have agreed to give the arbitrator the authority to convert discipline.

[54]508 F.2d 500, 88 LRRM 3205 (10th Cir. 1975).

[55]*Id.* at 504, 88 LRRM at 3207.

[56]*American Bosch Arma Corp. v. Electrical Workers, IUE, Local 794*, 243 F. Supp. 493, 494, 59 LRRM 2798, 2799 (N.D. Miss. 1965).

The Court responded more technically on the scope of the submission in *Automobile Workers, Local 1078 v. Anaconda American Brass Co.* [57] The parties had submitted for resolution the issue of whether the employer's "present operating practice" permitted the foremen to perform certain production work. Instead of answering this question "yes" or "no," the arbitrator ruled that the agreement was not violated "so long as the work involved does not occupy the major portion of the foremen's time." [58] The court vacated the award on the ground that the arbitrator had not responded to the submitted question and, hence, went beyond his authority.

Likewise, when an arbitrator held that technical employees were not covered by the labor agreement but that their work was governed by it, the court in *Sperry Rand Corp., Sperry Division v. Electrical Workers, IUE, Local 445* [59] modified the award to limit it only to the holding by the arbitrator that the technical employees were not covered by the labor agreement.

One court, *Newark Wire Cloth Co. v. Steelworkers,* [60] allowed greater latitude. The court said that the award technically went beyond the scope of the submission but since it fell within the general scope of the grievance and the labor agreement, it should be enforced.

Vacation for Error in Law

At common law, most courts refused to set aside an arbitrator's award because of an error in law. The following excerpt from a 1939 New York case is illustrative of many decisions to this effect:

> The courts are very much restricted in disturbing an award of an arbitrator. If he has kept within the jurisdiction of the agreement, the award will not be set aside because he may have erred in judgment either upon the law or the facts.... Where there was a fair and impartial hearing the arbitrator's determination as to law and facts is conclusive, and his award will not be set aside for mere errors of judgment if he is not guilty of fraud or other misconduct.... [61]

---

[57] 149 Conn. 687, 183 A.2d 623, 50 LRRM 2928 (1962).

[58] 149 Conn. 687, 689, 183 A.2d 623, 625, 59 LRRM 2926, 2928 (1962).

[59] 80 LRRM 2061 (N.Y. Sup. Ct. 1971), *aff'd,* 345 N.Y.S.2d 972, 24 A.D.2d 691, 84 LRRM 2336 (1973), *motion for leave to appeal denied,* 33 N.Y.2d 517, 85 LRRM 2256 (1973).

[60] 339 F. Supp. 1207, 80 LRRM 2094 (D. N.J. 1972).

[61] *In re Pioneer Watch Case Co.,* 4 LRRM 810, 811 (N.Y. Sup. Ct., 1939). *Accord, Harris v. R.C. Havener,* 169 Cal.2d 531, 337 P.2d 832 (1969); *Fischer v. Guaranteed Concrete Co.,* 276 Minn. 510, 151 N.W.2d 266, 65 LRRM 2493 (1967); *Engineers, District 2 v. Isbrandtsen Co.,* 36 Misc.2d 617, 233 N.Y.S.2d 408 (Sup. Ct. 1962); *Kesslen Bros. Inc. v. Board of Conciliation and Arbitration,* 339 Mass. 301, 158 N.E.2d 871, 32 LA 859 (1959); *Aster v. Jack Aloff Co.,* 190 Pa. Super. Ct. 615, 155 A.2d 627 (1959).

In *Publishers Ass'n of New York City v. New York Typographical Union No. 6*,[62] it was held that the award of an arbitrator was not to be vacated for misconception of the law, since errors, mistakes, and departures from strict legal rules are all included in the arbitration risk. The Fifth Circuit emphasized in *Safeway Stores v. Bakery & Confectionery Workers, Local 111*,[63] "even if perhaps erroneous" as to an interpretation of law, the arbitrator's award should not be overturned, with the exception that "if the reasoning [of an arbitrator] is so palpably faulty that no judge, or group of judges, could ever conceivably have made such a ruling then the Court can strike down the award."[64] The court held:

> We emphasize again and again, as we have before, . . . that cases of the type pressed so heavily on us by the Employer must not be read to justify the court resuming its traditional role of assaying the judicial acceptability of the award had it been a court judgment.
>
> As these admonitions are addressed primarily to ourselves as Judges on the trial and appellate fronts we should heed them by resisting the temptations to "reason out" a la judges the arbiter's award to see if it passes muster. So it is here. But even under these self-imposed wraps this award shows on its face two things. First, the arbiter was drawing on the collective bargaining agreement as the source both of the dispute and its solution. Second, the award put forward a passably plausible—even if perhaps erroneous—analysis of the interplay of the contractual wage-minimum-day-week provisions, especially in the light of the Employer's long practice of wage payment to the very eve of payment day with no withholding of earned wages.
>
> If such a result is unpalatable to an employer or his law-trained counsel who feels he had a hands-down certainty in a law court, it must be remembered that just such a likelihood is the by-product of a consensually adopted contract arrangement—a mechanism that can hold for, as well as against, the employer even to the point of outlawing labor's precious right to strike. . . .
>
> The arbiter was chosen to be the Judge. That Judge has spoken. There it ends.[65] [Footnotes omitted.]

The interplay between federal substantive law and arbitration awards has increasingly been the subject of court review. As one court noted, arbitrators, as well as courts, must correctly apply federal substantive laws:

---

[62]168 Misc. 267, 5 N.Y.S.2d 847, 2 LRRM 809 (Sup. Ct. 1938); *see also Phillips v. American Casualty Co. of Reading, Pa.*, 198 N.Y.S.2d 538 (Sup. Ct. 1960); *Delma Engraving Corp. v. Johnson Contracting Co.*, 45 N.Y.S.2d 913 (Sup. Ct. 1944); *In re Wilkins*, 169 N.Y. 494 (Sup. Ct. 1902).

[63]390 F.2d 79, 67 LRRM 2646 (5th Cir. 1968).

[64]*Id.* at 82, 67 LRRM at 2648.

[65]*Id.* at 83, 67 LRRM at 2648-49.

[I]t is true that Federal substantive law must be applied by the arbitrator and the State Courts in decisions involving contract violations between an employer and a labor organization representing employees in an industry affecting commerce....[66]

Nevertheless, some courts continued to hold that an arbitrator's "misinterpretation of the law" does not mandate vacation of the award because vacation should only occur when the award is in "manifest disregard" of the law.[67] One district judge said:

Manifest disregard of the law "must be something beyond and different from a mere error in the law or failure on the part of the [arbitrator] to understand or apply the law".... In order to have an award vacated on this ground, the complaining party must establish that the arbitrator understood and correctly stated the law but proceeded to ignore it....[68]

In this vein, courts grappled with the numerous attacks on arbitration awards based on alleged conflicts with federal law. On more than one occasion, awards enjoining work stoppages were upheld even though it was argued that the result conflicted with the prohibitions of Norris-LaGuardia.[69] In another case, an alleged conflict with Interstate Commerce Commission regulations did not cause the court to vacate an award because the award dealt carefully with the statutory question.[70] In still another case, the union claimed that the award,

---

[66]*Ryan Aeronautical Co. v. Automobile Workers, Local 506*, 179 F. Supp. 1, 4–5 (S.D. Cal. 1969), citing *Textile Workers v. Lincoln Mills*, 353 U.S. 448, 40 LRRM 2113 (1957). Arbitrators Russell A. Smith and Dallas Jones concur with the view that courts should be able to review and correct an arbitrator's errors in the application of federal substantive law:

The basic question is whether the Court, in discharging its role of superintendent of the development of emerging federal law concerning the collective bargaining agreement, will determine for reasons of policy that arbitral as well as judicial decisions should be in conformity with principles approved by the Court. An affirmative view would place issues of this kind in a special category to be differentiated from other kinds of alleged errors of contract interpretation, fact, or law with respect to which the orthodox rule of non-reviewability would obtain.

Smith and Jones, *The Supreme Court and Labor Dispute Arbitration: The Emerging Federal Law*, 63 MICH. L. REV. 751, 806 (1965). *See also* Jay, *Arbitration and the Federal Common Law of Collective Bargaining Agreements*, 37 N.Y.U.L. REV. 448, 457–58, 468 (1972).

[67]*Metal Products Workers, Local 1645 v. Torrington Co.*, 242 F. Supp. 813, 59 LRRM 2267 (D. Conn. 1965), *aff'd*, 358 F.2d 103, 62 LRRM 2011 (2d Cir. 1966).

[68]*Bell Aerospace Co., Div. of Textron, Inc. v. Automobile Workers, Local 516*, 356 F. Supp. 354 (W.D. N.Y. 1973), *aff'd in pertinent part*, 500 F.2d 921, 86 LRRM 3240 (2d Cir. 1974); *accord*, *Amerada Hess Corp. v. Federal Labor Union, Local 2206*, 385 F. Supp. 279, 87 LRRM 2698 (D. N.J. 1974).

[69]*Pacific Maritime Ass'n v. Longshoremen & Warehousemen*, 304 F. Supp. 1315, 71 LRRM 3117 (N.D. Cal. 1969); *New Orleans Steamship Ass'n v. Longshoremen, ILA, Local 1418*, 389 F.2d 369, 67 LRRM 2430 (5th Cir. 1968), *cert. denied*, 383 U.S. 828, 69 LRRM 2434 (1968); *General Dynamics Corp. v. Marine & Shipbuilding Workers, Local 5*, 469 F.2d 848, 81 LRRM 2746 (1st Cir. 1972); *United States Steel Corp. v. Mine Workers, UMW*, 519 F.2d 1236, 90 LRRM 2539 (5th Cir. 1975), *cert. denied*, 428 U.S. 910, 92 LRRM 3006 (1976).

[70]29 U.S.C. § 101 *et seq.* (1976); *International Auto Sales & Service, Inc. v. Teamsters, Local 270*, 311 F. Supp. 313, 73 LRRM 2829 (E.D. La. 1970).

upholding the discharge of an employee, was at odds with the Jones Act[71] but it was not vacated because the Court found the arbitrator's ruling was not "totally inconsistent."[72]

More recently, where conflicts between awards and applicable law are demonstrated, the courts are more likely to refuse to enforce the award. For example, in *Glendale Manufacturing Co. v. Garment Workers, Local 520*,[73] the Fourth Circuit affirmed a district court's refusal to enforce an award (a vacation) that would have required an employer to commit an unfair labor practice. In *Carpenters, Puerto Rico District Council v. Ebanisteria Quintara*,[74] the court vacated part of an award on the ground that compliance with it would have required a violation of the National Labor Relations Act.[75]

In *General Telephone Co. of Pennsylvania v. Locals 1635, 1636, & 1637*[76] the conflict between an arbitrator's award and the law came into sharp focus. The labor agreement provided that no sick pay benefits would be provided during an absence from work due to pregnancy. The arbitrator, however, found that such failure to pay during an absence for pregnancy was unenforceable because the exclusion was an unlawful sex discrimination.[77] He explained that the "overwhelming majority" of district courts and courts of appeal had interpreted Title VII of the Civil Rights Act of 1964 to mean that a pregnancy absence must be considered a sickness and that the sick pay described in the labor agreement must be paid during a pregnancy absence to avoid a violation under Title VII. The arbitrator's award was submitted to the district court for vacation on the ground that the award was inconsistent with clear words in the labor agreement and, hence, "did not draw its essence" from the labor agreement. The district court judge was unsure of the law and stayed the case until the Supreme Court rendered its decision in *General Electric Co. v. Gilbert*.[78] Then the district court decided that sick pay benefits need *not* be paid during an absence due to pregnancy, and vacated the ar-

---

[71]46 U.S.C. § 688 (1976).

[72]*Maritime Union v. Federal Barge Lines, Inc.*, 304 F. Supp. 256, 72 LRRM 2942 (E.D. Mo. 1969).

[73]283 F.2d 936, 47 LRRM 2152 (4th Cir. 1960), *cert. denied*, 366 U.S. 950, 48 LRRM 2323 (1961).

[74]56 LRRM 2391 (D. P.R. 1964). To the contrary is a reasonably similar situation where an award directed the employer to pay contributions on his total payroll (which included nonunion workers) to the union's health, welfare, and retirement funds; it was enforced in spite of the employer's contention that the payment violated § 302(a) of the Taft-Hartley Act because non-union members would receive no benefits from the funds. *Kreindler v. Clarise Sportswear Co.*, 184 F. Supp. 182 (S.D. N.Y. 1969).

[75]29 U.S.C. § 186(c)(4) (1970).

[76]427 F. Supp. 398, 95 LRRM 2899 (W.D. Pa. 1977).

[77]*Id.* at 399, 95 LRRM at 2899.

[78]429 U.S. 125, 13 FEP Cases 1657 (1976).

bitrator's award on the ground that it was inconsistent with the labor agreement, even though the judge added that if the Supreme Court had followed the "unanimous holdings of the United States Courts of Appeal," he would not have vacated the award.[79] This ruling that a pregnancy absence was not a sickness was reversed when Congress passed the Pregnancy Discrimination Act[80] in 1978.

During this period of change, Arbitrator Z. S. Rice, in *Muskego-Norway School District*,[81] was asked whether an absence due to pregnancy was a sickness and, if so, whether the nonpayment of sick pay during a pregnancy was a Title VII sex-based discrimination. Arbitrator Rice concluded (1) that the state law made it unlawful to discriminate against an employee on the basis of sex; (2) that the state supreme court had decided that an employee absent during maternity was entitled to such payments if sick pay benefits were provided under an agreement with the employer; and (3) that the provision in the labor agreement that denied pay benefits during maternity periods was *contra* to the law. He came to this conclusion even though his award was rendered after *General Electric Co. v. Gilbert*,[82] and before Congress passed the Pregnancy Discrimination Act.

Arbitrator William Rentfro in *American Postal Workers*[83] reinstated with back pay a grievant who had been terminated by the employer because he participated in a strike in violation of the labor agreement. The arbitrator did this because he believed there were mitigating circumstances in the grievant's case. However, he ignored the law that prohibits individuals who have struck against the government from being employed by the government. The district court held that the award reinstating a striker was an illegal act and that it could not be enforced.[84] This vacation of the award was affirmed by the Ninth Circuit.[85] Judge Wallace wrote: "The courts cannot enforce an arbitrator's award if it requires the performance of an illegal act."[86]

An award by Arbitrator Charles Morris was vacated by the Fifth Circuit in *Teamsters, Local 757 v. Standard Brands*.[87] The arbitrator had concluded that the company violated the labor agreement when it closed the Dallas plant and opened a new one about seventy-five miles away in Denison, Texas without first bargaining with the union over the

---

[79]427 F. Supp. at 399, 95 LRRM at 2899.
[80]42 U.S.C.A. § 2000e(k) (1981).
[81]71 LA 509 (Rice, 1978).
[82]*Id*. at 513.
[83]Award of December 31, 1979 (Rentfro), unreported.
[84]*Postal Workers v. U.S. Postal Service*, 104 LRRM 3115 (N.D. Calif. 1980).
[85]*Postal Workers v. U.S. Postal Service*, 682 F.2d. 1280, 110 LRRM 2764 (9th Cir. 1982).
[86]*Id.*. at 1286, 110 LRRM at 2768.
[87]579 F.2d 1282, 99 LRRM 2377 (5th Cir. 1978).

relocation. As a remedy the arbitrator set up seniority dates for the
laid-off Dallas plant employees in the new Denison, Texas plant, so
these employees could transfer to that plant and displace the
employees then working there. The Dallas plant employees, prior to
the closing, had been represented by the Teamsters and if the award
had been enforced, the Teamsters would have displaced the Machinists
as the representative at the Denison plant. The Fifth Circuit found Arbitrator Morris' award to be "repugnant to the law" and remanded
the award back to him, directing a revised award compatible with the
court's decision.

Arbitrator Max Meyer in *Western Union Telegraph Co.*[88] ordered
full back pay to eliminate disciplinary suspensions issued by the company to employees who had refused to handle international traffic as
part of a union-imposed boycott to assist a sister union then on strike.
The Arbitrator held that the refusal to handle such traffic was not a
violation of the "no strike" clause in the labor agreement because such
boycotts were an industry tradition. Justice Pecora subsequently confirmed the award, holding that the arbitrator had the authority to construe the labor agreement in "conformity with the practices of the industry."[89] Then the New York Supreme Court, Appellate Division,
reversed Justice Pecora, holding that the reinstatement of employees
who had refused to receive and transmit messages was not only a violation of an express provision of the labor agreement, but was also a
violation of the law:

> Sections 552 and 1423 of the Penal Law [of New York] makes [sic] it a
> crime punishable by fine and imprisonment for any employee of a
> telegraph company to wilfully delay messages or "wilfully refuse or neglect
> to transmit or deliver messages."[90]

The Second Circuit vacated an award on the ground that the provision in the labor agreement that the arbitrator had enforced violated
federal labor laws.[91] A district court in Pennsylvania vacated an award
which upheld the right of an employer to require employees to drive
vehicles which did not fully comply with Pennsylvania's Vehicle
Code.[92]

[88]2 LA 619 (Meyer, 1946).
[89]*In re Western Union Telegraph Co.*, 21 LRRM 2507 (N.Y. Sup. Ct. 1948).
[90]*In re Western Union Telegraph Co.*, 274 A.D. 754, 79 N.Y.S.2d 545, 22 LRRM 2237, 2238
(1948), *aff'd sub nom. Western Union Telegraph Co. v. American Communications Ass'n,* 299
N.Y. 177, 86 N.E.2d 162 (1949).
[91]*Vacated as moot sub nom. Robb v. Clothing Workers, New York Joint Board,* 506 F.2d
1246, 87 LRRM 3277 (2d Cir. 1974).
[92]*Teamsters, Local 249 v. Consolidated Freightways,* 464 F. Supp. 346, 100 LRRM 2699
(W.D. Pa. 1979).

Some courts have taken the view that the award must be so illegal that it is "a perverse misconstruction" of the law, not merely "an egregious error of law." In one case[93] the award was not vacated even though the award was inconsistent with law; the court's tolerance of a margin between an "egregious error" and the "perverse" misconstruction was simply an effort to create more finality to awards. The court said:

> [T]he perverse misconstruction must be more than an egregious error of law before it satisfies the statute; it must be one which is so divorced from rationality that it can be accounted for only by one of the kinds of misbehavior recited in the statute. In that event, the [vacation] is granted not for error of law or misconstruction of documents but for misconduct under one or more of the permitted categories, which misconduct has been established. Nothing like that was established in this case.[94]

The same tolerance was applied in *Coleman Co. v. Automobile Workers.*[95] The Kansas Supreme Court explained that vacation of awards should not be made too easy:

> [C]ertain grounds that would be sufficient in an appeal from a judgment would not be grounds for impeaching an award, for the reason that the contractual element is present in the award. Thus, the fact that the arbitrator made erroneous rulings during the hearing, or reached erroneous findings of fact from the evidence, is no ground for setting aside the award, because the parties have agreed that he should be the judge of the facts. Even his erroneous view of the law would be binding, for the parties have agreed to accept his view of law. Were it otherwise in either of these cases, arbitration would fail of its chief purpose; instead of being a substitute for litigation, it would merely be the beginning of litigation. Error of law renders the award void only when it would require the parties to commit a crime or otherwise to violate a positive mandate of the law.[96]

Vacation for Inconsistency With a Decision of the NLRB

Closely related to refusals of courts to enforce awards, or to vacate them, because of inconsistency with statutory law is the refusal by courts to enforce awards because they are inconsistent with a determination by the NLRB. This was well demonstrated in *New Orleans Typographical Union No. 17 v. NLRB.*[97] There, the Board had assigned

---

[93]*In re S & W Fine Foods, Inc.*, 30 LA 346 (N.Y. Sup. Ct. 1958), *rev'd*, 8 A.D.2d 130, 185 N.Y.S.2d 1021, 32 LA 660 (1959), *aff'd*, 7 N.Y.2d 1018, 200 N.Y.S.2d 59, 35 LA 649 (1960).

[94]32 LA 660, 8 A.D.2d 130 (1959).

[95]181 Kan. 969, 317 P.2d 831, 41 LRRM 2113 (1957).

[96]317 P.2d at 837, 41 LRRM at 2117.

[97]368 F.2d 755, 63 LRRM 2467 (5th Cir. 1966); *accord, Longshoremen, ILA, Local 854 v. W.L. Richeson & Sons*, 280 F. Supp. 402, 67 LRRM 2560 (E.D. La. 1968).

certain disputed work to employees represented by one of the two contesting unions, but the arbitrator assigned the work to employees represented by the other union. The court found that the Board's determination, which was contrary to the arbitrator's subsequent award, took precedence. The Supreme Court in *Carey v. Westinghouse Electric Corp.*[98] held that "[s]hould the Board disagree with the arbiter, . . . the Board's ruling would, of course, take precedence...."[99] Following this mandate, the Fifth Circuit refused to enforce the arbitration award because it was contrary to the Board's Section 10(k) ruling on the work jurisdiction dispute.[100]

In *In re Meyers*,[101] the court refused to enforce an arbitration award requiring that the employees working in the Pleasantville plant be covered by the labor agreement that covered the employees working in the Brooklyn plant. Because the United Automobile Workers had filed a petition with the NLRB and the Board had found that that union was the representative of the employees at Pleasantville, the award extending the agreement of Local 355 of the Amalgamated Union to cover the employees in the Pleasantville plant was vacated.

Vacations Based on Public Policy Considerations

The Supreme Court in *Hurd v. Hodge*[102] in 1948 explained that the power of the federal courts to enforce the terms of private agreements is at all times exercised subject to the restrictions and limitations of the public policy of the United States as manifested *"in the Constitutions, treaties, federal statutes and applicable legal precedents."* [Emphasis added.][103]

The Second Circuit in *Electrical Workers, IUE, Local 453 v. Otis Elevator Co.*[104] adopted the same definition of the meaning of the two words "public policy" when it held that when an arbitrator issues a "final and binding" decision on the grievance it cannot be vacated by a trial judge merely by saying that the award is "inconsistent with public policy." The arbitrator's award reinstated a grievant who had been discharged because he had distributed some gambling "policy slips" to fellow employees during working hours. The company sought

---

[98]375 U.S. 261, 55 LRRM 2042 (1964).
[99]*Id.* at 272, 55 LRRM at 2047. *See* vacation of an award by nondeferral to it by the NLRB in text associated with footnotes 217 *et seq. infra.*
[100]*New Orleans Typographical Union No. 17 v. NLRB*, 368 F.2d 755, 63 LRRM 2467 (5th Cir. 1966).
[101]32 A.D.2d 266, 301 N.Y.S.2d 171, 72 LRRM 2064 (1969).
[102]334 U.S. 24 (1948).
[103]*Id.* at 34–35.
[104]314 F.2d 25, 52 LRRM 2543 (2d Cir. 1963), *cert. denied*, 373 U.S. 949, 53 LRRM 2394 (1963).

vacation on the ground that the reinstatement of an employee who engaged in such activity was contrary to public policy, and the district court agreed. The Second Circuit reversed the decision, saying:

> It is no less true in suits brought under § 301 to enforce arbitration awards than in other lawsuits that the "power of the federal courts to enforce the terms of private agreements is at all times exercised subject to the restrictions and limitations of the public policy of the United States...." *Hurd v. Hodge*, 334 U.S. 24, 34-35, 68 S.Ct. 847, 852-853, 92 L.Ed. 1187 (1948). The public policy to be enforced is a part of the substantive principles of federal labor law....[105]

The Second Circuit cited *Hurd v. Hodge, supra,* the Supreme Court decision that had set up the four sources of public policy (the Constitution, treaties, federal statutes and applicable legal precedents), and held that the district judge could not vacate the award merely because *he* believed the award was contrary to public policy. The New Jersey Supreme Court, similarly defining the meaning of the words "public policy," said:

> It has frequently been said that such public policy is a composite of constitutional provisions, statutes, and judicial decisions, and some courts have gone so far as to hold that it is limited to these.[106]

And the Kentucky Court of Appeals in *Smith v. Hillerich & Bradsby Co.*[107] also explained that a claim that an award is inconsistent with "public policy" will support a vacation only if the award will require illegal activity (see discussion of vacation for illegality *supra*). In this case, a group of employees had engaged in a "wildcat" strike and the employer discharged four strikers on the ground they had breached a "no strike" provision in the labor agreement. A grievance was filed and the arbitrator reinstated the four grievants because other employees had participated in the wildcat strike and were not discharged and, hence, the discipline of the four was not equal to that of others involved in the same breach. The trial court vacated the award (refused to enforce it) on the ground that it was "contrary to public policy." The Kentucky Court of Appeals reversed, explaining:

> The law favors and encourages the settlement of controversies by arbitration, and arbitrators are not expected or required to follow the strict rules of law, it being sufficient that they have due regard for natural justice. If the parties wanted exact justice administered according to the forms of law they should not have agreed to substitute a private forum for a court of law....

---

[105] 314 F.2d at 29, 52 LRRM at 2546.
[106] *Allen v. Commercial Casualty Ins. Co.*, 131 N.J.L. 475, 37 A.2d 37, 154 ALR 834 (1943).
[107] 253 S.W.2d 629, 19 LA 745 (Ky. 1952).

The record discloses no gross mistake of law or fact on the part of the arbitrator such as would evidence partiality or fraud on his part....

Although Federal policy, as formulated under the National Labor Relations Act ... condones discharges of some employees while reinstating others who have participated in an unauthorized strike, this did not have the binding effect of law upon the arbitrator. The parties could have left such disputes to the N.L.R.B. or to the courts to decide, but chose voluntary arbitration instead.[108]

The court of appeals enforced the award, even though the trial court had decided the award was "contrary to public policy," because the award was not shown to be a gross mistake of the law.

The first vacation of a labor arbitration award because the court concluded the award was "inconsistent with public policy" but did not require any showing that the award would produce an illegal result was by the Supreme Court of California in *Black v. Cutter Laboratories*[109] in 1955. Four out of seven of the justices determined that reinstating a communist after the individual was discharged was sufficiently "inconsistent with public policy" to vacate the award. This California decision was mentioned in a footnote in a Third Circuit decision[110] in 1969, and was considered by the Third Circuit to be contrary to the Second Circuit's decision in *Otis Elevator, supra*. The California decision was not used as a precedent in either state or federal courts for thirty-five years and was generally considered asleep until in 1981 a district judge in Wisconsin in *Meat Cutters, Local P-1236 v. Jones Dairy Farm*[111] vacated an award on the ground that he believed the award was "inconsistent with public policy," without any showing that an enforcement of the award would produce an illegal result.

This district court decision becomes very significant for two reasons: first, because it holds that the court has the right to review an arbitration award if the award was challenged as "inconsistent with public policy" and, second, because it supports this view by an analogy to the

---

[108]*Id*. at 630, 19 LA at 746.

[109]43 Cal.2d 788, 278 P.2d 905, 23 LA 715, 35 LRRM 2391 (1955), *cert. denied*, 351 U.S. 292, 38 LRRM 2160 (1956).

[110]*Ludwig Honold Mfg. Co. v. Fletcher*, 405 F.2d 1123, 1128 n. 27, 70 LRRM 2368, 2371 n. 27 (3d Cir. 1969). Whether or not it could have been urged upon a trial judge in the Third Circuit's jurisdiction that this footnote meant the judge could vacate an award if he or she believed the award was contrary to public policy, even when enforcement would not generate illegality, the footnote can no longer be the basis for such a claim because in *Kane Gas, Light & Heating Co. v. Firemen & Oilers*, 687 F.2d 673, 681 n. 11,111 LRRM 2094, 2099 n. 11 (1982), the Third Circuit said: "We have serious questions about the continued vitality of the majority opinion in *Black v. Cutter*.... In our view Justice Traynor's dissent in *Black* represents a far more reasoned approach." *See* discussion of Justice Traynor's dissent in text associated with note 126 *infra*.

[111]519 F. Supp. 66, 108 LRRM 2129 (W.D. Wis. 1981).

Supreme Court decision in *Alexander v. Gardner-Denver*.[112] In that decision, a grievant is given the right to have an arbitration award reviewed by a judge if the award could be said to "touch" the Civil Rights Act (Title VII).

The district court judge related his decision to the *Alexander v. Gardner-Denver* decision by incorporating this quotation from *Alexander*:

> As the proctor of the bargain, the arbitrator's task is to effectuate the intent of the parties. His source of authority is the collective-bargaining agreement, and he must interpret and apply that agreement in accordance with the "industrial common law of the shop" and the various needs and desires of the parties. The arbitrator, however, has no general authority to invoke public laws that conflict with the bargain between the parties.... [T]he arbitrator has authority to resolve questions of contractual rights....
>
> ...
>
> ... Parties usually choose an arbitrator because they trust his knowledge and judgment concerning the demands and norms of industrial relations. On the other hand, the resolution of statutory or constitutional issues is a primary responsibility of courts....[113]

The *Alexander* decision and its progeny have punched big holes in labor arbitration finality. These significant changes are discussed extensively in the next chapter, and the Wisconsin District Court decision in *Jones Dairy Farm, supra,* affirmed by the Seventh Circuit,[114] should be considered another significant reduction in labor arbitration finality.

These "two alliteration words [*public policy*] ... often used as if they had a magic quality and were self-explanatory," as Corbin wrote,[115] have now been reinserted into labor arbitration vacation jargon. Corbin added this about these two alliterative words: "What is *public policy* and who knows what it requires? Does a judge know this by virtue of becoming a judge?"[116] Because of the reawakening of the "contrary to public policy" basis for a vacation of a labor arbitration award, a basis that had been asleep for twenty-six years, it is appropriate to review quite carefully the two arbitrations that have been vacated by the use of these "magic" words to determine as best we can what these words mean. The awards that were vacated because the judges determined they were contrary to public policy[117] were those

---

[112]415 U.S. 36, 7 FEP Cases 81.

[113]*Id.* at 53–54 and 56–57, 7 FEP Cases at 87, 89.

[114]680 F.2d 1142, 110 LRRM 2805 (7th Cir. 1982).

[115]6A Corbin § 1375 at 219 (1962).

[116]6A Corbin § 1375 at 219 (1962), quoted in *Meat Cutters, Local P-1236 v. Jones Dairy Farm*, 519 F. Supp. 1366, 108 LRRM 2129 (W.D. Wis. 1981).

[117]*Black v. Cutter Laboratories*, 43 Cal.2d 788, 278 P.2d 905, 23 LA 715, 35 LRRM 2391 (1955), *cert. denied*, 351 U.S. 292, 38 LRRM 2160 (1965), and *Jones Dairy Farm, supra*.

written by Arbitrators Hubert Wyckoff and Paul Heide (the majority
of a panel) in *Cutter Laboratories*[118] in 1950 and by Arbitrator
Maslanka in *Jones Dairy Farm*[119] in 1979.

Arbitrators Wyckoff and Heide had reinstated a grievant discharged
by the company because of some omissions and falsifications in the
grievant's employment application and because she was a communist.
The majority of the arbitrators found that since the employer knew of
the omissions and falsifications on the employment application and of
the fact that the employee was a communist for over two years, the
failure of the employer to act promptly after having learned these facts
caused them to be waived as a "proper cause" for discharge. The arbitrators wrote:

> It is a familiar principle of law, industrial relations and commonsense
> that the existence of a right may be doubted or lost by reason of an un-
> justifiable failure to assert it. . . . [I]t is established to our satisfaction, by
> admissions of the company and by proof, that the reasons assigned in 1949
> by the company for the discharge were both known and believed by the
> company in 1947.[120]

Those arbitrators also found in their award that the discharge of the
grievant was in fact in retaliation for the grievant's *lawful* union activities and that the company used these *stale* facts as the excuse for
her termination.

The company filed a suit in the Superior Court in San Francisco[121]
for vacation of the reinstatement award but the vacation was not
granted. Judge Molkenbuhr wrote:

---

[118]15 LA 431 (Wyckoff and Heide, 1950).

[119]*In the Matter of Arbitration Between Jones Dairy Farm and Amalgamated Meat Cutter
and Butcher Workmen of North America AFL-CIO No. P-1236* (Maslanka, May 21, 1979),
unreported.

[120]15 LA at 443; *see, e.g., Niagara Frontier Transit Systems, Inc.*, 26 LA 575 (Thompson,
Chmn., 1956) and Comment, 6 UCLA Rev. 603, 674 (1959). Membership in the communist
party was basic to various discharges of employees and the arbitrators in the following cases
reinstated the grievants: *Foote Bros. Gear & Machine Corp.*, 13 LA 848 (Larkin, 1949); *Curtiss
Wright Corp.*, 9 LA 77 (Uible, Chmn., 1947); *Spokane Idaho Mining Co.*, 9 LA 749 (Cheney,
1947). If an authorized government security agency denied the grievant access to classified information, the question before the arbitrator became whether the company could find work for the
employee which did not involve access to classified information; if the company could not,
discharge was upheld. *See, e.g., Wisconsin Telephone Co.*, 26 LA 792 (Whelan, Chmn., 1956);
Liquid Carbonic Corp., 22 LA 709 (Baab, 1954); *Rudolf Wurlitzer Co.*, 18 LA 648 (Thompson,
1952); *Bell Aircraft Corp.*, 16 LA 234 (Shister, Chmn., 1951). A labor agreement clause which
permits suspension of an employee upon denial of clearance has been construed to apply to a
government denial of clearance, not to an employer denial. *See, e.g., Arma Corp.*, 22 LA 325
(Shake, 1954); *see* dissent of Justice Traynor in *Black v. Cutter Laboratories* in text associated
with note 126 *infra*.

[121]*Cutter Laboratories v. Office & Professional Workers, Bio-Lab Union, Local 225*, 16 LA
208 (Cal. Super. Ct. 1951).

The law of arbitration is well settled. It is not in the province of the court
to substitute its conclusions or opinion for the award of arbitrators nor is
the award subject to judicial review unless the award was (1) procured by
corruption... ; (2) there was corruption in the arbitrators; (3) the arbitrators were guilty of misconduct... ; (4) the arbitrators exceeded their
powers.... [122]

The company then appealed this decision to the California District
Court of Appeals[123] and the decision below was affirmed. Justice
Peters, with Justices Brag and Wood concurring, wrote:

There is ... a strong public policy in favor of arbitration, of settling arbitrations, particularly labor arbitrations, speedily and with a minimum
of court interference, and of making the awards of arbitrators final and
conclusive.... [124]

Then the company appealed to the California Supreme Court[125] and
four of the seven justices agreed that the reinstatement award of the
grievant should be vacated because it was contrary to public policy
because a communist was being reinstated. Justice Traynor, joined by
two other justices, issued a strong dissent. He said there was no
governmental decision or statutory rule that a member of the Communist Party should be deprived of work opportunities and that the
four justices who became the majority of the court were imposing their
own belief that communists should be excluded from employment,
merely labeling their views "public policy." In addition, Justice
Traynor pointed out that the important "public policy" that favors
final settlement of disputes by arbitration is simply defeated if judges
can upset the award by merely asserting that the award is inconsistent
with "public policy":

By sanctioning these violations of Cutter's contract [the arbitrators had
held that the discharge was a violation of the labor agreement] this court
[the four justices in majority] not only defeats ... the public policy in favor
of the settlement of disputes by arbitration ... but needlessly introduces
confusion into a field in which Congress has already undertaken to formulate a workable policy.[126]

There were seven judges in the California judiciary who believed
that a labor arbitration award should not be vacated when a judge
asserts the magic words "contrary to public policy," whereas four

[122]*Id*. at 210.
[123]*Black v. Cutter Laboratories*, 266 P.2d 92, 22 LA 4 (Cal. Dist. Ct. App. 1934).
[124]*Id*. at 102, 22 LA at 12.
[125]*Black v. Cutter Laboratories*, 43 Cal.2d 788, 278 P.2d 905, 23 LA 715, 35 LRRM 2391
(1955).
[126]278 P.2d at 920, 23 LA at 727, 35 LRRM at 2403.

believed that such an assertion was sufficient. It took five years of litigation before the company could reach the four judges, who finally agreed with the vacation.[127]

The arbitration award that was vacated by the Wisconsin District Court was rendered by Arbitrator Maslanka in *Jones Dairy Farm*.[128] He denied a grievance that had been filed by the local union president of the Amalgamated Meatcutter and Butcher Workmen of North America, who worked in the company's plant where meat products were being manufactured. Inspectors of the U.S. Department of Agriculture were always in residence at the plant inspecting the quality of the meat and the union president began to by-pass his supervisor and report directly to the inspectors about conditions he believed were below the required sanitary standard. The management chastised him for this practice in a letter and promulgated a new rule that required employees to follow the normal communication route and report any such claims to their supervisors:

> "Employees must deal through supervisors or designated plant management rather than directly with USDA government inspectors."
> Any deviation from this rule will result in appropriate disciplinary action.[129]

The union official filed a grievance on August 30, 1978, asserting that the rule violated the labor agreement and the First Amendment of the Constitution and was against public policy. The grievance record was set forth in the award:

> The Union demands that the Company remove from its list of Rules and the Company bulletin board the rule regarding the USDA. . . . The Union contends that this rule is unjust. It is the Union's position that employees *have a right* to tell USDA inspectors of possible problems. [Emphasis added.]

The company's answer to this grievance was as follows:

> The rule is just. Employees have no *right* to contact U.S.D.A. inspectors on [sic] problems[130] [Emphasis added.]

Arbitrator Edward T. Maslanka in his award set forth the question he was asked to answer:

---

[127]The U.S. Supreme Court accepted a writ of *certiorari* but after hearing arguments, the Justices decided that the Supreme Court of California's decision did not raise a substantial federal question (351 U.S. 292, 38 LRRM 2160 (1956)).

[128]*See* note 119 *supra*.

[129]*Meatcutters, Local No. P-1236 v. Jones Dairy Farm*, 519 F. Supp. 1362, 1365, 108 LRRM 2129 (W.D. Wis. 1981).

[130]*See* note 119 *supra* at p. 2.

"Did the Company violate the contract by establishing a rule which prohibits employees from reporting or dealing directly with the U.S.D.A. inspectors?"[131]

Arbitrator Maslanka also reported that the union had filed an unfair labor practice charge based on this rule with the Milwaukee NLRB office, and that the regional director on October 12, 1978, dismissed this charge with this comment:

Based on the investigation, it does not appear that further proceedings are warranted as to the above rule inasmuch as it does not appear that the rule, as posted by the Employer, constitutes a violation of employee rights under Section 7 of the Act even though it restricts employees from reporting product sanitation or related problems to agents of a Federal regulatory body. Rather it appears that the duties and responsibilities of the USDA inspectors are strictly product-oriented (i.e., to insure that USDA standards are followed in the processing of meat) and that the type of complaints taken to the inspectors in the past, by employees, were again product-oriented and did not directly concern safety, working conditions or other terms or conditions of employment. Contrasting the role of the USDA with that of other Government agencies such as OSHA and EEOC, whose primary function is to protect employee rights, it appears that the USDA relation to Section 7 rights is too remote to warrant a conclusion that employee access to USDA inspectors should be covered by the Act.[132]

Arbitrator Maslanka then stated in his award:

... However, in view of the uncontradictory testimony of Company witnesses as to the motivation for the rule I find no evidence of arbitrary or unreasonable conduct in establishing the rule. In my view the rule can be seen as a reasonable method by which the Company can seek to insure that any possible violations of USDA regulations are brought to its attention for correction....

...

The Union also contends that the rule is against public policy. However the record ... contains no evidence that the rule has been utilized in any way to intimidate employees to prevent them from reporting matters to supervision or [that] once reported, supervision has in any way acted in an irresponsible manner....

I find therefore that based on the record as a whole ... the Company has not violated the contract in promulgating and enforcing the rule herein.

<u>AWARD</u>

The grievance is denied.[133]

---

[131]*Id.* at p. 1.
[132]*Id.* at p. 4.
[133]*Id.*

The company's explanation of why the new rule was issued was reported in the district court decision:

> It has long been the company's policy that employees must deal through supervision or designated plant management rather than directly with U.S.D.A. government inspectors in reporting real or alleged deficiencies, deviations, violations, or other plant problems.
>
> There are very sound reasons for this policy. By regulation there must be a company designated individual in each department or area who is responsible for the sanitation program and compliance with regulations. The company must inspect the department and allow operations to be performed only when all requirements are attained. Plant management is responsible for training plant employees in proper procedures and compliance. Plant management through it's [sic] supervisors must actually guarantee to strictly conform to all Federal regulations. Plant management is responsible for producing wholesome products in a clean plant, utilizing hygienic procedures. It follows that supervisory awareness and following the "chain of command" can expedite solution of the problem, prevent disorder and misunderstanding, and thus minimize any interference with production. The supervisor is the person responsible for corrective action when a deficiency occurs.[134]

The district judge decided first that a Section 301 complaint seeking vacation of an award because it was "inconsistent with public policy" set up jurisdiction to relitigate. The judge explained:

> [I]t is clear that an arbitrator's sole authority is to construe and apply the collective bargaining agreement; his or her *sole responsibility* is to the parties to that agreement. Put another way, the arbitrator *lacks the power, and perhaps also the expertise, to rule on questions of federal law as they affect labor relations,* and to consider the interests of those who are not parties to the collective bargaining agreement. With respect to these questions and interests, then, deference to the arbitral process is not appropriate. [Emphasis added.]
>
> . . .
>
> . . .
>
> The arbitrator's construction of the underlying collective bargaining agreement must be accepted, but it is *for a court* to decide whether the resulting award is unlawful *or so contrary to important public policy* that it must be vacated or denied enforcement.[135] [Emphasis omitted; emphasis added.]

---

[134]519 F. Supp. 1362, 1365, 108 LRRM 2129, 2130.

[135]*Id.* at 1368, 108 LRRM at 2132-33. Judge Crabb supported his conclusions that (1) he had jurisdiction to review any claim that "the award was contrary to public policy," (2) he could determine the meaning of the words "public policy," and (3) he could vacate the award if, in his review, the award was contrary to public policy with a quotation from Summer, *Collection Agreement and the Law of Contracts,* 78 YALE L.J. 525, 556-57 (1969), which incorporated a quotation from Professor Corbin about public policy: "Public policy is an unruly horse and dangerous to ride. . . ." Professor Summer added this comment: "We may criticize the courts

The judge went on to state that the Seventh Circuit Court (and apparently no other federal court) had considered a vacation of an award because it was "contrary to public policy." The judge wrote:

> The court of appeals for this circuit has not yet ruled on this question. In one case in which it was faced with a public policy challenge to an arbitration award, that court found that no federal or state policy was violated by the challenged arbitration award.[136]

The judge then evaluated the rule posted by the company which caused the grievance, the arbitration, and the relitigation at the district court.

> There is no merit to plaintiff's [union's] argument that it is a violation of public policy to require employees to report problem conditions to supervisors. To the contrary, it is in the public's interest that problems identified by line workers be brought to the attention of those who are responsible for remedying them. As defendant accurately stated in its notice of the rule:
>
> > Plant management is responsible for producing wholesome products in a clean plant, utilizing hygienic procedures. It follows that supervisory awareness and following the "chain of command" can expedite solution of the problem, prevent disorder and misunderstanding, and thus minimize any interference with production.[137]

The judge stated that the posted rule was not contrary to public policy *per se* but since the rule did not also give an employee a right to go directly to the Agriculture Department inspectors *if a serious problem remained uncorrected for an unreasonably long period of time after management has been informed of it,* the rule might possibly confuse employees.[138] The judge not only vacated the award, but also enjoined the enforcement of the rule.

---

for their horsemanship, but not for riding the horse on which contract principles place them." *Id.* at 1372, 108 LRRM at 2135. Professor Corbin's source for "Public policy is an unruly horse and dangerous to ride" is a quote from Burrough, Justice, quoting Hobart, Chief Justice, reported in 6A Corbin § 1375 at pp. 11-12 n. 9. Corbin then quotes Judge Cave in *Mogul S.S. Co. v. McGregor* (1892) AC 25 (Law Reports Appeal Cases (Eng.)): "Certain kinds of contracts have been held void at common law on the ground of public policy; a branch of the law which certainly should not be extended, as judges are more to be trusted as interpreters of the law than as expounders of what is called 'public policy.' " The Eleventh Circuit in *Loveless v. Eastern Air Lines, Inc.*, 681 F.2d 1272, 111 LRRM 2001 (1982) reviewed various decisions to determine the scope of the "essence" test (*Id.* at 1279, 111 LRRM at 2006) and reversed a vacation by the district court because while the arbitrators "went behind the contractual language" to reach a result opposite to the "superficially clear and unambiguous" words, they did so because of the "[arbitration] panel's perception of the true intent of the parties" and, hence, the panel's determination drew its essence from the agreement.

[136]519 F. Supp. at 1369, 108 LRRM at 2133.
[137]*Id.* at 1371, 108 LRRM at 2134.
[138]*Id.* at 1372, 108 LRRM at 2135-36.

When the award reached the Seventh Circuit, that court said that "While it is beyond dispute that insuring sanitary conditions in meat packing plants is an important public policy, that policy is not necessarily violated by a rule which requires employees to first report violations of the law to the. Company.[139] Then, in spite of the finding that the rule did not violate public policy, the Seventh Circuit affirmed the vacation and the injunction because the rule "fails to allow for exigent circumstances."[140] The court added that its holding did not preclude the Company from promulgating a rule that required employees to first report violations to the management if it also permitted employees to report directly to USDA inspectors *"if the conditions remain uncorrected for a specified time."*[141] [Emphasis added.]

It was the view of District Judge Crabb in *Jones Dairy Farm, supra,* that labor arbitrators should *not* be concerned with "public policy" matters because they are exclusively the concern of the courts. In sharp contrast, Alfred W. Blumrosen, in his article *Public Policy Considerations in Labor Arbitration,* [142] catalogued twenty-one years earlier the many arbitration awards that turned on public policy considerations. His article has the following headings: public policy concerns in physical and property safety;[143] public policy concerns in the protection of persons and property from violence;[144] public policy supporting continued production;[145] public policy in connection with criminal proceeding;[146] public policy to create national security;[147] public policy toward mental illness;[148] public policy toward marriage;[149] public policy of allowing access to the courts;[150] and public policy toward health.[151] The last of the list of public policy determinations by arbitrators reviewed by Blumrosen involved the public policy con-

---

[139]680 F.2d 1142, 1144, 110 LRRM 2805, 2808 (7th Cir. 1982).

[140]*Id.*

[141]*Id.* The Third Circuit, in *Kane Gas, Light & Heating v. Firemen & Oilers*, 687 F.2d 673, 111 LRRM 2094 (1982), held, in contrast to the Seventh Circuit decision in *Jones Dairy Farm*, discussed *supra*, that "only if upholding an award would amount to 'judicial condonation' of illegal acts, should the award be vacated on grounds of inconsistency with public policy." 687 F.2d at 682, 111 LRRM at 2100. This decision makes it clear that vacation of an award for the two reasons that enforcement (1) would generate illegality and (2) would be inconsistent with public policy actually is vacation for one and the same reason (see text associated with notes 102–108) and is directly contrary to the Seventh Circuit affirmation of the Wisconsin District Court decision in *Jones*.

[142]RUTGERS L. REV., Vol. 14, No. 2 (1960), p. 217.

[143]*Id.* at pp. 221–27.

[144]*Id.* at pp. 227–28.

[145]*Id.* at pp. 228–30.

[146]*Id.* at pp. 230–31.

[147]*Id.* at pp. 232–33.

[148]*Id.* at p. 234.

[149]*Id.*

[150]*Id.* at pp. 234–35.

[151]*Id.* at p. 235.

sideration similar to the public policy that meat products should be produced in a sanitary environment discussed in *Jones Dairy Farm, supra.* Blumrosen set out five conclusions, following his extensive study of the public policies that have been absorbed by labor arbitrators. He wrote:

> What conclusions can be drawn from this survey of arbitrators' opinions?
>
> (1) Arbitrators consider it their duty to take account of public policy considerations involved in labor-management relations. In not a single case has it been suggested that the employer-union relationship is a private affair, and that public interests should not affect a decision by a person privately selected by the parties to resolve some of their private disputes. The argument might be made that an arbitrator, not being a judge, does not represent the public, and ought not to concern himself with the implications of his decision for the public interest. Rather, he ought to focus on the purely private considerations affecting the parties to the dispute, leaving public policy considerations to the courts. This argument is foreign to the body of labor arbitration decisions. It has no place in developing arbitration law. The decisions assume that labor arbitrators are to determine the public policies involved in their cases, and the impact of these policies on the issues before them.
>
> (2) Arbitrators are not blinded by the importance of policy considerations into an ill-considered weighing of evidentiary factors. The strongest policy argument is not availing if the factual context does not call it into play. Thus we can say that, while arbitrators are sensitive to policy problems, they are not so overwhelmed as to ignore the other facets of the case before them.
>
> (3) In most cases the weight arbitrators accord to public policy considerations parallels that of the legal system. Where the law is clear, arbitrators tend to agree; where the law is clouded, the arbitrators diverge.
>
> (4) Because of their non-governmental position, and the fact that the contractual language to be construed is broad, the arbitrators have an opportunity to refine the public policy considerations in cases before them to a degree not always open to other tribunals....
>
> (5) The decisions suggest intelligent, rational handling of difficult problems. Some of the opinions are masterpieces. In the main, they reflect the men who wrote them, who have over the last fifteen years created an intelligible industrial jurisprudence from the raw matrix of labor relations and whose continued activity depends upon convincing both labor and management of the integrity and wisdom of their judgments. The impression created is a group whose judgment can be trusted to adequately weigh matters of public concern within the labor arbitration framework.[152]

Blumrosen also explained that the public policy concerns of arbitrators are *external* to the provisions set out in the labor agreement:

---

[152]*Id.* at pp. 232–33.

Is this search for the thread of public policy in arbitration opinions doomed to futility because each case involves a particular contract, and it is the contract, not the public policy, which guides the arbitrator to his decision? The answer is no, on two grounds. First, most of the problems involve discharge or discipline of employees and the contractual language does not vary significantly from case to case. The question put to the arbitrator is this: Was this employee discharged or disciplined for "just cause?" Such language invites a consideration of policy factors. Secondly, the line between the construction of such language in a labor agreement and a decision based on public policy is not at all clear. An arbitrator might construe the contract in light of public policy considerations. His decision simultaneously involves public policy and a construction of the particular contract.[153]

The Supreme Court explained that arbitrators use what is called the "law of the shop" when they approve or disapprove actions of employers after they consider matters that are *external* to the words found in the labor agreement, stating: " '[A]rbitrator's source of law [includes] the industrial common law—the *practices* of the industry and the shop. . . .' "[154] [Emphasis added.] The Court gave this source of law more meaning when it said "that the specialized competence of arbitrators pertains primarily to the law of the shop."[155] Since the "law of the shop" is acquired out of the special competence of arbitrators, who learn the practices of the industry and the shop, this law is not *statutory* or *common* law and it can quite properly be some accepted codification of the *policies* that have been accepted generally by arbitrators as they resolve disputes and can well be referred to as the *public policy* of labor relations developed slowly by arbitrators.

Alfred Blumrosen's article, codifying the "public policies" enunciated by various arbitrators, was written in 1960, the same year that the phrase "law of the shop" was introduced into labor arbitration jargon by the Supreme Court.[156] It is only when the arbitrator goes beyond the scope of the "law of the shop" or, in other words, beyond the scope of accepted labor relations policies that the award becomes vulnerable on the ground that it is "his own brand of industrial justice."[157]

Since public policy concerns by a labor arbitrator can properly be

---

[153]*Id*. at p. 221.

[154]*Steelworkers v. Warrior & Gulf Navigation Co.*, 363 U.S. 574, 581-82, 46 LRRM 2419 (1960), cited and quoted in *Arco Polymers, Inc. v. Oil, Chemical & Atomic Workers, Local 8-74*, 671 F.2d 752, 758, 109 LRRM 3157, 3162 (3d. Cir. 1982).

[155]*Steelworkers v. Warrior & Gulf Navigation Co.*, 363 U.S. 574, 581-83, 46 LRRM 2416, 2418-19 (1960).

[156]*Id*.

[157]*Steelworkers v. Enterprise Wheel & Car Corp.*, 363 U.S. 593, 597, 46 LRRM 2423, 2425 (1960).

referred to as the "law of the shop" and since the Wisconsin District Court has held in *Jones Dairy Farm, supra,* that a claim that the award is "contrary to public policy" gives it jurisdiction to reexamine and redetermine the award, it seems to follow that the district court took over the right to review "law of the shop" concerns of a labor arbitrator, which the Supreme Court said constituted the area of "specialized competence"[158] of labor arbitrators. The Supreme Court also said, "Parties usually choose an arbitrator because they trust his knowledge and judgment concerning the demands and *norms of industrial relations.*"[159] [Emphasis added.] "Norms of industrial relations" is actually another description for the industrial relations policies that are also called the "law of the shop." The district court decision in *Jones Dairy Farm* might have been passed by, but because of the Seventh Circuit Court's affirmance, many disappointed grievants will rush to the district courts attempting to use "contrary to public policy" as a new route into a court seeking a vacation.

Another concern that might be expressed in regard to *Jones* is that the Seventh Circuit seems to have believed that Arbitrator Maslanka based *his award on public policy considerations.* The court said:

> When an arbitrator bases his award on public policy considerations, he has overstepped his authority and the court may review the substantive merits of the award.[160]

This finding is quite at variance with Arbitrator Maslanka's statement in his award:

> As an arbitrator, my authority is limited to and derived from the contract.[161]

The arbitrator pointed out that it was the union representative who raised the "public policy" consideration:

> The union also contends that the rule is against public policy. However the record as noted above contains no evidence that the rule has been utilized in any way to intimidate employees to prevent them from reporting matters to supervision or that once reported, supervision has in any way acted in an irresponsible manner.[162]

In spite of the fact that Arbitrator Maslanka did not predicate his award on any "public policy" consideration, the Seventh Circuit wrote:

---

[158]*See* note 154 *supra.*

[159]*Alexander v. Gardner-Denver,* 415 U.S. 56, 57, 7 FEP Cases 81 (1974).

[160]*Meat Cutters, Local P-1236 v. Jones Dairy Farm,* 680 F.2d 1142, 1144, 110 LRRM 2805, 2807 (1982).

[161]*See* note 119 *supra,* at p. 4.

[162]*Id.*

The district court was correct in concluding that it had the authority to review the award on the basis of public policy considerations.

. . .

Public policy considerations are wholly independent of the collective bargaining agreement. When an arbitrator bases his award on public policy considerations, he has overstepped his authority and the court may review the substantive merits of the award.[163]

An arbitrator who merely rejects a "public policy" claim raised by the union at the arbitration hearing should not by that rejection have initiated a vacation of his or her own award. It is, however, suggested that, while the situation discussed above continues, in any arbitration case in the jurisdiction of the Seventh Circuit Court the arbitrator should not report in his or her award that he or she rejects the union's "public policy" contention.

Another consideration in regard to *Jones* is the following: The Commissioners on Uniform State Laws adopted, and the American Bar Association House of Delegates approved, a Uniform Arbitration Act in 1953. Section 12(a) provided:

Upon application of a party a court shall vacate an award where: ... (3) arbitrators exceeded their powers and rendered an award contrary to public policy.[164]

The National Academy of Arbitrators subsequently criticized the reference to "public policy" in the Uniform Act, and that reference was stricken in a later version.[165]

Vacation for Error in Fact

A claim that an award should be vacated because the arbitrator did not base the award on all the evidence usually has been an insufficient reason for vacation unless there also exists some evidence of fraud. Consistent with this view, the Fifth Circuit in *Safeway Stores v. Bakery & Confectionery Workers, Local 111*[166] held that an arbitrator's decision should be enforced "even if perhaps erroneous" and even if the

---

[163]680 F.2d at 1144, 110 LRRM at 2807.

[164]24 LA 886, 887 (1955).

[165]27 LA 910 (1957); *see also Report of Committee on Law and Legislation*, Management Rights and the Arbitration Process, Proceedings of the Ninth Annual Meeting, National Academy of Arbitrators, J. McKelvey, ed. (Washington: BNA Books, 1956), p.201; *The Proposed Uniform Arbitration Act: A Panel Discussion*, Critical Issues in Labor Arbitration, Proceedings of the Tenth Annual Meeting, National Academy of Arbitrators, J. McKelvey, ed. (Washington: BNA Books, 1957), p. 112.

[166]390 F.2d 79, 67 LRRM 2646 (5th Cir. 1968). *See* quotation from the same decision in text related to note 63 *supra*.

court would have arrived at a different decision.[167] However, the court did say, "We may assume, without here deciding, that if the reasoning is so palpably faulty that no judge or group of judges, could ever conceivably have made such a ruling then the Court can strike down the award."[168]

In *Electronics Corp. of America v. Electrical Workers, IUE, Local 272*,[169] the grievant had been discharged for continuing to falsify time tickets after the company had (1) repeatedly given the grievant oral warnings, (2) given him written warnings, and (3) suspended him for over four weeks. The arbitrator reinstated the grievant, reasoning that "industrial due process" had not been observed because no "suspension" had been given to the grievant before the discharge. It was explained to the district court that the grievant had previously been given a disciplinary suspension, but since the arbitrator's finding that no disciplinary suspension had occurred was an error of fact, the district court did not vacate the award. Then the First Circuit reversed the decision, holding that the employer's discharge should not be upset because of the arbitrator's misapprehension.[170]

Vacation for Fraud and Corruption

Courts make every legitimate presumption that favors the validity of the award, including the assumption that the award was made honestly and without fraud.[171] However, when there is evidence of *fraud* on the part of the arbitrator, courts always vacate the award, following the principles developed in the common law,[172] in the statutory law in

---

[167]*Id.* at 82, 67 LRRM at 2649. *See also Ludwig Honold Mfg. Co. v. Fletcher*, 405 F.2d 1123, 70 LRRM 2368 (3d Cir. 1969).

[168]*Id.*, 67 LRRM at 2648. *Cf. Marble Products Co. of Ga. v. Stone Workers, Local 155*, 335 F.2d 468, 56 LRRM 2967 (5th Cir. 1964) (award vacated where arbitrator's reading of the contract was "so unreasonable as to be arbitrary or capricious"); *In re Firestone Tire & Rubber Co.*, 168 Cal. App.2d 444, 335 F.2d 990, 32 LA 106 (1959); *Automobile Workers, Local 18 v. Eljer Plumbingware Div., Murrary Corp.*, (M.D. Pa. 1973), unreported.

[169]492 F.2d 1255, 85 LRRM 2534 (1st Cir. 1974); *see also Procter & Gamble Mfg. Co. v. Independent Oil & Chemical Workers*, 386 F. Supp. 213, 87 LRRM 3179 (D. Md. 1974); *Northwest Airlines, Inc. v. Airline Pilots Ass'n*, 530 F.2d 1048, 91 LRRM 2304 (D.C. Cir. 1976); *cert. denied*, 426 U.S. 942, 92 LRRM 2768 (1976); *NF&M Corp. v. Steelworkers, Local 8148*, 524 F.2d 756, 90 LRRM 2947 (3d Cir. 1975); *Western Elec. Co. v. Communication Equipment Workers, Inc.*, 409 F. Supp. 1616, 91 LRRM 2621 (D. Md. 1976), *aff'd*, 554 F.2d 135, 95 LRRM 2268 (4th Cir. 1977).

[170]492 F.2d at 1255, 85 LRRM at 2535.

[171]*See generally* Note, *Arbitration Awards Vacated for Disqualification of an Arbitrator*, 9 SYRACUSE L. REV. 56, 57–58 (1957). *But see* Hays, *The Future of Labor Arbitration*, 74 YALE L.J. 1019 (1965).

[172]*Withington v. Warren*, 51 Mass. 431 (1845).

620   PRACTICE AND PROCEDURE IN LABOR ARBITRATION

effect in a number of states,[173] and in the United States Arbitration Act.[174]

Justice Black, drawing upon the U.S. Arbitration Act, said in *Commonwealth Coating Corp. v. Continental Casualty Co.*[175] that an award should be vacated when there is merely the *appearance* of bias. In this case the *appearance* resulted from the fact that at the time of the arbitration hearing it had not been disclosed that the arbitrator and one party had enjoyed a long-term business relationship. Actual fraud or bias was not alleged by the party seeking vacation, but the court reversed the lower court's enforcement of the award and granted the vacation to protect that party from the *risk* of partiality. Prior to this decision, *bias* was considered one step below *fraud* and *corruption* and courts were unwilling to vacate for *bias* unless it was *blatant*. For example, one court refused to vacate an award when the union failed to prove that an arbitrator knew of, participated in, or benefited from any business dealings his cousin allegedly had with the employer,[176] and another court refused to vacate when an arbitrator had once been the legal representative for one of the parties.[177]

---

[173]Statutory provisions of the following states specify fraud or corruption in procuring the award as grounds for vacating the award: ALA. CODE § 6-6-14 (1975); ALASKA STATS. § 04.43.120 (1973); ARIZ. REV. STATS. ANN. § 12-1512 (1982); ARK. STAT. ANN. § 34-522 (1947); CAL. CIV. PROC. CODE § 1286.2 (West 1972); COLO. REV. STAT. § 13-22-214 (Supp. 1980); CONN. GEN. STAT. ANN. § 52-418 (1958); FLA. STAT. ANN. § 682.13 (West Supp. 1982); GA. CODE ANN. § 7-111 (1973 Rev.); HAWAII REV. STAT. § 658-9 (1976); IDAHO CODE ANN. § 7-912 (1979); ILL. ANN. STAT. Ch. 10 § 112 (1975); IND. CODE ANN. § 3-240 (Burns 1972); IOWA CODE ANN. § 679A.12 (West Supp. 1982-83); KAN. STAT. ANN. § 5-211 (1975); ME. REV. STAT. ANN. tit. 14 § 5938 (1964); MASS. GEN. LAWS Ch. 150C § 11 (Michie/Law Co-op. 1976); MINN. STAT. ANN. § 572.19 (West Supp. 1982); MISS. CODE ANN. § 11-15-23 (1972); MO. ANN. STAT. § 435.100 (1949); MONT. CODE ANN. § 93-201-7 (1964); NEV. REV. STAT. § 38.145 (1967); N.H. REV. STAT. ANN. § 542:8 (1974); N.J. REV. STAT. § 2A:24-8 (1952); N. M. STAT. ANN. § 447-7-12 (1978); N.Y. CIV. PRAC. LAW § 7511 (McKinney 1980); N.C. GEN. STAT. § 1-559 (1969); N.D. CENT. CODE § 32-29-08 (1976); VA. CODE § 38.01-580 (1950); W. VA. CODE § 55-10-4 (1981); WIS. STAT. ANN. § 298-10 (1958); WYO. STAT. § 1-36-114 (1977).

[174]9 U.S.C. § 10 (1976).

[175]393 U.S. 145 (1968); *accord, J.P. Stevens Co. v. Rytex Corp.*, 34 N.Y.2d 123, 312 N.E.2d 466, 356 N.Y.S.2d 278 (1974); *Amerada Hess Corp. v. Federal Labor Union, Local 22026*, 385 F. Supp. 279, 87 LRRM 2698 (D. N.J. 1974); *Newark Stereotypers Union No. 18 v. Newark Morning Ledger Co.*, 397 F.2d 594, 599, 68 LRRM 2561 (3d Cir. 1968), *cert. denied*, 393 U.S. 954, 69 LRRM 2653 (1968). A district court vacated an award because the appearance of unfairness arose when the neutral arbitrator had drinks with one of the firefighters. The circuit court reported that the court below had "stated there was nothing wrong with the result" and in reversing the vacation said that "unless the decision is arbitrary and capricious, the statute does not authorize its being set aside." *Firefighters, Local 1296 v. City of Kennewick*, 542 P.2d 1252, 92 LRRM 2118 (Wash. 1975). *See also Journal Times v. Typographical Union*, 409 F. Supp. 24, 92 LRRM 2818 (E.D. Wis. 1976); *Bethlehem Steel Corp. v. Fennie*, 383 N.Y.S.2d 948, 92 LRRM 3470 (N.Y. Sup. Ct. 1976), *aff'd*, 55 A.D.2d 1007, 95 LRRM 2099 (1977); *City of Hartford v. Police Officers*, 171 Conn. 420, 93 LRRM 2321 (Conn. 1976). *See Note, Disclosure by Arbitrators*, 3 HOFSTRA L. REV. 155 (1975).

[176]*Brewery Workers, Joint Local Executive Board of New Jersey v. P. Ballantine & Sons*, 83 LRRM 2712 (D. N.J. 1973).

[177]*Teamsters, Local 560 v. Bergen-Hudson Roofing Supply Co.*, 98 LRRM 3059 (N.J. Super. Ct. 1978).

Vacation for Lateness of the Award

A large number of labor agreements contain clauses establishing a time limitation on the rendering of an award by the arbitrator after final submission of a case by the parties.[178] The purpose of these provisions is generally to cause awards to be rendered promptly. Where a labor agreement provides a time limit for the rendition of an arbitration award, an award handed down after that time constitutes a violation of the agreement, regardless of the reasons for the delay.[179] A suit by an employer or a union to determine the effect of such a violation is a suit "for violation" of the labor agreement and within the literal language of Section 301, even though the violation was committed by the arbitrator.[180]

At common law, an award rendered after the expiration of such time limit was generally considered void.[181] There are, however, a number of more modern decisions to the contrary.[182] Some decisions have made a distinction between labor arbitration and commercial arbitration cases, holding that a late award in the former is not necessarily void.[183] For example, Arbitrator Milton H. Schmidt in *Bendix-Westinghouse Automotive Air Brake Co.*[184] disagreed when the union representative claimed the award was ineffective because it was rendered after excessive delay:

> The next question is whether the lateness of the award destroyed its validity. My answer to that question is "no". . . .

---

[178]Sometimes a time limit rule is adopted by the parties when they adopt the rules to govern an arbitration. Rule 37 of the 1979 *Voluntary Labor Arbitration Rules* of the American Arbitration Association provides:
The award shall be rendered promptly by the Arbitrator and, unless otherwise agreed by parties, or specified by the law, not later than 30 days from the date of closing the hearings, or if oral hearings have been waived, then from the date of transmitting the final statements and proofs to the Arbitrator.

[179]*See generally* Givens, *The Validity of Delayed Awards Under Section 301 Taft-Hartley Act*, 16 ARB. J. 161 (1961).

[180]*Id.*

[181]*Goerke Kirch Co. v. Goerke Kirch Holding Co.*, 118 N.J. Eq. 1, 176 A. 902 (1935); *General Metals Corp. v. Machinists, Precision Lodge 1600*, 183 Cal. App.2d 586, 6 Cal. Rptr. 910, 34 LA 851 (1960). *See* Annot., 154 A.L.R. 1392 (1945); Morse, ARBITRATION AND AWARD 223 (1972); Sturges, COMMERCIAL ARBITRATION AND AWARDS ¶ 83 (1930); 6 Williston *Contracts* ¶ 1929 (1938).

[182]*See Hegeberg v. New England Fish Co.*, 7 Wash.2d 509, 110 P.2d 182 (1941); *Damon v. Berger*, 191 Pa. Super. 165, 155 A.2d 388 (1959); *Rosenthal v. Tannhauser*, 279 A.D. 902, 111 N.Y.S.2d 221, *aff'd*, 304 N.Y. 812, 109 N.E.2d 470 (1952); *cf.* Note, *Procedural Requirements of a Grievance Arbitration Clause: Another Question of Arbitrability*, 70 YALE L.J. 611 (1961).

[183]*Teamsters v. Shapiro*, 138 Conn. 57, 82 A.2d 345, 350, 16 LA 671 (1951); *Danbury Rubber Co. v. Local 402*, 145 Conn. Supp. 230 (1953).

[184]36 LA 724, 729-31 (Schmidt, 1961); *see also Modernage Furniture Corp.*, 4 LA 314, 315 (Feinberg, 1946).

. . .

It seems to me a fair guess that had the award been more favorable to the union no attempt would have been made to nullify it—at least no attempt by the union. I cannot speculate what the company might have done in those circumstances. In my view it would be unfair and unreasonable to construe this Agreement to mean that the union (or for that matter, the company) could first look into the package, after asking that it be forwarded, and then decide that since it did not like the looks of the contents, the arbitrator was exceeding his authority when he sent it on. Such a privilege would be tantamount to seeing whether you are dealt a good hand before announcing that the deal is out of turn.

. . .

The principles of waiver which I have held to apply here are embodied in the proposed Uniform Arbitration law drafted and recommended by the National Conference of Commissioners on Uniform Laws (Section 8(b)), 9 U.L.A. pp. 76, 81 (1957), as well as in the proposed United States Arbitration Act adopted by the National Academy of Arbitrators in 1959 (Section 9(B)), 34 L.A. 942, 946.[185]

Arbitrator Schmidt's view appears to be in the mainstream of opinion on this subject: a delayed award should not be considered void. However, the arbitrator's jurisdiction may be severed if a challenge is made prior to the rendering of the award. After such a challenge the award usually is considered void because of lack of jurisdiction.[186] In *Machinists, West Rock Lodge 2120 v. Geometric Tool Co.,*[187] the Second Circuit held that the fact that the award had not been rendered within the mandatory sixty days required by the state statute did not justify its vacation. However, in so holding the court did describe the conditions that would justify a vacation of an award if rendered late. The court said:

> In adopting a uniform federal standard, we ought not to accept an arbitration rule which encourages post-award technical objections by a losing party as a means of avoiding an adverse arbitration decision. . . . Rather, we believe it to be a better rule that any limitation upon the time in which

---

[185]36 LA at 729-31.

[186]*Hotel Employees, Local 355 v. Fontainbleau Hotel Corp.*, 423 F. Supp. 83, 93 LRRM 2983 (S.D. Fla. 1976); *Seafarers v. Standard Oil Co. of Cal.*, 378 F. Supp. 1278, 83 LRRM 3114 (C.D. Cal. 1973); *Machinists, Local 701 v. Holiday Oldsmobile*, 356 F. Supp. 1325, 84 LRRM 2200 (D. Ill. 1972); *Machinists, Lodge 725 v. Mooney Aircraft*, 410 F.2d 681, 71 LRRM 2121 (5th Cir. 1969); *Machinists, District Lodge 71 v. Bendix Corp., Kansas City Div.*, 218 F. Supp. 742, 53 LRRM 2854 (W.D. Mo. 1963); *Nathan v. Jewish Center of Danbury*, 20 Conn. Supp. 183, 129 A.2d 514 (1955); *Campbell v. Automatic Dye & Products Co.*, 162 Ohio St. 321, 123 N.E.2d 401, 405 (1954); *In re Service Employees*, 60 N.Y.S.2d 811, 17 LRRM 829 (Sup. Ct. 1946); *In re Famous Realty*, 283 A.D. 957, 130 N.Y.S.2d 281 (1934); *Parks v. Cleveland Railway*, 124 Ohio St. 79, 177 N.E. 28, 29 (1931); *Fudickar v. Guardian Mutual Life Ins. Co.*, 62 N.Y. 392, 405 (1875).

[187]406 F.2d 284, 70 LRRM 2228 (2d Cir. 1968).

an arbitrator can render his award be a directory limitation, not a mandatory one, and that it should always be within a court's discretion to uphold a late award if no objection to the delay has been made prior to the rendition of the award or there is no showing that actual harm to the losing party was caused by the delay.

In arriving at this standard we are merely restating the rule that has been promulgated in the vast majority of statutes and cases.[188] [Citations omitted.]

Drawing upon this principle announced by the Second Circuit, the Third Circuit adopted it and drafted a rule:

The requirements of federal labor policy will be served by requiring that if the parties intend to provide for the automatic invalidation of a late award they must say so in unequivocal language. If they do not so provide, the authority of the arbitrator will expire after a reasonable time beyond the period originally fixed for the award has gone by. Where the parties consent to an extension of time for the award, they are not bound endlessly and one party may effectively terminate his consent before the award is handed down by giving reasonable notice, and of course, its reasonableness must be judged in the light of the surrounding circumstances, including any element of harm or prejudice.[189]

Vacation for Procedural Errors

The Supreme Court declared that the procedural flaws affecting the parties' contractual obligation to arbitrate are to be resolved by the courts, but that once the duty to arbitrate has been established, all additional procedural issues are to be left to arbitrator's judgment.[190] As an illustration of the former type of procedural infirmity, vacation occurred where the award was rendered against a non-party[191] and where the appointment of the arbitrator who rendered the award was not according to the procedure in the agreement.[192] Courts will usually

---

[188]*Id.* at 286, 70 LRRM at 2229-30.

[189]*Teamsters, Local 560 v. Anchor Motor Freight, Inc.*, 415 F.2d 220, 226, 71 LRRM 3205 (3d Cir. 1969); *accord, Teamsters, Local 604 v. Placke Chevrolet Co., Inc.*, 383 F. Supp. 1156, 87 LRRM 2193 (E.D. Mo. 1974).

[190]*John Wiley & Sons, Inc. v. Livingston*, 376 U.S. 543, 54 LRRM 2769 (1964). This distinction between procedure affecting substantive arbitrability and procedural matters affecting the arbitration proceeding itself cannot always be clearly drawn. *See, e.g., Procter & Gamble Mfg. Co. v. Independent Oil & Chemical Workers*, 386 F. Supp. 213, 221-22 (D. Md. 1974).

[191]*Livingston v. Cheney-Frantex, Longford-Weavers, Inc.*, 14 A.D.2d 518, 216 N.Y.S.2d 1011 (1961).

[192]*Hod Carriers, Local 277 v. Sullivan*, 221 F. Supp. 696, 54 LRRM 2548 (E.D. Ill. 1963); similarly in *Food Handlers, Local 425 v. Pluss Poultry, Inc.*, 260 F.2d 835, 43 LRRM 2090 (8th Cir. 1958), it was held that where each party must appoint one arbitrator to a panel pursuant to a contractual scheme, one party's failure to do so renders unenforceable an award achieved by the other party's unilateral initiation of the arbitral process; *cf. Tamari v. Conrad*, 552 F.2d 778 (7th Cir. 1977).

hold, however, that there has been a waiver of such defects if objection to the award on such a ground is made after the award is received.[193]

Vacation of awards because they were "tainted" by the negligence of the union representative who was assigned to represent the grievant and therefore caused a "breach of the duty to represent fairly" is discussed in Chapter XXIII, "Fair Representation Obligations."

Vacation Through the Bankruptcy Court

When a company is being administered by a bankruptcy judge, an arbitration procedure cannot produce an enforceable award unless the bankruptcy judge has granted prior permission for the arbitration. This created an interesting interplay between bankruptcy rules and labor law in *Teamsters, Local 807 v. Bohack Corp.*[194] The company in July 1974 had filed a petition under Chapter XI of the Bankruptcy Act and the judge allowed the company to operate its business as a debtor-in-possession. In December, the company decided to terminate most of its trucking operations at a particular location and subcontract the trucking. This subcontracting caused about sixty drivers to be displaced, and the union immediately filed a grievance contending that the company had violated the labor agreement. A joint committee decided that the company had violated the agreement and ordered the company to cease and desist the subcontracting of the trucking work, and the union then brought suit in a state court to confirm the award. The company had the case removed to the federal court and the union then instituted a strike to force the termination of the subcontracting. Then a temporary restraining order against the strike was issued by the bankruptcy judge and in response the union appealed the bankruptcy judge's restraining order to the district court. The district court judge vacated the restraining order of the bankruptcy judge and replaced it with one of his own. The judge also dismissed the union's petition to have the joint committee's decision confirmed because no permission for the arbitration had been obtained from the bankruptcy judge. Two years later another strike began. The Second Circuit then dissolved the district judge's restraining order against the strike and remanded the case to the bankruptcy judge, asking him to decide whether arbitration of the subcontracting dispute should take place.[195]

---

[193]*National Cash Register Co. v. Wilson*, 8 N.Y.S.2d 377, 171 N.E.2d 302 (1969); *but see In re Consolidated Carting Corp.*, 280 N.Y.S.2d 872, 65 LRRM 3069 (Sup. Ct. App. Div. 1967) and *Hellman v. Wolbron*, 298 N.Y.S.2d 540 (Sup. Ct. App. Div. 1969).

[194]541 F.2d 312, 93 LRRM 2001 (2d Cir. 1976).

[195]*Id.*

The Ninth Circuit in *Local Joint Executive Board v. Hotel Circle Inc.* [196] explained that a receiver in a bankruptcy is not the same entity as the pre-bankruptcy company and hence is not a party to an existing labor agreement. In addition, the receiver is not vested with authority to affirm or enter into a labor agreement without the bankruptcy court's approval. [197] And if an arbitration hearing takes place under the grievance procedure in a labor agreement, the award can be vacated by the bankruptcy court even if the debtor fully participated in the arbitration proceedings. [198]

CONFIRMING AN AWARD

Court confirmation of an award, theoretically, should not alter its *collateral estoppel* or *res judicata* effect [199] but as a practical matter, such confirmation does alter the effect because a confirmed award becomes an order of the court. Avco Lycoming Division of Avco Corporation discharged an employee who left work early on Friday for religious reasons and the award approving the discharge was confirmed by a Connecticut court. The discharged employee then initiated a proceeding before the Connecticut Commission on Human Rights and Opportunities and that tribunal decided that the employee had been discriminated against because of her religion and ordered her reinstated. The company then appealed the Commission's decision to the Connecticut court that had previously enforced the arbitration award and that Court declared that the decision of the Commission must be "annulled and set aside." [200] The court explained that a confirmed arbitration award became a *res judicata* decision and the Human Relations Commission could not effectively issue a contrary decision.

However, the Ninth Circuit rendered a contrary decision. [201] An employee had been discharged and a grievance was filed claiming the discharge was an improper discrimination because of religious reasons

---

[196] 613 F.2d 210, 103 LRRM 2423 (9th Cir. 1980). *See also NLRB v. Burns International Security Services*, 406 U.S. 272, 80 LRRM 2225 (1972).

[197] Bankruptcy Act, Chapter XI; Bankruptcy Rule 919(b), 11 U.S.C.A. §§ 1101 *et seq.* (1979).

[198] *Teamsters, Local 807 v. Bohack Corp.*, 541 F.2d 312, 93 LRRM 2001 (2d Cir. 1976). *See also In re Louis F. Sammarco Electric Co.*, 109 LRRM 3288 (1982); *In re Handy Andy Inc.*, 109 LRRM 3298 (1982).

[199] *Bohack Corp. v. Teamsters, Local 807*, 431 F. Supp. 646, 95 LRRM 3031 (E.D. N.Y. 1977). Confirmation is a simple proceeding. For example, it is mandatory in Ohio for the court to confirm and enforce the award. *Brennan v. Brennan*, 164 Ohio St. 29, 128 N.E.2d 89, 90 (1955).

[200] *Corey v. Avco Corp., Avco-Lycoming Div.*, 2 FEP Cases 738 (Conn. Super. Ct. 1970), *aff'd sub nom. Corey v. Avco-Lycoming Div.*, 163 Conn. 309, 307 A.2d 155, 4 FEP Cases 1028 (1972), *cert. denied*, 409 U.S. 1116, 5 FEP Cases 300 (1973).

[201] *Aleem v. General Felt Industries*, 661 F.2d 135, 27 FEP Cases 569 (9th Cir. 1981).

and hence not for "good cause"; the arbitrator dismissed the grievance, finding that the discharge was not a religion-based discrimination. Vacation was sought at the district court and the judge dismissed
the suit (confirmed the award). Then the grievant filed a charge with
the Equal Employment Opportunity Commission. A right-to-sue letter was issued, a suit was initiated at the same district court that had
confirmed the award approving the discharge, and the suit based on
the right-to-sue letter was dismissed. The grievant appealed the
dismissal to the Ninth Circuit Court. The company's attorney argued
that when the grievant first sought a vacation of the award at the district court which had approved the award and the award was confirmed, the grievant had received the *de novo* review of his discrimination claim by a court under the principles established by *Alexander v.
Gardner-Denver,* [202] and that the award had become a *res judicata*
decision and could not be relitigated. The Ninth Circuit disagreed, [203]
reversed the district court, and specifically criticized the Connecticut
court's decision discussed above.

In contrast a union that sought to relitigate the same issue that had
been decided by the arbitrator and then confirmed by the court at the
request of the employer had that court issue an injunction against the
relitigation of the same issue on the ground that such action was vex-
atious—another interesting gain obtained from a confirmation. [204]

A somewhat strange double statute of limitations rule was used in
Service Employees, Local 36 v. Office Center Services, Inc. [205] to prevent affirmative defenses from being raised in a confirmation of an
award proceeding. The Third Circuit said that since the employer had
three months to sue to have an arbitration award vacated and did not
do it, it could not raise affirmative defenses in a union's timely action
to confirm the award, because the statute on the confirmation suit was
one year (twelve months).

It had generally been assumed that when an employer does not
"win" a desired construction of the labor agreement provision the
employer had two options. First, the employer could refuse to accept
the arbitrator's construction and then explain the reasons for this refusal to the union representatives, who would (a) upon further reflection,
accept the employer's construction, (b) leave it in *status quo* pending
another arbitration hearing before a different arbitrator, or (c) file a
Section 301 suit asking for confirmation. In such a suit the employer

---

[202]415 U.S. 36, 7 FEP Cases 81 (1974); *see* discussion in Chapter XXII, *"De Novo* Reviews in
a Court."
[203]661 F.2d 135, 27 FEP Cases 569 (9th Cir. 1981).
[204]*Laursen v. Lowe,* 50 Ohio App. 103, 197 N.E. 597 (1935).
[205]670 F.2d. 404, 109 LRRM 2552 (3d Cir. 1982).

would then make the same arguments before the judge that the employer would have made in a suit for a vacation, hoping that the judge will not confirm. Or second, the employer could file a Section 301 suit asking for a vacation of the arbitration award. In that suit the argument on the two sides would be the same except that the defendant becomes the plaintiff.

Because of the difference in time barring a Section 301 suit to vacate and a suit to confirm in the state of Pennsylvania (three months for a vacation suit and twelve months for a confirmation suit), the employer lost the right to set out affirmative defenses in the suit to confirm. And where the differences in time affect the affirmative defenses, it is obvious that a union will stay quiet and not file the suit to confirm until the three months pass, and its suit will then of course be won because the defendant must then remain mute.

The Seventh Circuit allowed affirmative defenses by a defendant in an action to confirm[206] despite the passage of the three-month limitation period for motions to vacate, where the defenses would be the plaintiff's case in chief.[207] These differences mean a *caveat*.[208] To be certain the affirmative defenses are not blocked, one should take the "suit for vacation" step rather than hoping to be granted a time limitation waiver such as that discussed *supra*.

Judge Jerre S. Williams of the Fifth Circuit discussed another related situation.[209] A disappointed party did not seek to vacate the award but raised the same objections when they were presented in a subsequent arbitration involving an identical grievance before a different arbitrator. Judge Williams held that the failure to sue to vacate an award generated no waiver in a subsequent identical grievance arbitration case:

> The company urges, however, that the union waived its right to attack the Sabella award by not bringing a suit in court to set it aside. This assertion cannot prevail. The union elected to choose arbitration as the means of setting aside the Sabella award. Under the well established national policy favoring arbitration,[210] this was a proper decision to make. The

---

[206]*Teamsters, Local 135 v. Jefferson Trucking Co.*, 628 F.2d 1023, 105 LRRM 2711 (7th Cir. 1980), *cert. denied*, 449 U.S. 1125, 106 LRRM 2256 (1981). *See also United Parcel Service, Inc. v. Mitchell*, 451 U.S. 56, 107 LRRM 2001 (1981); *Kikos v. Teamsters, Local 299*, 526 F. Supp. 110, 108 LRRM 2787 (D. Mich. 1981).

[207]*See also Paul Allison, Inc. v. Minikin Storage of Omaha, Inc.*, 452 F. Supp. 573 (D. Neb. 1978); *Rikop Enterprises, Inc. v. Seattle Supersonics Corp.*, 357 F. Supp 521 (S.D. N.Y. 1973).

[208]*The Hartbridge*, 57 F.2d 672 (2d Cir. 1932), *cert. denied*, 288 U.S. 601 (1932).

[209]*W.R. Grace & Co. v. Rubber Workers, Local No. 759*, 652 F.2d 1248, 1258, 107 LRRM 3251, 3258 (5th Cir. 1981), *cert. granted*, 50 USLW 3998.18 (U.S. June 28, 1982) (No. 81-1314).

[210]Citation by the court, *United States Steel Corp. v. United Mine Workers*, 519 F.2d 1236, 1242 [90 LRRM 2539, 2542] (5th Cir. 1975), *reh'g denied*, 526 F.2d 376 [91 LRRM 2306] (1976), *cert. denied*, 428 U.S. 910, 96 S. Ct. 3221, 49 L. Ed.2d 1217 [92 LRRM 3006] (1976).

union had the right to choose this means of attacking the earlier award. As has been pointed out above, there are many instances of second arbitrations being pursued as a means of evaluating the validity of earlier arbitration awards. In *San Antonio Newspaper Guild, Local No. 25 v. San Antonio Light Div.* [481 F.2d 821, 83 LRRM 2728 (5th Cir. 1973)], this Court upheld as binding a second award which resolved issues left so unclear by a first award that we held the first award unenforceable. It is established that if a party to the contract demands a second arbitration to test the validity of the first arbitration, the courts will order the second arbitration because it is for the arbitrator to determine in the first instance whether the prior award is valid.[211]

Confirmations of award were previously made in state courts under the common law writ of *assumpsit,*[212] then under various state statutes, but now state courts as well as federal courts clearly have jurisdiction for confirmation suits under Section 301 of the Labor-Management Relations Act.[213] The suit must be filed in the state or federal court that is operating in the geographic district where the arbitration hearing took place.[214]

Actions to confirm awards have sometimes been stretched into actions to revise. When a union sought confirmation and enforcement of an award, confirmation of that portion of the award that provided for punitive damages was denied by the district court in Texas because the court found this portion of the award did not have its "essence" drawn from the agreement, but the court confirmed the remainder of the award.[215] In contrast the Fifth Circuit confirmed an award that included punitive damages, saying:

[A] collective bargaining agreement may not specify the relief required for every conceivable contractual violation, so the arbitrator must often rely on his own experience and expertise in formulating an appropriate remedy.[216]

---

[211]652 F.2d at 1258, 107 LRRM at 3258. Citation by the court, *Local 103, Int'l U. of Electrical, Radio and Machine Workers v. RCA Corp.* [516 F.2d 1336, 89 LRRM 2487 (3d Cir. 1975)]; *Avco Local Union No. 787 v. Int'l U. United Automobile, Aerospace & Agricultural Implement Workers of America,* 459 F.2d 968 [80 LRRM 2290] (3d Cir. 1972).

[212]BLACK'S LAW DICTIONARY (St. Paul: West Pub. Co., 1968), p. 157.

[213]*Harris v. Stroudsburg Fur Dressing Corp.*, 389 F. Supp. 226, 88 LRRM 3233 (S.D. N.Y. 1975).

[214]*Arthur Imerman Undergarment Corp. v. Garment Workers, Local 162*, 145 F. Supp. 14, 38 LRRM 2766 (D. N.J. 1956).

[215]*Operating Engineers, Local No. 450 v. Mid-Valley, Inc.*, 347 F. Supp. 1104, 81 LRRM 2325 (S.D. Tex. 1972).

[216]*Bakery & Confectionery Workers, Local 369 v. Cotton Baking Co., Inc.*, 514 F.2d 1235, 1237, 89 LRRM 2665, 2666-67 (5th Cir. 1975); *see also Peter Cooper Corp., U.S. Glue and Gelatin Div. v. Electrical Workers, UE, Local 1132*, 472 F. Supp. 692 (D.C. Wis. 1979).

VACATION BY NONDEFERRAL BY THE NLRB

In *Associated Press v. NLRB*, [217] the District of Columbia Circuit Court approved the Board's policy of deferring to arbitration, stating:

> We think it clear that submission to grievance and arbitration proceedings of disputes which might involve unfair labor practices would be substantially discouraged if the disputants thought the Board would give *de novo* consideration to the issue which the arbitrator might resolve. Such discouragement would be contrary to the Supreme Court's efforts to effectuate the congressional desire to support "administrative techniques for the peaceful resolution of industrial disputes." The Board does not abdicate its responsibilities to implement the National Labor Relations Act by respecting peaceful resolution of disputes through voluntarily agreed upon administrative techniques as long as it is assured that those techniques are procedurally fair and that the resolution is not clearly inconsistent with or repugnant to the statute. [218] [Footnote omitted.]

There are now two procedures which bring an arbitration award into review by the NLRB. The first has often been referred to as the *Spielberg* review [219] and the second as the *Collyer* review. [220]

Arbitrators often receive grievances which involve matters which could have been filed as an unfair labor practice charge in the appropriate general counsel's office of the NLRB. If a complaint is later issued, a hearing held before an administrative law judge covering the same matter would be a double litigation. The NLRB in recognition of Section 302(d) of the Labor-Management Relations Act [221] adopted, in the *Spielberg Manufacturing Co.* decision [222] in 1955, a policy of reviewing the previously issued arbitration award and deferring to it (accepting it) if the same factual situation that would be moved up to a Board decision meets five standards: (1) the arbitration hearing appears to have been fairly and regularly handled by the arbitrator; (2) all parties involved with the subsequent unfair practice charge have agreed to be bound by the award; (3) the award disposes of the unfair labor practice aspects in a manner that is not clearly repugnant to the Board's policies; [223] (4) the unfair labor practice aspects involved have

---

[217] 492 F.2d 662, 85 LRRM 2440 (D.C. Cir. 1974).
[218] *Id.* at 667, 85 LRRM at 2444.
[219] *Spielberg Mfg. Co.*, 112 NLRB 1080, 36 LRRM 1152 (1955).
[220] *Collyer Insulated Wire*, 192 NLRB 837, 77 LRRM 1931 (1971).
[221] 29 U.S.C. § 173(d) (1970).
[222] 112 NLRB 1080, 36 LRRM 1152 (1955).
[223] *Id.*

been "clearly decided" by the arbitrator; and (5) the arbitrator decided the issue "within his competence."[224]

If the unfair labor practice charge against the employer either was not presented in the prior arbitration proceeding or was not considered by the arbitrator, the Board staff can decide against recommendation of "deference." For example, in *General Warehouse Corp.*,[225] the arbitrator *did not* specifically state in his award that the grievant *had not* been discharged because he spoke out vociferously against the company's request that the employees waive cost-of-living increases due them under the agreement, but *did* state that the grievant had been discharged because of his extensive absentee record; the arbitrator concluded the grievant's record was "just cause" for his discharge. The NLRB staff did not recommend deference to the award because the arbitrator had not dealt with the unfair labor practice aspect introduced first in the charge. The vacation of the award by nondeferral and the Board's decision that the dischargee was to be reinstated was sustained by the Third Circuit.[226] Judge Aldisert dissented, stating that the failure to defer, causing the vacation of the award, resulted only because the arbitrator's failure to affirmatively reject the unfair labor practice claim subsequently made it an unfair labor practice charge:

> If the arbitrator's decision means that just cause *existed* for the discharge and also that the discharge was *for* just cause, then it must logically follow that the arbitrator implicitly considered and rejected [the employee's] argument that the discharge was *for* an illicit cause.[227] [Emphasis in original.]

In view of this discussion, an arbitrator may want to indicate negative findings as well as affirmative ones in preparing his or her award so that possible unfair labor practice aspects will be disposed of if the Board's staff subsequently is asked to review the discharge.[228]

A nondeference by the general counsel's staff members that caused a vacation of the award was considered by the Third Circuit to be an

---

[224]*Ford Motor Co.*, 131 NLRB 1462, 48 LRRM 1280 (1961); *Monsanto Chemical Co.*, 130 NLRB 1097, 47 LRRM 1451 (1961); *accord, La Prensa, Inc.*, 131 NLRB 527, 48 LRRM 1076 (1961); *Electric Motors & Specialties, Inc.*, 149 NLRB 131, 57 LRRM 1258 (1964).

[225]247 NLRB 1073, 103 LRRM 1294 (1980).

[226]*NLRB v. General Warehouse Corp.*, 643 F.2d 965, 106 LRRM 2729 (3d Cir. 1981).

[227]*Id.* at 974, 106 LRRM at 2735. Judge Merritt also warns in dissent in *NLRB v. Magnetics International, Inc.* that the Sixth Circuit has undermined arbitration finality because "the majority's rule encourages litigants . . . to withhold their unfair labor practice claims from arbitration proceedings and thereby preserve a 'second bite' before the Board, should the arbitrator's decision prove unsatisfactory." —— F.2d ——, ——, 112 LRRM 2658, 2666, (6th Cir. 1983).

[228]Incorporating significant "negative" considerations to assist the Board is similar to incorporating such "negative" considerations if the award might be submitted to a court. Incorporating the "negative" considerations will help eliminate relitigation. *See* discussion under "A Base for Court Reviews of Job Evaluation Awards Started in 1981" in Chapter XXII.

abuse of discretion in *NLRB v. Pincus Brothers, Inc.*[229] Arbitrator I. Herman Stern had sustained the discharge of a grievant because she had distributed leaflets during working time criticizing the employer's labor policy and the company products. The grievant's private attorney then filed a charge with the NLRB alleging that both the discharge and the award had violated Section 8(a)(1) of the Act. The administrative law judge recommended reinstatement, and vacation of the award, and the Board concurred. The Board's reinstatement order was then moved up to the Third Circuit, which said:

> In this case, the arbitrator found that [R——] was terminated for "cause" because she abused working time and wrote and distributed the leaflet. The Board concluded that [R——]'s leafletting activity was protected by Section 7 of the Act and declined to defer. We hold that the Board abused its discretion in refusing to defer to the arbitration award because [R——]'s leafletting was arguably unprotected activity and therefore not "clearly repugnant" to the Act.[230]

The court, in conclusion, pointed out the difference between a decision by an arbitrator and a decision of the Board where the complaint was being decided *de novo*:

> In holding that [R——]'s conduct was arguably unprotected we express no opinion on how this court or the Board would decide the merits of the unfair labor practice charge in a trial *de novo*. We hold only that where there are two arguable interpretations of an arbitration award, one permissible and one not permissible, the Board must defer to the decision rendered by the arbitrator.[231]

In contrast, the Seventh Circuit said the Board had not abused its discretion when it *did not* defer to an almost identical arbitration award.[232] The grievant had passed out leaflets condemning his supervisor and asking for the aid of his fellow employees in pursuing a grievance filed against the supervisor. The company discharged the employee on the ground that his action was an effort to circumvent the grievance procedure; a grievance was filed concerning the discharge and the arbitrator dismissed it. The Board did not defer. It found that the leaflet was designed to enhance and not circumvent the grievance process, suggesting that any grievant can distribute similar leaflets. Because the Board did not defer, the arbitrator's award was vacated and on review, the Seventh Circuit agreed with the Board that leaflet writing is proper and, hence, that the award sustaining the discharge was legally wrong.[233]

---

[229]620 F.2d 367, 104 LRRM 2001 (3d Cir. 1980).
[230]*Id.* at 375, 104 LRRM at 2005.
[231]*Id.* at 377, 104 LRRM at 2007.
[232]*Dries & Drump Mfg. Co., Inc. v. NLRB*, 544 F.2d 320 (7th Cir. 1976).
[233]*Id.*

PRACTICE AND PROCEDURE IN LABOR ARBITRATION

A criticism of the Board occurred when the Board did not defer to an arbitration award involving Douglas Aircraft Co.[234] The arbitrator had reinstated a discharged union grievance committeeman but without back pay because of his "hostile, abusive, profane and uncivil" conduct toward the management. After the award was issued, the grievant filed an unfair labor practice charge with the NLRB, claiming that he would have been reinstated much sooner if he had agreed to withdraw his charge before the Board and that the arbitrator, by not granting back pay, had, in fact, supported the economic pressure generated on the grievant by the company which, although not effective, had been designed to cause him to withdraw his charge. Before the charge reached the hearing, a request for clarification, submitted to the arbitrator jointly by the union and the company, was answered by the arbitrator, who said that his failure to award back pay was *solely* because of the abusive, profane and uncivil conduct of the grievant.[235] Although the administrative law judge recommended dismissal of the charge, the Board decided that the no back pay award had added unsuccessful economic pressure on the grievant-plaintiff and the award should be vacated and back pay ordered by the Board. On appeal, the Ninth Circuit court held that the nondeferral that caused the award to be vacated was an abuse of discretion by the Board, and the Board's decision was reversed. The Ninth Circuit set up this principle:

If the reasoning behind an award is susceptible to two interpretations, one permissible and one impermissible, it is simply not true that the award was "clearly repugnant" to the [National Labor Relations] Act.[236]

Furthermore, the Ninth Circuit picked up the earlier Third Circuit test and explained again that the Board should give arbitrators the benefit of the doubt and refrain from "overzealous dissection of opinions" written by arbitrators.[237]

In *Sea-Land Service, Inc.*[238] the arbitrator had reinstated a grievant but without back pay because the grievant made obscene remarks during a grievance meeting. Because back pay had not been ordered in the award, an unfair labor practice charge was filed and the award

[234]*Douglas Aircraft Co.*, 234 NLRB 578, 97 LRRM 1242 (1978).
[235]*Id.*
[236]*Douglas Aircraft Co. v. NLRB*, 609 F.2d 352, 354, 102 LRRM 2811, 2813 (9th Cir. 1979).
[237]*Id.*
[238]*Sea-Land Service, Inc.*, 240 NLRB 1146, 100 LRRM 1406 (1979); *see United States Stove Co.*, 245 NLRB 1402, 102 LRRM 1573 (1979) (Board non-deferral caused a vacation because arbitrator did not grant back pay because of obscene outbursts). *See also Hawaiian Hauling Service, Ltd. v. NLRB*, 545 F.2d 674, 93 LRRM 2952, *cert. denied*, 431 U.S. 965, 95 LRRM 2642 (9th Cir. 1976); *contra, Atlantic Steel Co.*, 245 NLRB 814, 102 LRRM 1247 (1979) (Board deferred to an award sustaining a discharge because of obscenity directed to a supervisor).

was not deferred to because, the Board panel concluded, the arbitrator had "fictionalized" the obscenity. Member Penello dissented, stating that the nondeferral was simply because the Board staff and a majority of the panel had disagreed with the arbitrator's factual finding, not because the award, based on those findings, would be repugnant to the National Labor Relations Act.

Another re-evaluation of facts that resulted in a nondeferral and hence a vacation of an arbitrator's award occurred in *Mason and Dixon Lines, Inc.* [239] The arbitrator sustained the discharge because the grievant's wages had repeatedly been garnished in amounts beyond the normal limits whereas the Board's review staff suspected that the grievant's discharge was because he, as a union representative, had been openly criticized by the union membership and a discharge by the employer for such a reason would be an unfair labor practice. The Board panel agreed.

In another case, Arbitrator Carl F. Stoltenberg in *Consolidation Coal Co.* [240] sustained the discharge of the local union president because he instigated a work stoppage of seventy employees in violation of the agreement but converted the discharge of two union committeemen to thirty-day suspensions. The arbitrator explained why he converted the discharges to suspensions:

> At first glance it might appear that [the committeemen's] transgressions were not greater than those of any other employee who participated in the Wildcat strike. However, an officer of a Local Union has a greater responsibility for observance of a no-strike rule than do the rank and file members.
> While [the committeemen's] actions did not constitute instigation of the Wildcat strike, they do serve to establish an abrogation of [each committeeman's] responsibility as a Local Union Officer.

The two committeemen who had been given thirty-day suspensions instead of a discharge filed charges with the NLRB and the Board vacated the award and ordered full back pay on the ground that the arbitrator could not properly award more discipline to the two committeemen than other participants because they were merely participants in the agreement-breaching strike. [241]

Chairman Van de Water and Member Hunter in a minority opinion concluded that the arbitrator could properly decide that the discipline given the two members in the strike in violation of the agreement could be converted from discharges to suspensions without generating an unfair labor practice, but Member Fanning, writing the majority

---

[239]237 NLRB 6, 98 LRRM 1540 (1978).
[240]Award of March 12, 1980 (Stoltenberg), unreported.
[241]*Consolidation Coal Co.*, 263 NLRB No. 188, 111 LRRM 1205 (1982).

decision, held that since the arbitrator had found that the two grievants were not instigators of the strike, a thirty-day suspension of them was improper disparate discipline when the employer had not disciplined the other sixty-seven participants. The award was not deferred to, resulting in its vacation. Arbitrators have recognized that requiring equal discipline for all employees who breach their agreement by engaging in a strike would make discipline difficult, if the plant was to be operated during the period of the suspension of all who participated.[242] Some arbitrators have concluded that once an employee breaches his or her agreement by participation in a strike, the employer can treat all participants as "quits," permitting recalls to be selective.[243] If the arbitrator had concluded that the no-strike commitment of the labor agreement negotiated by the union included within it an understanding, specific or by construction by the arbitrator, that the union officials had a special duty to refrain from participation in a strike in violation of the labor agreement, the circuit court decision in *Fournelle v. NLRB*[244] that reversed the Board's vacation of an arbitrator's award would be most pertinent. Member Hunter had based his dissent in that case on the ground that union officials had a higher duty to not participate in an illegal strike, to avoid its sanction by a union official. Member Fanning, however, writing the majority opinion, concluded that the arbitrator had not determined that the labor agreement, properly construed, included this higher duty and, hence, these members vacated the award that had reduced discharge to a thirty-day suspension for the two union leaders who had participated in the strike in violation of the agreement.

Sixteen years after the *Spielberg* decision,[245] wherein the policy of deference to arbitration awards was established, another deferral to arbitration was developed in *Collyer Insulated Wire*.[246] In that case, the company spokesman explained to the Board panel that, under the labor agreement, the union and company had agreed that: (1) man-

---

[242]*See* text associated with notes 41–43, 63 in Chapter XVIII, "Remedies."

[243]*See* text associated with note 43 in Chapter XVIII, "Remedies."

[244]670 F.2d 331, 109 LRRM 2441 (D.C. Cir. 1982), *denying in part* 252 NLRB 982, 105 LRRM 1441 (1980). The arbitrator in his award vacated by the Board in *Consolidation Coal Co.*, 263 NLRB No. 188, 111 LRRM 1205 (1982), did not construe the no-strike clause to require a higher obligation on the part of a union official to not participate in a strike in violation of that clause. Since he merely said that a union officer had a higher duty of nonparticipation without basing this on the words in the agreement, the majority ordered back pay. Only Member Hunter concluded in a dissent that "imposing harsher discipline on the union committeemen for failing to meet their duty, *inherent* in the *collective bargaining agreement's* no-strike obligation," was justified. 263 NLRB No. 188 at 55, 111 LRRM at 1221. (Emphasis added.) *See also Metropolitan Edison Co. v. NLRB*, 663 F.2d 478, 108 LRRM 3020 (3d Cir. 1981), *cert. granted*, 102 S. Ct. 2926 (1982).

[245]*Spielberg Mfg. Co.*, 112 NLRB 1080, 36 LRRM 1152 (1955).

[246]192 NLRB 837, 77 LRRM 1931 (1971).

agement could "unilaterally" determine "buy" or "make" decisions (subcontract); (2) an arbitrator, not the Board, should interpret provisions in the labor agreement; and (3) the arbitrator could also resolve any unfair labor practice claims related to any of the "buy" or "make" decision activity.[247] The Board accepted this view and transferred the unfair labor practice complaint to the arbitrator, converting the unfair labor practice charge to a grievance claim to be handled under the labor agreement grievance procedure.

Later, when the membership of the Board changed, more such charges were transferred as grievances to arbitrators. (These were sometimes called *Collyer* transfers.) The Board staff then would review the arbitrator's award to determine whether the award dealt properly with the unfair labor practice charge aspects. If the staff did not approve the award under the *Spielberg* standards, the award would be vacated and the original unfair labor practice complaint sent on to a *de novo* hearing before an administrative law judge.[248]

The Ninth Circuit in *Stephenson v. NLRB*[249] looked on the "other side of the coin" and decided that the deferral of the award by the Board staff, which caused the award not to be vacated, was a breach of discretion by the Board. The Ninth Circuit concluded there was evidence of some improper discrimination surrounding the discharge and hence the arbitrator's award was wrong and *should have been vacated by nondeferral.*

COURTS' REMANDS TO THE ARBITRATOR TO CLARIFY OR CORRECT AWARDS

Sometimes a party seeks a judicial review of an arbitrator's award alleging that the award is ambiguous or indefinite and that the court should correct it. In light of the philosophy of deferring to the arbitrator's award expressed in the *Steelworkers Trilogy,*[250] some courts have been reluctant to interpret and then correct awards, and if the court concedes that the award is ambiguous or indefinite and should not be enforced for that reason, the court will remand the award back to the

---

[247]*Id.*

[248]Examples are: *Ad Art, Inc.*, 238 NLRB 1124, 99 LRRM 1626 (1978); *NLRB v. Longshoremen & Warehousemen, Local 27*, 514 F.2d 481, 89 LRRM 2133 (9th Cir. 1975); *Wilson Freight Co.*, 234 NLRB 84, 97 LRRM 1412 (1978); *Marin Dodge, Inc.*, 206 NLRB 370, 84 LRRM 1341 (1973); *NLRB v. Owen's Maintenance Corp.*, 581 F.2d 44, 98 LRM 3299 (2d Cir. 1978).

[249]550 F.2d 535, 94 LRRM 3224 (9th Cir. 1977).

[250]*Steelworkers v. American Mfg. Co.*, 363 U.S. 564, 46 LRRM 2414 (1960); *Steelworkers v. Warrior & Gulf Navigation Co.*, 363 U.S. 574, 46 LRRM 2416 (1960); *Steelworkers v. Enterprise Wheel & Car Corp.*, 363 U.S. 593, 46 LRRM 2423 (1960).

arbitrator for clarification. A clarification usually cannot be obtained from the arbitrator on a request by *one* party, under the remnant of the *functus officio* doctrine that provides that the arbitrator's function is exhausted when he or she submits an award unless jurisdiction is reestablished by the two parties jointly.[251] However, the jurisdiction of the arbitrator is considered reestablished when a court directs the arbitrator to clarify the award. In *Hanford Atomic Metal Trades Council v. General Electric Co.*,[252] the Ninth Circuit remanded an ambiguous award to the arbitrator for clarification, stating:

> The award must be read in the context of the opinion and the findings of the board of arbitration. We share the view of the district court that the opinion required clarification and interpretation. We also share the view of the district court that this was a task to be first performed by the arbitration committee and not the court, and that the court properly remanded the matter to the arbitration committee for such clarification and interpretation. See *United Steelworkers of America v. American Manufacturing Co.*, 363 U.S. 564, 46 LRRM 2414 (1960), *United Steelworkers of America v. Warrior & Gulf Navigation Co.*, 363 U.S. 574, 46 LRRM 2416 (1960); and *United Steelworkers of America v. Enterprise Wheel & Car Corp.*, 363 U.S. 593, 46 LRRM 2423 (1960). It is appellant's position that once the arbitrators have acted, it is the duty of the court to interpret and enforce the award, rather than to send the matter back to the arbitrators, to the end that the further delay involved in sending the matter back can be avoided. We think, however, that all of the foregoing cases accept the philosophy that where the parties have elected to submit their disputes to arbitration, they should be completely resolved by arbitration, rather than only partially resolved. In some cases the carrying out of this philosophy will require remanding the matter to the arbitrators, and we think that this is such a case.

Courts have directed a hearing *de novo* before the same arbitrator where the award covered matters beyond the submission[253] (for example, when back pay was ordered for a time after the expiration date of

---

[251]*See* discussion under "Modification and Correction of an Award by the Arbitrator" in Chapter XX.

[252]353 F.2d 302, 307, 61 LRRM 2004, 2008 (9th Cir. 1965). *Accord, Electrical Workers, IBEW, Local 494 v. Brewery Proprietors*, 289 F. Supp. 865, 69 LRRM 2292 (E.D. Wis. 1968) (award remanded to board of arbitration for clarification and correction of arithmetic errors); *Todd Shipyards Corp. v. Marine & Shipbuilding Workers, Local 15*, 242 F. Supp. 606, 59 LRRM 2613 (D. N.J. 1965) (award remanded to arbitrator where there was reasonable ground for disagreement as to what was actually decided); *Machinists, Winnebago Lodge 1947 v. Kiekhaefer Corp.*, 215 F. Supp. 611 (E.D. Wis. 1963) (award remanded to the arbitrator because the formula for computing vacation payments under certain circumstances was not included); *see also Printing Pressmen 135 v. Cello-Foil Products, Inc.*, 459 F.2d 754, 80 LRRM 2309 (6th Cir. 1972). *See also* text associated with notes 34–46 *supra*.

[253]*Kollsman Instrument Corp. v. Machinists*, 24 A.D.2d 865, 264 N.Y.S.2d 354 (1965).

the agreement[254] or when the meaning of the award was unclear.)[255] Courts have directed, also, a hearing before a *new* arbitrator where proferred evidence was found by the court to be so relevant that its exclusion by the first arbitrator denied one party a fair hearing[256] and after an arbitrator issued a second "clarifying" award on remand and it was still ambiguous.[257]

ENFORCEMENT OF AN OLD AWARD RENDERED WITH SIMILAR FACTS

Arbitrator White issued an award involving Ethyl Corporation in 1973, holding that some work performed by a supervisor in the railroad yard area of the plant was a contract violation. In 1979, the union learned that six supervisors had been instructed to perform similar work in a different department. Rather than filing a grievance the union filed a suit directly in the district court, asserting that Arbitrator White's award issued six years previously construed the provisions of the labor agreement that limited work by supervisors but allowed work to be performed to (1) preserve plant safety, (2) provide instruction to employees, or (3) conduct research and development. The district court in *Oil, Chemical & Atomic Workers, Local 4-16000 v. Ethyl Corp.*[258] dismissed the suit on the ground that an enforcement of a prior award required "strict factual identity" between the prior award and the current enforcement suit. On appeal, the Fifth Circuit re-

---

[254]*Burt Bldg. Materials Corp. v. Teamsters*, 24 A.D.2d 897, 264 N.Y.S.2d 993 (1965).

[255]*Kennedy v. Continental Transportation Lines, Inc.*, 230 F. Supp 760, 56 LRRM 2663 (W.D. Pa. 1964); *Transport Workers Union of Philadelphia, Local 234 v. Philadelphia Transportation Co.*, 228 F. Supp. 432, 55 LRRM 3014 (E.D. Pa. 1964).

[256]The Sixth Circuit in *Grand Rapids Die Casting Corp. v. Automobile Workers, Local 159*, 684 F.2d 413, 111 LRRM 2137 (1982), vacated the award of an arbitrator because the award "did not draw its essence from the collective bargaining agreement and should not be enforced." Then the court said:

"The federal common law of labor has developed to give the courts power to remand to the arbitrator when appropriate.... A case such as this, where the arbitrator did not decide the question presented to him, is an appropriate one for remand to avoid the draconian choice of penalizing either the company or the employee for what is, after all, the arbitrator's failure. We suggest to the District Court that remand should be to *a different arbitrator*. The previous arbitrator's outburst against the language of the contract compromises the appearance of impartiality to which the parties are entitled. If the parties are unable to agree to a different arbitrator, the District Court is entitled to appoint a neutral arbitrator."

Id. at 416, 111 LRRM at 2139. (Emphasis added.) *See, to the same effect, Smaglio v. Fireman's Fund Insurance Co.*, 432 Pa. 133, 247 A.2d 577 (1968).

[257]*Textron, Inc., Bell Aerospace Div. v. Automobile Workers, Local 516*, 500 F.2d 921, 86 LRRM 3240 (2d Cir. 1974).

[258]479 F. Supp. 953, 107 LRRM 2414 (D. Tex. 1979); *accord, New Orleans Steamship Ass'n v. Longshoremen, Local 1418*, 626 F.2d 455, 468, 105 LRRM 2539 (5th Cir. 1980); *Fontainbleau Hotel Corp. v. Hotel Employees Union*, Local 255, 328 F.2d 310, 55 LRRM 2439 (5th Cir. 1964).

versed,[259] explaining that when the union claimed that the supervisors had violated a six-year-old award, the burden shifted to the employer to demonstrate that the supervisors' work fell under the safety, training, or research exceptions, and that if the work performed in 1979 violated the award issued in 1973, there was no reason to have a new grievance filed and submitted to a new arbitrator.

> If the defendant is unable to articulate, through evidence, legitimate reasons why the disputed conduct is even arguably exempt from the prohibition, then the court can conclude that the present conduct is substantially or materially similar to the company's previous actions and thereby constitutes a "like" violation of the bargaining agreement as condemned in the prior arbitration award. At that point, the court may issue an order fashioning an appropriate remedy to enforce the prior arbitration award.[260]

The judge did explain that he was, in this decision, "ploughing some new ground" in labor arbitration award enforcement:

> By relying on the "strict factual identity" test, the district court improperly granted defendant Ethyl's motion for summary judgment. We have closely heeded the warnings of peril advanced by both parties in this suit, and, by our Odyssey today, *have charted out a course to be followed by the district court on remand.* We feel this new course best preserves the integrity of the labor arbitration process and fosters the time-tested wisdom of the Supreme Court's Steelworkers' trilogy.[261] [Emphasis added.]

This enforcement of a prior award seems more similar to contract law than to labor arbitration law. Many labor agreements state that the two parties (the union and the company) agree to accept the decision of the arbitrator as final, but such acceptance does not mean that the theory or construction underlying the award then becomes attached to the labor agreement. The Fifth Circuit in *Ethyl Corp., supra,* applied an *old* award to somewhat different facts assuming that the prior award established a proper theory and construction of the provision involved:

> If, based on the evidence at trial it is not even arguable that the current facts fall outside the prohibition or within an exemption of the article in question, then a court can safely conclude that the defendant's conduct does not differ materially from the previously condemned actions and thus, that the defendant is committing a "like" violation of the bargaining agreement, *in violation of the prior arbitration award.*[262] [Emphasis in original.]

[259]*Oil, Chemical & Atomic Workers, Local 4-16000 v. Ethyl Corp.,* 644 F.2d 1044, 107 LRRM 2417 (5th Cir. 1981).
[260]*Id.* at 1052, 107 LRRM at 2423.
[261]*Id.* at 1055, 107 LRRM at 2426.
[262]*Id.* at 1053, 107 LRRM at 2422.

Speed in obtaining a final resolution of a grievance is a basic objective underlying labor arbitration, and because many parties accept awards rather than seek vacation—even if they do not accept the theory or construction used by the arbitrator—the acceptance should not cause a party to lose the right to reargue the original theory or construction before a different arbitrator in another arbitration case. If the party cannot do this, there will be an increase in the flood of cases to district courts.

Often a losing party has no right to seek vacation or *de novo* review in spite of the looser vacation and review principles. Neither can the losing party seek a rehearing before the same arbitrator. The policy of finality of awards and the resulting difficulty of obtaining a review was illustrated when the Parker Pen Company attempted to have Arbitrator Pearce Davis review one of ten awards that he issued at the same time.[263] The Company accepted nine awards without objection, but, with respect to the tenth, it filed a "Request for Determination That the Award Is Void" as follows:

> The Parker Pen Company, after careful consideration of the awards rendered by Pearce Davis as Arbitrator, received August 15, 1961, believes that the Arbitrator in Case No. 10 has rendered an award which has gone beyond the limits of his jurisdiction and hence is an award which would be considered illegal if reviewed by a Reviewing Court and hence should be declared void by this Arbitrator. The reasons for the conclusions of the Company are as follows:
>
> The Arbitrator's Jurisdiction Is Clearly Set Forth
> In the Labor Agreement
> In Article V, Section B(6) the Arbitrator's jurisdiction is described as follows:
> "The Arbitrator in rendering a decision shall be limited to the terms, conditions, and provisions set forth in this Agreement, or any written supplementary agreements made thereto. The Arbitrator shall have no power to add to or subtract from or modify any of the terms of this Agreement, or any written supplementary agreements made thereto. Further, the Arbitrator shall not rule proposed amendment to, or propose modifications of this Agreement, or its extinction or removal."
> On the Face of The Award it is Clear
> That the Contract Was Not Construed
> But Rather the Award was Based on
> Extraneous Considerations
> The Arbitrator stated in his opinion concerning the decision in Case 10: "The decision in this case cannot be made to turn on the applicable contract language."
> The Arbitrator can only make a decision based on contract language. In

---

[263]*Parker Pen Co.* (Davis, 1961), unreported.

his award he made it clear that he is not basing his decision on contract language and hence that he was exceeding his jurisdiction.[264]

Arbitrator Pearce Davis responded to this request:

> I received your recent memorandum requesting that I declare void my recent arbitration award, Case #10, Parker Pen Company and Federal Labor Union 19593.
> You indicated that you have sent copies of your petition to union representatives. I have waited for communication from them but none has been received. At this time I therefore conclude that the union does not join in the company's petition; there is no joint request for reconsideration of the award. This being so it is apparent that I have no jurisdiction to reconsider the validity of the award in Case #10. Once an award has been issued, that award is final and binding upon the parties and the arbitrator loses jurisdiction.[265]

The plant manager then reviewed Arbitrator Davis' response and informed the union that the company would accept the award in Issue 10 in view of the arbitrator's refusal to review it, but advised the union that its acceptance of the award in Issue 10 did not mean an acceptance of the theory or constructions used by the arbitrator. The plant manager wrote:

> [In] view of arbitrator Pearce Davis' awards in the ten cases referred to him for arbitration and Company counsel's subsequent letter to him dated 29 August 1961, with a copy to you, requesting the arbitrator to set aside his award in Case 10, it is clear that of the whole arbitration only Case 10 (Spin Finish) remains in question.
> In an effort to dispose of this one matter and thus conclude the whole arbitration, the Company will in this case, without prejudice to any future matter and without raising any question regarding counsel's right to action, agree to offer to employees on Polisher and Buffer, Job #1-508(A), preferential right to Spin Finish, Job #GW-5529.[266]

Subsequently, precisely the same issue was presented by the union in another grievance at Parker Pen and Arbitrator Reynolds C. Seitz, a teacher of law at Marquette University, was selected as the arbitrator. After reviewing both the company's objection to the prior award by Arbitrator Davis on Issue 10, and after analyzing the labor agreement language, Arbitrator Seitz released an award which was diametrically opposite to the prior Davis award.[267] He explained that an award by one labor arbitrator may be persuasive but is not binding upon another arbitrator in labor arbitration.

---

[264]Company correspondence.
[265]Company correspondence.
[266]Company correspondence.
[267]*Parker Pen Co.*, Grievance No. 251 (Seitz, 1962), unreported.

CONTEMPT ACTION FOR FAILURE TO COMPLY WITH AN AWARD

Thus far, relatively few examples of civil or criminal contempt against a party who did not comply with an award after it was approved and enforced by a court have been found. However, the Third Circuit faced this problem in *Philadelphia Marine Trade Ass'n v. Longshoremen, ILA, Local 1291,*[268] and affirmed a district court decree imposing a fine of $100,000 per day upon a union for failure to comply with an arbitrator's award. While there are many procedural aspects of contempt proceedings that have not been finally resolved, it would nevertheless appear to be clear that both state and federal courts have authority under Section 301 to find a party in contempt for failure to abide by an arbitration award previously enforced by the court.

Civil or criminal contempt is used to enforce an award confirmed by a court but not complied with by the company, and in one case an officer of a company was held to be personally in contempt and fined even though that officer was not personally involved in the arbitration hearing and the award did not name him.[269]

RECOVERY OF ATTORNEYS' FEES AND COSTS IN ENFORCEMENT OR VACATION SUITS

It is well established that courts have equitable power to award attorneys' fees in cases brought under Section 301 of the Labor Management Relations Act,[270] to enforce arbitration awards. In *Electrical Workers, IBEW, Local 494 v. Artkraft, Inc.,*[271] the court explained the reasons:

> [I]t is needed to compensate plaintiffs who must resort to the courts for this enforcement of arbitration awards. Granting attorney fees is also an appropriate way to enforce National Labor policy.... The standard which has been developed in §301 cases is whether the party acted "without justification" in refusing to abide by the arbitration award.

In *Parker v. Mercury Freight Lines, Inc.,*[272] the court did not allow attorneys' fees, believing that there was "not sufficient evidence that defendants acted arbitrarily and without some justification." In

---

[268]368 F.2d 932, 65 LRRM 2510 (3d Cir. 1966), *rev'd on other grounds*, 389 U.S. 64, 66 LRRM 2433 (1967).

[269]*Milano v. Hingham Sportswear Co., Inc.*, 366 Mass. 376, 318 N.E.2d 827 (1974).

[270]29 U.S.C. § 185 (1976).

[271]375 F. Supp. 129, 132-33, 86 LRRM 3111, 3114 (E.D. Wis. 1974). *See also Mine Workers, UMW, District 50 v. Bowman Transportation, Inc.*, 421 F.2d 934, 73 LRRM 2317 (5th Cir. 1970) (attorney's fees incurred by plaintiff union in enforcing award in the arbitration of a seniority dispute ordered to be paid by the company).

[272]307 F. Supp. 789, 797, 73 LRRM 2189, 2195 (N.D. Ala. 1969).

Wilson H. Lee Co. v. New Haven Printing Pressmen, Local 74,[273] attorneys' fees claimed under a provision of a state statute providing for payment of such fees were denied with this statement:

> [I]t would appear particularly inappropriate, absent specific Congressional authority, for this Court to graft on to the federal remedy a part of a state statute to provide attorney's fees, ... and to that extent undermining the Act's basic objective of a uniform national labor policy. [Emphasis omitted.]

One court said that when the company attempts to upset an award based on the "intrinsic merits" of the dispute, the company should pay the union's attorney. If the company makes the same attempt to upset the award on jurisdiction, the company need not pay the union attorney, even if it loses.[274] Another court refused to award attorneys' fees against a company when the company did not comply with an award, pending clarification of other applicable rules under the Economic Stabilization Act and Pay Board. The court stated that "The standard which has been developed in Section 301 cases is whether the party acted without justification in refusing to abide by the award."[275]

The Fifth Circuit said a district court did not abuse its discretion in awarding a union's costs and attorneys' fees against a company because the refusal to abide by the arbitrator's award was unjustified.[276] The arbitration award had ordered reinstatement of a discharged employee and the award was enforced by the district court. When an award of back pay or monetary damages is enforced, a court may also award interest on the amount owed, calculated from the date of the award until final payment is tendered.[277]

---

[273] 255 F. Supp. 929, 930, 62 LRRM 2727, 2728 (D. Conn. 1965).

[274] *Machinists v. Texas Steel Corp.*, 97 LRRM 2496 (N.D. Tex. 1978).

[275] *Electrical Workers IBEW, Local 494 v. Artkraft, Inc.*, 375 F. Supp. 129, 133, 86 LRRM 3111, 3114 (E.D. Wis. 1974). *See also Teamsters, Local 394 v. Associated Grocers of Iowa Corp., Inc.*, 263 N.W.2d 755, 98 LRRM 2140 (Iowa Sup. Ct. 1978); *General Telephone Co. of the Northwest v. Electrical Workers, IBEW, Local 89*, 554 F.2d 985, 95 LRRM 2810 (9th Cir. 1977).

[276] *Mine Workers, UMW, District 50 v. Bowman Transportation, Inc.*, 421 F.2d 934, 73 LRRM 2317 (5th Cir. 1970). *In Steelworkers v. Butler Mfg. Co.*, 439 F.2d 1110, 77 LRRM 2057 (8th Cir. 1971) the union was granted attorneys' fees in a suit to recover insurance premiums paid by the union as damages, largely on the basis of a finding that the company's defenses were in bad faith; *Electrical Workers, IUE v. Peerless Metals Corp.*, 489 F.2d 768 (1st Cir. 1973).

[277] *Electrical Workers, IBEW, Local 494 v. Artkraft, Inc.*, 375 F. Supp. 129, 86 LRRM 3111 (E.D. Wis. 1974); *Meat Cutters, Local 248 v. Packerland Packing Co.*, 411 F. Supp. 1280, 92 LRRM 2774 (E.D. Wis. 1976); *but see Western Electric Co. v. Communication Equipment Workers, Inc.*, 409 F. Supp. 161, 91 LRRM 2621 (D. Md. 1976).

CHAPTER XXII

De Novo Reviews in a Court

The Supreme Court in two cases, *Alexander v. Gardner-Denver*[1] in 1974 and *Barrentine v. Arkansas-Best Freight System*[2] in 1981, set up an automatic review of a labor arbitration award in a federal district court if the award touches the public law. The first of these two cases set up a review of an award only if a Civil Rights Act (Title VII)[3] problem was involved, but later, in the second decision, this review was extended because payments touching the Fair Labor Standards Act[4] were involved. By this decision the Supreme Court applied the right of review to labor arbitration awards if they involved any public law.[5]

The Supreme Court said first in *Alexander* that a labor arbitration award could be accepted into the record at the district court if the arbitration meets "procedural fairness" and "adequacy of the record."[6] The amount of "weight" to be given to the award in the district court proceeding is the amount of "weight" the district judge desires to give. The effect of these two matters—(1) "procedural fairness" and (2) the acceptance by a district judge of the arbitrator's findings of fact and analysis—to limit or allow avoidance of relitigation in the district court will be discussed in this chapter.

DE NOVO REVIEW WAS MADE AVAILABLE WHEN THE AWARD TOUCHED TITLE VII MATTERS

On October 1, 1969, Harrell Alexander, a United Steelworkers Union steward in the Gardner-Denver Co. plant in Colorado, filed a grievance stating, "I believe I have been unjustly discharged and ask that I be reinstated with full seniority and pay." No racial discrimina-

---

[1]415 U.S. 36, 7 FEP Cases 81 (1974).
[2]450 U.S. 728, 24 WH Cases 1284 (1981).
[3]42 U.S.C. §§ 1971, 1975a to 1975d, 200a to 200h-6 (1964).
[4]29 U.S.C. § 201–219 (1938).
[5]*See* discussion by Chief Justice Burger in his dissent in *Barrentine*, quoted and discussed in the text *infra* associated with note 26.
[6]415 U.S. at 60 n. 21, 7 FEP Cases at 90 n. 21.

tion clause was included in the labor agreement and Alexander made
no allegation of racial discrimination in his grievance.

At the arbitration hearing where Arbitrator Don W. Sears (a teacher
of law at the University of Colorado) was presiding, Alexander asserted
orally that he believed his discharge was a result of racial discrimination and that he had already filed a discrimination charge with the
Colorado Civil Rights Commission.[7]

On December 30, 1969, Arbitrator Sears stated in his award that
the discharge was for "just cause" because of Alexander's negligent
work and made no reference to deny the racial discrimination claim
raised only in an oral comment at the arbitration hearing.

A private attorney filed a Section 301 suit in the federal district
court asserting that Gardner-Denver had violated Alexander's legal
rights under Title VII. When the award by Arbitrator Sears was put
into the record the district court "deferred" to the award.[8] The Tenth
Circuit affirmed the district court opinion *per curiam*[9] and *certiorari*
was then granted by the Supreme Court.

Four years after the discharge of Alexander the Supreme Court remanded the decision of the district court to the same court,[10] instructing it not to *defer* to the arbitrator's award but to evaluate the award
de novo. The difference between these two approaches was that in the
second instance the district court judge was to review the award very
carefully and—unless he himself believed the award was sound as a
decision—the dispute should be reopened and relitigation commence;
but if the district court judge considered the award sound, he could
adopt the award as his decision and make the award final.

When the award by Arbitrator Sears was carefully reviewed by the
district judge the second time, the judge concluded that the "appellant was discharged for a legitimate nondiscriminatory reason,"[11]
thereby making the Sears award the decision of the judge. The district
court decision was approved by the Circuit Court[12] and the writ of *certiorari* was denied by the Supreme Court.[13] Arbitrator Sears' award
thereby became final six years after the grievance on behalf of a union
steward was filed by the United Steelworkers Union.

---

[7]*Id*. at 42, 7 FEP Cases at 83; *see also* the lower court's ruling at 466 F.2d 1209, 4 FEP Cases
1210 (10th Cir. 1972). The charge filed by Alexander with the Colorado Civil Rights Commission
was transferred to the federal Equal Employment Opportunity Commission (EEOC) six months
after the arbitration award of Arbitrator Sears was released (July 23, 1970). The EEOC denied
Alexander's claim, reporting that there was "not reasonable cause to believe that a violation of
Title VII . . . had occurred." 415 U.S. at 43, 7 FEP Cases at 83.

[8]*Alexander v. Gardner-Denver*, 346 F. Supp. 1012, 4 FEP Cases 1205 (D. Colo. 1971).

[9]466 F.2d 1209, 4 FEP Cases 1210 (10th Cir. 1972).

[10]415 U.S. 36, 7 FEP Cases 81 (1974).

[11]519 F.2d 503, 505, 11 FEP Cases 149, 151 (10th Cir. 1975).

[12]*Id*.

[13]423 U.S. 1058, 11 FEP Cases 1450 (1975).

This analysis of the various *Alexander v. Gardner-Denver* decisions demonstrates that a private attorney does not have an automatic opportunity to relitigate the grievance in the District Court. If the arbitration award is as well-reasoned and as well-supported by a complete record as was Arbitrator Sears' award, judges will accept the award as the decision and, if this is done in general, *de novo* review will become infrequent.

DE NOVO REVIEW WHEN AN AWARD TOUCHED THE FAIR LABOR STANDARDS ACT

For a period of time the only *de novo* reviews of an arbitration award were those which touched discrimination matters (Title VII). Grievants who were disappointed by awards that did not touch such a matter were unable to obtain a *de novo* review. For example, in 1974 a disappointed grievant wanted a review of an award that touched the Fair Labor Standards Act and fifty-eight other employees joined the suit as plaintiffs in the district court in *Satterwhite v. United Parcel Service, Inc.* [14] The arbitrator had decided that the company could pay straight time rather than time and one-half for the two and one-half hours a week which two fifteen-minute daily coffee breaks amounted to and which had been included into work time, extending the total work time to forty-two and one-half hours per week. [15] The employees' private attorney argued before the district court that the award was inconsistent with the Fair Labor Standards Act and that all the employees adversely affected by the award should be granted back pay. [16]

The circuit court pointed out that wage and hour claims are typical of grievances filed under labor agreements [17] because the language in the Fair Labor Standards Act is uniformly incorporated in such agreements:

> In many contracts the unions have foregone the right to strike and management has accepted compulsory arbitration.... The ever-present disputes over wages and hours are readily adaptable to arbitration. Resort to judicial process after arbitration *prolongs* the controversy and serves *no* good purpose when the arbitral and judicial proceedings *arise out of* and *must be decided on* the same factual background. [18] [Emphasis added.]

---

[14] 496 F.2d 448, 21 WH Cases 747 (10th Cir. 1974).

[15] *Id.* at 449, 21 WH Cases at 748.

[16] *Id.*

[17] *Id.* at 451, 21 WH Cases at 750.

[18] *Id.* at 451, 452, 21 WH Cases at 750; *see also Atterburg v. Anchor Motor Freight, Inc.*, 425 F. Supp. 841, 23 WH Cases 17 (D. N.J. 1977).

However, in *Marshall v. Coach House Restaurant, Inc.,*[19] an award similar to *Satterwhite, supra,* was submitted to the Federal District Court—not by a grievant with a private attorney but by the Secretary of Labor. In this case Judge Haight explained that Congress had empowered the Secretary of Labor to obtain a court review of an award determining matters touching the Fair Labor Standards Act, and since the Secretary of Labor was not one of the parties who had agreed in advance that the arbitration award would be the "final" disposition,[20] he was not barred from bringing suit.

Then in 1981, seven years after *Satterwhite,* the Supreme Court in *Barrentine v. Arkansas-Best Freight System*[21] significantly changed the law. Two truck drivers, L. Barrentine and J. N. Scates, had filed grievances against the Arkansas-Best Freight System in 1970. They arrived at the office of the Little Rock terminal and "punched in," and, after completing their paper work, "punched out" and proceeded to their assigned "rig" (a tractor and semi-trailer). Then they went through the Federal Highway Administration (FHA) start-up tests, which took a few minutes (operating the brakes, the steering mechanism, the lights and the windshield wiper; testing the tire pressure; activating the horn and aligning the rear vision mirror). On rare occasions, a driver would find a defect (a worn-out windshield wiper, for example) and would then drive to the repair station located within the terminal area, and there "punch in" again on a time clock. For the time spent waiting for the repair the drivers would receive an hourly rate.

The two grievants, Barrentine and Scates, however, claimed two additional hourly payments—*i.e.*, for the time involved in making the first FHA inspection, and then for the time involved in driving to the repair station on this comparatively rare occasion when a defect was discovered. These grievances were presented by the union representatives to "a joint grievance committee" consisting of three representatives of the union and three of the employer. The committee, by unanimous action, "rejected the grievances without explanation." The district court, and subsequently the Eighth Circuit, denied the claims of the grievants, considering the unanimous decision of the "joint committee" to be final.

The district court dismissed the suit on the ground that the grievants had agreed in the labor agreement that the joint committee arbitration board award would be the final decision between the grievants and the employer. This denial was affirmed by the Eighth Circuit.[22]

---

[19]457 F. Supp. 946 (D. N.Y. 1978).
[20]*Id.* at 952.
[21]450 U.S. 728, 24 WH Cases 1284 (1981).
[22]615 F.2d 1194, 24 WH Cases 545 (8th Cir. 1980).

The Tenth Circuit in *Satterwhite v. United Parcel Service, Inc.*[23] had explained the reasoning:

> In Gardner-Denver the [Supreme] Court reasserted the federal policy favoring arbitration of labor disputes.... This policy was offset against that established by the Civil Rights Act of 1964 .... [T]he Court said that in the Civil Rights Act "Congress indicated that it considered the policy against discrimination to be of the 'highest priority.'" The conclusion that the anti-discrimination policy rated higher than that favoring arbitration of labor disputes was determinative."

The court added:

> We find nothing in any pertinent legislative history or court decision to indicate that Congress, by the grant of a right to private suit under FLSA § 16 (b), intended to establish a policy preference for the determination of a wage dispute in judicial rather than arbitral proceedings ....[24]

However, the Supreme Court majority in *Barrentine v. Arkansas-Best Freight System*[25] explained that because the joint committee denied the grievance claim *"without explanation"* the disappointed grievants should have the right to have a federal district court decide whether the joint committee, by its unanimous action, had protected their rights under the Fair Labor Standards Act. The majority of the court concluded that the grievants should be able to ask a federal court to decide whether the arbitrator had applied the Fair Labor Standards Act properly, just as a grievance that involved rights under the Civil Rights Act was protected by court review. Justice Burger in his dissent said:

> It is hornbook law ... that there is a strong congressional policy favoring grievance committee procedures and arbitration as a method of resolving disputes.... The Court [majority] today pays lip service to that congressional policy but then—paradoxically—ignores it.
>
> ...
>
> By rejecting binding arbitration for resolution of this relatively simple wage claim the Court thereby rejects as well a policy Congress has followed arising under the Fair Labor Standards Act, for at least half a century throughout the field of labor relations and now being applied in other areas as well. To reach that strange result, the Court relies on our holding in *Alexander v. Gardner Co.*, 415 U.S. 36, 7 FEP Cases 81 (1974). But that case in no sense compels today's holding .... But there obviously is a vast difference between resolving allegations of discrimination under the Civil Rights Act and settling a relatively typical and simple wage dispute such as

---

[23]496 F.2d 448, 451, 21 WH Cases 747, 750 (10th Cir. 1974).
[24]*Id.*
[25]450 U.S. 728, 24 WH Cases 1284 (1981).

we have here when the parties have expressly agreed to resolve such grievances by arbitration.

. . .

This elementary wage dispute falls well within the scope of traditional
arbitration as it exists under countless collective-bargaining agreements,
which the Court now channels into the federal courts. . . .

Allowing one party to such an elementary industrial dispute unilaterally
to resort to the federal courts when an established, simplified, less costly
procedure is available—and desired, as here, by the employer and the employee's union—can only increase costs and consume judicial time unnecessarily. It makes neither good sense nor sound law to read the broad language of *Gardner-Denver*—written in a civil rights *discrimination* case—to
govern a routine wage dispute over a matter traditionally entrusted by the
parties arm's-length bargaining to binding arbitration.[26] [Emphasis in
original.]

The analysis by Justice Burger makes it clear that the scope of automatic *de novo* review established by the majority did not merely add
awards that touched Fair Labor Standards Act problems to the list of
awards that were entitled to *de novo* review—a list previously confined
to those that touched Civil Rights Act problems—but would permit
de novo review of awards that touch any public act. The logic that
de novo review was previously tightly limited to Title VII discrimination matters has changed, and any representative or labor arbitrator
must assume that an award that involves any public law may be pushed
up to the federal district court by some private attorney because the
grievant is disappointed.

The extent of this push can be illustrated in an award by Arbitrator
Leo Weiss in *Rohr Industries, Inc.*[27] He sustained the discharge of an
employee who had brought literature into the plant for distribution to
fellow employees in violation of a clear rule against such activity,
against the union representative's claim that the employer's rule about
no distribution of literature violated the grievant's free speech First
Amendment rights. Arbitrator Weiss, a lawyer, interpreted the public
law and concluded that the employer's rule was not inconsistent with
the First Amendment. Under the *Barrentine* decision, *supra*, would
the disappointed grievant who was not reinstated in this case have the
right to have a private lawyer present the award to a federal judge to
review the determination by Arbitrator Weiss because it involved the
U.S. Constitution, obviously a significant "public law"? It is not yet
sparklingly clear that there is an automatic review of such an award,
but some private lawyer will certainly try to obtain it.

---

[26]*Id*. at 747, 24 WH Cases at 1291–93.
[27]76 LA 273 (Weiss, 1980).

JOINT COMMITTEE GRIEVANCE HEARINGS
ARE NOT ARBITRATIONS

One interesting and surprising reason why the majority of the justices in *Barrentine v. Arkansas-Best Freight Systems*[28] decided that a grievant should have the right to have an automatic review of an arbitration award regarding wage determinations by the joint committee was that the Supreme Court was afraid that the committee might not fairly represent a grievant. The Court said:

> There are *two* reasons why an employee's right to a minimum wage and overtime pay under the FLSA *might* be lost if submission of his wage claim to arbitration precluded him from later bringing an FLSA suit in federal court. *First*, even if the employee's claim were meritorious, *his union might* ... decide not to support the claim vigorously in arbitration.... Since a union's objective is to maximize overall compensation of its members, not to ensure that each employee receives the best compensation deal available, ... a union *balancing* individual and collective interests might *validly* permit some employees' statutorily granted wage and hour benefits to be sacrificed if an *alternative expenditure* of resources would result in increased benefits for workers *in the bargaining unit as a whole.*[29] [Emphasis added.]

Robert Coulson, the President of the American Arbitration Association, explained that the majority of the Supreme Court was actually describing a collective bargaining process, and during such a process the rights of an individual may be *sacrificed in exchange for increased benefits for the total membership.* He put the Teamsters joint committee collective bargaining process under focus and said:

> The joint grievance committee system of arbitration found in Teamster contracts is so clearly defective as an impartial mechanism that it is not surprising that we keep seeing it tested in the courts, as in *Barrentine* .... I continue to be astonished that the Supreme Court refers to that system as "arbitration."[30]

At the end of several joint committee meetings at different levels, if a unanimous agreement between the committees is not reached, a right to strike arises. In sharp contrast in labor arbitration, the risk of a strike is removed because the neutral renders the decision.

The pressure of a strike risk that builds up after several committees

---

[28]450 U.S. 728, 24 WH Cases 1284 (1981).

[29]*Id.* at 742, 24 WH Cases at 1289.

[30]Address by Robert Coulson, read at the New York University National Conference on Labor. 114 DLR D-1 (June 14, 1981). Unless a grievance is resolved by an arbitrator (a neutral), the dispute can deadlock until the right to strike point is reached. Under this type of procedure, a court could not properly enjoin a strike under the principle enunciated in *Boys Markets, Inc. v. Retail Clerks, Local 770,* 398 U.S. 235, 74 LRRM 2257 (1970).

have deadlocked, will, of course, invite negotiation and trading at the next level.[31] Arbitrator David Feller, a professor of law at the University of California, Berkley, explained:

> Where there are a number of employers bargaining through an association, a grievance that is not settled with the individual employer can be referred to a joint committee consisting of representatives of the employer group and of the signatory union or unions. The agreements of the International Brotherhood of Teamsters establish a whole hierarchy of these joint committees at the local, state, area, and most recently, national levels. If the employer and union representatives on a committee agree, the settlement reached is said to be "final and binding." If they are deadlocked, the case is referred to the joint committee at the next higher level . . . .
>
> . . .
>
> Decisions by joint committees are therefore appropriately treated, as Mr. Justice Goldberg reasoned in *Humphrey*, as *agreements of the parties, not arbitration awards*. The accuracy of that classification is emphasized by the fact that in most Teamster agreements the failure to agree at the highest committee level *does not result in arbitration by a neutral but the right to strike.*[32] [Emphasis added.]

If a neutral had rendered a final decision in *Barrentine, supra,* and he was qualified—as was Arbitrator Don W. Sears, a teacher of law, in the *Alexander* case, *supra*—the majority of the Supreme Court would have been able to evaluate the analysis of the statutory rights of the employees in *Barrentine* and would not have been so troubled because the grievance had been "rejected without explanation."[33] However, in the *Barrentine* situation the court sent back to the district court a decision reached through bargaining between the two sides

---

[31]The inevitable "horse trading" in joint committee negotiations and decisions was discussed in *Longshoremen & Warehousemen, Local 13 v. Pacific Maritime Ass'n*, 441 F.2d 1061, 1067, 77 LRRM 2160, 2165 (9th Cir. 1971):

"[T]hey had a deal working on the belly-packing-sacks matter and the Pete Velasquez case, and they had to sacrifice Pete Velasquez to gain the belly-packing-sacks matter.... [T]hey had more at stake on the belly-packing-sacks matter than they had on the Pete Velasquez case which involved one man where the belly-packing-sacks issue involved many."

The Ninth Circuit indicated that in this "practical world," there are no absolutely "right" solutions and the court recognized that cases are often resolved by accommodation and trade-off.

[32]Feller, *A General Theory of the Collective Bargaining Agreement*, 61 Cal. L. Rev. No. 3, 663, 836–38 (May 1973). This analysis by Feller was cited in *Satterwhite v. United Parcel Service*, 496 F.2d 448, 21 WH Cases 747 (10th Cir. 1974). In *Humphrey v. Moore*, 375 U.S. 335, 55 LRRM 2031 (1964), the Supreme Court approved a joint committee agreement to integrate the seniority plans of two trucking companies after a merger. Justice Goldberg, himself a former union lawyer, in his concurring opinion in *Humphrey* expressed the view that once the joint committee reaches a unanimous agreement, it becomes either a final interpretation of the labor agreement or a final amendment to the labor agreement. Courts then have no power to approve or disapprove what the parties have established (*Id.* at 351, 55 LRRM at 2039).

[33]450 U.S. at 729, 24 WH Cases at 1285 (1981).

and apparently the Supreme Court was asking the district court judge to renegotiate a unanimous collective bargaining agreement.

The second reason in the *Barrentine* majority decision why a review of an "arbitration" award before a federal district judge should be made available is because the justices believed that "arbitrators" could not deal competently with the "law of the land."

> [T]he "specialized competence of arbitrators pertains primarily to the law of the shop, not the law of the land".... Although an arbitrator may be competent to resolve many preliminary factual questions, such as whether the employee "punched in" when he said he did, he may lack the competence to decide the ultimate legal issue whether an employee's right to a minimum wage or to overtime under the statute has been violated.[34]

In footnote twenty-one of the majority opinion is found this additional generalization about labor arbitrators: "We have noted that 'a substantial proportion of *labor arbitrators are not lawyers*'...."[35] (Emphasis added.) Then the opinion speculated that many arbitrators may not be conversant with public law considerations.

Such a conclusion about the lack of competence of arbitrators *as a class* on the ground that a substantial proportion of labor arbitrators are not lawyers comes from the fact that the justices are making generalizations about collective bargaining teams (joint committees) rather than about arbitrators. The author could not resist counting the arbitrators elected to the National Academy of Arbitrators who are licensed lawyers. There were 208 licensed lawyers out of 482 arbitrators (61 of these busy arbitrators are teachers in important law schools).[36] The other labor arbitrators in the Academy who are not licensed lawyers are generally Doctors of Philosophy or Doctors of Engineering, and usually are teachers in universities.

AWARDS THAT TOUCH OSHA OR ERISA CAN ALSO BE REVIEWED *DE NOVO* IF THE SECRETARY OF LABOR FILES A PETITION

If a grievant believes that an arbitration award is inconsistent with either the Occupational Safety and Health Act (OSHA)[37] or the

---

[34]*Id*. at 743, 24 WH Cases at 1290, quoting *Alexander v. Gardner-Denver*, 415 U.S. 36, 57, 7 FEP Cases 81, 89 (1974).

[35]*Id*.

[36]1978-79 membership directory of the National Academy of Arbitrators was cross-referenced with the *Arbitrators' Qualifications Report* (R. C. Simpsons, Inc.) to find the background information on these members. This analysis does exclude some active arbitrators, who are also lawyers, because they are not members of the Academy.

[37]29 U.S.C. § 660(a) (1973).

Employee Retirement Income Security Act (ERISA),[38] the award can be reviewed by having a private attorney file a Section 301 suit in the same way such suits are filed concerning other awards that touch public law discussed above. In addition, under each of these statutes, the award can be reviewed in a court if the Secretary of Labor files a petition to review.

In one case the Secretary of Labor sought a modification of an arbitration award so the grievant, reinstated by an arbitrator but without back pay, would be given back pay by the employer, Allen Wood Steel Company. The employer had discharged the grievant because he had been insubordinate to his supervisor when he refused on two occasions to operate a crane after being instructed to do so. The grievant had refused because he claimed that operating the crane would have exposed him to a safety hazard because of its disrepair. A grievance over the discharge was filed. The arbitrator reinstated the grievant because the proof of the first refusal was unclear, but no back pay was awarded because the second refusal was not justified because the asserted hazard was not established in the opinion of the arbitrator.

The Secretary of Labor sought an order from a district court under Section 11C of OSHA to require the employer to pay the back pay but the court held in the second of two decisions[39] that the Secretary had not proved that the refusal to follow instructions was justified by a safety hazard. The most significant decision is the first one[40] because there the court held that there was no policy to defer to an arbitration award even if it met the same standards that would cause the NLRB to defer to the award under the policy encouraging finality to awards. This construction of Section 11C created another reduction of finality in the labor arbitration process.

The Secretary of Labor filed another review in a district court (*Marshall v. N. L. Industries, Inc.*[41]) to obtain back pay for a grievant who had been reinstated by an arbitrator but without back pay. The Circuit Court stated that the *Gardner-Denver de novo* review principle applied to arbitration awards that involve aspects of the Occupational Safety and Health Act:

> [T]he controlling case in deciding this issue is *Alexander v. Gardner-Denver Co.*, 415 U.S. 36, 94 S. Ct. 1011, 39 L.Ed2d 147, 7 FEP Cases 81, in which the Supreme Court held that an arbitrator's decision under a collective bargaining agreement to deny relief does not bar a later suit in federal court under Title VII, even if the discrimination question was pre-

---

[38] 29 U.S.C. § 1132(a) (1974).

[39] *Usery v. Alan Wood Steel Co.*, 4 OSHC 1598 (E.D. Pa. 1976). *See* note 40 *infra* for prior order of the court.

[40] *Usery v. Alan Wood Steel Co.*, 30 OSHC 1654 (E.D. Pa. 1975).

[41] 618 F.2d 1220, 8 OSHC 1166 (7th Cir. 1980).

sented in the arbitration proceedings. That conclusion applies equally well for the Occupational Safety and Health Act. Like Title VII, this legislation was passed to mobilize the resources of the federal government in an effort to eradicate a specific group of problems confronting workers nationwide. See *Whirlpool Corp. v. Marshall*, __ U.S. at __, 100 S.Ct. at 890, 8 OSHC at 1003. Enacted after the Supreme Court developed its policies encouraging deference to arbitration in a pure collective bargaining context, the OSHA legislation was intended to create a separate and general right of broad social importance existing beyond the parameters of an individual labor agreement and susceptible of full vindication only in a judicial forum. As a result, giving preclusive effect or even requiring total deference to an arbitrator's decision in this context would be inconsistent with the statutory purpose.

... *Gardner-Denver* itself was a private suit filed in protest over a discharge. In short, that the legislation requires that an individual prime the statutory machinery with some personal grievance does not diminish the social value of the subsequent judicial decision granting relief.[42] [Footnote omitted.]

In another case in this area, Arbitrator Bert Luskin became involved with representatives of both the Department of Labor and the NLRB. Fred Hamer, an employee of Interlake Iron Corporation and also a union official, was suspended for failure to shut down some pumps after being instructed to do so by his foreman, and this failure caused an overflow of tar. Hamer objected to his suspension and filed a grievance claiming that he had been suspended because he (1) had filed a series of OSHA complaints and (2) had been a long-time active union leader. In addition to the grievance he filed, Hamer filed an unfair labor practice charge with the Chicago regional office of the NLRB. Because the charge had grievance aspects, the Board staff transferred the charge to Arbitrator Luskin even before Hamer's grievance reached arbitration. Both the union and the company accepted Luskin as the arbitrator to resolve the previously filed grievance as well as the charge Hamer filed with the Chicago office. In his award, Arbitrator Luskin in *Interlake, Inc.*[43] wrote:

[T]here is simply no evidence in this record that would support a contention that Hamer's [grievant's] activities as chairman of the coke plant's safety committee resulted in his becoming the subject of discriminatory acts on the part of members of supervision. The fact that Hamer may have registered complaints with OSHA concerning alleged safety violations in the plant would have had absolutely no bearing on the fact situation concerning Hamer's failures to carry out instructions and his failures to take steps necessary to protect company equipment from damage.

---

[42]*Id*. at 1222-23, 8 OSHC at 1167-68.
[43]Grievance Case No. 78-912 (Luskin, 1979), unreported.

Arbitrator Luskin's award was reviewed by the NLRB staff and it recommended that the award should be deferred to, dismissing the unfair labor practice charge. Then a private attorney filed a suit in the district court, claiming that discipline of the grievant was in retaliation for his filing of OSHA complaints, and sought a vacation of Arbitrator Luskin's award. Judge Marshall referred the claim back to the Secretary of Labor for completion of administrative investigation and after investigation the case was not reactivated within the proper time period.[44]

A BASE FOR COURT REVIEWS OF JOB EVALUATION AWARDS STARTED IN 1981

For many years, labor arbitrators have used the job evaluation methodology established by the company concerned because it was accepted either by the union by agreement or by usage. For example, an award by Arbitrator Charles O. Gregory in *Acme Steel Co.*[45] was issued in 1948 to resolve a grievance filed by the union on behalf of a "set up man in Department R-151," claiming that his wage rate placed by the company in job class 11 should have been placed in job class 13. Arbitrator Gregory resolved the dispute by reevaluating the degree values (points). He said with respect to the challenges of degree evaluations in Factors 1 and 2:

> First of all, the arbitrator is convinced that the Union has not proven its points with respect to Factors 1 and 2. He believes that the Company's determination of B 0.3 and E 1.6, respectively, are fair and that any higher rating in either case would not be justified.[46]

He did adjust the degree values for Factor 5, but approved the degree values selected by the employer under Factor 6:

> In short, then, the arbitrator believes that Factor 5 should be rated as D 1.6 and that Factor 6 was correctly stated as C 0.4.[47]

Then he discussed the value for Factor 9:

> The only remaining inquiry is with respect to Factor 9. This, it will be recalled, has to do with "Mental Effort."[48]

---

[44]*Fred L. Hamer v. Interlake, Inc.*, No. 79 C 3482 (N.D. Ill. January 9, 1980) (memorandum order by Judge Prentice Marshall).

[45]*United Steelworkers and Acme Steel Company*, "Classification of Setup in Department R-51," (Gregory, June 1948), unreported.

[46]*Id.*

[47]*Id.*

[48]*Id.*

The arbitrator concluded that in this case the degree value selected by the employer was correct and hence that factor's value was not changed. When he totalled the points for all the factors where degree determinations were in dispute he reported:

> This, on the final count, leaves the Union with 11.2—a total which the arbitrator understands to mean that the setup job in Department R-51 remains in job class 11.[49]

About thirty years later, Arbitrator Peter M. Kelliher in a *Calumet Steel Division*[50] award used the same methodology and adjusted some degree values which changed some factor values and some "job worth scores" for certain jobs using the company-union job evaluation plan. Arbitrator Kelliher reasoned:

> [E]xcept for the fact that the Scrap Burner burns railroad cars for scrap, the Scrap Burner and the Scrap Man work at the same location with the same tools and materials and perform the same kind of work; . . . based on the Parties' history, a well established practice in burning operations, and the Job Description and Classification Manual, the disputed Factor was properly coded as B.4.[51]

These two awards are thirty years apart, yet the analytical process is identical.[52] This is significant to this discussion because it points out that an arbitrator resolves the dispute using the company's job evaluation methodology. It is true that a labor agreement almost always contains a provision that the employer may not take discriminatory actions for reasons of sex, race, national origin or age, and that under such a provision a union representative could challenge the company's job evaluation plan if an application of the methodology generating some sex-based wage rate discriminations had been built into the plan or was involved in its application. Such challenges did not happen, however, because the job evaluation methodology that was used by the arbitrator was the methodology *agreed* upon by the union and the company as the method used to resolve the grievance.

However, a new "ball game" started in 1981. In and after that date private lawyers, representing disappointed female grievants, can, and certainly will, file a Section 301 suit in courts[53] claiming that some Title

---

[49]*Id.*

[50]Grievance No. 16-77 (May 19, 1978, Kelliher), unreported.

[51]*Id.*

[52]The job evaluation methodology used by Arbitrator Kelliher (1978) was developed through a joint effort by twelve basic steel companies and the United Steelworkers Union pursuant to an order of the War Labor Board issued in 1944. The industry-wide plan (applicable to 94 companies) is set out in the text associated with note 71 *et seq. infra*.

[53]Section 301 suits can be filed in state courts but since this type of suit can be removed to federal court, such suits generally are initiated there. In these cases, both the union and the company are sued for a breach for different reasons.

VII violation had been built into the job evaluation plan or results from its application, and will seek to upset the award and obtain from the court a change in a wage rate and some back pay for their client or clients. Not until 1981 could a complaint be filed in a court asserting that an arbitrator overlooked some aspect of a job evaluation matter and it was in fact a Title VII violation and should be vacated or modified by the court.

Before 1981 the only *prima facie* Title VII sex-based wage discrimination that could move into the court was a claim that a *female* was paid *less* than a *male* for performing the *same* work. If the section 301 complaint set out any other claim of sex-based wage discrimination the complaint would be dismissed because the factual assertion, if proven to be true, would not be a violation of the Equal Pay Act of 1963[54] and hence not a Title VII violation. Violations described in the Equal Pay Act of 1963 became the limitation on the scope of sex-based wage rate violations under Title VII due to a statutory construction principle called "*in pari materia*."[55] Because Congress enacted a statute describing a narrow, precise, and specific sex-based wage rate discrimination in 1963 (the Equal Pay Act) it could not have intended this statute to be submerged the next year by the Civil Rights Act of 1964, unless it was made clear by Congress that submerging the earlier statute by the general terms of Title VII was its intention. This construction was reinforced by an amendment, the Bennett Amendment, added to the Civil Rights Act of 1964.[56] It appeared to be a congressional edict that the specific limitation on the sex-based wage rate discrimination enacted in 1963 in the Equal Pay Act was to be a limitation on any Title VII sex-based wage rate discrimination enacted in 1964.

In *County of Washington v. Gunther*[57] the Supreme Court in 1981

---

[54]29 U.S.C. § 206(d) (1) (1976) provides in relevant part (stated in the negative): "No employer having employees . . . shall discriminate . . . between employees on the basis of sex by paying wages to employees in such establishment at a wage rate less than the rate at which he pays wages to employees of the opposite sex . . . for equal work in jobs the performance of which requires equal skill, effort, and responsibility and which are performed under similar working conditions . . . ."

[55]*Marshall v. Dallas Independent School District*, 605 F.2d 191, 21 FEP Cases 143 (5th Cir. 1979); *Di-Salvo v. Chamber of Commerce*, 568 F.2d 593, 596, 20 FEP Cases 825, 826–27 (8th Cir. 1978). See *Morton v. Mancari*, 417 U.S. 535, 550–51, 8 FEP Cases 105, 110–11 (1974); Crawford, THE CONSTRUCTION OF STATUTES § 231 (1940).

[56]H.R. 8898, 87th Cong., 1st Sess. (1961); H.R. 10226, 87th Cong., 2d Sess. (1962). See *Keyes v. Lenoir Rhyne College*, 552 F.2d 579, 15 FEP Cases 925 (4th Cir. 1977), cert. denied, 434 U.S. 904, 16 FEP Cases 501 (1977); *Orr v. Frank R. MacNeill & Son, Inc.*, 511 F.2d 166, 10 FEP Cases 697 (5th Cir. 1975), cert. denied, 423 U.S. 865, 11 FEP Cases 576 (1975); *Ammons v. Zia Co.*, 448 F.2d 117, 3 FEP Cases 910 (10th Cir. 1971); *Schultz v. Wheaton Glass Co.*, 421 F.2d 259, 9 FEP Cases 502, 9 FEP Cases 509 (3d Cir. 1970), cert. denied, 398 U.S. 905, 9 FEP Cases 1408 (1970).

[57]452 U.S. 161, 25 FEP Cases 1521 (1981). The Court said:
The Bennett Amendment does not restrict Title VII's prohibition of sex-based wage discrimination to claims for equal pay for "equal work." Rather, claims for sex-based wage

reconstrued the meaning of the Bennett Amendment and dissolved the *"in pari materia"* straightjacket that had been limiting the scope of Title VII sex-based wage discrimination violation suits to the specifics set out in the Equal Pay Act of 1963.[58] *Gunther* involved a claim of a sex-based wage rate discrimination against four female matrons who were not paid 95 percent of the rate for correction officers (male) and assistant sheriffs (male), although the supervising sheriff had recommended that the 95 percent rate be paid; only 70 percent of the male rate was approved by the county board. The Supreme Court sent back to the federal district court for trial the claim that the county board, when it refused to approve a wage increase for the four female matrons working in the jail, had *intentionally* engaged in sex-based discrimination in violation of Title VII.[59] Arbitrators had, for years, been applying the methodology set out in a job evaluation plan to evaluate the *relative* value of the jobs when a dispute over relative value arose. Job evaluation arbitration was and is *always* a *relative value* evaluation or a *"comparable worth"* evaluation and hence it could not be reexamined by a court on the ground that some Title VII issue was involved until the Supreme Court opened up the scope of sex-based wage rate discriminations in 1981.

A second significant decision was released in 1981. The Third Circuit in *Electrical Workers, IUE, v. Westinghouse Corp.*[60] dealt factually with job evaluation procedure and application because the plaintiff had claimed that a sex-based wage rate discrimination had been "built" into the job evaluation plan when the company added four additional labor grades to the job evaluation structure and slotted into these grades jobs predominantly performed by females when the Civil Rights Act became effective in 1964. It was admitted that when the plan was first installed in 1939 a lower cents-per-hour per-job evaluation point had been assigned to "female jobs" than to "male jobs," and even though all explicit sexual identifications in the job evaluation manual

---

discrimination can also be brought under Title VII even though no member of the opposite sex holds an equal but higher paying job, provided that the challenged wage rate is not exempted under the Equal Pay Act's affirmative defenses as to wage differentials attributable to seniority, merit, quantity or quality of production, or any other factor other than sex. Syllabus, 425 U.S. at 161.

[58]Title VII wage rate discriminations would become violations *not only* if the discrimination was based on sex, but also if it was based on race, national origin, or age. However, for brevity a Title VII violation will be referred to as a "sex-based wage rate discrimination" because the Title VII job evaluation problems that will be discussed in this section will generally involve claims of sex-based discrimination.

[59]452 U.S. 161, 165–66, 25 FEP Cases 1521, 1522. The recommendation of the sheriff and the rejection by the county board is reported in *Gunther v. County of Washington*, 20 FEP Cases 788 (D. Ore. 1976), *rev'd and remanded*, 602 F.2d 882, 891, 20 FEP Cases 792, 798 (9th Cir. 1979), *republished on denial of rehearing*, 623 F.2d 1303, 22 FEP Cases 1650 (9th Cir. 1980), *aff'd*, 452 U.S. 161, 25 FEP Cases 1521 (1981).

[60]631 F.2d 1094, 23 FEP Cases 588 (3d Cir. 1980).

had been stripped out in 1964, the increase in the number of labor grades from 9 to 13,[61] the union lawyers argued, was the original sex-based wage rate discrimination buried in the plan.[62]

The Third Circuit sent this claim back to the district court where the facts were to be assembled and possible violation of the company under Title VII determined. If the factual assertions of the union attorneys are proven, the wage rates established by the many arbitrators who had used the methodology set up under the Westinghouse plan in 1964 would be contaminated by the buried Title VII violation and the wage rates established by the various arbitrators could well be upset.

Judge Van Dusen of the Third Circuit reacted to the argument of the plaintiff (union) attorneys, causing him to issue a dissent. He explained that the only way to determine whether a historical sex-based wage rate discrimination had in fact occurred and had not been corrected would be to have "comparative worth" or "equal value" evaluations of the many jobs considered predominantly "male" and "female" and compare their numerical rankings. He said:

> [T]he Union's case can only be proved through evidence of the worth of *comparable work*. The Union's sole evidence of an express policy and discrimination at the Trenton facility is a statement from 1939. Although the Union acknowledges that there have been changes in the content of the various jobs and adjustments to the pay scales over the last 40 years, they argue that, with comparable work evidence, they can prove that the 1939 policy has been perpetuated. . . . Although the Union downplays the importance of the *comparable work* evidence, it is the sole evidence available to them to demonstrate that the discrimination has continued. Thus, the evidence of *comparable work* will be the central focus of the Union's case.[63]
> [Footnotes omitted. Emphasis added.]

A writ of *certiorari* was filed, but the Supreme Court rejected it, thereby sending the case back to the district court. The district court judge must decide whether the company violated Title VII because of an *intentional* sex-based wage rate discrimination.

Because the representatives on both sides and the arbitrators always accepted the job evaluation methodology used to resolve the dispute, they are *not* skilled in the *pro* and *con* arguments that are now lurking

---

[61]*Id*. at 1097, 23 FEP Cases at 590.

[62]The National Research Council report (*see* note 66 *infra*), printed as WOMEN, WORK AND WAGES: EQUAL PAY FOR JOBS OF EQUAL VALUE (Washington: National Academy Press, 1981), explained the effect of the increase in the number of labor grades in 1964:

> When these separate series were merged into a single series in 1965, however, the male grades 1 through 10 were simply relabeled 6 through 15, so that the sex differential in pay was preserved. The labor grades were not combined in such a way as to reflect the original evaluation of these jobs.

Id. at pp. 57–58.

[63]631 F.2d at 1108-9, 23 FEP Cases at 599.

in the wings suggesting that Title VII sex-based wage rate discriminations can be found in job evaluation methodologies.[64] New theories that might well support Section 301 job evaluation award suits have been articulated in various law reviews and elsewhere.[65] The most significant new theories are those articulated in the National Research Council (NRC) report, commissioned and financed by the Equal Employment Opportunity Commission (EEOC) and widely distributed as a book entitled *Women, Work and Wages: Equal Pay for Jobs of Equal Value*.[66]

If the supporting record to a job evaluation award does not contain the findings of fact that remove the theoretical basis for the various challenges that have been lurking in the wings, various job evaluation awards may be challenged in Section 301 suits. However, if the needed findings of fact are carefully set forth in the record, in the accompanying exhibits, and in the accompanying transcript, challenges may not be attempted, or, if they are attempted, the judge may be able to handle the challenges expeditiously and avoid opening the case at the court level to extensive evidentiary hearings.[67]

The following four subsections discuss questions that will bring out

---

[64]The variations of job evaluation plans were described in the National Research Council report, note 62 *supra*, at p. 63:

At the present time in the United States many large private companies, the federal government, and many state governments make use of some form of formal job evaluation as an aid to establishing pay rates for jobs. Although job evaluation systems differ in details of design and implementation, almost all conform to a common methodology and underlying logic.

[65]Thomsen, *Eliminating Pay Discrimination Caused by Job Evaluation*, Personnel (Sept.-Oct. 1978) at 11-12; Treiman, Job Evaluation: An Analytic Review, note 66 *infra*; Note, *Equal Pay, Comparable Worth and Job Evaluation*, 90 Yale L.J. 657; *see also* articles reported in notes 75, 86, and 87 *infra*.

[66]The report was commissioned by the Equal Employment Opportunity Commission in 1977 to determine if job evaluation procedures had any built-in bias against females that when used by employers constituted a violation of Title VII of the Civil Rights Act of 1964. The report (hereinafter referred to as the NRC report) was written by the Committee on Occupational Classification and Analysis, Assembly of Behavioral and Social Sciences, National Research Council, and was published in book form as Women, Work and Wages: Equal Pay for Jobs of Equal Value (Washington, D.C.: National Academy Press, 1981). The EEOC paid $200,000 for the report but the EEOC's then acting chairman V. Clay Smith said that the report did not necessarily reflect the official opinion or policy at EEOC. An interim report was delivered to the EEOC in 1979 and was published in book form as Treiman, Job Evaluation: An Analytic Review, Interim Report to the Equal Employment Opportunity Commission by the Committee on Occupational Classification and Analysis, National Research Council (Washington, D.C.: National Academy Press, 1979) (hereinafter referred to as the NRC interim report).

[67]A judge may find it quite difficult to brush aside the Title VII theoretical challenges set forth in the NRC reports in view of the fact these reports were commissioned by a government commission (the EEOC), unless the arbitrator discusses the theoretical challenges having any possible relationship to the particular case and sets forth all findings necessary to permit the court to deal with the challenges. Findings of facts by the arbitrator will be accepted as accurate in a *de novo* review; see discussion under "Title VII Presumptions Used in Arbitration" in Chapter XII.

some of the theories that may support a challenge and some of the factual matters that should be put in the record to prevent the filing of a challenge or to resolve it promptly if the challenge should surface.

Question 1. Is There a Title VII Violation in a Job Evaluation Plan Because Factor Weights Are Biased Against Females?

In the NRC report there is found a conclusion that (1) "market"-created wage rates for jobs normally performed by females are relatively lower than the wage rates paid males performing jobs of equal value and (2) these relatively low wage rates for females become the basis for the determination of the job evaluation points (degree and factor values), and that there is thus in these points or values a discrimination or bias against females in the weights given points or values to jobs wherein females are predominant. Three quotations from the majority report set out these theoretical conclusions:

> Many of the factor point job evaluation systems in use today were developed by using a firm's existing pay structure to statistically determine which attributes of jobs best predict their pay rates. In this approach a set of factors that is thought likely to be related to existing pay differences among jobs is identified—factors representing differences in skill, effort, responsibility, and working conditions. Each job is scored on each of the factors. . . . The factors and factor weights can then be used to assign pay rates for new jobs and to adjust the pay rates of existing jobs that are overpaid or underpaid relative to the predictions of the formula. This method provides an empirically derived underlying structure with which the pay rates of all jobs in a firm can be brought into conformity. This is sometimes called a "policy-capturing" approach—the implicit policy underlying the existing pay system is made explicit. Job evaluation plans developed in this way necessarily produce hierarchies of job worth that are closely related to existing pay hierarchies: that is what they are designed to do.[68]

Then the report added:

> The second major drawback of using existing wages to derive factor weights is that the weights will then necessarily reflect in turn any biases [against females] that exist in market wages. To the extent that existing wages incorporate the effects of discriminatory practices . . . the weights derived from these wages as well as the resulting job worth scores also incorporate those effects.[69]

And then the report added this conclusion:

> [J]ob worth scores are highly dependent on the choice of compensable features and the weights assigned to *them; since most job evaluation plans use*

---

[68]NRC report, note 66 *supra*, at p. 72.
[69]*Id*. at p. 76.

*market wage rates to establish factor weights, the weights will incorporate
the effects of any discrimination that exists in market wages.*[70] [Emphasis
added.]

However, if actual wage rates are not used in any way to develop the
numerical values (weights) for the factors used to evaluate the "job
worth scores" on jobs primarily performed by females, the plan and
wage rates established using its methodology cannot be challenged as
sex-based wage rate discriminations.

Many companies have "borrowed" job evaluation plans and have
taken over the numerical values for the factors and may not even know
the sources of these values. It is significant, however, that the source of
the numerical values in the job evaluation plan that is used in hundreds
of plants in the iron and steel industry and related activities is known.
The plan is called the Cooperative Wage Survey (CWS) plan. Its development started in 1944 due to a War Labor Board decision that applied
to ninety-six companies and the United Steelworkers Union.[71] Because
of the diverse work being performed in the many companies and their
plants, a joint committee composed of representatives of the twelve
largest companies and the union was designated the Central Committee and set to work in an office building in Pittsburgh, Pa. The eighty-
four smaller companies merely stood by until a plan was developed by
the Central Committee. The Central Committee described the work
content of over 1,000 jobs regularly performed in many of the plants of
the twelve largest companies. A job description is a listing of the regular
assignments given to the personnel classified in those jobs; this description is often referred to as the "work content" of the job. Once the
1,000-plus jobs were described, the committee set about to develop numerical values for twelve factors.[72] The numerical values assigned to
the various jobs first were determined and then these jobs were ranked.
Then the values were adjusted and the jobs were re-ranked. Then the

---

[70]*Id.* at p. 12.

[71]The National War Labor Board issued an order, referred to as the *Basic Steel Case*, No.
111-6230-D (14-1 *et al.*), November 25, 1944, that applied to 96 companies, directing them to
negotiate with the union stewardship and eliminate wage rate inequities using a job evaluation
procedure that the companies would develop through negotiations with the United Steelworkers
Union. The decision is found at 19 WAR LAB. REP. 568 (BNA); the order directing the develop-
ing of a job evaluation through joint negotiations is found at 19 WAR LAB. REP. 691–702. The
Cooperative Wage Survey plan (CWS), as it became known, is described in Seyfarth, Shaw,
Fairweather & Geraldson, LABOR RELATIONS AND THE LAW IN WEST GERMANY AND THE
UNITED STATES (Ann Arbor: U. Mich. Bus. Div. Res., 1969) at p. 263 and in LABOR RELA-
TIONS AND THE LAW IN BELGIUM AND THE UNITED STATES (Ann Arbor: U. Mich. Bus. Div.
Res., 1972) at p. 197, which report therein the degree values basic to factor values.

[72]The 12 factors and degree values (subdivisions) that were part of the CWS plan and used
throughout the industry are: (1) pre-employment training (3 degrees: A O, B .3, C 1.0); (2)
employment training and experience (9 degrees: A O, B .4, C .8, D 1.2, E 1.6, F 2.0, G 2.4, H
3.2, I 4.0); (3) mental skill (6 degrees: A O, B 1.0, C 1.6, D 2.2, E 2.8, F 3.5); (4) manual skill (5
degrees: A O, B .5, C 1.0, D 1.5, E 2.0); (5) responsibility for materials (5 degrees: A O, B .3 to

values were adjusted and the jobs were re-ranked over and over again until the committee as a group became satisfied that the key jobs were ranked "equitably."

One convention that was used in assigning factor values to a given job under the CWS plan required that the job be given the *highest* value (sometimes called skill points or degree values) that was applicable to any one given work assignment listed in the composite of the work assignments (referred to as the job's "work content"). The value for the one assignment that had the highest skill points assigned was accumulated under different tests: the mental skills, manual skills, training and experience, etc., that are needed to perform such an assignment satisfactorily. In addition, this convention provided that the frequency of the one assignment with the highest value (points) was of no consequence if such an assignment was sometimes required of an employee in the job classification by his or her supervisor in job classes. The values assigned each job—referred to as factor values developed from the job points, degree values, or worth scores (different names for the same measurement)—were established by the Central Committee.

This job description process created few disagreements unless one side of the committee attempted to sprinkle assignments that had relatively high skill points (causing a high factor value for the job) into the description, thereby increasing the job's slotting and increasing the wage rates for more jobs. Such disagreements would produce discussions with employees and supervisors and the participants would learn the effect of making infrequent work assignments that had high skill points, and the supervisors would begin to concentrate the work assignments with high skill points, reserving them for those employees who would inevitably be classified in jobs with high job class rankings because their regular assignments already would have high skill points. The supervisors, who could control the work assignments of the employees they supervised, began to move relatively infrequently assigned, high-skilled work to employees considered more skilled, removing from the mixture of assignment of generally low-skilled work some infrequent assignments of skilled work, to hold down the wage rates for those employees whose jobs otherwise would be given higher values.

The reason this history is incorporated here is to point out that the factor values used in slotting the jobs of thousands upon thousands of jobs in hundreds of plants were not developed out of the wage rates

---

2.3, C .5 to 3.7, D .8 to 8.5, E 1.2 to 10.0); (6) responsibility for tools and equipment (6 degrees: A O, B .2 to .5, C .4 to 1.0, D .7 to 2.0, E 1.0 to 3.0, F 1.5 to 4.0); (7) responsibility for operations (8 degrees: A O, B .5, C 1.0, D 2.0, E 3.0, F 4.0, G 5.0, H 6.5); (8) responsibility for safety of others (5 degrees: A O, B .4, C .8, D 1.2, E 2.0); (9) mental effort (5 degrees: A O, B .5, C 1.0, D 1.5, E 2.5); (10) physical effort (5 degrees: A O, B .3, C .8, D 1.5, E 2.5); (11) surroundings (5 degrees: A O, B .4, C .8, D 1.6, E 3.0); (12) hazards (5 degrees: A O, B .4, C .8, D 1.2, E 2.0).

actually paid employees in those plants and, hence, the assumption that job evaluation factor numerical values have a bias against females would not be valid. If in an arbitration hearing it is reported into the record that the plan being used by the arbitrator to resolve the disputes was the CWS plan or a comparable one, any challenge against the award because there is buried in the plan some discrimination against females in the factor values assigned jobs must dissolve. However, unless these facts are reported, an assumed bias against females may be presented to a court, using the NCR report, financed by a government commission, as the supporting exhibit, and the judge might consider himself or herself obligated to start evidentiary hearings to find out whether actual wage rates were or were not used.[73]

Question 2. Does a Sex-Based Title VII Discrimination Occur When Females Are Paid Less Than Males Yet Perform Work With the Same "Job Worth Scores"?

Judges may well be troubled when a wage rate in a plant for a job predominately performed by females is found to be lower than a rate for a job predominately performed by males, and the "job worth score" of the "female" job, developed in a job evaluation analysis, is equal to or higher than the score of the "male" job.[74] If there is such a lack of correlation between wage rates and scores, the wage determinations might well be challenged as a sex-based Title VII discrimination and

---

[73]Ernest J. McCormick, in his minority report within the NRC report (*see* note 66 *supra*), was critical of the majority report, saying that "the report of any committee that deals with a controversial subject typically reflects the composition of the committee" and that this committee had "no member who was a full-time practitioner in the field of job evaluation, and only a very few members had any specific experience with, or involvement with, practical job evaluation procedures or with job analysis processes that are basic to job evaluation and wage determination." *Id.* at p. 116. He also said that "in the report of the committee there are numerous statements that either directly, or by implication or inference, take issue with the principle that the prevailing rates of pay in the labor market should serve as the primary basis for the establishment of pay scales for jobs in specific situations" and that the "committee report implies that the determination of the comparability in worth between jobs should be independent of current wages and salaries found in the labor market. It is with these portions of the agreement that I am in disagreement, since it is my firm conviction that current wages and salaries are indeed one indication of the underlying relationships between jobs." *Id.* at p. 117. McCormick then said: "The most effective job evaluation system usually is one that accurately examines the content of jobs (skills, effort, responsibilities, activities, working conditions, etc.) and yields relative job values (usually point values) that correspond closely with (i.e. are correlated with) prevailing rates in the labor market...." *Id.* at p. 119. He declared that "use of structured job analysis procedures in this process seems to make it possible to document the content of jobs without regard to sex of the incumbent ... and fairly evaluate jobs without regard to sex of the incumbent." *Id.* at p. 123.

[74]The designations "female job" and "male job" could more accurately be stated as "jobs which are predominantly performed by males" and "jobs which are predominantly performed by females" to avoid any impression that female employees have been segregated in certain jobs, but for reasons of brevity the short form reference has been used.

upset an arbitrator's award. The theory basic to such a challenge has been articulated in law reviews and other sources[75] and is also found in the NRC report. The theory is that an employer must pay women as much as men for performing work of "comparable worth" or a discrimination in violation of Title VII is presumed. The debate has become so general that a new section entitled "Comparable Worth" has been added to Chapter XIII, "Equal Pay," of the second edition of the BNA book *Employment Discrimination Law*.[76] In this section one part of the "Recommendations to Employers on Minimizing Compensation Discrimination Exposure" states the following:

> An employer that utilizes a point-count-type job evaluation system companywide and then deviates from it obviously runs a severe risk in light of *Gunther*. For example, if a large employer evaluates its predominately female administrative assistant job at 410 points, and its largely male computer job at 405 points and then because of market conditions establishes a higher rate of pay for the computer operation position, plaintiffs could argue, based on *Gunther*, that conscious, intentional wage discrimination has been established.[77]

Then in this new section recommendations to plaintiffs who plan to bring a "comparable worth" challenge against the employer are set forth:

> Given the uncertain status of pure comparable worth suits, plaintiffs seeking to bring suits for discrimination in compensation should look for cases in which there *is* evidence of intentional discrimination in the setting of wage rates. Plaintiffs should seek cases: (1) where historically there was sex segregation between jobs, with the titles now changed but not the rates; (2) where there is evidence of discriminatory statements being made by employer officials; and (3) where employers have conducted job evaluations or wage surveys, and have then deviated from them.[78]

Job evaluation studies have been prepared by highly qualified experts at the request of, and financed by, unions, to prove that the employer was guilty of a sex-based wage rate discrimination that violates

[75]Blumrosen, *Wage Discriminations, Job Segregation, and Title VII of the Civil Rights Act of 1964*, 12 U. Mich. J.L. Ref. 397, 468 (1979); Mossholder, Nurick, Gordon & Pryor, *An EPA Exceptions Model—Cracking the Sex-Based Wage Differential*, Compensation Rev. (First Quarter 1979), p. 42; Nelson, Opton & Wilson, *Wage Discrimination and the "Comparable Worth" Theory in Perspective*, 13 U. Mich. J.L. Ref. 231, 293-96 (1980); Note, *Equal Pay, Comparable Worth and Job Evaluation*, 90 Yale L.J. 657 (1981).

[76]Schlei & Grossman (Washington: BNA Books, 1983).

[77]*Id.* at p. 481, discussing *County of Washington v. Gunther*, 452 U.S. 161, 25 FEP Cases 1521 (1981).

[78]*Id.*

Title VII[79] because the wage rates and the "job worth scores" of jobs predominantly performed by females and those performed by males were not in proper correlation. In various of these situations the wage rates for "female" and "male" jobs had been established according to a "prevailing wage rate" formula required by government contractors under the Davis-Bacon Act[80] and in others because that formula has been adopted by the employer under the urging of the union representatives. The NRC report stated that a lack of correlation between the "job worth scores" of "female" and "male" jobs because the "prevailing wage rates" formula had been used is excused from discrimination as a violation of Title VII because the employer is not engaged in an *overtly discriminatory act*:

> By use of the "going wage" as a standard to set pay rates the wages of a (nondiscriminating) firm will be biased by the discrimination of other firms in the market. In the State of Washington case reviewed above, the cause of the "underpayment" of jobs held mainly by women was *not* a result of an *overtly discriminatory* act on the part of the employer but simple conformity to the *prevailing pay rate* of the private sector.[81] [Emphasis added.]

The NRC report then explains that if special competitive pressures push the wage rate of jobs predominantly performed by men above the "job worth scores" of the rates of jobs predominantly performed by females, the employers are also excused because their discrimination is not an *overtly discriminatory act*:

> For example, computer personnel are "overpaid" until enough workers can train for the position; workers in new oil fields are "overpaid" until more workers arrive . . . . "Equalizing" or "compensating" wage differentials are

---

[79] One union employed Norman Willes and Associates to make a job evaluation study and then claimed that the state of Washington had violated Title VII because the wage rates of females were lower, relative to the "job worth scores," than the wage rates paid males. NRC interim report, note 66 *supra*, at p. 59. The response to the lack of correlation was that the wage rates had been established under a "prevailing rate" formula. The American Federation of State, County and Municipal Employees Union asserted that there was a sex-based wage rate discrimination in violation of Title VII in the San Jose, California municipality wage rate when a Hayes Associates job evaluation found that rates for jobs performed predominately by females were up to 10% below the structure line whereas rates for jobs performed predominately by males were up to 15% above that line. 100 DLR A-3 (May 26, 1981); 128 DLR A-3 (July 6, 1981). Hayes Associates made a job evaluation for the plaintiffs who claimed a sex-based discrimination at the University of Northern Iowa. The study reported a similar lack of correlation. The Eighth Circuit set forth reasons why the lack of correlation between wage rates and "job worth scores" is not evidence of a Title VII violation; this is reported in text associated with note 83 *infra*.

[80] The AFL-CIO Building and Construction Trades Department argues that the "prevailing wage" rate formula set out in the Davis Bacon Act is the best for its members. Labor Law Reports No. 515, 100 DLR A-6 (May 26, 1981).

[81] NRC report, note 66 *supra*, at pp. 61–62, discussing *County of Washington v. Gunther*, 452 U.S. 161, 25 FEP Cases 1521 (1981).

also recognized by neoclassical theorists: risky, dirty, or unpleasant jobs are thought to earn premiums (relative to others requiring similar skills) in order to induce workers to be hired. Jobs that require long and costly training also command such premiums.[82]

The Eighth Circuit, in *Christensen v. Iowa*,[83] explained that when "market pressures" push up wage rates for certain jobs and when "prevailing rates" become the formula to respond to these market pressures so the employer can hire individuals who have the various skills, evidence that the employer failed to pay the same wage rate for work of "comparable worth" is not evidence of a Title VII sex-based wage rate discriminatory act. In this case, female employees performing administrative and teaching jobs at the University of Northern Iowa were paid relatively less than the university-paid males performing maintenance craft jobs even though the "job worth scores" on the predominantly female jobs were equal to or above the scores of the maintenance craft jobs. The "job worth scores" of the different types of jobs had been developed by the Hayes organization at the request of the plaintiffs and financed by them. The court explained:

> The record further discloses that the university, by adoption of the Hayes System, sought to remove pay disparities between occupations staffed by women and those occupations principally staffed by men. As we have noted, full adoption of the system became unrealistic economically, for some physical plant jobs commanded a higher wage scale in the community than those jobs were worth to the university under the Hayes System's evaluation. Thus, some disparities in wage scales persisted regardless of the values assigned work.[84]

The Eighth Circuit decided that the lack of correlation in female and male jobs between the "job worth scores" produced by the evaluation study and the actual wages paid was *not* evidence of a sex-based wage rate discrimination in violation of Title VII for another reason: the plaintiff females who were complaining about the sex-based wage rate discrimination were free to accept training and "bid up" to vacancies in the maintenance craft job and receive the higher rate but chose not to do so. This meant, in essence, that the relative lower wage rate of a female was her "fault" rather than the employer's "fault."

The district court had filed a special report with the appellate court setting forth a specific finding that the females had the right to "bid

---

[82]*Id.* at p. 51.

[83]563 F.2d 353, 16 FEP Cases 232 (8th Cir. 1977); *compare Lemons v. City & County of Denver*, 620 F.2d 228, 22 FEP Cases 959 (10 Cir. 1978), *cert. denied*, 449 U.S. 888, 23 FEP Cases 1668 (1980).

[84]563 F.2d at 356, 16 FEP Cases at 235.

up" to vacancies in the maintenance craft work jobs and the appellate court clearly relied on this finding in its decision to dismiss:

> The trial court specifically found that these higher pay-scale jobs, as well as all physical plant jobs, were open equally to all qualified applicants, men or women. This finding is not attacked.[85]

When females have the right to "bid up" to the vacancies in jobs where the wage rate is relatively high due to market pressures and they do not choose to do so, it is difficult to conclude that the employer is guilty of a sex-based wage rate discrimination. Statistics with respect to the "bidding up" of females compared with males should be made part of arbitration records in job evaluation cases to assist the judge determining whether the lack of correlation between "job worth scores" and actual salaries is evidence of a Title VII violation or of a difference in job choices by the females involved.[86]

A finding that females are not "locked in" to certain "jobs" is also significant. Various theorists have asserted that it is the segregation of females to certain types of jobs that causes them to be paid relatively less than males.[87] A blockage in the seniority bidding procedure might well be evidence of a sex-based wage rate discrimination, and evidence on this subject should be put "in the record." But if there is "open bidding," that fact should be reported if there is a lack of correlation between the "job worth scores" and the wage rates.

If the necessary facts needed to understand the lack of correlation are not in the record, a judge might merely find that the lack of correlation between the wage rates of females and males and the "job worth scores" is evidence of sex-based wage rate discrimination as the judge did in *Taylor v. Charley Brothers Co. and Teamsters, Local 30:*[88]

---

[85]*Id.* at 357, 16 FEP Cases at 236.

[86]A high refusal rate by females who could bid up results, many labor relations students believe, from the fact that many women believe their employment will not be continuous, and hence forego new employment experiences because the transfer will require them to accept training and enter a different and unfamiliar working situation. *See* the NRC report, note 66 *supra,* at p. 53; Kreps, SEX IN THE MARKETPLACE: AMERICAN WOMEN AT WORK (Baltimore: Johns Hopkins Univ. Press, 1971), pp. 44–45, Polachek, *Discontinuous Labor Force Participation and Its Effect on Women's Market Earnings,* SEX DISCRIMINATION, AND THE DIVISION OF LABOR, C. Lloyd, ed. (New York: Columbia Univ. Press, 1975), pp. 90, 111. This refusal also results from the fact that the career choices made by women are different from those made by men in high schools and that females generally do not obtain the same training at the high school level for use in large manufacturing plants. See Reubens & Reubens, *Women Workers, Nontraditional Occupations and Full Employment,* WOMEN IN THE U.S. LABOR FORCE, A. Cahn, ed. (New York: Praeger Publications, 1979), pp. 103, 121–123.

[87]Blumrosen, note 75 *supra;* Keyserling, *Women's Stake in Full Employment: Their Disadvantaged Role in the Economy—Challengers to Action,* WOMEN IN THE U.S. LABOR FORCE, note 86 *supra,* pp. 25, 29; Lloyd and Niemi, *The Economics of Sex Differentials* (New York: Columbia Univ. Press, 1979), pp. 237–38; *Oaxaca Male-Female Wage Differentials in the Telephone Industry,* EQUAL EMPLOYMENT OPPORTUNITY AND THE AT&T CASE, P. Wallace, ed. (Cambridge: MIT Press, 1976), pp. 17, 34.

[88]25 FEP Cases 602, 614 (D.C. Pa. 1981).

Defendant Charley Brothers intentionally discriminated against ... women in Department 2 by paying them substantially less than the men in Department 1 because they worked in a department populated only by women, and not because the jobs they performed were inherently worth less than the jobs performed by the men, all in violation of Title VII.

If computer operators or programmers, for example, are in short supply and their wage rates rise higher than the relative "job worth scores," carefully prepared exhibits should be put in the record to report the market level for this special skill to preclude any challenge that the employer was paying improper wage rates because some wage rates were "out of line" with the "comparable worth" of various jobs.

Question 3. When Structures in Job Evaluation Plans Are Not Based on a Single Straight Line and Wage Rates Do Not Correlate With "Job Worth Scores," Is There a Sex-Based Discrimination?

The preceding subsection suggests that when wage rates are not correlated with the "job worth scores," it has been asserted by some theorists that a sex-based wage rate discrimination has occurred unless the reasons for the differentials are clearly understood and unrelated to sex. This subsection extends the discussion to similar concerns by analyzing three different types of job evaluation plan structures.

It will be shown that two of the structures are *intentionally* designed to cause the wage rates to be *out of correlation* with the "job worth scores" and the third is *intentionally* designed to have the wage rates *in correlation.*

The *first* can be referred to as a *curved line* structure into which "notches" are created for labor grade levels, causing the cents-per-hour wage for each labor grade to increase proportionally *more* than do the job evaluation points ("job worth scores") for each labor grade. A curved line is developed in one of two ways. The first is by drawing a line through the cluster points of the wage rates plotted on a chart. (The job evaluation points are located on the base line and then the actual wage rate is located and plotted on the other axis.) The second method is use of a mathematical formula called "linear regression analysis" which sets up a smooth line that also takes into account the number of employees in the jobs in each cluster point.[89] The *second* type of structure, and the one that is most common, is based on a *straight line* that starts out at the minimum wage rate paid by the employer and then moves up

---

[89] An explanation of the mathematical retrogression formula and descriptions of the other different types of job evaluation structures are included in Maynard, INDUSTRIAL ENGINEERING HANDBOOK (New York: McGraw Hill, 1956) and in Benge, Burk & Hay, MANUAL OF JOB EVALUATION (New York: Harper Brothers, 1941); NRC interim report, note 66 *supra*; Stanway, APPLIED JOB EVALUATION (New York: Ronald Press, 1947), p. 8.

toward the wage rate for the job or jobs with the highest job evaluation points.[90] Along this straight line the same "notches" as in a curved line structure are created for wage levels for each labor grade; but with a straight line structure, the rate for each grade increases proportionately with the increase in the job evaluation points ("job worth scores") for each labor grade.

The job evaluation planners who advocate *straight line* structures assert that wage rates should increase logically as the job evaluation points increase. This simple logic is easily understood by the employees who are represented by the union officials and hence it is easier to reach an agreement with union representatives when a straight line structure is used. However, those job evaluation planners who advocate a *curved line* structure argue that when the wage rates rise in each successive labor grade step relatively *more* than do the job evaluation points, individuals who must spend years in apprentice and other training courses receive the needed financial incentive to continue the training. These advocates for the *curved line* structure look back on the many special negotiated wage rate additions to each labor grade to make the "straight line" structure adopted with the CWS plan, *supra*, steeper and steeper. (A specific amount of cents per hour to be multiplied by the labor grade number was added in various negotiations; for example, a two-cent addition to be multiplied by the number of labor grades would increase the wage rate for the thirty-second labor grade by sixty-four cents per hour.) Thus, year after year the special job evaluation "extra" for each labor grade was merely the recreation of the needed "bonus" for the skilled workers that had disappeared when the original straight line structure was adopted when the CWS plan first was introduced.[91]

The third type of structure discussed here is quite unusual. It is built on a *double line* and the difference between these lines becomes a premium paid to some employees above the normal "job worth score" of others to produce the bonus needed to increase a certain work force or draw certain skills. Massey Ferguson set up such a *double line* job

---

[90]The CWS straight line started at the uniform minimum rate and ran toward the "higher" wage rates, but not to the highest wage rate in a particular company. *See* note 71 *supra*.

[91]Negotiation each year of an extra "labor grade increase" multiplied times the number of labor grades, which totalled 32, caused the wage rates for the highly skilled employees to rise rapidly relative to the wage rates for the employees with low or mid-level skills, who often received an incentive bonus of their own not paid skilled employees. The problem that develops with the premium for "high skilled" jobs is illustrated by one fact and one comment as follows: 2,500 journeymen tool and die makers were needed as of 1981, but in 1980 only 925 individuals commenced apprentice training. The U.S. Department of Labor forecasts that by 1990 about 31,000 tool and die workers will be needed each year but trained employees will not be available in sufficient numbers. Bruno Fisher, a shop superintendent, explained the shortage of skilled employees: "[T]hey don't want to put the effort into it. It's funny. They'll say, I'll drive a truck and make more money." Chicago Suburban Sun Times, Sept. 4, 1981.

evaluation structure to create premiums to draw both males and females into a needed work force to train them to rivet and weld ships, tanks, and trucks during World War II. The premium provided was intentional and the amount of "extra" paid for "comparable worth" work was built into the job evaluation plan.[92] Similarly, a *double line* structure was set up to create premiums to draw computer operators and planners into Massey Ferguson plants after the war. These premiums, intentionally created by the use of a *double line* structure, were set up for essentially the same reasons when Northern Iowa University paid a premium to draw into university employment individuals who had been trained on maintenance craft-type jobs in the private sector in the surrounding labor market area.[93]

In sharp contrast, however, the use of a *double line* job evaluation structure was found to be an illegal sex-based wage rate discrimination at the government arsenal in Liege, Belgium. The wage rates for jobs predominantly performed by females were calculated from the lower line and the rates for jobs predominantly performed by males were calculated from the higher line. The difference in these wage rates was simply a wage discrimination against females and was considered to be an illegal violation when Belgium adopted the International Labour Convention outlawing wage rate sex discrimination in 1966.[94]

This discussion of the three different types of job evaluation structures and the reasons why different structures are used is incorporated here to cause representatives to introduce evidence in the arbitration hearings so there will be in the records the necessary facts to reduce confusions if the award is subsequently challenged in a court.

Question 4. Does the Reduction of Female Wage Rates Associated With an Installation of Job Evaluation Cause a Sex-Based Wage Rate Discrimination?

The last question for discussion is the reason why changes in the pattern of regular work assignments sometimes occur in connection with a job evaluation analysis, and whether evaluating more jobs as having lower "job worth scores" causes a sex-based wage rate dis-

---

[92]Seyfarth *et al.*, LABOR RELATIONS AND THE LAW IN WEST GERMANY AND THE UNITED STATES, note 71 *supra*, at p. 259.

[93]*See* note 79 *supra*.

[94]Seyfarth *et al.*, LABOR RELATIONS AND THE LAW IN BELGIUM AND THE UNITED STATES, note 71 *supra*, at p. 213; *see also* Plaintiffs' Memorandum in Opposition to Motion for Partial Summary Judgment *re* National Compensation Claims, Exhibit C, *National Organization for Women v. Minnesota Mining & Mfg. Co.*, Civ. No. 4-74-555 (D. Minn. filed Aug. 4, 1980), at pp. 79-80 (employer allegedly used separate wage curve to establish lower pay for women's jobs than for men's jobs with equal job evaluation scores). *See also* text associated with notes 60-63 *supra* wherein the *Westinghouse* case is discussed.

crimination when females are assigned to such jobs. When job evaluation analysis commences, the regular work assignments of the employees working in a particular department are described and the work content is then evaluated and job evaluation points are assigned. For convenience, many foremen, directing employees in departments where work flow can be interrupted by lack of parts, machine breakdowns, etc., train the employees to be interchangeable—that is, to accept work assignments that involve high skills and those that involve low skills—so transfers can take place easily. When the description of the regular work assignments becomes the work content of a job in a department, it becomes clear that occasional assignment of work that involves high skills causes the job evaluation points (mental skill, manual skill, pre-employment training, employment and experience, responsibility for tools and equipment, etc.) of the job to be higher than they would be if the work assignment pattern were changed so that the low-skilled work *regularly* is assigned to certain employees and the high-skilled work *regularly* is assigned to others. (The increase in the frequency of skilled work assignments to certain employees does not increase the job evaluation points of the job, since the points are determined by the most skilled work assigned, whereas eliminating occasional skilled work assignments to other employees will sharply reduce the job evaluation points for the jobs wherein such employees are classified.) A statement making it clear that the content of a job can be changed and a new description issued with a new evaluation was set forth in one of the early editions of the CWS manual:

> The job description and classification of each existing job shall continue in effect unless Management, at its discretion, changes the job content (job requirements as to training, skill, responsibility, effort and working conditions) to the net extent of one full job class or more. If the content of a job is changed to the extent that the sum of the numerical values assigned to each of the twelve factors is changed by one whole number or more, a new description and classification shall be established and installed, subject to the provisions of the Basic Labor Agreement between the Company and the Union. In the determination of the effect of new or changed job requirements on the classification of the job, only the factors which are affected by the change shall be considered.[95]

In connection with a plant-wide job evaluation analysis, the Maytag Company superintendents and foremen were asked to work with the company job evaluation representatives and replan the work assignment patterns to cause the work requiring high skills to be given to

---

[95] Seyfarth *et al.*, LABOR RELATIONS AND THE LAW IN BELGIUM AND THE UNITED STATES, note 71 *supra*, at p. 204. *See also* COMPENSATION, R. Sibson, ed. (New York: Am. Mgmt., 1974), p. 37; Belcher, COMPENSATION ADMINISTRATION (New Jersey: Prentice Hall, 1974). p. 88.

those employees already classified in jobs with high points and to cause the work requiring lower skills to be assigned regularly to other employees who could then be classified in newly-described jobs that could be evaluated much lower.

The effect of the change in the work assignment patterns caused a grievance to be filed on February 25, 1955, by a group of females who had their wage rates established in Wage Group B (second grade) because on a regular eight-hour basis they would merely pull a handle and drill four holes in a block of wood that had been inserted in a fixture on the drill press. Since this low-skilled work became the regular eight-hour assignment described and was evaluated as a separate job entitled "drill press—wood block drilling" and placed in Wage Group B (second grade), the females complained, saying in their grievance that they should be classified in the "woodworkers" job category, Wage Group E (fifth grade), because prior to the job evaluation analysis some of the employees classified as "woodworkers" had been assigned to "fill in" by drilling holes in the wooden blocks using a drill press. After the work assignment pattern had been changed, the employees classified as "woodworkers" in Wage Group E were assigned regularly high-skilled work evaluated as being in Wage Group E. Employees classified in jobs evaluated in Wage Group B entitled "drill press—wood block drilling" were assigned *only* to low-skilled work. Arbitrator George Gorder in his award set forth the issue:

> Does the Company have the right to take any portion of a job away and reevaluate it into a lower wage group?[96]

Then in his award he explained:

> Employees classified as "Woodworkers" possess and use skills required to operate relatively complex machines such as planners, dado machines, saws, joiners, and others, which are used to build a variety of items such as finished cabinets, racks, storage bins, shelves, racks for cribs, etc., from sketches and blueprints. The drilling of a hole in a wooden block does not involve similar skills.
> . . .
> Since the Company has a right to combine duties of different skill values, it has a right to separate them out of the regular duties of a classification and transfer them to other classifications or set them up in a new classification under the wage structure on the plant. . . . An employer . . . [who] subtracts certain elements from a job, is justified in reducing the rate of the segregated operation where the new rate is set by recognized sound evaluation methods in accordance with the provision of the contract.[97]

---

[96]*Maytag Co.* (Gordon, February 23, 1955), unreported.
[97]*Id.*

Since sex-based wage rate discrimination under Title VII was not a concern of arbitrators until 1981, the Gorder award rendered in 1955 did not reflect any of these concerns. It is, however, an illustration of how a job evaluation analysis causes management to realize that by carefully planning the work assignments to concentrate assignments of low-skilled work to employees in lower paid jobs, the average wage cost in the department will become lower. Since more females have low "length of service" points, they will be assigned the lower-skilled work under the seniority provision set out in the labor agreement.[98] This shift of the average wage rates of females downward may be challenged as a sex-based wage rate discrimination on the part of the employer, but the shift comes from the seniority rules, not from the job evaluation plan. However, if the facts are similar to those in the Gorder award (i.e., the shift in the work assignment patterns causes the work content to be redescribed and the job evaluation points, for some jobs, to drop, and because of the difference in length of service of females and males in the department the females are transferred to classifications with lower wage rates), the reasons should be carefully described in the "record" to avoid confusion when judges and their magistrates meet up with job evaluation methodology the first time.

The same methodology, with a different result, was used by Arbitrator Anthony V. Sinicropi in *Sanyo Manufacturing Corp.*[99] When a new line of nineteen-inch portable sets was introduced, it was discovered that the chassis of the new model weighed only seven instead of twenty-eight pounds. The job at the inspection and repair station was re-evaluated, downgrading it from "heavy assembler" to "general operator." Arbitrator Sinicropi conceded that the decrease in the weight caused the "physical demand" factor to drop from degree three to degree two but the degree values for "initiative and ingenuity exercised," "the responsibility for material or product," "the responsibility for the safety of others" or "the unavoidable hazards attendant to the job" did not drop, he concluded, and hence he determined that the total amount of points was 154, and the job was to remain in labor grade two as that of a "heavy assembler." This award is described here to point out that job evaluation methodology does not always cause the wage rates to drop when technological changes occur.

---

[98]There are many reasons why women do not have, on the average, as much "length of service" as males and do not "bid up" to higher skilled jobs with higher rates as often as do males. Five separate reasons for this are set forth in the NRC report, note 66 *supra*, at p. 53. The reasons for the higher refusal rates of females when offered promotions are discussed in Kreps, note 86 *supra*; Polachek, note 86 *supra*; Reubens & Reubens, note 86 *supra*. Many companies collect the statistics on refusals by eligible bidders to bid on higher jobs and such statistics should be added into the arbitration record if it involves matters of the type discussed in the text associated with note 87 *supra*.

[99]80-1 ARB § 8150 (Sinicropi, 1979).

The above four subsections should not be considered to be discussions of all of the Title VII challenges that can develop around a job evaluation labor arbitration dispute, but they illustrate the new vista that was opened when *de novo* review began in 1981. Representatives should put into the record the significant facts to assist a reviewing judge and his or her magistrates to resolve a Title VII challenge without starting up evidentiary hearings just as the district court did when it sent up to the Sixth Circuit special findings that enabled the appellate court to resolve the Title VII challenge that was involved in *Christensen v. Iowa*.[100]

THE "WEIGHT" TO BE GIVEN A LABOR ARBITRATOR'S AWARD IS DETERMINED BY THE JUDGE

The Supreme Court explained in *Alexander v. Gardner-Denver*[101] that if the arbitration award is rendered with "procedural fairness" and "adequacy of the record," the award can be added into the record in the district court case.[102] Once the arbitration award can be properly added, the amount of weight to be given the award is completely within the control of the district judge. The Court said:

> We adopt no standards as to the weight to be accorded in arbitral decision, since this must be determined in the court's discretion with regard to the facts and circumstances of each case.[103]

This same view was also expressed in *Barrentine v. Arkansas-Best Freight System:*

> We do not hold that an arbitral decision has no evidentiary bearing on a subsequent FLSA action in court. As we decided in *Gardner-Denver,* such a decision may be admitted into evidence, but "[w]e adopt no standards as to the weight to be accorded an arbitral decision, since this must be determined in the court's discretion with regard to the facts and circumstances of each case."[104]

Labor arbitrators should want to know what "weight" federal judges will give their awards if the awards are filed in the federal

---

[100]563 F.2d 353, 16 FEP Cases 232 (8th Cir. 1977).

[101]415 U.S. 36, 44, 7 FEP Cases 81 (1974). The joint committee decision referred back to the district court in *Barrentine v. Arkansas-Best Freight System*, 450 U.S. 728, 24 WH Cases 1284 (1981), was not an arbitration award and yet the court described it as one and sent it to the district court for review. The decision did not meet the "procedural fairness" and "adequacy record" standard discussed in the *Gardner-Denver* opinion; *see* discussion in text *supra*, associated with notes 21–26.

[102]*Id*. at 1025, 7 FEP Cases at 90.

[103]*Id*. at 60 n. 21, 7 FEP Cases at 90 n. 21.

[104]450 U.S. 728, 743 n. 22, 24 WH Cases 1284, 1290 n. 22.

district court for review and what they could do to increase the "weight" of their awards if so filed so relitigation would be avoided. It is to be assumed that labor arbitrators have pride and do not want their "effect to go to naught."

When the *Gardner-Denver* decision, *supra,* was referred back to the district court judge, directing him to change the handling of the award from *defer* to *de novo* review of the arbitration award, his decision remained the same, with no articulating reasons. Later, in two arbitration awards, filed in two different district courts in Michigan, the judges did articulate the weight they, as judges, should give a labor award. In *Becton v. Detroit Terminal of Consolidated Freightways,* [105] the suit was a claim that the company and Local 299 of the Teamsters had violated Title VII by improperly discharging the plaintiff for racial reasons. Then three analytical steps occurred: (1) the plaintiff lawyers produced enough evidence to satisfy the initial burden, (2) the defendant lawyer filed the arbitration award to articulate the non-discriminatory reason for the discharge, and (3) the plaintiff asserted that the nondiscriminatory reason was a pretext. In evaluating the weight to be given the award in connection with (1) and (2) the judge wrote:

> The case at bar presents a situation which is different from that presented in *Gardner-Denver* in a way that gives this court an opportunity to examine the outer limits of the doctrine announced in *Gardner-Denver* and to continue the process of developing the appropriate relationship between "arbitration" (based on private contracts) and judicial litigation (based on congressional action). Here, the "arbitrator" was not presented with and made no decision concerning the question of whether or not race was a factor in the employer's decision in this instance. All that the "arbitrator" was asked to do and did do was to examine the facts along with the provisions of the collective bargaining contract between the company and the plaintiff's union and to decide whether the action taken by the company was justified.
>
> The court is not called upon in this case to abdicate its duty to make the ultimate decision as to the existence of racial discrimination; it is asked only to defer to the arbitral determination on the issue of just cause when an "arbitrator" has determined that there was just cause under the contract for the plaintiff's termination. *Gardner-Denver* stands for the proposition that a court may not let an "arbitrator" decide for it the issue of discrimination; neither the words of the opinion nor the reasoning behind it would justify the extension of the rule applied there to cover the situation presented here, where findings essential to the "arbitral" determination did not directly involve a finding of discrimination or no discrimination.
>
> To rule that the court must consider the issue of just cause for termination on a *de novo* basis in this case would be to needlessly emasculate the

---

[105] 490 F. Supp. 464, 22 FEP Cases 1655 (E.D. Mich. 1980).

arbitral process and to pass up an opportunity to conserve judicial resources.

When the parties to a dispute have, by virtue of the collective bargaining process, agreed to a contract calling for "arbitration" of grievances, the law has looked with favor at arbitration as the final arbiter. As is evidenced by the Steelworkers Trilogy, this tradition has the unabashed approval of the Supreme Court.[106]

The court concluded:

For these reasons, the court need not consider the evidence presented to it on this issue. To the extent that the defendant has been called upon to produce evidence of just cause for termination, the arbitral decision will suffice. The inquiry now turns to the question of whether the plaintiff has shown that the just cause that did exist was merely a pretext to cover up what was in reality a racially discriminatory termination. Only by such a showing can the plaintiff prevail in this action.[107]

Then the judge disposed of the third analytical step as follows:

The court finds from the evidence produced in this case that the discharge was not a pretext to cover up racial discrimination nor was racial animus involved in the discharge.[108]

In *EEOC v. Union Camp Corp.*,[109] the award of Arbitrator Keith Grotz[110] was filed by the defendant (employer) with the district court to demonstrate to the court that Arbitrator Grotz had sustained the discharge of the grievant under the "just cause" standard of the labor agreement. The underlying articulation and conclusion of the arbitrator was filed to rebut the *prima facia* case of racial discrimination presented to the court by the plaintiff (EEOC) in its case in chief. Even though the arbitrator set forth in his award careful "findings and conclusions" disclosing seven separate incidents in four typed pages, including detail about the refusal of the grievant to wear a hairnet required by OSHA regulations when the hair of an employee extends more than two inches below the ear, Judge Miles of the Western District of Michigan did not accept these findings. He said he made a complete *de novo* reexamination of the evidence—that he had "reviewed all the testimony and other evidence in this record concerning the incident on February 10, as well as [the employee's] entire history of employment with defendant." These comments make it clear that he concluded that under a *de novo* review, he was obligated

---

[106]*Id*. at 465–66, 22 FEP Cases at 1657–58.
[107]*Id*. at 467, 22 FEP Cases at 1659.
[108]*Id*. at 467–68, 22 FEP Cases at 1659.
[109]27 FEP Cases 1393 (W.D. Mich. 1981).
[110]*Union Camp Corp.*, Case No. 54-30-0863-76 (Grotz, 1976), unreported.

to review the factual basis for the arbitrator's findings and "just cause" determination that he had issued.

Judge Joiner of the Eastern District of Michigan, on the other hand, said in *Becton, supra,* that a judge should *not* reexamine the factual basis of the arbitrator's findings, articulation, and conclusion because to do so would "emasculate the arbitral process." He followed this up by saying that "the court need not consider the evidence presented to the arbitrator on this [just cause] issue" and "the [filing of] the arbitral decision will suffice."[111]

However, both judges stated clearly that they were obligated to carefully examine the factual basis of the claim that the discharge was merely a "pretext" to "cover up what was, in reality, a racially discriminatory termination." Judge Miles discussed Judge Joiner's two steps in a footnote. In the last sentence of his note, he made it clear that he and Judge Joiner had the same view that when a *de novo* review is filed, the judge must examine the facts underlying the Title VII (Civil Rights Act) aspect of the case:

> Defendant has argued that this court's *de novo* review of plaintiff's discrimination claim should be limited in scope, giving great weight to the decision rendered by an arbitrator to whom [S____'s] grievances were taken under the terms of the collective bargaining agreement. In *Alexander v. Gardner-Denver Co.,* 415 U.S. 36, 7 FEP Cases 81 (1974), the court held that the courts should consider employees' Title VII claims *de novo,* giving such weight as is deemed appropriate to any prior arbitral decisions. 415 U.S. at 60. *Becton v. Detroit Terminal of Consolidated Freightways,* 490 F. Supp. 464, 22 FEP Cases 1655 (E.D. Mich. 1980), in construing *Gardner-Denver,* held that an arbitral determination that just cause supported an employer's actions was binding on the court in a subsequent Title VII action. Defendant urges this court to follow *Becton,* and therefore to find that the arbitration adverse to [S____] has the effect of compelling this court to reach a like result. A close reading of *Becton*, however, reveals that the binding effect given the arbitral decision went only so far as the issue of whether the employer had met its burden of articulating a legitimate nondiscriminatory basis for its actions. After acknowledging

---

[111]*Becton v. Detroit Terminal of Consolidated Freightways*, 490 F. Supp. 464, 22 FEP Cases 1655, 1659 (E.D. Mich. 1980). Judge Joiner supported his conclusion on the lack of necessity for a factual review *de novo* of the arbitrator's findings with this comment:
To chip away at the finality of arbitral decisions any more than is made necessary by the legislature would be to lessen the importance of arbitration in the labor area and thus to destroy part of the carefully constructed system through which labor disputes are resolved. As the Steelworkers Trilogy pointed out, a system based upon arbitration will function smoothly only if the people involved have confidence in the decisions of the arbitrators, and this confidence will exist only to the extent that the arbitral decisions are given finality by the courts. *Id.* at 468, 22 FEP Cases at 1658.

itself so bound, the *Becton* court turned to "the question of whether the plaintiff has shown that the just cause that did exist was merely a pretext to cover up what was in reality a racially discriminatory termination," 490 F. Supp. at 470, upon which the court made its own determination, albeit a terse one. Likewise, in the instant case the issue of pretext must be decided by the court, which is not bound by the arbitrator's decision.[112]

The factual analysis used by Judge Miles to determine the claim of "pretext" was to compare the disciplines issued by employees who had different racial origins and had similar employment faults to determine whether the discipline was different, explainable only because of the difference in race.

Since no other employees with different racial origins had been treated differently in the enforcement of the hairnet rule, no unequal enforcement of discipline for racial reasons could be established and Judge Miles dismissed the Title VII claim. He did not articulate the same "pretext" analysis as did Judge Joiner but since he did not vacate the discharge award, he was following the same path.

A COURT CAN ORDER THE PLAINTIFF TO PAY THE DEFENDANT'S LEGAL FEES IN A FRIVOLOUS *DE NOVO* REVIEW

In addition, Judge Miles, in a second opinion[113] involving the same parties, ordered the plaintiff, the EEOC, to pay to the defendant (the employer) the legal fees ($28,541.50) the defendant paid defending itself against the Section 301 *de novo* review suit filed by the Commission.[114] Judge Miles wrote in the second opinion:

> The exercise of the court's discretion in awarding an attorney's fee to a prevailing plaintiff is tightly circumscribed as to both award and amount.... These cases, however, do not control the question of attorney's fees to a prevailing defendant.... A prevailing defendant may recover attorney's fees either under the Court's inherent equity power where the prosecution is in bad faith, or under 42 U.S.C. §2000e(5)(k) only where the court finds "that the plaintiff's action was frivolous, unreasonable, or without foundation, even though not brought in subjective bad faith," [*Christiansburg Garment Co. v. EEOC*, 16 FEP Cases 502 (1978)] 434 U.S. at 421.
>
> [1] Having considered the parties' four briefs on attorney's fees, the Court does not know and will not speculate as to whether this case was brought in subjective bad faith. However, the Court is persuaded, based upon the record, files, and four day trial, that this case was frivolous, un-

---

[112]27 FEP Cases at 1395 n. 2.

[113]*EEOC v. Union Camp Corp.*, 536 F. Supp. 64, 27 FEP Cases 1400 (W.D. Mich. 1982).

[114]42 U.S.C. § 2000e(5) (k).

reasonable, and without foundation. An award of attorney's fees is therefore appropriate.[115]

Judge Miles went on to say:

Here the charging party cries discrimination and the EEOC, despite an utter lack of evidence, sympathetically files suit, hoping that defendant will surrender rather than go to trial. When, as here, defendant refused to knuckle under, EEOC goes to a lengthy trial, tries the case poorly, loses, and hopes a lesson has been taught. A better case for an award of attorney's fees could not be made.[116]

This award for fees relates to an attempt by a plaintiff to vacate an award. Litigation over attorneys' fees related to the arbitration process is discussed *supra*.[117] The rationale against transferring legal fees to the other party in the arbitration process is quite different from the rationale involved with the transfer of legal fees when one party is attempting to have an award vacated for the various reasons discussed in the prior chapter and for a *de novo* review when such is desired when the award touches Title VII (Civil Rights Act) or other public statutes. In this regard, one may cite Chief Justice Burger's concerns that are resulting from the rush to court when the grievant is disappointed in an award. This rush may slow down if the legal fees of the defendant can be switched to the plaintiff when the suit is shown to be a harassment of the defendant or an attempt to set the stage for bargaining for a modification by the defendant merely to avoid the defendant's legal costs.[118]

THE ARBITRATION AWARD REVIEW PROCEDURE IS ESTABLISHED BY THE JUDGE

In some of the footnotes and scattered references in the text in *Alexander v. Gardner-Denver*[119] and *Barrentine v. Arkansas-Best Freight System*[120] it is clear that the Supreme Court has explained that the district court judge should examine the "procedural fairness" and the "adequacy of the record" in the labor arbitration process and that if the award meets this test, the judge is free to determine what weight he will give to the findings set fourth in the labor arbitration award. Since the weight to be given is only if the "procedural fairness" and "adequacy of the record" standards have been met, these standards that

---

[115]536 F. Supp. at 65, 27 FEP Cases at 1401.
[116]*Id*. 66, 27 FEP Cases at 1402.
[117]"Awarding of Attorneys' Fees" in Chapter XVIII.
[118]Burger, *Isn't There a Better Way?* (1982 report on the state of the judiciary), 68 A.B.A. J. 274.
[119]415 U.S. 36, 7 FEP Cases 81 (1974).
[120]450 U.S. 728, 24 WH Cases 1284 (1981).

have been drilled into district court judges will become the accepted ones that the district court judges will use.

First, the Administrative Procedure Act[121] standards will be applied by the judges and hence labor arbitrators should understand, at least in outline, the procedural standards contained therein. That Act provides that when the court is being asked to set aside any action of a deciding tribunal (an administrative agency), "the court shall review the *whole* record or such portions thereof as may be cited by any party."[122] (Emphasis added.) The "whole record" requirement is not satisfied if the court receives a contracted record that would require the judge to evaluate evidence in isolated amounts.

Evidence which may be logically substantial in isolation may lose its logical relevance, even its claim to credibility, in context with other evidence.[123]

Thus if a labor arbitration award is to be reviewed by a district judge, a *whole* record (not complete, but connected, *i.e.*, not in isolated pieces) should accompany the award. If not, the district judge should not give the award any more weight than he or she should give to any decision by an administrative law judge (*e.g.*, a decision in a tax matter or bank merger).[124]

Masters' and magistrates' reports[125] are another guide that will certainly be used by federal district court judges when they are asked to determine whether labor arbitration awards should be accepted into the record. The findings and report that a judge receives from a master or a magistrate must meet certain standards.[126] Masters and magistrates are the agents of the judge and the judge explains to them

---

[121]5 U.S.C. § 551 *et seq.*
[122]*Id.*
[123]Jaffee, JUDICIAL CONTROL OF ADMINISTRATIVE ACTION (Boston: Little, Brown, 1965), p. 600.
[124]*Id.* at 601.
[125]The Federal Rules of Civil Procedure permit the appointment of a special master in cases that are especially burdensome or require unique expertise. FED. R. CIV. P. 53(b); masters have been appointed frequently in Title VII cases. *See, e.g.*, *Thompson v. Boyle*, 499 F. Supp. 1147, 1167, 22 FEP Cases 1500 (D. D.C. 1980); *Kohne v. Imco Container Co.*, 480 F. Supp. 1015, 1039, 21 FEP Cases 535 (W.D. Va. 1979). Justice Burger, in his dissent in *Barrentine v. Arkansas-Best Freight System*, 450 U.S. 728, 24 WH Cases 1284 (1981), reported that the number of civil findings in fiscal year 1960 was 52,284; this number rose in 1980 to 168,739, which represents an increase of 184.7%. Even with the increase in the numbers of judges, the number of cases per judge had risen 35.1% (from 183 to 327). The cases docketed in the courts of appeals in the same period rose from 3,446 to 23,200, an increase of 495.0%, and the case load per panel increased from 184 to 527, a 206.4% increase.
[126]During the last two decades, due to the growth in the judicial load, an Office of United States Magistrates was added in 1971. Magistrates are being employed to assist the judges. A magistrate must be a lawyer and receives 75% of the district judge's compensation. As the case load rises, more magistrates have acted as special masters in appropriate civil actions. *See* the Federal Magistrate Act of 1968, 28 U.S.C. § 636 (Supp. IV 1981) modified both in 1976 and in 1979.

what the judge believes he or she needs to cause him or her to accept a report without accepting additional evidence and making substantial revisions. The minimum level for acceptance of such a report is found in the Federal Rules of Civil Procedure and in various circuit court decisions.[127]

If oral testimony is basic to the master's report, a transcript of the oral testimony must be attached to the report, but under the Rules of Civil Procedure, the judge should not change the factual findings of a master (or magistrate) based on oral testimony unless the findings are "clearly erroneous."[128] This rule suggests that if the findings of the labor arbitrator are based on oral testimony and the testimony was received in compliance with the Rules of Civil Procedure, the district judge cannot ignore the findings set forth by the arbitrator. Since arbitrators want their awards to stand up if a *de novo* review by a district court judge commences, they will undoubtedly tighten up their oral testimony rulings. This means that representatives presenting evidence to arbitrators should reread the Rules of Civil Procedure and attempt to present the evidence in compliance with them.

Although the findings of fact of the master or magistrate based on testimony should not be changed by the judge unless "clearly erroneous," the judge still has the power to modify a master's report in any particular. Therefore, the labor arbitrator's award will be modified in any particular by the judge if the judge decides that he or she should do so. A judge will react adversely to an award that is unclear or inadequate just as a judge will react adversely to a report by a master or magistrate that is unclear or inadequate. In this connection, it is interesting to note that when Title VII (discrimination) complaints have been filed in district courts, the cases have been referred to magistrates with, and, more recently, without, the parties' consent and then

---

[127] Rule 53(e)(I) of the Federal Rules of Civil Procedure states in part:

(I)*Contents and Filing.* The master shall prepare a report upon the matters submitted to him by the order of reference and, if required to make findings of fact and conclusions of law, he shall set them forth in the report. He shall ... file with it a transcript of the proceedings and of the evidence and the original exhibits.

Judge Evans, speaking for the Seventh Circuit, explained in *Carter Oil v. McQuigg*, 112 F.2d 275, 279 (7th Cir. 1949):

Where the question is one of veracity it is clear that the appellate court should give controlling weight to the trier of fact who saw and heard the witnesses. This is well established. Where the testimony consists of documentary evidence and depositions, the master is in no better position to determine an issue of fact than a reviewing court. The District Court's findings on such evidence is likewise subject to free review unaffected by presumptions which ordinarily accompany their findings on controverted issues.

See also Krinsley v. United Artists Corp., 225 F.2d 579, 582 (7th Cir. 1955).

[128] Rule 53(e)(II) states in part:

(II) *In Non-Jury Actions.* In an action to be tried without a jury the court shall accept the master's findings of fact unless clearly erroneous. ... The Court after hearing may adopt the report or may modify it or may reject it in whole or in part or may receive further evidence or may recommit it with instructions.

the magistrate's report is sent to the judge for a *de novo* review.[129] If the judge signs the report, with or without modifications, the report becomes the judge's decision. In one case, the trial court decision was vacated on appeal and remanded back to the district court because the judge had signed the magistrate's findings and report without reviewing the transcription of the oral portions of the magistrate's proceeding.[130]

ARBITRATORS HAVE BEEN APPOINTED AS MASTERS

As noted earlier, when a federal judge accepts an arbitrator's award as his or her product, with or without modification, a *"de novo"* review has taken place and relitigation has been avoided. Quite obviously, when an arbitrator is appointed as a "court administrator" by the district court judge, the arbitrator will be performing a task closely related to the task performed for the judge by a master or magistrate. Furthermore, when a district judge asks an arbitrator to perform such a task, the judge is recognizing the "special expertise" of the arbitrator.

The district court judge in *United States v. Steamfitters, Local 638*[131] appointed Arbitrator George Moskowitz to be the "court administrator" charged with the responsibility for devising and installing an affirmative action program to adjust the rate of training of journeymen so 30 percent of them would be minority members. The court asked the arbitrator-administrator to supervise the testing procedures of the minority applicants and then to supervise the referral system.

Another arbitrator was appointed by a district court judge as an administrator in *Foreman v. Wood, Wire and Metal Lathers.*[132] The plaintiffs then claimed that the district court decision should have been vacated on the ground that the court simply accepted the award of the arbitrator without providing a *"de novo"* hearing before the judge as required by the *Gardner-Denver* opinion, *supra*. Significantly, the court of appeals stated that the acceptance and approval of the special arbitrator's report caused that report to be a *"de novo"* review by the judge and no hearing before the judge was necessary if the judge was satisfied with the report.

[129]*Muhich v. Allen*, 603 F.2d 1247, 20 FEP Cases 551 (7th Cir. 1979); *Livas v. Teledyne Movible Offshore, Inc.*, 607 F.2d 118, 21 FEP Cases 505 (5th Cir. 1979). In another case, the Ninth Circuit held that a claimant who appeals a magistrate's decision recommending dismissal of case under Title VII is entitled to a free transcript of the proceedings "[b]ecause Title VII cases, unlike most other cases, *can be referred to magistrates for trial without consent of the parties....*" [Emphasis added]. *Spaulding v. University of Washington*, 676 F.2d 1232, 1235, 28 FEP Cases 995, 997 (8th Cir. 1982).
[130]*Livas v. Teledyne Movible Offshore, Inc.*, 607 F.2d 118, 21 FEP Cases 505 (5th Cir. 1979).
[131]347 F. Supp. 164 (D. N.Y. 1972), *decision on merits*, 360 F. Supp. 979, 6 FEP Cases 319 (D. N.Y. 1973), *rem'd and modified and aff'd sub nom. Rios v. Steamfitters, Local 638*, 501 F.2d 622 8 FEP Cases 293 (2d Cir. 1974).
[132]557 F.2d 988 (5th Cir. 1977).

A job evaluation dispute always involves a comparison of wage rates assigned to covered work activities that are different from the work activities in the job in question. The dispute can now be called a "comparable worth" or "equal value" dispute. If an arbitrator's resolution of such a dispute is then submitted to review by a judge, the judge will seek assistance from his or her magistrates and from special masters, etc., as the judge struggles with the completely new language and concepts that have developed around job evaluation practice and that now have been articulated about job evaluation by those probing for female bias in the plans or sex-based wage rate discrimination in the application of job evaluation methodology.

One judge received from a special master a report that informed the judge about the job evaluation plan (its structure factors, degrees, etc.), but then also advised him of the facts in the record that supported or rebutted the challenges against the plan and its application. Assertions that there existed some Title VII violations were in the information in the master's report. The judge in *Durant v. Owens-Illinois Glass Co.*[133] said:

> It is possible that certain influences exist at the plant which tend to discourage women from applying for better-paying jobs. However, plaintiffs have been unable to uncover any of a serious nature. *They argue from some isolated fragments of evidence, much of it now seriously dated, and from testimony of an expert who has never studied the plant and may well not be an expert in the field that the defendants discouraged women from bidding for jobs outside of the Selecting and Quality-and-Specifications Departments.* Defendants demonstrated that the openings at the plant were posted in the main hallway and awarded on the basis of a sex-neutral seniority system. *The weak evidence of "formal and informal systems" of sex discrimination offered by plaintiffs is insufficient to overcome that showing.* [Emphasis added.]

Another example of the importance of making available the facts needed to evaluate the Title VII claims related to a job evaluation dispute is the special fact-finding report sent by the district court to the appellate court that permitted that court to dispose of a Title VII violation claim in *Christensen v. Iowa*[134] discussed earlier in this chapter.

If females are involved in a job evaluation award the arbitrator should assist the judge with the significant facts, some discussed previously,[135] to avoid extensive hearing costs and confusions if a review is sought. The reason these special findings are significant when females are involved is that until 1981 no Title VII sex-based wage rate dis-

---

[133]517 F. Supp. 710 (E.D. La. 1980), *aff'd*, 656 F.2d 89 (5th Cir. 1981).
[134]563 F.2d 353, 16 FEP Cases 232 (8th Cir. 1977).
[135]*See* text associated with notes 68 to 98 *supra*.

crimination could be litigated before a court unless the challenge was limited to a claim of a lower wage rate for the same work.[136]

EFFECT OF EQUAL EMPLOYMENT OPPORTUNITY COMMISSION RULINGS

Another event that increases the "weight" of an arbitrator's award in the record before the district judge occurs when the Equal Employment Opportunity Commission has also concluded after investigation that there is "no reasonable cause" to believe a Title VII violation report. Busy federal district judges do not want to open a *"de novo"* review case for relitigation if the Commission has found "no cause" and an arbitrator, in a carefully handled case, also has found "no discrimination" under the standards in the labor agreement. It should be recalled that the district court judge accepted the award by Arbitrator Sears in *Alexander v. Gardner-Denver*[137] as his decision and in that case a discrimination charge filed by grievant Alexander caused the Equal Employment Opportunity Commission's Denver, Colorado office to investigate the matter; it found "no reasonable cause to believe that a violation of Title VII had occurred."[138] The district judge in *Fort v. TWA*[139] discussed this aspect of his acceptance of the arbitrator's award as his decision:

> Although there is no indication in the arbitral decision that plaintiff's grievance was cast in the form of a Title VII claim, it is apparent that the history of plaintiff's unsuccessful attempts at promotion was well-developed before the [arbitration] board. Further, plaintiff submitted her claims of race discrimination and retaliation to the Equal Employment Opportunity Commission ... which determined there was not reasonable cause to credit them.... Applying the standards set forth in *Alexander v. Gardner-Denver Company*, ... the Court is inclined to give considerable weight to the combined determinations of the arbitration board and EEOC, especially in the absence of direct or other persuasive evidence of discrimination against plaintiff."

A PERSONAL REPRESENTATIVE'S PRESENCE AT THE ARBITRATION HEARING ENCOURAGES ACCEPTANCE OF AWARDS APPEALED *"DE NOVO"*

When the individual grievant is given the right to have private counsel present facts, cross-examine witnesses, and present an argument to

---

[136]*See* text associated with notes 53 to 56 *supra.*
[137]415 U.S. 36, 7 FEP Cases 81 (1974).
[138]*See* note 7 *supra.*
[139]14 FEP Cases 208, 213 (N.D. Cal. 1976).

the arbitrator at the arbitration hearing, one of the important concerns that caused the *"de novo"* review procedures to be introduced by the Supreme Court disappears. Again, the Justices in *Alexander v. Gardner-Denver*[140] were simply afraid that the union representative who represents a grievant may have conflicts that cause the interests of the grievant to not be fully protected. In a significant footnote the Supreme Court said that the individual grievant's rights in the arbitration process may be weakened by the fact that the grievant does not have personal counsel:

> A further concern is the union's exclusive control over the manner and extent to which an individual grievance is presented. . . . In arbitration, as in the collective bargaining process, the interests of the individual employee may be subordinated to the collective interests of all employees in the bargaining unit. . . . Moreover, the harmony of interest between the union and the individual employee cannot always be presumed, especially where a claim of racial discrimination is made. . . . And a breach of the union's duty of fair representation may prove difficult to establish.[141]

The federal district judge in *Burroughs v. Marathon Oil Co.*[142] accepted an arbitrator's award as "his" award on a *de novo* review because, among other things, the grievant-plaintiff was represented at the arbitration hearing by competent counsel:

> This Court finds that the provisions in the collective bargaining agreement between defendant and Teamsters Local Union No. 283 parallel the language of Title VII, that plaintiff was given procedural fairness in the arbitral forum, *that he was represented by competent counsel and was given full opportunity to present his case and cross-examine witnesses,* that the issue of discrimination was a central issue in the arbitration proceedings, and that the arbitrator's decision fully and completely dealt with the issue of discrimination.[143] [Footnote omitted. Emphasis added.]

Arbitrator William B. Gould in *Basic Vegetable Products, Inc.*[144] described the agreement that was worked out to permit private representation if the grievance involved a Title VII matter, to reduce the rapidly developing *de novo* review problems being attached to labor arbitration.

> [I]t seems to me that an exclusion of employment discrimination cases from the grievance arbitration machinery and their relegation to the courts

---

[140]415 U.S. 36, 7 FEP Cases 81 (1974).

[141]*Id.* at 59 n. 19, 7 FEP Cases at 89 n. 19.

[142]446 F. Supp. 633, 17 FEP Cases 612 (E.D. Mich. 1978). *See also Kornbluh v. Stearns & Foster Co.*, 73 F.R.D. 307, 14 FEP Cases 847 (S.D. Ohio 1978).

[143]446 F. Supp. at 636-37, 17 FEP Cases at 614.

[144]64 LA 620 (Gould, 1975). *See also Mason & Dixon Lines, Inc.*, 237 NLRB 6, 98 LRRM 1540 (1978); *Versi Craft Corp.*, 227 NLRB 877, 94 NLRB 1207 (1977); *Jo Jo Management Corp.*, 225 NLRB 1133, 93 LRRM 1475 (1976); *Sabine Towing & Transportation Co., Inc.* 224 NLRB 941, 92 LRRM 1562 (1976).

would have a deleterious impact inasmuch as it would segregate the claims of racial minorities and women from the mainstream of plant level adjudication. This segregation seems undesirable.... I believe that the Supreme Court in *Alexander v. Gardner-Denver* ..., while properly noting that the Courthouse door cannot be barred by an arbitrator's award, encouraged the parties to collective bargaining relationships to do what they have done in the instant case. The Court in *Gardner-Denver* noted the fact that an attempt to resolve disputes prior to litigation is salutory and, in many instances, may bind up the wounds which would otherwise fester in complicated judicial proceedings.... I am of the view that the parties in the instant proceeding have diligently attempted to bring themselves within the guidelines established by the Court in footnote 21, and to accomplish equal opportunity without resort to the judiciary. One would hope that others would follow suit.[145]

Specifically, with respect to the agreement between the union and the company private attorneys selected by the grievant were permitted to be active at the hearing if the grievant desired such "protection." Arbitrator Gould said:

I commend the parties for entering into this novel and important agreement. It seems to me desirable that employment discrimination cases be heard by arbitrators wherever possible because of the complicated and time-consuming nature of Title VII litigation in the Federal Courts and the huge backlog with which the Equal Employment Opportunity Commission is now confronted. Delay and protracted litigation permit open wounds to fester.... [I]t should be noted that the parties have wisely permitted third party intervention.[146]

In various arbitration cases where there has been some possibility that the grievant and the union representatives may have differences or assumed differences, the two parties and the arbitrator have been willing to agree to the participation of personal counsel for the grievant. Union representatives are often willing because a refusal to do so could set up a claim of improper representation or lack of fair representation.[147]

When private counsel is invited to participate in the arbitration hearing at the request of the grievant, it is normal that the grievant pays the fees of the private counsel. This fact may cause many grievants not to have private counsel. However, the fact that the grievant has the opportunity to have a private counsel reduces the concerns that were reflected in the *Gardner-Denver* Supreme Court decision.[148]

---

[145]64 LA at 625.

[146]*Id.* at 624-25.

[147]Suits involving charges of lack of fair representation are discussed in Chapter XXIII, "Fair Representation Obligations."

[148]415 U.S. 36, 59 n. 19, 7 FEP Cases 81, 89 n. 19. *See also Burroughs v. Marathon Oil,* 446 F. Supp. 633, 636-37, 17 FEP Cases 612 (E.D. Mich. 1978).

Whenever the grievant files a suit in the district court to have an award reviewed the grievant must retain a private attorney.

THE POSSIBLE WAIVER OF *DE NOVO* REVIEWS OF AWARDS

The Supreme Court held in *Alexander v. Gardner-Denver*[149] that a grievant cannot waive his or her right to have the district court review the discriminatory facts underlying the grievance *unless* the grievant has made an intelligent waiver.[150] The Fifth Circuit, in *U.S. v. Allegheny-Ludlum Industries, Inc.*[151] also relied on the concept of an intelligent waiver:

> [I]n order to delineate more precisely the contours of the applicable rule of law, we hold that the employee may release not only claims for additional back pay, but also claims for other relief—including injunctive—provided the released claims arise from antecedent discriminatory events, acts, patterns, or practices, or the "continuing" or "future" effects thereof so long as such effects are casually rooted—in origin, logic, and factual experience—in discriminatory acts or practices which antedate the execution of the release, and provided, of course, that the release is executed voluntarily and with adequate knowledge....

Thus, the *Allegheny* court developed further the *Gardner-Denver* proposition that a grievant may waive the *de novo* review before a federal judge if the grievant does so with adequate knowledge of his or her right to have the review. This means that when an arbitrator discovers that matter involving the Civil Rights Act or Fair Labor Standards Act or other public law develops at the arbitration hearing, the arbitrator could quite properly inquire whether the award will be considered final by both parties or merely a first step to the district court if the grievant is disappointed in his or her award. The court in *Allegheny* explained:

> Very frankly, we cannot conceive of how any employment discrimination dispute could ever be resolved outside, or indeed inside, the courtroom, if defendants were forbidden to obtain binding, negotiated settlements. No defendant would ever deliver money, promises, or any other consideration—not even a peppercorn—except after entry of a contested, final court order, and even this, on appellants' reasoning, might not end the matter. The EEOC and judicial caseload would swell....[152]

---

[149]415 U.S. 36, 7 FEP Cases 81 (1974).
[150]*Id.* at 51-52, 7 FEP Cases at 86-87.
[151]517 F.2d 826, 853, 11 FEP Cases 167, 187 (5th Cir. 1975).
[152]*Id.* at 858-59, 11 FEP Cases at 193.

A waiver of a right to a *de novo* review of an arbitration award was approved by a district court because the grievant was reinstated by the arbitrator but without back pay. The grievant then accepted the award by returning to work without back pay. The company established to the arbitrator's satisfaction that the kettle in which lead was being melted was not so hot that the work could not have proceeded safely.[153] The Secretary of Labor filed a suit in the district court for back pay for the reinstated employee. The district court granted summary judgement for the company (defendant) because the grievant had returned to work without back pay, making the award dispositive, thereby waiving the *de novo* review.

The Secretary of Labor filed an appeal and the Seventh Circuit held that the acceptance of the reinstatement without back pay did not generate a waiver of the right to the review:

> *Gardner-Denver* does except from the general rule those cases in which the employee has voluntarily waived his right to judicial relief. As noted, the district court viewed this case as falling within this exception. Yet the exception looks to cases in which the employee and employer have reached a voluntary settlement (see *Marshall v. General Motors Corp.* [6 OSHC 1200]), while *Gardner-Denver* specifically states that the mere submitting of a grievance to arbitration does not itself constitute a waiver. In *Gardner-Denver*, the arbitrator had decided against the grievant. We fail to see why the arbitrator's decision in this case awarding [the grievant] reinstatement but denying the rest of his claim should be treated differently. An employee should not have to refuse reinstatement ordered by an arbitrator and thereby risk losing his job permanently in order to exercise his statutory right to seek judicial relief with all the risks that it may entail. Such a rule would undermine the statutory purpose. Accordingly, short of some other proof that the employee actually intended to waive his statutory right, his acceptance of the benefits of the arbitrator's decision does not preclude his action here.[154]

If the employer, the union, and the grievant all believe a waiver of a federal court review is wise, a waiver of the *"de novo"* review can be accomplished in a separate and complete arbitration agreement. The only practical reason for the waiver in advance of the arbitrator's award is that the award may be acted upon more expeditiously once it

---

[153]*Marshall v. N.L. Industries, Inc.*, 618 F.2d 1220, 8 OSHC 1166 (7th Cir. 1980). In *Marshall v. Whirlpool Corp.*, 593 F.2d 715 (6th Cir. 1978), (*aff'd*, 445 U.S. 1, 8 OSHC 1001, 1980). it was clear that an employee does not have a right to walk away from a job based on a belief there is a safety risk without calling for an OSHA inspector except under the following conditions: (1) there is insufficient time to resort to the established OSHA channel; (2) the danger is imminent and objectively reasonable (*i.e.*, any reasonable person would agree that such condition exists); (3) the employee's motivation in refusing to perform the job is based on safety considerations, not a desire to receive more pay or to harrass the management; and (4) the employee cooperates with management to eliminate the hazard.
[154]618 F.2d 1223, 8 OSHC at 1168.

is rendered. The key to any waiver is the employee's consent to the it—before the award or settlement, or after the award, with full recognition by all that the employee's consent to the settlement was voluntary and knowing.[155] The employee-grievant should waive not only his or her review under Title VII to the federal district court but also his or her review before any other forums. This special agreement must involve the union so that the employer retains the right to enjoin a strike if one arises to protest alleged discriminatory practices.[156]

DE NOVO REVIEW RIGHTS WILL
INCREASE PROCEDURAL TECHNICALITIES

As mentioned earlier, the arbitrators and the parties have developed their procedural rules, and different arbitrators working with different parties have created different procedural rules. For example, Arbitrator Ralph Seward developed more formal procedures for arbitration involving General Motors and the United Automobile Workers, whereas less formal procedures were developed by Arbitrator Harry Schulman for arbitration involving Ford Motor Company and the same union. Under the more formal procedures of General Motors, careful opinions were prepared and used for training supervisors and union committeemen, whereas under the early Ford Motor procedures only oral presentations about grievances were made to Arbitrator Schulman and he would promptly respond with an oral opinion without any backup of transcripts or briefs. Between these extremes were the procedures developed by Arbitrator David Wolff at International Harvester for arbitration involving the same union. He asked the parties to submit, in advance, a written "prehearing statement of facts." At the hearing he would identify the areas of factual differences and then he would elicit testimony recorded on a transcript, but limited to the areas where a factual difference had been identified. The parties would also be asked by Arbitrator Wolff for fact stipulations covering areas where there was no real factual dispute to eliminate long cross-examination. Extensive background testimony was not necessary to inform Arbitrator Wolff when a similar grievance was presented because he had acquired the background and could be filled in by oral stipulations that would reduce the time involved in a hearing. A court reporter would take the testimony when it was in conflict so the permanent arbitrator was not burdened with elaborate note-taking and

---

[155]*U.S. v. Allegheny-Ludlum Industries, Inc.*, 517 F.2d 826, 11 FEP Cases 167 (5th Cir. 1975).

[156]*Boys Markets, Inc. v. Retail Clerks, Local 770*, 398 U.S. 235, 74 LRRM 2257 (1970); the Norris-LaGuardia Act injunction prohibition is not applicable to a strike in breach of contract when the underlying dispute is arbitrable.

could have the oral stipulations covering the facts that were not in conflict carefully recorded. When either party wanted to add a brief post-hearing statement in addition to the pre-hearing statement, the arbitrator would require such statement to be filed within a short time limit. Under this procedure, four grievances could generally be heard in a single arbitrator hearing day.

Since Arbitrator Wolff was a pre-selected umpire, no delay was involved in the choosing of an arbitrator and hearing days would be scheduled months in advance with the grievance numbers listed later so there would be no delays. Such an expedited procedure usually was developed by the parties working with the permanent arbitrator when a high volume of arbitration was expected and the arbitrator, usually referred to as an umpire, remained the same.

> In these early days of labor arbitration, the whole process was itself expedited. Arbitrators were selected, hearings were held, and awards were rendered within a matter of days, even hours. Speed has always been an important advantage of arbitration to both unions and employers and as the use of labor arbitration spread, the parties began to make specific written provisions to insure speedy procedures .... [157]

Later, the words "expedited arbitration" became associated with a write-up of the procedures in a particular article in the labor agreement or in an appendix attached thereto. The earlier "expedited arbitration" procedures were developed in conjunction with the permanent arbitrator (or umpire) and were understood by the representatives of both sides but were not developed by the collective bargaining negotiators who were negotiating the agreements. The first "expedited arbitration" procedures negotiated during the collective bargaining period were set out as a uniform procedure in Appendix L to the nationwide agreement negotiated between the United Steelworkers and the "Big Nine" steel producers in 1971.[158] Later, similar provisions were incorporated in the labor agreements between the United Steelworkers and Reynolds Metals, National Can, Libby, McNeill & Libby, Kennecott Copper, and other companies.[159]

The words "expedited arbitration" also became associated with the

---

[157]Address by Michael F. Hoellering, Vice President, Case Administration, American Arbitration Association, given at New York University Twenty-Eighth Annual Conference on Labor (1976), reprinted at CBNC 17:41 *et seq.* (1977).

[158]Reprints of articles from the United Steelworkers newspaper *Steel Labor* describing the expedited arbitration adopted by all of the "Big Nine" steel-producing companies in 1971 are collected at CBNC 17:31 *et seq.* (1977). The full text of the grievance procedure is included in Section 29 of the agreement between the U.S. Steel Corp. and the Steelworkers. *See also* Murray & Griffin, *Expedited Arbitration of Discharge Cases,* 31 Arb. J. No. 4 (1976), p. 263; Fisher, *Arbitration: The Steel Industry Experiment,* 95 Monthly Lab. Rev. 7–10 (Nov. 1972); Cohen, *The Search for Innovative Procedures in Labor Arbitration,* 29 Arb. J. No. 2 (1974), p. 104.

[159]CBNC at 17:42 (1977).

Expedited Labor Arbitration Rules set out by the American Arbitration Association,[160] designed in 1972. These rules permitted parties to speed up the selection of arbitrators and, also, to adopt some procedures they believed would reduce costs and increase speed. International Paper Co. and the United Paperworkers; the United Transportation Union and Long Island Railroad; New York State and various unions; and the U.S. Postal Service and the Postal Unions incorporated similar rules in their agreements in 1972, 1973, and 1974.[161]

Some observers have stated that the expedited arbitration procedures set out in labor agreements or in the appendices attached thereto were a new development that would have significant impact on labor arbitration,[162] whereas others pointed out that permanent labor arbitrators (umpires) had been reaching expedited arbitration procedure agreements for years but they had not recorded them in the text of the labor agreement itself or in an appendix attached thereto. One arbitrator said:

> What is called "expedited arbitration" of a grievance should instead be identified as "normal arbitration" in my opinion. The cumbersome kind, with a transcript, briefs, and all the trimmings should be denominated "protracted arbitration".... [163]

The 1971 agreement between the Steelworkers and the steel companies provided:

> The hearing will be informal. No briefs will be filed or transcripts made, and there shall be no formal evidence rules. The arbitrator shall have the obligation of assuring that all necessary facts and considerations are brought before him.... [164]

Some of these rules set up in labor agreements have generated *contra* reactions by the courts, particularly when the expedited procedures provided for no transcript of the controverted facts basic to an award. When no transcripts of controverted oral evidence and no findings of fact were associated with an award, personal lawyers would rush into court or to the NLRB seeking relitigation. The trial court judges and the administrative law judges, who had to review the awards, did not have sufficient evidence to prevent the duplication, and the grievance would be relitigated.[165]

The federal judges working within the legal system, when they learned

---

[160] Reprinted at CBNC 17:71 *et seq*. (1979).

[161] *Id*. at 17:43, 44, 17:46.

[162] *Id*. at 17:46.

[163] *Id*. at 17:43.

[164] *Id*. at 17:34.

[165] Section 301 suits to obtain a *de novo* review or fair representation trial are discussed in this chapter and in chapter XXIII, "Fair Representation Obligations."

about some of the procedural informalities that operate in *some* labor arbitration procedures, concluded that these informalities were typical and pushed the challenged award toward relitigation. One U.S. Supreme Court Justice stated his criticism of the procedures he considered typical of some "expedited procedures":

> The record of the arbitration proceeding is not as complete as in a court proceeding—the usual rules of evidence do not apply, the rights and procedures common to civil trials such as discovery, compulsory process, cross-examination, testimony under oath are often severely limited or unavailable. And as this Court has recognized, "[a]rbitrators have no obligation to the court to give their reasons for an award."[166] [Citations omitted.]

After the 1974 decision of the Supreme Court in *Alexander v. Gardner-Denver, supra,* John Zalusky, an economist working for the AFL-CIO Department of Research, wrote in 1976 that the "no record" procedures that were being forced upon labor arbitration by adopting the more extreme "expedited arbitration" procedures would have to be relaxed. He said:

> In 1974, in *Alexander v. Gardner-Denver,* the U.S. Supreme Court ruled that an arbitration resolution to a civil rights discrimination grievance does not prevent the aggrieved worker from bringing up the same issue through the provisions of the Civil Rights Act. This decision is bound to have an effect on the arbitration process. The parties and the arbitrator probably will find it necessary to add even more procedural formalities so that the entire proceedings can stand judicial review in court.[167]

The General Counsel of the NLRB said that *Collyer* and *Spielberg* procedural standards would probably require relaxation of the more restrictive procedural rules:

> The third pertinent issue is what impact this requirement will have upon the process of arbitration; that is, will *verbatim transcripts*, extensive legal briefs, and detailed written decisions become more prevalent, thus complicating, extending, and making more expensive the arbitration process? Again, the impact of Board deferral prior to arbitration makes this question even more valid today than it was in the past when *Spielberg* review was only a remote possibility.
>
> The most candid answer I can give to the question is "probably".... [168] [Emphasis added.]

---

[166]*Alexander v. Gardner-Denver,* 415 U.S. 36, 56, 7 FEP Cases 81, 89 (1981), quoting *Steelworkers v. Enterprise Wheel & Car Corp.,* 363 U.S. 593, 46 LRRM 2423, 2425.

[167]Zalusky, *Arbitration: Updating a Vital Process* (AFL-CIO Department of Research, 1976).

[168]Nash, *The NLRB and Arbitration: Some Impressions of the Practical Effect of the Board's Collyer Policy Upon Arbitrators and Arbitration,* ARBITRATION—1974, Proceedings of the Twenty-Seventh Annual Meeting, National Academy of Arbitrators, B. Dennis and G. Somers, eds. (Washington: BNA Books, 1975), p. 118.

John Zalusky was intensely critical of the costs involved in the taking of a stenographic transcript in labor arbitration hearings. He said, in 1976, that the cost was $2.75 per page (now it would be much higher) and he seems to have justified the "no transcript" in labor arbitration procedure simply because of its cost.[169] Unions need not share in the stenographic record cost unless they ask for a copy and, for this reason, the cost of a stenographic record should not be considered a necessary union cost. What is more significant, however, is that many arbitration hearings have the controverted testimony and oral stipulations recorded on an electronic tape—a low-cost procedure—and then the testimony is not converted into typed pages unless one party or the grievant's private attorney requests it.[170] The arbitrator can replay the tape if he or she desires to hear the testimony again, and this replay creates no delay such as that caused when the stenographic symbols have to be transcribed to produce a typed transcript. Receipt of a written transcript is not a requirement in court proceedings and even when a party retains a court reporter to protect that party, the judge may issue a final order from the bench at the end of the hearing, as in an injunction case. Parties who desire to adopt the expedited procedures that are described in injunction cases could adopt them, and some courts are now dispensing with court reporters and are using electronic tapes under the supervision of deputy clerks to reduce the cost attendant to the preservation of testimony if one or another party seeks review in an appellate court.[171]

If there is a *de novo* review or fair representation suit, the record on appeal that the plaintiff would be required to produce would be the same that an appellant would be required to produce if he or she was filing an appeal from the trial court decision if that court is to act as an appellate court and review the award. Rule 10(b) of the Federal Rules of Appellate Procedure provides that the appellant is to order from the

---

[169]Zalusky, note 167 *supra*.

[170]In Rodebaugh, *Sound Recording in the Courtroom, A Reappraisal*, A.B.A. J. 1185 (1961), the author explained that the Judicial Conference of the United States Courts, following a study completed in 1959, recommended that the Administrative Office be instructed, wherever possible and agreeable to the judges concerned, to supply electronic recording systems for use in the United States district courts whenever a vacancy occurred in the office of the existing reporter. The state courts of Alaska began to function on February 20, 1960, with no shorthand reporters but with tape recorders of the type tested by the Administrative Office and under the supervision of deputy clerks. Warren Olney III, Director of the Administrative Office, issued a report on February 20, 1961, saying that electronic reporting produces "a more accurate and complete record, a record which need not be transcribed to be useful; that it reduces delay in transcription, and is less costly...." *Id.* at 1186. In addition, Rule 20003(c) of the Suggested Interim Bankruptcy Rules released August 13, 1979, provides on page 19: "Record of Proceeding. Electronic sound recording equipment shall be used by the clerk of the bankruptcy court to record the meeting of creditors or equity security holders." Interim Bankruptcy Rules Special Pamphlet (St. Paul: West, 1982). *See* "Use of Transcripts and Tapes in Arbitration Hearings" in Chapter VIII.

[171]*See* fair representation trials discussed in Chapter XXIII, "Fair Representation Obligations."

court reporter such parts of the proceedings not already on file that the appellant deems necessary for inclusion in the record, and, if less than the entire transcript is ordered, Rule 10(b) makes provisions for designations and counter-designations of what shall be transcribed.[172]

In the rare situation when no report of the evidence or proceedings at the hearing or trial is available, Rule 10(c) provides that "the appellant may prepare a statement of the evidence or proceedings from the best available means, including his recollection" and the appellee has 10 days after service of the appellant's statement to "serve objections or propose amendments thereto."[173]

The reason the appellant develops a record incorporating a complete or partial transcript from the court reporter's symbols or from the electronic tape is to have the facts in the record that could be used to upset the findings of fact and conclusions of law of the trial judge. The text of Rule 52(a) of the Rules of Civil Procedure for the United States District Courts states:

> In all actions tried upon the facts without a jury or with an advisory jury, the court shall find the facts specially and state separately its conclusions of law thereon, and judgment shall be entered pursuant to Rule 58; and in granting or refusing interlocutory injunctions the court shall similarly set forth the findings of fact and conclusions of law which constitute the grounds of its action. Requests for findings are not necessary for purposes of review. Findings of fact shall not be set aside unless clearly erroneous, and due regard shall be given to the opportunity of the trial court to judge the credibility of the witnesses. The findings of a master, to the extent that the court adopts them, shall be considered as the findings of the court. If an opinion or memorandum of decision is filed, it will be sufficient if the findings of fact and conclusions of law appear therein....[174]

Certainly, labor arbitrators do not want their activities to become merely preliminary steps in expensive court and NLRB relitigation because they fail to record their findings of fact and conclusions in their awards. Because *de novo* review rights have spread so far, one can no longer discuss labor arbitration separately from these simple yet formal legal procedures. Fair representation litigation started up slowly but now such cases and *de novo* review activities are filling up the calendars of the trial courts.[175] Chief Justice Warren Burger has

---

[172]Wright, Miller, Cooper & Gressman, Federal Practice and Procedure (St. Paul: West, 1977), Vol. 16, § 3956, p. 386.

[173]*Id.* at 387.

[174]*Id.*, Vol. 9, § 2571, p. 677.

[175]*See generally* Rosen, *The Individual Worker in Grievance Arbitration: Still Another Look at the Problem,* 24 Md. L. Rev. 233, 258 (1964); Smith, *The Question of "Arbitrability"—The Roles of the Arbitrator, the Court and the Parties,* 16 Sw. L.J. 1 (1962); Weiss, *Labor Arbitration in the Federal Courts,* 30 Geo. Wash. L. Rev. 285, 293-301 (1961); Van De Water, *Growth of Third Party Power in the Settlement of Industrial Disputes,* 12 Lab. L.J. 1135, 1143-49 (1961).

pointed to the problem.[176] One way to slow down the race to the courts is to have arbitrators put in their awards the facts and conclusions that are needed to help a judge resolve the challenges without reopening of the record if a suit is initiated. Such care will also discourage plaintiffs' lawyers, because their opportunity to win will shrink.

---

[176]*See* comments in preface and detailed discussion, Burger, *Isn't There a Better Way?* (1982 report on the state of the judiciary), 68 A.B.A. J. 274.

CHAPTER XXIII

Fair Representation Obligations

The National Labor Relations Act provides that when a union wins a representation election by a majority of employees, the union wins, as a matter of law, the right to represent not only those employees who voted for the union (the majority), but also those who did not (the minority). Any labor agreement negotiated by a union and a company applies to the minority as well as to the majority. The courts became concerned over possible abuse of the power of the union representatives when they made decisions that affected their representation of the minority group. In 1944, the special "duty of fair representation" applicable to union representation of members came into being.[1]

However, Congress did not vest exclusive representation control over the individual employees, insofar as grievances against the company were concerned, because of a significant proviso in the act which says:

> Representatives designated or selected for the purpose of collective bargaining by the majority of the employees in a unit appropriate for such purposes, shall be the exclusive representatives of all the employees in such unit for the purposes of collective bargaining in respect to rates of pay, wages, hours of employment, or other conditions of employment: *Provided*, That any individual employee or a group of employees shall have the right at any time to present grievances to their employer and to have such grievances adjusted, without the intervention of the bargaining representative, as long as the ad-

---

[1] *Steele v. Louisville & Nashville R.R. Co.*, 323 U.S. 192, 15 LRRM 708 (1944); *see also Wallace Corp. v. NLRB*, 323 U.S. 248, 15 LRRM 697 (1944) and *Ford Motor Co. v. Huffman*, 345 U.S. 330, 31 LRRM 2548 (1953); Railway Labor Act, 45 U.S.C. §§ 151-188 (1976); National Labor Relations Act, 29 U.S.C. §§ 151-169 (1976). *See, e.g.*, Cox, *The Duty of Fair Representation*, 2 VILL. L. REV. 151 (1957); Feller, *A General Theory of the Collective Bargaining Agreement*, 61 CALIF. L. REV. 663 (1973); Lewis, *Fair Representation in Grievance Administration: Vaca v. Sipes*, 1967 SUP. CT. REV. 81; Summers, *Individual Rights in Collective Agreements and Arbitration*, 37 N.Y.U. L. REV. 362 (1962); Note, *Statute of Limitations Governing Fair Representation Action Against Union When Brought With Section 301 Action Against Employer*, 44 GEO. WASH. L. REV. 418 (1976); Comment, *The Duty of Fair Representation: A Theoretical Structure*, 51 TEX. L. REV. 1119 (1973); Comment, *Exhaustion of Grievance Procedures and the Individual Employee*, 51 TEX. L. REV. 1179 (1973).

justment is not inconsistent with the terms of a collective-bargaining contract or agreement then in effect: *Provided further*, That the bargaining representative has been given opportunity to be present at such adjustment.[2]

This clearly reserved for the individual employee the right to have his or her grievances against the company presented in private and adjusted without intervention of the union representative, subject to the right of the union representative to be given the opportunity to be present when a grievance is adjusted.

These two overlapping provisos would conflict considerably if it were not for the fact that the employees, when they approve the labor agreement, accept its terms, and the language in the agreement removes the ambiguity of when and how a grievance is submitted to the company; when and how the grievance is negotiated in a series of grievance meetings; and whether and how unresolved grievances are introduced into the arbitration process designed to resolve the grievance of the employee expeditiously and at a low cost.

By the provisions set out in the labor agreement the union continues to represent all the individual employees insofar as their grievances are concerned, and hence the duty to fairly represent employees with respect to their grievances results from the exclusivity of the union's representation in grievance matters that is established in the labor agreement,[3] not in the statute. The statute does grant to the union exclusive bargaining rights for all employees in the appropriate unit, and once the union secures an agreement, the right to exclusivity in repre-

---

[2]Section 9(a), 29 U.S.C. § 159(a) (1976).

[3]The district court in *Laney v. Ford Motor Co.*, 95 LRRM 2002 (D. Minn. 1977), pointed out that Section 9(a) of the Labor Management Relations Act, 29 U.S.C. § 159(a), does not give an employee a right to be represented by an independent counsel in disciplinary and grievance hearings because "the Collective Bargaining Agreement does not provide for the assistance of counsel at those hearings." *Id.* at 2003. The right of the union to be the exclusive grievance representative for grievants comes out of the labor agreement. The court recorded the argument of the company:

Ford also argues that to require it to deal with independently retained counsel at the procedures would violate the terms of the Collective Bargaining Agreement. The Agreement provides that

the Union shall, in the redress of alleged violations by the Company of this Agreement or any local or other agreement supplementary thereto, be the exclusive representative of the interests of each employee or group of employees covered by this Agreement, and only the Union shall have the right to assert and press against the Company any claim, proceeding or action asserting a violation of this Agreement. Section 1 of Article VII, Grievance Procedure.

Id. To the same effect, see *Seymour v. Olin Corp.* 666 F.2d 202, 109 LRRM 2728 (5th Cir. 1982), where the court explains that the union's exclusivity in the selection of the representative for a grievant comes from the labor agreement rather than from the statute. Because the exclusivity comes from the labor agreement, some corrective suggestions are discussed in the text *infra* associated with notes 86–91.

sentation of the employee during the grievance process comes from the agreement, not from the Act.[4]

A TANDEM: A FAIR REPRESENTATION ACTION AGAINST THE UNION AND THE EMPLOYER LIFTS THE FINALITY PROVISIONS

A fair representation action is a tandem suit by a grievant (1) against the union claiming that the grievant's grievance was not handled properly, and (2) against the company, if the grievant has been discharged, on the ground that it breached the "just cause" commitment in the labor agreement, and that the arbitrator would undoubtedly have reinstated the grievant if the grievance had been processed properly.

Since the suit is against the union, the grievant must employ a private attorney to present the evidence that the union breached its duty to the grievant because the union representative handled the matter negligently or in an arbitrary manner and the employer did so also for different reasons. The jury will determine whether these different breaches are true.

When in a Section 301 suit it is established that the union engaged in a breach, the alleged breach of the employer (the allegation that the discharge was not for "just cause") is not then sent to a new arbitrator or to the one previously appointed because (1) the plaintiff has a constitutional right to have the facts and damages determined by a jury;[5] (2) if the discharge grievance were sent back to an arbitrator he or she could not rectify the losses to the plaintiff due to the union's breach; and (3) the jury can assess not only back pay but also prospective damages instead of reinstatement and money damages, making this route more attractive to the grievant and his or her attorney.

The number of these Section 301 tandem suits is increasing. They are backing up on the trial courts' calendars because it is now much easier for a private attorney to persuade a jury, particularly when the standard for determining a breach dropped from "in bad faith" to "negligence," "perfunctory" or "arbitrary."[6] When the company becomes involved with damages, the back pay portion may have reached a high total

---

[4]Various labor agreements provide different procedures for the resolution of grievances. For example, a grievance can first be reviewed by a "joint arbitration board" and then, if a deadlock occurs, an impartial arbitrator is added as the "tie-breaker"; other labor agreements do not provide for a final resolution, and if the joint arbitration board deadlocks, the grievance has been presented directly to a court to be resolved, using quite normal breach of contract procedures. *Black-Clawson Co. v. Machinists, Lodge 355, District 137*, 313 F.2d 179, 52 LRRM 2038 (2d Cir. 1962); *Smith v. Evening News Ass'n*, 371 U.S. 195, 51 LRRM 2646 (1962).

[5]*See* text *infra* associated with notes 48–54.

[6]*See* discussion under "Shifts From 'Bad Faith' to 'Negligence' Adversely Affect Arbitration" *infra*.

because of the long delay, and then the jury can assess prospective damages causing the damages to inflate. Some company attorneys become quite willing to settle rather than to "battle up to the last bridge." In addition, the longer the battle, the higher the fees due the private attorney.[7]

A basic legal complication from the company's point of view is that the statute of limitations built into the labor agreement does not bar these Section 301 suits. The Supreme Court explained in *Hines v. Anchor Motor Freight, Inc.* [8] that, when a negligent union representative is guilty of a breach of representation, the labor agreement "statute of limitations" is lifted:

> The union's breach of duty relieves the employee of an express or implied requirement that disputes be settled through contractual grievance procedures and if it [the union's breach] seriously undermined the integrity of the arbitral process the union's breach also removes the bar of the finality provisions of the contract.

In this case the Supreme Court explained that the truck drivers, who were the plaintiffs, would be precluded from the relief they actually sought (reinstatement) if relief was barred by the time limits set up in the labor agreement, since in this case there was not, examined by hindsight, "just cause" for the discharge of the plaintiffs.[9] The Court extended its reasoning by explaining "it was Anchor [the Company] that originated the discharges for dishonesty. If those charges are in error, Anchor has surely played its part in precipitating this dispute" and hence the built-in statute of limitations that would otherwise bar suits and the finality rule applicable to arbitration awards against the employer legally are lifted.[10] Justice Stewart did explain in his concurring opinion that an employer who relied in good faith on a favorable arbitration award in a discharge case should not be liable for back pay damages after the date of that award and that the intervening wage loss should fall upon the union.[11] Justice Rehnquist and Chief Justice

---

[7]*Scott v. Teamsters, Local 377*, 548 F.2d 1244, 94 LRRM 2505 (6th Cir. 1977), *cert. denied*, 431 U.S. 968, 95 LRRM 2643 (1977), *on remand*, 96 LRRM 2903 (N.D. Ohio 1977); *Emmanuel v. Omaha Carpenters District Council*, 560 F.2d 382, 92 LRRM 2504 (8th Cir. 1977); *Ruzicka v. General Motors Corp.*, 96 LRRM 2822 (E.D. Mich. 1977).

[8]424 U.S. 554, 567, 91 LRRM 2481, 2486 (1976).

[9]*Id.* at 554, 91 LRRM at 2481.

[10]*Id.* at 571, 91 LRRM at 2487, where the court also said:
In our view, enforcement of the finality provision [in the labor agreement] where the arbitrator has erred is conditioned upon the union's having satisfied its statutory duty fairly to represent the employee in connection with the arbitration proceedings. Wrongfully discharged employees would be left without jobs and without a fair opportunity to secure an adequate remedy.

[11]*Id.* at 573, 91 LRRM at 2488; *see also Zipes v. Trans World Airlines, Inc.*, 455 U.S. 385, 28 FEP Cases 1 (1982), where the Supreme Court granted retroactive seniority to persons even though their claims were time-barred. The union contended that retroactive seniority ad-

Burger dissented, arguing that a company that acts in good faith throughout the grievance-arbitration proceedings should not be subjected to a Section 301 damage suit because of a union's breach.

SHIFTS FROM "BAD FAITH" TO "NEGLIGENCE" ADVERSELY AFFECT ARBITRATION

The standards for a breach of the duty of fair representation began to shift dramatically in 1964. A private attorney had attacked the fairness of the union members of an arbitration board after they agreed that it was quite normal to use the "dovetail" formula to establish the seniority list of the drivers when two trucking companies merged into one. Since the number of drivers needed was smaller after the merger, a few were laid off and those who were, hired a private attorney. He filed a breach of fair representation suit in a Kentucky state court and this court concluded that the union had breached its duty to the laid-off plaintiffs, and approved the jury verdict that the union pay substantial amounts to the laid-off drivers. The union's attorneys appealed the case to the Kentucky Court of Appeals and the decision below was upheld. [12] But after a writ of *certiorari* to the U.S. Supreme Court was accepted, the Court reversed the Kentucky Court of Appeals decision, explaining that the union members of the arbitration board had not acted "capriciously or arbitrarily." [13] Even though the union won, many readers found in this decision a momentous change. The Court, they said, would uphold a breach of the union's duty if it decided, by hindsight, that the union representative had acted "capriciously or arbitrarily" in the grievants' representation.

In *Vaca v. Sipes* [14] the union also won. The U.S. Supreme Court reversed a decision by the Supreme Court of Missouri [15] that the failure to process a discharge grievance constituted a breach of the union's duty to fairly represent the grievant. The grievance had been filed because Grievant Owens had not been recalled at the end of a period of

---

justments contrary to the later agreement should not be awarded over the objection of the union that has not itself been found guilty of discrimination. Justice Powell, joined by Chief Justice Burger and Justice Rehnquist, expressed concern that the Court's decision with respect to retroactive seniority credits is inconsistent with the *bona fide* seniority system rule in Title VII.

[12] *Moore v. Teamsters, Local 89*, 356 S.W.2d 241, 49 LRRM 2677 (Ky. 1952), *rev'd*, 375 U.S. 335, 55 LRRM 2031 (1964).

[13] *Humphrey v. Moore*, 375 U.S. 335, 55 LRRM 2031 (1964). An alternate formula often used to set up the seniority list is referred to as "end tail." Under this formula, the prior seniority list of one group of employees is merely added *after* the prior seniority list of the other group. *Barton Brands, Ltd. v. NLRB*, 529 F.2d 793, 91 LRRM 2241 (7th Cir. 1976).

[14] 386 U.S. 171, 64 LRRM 2369 (1967).

[15] *Sipes v. Vaca*, 397 S.W.2d 658, 61 LRRM 2054 (Mo. 1965), *rev'd*, 386 U.S. 171, 64 LRRM 2369 (1967).

sick leave on the ground that he was not physically able to return to work. The union representative, who had filed the grievance and was processing it up the steps of the grievance procedure, asked Grievant Owens to have the union's doctor evaluate this physical ability to return to work. The union doctor concluded that Owens was *not* yet well enough and, after receiving this medical advice from the union's doctor, the union representative did not appeal the grievance. The representative concluded that the arbitrator certainly would not order reinstatement of Owens when the doctor, selected by the union, would testify that Owens was not physically able to report to work.

Because the union representative did not appeal the grievance to arbitration, Owens hired a private attorney and sued the union for a breach of the duty of fair representation. The jury decided Owens was well enough to return to work and assessed damages against the union for this "breach," and the Supreme Court of Missouri affirmed the verdict. The U.S. Supreme Court, however, accepted the writ of *certiorari* and then reversed, holding that a breach of the duty of fair representation had not been established in spite of the jury's decision. In this U.S. Supreme Court decision Justice White attempted to clarify the standards. He said that a representative "may not *arbitrarily* ignore a meritorious grievance or process the grievance in a *perfunctory* fashion"[16] and that a "breach" can occur when the Union representative's "conduct toward a member . . . is arbitrary, discriminatory, *or* in bad faith."[17] [Emphasis added.] The introduction of the words in the disjuncture seemed to mean to many that, to win, the private attorney clearly did not have to prove that the union representative acted in *bad faith* but only that the representative acted *"arbitrarily or perfunctorily."*[18] [Emphasis added.]

Later it appeared that some of the justices of the Supreme Court were attempting to move the standard back somewhat—toward the "bad faith" standard. Justice Harlan wrote, in *Transit Union v. Lockridge*,[19] that before a union can "breach" its duty, there must be " 'substantial evidence of fraud, deceitful action or dishonest conduct' "[20] on the part of the union representative. Almost immediately the circuit courts followed Justice Harlan's lead and returned to the requirement that there must be evidence of bad faith and hostile intent before a "breach" can be proven.[21]

---

[16]386 U.S. at 190, 64 LRRM at 2377.
[17]*Id.*, 64 LRRM at 2376.
[18]*Id.* at 194–95, 64 LRRM at 2378.
[19]403 U.S. 274, 77 LRRM 2501 (1971).
[20]*Id.* at 1924, 77 LRRM at 2511, quoting *Humphrey v. Moore*, 375 U.S. 335, 348, 55 LRRM 2031 (1964).
[21]*Brock v. Bunton*, 512 F.2d 720, 88 LRRM 3002 (8th Cir. 1975); *Freeman v. Grand*, 493 F.2d 628 (5th Cir. 1974); *Bruen v. Electrical Workers, IUE, Local 492*, 425 F.2d 190, 74 LRRM

Then the swing went the other way. In the Supreme Court decision in *Hines v. Anchor Motor Freight, Inc.* [22] the claim that the union was guilty of a breach was upheld by the Court of Appeals and again by the Supreme Court. In that case, two truck drivers had been discharged by the company after a company investigator found in the motel records that room bills sent in by the drivers and paid by the company were in excess of the actual amounts credited on the motel receipt records. The drivers denied that they had personally pocketed the difference, leaving the motel clerk the only alternative culprit. The drivers asked their union grievance representative to make a careful investigation of the bill-paying procedures at the motel but at the arbitration hearing he presented no new evidence and the discharge of the drivers was sustained.

The discharged drivers then retained a private attorney and by taking depositions of the motel clerk the private lawyer was able to prove that he, the clerk, had pocketed the difference. A rehearing before the arbitration board was requested but was denied; then a combined suit against both the union and the company was commenced. The district court dismissed it; the appellate court agreed but then after a *certiorari* writ was filed the Supreme Court reversed the decisions below. In doing so the Court decided that the labor agreement's time limitation on the grievance review should be lifted because of the breach of fair representation. The court explained that even though there was no evidence that the union representative had acted in *"bad faith"* but only had been *"arbitrary,"* [23] the limitation bar was still removed. [Emphasis added.] When this "swing back" occurred, a new rash of circuit court opinions were released holding that the "breach" occurred when the union grievance representative was found to be "arbitrary" even if the representative was not found to be acting in "bad faith."

Then the Supreme Court reviewed *Electrical Workers, IBEW v. Foust* [24] and dropped the standard farther—from "arbitrary" down to "negligent." A union representative had failed to process a grievance within the time limit set up in the labor agreement; the district judge had allowed the claim of breach of duty to go to the jury and the jury awarded actual damages of $40,000 and punitive damages of $75,000 against the union. The Supreme Court reversed the award of punitive damages but upheld the award of actual damages. One commentator

---

2169 (3d Cir. 1970); *Longshoremen & Warehousemen, Local 13 v. Pacific Maritime Ass'n*, 441 F.2d 1061, 77 LRRM 2160 (9th Cir. 1971), *cert. denied*, 404 U.S. 1016, 79 LRRM 2182 (1972); *Jackson v. Trans World Airlines, Inc.*, 457 F.2d 202, 80 LRRM 2362 (2d Cir. 1972); *Hiatt v. N.Y. Central R.R.*, 444 F.2d, 77 LRRM 2880 (7th Cir. 1971).

[22] 424 U.S. 554, 91 LRRM 2481 (1976).
[23] *Id.* at 571, 91 LRRM at 2487.
[24] 442 U.S. 42, 101 LRRM 2365 (1979).

was impelled to assert that this decision was a "sub silentio" acceptance of the principle that the *perfunctory* or *negligent* processing of a grievance by a union grievance representative constituted a breach by the union of its duty of fair representation because the union had selected a "perfunctory" or "negligent" representative.[25]

In *Ruzicka v. General Motors Corp.*,[26] the Sixth Circuit related the word "arbitrary" to "negligent" when it reversed a district court's dismissal, noting that "arbitrary" conduct can breach the duty without a showing of "bad faith," and that in this case there was "negligent handling," a "clear example of arbitrary and perfunctory handling of a grievance."[27] In *Ruzicka*, the plaintiff had been discharged for drunken and threatening behavior. The private attorney representing Grievant Ruzicka did not challenge the facts leading up to his discharge but argued that discharge was an excessive penalty, inconsistent with previous arbitration decisions, and for this reason the union grievance representative was "negligent" when he failed to appeal on time, despite two extensions granted by the company.

The Seventh Circuit in *Hoffman v. Lanza*[28] "parted company" with the Sixth Circuit in *Ruzicka, supra.* In *Hoffman*, the union representatives "forgot" to file a timely arbitration demand but this forgetfulness was not a breach of the duty of fair representation, said the court, because to establish unfair representation, the union representative must "intentionally cause harm" and there must be "evidence of fraud, deceitful action or dishonest conduct,"[29] a standard not met by the unexplained union inaction.

In contrast in *Dutrisac v. Caterpillar Tractor Co.*,[30] the Northern District Court of California several months earlier found the failure of the union representation to submit a grievance to arbitration within the time limit to be so egregious as to be arbitrary, because only the union representation could file for arbitration and since the loss to the employee was severe, the failure to file amounted to more than "mere" negligence.

The Fourth Circuit has said that when a union representative in

---

[25]*See* Address by Paul H. Tobias in panel discussion titled "The Duty of Fair Representation—Current Dimensions" at 1979 American Bar Association annual meeting, reported in *Current Views on the Duty of Fair Representation*, Labor Relations Yearbook—1979 (Washington: BNA Books, 1980), pp. 58–59. The conclusion goes squarely against the NLRB's conclusion in *Truck Drivers, Local 692 (Great Western Unifreight System)*, 209 NLRB 442, 85 LRRM 1385 (1974). There, too, the union's negligence in processing a grievance within the contractual time limits barred an otherwise meritorious grievance from coming to arbitration.

[26]523 F.2d 306, 90 LRRM 2497, *reh'g denied*, 528 F.2d 912, 91 LRRM 3054 (6th Cir. 1975). *See also Ruggirello v. Ford Motor Co.*, 411 F. Supp. 758 (E.D. Mich. 1976).

[27]*Id.* at 310, 90 LRRM at 2500.

[28]658 F.2d. 519, 108 LRRM 2311 (7th Cir. 1981).

[29]*Id.* at 522-23, 108 LRRM at 2314.

[30]511 F. Supp. 719, 107 LRRM 2195 (N.D. Cal. 1981).

"complete good faith" pursues an *unreasonable* course of action, "he is guilty of a breach";[31] the Ninth Circuit said a union representative does not satisfy the duty standard merely by "refraining from wrongful conduct," when by hindsight the court concluded that the union representative treated a "meritorious claim arbitrarily";[32] the Fifth Circuit said "negligent conduct may be a breach";[33] the Tenth Circuit said that "dilatory forwarding of a grievance claim" is evidence of "arbitrariness and capriciousness" and "processing in a perfunctory manner";[34] the First Circuit said "arbitrary treatment by a union representative is a breach";[35] and the Second Circuit said that the failure to respond within the required time is a "negligent breach."[36]

This review reveals that the courts have lowered the standard for a breach of the duty to fairly represent from "bad faith" to "negligence." The courts then became deeply involved in semantics.[37] Some judges would draw a distinction between "arbitrary" and "imprudence and poor judgment"[38] and some would not, in a weak counteraction against the swing from the "bad faith" standard down to "negligence."

JURIES ARE CHANGING THE ARBITRATION RULES

Juries are composed of a randomly selected group of citizens and they are asked in these Section 301 suits to make findings concerning two

---

[31]*Griffin v. Automobile Workers*, 469 F.2d 181, 183, 81 LRRM 2485, 2486 (4th Cir. 1972).

[32]*Retana v. Apartment, Motel, Hotel & Elevator Operators, Local 14*, 453 F.2d 1018, 79 LRRM 2272 (9th Cir. 1972).

[33]*Connally v. Transcon Lines*, 583 F.2d 199, 99 LRRM 3102 (5th Cir. 1978).

[34]*Foust v. Electrical Workers, IBEW*, 572 F.2d 710, 97 LRRM 3040 (10th Cir. 1978), *aff'd in pertinent part*, 439 U.S. 892, 101 LRRM 2365 (1979).

[35]*De Arroyo v. Sindicato de Trabajadores Packinghouse*, 425 F.2d 281, 74 LRRM 2028 (1st Cir. 1970), *cert. denied*, 400 U.S. 877, 75 LRRM 2455 (1970).

[36]*Holodnak v. Avco Corp.*, 514 F.2d 285, 88 LRRM 2950 (2d Cir. 1975), *cert. denied*, 423 U.S. 892, 90 LRRM 2614 (1975); *see also to the same effect, Schum v. South Buffalo Ry.*, 496 F.2d 328, 86 LRRM 2459 (2d Cir. 1974).

[37]When the Supreme Court imported the word "arbitrary" into the "breach" cases in *Vaca v. Sipes*, 386 U.S. 171, 190, 194-95, 64 LRRM 2369, 2376, 2378 (1967), the private lawyers must have rushed back to read the word "arbitrary" in Black's Law Dictionary. There it means "...without adequate determining principle; not founded in the nature of things; nonrational; not done or acting according to reason or judgment...." *Id.* at 134. The judge in *Electrical Workers, IBEW v. Foust*, 572 F.2d 710, 714, 97 LRRM 3040, 3043 (10th Cir. 1978), seeking for the Supreme Court's standard, undoubtedly also read Black's because he defined "arbitrary" as an "act done without adequate principle or an act not done according to reason and judgment." One should recall the wise counsel when Humpty Dumpty said to Alice, "When *I* use a word ... it means just what I choose it to mean—neither more nor less." (Emphasis in original.) Carroll, Alice in Wonderland and Through the Looking Glass (New York: Grossett & Dunlap, 1946), p. 238.

[38]*Douillette v. Rumsford Press, Inc.*, 95 LRRM 2555 (D. N.H. 1977); *Bantley v. Lucky Stores, Inc.*, 95 LRRM 3232 (N.D. Cal. 1977); *Besedich v. Missile & Space Div. of LTV Aerospace Corp.*, 433 F. Supp. 954, 95 LRRM 2768 (E.D. Mich. 1977); *Hayes v. Kroger Co.*, 92 LRRM 3503 (S.D. Ohio, 1976).

defendants—one a union and one a company—complicated by the fact that before the second defendant (the company) can be found guilty, the first (the union) must be found guilty. In *Barrett v. Safeway Stores*,[39] the jury got mixed up. It found the union was not guilty of a "breach of the duty of fair representation," but that the company was guilty of the breach of the "just cause" provision in the labor agreement even though the discharge case had not gone through arbitration and the time limit had passed. The court held that the time limit rule in the labor agreement could not be lifted unless the union was found guilty of a breach, and the verdict against the company was then set aside. In addition, the court criticized the jury verdict on the ground that it was inconsistent with a provision in the labor agreement that had been applied by the company and the union for over twenty-two years.[40] The court was essentially saying that practice was part of the "law of the shop" used to construe the provisions of the labor agreement. Arbitrators accumulate the meanings on the "law of the shop" over many years. The Supreme Court has pointed out that the "law of the shop" is different from the "law of the courts"[41] and quite obviously juries would find these distinctions difficult.

A good example of the difference between a jury verdict and a "law of the shop" concept occurred in *Lowe v. Pate Stevedoring Co.*,[42] with the jury reinstating John Lowe after he had been discharged for attacking his foreman in anger and knocking him down. Lowe had asked his union representative to file a grievance against Pate Stevedoring Company requesting reinstatement and back pay, but the union representative told him that he would not file one because, when an employee physically attacks his supervisor, no arbitrator would reinstate him, let alone order the employer to pay him back pay.

Lowe then hired a private attorney, who filed a Section 301 complaint with the federal court, claiming that the refusal to file the grievance was a breach of the duty of fair representation and that the "discharge" by the company had not been for "just cause." The jury ordered reinstatement and awarded $25,500 damages to Lowe; the district court judge reversed the jury's verdict on the grounds that a physical attack upon a supervisor in anger is *per se* "just cause" for discharge; but, on appeal, the Fifth Circuit felt compelled to reverse, holding that knifings, shootings, and baseball bat beatings on the Tampa wharves were common

---

[39]538 F.2d 1311, 92 LRRM 3406 (1976).

[40]*Id.* at 1313–14, 92 LRRM at 3408. *See also* similar jury confusions in *Petersen v. Rath Packing Co.*, 461 F.2d 312, 80 LRRM 2833 (8th Cir. 1972); *Steinman v. Spector Freight System, Inc.*, 441 F.2d 599, 77 LRRM 2412 (2d Cir. 1971).

[41]*Steelworkers v. Warrior & Gulf Navigation Co.*, 363 U.S. 574, 580, 46 LRRM 2416, 2418–19 (1960).

[42]*Lowe v. Pate Stevedoring Co.*, 558 F.2d 769, 96 LRRM 2205 (5th Cir. 1977).

enough to permit the jury to find that discharge of Lowe for his attack on his foreman was not for "just cause." Somewhat sarcastically, one judge dissented:

> Today, this Court stamps as legally permissible a criminal assault by a long-shoreman upon his supervisor because knifings, shootings and baseball bat beatings occur with regularity on the Tampa wharves. If the unprovoked, malicious assault of a supervisor is not "just cause" for a management decision to eliminate the attacker from that supervisor's "gang," I missed a turn in the road. If it is not universally recognized as constituting just cause *per se*—it should be! ... Instead [of punishing Lowe for the crime he admits committing,] our judicial system rewards him with $25,500. [43]

Juries second-guess the judgment not only of union representatives but also of arbitrators after the award has been rendered. An example of this is found in *Smith v. Hussmann Refrigerator Co.* [44] During April and May, 1975, a foreman posted "bids" from employees who might desire to be promoted to a vacancy in a "maintenance pipefitter" job, and four out of twenty-five bidders were selected after he (the foreman) carefully reviewed the backgrounds of all the "bidders." Under the labor agreement, it was provided that employees with less length of service could be promoted over those with longer service if they had more "skill and ability."

Four bidders with greater service asked the union representative to file grievances on their behalf because they believed that they should have been selected by the foreman rather than the four he selected. At the hearing, the foreman told the arbitrator why he selected the more junior bidders. He said they had greater "skill and ability" than the grievants. The grievants responded, explaining that their "skills and abilities" were at least comparable to those of the employees selected by the foreman. The union representative argued to the arbitrator that length of service (seniority) is the most equitable standard for making promotions. The arbitrator, in his award, promoted two of the grievants out of the four, requiring two of the previously selected employees to be demoted. The arbitrator disagreed with the foreman. He said that two of the grievants had "skill and abilities" comparable to those of the promoted employees.

The two employees who were *demoted* by the arbitrator then hired a private attorney, who filed a Section 301 suit against the union (claiming negligence by the union representative because he argued too hard for the grievants) and against the company (claiming that the award by the arbitrator was tainted by the union representative's negligence).

---

[43]*Id.* at 773, 96 LRRM at 2208.

[44]619 F.2d 1229, 103 LRRM 2321, 2976 (8th Cir. 1980), *cert. denied*, 449 U.S. 839, 105 LRRM 2657 (1980). *See* a similar factual case in *Washington-Baltimore Newspaper Guild (CWA)*, 239 NLRB 1321, 100 LRRM 1179 (1975).

The trial judge then struck down the jury's verdict reinstating the two selectees and granting $6,500 to one and $2,500 to the other.

The trial judge's decision was appealed to the Eighth Circuit.[45] There the company argued that the jury's determination of damages of $6,500 in favor of one plaintiff and $2,500 for another indicated that the jury was confused and impassioned. However, the appellate court reversed the trial judge and reinstated the jury verdict.[46]

Various trial judges, when suits claiming breach of the duty of fair representation were first being filed, would automatically strike a "jury demand" from the Section 301 complaint usually for four reasons: (1) the suit was based on "equity" instead of "law"—an original distinction between lawsuits handled by judges and those handled by juries; (2) the right of a plaintiff to have a jury involved only lawsuit issues that were part of the "common law"; (3) the presence of two defendants being charged with different types of breaches made determinations for juries too complicated; and (4) legal constructions of provisions in labor agreements were not matters that should be decided by juries.[47]

This normal striking of the jury demand from a Section 301 complaint began to cease after 1973 when a federal district judge in Michigan[48] picked up a Supreme Court ruling and stated that plaintiffs had a constitutional right to have a jury make the various determinations. He explained:

[T]his Court must conclude that plaintiffs' claim for damages because of defendant union's alleged breach of its duty of fair representation is comparable to the words "action of law" which were used prior to the merger of law and equity in the federal courts.

. . . [T]he nature of the remedy . . . also indicates that plaintiffs are entitled to a jury trial. This conclusion is supported by the fact that the Seventh Amendment entitles the parties to a jury trial in an action for damages which resulted from an alleged breach of a legal duty which was owed to a person . . . .

. . .

This Court by using the before mentioned (Ross) test [Ross v. Bernhard, 396 U.S. 531 (1970)] has reached the conclusion that plaintiffs' claim for

[45]619 F.2d at 1246, 103 LRRM at 2333, citing Chicago & Northwestern Railway Co. v. Minnesota Transfer R.R. Co., 371 F.2d 129, 130 (8th Cir. 1967).

[46]619 F.2d at 1246, 103 LRRM at 2333. Cf. Richardson v. Communications Workers, 486 F.2d 801, 806, 84 LRRM 2617 (8th Cir. 1973) and Richardson v. Communications Workers, 443 F.2d 974, 982-85, 77 LRRM 2566 (8th Cir. 1971).

[47]Harrison v. Chrysler Corp., 60 F.R.D. 9, 85 LRRM 2141 (S.D. Ind. 1973); Acheson v. Bottlers, Local Union 896, 17 F.R. Serv.2d 1599, 83 LRRM 2845 (N.D. Cal. 1973); Nedd. v. Thomas, 316 F. Supp. 74, 75 LRRM 2699 (M.D. Pa. 1970); Brady v. Trans World Airlines, Inc., 196 F. Supp. 504, 48 LRRM 2761 (D. Del. 1961), aff'd on other grounds, 401 F.2d 87, 69 LRRM 2048 (3d Cir. 1968), cert. denied, 393 U.S. 1048, 70 LRRM 2249 (1969).

[48]Rowan v. Howard Sober, Inc., 384 F. Supp. 1121, 86 LRRM 2674 (1973).

damages because of the company's alleged breach of the collective bargaining agreement, also entitles them to a jury trial. In support of this conclusion, the court considered the fact that (1) the breach of a collective bargaining agreement in which the employee is seeking damages is merely an action for breach of contract, an action which has been traditionally recognized as a legal action. . . .

. . .

. . . The Court, however, finds that it, without the aid of a jury, must decide whether plaintiffs are entitled to receive any equitable relief. The Court also finds that it will make a determination on the requested equitable relief only after the jury has decided the legal claims. [49]

Later, in 1974, the Supreme Court repeated its prior view that the jury demand cannot properly be stricken from a complaint in *Curtis v. Loether.* [50] In this case the jury demand was made to determine whether there was a breach of fair housing under Section 8 of the Civil Rights Act. [51] Then a Pennsylvania federal court followed this Supreme Court decision, holding that a plaintiff has the right to have a jury to determine facts and set damages in private attorney litigation under statutes that deal with "fair" conduct; [52] then a Northern Indiana federal court followed with one opinion [53] and the Fifth Circuit followed with three. [54] This sequence of opinons "riveted in" the right of the plaintiff to have the jury make the findings in suits charging breach of the duty of fair representation and this, therefore "riveted in" an erratic influence juries have on grievance determination before and after arbitration.

Another very difficult factor that is now interacting between determinations by arbitrators and those by juries is the calculation of damages. After an arbitrator finds a discharge was not for "just cause," the arbitrator will grant back pay and reinstatement. Now juries, on the other hand, will determine that the discharge was not for "just cause" and then award back pay and prospective money damages but not reinstate-

---

[49]*Id.* at 1124–25, 86 LRRM at 2676.

[50]415 U.S. 189 (1974). *See also Pernell v. Southall Realty*, 416 U.S. 363 (1974).

[51]29 U.S.C. § 185 (1964).

[52]*Lucas v. Philo-Ford Corp.*, 380 F. Supp. 139, 87 LRRM 2176 (E.D. Pa. 1974).

[53]*Steele v. Brewery Workers, Local 1162*, 432 F. Supp. 369, 96 LRRM 2935 (N.D. Ind. 1977).

[54]*Minnis v. Automobile Workers*, 531 F.2d 850, 91 LRRM 2081 (5th Cir. 1974); *Cox v. C.H. Masland & Sons, Inc.*, 607 F.2d 138, 102 LRRM 2889 (5th Cir. 1979); *Smith v. Hussman Refrigerator Co.*, 619 F.2d 1229, 103 LRRM 2321, 2976 (8th Cir. 1980). The court in *Smith* said:
[4] First, the union argues that plaintiffs had no right to a jury trial, although it candidly concedes that the law in this circuit is contrary to its position. *Minnis v. International Union, United Automobile, Aerospace and Agricultural Implement Workers of America, UAW*, 531 F.2d 850, 91 LRRM 2081 (8th Cir. 1975), explicitly held that plaintiffs charging a breach of the duty of fair representation are entitled to a jury trial. In view of the union's failure to show any error in the analysis made in *Minnis*, we decline to overrule its holding."
Id. at 1244, 103 LRRM at 2331.

ment. Since these prospective money damages may be substantial, the grievant, and possibly more often the private attorney, will prefer the money over the reinstatement. In *Seymour v. Olin Corp.* [55] the jury ordered the company to pay $139,177.02 *prospective* damages to Seymour. Seymour did not request reinstatement, only back pay, and the jury set up a *prospective* damage for what it had just determined was a wrongful discharge. The Fifth Circuit pointed out that back pay up to date of reinstatement was the remedy provided when the arbitrator finds a discharge was not based on "just cause." But the court approved the prospective money damages set by the jury rather than the normal arbitrator's reinstatement remedy, saying:

> The parties concede that when wrongful discharge suits are submitted to arbitration, the normal remedy is reinstatement with back pay. In § 301 suits, however, it is clear that the federal courts have the power to order either reinstatement or prospective damages. . . .
>
> Olin argues that where a company is found to have wrongfully discharged an employee, the court must award reinstatement unless it would not be feasible for the employer to reinstate the employee. The question of whether prospective damages can be awarded only where the equitable remedy of reinstatement is unavailable has not been squarely addressed in this circuit. A strong argument can be made that reinstatement should be awarded where possible since that is the normal practice in arbitration and since it is often difficult to value future earnings. However, some courts have characterized reinstatement as the more drastic and therefore less favored remedy in § 301 suits. In the instant case, we need not decide this issue. We assume *arguendo* that standard urged by Olin—i.e., that prospective damages may be awarded only if reinstatement is impractical—but even under this standard the district court in the present case did not abuse its discretion in allowing the jury to award prospective damages. [56] [Footnote omitted.]

THE DILEMMA OF UNION
GRIEVANCE REPRESENTATIVES

Previously in this chapter it was pointed out that "negligence" by a union representative in a discharge grievance case permits a Section 301 tandem suit to be started against both the union and the company for different breaches. The use of a jury has added troublesome dilemmas for a union's grievance representative when different members

---

[55] 666 F.2d 202, 109 LRRM 2728 (5th Cir. 1982). *See also Lowe v. Pate Stevedoring Co.*, 558 F.2d 769, 96 LRRM 2205 (5th Cir. 1977); *Scott v. Teamsters, Local 377*, 548 F.2d 1244, 94 LRRM 2505 (6th Cir. 1977); *Emmanuel v. Omaha Carpenters District Council*, 422 F. Supp. 204, 93 LRRM 2929, *aff'd*, 560 F.2d 382, 92 LRRM 2504 (8th Cir. 1977); *Ruzicka v. General Motors Corp.*, 96 LRRM 2822 (E.E. Mich. 1977).

[56] 666 F.2d at 211, 109 LRRM at 2734.

have different interests in a particular grievance case.[57] A jury's findings and the damage determinations it makes are quite strange when judged against labor arbitration practice.[58]

These erratic verdicts of juries, which lack a pattern, make it sometimes difficult for representatives to determine whether a grievance should be "closed out" before arbitration or not, even after the representatives have carefully investigated the facts and even though the union representative believes the grievance claim against the employer is not valid, because of the risk of a suit for "breach of the duty to fairly represent." Pursuing claims that otherwise would be dropped will breed misunderstandings and frictions between the company and union officials, impose upon busy arbitrators, and place unnecessary high costs upon the union. Some suggestions that have been distilled from various "breach of the duty to fairly represent" decisions may be helpful to reduce and evaluate the risks.

Breach Risks Before a Grievance Reaches the Arbitration Hearing

(a) *Once a grievance against the employer is claimed by a member-employee, the representative should write it up promptly and carefully.* Then the form on which the grievance is described should be signed by the grievant[59] to reduce disagreements with the union grievance representative that may occur if the grievance is maintained on a verbal basis. This suggestion would be contrary to the views of some that grievances should be handled orally and informally for as long as possible to avoid the development of rigidity of position.

(b) *A written grievance need not be presented for every complaint* if (1) similar grievances have been denied by arbitrators; (2) no provision in the labor agreement covers the complaint; (3) a company practice considered by the grievant to be the basis of the complaint is not clear or uniform; and (4) the advice to the employee that the complaint will not

---

[57]The negligence of a union representative in one case was established because the jury found one or a combination of the following actions:

(1) too great an advocacy of use of the length-of-service policy in promotions;
(2) failing to notify the selectees to attend the arbitration hearing to contest the position of the grievants;
(3) resubmitting the arbitrator's award by joint agreement with the company representative after the parties had agreed to changes in the labor agreement; or
(4) failing to accept grievances on behalf of the selectees, causing them not to become parties in the arbitration prior to joint resubmission of the award to the arbitrator.

Smith v. Hussmann Refrigerator Co., 619 F.2d 1229, 103 LRRM 2321 (8th Cir. 1980). *See* discussion of this case in text associated with notes 44–46 *supra*.

[58]*Lowe v. Pate Stevedoring Co.*, 558 F.2d 769, 773, 96 LRRM 2205, 2208 (5th Cir. 1977).

[59]*Retana v. Apartment, Motel, Hotel & Elevator Operators, Local 14*, 453 F.2d 1018, 79 LRRM 2272 (9th Cir. 1972). *See also* the discussion concerning the reduction of risks by improving grievance forms in text associated with notes 96–114 *infra*.

be filed is given promptly and clearly so he or she can seek advice from a private attorney or attorneys before any time limit runs out.[60]

(c) *A refusal to allow a private attorney to act as the representative is not itself a "breach."* If a private attorney is given permission to participate as a collaborating representative to reduce the risk, the extent of such participation should be set forth in writing to avoid misunderstanding.[61]

(d) The failure to have the union representative defend a discharged nonmember, who ultimately "lost" the grievance, because he had retained a private attorney to represent him is a failure to fairly represent. The Court upheld a jury award of $35,000, the actual and reasonable fees paid the private attorney.[62]

(e) *A non-filing of a grievance is not a breach if the employee-member delays notifying the representative before the time limit runs.* For example, in one case a member delayed for forth-three days after his discharge before notifying the representative when the labor agreement time limit on the filing of a grievance on a discharge was seventy-two hours.[63]

(f) *Withdrawal or non-appeal of a grievance must be with the grievant's knowledge and the reasons for this should be communicated.* Once the union commences to represent a grievant, the union must act as a strong advocate[64] and any "withdrawal" or "non-appeal" should be supported with clear reasons set forth by the union grievant representative in writing.[65]

---

[60]*Robesky v. Quantas Empire Airways*, 573 F.2d 1082, 98 LRRM 2090 (9th Cir. 1978); *Lewis v. Greyhound Lines-East*, 555 F.2d 1053, 95 LRRM 2449 (D. D.C. 1977); *cert. denied*, 434 U.S. 997, 96 LRRM 3320 (1977); *Beriault v. Longshoremen & Warehousemen, Local 40*, 501 F.2d 258, 87 LRRM 2070 (9th Cir. 1974); *Retana v. Apartment, Motel, Hotel & Elevator Operators, Local 14*, 453 F.2d 1018, 79 LRRM 2272 (9th Cir. 1972). Under NLRB law, the union also has a right to disclaim further representation if the members' rights are properly protected. *See, e.g., Steinmetz Electrical Contractors Ass'n*, 234 NLRB 633, 97 LRRM 1263 (1978); *Seymour v. Olin Corp.*, 109 LRRM 2728 (5th Cir. 1982).

[61]*Laney v. Ford Motor Co.*, 95 LRRM 2002 (D.C. Minn. 1977); *Seymour v. Olin Corp.*, 109 LRRM 2728 (5th Cir. 1982).

[62]*Del Casal v. Eastern Airlines, Inc.*, 634 F.2d 295, 106 LRRM 2276 (5th Cir. 1981), *cert. denied*, 454 U.S. 892, 108 LRRM 2656 (1981).

[63]*Franklin v. Crosby Typesetting Co.*, 568 F.2d 1098, 97 LRRM 3009 (5th Cir. 1978), *cert. denied*, 439 U.S. 847, 99 LRRM 2601 (1978). *See Beverly Manor Convalescent Center, et al.*, 229 NLRB 692, 95 LRRM 1156 (1977); *P & L Cedar Products*, 224 NLRB 244, 93 LRRM 1341 (1976); *Lewis v. Greyhound Lines-East*, 555 F.2d 1053, 95 LRRM 2449 (D.C. Cir. 1977), *cert. denied*, 439 U.S. 847, 96 LRRM 3320 (1977).

[64]*Associated Transport, Inc.*, 209 NLRB 292, 86 LRRM 1119, *aff'd sub nom. Kesner v. NLRB*, 532 F.2d 1169, 92 LRRM 2137 (7th Cir. 1976), *cert. denied*, 429 U.S. 983, 93 LRRM 2843 (1976).

[65]*Curth v. Faraday, Inc.*, 401 F. Supp. 678, 90 LRRM 2735 (E.D. Mich. 1975). "[T]he union does not breach its duty of fair representation by deciding on the basis of a rational and objective criteria" to not arbitrate a grievance. *Id.* at 681, 90 LRRM at 2737. *See also Robbins v. George W. Prescott Publishing Co., Inc.*, 614 F.2d 3 (1st Cir. 1980); *Kleban v. Hygrade Food Products Corp.*, 102 LRRM 2773 (E.D. Mich. 1979); *Besedich v. LTV Aerospace Corp., Missile & Space*

(f) *A withdrawal of a grievance when it can be shown that the grievant has not cooperated is not a breach.*[66] The evidence of non-cooperation should be recorded by the union grievance representative in writing.

(g) *Any language barrier between the union representative and a member should be removed by use of a translator to avoid misunderstandings.* If the member does not speak or understand English, a translator, who may be another member, should become involved to explain to the grievant: (1) the meaning of a written grievance; (2) that a grievance will not be filed unless the asserted facts, if true, would be a violation of the labor agreement; and (3) the meaning of the grievance as written in English before the member signs it.[67]

(h) *Delays in grievance processing must be avoided.* Courts have said that delay in handling grievances through the processing steps, even where time limits are not provided, is evidence of "perfunctory" handling.[68] Since some labor agreement grievance procedures do not have time limits on appeals into arbitration, many grievances cluster at the "last step." If a member believes that his grievance has merit and could become lost or "traded out" in the resolution of such a cluster of grievances, the risk of a Section 301 suit increases. Therefore grievances appealed should be pushed into arbitration to avoid "clusters."

(j) *The investigating by a representative should not be superficial.* An allegation of "inadequate investigation" standing alone does not state a cause of action for a suit for breach of the duty of fair representation.[69] However, if the grievant's version of what occurred differs mate-

---

Division, 433 F. Supp. 954, 957–59, 95 LRRM 2768 (E.D. Mich. 1977); *Ludovico La China v. Dana Corp., Parish Frame Division*, 433 F. Supp. 430 (E.D. Pa. 1977); *Turner v. Air Transport Dispatchers Ass'n*, 468 F.2d 297, 81 LRRM 2471 (5th Cir. 1972); *Encina v. Tony Lama Co.*, 316 F. Supp. 239, 75 LRRM 2012 (W.D. Tex. 1970), *aff'd per curiam*, 448 F.2d 1264, 78 LRRM 2382 (5th Cir. 1971); *Bazarte v. United Transportation Union*, 429 F.2d 868, 75 LRRM 2017 (3d Cir. 1970).

[66]*In Hicks v. J. H. Routh Packing Co.*, 95 LRRM 2814 (N.D. Ohio 1977), plaintiff, returning from a medical leave of absence, refused to provide his medical records for review by the company's representative. Although he did submit to a physical examination by the company's doctor, plaintiff refused to produce an "able to work" slip from his own treating physician. The court held that plaintiff's refusal to furnish his medical records justified the union representative's withdrawal of his grievance. *See also Williams v. Dana Corp.*, 86 LRRM 2371 (E.D. Mich. 1973).

[67]*Retana v. Apartment, Motel, Hotel & Elevator Operators, Local 14*, 453 F.2d 1018, 79 LRRM 2272 (9th Cir. 1972).

[68]*Robesky v. Quantas Empire Airways*, 573 F.2d 1082, 98 LRRM 2090 (9th Cir. 1978); *De Arroya v. Trabajadores Packinghouse*, 425 F.2d 281, 74 LRRM 2028 (1st Cir. 1970); *Griffin v. Automobile Workers*, 469 F.2d 181 (4th Cir. 1972); *Archie v. Teamsters*, 585 F.2d 210, 99 LRRM 2586 (7th Cir. 1978); *Ruzicka v. General Motors Corp.*, 523 F.2d 306, 90 LRRM 2497 (6th Cir. 1975); *Foust v. Electrical Workers, IBEW*, 572 F.2d 710, 97 LRRM 3040 (10th Cir. 1978), *aff'd*, 439 U.S. 892, 101 LRRM 2365 (1979).

[69]*Hughes v. Teamsters, Local 683*, 554 F.2d 365, 95 LRRM 2652 (9th Cir. 1977); *Hershman v. Sierra Pacific Power Co.*, 434 F. Supp. 46, 95 LRRM 3294 (D. Nev. 1977); *Patterson v. Bialystoker & Bikur Cholim*, 95 LRRM 3115 (S.D. N.Y. 1977); *Barhitte v. Kroger Co.*, 99 LRRM 2663 (W.D. Mich. 1978).

rially from the employer's response, the employer's version should be thoroughly investigated before the grievance is "closed out" or "not appealed" within the time limit.[70]

(k) *A withdrawal of a grievance by the representative in return for a negotiated compromise settlement is not a breach* if the grievant is advised of the settlement promptly and the reasons are explained.[71]

(l) *The failure of a union representative to file an appeal of an award to the court is not a breach.* The union represented the grievant at the arbitration hearing but the grievance was not upheld.[72]

(m) *A deviation from the grievance processing procedures need not be a breach* if the grievant is informed promptly and the reasons for a deviation explained.[73]

(n) *The failure of the representative to participate in selection of an arbitrator within the necessary time limits creates a substantial risk of a breach.* A court said that the failure to select an arbitrator within the time limit was a union strategy to dispose of grievances over the discharge of employees who had engaged in an improper strike and was an "arguable flaw" in the fairness of the representation but, under the particular circumstances, not sufficient "breach" to have financial liability imposed on the union.[74]

Breach Risks After the Grievance Enters the Arbitration Hearing

Once a case has been processed to arbitration, the inquiry into any breach of the union's duty to represent fairly focuses on the adequacy of the union representative as an advocate supporting the grievance at the hearing. In this area the courts have had difficulty determining the precise level of professionalism that is required; at one extreme, courts have not attempted to second guess trial tactics;[75] at the other, courts

---

[70]*Hines v. Anchor Motor Freight, Inc.*, 424 U.S. 554, 91 LRRM 2481 (1976).

[71]*Robesky v. Quantas Empire Airways, Ltd.*, 573 F.2d 1082, 98 LRRM 2090 (9th Cir. 1978). Unions are not precluded from withdrawing a grievance simply because a grievant rejects a negotiated settlement. *See Douillette v. Rumsford Press*, 95 LRRM 2555 (D. N.H. 1977); *Simberlund v. Long Island R.R. Co.*, 421 F.2d 1219, 73 LRRM 2451 (2d Cir. 1970); *Longshoremen & Warehousemen, Local 13 v. Pacific Maritime Ass'n*, 441 F.2d 1061, 77 LRRM 2160 (9th Cir. 1971), *cert. denied*, 404 U.S. 1016, 79 LRRM 2182 (1972); *Miller v. Greyhound Lines, Inc.*, 95 LRRM 2871, 2873-74 (E.D. Pa. 1977); *Besedich v. LTV Aerospace Corp., Missile & Space Division*, 433 F. Supp. 954, 95 LRRM 2768 (E.D. Mich. 1977); *Atwood v. Pacific Maritime Ass'n*, 100 LRRM 2614 (D. Ore. 1979); *Johnson v. Teamsters, Local Union 89*, 488 F.2d 250, 84 LRRM 2961 (6th Cir. 1973); *Atwood v. PMA*, 100 LRRM 2614 (D. Ore. 1979).

[72]*Sear v. Cadillac Automobile*, 654 F.2d 4, 107 LRRM 3218 (1st Cir. 1981).

[73]*See Marietta v. Cities Service Oil Co.*, 414 F. Supp. 1029, 92 LRRM 2867 (D. N.J. 1976).

[74]*Walker v. Steelworkers, Local 7857*, 98 LRRM 2463 (E.D. Ky. 1978).

[75]*See, e.g., Ness v. Safeway Stores, Inc.*, 598 F.2d 558, 101 LRRM 2621 (9th Cir. 1979); *Hardee v. N. C. Allstate Services, Inc.*, 537 F.2d 1255, 92 LRRM 3342 (4th Cir. 1976); *Bentley v. Lucky Stores, Inc.*, 95 LRRM 3232 (N.D. Cal. 1977); *Martin v. Terminal Transport Co.*, 90 LRRM 3188 (M.D. Tenn. 1975); *Bell v. Mercury Freight Lines, Inc.*, 388 F. Supp. 1, 88 LRRM 3373 (S.D. Tex. 1975).

have inquired into them with vigor and consider inept preparation a "breach."[76] Some suggestions that have been distilled from cases wherein the "breaches" arise during the arbitration process are:

(a) *The representative should not fail to give a written notice of the date and location of the hearing to the grievant.* The grievant should always be invited to be present at the hearing and should be given the right to present his or her own comments so as to foreclose after-the-fact claims that the representative did not present the grievance claim completely.

(b) *The representative should obtain the names of all possible rebuttal witnesses and interview them.* A failure to interview individuals who might become rebuttal witnesses does not constitute a breach *per se*,[77] but such a failure sets up a substantial risk. In addition, selected witnesses should receive written notices of the date and location of the hearing and the company should be advised of this in advance so the excuses from work will be provided and replacements can be scheduled.

(c) *The use of a lawyer at the hearing does not insulate the union from the risk.* One court said that no lawyer can merely "step in" and properly represent an employee in view of the fact that labor arbitrations have become so complicated. Any lawyer who becomes a representative must understand the related labor agreement provisions, their negotiation background, and the related prior arbitration decisions, and obtain information from the grievant and other sources, through means including the discovery requests to obtain information from the company at a reasonable date before the hearing.[78]

(d) *Not using a lawyer as the representative is not a breach.* One court said an arbitration hearing is not a court of law and "neither lawyers nor strict adherence to judicial rules of evidence are necessary."[79]

(e) *A representative should refrain from offensive or irrelevant criticisms of the grievant and obtain from him or her compliments if possible.* Evidence of comments to the grievant about his or her political and

---

[76]*See, e.g., Allsbrook v. Consolidated Freightways*, 96 LRRM 2628 (E.D. Pa. 1977); *Marietta v. Cities Service Oil Co.*, 414 F. Supp. 1029, 92 LRRM 2867 (D. N.J. 1976); *Holodnak v. Avco Corp.*, 381 F. Supp. 191, 87 LRRM 2337, *modified on other grounds*, 514 F.2d 285, 88 LRRM 2950 (2d Cir. 1975), *cert. denied*, 423 U.S. 892, 90 LRRM 2614 (1975).

[77]*Hardee v. N.C. Allstate Services, Inc.*, 537 F.2d 1255, 92 LRRM 3342 (4th Cir. 1976); *Minnis v. Automobile Workers*, 531 F.2d 850, 91 LRRM 2081 (8th Cir. 1975); *Thompson v. Machinists*, 258 F. Supp. 235 (E.D. Va. 1966); *Mangiaguerra v. D&L Transport, Inc.*, 410 F. Supp. 1022, 92 LRRM 2426 (N.D. Ill. 1976); *Marietta v. Cities Service Oil Co.*, 414 F. Supp. 1029, 1039, 92 LRRM 2867 (D. N.J. 1976).

[78]*Holodnak v. Avco Corp.*, 381 F. Supp. 191, 195-96, 200, 87 LRRM 2337, 2341, 2346 (D. Conn. 1974), *modified on other grounds*, 514 F.2d 285, 88 LRRM 2950 (2d Cir. 1975), *cert. denied*, 423 U.S. 892, 90 LRRM 2614 (1975).

[79]*Walden v. Teamsters, Local 71*, 468 F.2d 196, 197, 81 LRRM 2608, 2609 (4th Cir. 1972).

social views have supported the finding of a breach of duty to fairly represent.[80] To the contrary, when a grievant said on the record that he had received good representation, this is evidence that no breach occurred.[81]

(f) *A representative's failure to object to the introduction of evidence is not a breach.*[82]

EXHAUSTING INTRA-UNION REMEDIES

The union constitution and local by-laws typically include the requirement that an employee, before resorting to judicial remedies, appeal through internal channels the union's alleged failure to properly represent him or her. Both employers and unions argue that such an exhaustion requirement would promote the goals of national labor policy by encouraging private resolution of disputes arising from labor agreements.

When a Section 301 breach of fair representation complaint is filed (a tandem suit against the company and the union), the company defense attorneys will inspect the complaint and, unless it alleges that the intra-union remedy procedure available to the grievant had been exhausted, a motion to dismiss would be filed by both union and company attorneys in some courts, by the union attorney unilaterally in others,[83] and by the company attorney unilaterally in others.[84] However, the fil-

---

[80]381 F. Supp. at 196, 197, 200, 87 LRRM 2337.

[81]*Hart v. National Homes Corp.*, 668 F.2d 79, 109 LRRM 2938 (5th Cir. 1982).

[82]*Walden v. Teamsters, Local 71*, 468 F.2d 196 (4th Cir. 1972); *Bantley v. Lucky Stores, Inc.*, 95 LRRM 3232, 3235 (N.D. Cal. 1977).

[83]*Geddes v. Chrysler Corp.*, 608 F.2d 261, 102 LRRM 2756 (6th Cir. 1979); *Clayton v. ITT Gilfilian*, 623 F.2d 563 (9th Cir. 1979); *Miller v. Local 50*, 468 F. Supp. 193, 104 LRRM 2118 (D. Neb. 1978); *Baldini v. Automobile Workers, Local 1095*, 581 F. 2d 145, 99 LRRM 2535 (7th Cir. 1978); *Fizer v. Safeway Stores*, 586 F.2d 182, 99 LRRM 3116 (10th Cir. 1978); *Manica v. Chrysler Corp.*, 97 LRRM 2679 (E.D. Mich. 1978); *Winter v. Teamsters, Local 639*, 569 F.2d 146, 97 LRRM 2372 (D.C. Cir. 1977); *Orphan v. Furnco Construction Corp.*, 466 F.2d 795, 81 LRRM 2058 (7th Cir. 1972); *Petersen v. Rath Packing Co.*, 461 F.2d 312, 80 LRRM 2833 (8th Cir. 1972); *Retana v. Apartment, Motel, Hotel & Elevator Operators, Local 14*, 453 F.2d 1018, 79 LRRM 2272 (9th Cir. (1972).

[84]*Gerb v. Boeing Co.*, 102 LRRM 2854 (E.D. Pa. 1979); *Dezura v. Firestone Tire & Rubber Co.*, 470 F. Supp. 121, 101 LRRM 2849 (E.D. Pa. 1979), *aff'd*, 612 F.2d 571 (3d Cir. 1979); *Kobielnik v. Teamsters*, 470 F. Supp. 125, 101 LRRM 2541 (E.D. Pa. 1979); *Neiger v. Sheet Metal Workers*, 470 F. Supp. 622, 101 LRRM 2713 (W.D. Mo. 1979); *Johnson v. Wilson Foods*, 102 LRRM 2149 (D. Kan. 1978); *Ditzler v. Machinists, Local Lodge 1984*, 453 F. Supp. 50, 98 LRRM 3018 (E.D. Pa. 1978); *Niepert v. Arthur G. McKee & Co.*, 448 F. Supp. 206, 98 LRRM 2152 (E.D. Pa. 1978); *Hedge v. Deere*, 99 LRRM 3401 (S.D. Ill. 1978); *Pullen v. General Motors Corp.*, 444 F. Supp. 87, 97 LRRM 2757 (E.D. Mo. 1978); *Pawlak v. Teamsters, Local 764*, 444 F. Supp. 807, 95 LRRM 2263 (M.D. Pa. 1977), *aff'd*, 571 F.2d 572, 98 LRRM 2438 (3d Cir. 1978); *Ratleff v. Ford Motor Co.*, 98 LRRM 2699 (E.D. Mich. 1978); *Coffey v. Teleprompter, Inc.*, 95 LRRM 2561 (N.D. Ala. 1977); *Adams v. Automobile Workers, Local 1193*, 96 LRRM 2867 (M.D. Pa. 1977); *Bradley v. Ford Motor Co.*, 417 F. Supp. 23 (N.D. Ill. 1975); *Fleming v. Chrysler Corp.*, 416 F. Supp. 1258, 98 LRRM 2967 (E.D. Mich. 1975), *aff'd*,

ing of such a motion does not mean dismissal. Out of concern for the grievant, the Supreme Court in *Clayton v. Automobile Workers, etc.*[85] set up three tests; if the internal channel procedure was inconsistent with any of them, the Section 301 fair representation suit would not be dismissed, so the suit in court could proceed.

Both the union and employer raised as a defense the plaintiff's failure to exhaust internal union appeals procedures contained in the union's constitution and by-laws. Under these procedures, union members are required to exhaust internal remedies before seeking redress from a "civil court or governmental agency." Under *Clayton*, the three relevant factors to be considered by lower courts in exercising this discretion in accepting or rejecting failure to exhaust internal procedures as a valid defense are

> first, whether union officials are so hostile to the employee that he could not hope to obtain a fair hearing on this claim; second, whether the internal union appeals procedures would be inadequate either to reactivate the employee's grievance or to award him the full relief he seeks under Section 301; third, whether exhaustion of internal procedures would unreasonably delay the employee's opportunity to obtain a judicial hearing on the merits of his claim.[86]

If any one of these factors is found to exist, failure to exhaust may be excused, said the court.

Once the time limits have run at any step in the grievance procedure, the second test can not be satisfied by the union—*i.e.*, ability to reactivate the employee's grievance. It is only the employer who can waive the time limit bar to allow the grievance to be reactivated by the union representative. The grievant-plaintiff in *Clayton* had been discharged for violating a plant rule promulgated by the employer. The union filed a grievance protesting the discharge and pursued the grievance through the third step of the procedure; a timely request for arbitration was made, but the union subsequently withdrew the grievance and did not notify the grievant of the withdrawal until after the contractual time

---

575 F.2d 1187, 98 LRRM 2973 (6th Cir. 1978); *Aldridge v. Ludwig-Honold Mfg.*, 385 F. Supp. 695, 87 LRRM 3048 (E.D. Pa. 1974), *aff'd*, 517 F.2d 1397 (3d Cir. 1975), *cert. denied*, 423 U.S. 937, 96 LRRM 2748 (1975); *McCloskey v. General Motors Corp.*, 88 LRRM 2414 (N.D. Ohio 1974); *Brookins v. Chrysler Corp.*, 381 F. Supp. 563, 87 LRRM 3024 (E.D. Mich. 1974); *Davis v. Laborers, Local 242*, 84 LRRM 2544 (D. Wash. 1973); *Imbrunnone v. Chrysler Corp.*, 336 F. Supp. 1223, 77 LRRM 2690 (E.D. Mich. 1971); *Harrington v. Chrysler Corp.*, 303 F. Supp. 495, 72 LRRM 2248 (E.D. Mich. 1969); *see also Harrison v. Chrysler Corp.*, 558 F.2d 1273, 95 LRRM 2953 (7th Cir. 1977); *Orphan v. Furnco Construction Co.*, 466 F.2d 795, 81 LRRM 2058 (7th Cir. 1972); *Morin v. Buick Motor Division*, 91 LRRM 2578 (E.D. Mich. 1976); *Generales v. Hotel Employees, Local 25*, 92 LRRM 3668 (D. D.C. 1975); *Willetts v. Ford Motor Co.*, 93 LRRM 2832 (E.D. Mich. 1976); *Frank v. Volgswagenwerk A.G. of West Germany*, 522 F.2d 321, 327–28 (3d Cir. 1975).

[85] 451 U.S. 679, 107 LRRM 2385 (1981).

[86] *Id.* at 689, 107 LRRM at 2389.

limits for requesting arbitration had expired. The grievant became the plaintiff and filed suit under Section 301, alleging that (1) the employer had breached the labor agreement by discharging him without just cause and (2) the union had breached its duty of fair representation by arbitrarily refusing to pursue his grievance.

Clayton undermines completely an employer's ability, *albeit* right, to rely on collectively bargained contractual time limits for processing grievances and demands for arbitration. Employers are faced with a Hobson's choice:[87] they may either waive contractual time limitations and start up an arbitration that had been closed, and remove for all time the practical termination effect of the time limits, or they may enforce the time limitations and face the grim prospect of joining the union as a defendant in a lengthy, expensive Section 301 duty of fair representation suit.

Anderson v. Field Enterprises, Inc.[88] is the first case to apply the *Clayton* rationale. The plaintiff argued that the presence of two of the three *Clayton* factors, union hostility and insufficiency of union remedies, excused his failure to exhaust internal union procedures. The court dismissed the suit because Anderson "made no attempt to exhaust his internal Union remedies and the evidence of hostility or futility submitted by plaintiff is far from the clear, specific and convincing showing necessary to excuse exhaustion."[89]

THE UAW PUBLIC REVIEW BOARD

The United Automobile Workers Union set up a UAW Public Review Board consisting of highly experienced arbitrators to review "breach of duty to fairly represent" suits filed against the union. If the Review Board then concludes that there is evidence of some negligence and that the award could be upset and the plaintiff could possibly obtain financial relief from a jury, the Review Board may offer a financial payment in return for the withdrawal of the case so the claim of breach will not go to the jury. In *Pfeiffer v. United Automobile Workers, Local 556*,[90] the UAW Public Review Board explained that it would apply very rigid standards to determine if, in its judgment, the union

---

[87]The application of Hobson's choice to the Supreme Court tests comes from Ferguson and Desruisseaux, *The Duty of Fair Representation: Exhaustion of Internal Union Remedies*, EMPLOYEE RELATIONS L.J., Vol. 7, No. 4 (1982), p. 610. Arbitrator W. Gould commented:
> [S]hould employers feel compelled to adopt this course of action and permit waiver of contractual time limits, the enforcement of contractual time limitations in this context "would soon become the exception rather than the rule."

Address at meeting of ABA Section of Labor and Employment Law, reported in "News and Background Information," 107 LRR 358 (1981).

[88]No. 80-C-4072 (N.D. Ill. July 17, 1981), slip opinion by Judge George N. Leighton.

[89]*Id.*

[90]Case No. 192 (Decision of UAW Public Review Board, October 18, 1968), reported in 216 DLR D-1 (November 4, 1968).

breached its duty to represent fairly. In *Pfeiffer*, the union declined to take the grievant's case to arbitration because a union attorney predicted the chance of winning was only fifty-fifty. The Review Board offered to award the grievant several thousand dollars in lost wages.

REDUCING RISKS BY USING REVISED GRIEVANCE FORMS AND KEEPING RECORDS MUTUALLY

A suggestion that will generate considerable controversy from both union and company representatives is that the union's exclusive right to select the representative who will represent a grievant during the grievance procedure up through arbitration be removed and an option set up in the grievance procedure in the labor agreement so the grievant can either (1) affirm the union's selection as his or her selection or (2) select a private attorney who will then be privileged to collaborate with the union's selected representative.

If the grievant *does not have this option,* obviously the union has *complete* authority over the selection of the grievant's representative. It is because of this fact that the *special* duty of careful handling of the grievant's case arises. If the union has complete authority over the selection of the representative and that representative turns out, by hindsight, to be negligent, and the grievant, without this negligence, might have won but did not, the union has "breached" this special duty. If there is *any* evidentiary basis for the claim of negligence, the judge will ask the jury to make the determination (1) as to whether there was a breach and (2) as to the damages to be paid the grievant.

On the other hand, if the grievant *had the option* to choose a personal attorney to *collaborate* with the union representative, possibly to reinforce his chances of winning, it cannot be stated in the Section 301 complaint that the union had the *exclusive* right to select the grievant's representative which is a necessary fact to set up the special duty.[91] If the grievant *did exercise* the option and had a personal attorney acting with the union representative as a collaborating attorney and the grievance then was not sustained and, by hindsight, the grievant claims that the two representatives were jointly "negligent" or "incompetent," at least one of them was selected by the grievant and he or she must accept the blame.

The theory that the union becomes liable to the grievant when it selects a representative who turns out to be "negligent" or "incompetent" is close to the *respondeat superior* responsibility obligation that places the damages on the trucking company, for example, when a truck driver becomes involved in an accident due to his or her negligence. This shift of liability to the trucking company is because it

---

[91] In the first section of this chapter, it was explained that the exclusivity of the union in selection of the grievant's representative is found in the labor agreement, not in the law.

breached its duty to select and hire careful drivers, because the trucking company had exclusive control over the selection process.

That exclusive selection is a foundation for the *respondeat superior* liability is clearly expressed in *Corpus Juris Secundum*:

> In order that the relation of master and servant may exist for the purpose of fixing liability under the doctrine of *respondeat superior*, the alleged master must have the right to select, direct, control, and discharge the alleged servant.[92]

Once the grievant is, or has the option to become, involved in the selection of his or her representative, the risk of a union breaching its special duty to the grievant to select "non-negligent" representation because of its exclusivity in the selection process would seem to disappear. Any negligence that might have occurred can then be traced in *two* directions, and one is toward the grievant.

In normal litigation, if the plaintiff does not win and, by hindsight, it is clear that the loss was due to the negligence of the plaintiff's lawyer, the plaintiff has no right to sue the defendant again under the "no double jeopardy" rule. This rule should protect an employer defendant if the grievant *selects* a negligent advocate and for this reason does not win his or her grievance. The application of this rule would be consistent with the national policy that encourages prompt and final grievance resolution and discourages long, drawn out, expensive grievance litigation.[93] The Supreme Court lifted the labor agreement "statute of limitations" that protects the employer and is consistent with prompt and final resolution only because in a situation where a grievant loses his or her grievance when there is a negligent union representative and the union has exclusivity over the selection, the grievant has no ability to become involved in the selection and, hence, no way to protect his or her interests. However, if a grievant has a way to protect himself or herself by becoming involved in the selection, the national labor policy of desiring prompt and final resolution of labor grievance disputes should be strong enough to *not* lift the time limitation rule built into the labor agreement when the representative selected by the grievant is involved with the negligence.

The Fifth Circuit strongly suggests that maintaining exclusivity in the selection of the grievance representative, particularly where the grievant has been discharged for reasons that have criminal overtones, could be a questionable practice. The court said:

---

[92]C.J.S. *Master and Servant* § 563.

[93]*In McQuay v. Bethlehem Steel Corp.*, 109 LRRM 2159 (D. Md. 1981), the statute of limitations that was selected in unfair representation suits was the 30-day period used for vacating arbitration awards rather than the 6-year breach of contract limitation because of the federal policy of "rapid disposition of labor law disputes." *But see* remand from the U.S. Supreme Court to the New York Appellate Court in *United Parcel Service, Inc. v. Mitchell*, 451 U.S. 56, 107 LRRM 2001 (1981).

The exclusive right to represent employees in the grievance process allows the Union to limit the participation of privately retained counsel in grievance proceedings. However, we need not decide the outer limits on the Union's ability to insulate the grievance process from outside counsel, for whatever powers are conferred upon the Union by statute or the collective bargaining agreement, the Union has no permissible interest in prohibiting employees from retaining private counsel merely for the purpose of consultation.[94] [Footnote omitted.]

In an accompanying footnote the court stated:

Delimiting the full extent of this power of the Union would require answering such questions as whether the Union may prohibit the mere presence of private counsel at grievance proceedings or meetings, even when the attorney takes no active role. This issue is, of course, further complicated when there is a potential for criminal proceedings arising out of the incident that gives rise to the grievance, as in this case. In most instances, a union's power in this regard can only be determined by an analysis of the collective bargaining agreement and the particular facts presented by the individual case. We leave the decision of such difficult questions to another day.[95]

The court went on to say:

. . .[A] union's ability to represent all its employees is not compromised by the mere fact that an employee is consulting with an attorney regarding matters related to his discharge.

There are important policy concerns which strongly support this rule. Attorneys play an important role in advising individuals who are not versed in the complexities of the law. Members of our society often require information and guidance of a nature that lawyers are uniquely capable of conferring. The intricacies of our labor law often will mean that a layman will be either confused by or wholly ignorant of its provisions. Employees have a legitimate interest in discussing their rights and obligations under the law with an informed but neutral third party. This is especially true where the interests of the union might deviate from those of an individual employee.[96]

If the suggestion for a change away from union exclusivity is now wise, a change in the grievance forms is the follow-up suggestion. The following statement would be printed prominently on the grievance form whereon the written grievance against the company is first written and under which the grievant signs his or her name:

If the union member desires to have a private attorney help process the grievance during the step-by-step procedure set up in the labor agreement, he need only to promptly advise the assigned union representative in writing of the name and address of the private attorney. He will then be sent the location and time for the first grievance meeting with the grievance number listed on the meeting agenda.

---

[94]*Seymour v. Olin Corp.*, 666 F.2d 202, 109 LRRM 2728, 2733 (5th Cir. 1982).
[95]*Id.* n.5.
[96]*Id.*

If the member's grievance is not settled during the step-by-step procedure and will be appealed to arbitration by the union representative, the private attorney as a collaborating representative may attend the hearing and, with prior arrangement with the union representative, present evidence and question witnesses and present an oral or written statement to the arbitrator with the understanding that the arbitrator has complete control over the proceedings at the arbitration hearing.

Any fees or expenses of such private attorney shall be exclusively the responsibility of the member retaining such private attorney.

If the grievant signs this form, the grievant will be accepting the representative selected for the grievant or will be accepting the option of selecting a private attorney to collaborate with the union-selected representative, believing that such collaboration will increase the chance of a win against the company by decreasing the chance the representative's strategy will be poor or negligence will occur. The grievant will most likely not hire a personal attorney to act as a collaborating lawyer, because the cost of this service will fall on the grievant, unless the grievant believes *he* wants to reinforce his winning chances and is willing to pay the cost involved, which is the cost that would be placed on any plaintiff in most other legal representation arrangements.[97]

If it is considered wise to modify the union's exclusivity by permitting a collaborating private lawyer to become involved (if the grievant wants one), a suggested statement as set forth above could be printed on the grievance form, but not until an appropriate modification is incorporated into the labor agreement. In *Seymour v. Olin Corp.*[98] the Fifth Circuit explained that a private attorney, on behalf of Seymour, had requested a meeting with Olin to discuss the discharge of his client and Olin had responded that negotiations over grievances would be conducted only with the union representative.[99] The court explained that "the terms of Articles 8 and 9 of the contract [labor agreement] appear to contemplate that the Union will be the party with whom the Company will deal in the grievance process."[100] In a footnote the court explained exclusivity was generated by the agreement, not by the law:

Under § 9(a) of the National Labor Relations Act, 29 U.S.C.A. § 159(a) (West 1973), Seymour could seek redress for grievances without the assistance of the Union where such action is not inconsistent with the collective bargaining agreement. However, the employer is not required to entertain such a presentation and can insist upon handling grievances exclusively with the Union pursuant to the collective bargaining agreement.[101]

---

[97]Note the cost in *Seymour v. Olin Corp.*, discussed in the text associated with note 105 *infra*.
[98]666 F.2d 202, 109 LRRM 2728 (5th Cir. 1982). *See also Laney v. Ford Motor Co.*, 95 LRRM 2002 (D. Minn. 1977).
[99]*Id.* at 209 n.6, 109 LRRM at 2733 n.6.
[100]*Id.* at 209, 109 LRRM at 2732.
[101]Id. at 207 n.2, 109 LRRM at 2731 n.2. *See also Emporium Capwell Co. v. Western Addition Community Organization*, 420 U.S. 50, 61 n.12, 88 LRRM 2660, 2665 n.12.

In this case the union representative had told the grievant that "under the union rule, there was nothing that the union could do for him unless he got rid of his lawyer and that if he was going to do so he had better hurry up, since his time to file a grievance was running out."[102] Because Seymour did not terminate his relationship with this private lawyer,[103] the union representative filed no grievance with the company[104] and the failure to file one for this reason was held to be a breach of the duty of fair representation. After the District Court processed the Section 301 suit through the jury, Olin was required to pay $139,000 in back pay and prospective damages to Seymour and the union was required to pay him $39,000 to permit him to pay the fee of his private lawyer.[105]

This case is significant, not because the court said the grievant has an option to retain a consulting attorney, but because the union's attempt to exclude the consulting attorney generated a union breach which led to a damage award by a jury against both the company and the union. The court announced the general rule and applied it in this case:

> "In this case, even if the union had breached its duty, all or almost all of [the employee's] damages would still be attributable to his allegedly wrongful discharge by [the employer]."[106]

The second suggestion for changes in the grievance forms arises from the fact that most grievance forms (many printed by unions) are too simplistic. For example, they permit one grievance form to be used to describe the grievance and then to appeal it up through the grievance procedure and into arbitration by merely marking an "x" in a box. An "x" in a box does not produce any evidence that the union grievance representative was acting thoughtfully or not thoughtfully by appealing or not appealing the grievance, etc.

One company that has handled grievances with the United Automobile Workers for some years reached a mutual agreement[107] to dispense with the overly simplistic, one-sheet grievance forms and de-

---

[102]666 F.2d at 206, 109 LRRM at 2730.

[103]*Id.*

[104]Under § 9(a) of the National Labor Relations Act, 29 U.S.C.A. § 159(a) (West 1973), the grievant could have filed a grievance personally but he did not do so.

[105]If the fees of a private "consulting" lawyer can be assessed against the union, the incentive for the grievant to accept the union grievance representative as the grievant's sole representative, discussed in the text associated with note 97 *supra*, would tend to diminish.

[106]*Seymour v. Olin Corp.*, 666 F.2d 202, 109 LRRM 2728, 2736 (5th Cir. 1982); the quotation was incorporated into the opinion with the brackets from *Vaca v. Sipes*, 386 U.S. 171, 197-98, 64 LRRM 2369, 2380 (1967). Back pay apportionment by the union and employer developed by the Supreme Court is discussed on p. 725 *infra*.

[107]The description of these forms is based on the two-form procedure developed in negotiations between Rockford Division, Borg-Warner Corporation, and the United Automobile Workers. These forms at first appeared to be cumbersome but they have been used long enough to be tested and found basic to good recordkeeping and risk control.

velop a two-step grievance form arrangement in the hope that this procedure would allow the grievance procedure to operate without a flaw.

An illustration of the risk that is involved if there are flaws in record-keeping is the $15,000 award granted by a jury to a Jersey City postal worker because his grievance file simply disappeared from the New York City office of the Metro Area Postal Union.[108] Because of this his grievance was not processed. The discharged grievant hired a private attorney and he filed a breach of duty of fair representation suit in the district court. There the jury restored the plaintiff to duty and placed damages on both the Union and the Company[109] even though the Union (defendant) argued that "the claim must be dismissed because the original discharge was for cause."[110] Judge Ward responded to this argument by saying that whether or not the original discharge was with or without cause was, in the court's view, not determinative. What was determinative was the undue length of time that was consumed before the plaintiff was "restored to duty" *by the jury.*

The new forms, designed to permit no-flaw grievance processing, also were designed to build in evidence that the union grievance representative had handled each grievance carefully, giving the grievant sound and thoughtful representation, so any claim of negligence could be defeated. The first form is a multi-copy one on which the grievance is described in writing, with the section or sections of the labor agreement involved recorded. The grievant signs this form, reducing the risk that the grievant can later claim the grievance processed was really not the grievance the grievant thought should have been processed. One copy of this first form is then given to the grievant, one is retained by the union representative and two are sent to the mutual grievance record office though the plant mail. Upon receipt by the office the form is stamped, proving the time of receipt. On each copy of the multi-copy form appears the *same* sequential printed number. The grievance number is set forth in a grievance record chart on which is set forth the name of the union representative, the name of the grievant(s), the date of the filing, the date the company's answer should be mailed, and the date the first time limit will run if an answered grievance is not processed by the union grievance representative up through the grievance procedure. This ensures a telephone call will be made to the union representative if the next processing step is not taken by that representative within a fixed amount of time in advance of the date of the time limit.

A company's written answer to the grievance is filled in on the grievance report and one copy and several photocopies with references to pertinent arbitration awards are sent back to the union grievance representative. Then that representative discusses the company's answer

---

[108]*Reid v. New York Metro Area Postal Union*, 109 LRRM 3065 (S.D. N.Y. 1982).
[109]*Id.* at 3067.
[110]*Id.* at 3067.

with the grievant and determines whether the grievance is to be appealed into the first grievance meeting procedure or "closed out" because the company's answer has satisfied the grievant.

If the grievance is to be appealed, a space on the second form, the "Grievance Appeal or Closeout" form, asks that the following statement be filled in:

The Foreman's answer to this grievance is unsatisfactory because _____
_____.[111]

If no reason for lack of satisfaction can be set out in response after the grievant and the union grievance representative have discussed the answer, the form has a space for the other option—i.e., to "close out" the grievance. At this point, the union grievance representative can close out the grievance, even if the grievant does not agree and will not sign. If the grievant will not sign, the union grievance representative in an appropriate space sets forth a brief statement of the reasons why the union grievance representative is "closing out" the grievance.

It was stated clearly in *Blevins v. General Electric Co.*[112] that the decision not to submit a grievance to arbitration rests with the union representative and not with the employee. The employee's grievance had been reviewed by the union and company representatives at three levels in the grievance procedure, and the discussion revealed that the union representative had not acted "arbitrarily, discriminatorily or in bad faith" when he decided not to move the grievance up to arbitration.

When the grievant is not satisfied when the grievance is not processed to arbitration, there should be evidence that the union representative did evaluate the facts and had nonarbitrary reasons for not moving up the grievance, to rebut the claim of unfair representation if one is filed in a court. The needed evidence should be available if a notation of the reasons for not moving up the grievance is set forth on the grievance form which had been sent by plant mail to the grievance record office and there time stamped. This form should supply proof that an appeal by the union grievance representative was considered and that the representatives had reasons for the non-appeal before the appeal time limit had expired.

If the grievance form is not received a few days before the time limit period ends, the grievance record supervisor should telephone the union representative to insure against inadvertent (negligent) failure to appeal. Once an appeal is recorded, the grievance is scheduled by number for discussion at the next available open grievance meeting; copies of the agenda are distributed to all union grievance representatives with a separate notice to the grievant. If the grievant does not attend, he or she can hardly claim negligence if the grievance is not

_____

[111]*See* note 107.
[112]491 F. Supp. 521, 525, 105 LRRM 3242 (W.D. Va. 1980).

sustained at the meeting.[113]

Use of the double set of forms may appear to be a complication, but it will produce the needed information, eliminate the risk of procedural flaws, and generate a complete record of positions taken by the two sides within each time limit. A personal attorney considering filing a suit for a disappointed grievant can obtain a copy of the record from the grievance record office and will know that the judge will know about the union representative's diligence, even when the grievance is withdrawn, not appealed, or lost in arbitration, and may then decide not to file a suit.

Bowen v. United States Postal Service[114] should generate support for the suggested revised forms and mutual recordkeeping procedures described above. In *Bowen* the national union office, for no apparent reason, did not pursue a discharge case, even though union representatives below had recommended this. The lack of apparent reason established the breach needed to lift the time limit so the Section 301 suit could proceed. If some reasonable reason had been recorded by the national office, there would have been no basis for lifting the agreement's time limit. The Court also pointed out that if the grievant had been able to individually pursue his grievance and had not done so, the time limit would not have been lifted and the grievance would have been disposed of.[115]

Justices Powell, Burger, Brennan, Stevens, and O'Connor (five out of nine) required the union to pay the grievant back pay that accumulated after the hypothetical date the arbitrator would have issued the reinstatement order. These justices rejected the view that the employer should be solely liable for accumulated back pay. Such liability is not "governed by traditional common law" principles because the agreement creates "relationships and interests under the federal common law of labor policy." The Court reapportioned the liability of the employer and union according to the damages caused by the fault of each, ordering the union to pay $30,000 of the back pay even though the discharge was caused exclusively by the employer.[116] The obligation to impose *apportioned* liability in such cases should provide a strong incentive for both unions and employers to mutually administer the grievance procedure carefully to avoid the union fault that will lift the time limit in the labor agreement that protects the employer.

---

[113]In *Harris v. Schwerman Trucking Co.*, 668 F.2d 1204, 109 LRRM 3135 (11th Cir. 1982), the fact that a union representative was assisting the grievant at a grievance meeting was evidence that there was no merit to the grievant's claim that the union breached its duty of fair representation by "perfunctorily" representing the employee's discharge grievance.

[114]____ U.S. ____, 112 LRRM 2281 (1983).

[115]*Id.* See *Czosek v. O'Mara*, 397 U.S. 25, 73 LRRM 2481 (1970), discussion in *Bowen*.

[116]Reaffirming the trial court's union portion of back pay, 470 F. Supp. 1127, 1129, 103 LRRM 2366 (W.D. Va. 1979), that the Fourth Circuit had eliminated, 642 F.2d 79, 106 LRRM 2701 (1981).

CHAPTER XXIV

Special Arbitration Procedures

The previous chapters have dealt with labor arbitration practice and procedure as they have been shaped by courts and arbitrators during the last forty-five years. As has been shown, notions of "due process" must be incorporated into the procedure if the arbitration award is to be sustainable by a court, or if the award is to be deferred to by the NLRB.[1] Loosely described, "due process" means that evidence is presented to the arbitrator through witnesses, with the opposing party having the right to cross-examine, or in agreed stipulations of facts; and the determination of the arbitrator is based upon the evidence contained in the record.

Despite the courts' insistence that labor arbitration hearings conform to "due process" standards, there are certain "labor arbitrations" which do not fit into this mold. No discussion of arbitration practice and procedure would be complete without at least a brief discussion of these different and, hence, special, types of arbitration procedures.

SPECIAL PROCEDURES TO RESOLVE EQUAL EMPLOYMENT OPPORTUNITY DISPUTES

The American Arbitration Association has announced that the AAA has developed a new system of rules and procedures designed especially for arbitration of equal employment opportunity disputes. Arbitration of such issues would be based not on a labor agreement but on "a submission agreement drafted by an attorney for an employee and an attorney for an employer."[2] The agreement would identify the disputing parties, define the claims, clarify criteria to be considered by the arbitrator, specify the method for selecting the arbitrator, select appropriate hearing procedures, and confirm that the award is to be

---

[1]*Spielberg Mfg. Co.*, 112 NLRB 1080, 36 LRRM 1152 (1955). *See also Collyer Insulated Wire*, 192 NLRB 837, 77 LRRM 1931 (1971).

[2]*Employment Dispute Arbitration Rules of the American Arbitration Association* (effective June 1, 1978), published in EMPLOYMENT ARBITRATION: PLAIN AND FANCY (New York: AAA, 1979).

conclusive. The AAA has assembled a panel of arbitrators familiar with EEO law. The goal is to develop a truly voluntary arbitration of Title VII disuptes by qualified and experienced arbitrators as an alternative to court litigation. There has been considerable discussion of grievances that include discrimination claims in prior chapters. The mention of this special procedure developed by the American Arbitration Association is to inform the reader of a new mechanism that is available to resolve such claims.

RESOLUTION OF MEDICAL QUESTIONS

Special labor arbitration procedures have most often been developed to resolve disputes over medical questions. Basically, they provide that a doctor, or clinic, investigate the facts in dispute and then determine the ultimate question *de novo*. The arbitrators obtain the facts, not at a hearing, but privately, and only a minimal factual record of their private investigation is made.[3] Such a procedure, using a clinic to resolve disputes over medical facts, is as follows:

> If an employee returns after a sick leave or layoff of thirty days or more, or from any absence due to an occupational injury or occupational illness, or from any absence during which he has been hospitalized, he may be required to take a physical examination by the company's doctor....
>
> ... [A]ny claim that the company has improperly concluded that reinstatement of the employee in active employment in his regular job classification causes an abnormal health risk ... shall be resolved ... by an examination at the diagnostic clinic of the ... University Hospital.
>
> If the employee is sent to such ... clinic, a jointly agreed upon detailed description of the work in the classification or classifications that the employee would perform if he was returned shall be submitted to such doctor or clinic as a basis for a determination of whether the company's action in returning the employee or refusing to return the employee was reasonable. The company doctor and the employee's doctor may submit a statement and copies of medical records or findings to such doctor or such clinic. The costs of such medical examination by such doctor or such clinic shall be paid by the company.
>
> The findings of such doctor or clinic shall be binding on the company, the union and the employee involved.

---

[3]Simkin, *The Arbitration of Technical Disputes*, NEW YORK UNIVERSITY SIXTH ANNUAL CONFERENCE ON LABOR, E. Stein, ed. (Albany: Mathew Bender & Co., 1953), p. 181. *See also* Lohoczky, *Industrial Engineering and Collective Bargaining*, 17 LAB. L.J. 393 (1966); Presgrave, *Grievance Arbitration and the Industrial Engineer*, 18 J. IND. ENG'G. 605 (1967); Sherman, *Arbitrator's Analysis of Job Evaluation Disputes*, 43 PERSONNEL J. 365 (1964); Werner, *Industrial Engineers, Incentive Systems, and the Contract*, 11 J. IND. ENG'G. 231 (1960).

Another example, where the independent diagnostic skill of the neutral doctor is made final, is the following:

> If the two examining physicians disagree concerning whether the employee or pensioner is permanently incapacitated, the question shall be submitted to a third physician selected by such two physicians. The medical opinion of the third physician, after examination of the employee or pensioner and consultation with the two physicians, shall decide such questions, and such decision shall be binding upon all interested parties. The fees and expenses of the third physician shall be shared equally by the employer and the local union representing the employee or pensioner.

Arbitrator Murray M. Rohman, in *Union Carbide Corp., Linde Division,*[4] an interim award, directed that the grievant, who had undergone back surgery, be examined by an orthopedic physician to resolve conflicting medical evidence concerning the risk to the grievant if he performed certain work. Thus, this arbitrator obtained the aid of a special medical "adviser" or "fact-finder" by his own order in an interim award.

RESOLUTION OF INCENTIVE MEASUREMENT QUESTIONS

Some procedures used to resolve industrial engineering disputes actually mix the normal type of arbitration procedure and special fact-finding procedures. Under such procedures, an arbitrator sometimes is permitted to retain an industrial engineer or doctor, not associated with either party, to act as his or her technical assistant, adviser,[5] or fact-finder.[6] Sometimes an arbitrator will ask an industrial engineer to make an independent measurement of the time required to perform an operation and then, by a subjective judgment, to "level" the "measured time" and report an "allowed time" to the arbitrator.

When such a procedure is used in a situation where the dispute is over the "leveling" of "measured time" by the company's industrial engineer, and the arbitrator's industrial engineer or fact-finder uses a different method to measure the performance time or to "level" it, a different allowed time usually will result. This procedure merely substitutes a judgment determination of the arbitrator's industrial engineer for that of the company's industrial engineer. A variation in the allowed time determinations merely proves that such determinations may differ

---

[4]72-2 ARB ¶ 8382 (Rohman, 1972).

[5]Gomberg, *Arbitration of Disputes Involving Incentive Problems: A Labor View*, CRITICAL ISSUES IN LABOR ARBITRATION, Proceedings of the Tenth Annual Meeting, National Academy of Arbitrators, J. McKelvey, ed. (Washington: BNA Books, 1957), p. 85; Unterberger, *Technicians As Arbitrators of Wage Disputes*, 4 LAB. L.J. 433 (1953).

[6]Haughton, Discussion of Gomberg, note 5 *supra*, p.94.

and does not prove that the incentive standard as originally established was arbitrarily or capriciously established, which is the standard usually applied before a management decision is upset.[7]

When the time required to perform the manual elements of an operation is determined by totaling predetermined times for each motion used by the employee performing the operation, the dispute is much easier to resolve than when judgmental leveling is used. Well-known procedures for determining the "allowed time" by totaling predetermined times are "Methods Times Measurement" and "Work Factor." When these procedures are used, no stop watch need be used and, hence, no subjective judgment concerning the work pace of an employee being observed need be made and such judgments do not become involved in the dispute. When predetermined time techniques are used, the normal arbitration procedure can be employed to resolve the dispute. The "allowed time" can be reanalyzed by the arbitrator through a review of the motions and a totaling of the predetermined time values for each motion that are taken from the motion time chart used with the particular predetermined time system. It is true that the selection of the proper time value from the motion time chart for a particular motion will involve some judgment, but the possible difference is much less than when a stop-watch reading is made by different observers timing performance of the task by different employees at different times and when the recorded time then is adjusted by the industrial engineer by the use of his or her subjective judgment.

The following is an example of a special incentive dispute arbitration procedure designed to minimize the dispute area in the arbitration proceeding by requiring the arbitrator or the arbitrator's technical assistant or fact-finder to use the same methods to produce the leveled time. Under the following procedure, the industrial engineer-arbitrator is required to use the same methods for measuring and leveling the time that were used by the company's industrial engineer. Essentially the industrial engineer-arbitrator's role is to determine whether the company's industrial engineer *properly* used the time measurement procedures which are regularly used *at that plant* to determine the allowed time:

(a) The Special Arbitrator shall study the entire operation or operations involved, unless it is mutually agreed otherwise. He shall have only the right to determine whether the labor standard was or was not established within

---

[7]*See* Chapter XI, "Amount of Proof." In regard to the quotation describing the special arbitration procedure for incentive disputes, in text *infra*, the arbitrator can change the incentive standard only if he or she finds the standard in dispute was erroneous beyond "the limits of industrial engineering accuracy." What is meant by this tolerance is discussed in Fairweather, *Arbitration of Disputes Involving Incentive Problems: An Industry View*, CRITICAL ISSUES IN LABOR ARBITRATION, note 8 *supra*, pp. 61, 68.

the limits of industrial engineering accuracy, to be determined by using the
following tests:

(1) If the element to be measured was established by the Company by a
predetermined time value procedure or by a standard data procedure, the
Arbitrator shall be required to use the same procedure. If the element to
be measured was established by the Company by a stop watch observation, the Arbitrator shall be permitted to level a stop watch observation to
daywork pace.

(2) If the element to be measured is a machine or process-controlled
element, the time value shall be established by the determination of the
elapsed time required for the machine or process cycle plus a 20 percent
process control allowance.

Sometimes the parties will ask an industrial engineer, acting as an
arbitrator, to render an award which will set up a fair incentive bonus.
Where an arbitrator was given this special power, his award requiring
bonus standards to be calculated by a method different from the system
previously used by a company and a union for many years was correct.[8]

JOINT UNION-MANAGEMENT COMMITTEES FOR SENIORITY
GRIEVANCE RESOLUTION

In one case a joint union-management committee was set up by the
two parties to establish the final seniority determinations. Seniority
grievances would not be processed if agreement not to do so was unanimous. The seniority determinations based on this special arrangement
were challenged as a "breach of fair representation." The court, however, said "No."[9] Similarly, a joint committee approved some new productivity standards, replacing some prior looser standards, and would
not present employee complaints as grievances. This procedure was
challenged as a "breach of fair representation" and the court said
"No."[10]

A joint union-management committee should not be referred to as a
labor arbitration procedure. That procedure should contain a neutral
who will make the final decision and produce a resolution. Unless there
is a neutral in the process, the "failure to agree" on the part of the two
parties leaves a strike the other option. The failure of the Supreme
Court to point out the difference between joint union-management
committees and labor arbitration was discussed in Chapter XXII.

---

[8]*Litton Business Systems, Inc., Cole Div. v. Steelworkers, Local 4407*, 441 F. Supp. 1346, 99
LRRM 2258 (M.D. Pa. 1977).

[9]*Walters v. Roadway Express*, 557 F.2d 521 (5th Cir. 1977).

[10]*Teamsters, Local 30 v. Holms Express, Inc.*, 97 LRRM 2798 (W.D. Pa. 1978).

RELATIONSHIP BETWEEN SPECIAL AND REGULAR PROCEDURES

These descriptions of the special arbitration procedures used in disputes involving medical and industrial engineering questions should not cause one to conclude that such disputes are not usually presented for resolution to a regular arbitrator. When they are, the technical aspects of the case are often introduced by industrial engineers or doctors, who are called as witnesses by the parties. Those witnesses are then subject to cross-examination by the representatives of the other party, incorporating the minimal due process which courts require in labor arbitration procedures.[11] Arbitrator William Waite expresses a widely-held view that an experienced arbitrator should be able to understand and determine disputes involving these questions if the arbitrator can obtain from expert witnesses the technical information he or she needs:

> Common sense is still the foremost requirement for an arbitrator, and if he possesses an optimum amount of this quality he need not fear to step in, regardless of technical shortcomings. Common sense should also tell him when he is over his head, and when to go for help if he needs it.[12]

Arbitrators, in the evaluation of evidence in industrial engineering disputes, have developed certain presumptions. For example, they have learned to refrain from being influenced by earnings information when an incentive standard is under attack. Obviously, when the employees performing the operation are claiming that they are working with incentive effort but cannot make the expected level of earnings, they will not "lose their case" by not holding down their effort, causing their earnings to reach or exceed the expected level. For example, Arbitrator Ralph Seward in *Bethlehem Steel Co.*[13] said, concerning a situation where the employees were not making the expected earnings:

> Such earnings, it is true [measured against an expected earnings level], have not been realized in actual practice. The Umpire has given the Union every opportunity to analyze the time studies and line speed studies on which the rates were based and to point out errors or defects in those studies which would account for the failure to reach target earnings. The Union has failed to make such an analysis or to demonstrate any inadequacy in the studies or any errors in the assumptions which the Company based upon those stud-

---

[11]Miller, *Expert Medical Evidence: A View from the End of the Table*, Arbitration and Social Change, Proceedings of the Twenty-Second Annual Meeting, National Academy of Arbitrators, G. Somers, ed. (Washington: BNA Books, 1970), pp. 138–39.

[12]Waite, *Problems in the Arbitration of Wage Incentives*, Arbitration Today, Proceedings of the Eighth Annual Meeting, National Academy of Arbitrators, J. McKelvey, ed. (Washington: BNA Books, 1955), p. 25.

[13]20 LA 38, 42–43 (Seward, 1953). *See also Wolverine Shoe & Tanning Corp.*, 15 LA 195, 196 (Platt, 1950).

ies. . . . It has offered the Umpire no grounds for holding that the reason for the failure to reach target earnings lay with the rates rather than with the employees themselves.

Under these circumstances, the Umpire has no alternative but to hold that the Union has failed to establish that the incentive rates . . . are not in equitable relationship to the old rates and to deny the grievances on that basis.

Similarly, Arbitrator Fred Kindig in *Fenestra, Division of the Marmon Group*,[14] expressed and applied the normal burden-of-proof concepts so often applied by arbitrators in deciding an industrial engineering dispute:

The primary question then is as proposed by the parties. Regardless of the validity of the previous standards, do the new standards provide an incentive opportunity of 125 per cent? The Arbitrator agrees with the Company that the burden of proof is with the Union; that a standard created by management should not be overriden by an arbitrator in the absence of clear proof of arbitrariness; that low earnings do not necessarily establish the incorrectness of incentive standards; and that the Arbitrator has no authority to establish a different method of compensating employees, such as, for unavoidable delays.

When normal arbitration procedures are used, the same burden usually is placed upon the union to show that a medical determination of a company physician was clearly erroneous, before it will be upset.[15]

When disputes over "allowed time determinations" of "medical judgments" are resolved by special procedures, the judgment of the special arbitrator (special industrial engineer, doctor, clinic) is final. The fact-finder's investigation is private; no evidence is presented in the normal way and there are no witnesses who can cross-examine the agreed upon "expert"[16] and his or her determination is *de novo*.

This final chapter is not an attempt to catalog all of the variations of procedure that are used by companies and unions to handle special types of disputes, but merely to record the fact that there are special procedures and to note the essential differences between them and those used in the normal labor arbitrations discussed in the various other chapters in this book.

---

[14](Kindig, 1970), unreported, at pp. 17–18.

[15]*Ideal Cement Co.*, 20 LA 480, 482 (Merrill, 1953); *International Shoe Co.*, 14 LA 253, 255 (Wallen, 1950); *Great Lakes Spring Corp.*, 11 LA 159,160 (Gregory, 1948).

[16]As noted elsewhere in this volume, the NLRB will defer to an arbitration award if the due process safeguards were followed and the statutory issue raised and determined. One can only speculate what the Board would do if an employee active in organizing a union claimed he was discharged for his union activities and that his discharge violated § 8(a)(3) of the National Labor Relations Act, and the company defended itself on the ground that a clinic determined he was physically unsuited for the work pursuant to a procedure in a labor agreement which did not provide for the making of a factual record or for the cross-examination of the examining physician.

TABLE OF AWARDS
(By Arbitrator)

This Table reports the names of arbitrators in alphabetical order (with initials when different arbitrators have the same last name) and the page and footnote in each chapter where the award is cited. This Table may be of assistance to representatives when they are evaluating arbitrators in connection with the ranking of a selection panel or may find awards of particular arbitrators of interest during a hearing or in connection with writing a brief. It also may be helpful to arbitrators in award preparation. There is a separate Table for each chapter to cross-reference the arbitrator with the subject matter. Page numbers are in roman type; footnote numbers are in italics.

Chapter II The Submission of a Case to Arbitration

Amis 19:*37*
Begley 13:*11*
Belkin 19:*36*
Block, H. S. 26:*79*; 26:*80*; 27:*86*
Blue 19:*39, 40*
Carmichael 18:*33*
Crawford 24:*71*
Davis 17:*30*
Duff, C. V. 18:*33*
Dworkin, H. J. 17:*30*; 19:*37*; 22:*56*; 22:*57*
Dybeck 17:*30*
Emery 22:*58*
Feinberg 25:*77*; 27:*86*
Fischer 19:*36*
Fleming 18:*33*; 18:*35*; 27:*86*
Fuller 19:*36*
Gentile 17:*30*; 26:*79*
Gibson 26:*79*
Gootnick 14:*15*
Graham 14:*15*
Hebling 27:*86*
Jones, E. A. 26:*82*
Jones, F. E. 26:*81*; 27:*84*

Keefe 19:*36*
Koven 27:*86*
Larson 19:*37*
Lazarus 27:*86*
Lippman 17:*30*
Lockhart 19:*37*
Loucks 24:*71*
Luskin 19:*36*
Malinowski 19:*41*
Marshall 19:*37*
McCoy 17:*30*
McIntosh 17:*30*
Morvant 20:*43*
Norton 18:*34*
O'Malley 19:*37*
Platt 27:*86*
Porter 19:*37*
Prasow 14:*15*
Ray 18:*33*
Rock 15:*20*
Rubin 19:*37*
Sanders 15:*18*
Schedler 20:*42*; 27:*86*
Seinsheimer 18:*33*; 20:*42*; 22:*55*

Chapter VII   Obtaining the Evidence

Chapter XI   Amount of Proof

Chapter XII   Rules of Evidence

Chapter XII—*Contd.*

Chapter XIII Due Process Considerations

Chapter XIV   Polygraphy in Labor Arbitration

Chapter XV   The "Duty" to Cooperate With Polygraph Testing Versus the Right to Refuse

Chapter XVIII   Remedies

Chapter XVIII—*Contd.*

Chapter XIX   Post-Hearing Procedures

Chapter XX The Award

Chapter XXI Vacation, Enforcement, or Correction

Chapter XXII *De Novo* Reviews in a Court

Chapter XXIV   Special Arbitration Procedures

TABLE OF CASES

U.S. Supreme Court Cases

747

Federal Circuit Court Cases

Federal Circuit Court Cases—*Contd.*

Meat Cutters (see also Food Handlers)
Dist. Local 540 v. Neuhoff Bros. Packers, Inc. 579
Local 405 v. Tennessee Dressed Beef Co. 54
Local 540 v. Neuhoff Bros. Packers, Inc. 260, 420
Local 641 v. Capitol Packing Co. 589
Local P-1236 v. Jones Dairy Farm 617
Mercury Oil Refining Co. v. Oil, Chemical & Atomic Workers 580
Metropolitan Edison Co. v. NLRB 634
Metropolitan Paving Co. v. Operating Engineers 535, 538, 539
Mine Workers, UMW
District 5. v. Consolidated Coal Co. 489
District 50 v. Bowman Tranportation, Inc. 53, 641, 642
Local 12405, District 50 v. Martin Marietta Corp. 44
Local 12934, District 50 v. Dow Corning Co. 59
Minnis v. Automobile Workers 708, 714
Minute Maid Co. v. Citrus, Cannery, Food Processing, and Allied Workers, Local 344 512, 513 592
Mogge v. Machinists 589
Molders, Local 239 v. Susquehanna Casting Co. 63
Monroe Sander Corp. v. Livingston 31, 50, 66
Montgomery Ward & Co. v. NLRB 335
Muhich v. Allen 682
Muko, Larry V., Inc. v. Building & Const. Trades Council (Southwestern Pennsylvania) 492
Muskegon Motor Specialties Co. v. Davis 50

N

NF&M Corp. v. Steelworkers, Local 8148 619
NLRB (see name of opposing party)
Napa Pittsburgh, Inc. v. Chauffers, Local 926 63
National Parks & Conservation Ass'n v. Kleppe 157
Ness v. Safeway Stores, Inc. 713

New Orleans Steamship Ass'n v. Longshoremen, ILA, Local 1418 544, 599, 637
New Orleans Typographical Union No. 17 v. NLRB 602, 604
Newark Stereotypers' Union v. Newark Morning Ledger 181, 266, 620
Nix v. Spector Freight Systems, Inc. 577
North River Energy Corp. v. Mine Workers, UMW 534
Northwest Air Lines, Inc. v. Airline Pilots Ass'n 619

O

Office Employees, Local 95, NEPCO Unit v. Nekoosa-Edwards Paper Co. 75
Oil, Chemical & Atomic Workers
v. American Maize Products Co. 37, 52
Local 8-831 v. Mobil Oil Corp. 30
Local 4-16000 v. Ethyl Corp. 638
Oliver; U.S. v. 392, 393
Operating Engineers
Local 3 v. Crooks Bros. Tractor Co. 75
Local 150 v. Flair Builders, Inc. 56
Local 279 v. Sid Richardson Carbon Co. 59
Orphan v. Furnco Construction Corp. 715, 716
Orr v. Frank R. MacNeill & Son, Inc. 656
Owen's Maintenance Corp.; NLRB v. 635

P

Pacific Northwest Bell Tel. Co. v. Communications Workers 69
Packinghouse Workers, Local 156 v. Du Quoin Packing Co. 67
Painters
District Council 38 v. Edgewood Contracting Co. 493
Local 1179 v. Welco Mfg. Co. 588
Palestine Tel. Co. v. Electrical Workers, IBEW, Local 1506 34, 56
Parade Publications, Inc. v. Philadelphia Mailers Union, Local 14 63
Petersen v. Rath Packing Co. 705, 715

Federal Circuit Court Cases—*Contd.*

Seattle Times Co. v. Mailers Union No. 32   535

Selb Mfg. Co. v. Machinists, District 9   496, 549

Service Employees, Local 36 v. Office Center Services, Inc.   626

Seymour v. Olin Corp.   697, 709, 711, 720, 721, 722

Sheet Metal Workers, Local 223 v. Atlas Sheet Metal Co. of Jacksonville   535, 537, 538, 539

Shell Oil Co. v. NLRB   152

Shoe Workers, United, Local 127 v. Brooks Shoe Mfg. Co.   525, 532

Simberlund v. Long Island R.R. Co.   713

Sinclair Refining Co. v. NLRB   151

Sine v. Teamsters, Local 992   8

Smith v. Hussmann Refrigerator Co.   706, 708, 710

Smith Steel Workers v. A.O. Smith Corp.   59

Soap Workers v. Proctor & Gamble   69

Southbridge Plastics Div. v. Rubber Workers, Local 759   465

Southwestern Electric Power Co. v. Electrical Workers, IBEW, Local 738   66

Spaulding v. University of Washington   682

Stage Employees, Local 771 v. WOR Div., RKO General, Inc.   54

Steelworkers
  v. NLRB   63
  v. United States Gypsum Co.   49, 125, 437, 497
  Local 1617 v. The General Fireproofing Co.   31
  Local 4377 v. General Electric Co.   74
  of W. Pa. v. Butler Mfg. Co.   537, 642

Steinman v. Spector Freight System   705

Stephenson v. NLRB   635

Storer Broadcasting Co. v. Television & Radio Artists (AFTRA), Cleveland Local   592

Strauss v. Silvercup Bakers, Inc.   70

Street, Electric Ry. & Motor Coach Employees v. Greyhound Corp.   479

Sunrise Lumber & Trim Corp.; NLRB v.   195

T

Taft Broadcasting Co.
  v. Radio Broadcasting Technicians, Local 253, (IBEW)   67

Taft Broadcasting Co.
  WDAF AM-FM-TV v. NLRB   31

Tamari v. Conrad   623

Teamsters (see also General Drivers, Ice Cream Drivers, Truck Drivers & Helpers)
  v. Blue Cab Co.   69
  v. Kroger Co.   37
  Local 70 v. Consolidated Freightways Corp.   76
  Local 94 v. Humko Co.   537
  Local 135 v. Jefferson Trucking Co.   627
  Local 251 v. Narragansett Improvement Co.   6, 166, 181, 589
  Local 290 v. Oolite Concrete Co.   493
  Local 396; NLRB v.   86
  Local 560 v. Anchor Motor Freight, Inc.   569, 570, 623
  Local 745 v. Braswell Motor Freight Lines, Inc.   50
  Local 757 v. Borden, Inc.   63
  Local 757 v. Standard Brands   601
  Local 782 v. Blue Cab Co.   67
  Local 784 v. Ulry-Talbert Co.   590
  Local 807 v. Bohack Corp.   624, 625

Tenney Engineering, Inc. v. Electrical Workers, IUE, Local 437   76

Texaco, Inc. v. NLRB   153

Textile Workers, TWUA
  v. American Thread Co.   234
  v. Cone Mills Corp.   584

Textile Workers, UTW, Local 120 v. Newberry Mills, Inc.   63

Textron, Inc., Bell Aerospace Div. v. Automobile Workers, Local 516   637

Timken Co. v. Steelworkers, Local 1123   503

Timken Roller Bearing v. NLRB   151

Tobacco Workers, Local 317 v. Lorillard Corp.   36, 56

Torrington Co. v. Automobile Workers, Metal Products Workers Local 1645   30, 66, 437, 579, 588

Town & Country Mfg. Co. v. NLRB   471

Federal District Court Cases

Federal District Court Cases—*Contd.*

American Bosch Arma Corp. v. Electrical Workers, IUE, Local 794 16, 495, 596

American Can Co. v. Papermakers & Paperworkers, Local 412   20

American Home Assurance Co. v. American Fidelity   86

American Sterilizer Co. v. Automobile Workers, Local 832   20, 21, 25

Anaconda Co. v. Great Falls Mills & Smeltermen's Union   589

Anderson v. Field Enterprises, Inc. 717

Arco Polymers, Inc. v. Oil, Chemical & Atomic Workers, Local 8-74 595

Armstrong-Norwalk Rubber Corp. v. Rubber Workers, Local 283 63

Asbestos Workers, Local 166 v. Leona Lee Corp.   142

Atomic Uniform Corp. v. Garment Workers, ILGWU   549

Atwood v. Pacific Maritime Ass'n   713

Austin Mailers Union No. 136 v. Newspapers, Inc.   4, 37

Automobile Mechanics, Local 701 v. Holiday Oldsmobile   166
  v. Robertshaw Controls Co.   20

Automobile Workers
  v. Tri-State Plastic Molding Co. 38
  v. Waltham Screw Co.   173
  v. The Weatherhead Co.   577
  v. White Motor Corp.   37
  Local 463 v. Weatherhead Co.   68, 73
  Local 586 v. Federal Pacific Electric Co.   485
  Local 600 v. Ford Motor Co.   485
  Local 985 v. Chace Co.   438
  Local 1645 v. Torrington Co.   4

Avco Corp. v. Automobile Workers, Local 787   43

B

Bakery Workers
  Local 464 v. Hershey Chocolate Corp.   59
  Local 719 v. National Biscuit Co. 584

Bantley v. Lucky Stores, Inc.   704, 713, 715

Barhitte v. Kroger Co.   712

Becton v. Detroit Terminal of Consolidated Freightways   675, 677

Bell v. Mercury Freight Lines, Inc.   713

Bell Aerospace Co., Div. of Textron, Inc. v. Automobile Workers, Local 516   6, 589, 599

Bennun v. Bd. of Governors of Rutgers 269

Bergen Shipping Co., Ltd. v. Japan Marine Services, Ltd.   141

Besedich v. LTV Aerospace Corp., Missile & Space Div.   704, 711, 713

Bethlehem Mines Corp. v. Mine Workers, UMW   30

Blevins v. General Electric Co.   724

Bigge Crane and Rigging Co. v. Docutel Corp.   143, 146

Boeing Co. v. Automobile Workers, Local 1069   72

Bohack Corp. v. Truck Drivers (Teamsters), Local 807   38, 625

Boot & Shoe Workers, Local 149 v. Faith Shoe Co.   76

Boston Printing Pressmen's Union No. 67 v. Potter Press   39

Botany Industrial, Inc. v. New York Joint Bd.   449

Bowen v. Eyman   392, 424

Bradley v. Ford Motor Co.   715

Brady v. Trans World Airlines, Inc. 707

Brewery Workers
  v. Stigmaier Brewing Co.   44
  Joint Local Executive Bd. of New Jersey v. P. Ballantine & Sons 620
  Local 366 v. Adolph Coors Co.   54, 55

Brookins v. Chrysler Corp.   716

Brown v. Lithographers, Local 17   486

Bullard Contracting Corp., In re   492

Burroughs v. Marathon Oil Co.   685, 686

C

Cahn v. Garment Workers, ILGWU 96

California Trucking Ass'n v. Corcoran 41

Capital City Telephone Co. v. Communication Workers   13

Federal District Court Cases—Contd.

Old Dutch Farms, Inc. v. Milk Drivers
& Dairy Employees, Local 584
(Teamsters) 77
Operating Engineers
v. Corley Builders 27
Local 139 v. Carl A. Morse, Inc. 5
Local 450 v. Mid-Valley, Inc. 628
Ostrofsky v. Steelworkers 39
Ourisman Chevrolet Co., Inc. v. Ma-
chinists, Automotive Lodge
1486, District Lodge 67 547

P

Pacific Maritime Ass'n v. Longshore-
men & Warehousemen 544,
599
Pacific Tel & Tel Co. v. Communications
Workers 202
Packinghouse Workers, Local 52 v.
Western Iowa Pork Co. 583
Palacios v. Texaco Puerto Rico, Inc.
589
Papermakers & Paperworkers
v. Penntech Papers, Inc. 49
Local 463 v. Federal Paper Board
Co. 41, 76
Paramount Bag Mfg. Co., Inc. v. Rub-
berized Novelty and Plas-
tic Fabric Workers Union, Lo-
cal 98 (Garment Workers,
ILGWU) 68
Paramount Transport Systems v. Team-
sters, Local 150 573
Parker v. Mercury Freight Lines, Inc.
641
Partin; U.S. v. 58
Patrick v. I.D. Packing Co. 526
Patterson v. Bialystoker & Bikur Cholim
712
Pawlak v. Teamsters, Local 764 715
Penn Tanker Co. of Delaware v. C.H.Z.
Rolimplex, Warszawa 145
Pepsico, Inc. v. Brewery Workers Local
812, Soft Drink Workers Union
5
Pesola v. Inland Tool & Manufacturing,
Inc. 101
Pharmaceutical Mfrs. Ass'n v. Wein-
berger 157
Philadelphia Leather Workers, Local 30
(Meat Cutters) v. Brodsky &
Son 65
Philadelphia Photo-Engravers Union 7
v. Parade Publications, Inc.
66

Piano & Musical Instrument Workers v.
W.W. Kimball Co. 34, 37
Piggly Wiggly Operator's Warehouse,
Inc. v. Teamsters, Local 1
588
Piper v. Meco, Inc. 37
Pittsburgh Railways Co. v. Street, Elec-
tric Ry. and Motor Coach Em-
ployees, Division 85 31, 577
Playboy Clubs International v. Hotel &
Restaurant Employees 70,
99
Plumbers, Local 702 v. Nashville Gas
Co. 67
Pock v. New York Typographical Union
No. 6 4, 60
Postal Workers v. U.S. Postal Service
601
Printing Pressmen, Local 210 v. Times
World Corp. 55
Procter & Gamble Mfg. Co. v. Indep.
Oil & Chem. Workers 15,
589, 619, 623
Public Service Production of Mainte-
nance Employees, Local 1057
v. Transit Management of
Laredo, Inc. 37, 52
Pullen v. General Motors Corp. 715

Q

Quadrini v. United Aircraft Corp., Sikorsky Aircraft Div. 158

R

Railway, Airline & Steamship Clerks,
Local 1902 v. Safety Cabs, Inc.
584
Railway Conductors & Brakemen v.
Clinchfield R.R. Co. 79
Ratleff v. Ford Motor Co. 715
Red Ball Motor Freight, Inc. v. Team-
sters, Local 961 584
Redling; U.S. v. 358, 391, 397, 424
Reece v. Westmoreland Coal Co. 499,
502
Reid v. New York Metro Area Postal
Union 723
Repeatermen and Toll Test-Boardmen,
Local 1011 (Electrical Work-
ers, IBEW) v. Bell Tel. Co. of
Nevada 69, 72
Retail Clerks
v. Lane County Independent Gro-
cery Employers Committee
554

State Court Cases

State Court Cases—*Contd.*

NLRB Cases

NLRB Cases—_Contd._

O

Operating Engineers
    Local 9   197
    Local 18   23
    Local 926   282
Oregon Teamsters Security Plan Office 326
Oscherwitz, I., & Sons   175

P

P & L Cedar Products   711
Plumbing Contractors Ass'n   479
Postal Service, U.S.   326
Precision Fittings, Inc.   164
Progress Bulletin Publishing Co.   68

Q

Quality Mfg. Co.   332

R

Raffman, Edward Axel, Associates, Inc.   24
Raytheon Co.   167, 175
Retail Clerks Union   25
Roadway Express, Inc.   88, 164, 334

S

Sabine Towing & Transportation Co., Inc.   685
Sea-Land Service, Inc.   632
Sidele Fashions, Inc.   472
Speilberg Manufacturing Co.   23, 88, 131, 163, 501, 629, 634, 726
Steinmetz Electrical Contractors Ass'n 711

T

Taft Broadcasting Co.   38
Tanner Motor Livery, Ltd.   154
Teamsters, Local 788   187
Terminal Transport Co., Inc.   88, 501
Time-DC, Inc.   25
Town & Country Mfg. Co.   471, 472
Truck Drivers, Local 692 (Great Western Unifreight System)   703
Tulsa-Whisenhunt Funeral Homes, Inc.   88
Tyee Construction Co.   88

U

United Parcel Service, Inc.   88
United States Steel Corp.   151
United States Stove Co.   632

V

Versi Craft Corp.   685

W

Walton Mfg. Co.   341
Warm Springs Lumber Co.   24
Washington-Baltimore Newspaper Guild (CWA)   706
Weingarten, J.   332
Westinghouse Electric Corp.   25, 59, 152, 153
Wilson Freight Co.   635

XYZ

Youngstown Cartage Co.   88

INDEX

A

Accomplices, credibility of testimony 316–318
Ad hoc arbitrators   79, 80, 82
Administrative Procedure Act   680
Admissions of guilt   314–318
Adverse witnesses   187–189
Advocates (*see* Attorneys)
Affirmative action plans   459–460
Affirmative relief   520–521
AFL-CIO Internal Disputes Plan   28
Aggrieved employees (*see* Grievants)
Agreed awards   348–351
Agreement to be bound by award 22–24
Agreements for polygraph testing 401–405, 431–433
Agreements to arbitrate, enforcement of   3–4, 29
  absence of agreement, and arbitrator's jurisdiction   123–127
  by aggrieved employee   51–52
  compliance with grievance procedures as prerequisite for 34–36
  as not determining merits of dispute   33–34
  disputes over new contract terms 39
  existence of agreement and   29–32
  by local union   44–45
  by NLRB   53
  revocability of agreement   1–2
  by signatory employer   40–43
  by signatory union   39–40
  by and against successor employer 45–50, 125–127
  by successor union   44
  termination of contract and   36–39
  by third parties   52
Airline industry   238–240
"Alter ego" concept   125–126, 379
Ambiguous language, construing of 201–210

American Arbitration Association (AAA)   82–84, 91–92, 96, 178, 191, 348, 568, 691, 726–727
  Employment Dispute Arbitration Rules   726–727
  Voluntary Labor Arbitration Rules 10, 84, 92, 137, 139–141, 145, 149, 161–163, 168, 173, 174, 176, 190, 265–266, 557, 560, 567
American Bar Association   196, 618
Amount of proof   251, 256–263
Antitrust, and subcontracting limitations   490–493
Appeals, taken after denial of stay of arbitration   77
Application for employment, falsification   110–111, 529
Appointing agencies
  disclosure duty of   95–96
  procedures for selecting arbitrators 82–85
Apprentice arbitrators   149
Arbitrability
  absence of contract to interpret and 123–127
  bargaining agreement as basis for 99
  bargaining history as basis for 69–70
  changing of issue and   112–116
  court's finding, effect on arbitrator's authority to decide arbitrability   97–98
  of employer damage claims for breach of no-strike clause 41–43, 76–77, 100
  jurisdiction of arbitrator, procedures for challenging   132
  of jurisdictional disputes   25–26
  lack of grievant or addition of unnamed grievants   117–120
  late filing of grievance and   101–105

773

B

Back pay
  amount due   517–518
  arbitrator's authority to award
    512–513
  award of from date grievance filed
    103
  as compensatory damages   513
  interest on   518–520, 642
  and interim earnings   514
  laches defense   111
  medical basis for discharge   516–
    517
  and misconduct after discipline inci-
    dent   305–306
  as punitive damages   513, 725
  reductions in amount of   513–517
  reinstatement without   590–596
  and suspicion of intoxication
    517
  and unemployment compensation
    515–516
Bankruptcy
  and stays of arbitration   77
  successor entities as not bound by la-
    bor agreement   50, 625
  and vacation of arbitration award
    624–625
Bargaining agreements (*see* Collective
    bargaining agreements)
Bargaining history
  use to construe ambiguous lan-
    guage   207–210
  use to determine arbitrability   69–
    70
Bargaining units   67
Beneficial working conditions, clause
    343
Benefits (*see* Employee benefits)
Bennett Amendment   656–657
"Best evidence" rule   291–293, 342
Bethlehem Steel Corp.   508–509,
    526
"Beyond a reasonable doubt" stan-
    dard   257–263
Bidding disinclination   288n
Board of arbitrators   12, 85–90
Bonuses   68
Boycotts, secondary   487, 490–491
Breach of contract (*see* No-strike clause,
    breach of)
Breach of fair representation duty (*see*
    Fair representation duty)
Breath analyzer tests   322, 415
Briefs, post-hearing   563–565
Broad clauses (*see* Stays of arbitration)
Burden of proof   250–256, 287

Bureau of Labor Statistics   85
Business records as evidence   293–
  294

C

Canadian Arbitration Board   304
Carbon copies   293
Cardiologists   361
Chicago Tripartite Committee   189,
    192, 194, 290, 291, 308
Civil law standards   257, 261–262
Civil Rights Act of 1964   438
  Title VII   51, 286–289, 568, 607,
    643–645, 656–674
Civil rights groups, as lacking standing
    to compel arbitration   52
Claim of reservation   23
Class actions   35
Classified information, as privileged
    309
Clayton Act   491
"Clear and convincing evidence" stan-
    dard   261–263
Closed-circuit television surveillance
    343–345
Clothing industry   486
Code of Ethics and Procedural Stan-
    dards for Labor-Manage-
    ment Arbitration   348
Code of Federal Regulations, FMCS
    92, 93
Code of Professional Conduct for Labor
    Mediators, FMCS   92–93
Code of Professional Responsibility for
    Arbitrators of Labor-Man-
    agement Disputes   90–92,
    178, 265
Collateral estoppel   269–272, 625
Collateral proceedings, theft cases
    279–280
Collective bargaining agreements
  affirmative action requirements vs.
    seniority provisions   459–468
  and agreement to arbitrate   29–
    32, 36–39, 123–127
  as basis for arbitrability determina-
    tion   99
  construction principles (*see* Parol evi-
    dence)
  discharge procedures   352
  employer denied access to grievance
    procedures   41–43, 76–77,
    99–100
  ex parte arbitration proceedings
    173

Interest groups, as lacking standing to compel arbitration	52
Interpleader orders	26–28
Interrogation, and right of union representation	314–316, 331–341

J

Job assignments	67, 212–213, 236, 252
Job classifications	66, 67, 75, 212
and implied subcontracting limitations	480–482
Job evaluations	138, 236
judicial review of arbitration awards based on	654–674, 683
Joint arbitration	27
Joint committee grievance hearings	649–651, 730
Jones, Edgar A., Jr.	133–135, 151–152, 357, 367, 373–374, 400, 411–413, 430, 431
Judical notice	295–296
Judicial review of awards (see Awards)
Judiciary (see Courts)
Jurisdiction of arbitrator (see Arbitrability; Authority of arbitrator)
Jurisdictional disputes	25–28, 56–59
Jury trials, for breach of fair representation duty	704–709
Just cause (see Discipline and discharge)
Justice Department	423

L

Labor agreements (see Collective bargaining agreements)
Labor arbitration (see Arbitration)
Labor Management Relations Act (LMRA)	3, 23n, 28, 452, 566
Sec. 301	3–6, 29, 144–147, 158, 284, 584–585
Laches	36, 56, 110–111
Language
ambiguous, construing of	201–210
profane, against supervisor	228
of written grievance	712
Lateness, employee penalty	529
Law (see also State statutes)
external to agreements (see Collective bargaining agreements)
"law of the shop"	224–225, 616–617
source of, in arbitration	1–9

Lawyers (see Attorneys)
Layoffs	74, 252
Leave time	74
Legal supremacy clauses	447–448
Liability
of arbitrators	96
for breach of no-strike clause	282–284, 540
Licensure of polygraphers	365–367
Lie detector testing (see Polygraph testing)
Litigation
arbitration compared	133–134, 145, 170, 197, 309, 312–314
Sec. 301 suits for breach of fair representation duty (see Fair representation duty)
Local unions, enforcement of agreement to arbitrate	44–45
Local working conditions, clause	224
Location of hearing	161–163

M

Magistrates' reports	680–682
Management
burden of proof on	254–256
damage claims for breach of no-strike clause	41–43, 76–77, 99–100
employees as company witnesses	182–183
employer-union communications as not privileged	309
enforcement of agreements to arbitrate	40–43, 45–50
protection of informants from reprisal	183–187
Management rights	65–66
and arbitrator's jurisdiction	232–240
"just cause" for discharge	224–232, 240–245, 249–250
limitation by imposition of criminal standards in discharge cases	260–261
nonarbitrability of	72–74, 127–130
parol evidence rule and	199, 210–213
subcontracting (see Subcontracting limitations)
supervision methods, right to change	343–344
Maryland	8
Masters' reports	680–684
Materiality of evidence	310

U

Umpires (*see also* Arbitrators)   690
Undisclosed evidence   297–300
Unemployment compensation, and back pay award   515–516
Unfair labor practices   486, 487
Uniform Arbitration Act   146–148, 166, 191, 580, 618
Uniform Business Records as Evidence Act   293, 321
Unions (*see also* Fair representation duty)
   breach of no-strike clause
      money damages   532–542
      nonliability of members   284, 540
      responsibility for   282–284, 540
   burden of proof on   252–254
   communications as not privileged   309
   discipline by   61
   education of members concerning plant rules   281–282
   enforcement of agreements to arbitrate   39–40, 44–45
   exclusive representation right   28, 52
   officials as witnesses   182–183
   and removals in stay litigation   77–78
   representation right at employee interrogations   314–316, 331–341
   as third party in arbitration hearing   24–28
Unit for bargaining   67
United Automobile Workers (UAW)   717–718, 722–723
United Mine Workers   534
United Shoe Machine Co.   460–462
United States Arbitration Act   3–6, 29, 93, 94, 143, 145–146, 177, 620
United Steelworkers of America   134, 352, 460–462
Unlawful searches   321–322, 324–331
Unnamed grievants   114, 117–120
"Unreasonable, arbitrary, or capricious" test, for discipline   233–237, 244

V

Vacation of award (*see* Awards)
Vacation pay   66, 74
Vacations
   during plant shutdowns   127–128
   rescheduling by employer   526

Valdez formulations   394
Veterans, seniority preference   451–452
Violence, as just cause for discharge   225
Visual surveillance (*see* Industrial surveillance)
Vocational Rehabilitation Act   438
Voir dire examination of polygraphers   363–368, 394, 396
Voluntary Labor Arbitration Rules, AAA   10, 84, 92, 137, 139–141, 145, 149, 161–163, 168, 173, 174, 176, 190, 265–266, 557, 560, 567
Voucher rule   395

W

Wages
   arbitrability of   67, 75, 129
   interim earnings, and back pay awards   514
   sex-based wage discrimination   654–674, 683
Waiver
   of *de novo* review of arbitration award   687–689
   of objection to lack of formal notice of hearing   163
   of time limit objections   104, 105, 108–109
Walk-offs   67
War Labor Board   436, 500
Warnings, written, as evidence   281
Weapons carrying, search to determine   322
Wildcat strikes (*see* No-strike clause, breach of)
Wiretapping (*see* Industrial surveillance)
Wisconsin   5
Witnesses
   accomplices as, and credibility of testimony   316–318
   advocate-witness exclusion rationale   195–198
   attorney-witness communications as privileged   309
   cross-examination of   191–194
   employees as company witnesses   182–183
   evidentiary depositions from   146
   exclusion of during testimony of others   164–165, 190–191
   expert witness testimony   158–159, 290–291, 731